DATE DUE

			PRINTED IN U.S.A.

Epics
for Students

Epics
for Students

Presenting Analysis, Context, and Criticism on Commonly Studied Epics

Volume 2

Elizabeth Bellalouna, Editor

Foreword by Helen Conrad-O'Briain, School of English, Trinity College, Dublin

GALE GROUP

Detroit
New York
San Francisco
London
Boston
Woodbridge, CT

Epics for Students

Staff

Editor: Elizabeth Bellalouna.

Contributing Editors: Anne Marie Hacht, Kimberly Hazelmyer, Michael L. LaBlanc, Mark Milne, Jennifer Smith.

Managing Editor: Dwayne Hayes.

Research: Victoria B. Cariappa, *Research Manager*. Cheryl Warnock, *Research Specialist*. Tamara Nott, Tracie A. Richardson, *Research Associates*. Nicodemus Ford, Sarah Genik, Timothy Lehnerer, *Research Assistants*.

Permissions: Maria Franklin, *Permissions Manager*. Sarah Tomasek, *Permissions Associate*.

Manufacturing: Mary Beth Trimper, *Manager, Composition and Electronic Prepress*. Evi Seoud, *Assistant Manager, Composition Purchasing and Electronic Prepress*. Stacy Melson, *Buyer*.

Imaging and Multimedia Content Team: Barbara Yarrow, *Manager*. Randy Bassett, *Imaging Supervisor*. Robert Duncan, Dan Newell, *Imaging Specialists*. Pamela A. Reed, *Imaging Coordinator*. Leitha Etheridge-Sims, Mary Grimes, *Image Catalogers*. Robyn Young, *Project Manager*. Dean Dauphinais, *Senior Image Editor*. Kelly A. Quin, *Image Editor*.

Product Design Team: Kenn Zorn, *Product Design Manager*. Pamela A. E. Galbreath, *Senior Art Director*. Michael Logusz, *Graphic Artist*.

Copyright Notice

Table of Contents

Guest Foreword

I am reliably informed that no one ever reads introductions these days, but then it wasn't so very long ago that I was reliably informed that no one reads epics either. Still here before us both, writer and reader, is the second volume of *Epics for Students*, and I cannot help but feel a certain hopefulness that if the epic still exerts a pull on modern tastes and imagination, perhaps the introduction as a form has not quite lost its appeal either.

So why should anyone, in a world where entertainment that doesn't even require anything so strenuous as holding a book or turning a page, sit down and read an epic? The ancient Greeks had a theory that all literary genres, even oratory and the various forms of lyric poetry, had their origins in the epic. There is a certain truth to this, even if scholars dispute it on a technical level. Greek literature, philosophy and science, even the collection of historical and geographical material begin almost as footnotes to the *Iliad* and the *Odyssey*. Literary criticism, and the methods used to establish a correct text were invented by the librarian scholars of Alexandria to deal with the *Iliad* and *Odyssey*. The simple fact you are studying literature goes back to the importance the Greeks placed on the Homeric epics. But Homer and his descendants are not the whole of the tradition, nor is he even the earliest. The Mesopotamian epic of *Gilgamesh* was old when the Greeks dragged their ships out of the wine dark sea onto the beaches of the Troad. In the Indian sub-continent the epic impulse produced the *Rámayana* and the *Mahábhárata*; works as important to the Indian subcontinent and the peoples it influenced as Homer's works have been to the West. The epic has claim to the breadth of narrative that sees the larger patterns which run through history, patterns which seem to exist by nature of our humanity and our changeable world. In it characters may seem bigger than our daily experience of men and women, not because they are superhuman, but because they are intensely human. There are only so many stories in the world, and all of them are rooted in the epic. The epic was born in an age when literature, however entertaining, was didactic. It was meant to leave the audience with something important, a way of looking at the world, a method for meeting life with dignity. Sometimes it held a warning, sometime it made an ideal live. Always it lead back to life, not away from it. And that is why, despite all the fashions in literature, readers and writers return to the epic.

And this is important to you picking up this book. The epic lives. It is by no means dead, although at times in the last three hundred years it has seemed to be resting. Having turned the novel to good account in the nineteenth and twentieth century, it has moved on to the film. There, it has not only transposed preexisting works, from Fritz Lang's silent movies based on the Volsung Saga to the live action trilogy of films based on Tolkien's *Lord of the Rings* now in production, but it has spawned new epics, using new methods of visual storytelling, which are the children of its traditional verbal techniques.

Some critics, particularly when facing the epic's modern manifestations, will say that its popularity is based on escapism, the happy ending, the clear cut good guys and bad guys, the simple certainties. But, in fact, this is just what the epic is not about. We live in an age of hypersensitivity in some areas and moral numbness in others. The epic writer, always struggling to define what is noble, what is excellent among our limitations and expectations, has always reminded us of the flawed but limitless potential of our nature, not in terms of things but in terms of spirit. The epic seldom has a happy ending, although the epic spirit does not refuse the possibility of happiness. Can we deny Homer's *Odyssey* the status of great literature, let alone an epic, because Odysseus not only reaches home, but his wife still loves him, his old dog dies wagging his tale at him, and he saves the family farm, so to speak? Epics are not escapist; under the action and the apparent victories, there are the passions built into human nature, there are the simple, inexorable physical laws of the earth or the galaxy, even a galaxy far, far away, which set the action in motion. These never go away, and they are never defeated, only contained. The Ring or the Death Star are destroyed, but not the greed for power. Fame may last forever, but it will not bring back even the glorious dead. Lover finds beloved, but even love must live in an imperfect world. Victory is never final, only an interim solution, because hate and fear, loss and change, seem to have entered the universe, even the mirror universes of literature, with the laws of physics. Odysseus makes it home, but in the process, the poet has never let us forget that the earth will never see the end of the homeless man on the doorstep.

Epics are somehow profoundly pessimistic and profoundly optimistic at the same time. The fight may be endless, the solutions only for a moment, at best only for a lifetime, but the process of simply keeping the darkness at bay creates or finds its own energy and exuberance. The epic, for all its grandeur, big setting, and ideal, takes us back into the larger patterns of life that every day possesses, but which we cannot always see. Epics may, and probably will, force us to consider ways of understanding and evaluating experience which are not our own, but they will not always be anchored just in their maker's own day. Somehow the epic forces its creator down into some bedrock where the human heart finds a small worn place to rest and say, I

know these people, this looks like home. And from this bedrock of recognition the epic will enlarge, rather than contract your sympathy. The far away, the long ago are no longer alien, but human and near. Pick up any of the texts whose introductions you will find in this book. You will be swept into another world, contiguous to our own, but one which brings our own greater clarity even as we look on the other. The epic does not ignore the everyday, the trivial. Somehow it provides a context in which triviality is banished. Small things we brush past in our daily lives can be given back their rightful beauty in the epic. Read Lucretius and you will never again fail to look at dust dancing in the sunlight and wonder at its implications. The epic attitude that there is more to life than the immediate insures that the immediate is filled with meaning, that the good things in life are good.

Sounds a bit bleak, doesn't it, just what you would expect from a class assignment, all duty and decisions, simple pleasures and the dying of the light with a 5,000 word paper at the end of it. There are many ways of reading the epics which follow, and all of them in a way are the right way. I often think it is unfortunate that we usually first read these works as school assignments with an eye to papers and exams. We seldom read them for immediate personal enjoyment. But anyone who has ever by design or luck simply sat down and let an epic sweep them away knows that however much things may stay with you long after you have read them, making you think, changing your perspective if only for a moment, the reason why you do think of them is because the best epics are a verbal rush of adrenaline. If literature is vicarious experiences, there are few experiences to match the epic. There are armies like forces of nature, winters that bring conquerors to their knees. There are lovers who cross death itself for the beloved. There are places of breathtaking beauty, places of stomach-wrenching horror and you don't even have to take a jacket. I was twelve when I first read Spenser's *Faerie Queen*. It was one amazing convoluted adventure after another, and I loved it. Later I taught it for nearly ten years. Year after year, I found something more, something profound, something that forced me to reevaluate my own convictions and lack of them, but I could never teach the zest that comes of reading it for the first time, for the sheer excitement of the narrative, the moments when a particularly well-written line or puzzling idea will jump out and catch you forever. Those are the ideas that you will chew over for years and which will, as you attempt to understand them, transform you in the process. The great epics pull you along, they pull you in, they pull you through, and when you finish them the only thing you regret is that however many times you will read them, it will never again be the first.

Helen Elizabeth Conrad-O'Briain
Research Associate
School of English
Trinity College, Dublin

Introduction

Purpose

Epics for Students (*EfS*) is designed to provide students with a guide to understanding and enjoying epic literature. Part of Gale's ''For Students'' Literature line, *EfS* is crafted to meet the curricular needs of high school and undergraduate college students and their teachers, as well as the interests of general readers and researchers. This volume contains entries on the works of epic world literature that are most studied in classrooms.

Coverage

Each entry includes an introduction to the epic and its author, when known, and discussion of authorship controversies or speculation in the case of anonymous works. A plot summary helps readers follow the often complicated series of events in the epic. Character sketches include explanation of each character's role in the epic and relationships with other characters. Separate essays provide analyses of important themes and of literary techniques.

In addition to this material, which helps readers understand and analyze the epic itself, students are provided with meaningful information on the literary and historical background of each work. This includes an essay on the historical context of the epic, comparisons between the time and place of the epic's setting and modern Western culture, an overview essay surveying the course of commentary about the work, and excerpts from critical essays on the epic.

Special Features

EfS includes a foreword by Helen Conrad-O'Briain, Trinity College Dublin, University College Dublin. This essay provides an enlightening look at how readers interact with literature and how teachers and students can use *Epics for Students* to enrich their own experiences with epic literature.

A unique feature of *EfS* is a specially commissioned essay on each epic by an academic expert, usually one who has taught the work extensively, targeted to the student reader.

To further aid the student in studying and enjoying each epic, information on media adaptations is provided, as well as reading suggestions for works of fiction and nonfiction on similar themes and topics. Each entry also features illustrations, such as maps and depictions of key scenes. Classroom aids include ideas for research papers and lists of critical sources that provide additional scholarly information on each work.

Organization

Each entry in *EfS* focuses on one work. The heading lists the title of the epic, the author's name (when known), and the date that the epic first appeared. In some cases, this date is known; in others, a range of dates is provided. The following elements appear in each entry:

- **Introduction:** A brief overview which provides general information about the epic, such as its place in world literature, its significance within its national culture, any controversies surrounding the epic, and major themes of the work.

- **Author Biography:** Includes basic facts about the author's life. In the case of anonymous works, speculative scholarship about the anonymous author or authors is summarized here.

- **Plot Summary:** A description of the major events in the epic, with interpretation of how these events help articulate the primary themes.

- **Characters:** An alphabetical listing of the epic's main characters. Each character name is followed by a description of that character's role, as well as discussion of the character's actions, relationships, and motivations.

- **Themes:** A thorough overview of how the principal themes, topics, and issues are addressed within the epic.

- **Style:** This section addresses important stylistic elements, such as setting, point of view, and narrative method, as well as literary devices such as imagery, foreshadowing, and symbolism. Literary terms are explained within each entry and can also be found in the Glossary.

- **Historical and Cultural Context:** This section outlines the social, political, and cultural climate in which the author lived and the epic was created. Descriptions of related historical events, pertinent aspects of daily life in the culture, and the artistic and literary sensibilities of the time in which the work was written are provided here.

- **Critical Overview:** Supplies background on the critical and popular reputation of the epic. Offers an overview of how the work was first received and how perceptions of it may have changed over time.

- **Sources for Further Study:** Alphabetical list of critical material quoted in the entry and other critical sources useful to the student who wants to read more about the epic. Full bibliographical information and descriptive annotations are provided for each source.

- **Criticism:** This section begins with an essay commissioned for *EfS* designed to introduce the epic work to the student reader. This section also

includes excerpts from previously published criticism that has been identified by subject experts as especially useful in explicating each work to students.

- **Media Adaptations:** A list of film and television productions of the epic, as well as information about stage adaptations, audio recordings, and musical adaptations.

- **Compare and Contrast Box:** ''At-a-glance'' comparison of some cultural and historical differences between the epic's time and culture and late twentieth-century Western society.

- **What Do I Read Next?:** A list of works that complement the featured epic or serve as a contrast to it. This can include works by the same author and works from other authors, genres, cultures, and eras.

- **Study Questions:** Questions designed to spark classroom discussion or research paper topics. This section includes questions related to other disciplines, such as American history, world history, science, math, government, business, geography, economics, and psychology.

Indexes

A **Cumulative Author/Title Index** lists the authors and titles covered in the volume.

A **Nationality/Ethnicity Index** lists the authors and titles by nationality and ethnicity.

A **Subject/Theme Index** provides easy reference for users studying a particular subject or theme within epic literature. Significant subjects and themes are included. Boldface entries in this index indicate in-depth discussion of that subject or theme.

Each entry features **illustrations,** including author portraits, depictions of key scenes, and maps.

We Welcome Your Suggestions

The editors of *Epics for Students* welcome your comments and ideas. Readers who wish to suggest epic works to appear in future volumes, or who have other suggestions, are cordially invited to contact the editor. You may write to the editor at:

Editor, *Epics for Students*
Gale Group
27500 Drake Road
Farmington Hill, MI 48331–3535

Literary Chronology

94 B.C.: Titus Lucretius Carus, known as Lucretius, the author of the six-volume epic poem *De rerum natura* is born in Rome.

58 B.C.: Lucretius writes *De rerum natura*.

55 B.C.: Lucretius commits suicide.

39 B.C.: Marcus Annaeus Lucanus, better known as Lucan, is born in Cordova, Spain on November 3.

65: Lucan writes the epic *Pharsalia*.

65: Lucan commits suicide at the order of the emperor Nero on April 30 following a failed assassination attempt on the Roman leader.

800–1100: The thirty-nine poems that comprise the *Elder Edda* are written by author or authors unknown.

973: Lady Murasaki Shikibu is born in Koyto, Japan.

1000: Shikibu's epic-length novel, *Tale of Genji,* is written.

1030: Shikibu dies.

1150–1250: The *Elder Edda* is first written down.

1185: *The Song of Igor's Campaign* is written.

1270: Thirty-four of the poems in the *Elder Edda* are copied into the *Codex Regius* (King's book), in Iceland.

1410: Thomas Malory, traditionally believed to be the author of *Le Morte d'Arthur*, is born.

1470: Malory completes *Le Morte d'Arthur* while imprisoned for numerous criminal acts.

1471: Malory dies and is buried in Newgate, just outside of London, England.

1485: William Caxton first publishes Malory's *Le Morte d'Arthur*.

1544: Torquato Tasso is born in Sorrento, Italy, on March 11.

1552: Edmund Spenser is born in London, England.

1562: Tasso begins writing his epic poem *Gerusalemme Liberata*, which will take him thirteen years to complete.

1579: Tasso's *Gerusalemme Liberata* first appears in a pirated edition.

1590: Spenser publishes the first three books of *The Faerie Queene*.

1595: Tasso dies in the convent of Saint Onofrio in Rome on April 25 following a serious illness.

1599: Spenser dies in London, England, (some say of starvation) on January 13.

1643: The *Codex Regius* containing the *Elder Edda*, comes into the possession of Bishop Brynjólfr Sveinsson.

1795: *The Song of Igor's Campaign*, written much earlier by an anonymous author, is discovered.

1802: Victor Hugo is born in Besançon, France.

1828: Leo Tolstoy is born to an upper-class Russian family at the family's estate in Tula province, Russia, on September 9.

1862: Hugo publishes *Les Misérables* during a nineteen-year exile on the Isle of Guernsey in the English Channel.

1866: Tolstoy publishes *War and Peace*.

1885: Ezra Pound is born in Idaho.

1885: Hugo dies in France.

1892: J. R. R. Tolkien is born January 3 in South Africa.

1910: Tolstoy dies of pneumonia on November 20.

1917: Pound begins work on his epic poem *The Cantos*, comprised of 120 shorter poems, which he will work on for over fifty years.

1936: Tolkien publishes *The Hobbit*, a story he writes for his children.

1954: Tolkien publishes *Lord of the Rings*.

1972: Pound dies in Venice, Italy.

1973: Tolkien dies in England on September 2.

1997: *Lord of the Rings* is voted the greatest book of the twentieth century in a poll run by major British booksellers.

Acknowledgments

The editors wish to thank the copyright holders of the excerpted criticism included in this volume and the permissions managers of many book and magazine publishing companies for assisting us in securing reproduction rights. We are also grateful to the staffs of the Detroit Public Library, the Library of Congress, the University of Detroit Mercy Library, Wayne State University Purdy/Kresge Library Complex, and the University of Michigan Libraries for making their resources available to us. Following is a list of the copyright holders who have granted us permission to reproduce material in this volume of *Epics for Students (EfS)*. Every effort has been made to trace copyright, but if omissions have been made, please let us know.

COPYRIGHTED EXCERPTS IN *EFS*, VOLUME 2, WERE REPRODUCED FROM THE FOLLOWING PERIODICALS:

The Christian Century, v. 110, February 24, 1993. Copyright Christian Century Foundation 1993. Reproduced by permission.—*CLA Journal*, v. XX, December, 1976. Copyright, 1976 by The College Language Association. Used by permission of The College Language Association.—*Classical Antiquity*, v. 13, October, 1994; v. 15, October, 1996. © 1994, 1996 by The Regents of the University of California. Both reproduced by permission.—*Classical Philology*, v. 90, January, 1995. © 1995 by The University of Chicago. All rights reserved. Reproduced by permission.—*The Econo-mist*, December 25, 1999. © 1999 The Economist Newspaper Group, Inc. Reproduced with permission. Further reproduction prohibited.—*English Language Notes*, v. XXII, September, 1984. © copyrighted 1984, Regents of the University of Colorado. Reproduced by permission.—*English Literary Renaissance*, v. 26, Spring, 1996. Copyright © 1996 by English Literary Renaissance. Reproduced by permission.—*The Explicator*, v. 54, Summer, 1996; v. 57, Summer, 1999. Copyright 1996, 1999 by Helen Dwight Reid Educational Foundation. Both reproduced with permission of the Helen Dwight Reid Educational Foundation, published by Heldref Publications, 1319 18th Street, NW, Washington, D.C. 20036–1802.— *Forum for Modern Language Studies,* v. 18, 1982 for "Appearances and Reality in 'La Mort le Roi Artu'" by Donald C. MacRae. Reproduced by permission of the publisher and the author.—*The French Review*, v. 67, December, 1993. Copyright 1993 by the American Association of Teachers of French. Reproduced by permission.—*Maal Og Minne*, 1988. Reproduced by permission.—*Modern Language Review*, v. 69, January, 1974; v. 71, January, 1976. Both reproduced by permission.—*Mosaic: A Journal for the Interdisciplinary Study of Literature,* v. XIX, Summer, 1986. © Mosaic 1986. Acknowledgment of previous publication is herewith made.—*Ramus—Critical Studies in Greek and Roman Literature*, v. 24, 1996. Reproduced by permission.—*Renaissance Quarterly*, v. 31, Spring, 1978. © 1978 Renaissance

Society of America. Reproduced by permission.—*Russian Literature*, v. 42, 1997. © 1997 Elsevier Science B. V. All rights reserved. Reproduced with permission from Elsevier Science.—*The Russian Review*, v. 56, October, 1997. Reproduced by permission.—*Slavic Review*, v. 39, June, 1980. Copyright © 1980 by the American Association for the Advancement of Slavic Studies, Inc. Reproduced by permission.

COPYRIGHTED EXCERPTS IN *EFS*, VOLUME 2, WERE REPRODUCED FROM THE FOLLOWING BOOKS:

Bartsch, Shadi. From *Ideology in Cold Blood: A Reading of Lucan's Civil War*. Harvard University Press, 1997. Copyright © 1997 by the President and Fellows of Harvard College. All rights reserved. Reproduced by permission.—Brand, C. P. From *Torquato Tasso: A Study of the Poet and of His Contribution to English Literature*. Cambridge at the University Press, 1965. © Cambridge University Press 1965. Reprinted with permission of Cambridge University Press and the author.—Cerisola, Anne-Sophie. From "'Les Miserables': Criticism" in *Novels for Students, Vol. 5*. Edited by Sheryl Ciccarelli and Marie Napierkowski. Gale Group, 1999. Copyright © 1999 by The Gale Group. Reproduced by permission.—Hollander, Lee M. From *The Poetic Edda*. Revised edition. Translated by Lee M. Hollander. University of Texas Press, 1962. Copyright © 1962, renewed 1990. By permission of the University of Texas Press.—Kay, Sarah. From "Adultery and Killing in 'La Mort le Roi Artu'" in *Scarlet Letters: Fictions of Adultery from Antiquity to the 1990s*. Edited by Nicholas White and Naomi Segal. Macmillan Press Ltd., 1997. Editorial matter and selection © Nicholas White and Naomi Segal 1997. Text © Macmillan Press Ltd. 1997. All rights reserved. Reproduced by permission.—Kelly, Patricia. From "The Tain as Literature" in *Aspects of the Tain*. Edited by J. P. Mallory. December Publications, 1992. © J. P. Mallory and others, 1992. Reproduced by permission.—Kenner, Hugh. From "Pound and Homer" in *Ezra Pound among the Poets*. Edited by George Bornstein. University of Chicago Press, 1985. © 1985 by The University of Chicago. All rights reserved. Reproduced by permission.—Knowles, A. V. From "'War and Peace': Overview" in *Reference Guide to World Literature, second edition*. Edited by Lesley Henderson. St. James Press, 1995. Reproduced by permission.—Porter, Laurence M. From *Victor Hugo*. Twayne Publishers, 1999. Copyright © 1999 by Twayne Publishers. All rights reserved. Reproduced

by permission.—Ross, Charles. From *The Custom of the Castle: From Malory to Macbeth*. University of California Press, 1997. Copyright © 1996 The Regents of the University of California. Reproduced by permission.—Rowe, William W. From *Leo Tolstoy*. Twayne Publishers, 1986. Reproduced by permission.—Shipley, T. A. From *The Road to Middle-Earth*. George Allen & Unwin, 1982. Copyright © Tom Shippey 1982. Reproduced by permission of HarperCollins Publishers Ltd.—Terrell, Carroll F. From "Pound, Ezra" in *The Reader's Companion to American History*. Edited by Eric Foner and John A. Garraty. Houghton Mifflin Company, 1991. Reproduced by permission.

PHOTOGRAPHS AND ILLUSTRATIONS APPEARING IN *EFS*, VOLUME 2, WERE RECEIVED FROM THE FOLLOWING SOURCES:

Anglo-Saxon Viking, illustration. Picture Collection, The Branch Libraries, The New York Public Library.—Beowulf, photograph.—Caesar, (Gaius) Julius, painting. The Library of Congress.—Cato, Marcus Porcius, engraving. The Library of Congress.—From a painting by E. Wallcousins in "Celtic Myth and Legend" by Charles Squire. Mary Evans Picture Library. Reproduced by permission.—"Chronicle of the Crusades," photograph. © Gianni Dagli Orti/CORBIS. Reproduced by permission.—Commemoration of the Storming of the Bastille, photograph. © Hulton-Deutsch Collection/CORBIS. Reproduced by permission.—Confucius, drawing. Archive Photos/Popperfoto. Reproduced by permission.—"The Death of Balder," painting by Dorothy Hardy.—Design of new 2,000 yen bill, photograph. © Reuters Newmedia Inc./CORBIS. Reproduced by permission.—Elizabeth I, photograph. © Bettmann/CORBIS. Reproduced by permission.—Epicurus, 1810 engraving by George Cooke. The Library of Congress.—Title page from "Faerie Queen" by Edmund Spenser, photograph. © Bettmann/CORBIS. Reproduced by permission.—Forum Romanum, Rome, photograph. New York Public Library Picture Collection.—Harris, Richard and Vanessa Redgrave, in the film "Camelot," 1967, photograph. The Kobal Collection. Reproduced by permission.—Hugo, Victor, drawing. French Embassy Press and Information Division.—King Arthur (being transported to Avalon after his death), photograph. © Bettmann/CORBIS. Reproduced by permission.—King Arthur, photograph. © Francis G. Mayer/CORBIS. Reproduced by permission.—Lucretius, engraving. The Library of Congress.—March, Frederic, in the film "Les

Miserables,'' 1935, photograph. The Kobal Collection. Reproduced by permission.—Medieval Russian clergy (standing in cluster), photograph. © Austrian Archives/CORBIS. Reproduced by permission.—Mussolini, Benito, photograph. © Bettmann/CORBIS. Reproduced by permission.—''Napoleon on Horseback at the St. Bernard Pass,'' painting by Jacques-Louis David, 1801, oil on canvas. Corbis/Francis G. Mayer. Reproduced by permission.—Nero, Emperor of Rome, engraving. Corbis-Bettmann/Michael Nicholson. Reproduced by permission.—Norse Goddess Frigga, illustration. Corbis-Bettmann. Reproduced by permission.—Norse Gods Loki and Hodur, sculpture by C. G. Qvarnstrom.—Odin (seated on throne), photograph. Christel Gerstenberg/CORBIS. Reproduced by permission.—Poole, John W. (addressing crowd), photograph. © Hulton-Deutsch Collection/CORBIS. Reproduced by permission.—Pound, Ezra, photograph. The Library of Congress.—Prince of Kiev (reigned 1078–1093), c. 1090, photograph. © Archive Photos/Hulton Getty. Reproduced by permission.—''Queen Maeve and the Druid,'' photograph. Mary Evans Picture Library. Reproduced by permission.—''Queen Maeve,'' photograph. Mary Evans Picture Library. Reproduced by permission.—Roman de Tristan, manuscript. © Archivo Iconografico, S. A./CORBIS. Reproduced by permission.—Russian Medieval nobles, photograph. © Austrian Archives/ CORBIS. Reproduced by permission.—''Saint George Slaying the Dragon,'' painting by Bernardo Martorll. © Archivo Iconografico, S. A./CORBIS. Reproduced by permission.—''The School of Athens'' (many men inside structure with archways and marble statues), mural, painted by Santi Raphael, photograph by Erich Lessing. Erich Lessing/Art Resource, NY. Reproduced by permission.—Second attack of the Crusaders on Jerusalem, photograph. © Bettmann/CORBIS. Reproduced by permission.—Spenser, Edmund (in dark shirt with Elizabethan ruff), drawing.—Strzhelchik, Vladislav, in the film ''War and Peace,'' 1968, photograph. The Kobal Collection. Reproduced by permission.—Illustration from the Yugao Chapter from the ''Tale of Genji,'' woodblock print by Buemon Akiyama Tsukioka Yoshitoshi, photograph. © Asian Art & Archaeology, Inc./CORBIS. Reproduced by permission.—Scene from the ''Tale of Genji,'' photograph. © Archivo Iconografico, S. A./CORBIS. Reproduced by permission.—Tasso, Torquato, photograph. Archive Photo, Inc. Reproduced by permission.—Thor, illustration. Corbis-Bettman. Reproduced by permission.—Tolkien, J. R. R., 1973, photograph. AP/Wide World Photos. Reproduced by permission.—Tolstoy, Leo, 1897, photograph. The Library of Congress.—''Venus de Milo,'' sculpture, arms broken off, photograph. AP/Wide World Photos. Reproduced by permission.

Contributors

Bryan Aubrey: Aubrey holds a Ph.D. in English Literature from the University of Durham, England. Entry on *Song of Igor's Campaign*. Original essay on *Song of Igor's Campaign*.

Greg Barnhisel: Barnhisel holds a Ph.D. in American Literature from the University of Texas at Austin. He has taught English as Assistant Professor at Southwestern University in Georgetown, Texas and has worked as a freelance writer and editor. He has published other articles on Ezra Pound. Entry on *The Cantos*. Original essay on *The Cantos*.

Jennifer Bussey: Bussey holds a bachelor's degree in English literature and a master's degree in interdisciplinary studies; she is an independent writer specializing in literature. Entry on *De rerum natura*. Original essay on *De rerum natura*.

Anne-Sophie Cerisola: Cerisola is a former teacher at the Lycee Francais de New York and a current instructor at New York University. Original essay on *Les Misérables*.

Helen Conrad O'Briain: Conrad O'Briain holds a Ph.D. from Trinity College, Dublin, where she is a research associate and departemental librarian for the School of English. She also teaches Old English and has published on early insular theology and the use of Virgil in early Anglo-Latin literature. Entries on *Elder Edda*, *Lord of the Rings*, *Pharsalia*, and *Táin Bó Cúailnge*. Original essays on *Elder Edda*, *Lord of the Rings*, *Pharsalia*, and *Táin Bó Cúailnge*.

Donald G. Evans: Evans is an adjunct professor at Hamilton College in Cedar Rapids, IA, as well as a free-lance writer for *Advertising Age* and editor for *Story Quarterly*. Entry on *Tale of Genji*. Original essay on *Tale of Genji*.

David J. Kelly: Kelly is a professor of English at College of Lake County, IL. Entry on *War and Peace*. Original essay on *War and Peace*.

Sheri Metzger: Metzger is a freelance writer, has a Ph.D., and is an adjunct professor in the Department of English at the University of New Mexico in Albuquerque, NM. Entries on *The Faerie Queene* and *Le Morte d'Arthur*. Original essays on *The Faerie Queene* and *Le Morte d'Arthur*.

Gail Nelson: Nelson holds a master's degree from the University of Chicago and is a freelance writer and editor in San Francisco. Entry on *Les Misérables*.

Michael Rex: Rex is an adjunct professor at the University of Detroit-Mercy, MI. Entry on *Gerusalemme Liberata*. Original essay on *Gerusalemme Liberata*.

The Cantos

EZRA POUND

1917—1968

The difficult, sometimes frustrating, often moving, occasionally brilliant epic poem *The Cantos* is Ezra Pound's most significant contribution to world literature. The poem, though, is rarely read all the way through, and Pound is better remembered for his short poems, his early theoretical writings and manifestoes, and his turbulent personal history. This is unfortunate, because in *The Cantos* are some of the most beautiful and powerful passages in twentieth-century poetry. Written over more than fifty years, the poem is a document of the rise, reign, and fall of a literary style, a generation of artists, and a way of life. Pound was perhaps the central figure in the development of modernism, not only in literature but in fiction, drama, sculpture, and even music, and in *Cantos* so many of his enduring concerns and artistic innovations are present, both as prefigurations and reminiscences of the heady days of the 1920s and 1930s. Although the poem is erratic, difficult, and at times willfully obscure, it merits careful attention and has much to reward the patient reader.

AUTHOR BIOGRAPHY

One of the most significant literary figures of the twentieth century, Ezra Loomis Pound was born in Idaho in 1885. His family soon moved to the suburbs of Philadelphia, where Pound grew up. In college at the University of Pennsylvania, he met

Hilda Doolittle and William Carlos Williams. Pound and these two poets became friends and colleagues in the burgeoning "Modernist" movement. Pound transferred to Hamilton College before returning to the University of Pennsylvania for postgraduate studies in Provencal.

Pound never received his Ph.D., and after one disastrous year of teaching college in Indiana he moved to Europe in 1908. Settling in Venice, Pound published his first book of poems, *A Lume Spento*, there before moving on to London. In London, Pound used his forceful personality to insert himself into the avant-garde literary scene. In the twelve years he spent in London, Pound helped wrest literature from the fusty Georgian style of such writers as Swinburne and Henry James (both of whom he admired greatly), forging the lapidary, dynamic modernist style. In the process, he befriended W. B. Yeats, T. S. Eliot, James Joyce, Wyndham Lewis, Henri Gaudier-Brzeska, Richard Aldington, and many others.

World War I was a great tragedy for Pound, and he felt that after the war ended the atmosphere of literary experimentation that dominated pre-war London had died. He wrote his great cycle "Hugh Selwyn Mauberley" as a farewell to the city in 1920, and left. Moving briefly to Paris, Pound found that city not to his liking—probably because his role as impresario and dominant personality was already held by Gertrude Stein—and came to Italy in 1924. He stayed in Italy for twenty-two years, during which time he came to greatly admire Mussolini and Italian fascism. In these years, Pound was studying economics and history but had also thrown himself fully into the composition of *The Cantos*, his epic "tale of the tribe" that he would never complete. During World War II, Pound, who had grown increasingly convinced that the American economic system was harmful, made radio broadcasts on Italian state radio and was indicted for treason in the United States. After Mussolini fell, Pound was captured and held in the U. S. Army's Disciplinary Training Center in Pisa, Italy.

Pound was returned to America and, because the authorities felt that he was mentally unfit to stand trial, was incarcerated in St. Elizabeth's mental hospital in Washington, D. C., for thirteen years. During this time Pound continued to write and to collect disciples—admirers, poets, critics, sycophants, and crackpots. He was released in 1958 and returned to Italy. After an initial burst of activity, Pound grew depressed and fell into a silence. He made few public appearances in the 1960s, contenting himself with living in Venice, and died there in 1972.

PLOT SUMMARY

The Cantos really has no plot. The poem consists of approximately 120 shorter poems (themselves called "cantos," after the sections into which Dante divided each book of his *Divine Comedy*), some of which tell unified stories and some of which are simply collections of musings, observations, memories, and exhortations. To summarize the "plot" of *The Cantos*, therefore, it is probably best to describe the poem in terms of sections.

Although the first draft of the first three cantos appeared in *Poetry* magazine in 1917, these three cantos were significantly changed for their first appearance in a book. This book, *A Draft of XVI Cantos,* appeared in 1925. Ten other installments followed, ending with *Drafts and Fragments of Cantos CX-CXVII* in 1968 (a publication that was prompted by an illegal "bootleg" edition of the same poems). Pound never lived to complete the entire 120-poem cycle that he envisioned, but as it stands today the complete *Cantos* includes 116 complete cantos and fragments of the remaining four.

A Draft of XVI Cantos

The first installment of cantos appeared just as Pound was leaving Paris. Published in a small, limited, expensive edition with medieval-looking illuminated capitals, the book was self-consciously aimed at an exclusive public. In these first sixteen poems, Pound introduces the themes that he intends to pursue throughout his long "poem containing history."

The first canto, certainly one of the finest, is both a retelling of the story of Book 11 of Homer's *Odyssey* and a modeling of the "palimpsestic" mode of the construction of poetry that Pound uses throughout *The Cantos*. A palimpsest is an ancient piece of paper or parchment that has been written on a number of times at different points in history. On a palimpsest, the traces of the earlier writing are incompletely erased and are visible. Pound was fascinated by this idea. In this first canto, Pound uses a number of "texts." Obviously, Homer is the most important—it is his book that is the source text—but we learn at the end of the canto that Pound has found his text of Homer in a Latin translation from 1538. Pound's own translation (of a translation) sounds less like Latin or Greek or contemporary English than it sounds like his earlier translation of the Anglo-Saxon poem "The Seafarer." So here we have an Anglo-Saxon sounding version of a Latin version of a Greek poem that Pound found in a book on the banks of the Seine in Paris.

Much of the rest of this installment continues in this vein. From Homer we go immediately to the Provencal troubadours' stories as retold by the Victorian English poet Robert Browning, to China, and back to Homer. The third canto takes us to Pound's own life, recently arrived in Venice and sitting "on the Dogana's steps." Canto IV reels around the Mediterranean as it goes from the smoking stones of destroyed Troy to the ruins of a Roman arena in Verona, Italy. These cantos, through number seven, introduce Pound's themes: history, the persistence of the image, the senselessness of violence and destruction, the beauty of human accomplishments.

In Cantos VIII through XI, Pound tells his version of the story of the Renaissance Italian condottiere Sigismondo Malatesta, the lord of Rimini who fought as a mercenary and was condemned by the Pope to burn in hell. Pound's attraction to Malatesta was complicated, but he was particularly struck by how Malatesta used his power not to amass more power or money but to create a court of artistic and intellectual accomplishment—the "Tempio Malatestiano," a church in Rimini that is more dedicated to Malatesta and his wife, Isotta, than to God or a saint, remained one of Pound's favorite artistic accomplishments.

Canto 13 introduces the Chinese and Confucian theme that will dominate much of the Cantos, and in its quiet beauty could not contrast more with the cantos that follow it, the so-called "Hell Cantos." In these cantos, Pound's predecessor becomes Dante (it has already been Homer, Browning, and Confucius), but Pound's hell is not a place of unholiness but of money-worship and the befoulment of art and artists. This first installment ends, in Canto 16, with hell brought forward to the twentieth century.

A Draft of the Cantos 17–27

The second installment of cantos appeared in 1928, published by another small press (John Rodker's). Instead of beginning with Homer, in these poems Pound begins with a vision from Ovid and a glimpse, following the horrific Hell Cantos that ended the previous installment of his "paradiso

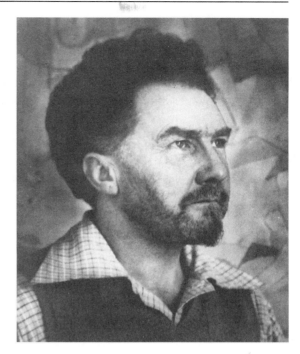

Ezra Pound

terrestre," his earthly paradise. In these cantos, Pound begins in earnest to examine the history of banking and finance, concentrating on the Florentine state and on the industrialization of America, and especially focuses on the links between banking and war.

A Draft of XXX Cantos

A limited edition of this book appeared from the Hours Press in Paris in 1930, but in 1933 the American trade publisher Farrar & Rinehart published Pound's cantos for the first time in the United States (and T. S. Eliot's company, Faber & Faber, published the book in a trade edition in Britain at this time). This book reprinted the poems of the first two installments and added three cantos, ending with the short Canto 30. In this final canto, Pound brings us back to the Greek world where we started, but moves in and out of the Italian Renaissance (mentioning Cesare Borgia and the Malatesta). The book ends with the death of Pope Alessandro Borgia, who represents both the intrigue and the culture of the Renaissance.

Eleven New Cantos

Soon after Pound's *A Draft of XXX Cantos* appeared in the U. S. and Britain, Pound published the next eleven cantos with the same publishers. This 1934 volume reflects Pound's increasing concern with economics and his growing fascination with and admiration for Mussolini. Canto 31 is based on the correspondence between Thomas Jefferson and John Adams. In fact, much of this volume consists of Pound's version of early American history and the Bank of the United States controversy, always with an eye to the Italian Renaissance and as a prefiguration of the twentieth century. One of the most important cantos of the whole collection, however, is Cantos 36, Pound's translation of the troubadour Guido Cavalcanti's poem "Donna mi prega." Here, Pound's enduring love of the Provencal language and the troubadour period finds its greatest expression.

The Fifth Decade of Cantos

Still consumed by economic history, Pound published his next installment of cantos in 1937. The book moves from the Monte dei Paschi di Siena, a Renaissance bank that Pound greatly admired, to a medieval-sounding litany about "usura," to more representations of Greek myths. By this point in his long poem, Pound was being asked about how the work as a whole was structured, and responded that it was much like a "fugue: theme, response, contrasujet." Readers and critics have continued to look for the underlying structural principles in the work, and generally have concluded that it is structured much like the musical form to which Pound alludes.

Cantos LII-LXXI

Appearing in 1940, just as the war in Europe was beginning, these cantos received little notice and are generally considered the weakest installment. The first ten recount millenia of Chinese history, then Pound switches focus when he reaches 1776 and returns to America for the final ten poems.

The Pisan Cantos

These cantos were written largely while Pound was held in the U. S. Army's Detention Training Center in Pisa, Italy, and are generally considered to be the most successful of the individual collections. Amid much controversy, the book won the first Bollingen Prize for Poetry from the Library of Congress, just when Pound was being held in an asylum for the criminally insane. (The book starts at Canto 74, omitting 72 and 73, Fascist-themed Italian language cantos that Pound's publisher has now included in the complete edition of the poem.) Pound's study of philosophy appears in this book, for he was preparing to take his poem on an ascent into paradise, just as Dante did. However, these flights are accompanied by the most personal of details: reminiscences of Pound's days in London, impressions of Fascist Italy, mentions of Pound's fellow prisoners in the DTC. The book manages, better than any of the previous installments, to express Pound's ideas of the "Periplum," the wholeness of a man's life as contextualized in history, art, and politics.

Section: Rock-Drill and Thrones

Pound wrote little in his first years in St. Elizabeths hospital, but near the end of his time there he returned to the cantos. In these two volumes—one published in 1955 and the second in 1958—Pound's focus is on his method: how does one read these difficult poems? His ideal reader would have to be not just incredibly well-educated, but well-versed in a number of extremely obscure texts and ideas, not to mention competent in five or six languages. These two installments ask the reader not as much to understand as to join in Pound's "imaginative habits and the energy of his mind," in the words of Northrop Frye. Readers can enjoy the beauty of many of the images and of the command of the poetic line that always was one of Pound's greatest strengths even if one cannot understand the subject matter.

Drafts and Fragments of Cantos CX-CXVII

This book, appearing in 1968 as a response to a "bootleg" publication of the same poems, collects a few finished and a few unfinished cantos. In these poems, the tone has shifted drastically from the previous two installments. The tone of erudite confidence and the sense of haranguing are gone; instead, we return to the contemplative, sad, meditative tone that characterized much of *The Pisan Cantos*. In the eleven years between the publication of *Thrones* and this volume, Pound fell into a depression and silence. He began to regret much of what he had done and said during his life, writing "Let those I love try to forgive / what I have made." But these are the most beautiful of the Cantos: his light touch with Greek myth and with a striking image of man-made beauty illuminated by the natural light is never more notable.

CHARACTERS

John Adams

John Adams (1735–1826) was the second president of the United States. His correspondence with Jefferson forms the basis for many of the middle cantos.

The Boss, Muss

See Benito Mussolini

Confucius

See Kung Fu-tse

Isotta degli Atti

Isotta degli Atti (1430?–1470) was Sigismondo Malatesta's mistress and, later, his third wife. His love for her is demonstrated all over the Tempio Malatestiano by the intertwined initials S and I.

Kung Fu-tse

Confucius (551–479 B.C.) is the moral anchor of *The Cantos*. Pound compares the moral precepts of the West, especially those of Aristotle, against Confucian ideals and finds the West's lacking. Perhaps the most important dictum of Confucius for Pound's poem is his insistence on exact terminology; Pound feared and hated the inexact use of language, and *The Pisan Cantos* are suffused with Pound's regretful sense that he violated this precept in his wartime broadcasts.

Ixotta

See Isotta degli Atti

Thomas Jefferson

The third president of the United States, Jefferson (1743–1826) was a proponent of agrarian democracy and opposed centralized banking systems.

Sigismondo Malatesta

Sigismondo Pandolfo Malatesta (1417–1468) was the lord of the Italian city of Rimini and a famous "condottiere," or Renaissance courtier. By the time he was 13, Malatesta was fighting in the field, leading his troops against Papal armies—and winning. These experiences were the prelude to a violent life in which Malatesta struggled against the Popes Pius II and Paul II. Malatesta held his own, and at the same time built a court in Rimini. This court, for Pound, was an example of enlightened governance, bringing the artists Agostino di Duccio

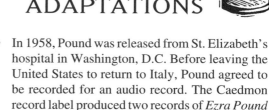

MEDIA ADAPTATIONS

- In 1958, Pound was released from St. Elizabeth's hospital in Washington, D.C. Before leaving the United States to return to Italy, Pound agreed to be recorded for an audio record. The Caedmon record label produced two records of *Ezra Pound Reading His Poetry*, both of which have extensive selections from *The Cantos*.

and Piero della Francesca to Rimini to help in the decoration of the church of San Francesco, also known as the Tempio Malatestiano.

Benito Mussolini

The Fascist party leader and Italian dictator Benito Mussolini (1883–1945) was Pound's contemporary and one of his idols. Pound met with him once, in 1933, having sent "il Duce" an economic program, and felt that he could sense Mussolini's intelligence in their brief encounter. He retells this story in Canto 41. Mussolini returns in Canto 74, the first of the Pisan series, when we see him and his mistress Clara hung "by the heels at Milano." After the Italian fascist state fell, the Nazis took Mussolini to the northern Italian city of Salo and set up a puppet government there. As the Allied forces penetrated northward, the Italian partisáns captured Mussolini, executed him, and displayed his body in the main square of Milan.

Siggy

See Sigismondo Malatesta

THEMES

The Cantos is one of the most difficult and erudite of the epic poems. Attempting to rewrite Dante's journey from hell to paradise, Pound chooses the form of a fugue in which to write his poem. The work is suffused with history, myth, crosscultural allusions,

TOPICS FOR FURTHER STUDY

- In many of the middle cantos, Pound focuses on the correspondence between Thomas Jefferson and John Adams. He is also interested in the establishment of the first and second Banks of the United States, and on how these two early presidents clashed with Alexander Hamilton on economic policy. What was the purpose of the Bank of the U.S.? What were Jefferson's and Adams' opinions of it? What is Pound's opinion?

- Beginning in Canto 13, Pound examines the thought of the ancient Chinese philosopher Kung Fu-tse, or Confucius. What are some important Confucian ideas? How has Confucianism influenced Chinese society over the centuries? What is the current Chinese government's attitude toward Confucian thought?

- Ezra Pound greatly admired the Italian dictator, Benito Mussolini, and Mussolini makes appearances in *The Cantos*. What was Mussolini's government like? How did he rise to power? What relationship was there between Fascist Italy and Nazi Germany in the 1930s and 1940s?

- An important cultural moment for Pound, one that informed the conception of *The Cantos*, is the Provencal or troubadour culture. Where did these people live? What language did they speak? How was their society organized? What does the word ''troubadour'' mean?

striking images, pedantry, and a deep love for humanity. However, the poem also expresses many opinions that are almost medieval in their ignorance and hatefulness. Pound's poem makes us confront questions of whether truly great art can express abhorrent viewpoints.

The Palimpsest

A palimpsest, most simply, is a piece of paper or parchment that has been written on a number of times and on which the earlier writing has been only partially effaced. But the term also designates a building that incorporates an earlier building, especially one from a previous historical period. The image of the palimpsest is both a structural principle for *The Cantos* and one of its most important themes. Pound began his adult life as a scholar of Provencal, the Latinate language spoken in southern France, and in his early years in Europe he traveled extensively in the Provence region. In that part of France, as in much of Europe, cultures are laid on top of each other both metaphorically and literally. Roman architecture and literature were important influences for the Provencals, and the

Romans, of course, appropriated Greek themes and religion. Pound loved Provence and Provencal troubadour literature, but he traced its influence forward, to Dante and from there to the Italian Renaissance and to modern times.

Pound strongly believed in the idea, most pithily stated by the American novelist William Faulkner, that the past is not gone—it is not even past. Throughout *The Cantos* Pound argues how the past underlies our present beliefs and practices. He felt, for instance, that one could not understand modern war and finance without carefully studying the foundations of modern banking in Florence and Siena. His obsession with the idea of the image or the "luminous detail" found a correlative in his study of the Chinese ideogram, in which he felt that the very ideas at the base of language itself were expressed in pictorial and verbal form. In an early poem, "The Return," he writes of the ancient gods of the classical world waking up in modern times and returning to active life. They are not dead, he felt; they are just dormant, but their influence lives. Perhaps the most striking palimpsest in the poem is the first canto, in which Pound translates into Anglo-Saxon sounding English a Latin translation of a Greek text that he found at a Paris bookstall.

Beauty

Although Pound is often faulted for how his *Cantos* so often consist of transcribed historical documents and are thus barely artistic, much of the poem is concerned with the search for beauty. Pound was not a nature poet and did not find beauty to reside solely in nature, as did the early Romantics. For Pound, the collaboration of human creation and natural forces—especially light—create the greatest beauty. He is fascinated with the strong sunlight of the Mediterranean as it illuminates the ruins of ancient cultures, and he imagines those cultures when they were young. Human striving is not vain, for Pound. He admires strong historical figures who seek to create both beauty and justice. Unfortunately, Pound often set forth as models historical personages whom we have come to understand were cruel people—Benito Mussolini, most notably, but also Sigismondo Malatesta, Pope Alessandro Borgia, and others. But he also admires Confucius, Dante, Guido Cavalcanti, John Adams, and like men who wanted to create cultures in which art and governance worked together, not in opposition.

But the strongest parts of Pound's poem are his descriptions of beauty. In haunting lines, Pound describes images that strike us as beautiful but that, for the poet, also exemplify good governance and healthy culture. Such passages as "Seal sports in the spray-whited circles of cliff-wash," "Gods float in the azure air, / Bright gods and Tuscan, back before dew was shed," or "Thus the light rains, thus pours, *e lo soleills plovil* / The liquid and rushing crystal / beneath the knees of the gods" from the first installment of cantos remain in the memory. In later installments, the same kinds of images return: "To build the city of Dioce whose terraces are the color of stars," he says in canto 74, and in one of the final cantos he concludes with the memorable line "A little light, like a rushlight / to lead back to splendour."

Time and History

Time is a constant theme in *The Cantos*, and history is the poems' most important element. As he conceived of his epic, Pound described it as "a poem containing history" and as "the tale of the tribe." Pound mixes together diverse times constantly, often in adjacent lines. Almost all of the cantos jump wildly around in time. Rather than using chronology to construct his poem, Pound structures his poem with ideas and images, and he can move easily through history and geography, connecting ancient China to the nascent American republic, for instance. His ideas of time are related to Faulkner's, for both men feel that the past is not, in fact, past. But where Faulkner examines one small area of the United States and focuses on how the past is never dead in or for that area's inhabitants, Pound follows concepts and relations, comparing them in vastly different periods.

STYLE

The construction of *The Cantos* is extremely complex. It is an epic, so it involves a journey, but unlike the *Odyssey* or the *Aeneid* the journey is not through space but through history. Pound initially thought of his poem in terms of Dante's medieval epic the *Divine Comedy*, in which the poet journeys from earth to the depths of hell, then ascends through purgatory to the heights of Heaven. But Pound's poem does not do this in any linear fashion. The first canto presents, in Pound's translation of a translation, Odysseus' preparations to journey into the underworld, and in these early cantos, Sigismondo Malatesta braves terrestrial and spiritual hells. The first section of cantos ends with the famous "Hell Cantos," which present images as horrific as anything since Dante.

But after the first sixteen cantos, the Dantean structure fades. Pound provides the reader the occasional glimpse of what he called his "pdiso terrestre," the earthly paradise, especially in his descriptions of light glinting off artworks such as the mosaic over the doorway in the church at Torcello, Italy, but for the most part the bulk of the cantos are concerned with what might be "purgatorio," or the world of history. Entire cantos are enumerations of Chinese rulers or of the correspondence between Thomas Jefferson and John Adams. Only in the last few cantos does Pound begin to concern himself fully with what is in his paradise, and over the fifty years he spent writing the poem he seems to have come to the conclusion that paradise is both fleeting and the most simple of things: "Do not move / let the wind speak / that is paradise," he says in a fragment for one of the final cantos.

Perhaps the best description of the structure of the poem is Pound's. At times, he told friends that he had built the poem to mirror the construction of the musical fugue, a form that consists of the announcement of a theme in one voice, the echoing of that theme from other voices, and the contrapuntal development of that theme. Pound diagrammed this in 1927 as "A. A. Live man goes down into world of Dead. C. B. The 'repeat in history.' B.C. The 'magic moment' or moment of metamorphosis, bust through from quotidian into 'divine or permanent world.'" He wrote in 1944 that his epic "begins 'In the Dark Forest' crosses the Purgatory of human error and ends in the light."

On a lower level, the individual cantos are structured not as coherent narratives but as details linked together imagistically. Canto 3, for instance, begins in Venice, where Pound "sat on the Dogana's steps / For the gondolas cost too much, that year." He muses on the appearance of Venice in 1908, talking about such specifics as the Buccentoro rowing club and the citizens "howling 'Stretti,'" a line from a popular song, but quickly moves to the baths at Baden, Switzerland, and from there to Burgos, Spain. These details are linked by images and concepts: the air and colors of Venice make Pound think of Tuscany, which makes him think of the ancient gods and nymphs. From that fleshy, earthly image he jumps to a Roman text about the baths where young women bathe nude. For Pound, the image was the basis of all poetry, and communicated not just a picture in the mind but "presents an intellectual and emotional complex in an instant of time," in his words of 1912.

HISTORICAL CONTEXT

Pound wrote his *The Cantos* over a long period of time—the first canto was published in 1917 and the final installment to be published during Pound's lifetime appeared in 1968. Needless to say, these years were turbulent; they constitute the majority of the last century. But Pound's poem is especially steeped in history: his own description of the poem as he formulated it was "a poem containing history." History, therefore, both formed the raw material for the poem and impinged upon its construction and creation.

When Pound first thought of writing his "tale of the tribe," he was living in London and had gained a great deal of fame as a literary impresario and provocateur. From the time that he arrived in London—1909—he had set himself the task of wresting art and literature from the nineteenth century into the twentieth. To achieve this end, he did everything: he served as a foreign editor for American publications, he "discovered" such writers as T. S. Eliot, he edited anthologies, he promoted operas, he gave money and materials to sculptors, he harangued and wrote and dashed about the city, an unforgettable figure in his pointy beard and cape.

But by 1920, Pound had tired of London. WWI had taken its toll on the writers and artists he sponsored, and London's openness to artistic experimentation was waning. Pound wrote his well-known *"Hugh Selwyn Mulberry"* poem cycle in 1920 and moved to Paris. He only stayed there a few years, though, feeling that Italy was a better place for him to be to work on *The Cantos*, the poem that now consumed his energies. In the 1920s, as Pound finished the first thirty cantos, he grew increasingly interested in European and American history and economics, subjects that supplemented his already extensive knowledge of Chinese and Provencal history and art and of classical civilization. *The Cantos* began to be Pound's "tale of the tribe," the "tribe" being intelligent, artistic, culturally-minded people. In his historical research, Pound came across a number of men who brought together what he saw as political justice, economic wisdom, and an artistic temperament and *The Cantos* quickly became a tale of how those men—Jefferson and Adams, Confucius, Malatesta—had to fight against the venality and stupidity of their contemporaries.

Unfortunately for Pound, though, he felt that his time's answer to these "factive personalities" was the Italian fascist dictator Benito Mussolini. Through the late 1920s and the 1930s, Pound began to write more and more on economics and argued that Mussolini's programs epitomized the kind of humane system that Pound hoped to see succeed in the world. In Cantos 42 through 71, Pound wrote extensively on Chinese and American history, but Mussolini's name and ideas come up more and more often. Even more disturbing is a growing anti-Semitism in the poems. Consumed by a hatred of banks and always possessed of an affection for medieval times, Pound concluded that powerful Jews were behind the world banking system. Exacerbating Pound's fascist and anti-Semitic sympathies were his very real mental problems—by the late 1930s Pound was showing clear signs of paranoia.

COMPARE
&
CONTRAST

- **1920s:** The United States, fresh from its success in World War I, enjoys the "Roaring Twenties," a period of economic expansion and artistic experimentation. Many prominent American artists and writers, though, are living in Paris, fleeing what they see as American bourgeois provincialism.

  1990s: The United States enjoys an unprecedented period of economic expansion and the creation of wealth. During these years, however, many experimental artists find themselves in conflict with conservative American values. Such artists as Robert Mapplethorpe, Karen Finley, Andres Serrano, and Chris Ofili see their esoteric, avant-garde work become the subject of impassioned public debate because of its perceived immorality or blasphemy.

- **1930s:** Europe sees the rise of fascist, military-dominated states such as Spain, Italy, and Germany. America remains "isolationist," tending to its own affairs, while Americans in Europe warn of an impending conflict.

  2000: After the fall of the Soviet empire, the former Eastern Bloc states create their own destinies. Some, like the Czech Republic and Poland, are stable and improve their citizens' economic lives. Others, such as Yugoslavia, break apart. In 1999, the United States gets involved in an ethnic conflict in the former Yugoslavia, bombing targets in Serbia in an effort to convince the Serbian leader to end his war on the people of Kosovo.

- **1940s:** World War II, the greatest and most destructive conflict the world has ever seen, kills millions. Europe, Japan, and much of the South Pacific and Southeast Asia are devastated. In response, the victorious powers help the defeated nations rebuild, but dictate the rebuilding of the political systems of their former foes.

  2000: The United States, NATO, and the UN keep their eyes on two nations: Iraq and Serbia. Each of these countries was recently defeated in military action by the United States and its allies, but neither fully capitulated, and the countries regard each other with wary hostility.

Pound returned to the United States briefly in 1939 and gave a few speeches, but managed only to convince his audiences that he was a crank or just mad. When war broke out in Europe, Pound was forced to remain in Italy, and for the duration of the war he lived there. To earn money, he made broadcasts on Italian state radio, broadcasts filled with anti-Semitism and venom directed at President Roosevelt. In 1943, Pound was indicted for treason in the United States, and as the war was ending he was captured by Italian partisans and turned over to the U.S. Army. He was kept in a cage in Pisa for a while before being returned to the U.S. to stand trial.

Upon his arrival in Washington, D. C., Pound was found mentally unfit for trial and sentenced to detention in a mental hospital. However, at this same time, a collection of the poems that he had written while held by the Army, *The Pisan Cantos*, appeared, and to many readers they were the best poems Pound had ever written. As ever, they were difficult and relied on an enormous body of crosscultural knowledge, but for the first time Pound shows weakness, doubt, and regret about his actions and beliefs. In these poems, he is as honest with himself as he had ever been. While in the hospital, he published one other set of cantos before his 1958 release.

When he was released, he returned to Italy to live out the rest of his life quietly. But Pound's epic engendered many difficult questions for American culture about the relative places of art and politics. Should a traitor be lauded by his nation for his poetic accomplishments, as Pound was when he won the Library of Congress' Bollingen Prize in

---

1949? Can a man with abhorrent beliefs write great poetry? Can that poetry be great when it expresses those beliefs? Pound's *The Cantos* continues to cause critics and general readers to examine their ideas about these complex issues.

CRITICAL OVERVIEW

Critical opinion on Pound's *The Cantos* is more divided than is the critical opinion on any other important modernist work, and the epic's critical fortunes have risen and fallen with time. Even during the half-century during which the work appeared in installments, readers and critics were widely divided on the poem's merits. As the critical literature on *The Cantos* is vast, here we will look only at how some of the most prominent writers and critics have felt about Pound's epic.

As the poem was being composed, even Pound's close friends and admirers were unsure about the structure of the poem—how it fit together and what it would look like as a whole. The Irish poet William Butler Yeats wrote in 1936 that "the relation of all the elements to one another, repeated or unrepeated, is to become apparent when the whole is finished. . . Like other readers I discover at present merely exquisite or grotesque fragments." Yeats felt that the poem had "more style than form; at moments more style, more deliberate nobility and the means to convey it than in any contemporary poet known to me, but it is constantly interrupted, broken, twisted into nothing by its direct opposite, nervous obsession, nightmare, stammering confusion."

T. S. Eliot echoed Yeats' criticisms, writing in 1946 that "*The Cantos* there is an increasing defect of communication, not apparent when he is concerned with Sigismondo Malatesta, or Chinese dynasties, but, for instance, whenever he mentions Martin Van Buren. Such passages are very opaque: they read as it the author was so irritated with his readers for not knowing all about anybody so important as Van Buren." Eliot praised Pound's influence in the highest terms, but was less enthusiastic about his most important poem.

In 1950, the prominent English critic F. R. Leavis responded to Eliot's opinions on Pound. Like Eliot and Yeats, Leavis felt that Pound did not use the historical sources well. "Pound's various

addictions,'' he wrote, "speak the amateur: one cannot doubt his enthusiasm, but something else, surely was needed to impel significant innovations in poetry." But where Eliot felt that Pound's importance as an influence was immeasurable, even if the meaning of his poem was opaque, Leavis felt that this "limited very drastically the kind of importance that can be attributed to *The Cantos*."

Pound's greatest defender among literary critics has been the Canadian Hugh Kenner, who wrote the first book-length study of Pound's work, *The Poetry of Ezra Pound*, in 1951, and who contributed the single greatest work of Pound scholarship, *The Pound Era*, twenty-one years later. In *The Poetry of Ezra Pound* Kenner forcefully answered Pound's critics. After the appearance of the Pisan section of cantos in 1948, he wrote, "it is no longer easy. . . to dismiss *The Cantos* as either formless or irrelevant. Pound impinges upon the citizen of A.D. 1950 or whenever, not via his psychological tensions. . . but through a rational amalgam of morals and politics." Kenner's book was the first to argue that the epic was in fact an epic with form; Kenner made it possible for a large group of scholars to write on Pound without having to defend the poet on charges of formlessness or sloppiness. For Kenner, "Pound's structural unit in *The Cantos* is not unlike the Joycean epiphany: a highly concentrated manifestation of a moral, cultural, or political quiddity [the essential quality of a thing, its 'suchness']."

Although *The Cantos* were constantly criticized for being formless—and Kenner's work only provided a means of defense, it did not dispel all of the objections to Pound's poem—few critics ever took issue with Pound's poetic strengths. Perhaps Pound's most important innovation was in his use of the line. Pound's close friend William Carlos Williams admired *The Cantos* primarily for Pound's command of the poetic line. "Pound's line is the movement of his thought. . .they have a character that is the parcel of the poem itself," he wrote. Eliot, Leavis, and others all praised this aspect of *The Cantos* and of Pound's work in general.

The Cantos, for all of its difficulty, was an important inspiration for a number of other poets who saw in Pound's long "poem containing history" a different model for the epic. John Berryman's *Dream Songs*, Louis Zukofsky's *A*, and Charles Olson's *Maximus Poems* all were deeply influenced by Pound's innovations. In the 1960s, more criticism was written on Pound than on almost any other

American poet, and many of the young poets of the period, ranging from the Buddhist poet Gary Snyder to the southern nature poet Charles Wright, saw Pound as their most important ancestor. In recent decades, with the decline of the "New Critical" method that studied poems in isolation from their context, Pound's poems have come under increasing criticism. Even as readers and critics discover Pound's innovations and inventions, they also have come to understand just how central Pound's disturbing political opinions have to do with the poem. This attention to Pound's biography and beliefs, coupled with *The Cantos'* inherent and undeniable difficulty, have made the poem almost disappear from college poetry surveys. But at the same time, this increasing attention to Pound's biography and beliefs is also "rehabilitating" him, showing that he was indeed a good friend to hundreds of artists of all kinds and that he was perhaps the central figure in literary modernism.

CRITICISM

Greg Barnhisel

In this essay, Barnhisel looks at the Cantos *in their historical context. He argues that the poem became the focal point for a debate in American culture whose ramifications went far beyond the poem, Pound, or even literature.*

Ezra Pound's *Cantos*, the masterpiece of one of modernism's central figures, is perhaps the least read of any of the great works of modernism. The poem is difficult, certainly. It asks the reader to come to it with a vast array of knowledge of languages, historical events, and mythologies. It is written imagistically, as a string of images and fragments strung together by a logic that is hard to decipher. It expresses opinions that are unfamiliar and foreign at times and at other times are disturbing and offensive. For these and other reasons, few college poetry courses bother to include more than a few excerpts from *The Cantos* and few readers outside of academia bother with the poem.

Yet many critics feel that the poem is the great epic of modernist poetry, and some feel that it, not James Joyce's *Ulysses*, is the greatest work of modernism. Pound was a central figure in the development of modernism, both in terms of facilitating

The influence of the Chinese teacher and philosopher Confucius is evident throughout the poem, especially in the segment beginning with Canto 42, where Pound gives a Confucian digest of the history of China.

the careers of other artists and writers and of developing the techniques that would become the hallmarks of modernism. Pound's lifelong dictum was "Make it New!" and the drive for innovation inspired most of his artistic endeavours. His early poems are some of the most familiar works of literary modernism and almost no course in American poetry omits such poems as "In a Station of the Metro," "Sestina: Altaforte," or "The River-Merchant's Wife."

But the issue of *The Cantos'* difficulty is really not the central one when we ask ourselves why the most important poem by one of the most important figures in modernism is rarely read. After all, T. S. Eliot's "The Waste Land" remains popular and is hardly easier than *The Cantos*. Today, students learn a little bit about Pound early; high school English classes often read "In a Station of the Metro" to illustrate metaphor, and freshman literature survey courses read a few of his poems in their modernist units. But if the reader wishes to venture any further into Pound's work, he or she is immedi-

WHAT DO I READ NEXT?

- Pound's earlier and shorter poetry is collected in the volume entitled *Personae*. Although none of the poems in this book were written after 1920, they give an important introduction to the methods that *The Cantos* use: the centrality of the image, free verse, and the speaking voice. In addition, many of the poems prefigure the themes that Pound addresses more expansively in *The Cantos*.

- In the *Literary Essays of Ezra Pound* and *Ezra Pound: Selected Prose 1909–1965*, the New Directions publishing house collected almost all of Pound's important writings on literary, political, and economic topics. (Pound was such a prolific writer that a collection of all of his writings would fill dozens of books.) The *Literary Essays* contain important statements that illuminate Pound's use of the image and his opinions of literary predecessors. *Selected Prose*, by contrast, includes many of Pound's most controversial statements on politics and economics.

- Pound got most of his ideas about the power of Chinese and Japanese poetry from the short book *The Chinese Written Character as a Medium for Poetry* by Ernest Fenollosa. This book deeply influenced the composition of *The Cantos*, even if many of Fenollosa's ideas have been shown to be wrong.

- If *The Cantos* were only a moderate success critically, a poem that Pound helped author was his greatest public success. T. S. Eliot's poem "The Waste Land" was a sprawling mass of observations when Eliot gave the poem to Pound to edit. Pound cut almost four-fifths of the poem and suggested a number of changes—most importantly, changing the name from "He Do The Police In Different Voices"—that should qualify him as Eliot's co-author.

- Stephen Kern's scholarly study *The Culture of Time and Space* is an excellent overview of the vast cultural, social, and technological changes that influenced modernist art. Many of the developments that Kern describes have been essentially forgotten, but his book lays out, in great detail, how the late nineteenth century was having its entire worldview altered by such massive ideas as Darwin's and such seemingly petty developments as the widespread use of pocket watches.

---

ately confronted by the "big issues" of Pound's life and beliefs. This is neither a conspiracy on the part of Pound-haters nor is it unjustified: in order to understand *The Cantos*, one must be conversant with the historical events, personages, and economic ideas that really are the central subject of the poem. But acquaintance with what Pound did in his life and what he thought, combined with the difficulty inherent in reading *The Cantos*, makes students reluctant to undertake the project.

The relationship of Pound's ideas to his poetry is a topic that has been central to public understanding of the poet since at least the late 1920s. Cultures have always tried to balance out the competing claims of aesthetic value and a "good message" in art. In the fifth century before Christ, Plato banished the poets from his imaginary "Republic" because art encouraged dissent and disreputable ideas. In the seventeenth century, John Milton tried to use art to rally English people against the abuses of royalty while at the same time the elites were creating aesthetically rarefied art for themselves. The essential question for all of these writers and thinkers was whether art can be viewed entirely aesthetically, or solely in terms of its artistic and creative attributes, or whether art always bears some traces of, comment on, and responsibility to the society that produced it.

Pound's *Cantos*, with its attacks on Roosevelt and Alexander Hamilton and their advocacy of

Italian fascism and anti-Semitism, was a problematic poem in this context. During the 1930s, while most readers had begun to just ignore Pound, many critics felt that the poem would indeed be a great work if Pound could ever come up with a coherent structure for it. But how could literary critics ignore the admiration of Mussolini? how could they dismiss as unimportant the poem's attacks on Jewish bankers? The answer lies in the profound changes that occurred among American cultural intellectuals between the 1930s and the 1950s.

After the Great Depression, in the 1930s Socialist and Communist movements met some success in the United States. On the East Coast and especially in New York City, many young intellectuals, most of whom were from Jewish immigrant families that had labored in poverty, gravitated to Communism. Communist groups published magazines and newspapers, including poems, fiction, and literary criticisms by these young intellectuals. But by the late 1930s, a small group of Jewish intellectuals from New York grew tired of the strict rules the Communist Party of the USA (CPUSA) had set regarding the art and literature that should be supported. Adhering to the Soviet line, the CPUSA advocated so-called "Socialist Realism," realistic art that exalted workers and their struggles.

This group of breakaway critics (who became known as the New York Intellectuals) disagreed. They sought out art that was more daring, more abstract and experimental. Forming their own journal, *Partisan Review*, the New York Intellectuals forged their own kind of cultural criticism: strongly left-wing, anti-Nazi but also anti-Soviet, seeking out new and avant-garde art as a way to undermine the bourgeois complacency of the United States. This group included Mary McCarthy, Delmore Schwartz, Philip Rahv, Irving Howe, Clement Greenberg, Lionel Trilling, and many others. They felt that art had a responsibility not just to society, as the Socialist Realism doctrine held, but also must seek aesthetic goals that have nothing to do with morals or ethics or societal aims. James Joyce, T. S. Eliot, James Baldwin, and the abstract expressionist painters were some of the artists favored by the New York Intellectuals. However, as most of this group was Jewish, they were very suspicious of Pound.

As the New York Intellectuals were going through their educations and growing more independent, another important group of critics was forming, this one in the South. The "Fugitive Group,"

> **"** The essential question for all of these writers and thinkers was whether art can be viewed entirely aesthetically, or solely in terms of its artistic and creative attributes, or whether art always bears some traces of, comment on, and responsibility to the society that produced it. **"**

named after their literary journal, consisted of Southern literary men who looked back to the Old South and saw in it culture, refinement, and an artistic sensibility. Although they initially linked their literary program strongly with the South, they quickly developed a more general methodology for studying literature of all kinds. By the 1940s, these writers (who included John Crowe Ransom, Cleanth Brooks, Robert Penn Warren, and R. P. Blackmur) were becoming known as the "New Critics." Their approach to literature centered on close reading: poems should be read not with an eye to the biography of the poet, not with attention to the political beliefs of the poet or of his time, but with the greatest emphasis placed on the inner workings of the poem. The New Critics sought out tension, ambiguity, irony within the poem, and paid extremely close attention to each individual word and all of its connotations. For them, the social value of literature—if any—was that it developed an aesthetic sensibility in readers, which would make them more sensitive and perceptive citizens.

Both the New Critics and the New York Intellectuals, therefore, believed that literature should not be judged primarily by the ideas it expresses. The form and structure of a poem, its sound, its imagery, and its innovations should be its most important attributes, and critics should pay attention to those aspects of a poem rather than to what lessons a poem teaches or what kind of man the poet is. In 1949, just as these groups were becoming the most prominent cultural intellectuals in America, they were called upon to defend these claims about how to judge art.

Ezra Pound was brought back to the United States soon after the war and was quickly put on trial. Knowing that he would be found guilty and most likely executed, his lawyer, Julian Cornell, sought to have Pound found mentally unfit to stand trial, and the judge agreed. Pound was incarcerated in St. Elizabeth's Hospital in Washington, D. C. The U.S. reading public was disgusted with Pound and, to make matters worse, had essentially stopped buying his books. Pound seemed destined to fade into irrelevance. But in 1948, Pound's collection *The Pisan Cantos* appeared. The book received largely positive reviews, and many readers who had dismissed Pound now began to feel again that he was a great poet. The following year, the book won the first Bollingen Prize, an award given by the Library of Congress to the year's best book of poetry.

Predictably, much of the public was outraged. How could a man be lauded by his country just three years after that country had sought to execute him for treason? The *Pisan Cantos* themselves were not innocent of those acts and beliefs for which Pound had earned such opprobrium: in the poems he laments the death of Mussolini and talks about his wartime radio broadcasts. In the *Saturday Review of Literature*, the most important mainstream book review magazine in the country, a poet named Robert Hillyer published two attacks that took as their targets Pound, T. S. Eliot, literary modernism, the Bollingen foundation, and the New Criticism. How could these people, Hillyer asked, reward art that held positions that were so inimical to the values for which America had just fought a terribly destructive war?

The Bollingen committee, which included T. S. Eliot and a number of New Critics, responded to Hillyer's objections in terms that would determine academic approaches to Pound's poetry for decades. In a communique, the committee cited the "objective perception of value," arguing that aesthetic and artistic value could be judged entirely separately from moral or social standards. Surprisingly, the New York Intellectuals agreed with the Bollingen committee. In a forum convened for *Partisan Review*, most of the contributors supported the Bollingen award. One notable exception was the poet Karl Shapiro, a member of the Bollingen

committee, who stated frankly that he voted against awarding the prize to Pound because "I am a Jew and I cannot honor anti-Semites."

This cultural moment was the coalescing of a strange and unpredictable alliance. The left-wing, cosmopolitan, nonacademic, largely Jewish New York Intellectual group came together with the right-wing, agrarian, academic, largely Southern New Critics to argue that art must be judged first and foremost on aesthetic standards. As a result of this endorsement, Pound's popularity, sales, and critical respect slowly but steadily grew over the next ten years and then grew dramatically during the 1960s. *The Cantos* had the endorsement of the leading critics of the day, and readers were given license to read the poems as strictly aesthetic artifacts.

Source: Greg Barnhisel, for *Epics for Students*, Gale, 2001.

Ezra Pound

This biographical entry of Ezra Pound in The Readers Companion to American History *describes Pound as a "catalyst for all serious artists" fighting to make their work new and describes how his work affected unknowable changes.*

Until age twenty-two Pound lived and attended schools in New York and Pennsylvania. In 1901 at the University of Pennsylvania he began a lifelong friendship with William Carlos Williams. He transferred to Hamilton where in 1905 he received a Ph.B.—a degree the school invented for him (and never offered before or since) to fit the assortment of courses he insisted on taking. He then returned to Penn. Money problems in 1907 forced him to take a job at Wabash College, Indiana, but after four months he was fired for being "a Latin Quarter type." The next year he went by cattle boat to Spain, crossed to Venice, stayed for three months, and then went to London where William Butler Yeats was and the action should be. There he became a catalyst for all serious artists who fought to realize their élan and "make it new": T. S. Eliot, James Joyce, Ford Madox Ford, Wyndham Lewis, and H. D., among others. In 1914 he married Dorothy Shakespear. She had a small income; he supported himself by writing.

His major works include, in poetry: *A lume spento* (1908), *Cathay* (1915), *Lustra* (1916), *Quia pauper amavi* (1919), and *The Cantos* (1917–1961);

Cantos 71–72, written in Italian, defend the fascist ideals of dictator Benito Mussolini.

in prose: *The Spirit of Romance* (1910), *Noh* (1916), *Instigations* (1920), *ABC of Reading* (1934), *Guide to Kulchur* (1938), and *The Classic Anthology Defined by Confucius* (1954). Concurrently, he translated volumes of poetry, prose, and drama from Greek, Latin, Provençal, Japanese, and Chinese. Tirelessly, he fought Western provincialism and celebrated the great art of China, Japan, and Africa.

From Rapallo, Italy, where he lived after 1924, he conducted a worldwide correspondence with all who sought his help. But he became increasingly controversial, partly because his critics didn't know what he meant by words such as *illumination*. That word, which he said he used "in a technical sense," is the key to his life and his work and marks him as a visionary and a mystic in the Neoplatonic-Blake-Whitman tradition.

Pound's major work, *The Cantos*, expresses this tradition, as did all his acts and opinions. According to Pound, *The Cantos* was a poem containing history and concerning humanity's progress out of tribal darkness toward the light of *paradiso terrestre* to come in the future. All mystics find that the major world religions manifest tribal darkness, which they express by war and dogma, and "dogma" is the "bluff" of "tax-gathering priests" based on "ignorance." Of Christ himself he said, "He is hardly to be blamed for the religion that has been foisted upon him." The coming of paradiso terrestre is deterred mainly by the love of money, for money is power and power corrupts. Thus avarice was a central theme of *The Cantos*, in which bankers and munition makers create wars. He became known as anti-Semitic though he wrote, "Inasmuch as the Jew has conducted no holy war for nearly two millennia, he is preferable to the Christian and the Muhammadan." His anti-Semitism was due not to his opinions on race or religion but to what Pound saw as the corrupting force of money and power.

In 1945 he was arrested for treason because of radio broadcasts he made from Italy in 1941. He spent six months at the Disciplinary Training Center in Pisa and was then flown to the United States. Being found unfit to stand trial, he was remanded to St. Elizabeth's where, before his release and return to Italy, he stayed for thirteen years. Being thus relieved of the need to make a living, he practiced his art and produced his greatest work. All his life, he had said the state should provide its artists with a "competence": money enough to exist on so they could create. Ironically, at St. Elizabeth's the state provided that competence. Even better, Congress founded the National Endowment for the Arts, which brought us a little closer to the light of paradise-on-earth when, as the final lines of *The Cantos* say, we will enter "arcanum" "To be men not destroyers."

Source: Carroll F. Terrell, "Ezra Pound," in *The Reader's Companion to American History*, edited by Eric Foner and John A. Garraty, Houghton Mifflin Company, 1991, pp. 857–8.

Hugh Kenner

Hugh Kenner relates Ezra Pound's connection with Homer and how this association both inspires and informs his Cantos.

No exertion spent upon any of the great classics of the world, and attended with any amount of real result, is really thrown away. It is better to write one word upon the rock, than a thousand on the water or the sand.
—W. E. Gladstone, Studies on Homer and the Homeric Age

Homer is the West's six trillion dollar man. For two millennia and a half at least we have kept him alive and vigorous with an increasingly complex and costly life-support system that from earliest times has drawn on all the technology around. To make papyrus in Egypt, then construct and navigate a ship to take it to Athens, entailed most of the chemistry, the metallurgy, the carpentry, and the mathematics accessible to Mediterranean men of the fifth century B.C. What Athenians did with papyrus was, of course, write out on it the two big books of Homer.

Parchment came later, and parchment Homers were precious spoil from Byzantium, 1453. Renaissance architects designed libraries that housed hand-made copies; blacksmiths forged chains to keep them where they belonged. As soon as there were printing presses in Italy, there was a folio Homer, two volumes, printed in Florence about 1480. The next need was for a Homer you could carry around. That meant both smaller sheets and smaller type. Pound's Canto 30 shows us Francesco da Bologna incising dies with the Greek letters they'd need for the pocket Aldine Homer. To aid comprehension scholars made Latin versions, their printings embellished by the newly designed Italic characters. Readers of Canto 1 will remember one such version of the *Odyssey*, Divus's, dated 1538. And all over Europe lens-grinders were enabling presbyopic and myopic eyes to scan Homer's lines.

Our own silicon technology stores Homer and retrieves him, catalogs his words and cross-references them, relying on magnetic disks, on air conditioners, on central processing units, on central generating stations, and also on toil and ingenuity in California and Japan, to keep alive an old poet whose very existence has been repeatedly questioned. We have no such continuous record of commitment to any other part of our heritage save the Bible. The six trillion dollars I hazarded was rhetorical; what eighty generations have invested in Homer, directly and indirectly, eludes computation and nearly defies comprehension.

For we've not even settled what the Homeric poems *are*; something more than Bronze-Age entertainments, surely? Our efforts to assure ourselves that we know what we're valuing have constituted much of the history of our thought. At one time the *Iliad* and *Odyssey* were esteemed as a comprehensive curriculum in grammar, rhetoric, history, geography, navigation, strategy, even medicine. But by the mid-nineteenth century A.D. they no longer

Pound discusses the monopolies on credit and interest rates perpetuated by banks at the time he was writing The Cantos. *In this 1931 scene, the president of the Federal American Bank in Washington, D. C., addresses a crowd of depositors angry over the bank's restrictive practices.*

seemed to contain real information of any kind at all. Had there ever been a Trojan War? Scholars inclined to think not, much as connoisseurs of the West's other main book were doubting that there had been a Garden of Eden with an apple tree, or that planks of an Ark might have rotted atop Mount Ararat. Both books got rescued by identical stratagems; the Bible was turned into Literature, and so was Homer. That entailed redefining Literature, as something that is good for us, however

unfactual. That in turn meant Nobility, and also Style. It also required that Longinus supplant Aristotle as the prince of ancient critics, and that Matthew Arnold become the Longinus of Christian England. He said that Homer was rapid and plain and noble: by Longinian standards, Sublime. Those were the qualities a translator should reach for, in part to sweep us past mere awkward nonfact. The Bible in the same way was edifying if you knew how to go about not believing it.

"Pound yielded to no one in his respect for fact, but for him the 'fact' was apt to be whatever he could find right there on the page. . ."

In 1861, while British ink was drying on printed copies of Arnold's three lectures on translating Homer, Heinrich Schliemann was nourishing a dream. He had dreamed it since boyhood. He was going to find Troy! By 1870 he had found it, yes he had, at a place the maps called Hissarlik, found traces, too, of the great burning, and he photographed his wife Sophie wearing what he thought were Helen's jewels. (A photograph, no light undertaking in 1870, was merely the most recent of the technologies mankind's Homeric enterprise keeps conscripting.)

The story, as so often, now slips out of synch. Andrew Lang, the folklorist, published with one collaborator an English *Odyssey* in 1879, with two others an English *Iliad* in 1883. These, for various reasons not excluding the fine print of copyright law, remained the standard English versions as late as the mid twentieth century—even the Modern Library used to offer them—and they were already obsolete when they appeared. For Lang and Butcher, Lang, and Leaf and Myers had fetched their working principle from pre-Schliemann times. The way to translate Homer, they thought, was to make him sound like the King James Bible, the idiom of which has great power to ward off questions about what details mean. But what details mean—in particular what many nouns meant—was being settled year by year as men with spades ransacked Troy and Mycenae for such cups and golden safety pins as Helen and Hector knew.

Ezra Pound was born in 1885, just two years after the Butcher and Lang *Odyssey*. One unforgotten day when he was twelve or so, enrolled at the Cheltenham Military Academy in Pennsylvania, a teacher chanted some Homer for his special benefit. After four dozen years, from amid the wreckage of Europe, the man's name merited preserving:

and it was old Spencer (H.) who first declaimed
      me the Odyssey

with a head built like Bill Shepard's
on the quais of what Siracusa?
or what tennis court
near what pine trees?
(C 512)

It was from "Bill Shepard" at Hamilton that he'd picked up his first Provençal enthusiasm, so the heads of these two instigators made a fit rhyme. And hearing Homer declaimed, he testified, was "worth more than grammar." Though all his life a great connoisseur of detail, he was never easy with schoolmasters' grammar. It screened out what he thought crucial, the tang of voices.

That would have been about 1897, when it was just beginning to look as though the wanderings of Odysseus, too, might mirror an order of factuality analogous to that of the new historic Troy. In 1902 Schliemann's architectural adviser, Wilhelm Dörpfeld, explained the topography of Ithaka; in the same year, Victor Berard published the book Joyce was to use so copiously, about the origins of the *Odyssey* in Phoenician *periploi*, a noun Pound was to gloss:

periplum, not as land looks on a map
but as sea bord seen by men sailing.
(C 324)

Those are arguably the most important lines in the *Cantos*. It is characteristic of the poem's way of working that we find then embedded in a narrative about seventeenth-century China. And the word on which they turn came from the edges of the new Homeric scholarship.

The *periplous* (a Greek noun Pound transmuted into an unrecorded Latin form, *periplum*) registers the lay of the land the way it looks now, from here.

Olive grey in the near,
far, smoke grey of the rock-slide,
… … … …
The tower like a one-eyed great goose
cranes up out of the olive-grove.
(C 10)

That is an Imagist detail, also "sea bord seen by men sailing": a detail from some imagined *periplous*. If you were sailing in the track of that skipper you might not find the color useful—light shifts day by day—but "the tower like a one-eyed great goose" would help you be sure of your position: such an apparition is not easy to mistake for some other tower. Likewise the Homer we encounter in the first canto is not to be taken for Pope's or Lattimore's. Homer mutates down the centuries; we can only begin to savor the mutations when translators begin to record what they can of them.

And translators only began their notes on the *periplous* past Homeric capes and shoals when they had Homer's text to translate, some time after Byzantine scholars had carried the precious manuscripts to Italy. The first canto reminds us just what Andreas Divus did: he mapped the words in blind fidelity. The canto's resonant "And then went down to the ship" follows Divus's "Ad postquam ad navem descendimus," which in turn follows Homer's "Autar epei hr' epi nea katelhomen": *Autar*, and; *epei*, then; *epinea*, to the ship; *katelthomen*, we went down. In placing "descendimus" where he did, Divus even kept the order of Homer's words, putting the Greek into Latin, as he says, *ad verbum*, the way one inflected language can map another. With his page-by-page, line-by-line, often word-by-word fidelity, Divus was making a crib a student in the sixteenth century could lay open beside the Aldine Greek, to get guidance you and I might seek in a dictionary. When Ezra Pound thought his Latin "even singable," he was suggesting what much later he would suggest of a fiddle rendition of Clement Janequin's *Canzone degli ucelli*, that sheer note-by-note fidelity had kept the song audible.

Can sheer blind fidelity be faithful to so much? We have come to something fundamental. A while ago we were talking of fact, the order of Homeric fact archaeologists were producing, to supplant the circumlocutions of the lexicons. Pound yielded to no one in his respect for fact, but for him the "fact" was apt to be whatever he could find right there on the page: whatever Dante might have meant by "the literal sense": mere letters, queer sounds, or even just lexicon entries. Letters, sounds, tagmemes: from the 1930s till he died he would love the Chinese character out of conviction that alone among the scripts of civilized men it collapsed all of these, shape, sound, and referent, into a sole inscrutable polysemous sign. The Chinese ideogram for "man" is a picture of a man; the Chinese spoken word for "cat" is what all cats say, "mao." If you say that "with a Greek inflection," you are saying the Greek for a catly thing, "I am eager." That's a detail we find in Canto 98 (C 686); in the late cantos especially we see words *exhibited*: isolated words, including a few of Homer's words, set off on the page by white space. Such words, though no taller than a printed line, are aspiring to the status of the ideogram. They are centers of radiance. We may think of them as opportunisms, like Shakespeare's when he rhymed "dust" with "must," mortality with necessity.

Such opportunisms irradiate the "Seafarer" of 1911. "Blaed is genaeged" says, word by word,

"glory is humbled." Pound looked at "blaed," saw a sword-blade, and wrote "The blade is laid low." There's no arguing with that, and no justifying either. Nor can we argue when, in Canto 1, by a triumph of the literal, English words map Divus' words which map Homer's words and the whole goes to "Seafarer" cadences. He is following Divus because for one thing, he wants to celebrate the occasion when, thanks partly to Aldus and Divus, Homer was recovered for the West; for another because he was himself a man of the Renaissance in having been well-taught his Latin and ill-taught his Greek. Latin, even Latin verse, Pound could read at sight. Greek, even Homer's, he'd pick at, with a crib. Divus might have labored with Ezra Pound in mind. No one in four hundred years has owed him so much.

Now though Divus intended a drudgelike fidelity, still he, too, invented a Homer: whether by sheer human exuberance, or by inadvertence, or via textual error we can't always say. Now and then his Homer is not the Greek scholars' Homer. For listen:

> And then went down to the ship,
> Set keel to breakers, forth on the godly sea and
> We set up mast and sail on that swart ship....
> (C 3)

"On the godly sea?" Yes, it's alive with gods. But any modern crib, for instance, the Loeb, says, "on the *bright* sea," and for the good reason that the Greek word is "dian," a form of "dios," one of Homer's favorite epithets, especially for the sea you push a ship into. "Eis hala dian," reads *Odyssey* 11.2: "into the bright sea." It's a formulaic phrase at the *Odyssey*'s numerous launchings.

But what does Divus have? He has "in mare divum," as if he were distracting us by a play on his own name. *Divus,* says the Latin lexicon, "of or belonging to a divinity; divine." A contracted neuter form would be *dium,* perhaps close enough to *dian* to have caused confusion in a shaky time for classical understanding. How did someone, in those days before lexicons, collect equivalences between Greek and Latin words? About Divus we seem to know nothing save that he may have come from East Asia Minor, a better place for Greek than for Latin. But however *divum* arrived on Divus's page, Ezra Pound followed him faithfully, and wrote "the godly sea":

> periplum, not as land looks on a map
> but as sea bord seen by men sailing

—here, as seen by a man who sailed four centuries ago, and whose compass was not wholly reliable. It is an interesting rule, that in the presence of a textual crux Ezra Pound is apt to be utterly literal. Those are just the places where credentialled scholars guess. But Pound would only guess when the text was foolproof. When he didn't understand the words, or when they diverged from convention, then he'd presuppose someone else who'd known better than he; as Divus had, in prompting him to write "godly."

"Of Homer," Pound wrote as long ago as 1918, "two qualities remain untranslated: the magnificent onomatopoeia, as of the rush of the waves on the sea-beach and their recession in

para thina poluphloisboio thalasses

untranslated and untranslatable; and, secondly, the authentic cadence of speech; the absolute conviction that the words used, let us say by Achilles to the 'dog-faced' chicken-hearted Agamemnon, are in the actual swing of words spoken." When men speak, not by the book but as they are moved to, uncounterfeitable rhythm asserts itself—"the actual swing." It eludes the dictionary, eludes mappings of "meaning": the translator has to leap for it, with his own time's live speech in his ears. Only if he makes that leap has he a chance of making us hear.

Hughes Salel, 1545, called Odysseus "ce ruse personage": that is one French way to look at *polytropos*, the *Odyssey*'s first epithet, and from our own century we might use "that tricky bastard" as a sightline on Salel. (Yes, "bastard" is extreme, but it's part of an idiom.) Andreas Divus, 1538, has "multiscium," much-knowing, as it were "savvy." Thereafter the reality fades, and the renderings decline. Butcher and Lang, 1879, offer "so ready at need," like a detail from a hymn. A. T. Murray in the 1919 Loeb tries "man of many devices," and Liddell and Scott in their lexicon make a stereophonic mumble, "of many counsels *or* expedients." "That man skilled in all ways of contending," says the often admirable Robert Fitzgerald, here smothering perception with poetic dignity. Nobody speaks phrases like those.

You cannot cut such a knot with a trick of idiom, not even one as stolidly idiomatic as W. H. D. Rouse's "never at a loss." The problem goes far too deep. It has been hard for many centuries to imagine what Odysseus was really being commended for. We have all inherited the Roman distrust for quick Greek intelligence—we associate it with huckstering—and translators, being men of literary cultivation, have additionally been infected with the changed attitude to our hero that set in when his name became Ulixes ("Ulysses") and he got tarred

with the brush of fatal deviousness. Dante did much to propagate the tricky Ulysses. We need not blame Dante. Though he placed Ulysses in the hell of the false counselors, he had the excuse of never having read Homer. He had read Dictys and Dares, second-century popularizers who turned the designer of the wooden horse and vanquisher of the Cyclops into (says W. B. Stanford) "an anti-hero."

Pound read Homer's Greek slowly, Dante's Italian fluently, and it is unsurprising that the way he conceives Odysseus owes as much to Dante as it does to Homer. Luckily, he was also misreading Dante, to the extent that he was thrilling to the eloquent speech and disregarding the great flame in which the evil counselor is imprisoned. So he stressed what the speech stresses, an urgent thirst after novelty, and read it back into Homer where it is not to be found. It is Dante, not Homer, whose Ulysses grows bored in Ithaca, where no amenity, no, not the bed of Penelope,

Could conquer the inward hunger that I had
To master the earth's experience, and to attain
Knowledge of man's mind, both the good and bad.

That was where Tennyson had found a Ulysses

… yearning in desire
To follow knowledge like a sinking star
Beyond the utmost bound of human thought,

and that is what Pound is echoing in his own way:

Knowledge the shade of a shade,
Yet must thou sail after knowledge.

In its place in the *Cantos* that is a doom laid on Odysseus, spoken in the regretful voice of Circe. In making it a doom Pound is faithful to one aspect of Homer, whose Odysseus thought nothing was worse for mortal man than wandering and for whom no place was sweeter than home. That is Pound's way of compromising Homer as little as possible, all the while he is handling the hero's need to sail after knowledge, weaving it right back into a scene in Homer's tenth book, where the Greek is innocent of any such motif. Odysseus is pleading with Circe in her bedroom to be let go to continue his voyage home, and in Canto 39 the crucial six lines of her response are reproduced in the Greek, word for word and accent for accent (a printer lost one line, but Pound gives the line numbers, and they show what he intended). No other passage of Homer gets transcribed in full anywhere in the long poem.

Possible English for what her Greek says might run: "But first you must complete another journey, to the house of Hades and dread Persephone, to seek the shade of Tiresias of Thebes, the blind seer, whose mind stays firm. To him in death Persephone has given mind, he alone unimpaired while the rest flit about as shades." That is exactly all, and in Canto 39 we see it on the page in Homer's very words. But eight cantos later we encounter it again, memorably paraphrased and amplified:

> Who even dead, yet hath his mind entire!
> This sound came in the dark
> First must thou go the road
> to hell
> And to the bower of Ceres' daughter Proserpine,
> Through overhanging dark, to see Tiresias,
> Eyeless that was, a shade, that is in hell
> So full of knowing that the beefy men know
>   less than he,
> Ere thou come to thy road's end.
> Knowledge the shade of a shade,
> Yet must thou sail after knowledge
> Knowing less than drugged beasts.

(C 236)

That seems to make sailing after knowledge a theme of the *Odyssey*, as it was certainly a theme for Ezra Pound. It has been recognizably a theme for Americans, in a country whose Enlightenment heritage sets knowing anything at all above not knowing it. (Never mind knowing what; there is an American book on how to win at Pac Man.) Quoting, in another connection, "Who even dead, yet hath his mind entire!" Pound hoped he had done sufficient homage to the Greek veneration of intelligence above brute force (GK 146).

Let us concede, though, that there is intelligence and intelligence, and credit Pound with having intended more than bric-à-brac knowingness. "Who even dead, yet hath his mind entire!" That resonant line is drawn from five words of Homer's, where "mind" is *phrenes*, the whole central part of the body, where you know that you are yourself and not a shade, and "entire" is *empedoi*, meaning firm on the foot, not slipping. Both are body-words: the midriff, the foot. The intelligence is in the body the way the meaning is in the ideogram: intrinsic and manifested, independent of lexicons, not deconstructible. To have merely one's "mind" entire is a later and less substantial concept. Pound lends it body as best he can with a weight of monosyllables and a stark contrast with how it is to be dead. Homer's word for how the dead flit about, *aissousin*, held his attention; it is a word he places on show twice in the *Thrones* cantos (C 675, 730). Disembodied, they have no minds; they flutter. If intelligence is in them, it is in the way it is in dictionaries. ("The trouble with the dictionary," Louis Zukofsky liked to say, "is that it keeps changing the subject.") A flitting, a fluttering: that was the Greek sense of disembodiment, and it fascinated Pound, and it was not intelligence. ("Butterflying around all the time," he said once, of aimless speculation. He was speaking of Richard of St. Victor's *cogitatio*, to be distinguished from *meditatio* and the highest thing, *contemplatio*.)

So we are learning how to take the stark physicality of the rites in the first canto, in particular how to take the need of the shades for blood. They need blood to get what is peculiar to the body, hence to the *phrenes*, the totally embodied intelligence. Without blood, the shades cannot so much as speak. Canto 1 draws on the part of the *Odyssey* Pound judged "older than the rest": Ronald Bush suggests he may have been following Cambridge anthropology here—the tradition of studies that, following on *The Golden Bough*, made Greek intuitions seem so much less cerebral than they had been for Flaxman and Arnold. Or—since I don't know whether he so much as read such a book as Jane Harrison's *Themis*—it is conceivable that in ascribing the underworld journey to "fore-time" he was trusting sheer intuition. It implies, anyhow, the Homeric sense of "intelligence," of "knowledge," something so remote from "ideas"—a word whose Greek credentials are post-Homeric—as to have drawn the snort, "Damn ideas, anyhow … poor two-dimensional stuff, a scant, scratch covering."

To sail after knowledge, then, is to seek what cannot be found in libraries, no, a wholeness of experience. I hope I have suggested that in weaving that phrase back from Dante into Homer, Pound was embellishing less than we may have thought. And it brought him to the superbly colloquial words of Zeus, who, admiring Odysseus, says (in Ezra Pound's English), "With a mind like that he is one of us". That consorts with a fact that has given scandal but need not, that Homer's gods are superbly physical, embodied. Odysseus, for such a god, is "one of us," precisely in having not a Ph.D. but *phrenes*: "the embodiment," said Pound's classmate Bill Williams, "of knowledge."

Having sailed a long circuit after the colloquial, we will not need a second for the other thing Pound wanted, "the magnificent onomatopoeia." Though "untranslated and untranslatable,"

para thina poluphloisboio thalasses

may serve as our terminal emblem: not boom rattle and buzz but the rare identity of words with whatever they signify, achieved with the signifying sound the way Chinese calligraphers achieved it with a signifying outline. Pound listened and heard the wave break, and in the sibilants of *thalasses* heard "the scutter of receding pebbles" (L 274): that whole mighty recurrent phenomenon incarnated in a few syllables represented by a few marks. The way into understanding this is like the way into understanding Homeric intelligence, something only there when it is embodied. So meanings are only there when the words embody them; otherwise, like the dead, they flutter, *aissousin*. And we are back, in a circle, to "the actual swing of words spoken," the other stamp that can authenticate language. Pound first encountered Homer through a man speaking: Mr. Spencer, at the Cheltenham Military Academy, the man "who first declaimed me the *Odyssey*," and was remembered for that after forty years.

Scholars now imagine an "oral-formulaic" Homer, a poet continually speaking, but speaking with the aid of formulae to fill out the meter. When Pound, aged eighty-four, heard an exposition of that, he responded that it did not explain "why Homer is so much better than everybody else." That was very nearly all that he said that day. Why Homer is so much better than everybody else is a thing there's no way to explain; nor why, having sailed after knowledge and turned astray, Ezra Pound should have fulfilled Dante's image with such precision: transmuted after so much eloquence into a tongue of flame, and a tongue that went silent.

Source: Hugh Kenner, "Pound and Homer," in *Ezra Pound Among the Poets*, edited by George Bornstein, University of Chicago Press, 1985, pp. 1–12.

T. S. Eliot

In his essay "Retrospect," Pound gives advice to new poets, detailing his opinions, approach, and ideas regarding the craft.

There has been so much scribbling about a new fashion in poetry, that I may perhaps be pardoned this brief recapitulation and retrospect.

In the spring or early summer of 1912, 'H. D.', Richard Aldington and myself decided that we were agreed upon the three principles following:

1. Direct treatment of the 'thing' whether subjective or objective.

2. To use absolutely no word that does not contribute to the presentation.

3. As regarding rhythm: to compose in the sequence of the musical phrase, not in sequence of a metronome.

Upon many points of taste and of predilection we differed, but agreeing upon these three positions we thought we had as much right to a group name, at least as much right, as a number of French 'schools' proclaimed by Mr. Flint in the August number of Harold Monro's magazine for 1911.

This school has since been 'joined' or 'followed' by numerous people who, whatever their merits, do not show any signs of agreeing with the second specification. Indeed *vers libre* has become as prolix and as verbose as any of the flaccid varieties that preceded it. It has brought faults of its own. The actual language and phrasing is often as bad as that of our elders without even the excuse that the words are shovelled in to fill a metric pattern or to complete the noise of a rhyme-sound. Whether or no the phrases followed by the followers are musical must be left to the reader's decision. At times I can find a marked metre in 'vers libres', as stale and hackneyed as any pseudo-Swinburnian, at times the writers seem to follow no musical structure whatever. But it is, on the whole, good that the field should be ploughed. Perhaps a few good poems have come from the new method, and if so it is justified.

Criticism is not a circumscription or a set of prohibitions. It provides fixed points of departure. It may startle a dull reader into alertness. That little of it which is good is mostly in stray phrases; or if it be an older artist helping a younger it is in great measure but rules of thumb, cautions gained by experience.

I set together a few phrases on practical working about the time the first remarks on imagisme were published. The first use of the word 'Imagiste' was in my note to T. E. Hulme's five poems, printed at the end of my 'Ripostes' in the autumn of 1912. I reprint my cautions from *Poetry* for March, 1913.

A Few Don'ts

An 'Image' is that which presents an intellectual and emotional complex in an instant of time. I use the term 'complex' rather in the technical sense employed by the newer psychologists, such as Hart, though we might not agree absolutely in our application.

It is the presentation of such a 'complex' instantaneously which gives that sense of sudden liberation; that sense of freedom from time limits and space limits; that sense of sudden growth, which we experience in the presence of the greatest works of art.

It is better to present one Image in a lifetime than to produce voluminous works.

All this, however, some may consider open to debate. The immediate necessity is to tabulate A LIST OF DON'TS for those beginning to write verses. I can not put all of them into Mosaic negative.

To begin with, consider the three propositions (demanding direct treatment, economy of words, and the sequence of the musical phrase), not as dogma—never consider anything as dogma—but as the result of long contemplation, which, even if it is some one else's contemplation, may be worth consideration.

Pay no attention to the criticism of men who have never themselves written a notable work. Consider the discrepancies between the actual writing of the Greek poets and dramatists, and the theories of the Graeco-Roman grammarians, concocted to explain their metres.

Language

Use no superfluous word, no adjective which does not reveal something.

Don't use such an expression as 'dim lands *of peace*'. It dulls the image. It mixes an abstraction with the concrete. It comes from the writer's not realizing that the natural object is always the *adequate* symbol.

Go in fear of abstractions. Do not retell in mediocre verse what has already been done in good prose. Don't think any intelligent person is going to be deceived when you try to shirk all the difficulties of the unspeakably difficult art of good prose by chopping your composition into line lengths.

What the expert is tired of today the public will be tired of tomorrow.

Don't imagine that the art of poetry is any simpler than the art of music, or that you can please the expert before you have spent at least as much effort on the art of verse as the average piano teacher spends on the art of music.

Be influenced by as many great artists as you can, but have the decency either to acknowledge the debt outright, or to try to conceal it.

Don't allow 'influence' to mean merely that you mop up the particular decorative vocabulary of some one or two poets whom you happen to admire.

A Turkish war correspondent was recently caught red-handed babbling in his despatches of 'dove-grey' hills, or else it was 'pearl-pale', I can not remember.

Use either no ornament or good ornament.

Rhythm and Rhyme

Let the candidate fill his mind with the finest cadences he can discover, preferably in a foreign language, so that the meaning of the words may be less likely to divert his attention from the movement; e.g. Saxon charms, Hebridean Folk Songs, the verse of Dante, and the lyrics of Shakespeare—if he can dissociate the vocabulary from the cadence. Let him dissect the lyrics of Goethe coldly into their component sound values, syllables long and short, stressed and unstressed, into vowels and consonants.

It is not necessary that a poem should rely on its music, but if it does rely on its music that music must be such as will delight the expert.

Let the neophyte know assonance and alliteration, rhyme immediate and delayed, simple and polyphonic, as a musician would expect to know harmony and counterpoint and all the minutiae of his craft. No time is too great to give to these matters or to any one of them, even if the artist seldom have need of them.

Don't imagine that a thing will 'go' in verse just because it's too dull to go in prose.

Don't be 'viewy'—leave that to the writers of pretty little philosophic essays. Don't be descriptive; remember that the painter can describe a landscape much better than you can, and that he has to know a deal more about it.

When Shakespeare talks of the 'Dawn in russet mantle clad' he presents something which the painter does not present. There is in this line of his nothing that one can call description; he presents.

Consider the way of the scientists rather than the way of an advertising agent for a new soap.

The scientist does not expect to be acclaimed as a great scientist until he has *discovered* something. He begins by learning what has been discovered already. He goes from that point onward. He does not bank on being a charming fellow personally. He does not expect his friends to applaud the results of his freshman class work. Freshmen in poetry are unfortunately not confined to a definite and recognizable class room. They are 'all over the shop'. Is it any wonder 'the public is indifferent to poetry?'

Don't chop your stuff into separate *iambs*. Don't make each line stop dead at the end, and then begin every next line with a heave. Let the beginning of the next line catch the rise of the rhythm wave, unless you want a definite longish pause.

In short, behave as a musician, a good musician, when dealing with that phase of your art which has exact parallels in music. The same laws govern, and you are bound by no others.

Naturally, your rhythmic structure should not destroy the shape of your words, or their natural sound, or their meaning. It is improbable that, at the start, you will be able to get a rhythm-structure strong enough to affect them very much, though you may fall a victim to all sorts of false stopping due to line ends and cæsurae.

The Musician can rely on pitch and the volume of the orchestra. You can not. The term harmony is misapplied in poetry; it refers to simultaneous sounds of different pitch. There is, however, in the best verse a sort of residue of sound which remains in the ear of the hearer and acts more or less as an organ-base.

A rhyme must have in it some slight element of surprise if it is to give pleasure; it need not be bizarre or curious, but it must be well used if used at all.

Vide further Vildrac and Duhamel's notes on rhyme in '*Technique Poétique*'.

That part of your poetry which strikes upon the imaginative *eye* of the reader will lose nothing by translation into a foreign tongue; that which appeals to the ear can reach only those who take it in the original.

Consider the definiteness of Dante's presentation, as compared with Milton's rhetoric. Read as much of Wordsworth as does not seem too unutterably dull.

If you want the gist of the matter go to Sappho, Catullus, Villon, Heine when he is in the vein, Gautier when he is not too frigid; or, if you have not the tongues, seek out the leisurely Chaucer. Good prose will do you no harm, and there is good discipline to be had by trying to write it.

Translation is likewise good training, if you find that your original matter 'wobbles' when you try to rewrite it. The meaning of the poem to be translated can not 'wobble'.

If you are using a symmetrical form, don't put in what you want to say and then fill up the remaining vacuums with slush.

Don't mess up the perception of one sense by trying to define it in terms of another. This is usually only the result of being too lazy to find the exact word. To this clause there are possibly exceptions.

The first three simple prescriptions will throw out nine-tenths of all the bad poetry now accepted as standard and classic; and will prevent you from many a crime of production.

'... *Mais d'abord il faut être un poète',* as MM. Duhamel and Vildrac have said at the end of their little book, '*Notes sur la Technique Poétique.'*

Since March 1913, Ford Madox Hueffer has pointed out that Wordsworth was so intent on the ordinary or plain word that he never thought of hunting for *le mot juste.*

John Butler Yeats has handled or man-handled Wordsworth and the Victorians, and his criticism, contained in letters to his son, is now printed and available.

I do not like writing *about* art, my first, at least I think it was my first essay on the subject, was a protest against it.

Prolegomena

Time was when the poet lay in a green field with his head against a tree and played his diversion on a ha'penny whistle, and Caesar's predecessors conquered the earth, and the predecessors of golden Crassus embezzled, and fashions had their say, and let him alone. And presumably he was fairly content in this circumstance, for I have small doubt that the occasional passerby, being attracted by curiosity to know why any one should lie under a tree and blow diversion on a ha'penny whistle, came and conversed with him, and that among these passers-by there was on occasion a person of charm or a young lady who had not read *Man and Superman*; and looking back upon this naïve state of affairs we call it the age of gold.

Metastasio, and he should know if any one, assures us that this age endures—even though the modern poet is expected to holloa his verses down a speaking tube to the editors of cheap magazines—S. S. McClure, or some one of that soft—even though hordes of authors meet in dreariness and drink healths to the 'Copyright Bill'; even though these things be, the age of gold pertains. Imperceivably, if you like, but pertains. You meet unkempt Amyclas in a Soho restaurant and chant together of dead and forgotten things—it is a manner of speech among poets to chant of dead, half-forgotten things, there seems no special harm in it; it has always been done—and it's rather better to be a clerk in the Post Office than to look after a lot of stinking, verminous sheep—and at another hour of the day one substitutes the drawing-room for the restaurant and tea is probably more palatable than mead and mare's milk, and little cakes than honey. And in this fashion one survives the resignation of Mr Balfour, and the iniquities of the American customs-house, *e quel bufera infernal*, the periodical press. And then in the middle of it, there being apparently no other person at once capable and available one is stopped and asked to explain oneself.

I begin on the chord thus querulous, for I would much rather lie on what is left of Catullus' parlour floor and speculate the azure beneath it and the hills off to Salo and Riva with their forgotten gods moving unhindered amongst them, than discuss any processes and theories of art whatsoever. I would rather play tennis. I shall not argue.

Credo

Rhythm.—I believe in an 'absolute rhythm', a rhythm, that is, in poetry which corresponds exactly to the emotion or shade of emotion to be expressed. A man's rhythm must be interpretative, it will be, therefore, in the end, his own, uncounterfeiting, uncounterfeitable.

Symbols.—I believe that the proper and perfect symbol is the natural object, that if a man use 'symbols' he must so use them that their symbolic function does not obtrude; so that *a* sense, and the poetic quality of the passage, is not lost to those who do not understand the symbol as such, to whom, for instance, a hawk is a hawk.

Technique.—I believe in technique as the test of a man's sincerity; in law when it is ascertainable; in the trampling down of every convention that impedes or obscures the determination of the law, or the precise rendering of the impulse.

Form.—I think there is a 'fluid' as well as a 'solid' content, that some poems may have form as a tree has form, some as water poured into a vase.

That most symmetrical forms have certain uses. That a vast number of subjects cannot be precisely, and therefore not properly rendered in symmetrical forms.

'Thinking that alone worthy wherein the whole art is employed'. I think the artist should master all known forms and systems of metric, and I have with some persistence set about doing this, searching particularly into those periods wherein the systems came to birth or attained their maturity. It has been complained, with some justice, that I dump my note-books on the public. I think that only after a long struggle will poetry attain such a degree of development, or, if you will, modernity, that it will vitally concern people who are accustomed, in prose, to Henry James and Anatole France, in music to Debussy. I am constantly contending that it took two centuries of Provence and one of Tuscany to develop the media of Dante's masterwork, that it took the latinists of the Renaissance, and the Pleiade, and his own age of painted speech to prepare Shakespeare his tools. It is tremendously important that great poetry be written, it makes no jot of difference who writes it. The experimental demonstrations of one man may save the time of many—hence my furore over Arnaut Daniel—if a man's experiments try out one new rime, or dispense conclusively with one iota of currently accepted nonsense, he is merely playing fair with his colleagues when he chalks up his result.

No man ever writes very much poetry that 'matters'. In bulk, that is, no one produces much that is final, and when a man is not doing this highest thing, this saying the thing once for all and perfectly; when he is not matching . . . 'Hist—said Kate the Queen', he had much better be making the sorts of experiment which may be of use to him in his later work, or to his successors.

'The lyf so short, the craft so long to lerne.' It is a foolish thing for a man to begin his work on a too narrow foundation, it is a disgraceful thing for a man's work not to show steady growth and increasing fineness from first to last.

As for 'adaptations'; one finds that all the old masters of painting recommend to their pupils that they begin by copying masterwork, and proceed to their own composition.

As for 'Every man his own poet', the more every man knows about poetry the better. I believe in every one writing poetry who wants to; most do. I believe in every man knowing enough of music to play 'God bless our home' on the harmonium, but I do not believe in every man giving concerts and printing his sin.

The mastery of any art is the work of a lifetime. I should not discriminate between the 'amateur' and the 'professional'. Or rather I should discriminate quite often in favour of the amateur, but I should discriminate between the amateur and the expert. It is certain that the present chaos will endure until the Art of poetry has been preached down the amateur gullet, until there is such a general understanding of the fact that poetry is an art and not a pastime; such a knowledge of technique; of technique of surface and technique of content, that the amateurs will cease to try to drown out the masters.

If a certain thing was said once for all in Atlantis or Arcadia, in 450 Before Christ or in 1290 after, it is not for us moderns to go saying it over, or to go obscuring the memory of the dead by saying the same thing with less skill and less conviction.

My pawing over the ancients and semi-ancients has been one struggle to find out what has been done, once for all, better than it can ever be done again, and to find out what remains for us to do, and plenty does remain, for if we still feel the same emotions as those which launched the thousand ships, it is quite certain that we come on these feelings differently, through different nuances, by different intellectual gradations. Each age has its own abounding gifts yet only some ages transmute them into matter of duration. No good poetry is ever written in a manner twenty years old, for to write in such a manner shows conclusively that the writer thinks from books, convention and *cliché,* and not from life, yet a man feeling the divorce of life and his art may naturally try to resurrect a forgotten mode if he finds in that mode some leaven, or if he think he sees in it some element lacking in contemporary art which might unite that art again to its sustenance, life.

In the art of Daniel and Cavalcanti, I have seen that precision which I miss in the Victorians, that explicit rendering, be it of external nature, or of emotion. Their testimony is of the eyewitness, their symptoms are first hand.

As for the nineteenth century, with all respect to its achievements, I think we shall look back upon it as a rather blurry, messy sort of a period, a rather sentimentalistic, mannerish sort of a period. I say this without any self-righteousness, with no self-satisfaction.

As for there being a 'movement' or my being of it, the conception of poetry as a 'pure art' in the sense in which I use the term, revived with Swinburne. From the puritanical revolt to Swinburne, poetry had been merely the vehicle—yes, definitely, Arthur Symon's scruples and feelings about the word not withholding—the ox-cart and post-chaise for transmitting thoughts poetic or otherwise. And perhaps the 'great Victorians', though it is doubtful, and assuredly the 'nineties' continued the development of the art, confining their improvements, however, chiefly to sound and to refinements of manner.

Mr Yeats has once and for all stripped English poetry of its perdamnable rhetoric. He has boiled away all that is not poetic—and a good deal that is. He has become a classic in his own lifetime and *nel mezzo del cammin*. He has made our poetic idiom a thing pliable, a speech without inversions.

Robert Bridges, Maurice Hewlett and Frederic Manning are in their different ways seriously concerned with overhauling the metric, in testing the language and its adaptability to certain modes. Ford Hueffer is making some sort of experiments in modernity. The Provost of Oriel continues his translation of the *Divina Commedia*.

As to Twentieth century poetry, and the poetry which I expect to see written during the next decade or so, it will, I think, move against poppy-cock, it will be harder and saner, it will be what Mr Hewlett calls 'nearer the bone'. It will be as much like granite as it can be, its force will lie in its truth, its interpretative power (of course, poetic force does always rest there); I mean it will not try to seem forcible by rhetorical din, and luxurious riot. We will have fewer painted adjectives impeding the shock and stroke of it. At least for myself, I want it so, austere, direct, free from emotional slither.

What is there now, in 1917, to be added?

Re Vers Libre

I think the desire for vers libre is due to the sense of quantity reasserting itself after years of starvation. But I doubt if we can take over, for English, the rules of quantity laid down for Greek and Latin, mostly by Latin grammarians.

I think one should write vers libre only when one 'must', that is to say, only when the 'thing' builds up a rhythm more beautiful than that of set metres, or more real, more a part of the emotion of the 'thing', more germane, intimate, interpretative than the measure of regular accentual verse; a rhythm which discontents one with set iambic or set anapaestic.

Eliot has said the thing very well when he said, 'No *vers* is *libre* for the man who wants to do a good job.'

As a matter of detail, there is vers libre with accent heavily marked as a drum-beat (as par example my 'Dance Figure'), and on the other hand I think I have gone as far as can profitably be gone in the other direction (and perhaps too far). I mean I do not think one can use to any advantage rhythms much more tenuous and imperceptible than some I have used. I think progress lies rather in an attempt to approximate classical quantitative metres (NOT to copy them) than in a carelessness regarding such things.

I agree with John Yeats on the relation of beauty to certitude. I prefer satire, which is due to emotion, to any sham of emotion.

I have had to write, or at least I have written a good deal about art, sculpture, painting and poetry. I have seen what seemed to me the best of contemporary work reviled and obstructed. Can any one write prose of permanent or durable interest when he is merely saying for one year what nearly every one will say at the end of three or four years? I have been battistrada for a sculptor, a painter, a novelist, several poets. I wrote also of certain French writers in *The New Age* in nineteen twelve or eleven.

I would much rather that people would look at Brzeska's sculpture and Lewis's drawings, and that they would read Joyce, Jules Romains, Eliot, than that they should read what I have said of these men, or that I should be asked to republish argumentative essays and reviews.

All that the critic can do for the reader or audience or spectator is to focus his gaze or audition. Rightly or wrongly I think my blasts and essays have done their work, and that more people are now likely to go to the sources than are likely to read this book.

Jammes's 'Existences' in '*La Triomphe de la Vie*' is available. So are his early poems. I think we need a convenient anthology rather than descriptive criticism. Carl Sandburg wrote me from Chicago, 'It's hell when poets can't afford to buy each other's books.' Half the people who care, only borrow. In America so few people know each other that the difficulty lies more than half in distribution. Perhaps one should make an anthology: Romains's 'Un Etre en Marche' and 'Prières', Vildrac's 'Visite'. Retrospectively the fine wrought work of Laforgue, the flashes of Rimbaud, the hard-bit lines of Tristan Corbière, Tailhade's sketches in 'Poèmes Aristophanesques', the 'Litanies' of De Gourmont.

It is difficult at all times to write of the fine arts, it is almost impossible unless one can accompany one's prose with many reproductions. Still I would seize this chance or any chance to reaffirm my belief in Wyndham Lewis's genius, both in his drawings and his writings. And I would name an out of the way prose book, the '*Scenes and Portraits* ' of Frederic Manning, as well as James Joyce's short stories and novel, 'Dubliners' and the now well known 'Portrait of the Artist' as well as Lewis' 'Tarr', if, that is, I may treat my strange reader as if he were a new friend come into the room, intent on ransacking my bookshelf.

Only Emotion Endures

'Only emotion endures.' Surely it is better for me to name over the few beautiful poems that still ring in my head than for me to search my flat for back numbers of periodicals and rearrange all that I have said about friendly and hostile writers.

The first twelve lines of Padraic Colum's 'Drover'; his 'O Woman shapely as a swan, on your account I shall not die'; Joyce's 'I hear an army'; the lines of Yeats that ring in my head and in the heads of all young men of my time who care for poetry: Braseal and the Fisherman, 'The fire that stirs about her when she stirs'; the later lines of 'The Scholars', the faces of the Magi; William Carlos Williams's 'Postlude', Aldington's version of 'Atthis', and 'H. D.'s' waves like pine tops, and her verse in 'Des Imagistes' the first anthology; Hueffer's 'How red your lips are' in his translation from Von der Vogelweide, his 'Three Ten', the general effect of his 'On Heaven'; his sense of the prose values or prose qualities in poetry; his ability to write poems that half-chant and are spoiled by a musician's additions; beyond these a poem by Alice Corbin, 'One City Only', and another ending 'But sliding water over a stone'. These things have worn smooth in my head and I am not through with them, nor with Aldington's 'In Via Sestina' nor his other poems in 'Des Imagistes', though people have told me their flaws. It may be that their content is too much embedded in me for me to look back at the words.

I am almost a different person when I come to take up the argument for Eliot's poems.

Source: T. S. Eliot, "A Retrospect," in *Literary Essays of Ezra Pound*, edited by T. S. Eliot, New Directions, 1965, pp. 3–14.

M. L. Rosenthal

In the following essay, M. L. Rosenthal discusses Pound's Cantos *as a work that must be read "experientially" rather than "schematically" and how this reading exposes its historical scope and its multiple voices.*

Space forbids our going into the *Cantos* in even as much detail as we have into *Mauberley*. We have already, however, noted some of the leading ideas behind this more involved and ambitious work, and though we cannot here trace their handling throughout its winning, Gargantuan progress, a few suggestions concerning its character as a poetic sequence may be useful. First of all, we may take as our point of departure the fact that in motivation and outlook the *Cantos* are a vast proliferation from the same conceptions which underlie *Mauberley*. The difference lies partly in the multiplicity of "voices" and "cross-sections," partly in the vastly greater inclusiveness of historical and cultural scope, and partly in the unique formal quality of the longer sequence; it is by the very nature of its growth over the years a work-in-progress. Even when the author at last brings it to conclusion, reorganizing it, supplying the withheld Cantos 72 and 73, completing his revisions, and even giving his book a definitive title, it will remain such a work. Each group of cantos will be what it is now—a new *phase* of the poem, like each of the annual rings of a living tree. The poet has put his whole creative effort into a mobilization of all levels of his consciousness into the service of the *Cantos*; there has been a driving central continuity, and around it new clusters of knowledge and association linked with the others by interweavings, repetitions, and overall perspective. Pound has staked most of his adult career as a poet on this most daring of poetic enterprises; literary history gives us few other examples of comparable commitment.

The *Cantos* has been called Pound's "intellectual diary since 1915," and so it is. But the materials of this diary have been so arranged as to subserve the aims of the poem itself. Passage by passage there *is* the fascination of listening in on a learned, passionate, now rowdy, now delicate intelligence, an intelligence peopled by the figures of living

tradition but not so possessed by them that it cannot order their appearances and relationships. Beyond the fascination of the surface snatches of song, dialogue, and description, always stimulating and rhythmically suggestive though not always intelligible upon first reading, there is the essential overriding drive of the poem, and the large pattern of its overlapping layers of thought. The way in which the elements of this pattern swim into the reader's line of vision is well suggested by Hugh Kenner, one of Pound's most able and enthusiastic interpreters:

> The word "periplum," which recurs continually throughout the *Pisan Cantos* [74–84], is glossed in Canto LIX:
> periplum, not as land looks on a map
> but as sea bord seen by men sailing.

Victor Brerard discovered that the geography of the *Odyssey*, grotesque when referred to a map, was minutely accurate according to the Phoenician voyagers' *periploi*. The image of successive discoveries breaking upon the consciousness of the voyager is one of Pound's central themes.... The voyage of Odysseus to hell is the matter of Canto I. The first half of Canto XL is a periplum through the financial press; "out of which things seeking an exit," we take up in the second half of the Canto the narrative of the Carthagenian Hanno's voyage of discovery. Atlantic flights in the same way raise the world of epileptic maggots in Canto XXVIII into a sphere of swift firm-hearted discovery.... The periplum, the voyage of discovery among facts,... is everywhere contrasted with the conventions and artificialities of the bird's eye view afforded by the map....

Thus, the successive cantos and layers of cantos must be viewed not so much schematically as experientially. Here we see how the early Pound's developing idealization of the concrete image, the precise phrase, the organically accurate rhythm are now brought to bear on this vast later task. The many voices, varied scenes and *personae*, and echoes of other languages and literatures than English reflect this emphasis on experience itself: something mysterious, untranslatable, the embodied meaning of life which we generalize only at peril of losing touch with it. So also with Pound's emphatic use of Chinese ideograms, whose picture-origins still are visible enough, he believes, so that to "read" them is to think in images rather than in abstractions. His use of them is accounted for by the same desire to present "successive discoveries breaking upon the consciousness of the voyager." The first effect of all these successive, varied breakings is not intended to be total intellectual understanding, any more than in real experience we "understand" situations upon first coming into them. But by and by the pattern shapes up and the relationships clarify themselves, though always there remains an unresolved residue of potentiality for change, intractable and baffling.

Pound's "voyager," upon whose consciousness the discoveries break, is, we have several times observed, a composite figure derived first of all from the poet-speaker's identification with Odysseus. A hero of myth and epic, he is yet very much of this world. He is both the result of creative imagination and its embodiment. He explores the worlds of the living, of the dead, and of the mythic beings of Hades and Paradise. Lover of mortal women as of female deities, he is like Zagreus a symbol of the life-bringing male force whose mission does not end even with his return to his homeland. Gradually he becomes all poets and all heroes who have somehow vigorously impregnated the culture. He undergoes (as do the female partners of his procreation and the *personae* and locales in time and space of the whole sequence) many metamorphoses. Hence the importance of the Ovidian metamorphosis involving the god Dionysus, the sea (the female element and symbol of change), and the intermingling of contemporary colloquial idiom and the high style of ancient poetry in Canto 2. The first canto had ended with a burst of praise for Aphrodite, goddess of love and beauty, and in language suggesting the multiple allusiveness of the sequence: to the Latin and Renaissance traditions, as well as the Grecian-Homeric, and to the cross-cultural implications suggested by the phrase "golden bough." The second canto takes us swiftly backward in the poetic tradition, through Browning, then Sordello and the other troubadours, and then to the classical poets and the Chinese tradition. All poets are one, as Helen and Eleanor of Aquitaine and Tyro (beloved of Poseidon) and all femininity are one and all heroes are one.

In the first two cantos, then, the "periplum" of the sequence emerges into view. Three main value-referents are established: a sexually and aesthetically creative world-view, in which artistic and mythical tradition provides the main axes; the worship of Bacchus-Dionysus-Zagreus as the best symbol of creativity in action; and the multiple hero— poet, voyager, prophet, observer, thinker. The next four cantos expand the range of allusiveness, introducing for instance the figure of the Cid, a chivalric hero, to add his dimension to the voyager-protagonist's consciousness. Also, various tragic tales are brought to mind, extending the initial horror of Odysseus' vision of the dead and thus contributing to the larger scheme of the poet in the modern wasteland. In absolute contrast, pagan beatitudes are clearly projected in Canto 2 in the pictures of Poseidon and Tyro:

> Twisted arms of the sea-god,
> Lithe sinews of water, gripping her, cross-hold,
> And the blue-gray glass of the wave tents them....

and, at the scene's close, in the phallic "tower like a one-eyed great goose" craning up above the olive grove while the fauns are heard "chiding Proteus" and the frogs "singing against the fauns." This pagan ideal comes in again and again, sharp and stabbing against bleak backgrounds like the "petals on the wet, black bough" of the "Metro" poem. Thus, in Canto 3:

> Gods float in the azure air,
> Bright gods and Tuscan, back before dew
>   was shed.

In Canto 4:

> Choros nympharum, goat-foot, with the pale foot
>   alternate;
> Crescent of blue-shot waters, green-gold in
>   the shallows,
> A black cock crows in the sea-foam....

In 4 and 5 both there are deliberate echoes of such poets as have a kindred vision (Catullus, Sappho, and others), set against the notes of evil and damnation. The lines from Sordello in 6 serve the same purpose:

> "Winter and Summer I sing of her grace,
> As the rose is fair, so fair is her face,
> Both Summer and Winter I sing of her,
> The snow makyth me to remember her."

The Lady of the troubadours, whose "grace" is a secularized transposition from that of Deity, is another manifestation of "the body of nymphs, of nymphs, and Diana" which Actaeon saw, as well as of what Catullus meant: " 'Nuces!' praise, and Hymenaeus 'brings the girl to her man....' "

After these archetypal and literary points of reference have been established, Cantos 8–19 move swiftly into a close-up of the origins of the modern world in the Renaissance, and of the victory of the anticreative over the active, humanistic values represented by Sigismundo Malatesta and a few others. (Canto 7 is transitional; in any case we can note only the larger groupings here.) The relation between the "Renaissance Cantos" (8–11) and the "Hell Cantos" (14–16), with their scatological picturings of the contemporary Inferno, is organic: the beginning and the end of the same process of social corruption.

The beautiful dialogue on order in 13 provides a calm, contrasting center for this portion of the sequence, and is supported by the paradisic glow and serenity of Elysium, revealed in 16 and 17. The earlier cantos had given momentary attention to Oriental poetry and myth and, as we have seen, Elysian glimpses also. Now these motifs are expanded and related to a new context, bringing the sequence into revised focus but carrying all its earlier associations along. This leaping, reshuffling, and reordering is the organizational principle behind the growth, the "annual rings," of the *Cantos*.

The next ten cantos interweave the motifs of these first two groups and prepare us for the next leap (in Cantos 30–41) of perspective. There are various preparations for this leap, even as early as Canto 20, in which there is a moment of comment from the "outside" as if to take stock before hurtling onward. From their remote "shelf," "aerial, cut in the aether," the disdainful lotus-eaters question all purposeful effort:

> "What gain with Odysseus,
> "They that died in the whirlpool
> "And after many vain labours,
> "Living by stolen meat, chained to the
>   rowingbench,
> "That he should have a great fame
> "And lie by night with the goddess?…"

Is the question wisdom or cynicism? No matter. The poem, given the human condition and the epic tasks that grow out of it, is held in check but an instant before again plunging ahead. The *Cantos* accepts the moral meaning and the moral responsibility of human consciousness. The heroic ideal remains, as on the other hand the evil of our days remains even after the goddess' song against pity is heard at the beginning of 30.

The new group (30–41) is, like the later Adams cantos (62–71), in the main a vigorous attempt to present the fundamental social and economic principles of the Founding Fathers as identical with Pound's own. Adams and Jefferson are his particular heroes, and there is an effort to show that Mussolini's program is intended to carry these basic principles, imbedded in the Constitution but perverted by banking interests, into action. Pound works letters and other documents, as well as conversations real and imagined, into his blocks of verse, usually fragmentarily, and gives modern close-ups of business manipulations. The method has the effect of a powerful exposé, particularly of the glimpsed operations of munitions-profiteers. The cantos of the early 1930's have, indeed, a direct connection with the interest in social and historical documentation and rhetoric that marks much other work of the same period, and at the end of Canto 41 (in which Mussolini is seen) we should not be surprised to find an oratorical climax similar in effect to that of Poem IV in *Mauberley* (1919). As in the earlier groups, however, we are again given contrasting centers of value, especially in Canto 36 (which renders Cavalcanti's *A lady asks me*) and in Canto 39, whose sexually charged interpretation of the spell cast over Odysseus and his men on Circe's isle is one of Pound's purest successes.

The Chinese cantos (53–61) and the Pisan group (74–84) are the two most important remaining unified clusters within the larger scheme. Again, the practical idealism of Confucianism, like that of Jefferson and Adams, becomes an analogue for Pound's own ideas of order and of secular aestheticism. Canto 13 was a clear precursor, setting the poetic stage for this later extension. "Order" and "brotherly deference" are key words in Confucius' teachings; both princes and ordinary men must have order *within* them, each in his own way, if dominion and family alike are to thrive. These thoughts are not clichés as Pound presents them. We hear a colloquy that has passion, humor, and depth, and what our society would certainly consider unorthodoxy. Kung "said nothing of the 'life after death,'" he considered loyalty to family and friends a prior claim to that of the law, he showed no respect for the aged when they were ignorant through their own fault, and he advocated a return to the times "when the historians left blanks in their writings, / I mean for things they didn't know." The Chinese cantos view Chinese history in the light of these principles of ordered intelligence in action, with the ideogram *ching ming* (name things accurately) at the heart of the identity between Confucian and Poundian attitudes. "The great virtue of the Chinese language," writes Hugh Gordon Porteus, "inheres in its written characters, which so often contrive to suggest by their graphic gestures (as English does by its phonetic gestures) the very essence of what is to be conveyed." The development of Pound's interest in Chinese poetry and thought, as well as his varied translations from the Chinese, is in itself an important subject. This interest, like every other to which he has seriously turned his attention, he has brought directly to bear on his own poetic practice and on his highly activistic thinking in general.

With the *Pisan Cantos* and *Rock-Drill* we are brought, first, into the immediately contemporary world of the poet himself, in Fascist Italy toward the close of World War II, in a concentration camp at Pisa, during the last days of Mussolini; and second, into a great, summarizing recapitulation of root-attitudes developed in all the preceding cantos: in particular the view of the banking system as a scavenger and breeder of corruption, and of ancient Chinese history as an illuminating, often whole-somely contrasting analogue to that of the post-medieval West. Even more than before, we see now how the *Cantos* descend, with some bastardies along the line, from the Enlightenment. They conceive of a world creatively ordered to serve human needs, a largely rationalist conception. Hence the stress on the sanity of Chinese thought, the immediacy of the Chinese ideogram, and the hardheaded realism of a certain strain of economic theory. The *Pisan Cantos* show Pound's vivid responsiveness as he approached and passed his sixtieth birthday; his aliveness to people his Rabelaisian humor, his compassion. The lotus-eaters of Canto 20, aloof and disdainful, have missed out on the main chances. Canto 81 contains the famous "Pull down thy vanity" passage in which the poet, though rebuking his own egotism, yet staunchly insists on the meaning-fulness of his accomplishment and ideals. As the sequence approaches conclusion, the fragments are shored together for the moral summing-up. In the *Rock-Drill* section, Cantos 85–95, the stocktaking continues and we are promised, particularly in Canto 90, an even fuller revelation than has yet been vouchsafed us of the Earthly Paradise.

Cantos 96–109 begin to carry out this promise, though after so many complexities, overlappings, and interlocking voices it must be nearly impossible to bring the work to an end. It is essentially a self-renewing process rather than a classical structure, and there is no limit to the aspects of history and thought the poet has wished to bring to bear on the poem. Canto 96, for instance, touches on certain developments after the fall of Rome, especially two decrees in the Eastern Empire by Justinian and Leo VI concerning standards of trade, workmanship, and coinage. The special emphasis in this canto on Byzantine civilization is particularly appropriate because of Byzantium's historical and geographical uniting of East and West as well as its mystical associations pointing to a new and dramatic paradisic vision. Although the memory of earlier glimpses of "paradise" and the recapitulative, self-interrupting method militate against an effect of a revelation overwhelmingly new, the pacing of the whole sequence has made this difficulty at the end inevitable. Pound's conclusion must be introduced as emergent from the midst of things, still struggling from all in life and consciousness that makes for disorder.

Source: M. L. Rosenthal, "The Cantos," in *A Collection of Critical Essays*, edited by Walter Sutton, Prentice-Hall, Inc., 1963.

SOURCES

Kenner, Hugh, *The Poetry of Ezra Pound*, University of Nebraska Press, 1985 (reprint).

Partisan Review, May 1949, p. 518.

"Poetry's New Priesthood," in *Saturday Review of Literature*, June 18, 1949, pp. 7–9, 38.

Sutton, Walter, *Ezra Pound: A Collection of Critical Essays*, Prentice-Hall, 1963.

"Treason's Strange Fruit: The Case of Ezra Pound and the Bollingen Award," in *Saturday Review of Literature*, June 11, 1949, pp. 9–11, 28.

FURTHER READING

Carpenter, Humphrey, *A Serious Character: The Life of Ezra Pound*, Faber & Faber, 1988.
    Carpenter's biography is the most extensive and detailed of the many books that tell the story of Pound's life.

Casillo, Robert, *The Genealogy of Demons*, Northwestern University Press, 1988.
    Casillo confronts Pound's ugliest side: his fascist and anti-Semitic ideas.

Kenner, Hugh, *The Pound Era*, University of California Press, 1971.
    Many consider this to be the definitive book not only on the Cantos but on Pound's contribution to twentieth-century literature and culture.

Rainey, Lawrence, *Ezra Pound and the Monument of Culture*, University of Chicago Press, 1991.
    Rainey's book examines in close detail the historical and artistic sources behind the "Malatesta cantos" (8–11).

Terrell, Carroll F., *A Companion to 'The Cantos' of Ezra Pound*, University of California Press, 1980.
    Terrell compiles an incredibly detailed and helpful annotation of almost every proper name, place, historical event, and foreign word used in Pound's poem.

De rerum natura

(TITUS) LUCRETIUS (CARUS)

58 B.C.

Lucretius' scientific epic *De rerum natura* is considered a masterpiece of Epicurean philosophy. Epicurus taught that the world could be understood by reason and that religion only arouses unnecessary fear. Lucretius denounced popular beliefs in deities and supernatural creatures. He viewed humans as ignorant creatures who fabricated the powers of the gods, only to live in fear of them. In his epic, Lucretius appeals to reason in order to enlighten his readers and persuade them to accept his belief system. Because of its atheistic ideals, *De rerum natura* almost faded into obscurity as Christianity gained momentum. During the Renaissance, however, Lucretius's epic was rediscovered, and it continues to be translated and studied today.

As a poem, *De rerum natura* is remarkable. First, it is a lyrical presentation of what would otherwise be tedious information. Second, it is the earliest known work of Latin hexameter verse. (Hexameter verse is poetry in which each line has six "feet," or units of rhythm.) The fact that it is such a lengthy example secures its distinction as an important work. Although a rumor persists that Cicero edited the epic, history better supports the idea that Cicero's brother Quintus directed its publication.

De rerum natura is praised for its depiction of nature as a source of life, death, joy, peace, and terror. It is not a poem strictly about the physical world, as Epicureanism also offers guidelines for

human conduct and relationships. Lucretius's philosophy of how human beings should live dictates pursuing friendship and avoiding war. In the introduction to his translation of *De rerum natura*, Anthony M. Esolen comments that Lucretius "really believes that in Epicureanism lies our best hope for happiness, and he very much wants to let us in on the secret, so that we may be as happy as is possible in a world imperfectly suited for our existence."

AUTHOR BIOGRAPHY

Titus Lucretius Carus, known as Lucretius, was born in Rome circa 94 B.C. Little is known about his life apart from the beliefs and values he describes in his epic scientific poem, *De rerum natura*, or *On the Nature of Things*. Unfortunately, nothing is known about Lucretius' schooling, family, or literary development. There is confusion regarding his social standing, as the name "Carus" suggests servitude, while "Lucretius" indicates aristocracy. Scholars believe that his six-book masterpiece, *De rerum natura*, is unfinished. In this epic, he repeatedly discourages the reader from fearing death, advice Lucretius apparently embraced when he committed suicide in about 55 B.C. According to a long-standing (although questionable) rumor reported by the historian Jerome, Lucretius was driven insane by a love potion given to him by his wife.

Throughout his life, Lucretius was surrounded by political upheaval and war. He saw firsthand the cruelty and domination of dictators, along with the instability of such rule. He saw the decline of Rome's republican government and died before stability was restored. He was a man who felt deep compassion for the human race, which he perceived as living in fear and ignorance. He criticized religious leaders who instilled terror in order to bring about moral living. Lucretius was a follower of Epicurus and his scientific, rational way of understanding the world. In turn, Lucretius became a strong influence on later writers such as Virgil and Ovid.

PLOT SUMMARY

Book One

Lucretius begins by invoking the name of Venus as a creative force, appealing to Memmius (to whom the work is addressed), and then praising his master Epicurus. (Scholars have noted the seeming inconsistency in Lucretius' invoking Venus at the beginning of a work that disclaims the gods' involvement with human life. The solution most commonly offered is that such a invocation was standard in the literature of the time, and that by keeping to the standard Lucretius hoped to win the trust and continued attention of readers.) Lucretius states that religion teaches fear, while science teaches fact. He recounts the story of Agamemnon, who was willing to sacrifice his daughter Iphigenia for the good will of the gods. This is not piety, Lucretius says, but rather wickedness demanded by religion.

Next, Lucretius sets about describing atoms as the building blocks of every object and living thing in the world. Nothing comes from nothing, and no object can ever be reduced to nothing. Although atoms cannot be seen, their presence can be felt in the wind, evaporation and humidity, and sensory experience. The entire world is composed of atoms and space, or void. Void is what allows motion because atoms can move through space without interference. Lucretius asserts that atoms are indivisible, solid, and indestructible, as each one moves from thing to thing.

In anticipation of protests, Lucretius disclaims the theories of the philosophers Heraclitus, Empedocles, Anaxagoras, and the Stoic objectors. Next, Lucretius explains that the universe is infinite. He illustrates this point by asking what would happen if a man went to the edge of the earth and threw a spear. The spear would, of course, go somewhere. Consequently, he reasons, atoms and void are infinite.

Book Two

Lucretius explains that the differing properties of things are accounted for by the different properties of atoms. For example, substances with a bitter or harsh taste have sharper atoms than substances that have pleasant tastes. The same is true for aromas. A disagreeable scent irritates the nose as its atoms pass through, while pleasant scents are composed of smooth atoms. There are a fixed number of atomic shapes even though there are infinite atoms. Atoms are also colorless. He stresses that atoms are indestructible, but their compulsion to move on to other things creates instability in the world. He describes atomic motion as swerving. If atoms simply moved straight down, he explains, they would never collide and hence would never create anything at all.

All things must die, despite the fact that the atoms that make up a person came from another source and will become something else when the person dies. Earth provides everything humans need to live, but not forever. Lucretius concludes with the idea that there are other worlds like this one, subject to the same laws of atoms.

Book Three

The atomic theories are applied to humankind as Lucretius considers the nature of the soul (which he equates with the mind). He argues that even the soul is subject to death because it is composed of atoms, which are only present temporarily. Lucretius sets out four elements of the soul's atomic composition—air, breath, warmth, and an unnamed fourth element. He claims that the soul resides in a person's chest and is really a body part, except that the soul cannot exist without the body and vice-versa. Lucretius likens the body to a jar holding the soul; if the jar is dropped and shatters, the soul leaks out. Lucretius ends the book by reproaching those who fear death. After all, there is nothing after death, so why live in fear of nothingness? Death brings about the end of desire and is not to be mourned. Lucretius adds that all the great men who have gone before have died, so it is approaching arrogance to feel uncomfortable about following their paths. Living one's entire life in fear of death serves only to ruin what chance of happiness and peace there may be.

Book Four

Sense perception and visions are accounted for in Book Four. Lucretius explains that objects constantly give off atoms that can be perceived by the senses. These are called "films" or "peels." He adds that the senses are completely reliable, although interpretations of what is sensed are not always accurate. As an example, he writes that there are no such things as Centaurs, yet people have seen them because they perceive a film of a man and a film of a horse stuck together and interpret this as a single creature. Because people can be fooled by films that produce, what seems to be, images of Centaurs and other non-existent creatures, they feel compelled to create mythologies about them. This is how woodland gods, spectres, and dreams come into being in the mind.

As Lucretius approaches the end of this book, he begins a fiery section about love and lust. He describes romantic love as an emotional state to be avoided, as it is destructive and causes men and women to make poor decisions and lead themselves into ruin. Oddly, he includes a discussion of infertility and explains why it happens and how it can be corrected. He concludes with a brief description of true love. "Habit is the recipe for love," he says, suggesting that true love is not found in sudden passion but, instead, develops over time.

Book Five

In Book Five, the longest of the six books, Lucretius offers an account of how the world began and how civilization developed. He again emphasizes the futility of fearing gods or death, and he praises the virtues of friendship and peace.

First, Lucretius establishes that his telling of the creation of the world is not blasphemous because the gods are remote and unconcerned with human dealings. Besides, the gods have nothing to do with the creation of the world; nature is solely responsible. Explaining the wonders of celestial bodies, he returns to the assertion that everything is mortal and is subject to decay. The sun and moon are about the same size as they appear to the eyes and celestial bodies move because of gusts of heavenly winds. He describes the destructive nature of the elements and how they often battle each other.

Next, Lucretius describes life for early people as difficult and dangerous, but free of war between tribes. Early in human history, there were freakish beings that failed to continue in existence because they were unable to survive into adulthood, find food, or procreate. He explains that whenever a new idea came about, it was shared so that the other people could benefit by it. Humankind comes to discover fire, create language and music, develop medicine, establish law, and, upon discovering metal, makes progress in farming. Warfare is also raised to new heights with the creation of metal weapons.

Book Six

Lucretius opens Book Six with an extended speech about Epicurus, which many scholars view as a eulogy. In the final book of his epic, Lucretius intends to cast away any doubt in his reader's mind that there exist deities that meddle in human affairs. Natural occurrences such as high winds, volcanic eruptions, lightning, and earthquakes have nothing to do with divine activity. Only nature has the power to make these things happen, and to assume that the gods create them is ridiculous. Further, worshipping the gods does not prevent catastrophe. By discussing each type of natural disaster (and phenomena such as magnetism and rainbows), Lucretius hopes to reveal the folly of superstition so prevalent in his society.

Lucretius tells of the Athenian plague of 430 B.C., during which there was no comfort for the afflicted or for the survivors. Lucretius supposes that the Athenians failed to realize that there are limits to both pleasure and pain, otherwise they would know that nature does not give death without also giving life. This story brings the epic to a fitting close, as Lucretius began with the figure of Venus as a creative and life-giving force. Throughout the poem, Lucretius emphasizes the fleeting quality of life, and he supports his argument by constructing his poem in such a way that it begins with life and ends with death.

CHARACTERS

Epicurus

Epicurus is the father of the philosophy embraced in *De rerum natura*. Throughout the work, Lucretius praises Epicurus as "the founder of that way of life called 'wisdom'," "glory of Greece," "founder of truth," and "the first to stand firm in defiance" of popular religion.

(Gaius) Memmius

De rerum natura is addressed to Memmius. Lucretius writes to him as to a student, a convention that allows Lucretius to speak authoritatively as an instructor to all his readers. Memmius was a contemporary of Lucretius who wrote erotic verse. He became involved in questionable political activities and was eventually exiled. Many historians believe that Lucretius received financial patronage from Memmius.

THEMES

In *De rerum natura*, Lucretius discusses the qualities of atoms and space and how they make up the world and its inhabitants. He also describes how people should conduct themselves in their relationships with each other and with nature.

War and Friendship

As an Epicurean, Lucretius opposes war and values friendship and cooperation. He carries out these twin themes in *De rerum natura*, painting dreadful, gruesome pictures of war and pleasant pictures of people enjoying each other's company and supporting each other. Lucretius frequently uses war imagery to illustrate scientific points about atoms and nature. Describing the occurrence of accidents, he introduces the story of Helen of Troy and the Trojan War that resulted from her abduction. In Book Three, Lucretius explains that there is no reason to fear death, using an illustration from the Peloponnesian Wars to make his point. He writes that during these horrific wars, everyone lived in fear of which side would triumph and who would subsequently rule them. According to Lucretius, this is how most people view death. Letting go of one's fear of death, however, means releasing the fear of which "side" (life or death) will win.

Complementing Lucretius' view of war is the Epicurean view of friendship. The Epicureans regarded friendship as one of the greatest and most worthwhile experiences humans can pursue in life. This idea is not, however, carried over into the realm of romantic love. Lucretius denounces surrendering to this kind of love, as it only leads people to make unwise decisions and squander their fortunes, and leaves them vulnerable to jealousy and rejection.

Religion and Science

The Epicurean rejection of religion in favor of reason and science permeates *De rerum natura*. Lucretius explains that people have been too quick to believe that the movements and events of nature are dictated by the gods. On the contrary, Lucretius depicts the gods as remote beings living in total peace and tranquility. They have no reason to be interested in human affairs, so it is no use to worship them or make sacrifices to them. By telling the tragic story of Agamemnon willingly sacrificing his own daughter to win the favor of the gods, Lucretius demonstrates that what humans understand to be piety is actually senseless cruelty.

Science, on the other hand, is the path to truth. Lucretius maintains that the senses are unfailing and that, combined with experience, they have the power to teach people how the world truly operates. He appeals to reason and makes methodical arguments that not only tear down existing belief systems about natural occurrences, but also seek to replace them with reasonable explanations. For Lucretius, the only worthy religion is reverence toward nature. In Book Two, he goes so far as to assert that Earth is the only true creative divinity: "So Earth alone is

TOPICS FOR FURTHER STUDY

- Conduct general research on what modern-day physicists know about atoms (size, properties, visibility, etc.). Compare your findings to Lucretius' version of atomic theory. In what ways was he correct? In what ways was he mistaken? What can you conclude about Lucretius' ability as a scientist and observer of the world?

- Choose a partner. Think about a subject matter about which you are knowledgeable. Teach your partner about this topic using three analogies, just as Lucretius uses analogies to clarify his points to his readers. Then trade roles, with your partner acting as teacher and yourself as student.

- Review the passage in Book Five that begins with Line 852. What parallels can you draw between Lucretius' statements and evolutionary theory? Also, Lucretius writes, ''And many have been entrusted to our care, / Commended by their usefulness to us.'' Is there anything in this passage that reminds you of the creation narrative in Genesis?

- In Book Five, Lucretius states, ''But if true reason governs how one lives, / To have great wealth means to live sparingly, / With a clear heart: small wants are always met.'' Consider the philosophies of Henry David Thoreau and Ralph Waldo Emerson. Could you say that Lucretius was a Romantic or a Transcendentalist? Why or why not?

- Take into account Lucretius' views on death and write an Epicurean eulogy for him.

---

called 'Great Mother of Gods' / And 'Mother of Beasts' and 'She Who Formed Our Flesh.'''

Nature's Cyclical Rhythms

Throughout the poem, Lucretius affirms that nature functions in ongoing, predictable cycles. There is no death without birth, and every atom moves through a series of cycles as it converges with other atoms to create different things. In Book One, Lucretius writes, "Nothing returns to nothing; when things shatter / They all return to their constituent atoms. . . . / Nature restores / One thing from the stuff of another, nor does she allow / A birth, without a corresponding death." In Book Two, he comments, "So the / Whole is ever / Renewed, while mortal things exchange their lives." The cycles of nature are also apparent in the movements of the sun, moon, and stars.

Fear and Ignorance

Perhaps Lucretius' greatest goal in writing *De rerum natura* was to bring readers out of a state of superstition and needless fear into a state of rationality and understanding. He renounced fear in all six books, viewing it as a limitation on human life. In Book Three, he blamed fear for urging men to betray their countrymen and their own families, for generating envy, and for ruining friendships. Because life is relatively short and there is nothing afterwards, Lucretius sees no reason to spend one's life in constant fear of the wrath of the gods or of death. Ultimately, he contends, whatever will happen cannot be averted or in any way controlled by a person, so it is best to pursue simple pleasures and a carefree lifestyle.

The harshest realization, according to Lucretius, is that most fear is human-made. Unable to explain the world around them and aware of the presence of the gods (Lucretius says these people could see the gods), early people devised stories about divine intervention. This provided an explanation of the workings of nature and their own fates. Unfortunately, the result was that people learned to live in fear of seemingly all-powerful and fickle gods. From fear comes misery, as well as barbaric practices such as sacrifice, and senseless practices such as kneeling and burning incense. In Book One, Lucretius writes that "before our eyes man's life lay groveling, prostrate, / Crushed to the dust under the burden of Religion. . . . " Lucretius hoped that by explaining how nature really works, he would be able to lift the veil of ignorance and fear so that people could live fully, happily, and educated. Praising Epicurus in Book One, he proclaimed, "Religion now lies trampled beneath our feet, / And we are made gods by the victory."

STYLE

Epic Features

De rerum natura is a very unusual example of an epic. It lacks many of the epic's typical features, including an expansive setting, a heroic and adventurous figure, and praise for the gods. Still, the language is lofty and lyrical, and Lucretius often utilizes analogies and metaphors to convey his ideas. While he makes frequent allusions to the works of other philosophers, he generally does so to refute their positions rather than to align his work with theirs, as most epics do.

Audience

Lucretius claims that his audience is Memmius, the person to whom the epic is dedicated and addressed. In reality, however, the work is written for those who falsely believe in divine intervention and fear death. In short, his audience is his contemporaries and others who would come after him. His intention was to enlighten his readers in order to free them from a life of needless fear.

Didactic and Methodical Approach

In presenting his scientific ideas, Lucretius adopts a fitting writing style to complement his ideology. He explains the laws of physics in a methodical, organized manner that gives the reader the feeling that Lucretius is an instructor who is teaching a straightforward lesson. He proves one point, only to build on that point in a later discussion. The poem is didactic—intended to teach, not to inspire emotions or profound thoughts. Throughout the text, he makes statements of absolute truth as one who speaks with authority. In Book Two, for example, he proclaims, "Apply your mind now, hear the truth of reason!" To further establish himself as a reliable expert, he constantly denounces those who would disagree with him. In Book Four, he writes, "Lend me your subtle attention and keen mind, / And don't shout 'That can't be!' at what I

say. . . . " Typical of his comments regarding opposing theories, he writes in Book Five, "This far-fetched nonsense reason must reject."

Analogies

In order to make his scientific explanations accessible to a wide range of readers, Lucretius relies on analogies. He likens his scientific verse to honey-rimmed glasses of foul-tasting wormwood given to children by doctors. As he discusses the lightness of the soul's atoms in Book Three, he tells the reader that the fact that the soul cannot be felt by touch does not deny its existence. To illustrate this idea, he reminds the reader that chalk settling on the skin cannot be felt, fog cannot be felt, and a cobweb drifting onto one's head cannot be felt, yet all of these things exist.

Repetition

Just as Lucretius employs analogies to make certain his reader understands his ideas, he uses repetition to ensure that they do not forget what he has taught them. Numerous times and in numerous ways, for example, Lucretius emphasizes that nature operates in cycles that cannot be altered. He believes it is essential that his audience understand this point, so he inserts it in various forms throughout the text. The same is true for his views on fear. At every opportunity, he reiterates the wastefulness of living in fear.

HISTORICAL CONTEXT

Political Turmoil

During Lucretius' life (94 B.C. to 55 B.C.), Rome suffered a great deal of political upheaval in the struggle for power. In 88 B.C. civil war erupted between the aristocrat Lucius Cornelius Sulla and the populist Gaius Marius. When Marius marched against Rome, he was cruel and vindictive, seeking vengeance on the aristocracy with indiscriminate killing sprees. When Lucretius was a teenager, Sulla returned to Rome to be its dictator, seeking retaliation against those who had opposed him in the earlier conflict. Lucretius also saw the decline of the republican government that had been in place for much of his life. Although unstable, at least the republican government was familiar to the people and they did not have to live in constant fear of what

COMPARE
&
CONTRAST

- **First century B.C.:** Lucretius' *De rerum natura* describes atoms as the invisible, solid, indivisible building blocks of all matter.

  Sixteenth and seventeenth centuries: Experimental science gains popularity, and atomic theory begins to make important strides. Chemists discover that matter can be identified by its separate components. For example, water can be identified as being composed of hydrogen and oxygen.

  1930s: The electron microscope is developed, a tool that would eventually allow scientists to see particles as small as atoms.

- **First century B.C. Rome:** Most Romans believe that gods and goddesses govern natural occurrences and manipulate human affairs. In order to appease the gods and goddesses and win their favor, worshippers must create altars and, sometimes, make sacrifices.

  Twentieth-century United States: Statistics compiled in 1996 by the United States Census indicate that 56% of Americans practice Protestantism, 25% practice Roman Catholicism, and 11% practice no religion. These numbers suggest that most modern Americans believe in a single god.

- **First century B.C.:** Rome is under an unstable republican government.

  1789: The United States ratifies its Constitution, establishing a constitutional republic. The Constitution continues to form the basis of American government today.

---

kind of oppressive military regime would rule them next. A consequence of the fall of the republic was a shift in loyalty from the government to individual military leaders and political figures. The decline of the republican spirit among the people also weakened the Romans' traditional commitment to the family and state. In addition, many Romans were beginning to call into question the mythology that had guided their religious beliefs for so long. All of these factors created a cultural transformation and uncertainty.

The ongoing struggle for power among Pompey, Crassus, and Julius Caesar was underway throughout much of Lucretius' youth. Although the three formed a triumvirate (a political coalition intended to help each get what he wanted), power was abused and internal conflict eventually destroyed the compact. Shortly after Lucretius' death, Crassus died, which brought Pompey and Caesar into direct conflict with each other. In 52 B.C. the Senate made Crassus sole consul in an effort to defeat Caesar. Caesar returned to Rome in 49 B.C. and was soon ruling all of Italy. Lucretius' death came before Caesar brought the hope of stability to Rome.

Many scholars contend that the extreme political conditions in which Lucretius lived account for his adherence to Epicureanism. Faced with ongoing war and strife, he found Epicureanism to be a peaceful, pleasurable, moral way to live his life. His horrific depictions of war throughout *De rerum natura* can certainly be attributed to the political environment in which he lived. In addition, Lucretius admired the Epicurean pursuit of friendship. Having witnessed the massacres and bloodshed of power struggles, it is little wonder he would so fervently believe that people should seek to befriend and help each other.

Religious and Philosophical Crossroads

During Lucretius' time, educated Romans were beginning to feel uncertain about the elaborate mythologies in their religion. They began to doubt that gods and goddesses were really so active in human affairs that they would involve themselves in everything from love to mildew. The absence of a clear relationship between natural occurrences (volcanic eruptions, earthquakes, rain, etc.) and deity worship was a problem. Still, Romans continued to run colleges offering religious training, to worship the deities, and to dedicate sports events to the gods. The growing unwillingness to believe in the complicated mythology of the Roman gods may explain why, a century later, Romans would begin deifying their emperors. This practice not only personified Roman gods, but also discouraged the cults that were gaining popularity.

As an Epicurean, Lucretius was a philosophical outsider. Aristotle and Plato, though offering different views of the world and the universe, were the accepted thinkers of the time. They disagreed about certain key philosophical questions, such as the origin of the universe. Plato claimed that the universe was intentionally created by a divine being he named "The Craftsman." Aristotle, on the other hand, asserted that there was no beginning to the universe because it had always been in existence. Despite their divergent philosophies, Plato and Aristotle both claimed that the world is unique in the cosmos (i.e., that there are no other worlds like Earth) and that humans live in an intentional and ordered world. Lucretius, on the other hand, believed that there were more worlds like ours, and he states throughout *De rerum natura* that the world was created neither by gods nor for humans. In Book Five, he writes, "I'd dare assert / And prove that not for us and not by gods / Was this world made. / There's too much wrong with it!" This assertion directly opposes the notion of an ordered world created by a deity according to a design.

The teachings of Plato and Aristotle rose to prominence among the cultured citizens of Greece, after which the view of an ordered world was adopted by the Stoics in Rome. This happened around the time that Lucretius was writing *De rerum natura*. The teachings of the Stoics were the dominant philosophy in Rome at the time, which positioned Lucretius squarely in opposition to the accepted cosmological view.

CRITICAL OVERVIEW

As the oldest known example of Latin hexameter poetry, Lucretius' *De rerum natura* continues to be the subject of much scholarly debate. Entire journal articles focus on the translation of single excerpts, and an accepted "standard" translation is yet to be published. The challenge lies not only in translating the work, but also in preserving its rhythms and imagery in a way that is meaningful to contempo-

rary readers while maintaining the integrity of the text. Scholars and students of classicism admire the text for its lyrical presentation of scientific models. It is also an important text because it is the best single presentation of Epicurean ideals and classical atomic theory that is available. Although the hard science behind Lucretius' assertions concerning the physical world is somewhat naive, there are many ideas that have either been proven or are related to later, more sophisticated theories. In a review for *Free Inquiry*, Gordon Stein notes, "Granting his lack of equipment to measure things of an atomic (or even galactic) size, we must still marvel at how close his speculations came to the findings of modern science." As for Lucretius' religious beliefs (or lack thereof), critics find that the epic is still relevant to modern-day atheistic and agnostic beliefs.

One of Lucretius' major themes in *De rerum natura* is death. The ending of the poem, with its extended description of a plague that terrorized Athens, strikes many readers as abrupt and dark. The ending has, therefore, been fertile ground for critical debate. For a time, many scholars maintained that the sudden ending was evidence that the epic was incomplete. They argued that Lucretius intended to return to his masterpiece and finish it. Today, most scholars agree that the work is unfinished, but not because of the ending. In various places in the poem, Lucretius alludes to a later discussion of the gods and their living conditions, yet at the close of the work, he has not addressed this.

Although the ending seems abrupt, critics have devised various arguments to explain why Lucretius wanted his epic to end as it does. To some, the ending presents a sort of test for the reader. Having read Lucretius' account of death and the cyclical nature of the world, the reader has a choice. The reader either can be horrified at the scope of this historical event of human suffering; or can take comfort in the knowledge that with death comes life and the afflicted have nothing to fear because there is nothing beyond death—no judgment, no hell, and no desire. J. L. Penwill, in an article for *Ramus— Critical Studies in Greek and Roman Literature*, applies Lucretius' worldview to contemporary situations: "The victims of the plague are . . . innocent. And in the pain of an individual death from cancer or AIDS, or in the face of natural disasters such as fire, flood, and earthquake, or even of ones that can be ascribed to human causes such as ethnic cleansing in Bosnia or genocide in Rwanda, the undeserved suffering again and again forces the anguished cry, 'Why does God let this happen?' The

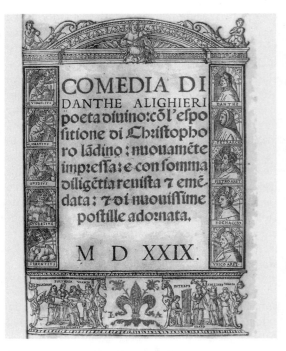

Manuscript page with writings by Lucretius.

answer is simple. God has no interest in the matter. That is the way things are." Granted, this is a harsh view that clashes with popular religious belief systems, but later in the same article, Penwill offers an insight that reveals Lucretius' tenderness toward people: "Unlike the gods, human beings possess the quality of compassion."

Also related to Lucretius' theme of death is a seeming contradiction in the text. His Epicurean ideals dictate that there is nothing beyond death, and so people should neither fear it nor seek immortality. He states that the pursuit of immortality leads men into ruin as they become creatures of envy, cruelty, and selfishness. Still, Lucretius claims that he will secure poetic immortality through his great work. In Book One, for example, he states, "Let the fame be mine, for I teach great things, stride forth / To free the soul from the stranglehold of religion; / Also, I sing dark matters into the light, / Spicing all with the grace of poetry." One school of thought argues that there is a difference between subjective and objective views of survival. The poet is the objective component that will eventually die. This is what Lucretius teaches should not be feared. Poetry and philosophy, however, have the subjective ability to survive the writer and continue into

existence without their creators. In an article for *Harvard Studies in Classical Philology*, Charles Segal expressed his doubt that this resolution is realistic. Believing that Lucretius did not differentiate between two types of immortality, he wrote, "Perhaps, then, to be a great poet means, ultimately, to be less of an Epicurean. Perhaps for all his philosophical acceptance of the power of death, something in Lucretius the poet has not given up 'hoping' what every poet since Homer had seen as his goal and his right."

Lucretius also addresses love in his epic. He opens by invoking Venus as his creative muse, but later delivers an impassioned section denouncing love as a wasteful and destructive distraction in people's lives. Although questionable, the rumor regarding Lucretius' wife giving him a love potion that eventually drives him mad has led some scholars to claim that his wife's conniving is what brought about his anti-love lecture. Still others, including William Fitzgerald in an article for *The Classical World*, contend that for Lucretius love and death are the "enemies of mental health: both the fear of death and the torments of love derive from a mind fettered to its own or another's unique individuality." Both force otherwise rational people to behave in ways that create confusion and pain for themselves. As an Epicurean, Lucretius valued pleasure and freedom, but in romantic love, these two seem to be mutually exclusive.

CRITICISM

Jennifer Bussey

In the following essay, Bussey defines Epicureanism and demonstrates how Lucretius upholds its basic tenets.

Lucretius' masterpiece *De rerum natura* is acknowledged as the preeminent presentation of Epicurean philosophy. How Lucretius came to learn about Epicureanism is uncertain, and there is no evidence of a specific teacher who guided Lucretius' philosophical development. Because Greek professors lectured on the teachings of Epicurus in Rome at the time, however, it is clear that he was well instructed. Epicureanism is based on four central ideas, which are that the gods are not frightening, there is nothing to fear in death, good is accessible, and bad is

WHAT DO I READ NEXT?

- Aristophanes' *The Complete Plays*, c. 300 B.C., compiles the humorous plays of the ancient Greek playwright Aristophanes. These plays demonstrate the satire and humor that delighted playgoers in ancient Greece.

- Mike Corbishley's *What Do We Know about the Romans?*, 1992, gives students a cultural and social context for studying Roman arts and literature.

- Dante's classic *The Divine Comedy*, 1307, offers a thorough, unique, and compelling look at the afterlife. Guided first by Virgil and then by Beatrice, Dante travels through hell, purgatory, and heaven, witnessing the consequences and rewards of decisions made in life.

- *The Iliad*, c. 850 B.C., is one of Homer's great epics. In the spirit and form of a classic epic, it is a story of adventure, the Trojan War, the gods, and great heroes.

- Shakespeare's *Julius Caesar*, 1599, is one of The Bard's greatest plays. It is the story of the rise and fall of Julius Caesar in Roman politics.

---

bearable. Epicurus and his followers formed small communities of like-minded friends who gathered in gardens to study and discuss philosophical issues. Historians note that these communities were especially noteworthy for their surprising inclusion of women and slaves. Studying science and the physical world, Epicurus found support for his ideas in nature. In his epic poem, Lucretius brings together Democritus' and Leucippus' theories of "atomism" (which guided Epicurus' philosophies regarding the physical world) and Epicurus' teachings on atomic properties and moral living. Lucretius' achievement is in bringing these ideas together into a coherent philosophy of rationalism and a virtuous lifestyle.

Central to Epicurean thought is atomic theory. Epicurus learned much from the early scientific theorists Democritus and Leucippus after realizing that their physics supported his beliefs about the absence of divine intervention. This, in turn, had a profound effect on his beliefs regarding morality. The atomists also taught that reality is accessible to anyone through sense perception; the world can be understood without resorting to divine explanations for natural occurrences. The Epicureans' major contribution to atomic theory was the notion of an imperceptible movement called "swerve." Lucretius explains in *De rerum natura* that atoms do not fall straight down to the earth, but fall in a swerving path. This allows them to collide and combine with each other, resulting in the creation of objects and beings. In Book Two, Lucretius explains, "When the atoms are carried straight down through the void by their own weight . . . they swerve a little. . . . For if atoms did not tend to lean, they would / Plummet like raindrops thorough the depths of space, / No first collisions born, no blows created, So / Nature never could have made a thing." Unfortunately, there is no explanation of why or how atoms swerve.

From Epicurus' cosmology came his views on morality and ethical living. In order to live fully, he claimed, it was necessary to observe and study one's natural surroundings. Epicurus designated three types of desire, the first and most important of which is natural and essential desire. This is desire for necessities, such as food, shelter, and clothing. Necessary desires are generally the easiest desires to fulfill. The second type is natural and unnecessary desire, such as sexual desire. The third type is unnatural desire, which includes luxury, power, wealth, and popularity. People who pursue these desires are often miserable because they fail to understand that what they desire is unnecessary. At the end of Book Three, Lucretius writes, "What vicious yearning for life, then, makes us hurry / In such a panic, attacked by doubts and dangers? . . . / Whatever we lack, we want, we think it excels / All else, but when we've grabbed it something new / We thirst for, always panting after life."

> *Epicureanism is based on four central ideas, which are that the gods are not frightening, there is nothing to fear in death, good is accessible, and bad is bearable."*

Epicureans pursued pleasure in life, although not to excess. In the opening of Book Two, Lucretius proclaims, "Our nature yelps after this alone: that the body / Be free of pain, the mind enjoy the sense / Of pleasure, far removed from care or fear!" Avoiding the excess of passions allows a person to remain in calm control and avoid the torments of being overly emotional. The Epicureans believed that pleasure was the natural standard that enables people to assess what is good and what is bad. From infancy, people recognize pleasure, but what must be learned is how to find pleasure in the right things. In other words, Epicurus taught that it is not adequate to seek immediate pleasure at every passing moment of life, but rather to strive to maximize pleasure over the long term. Along the same lines, Epicureans understood that they must sometimes endure pain and discomfort in order to enjoy pleasure later. Friendship is important in the Epicurean way of life because it provides pleasure, facilitates philosophical pursuits, and helps to avoid pain by creating a supportive community of allies. By extension, it is no surprise that the Epicureans, and Lucretius in particular, despised war.

The Epicurean fascination with atomic theory comes from the need to explain natural wonders in order to refute existing beliefs about the activities of the gods and goddesses. The result is important to Epicurean doctrine—the removal of fear of the deities. In essence, the Epicureans apply philosophy as a remedy for fear and worry. Lucretius' presentation of religion in *De rerum natura* almost resulted in the epic's permanent rejection. As Christianity grew, Epicurean assertions of mortal souls and a god absent from the world were almost forgotten. Further, Lucretius' depiction of religion as a great monster, choking humankind and inciting it to cru-

elty, was unacceptable among Christians. In fact, were it not for the beauty of the verse and the poetic art of the work, the epic would very likely be obscure today. Scholars, however, began to revisit the epic for its achievement in hexameter and language, which is what ultimately saved it from being forever lost.

The Epicureans were not atheists, despite the fact that atheists often share many of their beliefs. While Epicureans claimed that the gods had no hand in human life or in the creation or maintenance of the world, they never denied their existence. Nature alone is responsible for life. Consequently, the role of the gods in human life is simply to be admired, but not worshipped. Many scholars have noted that Lucretius' description of the gods' world very much resembles Epicurus' philosophical garden community of friends.

According to the Epicureans, the gods lived together in complete peace and happiness. They were remote from the activity of the world and had no reason to become the least bit involved in human affairs. To do so would only disrupt their perfect world and bring unnecessary turmoil upon themselves. In Book One, Lucretius describes the gods: "For by necessity the gods above / Enjoy eternity in highest peace, / Withdrawn and far removed from our affairs. / Free of all sorrow, free of peril, the gods / Thrive in their own works needing nothing from us, / Not won with virtuous deeds nor touched by rage." Later in the same book he addresses the human tendency to fear the gods out of ignorance and writes, "Fear grips all mortal men precisely because / They see so many events on the earth, in the sky, / Whose rational causes they cannot discern—/ So they suppose it's all the will of the gods."

Epicureanism attributes most human fear and anxiety to the basic fear of death. Lucretius blames the fear of death for greed, cruelty, and selfishness in the world. Understanding and accepting death is pivotal in Epicurean thought. Once liberated from the fear of dying, people can live in *ataraxia*, a state of peaceful serenity. Although people live their lives terrified of dying and of what happens beyond life, the Epicureans taught that there is, in fact, nothing beyond death. This conclusion is drawn from atomic theory, which claims that only what can be sensed is real. Interestingly, Lucretius offers an explanation that the soul is composed of atoms and is, therefore, mortal. He argues that the body and soul cannot exist without each other, and because the soul is a collection of atoms, it dies with the body. Of course, for Epicureans, dying means that the body and soul cease to be in a particular state and so move on to another form. The atoms are immortal although the form they take is not.

The idea that there is nothing beyond death is not necessarily comforting, so the Epicureans offer another way of considering death. Before people are born, they feel nothing, and thinking about non-existence prior to birth does not seem to upset people. Therefore, the Epicureans reason, there is no need to worry about non-existence after life. Lucretius expresses the Epicurean idea that if a person lived a happy life, then when it is time to die, he or she should simply go like a guest leaving the dinner table. If, however, life was unpleasant, the person should consider that there is little to be lost in death.

Although Lucretius was an Epicurean, he was also an independent thinker. He possessed qualities that were un-Epicurean, the most notable of which was his desire for poetic glory. Epicurus himself advised against writing poetry, yet Lucretius was compelled to write a sweeping epic poem focused on Epicurus' own philosophies. Lucretius lapses into passages surging with emotional force (such as his passage on the pitfalls of love), even though the Epicurean way is one of calmness and serenity. Despite his few Epicurean shortcomings, Lucretius will be forever known as the great epic poet who preserved Epicureanism for centuries of students, scholars, historians, and scientists.

Source: Jennifer Bussey, for *Epics for Students*, Gale, 2001.

J. L. Penwill

Penwill views the ending of Lucretius' Book 6 *as a representation of the ending process of life, which leads to an explanation of the abrupt ending.*

That Lucretius should choose to end his Epicurean representation of the world with a long and harrowing account of the plague that struck Athens in 430 B.C.E. is certainly one of the more remarkable facts in classical Roman poetry. More remarkable still is the suddenness of the ending. The poem simply breaks off as one critic says 'almost in mid-sentence'; and even if we follow this same critic in tidying up the end by transferring 6.1247–51 to follow 1286 we are still left very much *in mediis*

The poem begins and ends with an invocation to Venus, the Roman goddess of love.

rebus, with the plague at its height and death and misery all around. Our initial response is one of surprise and puzzlement as we feel cheated of a sense of an ending; this in turn leads to questions about overall design and authorial intent. Why does the poem end this way? Indeed, has it ended at all?

This was for a long time the accepted answer; there is no ending, because the poem is unfinished. The supposedly unfulfilled promise to write at greater length about the abodes of the gods at 5.155 was cited in support of this view, together with the

> " For one of the basic messages of the <u>DRN</u> is surely that we, the human race, are part of nature. . . .Attempts to transcend this limitation are futile, and lead inevitably to frustration and despair: to look for a better existence for the soul after death is to invent the worry of a worse one. . ."

sensationalist tradition that Lucretius was driven mad by a love-potion and that the (by implication unfinished) poem was published posthumously. But even if Lucretius died before the poem was completed and so was unable to tie up or remove the loose ends, it does not follow that the present ending is not the one he planned for it; the *Aeneid* too was published posthumously and it too has a problematic ending, but surely no-one these days tries to argue that had Virgil lived he would have added a further section to move the spotlight away from Aeneas' signal failure to live up to Anchises' ideal. Both the *DRN* and the *Aeneid* have endings which are deliberately provocative; they require the reader to make sense of the work which s/he has just read as a work which ends in the way it does. The challenge is to work out what the poet means by ending this way, not to rewrite the poem.

Modern criticism has by and large accepted this challenge. Minadeo has offered a systematic study of the cycle of creation and destruction that pervades the poem; and while some of his formulations have a Procrustean air, there can be no doubt that in the case of the poem as a whole and of the major sections of it he is right. The poem itself reflects the cycle it describes; every atomic construct goes through the process of coming to be and passing away, and so does the poem: the invocation to *Venus genetrix* in the proem to Book 1, replete with images of fertility, joy, and the exuberance of new

life, is neatly answered by the epilogue to Book 6, with its emphasis on sickness, despair, and the awfulness of death. Indeed, Bright's transposition of 6.1247–1251 to the end of the poem makes the antithesis particularly neat:

> lacrimis lassi luctuque redibant; inde bonam partem in lectum maerore dabantur. nec poterat quisquam reperiri, quem neque morbus nec mors nec luctus temptaret tempore tali.

> Wearied by tears and grief they would return; then for the most part they would give themselves to their beds from sorrow. Nor could anyone be found whom neither disease nor death nor grief was attacking in such a time.

The despondency of the mourners who have disposed of their dead in whatever way they could stands in stark contrast to the laughter and joy which permeates the first 20 lines of Book 1 as the world bursts into life at the advent of Venus; and the sequence 'disease, death, grief' baldly listed in the final couplet (if such it be) together with the image of the mourners taking to their beds to grieve in silence and solitude is the complete reverse of the expansive and syntactically complex description of the energy, vitality and *joie de vivre* of the creatures inspired by Venus to love-making and the creation of new life.

While this is an attractive and persuasive account of the overall design of the poem, it does not in my view constitute a sufficient explanation for the way in which the poem ends. Certainly there is balance, which functions as both demonstration and fulfilment of the Epicurean doctrine of *isonomia*; but this does not of itself account for the fact that Lucretius has chosen to end his poem with 130 lines of unrelieved horror in which he has taken care to edit out whatever vestiges of hope there are in Thucydides' bleak narrative of the same event. This, what is more, in a poem which has the stated purpose of removing those fears which perturb the mind of human beings, one of which is the fear of death. Can we still face death with equanimity after reading the end of Book 6? With this closure ringing in our ears, can we still be convinced by what had heretofore seemed so compelling but now so theoretical a series of arguments against the fear of death in Book 3? And how does this final passage accord with the author's earlier defence of the (un-Epicurean) use of poetry?—

> id quoque enim non ab nulla ratione uidetur; sed ueluti pueris absinthia taetra medentes cum dare

conantur, prius oras pocula circum contingunt mellis dulci flauoque liquore, ut puerorum aetas inprouida ludificetur labrorum tenus, interea perpotet amarum absinthi laticem deceptaque non capiatur, sed potius tali pacto recreata ualescat...

For this too seems not to be without purpose; but as doctors, when they are trying to give bitter worm-wood to children, first coat the rim around the cup with the sweet yellow liquid of honey, so that in their youthful thoughtlessness they will be fooled as they taste it, drink down the bitter juice of the wormwood and be deceived, not cheated, since in this way they will be restored to health...

Honey may certainly be a suitable image for the invocation to Venus in Book 1; but the description of the plague is unadulterated wormwood. The comparison of the unenlightened to children, famil-iar also from the 'for just as children tremble and fear everything' formula, is grimly recalled in the picture of children's corpses:

exanimis pueris super exanimata parentum corpora nonnumquam posses retroque uidere matribus et patribus natos super edere uitam.

Sometimes you could see the lifeless bodies of parents lying on their lifeless children, and again children giving up their lives on their mothers and fathers.

Medicine for these children is an irrelevance; indeed, medicine has been reduced to silence (*mussabat tacito medicina timore*, 'medicine mut-tered in silent terror', 6.1179). Again we ask, why end on this note?

Some critics draw attention to what they see as an ethical dimension to this ending. Throughout the poem, Lucretius has been drawing attention to the difference between the Epicurean and non-Epicu-rean world-views, depicting the latter as productive of anxiety and unhappiness. The earlier part of Book 6 has been particularly strong on this, dealing with meteorological and terrestrial phenomena that the unenlightened ascribe to the intervention of the gods; but as the syllabus to this book makes clear, that attitude is fraught with danger:

quae nisi respuis ex animo longeque remittis dis indigna putare alienaque pacis eorum, delibata deum per te tibi numina sancta saepe oberunt.

If you do not spit these ideas out of your mind and put far away from you thoughts unworthy of the gods and inconsistent with their tranquillity, the holy godhead you have diminished will often come against you.

The threat is not that god will hurl a thunderbolt at you if you do not worship him in the right way or if you deviate from religious orthodoxy, but rather that false belief will set up motions in your soul which will prevent you from receiving and correctly interpreting the *simulacra* ('images') that emanate from the gods. The state of the unenlightened is thus one of self-inflicted psychological sickness. Noting that one of the ways in which Lucretius has modi-fied Thucydides is to increase the emphasis on the psychological malaise experienced by the sufferers of the plague, Commager suggests that the whole episode is in a sense symbolic: the sufferings of the Athenians in 430 B.C.E. are generalised and ren-dered emblematic of the spiritual state of the unenlightened. Smith in his revision of the Loeb Lucretius adopts the same position.

The verbal parallelisms between the poem, with its emphasis on moral sickness and health, and the final passage confirm that Lucretius views the Athenian plague as a physical disaster that involved moral disaster as well, and as symbolising the moral condi-tion of unenlightened mankind.... The truth is that the prospect of salvation and of a heaven on earth which Lucretius offers in the *DRN* shines with a brighter and stronger light on account of this dark and hellish picture of what life is like without the guidance of Epicurus.

Now it is true that the unenlightened are termed *aegri,* 'sick', in the opening line of Book 6; it is also true that Athens is hailed in the proem to this same book as the home of Epicurus and the source of his *diuina reperta* ('divine discoveries', 6.7), and this framing of the book could lend some support to the idea that a contrast is being set up between the pre- and post-Epicurean city. But if this is what Lucretius is trying to do, he has been singularly and unusually reluctant to inform the reader of the fact. Lucretius' normal practice is to make his moves abundantly clear, as in the image of the man gazing out to sea in the proem to Book 2 (to which I shall return) or in the case of the sacrifice of Iphigenia at 1.80–101. And while both Commager and Bright are right in drawing attention to Lucretius' interest in the psy-chological impact of the plague, the emphasis has not in any way been removed from the physical. The context in which the modifications towards the psychological should be viewed is not so much that of the proem's outline of the spiritual malaise of the unenlightened but rather that of the arguments for the mortality of the soul in Book 3. One thinks particularly of 3.429–525, where the fact that men-tal derangement often accompanies physical ill-ness—indeed is itself part of that physical illness, in that it too is a consequence of the behaviour of the material particles of which the human organism is composed—is cited as evidence that the mind is subject to disease as much as the body and is therefore just as mortal. The sickness of soul experienced by the victims of the plague is thus not due to their unenlightened state but to the nature of the disease, which attacks all parts of the organism. Moreover, one of the effects of the plague is to break down religious observance:

> nec iam religio diuom nec numina magni pendebantur enim: praesens dolor exsuperabat.

> Now neither religion nor the gods were regarded as of any importance; the present anguish overwhelmed them.

It is as if the plague has effected what Lucretius' entire argument—and particularly the argument in Book 6—has been directed towards: a realisation that the gods have no interest in human affairs. On the one hand this is hardly an image of unenlightenment; on the other, we have to ask whether an Epicurean would be any better off than a non-Epicurean in coping with a disease that affects the mind to the extent that this one does.

Above all we need to remember that we are dealing here not with a generalised image but with a historical event. This is not an imagined scene of a man driving his chariot to the country and then coming home again, nor of a cow searching for her lost calf, but a record of an actual occurrence; and the poet has made this clear to the educated readership for which he is writing by the conspicuous use of Thucydides to which I have already alluded. Elsewhere when he alludes to or describes particular events, Lucretius explicitly draws the moral, as with the already mentioned sacrifice of Iphigenia in Book 1 or the death of major historical figures at 3.1025–44. But nothing of the kind is found here; the description is introduced as a particular example (*haec ratio quondam morborum*, 'this cause of diseases on one occasion …', 6.1138) to illustrate the nature of disease and runs to its end without comment. Indeed, if we compare Lucretius with Thucydides, we might conclude that it is the historian who is making the moral point in juxtaposing the account of the plague to Pericles' Funeral Speech, and so contrasting the ideal of the civilised city with the sordid reality of human nature reduced to its basics. Lucretius offers no such correlative; true, there is the reference to Athens as the home of Epicurus at the beginning of the book, but after line 5 the focus switches from city to philosopher, the

verbs become third person singular instead of third person plural, and Athens, named but once (line 2), is quickly forgotten. The notion that the plague is somehow symbolising the state of unenlightened, pre-Epicurean humankind is, in my view, untenable. The answer does not lie here.

Another view, put forward most forcefully by Clay, is that the description of the plague is presented as a kind of test:

> So Lucretius' reader arrives at the end of *De rerum natura* to face a spectacle of disease and disturbance and also to face the final test of his mastery of the poem. He is left to contemplate the ugliest face of an indifferent nature that destroyed, even as it created, the highest form of human civilisation.

The correct response on the part of the reader who has achieved the required grade of philosophical wisdom would presumably then be that of the watcher on the seashore:

> suaue, mari magno turbantibus aequora uentis, e terra magnum alterius spectare laborem; non quia uexari quemquamst iucunda uoluptas, sed quibus ipse malis careas quia cernere suauest.

> Sweet it is, when the winds are creating great rollers on the sea, to view from land the great toil of another; not because there is any pleasure in the fact that someone is in trouble, but because to look upon evils from which you yourself are free is sweet.

The poet goes on to make clear that by this image he is bringing to our minds the enlightened individual who has detached himself from the mad pursuit of wealth and power which is responsible for so much human unhappiness. He is in the fortunate position of being able to stand back and watch, and to experience the pleasure of knowing that he is no longer enmeshed in the toils of the rat-race. But this is merely to congratulate oneself on avoiding humanity's self-inflicted wounds and to engage in little more than poetic/philosophical/satiric commonplace. Reason can tell us that the desire for wealth and power, *auri sacra fames*, is a destructive force, that allowing oneself to succumb to sexual passion will ultimately bring more pain than joy (we've all seen some version of *Phaedra* or read the neoterics), that the doctrines of conventional religion, with their emphasis on interventionist gods and the bogey of eternal punishment for those who step out of line, are not worthy of belief; these are the 'storms' from which the philosophic mind can free itself in the quest for *ataraxia* . But are we as readers of the *DRN* being invited to adopt a similar attitude when it comes to the plague? Are we the watchers on the seashore experiencing the *suauitas* of not being embroiled in these horrors? Is Lucretius expending the full force of his poetic talent to create a picture of devastation and misery in order to give us *pleasure*? Is that the challenge of this final scene? If we view the plague as a test of Epicurean correctness as Clay would have us do, then that is the only conclusion we can come to. After all, the gods who constitute the ataraxic ideal do not care; and as for us, we are as remote from these events as we are from those of the Second Punic War, of which, as the poet triumphantly tells us (3.832ff.), we felt nothing.

The problem with this is that the gods neither perceive what takes place on earth nor read poetry; we are human beings and do both. Further, the idea that we are supposed to respond to the account of the plague with indifference would set up an impossible tension between invited and expected response, with the poetic voice immersing us in horror and the didactic voice counselling calm detachment. Poetry works through engaging the emotions, and Lucretius does this throughout, the fascination of this text lies in the fact that from first to last it demands involvement, drawing the reader in to experience the intensity of its representation of and response to *natura*. We may be able to congratulate ourselves on escaping from error; from *natura* there can be no escape.

So pedagogically attractive as it may be, the model of the *De Rerum Natura* as a course of instruction culminating in a final examination paper does not altogether appeal. The description of the plague is not an appendix or epilogue, any more than Virgil's account of the final confrontation between Aeneas and Turnus is to the *Aeneid*; rather it is central to the poem's thematic design, as Minadeo's analysis makes clear. We are not being asked to use the whole poem in order to 'master' one of its parts; rather we are being challenged to integrate this, the most problematic of its parts, into the overall structure of the work. This is what I shall be attempting to do in the remainder of this essay.

Let us consider the plague in its more immediate context, Books 5–6. The basic argument of these books is that everything is explicable in material terms, and so by applying the principle of Occam's razor we can exclude the hypothesis that the gods have any role to play. It is no accident therefore that Book 5 opens with that remarkable proem in which Epicurus is virtually deified:

> nam si, ut ipsa petit maiestas cognita rerum, dicendum est, deus ille fuit, deus, inclute Memmi, qui princeps uitae rationem inuenit eam quae nunc appellatur sapientia…

> For if we may speak as the perceived greatness of the matter itself demands, he was a god, a god, noble Memmius, who first discovered that rationale of life which is now called wisdom.

The sentiment is repeated at 5.19–21; we also hear echoes of it in the divinity ascribed to Epicurus' doctrines in the proem to Book 6:

> cuius et extincti propter diuina reperta diuolgata uetus iam ad caelum gloria fertur.

> Even though he is now dead, his fame, spread abroad of old, is now carded to the skies on account of his divine discoveries.

The only 'god with us' in this system is the philosopher; it is he who brings us the means to achieve happiness, and it is he who is the only true culture-hero. The world in which we live and of which we are a part is neither divine nor sentient; the notion of Mother Earth, presented particularly forcefully at 5.795ff., arises from our perception of the earth's fertility now and what *ratio* tells us about the origin of living things. But we must not allow ourselves to be carried away by this image to the extent of actually regarding the earth as a mother goddess; that would be both false and dangerous. The argument in Book 6, with its concentration on meteorological and terrestrial phenomena which have traditionally been ascribed to divine agency (thunder, lightning, thunderbolts, earthquakes, volcanoes and the like), not only stresses that all such occurrences may be explained in material terms (even though we may not be able to pinpoint precisely what that explanation is) but also, by the very explanations it offers, draws attention to the fact that earth is an unstable atomic construct, which will itself one day fall apart. Lucretius explicitly draws the conclusion:

> et metuunt magni naturam credere mundi exitiale aliquod tempus clademque manere, cum uideant tantam terrarum incumbere molem. quod nisi respirent uenti, uis nulla refrenet res neque ab exitio possit reprehendere euntis.

> And they fear to believe that the nature of the great world is awaiting a certain time of destruction and a disaster, although they see the great mass of lands leaning down. But if the winds did not pause for breath, no force would rein things in nor be able to hold them back from destruction in their onward rush.

Not only is the world not divine but it is subject to the same process as all other compounds, passing through the stages of birth, growth, maturity, decline and death. The individual human being is also subject to this process; and the essential similarity between earth and individual, macrocosm and microcosm, is shown by the recycling of the language of 3.806–18 (proof that the soul is mortal because it is a compound) to prove that the earth itself is mortal at 5.351–63.

One of the functions of the section on disease with which Book 6 concludes is to underscore this relationship between microcosm and macrocosm. In a passage just after the one to which I have just referred, Lucretius makes the point that compounds are subject to dissolution as a result of bombardment by particles from without:

> neque autem corpora desunt, ex infinito quae possint forte coorta corruere hanc rerum uiolento turbine summam aut aliam quamuis cladem inportare pericli…

> Nor are bodies lacking that can by chance come together out of the infinite and overwhelm this sum of things in violent storm, or bring in some other destructive calamity.

Particles from without are likewise the cause of disease, both generally (6.1090ff.—note particularly the recurrence of the phrase *forte coorta* at 1096) and in the particular case of the plague at Athens, where Lucretius follows Thucydides in saying that the infection came from Egypt (6.1141). The graphic details in the description of the plague are a telling illustration of the effect of noxious particles, which the principle of *isonomia* shows must be as numerous as beneficent ones (see esp. 6.1093ff.). The emphasis in the account of physical symptoms is on the internal organs; see especially 6.1163ff., where the poet states that the burning sensation could not be perceived by touching the skin: it affected only the *intima pars* ('innermost part', 1168), and the enormity of the suffering caused could only be judged by observation of behaviour. These are *corpora caeca* at work; and as death is the end result for the individual in the grip of plague, so will it be for the world as a whole as its *moenia* ('defences') are finally beaten down (*expugnata*, 2.1145) by the destructive particles that continually bombard them.

By concluding with the plague, Lucretius is also providing evidence for another argument introduced earlier in Book 5, namely that the world could not possibly have been made for mankind by the gods because there is too much wrong with it—or rather, so much of it is unsuitable or downright dangerous for human habitation. Disease is in fact adduced as one of the aspects of this unsuitability (*cur anni tempora morbos/adportant?*, 'why do the seasons of the year bring forth diseases?', 5.220f.). The general section on disease in Book 6 shows that many regions of the world are hotbeds of infection; as inhabitants of this world, we are subject to those infections just as birds are to the particles that emanate from the Avernian regions. We cannot escape the limitations of our human existence; for us too there is that *alte terminus haerens* ('deep-set boundary stone') which marks off what can be and what cannot within the whole of nature. A salutary reminder of this fact constitutes a suitable ending for the poem as a whole, as well as a fitting climax to the arguments presented in the final two books.

For one of the basic messages of the *DRN* is surely that we, the human race, are part of nature. Like everything else, we are compounded of primary particles, and are ourselves subject to the same eternal process of coming-to-be and passing-away. Attempts to transcend this limitation are futile, and lead inevitably to frustration and despair: to look for a better existence for the soul after death is to invent the worry of a worse one; to try to establish a link with some transcendent deity is to subject ourselves to the tyranny of a Big Brother who is always watching; to pretend that we are somehow different, that we are apart from rather than part of the natural world, is to create a poisoned physical and psychological environment. The 'progress' of civilisation outlined in the latter stages of Book 5 shows a progressive alienation from nature, nowhere more tellingly illustrated perhaps than in the account of the use of animals in warfare at 5.1297–1349. The poetic power of Lucretius' description of the world around us, which the philosophic voice describes as the honey round the cup, drags us back to the natural world and forces us to recognise that that is where we belong. We are part of a world, a scheme of things, which has both a creative and destructive aspect, a fact that we must comprehend and learn to live with. It is one thing to produce a string of arguments against the fear of death as a concept; it is quite another to face the reality of the death-process in all its grim, sordid, squalid detail. The ulcerated corpses at the end of the work are the ultimate condition of all of us, the end towards which our lives proceed as each of us lives through the cycle that all things must follow; and the nature of this end is in the vast majority of cases something over which we have no control. The poet of nature confronts the reader with the most uncomforting reality of all not as a test but as a statement; to write *de rerum natura* entails a duty to tell it how it is. Like Tannhäuser, we must quit the seductive delights of the *Venusberg* and face the truth.

We have come some way I think in accounting for this poem's ending. It is the final response to the dilemma faced by all at some stage in their experience of the world: how to cope with the fact of natural catastrophe and undeserved suffering. The world is a violent place: it may not be Jupiter who wields the thunderbolt, but thunderbolts still exist; indeed, it is the very fact that they strike down the innocent as well as the guilty that proves there is no divine hand guiding them:

> et potius nulla sibi turpi conscius in re uoluitur in flammis innoxius inque peditur turbine caelesti subito correptus et igni?

> Why rather is someone who is conscious that he is guilty of no wrongdoing engulfed in flames, an innocent victim wrapped around by a tornado from heaven and seized by sudden fire?

The victims of the plague are similarly innocent. And in the pain of an individual death from cancer or AIDS, or in the face of natural disasters such as fire, flood and earthquake, or even of ones that can be ascribed to human causes such as ethnic cleansing in Bosnia or genocide in Rwanda, the undeserved suffering again and again forces the anguished cry, 'Why does God let this happen?' The answer is simple. God has no interest in the matter. That is the way things are.

Such is the place of the plague in the poem as statement of the Epicurean position. It has in addition another function, related to that aspect of the poem on which Minadeo concentrates: its patterning around the creation/destruction cycle to which I referred earlier. In his analysis of individual books, Minadeo correctly observes that what he calls the *leitmotif* of the poem, the commencement of each book on a note of creation and its conclusion on a note of destruction, is broken in the proem to Book 2 and in the conclusion of Book 5; he errs in my view in trying to impose it on the sections of the work to which these passages are juxtaposed, namely the conclusion of Book 1 and the proem to Book 6. Certainly Book 1 ends on a seemingly destructive note as Lucretius demonstrates the absurdity of the centripetal theory of matter adopted by the Stoics,

showing that on this view the world would simply fall apart. But unlike the conclusion to Book 2, where the eventual destruction of the world is argued for in terms of Epicurean theory, this is based on a false premise; and in fact Book 1 concludes not with a vision of the world's end but with a celebration of the transition from error to enlightenment:

> namque alid ex alio clarescet, nec tibi caeca nox iter eripiet quin ultima naturai peruideas: ita res accendent lumina rebus.

> For one thing will grow clear out of another, and blind night will not snatch from you the path so as to prevent you seeing the ultimate realities of nature: thus truths will kindle torches for truths.

In fact the tone of the book is wholly creative: it opens with the wonderful image of *Venus genetrix*, a Venus who overcomes Mars the god of war, and proceeds to establish the basic postulates, to declare the poet's mission and to expose the deficiencies of rival theories. It is in fact the triumphal procession following the victory of the *Graius homo* celebrated at 1.62ff., parading both the spoils of the campaign (knowledge of the true nature of things) and the defeated prisoners (discredited alternative views). The sixth book, on the other hand, presents a mounting crescendo of destruction. True, there is that celebration of Epicurus and his *diuina reperta* in the proem (for which compare the openings of Books 3 and 5), but the content is unusually dark. It is here that we get the image of the corruption in the jar (against which we may contrast the honey round the cup of the poet's mission statement), recalling the negative observations on human life in the prologue to Book 2 which led Minadeo to exclude it from his general schema. Also in the prologue to Book 6 we are given the information that part of the Master's teaching has to do with coping with natural disaster:

> quidue mali foret in rebus mortalibus passim quod fieret naturali uarieque uolaret seu casu seu ui, quod sic natura parasset, et quibus e portis occurri cuique deceret.

> [He taught] what evil there was everywhere in human affairs, which comes about and flies around in different ways by natural force or chance, because nature has so provided, and from what gates one should sally forth to meet each one.

And the subject-matter of the book, while ostensibly supporting the thesis that the gods need not be feared because they have no part to play in the operation of the world, concentrates on those aspects of the earth and its surrounds which are indexes of its fragility and thus keeps before our minds the inevitability of its eventual collapse. Everything is hollow, everything is in motion, the force of moving matter tears objects apart.

This accounts for one of the more curious passages of this final book. Immediately prior to the section on disease, Lucretius devotes 184 lines to a discussion of the magnet, a seemingly innocuous phenomenon. As far as the syllabus of the book is concerned, it is presumably there because of its connection with the first philosopher, Thales, and his proposition that all things are full of gods; another example of the human tendency towards erroneous hypothesising of divine causation. But again it is the explanation which is thematically significant and makes the positioning of this section appropriate. In the middle of his account of the magnet, Lucretius places a long digression, in which two principles are stressed: first that there is a constant efflux of particles from all physical objects and secondly that everything is porous. Both these principles are invoked to explain the action of the magnet; and both are intimately linked to the theme of destruction. For (a) it is when more particles are given off than taken in that decline sets in and (b) the fact that 'there is nothing that presents itself to us except body mixed with void' (*nil esse in promptu nisi mixtum corpus inani*, 6.941; cf. 936f. and 958, where the fifth foot *raro corpore* takes on a distinctly formulaic ring) is a clear indication of the instability of the world around us. Contemplation of the magnet is thus not as it was for Thales a reminder of the fact that all things are full of gods; rather it is a *memento mori*. Stone and iron are two of the most solid and stable substances that we know of; but the capacity of this 'stone' (*lapis*, 907) to interact with iron shows how deceptive this seeming solidity is. And the very diversity that Lucretius so often celebrates as part of the richness and beauty of the phenomenal world is likewise drawn on in the context of this argument as index of its impermanence and instability: efflux of particles 959–78; porosity 979–97. The creatures and landscapes of Venus' processional are already pregnant with the seeds of their own destruction.

So in its movement from Venus to the plague, from coming-together to falling-apart, the *De Rerum Natura* itself constitutes an image of the world it describes. This aspect of the work has long been recognised; and it is its fusion of form and content, medium and message, that marks this poem as one of the great artistic achievements in the western cultural tradition. The very words on the page image the atomic process at work:

> quin etiam refert nostris in uersibus ipsis cum quibus et quali sint ordine quaeque locata; namque eadem caelum mare terras flumina solem significant, eadem fruges arbusta animantis; si non omnia sunt, at multo maxima pars est consimilis; uerum positura discrepitant res. sic ipsis in rebus item iam materiai concursus motus ordo positura figurae cum permutantur, mutari res quoque debent.

> Indeed, in these very verses of mine it matters with which and in what order each [letter] is placed; for the same [letters] signify sky, sea, earth, rivers, sun, and the same crops, trees, living things. Even if not all [these letters] are alike, yet by far the greatest part of them are; it is by their position that things sound different. So too in the case of actual objects, when the coming together, the motion, the order, the position, the shape of matter are changed, the objects too must change.

Words are the microcosm to the poem's macrocosm; words represent things and things in a process of change (cf. in particular the *lignum/ignis* illustration at 1.912–14), while the poem represents the world as a whole as it traverses through the cycle of generation and destruction. Beginning, middle, end: truly an Aristotelian *mimesis*.

And a *mimesis* that evokes the very emotions which Aristotle identified as aroused by the tragic experience: fear and pity. Let us accept that the gods have no role to play in meteorological upheavals or natural disasters; but this does not mean that such disasters are any the less fearful in themselves. Earthquakes:

> ancipiti trepidant igitur terrore per urbis: tecta superne timent, metuunt inferne cauernas terrai ne dissoluat natura repente, neu distracta suum late dispandat hiatum idque suis confusa uelit complere ruinis.

> And so they panic through the cities in twofold terror: they fear the roofs above, and they dread the caverns below lest the nature of the earth should suddenly break up, or be drawn asunder and widely spread her gaping jaws, which she may seek to fill with her own ruins.

Volcanoes, too:

> finitimis ad se conuertit gentibus ora, fumida cum caeli scintillare omnia templa cernentes pauida complebant pectora cura, quid moliretur rerum natura nouarum.

[Etna] drew towards itself the faces of neighbouring tribes, when perceiving smoke and sparks in all the regions of the sky they filled their breasts with terror and anxiety as to what kind of cataclysm nature was working towards.

In a universe in which the forces of creation and destruction are evenly balanced and a world in which nothing is inherently stable, we are at the mercy of thunderbolts, earthquakes, volcanoes, fire, flood—and those unseen particles that bring disease. To fear these is a natural human reaction; to avoid their depredations by moving from the vicinity of Etna, not going outside in a thunderstorm or boosting our immune system is regarded as perfectly reasonable behaviour. But there is no escape: death is the inevitable and necessary consequence of birth, and the chance of dying being a pleasant process is slim indeed. To pity those in the final stages of this process is also a natural human reaction:

> illud in his rebus miserandum magnopere unum
> aerumnabile erat…

> One thing in particular that was most pitiful and
> distressing in these circumstances…

The horrific description of the suffering of these innocent victims, whose only *hamartia* was a combination of having been born and being in the wrong place at the wrong time, brings us to the true heart of darkness—the 'supreme moment of complete knowledge' to which the only appropriate response is Kurtz's final cry, 'The horror! The horror!' Can we still claim that 'death is nothing to us' after reading the last 150 lines of Book 6? Is it *nothing* to you, all ye who pass by?

We have a sense of an ending, here, and the ending is a tragic one. Classical tragedy tended to portray the downfall of an individual who sought to transcend the limits of human existence, to make him-/herself as god, an arrogance which the Greeks termed *hubris*. Such was the case with Oedipus, whose attempt to avoid the necessary consequences of his birth achieved no more than the fulfilment of those consequences. Such too was the case of Athens in Thucydides' history, to which Lucretius' ending so clearly alludes. For Lucretius, the tragedy is that of the common man, the person most truly 'undeserving' and 'like ourselves'—because s/he *is* ourselves. We may follow our Greek hero beyond the *flammantia moenia mundi* ('flaming ramparts of the world', 1.74) and defiantly thumb our noses at *religio* by committing the ultimate act of hubris in declaring ourselves the equal of god; we may feel

that we have triumphed over death as a concept, and we may congratulate ourselves for doing so; we may even delude ourselves that our superior knowledge somehow gives us the power to overcome *natura*; but *natura* will have the last word. And here the 'last word' is not the satire with which she berates those who object to having to die in Book 3 but the awfulness of the death agony itself. It is noteworthy that Lucretius does not choose to refer to the thoroughly 'philosophical' way in which Epicurus dealt with his own painful death as Diogenes Laertius does; he deliberately eschews anything that might enable us to feel that this is something we can face with equanimity. For the victims of this disaster, philosophy is to be no consolation, nor to us, who can only respond to their plight in human terms. Unlike the gods, human beings possess the quality of compassion.

In the course of his laudatory account of Epicurus, Diogenes Laertius writes of his [unknown word]('goodwill to all', 10.9) and [unknown word]('benevolence/feeling of friendship towards all', 10.10). This reflects the fact that . . .'friendship'. . . is for Epicurus one of the great human virtues:

> . . . .

> The same understanding both makes us confident
> about nothing terrible being everlasting or of long
> duration and perceives that even in this limited state
> the most complete security is that of friendship.

But this reliance on the security . . . that friendship brings comes at a price; if we have friends, if we emulate the Master. . . then to share the pain of our fellow human beings is a necessary consequence:

> nam et laetamur amicorum laetitia aeque atque nostra
> et pariter dolemus angoribus.

> For we both rejoice at the joy of our friends as much as
> at our own, and are equally pained by their sorrows.

The irony, and it would not be inappropriate to call it *tragic* irony, is that that very bonding we feel towards our fellow *mortales aegri*, our main means of defence against the harshness of our existence in the world, renders indifference to their suffering impossible. The godlike detachment envisaged in the prologue to Book 2 is revealed as essentially unattainable. Philosophy can enable us to understand the physical processes involved in natural disasters, and to accept that these disasters are not to be seen as an act of divine vengeance. But it cannot destroy our feeling of compassion for our fellow human beings; and so, despite confident assertions such as 1.78f. and 3.319–22, it does not, cannot, make us equals of the gods. The insight is as old as Homer:

. . .

> For so did the gods spin fate for wretched mortals, that they should live unhappy; they themselves are free from pain.

So too for Lucretius: between us and the gods there is a great gulf fixed (*diuom natura...semota a nostris rebus seiunctacque longe,* 1.46 = 2.648), and their peace of mind is contingent on the fact that they are 'free from all pain and free from dangers' (*priuata dolore omni, priuata periclis,* 1.47 = 2.649); 'the heartache and the thousand natural shocks/that flesh is heir to' are the lot of human beings. The only difference now is that it is not the gods who are responsible for this but *natura*. The tragic consequences remain: we are on this treadmill; the gods are not.

Thus the *De Rerum Natura*, as Book 6 moves through its account of meteorological and terrestrial phenomena to its grim conclusion, enables us to perceive, as tragedy does, what is truly pitiable and fearful in the human condition. Like the fate of Oedipus, the plague serves as a reminder that our claims to possess the mental capacity to solve all problems are essentially hubristic; we may have minds that can soar above and beyond the *flammantic moenia mundi,* but as organisms compounded of atoms we are subject to the same process of creation and destruction as the most insignificant life-form. And while the Epicurean argument shows that (*un*like Oedipus) we have nothing to fear from the gods in elevating ourselves to their level, their lack of concern puts us completely at the mercy of *natura*. The plague is final and conclusive evidence that we do not live in a world ruled by any kind of moral principle; the conquest of our Greek hero has left us on our own in an unfeeling and indifferent universe. All we can do is bury our dead and learn how to draw on our own resources for the 'enduring spirit' that we need to retain our sanity. That is all that philosophy can offer.

It is not a comfortable or comforting ending; there are no last words of hope, no *Letter to Idomeneus* for the disciples to treasure. Lucretius is not making a work of art out of the life of Epicurus, but out of the life of the world and the individuals within it. And it is this, I think, that enables us to understand not only the content but also the suddenness of the closure. In the title of this essay I make allusion to Frank Kermode's *The Sense of an Ending,* which deals (among other things) with the ways in which the closed system of a work of fiction relates to the open system of the world:

> Men, like poets, rush...*in medias res* when they are born; they also die *in mediis rebus,* and to make sense of their span they need fictive concords with origins and ends, such as give meaning to lives and to poems.

The *De Rerum Natura*—whose ultimate fiction is that it is a philosophical text masquerading as a work of art rather than a work of art representing the world as experienced—is such an attempt to establish 'fictive concord'. For in its progress from birth to death, from the mother-figure of Venus (*Aeneadum genetrix,* 1.1), whose function is to bring male and female together to procreate, to the corpses that choke the sanctuaries of plague-stricken Athens, the poem images not only the cycle of the world but also—and more importantly—that of the individual human being. Macrocosm becomes the symbol of microcosm. It is we who make the journey from joyful childhood to painful death; and in this journey the tools we have for making sense of the world in which we find ourselves are our sense-perceptions, the motions within the soul to which these gives rise, and our feelings of pleasure and pain in response to them. Death is the ending of sense as it is of the poem. The plague represents the process of dying: infection (the invasion of noxious particles), multiplication of symptoms, physical pain, increasing mental derangement (be it delirium or senility), increasing solitude as one loses contact with those around, and finally the moment of death itself, which ends it all. The abrupt ending of the poem captures the ending of life precisely. After death there is no more sensation, no more feeling, no more words. The rest is silence.

Source: J. L. Penwill, "The Ending of Sense: Death as Closure in Lucretius Book 6," in *Ramus—Critical Studies in Greek and Roman Literature,* Vol. 25, No. 2, 1996, pp. 146–65.

Kirk Summers

Author Kirk Summers discusses Lucretius' ideas on the religious traditions of his time.

Epicurus' paradoxical attitude toward religious observances has fascinated scholars for a long time now. Although he dismissed most of the popular notions about the gods and their involvement in human affairs, he still encouraged his followers to participate in the traditional cults of their countries. He believed that, by engaging in popular religious activities, they would strengthen their own mental conception of the gods and thereby be better able to imitate and experience the divine blessedness. Yet, even when keeping this doctrine of imitation in view, one formidable inconsistency remains: How can an Epicurean maintain his [lack of disturbance] while praying, sacrificing, and making vows to gods who neither heed such ritualistic expressions nor are moved by them? In other words, would not the constant exposure to incorrect views about the gods and involvement in wrongheaded rituals corrupt the Epicurean's purified conception of the gods?

Many find a resolution to the problem in Lucretius' *De Rerum Natura*. Since there Lucretius sharply criticizes specific procedures of religious observance, some infer that Epicurus must have encouraged his followers to take part in cults in general terms, but discouraged participation in certain rituals. Numerous passages in Philodemus. . . however, disprove this inference. Philodemus draws heavily upon the words and actions of Epicurus, Hermarchus, Polyaenus, and Metrodorus to argue for full participation in traditional cults, thus presenting the school's orthodox position. Lucretius, on the other hand, by criticizing the specific details of religious practice, particularly Roman religious practice, represents a deviation from his master's original intent on the matter. It will be argued here that the religious ideas of Epicurus, especially as expressed by Philodemus, cannot be harmonized with the more revolutionary ones of Lucretius.

LUCRETIUS 5.1198–1203

For Lucretius' contemporary Cicero, *superstitio* is the groundless fear of the gods, while *religio* is the pious worship of them. Elsewhere he defines *religio* in practical terms by *cultus deorum* instead of a set of doctrinal statements. Whereas the exact nature of the gods remained nebulous, every Roman knew his or her duty regarding the traditional rituals that constituted *religio*. *Religio* meant fulfilling an understood contractual relationship with the gods. It involved acts, rather than beliefs; it centered on cult, instead of theology.

Therefore, when in the following passage Lucretius inveighed against the outward modes of

Lucretius subscribed to the belief system of the Greek philosopher Epicurus, whose ideals are evident throughout the poem.

worship, he struck at the heart of religion as the Romans knew it: few could have appreciated, as their primary expression of religion, the emphasis he was putting on meditation:

> nec pietas ullast velatum saepe videri
> vertier ad lapidem atque omnis accedere ad aras,
> nec procumbere humi prostratum et pandere palmas
> ante deum delubra, nec aras sanguine multo
> spargere quadrupedum, nec votis nectere vota,
> sed mage placata posse omnia mente tueri.

Cyril Bailey's comments on this passage exemplify the perplexity Lucretius' brief diatribe against religion has aroused. He remarks that Epicurus observed religious ceremonies and performed blood sacrifices and called on others to do likewise to prove their piety; he adds, "it is not the act of worship which the Epicurean thinks wrong, but its motive." It is important to note, however, that Bailey generalizes about Epicureans rather than attributes the view to Lucretius, since the passage at hand would contradict his assertion. The rest of his arguments exhibit the same unwarranted blending of Epicurean and Lucretian ideas. Lucretius is pious, he thinks, like Epicurus, and not at all against the worship of the gods; Lucretius only resents

> "...Lucretius emphasizes that religion has its origin in fear and intimidation, and that many of its cultic acts still depend on those ideas. Accordingly he derides current religious practice, with all of its browbeating and contractual requirements."

sacrifices and religious ceremonies, since they derive from superstition, that is, false fears stemming from false beliefs about the gods. Yet it cannot be, as Bailey says, that Lucretius is pious *like* Epicurus if Lucretius disparages the very sacrifices and ceremonies that Epicurus encouraged. Still he continues this train of thought: true piety for the Epicurean, he says, is the blissful contemplation of divine mental images. But does Lucretius' *placata posse omnia mente tueri* really have a parallel in Epicurus? Is "true piety" for Epicurus the same as for Lucretius? The texts suggest otherwise.

In analyzing this passage and others of the *De rerum natura* in detail I want to show that Lucretius writes about current Roman religious practice, and that the Romans who read (or heard) his poem would have recognized the elements of their own religion in it. Furthermore, Lucretius' attack on Roman cult is comprehensive; he attacks the totality of the Roman religious experience, including both *publica sacra* and personal acts of piety. Although Lucretius never explicitly forbids participation in cult, the hostility he shows throughout his poem to specific acts of traditional Roman piety and the confidence he places in reason suggest that he envisioned a religious experience different from that of Epicurus. He gives no indication, as Epicurus often did, that participation in standing cultic rituals offered benefits to one with a right attitude. Instead, Lucretius emphasizes that religion has its origin in fear and intimidation, and that many of its cultic acts still depend on those ideas. Accordingly he derides current religious practice, with all of its browbeating and contractual requirements.

Lines 5.1198–1203 belong to the larger context of Lucretius' discussion of the origins of religious beliefs and rites among mankind (5:1161–67):

> Nunc quae causa deum per magnas numina gentis pervulgarit et ararum compleverit urbis suspiciendaque curarit sollemnia sacra, quae nunc in magnis florent sacra rebu' locisque, unde etiam nunc est mortalibus insitus horror qui delubra deum nova toto suscitat orbi terrarum et festis cogit celebrare diebus.

Nations have filled their cities with temples, he says, and have instituted sacred rites for holy days, because they have ascribed to the anthropomorphic images of the gods, which come to them intuitively both when awake and in dreams, human attributes that do not belong to them. Furthermore, since these mental images of the gods appear nobler, stronger, and happier, and since these gods seem to accomplish many miracles, people suppose that they control the events in the heavens.

Several points are worth noting from this larger context, 5.1161–93, before analyzing 5.1198–1203. Despite the broad historical (*pervulagarit, compleverit,* and *curarit*) and universal (*toto orbi*) scope applied to the discussion of *religio,* Lucretius' real interest in the here and now—contemporary Rome—permeates the passage. Thus he quickly dismisses the past tenses (1162–63) for the present tenses in the lines that follow: *florent, est, suscitat,* and *cogit.* He reiterates the *nunc* of 1164 in 1165 to emphasize the present, and then adds *nova* in 1166 to show that these habits persist. The phrases *sollemnia sacra, delubra suscitat,* and *festis diebus* are general enough that no Roman would have pictured, say, Egyptian or Jewish practices, but rather his own religion.

Regarding the next section (lines 1169–93), Bailey rightly notes that Epicureans viewed the initial cause of religious feeling in man, that is, the constant stream of divine images, as legitimate and pure. Religion became distorted only when mankind misinterpreted those images by attaching to them limitless power and the will to intervene in human affairs. Bailey recognizes that lines 1198–1203 (*nec pietas ullast ...*) relate to this later distortion, but he does not carry the point through to its conclusion. Lucretius transforms the idea of what piety is for a Roman by rejecting rituals that perpetuate a belief in a reciprocal contract between gods and men. He opts instead for a rational meditation of the workings of nature, which alone can ease fears. Clearly, Lucretius thinks that the implied

'The School of Athens' by Renaissance artist Raphael depicts the discussions that took place among philosophers like Lucretius and his forefather, Epicurus.

threats and anxiety inherent within traditional Roman religion inhibit the attainment of this goal.

In 1198–99, *velatum saepe videri/vertier ad lapidem,* the word *velatum* connotes a specific Roman custom, as opposed to a Greek one. Pierre Boyancé has suggested that *velatum* refers not to the subject of *vertier,* as commonly taken, but to *lapidem,* which were sometimes garlanded. He bases his argument on the grounds that veiling the head is, according to him, properly *ritu Graeco;* however, exactly the opposite is true. Whether an official priest or priestess acting on behalf of the State, or a

private citizen sacrificing for his own purposes, the Roman commonly worshipped *capite velato.* Commentators have drawn the parallel with Vergil *Aeneid* 3.405–7, where Helenus tells Aeneas and his companions,

> purpureo velare comas adopertus amictu ne qua inter sanctos ignis in honore deorum hostilis facies occurrat et omina turbet …

Helenus then bids Aeneas to make this a traditional part of their religion. Ovid mentions Numa *caput niveo velatus amictu.* The purpose of the veil, according to Virgil's Helenus, is to keep the worshiper from seeing *hostilis facies* lest they disturb the *omina.* Various Roman coins and statues however, show that the eyes were not covered during the ceremony (see discussion below). On the *Ara Pacis* (voted 13 B.C., completed 9 B.C.), erected by Augustus, Aeneas (together with Vestal Virgins, priests, and magistrates) is represented in the act of sacrificing with his head veiled, yet eyes uncovered. Perhaps the veil only demonstrates the readiness to cover the eyes if evil visages should appear in the sacred flames and therefore was not always pulled over the eyes.

In particular, coins depict the head of *Pietas* herself wearing a veil (Herennius, Caesar, Hirtius, Tiberius) or her full figure with veiled head and in the act of sacrificing (Caligula, Galba, Hadrian, Antoninus Pius). Specifically, Caligula's coin shows a veiled *Pietas* seated and holding out a patera on the verse; the obverse portrays a veiled Caligula sacrificing a bull in the temple of *Divus Augustus* and holding out a patera. The extended patera, as well as the veiled head, connects Caligula with the *Pietas* on the reverse, suggesting both the piety of his sacrifice and the piety he offers to his subjects. On Galba's coin *Pietas* stands veiled at an altar on which is a relief with Aeneas, Anchises, and Ascanius; the legend around *Pietas* reads *Pietas Augusti, S.C.* The coin of Hadrian shows a standing, veiled *Pietas* on the reverse, holding her hands upward with an offering or in a praying gesture. On the reverse of Antoninus Pius' coin, *Pietas,* her head veiled, scatters grains of incense on an altar. These numismatic types derive from the numerous Roman statues, from all periods, of *Pietas* and similar goddesses wearing a veil.

Although the personification of *Pietas* most often signifies the devotion of child to parent, it also signifies the devotion of the citizen to the gods, as the many depictions of *Pietas* before the altar make clear. In the same way, Aeneas is *pius* both because he rescued his father from Troy and because he brought with him the household gods. I mention these depictions of *Pietas*, not because I think Lucretius refers here to the personified deity (he does not), but to demonstrate the wide gulf between his concept of piety and the prevailing Roman view: in the latter view, piety entailed most certainly worshipping the gods at the altar with veiled head; the deity herself personified the importance of wearing the veil before the altar. The average Roman must have clearly grasped that Lucretius had made a radical departure from religious custom when he asserted *nec pietas ullast velatum saepe videri.*

The precise connotation of *lapis* in 1199 has troubled many. If we take 1198–1202 to refer to one ceremony, then Lucretius depicts a typical worshiper who veils his head, turns toward the god's statue (*lapis*), and then prostrates himself. An attractive parallel, often adduced by commentators, is Suetonius *Vitellius* 2. Here Vitellius flatters Caligula by worshipping him as he would a god: *capite velato, circumvertensque se, deinde procumbens.* In view of this parallel, Lucretius' use of *lapis* for the image of the god would be contemptuous and derogatory. Yet two factors preclude us from taking *lapis* to mean "statue": first, Lucretius does not trace the steps of any one rite here, so that we can draw parallels to the descriptions of ceremonies in other authors; rather, he combines elements from several ceremonies to make a generalization about *pietas.* Second, he does not employ derisive imagery in the passage to represent the other cultic objects or acts that he mentions; to the contrary, he describes the rites in straightforward terms. Indeed, the passage makes perfect sense if *lapis* simply means "stone," without further connotation.

A Roman would not have considered *lapis* to be a derogatory word in the same way as someone with a Judaeo-Christian perspective. There were many instances in which Romans revered *lapides,* probably aerolites, which they believed Jupiter hurled from heaven. The stones represented either the divinity itself or some aspect of its personality and function. For example, the Romans considered the relocation of the black Cybele stone from Pessinus to Rome in 204 B.C. to be equivalent to transferring the goddess herself. Both Munro and Bailey think that if *lapis* is not disparaging then it probably means either the *termini* stones or stones "set up in the streets and roads, etc. occurring so often all periods," which were said to be *sacer.* The former did indeed involve an elaborate worship service (including veiling and sacrificing) out in the country. As for the latter category of stones, I cannot find solid evidence that indicates what they were or even that they were venerated.

We have to wonder why Lucretius chose the singular over the plural (cf. the plural forms *aras, delubra,* and *vota*). One possible answer is that he intends to say *the* stone instead of *a* stone. If so, a better parallel is found in a letter of Cicero to his friend Trebatius who has recently converted to Epicureanism. Cicero complains that as an Epicurean Trebatius can no longer function properly in public life, since Epicurean principles so often contradict Roman laws that promote fairness and selflessness among the community. Furthermore, Cicero implies that as an Epicurean Trebatius will not be willing to swear by the Jupiter-stone: "Quo modo autem tibi placebit 'Iovem Lapidem iurare,' cum scias Iovem iratum esse nemini posse?" The Romans had two ceremonies involving a stone and an oath. In one instance the stone represents the perjurer, while the priest acts as Jupiter. The participants take their oath, and then the priest casts away the stone to show what will happen to the one who breaks the oath. The *locus classicus* of this ceremony is Polybius 3.25. In the second instance, the stone is an extension of Jupiter, representing his thunderbolt, which the priest uses to strike a pig, the perjurer. Livy explains the details of that ceremony. Possibly the same stone is at issue, viewed from two different perspectives: Jupiter either cast the stone (assuming it was an aerolite) out from heaven as a perjurer, or hurled it from heaven against perjurers. From either perspective, the stone served as a sacred symbol of Jupiter's wrath against the practitioners of deceit.

A few other stones worshipped by the Romans could be mentioned here, but it should be evident by now how uncomfortable the phrase *nec pietas ullast ... vertier ad lapidem* must have made the average Roman, since he could immediately think of several instances in which he himself revered a stone. And perhaps Lucretius consciously intended to be vague, to leave each contemplating whatever instance came first to mind. Any Roman would have recognized himself in Lucretius' *vertier ad lapidem,* not because of the stone's intrinsic connection with statues of Jupiter and the like, but because sometimes the gods appeared as stones.

It is tempting to relate the phrase *omnis accedere ad aras* of 1199 to the *supplicatio*, which became an important Roman ritual around the third century B.C. We know from Ceasar and Cicero that Romans practiced it during the late Republic, and Livy describes the features of the ceremony as practiced during the Punic Wars: "undique matronae in publicum effusae circa deum delubra discurrunt crinibus passis aras verrentes, nixae genibus, supinas manus ad caelum ad deos tendentes." The *supplicatio* was an opportunity for the general Roman public, in times of peril and thanksgiving, to worship numerous gods at once, since images of them would be placed out on the lawn, often on couches, and there worshipped with kneeling or prostration. Lucretius' description of prostration, immediately followed by opening of the palms, along with the phrase *ante deum delubra* at 1201, resembles Livy's account.

But the passage of Livy suggests that the participants of the *supplicatio* wore laurel wreaths rather than veils, although one could argue that the veiled women portrayed on the Altar of Manlius are engaged in a *supplicatio*.

The *supplicatio* afforded the opportunity for Romans to express intense piety. Latte remarks, "The participation of the people as a whole in a religious act, and the intensification of feeling produced thereby, had previously been unknown in Roman religion. Instead of formulaic prayers consisting of wishes, we now have supplication that found words in the mood of the moment." Plautus illustrates this in the *Rudens* when he says "facilius si qui pius est a dis supplicans / quam qui scelestust invenient veniam sibi". Thus the act of "approaching every altar," at least in the context of the *supplicatio*, was for the Romans a unique experience. No fixed ritual or formulaic prayers existed to stifle the spontaneous outpouring of feeling to the gods. The gods were exposed for all to express personal heartfelt thanksgivings or unrehearsed petitions. In the mind of the Romans the act of "approaching every altar" would have been an especially pious one; certainly Lucretius' phrase, among other things, would have made the average Roman think of the *supplicatio*, and undoubtedly in that regard he would have felt deeply the import of *nec pietas ullast.*

At 1200–1201, the phrase "nec procumbere humi prostratum et pandere palmas / ante deum delubra" could again have many significations. In fact, it has been argued thus far that Lucretius intended to be vague, although the *supplicatio* may have served roughly as the archetypal cultic practice. Nevertheless, some parallels shed light on how a Roman might have understood the phrase.

Stretching oneself out on the ground before the images of the gods provided the outward manifestation of the inward intensity of one's emotions. Ovid's wife falls prostrate before the Penates in an earnest plea for her husband: *Ante Lares sparsis prostrata capillis.* Similarly in Livy, the prostrate women, sweeping the temple floors with their hair, implore mercy from the gods to stop the pestilence.

Cicero also sheds light on the meaning of prostration, although his example is of a nobleman before the Roman people: "ut, cum minus valuissent suffragiis quam putassent, postea prolatis comitiis prosternerent se et populo Romano fracto animo atque humili supplicarent." This action accords with the Roman concept of piety: there is an understanding of one's role in an implied contractual relationship, as well as the expectation of a return. In other words, piety is the humble acknowledgement of reliance on the will of another, with an offer of devotion to gain favor; prostration, as a part of that piety, expresses humility and dependence.

A passage of Tibullus will illustrate the point. While writing about troubles with a certain girl, Tibullus complains of his innocence, but concedes that, if guilty of some crime, he will beg for forgiveness: "non ego, si merui, dubitem procumbere templis / et dare sacratis oscula liminibus, … supplex …". Whereas Christian theology views worship as a response to the majestic nature of the deity, Romans prostrate themselves in worship to bargain with gods, asking them either to forgive a past crime (hence the sacrifice or vow) or to procure a future benefit. The Christian idea of glorification for its own sake was foreign to the Romans. A Roman did not prostrate himself to adore the gods, but to ask something from them.

Thus, since piety involved a certain amount of dealing and expectation, and since prostration was symbolic of the supplication, Lucretius rejected the prevailing concept of *pietas* by applying Epicurus' doctrine in a logical way. Epicureanism taught that the gods did not stoop to make bargains; therefore prostration was ridiculous.

Closely connected with the act of prostration is the act of praying, which Lucretius represents here through the phrase *pandere palmas*. Ovid reveals the meaning of the outstretched arms or open palms concisely when he writes *ad vatem vates orantia bracchia tendo*. The poet as *vates* performs a religious act. Seneca, in a strange mixture of Epicureanism and Stoicism, also combats this expression of Roman piety (though unlike Lucretius he means to retain the prayerful communication with an inner god): "Non sunt ad caelum elevandae manus nec exorandus aeditus, ut nos ad aurem simulacri, quasi magis exaudiri possimus, admittat; prope est a te deus, tecum est, intus est". Aeneas prays in distress over the storm sent by Aeolus: "ingemit, et, duplicis tendens ad sidera palmas". Piety, Lucretius is saying, does not involve praying to the gods.

Little needs to be said about the act of sacrificing, since it was a common expression of piety in the ancient world. Possibly Lucretius continues to use the model of the *supplicatio,* since Romans did sacrifice during that ceremony. He had already censured the sprinkling of altars with blood when he

described the efforts of men to secure divine aid in making their wives pregnant

> multo sanguine maesti conspergunt aras adolentque altaria donis, ut gravidas reddant uxores semine largo.

Although the term *pietas* does not appear here, the concept is as much at issue as in 5.1201–2. Line 4.1239 begins with *nequiquam*, a hint of the *nec pietas ullast* to come. Sacrificing and other modes of ritual are not impious: they are vain, if not emotionally harmful, because they come from a misunderstanding of the nature of things. Taken together, then, these passages constitute a forceful denunciation of the Roman's view of reality, a conception that was reflected in the way they worshipped.

The offering and fulfilling of vows was a practice shared by most ancient Mediterranean peoples, yet for the Romans it had greater significance than for most: since they couched the language of their vows in juristic terms, which was for them "the strongest form of obligation," the vow served as a visible sign of their *iustitia* toward the gods. The hundreds of inscriptions in the *CIL* that contain the abbreviation *v.s.l.m.* (*votum solvit libens merito*) attest to the prevalence of the practice. Its importance within the Roman experience is evinced by its frequent mention in a wide variety of genres, including history, myth, poetic imagery, novel, satire, and autobiography. Cicero includes a provision for vows in his sketch of the ideal set of religious laws. In contrast, Lucretius believes that people make vows in vain. Striking evidence is that all the same they are driven onto the shallows by a sudden gale.

One final comment needs to be made on the idiomatic use of *necto* here. Lambin is uncharacteristically silent on the matter, whereas Munro (ad loc.) says "*vota* are here the *votivae tabulae* or *tabellae*, hung up on the wall of a temple or elsewhere," and equivalent to *votivas*, as in Vergil *Aeneid* 3.279: *votisque incendimus aras*. By this Bailey has understood Munro to mean "to string votive-tablets together," which he considers unlikely. But Munro's interpretation of *vota* (= *votivas*) makes sense if we take the following *votis* to mean "vows," and *nectere* to be Lucretius' poetic way of expressing obligation. Thus the whole phrase reads in English: "It is not piety … to make oneself responsible for a votive-offering by making a vow."

The next line, "sed mage placata posse omnia mente tueri," sums up all that Lucretius has been trying to say thus far. The word *tueri* anticipates what follows in lines 1204–40, but no one to my knowledge has recognized how they link with 1198–1203. Lucretius is proposing that the ignorance that he describes at 1204–40 is the reason for certain Roman religious practices, thus showing how futile they really are. In ignorance men and women veil their heads and prostrate themselves because they feel small in the face of what they presume to be the immeasurable power of the gods and their eternal natures; people sacrifice because they shiver before displays of their anger and want to win their favor; they pray and make vows because they imagine the gods can turn storms to calm, and generally that they govern the world. Again we find the word *nequiquam*, which we may assume now sums up Lucretius' opinion on the activity of religion.

Thus, in stark contrast to Epicurus' tack, Lucretius has undermined theologically and rationally the reasons for performing customary rituals. And lest any Roman still not recognize his own religion in all of this, Lucretius adds,

> usque adeo res humanas vis abdita quaedam obterit, et pulchros fascis saevasque secures proculcare ac ludibrio sibi habere videtur.

It is none other than Roman glory that religion diminishes.

As a final argument showing that Lucretius is attacking current religious practice in this passage, I adduce Lucretius' own anticipation of this passage at 5.73–75. Lines 55–90 serve as a unit in which Lucretius outlines the order of his arguments in book 5. He sums up 5.1193–1203 with the following:

> et quibus ille modis divom metus insinuarit pectora, terrarum qui in orbi sancta tuetur fana lacus lucos aras simulacraque divom.

Clearly Lucretius has taken his criticism of specific ritualistic procedures further than Epicurus ever did. Rather than stressing the possibility of compromising with current practices, as Epicurus did, Lucretius points out in the strongest terms that mankind created the holy shrines, pools, groves, altars, and statues out of a false fear of the gods; his subsequent call to a "peaceful contemplation of the true nature of things" might take place in a holy place, such as a temple, but Lucretius never says so.

In analyzing this passage I have been attempting to reconstruct what a Roman would have thought when he read it. In some sense Lucretius' passage is general enough that it could have affected other peoples similarly, especially the Greeks, but not so thoroughly. A Greek, for example, would have agreed that veiling the head and prostrating oneself did not signify piety, since Greek religious practice did not entail either one. The fact is, Lucretius has aimed his attack on piety specifically at Romans and the way they practice religion. Nor should we underrate the force of Lucretius' passage: he hits right at the heart of Roman religion and everyday expressions of Roman piety.

Undoubtedly a contemporary Roman reader would have had a much different reaction to what Lucretius writes than we do today. He or she would have perceived much more of their own religious life in the very words and phrases that we now consider well-justified attacks on paganism. Yet because Lucretius' attacks seem less harsh today, many have resisted seeing the anti-religious elements of his poem. Lines 5.1198–1203 are the most open censure of Roman religion, but the poem is full of echoes of ordinary piety in late republican Rome and contains a redefinition of the conception of piety.

Lucretius considered his task to be one of liberation: "primum quod magnis doceo de rebus et artis / religionum animum nodis exsolvere pergo." He wanted to free his captive compatriots from their own religion, which functioned for them as an ordering of life at home, in public, and in the individual heart. When they learned the ways of nature, he thought, they would see that there was no need for elaborate burial rites, because the self dies with the body. This, of course, has negative implications for the Lar familiaris: "certe ut videamur cernere eum quem / rellicta vita iam mors et terra potitast." No longer will the happy home and wife and children receive the father, because he feels nothing and craves nothing; he cannot even be a *praesidium* for his own.

Exposing false fears about death also removes the need for the *Parentalia*:

> et quocumque tamen miseri venere parentant et nigras reactant pecudes et manibu' divis inferias mittunt multoque in rebus acerbis acrius advertunt animos ad religionem.

But this worship of the dead was one of the oldest of the Roman rites, with both communal and private expressions. It was based on the notion that the ancestors continued to be a part of the family with a new life outside the walls of the city. For Lucretius these concerns over death and the dead were ridiculous misunderstandings of nature and a major cause of evil among men.

Lucretius does not only attempt to alter the way Romans think about themselves; he also challenges the way they think about divine activity. The gods do not rule the universe, nor do they involve themselves in its development or destruction. The crops grow and creatures reproduce without them; and even the calendar itself precludes their interest in us. The gods do not send birds or lightning as omens of their will. To all such interpretations of reality, so deeply rooted in the Roman way of life and so much a basis of Roman religion, Lucretius throws down the gauntlet of his challenge. Death, crops, animals, seasons, weather, all have natural explanations and causes; the best religion is not traditional religion at all, but a contemplation of how the various phenomena of life and death fit into nature's great mechanism without divine involvement. It is a revolutionary proposition that no conservative Roman could have taken lightly.

The Religious in Lucretius

Lucretius' derisive stance toward cult at 5.1198–1203 diverges so starkly from Epicurus' attitude about religion that many consider it a temporary aberration. Other passages in *De rerum natura* seem to reveal the poet's admiration for those same rites and ceremonies that he elsewhere despises, or, as Bailey said, to indicate "something like a personal affection for their details." Nevertheless, I will argue that none of those so-called religious passages provide evidence that Lucretius encourages his readers to continue participating in the traditional worship of the gods; instead, in each case the poet either follows his description of a religious practice with some qualification, or contrasts the fear that marks the practice to the *pax* that comes through the rational contemplation of nature.

Those who want to see in Lucretius a religious sensitivity most often turn to 6.68–79:

> quae nisi respuis ex animo longeque remittis dis indigna putare alienaque pacis eorum, delibata deum per te tibi numina sancta saepe oberunt; non quo violari summa deum vis possit, ut ex ira poenas petere imbibat acris, sed quia tute tibi placida cum pace quietos constitues magnos irarum volvere fluctus, nec delubra deum placido cum pectore adibis, nec de corpore quae sancto simulacra feruntur in mentis hominum divinae nuntia formae suscipere haec animi tranquilla pace valebis.

H. Scullard relies on this single passage to support his view of Lucretius: "Lucretius seems to envisage some continuation of traditional worship when he says that unless you reject all erroneous ideas from your mind, 'you will not be able to approach the shrines of the gods with quiet heart.'" Since Lucretius specifically refers to our state of mind when approaching shrines, it seems *prima facie* that Lucretius not only condones approaching

the shrines, but encourages it. Yet the context cautions against such a conclusion, since the emphasis of the entire passage is on how religious fear disturbs mental tranquility (*pax*), not on the specific details of worship. In the immediately preceding lines Lucretius discusses how the events in the ethereal regions cause people to be afraid and to engage in old modes of worship (*rursus in antiquas referuntur religionis,*) that is, to appease the gods and win their favor, which is the core of Roman religious practice (as at 5.1161–1204). All such activity is based on the mistaken notion that the gods have regard for people and exercise an active sovereignty over the universe. Furthermore, the phrases *placido cum pectore adibis* and *suscipere haec animi tranquilla pace valebis* recall Lucretius' redefinition of *pietas* at 5.1203 (*sed mage placata posse omnia mente tueri*), which follows immediately upon his expression of scorn for specific rites. *Pax* and its cognates in these two passages are equivalent to Epicurus' concept of. . . something the gods possess (*pacis eorum,* 6.69; *placida cum pace quietos*), and Epicureans desire. Lucretius wants his readers to understand that they can never achieve the *pax* of the gods if they continue to harbor and act on false notions about them. One of the false notions that causes the most harm, according to Lucretius, is the belief that the gods "roll forth great waves of anger" and are eager to exact punishment. After undermining the intent behind religious practice, he cannot then in line 75 be encouraging his readers to carry on their religion as before. Thus he must be underscoring the impossibility of approaching the *delubra deum*. . . since the rites to be performed there have their basis in fear.

Even if Lucretius advocates approaching the shrines here, he does not advocate prayer, repentance, or sacrifice. I do not think, however, that Lucretius imagines his followers will need to continue going to the shrines. He has argued already that *pax* is achieved through a correct understanding of physical laws (first and foremost of which is that the gods do not control them), which is hardly promoted by the rites in the *delubra*. In 5.1203, he envisions a kind of mental focusing (*omnia mente tueri*) as the surest means to *pax*. Likewise, the emphasis in 6.68–79 is on the peace that the mind itself can secure, even in respect to the gods. The *simulacra* of line 76 are not the solid images or statues of the gods inside the *delubra* of 75, which would create visual images directly affecting the outer senses of the worshippers. The *simulacra* spoken of here are brought directly *in mentes hominum*, a notion that mirrors Epicurus' [application of understanding] that is, the idea of a direct, mental apprehension of certain fine or subtle images, which in the case of the gods come to us directly from the intermundane regions during dreams or moments of meditation. This accords with an earlier statement of Lucretius, that the gods do not visit their own temples anyway.

In the major religious passages Lucretius continually shifts the focal point of truly pious activity away from the holy temples of the gods into a mental sphere. Other passages in Lucretius progressively reveal a similar contempt for the temples and statues of the gods. At 5.306–10 he tells how, like the wearing away of stones with time, *delubra deum simulacraque fessa fatisci*. At 6.417–20 he challenges the notion that the gods send thunderbolts since these bolts often smash the *bene facta deum ... simulacra* and shatter the *sancta deum delubra*. Finally, in his description of the Athenian plague at 6.1272–77, he describes how people hope for salvation from the gods, but in vain. The telltale sign of the impotency of their shrines and statues was when the reality of nature forced people to stop worshipping at the *caelestum templa* and crowd them instead with dying bodies, because *praesens dolor exsuperabat*. Rather than being a haven for life and health, they became, fittingly, a place of decay and suffering.

Lastly, Diskin Clay has made an interesting observation on 6.68–79 that supports the thesis that Lucretius does not encourage his followers to approach the shrines and altars. The *tute tibi* of 6.73 strongly indicates a self-sufficient piety consisting of the contemplation of nature. This, I would add, to Lucretius' mind is best achieved apart from the gloomy and intimidating atmosphere of his native country's religious rites. The rites either foster fear or stem from it, thereby disturbing the mind and preventing it from discovering the true nature of the universe.

Venus and Cybele

Two other connected passages must be treated here, because they seem to indicate a use for traditional religious rites: 1.1–43 about Venus, and 2.600–660 about Cybele. The former passage especially has generated much debate. Most arguments reveal a reluctance on the part of scholars to accept that Lucretius could advocate a form of [reverence towards the gods] that deviated from what Epicurus recommended. Indeed, Lucretius appears to be striking a religious chord from the prologue of his poem.

Nevertheless, nothing in the invocation to Venus calls the reader to traditional religion, nor does the passage itself contradict Lucretius' overall teaching on piety.

Recently Diskin Clay has asserted that Lucretius introduces the goddess only to reject her later. Lucretius is, according to Clay, entering into the world of his audience and taking them on a journey from an incorrect conception of the universe to a right contemplation of nature. He points out that an uninitiated reader, reading the poem from start to finish, would need to be immersed in doctrines so unfamiliar gradually. Thus it makes sense for Lucretius to meet his audience where they are.

I agree with Clay's argument that Lucretius does not really reject Venus, but rather treats the same topic later in technical, atomistic terms. He couches his invocation in strikingly religious terms because that is what a Roman expects to hear. Religious language retains its value for Lucretius as a kind of vernacular observation on reality; it is simply the way a Roman communicates about the universe, and it is too deeply a part of the Romans' shared cognitive experience to disregard. Occasionally throughout the poem, Lucretius lifts the veil of this metaphorical, religious language to reveal certain truths about the nature of the universe that underlie it. In the end the language can remain the same, but the words must take on new significations.

In his invocation to Venus Lucretius is primarily concerned with Venus and Mars as symbols for constructive (or conservative) and destructive forces of the universe, respectively. The underlying Epicurean doctrine that informs Lucretius' representation of these creative and destructive forces through Venus and Mars is that of ...equilibrium, a doctrine that Lucretius discusses at 2.569–80. There Lucretius calls the destructive forces *motus exitiales* and the conservative and constructive forces *genitales auctificique*. Usually the two forces balance each other, although in their war, as it were, sometimes one obtains the upper hand, sometimes the other. They do not influence the gods, but only the *creata*.

In 2.569–80 Lucretius shows that there are natural creative and destructive forces within the universe, but he is unwilling to attribute the activities to personal beings. Whenever he speaks of the forces of growth and decay, or conservation and destruction, he quickly adds that the immortal gods are free from such concerns. The gods are not responsible for the action of *servare*; the law of equilibrium is. The Venus whom Lucretius invokes can be no goddess at all since the gods are not influential forces. They are antisocial, inactive, and motionless; they do not engage in love affairs, nor is there any contention among them; they do not grow angry, they do not protect or give aid, nor do they respond to prayers. When the poet invokes a Venus able to do all these things, some poetic personification of an insentient force must be at work. Lucretius hopes that the creative and conservative forces of the universe will predominate long enough for him to explain the teachings of Epicurus. In other words, in a time of civil strife, he prays for peace.

Certain parallels between Lucretius' opening invocation and his description of equilibrium further indicate that Venus stands as a symbol for the positive aspect of this principle. In the first 20 lines of the invocation Lucretius alludes to new life, creativity, and fertility in nearly every other genus omne animantum concipitur visitque exortum lumina solis. . . . Venus herself is called *genetrix, voluptas,* and *alma.* She fills (*concelebras*) the world with her presence, and by her "genus omne animantum concipitur visitque exortum lumina solis." Similarly at 2.571 the constructive forces are said to be *rerum genitales,* and at 2.576–77 the creative influence likewise brings children to the light of day: "miscetur funere vagor / quem pueri tollunt visentes luminis oras." The imagery of productivity is hinted at again in *navigerum* and *frugiferentis,* followed later by *frondiferas* in line 18. Lucretius pictures the world responding to the advancing Venus with light, warmth, and regeneration: the world basks again in the sunlight ("tibi rident aequora ponti / placatumque nitet diffuso lumine caelum"), as the life-giving springtime (*species ... verna diei*) returns and the productive (*genitabilis*) breeze of the west wind grows strong (*viget*). Likewise at 2.575 Lucretius says that a certain vitality takes hold of the world in the cycle of the constructive and destructive forces: "nunc hic nunc illic superant vitalia rerum." Finally, in the invocation we are presented with a string of sexually suggestive words and phrases: *capta lepore, cupide, virentis, incutiens blandum ... amorem*, and *propagent*, all of which are summed up at 2.571 in the one word *auctifici.*

From this beautiful personification of the productive forces, Lucretius can turn in the next verses to appeal for a measure of poetic creativity. Significantly he uses the word *gubernas* in line 21 to describe Venus' activity, a word that he will later apply to the productive activity of nature contrasted with the inactivity of the gods:

praeterea solis cursus lunaeque meatus expediam qua vi flectat natura gubernans, ne forte haec inter caelum terramque reamur libera sponte sua cursus lustrare perennis, morigera ad fruges augendas atque animantis, neve aliqua divom volvi ratione putemus.

Crops grow and animals reproduce apart from some plan of the gods, because the gods pass their time without caring for our reality: *deos securum agere aevom.* The correspondence with 1.44–49 is close. A failure to understand this law of how "heaven and earth traverse their yearly courses" and how things grow and animals reproduce, leads one to return again *in antiquas ... religiones* and to take to oneself *dominos acris,* that is, to look for help in the forms and gods of traditional religion.

To Lucretius, myths reflect a popular wisdom and owe their origin to ignorance of the nature of reality:

cetera, quae fieri in terris caeloque tuentur mortales, pavidis cum pendent mentibu' saepe, et faciunt animos humilis formidine divum depressosque premunt ad terram propterea quod ignorantia causarum conferre deorum cogit ad imperium res et concedere regnum.

The fears of mankind stem from the belief that the gods are active in the universe, when in fact they are not. Lucretius' message is that people will find peace only when they attribute to the natural interchange of atoms and void what they previously imputed to divine intelligence. Even so, he still views myth as a colorful and even useful shorthand for talking about natural phenomena, as evidenced by his frequent reliance on it. Also, the well-known passage on the symbolic uses of names like Neptune, Ceres, and Bacchus indicates that he allowed the allegorical use of myth under certain conditions.

In his poem, Lucretius slides between mythological glitter and bitter philosophical medicine with a remarkable dexterity. He has found a way to retain some of the outward linguistic trappings of religion. Lucretius may have been trying to give a temporary impression of religiosity by his invocation of Venus, as Clay suggests, but every other use of myth and every other mention of religion in the poem is either clearly allegorical or sharply negative. Since the *prooemium* corresponds so closely to Lucretius' own teachings about the creativity and destruction in the universe, it is safe to assume that he is allegorizing those principles through myth rather than promoting traditional religion.

The description of the magna mater cult

The invocation to Venus has many interesting parallels with the description of the Magna Mater cult at 2.600–660. Lucretius applies the term *genetrix* to describe both Venus and the Great Mother at 1.1 and 2.599 respectively, although he does not exactly equate the two. He views Cybele as an agent or instrument of the constructive force of Venus. Mother Earth produces her fruit in response to the approach of Venus (*tuum initum*) and because her body holds *primordia,* the first beginnings of things. She provides the material through which Venus works. Therefore she can be called *una genetrix,* but only in the sense that she is the parent *nostri corporis.*

The idea of agency connects the Magna Mater passage with Lucretius' major discourse on the forces of equilibrium in the previous lines. His argument from line 522 onward has been that there must be an infinite number of any given type of atom in order to supply various objects in the universe. Without this unlimited abundance of each kind of atom, he says, there would be no chance that in this vast universe like atoms could meet and make shapes. He concludes at lines 567–68: "esse igitur genere in quovis primordia rerum / infinita palam est unde omnia suppeditantur." From this passage Lucretius will move on to argue that every object depends on a supply of atoms that is both infinite and varied. It follows, then, that a major supplier of this great variety of atoms is the earth (*tellus habet in se corpora prima*), since so many different things come from her body. So while there is an infinite number of these *primordia,* the variety, so far as it is important for our existence, comes from earth herself: "terra quidem vero caret omni tempore sensu / et quia multarum potitur primordia rerum / multa modis multis effert in lumina solis".

Lucretius interrupts these two passages on the supply of the *primordia,* in one instance infinite, in the other various, with the description of the constructive and destructive forces. These kinetic forces are distinct from mother earth in that they act to combine and dissolve *primordia,* whereas she only supplies the needed material. Earth's role as a material supplier is clearly defined in lines 2.589–96:

> Principio tellus habet in se corpora prima unde mare immensum volventes frigora fontes adsidue renovent, habet ignes unde oriantur; nam multis succensa locis ardent sola terrae, ex imis vero furit ignibus impetus Aetnae. tum porro nitidas fruges arbustaque laeta gentibus humanis habet unde extollere possit, unde etiam fluvios frondes et pabula laeta montivago generi possit praebere ferarum.

Those words and phrases, which draw their meaning from the notion that mother earth "holds in herself the first bodies (i.e., the atoms)," deserve

special note. It is because she is a storehouse of different atoms that we have springs, seas, fires, crops, animals, and people (the source being indicated by the *unde*'s of 590, 591, 595, and 596). She has the ability or the means (*possit,* 595 and 597) to raise up and produce these things. However, her quality of *genetrix* rests solely in her being a "storehouse" or a "supplier." Allegorically speaking, then, Venus, the universal *genetrix,* acts upon and through mother earth, the materialistic *genetrix* of our immediate reality, to generate the creatures and objects (*creata* of 2.572) on earth.

Other echoes between the hymn to Venus and the Magna Mater passage support their connection. In addition to the *pabula laeta,* the passages share descriptions of wild beasts (1.14 *ferae pecudes* and 2.597 *ferarum*), mountains (1.17 *montis* and 2.597 *montivago*), rivers (1.15 *rapidos amnis,* 1.17 *fluviosque rapacis* and 2.596 *fluvios*), seas (1.17 *maria* and 2.590 *mare immensum*), and green leaves (1.18 *frondiferas* and 2.596 *frondes*). Finally, line 2.654 "multa modis multis effert in lumina solis" corresponds to the words in 1.4–5: "per te quoniam genus omne animantum / concipitur visitque exortum lumina solis." Taken together these parallels reveal an earth who is responsive to the constructive forces of Venus by virtue of her great variety of *primordia.*

Lucretius describes the cult of the Magna Mater in a way that the Romans would have known well. He did not simply copy from a Greek source now lost. Coins of the late Republic that depict various aspects of the Cybele cult and iconography bear a striking resemblance to his description of the cult. Lucretius intended to show his reader that, while the cult of Cybele that he or she observes illustrates beautifully and allegorically many of the truths about the earth that he has been discussing, it reveals nothing about the nature of the gods ("Quae bene et eximie quamvis disposta ferantur, / longe sunt tamen a vera ratione repulsa," 644–45). In fact, the cult functions primarily to terrify and coerce the crowds into, among other things, respecting their parents and defending their motherland. In his description of the historical development of religion the only time that there was an ideal understanding of the nature of the gods was before religious rites started, when people depended on the gradual influx of the divine images during their sleep for their knowledge about them. The sacred rites began, and temples and altars were erected, when people could not discover the causes of certain phenomena, and therefore were afraid. Likewise here Lucretius emphasizes over and over again the fearsomeness of the Cybele cult. At 610 he speaks of the dreadful nature of her procession (*horrifice fertur divinae matris imago*). He says she is accompanied by threatening music (*raucisonoque minantur cornua cantu,* 619) and by attendants who brandish weapons (*telaque praeportant, violenti signa furoris,* 621) and strike fear in the hearts of the spectators (*conterrere metu,* 623); they rejoice in the blood from the castration that their goddess demanded, and shake their helmets to add to the terror (*sanguine laeti, / terrificas capitum quatientes numine cristas,* 631–32). It is this use of intimidation, which to his mind is a main feature of all cultic practice, that invalidates religion.

The words that occurred at 1.44–49 reappear at 2.646–51 for the same reason as before. Again, the gods, who are called *semota* and *seiuncta,* could not be part of the creative activity that Mother Earth engages in, since they neither create nor provide the material of our creation. Furthermore, within the confines of their *intermundia* their needs are always met and their loss of atoms continually replaced (*ipsa suis pollens opibus* and *nil indiga nostri*), thus they have no need of our votive offerings, or sacrifices, or incense, inasmuch as these are seen to be *nourishment* for the gods. So, although he concedes that the mythic names of gods may be used as a colorful way of referring to natural concepts (as in the prologue he used the name "Venus" for "constructive force"), he advises his reader not to disturb their peace with terrifying cultic practices: "dum vera re tamen ipse religione animum turpi contingere parcat".

The programmatic passage: 1.62–78

The idea that fear is inherent to religion pervades, as we have seen, all Lucretius' poem. Not surprisingly, then, in the programmatic passage of the whole poem, a passage that sets the tone for the rest of the work, Lucretius treats religion as a tyrant to be deposed: "Humana ante oculos foede cum vita iaceret / in terris oppressa gravi sub religione ..." Fundamental to the understanding of the passage is the exact sense of *religio* here: it may mean either a feeling of awe or dread, or the established routine of rituals, prayers, and sacrifices. Because Lucretius assails *religio* so vigorously and crushes it so utterly in this passage, scholars have traditionally preferred the former meaning. They emphasize that here Lucretius disparages the fear of the divine, while remaining consistent with Epicurus' views on piety, that is, the actual worship of the gods. Cyril Bailey,

for example, introduces this section by noting that the lines "introduce the main purpose of the poem, to free men's minds from the *terrors* of religion" (ital. mine). He admits that elsewhere *religio* signifies the rites of worship, but in this passage Lucretius means "the dread of the intervention of the gods in the affairs of the world, and the fear of death and the punishment of the soul after death." Similarly H. Munro substitutes "fear of the gods and fear of death" for *religio* in his discussion of the passage.

These interpretations weaken the impact of the passage by separating religion from the fear it propagates. Lucretius makes no such distinction. The imagery he attaches to *religio* here is that used of the original giants or monsters of primitive mythology. In a similar vein Vergil described *Fama,* the last child of Mother Earth and sister to Coeus and Enceladus, as striding the earth and burying her head among the clouds (*ingrediturque solo et caput inter nubila condit, Aen.* 4.177). Mother Earth bore her because she was angry at the gods for slaying her children. She is a *monstrum horrendum,* who feeds on fear and *magnas territat urbes.* Lucretius, like Vergil, probably draws on Homer's description of Eris [the goddess Strife] at *Iliad* 4.440–45 Thus *religio,* which has its origin in mankind's primitive misunderstanding of the nature of the universe, is herself the terrorizing giant.

When Epicurus makes his assault on the heavens he does not do so to tame religion or a part of religion that causes fear (*superstitio*); he "conquers" the mysteries of nature herself, and brings back the truth about nature as a prize. To scale the heights Epicurus had to learn to ignore (or escape from) religion altogether: He ignores the myths about the gods (*fama deum*), their supposed power (*fulmina*), and their warnings (*minitanti murmure*), all of which in the following passage lead to the sacrifice of Iphigenia (*tantum religio potuit suadere malorum*). Traditional religion, which encourages mankind to appease the gods with sacrifices, to invoke their aid through prayer, and to learn their will through signs, is challenged *in toto.* Significantly, Lucretius does not cause Epicurus to revitalize or reorganize religion upon his return: giants have to be crushed under volcanoes or chained in Tartarus. In the end Epicurus achieves victory by replacing traditional religion with the truth about nature. Therefore, Lucretius advises his readers that if they hope to contemplate rationally and calmly the workings of nature, they will have to abandon the religious rites that distort the truth.

Commentators have exerted so much effort into making *religio* mean "fear" or "superstition" in this passage that they have obscured its total annihilation. The word *vicissim* in line 78 creates a ring structure for the entire passage: the situation of lines 62–63, "Humana ante oculos foede cum vita iaceret / in terris oppressa gravi sub religione," is reversed in 78–79, "quare religio pedibus subiecta vicissim / obteritur." Epicurus has turned the tables, so to speak, on religion. Therefore, the key to understanding the annihilation of religion lies in the nuances of the terms used to describe the former state when religion dominated and before the situation was reversed: *ante oculos, foede, iaceret, oppressa,* and *gravi.*

Scholars have ignored the phrase "humana ante oculos foede cum vita iaceret," except to point out that it means "plain for all to see" and to draw weak parallels to 3.995 and Sen. *Controv.* 1.1.16. When the phrase occurs with a form of *iacere,* as in this passage, it invariably connotes humiliating defeat and subjugation, hence, "to lie humiliated before" (Curtius Rufus *Alex.* 3.9, Cic. *Fam.* 4.5.4, cf. Verg. *Aen.* 11.310–11; Sen. *Troad.* 238, cf. Verg. *Aen.* 2.531–32). *Foede* heightens the aura of mankind's disgrace and subjugation, while also adding irreligious undertones to the act of domination by *religio.* It signifies that *religio* herself is the impious polluter of mankind's existence. *Foede* at *DRN* 1.62 anticipates the impious act of pollution at lines 1.84–86:

> Aulide quo pacto Triviai virginis aram Iphianassai
> turparunt sanguine foede ductores Danaum delecti,
> prima virorum.

The repetition of *foede* links the two passages together, so that Agamemnon's immolation of his daughter is viewed, not as an anomaly caused by fear, but as the natural consequence of the domination of *religio.* Agamemnon performed properly what *religio* demanded of him and Diana was pleased with the sacrifice: *exitus ut classi felix faustusque daretur* (1.100). By the term *oppressa* Lucretius conjures up an image of a *religio* that threatens, pollutes, and cruelly subjugates human life like a despot lording it over his subjects.

Fittingly, Lucretius makes intimidation the *modus operandi* of tyrannous *religio.* Before Epicurus mankind feared to raise its eyes, for *religio* towered threateningly overhead with frightful visage (*horribili super aspectu mortalibus instans,* 1.65). The words of the prophets strike terror in men (*vatum /terriloquis victus dictis,* 1.102–3), and the deafening cracks of lightning make men cower and fear the gods' anger (*fulminis horribili ... plaga,* 5.1220). For Lucretius,

what is currently believed about the gods causes fear. Never is *religio* distinct from its fear, and never is the possibility of a *religio* free from it entertained; rather, fear is a natural consequence of the tyrant *religio.* The following lines, often used to show that Lucretius is only interested in destroying fear and superstition, actually prove the opposite:

> quippe ita formido mortalis continet omnis, quod multa in terris fieri caeloque tuentur quorum operum causas nulla ratione videre possunt ac fieri divino numine rentur. quas ob res ubi viderimus nil posse creari de nilo, tum quod sequimur iam rectius inde perspiciemus, et unde queat res quaeque creari et quo quaeque modo fiant opera sine divum.

Fear ends when mankind learns that *religio*'s lessons are false. The gods do not really create, or become angry, or communicate through lightning.

Thus, when Epicurus dares to ignore the teachings of religion and to contemplate the true nature of reality, the tables are turned on *religio,* so that she is deposed and crushed the way she once crushed mankind. *Vicissim* creates the ring structure. The phrase *religio pedibus subiecta ... obteritur* of lines 78–79 recalls its counterpart *oppressa gravi sub religione* in line 63, while *nos exaequat victoria caelo* counters the humiliation indicated by *Humana ante oculos foede cum vita iaceret / in terris* in lines 62–63.

These lines are programmatic and forebode further invectives against *religio.* Nothing in them causes the reader to believe that only superstitious fear is at issue; at stake is traditional religion as practiced before the temple altars, at home before the hearth, and at the ancestral graves. Lucretius promises that this religion, deeply embedded in the Roman way of life, will be eliminated and replaced, but it must not have been clear to the average Roman what would take its place. Even so, Lucretius retains a genuine religious sensibility throughout his poem. Yet instead of capitulating in matters of practice, as Epicurus did, he directs his feelings of devotion and awe toward the knowledge of nature's workings and principles, and toward its vaunted discoverer, Epicurus. His religion, if such it can be called, is full of caveats and qualifications, and his piety characterized by redefinitions. Certainly there is nothing in Lucretius to merit Cotta's taunt, *novi ego Epicureos omnia sigilla venerantes.* Lucretius has set aside Epicurus' justification of continued traditional worship and resculpted his master's piety into what may seem a more consistent call to a mystical-transcendental contemplation of the workings of atoms, void, and swerve.

Source: Kirk Summers, "Lucretius and the Epicurean Tradition of Piety," in *Classical Philology,* University of Chicago Press, Vol. 90, No. 1, January, 1995, pp. 32–58.

SOURCES

Esolen, Anthony M., "Introduction" in *De rerum natura: De rerum natura*, Johns Hopkins University Press, 1995.

Fitzgerald, William, "Lucretius' Cure for Love in the "'De rerum natura,'" in *The Classical World*, Vol. 78, No. 2, 1984, pp. 73–86.

Penwill, J. L., "The Ending of Sense: Death as Closure in Lucretius Book Six," in *Ramus—Critical Studies in Greek and Roman Literature*, Vol. 25, No. 2, 1996, pp. 146–65.

Segal, Charles, "Poetic Immortality and the Fear of Death: The Second Proem of the 'De rerum natura,'" in *Harvard Studies in Classical Philology*, Vol. 92, 1989, pp.193–212.

Stein, Gordon, Review in *Free Inquiry*, Vol. 16, No. 1, 1996, p. 571.

FURTHER READING

Grant, Michael, *Greek and Latin Authors, 800 B.C.–A.D. 1000: A Biographical Dictionary*, H. W. Wilson, 1979.
    Provides profiles of 376 early Greek and Latin authors.

O'Hara, James J., "Venus or the Muse as 'Ally,'" in *Classical Philology*, Vol. 93, No. 1, 1998, pp. 69–76.
    Explores the influence of the Greek poet Simonides on Lucretius' *De rerum natura*.

Summers, Kirk, "Lucretius and the Epicurean Tradition of Piety," in *Classical Philology*, Vol. 90, No. 1, January, 1995, pp. 32–58.
    Lucretius' religious stance, central to his great epic, differs from that of his master Epicurus.

Thomas, Edmund J., and Eugene Miller, *Writers and Philosophers*, Greenwood Publishing Group, 1990.
    Offers information on 123 writers who are frequently anthologized, and explains their literary influence. Also, seventy-five philosophers are profiled with brief explanations of their teachings.

Elder Edda

ANONYMOUS

800

The *Elder Edda* is not a single continuous narrative, but a collection of poems, most of which are preserved in the *Konungsbók*, or *Codex Regius* (King's Book), copied in Iceland about A.D. 1270. The poems are the work of many poets. Their language suggests that they were composed between 800 and 1100 A.D. and first written down between 1150 and 1250 A.D. The poems are a rich source of information for culture and belief among the Vikings. They are not, however, purely Scandinavian. Christian Irish influence is likely, while the Sigurd story draws on actual events among the tribes that invaded the Roman Empire between 350–600 A.D.

The *Elder Edda* first came to scholarly attention in the seventeenth century as antiquarian interest in the non-classical past was growing in Europe. It was published in its entirety just as intense romantic and nationalistic interest in the perceived tribal ancestors of the European nation states emerged towards the end of the eighteenth century. This interest, combined with the new science of philology, ensured popular and scholarly interest in texts like the *Elder Edda*. Some of the lays were available in bowdlerized versions even for children by the later nineteenth century. In the hands of Richard Wagner, the *Elder Edda* became the foundation of one of the century's masterpieces. While northern legends and the scholarship based on it were misused by the Nazis to develop and further their ideas of race, they are seriously misrepresented by such ideas. In the 1960s, the poet W. H. Auden in

collaboration with an Old Norse scholar, Paul B. Taylor, produced a translation of sixteen of the poems.

AUTHOR BIOGRAPHY

The *Elder Edda* is not a continuous narrative, but a collection of thirty-nine poems of varying lengths and genres, including short narratives or lays, traditional wisdom including what amounts to a manual of good behavior, and several dialogues in which the question and answers provide a glossary of poetic terms and myth. They form a history of the world from creation to apocalypse, and like the Shakespearean canon, high tragedy exists side by side with bumptious comedy. Thirty-four are preserved in the *Konungsbók*, or *Codex Regius* (King's book), copied in Iceland about A.D. 1270, now in the Royal Library in Copenhagen. The language of the poems as preserved in that manuscript suggests that they were composed between 800 and 1100 A.D. but were first written down between 1150 and 1250 A.D. The poems are the work of many poets and some draw on historical traditions reaching back to the fourth century. Nevertheless, however northern and pagan they may appear to be, they contain much that suggests an interaction with both Greco-Roman and Judeo-Christian culture.

It is not known where in Iceland the *Codex Regius* was copied. The elegance of the scribe's writing and its similarity to those of at least two other Icelandic scribes of the period suggest its copyist was connected with a fairly large scriptorium with high standards. Despite early attempts to connect the *Elder Edda* as a collection with a legendary Icelandic scholar, Saemundur Sigfússon the Learned, (1056–1133), none of the poems can be connected with a named individual and were probably collected together only in the thirteenth century, perhaps only a generation before the production of the *Codex Regius*.

Nothing is known of the manuscript until the year 1643 when it came into the possession of Bishop Brynjólfr Sveinsson. It was already damaged then, and no copy was made of it before the missing leaves were lost. In 1662 the bishop gave the manuscript to the king of Denmark. In 1665 the two mythological poems *Völuspa* and *Hávemál* were published by the Danish scholar Peder Hansen Resen as part of an edition of Snorri Stulason's *Prose Edda*. The first full edition was prepared by the Arnamagnaean Commission in Copenhagen between 1787 and 1828.

PLOT SUMMARY

The Sibyl's Prophecy

At Odin's request, a prophetess predicts the future from creation to fall and renewal. She begins with a time when nothing existed; heavens and earth come into existence, but in chaos. The gods, who create the arts and crafts, social life, and finally, mankind, impose order. She prophesies the war between the Aesir and the Vanir and their conciliation, the death of Balder through Loki's trickery, Loki's punishment, the dwarves's golden home, the realm of the dead, and the punishment of the wicked. She foresees the final battle between gods and giants that will end in their mutual destruction. Sun and stars fail, the earth sinks beneath the sea, but in the final stanzas, she describes a second green earth rising from the waters. Balder and Hod, his blind brother who accidentally killed him, will come again to rule. Then a mighty one, sometimes identified as Christ, will come down to bring the deserving to a hall more beautiful than the sun.

The Sayings of the High One

This is a composite poem in which only stanzas 111–64 are in the voice of Odin the 'High One.' It begins with practical advice on behavior and attitude: "It takes sharp wits to travel in the world / they're not so hard on you at home—Better to be alive than to be lifeless / the living can hope for a cow." Even among such homely advice, however, is fame, so important to the epic attitude: "Cattle die, kinsmen die, / One day you die yourself; but the words of praise will not die." The poem ends with Odin's advice addressed to a young man called Loddfafnir.

The Lay of Vafthrudnir

Odin has a contest with the giant Vafthrudnir to determine who has the greater knowledge of the gods, creation, and the future. Odin wins because he alone knows what he whispered in Balder's ear as he lay on his funeral pyre. The lay serves as a glossary of the metaphors and images used in early Norse poetry.

The Lay of Grimnir

Hunding had two sons: Agnar and Geirrod. They were fishing from a rowboat and were swept out to sea. When they made land, a farmer took them in until spring came. When they arrived back home, Geirrod jumped out of the boat and pushed it and his brother back out to sea. Geirrod became king. Later, Odin and Frigg, his wife, were looking down at earth. Odin teased Frigg that Geirrod, whom he favored, was king while Agnar, whom Frigg favored, lived in the wilds. Frigg answered that Geirrod was stingy. Odin bet her he would find him generous to strangers. Frigg sends a message to Geirrod to beware of a wizard coming to his court, describing Odin in disguise. Odin arrives and when he refuses to give more than an assumed name, Grimnir, he is seated between two fires to make him speak. Geirrod's son Agnar thinks it wrong to mistreat a guest and brings him a drink. For this act, Odin blesses the boy and tells him his real name. When the king hears, he jumps up to take him away from the fires, but stumbles and falls on his own sword.

Skirnir's Journey

This lay tells of the god Frey who saw and loved a giant's beautiful daughter. He sent his servant Skirnir to persuade her to accept him as her lover. Skirnir cajoles and threatens her until she finally accepts Frey.

The Lay of Harbard

The first of the comical lays. Odin disguised himself as a ferryman and engaged Thor in a duel of words. Thor loses badly.

The Lay of Hymir

The gods are feeling like a party and ask the giant Aegir to brew beer for it. Thor unfortunately annoys Aegir. Aegir tells Thor he must borrow the giant Hymir's brewing vat. Thor and Tyr, Hymir's son, set out for Hymnir's home where Hymnir's young mistress welcomes them. She warns them Hymnir does not like guests and makes them hide when he comes. She tells Hymnir that his son has come with a friend. Three bulls are cooked for dinner. Thor eats two of them. Hymnir tells his guests that they will go out hunting for supper. Thor suggests that he will take a boat out and fish if Hymir provides the bait. Thor rows out, baits his hook with an ox's head, and catches the serpent that encircles the earth, drags it up into the boat, but thankfully, throws it back. Hymir then challenges Thor to crack his cup. Thor flings it; columns crash and stone splinters, but the cup is unbroken. At the mistress's suggestion, he flings it at the giant's head and it breaks. Thor grabs the kettle and kills the pursuing giants. Aegir brews the beer.

The Insolence of Loki

Loki infuriates the assembled gods and goddesses by bringing up past scandals. His stories grow more and more vile until he is finally frightened into leaving with the threat of Thor's hammer. He curses the gods as he leaves.

The Lay of Thrym

Thor's great hammer, Mjollnir, is stolen. Loki discovers that the giant Thrym has it. Thrym tells Loki that he will give it back only if he can marry Freyja. Not surprisingly, Thor has no luck in convincing Freyja that she should marry a giant. A council of the gods and goddesses is convened and Heimdal suggests that they dress Thor as a bride with Loki as her maid. Thor does not like it, but he must have his hammer to keep the giants out of Asgard. Thrym is beside himself with joy when they arrive, but after a comical passage in which Loki has to explain the bride's incredible appetite and frightening eyes, Thor gets his hands on his hammer and kills his prospective in-laws.

The Lay of Volund

Volund, the most famous smith of the north, is taken prisoner by Kind Nidud who lames him. Volund makes himself wings, avenges himself by murdering Nidud's sons and raping his daughter, and flies away.

The Lay of Alvis

The dwarf Alvis tries to steal Thor's daughter, but is tricked into such a lengthy display of his knowledge, which amounts to a catalogue of poetic synonyms, that he is caught by dawn and dies from exposure to sunlight.

Balder, whose death is depicted here, was the son of Odin and Frigg and a favorite of the gods. The blind god Hod, deceived by Loki, killed Balder by hurling mistletoe, the only thing that could hurt him.

The First and Second Lays of Helgi Hunding's Bane and The Lay of Helgi Hjorvar's Son

The Helgi lays are incomplete and confused. Taken with the notes attached to them, they recount a story of two lovers who are reborn again and again. The first and second lays are the story of Helgi, Sigmund's son. Helgi is loved and protected by the Valkyrie, Sigrun. Helgi must fight Sigrun's father, brothers, and suitor to save her from an unwanted marriage. He kills them all except for her brother Dag, whom he spares. Dag swears peace with Helgi, but sacrifices to Odin for vengeance. Odin lends him his spear, and Dag kills Helgi. Sigrun is inconsolable. A maid tells her Helgi's spirit is in his burial mound. Sigrun goes to his grave to be with him one last night, dying of grief soon after. Later, they are both reborn, as Helgi Hunding's Bane and Kara. In the 'The Lay of Helgi Hjorvar's Son' another Helgi is loved by a Valkyrie, Svava, who marries him. His brother Hedin confesses that he made a drunken vow to marry Svava. Helgi replies that his vow may be good for both of them; he is about to go into battle and does not expect to survive. Helgi, as he foresaw, is mortally wounded.

Dying, he asks Svava to marry Hedin. She refuses, but Hedin promises her he will avenge Helgi. The lay breaks off in the manuscript with a note that "It is said of Helgi and Svava that they were born again."

The Prophecy of Gripir

Ironically, the only straightforward version of Sigurd and Brynhild's story is in the form of a prophecy. Sigurd asks his uncle what he sees in store for him. Gripir tells him that he will be a great hero. Sigurd questions Gripir further. Gripir tells him he will avenge his father, kill Fafnir the dragon, the evil Regin, and win Fafnir's treasure. He will wake a sleeping Valkyrie and learn her wisdom. Gripir then breaks off. Sigurd asks him if he sees something shameful. Gripir reassures him and finally continues. Sigurd will fall in love with Brynhild. They will swear to be faithful, but Sigurd will betray her, because of Queen Grimhild who wants Sigurd married to her daughter, Gudrun, and Brynhild to her son, Gunnar. Sigurd will forget Brynhild and promise Gunnar and Hogni that he will win her for Gunnar. Sigurd will live happily with Gundrun, but Brynhild will plot her revenge for his betrayal. Gunnar and Hogni will fall in with her plans and murder Sigurd. Gripir consoles his nephew that at least he will be fortunate in his fame. Sigurd leaves saying, "You would have been glad to say good things of what is coming if you could."

The Lay of Regin

This lay begins with the history of Fafnir and his hoard. Regin takes Sigurd as his foster son, forges him a mighty sword, and urges him to kill the dragon Fafnir. Sigurd insists on avenging his father first.

The Lay of Fafnir

Sigurd, returning after avenging his father, kills Fafnir. The dying dragon warns Sigurd that his treasure is cursed and that Regin means to kill him. Sigurd roasts and eats the dragon's heart and finds he understands the birds talking about Regin's plans to kill him. Sigurd kills Regin.

The Lay of Sigdrifa

Sigurd has learned from the birds about a Valkyrie lying in an enchanted sleep. He wakes her, and she shares her wisdom with him.

Fragmentary Lay of Sigurd

A dramatic fragment dealing with the murder of Sigurd.

The Lay of Gudrun

Gudrun grieves for Sigurd while various noblewomen attempt to comfort her. Brynhild commits suicide to be with Sigurd in death.

The Short Lay of Sigurd

This is Sigurd's story from Brynhild's point of view. After the tale of her betrayal and revenge is told, she makes plans for her funeral and warns Gunnar what the future holds for him and for Gudrun.

Brynhild's Journey to Hel

Brynhild, on her way to meet Sigurd in the land of the dead, encounters a giantess who accuses her of murder and fickleness. Brynhild justifies her behavior to her.

The Second Lay of Gudrun

Gudrun tells of Sigurd's murder, of her brother's duplicity, and her marriage to Atli.

The Third Lay of Gudrun

Gudrun is suspected of being unfaithful to Atli. She proves her innocence by putting her hand into boiling water and withdrawing it unhurt.

Oddrun's Lay

Atli's sister, Oddrun, tells of her grief for Gunnar. After Brynhild's death, Gunnar wanted to marry her, but Atli forbade it. Oddrun and Gunnar met secretly. Atli learned of this and murdered Gunnar and Hogni.

The Lay of Atli

Gunnar and Hogni, despite forebodings, visit their brother-in-law, Atli, where they are murdered in Atli's attempt to extort Andvari's treasure from them. Gundrun avenges her brothers, murdering her sons by Atli, and feeding them to their father. She then burns Atli and his men in their hall.

The Greenland Lay of Atli

Another version of Gundrun's revenge for her brothers's murders.

Gudrun's Chain of Woes

Gudrun urges her sons by her third husband, Jonacr, to avenge their half sister, murdered by her husband Jormunrek.

The Lay of Hamdir

Hamdir and Sorli, the sons of Jonacr and Gundrun, set out to avenge their half-sister, Swanhild. On the way, they meet and murder their half-brother, Erp. When they reach Jormunrek's court, they fail to avenge their sister for the lack of his help.

Balder's Dreams

Odin consults a prophetess to learn the fate of his beloved son Balder.

The Mill Song

King Frodi had two captive giant girls. He put them to work grinding out gold and peace at a magic hand mill. They prophesy his downfall.

The Waking of Angantyr

Hervor, Angantyr's daughter, goes to his grave to demand his sword, Tyrfing, so she can avenge him. Angantyr's ghost, who knows Tyrfing is cursed to kill every one who uses it, tries to dissuade her, but she will not be persuaded. He allows her to take it.

CHARACTERS

Aesir

Aesir are the Norse gods, more particularly, the race of sky gods who first fought and then joined the Vanir gods of fertility and the earth. They lived in Asgard, home of the gods, reached by a rainbow bridge. The Aesir include Odin (ruler of the gods), Balder, Frigg, Tyr, and Thor.

Agnar

1. The son of King Hunding and the brother of King Geirrod. Patronized by the goddess Frigg, he still lost his place to his younger brother and lived as an outcast. 2. The son of King Geirrod who brought Odin a horn of wine when his father was torturing the disguised god between two fires. Odin rewarded Agnar with a successful reign.

All-Father

See Odin

Alvis

In the poem *The Lay of Alvis*, Alvis the dwarf attempts to steal the god Thor's daughter away to marry her as the price of Thor's great hammer, Mjollnir. Thor, however, catches him and insists that only if Alvis answers correctly a series of questions can he marry his daughter. Alvis answers the questions correctly, but Thor has kept him above ground until sunrise and he turns to stone. The series of questions and answers amounts to a catalogue of literary synonyms.

Andvari

Andvari is a dwarf who was fated to take the shape of a pike. Andvari's treasure plays a pivotal role in a series of lays. In *The Lay of Regin*, his gold is stolen by Loki to pay compensation for the unwitting murder of a man called Otter, killed while in the shape of an otter. Andvari curses the treasure. The gods pay Otter's father, Hreidmar, and brothers, Fafnir and Regin, compensation with the stolen gold. Fafnir murders his father for the treasure, beginning the series of disasters that follow the treasure from owner to owner.

Angantyr

Angantyr's father, Arngrim, won in battle a sword called Tyrfing that had the quality that wounds made by it never healed. The sword, however, had been stolen from the dwarves. The dwarves laid a curse on the blade so that it would always bring death to whomever carried it. Angantyr and his eleven brothers were killed together and buried in the same mound. When Agantyr's daughter found out the identity of her father, she was determined to avenge him and took Tyrfing from her father's grave despite his ghost's attempt to dissuade her.

Atli

Atli is the ruler of the Huns, the son of Budli, and brother of Brynhild. The character has its origin in the historical Atli, but the poets have made him and his people a Germanic tribe. Atli is not always a negative figure in northern legends, but in the *Elder Edda* he is a vicious, greedy ruler who murders his brothers-in-law for the sake of Andvari's treasure.

Balder

Balder is the favorite son of Odin and Frigg, and a favorite among all the gods. Frigg asked every living thing and all objects of metal, wood, or stone to swear never to harm him. The gods amused themselves by hurling weapons at him certain he could not be harmed. Loki, however, learned that Frigg had forgotten to ask the mistletoe. He made it into a dart and urged Balder's brother, the blind god Hod, to join in the game. The dart killed Balder. Balder's brother Hermod rode to the land of the dead and begged Hel, goddess of the dead to release him. She agreed if every person and thing in the world would weep for him. All did, except one giantess, believed to be Loki in disguise.

Bodvild

Bodvild is the daughter of King Nidudd. She was raped by Volund in revenge for his imprisonment and maiming by King Nidudd.

Borghild

Borghild is Sigmund's wife and Helgi Hunding's Bane's mother.

Bragi

Bragi is the god of poetry.

Brynhild

Many scholars believe Brynhild (also known as Sigdrifa) is based on a historical character, a sixth-century Visigothic princess, married to a Frankish king. Brynhild is Atli's sister and a Valkyrie. She was betrothed to Sigurd. In the *The Lay of Sigdrifa*, Odin has decreed she will no longer be a Valkyrie but must marry because she had disobeyed him and fought for a hero he had doomed. She swears she will only marry a man who does not know fear. Odin pricked her with a sleep thorn and she slept until wakened by Sigurd. They pledge themselves to marry each other, but Sigurd is given a magical drink at the court of Gunnar, forgets her, and marries Gunnar's sister, Gudrun. In return for Gudrun, Sigurd promises to win Brynhild for Gunnar and unwittingly breaks his oath and betrays her. Brynhild loves Sigurd deeply, but believes that he has cold-bloodedly wronged her. She sets in motion Sigurd's death. When he is dead, she kills herself to join the man she considers her real husband in the land of the dead.

Dag

Dag is the son of Hogni and Sigrun's sister. He kills Helgi in revenge for his father.

Dvalin

Dvalin is a dwarf. Angantyr's cursed sword, Tyrfing, is described as Dvalin's weapon.

Ermanrik

See Jormunrek.

Erp

Erp is the son of Atli and Gudrun. He was murdered by his half brothers Hamdir and Sorli on the way to Jormunrek's court to avenge their sister. His death doomed their plans since his blow would have silenced the old king.

Eylimi

In *The Lay of Helgi Hjorvards's Son* Eylimi is the father of the Valkyrie Svava, wife of Helgi Hjorvard's son. In the *Prophecy of Gripir*, he is Gripir's father, Sigurd's maternal grandfather.

Fafnir

Fafnir is the son of Hreidmar and brother of Otter and Regan. He murders his own father for Andvari's treasure. Fafnir turns into a dragon to better guard the treasures. As a dragon, he is killed by Sigurd. In both Roman and Germanic tradition, the dragon was a symbol of greed.

Father of the Slain

See Odin.

MEDIA ADAPTATIONS

- The *Elder Edda* was a primary source for Richard Wagner's cycle of musical dramas *The Ring of the Nibelungen*, four interconnected operas, *Rhinegold*, *The Valkyries*, *Siegfried*, and *The Twilight of the Gods*. Wagner adapted the mythical and legendary world of the *Elder Edda* to express his own disquiet with the industrial revolution and political movements and developments in nineteenth-century Germany.

- Two of the most important German movies of the silent era are Fritz Lang's *Siegfried* (1924) and *Kriemhild's Revenge* (1924).

- The Swedish poet Victor Rydberg in *Den nya Grottasongen* (1891) transformed the lay of Frodi's mill into a picture of the excesses of industrialism and capitalism, and its cynical exploitation for human beings.

Fenrir

Fenrir is the great wolf, the son of Loki and a giantess. He is bound by the gods until Ragnarok when he will break his chain and devour Odin.

Frey

Frey is a Vanir and a fertility god.

Freyja

Freyja is a Vanir and the goddess of love.

Frigg

Frigg is the Aesir goddess of love, Odin's wife, and the mother of Balder.

Frodi

Frodi is the king of a golden age of peace and prosperity. He owned a magic stone quern or hand mill that, when turned by two captive giantesses, ground out gold and peace. Unfortunately, he drives the the giantesses too hard and they rebel, breaking the quern.

Gagnrad

See Odin

Gangleri

See Odin

Garm

Garm is the hound of the goddess Hel, ruler of the land of the dead.

Geirod

Geirod is the son of king Hunding. He supplants his older brother Agnar and rules until Frigg tricks him into mistreating the disguised Odin against all rules of hospitality. He trips and dies on his own sword as he runs to release Odin when he realizes his mistake. His son Agnar had comforted and brought Odin a horn of wine against his father's wishes and was rewarded by the god.

Gerd

Gerd is a giantess, daughter of Gymir, and loved by Frey. Frey sends his servant Skirnir to woo her. Skirnir has to threaten to curse her with degradation and disgrace before she will meet Frey.

Gjuki

Gjuki is the king of the Burgundians, husband of Grimhild, and father of Gunnar, Hogni, and Gudrun. He is apparently dead by the time Sigurd reaches the Burgundian court.

Glaumvor

Glaumvor becomes Gunnar's wife after Brynhild's death.

Gram

Gram is Sigurd's sword. Naming swords, at least in heroic tales, was not uncommon.

Grani

Grani is Sigurd's horse.

Grimhild

Grimhild is the queen of the Burgundians, wife of Gjuki, and mother of Gudrun, Gunnar, and Hogni. There seems to be a hint of the witch or sorceress about her. She is the mastermind of the plot to drug Sigurd into forgetting his vow to Brynhild, marrying Gudrun, and helping Gunnar win Brynhild.

Grimodin

See Odin

Gripir

Gripir is the brother of Hjordis and Sigurd's maternal uncle. In northern heroic literature, the son of a man's sister was his closest male relative. In the *Gripisspé* (The Prophecy of Gripir), he has the gift of prophecy and tells his young nephew all that lies before him. He ends his prophecy with the promise that Sigurd will be 'fortunate in his fame' that no man will surpass. Sigurd is the greatest hero of the north. His exploits color the images and metaphors of the traditional skaldic poetry and Icelandic saga literature.

Gudrun

Gudrun is the daughter of Grimhild and Gjuki. Sigurd, under the influence of Grimhild's potion, marries Gudrun. Gudrun knows both of Sigurd's relationship to Brynhild and the plot to use a potion on Sigurd. It is she who provokes Brynhild into revenge. After Sigurd's death, Gudrun is persuaded to marry Atli, king of the Huns. She eventually murders him and his men to avenge his murder of her brothers. Her third husband is Jonacr by whom she has twin sons, Hamdir and Sorli.

Gungnir

Gungnir is Odin's spear. It is mentioned in many of the lays and sagas but is named only in the *Lay of Sigdrifa*.

Gunnar

King of the Burgundians after Gjuki and the son of Grimhild and Gjuki. His character changes between the lays involving Sigurd and Brynhild and those involving Atli. In the former, he is a deceiver, a breaker of oaths, and a murderer, led first by his mother and then by his wife, but always by his greed. In the later, he is a king who knows himself to be doomed but who will use the most unlikely tool for a hero, his and his brothers' deaths, to deny Atli Andvari's treasure.

Gunnlod

Gunnlod is the giantess who guards the mead of poetry.

Guthorm

Guthorm is the son of King Gjuki and a step-brother of Gunnar.

Hagal

Hagal is the foster father of Helgi Hunding's Bane.

Hamdir

Hamdir is Gudrun's son. He dies avenging his sister Swanhild's death on Jormunrek, King of the Goths.

Heimdal

Heimdal is the 'radiant' god and the gods' watchman. His horn is called Gjallarhorn.

Hel

Hel is the land of the dead and also the name of its goddess. She is the daughter of Loki.

Helgi Hjorvard's Son

See Helgi Hjorvard's Bane.

Helgi Hunding's Bane

Helgi Hunding's Bane is the son of Sigmund Volsung and Borghild and the hero of *The First Lay of Helgi Hunding's Bane* and *The Second Lay of Helgi Hunding's Bane*. His wife was Sigrun, the Valkyrie who had watched over him in battle. Sigrun chose Helgi, but her family had engaged her to King Hodbrodd. In the battle that followed, her father and all her brothers, but one, Dag, were killed. Sigrun and Helgi lived happily and deeply in love, despite her grief for her kinsmen, but eventually Dag killed Helgi in revenge for his father. Helgi and Sigrun loved each other so much that they were allowed to have one last night together in Helgi's burial mound. A note at the end of the lay says that she died young of grief for her husband. In the *Codex Regius* at the end of *The Lay of Helgi Hjorvard's Son* and at the end of *The Second Lay of Helgi Hunding's Bane* are references to a tradition that Helgi and Sigrun were reborn three times: once as Helgi Hjorvard's Son and Svava the Valkyrie, then as Helgi Hunding's Bane and Sigrun, and finally as Helgi Hadding's Bane and Kara the Valkyrie.

Hervard

Hervard is a brother of Angantyr. He was killed and buried with him.

Hervor

1. The daughter of Angantyr who retrieves her father's sword from his grave, much against his wishes, to avenge his death. 2. The Wise, King Hlodver's daughter, a Valkyrie and Volund's wife.

Hjalmar

Hjalmar is the slayer of Angantyr.

Hjalperk

Hjalperk is Sigurd's foster father.

Hjordis

Hjordis is Sigmund's second wife and the mother of Sigurd.

Hjorvard

Hjorvard is another brother of Angantyr who was also killed and buried with him.

Hoddmimir

See Mimir

Hogni

1. The father of Sigrun. Helgi kills him in a battle fought to prevent Sigrun's marriage to another man. Hogni is avenged by his son Dag who uses Odin's spear. 2. A Burgundian prince, brother of Gunnar and Gudrun. He dies rather than reveal the whereabouts of Andvari's treasure.

Hrani

Hrani is also a brother of Angantyr who was killed and buried with him.

Hreidnar

Hreidnar is the father of Regin, Fafnir, and Otter. He is given Andvari's treasure by Loki and Odin as compensation for their killing of his son Otter when he was in the shape of an otter.

Hunding

1. The father of Agnar and Geirrod. 2. A king killed by Helgi Hunding's Bane.

Jonacr

Jonacr is Gudrun's third husband and the father of Hamdir and Sorli.

Jormunrek

Jormunrek was the historical fourth-century king of the Goths who entered legend as the murderer of his young second wife Swanhild and his son who were falsely accused of adultery together.

Kostbera

In the *Greenland Lay of Atli*, Kostbera is Hogni's wife, a wise and learned woman who tries to make sense of Gudrun's runic warning and has a prophetic dream of disaster.

Loddfafnir

Loddfafnir is the recipient of Odin's wisdom in the *Sayings of the High One*.

Loki

Loki is an Aesir, but of doubtful allegiance. He is the trickster who is the preferred companion of the gods in tight corners, but whose advice usually involves morally questionable choices that create further problems for those who take it. His mischief becomes a pure destructive maliciousness over the course of the history of the gods.

Mimir

Mimir, also known as Hoddmimir, is the guardian of the well under the root of Yggdrasil, the Ash tree at the center of the universe.

Niflungs

Niflungs are essentially synonymous with Gjuking, the family and followers of King Gjuki.

Njord

Njord is the god of the sea.

Norns

Norns, also known as Urd, are the Scandinavian version of the Fates, who determined the destiny of the world and of individuals. They were of the race of giants.

Oddrun

Oddrun is the sister of Brynhild and Atli. She was originally promised to Gunnar. When Atli would not allow them to wed after Brynhild's death, they had a secret affair. Oddrun gave this as one of the reasons that Atli killed Gunnar.

Odin

For an almost-full list of Odin's names see *The Lay of Grimnir*, stanzas 12 and 13, which end "I've never been known by one name only/since I have wandered the world." (A brief listing of Odin's many names include: All-Father, Warfather, Father of the Slain, Gagnrad—'Counsel for Victory,' Gangleri, Grim and Ygg.) The king of the gods, known among the pagan English as Woden, the god of Wednesday, he was the god of battle, magic, poetic inspiration, and all those who die in battle. He was a shapeshifter and could appear as an old one-eyed man, dressed in a hooded cloak and broad hat, or as a wolf. He was usually accompanied by the so-called beasts of battle: two ravens, 'Thought' and 'Memory', and wolves. He sacrificed his eye and hung nine days and nine nights on *Yggdrasil*, the tree that supports the world, to gain wisdom. He is the Lord of runes and secret wisdom. Odin protected kings and encouraged heroes, largely to build up a fighting force in Valhalla the hall of the slain, for the great battle with the forces of darkness at the end of the world. When he thought the time was right, he would disarm even a protected favorite to bring about his death in battle. It has been suggested that Odin became important only during the period when the Germanic peoples were entering the former provinces of the Roman empire when, as a god of war bands, he attracted worshipers. Normal social and tribal bonds were under stress and were often replaced by new groups coalescing around successful warriors.

Otter

Otter is Regin and Fafnir's brother and Hreidnar's son. Andvari's treasure was handed over to his brothers and father as compensation for his murder while in the shape of an otter.

Ran

Ran is the goddess of the sea. Her husband and the god of the sea is Aeggir.

Regin

Regin is Hreidmar's son and the brother of Otter and Fafnir. He was twice cheated out of his part of Andvari's treasure. A dwarfish smith warped by thwarted greed, he takes Sigurd under his wing to train him to kill Fafnir, now in the shape of a dragon. Sigurd is warned of his treachery by both the dying Fafnir and the birds, and kills him.

Sif

Sif is Thor's wife.

Sigdrifa

See Brynhild

Sigmund

Sigmund is the son of Volsung and father, by different women, of Helgi, Sinfjotli, and Sigurd.

Signy

Siggeir, Signy's husband, murdered Sigmund and Signy's father and brothers. Signy sends her young sons to Sigmund hoping they will be able to help Sigmund avenge their family. When the boys prove to be less than the stuff of heroes, Signy, determined to have vengeance, changes shape with a sorceress, seduces her brother, and bears him a son Sinfjotli. Sinfjotli helps Sigmund in the vengeance. Sigmund only learns that he is his son and not his nephew when Signy tells him after they have set fire to Siggeir's hall. Signy then enters the burning hall because, as she says to her brother and their son in the *Volsung Saga*, "I have worked so hard to bring about vengeance I am by no means fit to live. Willingly I shall die with King Siggeir, although I married him reluctantly."

Sigrlinn

Sigrlinn is the daughter of King Svafnir and mother of Helgi in his first incarnation.

Sigrun

The three Helgi lays suggest that Sigrun, also known as Svava and Kara, was, like her beloved Helgi, reincarnated three times. In each incarnation, she was a Valkyrie who chose to protect and love Helgi, and eventually marry him.

Sigurd

Sigurd is the Siegfried of Richard Wagner's operas. In the *Elder Edda*, he is the son of Sigmund and Hjordis. He is the greatest warrior of his time. He kills the man-turned-dragon, Fafnir, and wins Andvari's treasure from him. Following this, he wakes the Valkyrie Sigdrifa/Brynhild, learns her wisdom and promises to marry her before he goes off to his fate at the hands of the wife and children of Gjuki. Sigurd is the type of honorable and courageous hero, who despite all his qualities, is manipulated into acting completely against his ideals.

Sinfjotli

Sinfjotli is the son of Sigmund and Signy his sister and the half-brother of Sigurd and Helgi. The story of his birth is not recorded in the *Elder Edda* where he is presented as helping his young half-brother Helgi.

Sorli

Sorli is the brother of Hamdir and son of Gudrun and Jonacr. He is killed on the expedition to avenge their half-sister, Swanhild.

Surt

Surt is the lord of the fire giants. He has given his name to a volcanic island off Iceland.

Svava

See Sigrun

Swanhild

Swanhild is the daughter of Sigurd and Gudrun. She is married to King Jormunrek of the Goths who executes her when she is falsely accused of adultery with her stepson.

Thor

Thor, also known as Ving-Thor and Veor, is the god of thunder. He is the son of the Earth (Fjorgyn), and with his great hammer, Mjollnir, he defended gods and men against the giants. He was the most popular of Norse gods. People wore little hammers much as Christians do crosses. Even after Christianity became common, some people would take no chances and keep up a quiet personal devotion to Thor as well as to Christ.

Thrym

A king of the giants, Thrym stole Thor's hammer, Mjollnir, in an attempt to force the gods to give him Freya as his wife. He and many of his family and wedding guests were killed when Thor got his hands back on his hammer.

Tyr

The god of war, he was apparently once a more important god, but lost most of his functions and popularity to Odin and Thor by the time the *Elder Eddas* were composed.

Urd

See Norns

Vanir

Vanirs were the gods of fertility who were at one time at war with the Aesir. They are often represented as having knowledge of the future.

Veor 'Holy, Defender of the Home'

See Thor

Ving-Thor

See Thor

Volsungs

Volsungs is the family name of Sigmund, Sinfjotli, and Sigurd.

Volund

Volund is the Weyland Smith of many English place names and the hero of the *Volundarqvitha* (The Lay of Volund). He was the son of a Finnish king famous for his ability to work iron, gold, and silver. He was captured and lamed by King Nidud who wanted to monopolize his skills. Volund made himself wings, and after killing Nidud's sons and raping his daughter, flew away from his captivity.

War Father

See Odin

Ygg

See Odin

Ymir

Ymir is a giant from whose body the earth, sea, and sky were made.

THEMES

The *Elder Edda* begins with the *Völuspa* or 'Sibyl's Prophecy,' a history of the world in the form of a prophecy. The poems following it give instructions for life, the fights and stratagems of the gods, and, finally, a series of heroic narrative poems and dialogues.

Divided Loyalties

Norse society was violent, as reflected in the *Sayings of the High One* "Don't leave your weapons lying about / behind your back in a field, / you never know when you may need / of a sudden your spear." In this society personal loyalties were everything, the only real basis of order and security. Nothing stood between order and chaos except the certainty that vengeance would be exacted for a wrong. The duty to defend family and lord was at the core too of personal honor and self-esteem. The man who did not take vengeance could expect neither mercy from his enemies nor sympathy from his friends. Neither love nor friendship nor practical expedience could stand in its way for long. Women would sweep aside all the commonplaces of love and gender roles to have it. The clash between competing loyalties and duties is perhaps the most important springboard of action in Old Norse literature.

Hospitality and Generosity

The "Sayings of the High One" paint a world where hospitality to the stranger as well as to the friend was a sacred duty. This idea was founded on the realities of Viking society. Populations were often small and scattered. In winter, it would be murder to deny a traveler a place at the fire. The man who welcomed a traveler to his home might soon be glad of a welcome himself. This idea was important. Odin himself was represented as checking an accusation of inhospitality. Even a child realized that mistreatment of a stranger is wrong and defied his father and king in *The Lay of Grimnir* to bring a horn of wine and a kind word to the disguised Odin. That small act was enough to win the little boy the lifelong favor of the god.

Generosity was the sign of nobility of spirit, of the regard of the giver for the person to whom the gift was given. It was one of the things that bound society together. If hospitality was born of a recognition of common humanity, gift giving was the specific recognition of the importance of one human being for another, whether between friends, lovers, or a king and his warrior.

Pessimism and Fatalism

Often, characters in the lays know exactly what lies before them and yet appear powerless to stop and make a conscious decision to snap the chain of events. This is a reflection of the belief that people's lives were laid out before them, just as Ragnarok (the end of time) lay before men and gods. The lays surrounding Sigurd and the royal house of the Burgundians are a reflection of this theory. He and they are swept up in a process started long ago, which centered on the cursed treasure that Sigurd won by killing the dragon Fafnir. The ultimate cause of the curse, the capricious slaying of Otter the dwarf by Loki, sets in motion a chain reaction of acts of vengeance and greed in which gods, giants, dwarves, and people suffer.

Ragnarok and Heroism

The opening poem of the *Elder Edda* describes the history of the world from creation to its destruction. The destruction of the world will take place at Ragnarok with the last, great battle between the gods and heroes on one side and the forces of evil on the other. It is in preparation for this battle that Odin sends his Valkyries to bring the spirits of men slain in battle to Valhalla, the hall of the slain. His need for heroes is so great that he will allow a warrior he has favored to be killed in battle rather than lose his help in the end time. Nevertheless, no matter what Odin and the gods may do, no matter how many heroes join their fight against the forces of darkness, the battle will end in defeat, or more specifically, the mutual destruction of the gods and their enemies. Ragnarok seems to be a symbol of the Vikings' view of their world. They knew that all things end. The world, flawed as it obviously was, could be no different. The important thing was to meet what came, good or bad, head on and unflinching. Man or woman, they must master events. Rather than allowing events to make them less than they were, events were the stage on which they could win the only immortality that mattered: fame. The certainty of defeat and death did not affect the will to fight. Defeat was not important; to endure, to live according to certain standards of loyalty and courage was important. To meet life courageously, however grim life might be, was to rob it of its fears.

Wisdom

Odin gave his eye for wisdom; Sigurd spent most of his courtship of Brynhild learning her supernaturally acquired wisdom. Heroes are expected to have discernment. They must be able to judge a situation and the character of the men and the women around them. The Norse poets gave wisdom, its acquisition, and transmission. The preoccupation with prophecy in the *Elder Edda* is a reflex of this pursuit of wisdom, even though it is a mixed blessing in a world overshadowed by pessimism and fate. To modern readers, this preoccupation may seem irrelevant and lacking in an aesthetic sense, but in Norse society it was an essential, defining poetic function. Elegance of diction, delicate metrical effects, creation of atmosphere, and emotional power were tools, not ends, for the Norse poet. In gnomic verse, poets distilled wisdom into memorable turns of phrase. In the narrative lays, poets provided embodiments of wisdom and foolishness in action. Experience is the source of wisdom.

Still there are limits to wisdom. The *Sayings of the High One* suggest that it is better not to know too much or to be too wise; perhaps the true nature of life would be too hard to carry. Most poignantly, however, it warns against knowing the future: "If you can't see far into the future, you can live free

TOPICS FOR FURTHER STUDY

- The Vikings opened trade routes down the rivers of Russia to Constantinople. Investigate the importance of Viking trade and trading posts to the development of the modern states of Russia and the Ukraine.

- Icelanders often boast of having the oldest parliament, the Althing, in existence. Investigate the origin and functions of the Althing and compare it to early attempts at self-government on the American frontier, beginning, perhaps, with the Plymouth Colony.

- Many of the heroes of the lays in the *Elder Edda* are not Scandinavian, but came from tribes as far apart as Burgundy and what is now the south west Russia and the Ukraine. Investigate the theories of how these heroes and their stories came to have such a wide and devoted audience.

- Norse raiding, trading and colonization could not have happened without the developments made by Scandinavian shipbuilding. Investigate Viking ships and their construction and the engineering and design principles behind their success.

from care." Discernment too could be thwarted by pull of other ideals and by magic. The betrayal that lies at the heart of Sigurd's tragedy is one induced by sorcery. Gudrun too knows disaster awaits in marriage with Atli, but she too succumbs to her mother's potions.

STYLE

Epic Characteristics

Leaving aside the *Sayings of the High One*, which has more in common with works like the biblical *Proverbs*, it appears that the *Elder Edda* is not an epic but materials for one. Here, for once, modern readers have the relatively short poetic narratives, or lays, which supposedly lie behind the epic. While the collection provides in the *Sibyl's Prophecy* a narrative from earth's creation through destruction and renewal, the majority of the poems fit only loosely into that scheme. There is no single hero, but rather a number of heroes ranging from the dim-but-effective god Thor to Gunnar, the treacherous brother-in-law of Sigurd, who, nevertheless, dies a hero while fighting the great tyrant of the age, Atli. Unlike the generic epic, the *Edda* has the obscenities of Loki in *The Insolence of Loki* and the broad humor of the Thor episodes—particularly the *Lay of Thrym*, an early example of that situation beloved of slapstick humor: the brawny man forced to pass himself off as the blushing girl.

Point of View

Each poem in the *Elder Edda* must be considered individually as to its narrator and point of view. The composite *Sayings of the High One* gives the impression of more than one narrator. The simple narratives use a third person point of view: except for the occasional lines like: "Hlorridi's heart leaped with laughter/ Then grew hard when he saw his hammer." Characters' thoughts and emotions are revealed entirely through their own words and actions. For example, Freyja's rage is clear from her actions in the *Lay of Thrym*: "Freyja snorted in such a fury / she made the hall of the Aesir shake." Two of the lays, the *Sibyl's Prophecy* and the *Prophecy of Gripir* by virtue of being prophecies, have an omniscient narrator. In some of the question and answer dialogues, for example, the *The Lay of Vafthrudnir*, the purpose is to provide specific information, but the dramatic and ironic interest that keeps the exchange from descending into a glossary is that while one character only appears to be omniscient the other truly is omniscient.

Setting

The characters's conduct in the *Elder Edda* is not greatly different from what we know of society in the Viking age. The physical setting of the lays stretches on the modern map from Scandinavia to southwestern Russia, home of the Goths before they entered the Roman empire in the late fourth century. The important Sigurd lays are centered on the Rhine valley in western Germany. The true setting of the *Elder Edda*, however, is a universe of nine worlds: Asgard, home of the gods in the center; Midgard, the home of men around it; and Utgard, containing Jötunheim, (giants), Alfheim (elves) Svartalfheim (dark elves) and possibly, the sources are not clear, Vanaheim, home of the Vanir gods. Under these

three is Niflhel, the realm of Hel, the goddess of the dead. The ninth world is possibly that of the dwarves, but its name and exact location are not certain. Asgard and Midgard are protected from Utgard by a body of water in which lives the Midgard serpent, so big that it encircles the whole of Midgard with his tale in its mouth. A rainbow bridge, Bifröst, connects Asgard and Midgard. The great world ash tree, Yggdrasil, has one root in Asgard, one in Utgard, and the third in Niflhel. Under the first root is the spring of Urd or Fate, under the second, the well of Mimir, the source of Odin's wisdom, and under the third is Hvergelmir, the source of all rivers. A dragon gnaws continually at its deepest root.

Allusions

The *Elder Edda* constantly alludes to a whole body of myth and legend that it only imperfectly preserves and that controls the imagery and symbolism of not only of the *Elder Edda*, but of Norse literature in general and Skaldic verse in particular. Even within the *Elder Edda*, there are poems that are essentially dramatic glossaries of allusions and metaphors: *The Lay of Alvis* and *The Lay of Vafthrudnir*.

Heiti and Kennings

The two most prominent poetic devices are heiti and kennings. Heiti are simply cultivated and unusual words for common things or concepts. They can be archaisms, lost from everyday speech, or common words used in a way peculiar to poetry, or poetic coinages. Kenning comes from the verb *kenna* to characterize or define. They consist of a noun plus a modifier in the possessive case, as 'the raven's feeder' for a warrior. Some rely on natural or everyday connections 'the bane of tinder' for fire or 'the giver of linen' for a lady. The most complex rely on allusions to legend or myth.

Prosody

The *Elder Edda* are typically in four line stanzas. Each line is divided by a *caesura* (pause). Each half-line contains two stressed syllables; the half lines are connected across the *caesura* by alliteration connecting a stressed initial sound in the first half of the line to a stressed initial sound in the second. Individual consonant sounds only alliterate with the same sound. All vowels alliterate with each other. There is no restriction on the position of the stressed syllables. *Fornyrdislag* (ancient verse) allows generally only two unstressed syllables per half-line:

Betty Bouncer bought a candle. *Málaháttr* (speech verse) allows three unstressed syllables per half-line: Sad little Susan, sought for a candle. In a third stanza form *ljódaháttr* (song measure) the first and fourth lines are in *Málaháttr*, the second and fourth have only three stresses.

HISTORICAL CONTEXT

The Vikings

The Vikings have entered popular imagination as bloodthirsty and immensely daring pirates, but they were first and foremost farmers and traders, raiding for treasure and slaves to accumulate capital to acquire status at home, or looking for lands abroad to colonize. Their raids, trading expeditions, and colonizing took them from Constantinople, modern Istanbul, to the coast of North America. They laid the basis of the Russian state with their trading posts along the Volga and Dneiper. They founded nearly all the cities of modern Ireland. The threat of their great raiding parties was crucial to the development of England as a unified state.

The society the Vikings came from was one of mixed farming, fishing and hunting, supplemented by trading. They would turn their hand to anything. The development of greatly improved ship designs towards the end of the eighth century gave the Scandinavians the finest ships in Europe. Their knorrs were the most effective cargo ships yet built. Their longships could cross the Atlantic or sail up the Seine to lay siege to Paris.

Beside their trading and manufacturing settlements in Ireland and settlements in England, the Vikings colonized the Isle of Man, the Orkneys, Iceland and Greenland. Many of the original settlers of Iceland were from Norway where the consolidation of the country under a central kingship was opposed by many noblemen and free farmers, used to handling their own affairs without outside interference. Others came from the Viking settlements in Ireland, always under pressure from the native Irish princes.

Viking Society

Scandinavia and her people were dominated by the sea. The landscapes of the three Nordic countries, Denmark, Sweden and Norway, are each distinct, but in all of them the terrain tended to separate communities, while the sea connected them. The people looked to the sea as naturally as to the land for opportunities.

The Scandinavians were farmers wherever the land was good enough. Rye, wheat, oats and barley were grown depending on local conditions. Cows, sheep, pigs, geese and chickens were kept. They supplemented agricultural production with hunting, fishing and gathering wild foods: honey, birds eggs and wild plants. Farms were family enterprises, and depending on the richness of the land, often at some distance from one another. Towns only began to emerge from trading posts and ritual centers towards A.D. 1000.

Control of land was the basis of wealth. Sons in a land-owning family increased its power since their wives' dowries would increase and consolidate their landholdings. The family itself in a legal sense and in terms of the various social obligations of Norse society was defined to the degree of third or fourth cousins recognizing a common great-great-great-grandfather. Obligations of one kind or another would also bind a man to the protection of a more powerful neighbor, whom he in turn would support at need. In a hard and violent age these mutual bonds were essential to the maintenance of order and to ensure access to justice.

Men worked their farms with the help of their family which might include two or three generations. Slaves were used for heavier labor by those who could afford them. Free laborers might work for their keep and a small wage. A rich landowner could afford to employ more help, giving him the leisure to go raiding and trading and with luck acquire the wealth necessary to maintain or enhance his status.

Viking Ships and Shipbuilding

The development of ship construction towards the end of the eighth century gave the Scandinavians the finest ships in Europe. They perfected sailing ships that had no need of deep water, safe anchorages or quaysides, but could cross the North Sea or the North Atlantic under sail, as well as be rowed up most of the major rivers of western Europe. These ships were slender and flexible. They had symmetrical ends and a true keel, the lengthwise structure along the base of a ship to which its ribs are connected. They were clinker-built, that is of overlapping planks riveted together. At times these planks would also have been lashed to the ribs of the ship with spruce roots to ensure the ship's

COMPARE
&
CONTRAST

- **Setting during** *The Elder Edda*: During the Viking era, raw material and slaves are the main resources of northern and western Europe. Tens of thousands of European men, women, and children are sold into slavery not only within Europe, but into Muslim Spain, North Africa, and the Middle East. Today, the tide of cheap labor has turned and thousands of North Africans are forced to seek a living in Spain and France.

  Medieval Iceland: Iceland is poor, with a small population, but it produces a vibrant and extensive literature in prose and poetry. Reading to the family group or to assembled neighbors is a common winter's entertainment into the nineteenth century in farming districts. Iceland still has one of the highest literacy rates in the world.

  Tenth and Twelfth Century: Norse colonies flourish in Greenland, which they found to be uninhabited and to have a climate good enough for stock-raising and their traditional way of life. Climactic change meant a return to the weather we see today and the Eskimo who had retreated north before the Vikings arrived. The colony finds it culturally impossible to adapt to the new conditions and disappears by the end of the fifteenth century.

flexibility in rough seas. They were steered with a side rudder fitted to the starboard side. One ship excavated in 1880 from a mound at Gokstad on the west side of the Oslo Fjord was 76 and 1/2 feet long. At its widest it was 17 and 1/2 feet. When fully laden it would have drawn only three feet of water: it could have been sailed deep into the heart of the Irish countryside or up to the gates of Paris. A copy was sailed across the Atlantic.

Treasure

However it was acquired, treasure, particularly silver, was important in Viking society. One function was display. Fine jewelry and ornamented weapons were an obvious indication of status and success. It was considered part of family wealth like land, and, despite legend, no more than one or two pieces of jewelry were buried with the dead. It was used to reward one's retainers and to provide lavish hospitality. Both of increased a man's standing in his society. Spent on land it raised a freeman's status. For a slave it could mean liberty.

On a practical level, because they did not have a coinage, silver had to be weighed and tested before transactions could take place. It was not necessary, therefore, to keep all one's silver in coins or even ingots. If, mid-deal, a man found himself a little short of cash, he need only throw in his cloak pin or a piece of a bracelet, properly weighed.

Iceland and its Professional Poets

Almost from the beginning of its settlement, Icelanders kept in constant touch with Ireland, England and their Scandinavian homelands. Icelanders with poetic skills found their services appreciated and well rewarded by Norse rulers or by rulers with Norse subjects. Indeed poetry became something of an Icelandic monopoly. For 350 years, from Egill Skalla-Grímson to Jón murti Egilsonn who composed for King Eiríkur Magnússon in 1299 there are records of 110 Icelandic court poets. Snorri was probably trying to keep alive a tradition which had proved useful not only to individual Icelanders, but to Iceland as a whole. A successful court poet would give his fellow countrymen access to the king's court, and keep distant Iceland's concerns from being completely forgotten.

CRITICAL OVERVIEW

The first indication of the *Elder Edda's* critical reception is the simple fact of its preservation in a quietly elegant manuscript, the *Codex Regius* with the explanatory prose passages interspersed among the lays. It is often assumed that, as Christianity reached the peoples of northern Europe, devout Christians, as well as the institutional church, automatically attempted to destroy the memory of the old gods and the human heroes whose activities, judged by Judeo-Christian standards, were often less than edifying. Nevertheless, the poems in *Elder Edda* were preserved, collected, and copied. This process can perhaps be most easily understood with reference to the work of the Icelandic scholar and politician, Snorri Sturlson (1179–1241), author of the treatise the *Prose Edda*, which laid the foundation for the analysis of Norse poetry. The stories preserved in the *Elder Edda* were part of the essential tools of the skalds, Norse poets who worked within complex metrical forms, using allusions and metaphors drawn from native heroic and mythological lays, much as Greek and Roman poets enriched their poetry with allusions to their god and heroes or Christian poets to the bible. A gifted skaldic poet could hope for patronage and advancement in the northern courts. Iceland in particular, poor in other resources, produced more than a few of these poets.

In the twelfth century, the ability to understand the older skaldic poetry and to compose in its manner was under threat from Church disapproval on one hand and new French-influenced popular poetry on the other. Christianity was probably the lesser threat. Once conversion was reasonably complete and real, references to Thor and Volund were generally considered as innocuous as references in Latin poetry to Hercules. The growing loss of the traditional material may indeed be reflected in the *Elder Edda* itself since the *Lay of Varthrudnir* and the *Lay of Alvis*, which function as dramatic glossaries of poetic terms and allusions. Snori attempted to reverse this loss with his *Prose Edda*, prose versions of the old stories together with a treatise on the complex metrical rules governing the composition of the various types of skaldic verse, and which provided an explanation of the ancient gods that turned them into clever Trojans, taking advantage of the gullible northerners. In a renaissance of the older literature, reflected in the work of Snorri, the lays of the *Elder Edda* were collected and copied.

There is no record of the *Elder Edda* before the *Codex Regius* came into the possession of Bishop Brynjólf Seinsson in 1643. The manuscript had lost a number of leaves by that time, and no copy exists that was made before the leaves were lost. In 1662, the bishop sent it to the ruler of Iceland, King

Frederick III of Denmark. The Renaissance had begun with a renewed interest in Greek and Roman literature and art. Before long, however, people in northern and western Europe, in emulation and partial reaction to this absorption, began to search for information about their own ancestors and their cultural life. This interest, fed by the political usefulness of national identities, lead to speculation about ancient monuments and the careful combing of Greek and Latin texts for information. It also meant that early vernacular writings now interested all those who felt it was their duty or in their interest to encourage scholarship and a sense of a shared national past. In 1665, the "Sibyl's Prophecy" and the "Sayings of the High One" from the *Elder Edda* were published together with Snorri Sturlson's *Prose Edda*. The full collection, however, was published only between 1787 and 1828. By this time, the romantic movement and the new study of philology, the study of the development and interconnection of languages, were ready to make full use of the texts. Scholars pored over them for linguistic clues to the development and interconnections of the Germanic branch of the Indo-European languages and ancient northern society. In England and Germany as the century progressed, the *Elder Edda*, along with the Icelandic Sagas (prose tales of fictionalized historical events and characters) were moving into the consciousness of the reading public at large. In Nordic countries, this assimilation was strikingly resisted on some fronts; in the nineteenth century, the traditional evening saga reading was discouraged in favor of the Bible in Iceland. The Danish scholar Grundtvig attempted to re-introduce the images, characters, and narratives of the *Elder Edda*, but with little success.

The *Elder Edda*, like many other early medieval epics, for example *Beowulf* and the *Táin Bó Cuáilgne,* were approached almost purely as philological lucky dips or archaeological artifacts well into the twentieth century. It can be no coincidence that Auden's translations, which helped bring the *Elder Edda* to the attention of late twentieth century readers, were dedicated to his former teacher Tolkien, whose own 1936 lecture, "*Beowulf:* The Monsters and the Critics" radically shifted the perception of the epic towards it first and essential existence as literature. Stylistic discussions of the poetry have begun to be discussed more, in the critical literature, even though Nordal's edition of the "Sibyl's Prophecy," revised in 1952 and printed in English translation as late as 1978, has nothing to say about the attributes of the poetry, which contains this mythology like insects and leaves in amber. Ursula Dronke's commentaries, particularly on the Atli lays, demonstrate both the richness of construction and the imaginative play of author with historical material.

CRITICISM

Helen Conrad-O'Briain

In the following essay, Conrad-O'Briain looks at the great romance of the Elder Edda *in an effort to understand its neglect by writers and critics.*

Seventeen of the lays in the *Elder Edda* concern the house of the Volsungs. Fifteen directly or indirectly point towards the Icelandic *Volsung Saga*, the Middle High German *Nibelungenleid*, and finally to Wagner's series of operas, *Ring of the Nibelungs*. They are part of one of the best case histories for the development of the epic from short lays or tales available. The other two "The First Lay of Helgi Hunding's Bane" and "The Second Lay of Helgi Hunding's Bane" could also be approached as points on a continuum of development, but a development that was somehow interrupted. The second lay has already begun the expansion. It adds incidents and treats them with greater complexity, even if it still relies, in true lay style, on the dramatic use of the characters' voices to create atmosphere and setting, direct the audience's sympathies, and propel the narrative. In that process of development, however, Helgi and his beloved Sigrun proved a dead end, while Sigurd and Brynhild became the star-crossed lovers of northern legend, the Viking answer to Lancelot and Guinevere or Tristan and Isolde.

Sigurd was not the only son of Sigmund to inspire the love a Valkyrie, but his elder brother Helgi and his Valkyrie, Sigrun/Svava/Kara and their love stretching across three lifetimes has never caught the popular fancy; even the extant lays in the *Elder Edda* are fragmentary. Their story must once have been popular. What happened?

In the second lay, as mentioned above, the story already incorporates events after Helgi's defeat and killing of Sigrun's father, brothers, and unwanted suitor. The audience now had both the beginning and end of their love, expanding Helgi's death into what might otherwise have been detached as a separate lay. Helgi's death by Dag, the brother-in-law he had spared, is of far less importance or interest to the poet than the love of Helgi and Sigurn. To express this love to the audience, the poet devoted slightly over a third of his lay to Sigrun's lament for Helgi and their meeting in his grave mound. He incorporated both the theme of the unquiet grave and an audacious reversal of the demon-lover motif.

Instead of being carried off unwillingly to the horrors of the grave as in the demon lover ballads and tales, Sigrun goes to the burial mound, arranges a bed, and insists "Here in the barrow we'll go to bed, released from sorrow, I will sleep, Helgi, safe in your arms the way I used to when you were alive." This material might serve to flesh out an epic, but placed on center stage, they seem more naturally the stuff of romance. This and the substitution in the second lay of the first's generalized hero's boyhood with Helgi's daring secret mission to spy on his family's enemies suggests a poet with a gift for narrative innovation. What then cuts off the development? Possibly the lack of a theme to support an extended narrative. The winning of Sigrun provided the center of a narrative lay, but the process was never given the emotional complexity to sustain a long narrative.

The core of the story, the unshakable love between Helgi and Sigrun, could not accommodate an emotional struggle between them to take the place of war. Such a change would rob the story of its essential character. In the second version, the scene in which, going over the battlefield, she first finds the despised Hodbrodd dying and then Helgi safe, might easily have become an extended episode. But when Helgi who says "'Sigrun I will grieve you by what I say . . . there fell this morning at Freka Stone, Bragi and Hogni; I was their bane.'" Her reaction does not give the society, which produced the *Volsung Saga* or *Njal's Saga*, much to work with to extend the conflict and therefore the narrative: "Then Sigrun wept. She said: 'Now I would wish those warriors alive, and still have your arms around me.'" Then, as the story says, they married and had sons, but "Helgi didn't live to grow old" and "grief and sorrow caused Sigrun to die young." Helgi had spared Sigrun's brother, Dag, who repays the oaths he has sworn with Odin's spear in vengeance for his father. When he confesses the slaying to his sister and offers compensation to her and her sons, she curses him, but she does not pursue vengeance. Her focus and the story's

WHAT DO I READ NEXT?

- Snorri Sturluson, *The Prose Edda: Tales from Norse Mythology*, trans. by Jean I. Young (1971), provides a lively translation of the most accessible parts of an encyclopedic thirteenth century prose collection of the myths and legends at the heart of the Norse poetic vocabulary.

- Magnus Magnusson, *Viking Expansion Westwards* (1973) is a lavishly illustrated history of the expansion of the Vikings from England to North America. Magnusson focuses on individuals like Aude the Deep-Minded and the realities of daily life, bringing the reader face to face with the people who wrote and listened to the *Elder Edda*.

- Lee Hollander, *The Skalds: A Selection of Their Poems* presents the poets of the Viking Age and a selection of their poetry whose incredibly elaborate lyric poetic language and imagery depends upon the myths and legends preserved in part in the *Elder Edda*.

- Magnus Magnusson and H. Pálsson, *The Vinland Sagas*. The vikings in North America in their own words, this might well be read in conjunction with *Viking Expansion Westwards*.

- Magnus Magnusson and H. Pálsson, *Njal's Saga*. This is perhaps the greatest of the Icelandic family sagas, set in the period when Icelandic society was slowly adopting Christianity and the cultural changes conversion required.

- Jesse L. Byock, *The Saga of the Volsungs: The Norse Epic of Sigurd the Dragon Slayer* (1990) is a prose retelling of the Sigurd story, written down between 1200 and 1270. It is closely related to the lays in the *Elder Eddas*, but presents all the Volsung stories as part of an integrated whole.

- A new collection of essays on *Elder Edda*, edited by Paul L. Acker, is promised for November, 2000. It is promised to apply new critical approaches to the mythological poetry in the *Elder Edda*.

---

focus remains love of Helgi rather than vengeance. She dares the terrors of the grave for him and dies of her grief; he comes back to her from the dead, from the halls of Odin.

Perhaps the most compelling scene, the one that might have offered the possibility of an extended narrative is Helgi's return from the dead to his wife for one night. It operates within the context of their inability to meet in the Norse afterlife. Since Sigrun is fated to die of grief, not in battle, she cannot join her husband in Valhalla. It is often overlooked by modern readers that Brynhild does not want Sigurd dead merely to punish him. She wants to ensure that she will have him in the afterlife. She does not kill herself out of guilt or remorse, but to join him in the kingdom of Hel. Sigurd must be killed treacherously, not merely because of his prowess, but because if he dies in battle he is lost to her forever. The

composers of the lays were very much alive to this. Their sensitivity to it is reflected in "Brynhild's Hel-ride."

The tale of Sigurd and Brynhild was a tale of thwarted love, but there is no adultery, no stolen meetings, none of the twists and turns of lovers's intrigue, only the cold frustrated fury of a woman who has been tricked into marrying a man she despises, having been betrothed to the one man she could respect and therefore love. Besides, the French romance as a genre was not invariably or even usually about adulterous love but a love that found its harbor in marriage.

The women of *Elder Edda* and of the saga literature in general are praised for the same qualities as the men. Modern readers tend to judge the medieval taste in heroines by Chaucer's, but Geoffrey Chaucer had a highly personal taste for the plaintive

> It is the nature of their love, their own natures, that they should find each other and nothing shall come between them, not even death itself, which is the meaning of the story . . . The center of their story is their love that propels them across death."

and helpless woman (usually married). Brynhild's character did not change substantially between the Norse and courtly version of her story. The ballad tradition is full of women who follow their lovers to war in disguise, often saving them.

The problem of the Helgi legends' dead end may lie exactly in the cleft stick of the Eddic traditions of the afterlife and the in the reincarnation motif. The great engine of the traditional development of the Helgi story, the narrative tool by which the story could be extended was that the lovers were reincarnated at least three times. The story never found a replacement. However much reincarnation may appeal to modern sensibilities, if only as a narrative tool, it was a bar to wider development of the story between the Vikings' conversion to Christianity and the end of the nineteenth century. It has been suggested that the statement at the end of "The Lay of Helgi Horvard's Son" may be a belated scribal attempt to link the old Helgi tradition to the Volsung-Helgi tradition." But, it seems unlikely that such an idea would have occurred to a Christian scribe out of nowhere, least of all to attract an audience. Keeping the interest in the story alive would have suggested suppressing or ridiculing such a heathen concept as reincarnation, as the prose passage at the end of "The Second Lay of Helgi Hunding's Bane": "In olden times it was believed that people could be born again, although that is now considered an old woman's tale." More likely to represent a scribal attempt to make the sequence more acceptable would be the prose introduction to "The Second Lay of Helgi Hunding's

Bane": "King Sigmund, the son of Volsung, married Borghild from Balund. They called their son Helgi, for Helgi Hjorvard's son." This at most suggests a subconscious recognition of their similar fate. The lines in "The Second Lay of Helgi Hunding's Bane"—"before she had ever seen Sigmund's son / she had loved him with all her heart"—is also suggestive of a love reincarnated.

Perhaps the problem is more fundamental. There simply wasn't enough material. Despite the great potential offered and already exploited by certain incidents, there were not enough of them. Even when fleshed out, there certainly were not enough tensions to make a convincing saga like that which formed around Sigurd. The tradition of their love offers only one possible tension between them: there is no meeting again for them after death. No writer after the conversion would be able to exploit the literary possibilities of either this endless loss or the alternative, the rebirth and repetition of the cycle of their love. There is no great object to be pursued. It is the nature of their love, their own natures, that they should find each other and nothing shall come between them, not even death itself, which is the meaning of the story. That is what differentiates them from the characters in the Sigurd material. The center of their story is their love that propels them across death. Their great sorrow, the thing that they must conquer, is their separation by death. That is a subject worthy of an epic, but not an epic that could have been written in the prevailing cultural atmosphere.

Source: Helen Conrad-O'Briain, for *Epics for Students*, Gale, 2001.

Lotte Motz

Lotte Motz argues that the pattern between Eskimo and Norse tradition is similar, which leads to understanding the "similarity of linguistic dynamics."

In his treatise on poetry, the so-called *Edda Snorra*, Snorri (1949:244) states that the human mind is periphrased in skaldic speech as 'the wind of troll-women' without offering an explanation for the unexpected image. We do find such kennings as . . . 'the storm of Járnsaxa (a giantess) in the meaning of 'courage', or *Herkju stormr*—'Herkja's (a giantess') storm' in the meaning 'mind'.

Snorri's puzzling statement has given rise to some scholarly interpretations. In his book on magic practices Dag Strömbäck assumed that the noun

The Norse god Odin is considered the mythological godfather of poets. The Elder Edda *includes a story about how Odin learned the runes, the alphabet of the ancient north Germanic tribes.*

hugr of Snorri's sentence (*Huginn skal svá kenna at kalla vind troll-kvenna*) relates to the force named *hugr*, which lives in men, and which may, according to Norse belief, detach itself and wander forth, corporeally, to attack and harm an enemy. Strömbäck (1935:175 ff) points out that witches or troll-women are often visualized as traveling in the wind. The 'trolls' wind' thus would be equated with the powerful and noxious force, named *hugr*.

Basing herself on folkbelief, Lily Weiser-Aall (1936:76–78) offered a somewhat different expla-

nation. The word *hugr* is, according to her, to be understood in its meaning of 'bodily affliction', the kind of sickness which may be brought on by a troll's breath or 'wind', as shown by the modern Norwegian nouns *trollgust, alvgust*—'trolls' wind', 'elves' wind', as names of a disease.

Concerning both interpretations we must note that the kenning 'trolls' wind' does not, in the instances which have been gathered, periphrase 'sickness' or 'attack'. The examples, cited by Rudolf Meissner, circumscribe the notions of 'cour-

> " . . .the equation 'mind—
> trolls' wind' of skaldic poetry
> had originated in its turn, as
> in the scenario of the Eskimos,
> in a belief, forgotten in its
> articulated form at the time
> of our texts, that to receive
> insight, strength, or vision, a
> man must attain close contact
> with the elemental powers."

age', 'mind', 'emotion', 'thoughts', which coincide with the standard meanings of the noun *hugr* — 'mind' 'feeling', 'desire', 'courage'. Snorri must have based his statement on his knowledge of skaldic diction. It is therefore not likely that he used *hugr* in the meaning 'sickness' or 'attack' if the metaphors consistently relate to the workings of the human mind. Strömbáck and Weiser-Aall apparently did not consider the material from which Snorri's conclusion was derived.

I shall, in my turn, seek to find the reason for linking witches' weather to human thoughts and emotions, and interpret Snorri's sentence, understanding *hugr* in its standard meaning of 'mind, emotion, consciousness', with the help of a non-Germanic parallel.

The parallel is found among the Eskimos. Their highest god, named Sila, Hila, or Tla, by the various groups, is a being of the outer air, of winds and storms, the great majestic, cosmic power before which men must bow in humbleness and awe. He is, as stated by an Eskimo, "A great spirit so mighty that his utterance to mankind is not through common words, but by storm and snow and rain and the fury of the sea; all the forces that men fear ..."

Surprisingly the name of this great force serves also as a designation of the human mind or human intelligence. In Greenlandic speech it may be said: *Siälihliuppa*—"Sila rained on him", and it may be stated about someone: "He has Sila," i.e. "He has intelligence." In Alaska the name Sla means 'weather' and the verb *slaugohaqtoa* means "I am thinking".

We may find an explanation for this duality of meaning by considering that among some of the Eskimo nations, for instance among the Caribou Eskimos, it is indeed from Hila that the shaman-magician, the central figure of religious life, receives his visionary powers. He has prepared himself for this profound experience by leaving the settlements of men and by the endurance of much suffering. Then in his loneliness he may hear the god's voice, be filled with god's presence, and thus himself become part of the secret workings of the universe. "All true wisdom," an Eskimo explained to the explorer Rasmussen, "is only to be learned far from the dwellings of men, out in the great solitudes".

In a recurrent tale from Greenland a poor orphan boy transforms himself into a mighty hero through his strength of will, and he too obtains his gifts through his experience of meeting Sila in the wilderness. If a man wishes to become an *angakoq* (shaman), we are told by an eighteenth century observer of Eskimo life, he must go a long way from his home to a field where there are no men; he must look for a huge stone, sit down on it, and call for Torngarsuk (the shaman's helping spirit with this group of Eskimos). The shock of the terrifying encounter will cause the man to fall into a stupor, and to lie like dead; but he will reawaken and return to his community as a shaman.

The examples given testify to a belief that to acquire knowledge of the secrets of the world one must meet and merge with the forces which are manifest in storm and winds.

Eskimo culture, as we know, remained for climatic reasons at a very early stage of economic development, i.e. that of hunters and of fishermen, until the most recent time, and preserved some extremely archaic forms of belief. It is reasonable to assume that these forms had at one time had a wider distribution and that some had stayed, vestigially, in more sophisticated environments.

I wish to show in this paper that the equation 'mind—trolls' wind' of skaldic poetry had originated in its turn, as in the scenario of the Eskimos, in a belief, forgotten in its articulated form at the time of our texts, that to receive insight, strength, or vision, a man must attain close contact with the elemental powers. If enough fragments of such a faith are still discernible, though in various altered forms, in our texts we may be able to assume the

The goddess Frigg (also known as Friia or Freya), Odin's wife and a promoter of marriage and fertility.

existence of such a pattern in Germanic lands. To arrive at this assumption we would have to be able to point to the following:

1. that in north-Germanic tradition inspiration may be gained by contact with the forces of untamed nature,

2. that trolls and giants (the names are interchangeable) represent such forces,

3. that trolls and giants are capable of dispensing knowledge and inspiration,

4. that humans have indeed gained inspiration through a meeting with the trolls in distant places.

The examples from the arctic environment, here cited, describe an initiatory experience from which the human arises with a new identity, a new dimension to his person, possibly a new conscious soul. We shall examine whether in the Germanic context the inspiration granted would be of an individual nature, pertaining to a certain task, the working of a poem, or the divining of the future, or to the more profound event of acquiring a new state of consciousness.

Inspiration through contact with the forces of untamed nature

The Icelandic noun *útiseta*—'sitting outside', designates the wizard's practice of staying outdoors for the night in the course of his profession. The act is performed to gather knowledge of the future—*eflaútiseta ok leita spádóms*—and is considered a felony or crime. And we may understand that the wizard of Germanic society reached in his lonely vigil contact with the superhuman as does the *angakoq* of the Eskimos, visited by Torngarsuk while 'sitting on a stone'.

Inspiration may also be gained by sitting on a mound—*sitja á haugi*. After a night of sleeping on a mound an Icelandic shepherd gained the gift of poetic creativity.

While the instances above depict techniques of seeking specific visions or knowledge the episode of an Eddic poem shows how a whole new form of being is granted to a man through forces that have come to him through wind and air. The lad was, in his early youth, mute and without a name. One day, while sitting on a mound, he noticed that a train of shining maidens was riding through the clouds; one of them came to him to bestow these gifts: a name, the power of speech, and a sword. That practices meant to gain manhood, i.e. a new state of consciousness, were associated in Norse tradition with a stay in uncultivated places may be surmised from a sentence of *Landnámabók*; here a man was led into a certain cave of Iceland before attaining the 'rank of man'.

2. Trolls and giants as representatives of nature

This point hardly needs belaboring. Trolls and giants are the powers of *úlgarthar*, for they dwell outside of the settlements of men in the stones and crags, the caves and glaziers of the mountainside. Theirs is an especially close alliance with the weather, with storms and snow, and frost and winds. In Norse myth the wind arises because a giant in the shape of an eagle flaps his wings. A saga giant will frequently manipulate the weather to gain his end; he thus may send a storm to wreck the boat of sailors near his shore. The troll-woman *Thorgerthr Hölgabrúthr* created a hailstorm so that her friend might win his battle (*The Saga of the Jomsvikings*). The giant Gusir was observed as he was moving in a whirl of snow (*Ketils saga hœngs*), and Thorri, a giant and a king in a legendary saga, sends snow for 'good skiing' if he is favorably inclined (*Hversu Noregr byggthist*).

Winds may rise and darkness fall, just before a human meets a giant. The young Icelandic lad Oddr thus found himself in darkness, frost, and drifts of snow as he was about to meet the giant Bárthr (*Bárthar saga Snæfellsáss*). Rain and hail descended just before the heroes Hjálmthér and Ölvir encountered the giantess Skinnhúfa (*Hjálmthés saga ok Ölvis*). The Icelander Thorsteinn experienced an agony of cold before he faced the giant Grámann (*Ármanns saga inn fyrri*). The modern German noun *Windsbraul* for 'whirlwind' shows that in folk belief storm and wind may be visualized in the form of a witch.

We may be quite sure that the giants speak to men, like Sila of the Eskimos, 'by storm and snow and rain and the fury of the sea'.

3. Trolls and giants as source of knowledge and inspiration

Óthinn learned nine important magic songs from the giant Bolborn, his maternal uncle (*Hávamál*). The goddess Freyja approached Hyndla, a troll-woman living in a cave, to learn from her the genealogy of her human friend Óttar. And she received the information (*Hyndlulióth*). Though the Eddic poem *Vafthrúthnismál* ostensibly presents a contest between Óthinn and a giant, much information, concerning matters of the cosmos, is dispensed by Vafthrúthnir in the course of the event.

Young Oddr acquired so much legal knowledge from the giant Bárthr that he became the greatest lawyer of his generation (*Bárthar saga Snæfellsáss*). The warrior Thorsteinn learned many skills from his giant mistress (*Thorsteins saga Geirneffjufóstra*), while another man, named Thorsteinn, was taught so well by a giant woman and her daughters in the arts of courtly accomplishment that none could rival him in these matters (*Ármanns saga inn fyrri*); and the giant Ármann offered valuable advice in the lawsuit of an Icelandic farmer (*Ármanns saga inn fyrri*). Bárthr, who himself was a giant, was introduced to magic skills, knowledge of genealogy, sorcerers' chants, and the old magic lore by the giant Dofri (*Bárthar saga Snæfellsáss*). This giant was also said to be the teacher of the historical king Harald Finehair and he in structed him in learning—*frœthi*—and accomplishments—*íthróttir*. The giantess Menglöth appeared to Ormr in a dream and advised him on his future battle (*Orms tháttr Stórólfssonar*), while the giantess Brana came to Hálfdan in a dream to remind him of a pledge he had forgotten (*Hálfdanar saga Brönufóstra*). The hero Hadingus was sent for his education to the giant Vagnhofthus and he increased much in strength and skill, as reported by Saxo Grammaticus.

Trolls and giants, who are themselves, as we have seen, wise and versed in magic crafts, thus appear in teaching and counseling, and, in dreams, in helping and admonishment.

4. The inspirational meeting between troll and human in the wilderness

The *útiseta*, the magician's stay outside of human dwellings, is performed, as it is overtly stated, so that the trolls may be aroused—*útisetur at vekja troll upp*. The trolls thus are, in this practice, the superhuman forces of the natural environment whom the Norse magician wishes to approach, as the *angakoq* wishes to approach the mighty Sila.

In most instances, cited under 3, knowledge is imparted and instruction conducted in the uncultivated space of the giant's realm. Oddr spent a winter in his teacher's cave. Thorsteinn lived with Geirnefja as her lover while she taught him, and the other Thorsteinn resided with three giant women. In a mountain cave young Bárthr became acquainted with the many magic powers and the wisdom of the giant Dofri. And young Harald, later king of Norway, spent five years in this giant's cave.

Frequently the hero gains, through his meeting with the troll, usually a troll-woman, a superhuman friend who will help him in time of need in his later adventures. The giantess Mána came to Sörli's rescue when he was threatened by the anger of a queen (*Sörla saga slerka*), and the giantess Fála rushed to fight at Gunnar's side against an entire horde of trolls (*Gunnars saga Keldugnúpsfífls*). The giantess Skinnhúfa killed a monstrous whale which had threatened her human friend (*Hjálmthés saga ok Ölvis*), and the giant woman Brana arrived to save Hálfdan from the fires of a blazing hall (*Hálfdanar saga Brönufóstra*). A troll-woman, riding on a wolf, offered to become the *fylgja*, the lifelong and loyal guardian force, of the warrior Heth inn.

After the encounter with the troll some heroes of the legendary sagas are given a new by-name as the fosterson of the respective spirit. In this way Hálfdan became the Fosterling of Brana, Illugi the Fosterling of Gríthr, and Thorsteinn the Fosterling of Geirnefja. King Harald Finehair was also known as the Fosterling of Dofri. It is clear that receiving a new name, which he will bear throughout his future

life, marks a decisive change in the being of a person, the reaching of a new stage, the acquisition of an altered identity. And this event is occasioned, in the cases cited, by the man's stay with the troll in the troll's environment.

Let us summarize our argument: we cannot doubt that in north-Germanic tradition men are believed to gain temporary or lasting wisdom or inspiration by meeting with forces of the wilderness (1); it is also clear that trolls and giants represent such forces, especially those of wind and weather (2); trolls and giants, themselves deeply versed in magic wisdom, may generously give of their knowledge (3); an encounter of a human hero with a troll, in the troll's environment, and its impact is also frequently noted in the Old Icelandic texts (4).

We may, however, raise some questions concerning the latest category and wonder if the Norse hero's friendship with the troll is indeed of the same kind as the Eskimo shaman's contact with his god. Let us consider these events more closely.

The Eskimo's experience in the solitude of the arctic waste initiates him into his craft. He leaves the place of contact as a profoundly altered being, a man with a new identity. The Norse hero's experience in a giant's cave also leaves him as an altered being. The possession of a helping spirit has added a new dimension to his person; he may, furthermore, be protected in his future adventures by a magic gift received from his superhuman friend, as is Hálfdan by the corselet *Brönunautr*. Sometimes, as in the case of Illugi Grítharfóstri, he goes forth as one whose mettle has been tested, for Illugi's courage did not falter even at the moment of the greatest peril. At times a new by-name marks him as a man tested or instructed by a superhuman creature in the wilderness.

The initiatory nature of the Norse episodes is also underlined by the events preceding the adventure. The Eskimo shaman cannot attain his visionary powers without enduring suffering so great that it may endanger his physical existence. The saga hero in his turn is subjected to hardship and to pain. His ship may have drifted aimlessly, for weeks or months, in fog and darkness, before it was shattered on the rocks; he may be the sole survivor on the cliffs (*Ásmundar saga Atlasonar*). He may have been wounded and lie close to death on the battle ground. He may be on the point of drowning, as was Thorsteinn of *Thorsteins saga Víkingssonar*, or worn to exhaustion by the cold as was Thorsteinn of *Ármanns saga inn fyrri*.

The initiatory pattern of the saga hero's adventure would allow us to place it generically with the initiatory encounter of the *angakoq*. We must admit, however, that the experience in the arctic ice is part of the tradition of a living faith while the *útiseta* of the sorcerer belongs with forbidden practices, and the episode concerning the Norse hero and the troll is embedded in fictional or semi-fictional tales. We may wonder in what way information from such sources may be related to religious beliefs. Clearly the magician's practices, though forbidden in Christian time, had been part of pre-Christian faith and its manifestations persisted, as we may note, after the conversion.

We do not know, however, to what extent the sagas mirror a believed reality. They clearly have preserved a tale of a man's meeting with an elemental power in the wasteland and its impact on his personality. To the extent to which there was belief in the actual existence of the hero there also must have been belief, at least at one time, in the reality of his adventures. That such a faith was likely and that it had, actually, not completely vanished, is supported by the fact that the medieval king Harald Finehair bore, among others, the title Fosterson of (the giant) Dofri. The assumption might have been that to be a real king or a real hero one must have had the tutelage of an elemental force of nature.

If the arguments brought forth allow us to understand that the thought pattern here discussed is, in essence, the same in Eskimo and in Norse tradition then we may also understand the similarity of linguistic dynamics, the equation of Sila with intelligence and the equation of the 'troll's wind' with the human mind, for in meeting with the troll the hero acquired his *hugr*, his aware and conscious soul. That the meaning 'courage' recurs among the kennings is in keeping with the destiny and role awaiting the young warrior of the northern lands.

Source: Lotte Motz, "The Storm of Troll-Women," in *Maal og Minne,* Vol. 1–2, 1988, pp. 31–41.

Lee M. Hollander

Lee M. Hollander, in this article from The Poetic Edda, *attributes the preservation of the Teutonic race's literary heritage to the early Christian missionaries, and specifically, to Iceland, whose inhabitants contributed greatly to capturing the wonders of the Viking Age, its sagas and Eddic lays.*

What the *Vedas* are for India, and the Homeric poems for the Greek world, that the *Edda* signifies for the Teutonic race: it is a repository, in poetic form, of their mythology and much of their heroic lore, bodying forth both the ethical views and the cultural life of the North during late heathen and early Christian times.

Due to their geographical position, it was the fate of the Scandinavian tribes to succumb later than their southern and western neighbors to the revolutionary influence of the new world religion, Christianity. Before its establishment, they were able to bring to a highly characteristic fruition a civilization stimulated occasionally, during the centuries preceding, but not overborne by impulses from the more Romanized countries of Europe. Owing to the prevailing use of wood for structural purposes and ornamentation, little that is notable was accomplished and still less has come down to us from that period, though a definite style had been evolved in wood-carving, shipbuilding and bronze work, and admirable examples of these have indeed been unearthed. But the surging life of the Viking Age—restless, intrepid, masculine as few have been in the world's history—found magnificent expression in a literature which may take its place honorably beside other national literatures.

For the preservation of these treasures in written form we are, to be sure, indebted to Christianity; it was the missionary who brought with him to Scandinavia the art of writing on parchment with connected letters. The Runic alphabet was unsuited for that task.

But just as fire and sword wrought more conversions in the Merovingian kingdom, in Germany, and in England, than did peaceful, missionary activity so too in the North; and little would have been heard of sagas, Eddic lays, and skaldic poetry had it not been for the fortunate existence of the political refuge of remote Iceland.

Founded toward the end of the heathen period (*ca.* 870) by Norwegian nobles and yeomen who fled their native land when King Harald Fairhair sought to impose on them his sovereignty and to levy tribute, this colony long preserved and fostered the cultural traditions which connected it with the Scandinavian soil. Indeed, for several centuries it remained an oligarchy of families intensely proud of their ancestry and jealous of their cultural heritage. Even when Christianity was finally introduced and adopted as the state religion by legislative decision (1000 A.D.), there was no sudden break, as was more generally the case elsewhere. This was partly because of the absence of religious fanaticism, partly because of the isolation of the country, which rendered impracticable for a long time any stricter enforcement of Church discipline in matters of faith and of living.

The art of writing, which came in with the new religion, was enthusiastically cultivated for the committing to parchment of the lays, the laws, and the lore of olden times, especially of the heroic and romantic past immediately preceding and following the settlement of the island. Even after Christianity got to be firmly established, by and by, wealthy freeholders and clerics of leisure devoted themselves to accumulating and combining into "sagas," the traditions of heathen times which had been current orally, and to collecting the lays about the gods and heroes which were still remembered — indeed, they would compose new ones in imitation of them. Thus, gradually came into being huge codices which were reckoned among the most cherished possessions of Icelandic families. By about 1200 the Danish historian, Saxo Grammaticus, already speaks in praise of the unflagging zeal of the Icelanders in this matter.

The greatest name in this early Icelandic Renaissance (as it has been called) is that of Snorri Sturluson (1178–1241), the powerful chieftain and great scholar, to whom we owe the *Heimskringla,* or *The History of the Norwegian Kings,* and the *Snorra Edda*—about which more later—but he stands by no means alone. And thanks also to the fact that the language had undergone hardly a change during the Middle Ages, this antiquarian activity was continued uninterruptedly down into the fifteenth and sixteenth centuries, when it was met and reinforced by the Nordic Renaissance with its romantic interest in the past.

In the meantime the erstwhile independent island had passed into the sovereignty of Norway and, with that country, into that of Denmark, then at the zenith of its power. In the search for the origins of Danish greatness it was soon understood that a knowledge of the earlier history of Scandinavia depended altogether on the information contained in the Icelandic manuscripts. In the preface to Saxo's *Historia Danica,* edited by the Danish humanist Christiern Pedersen in the beginning of the sixteenth century, antiquarians found stated in so many words that to a large extent his work is based on Icelandic sources, at least for the earliest times. To make these sources more accessible, toward the end of the sixteenth century, the learned Norwegian, Peder Claussön, translated the *Heimskringla,* which,

The whole is in one firm, legible hand which paleologists agree in assigning to an Icelander of the last half of the thirteenth century. He must have copied it from, it seems, at least two manuscripts for the nature of a number of scribal errors shows that he did not write from memory or from dictation."

with the kings of Norway in the foreground, tells of Scandinavian history from the earliest times down to the end of the twelfth century.

Since it was well known that many valuable manuscripts still existed in Iceland, collectors hastened to gather them although the Icelandic freeholders "brooded over them like the dragon on his gold," as one contemporary remarked. As extreme good fortune would have it, the Danish kings then ruling, especially Fredric III, were liberal and intelligent monarchs who did much to further literature and science. The latter king expressly enjoined his bishop in Iceland, Brynjólfur Sveinsson, a noted antiquarian, to gather for the Royal Library, then founded, all manuscripts he could lay hold of. As a result, this collection now houses the greatest manuscript treasures of Northern antiquity. And the foundations of other great manuscript collections, such as those of the Royal Library of Sweden and the libraries of the Universities of Copenhagen and Uppsala, were laid at about the same time.

This collecting zeal of the sixteenth and seventeenth centuries may almost be called providential. It preserved from destruction the treasures, which the Age of Enlightenment and Utilitarianism following was to look upon as relics of barbarian antecedents best forgotten, until Romanticism again invested the dim past of Germanic antiquity with glamor.

The god Thor, whose name means thunder, is probably the most well-known figure in all of Germanic mythology.

At the height of this generous interest in the past a learned Icelander, Arngrímur Jónsson, sent the manuscript of what is now known as *Snorra Edda* or *The Prose Edda* (now called *Codex Wormianus*), to his Danish friend Ole Worm. Knowledge of this famous work of Snorri's had, it seemed, virtually disappeared in Iceland. Its author was at first supposed to be that fabled father of Icelandic historiography, Sæmundr Sigfússon (1056–1133), of whose learning the most exaggerated notions were then current. A closer study of sources gradually undermined this view in favor of Snorri; and his authorship became a certainty with the finding of the *Codex Upsaliensis* of the *Snorra Edda,* which is prefaced by the remark that it was compiled by Snorri.

To all intents and purposes this *Edda* of Snorri's is a textbook—one of the most original and entertaining ever written. In it is set forth in dialogue form the substance and technique (as we should say) of skaldship, brought conveniently together for the benefit of those aspiring to the practice of the art. The first part, called "Gylfaginning" or "The Duping of Gylfi," furnishes a survey of Northern mythology and cosmogony; the second, called

"Skáldskaparmál" or "The Language of Skaldship," deals with the subject of "kennings," whose origin is explained by quotations from skaldic poems and other lore; the third, called "Háttatal" or "The Enumeration of *hættir* (metres)," contains Snorri's encomiastic poem, in 102 stanzas, on King Hákon and Duke Skúli, exemplifying as many metres employed in skaldship and giving explanations of the technical aspects of the skaldic art.

Among the scholars eagerly scanning this precious find the conviction soon made itself felt that the material in it was not original with Snorri: they saw that much of the first two books was on the face of it a group of synopses from older poetic sources which, in their turn, investigators ascribed to Sæmundr. Hence when that lucky manuscript hunter, Bishop Brynjólfur, discovered (about 1643) the unique and priceless codex containing what we now call *The Poetic Edda,* it was but natural that he should conclude this to be "The Edda of Sæmundr," whose existence had already been inferred theoretically. And this conclusion was unhesitatingly subscribed to by all, down to modern times. The fact is, though, that the connection of Sæmundr with *The Poetic Edda* has no documentary evidence whatever. Moreover, it is inherently improbable.

But, since the great bulk of poems which we have come to regard as "Eddic" is handed down precisely in this manuscript, and since we lack any other collective title, the name of *Edda,* which properly belongs to Snorri's work, has been retained for all similar works. We know with a fair degree of certainty that Snorri himself named his handbook of poetics "Edda"; but as to the meaning of this word we are dependent on conjecture.

Quite early, the name was taken to be identical with that of Edda, who was progenitress of the race of thralls according to "The Lay of Ríg," and whose name means "great-grandmother." This identification was adopted by the great Jakob Grimm who, with his brother Wilhelm, was one of the first to undertake a scientific edition of part of the collection. In the taste of Romanticism he poetically interpreted the title as the ancestral mother of mankind sitting in the circle of her children, instructing them in the lore and learning of the hoary past. However, as it happens, Snorri did not, in all likelihood, know "The Lay of Ríg"; nor does this fanciful interpretation agree at all with the prosy manner in which the Icelanders were accustomed to name their manuscripts, or—for that matter—with the purpose and nature of Snorri's work. It is altogether untenable.

Another explanation was propounded early in the eighteenth century by the Icelandic scholar, Árni Magnússon, and has been accepted by many. According to him, *Edda* means "poetics"—a title which (from a modern point of view) would seem eminently fitting for Snorri's work. Later scholars, who have provided a more solid philological under-pinning for this theory than Arni was able to, also point out that the simplex *óðr,* from which *Edda* may be derived, signifies "reason," "soul" and hence "soulful utterance," "poem," agrees excellently, etymologically and semantically, with the related Latin *vates* and the Old Irish *faith,* "seer," "poet." Nevertheless, this explanation does not quite sat-isfy, for the word "Edda" in the meaning "poetics" is nowhere attested before the middle of the four-teenth century.

The simplest theory, agreeing best with the matter-of-fact Icelandic style of naming their writ-ings, is the proposal of the Icelandic-English scholar, Eirík Magnússon. He reminded us that *Edda* may mean "the Book of Oddi." This was the name of the renowned and historic parsonage in southwest Ice-land which under that remarkable mind, Sæmundr Sigfússon, had become a center of learning whither flocked gifted youths eager for historical or clerical instruction. After his death, in 1133, the estate, continuing to prosper, kept up its tradition for learning under his two sons, and especially under his grandson, the wise and powerful chieftain, Jón Loptsson. It was he who fostered and tutored the three-year-old Snorri and under whose roof the boy lived until his nineteenth year. What is more likely than that Oddi with its traditions and associations played a profound role in Snorri's entire develop-ment? To be sure, whether Snorri wrote his work there in later years, whether he gave it the title in grateful recognition of the inspiration there re-ceived, or whether he wished thus to indicate an indebtedness to manuscript collections of poems owned at Oddi—these are mere surmises.

Magnússon, indeed, believed that Snorri, while in Oddi, had used a manuscript containing about all the lays comprised in the codex found by Bishop Brynjólfur, and from them made the synopses found in the "Gylfaginning." In this he was mistaken however; for it seems well-established now that Snorri could have had before him only "Voluspá," "Vafthrúonismál," and "Grímnismál."

Subsequent finds added a few lays of Eddic quality to those preserved in Brynjólf's codex, which thus remains our chief source for them. This famous manuscript, now known as *Codex Regius No. 2365* of the Royal Library of Denmark, is a small quarto volume consisting of forty-five sheets closely covered with writing. No distinction is made between prose and poetry, except that the beginning of every lay is marked off by a large colored initial, and every stanza, by a smaller one. The whole is in one firm, legible hand which paleologists agree in assigning to an Icelander of the last half of the thirteenth century. He must have copied it from, it seems, at least two manuscripts for the nature of a number of scribal errors shows that he did not write from memory or from dictation. Paleographic evi-dence furthermore shows that these postulated manu-scripts themselves cannot have been older than the beginning of the thirteenth century; also, that they must have been written by different scribes, for there is a distinct paleographic and orthographic boundary between "Alvíssmál," the last of the mytho-logical lays in *Regius,* and the heroic lays. We know nothing concerning the provenience of this priceless collection, not even where it was preserved when Bishop Brynjólfur found it. As to the date when the lays were first collected, various considerations make it probable that this occurred not earlier than the middle of the thirteenth century.

Next in importance to the *Regius* comes the manuscript *Fragment 748* of the Arnamagnæan Collection of the Copenhagen University Library, dating from the beginning of the fourteenth century. Among other matters it contains, in a slightly differ-ent form and in a divergent order, part of "The Lay of Hárbarth," "Baldr's Dreams" (for which it is the sole source), part of "The Lay of Skírnir," "The Lay of Grímnir," "The Lay of Hymir," and part of "The Lay of Volund ." For all the differences between the manuscripts, scholars are unanimous in holding that it derives, ultimately, from the same source as *Regius*. The different ordering of the two collec-tions may be due to the various lays having been handed down on single parchment leaves, which the scribe of *Regius* arranged as he saw fit. He no doubt was the author of the connecting prose links.

The large *Manuscript Codex No. 544* of the Arnamagnæan Collection, called *Hauksbók* from the fact that most of it was written by the Icelandic judge, Haukr Erlendsson, about the beginning of the fourteenth century, is important for Eddic study in that it supplies us with another redaction of "The Prophecy of the Seeress."

For "The Lay of Ríg" we are entirely dependent on the *Codex Wormianus* of the *Snorra Edda* (referred to above) written in the second half of the fourteenth century, where it is found on the last page.

The huge *Codex No. 1005* folio of the Royal Library, known as the *Flateyjarbók* because Brynjól-fur Sveinsson obtained it from a farmer on the small island of Flatey, is the source for "The Lay of Hyndla."

"The Lay of Grotti" occurs only in the *Codex Regius* manuscript *No. 2367* of the *Snorra Edda*, dating from the beginning of the fourteenth century, where the poem is cited in illustration of a kenning based on the Grotti myth.

There exists also a considerable number of paper manuscripts of the collection; but aside from the fact that some of them contain the undoubtedly genuine "Lay of Svipdag," not found in earlier manuscripts, they are of no importance since they all date from the seventeenth and eighteenth centuries and are essentially derived from the same source as *Regius,* if not from that collection itself. To be sure, they bear eloquent testimony to the continued interest of Icelanders in these poems.

The Eddic lays which are found in these manuscripts, utterly diverse though they be in many respects, still have in common three important characteristics which mark them off from the great body of skaldic poetry: their matter is the mythology, the ethical conceptions, and the heroic lore of the ancient North; they are all composed in a comparatively simple style, and in the simplest measures; and, like the later folk songs and ballads, they are anonymous and objective, never betraying the feelings or attitudes of their authors. This unity in apparent diversity was no doubt felt by the unknown collector who gathered together all the lays and poetical fragments which lived in his memory or were already committed to writing.

A well thought-out plan is evident in the ordering of the whole. In the first place, the mythic and didactic lays are held apart from the heroic, and those of each group disposed in a sensible order.

The opening chord is struck by the majestic "Prophecy of the Seeress," as the most complete bodying forth of the Old Norse conceptions of the world, its origin and its future. There follow three poems, in the main didactic, dealing chiefly with the wisdom of the supreme god, Óthin (the lays of Hár, of Vafthrúthnir, of Grímnir); then one about the ancient fertility god, Frey ("The Lay of Skírnir"); five in which Thór plays the predominant, or at least a prominent, part (the lays of Hárbarth, of Hymir, of Loki, of Thrym, of Alvís). The poems following in the present translation ("Baldr's Dreams," the lays of Ríg, of Hyndla, of Svipdag, of Grotti) are, it will be remembered, not contained in *Regius*.

The Heroic lays are found arranged in chronological order, as far as feasible, and joined by Prose Links so that the several smaller cycles form one large interconnected cycle. The procedure is especially clear in the case of the Niflung Cycle. Not only has the Collector been at pains to join the frequently parallel lays, but he tries hard to reconcile contradictory statements. Connection with the Helgi Cycle is effected by making Helgi Hundingsbani a son of the Volsung, Sigmund. The tragic figure of Queen Guthrún then links the Niflung Cycle with the Ermanarich lays ("Guthrún's Lament," "The Lay of Hamthir").

There has been a great deal of discussion as to the authenticity and age of the Prose of the Collection, but it is clear now that (excepting the piece about "Sinfjotli's Death," which no doubt is a prose rendering of a lay now lost) the Prose Links for the most part add nothing, or very little, of independent value—nothing, indeed, which could not have been inferred from the poems themselves. We shall hardly err in attributing these links to the intelligent, but not very gifted, compiler of the Collection.

The case is somewhat different, perhaps, with the narrative which binds together the fragments of "The Lay of Helgi Hjorvarthsson" and those of "The Second Lay of Helgi," and with the Prose Links of the Sigurth Cycle from "The Lay of Regin" to "Brynhild's Ride to Hel." Especially the latter group notably resembles in manner the genre of the *Fornaldarsaga* —prose with interspersed stanzas— a form exceedingly common in Old Norse literature and one which, for aught we know, may have been the original form in this instance. Still, even here the suspicion lurks that the Prose is but the apology for stanzas, or whole lays, imperfectly remembered: there is such discrepancy between the clear and noble stanzas and the frequently muddled and inept prose as to preclude, it would seem, the thought of their being by the same author.

Even greater diversity of opinion obtains concerning the age and home of the lays themselves. As was stated above, in sharp contradiction to our knowledge of skaldic poetry, we know nothing about the author of any Eddic poem. Nay, in only a very few, such as "The Lay of Grípir," or "The Third Lay of Guthrún," can one discern so much as the literary individuality of the authors. In consonance with medieval views, they were probably felt to be merely continuators, or elaborators, of legendary tradition. Thus, to illustrate by a very clear case: A Gothic lay about the death of Hamthir and Sorli is known to have existed already in the sixth century. So the person who indited or, perhaps, translated, or possibly, added to such a song could not well lay claim to be an "inventor" and hence worthy of being remembered. Skaldic art, on the other hand, may also deal with myth and legendary lore or allude to it; but—note well—skaldic poems do not narrate directly, though some do describe in detail pictorial representations of scenes from mythology or legendary history. Hence, there the author is faithfully recorded if we owe him but a single stanza; just as was the troubadour and the minnesinger, in contrast with the anonymity of the *chansons de geste* and the German folk epics.

Thus it is that we are entirely dependent on internal evidence for the determination of the age and the origin of the Eddic poems, individually and collectively. And here experience has taught that we must sharply differentiate between the subject matter of the poems and the form in which they have been handed down to us. Failure to do so was responsible for some fantastic theories, such as the uncritical notions of the Renaissance, that the poems harked back to the Old Germanic songs in praise of the gods of Tuisco and Mannus, or else to the *barditus*, as Tacitus calls the terrifying war songs of the ancient Teutons, and the speculations of the Age of Romanticism which claimed the Eddic poems as the earliest emanations of the Spirit of the Germanic North, if not of all German tribes, and would date them variously from the fifth to the eighth century.

It was not until the latter third of the nineteenth century, when the necessary advances in linguistic knowledge and philological method had been made, that it was established beyond contradiction that the Eddic poems have West Norse speech forms; that is, that they are composed in the language that was spoken only during and after the Viking Age (*ca.* 800–1050 A.D.), in Norway, Iceland, and the other Norwegian colonies in the Atlantic, and hence, in their present shape, could have originated only there. In the second place, they can under no circumstance be older than about 700 A.D.—most of them are much later—because it has been shown experimentally that the introduction of older (Runic) forms of the Old Norse language would largely destroy the metric structure. This date *a quo* is admirably corroborated by comparison with the

Loki the trickster, another commonly known Norse figure, is shown here helping Höd aim the arrow that caused the death of Balder.

language of the oldest skaldic poems, whose age is definitely known.

More general considerations make it plausible that even the oldest of the lays could hardly have originated before the ninth century. Of the Heroic lays precisely those which also appear in other ways to be the oldest breathe the enterprising, warlike spirit of the Viking Age, with its stern fatalism; while the later ones as unmistakably betray the softening which one would expect from the Christian influences increasingly permeating the later times. And the Mythical lays, by and large, bespeak a period when belief in the gods was disintegrating, thanks to contact with the same influences. In particular, "The Seeress' Prophecy" reads like the troubled vision of one rooted in the ancient traditions who is sorrowfully contemplating the demoralization of his times (which we know a change of faith always entails) and who looks doubtfully to a better future.

There is also the testimony of legendary development. To touch on only one phase of the matter: we do not know when the Volsung and Nibelung legends were first carried to Norway, but sparing allusions in the oldest skaldic verses from the early ninth century would point to the seventh or eighth century, thus allowing several generations for the complete assimilation and characteristic Northern transformation of the material. Some lays, however, show traits of a legendary development which had not taken place in Germany before the ninth century—in other words, they presuppose another, later, stratum of importation.

Contrary to views formerly held, we now understand that the lays about the gods are, on the whole, younger than some of the heroic lays, which in substance (except the Helgi lays) deal with persons and events, real or fictive, of the Germanic tribes from the Black Sea to the Rhine during the Age of Migrations. In general we may say that, although there is little unanimity among scholars as to the dating of individual lays, the composition of the corpus of Eddic poetry can safely be ascribed, not to a single generation, not even to a single century, but to three or four centuries at the very least.

Intimately connected with the question of the date is that of the home of Eddic poetry. There is fair agreement about only two poems. "Atlamál," which is generally allowed to be of Greenlandish origin, and " The Prophecy of Grípir," which no doubt was composed by an Icelander of the twelfth century or later who had before him a collection of the lays dealing with the Sigurth legends. But a strong diversity of opinion exists concerning the place of origin of the bulk of the lays.

For one thing, no evidence can be derived from the language because the Old West Norse of the *Edda* was spoken with scarcely a dialectal variation throughout the far-flung lands of the North Atlantic littorals and archipelagoes. Again, all attempts to seek definite and convincing clues in climatic or topographic references, or in the fauna and flora mentioned in the poems, have proved vain. Did they originate in the motherland, Norway, or in Iceland, or in the British or North Atlantic islands?

Those who claim the bulk of the Eddic poems for Norway have contended that the related Skaldic poetry flourished there especially throughout the tenth century, favored by a period of comparative calm following the organization of the realm by Harald Fairhair; whereas Iceland, from its first settlement down to the beginning of the eleventh century, was in a condition of constant turmoil which could not have favored the rise of a body of literature like that of *The Edda*. Undeniably, Norway furnishes the cultural background for the *Weltanschauung* of nearly all of the poems, mythologic, gnomic, and heroic. In every respect their milieu is that of a cold, mountainous land by the sea. One, "The Lay of Hyndla," may refer to a Norwegian princely race; another, "The Lay of Ríig," glorifies the institution of monarchy based on an aristocracy; both poems but poorly agree with Icelandic, republican conditions.

The theory of origin in the British Islands settled by Norwegians—the Orkneys, the Shetland Islands, the Hebrides, the Isle of Man, and the littoral of Ireland, Scotland, and Northern England, is based on several considerations. These regions furnish precisely the stage where the rude Vikings first came in contact with the cultural conditions of a more advanced kind already deeply infused with Roman and Christian elements. Indeed some Celtic influences are seen in the apparel, the architecture, and the wood carving of ancient Scandinavia. In literature the saga, and possibly also skaldic verse, were thought to owe their inception to Irish impulses. Also a small number of both mythical and heroic motifs occurring in the *Edda* may have congeners in the British Islands. Now, most of these claims are discounted by modern scholarship.

Those who argue Icelandic origin admit that Anglo-Celtic influences are evident, but insist that this can be amply accounted for by the fact that a very large proportion of Icelandic settlers had come from Norway by way of the North British Islands and littoral where they had sojourned for shorter or longer periods, frequently even wintering, and whence they had brought with them a goodly number of Celtic slaves and freedmen. Also, on their return journeys to the motherland they frequently touched at North British, and especially at Irish, trading towns, interchanging goods and ideas. As to the milieu being that of a cold, mountainous land, this holds of course also for Iceland. There, the general state of unrest attending the first times was by no means unfavorable to the intense cultivation of the skaldic art—witness such poets as Egil Skallagrímsson, Hallfrœth Óttarsson, Sighvat Thórtharson, not to mention scores of others—and hence probably was no more unfavorable to conditions for the inditing of Eddic lays. The first families of Iceland were notably proud of their origin from the princely races of the motherland—whence the aristocratic note of some lays. Indeed the whole people clung to their cultural traditions all the more tenaciously for being separated from their original homes. In general, the defenders of Icelandic origin would put the burden of proof on those who contend that the Eddic lays did not take at least their final, distinctive shape in the land where arose, and was perptuated, virtually all of Old Norse literature. Certainly, the later poems definitely point to Iceland. On the other hand this does not preclude a number of stanzas, particularly the gnomic ones representing the stored wisdom of the race, from having originated in Norway.

Of late the Norwegian paleographer Seip has endeavored to demonstrate, on the basis of a number of Norwegianisms in *Codex Regius*, that all the Eddic lays were originally composed in Norway. Other scholars would ascribe these to a pervading influence from the motherland, since several manuscripts of unquestionable Icelandic origin also show Norwegianisms.

All this raises the question as to the ultimate source, or sources, of the matter of the Eddic poems. Were they all or partly indigenous to Scandinavia?

With regard to the mythological poems we shall probably never know, though here and there we seem to glimpse a connection with classical or oriental legends. But in all cases the matter has undergone such a sea change that we never get beyond the verdict "perhaps."

With the Helgi poems we are on somewhat firmer ground. The Vendel Period of Scandinavian hegemony (550–800) in the north of Europe, attested by innumerable archeological finds in the western Baltic lands, may well have been accompanied by a flourishing poetic literature of which these lays (and *Bēowulf*) may be remnants.

The matter of the Niflung cycle undoubtedly is of German (Burgundian) provenience; and much has been made by German scholars of faint South and West Germanic traces in the style and language of the lays dealing with the Gjúkungs, Sigurth, and Atli. But whether these stories were transmitted to the North in poetic form or only there received their characteristic aspects, that is another question. The fact that only on Scandinavian soil did a rich literature actually arise as early as the ninth century, although its origins date even further back, would seem to speak for the latter assumption. But in the case of the retrospective and elegiac monologue poems it has been convincingly demonstrated that they share many motifs, phrases, even vocables, with what must have been the forerunners of the Danish ballads.

One of the distinguishing features of Eddic, as against skaldic, poetry is its comparative simplicity of style and diction. This is true notwithstanding the fact that we have to deal with poems different in subject matter and structure and composed by different poets working centuries apart. Essentially, the style is akin to that of the alliterative poetry of the other Old Germanic tribes, especially in the use of kennings and the retarding devices of variation and parenthetical phrases. It is to the employment, rather more extensive than usual, of these stylistic features that Old Norse poetic style owes its peculiar physiognomy which, in skaldic art, becomes most pronounced.

The figure of speech called a "kenning" is a kind of condensed metaphorical expression. It most often contains a real, or implied, comparison, or else defines a concept with reference to something else. Thus, a ship (which may be thought of as galloping over the waves) is called a "sailsteed"; a warrior, a "helm-tree" because, helm-clad, he stands proudly erect like a tree, braving the "shower-of-arrows" (as the battle is designated for obvious reasons). Or instead of naming a person or object directly, there is a reference to somebody, or something, else. Thór, for example, is called, simply, "Sif's husband," or "Hrungnir's bane," or in allusion to his typical activity, "Breaker-of-thurs-heads." Similarly, blood is termed "dew-of-wounds" or "dew-of-sorrow"; gold, "the burthen-of-Grani" (Sigurth's steed which bears away the Niflung hoard); a prince, most often "breaker-of-rings," "reddener-of-swords," or similar names, referring to the two qualities most highly admired in rulers—generosity and bravery.

Figures like these are common to the poetic speech of all races and all times. The important difference is that whereas elsewhere they are coined *ad hoc,* as the situation demands, and struck in the heat of poetic fervor, in Old Germanic, and particularly Old Norse, poetry they have become stereotyped; that is, entirely independent of the situation in hand, and hence are apt, at first, to appear to us farfetched and frigid, until by longer acquaintance we arrive at the deeper insight that they are part and parcel of a style, like the ever-recurring "dragon motif" of Scandinavian carvings.

In skaldic poetry the systematic and unlimited use of kennings marks that type of composition off from anything known elsewhere in world literature. Only two Eddic lays, "The Lay of Hymir" and "The First Lay of Helgi Hundingsbani," show a frequency of kennings approaching skaldic usage from afar. In "The Lay of Alvís" the express didactic purpose is to cultivate copiousness of diction by enumerating the "unknown names" (*heiti*) and kennings by which common objects may be designated.

Although somewhat less prominent, variation or parallelism is a stylistic device characteristic of all Old Germanic poetry—as it is, indeed, of the poetry of many nations. Only the more important features will be enumerated here, especially such as come out clearly in a somewhat faithful translation. There is variation of words, of conceptions, of verses; and there is refrain.

The variation of words (synonymic variation), more particularly found in gnomic poetry, is on the whole not frequent in *The Edda*. The following stanza will furnish an example:

> With his friend a man should be friends ever,
> and pay back gift for gift;
> laughter for laughter he learn to give,
> and eke lesing for lies.

More frequent, and also more characteristic, is the repetition of related, or contrasting, conceptions. These are usually joined by alliteration, and occasionally by rime, so as to form together a half-line. Thus: "bark nor bast," "he gives and grants," "shalt drivel and dote," "in wine and in wort," "whet me or let me."

Peculiar to Eddic poetry is the repetition, with or without variations, of entire half-lines. One example for many will suffice:

> I issue bore as heirs twain sons,
> as heirs twain sons to the atheling.

With variation:

> I saw but naught said, I saw and thought.

Repetition (with variation) of a full-line occurs in the so-called *galdralag* or "magic measure" of the *ljthaháttr* stanza:

> No other drink shalt ever get,
> wench, at thy will,
> wench, at my will.

Refrain—for example, the "know ye further, or how" of "The Seeress' Prophecy "—and incremental repetition—especially in the gnomic poetry—are occasionally used with telling effect.

Only less characteristic of skaldic art than the unlimited use of kennings is the employment of parenthetical phrases—usually containing an accompanying circumstance. In *The Edda* the device occurs infrequently, and most often in "The First Lay of Helgi the Hunding-Slayer," which also approaches skaldic art in the use of kennings; for example (Stanza 17):

> But high on horseback Hogni's daughter—
> was the shield-din lulled—to the lord spoke thus.

In contrast with Old West Germanic poetry, which is stichic, and quite generally uses run-on lines, Old Norse poetry is strophic, the stanzas as a rule being of four lines each. Each stanza is most commonly divided into two *vísuhelmings* or "half stanzas," by a syntactic cæsura.

This is the rule; but imperfect stanzas occur too frequently to be explained away in all cases by defective tradition. It is certainly worth pondering, however, that unexceptional regularity is found, on the one hand, in poems whose question-answer form offered a mnemotechnic help to preservation, and on the other, in those that belong to the youngest strata; whereas lays which, for a number of reasons, seem among the oldest—for example, "The Lay of Volund" and "The Lay of Hamthir"—are quite irregular in this respect. The inference seems plausible that stanzaic structure was a later and specifically Scandinavian development, the bulk of Old Norse monuments being younger, both chronologically and developmentally, than most West Germanic monuments.

Like the mass of Old Germanic poetic monuments, the Eddic lays are composed in alliterative verse; in verse, that is, whose essential principles are stress and concomitant alliteration.

The rhythmic unit of alliterative verse is the so-called "half-line," represented in metrics by convention as dipodic. These two feet, as will be seen, may be of very different lengths. In the normal half-line there are four or five syllables (very rarely three) two of which are stressed, the position of stress depending on the natural sentence accent. The rhythmical stress (and concomitant alliteration) generally requires a long syllable and is conventionally represented thus: $\perp$. However, it may also be borne by two short syllables ("resolved stress"). . ."a *salar steina*," where *salar* constitutes two short syllables; this may be paralleled by "that etin's beerhall," with *etin* reckoned as two shorts); or else by one short syllable immediately following a stressed long syllable. . . (see the discussion of rhythmic patterns below). In the unstressed syllable, quantity is indifferent, marked thus: x.

The juxtaposition of two stresses without intervening unstressed syllable, so rarely used in modern poetry, is not only permitted but is a distinctive feature in Old Germanic poetry. It gives rise to the rhythmic types C and D (see below), where a strong primary, or secondary, stress may fall on important suffixal or compositional syllables, and on stem syllables of the second member of compounds: for example, "es hann vaknathi" (C), "hatimbruthu" (D). The following may serve as English examples: "The sun knew not," "a hall standeth," "till trustingly."

Always, two half-lines, each an independent rhythmic unit, are joined together by alliteration to form the "long-line." Alliteration, or initial rime, consists in an initial consonant alliterating, or riming, with the same consonant (except that *sk*, *sp*, and *st* alliterate only with themselves), and a vowel alliterating with any other vowel; but—note well—alliteration occurs only at the beginning of *stressed syllables*. Because the verse is addressed to hearers, not to readers, "eye-rimes" are not permitted. Also, alliteration may be borne only by words of syntactic importance.

In Old Norse verse, alliterating initial sounds are called *stafir*, "staves," the one of the second half-line, *hofuthstafr*, "main-stave," governing the whole line. Somewhat greater latitude is allowed in Eddic poetry than in Old English poetry in the matter of the "main-stave" falling only on the first stress of the second half-line. In the first half-line, either stress, or both—they are called *stuthlar*, "props"—may receive the alliteration.

Beyond stating that alliteration is the bearing principle in their verse the ancients made no statement about how this verse is to be read. Simple observation shows that the alliteration is borne only by stressed syllables concomitant with the syntactic importance of the word, and also that the stress is borne predominantly by nominal elements—nouns, adjectives, and pronouns. As stated earlier, there is agreement among scholars that the half-line is dipodic. But there is divergence of opinion about the disposition and relative stress of the various elements of the half-line, that is, about its rhythm.

In view of the utter difference between Old Germanic verse and any modern or classic scheme of versification, an adequate comprehension of the principles of Old Germanic verse technique is essential for the correct reading and understanding—nay, for entering at all into the spirit—of Old Germanic poetry. It is hoped that the reader will acquaint himself with the facts set forth above before attempting to recite Eddic lays—and indeed he should recite them, for they are meant for the ear, not the eye.

In reciting the Eddic lays it should ever be kept in mind that the strongly expiratory nature of Germanic verse demands very strongly stressed syllables, and correspondingly weak or slurred unstressed syllables. Juxtaposed stresses must by no means be avoided; in fact, type C is of extremely common occurrence. We must ever be on the alert, guided by the alliteration, to ascertain which words or syllables bear the main stress and are, hence, syntactically predominant. Thus we must be careful to read not "wh*o* made M*i*thgarth," but "who m*a*de M*i*thgarth."

The translator has endeavored to follow faithfully the rules of Eddic metrics above explained—at least in spirit. Naturally, in an analytic tongue like English many more particles, pronouns, and prepositions must be used than in the highly inflected Old Norse. A liberal use of anacrusis (upbeats), to dispose of them, cannot well be avoided, and this use swells the number of syllables countenanced by the original. This should not, however, interfere with reading half-lines of the same metre in about the same time. Thus, "much that is h*o*arded and h*i*dden" should not occupy more time than the line "save *o*ne *o*nly."

I have followed Sophus Bugge's text in the main, but by no means always, because, for the purpose in hand, a somewhat constructive text is called for—one not fatuously sceptical of the results won by a century of devoted study. I can see no harm in adopting the brilliant emendations of great scholars, some of them guided by the poet's insight in solving desperate textual problems, always providing the emendations be shown as such. I have considered it unavoidable to transpose stanzas and lines for the sake of intelligible connection. In fact, this course must be chosen to accomplish an æsthetically satisfying translation of poems which, at best, are strange and difficult for the modern reader, both as to matter and manner. Naturally, not all, or even most, changes could be so indicated. Nor is that called for in a work intended, not as a critical text, but as an interpretation for the student of literature, of folklore and folkways. Still I have thought it wise to give warning whenever the terms of the translation might give rise to misconceptions.

I hope I shall not be criticized for confining myself to the body of poems generally considered as comprising *The Poetic Edda*. I am, of course, aware of the existence of other lays fully deserving to be admitted to the corpus; but neither in this respect nor in the ordering of the material was it my intention to rival Genzmer-Heusler's *rifacimento.*

As to the principles which I have endeavored to follow, I may be permitted to quote from my program, "Concerning a Proposed Translation of *The Edda*":

"… while scouting any rigorously puristic ideas, I yet hold emphatically that, to give a fair equivalent, Germanic material must be drawn upon to the utmost extent, and later elements used most sparingly and only whenever indispensable or unavoidable, and even then only after anxiously considering whether consonant with the effect of the whole. The stylistic feeling of the translator must here be the court of last instance; … At the same time I do not mean to be squeamish and avoid a given word just because it is not found in Anglo-Saxon before the battle of Hastings, or because I have preconceived notions about the relative merit of Teutonic and French-Latin elements. Any one who has given the matter thought knows that no amount of linguistic contortions will furnish Germanic equivalents in English for such oft-recurring words as: battle, hero, glory, revenge, defeat, victory, peace, honor, and the like. Still, wherever possible, Germanic words ought to be chosen … because of the tang and flavor still residing in the homelier indigenous speech material…

"Another difficulty: the old Germanic poetry, however scant in content, and in however narrow a circle it moves, is phenomenally rich in vocabulary, and shines with a dazzling array of synonyms for one and the same conception. Scherer has shown how this state of affairs was brought about by the very principle of alliteration. … *The Edda* shows almost all stages in this development short of the final consummation, from the austere art of the 'Volundarkvitha' to the ornate art of the 'Hymiskvitha.' It stands to reason that to approach this wealth of synonymic expressions even from afar, and to avoid the overhanging danger of monotony, all the resources of the English vocabulary ought to be at one's disposal. I have, therefore, unhesitatingly had recourse, whenever necessary, to terms fairly common in English balladry; without, I hope, overloading the page with archaisms.

"The proper rendition of Old Norse proper names presents a knotty problem to the would-be translator. Shall he translate them all, to the best of his knowledge—and that is a difficult task—or some only, and if so which? Or shall he leave all untranslated—much the easiest course. Or shall he try to render only those parts of proper nouns which are of more general significance? E.g., shall he call the dwarf, Alvís or Allwise; Thór, Sithgrani's son or Longbeard's son; the seeress, Hyndla or Houndling; the localities Gnipalund and Hátun, Cliffholt and Hightown? Shall we say Alfheim, Elfham, or Alfhome? Are we to render Skjoldungar, Ylfingar by Shieldings and Wolfings? I do not hesitate to say that on the translator's tact and skill in meeting this problem—for dodge it he cannot—will depend in large measure the artistic merit of his work and its modicum of palatableness to the modern reader."

For this reason, absolute consistency in this respect was not striven for or even thought desirable.

Source: Lee M. Hollander, "General Introduction," in *The Poetic Edda,* University of Texas Press, 1962, pp. iv–xxix.

SOURCES

Dronke, Ursula, "Art and tradition in *Skirnismal,*" in *English and Medieval Studies Presented to J. R. R. Tolkein,* edited by N. Davis and C. L. Wrenn, Allen and Unwin Ltd., 1962, pp. 250–268, repr. *Myth and Fiction in Early Norse Lands.*

———, "Classical Influence on Early Norse Literature," in *Classical Influences on European Culture, A.D. 500–1500.* edited by R. R. Bolgar, Cambridge University Press, 1971, pp. 143–149, repr. *Myth and Fiction in Early Norse Lands.*

———, "Eddic Poetry as a source for the history of Germanic religion," in *Germanische Religiosgeschichte. Quellen und Quellemprobleme,* edited by H. Beck, D. Elmers, and K. Schier, Walter de Gruyter, 1992, pp. 656–684, repr. *Myth and Fiction in Early Norse Lands.*

———, *Myth and Fiction in Early Norse Lands,* Variorum Collected Studies Series CS524, 1996.

———, "Pagan beliefs and Christian impact: The Contribution of Eddic Studies," in *Viking Revaluations. Viking Society Centenary Symposium,* edited by A. Faulkes and R. Perkins, Viking Society for Northern Research, 1993, pp. 121–127, repr. *Myth and Fiction in Early Norse Lands.*

———, *The Poetic Edda: Volume I Heroic Poems,* Clarendon Press, 1969.

———, "The Scope of the *Corpus Poeticum Boreale*" in *Úr Dölum til Dala. Guthbrandur Vigfússon Centenary Essays,* edited by R. McTurk and A. Wawn, Leeds Texts and Monographs New Series 11, Leeds Studies in English, 1989, pp. 93–111, repr. *Myth and Fiction in Early Norse Lands.*

———, "Völuspa and satiric tradition," in *Aion XXII, 1979: Studi per Mario Gabrieli Napoli,* Istituto Universitario Orientale, 1979, pp. 57–86, repr. *Myth and Fiction in Early Norse Lands.*

———, "Völuspa and Sibylline traditions" in *Latin Culture and Medieval Germanic Europe,* ed. R. North and T. Hofsta,

Germania Latina 1, Egbert Forsten, 1971, pp. 3–23, repr. *Myth and Fiction in Early Norse Lands.*

———, "The war of the Aesir and Vanir" in *Völuspá Idee, Gestalt, Geschichte. Festschrift Klaus von See,* edited by G. W. Weber, Odense University Press, 1988, pp. 223–238, repr. *Myth and Fiction in Early Norse Lands.*

Nordal, Sigurthur, ed., *Völuspa,* translated by B. S. Benedikz and John McKinnell, Durham and St. Andrews Medieval Texts 1, 1978.

Sturluson, Snorri, *The Prose Edda: Tales from Norse Mythology*, translated by Jean I. Young, University of California Press, 1966.

FURTHER READING

Byock, Jesse L., *The Saga of the Volsungs: The Norse Epic of Sigurd the Dragon Slayer,* University of California Press, 1990.
   A thirteenth century prose version of the Volsungs drawing upon the Edda lays. It will help the reader place the dramatic and allusive lays in a coherent narrative.

Dronke, Ursula, *The Poetic Edda: Volume I Heroic Poems,* Clarendon Press, 1969.
   This book is the most modern edition. The analysis of the poetry is designed for the advanced student but is the finest available.

Grahm-Campbell, James and Dafydd Kidd, *The Vikings,* British Museum Publications Limited, 1980.
   A magnificently illustrated book with a good but non-technical discussion of the Vikings at home and abroad.

Ker, W. P., *Epic and Romance,* Dover Press, 1957.
   A very old, but very engaging book. It has introduced generations to the excitement and beauty of Norse literature.

Magnusson, Magnus, *Viking Expansion Westwards,* The Bodley Head, 1973.
   This history of the Vikings from England to North America reads like a novel. It is full of lively portraits and the small happenings of everyday life as well as heroism and violence.

Sturluson, Snorri, *The Prose Edda: Tales from Norse Mythology*, translated by Jean I. Young, University of California Press.
   This text provides a lively translation of the most accessible parts of an encyclopedic thirteenth–century prose collection of the myths and legends at the heart of the Norse poetic vocabulary.

Taylor, Paul B., and W. H. Auden, tran., *The Elder Edda: A Selection translated from the Icelandic,* introduction by Peter H. Salus and Paul B. Taylor, Faber and Faber, 1969.
   Auden was a major twentieth century avant-garde poet who nevertheless maintained a lively interest in early medieval poetry. The introduction is particularly useful for the beginner.

Terry, Patricia, *Poems of the Vikings: The Elder Edda,* Bobbs-Merrill Company, 1969.
   A nearly complete and very careful translation of the *Elder Edda.* The introduction is clear and to the point.

Turville-Petr, E. O. G., *Myth and Religion of the North,* Holt, Rinehart and Winston, 1964.
   This book is still considered the best and most readable on the subject.

The Faerie Queene

EDMUND SPENSER

1590

The Faerie Queene is a romantic epic, the first sustained poetic work since Geoffrey Chaucer. In this work, Spenser uses the archaic language of Chaucer as a way to pay homage to the medieval poet. Spenser saw himself as a medievalist, but cognizant of his audience, he uses the modern pronunciation of the Renaissance. Spenser uses biblical allegory to tell his story, but the poem is much more than just a religious poem. Its purpose was to educate, to turn a young man into a gentleman. There are two levels of allegory present. One level examines the moral, philosophical, and religious and is represented by the Red Cross Knight, who represents all Christians. The second level is the particular, which focuses on the political, social, and religious, in which the Faerie Queene represents Elizabeth I. Spenser was not born to a wealthy household, as were so many of the other great Renaissance poets, such as Philip Sidney. This fact is important, since his work is colored by this lack of wealth. Spenser needed a patron to provide for his support while he worked, and patrons expect that the artists they support will write flattering words. This was certainly the case with Spenser's work, *The Faerie Queene*, which is meant to celebrate Elizabeth I and, oftentimes, flatter her. In this work, Spenser presents his ideas of what constitutes an ideal England. He also thought that he could use his text as a way to recall the chivalry of a past era, and thus, inspire such actions again. Spenser influenced many of the poets who followed, including John

Milton, Percy Shelley, John Keats, Lord Byron, and Lord Tennyson.

AUTHOR BIOGRAPHY

Edmund Spenser was born in London in 1552 or 1553. The Spenser household was working class, his father a tailor. Little is known about Spenser's family, although it appears he had a sister and a couple of brothers. As a child, Spenser attended the Merchant Taylor's Free School, where his education focused on the new humanist movement. Spenser received a bachelor's degree from Pembroke College, Cambridge in 1573 and a Master's degree in 1576. While at Cambridge, Spenser was a work study student, earning money to pay for his meals and lodging. After leaving Cambridge, Spenser worked as a secretary for the Bishop of Rochester, John Young. During this period, Spenser composed "The Shepheardes Calendar," which was printed in 1579. Also in 1579, Spenser went to work for the Earl of Leicester, where Spenser became acquainted with Sir Philip Sidney and Sir Edward Dyer, both of whom were part of the artistic circle at court. A year later, Spenser moved to Ireland as a secretary to the newly appointed Lord Deputy of Ireland.

Within the next few years, Spenser changed jobs a few more times, and in the process, acquired some property in Ireland, living there with his sister, Sarah. After Sir Walter Raleigh read through an early draft of *The Faerie Queene*, Spenser agreed to accompany Raleigh to court, where he was presented to Elizabeth I. At this time, Spenser published the first three books of *The Faerie Queene*. At this time, Spenser acquired a patron, which allowed him to remain in London. After some sort of scandal, Spenser returned to Ireland in 1591, marrying Elizabeth Boyle in 1594. To honor his new wife, Spenser wrote "Amoretti" and "Epithalamion" in 1595. "Astrophel" and "Colin clouts come home again" were also published in 1595. The next three books of *The Faerie Queene* were published in 1596, with Spenser once again back in London, although only temporarily. During this time, Spenser continued to work, writing "A vewe of the present state of Irelande," "Fowre

Edmund Spenser

Hymnes," and "Prothalamion." Spenser returned to Ireland, when he was unable to secure another patron at court.

In 1598, Spenser received an appointment as the Sheriff of County Cork, but the appointment did not last long. A rebellion in the area forced the Spenser family to flee to safety. Soon Spenser was sent back to London with messages for the Privy Council. Spenser died in London a few months later, apparently having starved to death, according to Ben Jonson. Spenser was immensely popular with other poets, who mourned his passing by throwing verses of their poetry into his grave. Spenser is buried in the Poets Corner at Westminster Abbey. It was never clear how a poet as popular as Spenser was allowed to die in such poverty, nor even if the story is true. Spenser was never wealthy, but he did earn a comfortable living, having years earlier secured a lifetime pension from the queen, in addition to his wife's dowry and his salary as sheriff. The facts surrounding Spenser's death, then, must be considered as undocumented. All that is known for certain is that he died on January 13, 1599. Spenser had always intended to publish another six books of *The Faerie Queene*; they were never found, nor is it known if Spenser ever completed the composition of the missing books.

PLOT SUMMARY

Book I

In this opening section, Spenser explains the legend of the Red Cross Knight and focuses on the importance of morality and holiness in man's life. This first book opens with the Red Cross Knight and Una journeying to destroy a dragon and rescue Una's parents. When a storm occurs, the knight and lady, accompanied by her dwarf, take shelter in a dark forest. Here they come across the monster, Error, who hates the light of truth, and her thousands of offspring. Error attacks the knight, who does not listen to Una's warnings. The Red Cross Knight must kill the monster to escape, cutting off her head. As the three continue their journey, they come across Archimago, an evil enchanter, who casts spells on the group as they sleep. The Red Cross Knight is given erotic dreams of Una, who is abandoned in the forest by the knight and dwarf, who believe the dreams. The Red Cross Knight continues on his journey where he foolishly releases the evil enchantress, Duessa, from her prison. The Red Cross Knight and Duessa continue on the journey, he still not knowing who she really is. As they journey, they arrive at a castle, inhabited by Lucifera, the mistress of Pride. She has six wizards: Idleness, Gluttony, Lechery, Avarice, Envy, and Wrath. Together, this group comprises the seven deadly sins. After a fight, which the Red Cross Knight wins, the knight leaves, still unaware that Duessa is not who she claims.

Meanwhile, Una, who has been abandoned in the forest, is searching for her knight. She encounters a lion, who is tamed by Una's beauty. The lion accompanies Una on her journey, guarding her. Archimago, who has disguised himself as the Red Cross Knight, finds Una, who is happy to be reunited with her knight. The group is attacked by Sans Loy, who does not recognize the disguised Archimago. The lion attempts to save Una but is killed by Sans Loy. Una successfully resists Sans Loy's attempts to seduce her, and she is quickly rescued by Fauns and Satyrs, the wood gods, who worship her as a god. Once again, Una is in need of rescue, and soon a woodsman, Satyrane, helps her to escape. As they journey, Archimago, now disguised as a traveler, tells them that the Red Cross Knight is dead. While Satyrane engages Sans Loy in a battle, Una flees. Meanwhile, Duessa catches up with the Red Cross Knight. As the knight drinks from an enchanted spring, the giant, Orgoglio, appears and attacks the knight. Duessa agrees to become the giant's mistress and the Red Cross Knight becomes the giant's prisoner. The dwarf takes the knight's spear, armor, and shield and leaves. He meets with Una and tells her of all that has happened. Next, Prince Arthur appears and assures Una that he will rescue the Red Cross Knight from Orgoglio. After a fierce battle, Arthur kills the giant and disarms Duessa, who has used her magic to try to kill Arthur. With the battle ended, Spenser takes a moment to tell Arthur's story and that he is on his way to the Queen of Faeries, whom he loves.

The Red Cross Knight, now freed, and Una continue on their journey to free her parents. They come to the cave of Despair, which tries to convince the Red Cross Knight to kill himself. Una reminds the knight of his duties and of the rewards of justice and mercy, and the two continue on their journey. Una brings the Red Cross Knight to the House of Holinesse to be healed. There, Reverence, Zeal, Fidelia (Faith), Charissa (Charity), Speranza (Hope), Patience, and Mercy work to heal the knight and restore him to his previous strength and valor. An old man, Contemplation, provides a vision to the Red Cross Knight that allows him to see his parentage and the future, in which he will be known as Saint George of England. Although reluctant to leave this happy place, the knight soon sets out with Una to fight the dragon. The battle is a long one, but eventually the knight slays the dragon and the King and Queen are freed. The Red Cross Knight is acclaimed a hero, and he and Una are married.

Book II

In this book, the main focus is on temperance and prudence. This section begins with Archimago free from the dungeon that had imprisoned him. He still wants to destroy the Red Cross Knight, and so, in disguise, he tells Sir Guyon, who is accompanied by the Palmer, that the Red Cross Knight has violated a virgin. Duessa pretends to be the virgin and identifies the Red Cross Knight as her attacker. Sir Guyon attacks the Red Cross Knight, but each knight recognizes the other's virtue, and together, their temperance prevents a tragedy. Next, the Palmer and Sir Guyon meet with a woman whose husband has been a victim of Acrasia and her Bower of Bliss. Sir Guyon swears vengeance for the damage that Acrasia has caused to this family and to the child, now orphaned. Since his horse is now missing, Sir Guyon continues on foot, carrying the child with him. Sir Guyon stops at a castle, wherein he meets Medina, whom he calls an image of the virgin queen. Sir Guyon leaves the orphaned child with her. Spenser includes a brief comic interlude with Braggadocchio (Windy Boasting) and his companion, Trompart. This section describes their meeting with the beautiful damsel, Belphoebe, who rejects the comic pair's attempts to woo her. Meanwhile, Sir Guyon is having many adventures, fighting Furor and Occasion and others, all of which teach him to beware of false pity. He also meets with Phaedria, who tempts men with idleness. Soon, Sir Guyon, now separated from his Palmer, meets Mammon, who represents financial greed. Mammon takes Sir Guyon on a tour of his riches; this place is hell.

When he returns from Mammon's hell, the Palmer is waiting with Prince Arthur, who must first battle with two paynim (heathen) knights. Sir Guyon tells Arthur that he, too, can be one of the Faerie Queene's knights, joining her Order of Maidenhead. Sir Guyon and Arthur continue on their journey together, and when they reach the Bower of Bliss, they destroy it.

Book III

This book focuses on virtue and chastity. Sir Guyon and Arthur continue on their journey, where an old squire and a young knight join them. The knight knocks Sir Guyon off his horse, and the Palmer stops the battle after he recognizes that the knight is Britomart, a chaste damsel, who is searching for her love, Artegall. Spenser spends some time telling Britomart's story and explaining how she came to be looking for Artegall, whose image was shown to her in Merlin's mirror. Meanwhile, Sir Guyon and Arthur are trying to rescue a damsel, Florimell, who is being chased by a forester. Arthur's squire, Timias, is wounded, and the fair Belphoebe treats him with herbs and heals him. When he awakens, Timias falls in love with Belphoebe. At the same time, a witch and her monstrous son are pursuing the beautiful Florimell, and soon an old fisherman is lusting for her. Spenser next turns again to Britomart's adventure. Britomart is told of Amoret, who has been held prisoner by a knight who tries to force her love. Britomart battles the two guards and frees Amoret, who joins Britomart in the search for their true loves.

Book IV

The focus of this section is on friendship and loyalty. Amoret thinks that Britomart is a man, since she was disguised as one when she rescued Amoret. But soon, Britomart reveals her identity after suc-

In Spenser's allegory, St. George is symbolic of England itself. Book I, 'The Legend of the Knight of the Red Cross,' relates a story analogous to the tale of St. George and the dragon.

cessfully defeating a knight during a tournament. After once again assuming the disguise of a man, the two young women continue on their journey. They soon encounter the disguised Duessa and participate in another tournament, of which Britomart is again the winner. One of the knights that Britomart defeated is her love, Artegall, whom Britomart is seeking. However, Artegall is also disguised, and so Britomart has no idea that she has unseated the man she loves. Soon things are set right, and Artegall learns that Britomart is a female. Amoret's true love, Scudamour, is also present and learns that Britomart is not a male, and thus, could not have dishonored Amoret. Amoret, though, is missing, having wandered off while Britomart was at rest, but after a wild monster seizes her, she is eventually rescued by Arthur. Soon, Amoret and Scudamour are reunited in the Temple of Venus.

Book V

In this section, Spenser focuses on justice, with Artegall to be the champion of justice. Artegall administers justice quite swiftly and with little indecisiveness. Most importantly, according to Spenser, is that Artegall has the power to enforce justice. Artegall has several successful encounters, but then he confronts a group of women about to hang a man, he hesitates when he sees their beauty and is captured. When Britomart learns of Artegall's capture, she sets out to rescue her lover. Britomart defeats the Amazons and Ertegall is freed to resume the journey that the Faerie Queene had sent him on—to free Irena (who represents Ireland) from Grantorto (who represents Spain). Artegall soon arrives at the trial of Duessa (representing Mary, Queen of Scots), at which Arthur is also present. Duessa is found guilty, although she is not sentenced. Belgae (who represents the Netherlands) also asks Arthur for help against Geryoneo (representing Spain). Arthur travels to Belgae's land and helps to free them from the Inquisition, slaying Geryoneo. After his success in freeing Belgae's land, Arthur joins Artegall in trying to help Irena. Artegall kills Grantorto and Irena is freed. With his mission ended, Artegall returns to the Faerie Queene.

Book VI

The focus of this final book is truth, honesty, and civility. These ideals represent the civilized world, as Spenser defines it. Calidore is the most gentle of knights, a man who represents these traits, which Spenser sees as so essential. Sir Calidore has many adventures, where in he teaches people the importance of courtesy and living in harmony. Arthur, who has finally been reunited with his squire, Timias, encounters the Blatant Beast. Meanwhile, Calidore is also pursuing the Blatant Beast. Calidore has a pleasant interlude in a pastoral paradise, where he is nearly distracted from his quest. However, he soon continues on his journey, where at last, Calidore meets and defeats the Blatant Beast.

Mutability Cantos

The Mutability Cantos are two small unfinished pieces, which Spenser had not completed. It is uncertain where Spenser intended to put these cantos, but they would have been intended for some section of the six books that Spenser intended but did not complete. These fragments deal with philosophical questions about nature. Mutability breaks the laws of nature, arguing that nature is changeable. However in a trial, Nature finds that Mutability's argument has flaws and finds against Mutability. According to nature, beings change but not from their first nature.

CHARACTERS

Acrasia

Acrasia is the mistress of the Bower of Bliss. She is Circe-like in her ability to lure men to their destruction. It takes both Sir Guyon and Prince Arthur to destroy her Bower.

Archimago

Archimago is an evil enchanter, a satanic figure who uses spells and disguises to lead his victims to sin. He represents Spain and the Roman Catholic Church. After the Red Cross Knight defeats the dragon, Archimago is arrested and thrown into a dungeon. Archimago reappears frequently, always in disguise, and always in an attempt to injure or tempt someone.

Artegall

Artegall is the Knight of Justice. Britomart has seen his face in a magic mirror and is seeking him. Eventually, Britomart and Artegall are united. Later, the Faerie Queene sends Artegall on a quest to rescue Irena (Ireland) from Grantorto (Spain).

Arthur

Prince Arthur appears initially as a rescuer of first Una, and later, the Red Cross Knight. Much of the Arthurian legend is incorporated, including the story of Merlin and his role in Arthur's birth. Arthur is in love with the Faerie Queene, whom he has dreamt of but never seen, and is on his way to find her when he encounters Una. After saving the Red Cross Knight and uniting him with Una, Arthur continues on his journey with Guyon. Later, Arthur will assist both Artegall and Calidore on their quests. Arthur is excessively moral and virtuous, serving the Faerie Queene with the same ardor as exists in the Arthurian legends.

Belphoebe

Belphoebe is a beautiful woman, as beautiful as the goddess Diana, who reared her, or the Queen of the Amazons. Bellphoebe is a virgin huntress, but she remains aloof from Timias, whom she has saved and who loves her.

Britomart

Britomart first appears disguised as a knight. And like a knight, she is brave and willing to risk her life to do the honorable thing. Britamart has seen a vision of the man she is to love in a mirror, which

Merlin has provided, and she is on a journey to find this man, Artegall. Britomart has several adventures, in which she proves that a woman can be as brave and moral as any man. She successfully defeats several men, including Artegall, while disguised as a man.

Calidore

Calidore is the last knight to appear. He is gentle and courteous, working during his quest to create harmony and to restore compassion to the world.

Contemplation

Contemplation is a hermit, who gives the Red Cross Knight a vision of the City of God and sends him back to complete his quest.

Duessa

Duessa is an evil enchantress, a partner of Archimago. She appears attractive on the outside, but inside, she is corrupt. Duessa represents several things: falsehood, the Roman Catholic Church, and Mary, Queen of Scots. She reappears in several disguises, but her duplicity is eventually recognized.

Dwarf

The dwarf accompanies Una and the Red Cross Knight on their journey to kill the dragon. The dwarf represents natural reason.

Error

Error is a monster, half woman and half serpent. She represents Eve and the serpent who deceived her. Error is surrounded by thousands of sucking offspring who gnaw at her. She cannot tolerate the light that is reflected from the Red Cross Knight's shield and she attacks him. After she is killed, her corpse vomits books and papers. Error is an important influence on John Milton who uses her as a model for Sin in *Paradise Lost*.

Gloriana

Gloriana is the Faerie Queene, who orders the Red Cross Knight to undertake a mission to rescue Una's parents. Gloriana is meant to represent Elizabeth I. She is a virgin queen and the knights who fight for her belong to the Order of Maidenhead. Although she has a small role, the Faerie Queene is the motivation for many of the knights' activities.

MEDIA ADAPTATIONS

- An audio cassette of *The Faerie Queene* (1998), with John Moffatt as reader, is available from Naxos of America. This recording, which is also available as a CD, contains selections from Spenser's text.

Guyon

Sir Guyon is a Knight of Temperance. He must be strong and uncompromising as he seeks to destroy Acrasia's power. Although he is tempted and frequently attacked, by using moderation, Sir Guyon is able to defeat his enemies and succeed in his quest.

Palmer

The black clad Palmer is Sir Guyon's companion and guide. He represents reason and prudence.

Red Cross Knight

The Red Cross Knight carries a shield that is dented and battered due to the many battles that he has fought. There is a cross on the shield that is the color of blood. The Red Cross Knight is a heroic figure, representing England's Saint George and the generic Christian man. The Red Cross Knight is impetuous and easily fooled, not always able to see beyond the obvious. He is confident of his abilities when he undertakes the mission, but after many confrontations, he is nearly suicidal. The Red Cross Knight is rescued by the teaching of the church in the House of Holiness. He is successful after a lengthy battle with the dragon and is married to Una.

Sans Foy

One of three knights who are Saracen knights that attack Una and her knight. Sans Foy represents lack of faith.

Sans Joy

One of three knights who are Saracen knights that attack Una and her knight. Sans Joy represents lack of joy.

Sans Loy

One of three knights who are Saracen knights that attack Una and her knight. Sans Loy represents lawlessness.

Timias

Timias is Arthur's squire, who is healed by, and falls in love with, Belphoebe. Disappointed by love, he becomes a hermit, but is finally healed by love and reunited with Arthur.

Una

Una is a beautiful woman, who is descended from the King and Queen of the West, a daughter of Adam and Eve. She represents truth and the true church. She requests the Faerie Queene's help in rescuing her parents. As she accompanies the Red Cross Knight, she rides a donkey, as did Christ when he arrived in Jerusalem. She also leads a lamb, the Paschal Lamb, a symbol of sacrifice. Una can advise the knight, but she cannot force him to listen to her wisdom, nor protect him from his own impetuous decisions. When she is deserted, she is assisted by the lion who willingly sacrifices his life for her. After Una is reunited with the Red Cross Knight and the dragon slain, she is married to the Red Cross Knight.

THEMES

Duty and Responsibility

Throughout the *The Faerie Queene*, Spenser emphasizes the importance of performing one's duty and accepting responsibility to complete the quest. Several heroic figures emerge during the course of the poem and each is given a question to undertake, a monster or demon to extinguish. Each time, the hero must overcome disadvantage and hurdles to succeed, but the importance of the quest is always the overriding concern. Although the Red Cross Knight must fight several demons and overcome despair, he always continues on the quest to rescue the King and Queen of the West. Similarly, Artegall must be rescued himself by Britomart. And although he really wants to continue with her, he must complete the quest of freeing Irena. Calidore is also momentarily distracted, enjoying a brief pastoral respite, but he also realizes that he must complete his quest in subduing the Blatant Beast. Throughout this epic, Spenser makes the same point

again and again: mankind must be responsible and fulfill the duties set before them.

Deception

For Spenser, deception is most often represented by the Roman Catholic Church and by Spain, which most clearly represents Catholicism in Britain. Archimago and Duessa represent how deception will attempt to prevent the honorable man from completing his journey and prevent him from meeting with god. During this period, the division between the Catholic world and Protestant world was filled with suspicion and animosity. Spenser uses this idea as a way to posit that an ideal Britain is one in which the true religion, the Anglican Church, defeats the monstrous Roman Catholic Church. This idea is personified by the Red Cross Knight's overcoming the tricks played by Archimago and Duessa. Since all good men will be tempted, these two characters reappear throughout the epic, thus requiring their defeat by several honorable knights. Spenser's audience would have easily identified Archimago and Duessa as representing the Catholic Church or key Catholic personages, such as Mary, Queen of Scots.

Friendship

The bond between all men, his relationship with everyone around him, is important to Spenser's work. None of the knights acts alone. The Red Cross Knight needs the help of Prince Arthur to succeed. And Arthur misses his squire, Timias, when he is lost. Arthur reappears frequently in the epic, each time to bond with another knight and help him in his quest. No knight works alone, with each one requiring the friendship of another to complete his quest. In addition to the friendships between men, friendship becomes the central focus of Book IV. The two women, Britomart and Amoret, continue the search together to find their true loves, illustrating the importance in women's friendships in achieving goals.

Humanism

Humanism was an intellectual movement of the Renaissance, beginning in Italy and quickly moving across Europe and into England. Sir Thomas More and Desiderius Erasmus were important authors of this movement, which promoted the education of a Christian gentlemen. Ideally, the education of Christian gentlemen emphasized, as a first concern, a preparation for public service. There was an emphasis on classical texts and on learning Latin language,

TOPICS FOR FURTHER STUDY

- The Cult of Elizabeth was an important literary force at the end of the sixteenth century. Because of a number of excessively flattering literary portrayals, Elizabeth, as a virgin queen, achieved goddess status. Discuss how Spenser's depiction of Elizabeth as Gloriana pays homage to this idea of Elizabeth, the goddess.

- Investigate the circumstances surrounding the British victory over the Spanish Armada, and discuss the impact of this event on Elizabethan society. Why was it so important for the British to defeat Spain, a Catholic country? Try to explore how a major victory during wartime contributes to national pride. Consider if this is a factor in Spenser's epic.

- Research the Catholic and Protestant conflict in England during the sixteenth century. Using what you discover, discuss the depiction of both Catholics and Protestants in Book I of Spenser's epic.

- The impact of Humanism on sixteenth century life was an important factor in how society functioned. Spenser saw the world of knights and religious quests as providing an effective model to teach people about truth, loyalty, and virtue. Select a modern text or film and discuss how this piece teaches its audience about these same attributes.

---

the language of diplomacy. Spenser's purpose in composing *The Faerie Queene* was to create a model for the ideal gentlemen. He sought to educate the public to chivalric ideals by recalling the medieval romance that he thought presented a better society. Spencer's text not only revives the classical epic, which in its purest form, had not been used since Virgil, but it emphasizes the ideals of charity, friendship, and virtue, which are the hallmarks of the Humanistic movement. Prior to the Reformation, Humanism embraced Catholicism as a representative ideal, as was the case with Sir Thomas More. But after the reformation, Protestantism became the ideal for Humanists in England, such as Spenser.

Justice

Justice is an important theme throughout *The Faerie Queene*, but in Book V, it is the central focus. Sir Artegall is the champion of Justice. As Spenser creates him, Artegall has the power to dispense justice, but he also discovers that justice can be a complex issue, with not every man receiving what is due him. Artegall discovers that what is right or fair is not always clearly defined. With Sir Sanglier, Artegall must use wit to devise a Solo-

mon-like decision to expose the guilty party. Later, Artegall must rule on the consistency of law when he settles a dispute between Bracidas and Amidas. Artegall also discovers, when dealing with the Amazons, that sometimes justice, tempered by pity, does not work well. The trial of Duessa, that completes Book V, illustrates that justice is effective when applied to solve problems.

Virtue

Virtue is a theme that runs throughout *The Faerie Queene*. According to Spenser, the virtuous will succeed at completing their journey or quest. Every knight who undertakes a quest for the Faerie Queen is forced to confront obstacles or deception. That each knight succeeds is a result of his inner strength, both his commitment to his quest, but just as importantly, his commitment to a moral life. The knights deserve to win because they are good, virtuous men. To contrast with a life of virtue, Spenser provides the example of virtue's enemies. In Book I, the Red Cross Knight meets with Lucifera, who is the mistress of Pride. Her six wizards are Idleness, Gluttony, Lechery, Avarice, Envy, and Wrath. These seven deadly sins constitute the opposite of the virtuous ideal. In Book III, four women must fight to preserve their chastity: Britomart, Florimell, Belphoebe, and Amoret. Spenser uses four different examples, and there are several others throughout the six books, to illustrate how important chastity is in a Christian life. Morality is essential to the chivalric ideal in other ways. When Arthur rescues Amoret, in Book IV, there is never any question that he will deliver her, unmolested to her destination. He is an honorable knight, as are Artegall, Guyon, and Calidore. Each man performs according to their code, which makes virtue, morality, and chastity, an essential part of each man's personality.

STYLE

Character

The actions of each character are what constitute the story. Character can also include the idea of a particular individual's morality. Characters can range from simple stereotypical figures to more complex multifaceted ones. Characters may also be defined by personality traits, such as the rogue or the damsel in distress. Characterization is the process of creating a life-like person from an author's imagination. To accomplish this task, the author provides the character with personality traits that help define who that character will be and how that character will behave in a given situation. Most of the characters in *The Faerie Queene* differs slightly from this definition, since each character is little more than a "type." The audience does not really know or understand the character as an individual. For instance, Una represents little more than a quality, not an individual. The audience understands that Una signifies truth, an essential component of an ideal world and a tenet of religious belief.

Epic

An epic is a long narrative poem, which presents characters and events of high position. There may be a central heroic figure, or, as in the case of Spenser's *Faerie Queene*, there may be several heroic figures, such as the Red Cross Knight, Prince Arthur, Sir Guyon, Sir Artegall, and Calidore. There is frequently a muse who inspires the writer to create a work that is inspired and magnificent in its scope. The epic most frequently recounts the origins of a nation or group of people. *The Faerie Queene* creates an ideal Britain, and it mythicizes Queen Elizabeth I, making her the ideal monarch. Epics usually share certain features: a heroic figure who is imposing in his greatness; a vast setting or great nation; heroic deeds; supernatural forces, such as miracles, gods, or angels; elevated diction and style; and an objective narrator. *The Faerie Queen* is an epic in the tradition of *The Odyssey*, creating an ideal world, filled with heroic deeds and people.

Genre

Genres are a way of categorizing literature. Genre is a French term that means "kind" or "type." Genre can refer to both the category of literature such as tragedy, comedy, epic, poetry, or pastoral. It can also include modern forms of literature such as drama, novels, or short stories. This term can also refer to types of literature such as mystery, science fiction, comedy, or romance. *The Faerie Queene* is an epic, but it has also been labeled a romantic epic.

Parable

A story intended to teach a moral lesson. The stories in *The Faerie Queene* are designed to teach people how to be better Christians and how to live a moral life. The bible is one of the most obvious sources of parables, since religion traditionally relies upon stories to teach lessons. This tradition stems from a period in which most men and women could not read, and the clergy found that stories were the most effective way to instruct moral lessons. Spenser uses his poetry in much the same way that the clergy uses the bible, to tell stories that teach a lesson.

Plot

This term refers to the pattern of events. Generally plots should have a beginning, a middle, and a conclusion, but they may also sometimes be a series of episodes connected together. Basically, the plot provides the author with the means to explore primary themes. Students are often confused between the two terms; but themes explore ideas, and plots simply relate what happens in a very obvious manner. In *The Faerie Queene*, Spenser creates a series of stories, and so, there are multiple plots. Sometimes, these many plots are unfolding at the same time, as characters and story lines jump from one idea to the next. But the themes include the need to prepare oneself for God and the importance of morality in creating an ideal world.

Romantic Epic

A romantic epic is a long narrative poem that combines the medieval romance and the classical epic. The poets who created romantic epics used many of the features of the classical epics but combined these features with stories of love and both romantic and religious. Spenser uses traditional romance, but he combines romance with love of God to create a blending of secular and religious love.

Setting

The time, place, and culture in which the action of the play takes place is called the setting. The elements of setting may include geographic location, physical or mental environments, prevailing cultural attitudes, or the historical time in which the action takes place. The location for *The Faerie Queene* is mostly Britain, but the time is in flux, with Spenser interjecting contemporary ideas into his work, which primarily recalls a period much earlier when knights and chivalry were common.

Stanza

A stanza is a grouping of two or more verse lines, which may be defined by meter, rhyme, or length. The stanza may also be considered as similar to a prose paragraph, exploring one element of the author's thoughts. The *Spenserian Stanza*, is nine lines, with a rhyme scheme of *abbabbcbcc*. Many other poets adopted the Spenserian Stanza for their work, including Shelley, Keats, Byron, and Tennyson.

HISTORICAL CONTEXT

Humanism and Education

Tudor England in the sixteenth century was a place of great change. There were significant social, religious, and political changes during this time, and together, these changes created an atmosphere of danger and tension. One of the earliest transformations was the way in which English boys and young men were educated. Education had always been an issue that focused on men, since there was little interest, nor perceived need to educate females, but as the fifteenth century drew to an end, the emphasis on education changed. Instead of educating boys and young men for a lifetime serving God, as members of the clergy, there was a new emphasis on careers in government, requiring a different sort of education. At the beginning of the sixteenth century, two men, the English Sir Thomas More and the Dutch Desiderius Erasmus, were cultivating an in-

tellectual movement that became known during the Renaissance as Humanism. According to the doctrine of Humanism, the education of a Christian gentlemen should be every society's primary concern. An important component of this education was a focus on the preparation of a young man for public service. As a way to achieve this goal, there was also a new emphasis on rhetoric and classical texts, and on a need to learn Latin grammar, the language of diplomacy. Latin had always been taught as necessary for the clergy, but now, it became clear there were other uses. Each country conducted its international business in Latin, and with international travel and trade, there was a greater need for men to assume these new duties. In this new world, there was a close connection between universities and the government. The sons of nobility attended colleges, but so too, did an increasing number of commoners, many of whom were destined for government service. Initially, humanism combined classical learning with Christianity or Catholicism. In humanism's early development, More was an enthusiastic supporter of Greek Classical texts, but he was also a Catholic who chose to die rather than agree to take the oath that acknowledged the king as head of the church in England. With the adoption of a new religion, the second-generation movement of humanism included Protestantism. Like many men of his period, Spenser was a strong advocate of Humanism, and so, one of his desires in composing *The Faerie Queene* was to create a model for the ideal gentlemen. Spenser was enamoured of chivalry and the medieval world, where men were honorable and where men adhered to a code of behavior that emphasized morality and truth. In composing his epic, Spenser sought to educate the public to chivalric ideals by recalling the medieval romance, which he thought presented a better society. Spencer's text not only revives the classical epic, which in its purest form, had not been used since Virgil, but it emphasizes the ideals of charity, friendship, and virtue, which are the hallmarks of the humanistic movement. In addition, Spenser uses allegory to tell his story, and allegory is a medieval tradition, which recalls the importance of allegory in biblical teaching. The setting of Spenser's epic is medieval England, but the topic is Renaissance in origin. As Philip Sidney argued in his *Defence of Poesy*, poetry has merit in its ability to make education sweeter and easier to swallow. Spenser accomplished this by resurrecting the medieval romance and the chivalric knight as instruments to demonstrate the righteousness of the Church of England.

COMPARE
&
CONTRAST

- **Sixteenth century:** In 1517, Martin Luther's actions grow into the Protestant reformation. This event has important ramifications for England, when King Henry VIII seeks a divorce from his wife. When the Pope refuses to grant a divorce, the king declares himself as leader of the English church. This act, in 1534, creates the Anglican Church and establishes Protestantism as the official church. In effect, it also outlaws the Roman Catholic Church, since Henry seizes all church property, using it as a source of revenue. Spenser uses this history to depict Una as Truth, the Anglican Church. Duessa represents falsehood, the Roman Catholic Church, which is attractive on the outside, but corrupt on the inside. This illustrates the English notion that Catholicism was all about performance and ornamentation and lacking substance inside.

  Late twentieth century: In many ways, the English still view the Catholic Church with suspicion. There are still laws that prohibit a member of the monarchy from marrying a Catholic, and the Anglican Church remains the official Church of England. No Catholic can inherit the throne.

- **Sixteenth century:** After Henry VIII and his only son, Edward VI, died, Mary I inherits the throne, and in 1555, she restores Catholicism to England and outlaws Protestantism. After marrying Spain's heir to the throne, Mary begins persecuting Protestants, burning those who fail to embrace the Catholic faith. Mary becomes known as ''Bloody Mary'' because of her actions. These persecutions lead to an enormous animosity between Protestants and Catholics, which Spenser depicts in his epic by having many evil characters portrayed as Catholic, such as Archimago, Duessa, and Error. In contrast, the good knights, such as the Red Cross Knight, are represented as Protestant,

  Late twentieth century: Not surprisingly, religion is still a source of conflict around the world. As it was in sixteenth-century England, the conflict between Protestants and Catholics still rages, accounting for bombings and deaths in both London and in Ireland. Each side still views the other as evil and destructive, much as they did when Spenser was writing his epic.

- **Sixteenth century:** In 1588, Elizabeth I defeats the Spanish Armada. The Spanish Armada, consisting of 132 vessels, sailed against England, with intent to invade and claim the country for the Catholic Church. The English rebuffed the invasion, and with the aid of a storm, destroyed more than half the ships. Elizabeth is seen as a heroic monarch, and thus her depiction in Spenser's epic as the Faerie Queene, the virginal queen who inspires such loyalty from her knights.

  Late twentieth century: The English have managed to successfully defend their small nation against invasion for the last four hundred years, defeating first Napoleon, and later, Hitler. The devotion to country and ideals that Spenser celebrated in his epic has continued to motivate the English to overcome overwhelming odds and defeat enemies, even when victory appeared out of reach.

- **Sixteenth century:** In 1587, Elizabeth I has her cousin, Mary, Queen of Scots, executed. Mary had been a prisoner since 1568, when she was forced to flee Protestant Scotland. While a captive of Queen Elizabeth, Mary was frequently the center of plots to overthrow the queen and place the Catholic Mary on the throne. The concern that the Protestants felt about Mary is depicted in Spenser's work. In Book V, Duessa is tried and found guilty. She represents the evil and deception that many English citizens felt that Mary represented.

  Late twentieth century: Although the English royalty are firmly entrenched on the throne, many other countries still bear witness to the possibility of a coup. This is unlikely in England, where the monarchy remains very popular, as it was when Spenser was writing.

Religious Turmoil

In *The Faerie Queene*, Spenser is reflecting the Renaissance emphasis of leading a life of beneficial action. At the same time, his text reflects the real-life tensions between the Roman Catholic Church and the Church of England, which was formally established by Elizabeth I in 1559. The pope's response to the queen's action was her excommunication in 1570, but officially, there was little notice of the pope's actions. After the formal establishment of the Anglican Church, some of the tension of the past twenty-five years dissipated, primarily because the queen was more tolerant of religious choice and less likely to endorse the extreme prosecution that Mary I favored. When Henry VIII dissolved the monasteries and abbeys in 1534, it was not because he would not tolerate dissenting religious views. Certainly he had no use for the Catholic Church, but that was primarily because the pope refused to permit his divorce. And, to assure the succession of any heir he might have after divorcing his first wife, Henry required that his citizens take an oath that recognized him as head of the Church of England. But Henry was never vehement about religion. The king dissolved the monasteries and abbeys to claim the land, buildings, monies, and expensive art and jewelry that lay inside. Henry VIII understood that eliminating the Catholic Church would make him rich; it was simply a sound economic move. After Henry died, his young son, Edward VI became king and for a while the religious component of Tudor life remained stable. But the young king did not live long, and at his death, his elder sister, Mary, became queen. During the brief years of Mary's reign, 1553–1558, religious intolerance and religiously inspired murder became commonplace. Mary, who was Catholic, immediately reinstated Catholicism as the official religion in England. Moving quickly, she outlawed Protestantism to please her new bridegroom, Philip of Spain. Protestants were persecuted, and hundreds were burned at the stake when they refused to convert to Catholicism. Mary's ruthlessness earned her the nickname, "Bloody Mary." In contrast to Mary's rule, Elizabeth seemed a refreshing new breath in the kingdom. She was young and beautiful, full of energy and vibrant. And although she quickly established Protestantism as the official religion, she manifested none of the intolerance of her older sister, Mary. The legacy of Mary's reign was a fear of Catholicism and a determination to permit no Catholic in government, nor should Catholics have any power. The immediate effect of Mary's reign was that any plotting that was discovered, any subversion that was detected, any unexpected crisis, could well be credited to Catholic sympathizers. Although Elizabeth's reign was prosperous and relatively peaceful, religion still remained a force that could divide the people. Spenser reflects these fears and determination in *The Faerie Queene*.

CRITICAL OVERVIEW

Edmund Spenser's *The Faerie Queene*, has had a lasting effect on the literary community. In some cases, it has been Spenser's nine line, Spenserian Stanza, that influenced poets such as Burns in *The Cotter's Saturday Night*, Shelley in *The Revolt of Islam* and *Adonis*, Keats in *The Eve of St. Agnes*, Tennyson in sections of *The Lotos-Eaters*, and Byron in *Childe Harold*. But Spenser's influence extends far beyond the construction of a stanza of poetry. John Milton's *Paradise Lost* draws from Spenser, especially in his development of Sin, who with her grotesque appearance and gnawing offspring, is taken from Spenser's depiction of Error in Book I. But Spenser influenced Milton in other ways. Spenser resurrected a classical literary genre that had been virtually ignored for hundreds of years. While there had been other compositions that were called epics, such as Thomas Mallory's *Le Morte D'Arthur*, most of these works did not draw on classical traditions. Mallory's epic is a collection of legends, assembled into one work. However, Spenser is returning to the Greek and Latin genesis of the epic, inspired by the works of Homer and Virgil. This recalling of the classical past also inspires Milton to create his own classically inspired epic. As a result, *Paradise Lost*, like *The Faerie Queene*, is modeled on the classical Greek origins of the genre.

In becoming such an important influence, it is easy to overlook Spenser's social and political contributions in composing *The Faerie Queene*. During Elizabeth's rule, there existed an aspect of her life that has been labeled the Cult of Elizabeth, which defines the literary treatment of women affected by the fact that the country was ruled by a virgin queen. Elizabeth was the object of enormous flattery. Her courtiers and poets provided her with adulation in language similar to that paid to a Petrarchan mistress. As a ruler, she was clothed in divinity because she was a woman and because she was a virgin. She was called Diana (the virgin goddess of the moon and of hunting), Cynthia (celebrated as the goddess of the moon), and Semele (mother of Dionysis). And, according to Spenser, Elizabeth was Glorianna in *The Faerie Queene*. Few women enjoyed the liberty and personal freedom of Elizabeth. Both traditional patriarchy and religion maintained that women were inferior; but as queen, Elizabeth could proclaim her superiority. As the ordained representative of god, the queen inverted the traditional claims of male superiority. Poets responded with exaggerated claims of her virtue, wisdom, and strength. The problem with the Cult of Elizabeth was that it provided little for ordinary women, who lacked God's endorsement of their adequacy. Whether it was because of the patronage system or just simple admiration for his queen, Spenser was a leading proponent of Elizabeth. As an anti-Catholic, nationalist, Spenser hoped to leave a legacy of national pride to inspire the sort of chivalry that he thought was missing from the Elizabethan world. Much of these emotions went into his epic. However, the patronage system was also an important factor in Spencer's glorification of Elizabeth. Simple economics influenced Spenser's work, as should be expected. With Elizabeth providing an income, a grateful poet might be expected to exaggerate his patroness' virtues, as well as the strengths of her court and couriers.

When Sir Philip Sidney wrote his *Defence of Poesy* in 1579, he saw little to admire in English poetry since the time of Geoffrey Chaucer. Spenser's letter to Sir Walter Raleigh, which opens *The Faerie Queene*, describes Spenser's intent to compose twenty-four books. The first twelve were to explore private virtues, and the last twenty-four were supposed to examine public virtues. Spenser died before he could complete the first twelve, but it is clear from this letter to Raleigh that Spenser intended to rectify the sad situation that Sidney described. Spenser envisioned becoming the sort of great poet that Sidney said England needed. Spenser wanted to create a great national literature, and did so with *The Faerie Queene*.

Most often, only the first book, or occasionally, the first three books of Spenser's epic, *The Faerie Queene*, are read by students. Spenser's use of archaic language is difficult for many students, as is the convoluted plot and the many characters, most of whom appear only briefly. In addition, the characters are only superficially defined, since they represent allegory. Often, characters reappear at random, with new roles and a new allegorical affiliation, such as Duessa and Archimago. Other characters appear only as needed, seemingly called, as if by telepathy, such as Arthur, who drifts in and out of the epic whenever he is needed. This perceived lack of continuity often intimidates first time readers, who are unprepared for the effort it takes to read and absorb *The Faerie Queene*. In spite of any difficulties, writers, from Spenser's death, through the end of the twentieth century, have found inspiration in Spenser's language. Students, too, have found that Spenser provides a wealth of characters and myths, each one worth the time to explore.

CRITICISM

Sheri E. Metzger

Metzger has a Ph.D., specializing in literature and drama at the University of New Mexico, where she is a Lecturer in the English Department and an Adjunct Professor in the University Honors Program. In this essay, she discusses Edmund Spenser's The Faerie Queene *and its contributions as a representation of the literary ideal, the usefulness of literature in educating man, and creating social change.*

Sixteenth-century England is framed by two fictional works that depict an ideal society. Sir Thomas More's *Utopia* (1516), which began the century, and Edmund Spenser's *The Faerie Queene* (1590), which ends the century, both create an ideal world where men behave with dignity and with truth and valor. This is a world in which personal values are more important than greed or lechery. When More creates his *Utopia*, he is responding to changes in English life, as English society moves from the Middle Ages into the Renaissance. In More's world, education is changing, as men are being educated for public service. In addition, the people are moving away from the church and a career in the clergy and into more secular interests. At the end of the century, when Spenser writes his epic, *The Faerie Queene*, England is once again facing change. Queen Elizabeth has ruled more than thirty years, nearly all of Spenser's life, and the country has begun to worry about an heir to the throne. Although the queen is healthy (she lives until 1603), the idea of a virgin queen has been losing its appeal for some time. Elizabeth has resisted all efforts, first to marry and give birth to an heir, and second, to name anyone as heir to her throne. In short, the Elizabethan world is on the cusp of change, just as More's Tudor world was eighty years earlier. As one way to

WHAT DO I READ NEXT?

- Edmund Spenser's "The Shepheardes Calendar" (1579) is a series of poems that celebrate the pastoral tradition and perfection of country life.

- John Milton's *Paradise Lost* (1667) is the story of the Fall of Man in the Garden of Eden. Milton derived many of his ideas from The Faerie Queene.

- Thomas Malory's *Le Morte D'Arthur* (1485) is the story of King Arthur. Spenser also uses many of the Arthurian legends in *The Faerie Queene.*

- Sir Philip Sidney's *Defence of Poesy* (1579) argues that poetry serves an important purpose in the education of people and maintains that poetry is superior to philosophy and history in teaching about virtue.

- Virgil's *The Aeneid* (30–11 B.C.) is a Roman epic that served as an important influence for Spencer's epic. The story of Aeneas and his journey establishes a history for the Roman people and the heroic behavior of Aeneas serves as a model for which men should strive.

- *The Cambridge Cultural History: 16th Century Britain* (1992) edited by Boris Ford, provides an accessible history of sixteenth century life, including: cultural and social life, architecture, literature, music, art, and Renaissance gardens.

respond to political and social tensions, Spenser illustrates the usefulness of literature, especially when combined with religion, history, and philosophy, as a means to effect social change.

In *The Faerie Queene*, Edmund Spenser presents his ideas of what constitutes an ideal England. In the letter to Sir Walter Raleigh that was published with Books I-III, Spenser states that his purpose in writing is to create a model for educating young men, but he is not simply providing an academic model. Spenser maintains that his purpose is to, "fashion a gentleman or noble person in vertuous and gentle discipline." To ease this learning, Spenser points out that his work will, "be most plausible and pleasing, being coloured with an historicall fiction, the which the most part of men delight to read." Spenser understands that his audience needs to find education palatable, and he continues in his letter to state that he has chosen King Arthur and his world as the topic of his epic because Arthur's story carries no political implications. In fashioning his epic as a means to teach valor and graciousness, Spenser is meeting the challenges set forth by Sir Philip Sidney only a few years earlier. In his *Defence of Poesy* (1579), Sidney argues that poetry creates pleasure and that pleasure makes learning more enjoyable. Sidney pointed out that men learn best when they want to learn, when they are eager to learn. Making learning pleasurable is one goal of the poet, according to Sidney: "he [the poet] doth not only show the way, but giveth so sweet a prospect into the way, as will entice any man to enter into it." The poet, says Sidney, has the power to make the distasteful, more agreeable: "even as the child is often brought to take the most wholesome things by hiding them in such other as have a pleasant taste." Thus the poet is akin to the mother who puts cherry flavoring in medicine to entice a child to swallow. For Spenser, the cherry flavoring is Prince Arthur and his knights, who teach honor and truth, through entertainment.

A classical epic, such as those composed by Homer or Virgil, requires a hero of imposing stature, one of national importance. Prince Arthur, the Red Cross Knight, Guyon, Artegall, and Calidore, fit this definition, since each knight engages in adventures and rescues damsels, requiring abilities far beyond the means of ordinary men. Their deeds are those of great valor, often demanding super human courage, just as the epic tradition requires. Spenser draws on England's legendary past, which recalls a time of greatness and of grandeur. He

Queen Elizabeth was the inspiration for Gloriana, to whom Spenser dedicated his epic poem. The queen is shown here on a visit to Hudson House.

implies that with these models to guide them, England's people can achieve this greatness again. In Spenser's world, there is sin and evil, balanced by virtue and goodness. Moreover, the manifestations of these qualities are interesting and alive, filled with plotting and deception, and the ability to create change. Spenser's heroes and villains are representative stereotypes. The Anglicans against the Catholics is a plot, really no different than the cowboys against the Indians of twentieth century cinema. An effective writer needs both heroes and villains to illustrate an idealized world. Unlike Sir Thomas More in *Utopia*, Spenser takes a chance and reaches back into England's history to appropriate his knights and their quests. Like More, Spenser was an apostle of humanism, but Spenser sought to use his text to educate the nobility to chivalric ideals, which he thought were superior to contemporaneous ideals. In his reading of Spenser, Graham Hough says that Spenser intended to educate the nobility to chivalric integrity by recalling the medieval romance that he thought represented a better society. Hough points out that there are no exact locations, with everything in Spenser's epic appearing rather dream-like. This vagueness of location adds to Spenser's ability to depict an ideal world and makes it safer for him to do so. He is not

competing with his own rather politicized world, and no one can condemn the poet for wanting to replace England with a dream—no matter how idealized.

In his work, Spenser is reflecting the Renaissance emphasis of leading a life of beneficial action. At the same time, his text reflects the real-life tensions between the Roman Catholic Church and the Church of England (established by Elizabeth I in 1559). Northrup Frye argues that Spenser saw *The Faerie Queene* as a means to reclaiming the virtue and education necessary to return fallen men to a higher level of nature in the upper world (Frye divides nature into four worlds and man should be closer to the top). Frye argues that education is the central theme of *The Faerie Queene*, pointing out that, "if we had to find a single word for the virtue underlying all private education, the best word would perhaps be fidelity: that unswerving loyalty to an ideal which is virtue, to a single lady which is love, and to the demands of one's calling which is courage." This emphasis on fidelity is the underlying ideal that motivates all of Spenser's heroes and heroines. For Spenser, the Anglican Church epitomizes this fidelity. Thus, Spenser's text relies on biblical allegory to present his perfect world. The imperfect world is represented by allusions to the Catholic Church. For instance, Archimago is first seen as a hermit singing Latin, the Ave Maria, the language of the Catholic Church. He represents evil and deception and the Pope. His accomplice, Duessa, is false, and at different times, she is Mary Queen of Scots, the Roman Catholic Church, and the Whore of Babylon. Her attempts to deceive the Red Cross Knight reveal the attempts of the Papacy to deceive the faithful. To serve as contrast to the evil of Archimago and Duessa, Una is truth, the Anglican Church. Red Cross Knight, the hero of Book I, represents St George, the Christian man who must rescue Una's parents and defeat hypocrisy. When he is driven to the brink of despair (a considerable sin in Renaissance life), only the teachings of the church (in the House of Holiness) restore him. In this epic, truth defeats the world (the House of Pride), flesh (Duessa at the fountain), and the devil (the cave of despair). Prince Arthur (ancestor to Elizabeth) defeats the giant, Orgolio, and the Catholic Church is defeated by the Anglican. The characters in Spenser's epic are allegorical representations of this tension between Protestant and Catholic belief. The setting is medieval England, but the topic is Renaissance in origin. As Sidney argued, poetry has merit in its ability to make education sweeter and easier to swallow. Spenser accomplishes this by resurrecting the medieval romance and the chivalric knight as instruments to demonstrate the righteousness of the Church of England.

Spenser's attempt to create an ideal world and to remind men of the importance of virtue was not a new idea. Sir Thomas More had attempted something similar at the beginning of the sixteenth century. The setting for More's *Utopia* (1516), is the ideal community that More wishes could be created in England. This is More's opportunity to criticize government and the ruling class in a less obvious way. If, as Horace argues (and later Sidney), the purpose of art is to educate, that must certainly be what More had in mind with *Utopia*. In this work, More offers political solutions disguised as fiction. Reform is at the center of More's design, and religious tolerance is his purpose. More felt that only an objective outsider could see the problems that plagued England. His work, then, is a guide for how to improve the world. *Utopia*'s ideal society is defined as a democracy of equal representation and equality of class. More envisioned the responsibilities of government being shared by the people—at least through their elective choices. Tyranny in a ruler would not be tolerated. In this sense, More is

> " The setting of The Faerie Queene may not be Renaissance England, but the content was still topical and important to that culture. By recapturing the past, Spenser has made the present more palatable, and he has instilled hope for the future."

echoing his own *History of Richard III*, with its condemnation of rulers who misuse power. He is nonpartisan in that text just as he is in *Utopia*. The *History of Richard III*, is not directed at one particular king but at the despotism of poor government.

Interestingly, More rejects the chivalry of the medieval period, which Spenser will embrace in *The Faerie Queene*. Because More is really on the cusp between the Middle Ages and the Renaissance, this omission is curious. Warriors have no place in his world. Perhaps More is saying that his Utopian people are better Christians than his contemporary Englishmen. Asking such questions in England could be dangerous, as it ultimately was for More. Because of this danger, More uses fiction and a fictional faraway location to ask serious questions and propose solutions to the domestic, political, and religious strife that defined English society. The problem with More's idealized world is that it is boring. There is no art, literature, or drama. There is no difference of opinion, and it is too safe. Why does man need god if his life is already perfect? This Utopian ideal contradicts human nature, which thrives on dissention and argument. Creativity and new ideas evolve out of conflict. Edmund Spenser appears to understand this, since his text, while presenting an idealized world, also makes a world that is rich in conflict and danger, full of risk, and offering the opportunity for redemption. Spenser's world still needs God and the Anglican Church to survive.

In each author's need to create an ideal world, there exists a desire to make England a better place. A heroic past, which emphasized honor and truth, was particularly important in a society where so much disorder had reigned. Peace and the end of the War of the Roses were only a century old. In addition, the reign of Mary, which was particularly bloody and painful, was still a recent memory. There had also been recent rumblings from Mary Queen of Scots and plots to seize the throne. Elizabeth I craved order, as did her subjects. Peace and order in the monarchy were too recent to be taken for granted. The setting of *The Faerie Queene* may not be Renaissance England, but the content was still topical and important to that culture. By recapturing the past, Spenser has made the present more palatable, and he has instilled hope for the future.

Source: Sheri E. Metzger, for *Epics For Students*, Gale, 2001.

John Vanderslice

John Vanderslice describes Amoret's rescue from Busirane by Britomart in The Faerie Queene *as one woman rescuing another from evil, but more importantly, aiding her in matters of the heart.*

The entrapment of the newly betrothed Amoret in the house of the magician Busirane in *The Faerie Queene*, book 4—and her extreme reaction to that place—has for decades sent readers scrambling for a satisfactory explanation. Why is she there? Whom should we hold responsible? Busirane has been seen as a presentation of the male sexual imagination "trying busily (because unsuccessfully) to dominate and possess woman's will". Scudamour, Amoret's aggressive new husband—who, while a complete stranger, abducted her against her will from her home in the Seat of Womanhood—is cited as the one responsible for engendering such terror in the young maiden toward this masculine force. It is he who reveals "the tension between husbandly love and its implicit antagonism to women". According to this reading, Scudamour, though he tries to rescue his wife from the magician's house, is, ironically, the one who put her there.

I, however, following Roche, find the source of Amoret's trials in her own character and upbringing. One must recall that Amoret was taken by Busirane during her wedding celebration, only hours before her marriage was to be consummated. In her blooming fear of her first sexual experience, she is blind to the difference between chaste love in a Christian marriage and lawless lust outside that institution: "Amoret makes no distinction between them, for her there is only the horror and enslavement of physical surrender".

Amoret, having spent time both in the Garden of Adonis, where she witnessed the beauty of natural generation, and at the Seat of Womanhood, where she learned the role of the virtuous lover, appears to have forgotten the lessons of the former and corrupted the lessons of the latter. For if Amoret, as most agree, stands for chaste affection, it can hardly be appropriate for her to withdraw from conjugal love with her presumably Christian husband. Even Paul, who thought the celibate state preferable for a Christian, taught: "Let the husband fulfill his duty to his wife, and likewise also the wife to her husband. […] Stop depriving one another, except by agreement for a time that you may devote yourselves to prayer" (Corinthians 7.3, 5).

Nor is Amoret the only character who makes this mistake. When the beautiful maiden is first grabbed by Scudamour in the Temple of Venus, the figure of Womanhood castigates him: "it was to knight vnseemly shame, / Vpon a recluse virgin to lay hold, / that vnto Venus seruices was sold". Here Womanhood is making what to Spenser would be a tragic, almost perverse, error: She is equating reclusive virginity with divine service. Representing only the civil, confined, retiring idea of woman, Womanhood is apparently unaware of the procreative nature of woman celebrated in the Garden of Adonis. That procreation, of course, is just as much a part of "Venus seruices" as Shamefastness and Obedience. It is unavoidable that if Amoret is destined to be married she must partake in both aspects of Venus; her education is designed to make the two complementary. Both aspects are necessary, yet neither can be regarded as sufficient in itself, or an end in itself; each can only find its completion and its harmony in the other. Womanhood, however, would deny "the lore of loue" that Amoret learned in the Garden and would argue for half an education—and half a responsibility—as a whole. She views any affection beyond that half as "vnseemly shame."

This is the attitude Amoret appears to have brought to her wedding. The polite circle of ladies in the Temple, then, because their tutelage expands beyond the designated half of Amoret's learning, is not merely a circle but a chain, restricting Amoret with links of fear and false notions of love. And given that Amoret is later trapped in the Cave of Lust, we should not dismiss the reality of her own sexual nature. It is not unthinkable that a portion of her fear and disgust is directed at her own sexual feelings, which she only begins to recognize after meeting Scudamour.

Busirane, then, cannot simply be regarded as a lust figure, or the overactive male sexual imagination. For regardless of Scudamour's claim that Busirane tortures his bride because "to yield him loue she doth deny", love—whether carnal or emotional—is hardly what Busirane seems to be after. He does not lust after Amoret in any way heretofore understood in the poem. Indeed, he looks nothing like the figure of Lust who later traps Amoret in his cave, or the more courtly lust figure Corflambo, who "cast[s] secret flakes of lustfull fire / From his false eyes". The poet actually gives us very little sense of Busirane's appearance, only that he is a "vile Enchaunter [...] Figuring straunge characters of his art".

What Busirane seems to be doing in removing the "living bloud" from Amoret's heart is not generating lust in her, or satisfying his own, but emptying her of the spirit of chaste affection, leaving a cold "dying heart" whose chastity is the brittle, life-denying kind which Spenser abhorred. It is the chastity that regards any and all forms of sexuality with suspicion and distaste; the chastity that denies the dual aspects of Venus and creates an Amoret who "cannot distinguish between the act of marriage and adulterous love".

The House of Busirane, therefore, should more rightly be termed the House of Fear. The reason Busirane is so vaguely described by Spenser is that the poet wishes to mimic the very formless and indecipherable nature of fear itself, which becomes more debilitating as one's apprehensions become less localized-and less justified. The reason Britomart must not merely kill Busirane but make him reverse his magic is that Amoret needs not only to shirk off her unwillingness to consummate her marriage, but also to be cured of the essential fear which caused her reluctance in the first place. The life blood of ideal chastity must be restored to her.

Britomart's rescue, then, should be regarded not simply as one woman rescuing another from the evils of male domination, but as a character more experienced in the trials of the heart helping another, who is much less so, to put aside wildly exaggerated and frightful notions. Britomart, who herself has felt the painful wound of love and been succored by Merlin's instruction that her affection is not an ignoble one, is the lone character in the poem, male or female, with the requisite sympathy, serenity, and power to free Amoret from her fear. After all, Dame Concord approved of Scudamour's

stealing his would-be bride from the safe, virginal Seat of Womanhood. Timid Amoret cannot possibly understand that benediction. Britomart can assure her of it.

Source: John Vanderslice, "Spenser's *The Faerie Queene*," in *The Explicator*, Vol. 57, No. 4, Summer, 1999, pp. 197–199.

Charles Ross

In this essay, Charles Ross examines Spenser's use of social practices and values in The Faerie Queene *and how he addresses the questions of tolerating others customs and staying true to one's own beliefs.*

The decrees of society are temporary ones. —Nabokov

In the first half of his *Faerie Queene*, published in 1590, Edmund Spenser generally looks to the distant past for those values that would fashion a gentleman to the ideals of chivalry. By the time he published the second installment of his poem in 1596, Spenser seems to have struggled more openly with the relationship between social practice and values: Should one tolerate customs of which one disapproves? What can be done when others condemn what one believes is right?

The allegory of Book VI, the legend of courtesy, foregrounds these questions. The hero of this section of Spenser's romantic epic is Sir Calidor, charged by the Faerie Queene to track down the Blattant (or Blatant) Beast, a houndlike creature that Spenser named after the *beste glattisant* that the pagan knight Sir Palomides tracks as hopelessly as he pursues the love of Isode in Malory's *Morte Darthur*. Calidor's quest is also incomplete, for he finds the baying animal but cannot muzzle it permanently.

The critical consensus that the Blattant Beast represents the inevitability of slander or detraction has not been matched by agreement over the way the rest of Book VI manifests the operation of courtesy. Hamilton's introduction finds no adequate social context for the story, declaring that "allegorical interpretation [is] entirely inadequate, irrelevant and disposable. Of all the books, Book VI seems closest to romance with its aura of manifold, mysterious meanings conveyed in a 'poetic' context and not at all in any abstract moral, philosophical, or historical argument." Most critics find the central theme of the legend in Calidor's vision of the Graces during the pastoral interlude in cantos 9 through 11.

What Hamilton and others attribute to the magic of romance, however, can be shown to be a deliberate vagueness that solves a problem that an enthusiastic reformer like Spenser could not avoid: how to establish good conduct, when too radical a theory of change will leave one's own system exposed to a similar revolution. Only by defining "custom" in general and universal terms as "courtesy" can Spenser open up the possibility for change and claim the prerogative to effect it. Faced with the problem that no simple rule or persuasive argument suffices to establish the priority of one of two competing moral systems, Spenser constructs a narrative solution in *The Faerie Queene* by drawing on the conventions of chivalric romance, which he read in ethical terms. Three times in the first half of Book VI, once at Crudor's Castle and twice at Sir Turpine's Castle of the Ford, Spenser uses the custom of the castle topos, a narrative structure in which clashing standards of behavior open a gap between moral knowledge and moral action. Spenser could have found the topos in many chivalric romances, but he certainly knew it from Malory's *Morte Darthur* and Ariosto's *Orlando Furioso*. In earlier books Spenser adopted the convention for the unchaste usage of Malecasta, the suffocating social arrangements of the Castle of Couples, and the injustice of Pollente's bridge. Unlike Britomart and Artegall, the heroes of Book VI find greater difficulty in countering charges of their own ill conduct, as first Sir Calidor, then Sir Calepine, and finally Prince Arthur face customs that someone else regards as proper. Their tribulation—the difference between what they think is right and what action they can effect—foreshadows Calidor's ultimate failure to eliminate detraction.

The narrative convention of the custom of the castle, as a model of moral uncertainty, allows the Book of Courtesy to make its point that courtesy is characterized by imprecision and vagueness. This lack of formal definition characterizes other virtues, but it seems more paradoxical in Book VI, since we usually associate courtesy with show and explicit forms of behavior. Red Crosse takes precise steps and learns fairly exact lessons (the seven acts of mercy) in the House of Holiness. But Spenser's letter to Walter Raleigh emphasizes what Spenser calls "the show" rather than "precepts … sermoned at large." Sir Calidor therefore properly enters a world of romance, pastoral woodlands and pirates, whose surface hides practical reasoning. For if good customs are merely equivalent to manners and fashion, then their social construction and relativity become embarrassingly obvious in the encounter with the Other. But if courtesy resides in the mind as some sort of universal ideal, then it can assume various outward forms.

The need for a general understanding of courtesy coincided with Spenser's early experience in Ireland. The flexible planning necessary to implement English social control over Ireland encouraged the optimistic attitude toward social change that Book VI explores. The other lesson of Book VI, that denigration accompanies accomplishment, warns that if a courteous knight wants to be a reformer, his reputation will fare better in Fairyland than in Ireland.

I

We first see Sir Calidor, a knight known for his "faire usage" (his moral habits), congratulating Sir Artegall, from whom he learns that Artegall's attempts to embody Justice in Book V have aroused Envy and Detraction and attracted the Blattant Beast. Artegall's perhaps misplaced certainty of his own virtue ("I that knew my selfe from perill free") contrasts to Calidor's perhaps overly pessimistic fore-knowledge that his quest is endless and without instruction ("an endlesse trace, withouten guyde"). Their encounter suggests that a clash of values may be resolved not by proving the invalidity of another culture (Artegall's task) but by striving to put one's own house in order. But few rules suffice for all occasions in the Book of Courtesy.

Sir Calidor attempts to apply the self-reliance Artegall preaches during his first adventure, when he confronts the foul customs of Briana and Crudor. The knight travels until by chance he finds a squire tied to a tree, who tells him about the local practice of exacting a toll (a form of custom) from passing knights and ladies:

> Not farre from hence, uppon yond rocky hill,
> Hard by a streight there stands a castle strong,
> Which doth observe *a custome lewd and ill*,
> And it hath long mayntaind with mighty wrong:
> For may no Knight nor Lady passe along
> That way, (and yet they needs must passe
>   that way,)
> By reason of the streight, and rocks among,
> But they that Ladies lockes doe shave away,
> And that knights berd for toll, which they for
>   passage pay.
> (my emphasis)

Calidor also learns that the source of the custom is Sir Crudor, who demands that Briana make a mantle "with beards of Knights and locks of Ladies lynd" to win his love. Calidor unbinds the squire and then rescues the squire's maiden by killing

Maleffort, who works for Briana. Calidor next invades Briana's castle and slays the porter. He is putting the castle to the sword, sweeping away the inhabitants like flies ("bryzes"), when Briana accuses the knight of courtesy of murdering her men—and of threatening to rob her house and ravish her. Hamilton hears an invitation in her declaration of helplessness, but surely the point of the scene is to force Calidor verbally to defend his attack on the custom of the castle. The rules of civility vary in different times and places. Spenser's scene therefore gives prominence not just to the difficulty but to the uneasiness that accompanies the establishment of civility. Briana's charge that the knight of courtesy has vilely murdered her men dramatizes the perception that one has a difficult responsibility when imposing upon the customs of others.

> False traytor Knight, (sayd she) no Knight at all,
> But scorne of armes that hast with guilty hand
> Murdred my men, and slaine my Seneschall;
> Now comest thou to rob my house unmand,
> And spoile my selfe, that can not thee withstand?
> Yet doubt thou not, but that some better Knight
> Then thou, that shall thy treason understand,
> Will it avenge, and pay thee with thy right:
> And if none do, yet shame shal thee with
>   shame requight.

Chagrin takes hold of Calidor, as he listens to Briana: "much was the Knight abashed at that word". Puttenham's term for this significant pause is "aporia," whose effect is to raise doubt, as "when by a plaine manner of speech wee might affirme or deny him." The nervous anxiety raised by the question of customary behavior gives a false edge to Calidor's response to Briana. First Calidor denies responsibility for what he has done. "Not unto me the shame, / But to the shameful doer it afford". Calidor's speech implies that good customs, which characterize civility, preexist the evil efforts of Briana and her people to negate them.

> Bloud is no blemish; for it is no blame
> To punish those, that doe deserve the same;
> But they that breake bands of civilitie,
> And wicked customs make, those doe defame
> Both noble armes and gentle curtesie.
> No greater shame to man then inhumanitie.

Briana, however, remains deaf to the "courteous lore" of Calidor, forcing him to fight Crudor.

The battle between Calidor and Crudor figures the particular strain felt by someone who alters the custom of others. Their lives are compared to castles, impenetrable, as each seeks entrance to the other. With no direction—no fixed rules of deportment—Calidor and Crudor "tryde all waies". Their battle mirrors Calidor's perennial pursuit of the Blattant Beast, "an endlesse trace, withouten guyde". The phrase tells us that no written manual of instruction exists. The duel of Crudor and Calidor therefore figures the wandering ways, the labyrinth of fairyland.

Calidor's strain and chagrin undercut his reformation of Crudor. The battle technically ends when Calidor reduces Crudor's pride and cruelty, imposing humility on the fallen foe whose life he spares. Calidor then lectures Crudor on the Golden Rule and demands that he marry Briana without a dowry. Glad to be alive, Crudor agrees to his terms. At once something snaps in Briana (her sudden "affect"). She quiets down and gives her castle to Calidor, who redistributes the property to the squire and lady to recompense their lost beard and hair.

The moral would seem to be that a rude population will offer up their property in grateful exchange for lessons in civility—a fit fantasy for an English colonist in Ireland—were not Crudor's reformation curiously incomplete. How can Calidor's lesson in chivalry ("Who will not mercie unto others shew, / How can he mercy ever hope to have?" guarantee a new mode of conduct? Pressured by the threat of death, forced to swear allegiance on his conqueror's sword and the holy cross, Crudor bends to superior power rather than to reason. Does his mind remain stubborn?

Spenser never lets us trust what we see as each quest of *The Faerie Queene* opens. Here, he casts doubt on the extent to which Crudor takes to heart the new custom of courtesy, for if Crudor arises as bidden, he does so "how ever liefe or loth". This episode is self-contained in the canto and never referred to again. Yet there are enough clues to the problems of reformation that we may suspect we are not violating the poem's artistic premises by wondering whether the new custom has indeed become customary, or whether Crudor's behavior may revert in an instant. Faced with a similar scoundrel, Boiardo's Brandimarte says, "A frog will never leave the mud!". Spenser's attitude is not devoid of such aristocratic disdain for the lower classes, but in contrast to Boiardo's rule of force in the face of hopeless intransigence and his appeal to a limited audience, Spenser's epic promises to fashion a gentleman without distinguishing whether he means to fashion one from scratch or merely to polish a gentleman born.

A spectacle, rather than specificity, solves the problem for one who, like Spenser, stands in the present and wonders what is the right thing to do today and how to ensure that pattern of behavior for the future. Cicero regarded eloquence as the source of civility, and we usually regard Spenser as promoting this humanist view. But the first custom of the castle scene in the legend of courtesy suggests that eloquence is a necessary but limited means of shaping social behavior. Calidor makes Crudor agree not to mistreat strangers. He tells him to help ladies, without explaining how. Crudor must marry Briana without demanding a dowry, but he receives no instructions on daily behavior. Such negative injunctions merely check the inclinations, including such selfishness as Crudor and Briana show. The purpose of the scene in the legend of courtesy is therefore not to promote Calidor or condemn Crudor and Briana, let alone to propose a blueprint for land appropriation or marriage settlements, but to explore social customs as a scene of contested values.

II

Spenser adopted the archaic mode of chivalric romance both for its essentially arbitrary form and to allow him to claim the authority of the past for those virtues he was keen to convey as guides for the future. But other people's customs represent formidable obstacles, because they too can claim the authority of the past. How can a reformer justify change without generating an uncontrollable force that can destroy the reformation process? To illustrate this issue, the custom of the castle motif operates as a dialectical structure in which social issues may take narrative form without our resorting to the ethical habit "of ranging everything in the antagonistic categories of good and evil" with the result that "what is bad belongs to the Other." The custom of the castle raises, as Jameson phrases it, "in symbolic form, issues of social change and counterrevolution."

There is, therefore, no bright line test for courtesy in *The Faerie Queene*. The Blattant Beast represents neither good nor evil but the way of the world: not just slander, but inevitable slander, from which no pastoral retreat provides protection. His bite seems arbitrary, like fashions or the complex set of duties determined by the rank of those one faces. Following the reformation of Crudor's castle, Spenser's narrative voice suggests that such courtesies are so bewildering that nature eases things for some people by making them naturally civil. Calidor, for example, has nature's gift, but Sir Calepine, Calidor's lesser image, is less fortunate in this respect, as the narrative proceeds to demonstrate.

The rude forest figures the uncertainty of moral guidelines by offering Calepine and his lover Serena opportunities for behavior that others—courtiers in a castle, for example—might regard as uncivil. Calepine and Serena are sporting in the forest when Calidor happens upon them, replaying a previous adventure in which a discourteous knight (slain by Tristram) stumbled on Aladine and Priscilla making love outdoors. Unlike the earlier knight, Calidor is too well heeled to stoop to jealous envy of their game; instead, he engages Calepine in conversation until they hear the screams of Serena, whom the Blattant Beast snatches in his jaws as she wanders away to make a garland for her head. The beast soon releases her, but Calidor continues chasing it, and we do not see him again until he begins his pastoral interlude in canto 9. Meanwhile, Calepine finds Serena wounded and travels with her till nightfall, when a "fair and stately place" beyond a river comes into view as they seek shelter.

The place is Turpine's castle, and its custom is discourtesy. Turpine refuses to help Calepine carry Serena across the ford. Calepine crosses anyway, then calls on Turpine to fight and justify his failure to lend assistance to those in need. When Turpine ignores him, Calepine calls him a coward, as Arthur will later. Turpine represents more than cowardice, however. He stands for the inevitability of social detraction when two competing sets of values confront each other.

Normally the foul custom of a castle is that one must fight for lodging rather than receive unquestioned hospitality. Turpine's custom adds a twist by setting this battle not in the present or future but in the past. The porter shuts the gates in Calepine's face and tells him

> that there was no place
> Of lodging fit for any errant Knight,
> Unlesse that with his Lord he *formerly* did fight.
> (my emphasis)

The custom doubly bars Calepine from entering since not only does Turpine fail to appear at his castle, but he has *already* refused to battle him at the ford. Turpine's barrier to entry is the kind of catch-22 or double bind that Spenser characteristically gives to villains who keep castles in Book III, the legend of chastity: the custom of Malecasta's Castle Joyous precludes any escape; Paridell will seduce Hellenore whether Malbecco watches jealously or not; and Amoret suffers whether she yields to or resists Busirane's black magic. Spenser does not label these practices as customs, but where a central personality organizes events, the pattern of behavior established by the moral habits of the individual symbolize those of an institution, as in the *Roman de la Rose*, the allegorical ancestor and source for medieval conventions of love.

Like the complex game of love that hinders access to the Rose in Jean de Meun's poem, the logic of Turpine's custom bewilders a naive Calepine. Turpine fails to abide not just by the rules of hospitality, but even by the normal foul custom of a castle, where a host insists on fighting his guests before giving them harbor. Calepine misses the point that he is therefore ineligible to enter. Sounding like Malory's Sir Dinadan, he tells the porter, who "no manners had," that he is weary, his lady is wounded, and he is in no mood to fight his host. He does not know that the man who refused to help him cross the ford also owns this castle. When he asks the porter for the name of the "Lord / That doth thus strongly ward the Castle of the ford", it seems that he has not conceived who and what he is up against. The custom of Turpine's castle finally forces Calepine and Serena to sleep outdoors, under a bush—appropriately for them, for they earlier made love outdoors "in covert shade".

Calepine's obtuseness reflects his incomprehension of the basis on which others disapprove of his conduct. The custom of Turpine's castle, which Calepine cannot overcome, therefore represents the larger social power that underlies the force of detraction. By keeping Calepine out, the society he faces robs him of his dignity. The custom of the castle distorts Calepine's reputation. Even Turpine's name infects the final syllable of "Calepine," which otherwise echoes Calidor as well as the generic Renaissance word for a dictionary: both Calepine and a word book are open to the inspection of others not familiar with their culture or language. They list rules for those not to the "manner" born. Moreover, Turpine causes not just mischief to Serena but inconvenience. English law distinguished an inconvenience from a mischief. An "inconvenience" results when the public is affected (*publicum malum*), while a "mischief" (*privatum damnum*) concerns private individuals. Serena inconveniences Turpine, in this public sense, so he refuses to admit her. Turpine's response is that of society—of those who believe the slander of the Blattant Beast, whose bite has wounded her.

As a "dark conceit" of detraction, Turpine continues his attacks after Calepine and Serena proceed on their way. Just as Calepine did not equate the knight at the ford with the keeper of the castle, so he does not realize that the knight who attacks him the next day is that lord of the castle whom he never saw the night before. The image of Calepine hiding behind "his Ladies backe" as Turpine attacks shows not a coward but someone who pays a social penalty for his actions. Calepine lacks awareness, as happens when one does not suspect the ill will of others. Turpine and his castle hold a distorting mirror up to the social reputation of whoever approaches them. They represent the sheer otherness of customs.

Detraction cannot harm one outside the society that circulates a slander. Once away from society, Calepine and Serena are safe. It is therefore fitting that "a salvage man" rescues them from Turpine. The savage's invulnerable skin, a romance image of his outsider status, makes him immune to the uncivil society Turpine represents. After chasing Turpine away, the savage invites Calepine and Serena to his forest home. Ensuing events suggest, indirectly, that Serena gives birth and Calepine arranges a foster family for the baby. When Calepine wanders away from her, he suddenly has an infant on his hands, which he gives to Matilda. Serena meanwhile is lodged in rustic solitude. She hurls herself down until her bleeding "did all the flore imbrew" as she lies "long groveling, and deepe groning". Spenser's romance uses uncertain, vague imagery and the temporal dislocations of *entrelacement* to avoid limiting the social allegory of Turpine's castle to a particular attitude about one issue, in this case the one raised by Serena's pregnancy. Serena's condition offers a specific but morally unnecessary reason why she and Calepine are not allowed inside Turpine's castle. The point is that the society of Turpine's castle, whatever one thinks of it, finds them unfit.

III

Spenser criticism is still reeling from the picture in Stephen Greenblatt's *Renaissance Self-Fashioning* of a poet participating in the cruder moments of colonization, repressing his sexual instincts in the name of a false civility, and helping himself to the wealth of a nation whose presence and practices provoked Spenser's deepest fears about his own stability. But the darkening of Spenser's world has the paradoxical effect of keeping his poem alive. For if Spenser's *View of the Present State of Ireland* and parts of Book V, the legend of justice, show us a man willing to starve a population or threaten it with the sword, Spenser's thought in *The Faerie Queene* depends on the narrative mode of romance.

The custom of the castle topos offered Spenser's romance a way to present social solutions without promoting specific programs. Arbitrary rules characterize the artificial castles where custom demands one's beard or locks or upper garments of travelers. Such rules also characterize the pastoral world that Sir Calidor enters in canto 9, where Calidor attempts to win Pastorella's love by his considerate treatment of his rival Coridon. Calidor gives Coridon a garland that he had himself obtained from Pastorella: "Then *Coridon* woxe frollicke, that earst seemed dead". Despite Coridon's delight, the garland seems like the sign of a loser, for Calidor gives Coridon another one after he throws him in wrestling. Boccaccio's *Filocolo* questions what it means for a lady to give someone a garland: is it a mark of favor, or a sign that the receiver is too poor to provide for himself? Boccaccio suggests that the meaning of the action can only be interpreted in terms of the customary behavior of lovers.

Such ambiguous images and courtly love games provided romances with materials to symbolize larger questions of how to conform to social customs: how to talk, eat, get ahead, or survive. Puttenham gives a nice example of how one must tailor one's actions to what others are doing when he discusses the trope of *hysteron proteron*. What he calls "the preposterous" occurs "when ye misplace your words or clauses and set that before which should be behind, & *è converso*, we call it in Englishe proverbe, the cart before the horse." Whether the sentence "I kist her cherry lip and took my leave" is a figure of speech depends on whether it is the custom to kiss first and then bid farewell, or to first take your leave and then kiss, thereby "knitting up the farewell," in which case the order of events is reversed. He wryly advises to "let yong Courtiers decide this controversie."

Spenser relies on romance images of arbitrary and symbolic behavior—bearding knights, denying hospitality, stripping upper garments—because he seeks a nonspecific picture of courtesy, conceived as a struggle to promote civic welfare. "Vertues seat," Spenser says, "is deepe within the mynd, / And not in outward shows, but inward thoughts defynd". A virtue that lies deep within the mind would create a problem for a mimetic poet precisely because the virtue cannot be seen. But nothing Spenser shows us in his nonmimetic mirror of chivalry need be courtesy itself.

When Spenser makes courtesy a mental phenomenon, he parts from Renaissance theorists like Erasmus and Bacon and Montaigne, who almost invariably defined custom as a form of pedagogy, the training of the individual to perform or to endure. Bacon's essay on custom amounts to a program based on the idea that one can get used to anything. His real subject is habit, which has a notable power of persuasion, as when Hamlet tells his mother she can overcome the "monster custom" to develop a taste for abstinence in her relations with his uncle. The first half of Montaigne's essay "Of Custom" is similar to Bacon's essay. It is about how habits developed since childhood create one's character. In the second half, Montaigne switches to public usages, which a strong educational system helps one adopt as personal habits.

In terms of fashioning a gentleman, Spenser's retreat to generality answers a paradox that Jacques Derrida identified in Rousseau's *Emile*: "Pedagogy cannot help but encounter the problem of imitation. What is example? Should the teacher make an example of himself and not interfere any further, or pile lesson upon exhortation? And is there virtue in being virtuous by imitation?" A measure of humility for the teacher is also involved, since as Descartes observed, "those who take the responsibility of giving precepts must think themselves more knowledgeable than those to whom they give them, and, if they make the slightest mistake, they are blameworthy." Descartes suggests a practical solution: a historical account or a fable may be allowed to contain examples one may follow as well as "others which it would be right not to copy." Philip Sidney's *Defense of Poetry* recommends fables over history for one who seeks to create role models. Spenser avoids the problem of constructing role models by adopting the form of nonimitative romance.

Vagueness, or generality, fittingly attends to the three goddesses who dance on Mt. Alcidale, near the end of the legend of courtesy. They are said to be the source of all civility, but they are not models for imitation. Euphrosyne, Aglaia, and Thalia offer no specific instruction in the general fields of "comely carriage, entertainment kynde, / Sweete semblaunt, friendly offices that bynde, / And all the complements of curtesie". Another hundred graces circle them to the tune played by Colin Clout, who represents Spenser in his role of inspired poet. They are said to be the "complements" (specific ceremonies) of courtesy, but Spenser does not name their qualities. The omission seems deliberate in a poem capable of listing every river in England and Ireland. The name of the goddess whom Colin calls the mother of the graces reinforces Spenser's representation of a wide picture of courtesy rather than a list of rules: She is Eurynome, and her name combines a suffix for laws, custom, or organization (*-nomy*, perhaps from *nomos*) with a modifier (*eury*) meaning broad. Her presence on Mt. Alcidale indicates that courtesy requires a wider ability than that of mastering rubrics in a handbook. Aladine and Calepine and Tristram, knights whose names come from books, never reach the standard of behavior of Calidor, whose generic name says that good conduct is a gift.

Spenser's fascination with transcending customs sets his romance beyond the clash of English and Irish cultures or the skeptical acceptance of a Montaigne or More or any of the Renaissance thinkers (Bacon is often cited) who realized that customs were a suitable instrument of social control. The mode of the poem mirrors the poet's mode of life. Spenser always operated with an eye to the future, conceiving plans for his career, organizing the vast project of *The Faerie Queene*, and eagerly participating in property speculation in Ireland. This latter activity gives us a clue to his imaginative association of courtesy and the spacious ways of romance as a literary form.

The Munster settlement in which Spenser participated in the late 1580s, as he finished the first three books of *The Faerie Queene*, raised the issue of any large entrepreneurial enterprise, how to plan when tomorrow brings change. The English resettlements gave this issue unprecedented scope. Elizabeth's privy council under Lord Burghley promoted settlement not under color of military conquest, though soldiers and their attendant violence were common, but through the subtler procedures of property development and social engineering. The result was a keen awareness of the difficulty of planning, of allowing for delays, disappointments, and competition. This activity gave Spenser a felt need for modes of conduct that would be both widely applicable and flexible.

The experience of the undertakers reinforced an axiom of anticipation that applies today. Where the future is uncertain, an employer, or undertaker, will find his or her interests best served not by constructing laws for his employees but by guidelines full of vague references to fairness and best efforts, to following standards according to the customs of others in similar enterprises, to duty and loyalty—in short, to equity and values. Equity is a judgment that depends on a total context, not strict rules. It offers open-ended flexibility. The drawback is that it courts uncertainty, especially in costs. Trying to account for activity in Ireland, the government regularly inquired into the exact numbers of English settlers transported to Ireland. Significantly, Sir Walter Raleigh was probably the most successful at settling large numbers of English tenants. But Raleigh's "short, rather vague, and detached" responses to the crown's 1592 inquiry were too imprecise to satisfy Burghley. According to MacCarthy-Morrogh, "Back came a letter demanding amplification upon a number of points including the English population: 'whose those be, or to what number, is not expressed, as the articles of the instructions did require.'" In fact, Raleigh raised working capital by offering land to Londoners whose goal was to profit by resale, not settlement.

The undertakers resorted to vagueness precisely because they bore the onus of day-to-day management and accountability, which belied the numbers Burghley might conjure up, sitting before his maps in his London chamber. Spenser must have felt the weakness of the settlement scheme as he wrote or revised Book VI during the 1590s. There should have been 1,575 armed settlers according to Burghley's covenants; in fact, there were hardly that many Englishmen in Munster, of whom perhaps three hundred were ready to fight, and there was lack of provision for enclosures or defensive buildings. In 1598, for reasons still obscure, the authorities suppressed publication of Spenser's analysis of what was wrong with the laws, customs, and religion of Ireland. The settlement plans failed completely that year, when the local Irish rebelled, and Spenser's castle at Kilcolman was burned. Spenser had become sheriff of Cork, but died in 1599 after sailing to London, paradoxically, to petition for help in controlling a society whose ways he knew as well as any man alive.

As romance versions of the Irish Other, Crudor and Turpine, Briana and Blandina base judgments on their own provincial terms, twisting the good intentions of Calidor, Calepine, and Prince Arthur. Turpine's detraction, in particular, stands for a "can't do" attitude, which must have been anathema to the poet who wrote the most mellifluous rhymed epic in English. Such an attitude never dies, but must be ignored by the successful undertaker, just as Turpine is not eliminated, only baffled, probably temporarily, like the Blattant Beast. That the conflict between another's views and one's own may seem preposterous (the key notion of Puttenham's definitions of *asteismus* and *hysteron proteron*) finds expression in the outcries of Briana and Blandina, in Serena's belated labor (*after* Calepine gives away a baby), and in Arthur's inability to punish Turpine because of slander that has always already occurred. The successful person, planning for tomorrow, learns to tolerate carping. The ultimate failure of Spenser's own career may disprove his message in particular but does not lessen the general power of courtesy conveyed by his chivalric romance.

IV

Prince Arthur offers an ambiguous solution to the problem of the uncivil social other when he confronts Turpine in the middle of the legend of courtesy. The ambiguity arises because, if Turpine represents society's judgment of others, Arthur is not only judged but discriminates too. The narrative raises the question of Arthur's opinion in a subtle way, by sending him to Turpine's castle not by chance but to "avenge th'abuses" that Serena complains of. Elsewhere in Arthurian romance, knights errant do not usually witness foul customs in operation before personally confronting them. In Spenser's poem, however, Calidor finds a squire tied to a tree and sees Maleffort tearing the hair from a maiden's head before he takes action. Serena suffers from Turpine's discourteous custom and then tells her story to Prince Arthur. The pattern continues when the narrator of *The Faerie Queene* mentions that Calidore once met Turpine ("that proud Knight, the which whileare/Wrought to Sir *Calidore* so foule despight"). Since we only see Calepine and Arthur, not Calidor, meet Turpine, this reference may be a misprint or a mistake. If "Calidor" is correct, however, it underscores the structural principle of the scene of Turpine's confrontation with Prince Arthur, who, it turns out, has heard yet another story about Turpine before he reaches his castle.

For Arthur accuses Turpine of despoiling knights and ladies of their arms or upper garments, although this practice is mentioned nowhere else in the poem. Turpine's counterpart in the *Morte Darthur* on this matter is Sir Turquin, or Tarquin, who beats his prisoners "with thorns all naked" as he goes about capturing King Arthur's knights during his search for Lancelot. Prince Arthur has such an act of public shaming in mind when he accuses Turpine of stripping his victims (also the practice of Ariosto's Marganorre, who short skirts ladies, and Malory's King Ryence, who collects beards and serves as a model for Sir Crudor). The public aspect that connects Turpine to Malory's Turquin is slightly roundabout, because we must consider the entire context of Turquin's story, but clear enough if we remember that the Turquin episode represents Lancelot's first appearance in the *Morte Darthur* and that Lancelot's reputation instantly becomes an issue. Because Lancelot rejects the sexual favors of four queens (Morgan, the queen of Northgales, the queen of Eastland, and the queen of the Out Isles) public speculation becomes so intense that "it is noised" that Lancelot loves Queen Guenevere. Lancelot denies the allegation but at the same time recognizes the logic of public infamy—"I may not warn people to speak of me what it pleaseth them". Public gossip makes it difficult for characters like Calepine, Serena, or Timias to alter the way of the world that Turpine represents.

Spenser added the motif of public opinion to the traditional topos of the custom of the castle to make Arthur's encounter with Turpine not a confrontation between right and wrong but a conflict between different opinions. That Arthur's own reputation may also be at stake at Turpine's castle helps explain his strange behavior there, for the strategy Arthur employs in attacking Turpine owes something to a trick Lancelot uses to defeat Sir Peris de Forest Savage, someone closely associated with Turquin in Malory's story ("For like as Sir Turquin watched to destroy knights, so did this knight attend to destroy and distress ladies, damosels, and gentlewomen"). In an unusual and seemingly ungallant maneuver, Lancelot sends a damsel before him while he keeps himself "in covert." When Sir Peris knocks the damsel from her horse, Lancelot rebukes him and cuts his throat. In *The Faerie Queene*, Prince Arthur easily passes through Turpine's gates, then, like Lancelot, he dissimulates. Arthur feigns distress to give Turpine's porter an opportunity to deny him hospitality, the usual foul custom of romance, just as Lancelot exposes Sir Peris by hiding while Sir Peris makes a damsel his victim.

Arthur's reformation of Turpine is inconclusive, as was Calidor's victory over Sir Crudor's custom early in Book VI, because in both cases the violence of the heroes distorts their intent. The savage man who accompanies Arthur tears Turpine's porter to pieces, while his attack on a biblical quantity of "forty" yeomen causes Turpine, like Briana, to blame Arthur for killing his people. Even though Turpine then attacks Arthur from behind and flees from room to room through his castle, he survives because he has used the issue of violence to cloud the moral certainty of Arthur's position. Arthur's sword twists in his hands, as happens in romances whenever the author wants to spare someone from the overwhelming force of a hero ("Yet whether thwart or flatly it did lyte, / The tempred steele did not into his braynepan byte"), while Arthur refrains from a second stroke because Blandina shrieks, shrouds Turpine, and entreats Arthur on her knees to spare him. Arthur calls Turpine a "vile cowheard dogge", then lectures him on social courtesy instead of killing him.

The prince of magnificence finds himself in a strangely unsettling situation—such as a foreign culture might offer—where he must abandon traditional notions of right and wrong as he instructs this allegorical figure of social detraction. Arthur accuses Turpine of cowardice, but at the same time, he oddly voices respect for Turpine's right to live as he pleases. We hardly believe Arthur when he informs Turpine that bravery in a bad cause is no vice ("for oft it falles, that strong / And valiant knights doe rashly enterprize, / Either for fame, or else for exercize / A wrongfull quarrell to maintaine by fight"). Turpine need not provide lodging for the wounded, Arthur says, as long as he does not attack secretly or from the back, since, even when defending bad causes, knights have "through prowesse and their brave emprize / Gotten great worship in this worldes sight. / *For greater force there needs to maintaine wrong, then right*" (my emphasis). Arthur means to persuade Turpine that it takes little pain to maintain what is right and that Arthur's own violent entry to the castle was of small moment compared to what it might have been had Arthur been in the wrong. Yet his message seems overly casuistic, ironically not forceful enough, since Arthur seems to praise the "greater force" needed to maintain wrong while he also he gives Turpine a choice how to behave. He seems to be saying, "your country, right or wrong," as long as you are strong. It is the colonizer's creed.

We recognize what is happening to Arthur from other examples of foul customs in chivalric romances. Normally a knight errant is trapped into upholding local law by the pressure of the population, a provision of the custom itself, or a double bind. Arthur succumbs to this literary tradition by agreeing to Turpine's practice of keeping people out. He ceases to reform the local inhabitants, an act figured by his calling off the savage, who kills yeomen downstairs while Arthur spares Turpine upstairs. Finally he settles down to a "goodly feast" and entertainment provided by Blandina, Turpine's wife, who hides her true aversion to his reform. At

Malory's Weeping Castle, Tristram and Galahalt find a way to "fordo" the foul custom when they submit to each other under the guise of sparing one another the shame of defeat. Arthur spends the night at Turpine's castle after seeming to achieve a similar resolution.

But it is not clear that Arthur makes the correct choice when he yields to Blandina's persuasions and spends the night, although two examples of the custom of the castle topos in Malory's *Morte Darthur* show that a knight may ignore the behavior of others and depart without fully reforming their foul ways: Sir Dinadan refuses to lodge where the custom of the castle is to joust for bed space, and Galahad rightly forsakes to kill the seven brothers who maintain the foul custom of the Castle of Maidens. Here, however, Arthur's reformation proves useless because it depends on a sense of shame that Turpine does not feel. The next morning Arthur leaves Turpine's castle intact, and Turpine continues his attacks.

According to the narrator, Turpine's problem lies in his "vile donghill mind". Using his wits, he convinces two knights to kill Arthur by telling them that Arthur ravished his lady, which distorts but does not totally falsify Arthur's sojourn with Blandina. Arthur's response depends on both prowess and deception. He kills one knight and forces the other, Sir Enias, to bring Sir Turpine to him. Then, in a ploy that seems designed to attack not just Turpine's practice but his mental attitude, Arthur falls asleep—and his savage page wanders off in the woods —as Sir Enias, whose name recalls the medieval reputation of Aeneas as the betrayer of Troy, fetches Turpine by tricking him into thinking Prince Arthur is dead. The ruse works, and when the prince wakes and grabs his sword, Turpine falls on the ground and holds up his hands for mercy.

All values need to be examined. Nothing Arthur does eliminates the social power that Turpine represents and that finds its cause in Turpine's intractable attitude. Arthur sets his foot on Turpine's neck "in signe / Of servile yoke, that nobler harts repine," but since Turpine's heart is not noble, he cannot "repine" or feel shame. The gesture is lost on him and once again Arthur fails to reform his ways. Arthur calls Turpine names and strips him of his "knightly bannerall," but he did essentially the same thing earlier in the castle, when he forbade him to bear arms and call himself a knight. Arthur's final act is to hang Turpine by his heels as a warning to others, but what warning can counter detraction? Puttenham translates what the Greeks called *asteismus* into English as the "merry scoff" or the "civil jest." He gives the example of one who knocked Cato on the head with a long piece of timber, then bade him beware. "What (quoth Cato) wilt thou strike me again?" The humor, Puttenham explains, arises because a warning should be given before, not after. Turpine's punishment is always too late because it comes after the fact: after his slander is already circulating. The "civil jest" reminds us that detraction is not just a court foible, but a deeply rooted confrontation with the Other, because reputations depend on someone else's point of view. Arthur's encounter with Turpine shows a poet concerned about reforming society for a better future but in no sense an idealistic dreamer of utopias.

Source: Charles Ross, "Spenser's Customs of Courtesy," in *The Custom of the Castle: From Malory to Macbeth,* University of California Press, 1997, pp. 83–103.

Katherine Eggert

In her analysis of Book 5 of The Faerie Queene, *Katherine Eggert makes the distinction that the book's shift from fiction to fact is in keeping with its concern of "transformations of kind" and how this shift includes the theme of female and poetic authority.*

To begin his discussion of the allegory of *The Faerie Queene*'s Book 5, A. C. Hamilton voices the private opinion of even Spenser's greatest admirers, that "Spencer's fiction seems to break down in Book 5. Probably for this reason the book is the least popular." A few pages later, however, Hamilton slightly revises his assessment of what happens to the poem's fiction in Spenser's Legend of Justice: not that the fiction has broken down, like some neglected machine in the garden, but that the fiction has been suppressed and restricted by Book 5's adherence to a nonfictional point of reference: "Throughout Book 5 the reader is aware of fact pressing down upon the fiction." As it turns out, "fact" for Hamilton, as for most readers, exerts its greatest pressure not on the whole of Book 5, but rather on the last five cantos, where the poem turns for the first time into a series of barely allegorized events in recent English history: the defeat of the Souldan (read Philip II and his Armada); the trial of Duessa (Mary Queen of Scots); Arthur's liberation of Belge; Burbon's fight for Flourdelis; and Artegall's rescue of Irena and subsequent slander by the Blatant Beast (read the adventures of Spenser's patron

in Ireland, Lord Gray). One of the most difficult tasks for critics attempting a traditional explication of Book 5's allegory has been to prove Hamilton wrong, and to demonstrate that even if fact seems to subsume fiction in these episodes, the reverse is actually the case, and history remains in the service of mythmaking and idealization. The trouble comes in contradicting centuries of readers' first and even second impressions to argue that what looks like mere fact is not mere fact, that history does not press down on fiction, but liberates it.

Of course "fact" in Spenser has, since Hamilton's complaint, enjoyed something of a critical renaissance. Insofar as Cantos 8 through 12 of Book 5 engage recent events, and especially in their interplay with the repressive and violent policies advocated in Spenser's *View of the Present State of Ireland*, they have recently attracted historicist commentary. At the same time, the episode of Book 5 featured just *before* the poem's turn to fact has increasingly drawn the attention of feminist critics—not because fiction is repressed, but because feminine authority is repressed. In this episode Britomart, the female knight who has been the intermittent focus of *The Faerie Queene* since the beginning of Book 3, rescues her fiancé Artegall by decapitating the Amazon queen Radigund, then rules Radigund's city-state for a time only to turn sovereignty over to Artegall. But little work has been done in either the New Historicist or the feminist mode to bridge the gap between the central and final sections of Book 5, to describe the killing of the Amazon queen and the turn to historical allegory as parts of versions of the same process or impulse. The discontinuous structure of Book 5— its sudden, unexplained, and unsatisfying shift in mode from fiction to fact—is replicated by a criticism that takes up Book 5 only in piecemeal fashion.

In my view, neither the traditionalist desire to paper over Book 5's structural shift nor the current tendency to treat Book 5 merely episodically does justice to a Book whose concern from the beginning is transformations of *kind*. The Proem to Book 5 not only dolefully announces that "the world … being once amisse growes daily wourse and wourse" (5.Pr.1), but also thinks of that decay in terms of materials once, but no longer, put to use:

> And men themselues, the which at first
>   were framed
> Of earthly mould, and form'd of flesh and bone,
> Are now transformed into hardest stone:
> Such as behind their backs (so backward bred)
> Were throwne by *Pyrrha* and *Deucalione*:
> And if then those may any worse be red,

They into that ere long will be degendered.

Breeding backward is the problem: it is also the solution. If humans have degenerated rather than evolved in kind, then a heroic poem must look backward for models and materials of literary types: "I doe not forme them to the common line/Of present dayes, which are corrupted sore". But Spenser's chronology deserves some examination here. In the second installment of *The Faerie Queene* the "present day" of the poem, the moment in which "form" has become so corrupt, has already been identified as the present *in which the poem is invented,* and in which the poem is therefore complicit: the "rugged forhead" of the Proem to Book 4 "[m]y looser rimes (I wote) doth sharply wite, / For praising loue, as *I haue done of late*" (my emphasis). In light of the rugged forehead's attack, Book 5's notoriously "tight" structure—especially, and especially in its last five cantos, its dispensing with the lush or knotty language, the odd twists of plot and identity beloved of Spenserians—seems a response to the "looseness" that *The Faerie Queene* has continued to perpetuate throughout Book 4. Book 5 begins with the degeneration of form through a history that turns out to be not only of humankind, but of the poem's production.

By using the word "degendered" rather than "degenerated" to describe the sorry pass to which form has and will come, Spenser not only easily catches a poststructuralist critic's eye, but also recasts the problem of form in the terms in which it will appear in Book 5: the problem of feminine authority. The Proem's stony men look forward to Artegall's subjection to hint that Book 5 might illustrate Freud's Medusa effect, where men are no longer men because they are "degendered" stones, castrated by the phallic woman. By the 1611 folio of Spenser's complete works, "degendered" in this stanza had become the more purely francophonic "degenered," a substitution that encourages us to make a more explicit connection between the end of feminine rule showcased in Book 5 and the shift in literary form that immediately follows. To reverse the effect of men becoming "degenered," enthralled by the Medusa or the Amazon, *The Faerie Queene* must confront the perception that the poem itself has become "degenered," debased in literary kind from its original epic intent. Book 5's repeal of feminine authority becomes both the motivation and the prerequisite for its turn toward the bleak new genre of historical allegory. If, as Fredric Jameson has contended, innovations in literary genre come about to address potentially discomfiting changes in poli-

Title page of the first edition of The Faerie Queene, *printed in London in 1590.*

tics and socioeconomics, then we should not be surprised that in this most self-conscious of poems, a shift in genre is baldly signalled by a shift in the gender of political regime. Britomart's returning the Amazons "to mens subjection" is an accomplishment labelled as "changing all that forme of common weale"; immediately thereafter, *The Faerie Queene* itself "changes all that form."

The genre in question for Jameson is romance, which expresses a nostalgia for "an organic social order in the process of penetration and subversion, reorganization and rationalization, by nascent capitalism, yet still, for another long moment, coexisting with the latter." But as Harry Berger reminds us, with *The Faerie Queene* matters of form are more complicated: if Spenser's poem expresses nostalgia for an earlier order, it does so with a canny awareness of the uses to which nostalgia can be put. As it turns out, romance in the poem is not itself a nostalgic mode, but rather an experimental mode that *induces* nostalgia—the poem's own display of nostalgia for a genre it occupied before, and other than, romance.

In *The Faerie Queene* order's "penetration and subversion" are laid explicitly at the feet not of Jameson's nascent capitalism, but rather of authoritative women. And implicitly, as Patricia Parker has demonstrated, order's penetration and subversion are laid at the feet of the genre of romance, which in Books 3 through 5 of the poem is intimately associated with those authoritative female figures and their characteristic modes of thought and action. Parker identifies romance and its failure to close off narrative as the foremost source of tension in *The Faerie Queene*, more recently, in a reading of Book 2 of the poem, she has identified that failure of closure with Acrasia's (and by extension any powerful woman's) ability to "suspend male instruments," holding men in thrall. Guyon's destruction of Acrasia's Bower has the effect of restoring narrative progress: "In Spenser, the 'suspended instruments' of Acrasia's male captives are recovered as the Bower itself is overcome, and as Guyon and his Mosaic guide move forward to the narrative 'point' or end of a Book of the Governor in which both a threatening female ruler and her suspect lyricism are finally mastered and surpassed." The genre of romance, the beauty of lush poetry, the power of a queen: all three elements that make the Bower so dangerously seductive are cancelled in Guyon's immoderate rampage toward conclusions. But as many critics have noticed, all three of these elements reemerge in Book 3, hold sway in Book 4, and linger stubbornly into the central cantos of Book 5. It is therefore Book 5's turn toward history, not romance, that carries the force of nostalgia: nostalgia for Guyon's antiromantic narrative thrust, which managed in its "rigour pitilesse" to conquer the effeminacy induced by both a desiring queen and an arrested, uncloseable poetics.

II

My first task, then, is briefly to track the history of the alliances between poetry and femininity proposed in Books 3 and 4, alliances that eventually necessitate Book 5's generic shifts. Because Book 5's attachment to history arises just as soon as its attachment to Britomart ends, it is worth remembering that Britomart's entry into *The Faerie Queene* came hard upon the heels of a gap in history. Near the end of Book 2, Arthur, in the castle of Alma, finds himself reading a chronicle of Britain, a chronicle that ends just after the name of Uther Pendragon, Arthur's father. Of course Arthur's name cannot be added to the chronicle because, in the time scheme of *The Faerie Queene*, he has not yet embarked upon the sequence of events that will lead him to the throne. Nevertheless, as Elizabeth Bellamy has pointed out, the chronicle's abrupt ending reveals that Arthur himself exists in an arrested moment, in a state of history that is not yet. Britomart's adventures, which commence as Book 2 ends and which inaugurate the poem's fullest experiment with the genre of Ariostan romance, therefore come to occupy that suspension of history, the breach made by Arthur's hesitation on the brink of his future.

Furthermore, Book 3 of the poem begins by taking the radical step of associating poetic power with feminine power, no matter how emasculating that power might be, no matter how it may dismay rather than fashion a gentleman. This extraordinary proposition is first voiced in the Proem to Book 3, which describes the "ravishing" power of Walter Ralegh's poem "The Ocean to Cynthia":

> But if in liuing colours, and right hew,
> Your selfe you couet to see pictured,
> Who can it doe more liuely, or more trew,
> Then that sweet verse, with *Nectar* sprinckeled,
> In which a gracious seruant pictured
> His *Cynthia*, his heauens fairest light?
> That with his melting sweetnesse rauished,
> And with the wonder of her beames bright,
> My senses lulled are in slomber of delight.

The dangling "that" clause of line 7 initially makes it possible that line 6's Cynthia, and not line 9's reader, is the one ravished by the poem. Yet Ralegh's verse ravishes by means of its "melting sweetnesse," a phrase that makes poetry a suspiciously liquid and hence potentially feminized medium. And the ravished receptor of that sweetness turns out to be not Cynthia at all, but instead the presumably male possessor of the "senses" in line 9 that "lulled are in slomber of delight." Feminized by a poetry that itself is feminine, Ralegh's reader rests passively in delightful "slomber." Book 3 here seems willingly to model itself after those moments in Books 1 and 2 that are most dangerous to the masculine integrity of both the adventuring knights and the male reader, as poetry becomes its most lush and enchanting exactly when it depicts an authoritative, seductive female and her hapless victim—Acrasia unmanning Verdant in her Bower, Duessa pleasuring and enfeebling Redcrosse at the fountain, false Una seducing Redcrosse in his dream. As a result Book 3's substantial investment of both moral virtue and poetic narrative in its female knight Britomart raises the stakes of assigning gender to poetic success. Can *The Faerie Queene* invest authority, moral or poetic, in the feminine without suspending heroic progress?

With Britomart, Spenser's narrative at first displays some easiness with the associations between feminine and poetic authority, partly because Britomart's ultimate fate is indeed a progressive one, to accomplish Spenser's aim of revivifying masculine epic in the modern world. As Merlin tells her.

> from thy wombe a famous Progenie
> Shall spring, out of the auncient *Troian* blood,
> Which shall reuiue the sleeping memorie
> Of those same antique Peres, the heauens brood,
> Which *Greeke* and *Asian* riuers stained with
>   their blood.

Although the woman is the bearer of epic destiny, in Merlin's prophecy she does not taint it with her femininity; rather, she reproduces epic as it ought to be. Moreover, Britomart's quest is prompted not by a desire to dominate or incapacitate men, but rather by a vision of her intended spouse that takes the form of a mental pregnancy, "To her reuealed in a mirrhour plaine,/Whereof did grow her first engraffed paine;/... That but the fruit more sweetnesse did containe,/Her wretched dayes in dolour she mote wast". With this visionary lying-in Britomart is allied with Spenser himself, who in the letter to Ralegh writes of having "laboured" to "conceiue" the person of Arthur and the shape of his adventures throughout *The Faerie Queene*. Her fate is also Spenser's project: to produce a succession of heroes, which when complete will end in Elizabeth—*The Faerie Queene*. This version of authorial conception and birth, however, is altered by the abrupt end of Merlin's narrative, which halts as Arthur's history does, with no end in sight. "But yet the end is not," says Merlin. This cutoff marks both the suspension of future male enterprise, which "yet...is not," and the beginning of Britomart's adventures, which immediately take the form of narrative digression, not lineal progression. As Britomart rides along she forges her own idea of her lover, one that departs from Merlin's prophecies: "A thousand thoughts she fashioned in her mind,/

And in her feigning fancie did pourtray/Him such, as fittest she for loue could find." Britomart's "image" of her goal becomes one that she authorially invents not as a singular heroic purpose, but as a set of multiple and interchangeably pleasurable possibilities. And from this moment, Book 3's narration itself begins its digressive turns, as if it too wished to fashion "a thousand thoughts." Unlike the severed genealogies of both Arthur's ancestors and Britomart's descendants, the romance adventures of Book 3 invest their energies not in the hope for a singular conclusion, but rather in potentially endless revisions of chase, discovery, reverie, and flight. By taking full advantage of Merlin's "but yet the end is not," Book 3 fully exploits as poetic form the feminized qualities attributed to Ralegh's verse. On the level not only of lyric but also of narrative structure, poetry in Book 3 becomes liquid, shifting, and diffuse, and these are the qualities meant to afford readerly delight.

Whether these qualities of a feminized poetic form *do* finally afford delight is quite another question, one that has recently engaged several Spenser critics in their evaluations of fulfillment and loss in Books 3 and 4 of *The Faerie Queene*. Maureen Quilligan and Lauren Silberman both read Book 3's Garden of Adonis, despite its elements of chaos, decay, and lamentation, as a privileged site of feminine production—of earthly forms, of chaste love and marital fecundity, and of a female reader's access to understanding. For them, Book 3's center celebrates a satisfying feminine poetic power. By contrast, in a turn that slightly predates Quilligan's and Silberman's gendered readings, Jonathan Goldberg draws from Derrida, Barthes, and Lacan to contend that the poetic pleasure offered by Books 3 and 4 is a writerly delight in castration and loss, in an excess of always-unfinished production. As Goldberg describes it, Book 3's revised 1596 ending, in omitting Amoret's reunion with Scudamour and thus emphasizing Britomart's unconcluded quest for her mate, acts as a template for the continued deferrals of Book 4. For Goldberg, the pleasure of the writerly text of the entire *Faerie Queene*, but particularly of Book 4, arises from its failure to engage in unitary poetic ending. It is instead "an 'endlesse worke' of substitution, sequences of names in place of other names, structures of difference, deferred identities. It plays upon a void; it occupies the place of loss—where Britomart's wound is extended to Amoret, where Amoret is 'perfect hole.'"

Although Goldberg does not otherwise share a critical agenda with Quilligan and Silberman, all three focus on the delight afforded by these Books' feminized (or at least effeminized) constructions. My own view is quite different. Beginning with its exit from the Garden of Adonis (and perhaps even within the Garden itself, as Harry Berger has pointed out) *The Faerie Queene* starts to expose its own feminized poetics as eminently unsatisfying, whether those poetics produce a full harvest of invention or whether they disjunctively cut off those inventions. And once again, that dissatisfaction is bound up with the fortunes of the poem's authoritative women.

We must remember that most of the primary female characters of Books 3 and 4 *are* in fact driving toward a particular conclusion, marriage. But as Books 3 and 4 progress, both the desirability and the conclusiveness of marriage become deeply compromised, and weddings are largely either delayed or evaded. The narrative therefore finds itself in a double bind. In order fully to exploit the female knighthood that, beginning with Britomart, the poem has delineated, marriage must be acknowledged as a legitimate ending to a heroic story. But in the view of the male characters who are the necessary partners in this enterprise, marriage seems largely to replicate the dangers to heroism embodied in Acrasia's bower: marriage does not sharpen knightly instruments, it suspends them. Aside from some marginal or deflected weddings (the curiously quadrangular union of Cambell, Cambina, Triamond, and Canacee; the morally suspect Poeana's wedding to the Squire of Low Degree; and the unnarrated vows of purely allegorical rivers), Book 4's narrative effort is spent eluding rather than concluding wedlock. This avoidance is jumpstarted, as Goldberg points out, by the 1596 revision of Book 3, which assigns not only Britomart but also Amoret to the category of frustrated brides. The abortion of Amoret's "conceiued" hope to find her husband rewrites her as a duplicate of the unhappy Britomart, who in the 1590 ending to Book 3 witnessed Scudamour's embrace of Amoret only to be reminded of her own incompletion: "In vaine she wisht, that fate n'ould let her yet possesse".

Considering that Britomart's quest was prompted by her conception of an envisioned Artegall, the 1590 ending's disjuncture of the "fate" of narrative from Britomart's wishful thinking signals the imminent demise of the feminine poetics that Britomart initially embodied. Although the 1596 ending leaves both Amoret and Britomart to "wend at will" while the narrator takes his breather, the female wanderings of Book 4 have little to do with women exercising will. Rather, women's thought and de-

sires in Book 4 seem largely to be displaced by happenstance and mistake. Britomart carelessly misplaces Amoret and untowardly jousts for the false Florimell; Belphoebe "misdeems" Timias' attentions to Amoret. And more significantly, Book 4's "middest," the analogue point to Book 3's superproductive, female-ruled Garden, seems pointedly to cancel Britomart's desired fulfillment. Britomart's encounter with Artegall in Canto 6 instead evades a permanent union of heroine and hero as Artegall immediately sues to leave upon his initial quest, "To follow that, which he did long propound". Artegall's ability to "propound," from *proponere* ("to put forward"), establishes him as the opponent of *post*ponement and delay, even though it is he who is postponing their marriage. But in the prevailing opinion of *The Faerie Queene*'s second half, marriage itself postpones rather than embodies masculine endings. What is a "conceiued" hope for Amoret or Britomart is, for Artegall, a return to Acrasia's bower. From the bridegroom's point of view marital union as the joining of man and woman—not as the barely mentioned preface to Book 2's patrilineal genealogies—is a kind of suspended animation. And a male hero's safe response in Book 4 is either to flee marriage (as in Canto 6's comic argument, where "Both Scudamour and Arthegall/Doe fight with Britomart,/He sees her face; doth fall in loue,/and soone from her depart") or to contemplate it only from several heavily mediated removes, as in the Temple of Venus, which hides its hermaphroditic goddess from view precisely *because*—as with man and wife become one flesh—she unites both sexes in one being:

> The cause why she was couered with a vele,
> Was hard to know, for that her Priests the same
> From peoples knowledge labour'd to concele.…
> But for, they say, she hath both kinds in one,
> Both male and female, both vnder one name

What must be covered up (and oddly so, in the Book that contains *The Faerie Queen*'s most famous union, the rivers' wedding) is the very definition of marriage: "Both male and female, both vnder one name." Wedlock and its results are threatening enough that Venus is thrice removed from direct experience, not only by her veil, but also by the pains her priests take to mystify the truth of her form, and finally by the narrative's revelation of her only indirectly, through Scudamour's tale of finding Amoret at Venus' feet. Meanwhile Amoret herself has mysteriously disappeared from the scene, as if the allegory of marriage can be recounted only when actual marriage has once again become impossible.

In my view, this revulsion from the feminine endings imagined by female authority accounts for the inconclusive structure of Book 4—its turns and returns, engagements and disengagements. Having devolved so much of its action upon anticipated wedlock, Book 4's ultimate evasions of marriage leave the poem confronting its own heroic void; notoriously lacking a unitary hero, a Guyon to break the Bower's thrall, Book 4 is seeded with ever-increasing narrative guilt for not properly ending things. The kinds of conclusions that Book 4 does feature are necessarily strained—not naturally arrived at, but arbitrarily imposed by the narrative voice. Canto 10, for example, reaches for completion by flatfootedly ending both Scudamour's tale and the canto that contains it with the word *end* ("So ended he this tale, where I this Canto end"). Elsewhere Book 4 begins to ask forgiveness for the cliff-hanger technique that *The Faerie Queene* has employed since Book 1. Canto II opens by apologizing that Florimell has been left "languishing in payne" since 3.8. And Book 4 itself ends on a hasty promissory note, a one-line uncompleted completion like the one Artegall effects by leaving Britomart: the marriage of Marinell and Florimell, "Which," says the narrative voice, "to another place I leaue to be perfected."

III

That "other place," that place of perfection, is Book 5, which in fact begins by once again shunting aside Florimell's and Marinell's wedding in favor of Artegall's mission to rescue Irena. Hence Book 5's narrative asserts openly what Book 4's indirections implied: that marriage is not perfection at all, and that it is at best a mere footnote to the glories of the heroic quest. Artegall attends the promised nuptials only as a brief stopover on his way to "his first adventure". The *firstness*, the originality, of that quest, as well as Artegall's often-repeated intent to continue upon that first quest despite minor skirmishes along the way, is a new emphasis for a knight of *The Faerie Queene*, and one that leads us to examine what is (literally) being prioritized in Book 5: what is the first intent to which both Artegall and the narrative must insistently refer? Artegall's task is to restore originary justice but in the reiterated word that describes Artegall's judiciary pronouncements, the word *doome,* we hear how that "first adventure" is dependent for its achievement of this restoration on a sense of ending, of final, irrevocable closure. And as we will see, the opening pretexts of Book 5 firmly

disenfranchise feminine authority from this return to finality.

Of all the proems in *The Faerie Queene*, Book 5's features the most cursory and oblique reference to Spenser's queen. After declaring that God's justice, delegated to earthly rulers, allows princes "To sit in his owne seate, his cause to end", the proem addresses Elizabeth in only one stanza, as the "Dread Souerayne Goddess" who initially seems to have the apocalyptic power of bringing about that doomsday:

> Dread Souerayne Goddesse, that doest highest sit
> In seate of iudgement, in th'Almighties stead,
> And with magnificke might and wondrous wit
> Doest to thy people righteous doome
>   aread (5.Pr.II)

Given Spenser's cunning hubris throughout *The Faerie Queene*, it is difficult not to read *aread* punningly: Elizabeth *areads* "righteous doome" not by discerning or pronouncing it herself, but by her act of a-reading Spenser's poem, which dispenses its own inspired judgments. The main action of Book 5 similarly weaves into its narrative structure a determination to achieve closure by substituting male for female authority. Just as the Proem addresses Elizabeth in the person of Astraea, a goddess whose naming here is prefaced on her absence from the poem and from the world, so too does Canto I go on to delineate Astraea's departure as the precondition for heroic action: only once she is reft from earthly sight can her foster child Artegall begin his career. Her removal from the poem therefore at last delivers narrative into the safekeeping of the masculine. As a substitute for herself Astraea leaves Artegall the iron man Talus, "And willed him with *Artegall* to wend,/And doe what euer thing he did intend". This absolute fulfillment of male intent seems a dream of narrative progress after the feminine postponements and beguilements of Books 3 and 4. Talus is never delayed or diverted on the way to a goal. Once he sets out after Sir Sanglier, for instance, he requires only three stanzas to find and bind his prey—a remarkable contrast to the pursuits in Books 3 and 4, some of which never end. Talus acts as an external manifestation of *doome*, with its connotations of finality as well as of certain judgment. In Cantos I-4 Artegall's *doome* extends even to narrative itself, as with the end of each canto an episode in his travels is firmly and finally concluded.

That conclusiveness, however, itself comes to an end as Book 5 approaches its center, a center we have learned in Books 3 and 4 to associate with realized or potential feminine arrestiveness, with marriage and feminine (re)production. Cantos 5 through 7 of Book 5 in fact stage in small the extensive, interwoven problematics of marriage and of a feminine poetics mounted at length through Books 3 and 4. Radigund's capture of Artegall externalizes what might be Artegall's nightmare of marriage to Britomart: not only do Radigund and Britomart resemble each other in looks and actions, as many critics have noticed, but Artegall crucially consents to his bondage, "to her yeelded of his owne accord". Moreover, Radigund catalyzes at the precise moment of Artegall's quasi-marital oath a regression to Book 3's literary model, in which a feminine poem equally effeminizes its reader. We witness this regression in a complex moment of reader-response that goes beyond the earlier instances of feminine ravishment it resembles, as Artegall unhelms Radigund and sees her features for the first time.

> But when as he discouered had her face,
> He saw his senses straunge astonishment,
> A miracle of natures goodly grace,
> In her faire visage

When he looks at her, he sees himself—and more than himself, his arrested self: "He saw his senses straunge astonishment." That reading of his own plight, of himself as Verdant in Acrasia's bower, causes him further to be emasculated, and finally further to emasculate himself by disarming: "At sight thereof his cruell minded hart/ Empierced was with pittifull regard,/That his sharpe sword he threw from him apart". At this point the *doome* that he has wielded until now returns upon himself, enforcing not masculine completion but effeminized thrall:

> So was he ouercome, not ouercome,
> But to her yeelded of his owne accord;
> Yet was he iustly damned by the doome
> Of his owne mouth, that spake so warelesse word,
> To be her thrall, and seruice her afford.

The effeminization of the knightly reader is accompanied by a similar regression to the effeminized narrative of Books 3 and 4. Unlike Cantos I through 4 of Book 5, Canto 5 ends with no ending; Artegall remains in bondage, and his release is postponed until another place, "Which in an other Canto will be best contayned". Worse yet, Canto 6 in fact fails to free Artegall, and he remains with knightly instruments suspended while Britomart makes her way to him. Thus, like Books 3 and 4, Book 5 has feminine authority at its heart. Significantly, Britomart in Book 5's "middest" Canto 6 rearms herself.

The dilemma of the arrested text begins to be resolved as Book 5 works its way out of this feminine center, a process encapsulated in Britomart's stay in the Temple of Isis. The Isis Church episode has proven especially troubling for critics trying to assert a unity of purpose in Book 5; as Clare Kinney has put it, the episode is one of those "exemplary union[s] of Justice and Mercy" that "seems oddly irrelevant to the actual narrative progress of Artegall and his automaton-slave Talus from one victory of *force majeure* to another." T. K. Dunseath, in contrast, has identified Isis Church as a necessary passageway to Britomart's restoration of Artegall's progress: "Once Britomart submits herself to Divine Providence in the Church of Isis, she discovers the true nature of her mission and is able to free her lover from woman's slavery." Chafing though Dunseath's condemnation of "woman's slavery" may now be, it is a condemnation shared by the poem at this point, and Isis Church becomes the site of the reiteration and recuperation of Artegall's stasis. This episode at first recalls and extends the state of overwhelming feminine power in which Artegall still lies languishing: Isis, as goddess of the moon, reminds us not only of Radigund, whose face was revealed "Like as the Moone in foggie winters night", but also of Britomart herself, whose own visage has borne the same comparison and whose chastity allies her with the moon-goddess. Moreover, the dream that comes to Britomart as she sleeps at Isis' feet consistently confuses her with Isis, using only "she" and "her," not a proper name, to describe the marvelous queen that subdues the crocodile. But unlike the close of Book 3, where Britomart's state of feminine dismay and incompletion bled over into the state of the narrative, this moment of feminine governance and of feminine conception is safely framed. At first Britomart's dream seems to rediscover her former authorial mode: whereas in Book 3 she set out fashioning "a thousand thoughts" of her lover, here as she awakens "long while she musing lay,/With thousand thoughts feeding her fantasie". The dream's aftermath of interpretation, however, reduces those thousand thoughts to orthodoxy. First of all, the ambiguous or oscillating gender identities inherent in the temple sort themselves out. Not only do the priests, once of uncertain gender, now become in the person of their spokesman an unambiguous "he", but the crocodile of Britomart's dreaming— which had been given both feminine and masculine pronouns, as well as variously hermaphroditic powers of tumescence, pregnancy, engulfment, and impregnation—is now unquestionably male, a figure of both Osiris and Artegall himself. And even though in the dream Isis/Britomart exerts phallic authority over that crocodile, "turning all his pride to humblesse meeke", Isis' priest rereads this episode for her as pointing not toward Britomart's subjection of men but toward her eventual marriage and male offspring. The priest thus reincorporates feminine power into masculine heroics as Merlin did when he traced the careers of Britomart's male descendants. But signally unlike Merlin's vision, the priest's explication runs without interruption, "vnto the end". From this point Britomart will step, not into a maze of digressive, self-made visions, but toward a certain closure of masculine heroics that she must internalize and enforce. As critics have often noticed, in Britomart's subsequent defeat of Radigund the two women warriors are scarcely distinguishable: the fray is described as a challenge between a tigress and a lioness. Britomart's task is evidently to subdue herself.

We can see in Britomart's subsequent reconstitution of Radigund's city-state the full consequences of Spenser's reading of Plutarch's "Of Isis and Osiris," although Book 5 does not explicitly refer to Isis' reconstitution of her dismembered husband. Unable to find Osiris' penis, Plutarch's Isis replaces it with a consecrated replica; and so too does Britomart reerect her husband's phallic power. She not only rearms him and restores the Amazons "to mens subiection"; she also establishes Artegall's thralldom as but a holiday aberration: "Ah my deare Lord, what sight is this (quoth she)/What Maygame hath misfortune made of you?". All of a sudden, and quite improbably, Artegall metamorphoses from an embarrassed, foolish Hercules to an epic Odysseus returning to his patient, waiting wife: "Not so great wonder and astonishment/Did the most chast *Penelope* possesse,/To see her Lord, that was reported drent". With Artegall's promotion to head of state, Book 5's curious catalogue of ways to abuse the human head—its elaborately grisly panoply of hangings, beheadings, scalpings, and even haircuts—begins to make sense: all these illegitimate mishandlings of the head are cancelled in one stroke, Britomart's decapitation of Radigund. From this moment, too, the narrative itself seems to know where it is heading. Artegall ventures forth once again with purpose upon his hitherto delayed quest: "He purposd to proceed, what so be fall,/ Vppon his first aduenture, which him forth did call". And he leaves Britomart behind.

We have heard Artegall's rededication to his "first adventure" before the end of Canto 7: signifi-

cantly, this resolution is repeated three times in quick succession in the brief interval between his attendance at Florimell's and Marinell's marriage, and his encounter with Radigund's crew. If first intent prevails only in the respite between weddings and Amazons, how could it hold up if Artegall stayed to marry his own Amazon-like fiancée? Artegall's second separation from Britomart in fact becomes an extended meditation upon the high stakes of avoiding feminine digression, both for Artegall and for the forward movement of narrative. After his announced departure at Canto 7's end, Canto 8 surprisingly begins not by portraying Artegall on his way, but by worrying again at the issue of female dominance:

> Nought vnder heauen so strongly doth allure
> The sence of man, and all his minde possesse,
> As beauties louely baite, that doth procure
> Great warriours oft their rigour to represse,
> And mighty hands forget their manlinesse

A comment on Artegall's recent imprisonment, it would seem—but as it turns out, the "louely baite" in question is not Radigund but Artegall's intended wife. Despite her recent role in suppressing female sway, Britomart still represents the "allure" that Artegall must resist if he is to escape the fate (says the narrator) of Samson, Hercules, and Mark Antony. Feminine rule of body and mind must be cut off, beheaded, as a way of propelling Artegall back upon his and the narrative's "first intent", the rescue of Irena.

IV

As Artegall's earlier dismissal of Britomart in Book 4 taught us, however, rejecting one version of feminine rule is not enough to restore with certainty either masculine heroics or a masculine model of poetic effect. More drastic measures are called for. To return to Goldberg's formulation: if Book 4 conforms to the poetics of castration—of excess compensation for loss—then in keeping with its obsessive decapitations of illegitimate authorities, Book 5 castrates the castrators, proposing a thoroughgoing revision of literary construction that ought for good and all to sever the poem from feminine influence. Feminine rule and feminized poetics are repealed in favor of the most straightforward mode that *The Faerie Queene* will ever assume, historical allegory. At this point the poem assumes a new literary mode as a way of galvanizing the sense of an ending, the *doome* that Artegall's adventures first promised before his digression into serving a queen.

I earlier suggested that Book 5's revision of form reaches back nostalgically for the completed heroic endeavors of Books 1 and 2; if Books 1 and 2 can legitimately (if broadly) be described as the epic segments of *The Faerie Queene*, then the nostalgia that Book 5 expresses is for epic over romance. But Book 5 in its last five cantos also audaciously construes itself as more uniformly heroic than even those earlier books of epic (not to mention than the *Aeneid* and the *Odyssey*, if not also the *Iliad*), since it thoroughly discounts feminine *otium* as holding any allure whatsoever, either for the poem or for its hero. None of the women of these cantos poses any sensual danger for Artegall or for the late-arriving Arthur. Adicia's malfeasance is described as sexual only *ex post facto*, once she has been banished "farre from resort of men". The female monster of the Inquisition's dual appearance of foul and fair briefly recalls Duessa's ("For of a Mayd she had the outward face,/To hide the horrour, which did lurke behinde,/The better to beguile, whom she so fond did finde"); but her implied weapon of seduction is never put to use. Even Duessa's sexual transgressions are described with extreme economy, not with either the seductive or the repulsive flourishes of Book 1. The prosecuting attorney at her trial, Zele, simply mentions "many a knight,/By her beguyled, and confounded quight". As well, these cantos decline to seduce their reader: their refusal of sensual appeal extends to their poetry, which Angus Fletcher may be alone in praising as "aesthetically lean and muscle-bound." Fletcher's personification of verse as a male warrior physique draws together precisely, if unintentionally, the aim of these cantos' poetic reformation, their expurgation of what Dunseath has called the poetic "suggestibility" we expect from Spenserian poetry.

I would argue that these cantos do not mean to be suggestive. Instead of dense wordplay and multiple allusiveness, their verse offers only a limited field of interpretation, a tunnel vision meant to afford narrative progress. Whereas *The Faerie Queene*'s poetry typically engages its reader by withholding conclusions—or as Fletcher puts it, by holding the ear "captive in the chains of suspense"— these cantos eagerly draw toward singular conclusions both poetic and narrative. When Canto 11 repeats the word "shield" thirteen times, for example (as Hamilton notes with irritation), not only do we get the message that a knight must never discard his shield, but we also get no other message. And when Canto 8 sketches Arthur's triumphal march upon defeating the Sultan in only seven parsimoni-

ous lines, the reader is also reminded not to wallow in celebratory glee. Arthur, Artegall, and the reader all move on to the next adventure "hauing stayd *not long*" (my emphasis). Book 5's last reiteration of Artegall's recall to his "first aduenture" clearly navigates where he and the poem are going: "on his first aduenture [he] *forward* forth did ride" (my emphasis).

What minimal figurative language and swift narrative conclusions do for these cantos in small, historical allegory does writ large; the first attachment of these cantos to easily recognizable political and military events serves to cordon off all but the most straitened avenues of interpretation. We might be allowed a bit of wiggle room in the form of some referents that are not merely unitary. As David Norbrook points out, for example, we must hear in the rescue of Irena a reference not only to Ireland, but also to the French philosopher of absolutism Jean Bodin, who "used the term [eirene] to describe the highest kind of justice." Kenneth Borris strenuously argues, too, that these cantos not only depict such said-and-done events as the Armada's defeat and Mary Queen of Scots's sentencing, but also voice a Protestant rewriting of history into the approach of the apocalypse. For Borris, Spenser "transforms the particulars of history into vehicles for the ostensibly prophetic revelation of cultural destiny." But Norbrook goes on to remind us that for Spenser as for others with more radical religious leanings, Protestant apocalyptics (like Bodin's political theory) were also a matter of historical event and analysis. If Book 5's Battle of Belge is seeded with allusions to radical Protestant apocalyptic commentary, it is because Spenser's hero Leicester sympathized with those Protestant factions, seeing his expedition in Belgium as a religious war as well as a containment of Spanish imperial ambitions. Spenser's portrayal of the battle for Belge as a resounding success runs counter to fact not because its eye is on the final victory at world's end, but arguably because Spenser was propagandizing in favor of continued military effort in the Low Countries, in hopes that Essex would be allowed to take up where Leicester had left off. Protestant messianics, far from being suprahistorical, circle back around into realpolitik, into strategic militarism and jurisprudence.

The relentlessly optimistic depiction of Belge's fate, however, like the redemption of Irena in Canto 12, finally uncovers the pitfall of these cantos' dependence on diachronic historical allegory. These two episodes patently do not depict accomplished historical victories at all, but rather revise past English engagements, some of them not at all successful, into future triumph. When Arthur recovers a city that looks suspiciously like Antwerp, we are asked to acquiesce in an event that in 1596 has not yet taken place (and in fact never took place). In the same way, Irena's rescue comes about as elegantly as a challenge to single combat—truly a kind of wishful thinking, on the order of Hal's flyting of Hotspur on the eve of Shrewsbury. Even in the poem (not to mention in late sixteenth-century Ireland) matters are not really so easy, for like Hal's England, Irena's realm sees considerable bloodshed before single combat is undertaken. Artegall's prosthetic Talus manages to massacre most of the barbaric hordes before Artegall calls him back, claiming a bit belatedly "that not for such slaughters sake/ He thether came". These intrusive details, these shadowy reminders that current uncompleted missions are not as neatly sewn up as famous past victories, expose the danger of engaging upon a historical allegory that extends from past to future. Standing in the road between past and future is the ineluctable present, where history's certain endings give way to the muddled and inconclusive status of recent current events, events that curtail any story of *doome.* Still the end is not.

In the end Book 5's historical episodes make the case that even when barren and driven poetry replaces seductive lyric, masculine heroism is still subject to an undirected feminine authority. The liberation of Belge and of Irena, both fantasies that expose their own frustration, are framed (and hence, in *The Faerie Queene*'s juxtapositional logic, arguably caused) by two dilatory queens and their tactics of diversion. In the first case, Mercilla's waffling pity for Duessa in Canto 9 is seemingly closed off by Artegall, whose judgment is accompanied by his usual epithet of first intent ("But *Artegall* with constant firme intent,/For zeale of Iustice was against her bent"). But Mercilla's wavering in a certain sense still carries the day, since the pronouncement of Duessa's final sentence is delayed until the beginning of the next canto, and even then her actual punishment is elided. Surprisingly enough in this book of beheadings, the poem remains silent on whether Duessa's means of demise also doubles Mary Queen of Scots's: most readers assume that Duessa is beheaded, but in fact the poem tells us only that Mercilla, having delayed judgment "Till strong constraint did her thereto enforce," then "yeeld[ed] the last honour to [Duessa's] wretched corse". In this light, Artegall's oddly gentle decapi-

tation of Grantorto ("Whom when he saw prostrated on the plaine,/He lightly reft his head, to ease him of his paine") is better read not as a somewhat extraneous detail, but as a displaced dropping of Duessa's unenacted deathstroke, as if Artegall must carry out somehow, anyhow, what Mercilla has postponed. If he finishes off Grantorto with unwonted mercy, it is because he is momentarily usurping Mercilla's role. The point is minor enough, except that this queenly stay of execution recurs when Artegall tries to conclude his final task. His mission is the same as Britomart's in Amazonia, "How to reforme that ragged common-weale", but "ere he could reforme it thoroughly" he is recalled to Gloriana's Faerie Court, "that of necessity/His course of Iustice he was forst to stay". Blocked in the course of first intent, Artegall turns aside toward his queen's command with a final reiteration of straightforwardness that is by now entirely ironic: "he for nought would swerue/From his right course, but still the way did hold/To Faery Court, where what him fell shall else be told". This promise of narrative closure is never kept. No *doome,* no end for Artegall; back to the demanding, static embrace of Venus, or Britomart, or Radigund, or Gloriana.

Gloriana's whim serves further to highlight the difficulty of constructing historical allegory as heroic accomplishment. Although depending on current events to endow narrative closure would be futile enough in any era, events in late sixteenth-century England seemed to many observers, especially those sympathetic to militant Protestantism, particularly recalcitrant to fostering masculine endeavor and its fruition. By the mid-1590s Spenser's queen had been perceived for several years as hindering a Protestant crusade on the Continent; in her canny ambivalence Elizabeth was never willing to commit the funds or the manpower for a full-scale effort against Spain. R. B. Wernham details "a secret agreement" in the Triple Alliance among England, France, and the United Provinces that "limited the English military contribution [to the Netherlands] to 2,000 men.... In fact, after 1594 England practically withdrew from the continental war, except for [these] forces in the Netherlands." Although Burleigh was partially if not primarily responsible for this policy, the Queen herself was blamed for womanish inconstancy and lack of will. J. E. Neale reports a story that circulated about the Queen's endless changes of mind: "the story of the carter who, on being informed for the third time that the Queen had altered her plans and did not intend to move on that day, slapped his thigh and said, 'Now I see that the Queen is a woman as well as my wife.'" Throughout her reign Elizabeth had used to her advantage the figuration of herself as her country's bride; in the 1590s certain factions within England found themselves wishing that, like Artegall upon his reunion with Britomart, they might simply ride away from the inaction their wife enforces. Such was the wish expressed by the Lincolnshire rector Henry Hooke, whose short manuscript treatise of 1601 or 1602 entitled "Of the succession to the Crowne of England" digresses from praising Elizabeth into desiring her replacement by a king whose "first intent" would overgo his predecessor's feminine stasis on the question of religious reform: "so the brightnes of [Queen Elizabeth's] daye … shineth still: and more & more may it shine vnto the perfect daye: that what corruptions in iustice, what blemishes in religion, the infirmitie, and inconueniency of woemanhead, would not permitt to discouer and discerne, the vigor, and conueniency of man sytting as king in the throne of aucthoritie; maye diligently search out, and speedylie reforme." Hooke's remarks couple a desire for the repeal of female authority with a hope for a new mode of monarchical endeavor entirely, one that brings heretofore unenacted intents to fruition.

But as Artegall's recall to Gloriana's court demonstrates, such a hope for reform in 1596 remains suspended, both in terms of English politics, where the anticipation of a king's succession only added to the internecine wrangling of Elizabeth's court, and in terms of *The Faerie Queene*'s ambitions as an activist poem. Book 5's revision of literary form might take the poem out of the realm of romance, but it cannot repeal the rule of queens, either of Elizabeth or of Gloriana. In this way Book 5 debunks the misogynist fallacy of *The Faerie Queene*'s earlier scenes of seduction and of wedlock: Artegall's recall reveals that heroic expeditions are delayed not in the private female world—not in the illicit bower or the sanctioned bridal chamber—but rather in the public world of political aspiration. And if the poem's opposition between romance (to which that feminized private world corresponds) and masculine heroism is shown to be a false opposition, then the nostalgia for an epic form that predated romance no longer holds any attraction.

Instead *The Faerie Queene* overpasses the uncompleted ending of Book 5 by engaging upon yet another generic experiment. Book 6's pastoral stands in contrast to Book 5 not only as a conspicuously anti-epic form, but also as a conspicuously

and innovatively *masculine* anti-epic form. Although Book 6 seems to accept with pleasure poetry's suspension of experience—as does the narrative voice, which in the Proem admits itself "nigh rauisht with rare thoughts delight" in Faery land's delightful ways—it does so in a way untainted by the interruptive demands of feminine authority. Queen Elizabeth's appearance in this Book is a pointed non-appearance, as on the revelatory Mount Acidale Colin Clout eliminates Gloriana from his configuration of the graces' dance, replacing her instead with "certes but a countrey lasse". In contrast to *The Shepheardes Calender*'s April eclogue, where Colin confidently fashioned his queen as an appropriate object for poetry, here Spenser's poetic alter ego apologetically but firmly defines poetry as that which takes shape when female rule is out of the way. Even more than splintering Elizabeth into "mirrhours more than one," displacing her entirely from consideration leaves room for poetic accomplishment.

Not that Book 6 is therefore marked by triumphant poetic closure. The "untimely breach" of Arthur's rent chronicle not only recurs as Calidore's comically blundering "luckelesse breach" in Colin's perfect vision, but also might be taken as the model for Book 6's narrative, which is hardly famous for its seamless conclusions. And Book 6's end is similarly not one of perfection, either promised or fulfilled. Like Artegall's recall to Gloriana's court, the Blatant Beast's present-tense rampage at the end of Book 6 wrenches poetry from the domain of the past(oral) to the unnatural shocks of the present day, so that conclusion once again is disrupted by uncertainty—in this case, uncertainty imposed by readers more willing to slander poetry than to be melted into sweetness by it: "Ne spareth [the Beast] the gentle Poets rime,/But rends without regard of person or of time". Books 5 and 6, although drastically different experiments in poetic form, thus share a mode of inconclusion. Both books play out fantasies of freeing politics and poetry from feminine rule; both envision a newly masculine poetics. And in the end both acknowledge those fantasies as fantasies, enacting the futility of imagining that a male-gendered mode, either of monarchy or of poetry, will bring about the wished-for consummation.

V

I come to this conclusion (or to *The Faerie Queene*'s non-conclusion), however, with my ear still cocked to Berger's warning: what we hear in Spenser's magnum opus as *argument*—as assertion, refutation, judgment, revelation, demonstration, or any other of those rhetorical certainties we so often attribute to Spenser's poetry—cannot be taken as "Spenser's" or even "the poem's" settled opinion, but rather must be viewed skeptically as one of the discourses that, like dummies at a ventriloquists' contest, voice the competing desires that prompt their speaking. In his challenge to Paul Alpers' thesis that Spenser's stanzas are "modes of address by the poet to the reader," Berger argues that "Alpers misdescribes the transaction as an empirical one between the author and actual readers, whereas I take it to be a virtual or fictive transaction, one that the poem actively represents and subtly criticizes, and therefore one that constitutes a rhetorical scene of reading from which actual readers can dissociate themselves." Hence we can undertake "an ideological reading of *The Faerie Queene* as a critique of the cultural discourses it represents." Berger's subtle argument describes *The Faerie Queene* as radical in ways that all its Elizabethan source materials and cultural commonplaces, rampant as they are in Spenser's poetic field, could never countenance. I would like to make use of his insights to examine the radical critique ultimately disclosed by the generic experiment of Book 5; not a critique of attempting closure by way of masculinized poetic form, but rather a critique of desiring closure in poetry at all. In particular, the failures of Book 5's final cantos unsettle the impulse toward closure that is, or at least can be, the impulse toward allegory. Allegory proposes that we can metonymically replace what is troublesome and undefinable by something that looks hermetically sealed: not sexuality, but Immoral Lust or Wedded Love; not savage massacres in Ireland, but a gratefully free Irena; not Elizabeth, but Gloriana. The problem of obtaining allegorical closure, however, is akin to the difficulties critics have had in plotting out Book 5's structural, mythical, or moral unity. To create a transcendent order, one must repress the messy and conflicting nature of the facts or events that are transcended. In this clunkiest portion of *The Faerie Queene*, then, Spenser anticipates how ballasted allegoresis of his poem can become, by showing how ballasted his own poetry can be when it succumbs to a fully allegorizing impulse. For that reason I think we should see Book 5's historical allegory not so much as a failed experiment, but as an experiment whose failure is allowed to stand for all failures to impose univocal meanings upon complicated poems. Like the nostalgia for an unsullied genre before romance, Book 5 shows us, so too is the desire for unsullied truth based on false premises. Just as the "problem"

of female authority precedes and enwraps and even motivates *The Faerie Queene*, and hence is not to be "solved" by backward glances to some golden age, so too are Spenserian irresolutions not to be wished away.

Book 5's demonstrated failure forewarns of the dangers of excess complacency toward the Mutabilitie Cantos, which most critics describe as the consummate enactment of allegorical closure. A. C. Hamilton's edition of the poem approvingly quotes a number of these judgments, including William Blissett's that the cantos are "a detached retrospective commentary on the poem as a whole, forming as they do a satisfactory conclusion to a foreshortened draft, a stopping place at which, after a seriatim reading, can be made a pleasing analysis of all." But as Gordon Teskey has recently pointed out, Blissett's essay also addresses the ways in which *Mutabilitie*, not so detached from its historical moment as it seems, in fact troubles itself again with the problematics of late-Elizabethan female rule. As Teskey paraphrases Blissett, *Mutabilitie* undertakes "the shocking representation, in the late 1590's, of Cynthia dethroned by Mutabilitie"; and Teskey adds the comment that "[c]riticism has yet to grapple with *Mutabilitie*'s being not only unpublished in Spenser's lifetime but unpublishable in Elizabeth's." In a brilliant analysis Teskey goes on to suggest that *Mutabilitie* does not transcend political struggle, but rather exposes that struggle by means of yet another Spenserian gap: in this case the gap is *Mutabilitie*'s omission of a Tudor-style myth of genealogical precedence, which we expect to be brought to bear against Mutabilitie's titanistic blood-claim to Jove's throne. Omitting that myth causes us to remember, rather than forget, the fact that Jove's rule, like Henry VII's, was brought about only by faction and bloodshed; and to remember, rather than forget, that the placid cycles of seasonal recurrence paraded in *Mutabilitie* were brought about only by Jove's thunderbolt. Teskey describes the thunderbolt's trajectory as the "least allegorical" moment of the myth: "it unmasks the foundation of world order in an absolute violence the forgetting of which *is* that foundation." Allegory's violent begetting, so easily passed over in *Mutabilitie*'s lovely pageant of times, is laid much more bare in Book 5's stark poetic reformation into historical allegory, which can be put into motion only by the "dreadfull sight" of Radigund's headless corpse.

No wonder, then, that *Mutabilitie*'s last stanzas admit a powerfully subversive reading. Most readers hear the narrator's declaration that Mutabilitie's argument "makes me loath this state of life so tickle,/And loue of things so vaine to cast away" as reaching toward the transcendence that allegory seems to offer. But Berger has given us an alternate cast to these lines that resists the allegorical temper: "I am loath to cast away this state of life and this love of things." The compounding in *Mutabilitie*'s final lines of *Sabbath* and *Sabaoth*—of peaceful rest and armed hosts—gives us reason to refuse what Susanne Wofford has called "figurative compulsion" in the poem, to evade allegorical conclusions for the "vain and tickle" present. Elizabeth Bellamy has pointed out that the prayer in these lines to "that great Sabbaoth God" disfigures Elizabeth's own name (Eli-sabbath, God's rest). That truncation, I would add, in turn enforces the "trunk-ation" of queens—Radigund's beheading, Britomart's abandonment—as the principle behind Mutabilitie's downfall and hence behind eternal rest. But if apocalyptic allegorical conclusions require the grim armed forces that brought about Book 5's historic ends, then the final downstroke of that "Sabbaoth God" to whom the narrator prays might show us that we have shaken off the powerful embrace of *The Faerie Queene*'s last seductive queen only to lie down with Talus, Artegall's right-hand iron man.

Source: Katherine Eggert, "'Changing all that forme of common weale': Genre and the Repeal of Queenship in *The Faerie Queen*, Book 5," in *English Literary Renaissance,* Vol. 26, No. 2, Spring, 1996, pp. 259–90.

Kathleen Williams

Author Kathleen Williams discusses the use of symbolism to create unity throughout the seven books of The Faerie Queene *in her essay.*

To give unity to so complex a poem as *The Faerie Queene* would seem a formidable task, and it was a task which Spenser left unfinished. Our loss, in the six unwritten books, is great; and all the greater because of the cumulative method by which the poem's meaning is revealed. The later books enrich the content of those which have gone before, so that from the first book to the fragmentary seventh the reader becomes increasingly aware of a clear and comprehensive vision, and of a steady purpose which impels him, through a mass of significant detail, towards a final unity.

That unity, at the court of Glory herself, was never reached, and without the unwritten books our appreciation of those we have must be incomplete. But even as it stands, half-finished and culminating in the fragment of the presumed seventh book, the poem is a unified whole. For the kind of unity which Spenser achieves, though cumulative, is not architectural; he works not by adding section to section so that the structure is meaningless until it is finished, but by revealing new levels of a structure which we thought complete at our first sight of it. Faeryland is only partially revealed, but it is unified and consistent as far as we know it, though if the poem had been completed it would be seen as only part of a greater unity and a fuller truth. The first book of *The Faerie Queene* has a simplicity which is proper both to its theme and to the plan of the poem; Spenser begins at the centre of his universe, with the proper conduct of man in relation to God, and the link which still exists between the world of mortality and the realm of eternal truth. Book II. shows, almost as simply, the control which is a necessary part of the good life. Themes so essential must be firmly and directly established, but in later books the concern is less exclusively with man, and the natural world too plays its part. Around the centre other and related themes appear, making a richer and more complex whole.

Yet Spenser's method is not a matter only of decorum or deliberate choice. As with any great poet writing seriously about the nature of man and of the universe, his method arises directly out of his vision. An eighteenth century poet, like Pope, will find it natural to write in contrasts, extremes whose balance will produce a truth more central than either. Spenser too sometimes uses a set framework of the Aristotelian mean and its two corresponding extremes, and finds it on occasion a useful piece of machinery; but it is not, as with Pope, his most natural way of seeing things. The living world of *The Faerie Queene* is not one of contrast and balance, but of analogy and parallel, with many kinds of life each complete in itself yet only fully comprehended when seen in relation to the rest. The full poetic effect cannot be contained in Spenser's own statement to Raleigh, "The generall end therefore of all the book is to fashion a gentleman or noble person in vertuous and gentle discipline." Man holds a place of prime importance in Spenser's vision of the world, but the conduct proper to mankind cannot be divined by looking at man alone. The other planes of existence must be comprehended too. So Spenser's is not a simple allegorical world of black and white, concerned only with the "twelve morall vertues as Aristotle hath devised." There are degrees and kinds of goodness, and these can be seen only when all the parallels are drawn, all the analogies completed. Allegory may present an

ideal of moral or political conduct, but beyond a
certain point the reader must, to apprehend all of
Spenser's vision, yield to the deepening effect of the
poem as a whole. The Aristotelian framework and
the allegory of the virtues, the vices, the parts of the
mind, form a pattern; one may fit together into
a satisfying unity the various kinds of chastity
as shown in Belphoebe, Britomart, Amoret, and
Florimell. But there is another and more organic
pattern, resulting from the inevitable ordering of the
material in accordance with Spenser's way of seeing the world, and developing from book to book to
a temporary culmination in the Cantos of Mutability. In this pattern, the shape of the poem is part of its
meaning, while characters like Belphoebe and
Florimell are symbols which release certain aspects
of Spenser's apprehension of life, and cast about
them "shadows of an indefinable wisdom."

Much of the significance of *The Faerie Queene*
is conveyed in the correspondences and parallels
which are gradually established throughout the poem,
and of course in the choice of symbol; and in both it
is the Platonic rather than the Aristotelian influence
on Spenser's mind which is most noticeable. For a
poet so much in tune with Neoplatonism it is natural
to express not personal reactions only but an interpretation of the universe by means of symbol. "All
things that are above are here below also," and
material things which more or less embody the
Ideas are themselves already latent symbols of those
Ideas. Spenser is always conscious of things as
deriving from, and partially embodying, their heavenly counterparts, and as bound together by their
common derivation, their common if varying possession of ideal truth. Chastity lives in heaven, but is
embodied and displayed in each chaste woman.
Shamefastness exists as the fountain of Guyon's
modesty, and is not a mere abstraction formed by
generalising the modesty of many individuals, as so
often in the personifications of later ages. Courtesy,
like all virtues, grows on Parnassus, but its "heavenly seedes" were planted on earth, while as a copy
among men of this heavenly process the Queen is an
ocean of courtesy, from whom all virtues proceed to
those who surround her, and to whom they return as
rivers to the sea.

Such an outlook enables the poet to see about
him a multiple unity which is embodied in the
development of his poem. There is no division
between literal and symbolic truth, for things exist
in an order of precedence which is valid in itself, but
they have at the same time a symbolic validity as
imperfect copies of the world of spirit from which

they take their source. In *The Faerie Queene* events
are never merely events; they partially show forth
something beyond themselves. Spenser's battles, it
has often been remarked, have less variety of incident and less actuality than Ariosto's or Tasso's, but
Spenser is interested in something else. Tasso's
Dudon strives three times to raise himself before he
dies, and there is a gain in suspense and dramatic
climax, but when Red Crosse falls three times to rise
again during his fight with the dragon Spenser is
concerned less with the dramatic effect of the particular event than with the greater struggle of which
it is a shadow. The four-fold repetition of "So
downe he fell," at the death of the dragon is again
not only dramatic, it is a solemn ritual repetition
meant to emphasize not the size of a dragon but the
terror of sin even at the moment of its defeat:

The knight himselfe even trembled at his fall.
Symbol and allegory, often difficult to separate, are
especially so in Spenser's case, for he often uses the
same figure now as part of a moral or political
allegory, now as a symbol of an indefinable truth.
His characters move freely from one plane to another, or exist simultaneously on more planes than
one, and that existence is at once both a means of
unifying the poem and a symbol of the multiple
unity of the world which—among other things—the
poem expresses.

Occasionally Spenser makes use of incidents or
figures which might support the definition of allegory quoted by W. B. Yeats: "Symbolism said
things which could not be said so perfectly in any
other way, and needed but a right instinct for its
understanding, while Allegory said things which
could be said as well, or better, in another way, and
needed a right knowledge for its understanding."
The giant of false justice, in Canto II, of Book V, is
such a contrived and limited figure, fitting one
occasion, but not suggesting others. But the Giant,
and those like him, serve to throw into relief the far
greater number of creatures in *The Faerie Queene*
who, like Wordsworth's monumental shepherds
and travellers, hint at the terrible greatness of the
events of this world. Nothing exists in isolation, but
draws with it an immense but controlled suggestion
of other occasions which are yet the same. Another
of the figures of Book V, the deceitful Malengin
who harries Mercilla's kingdom, may refer to the
guerilla warfare and treacherous behaviour of the
Irish, but this falsity is a part of, and a symbol of, all
deceit. The chase and the traditional beast transformations suggest the old menace of the covens, and
even the primal deceit of the devil; for Malengin is

killed as he changes into a snake, and his dwelling goes down to hell.

Malengin is one of the representatives of that evil which devil and man have brought into the world, and evil is shown here, as so often in Spenser, as deceit. Like the giant Orgoglio, who vanishes when Prince Arthur kills him, it is based upon nothingness, upon a false view of things. It tries to break the unity and shatter the truth of the universe, but it is doomed to defeat, for "Truth is One in All," and against that solid truth, present in some degree throughout the created world, evil can have no lasting force. It is seen as an alien intruder into the world of reality, and is embodied in the evil spirits which are used to make the false images of Una and Florimell, or in the devilish Malengin, Despair, and Archimago. To the clear sight of complete virtue it is irrelevant, but to a lesser goodness it is formidable indeed, for it is part of man's inheritance, making impossible for him the innocence of the natural world, and present in man alone. Nature may be involved in the fall and the suffering of man, but not through its own fault. It is only through the presence of a fallen angel that the snow which makes the false Florimell is corrupted.

The world of *The Faerie Queene* is one in which the values of Neoplatonism and of Christianity are familiarly blended, and of course it is very far from being peculiar to Spenser; but it is expressed in his poetry with a particular vitality. What other poets must show in the flash of an image, Spenser develops through the six Books of *The Faerie Queene* into a living and consistent universe. Through the growing pattern of the poem can be traced levels of being which extend from pure intelligences to inanimate nature, distinct but related by their common reference to the guiding and informing spirit which gives unity and order to a multiple world. It is not a dual world of pointless change contrasting with eternal changelessness; the changing world derives from, and returns to, unity, and each of its levels is good in its degree, being a reflection of the eternal. In ascending scale, created things are more beautiful because more pure—clearer manifestations of the spirit which informs them;

> Still as everything doth upward tend,
> And further is from earth, so still more cleare
> And faire it growes, till to his perfect end
> Of purest beautie, it at last ascend.

But though distance from the home of pure spirit, and involvement in matter, must lessen the purity and beauty of the creatures at certain levels,

all have their beauty and in Spenser's symbolism their goodness. All

> are made with wondrous wise respect,
> And all with admirable beautie deckt,

and in no part of Spenser's universe is the hand of God absent. His providence sustains and guides even the apparently lawless world of the beasts and the apparently aimless world of inanimate nature, but in this orderly universe springing from and guided by God the disruptive and unruly element is man. Spenser writes in Book V of the

> impotent desire of men to raine,
> Whom neither dread of God, that devils bindes,
> Nor lawes of men, that common weales containe,
> Nor bands of nature, that wilde beastes restraine,
> Can keepe from outrage, and from doing wrong.

Other created things are restrained by the laws proper to their being, and when Spenser considers evil the emphasis is, here as in An Hymne of Heavenly Love, on the sin of man, rather than on any sinfulness inherent in the whole material world. Our "sinfull mire," in which we endure fleshly corruption and mortal pain, is part of the inherited frailty of fallen humanity.

> We all are subject to that curse,
> And death in stead of life have sucked from
>   our Nurse.

Amavia, telling Sir Guyon the story of her husband's submission to Acrasia, accepts it as part of the weakness of man when faced by temptation through fleshly lusts:

> For he was flesh: (all flesh doth frailtie breed).

The same emphasis appears in the myth of Chrysogone and her two children. In the world of humanity, conception is involved in the "loathly crime" of the fall; but Chrysogone conceives in all the lustless innocence of the natural world, without sin and without pain:

> Unwares she them conceived, unwares she bore:
> She bore withouten paine, that she conceived
> Withouten pleasure.

Her children are born of sunshine and moisture, sharing the purity which characterises all the natural world when uncontaminated by the inherited sin of human flesh. Belphoebe is

> Pure and unspotted from all loathly crime,
> That is ingenerate in fleshly slime,

but Amoret too shares in the innocent birth, and the fruitful Garden of Adonis in which she is reared is presumably as much a symbol of primal innocence as are the cool chaste forests through which Belphoebe ranges.

The innocence and even holiness of nature, when considered without reference to the contamination of sin in the case of humanity, is one of the most noticeable features of Spenser's world, but there is nothing of that sentimental idealisation of the "natural" to which a later age was to fall victim. Spenser's clear vision of the ascending planes of existence prevents any loss of proportion, any concentration on a part of life to the detriment of the rest. The satyrs of Book I are innocent and, in their degree, good. Only the sacredness of the old religious rites is shown in their worship of Una, and they are an instrument of "eternall Providence exceeding thought," an example, like the noble lion of natural law who is killed by Sansloy, of the guidance of God even in the non-human world. But this is not the whole truth about the satyrs, for there is a parallel picture in Canto 10 of Book III, where Hellenore, garlanded like Una, is escorted by a similar band of dancing satyrs. Here the word used is not, as in Una's case, "queen," but "Maylady," and in the scenes which follow the license of the old nature cults, which the word suggests, is fully revealed. The satyrs have not changed; they are still charming, innocent, a "lovely fellowship," but Spenser is looking at them from a different point of view, and drawing an exact parallel with Una's story to make clear both the likeness and the difference in their good and our own. Hellenore is capable, as a human being, of a higher and more conscious goodness than that of the innocent brute world, and in entering that world she misuses it just as, with Paridell, she had misused the natural goodness and the sacred symbolism of wine.

There are many of these lesser planes in *The Faerie Queene*, and Spenser shows them in themselves and in relation to man. In forests and above all in the sea, we are shown kinds of being which, good in themselves, are not proper to mankind. The seas and forests are unknown, lacking by human standards in morality and in spirit. They can contain creatures of non-human goodness, like Belphoebe, but those who go there from man's world—Hellenore, the forester who pursues Florimell, the fisherman who attacks her—become brutalised. But nature, even at its most remote from man, has its share of the spirit which is the meaning of Spenser's world. The mutable is not necessarily the meaningless, but can "work its own perfection so by fate." What is meaningless and dead is the work of sin, of pride and distorted values, the places of Mammon or of Malecasta, where the lifeless glitter of gold and jewels is shown up in all its emptiness by the sudden reference to the stars in their order, reflections of mind and symbols of the steady life of the spirit,

> th' eternall lampes, wherewith high Jove
> Doth light the lower world.

It is, then, a universe with varying degrees of good, and evil which is a distortion, or sometimes a subtly distorted copy, of the good: the unnaturalness of Argante, Ollyphant, and the "damned souls" who capture Serena, or the magic and deceit of Acrasia, Duessa, and the false Florimell; and it is revealed partly by the gradual accumulation of correspondences between one kind of life and another. There are parallels between Una and Hellenore, Mercilla and Lucifera, the Garden of Adonis and the Bower of Bliss, Cleopolis and the New Jerusalem, the veiled Venus of Book IV, and the goddess Nature of Book VII. The virtues are seen, more and more, as various aspects of the same heavenly good, embodied in different ways in different kinds of life. "Truth is one in All," or to put it in another way,

> O goodly golden chaine, wherewith yfere
> The vertues linked are in lovely wize.

It is not a matter only of interlinked stories or of characters overlapping from one book into another. It is a linking, by symbol and allegory, of Justice with Constancy, Love with Courtesy; a deepening of content by reference to earlier themes so that nothing is lost, and so that certain passages, pre-eminently the Mutability Cantos, can call up by the briefest of references the more detailed treatment of earlier books, drawing all their diversity into unity.

One of the most far reaching of Spenser's series of inter-linked and expanding symbols is that of Florimell and Marinell, which stretches through three books and embraces many meanings and many characters. In the moral allegory, it is a story which displays Spenser's knowledge of humanity, and of the various temptations to which different natures will be subject. Florimell is one kind of chastity, the kind which maintains itself not by the awe which Belphoebe and Britomart inspire, but by fear and flight. Her temptation is not, like Amoret's, passion, but a timorous softness and gratitude. She escapes from her brutal pursuers by instinctive flight, but is disarmed by the protective kindness of Proteus, to be imprisoned by him as Amoret is imprisoned by Busyrane. On the same level of moral allegory, Marinell's is the nature which refuses to commit itself, and lives remote and self-sufficient, fearing the harm which may come to its own completeness by contact with others. But they are, both of them, more than this, for they play an important part in the network of symbol. Both seem to be creatures of the natural world which stands apart from the life of men but which yet, such is the unity of things, has its relevance to that life as it has to the life of pure spirit. The sea which is so intimate a part of their story is the remotest of all things from man, home of hydras and "sea-shouldring whales," and yet it is the most perfect of all symbols for the whole multiple, changing, but unified world, "eterne in mutabilitie." The sea can symbolize the character and meaning of the universe and so embodies a truth beyond itself, but it stands also, in its own right, for nature at its least formed and most nearly chaotic. It can show the thoughtless, blameless cruelty of nature, its blind suffering, and also the justice which works through it as through all creation. Such meanings play through the story of Marinell and Florimell, and the other stories which surround it, drawing even the Fifth Book, in which the justification of one man and one policy plays so large a part, into the scheme of the whole.

We meet first Florimell, "beautie excellent" and of a kind which delights the world,

> For none alive but joy'd in Florimell,

but apparently of a lesser order of being than that to which the great champions of virtue belong. Britomart, usually so prompt to relieve distress, refuses to join in the pursuit of Florimell, and she is clearly right. Britomart's

> constant mind,
> Would not so lightly follow beauties chace.

She remains faithful to her search for Justice and noble deeds, one aspect of that quest for ideal goodness to which her companions also, Guyon, Arthur, and Arthur's squire Timias, are in their various ways committed. In abandoning their quest, these others are leaving their proper sphere of spiritual endeavour, constancy to an unchanging truth, to pursue the fleeting charm of a mutable world. As a result, even the steadfast Prince Arthur finds himself at the mercy of passing events and emotions, and is perceptibly a lesser figure during this period of pursuit. Forgetting for the moment his vision of Gloriana, the true object of his quest, he gives way to confused fancies, wishing that Florimell were the Faerie Queene:

> And thousand fancies bet his idle braine
> With their light wings, the sights of
>   semblants vaine:
> Oft did he wish, that Lady faire mote bee
> His Faery Queene, for whom he did complaine:
> Or that his Faery Queene were such, as shee:
> And ever hastie Night he blamed bitterlie.

After a night of sleepless irritation, Magnificence itself becomes almost petulant:

> So forth he went,
> With heavie looke and lumpish pace, that plaine
> In him bewraid great grudge and maltalent.

Florimell's innocent beauty is too nearly empty of meaning for man to be other than harmful to high endeavour. She has little understanding of what is happening to her, but flies instinctively and suffers blindly, with the infinite uncomprehending pathos of nature. She has no place with the knights and ladies who represent human virtues but encounters, rather, creatures of nature like Satyrane and Proteus, and brutalized human beings who try to make use of her for their own ends. Yet this pathetic, fugitive creature, embodiment of transitory beauty, has her own element of constancy; her desire for union with Marinell, who is born of the sea, symbol of the source and home of all changing things. Her long flight and her suffering begin and end in her love for Marinell, and her story has its meaning, though to the world of men, of Arthur and of Britomart, it may seem to have none. Florimell's story is a parallel to that of Amoret, and their fates are compared at the beginning of Book IV, while Amoret alone can wear the girdle Florimell has lost. Both are held captive, and the tapestries portraying Jove's metamorphoses in the House of Busyrane are an echo and reminder of the transformations which Proteus undergoes earlier in the same book in his attempts to win Florimell.

It may be that in trying to define the meaning of such myths as these one can only rob them of their power. "Symbols are the only things free enough from all bonds to speak of perfection," and to limit them to a definable meaning is to bind them. Yet one may perhaps suggest, if only as one possible meaning among the many meanings which Spenser's myths contain, that Florimell is the prototype, in the world of inanimate nature, of the steadfast womanliness of Amoret. Both are saved by truth to the nobler and more constant elements of their own being, for Amoret overcomes enslavement to physical passion by the power of chaste and enduring love, while through her love for Marinell Florimell escapes from the mutable Proteus and so finds safety and the unchanging peace at the heart of a changing world. The two may be remote from one another, but they embody the same truth: that escape from bondage to what is fleeting and inessential can be achieved by a steadfast attention to eternal values, and that so we may work our own perfection. Man and nature both, apparently bound by the physical, subject to chance and change, have none the less their share in lasting truth. So Florimell's world and Marinell's can shadow the things above them, just as Cymoent's bower of hollow waves imitates the home of the gods, being vaulted

> like to the sky
> In which the Gods do dwell eternally.

Contemplating their life, we may "in those weaker glories spy Some shadows of eternity."

But it is a blind and innocent life, striving only for survival and self-protection through avoidance of danger, and unable to comprehend the decrees of fate and justice which work through it. Cymoent and Proteus have only faint inklings of the true meaning of the prophecy which Proteus himself makes. Yet justice works even by means of that blindness, and the sea, which is its instrument in ending the troubles of Florimell, forms a background still to the adventures of Artegall in Book V. Artegall himself enters the story of Florimell and Marinell when he deals justice at their wedding in the affair of the false Florimell, and the Book of Justice draws together some of the themes of earlier books. The Proem is another version of the theme which appears in so many guises in *The Faerie Queene,* and is hinted at in Florimell's story; that of change and constancy. Mutability in the natural world is paralleled by inconstancy and a lack of proper values in man, but beyond this instability Justice, the "most sacred vertue," lives unchanged,

> Resembling God in his imperiall might.

Artegall's reply to the giant in Canto II continues the theme, with its echoes of the Garden of Adonis and of Concord who holds the parts of the universe together

> As their Almightie Maker first ordained.

Concord persists even through the hostility of the world, and Providence works through apparent change and loss in the interests of a wider justice.

> What though the sea with waves continuall
> Doe eate the earth, it is no more at all:
> Ne is the earth the lesse, or loseth ought,
> For whatsoever from one place doth fall,
> Is with the tide unto an other brought:
> For there is nothing lost, that may be found, if sought.
> Likewise the earth is not augmented more,
> By all that dying into it doe fade.
> For of the earth they formed were of yore,
> How ever gay their blossome or their blade
> Doe flourish now, they into dust shall vade.
> What wrong then is it, if that when they die,
> They turne to that, whereof they first were made?
> All in the powre of their great Maker lie;

All creatures must obey the voice of the most hie.

The giant's notion of justice is presented as false not only in the case of human institutions but in relation to the whole of the created world, and it is the sea, symbol of ultimate unity and of the justice present in all things, which swallows the giant and all his works. The "mighty sea" is again the instrument of Providence in the episode of Amidas and Bracidas, for its "imperiall might" is a manifestation of the power which disposes of things justly for nature and man alike.

Spenser's interlinked themes are now so well established that in Book VI he is able to add to his symbols, but here too he writes much of nature, and of the exchanges of courtesy proper to it, for the charm of courtesy in man has its counterpart in the poetry of a pastoral world. Florimell has her place here too, for she was reared by the Graces on that same Acidalian mount on which they appear to Colin, where nature is at its loveliest and most fruitful, the heightened but still truthful nature of poetry. Spenser indicates the importance of the passage by his almost reverent preparation for it; and part of its importance may lie in the impression it gives of the order and unity of things as they appear to the shaping mind of the poet. The double circle of the dancing ladies moves, to Colin's piping, around his "countrey lasse," poetic symbol of all grace and virtue, while the imagery suggests earlier, related themes. The treatment of nature contrasts with that of the Bower of Bliss, the bridal imagery of Ariadne is a reminder of the Garden of Adonis and the Temple of Venus, and Florimell, child of the Graces, is also part of this ceremonious world of love, poetry, and natural grace. The passage is almost a copy in little of the widening circles of the poem and its meaning.

But the latest and fullest of such unifying passages as these is to be found in the fragment *Of Mutability*, a more explicit statement of the great theme which earlier books express chiefly by symbol and by arrangement of material. These two cantos, and the two final stanzas, are the culmination of the poem as it now stands, both unifying and illuminating it. Spenser's description of Nature, and Mutability's address to her, show her as the source— or rather as nearest to that source which man may know—of the conceptions in other books. She embodies Justice and Concord, she is veiled like Venus, and by her likeness to the transfigured Christ she suggests the Holiness of Book I. Mutability, on the other hand, is Corruption, sin, or the consequences of sin as seen in our world:

For she the face of earthly things so changed,
That all which nature had establish first
In good estate, and in meet order ranged,
She did pervert, and all their statutes burst:
And all the worlds faire frame (which
        none yet durst
Of Gods or men to alter or misguide)
She alter'd quite, and made them all accurst
That God had blest; and did at first provide
In that still happy state for ever to abide.

She is of mortal race, for it is this which saves her from the anger of Jove, and it is she who

death for life exchanged foolishlie;
Since which, all living wights have learned to die.

In her pride she has distorted what God had left in good order, has broken the laws of nature, justice, and policy, and has brought death into the world. She is a composite creature, for in her beauty can be seen the charm of Florimell's world of innocent partakers in the sorrows of man, but in her too is the guilt of man himself. The story of Faunus and Molanna is a pathetic and absurd parallel to the high seriousness of Mutability's trial and its theme of the effects of sin upon the world. Through the stupid presumption of Faunus the sacred Arlo hill, once the haunt of Diana and the setting chosen for Nature's court, becomes a place of desolation.

The issue of the trial is made clear. Mutability's claim to rule over the earth is allowed, but Jove retains his sway over "Heaven's empire," and is "confirm'd in his imperiall see." Indeed, once the realm of earth is left behind, and the higher places of the Universe are approached, Mutability's arguments lose much of their force. Her struggle with Cynthia in the sphere of the moon, traditionally the border of the regions of decay, is left unresolved, and her answer to Jove's claim that the gods control time and change is hardly conclusive. She begins with a flat denial:

What we see not, who shall us perswade?

and continues with a description of the changes of the moon and the motions of the planets which Nature has no difficulty in answering. The moon may have its phases, and the spheres move, but they return again to themselves.

They are not changed from their first estate,

for time and change are, as Jove has claimed, part of God's plan. But Nature's reply presumably deals with the whole of Mutability's case, including her claim to earth, and one may suppose that even there, where through sin and death she does now rule, the guidance of Providence is not absent. Even

there things "by their change their being doe dilate," and are being led to

that same time when no more Change shall be,
But stedfast rest of all things, firmely stay'd
Upon the pillours of Eternity.

On earth, the calm and orderly process through which the universe works it own perfection has been disrupted by sin, and is more difficult to perceive; but heaven can make use even of the disasters which sin has brought, and will at last bring the earth "to itselfe again," resolving change and death in eternal rest.

It is the world through which all the characters of *The Faerie Queene* can be seen to move, a world in which the linked orders of created things range from the least conscious and least spiritual upwards to the ranked angels

Singing before th' eternall majesty,
In their trinall triplicities on hye,

and in which God has ordained for each creature a steady movement towards its own perfection. Even in the life of man and of the hapless creatures which share in his fall, the remnant of this joyous order may still be seen in the justice and love which Spenser shows us at work in so many spheres and embodies in myth and symbol. Even now, if he is steadfast in devotion to truth, man may experience directly some part of the glory of eternity. Red Crosse, his quest over, delights in the company of Una,

Yet swimming in that sea of blisful joy,

and hears for a moment the songs of the angels themselves. All the virtues have their home in that Sabaoth, and on earth they are all—Holiness, Chastity, Temperance—made manifest by a constant attention to the unchanging truth. It is this proper movement of all the richness of created things towards the unity which produced them and works through them that the poem expresses, and by one of the fortunate chances of poetry it ends, as we have it, with the two great stanzas which sum up the Spenserian universe:

For, all that moveth, doth in Change delight:
But thence-forth all shall rest eternally
With Him that is the God of Sabbaoth hight:
0 that great Sabbaoth God, grant me that
        Sabaoths sight.

At the end of the poem, "the total life has suddenly displayed its source."

Source: Kathleen Williams, "'Eterne in Mutabilite': The Unified World of *The Faerie Queene*," in *ELH,* Vol. 19, No. 2, June, 1952, pp. 115–130.

SOURCES

Frye, Northrop, "The Structure of Imagery in *The Faerie Queene*," in *Edmund Spenser's Poetry*, edited by Hugh McClean, W. W. Norton, 1968, pp. 582–593.

Hough, Graham, "The Structure of *The Faerie Queene*," in *Edmund Spenser's Poetry*, edited by Hugh McClean, W. W. Norton, 1968, pp. 575–582.

Sidney, Philip, *The Defence of Poesy*, in *The Norton Anthology of English Literature*, Vol. I., 6th edition, edited by M. H. Abrams, W. W. Norton, 1993, pp. 480–500.

Spenser, Edmund, "A Letter of the Authors in *The Norton Anthology of English Literature*, Vol. I., 6th edition, edited by M. H. Abrams, W. W. Norton, pp. 516–519, 1993.

FURTHER READING

Berger, Harry Jr., *Revisionary Play: Studies in the Spenserian Dynamics*, University of California Press, 1988.
 Berger's book contains essays that he has written on Spenser's work. The essays span nearly twenty-five years of study of Spenser's poems and exam his work from several critical vantages.

Cavanagh, Sheila T., "Nightmares of Desire: Evil Women in *The Faerie Queene*," in *Studies in Philology*, Vol. 91, No. 3, Summer, 1994, pp. 313–338.
 Cavanagh examines the way women function in Spenser's epic, arguing that the dreams and visions of men suggest that women are dangerous.

Ferry, Anne, *The Art of Naming*, University of Chicago Press, 1988.
 Ferry's book is a rhetorical study of the language in Spenser's epic. Ferry makes connections between grammar and repetitions, etc., and then makes further connections to historical interpretations.

Fitzpatrick, Joan, "Spenser's Nationalistic Images of Beauty," in *Cahiers Elizabethains: Late Medieval and Renaissance Studies*, No. 53, April, 1998, pp. 13–26.
 Fitzpatrick examines Book I of Spenser's epic for representations of Irish Catholics in the demonic characters. Fitzpatrick argues that Spenser's demonization of the Irish appears in other Spenser work as well.

Frye, Susan, *Elizabeth I: The Competition for Representation*, Oxford University Press, 1996.
 Frye uses three separate episodes from Elizabeth's reign to explore her struggle for power. A significant portion of this text focuses on the queen's response to Spenser's epic.

Heninger, S. K. Jr., "Orgoglio," in *Edmund Spenser's Poetry*, edited by Hugh McClean, W. W. Norton, 1968, pp. 593–602.
 Heninger uses the giant, Orgoglio, as an example of Spenser's intention to conflate morality and history. Heninger maintains that Spenser uses classical mythology, the Book of Revelations, and recent politics in the Orgoglio episode to explore the connections between morality and history.

Summers, David A., *Spenser's Arthur: The British Arthurian Tradition and 'The Faerie Queene,'* University Press of America, 1997.
 Summers traces the history of the Arthurian legend through literature and examines its impact on British society.

Villeponteaux, Mary, "'Not as Women wonted to be' Spenser's Amazon Queen," in *Dissing Elizabeth: Negative Representations of Gloriana*, edited by Julia M. Walker, Duke University Press, 1998.
 Villeponteaux examines the representation of Elizabeth in the Amazon queen, Radigund.

Williams, Kathleen, "Spenser and Medieval Romance," in *Edmund Spenser's Poetry*, edited by Hugh McClean, W. W. Norton, 1968, pp. 555–563.
 Williams discusses the use of myth in Spenser's epic and argues that Spenser took old myths and made them contemporaneous with Elizabethan life.

Gerusalemme Liberata

TORQUATO TASSO

1581

When Torquato Tasso's *Gerusalemme Liberata* first appeared in a pirated edition in 1579, it was hailed as a great, albeit slightly flawed, art epic in the tradition of Dante and Virgil. Tasso, himself, was angry that the poem had appeared in print without his permission, especially since the manuscript had received some harsh criticism from its first readers. By the time the poem was printed in an authorized version, in 1581, its reputation as an uplifting, patriotic, influential, and brilliant examination of Christian Europe's heroic past was already established. Fellow Italians and other Europeans celebrated the poem's meaning and message. The English poets, especially those writing in the 1650s-1680s, were heavily influenced by Tasso's skill as a poet and word-crafter. Edmund Spencer and John Milton both credited Tasso's poem as an inspiration to their own epic poems, while literary critics such as John Dryden, Anne Dancier, and William Hayley all praised the work as the best modern epic poem before *Paradise Lost*. Although his poem achieved great success, Tasso either did not believe the praise or did not like the moral looseness of his characters. By 1591, he had drastically re-written the poem, eliminated all of the romance, magical, and adventure elements leaving only a moralistic and religious core. Tasso liked the finished product, but no one else did. Although few people read epic/heroic poetry for pleasure anymore, *Gerusalemme Liberata* continues to be one of the most important and influential works from the late Italian Renaissance.

AUTHOR BIOGRAPHY

Torquato Tasso, long regarded as the last great poet of the Italian Renaissance, was born in Sorrento, Italy on March 11, 1544. His father, also an epic poet, had political problems and was forced to move frequently; Tasso's mother died mysteriously when he was just twelve years old. Tasso, like most other poets of his time, sought patrons from among the wealthy aristocrats and churchmen that littered the Italian landscape. Tasso started the poem that would become *Gerusalemme Liberata* when he was sixteen and continued working on the poem until 1593. Most critics agree that all three of his major poems, *Rinaldo* (1562), *Gerusalemme Liberata (Jerusalem Delivered)* (1581), and *Gerusalemme Conquistata*, are essentially the same poem with different foci that mirror Tasso's emotional state at the time of each publication.

Rinaldo is an epic romance dealing with a young man in the spring of life. At the time, Tasso was enjoying some poetic success and working for Luigi, the Cardinal d'Este. His courtly love poetry addressed to the Cardinal's sisters, Lucrezia and Leonora d'Este, won him considerable praise. According to his letters, this was the happiest time of his life.

Heavily influenced by Ludovico Ariosto's *Orlando Furioso* and Matteomaria Bioardo's *Orlando Innamorato*, Tasso set out to write an epic poem that joined the adventure, magic, and intrigue of those works with the heroic, moral, and religious ideals of Dante's *Divine Comedy* and Virgil's *Aeneid*. Between 1562 and 1575, Tasso worked on *Gerusalemme Liberata* while living with Duke Alfonso II. This period of his life was a painful one. Tasso began displaying a mental disorder that drove him to paranoid delusions and to see conspiracies all around him. He had given his poem to several friends for comment and constructive criticism, but was stung by their harsh treatment of his masterpiece, and his grip on reality spun out of control. His behavior became so erratic that the duke was forced to imprison Tasso in a mental institution for seven years. While he kept in contact with the outside world, and even published his prose treaties on epic and heroic poetry, Tasso never really regained his sanity. Duke Alfonso did release Tasso in 1586, but he did not recover.

Tasso roamed Italy for the next nine years, never securing a stable patron or quieting the demons inside his mind. He rewrote *Gerusalemme*

Torquato Tasso

Liberata, removing all of the romance, intrigue, and chivalric elements, in order to reinforce the moral duty of Christians in an unchristian world. *Gerusalemme Conquistata* was published in 1593 much to Tasso's delight, but to his supporters' disappointment. His earlier works, especially *Gerusalemme Liberata* won him many admirers, but he no longer trusted anyone. In fact, Tasso's reputation was so respected and well-known that the pope named him the Poet Laureate for the Papal States in 1594. However, Tasso no longer cared for fame. On April 25, 1595, after a serious illness, Torquato Tasso died in the convent of Saint Onofrio in Rome. His work would go on to influence generations of poets, especially English poets like Edmund Spencer, John Milton, and Thomas Gray.

PLOT SUMMARY

Overview

Gerusalemme Liberata is, nominally, a poem about the First Crusade in the eleventh century CE. The First Crusade was ordered by Pope Urban II in 1094 as a way for European Christians to "liberate" Jerusalem from the Muslim Turks who had conquered the city several years earlier. The leader of the First Crusade was Godfrey of Bouillon (in modern-day Belgium) and he marched his multinational army across Europe, Asia Minor, and finally into the Middle East. He surrounded Jerusalem and eventually defeated the Turkish armies stationed there. He then set up the Latin Kingdom of Jerusalem so Christians could travel to the Holy Land without having to pay taxes. To the historical record, Tasso adds several knights, an enchantress, some Amazons, and a good deal of magic. The plot of the poem evolves around not only Godfrey's desire to capture the city, but also the love affairs of Clorinda, Tancred, and Erminia, and that of Armida and Rinaldo. The poem is divided into twenty cantos of varying lengths. Tasso suggests a four part structure in terms of the storyline.

Part I

The first section of *Gerusalemme Liberata* includes Cantos I, II, and III. Here, the groundwork for the developing plot surrounding the adventures of Godfrey and the various lovers is laid. Godfrey's campaign against the Turks is divinely inspired. God, much like the Greek and Roman gods in earlier epics did, selected Godfrey and told him to gather all the bravest Christian men together and to pick a leader. Godfrey's companions elect him leader and they all swear loyalty to him. Tasso uses this opportunity to introduce the major Christian characters, both historical and imagined. The army then sets out for the Holy Land. Their fame quickly precedes them and Aladine, the Turkish king, prepares for war. Tasso does mention the real reason for the Crusade in Stanza 84 when he suggests that Aladine eliminated the taxes on the Muslim population but kept them on the Christians.

Aladine, already described as a cruel king, decides to execute a couple of Christians, Sophronia and Olindo, because they have been accused by Ismen, a magician, of hiding the location of an idol that could destroy Godfrey's approaching army. Of course, they deny this and Aladine is going to execute them. They are saved by the arrival of Clorinda, a Persian Amazon warrior, who offers to lead the Muslim troops on the condition that Aladine spare the two lovers. He agrees to this arrangement.

Meanwhile, the Egyptian Muslims send ambassadors to Godfrey to find out what he wants. The Egyptians are bound by treaties to help Aladine and they want to avoid Godfrey's invasion altogether. However, Godfrey rejects their offer of peace and tells the ambassadors that as long as Jerusalem remains in the hands of "pagans," he will continue to fight. The ambassadors leave as Canto II closes.

Canto III finds the Christians at the walls of Jerusalem. Aladine brings in a refugee to identify the Christian knights. Erminia, niece of the dead king of Antioch, knows all of these knights since they were the ones who killed her uncle and destroyed her city. She points out each one, identifying the remaining characters. Clorinda proves her mettle as she leads the Muslims in the initial encounter. The Muslims win, a Christian knight named Dudon is killed, and the Christians lay siege. They set up their tents and start building the catapults, towers, battering rams, and other siege engines needed to destroy the city walls.

Part II

In the second group of cantos (IV–IX), the plot thickens, so to speak. Here, all kinds of problems get thrown in the Christians' way, most of them coming from Satan. Like most epics, the battles on earth are mirrored by battles on the cosmic scale. Here God is allowing Satan to torment and derail most of Godfrey's plans. In fact, Satan summons his fallen angels into a conference much like the one earlier in the poem. The result is an agreement to try to stop the Christians by any means necessary.

One of the most successful ways is through the use of sex. One of the devils devises a plan with Armida as the lynchpin. Armida is a beautiful enchantress who seeks out Godfrey's camp. She pretends to need his help, but in reality is trying to seduce as many of his men as possible. She is quite successful, especially after Godfrey refuses to help her.

Canto V muddies the waters even more. Rinaldo, one of Tasso's creations, is elected to replace the warrior killed earlier, but he is unpopular among some of the army. Rinaldo is the best fighter Godfrey has, yet Godfrey does not trust or believe him. The tension in the Christian camp is raised when Rinaldo kills Genrando for spreading lies about him. Rather than staying and explaining things to Godfrey, Rinaldo leaves. Meanwhile, Godfrey has allowed Armida to choose a few soldiers to help her get back home and they are chosen by lot. She departs taking her champions with her. Much to Godfrey's dismay, she has also "captured" a large number of other knights with her beauty and charm.

The problems in the Christian camp continue. Without Rinaldo, Godfrey cannot launch a full scale assault on the city and must settle for single combat. He does not have his greatest warrior, so he names Tancred as the Christian champion. Tancred is the second best warrior and he fights with the Muslim champion, Argantes. So well matched are they that their fight continues the entire day, ending only at night-fall. Both men are severely wounded and so the fight is a draw. However, the Muslim princess, Erminia, longs to nurse her beloved Tancred. She fell in love with him when he destroyed her city, Antioch. Unfortunately, she cannot go outside the city walls dressed as she is, so she borrows Clorinda's armor. Since no one would stop the leader of the Muslim army, Erminia is able to get outside the city walls. However, she is not a warrior and the guards recognize the armor and attack her, thinking she is Clorinda, who had killed one of the guards' fathers earlier. Erminia flees without ever seeing her beloved. Her appearance does help Tancred heal, though. He gets up from his sickbed because he thinks that the woman who came to him was his beloved, Clorinda. He had seen her in a dream much earlier in the poem and had fallen in love with her.

Canto VII, VIII, and IX follow several lines of the plot at once. Erminia gets away yet cannot get back to the city, and so ends up being taken in by some shepherds, while Tancred ends up being imprisoned in Armida's castle. Raymond then fights Argantes and almost wins. However, the demons fly in and disrupt the combat as a terrible storm drives the Christians back to their camp. Once they are back in their camp, they receive devastating news: their re-enforcements, Sven, Prince of Denmark, and his army, have been destroyed by Solyman. Solyman brutally murders Sven, who is a kinsman of Rinaldo and a survivor brings Sven's sword so that Rinaldo can take revenge. However, Rinaldo is no longer in the Christian camp. The news gets worse when news of Rinaldo's death reaches Godfrey's camp. Indeed, the entire Italian portion of the army threatens to pack up and go home. Godfrey is barely able to keep order. The only thing that prevents the entire disintegration of the Christian army is a nighttime raid by the Muslims. Solyman and Alecto attempt to destroy the Christians and they appear to be winning. However, God has had enough and forbids any further meddling by Satan and his demons. This breaks the spell Armida had put on the men who had followed her and they now return. Their return helps the Christians win the battle and Solyman flees back to the safety of Jerusalem.

Part III

The third part of *Gerusalemme Liberata* is the cantos that all the earlier action has been building up to. Here, Rinaldo and Godfrey are reconciled, the first assaults on the city are launched, the great battles are fought, and plans are laid.

Cantos X and XI deal with the plans for the first assault against Jerusalem. The Muslims plan their strategies inside, while the Crusaders celebrate mass and plan their attack. Godfrey is happy when he learns that Rinaldo is alive, and feels just a little justified when he finds out that Armida is an enchantress and not just some helpless maiden. The Crusaders attack Jerusalem at dawn and make a bloody day's work of it. Clorinda and Solyman lead the city's defenses and Tasso describes the fighting in heroic and chivalric terms. Godfrey is wounded and nightfall brings an end to the Christians' attack. The battle has proved to Clorinda that the siege machines that Godfrey built must be destroyed and, in Canto XII, she decides to burn them to the ground.

Before Clorinda can put her plan into action, she is told her earliest history. Instead of being born a Muslim, she was born a Christian and raised a Muslim. She finds this interesting, but it does not change her mind in anyway. She and a select few men steal out of the city and torch the wooden machines. On their way back to the city, Clorinda stops to kill a Christian soldier who has insulted her and so, gets locked out. She tries to blend in with the Christian troops, but she is recognized, not as herself, but as a Muslim. Tancred attacks her, not knowing who she is. He kills her and when he finds out who it is, he goes crazy with grief. Tancred does manage to baptize Clorinda before her death, but he is inconsolable. He even contemplates suicide, which was the only unforgivable sin for Renaissance Catholics, and is talked out of it by Peter the Hermit. The Muslims are now without a leader and Argantes swears revenge.

Cantos XIII and XIV deal with the reasons Godfrey reconciles with Rinaldo, while Cantos XV and XVI detail the trouble Godfrey goes through to get Rinaldo to come back. After Clorinda successfully burnt the siege machines, Ismen persuaded the devils and evil spirits to haunt the only nearby woods. Godfrey's people could not get rid of them. All of his heroes failed and finally, Godfrey had a dream. Peter the Hermit interpreted this dream as instructing Godfrey to send two men to find Rinaldo and bring him back. As much as Godfrey did not want to, he did what his advisor told him to do.

Charles and Ubaldo seek out Dame Fortune, who tells them about Christopher Columbus and directs them toward Armida's palace. After many hardships, they arrive and find Rinaldo. They convince him to come back with them and even Armida cannot get him to change his mind. Armida is a woman scorned; she destroys her palace and returns to Jerusalem angry and thirsty for vengeance.

Part IV

The last section of *Gerusalemme Liberata* deals with the final four cantos of the poem which describe the final assault on Jerusalem and record the deaths of all the major Muslim characters. Canto XVII sets the stage for the last battle. The Muslims are massing, including the armies of the King of Egypt, and backed by Armida and Emiren they march towards Jerusalem. Armida even offers to marry any man who brings her the severed head of Rinaldo. Meanwhile, Rinaldo arrives in the Holy Land and receives Sven's sword. He even takes a tongue lashing from several priests for abandoning his fellow Christians. The tension continues to mount as the attack proceeds. Rinaldo defeats the spirits in the woods and the Christians are able to build their machines again. Without Clorinda, the Muslims do not have a prayer. The Christians attack the city and claim control over parts of the walls. They slaughter the troops hiding in Solomon's temple and plant the Cross on the city walls. Canto XIX details a pitched battle within the city itself. All of the major characters are accounted for: Tancred kills Argantes, while Rinaldo and Godfrey pursue Solyman and Aladine from the Temple Mount to the Tower of David. The battle is suspended because Godfrey's spies have informed him of the approaching Egyptian troops. One of the spies, Vafrine, rescues Erminia and they find Tancred, almost dead, near Argantes's body. Erminia nurses Tancred in a portion of the city that the Christians control. After the crushing defeat of the Muslims in the following canto, Rinaldo and Armida declare their love for each other, she is baptized, and their engagement is announced.

Canto XX is the resounding crashing end to the battles and to the poem. The Egyptian and the Christian troops face each other and wreak great havoc on each other. Solyman attacks the Christians from the rear and kills a number of them. Tancred rallies the Christians and Solyman is killed by Rinaldo. Tancred and his group take the Tower of David and Aladine is killed. Godfrey pursues the Egyptian general and kills him as well. The battle is

over, the Christians have liberated Jerusalem. Godfrey hangs his weapons in Solomon's Temple.

CHARACTERS

Aladine

Aladine is the commander of the Saracen army in Jerusalem. His position mirrors Godfrey's in that he does not do that much fighting, leaving it to Clorinda, Solymon, and Argantes. He is killed by Tancred.

Argantes

Argantes is the Saracen second in command. He challenges the Christian knights to single combat and defeats most of them. He almost kills Tancred, which spells certain doom for the Christians. However, Tancred rises from his sickbed, rallies the Christians, kills Argantes, and saves the day.

Armida

She is the witch of the poem. Summoned by Satan to seduce and destroy Godfrey, Armida eventually seduces and captures over 30 knights including Rinaldo and Tancred. The majority of her captives escape or are rescued, but Rinaldo has fallen in love with her and she with him. On her island paradise in the Atlantic Ocean, Armida and Rinaldo spend much of the poem living in love. After Rinaldo is "rescued," Armida swears revenge, even offering a reward to any Saracen knight that brings her Rinaldo's head. After the battle, she realizes that Rinaldo still loves her and she accepts both her conversion to Christianity and his offer of marriage. Although Tasso is not exactly clear about her use of sexuality, most English translators suggest that while she uses her sexuality to kidnap men, she only consummates the act with Rinaldo, thus making her an acceptable wife for him.

Clorinda

Clorinda is the Princess of Damascus, an Amazon, and the most pivotal character in the poem. She is the leader of the Saracen attack forces and is a ruthless fighter. She is a brilliant military strategist as well as a tough woman. As long as she is alive, the Christians cannot hope to take Jerusalem. Several Christian heroes fall to Clorinda's sword, as well as most of their battle plans. She manages to destroy all of Godfrey's wooden siege equipment, which almost spells defeat for the Franks, and would have continued to reduce his army, but she is killed by the man who desperately loves her. Tancred does not realize that he has killed Clorinda until it is too late. He baptizes her as she lies dying and then loses his mind. Clorinda allows the baptism because she found out that she was born a Christian, but raised a Saracen. However, this knowledge does not change her dedication to the Turkish cause nor her loyalty to the Saracen king of Jerusalem. It is only after her death that Godfrey can gather his forces and defeat the Saracens.

Emiren

Emiren is the Saracen king of Jerusalem. He is killed by Godfrey.

Erminia

Erminia is the niece of the King of Antioch, who knows the Christian knights because they destroyed her city and killed her father and uncle before the poem opens. She tells the Saracen king who all the knights are in Canto II, thus introducing the characters to the readers. She is also desperately in love with Tancred. She watches his battles from the city walls and even tried to nurse him when he was wounded. She dresses in Clorinda's armor in order to sneak out of the city, but is recognized by the Christian guards and forced to flee without seeing Tancred. He follows her, but she escapes him. Their love affair is not resolved and her role as prize object or woman scorned is unclear.

Gildippe

She is the Christians' answer to Clorinda. Gildippe is a great Amazon warrior who, however, does not fight the Saracen Amazon, Clorinda. She is killed by Solymon.

Godfrey of Bouillon

Godfrey, modeled on the historical person, is one of the major characters in *Gerusalemme Liberata*. He is the French knight who is chosen by God and his fellow crusaders to lead the Christian armies against the Muslim Turks, called Saracens, who have taken Jerusalem. Godfrey does not actually fight in most of the battle, but rather directs the attacks and plans the siege. He is a character who has much in common with Thomas Malory's King Arthur and Homer's Agamemnon, which were two of Tasso's sources. Godfrey is the perfect Christian knight, in that he does not waver from his beliefs, yet will always obey the word of God. He banishes

Rinaldo for murder, but when Peter the Hermit tells Godfrey that only Rinaldo can defeat the spirits in the demonized forest, Godfrey recalls him and forgives him of his sins. Godfrey does participate in the final battle that "liberates" Jerusalem. He kills the last Saracen general and hangs his weapons in Solomon's Temple, showing that he only fights for honor and God.

Peter the Hermit

Peter plays the role of mystic advisor, much like Merlin in Malory's *Le Morte d'Arthur*. He advises Godfrey to recall Rinaldo. Throughout the epic, Peter delivers the word of God regarding the Christians' actions.

Rinaldo

Rinaldo is one of the major characters that Tasso inserted into his history of the First Crusade. Critics suggests that he is modeled on Tasso's patron at the time, Cardinal d'Este, and he is definitely one of the most important, heroic, romantic, and courteous characters in the poem. Rinaldo is a great warrior, chosen to succeed a fallen warrior as the leader of the calvary. After another knight spreads rumors about him, Rinaldo kills the man and is forced to flee Godfrey's camp. He is captured by Armida, who uses her magic to make him love her. They live happily in her enchanted garden for most of the poem, until Godfrey sends for him. Rinaldo is awakened from his magic spell and leaves Armida. His physical and spiritual strength allow him to defeat the Saracens and their allied demons. His love for Armida, however, is real and he convinces her of his passion. She then becomes a Christian and the poem ends with the plans for their wedding. Rinaldo, although not the leader of the Christians, is the only knight that can save the Christian army and get them to their goal.

Solymon

Solymon becomes the major Saracen warrior after Clorinda's death. He attacks and destroys the Prince of Denmark's army and does serious damage to the morale of the Christian troops. He also kills the great Christian warrior, Gildippe. He is killed by Rinaldo.

Tancred

Tancred is another Christian knight whom Tasso introduces to the First Crusade. He is a great warrior who loves Clorinda from afar. He worships her military ability as well as her beauty. He is captured by Armida, but escapes to lead the Christian army during Rinaldo's absence. After Clorinda has set fire to Godfrey's siege equipment and gets locked out of the city, Tancred fights this unknown warrior and kills her. Realizing his mistake, he is overcome by grief and is barely able to go on. He continues to fight for the Christians and lives through the horrific battle at the end of the poem. His affair with Erminia, however, is not resolved.

THEMES

Honor as Combat

One of the major themes in *Gerusalemme Liberata* is the idea of honor, or what makes someone a good person. The major element of honor is the character's ability to fight. Generally this applies to the male characters, with the exception being the two Amazons, Clorinda and Grildippe, since women's honor had to do with their sexual reputation and not an ability to fight. Godfrey, Rinaldo, and Tancred are examples of good and honorable men because they are able to fight when called upon and they are fighting for the side of the Christian God. Although Clorinda fights for the Saracens, she is a Christian by birth and does renounce Paganism, that is, Islam, right before her death. For Solyman, Argantes, and Aladine, honor is not obtainable since they are the bad guys. Their military victories are described as murders, while the military victories of the Christians are considered honorable acts.

Religious Truth as Justification

Tasso was writing his poem to a Christian audience who would not find anything wrong with his portrayal of the Muslims as pagans, Satan worshipers, or evil-natured brutes. The entire reason for Godfrey's attack on Jerusalem is the fulfillment of religious truth. From the moment Godfrey is nominated by God, the audience knows that Godfrey and the Christians are going to win. All of his actions, and those of his army, are justified by the truth of their religious beliefs. The question of whether they could be wrong does not even enter the picture. Tasso wants his readers to take the same surety that Godfrey and his comrades had and apply it to their own lives and struggles.

Transcendency of Love

In addition to the idea of religious truth, Tasso also emphasizes the idea of the transcendency of love. Love, as any good fairy tale says, conquers all and when love is mixed with honor and the "right" religion, it can be miraculous. Armida and Rinaldo discover that they truly love each other, even though she tricked him, he abandoned her, and she put a contract out on his life. She is willing to give up her religion, her powers, and her home for the man she loves, while he is willing to risk public scorn and humiliation for her. Even Tancred's relationships with Clorinda and Erminia display the all powerful aspects of romantic love. Tancred's affair with Clorinda may be one-sided, but it is enough to "save" her from eternal damnation to Hell, while Erminia displays the fidelity and faithfulness of, not only a good woman, but also that of Penelope, the model of wifely behavior. While Rinaldo and Armida announce their engagement at the end of the poem and Tancred is still mourning Clorinda, there is a suggestion that Erminia's love for Tancred and the idea of love in general will win in the end.

Might Makes Right

One of the major themes in almost every epic, whether poem or prose, is the idea of might establishing the rules. Whether this is the authors' intention or not, this theme seems recurrent throughout epic literature. Since the hero is the best fighter, by definition, his/her ability settles arguments and establishes how the society shall function. Godfrey gets to make the rules for how Jerusalem runs because he defeated the previous king. Aladine, the Saracen king, ruled Jerusalem and ran it his way. It is a simple matter of who is the better fighter. Tasso, as most epic authors do, makes his heroes absolutely the best, so there is no question of them being defeated, but none of these characters are able to legally or by any means other than feat of arms get what they want. So in the end, whether Tasso likes it or not, Military Ability (Might) makes the Rules (Right).

STYLE

Epic Features

In many ways, *Gerusalemme Liberata* is a perfect, rhetorically speaking, epic. Many of the

TOPICS FOR FURTHER STUDY

- Research the Crusades and compare the actions, behaviors, and outcomes of the historical record to the events, characters, and outcomes in Tasso's poem.

- Chivalry is an important element in the Renaissance art epic. After reading about chivalry, compare Tasso's treatment of the heroic ideal to the medieval chivalric code.

- Tasso suggests that his poem is an attempt to merge the Christian philosophy of Dante's work with the political ideology of Virgil's writings. After exploring Dante and Virgil, how well does *Gerusalemme Liberata* fulfill Tasso's goal?

- Women are not often thought of as warriors and historically not allowed to fight in most Renaissance European armies, yet the major warrior for the Saracens is female. What does Tasso say about women and evil by making Clorinda the head of the Turkish army?

- As a culture, American society does not glorify war, yet a lot of literature revolves around war and its consequences. How does Tasso resolve the conflict between the social needs for peace and the literary needs for war?

dominant features found in Greek and Roman epics are found in Tasso. He uses the idea of a perfect hero, Godfrey and Rinaldo, who is the salvation of his group. There is the use of military ability, the intervention of the supernatural (God verus Satan), and the trip to the underworld with Rinaldo's supposed death and re-birth. Tasso was actively following the successful models of Virgil, Dante, and Ariosto as epic authors. In his *Discourses on the Heroic Poem* (1594), Tasso suggests that there are four major elements to epic poetry that must be followed by all epic poets: the story or fable, the morality of the characters, the purpose behind the story, and the language. All of these elements could be manipulated in the extreme, but they have to be present for an epic poem to work. Tasso's definition of epic elements basically survived until the twentieth century.

Point of View

The point of view is a traditional third person unlimited narrator. All the characters' minds, wants, desires, and fears are laid open by the narrator. This is an essential part of epic poetry during this time period. Since epic characters were created to serve as examples of proper behavior, the motives and actions of those characters had to be easy to understand. A first person narration of the action would not work effectively for Tasso's purpose. A third person narrator also lends an air of finality or absoluteness to the poem.

Setting

Gerusalemme Liberata is set in Palestine, what is now Israel and the Occupied West Bank. Tasso acknowledges that this area is the religious homeland of the three major monotheistic religions: Judaism, Christianity, and Islam, but he does not recognize the political nature of the First Crusade. Tasso's Jerusalem bears almost no resemblance to the real city. Solomon's Temple was destroyed in 79 CE by the Romans, while the Tower of David has been a ruin since ancient times. There is also very little description of the countryside or the city itself. This is not important in a heroic epic. For heroic poetry, the where is not as important as the how. The fact that all these men fight and fight bravely is all that matters. The idea that all these knights, Christian or Saracen, fight by the same rules and in the same way takes precedence over any debt to reality. Tasso himself suggested the limits of using a real historical event, but he could not find a storyline that he liked better to explore his ideas on morality and heroics.

Figurative Language

The language of *Gerusalemme Liberata* depends mainly on the translation being used. Since very few Americans, relatively speaking, read Italian, most Americans experience the poem in translation. In fact, *Gerusalemme Liberata* was one of the more frequently translated epic poems. The earliest complete translation into English was that of Edward Fairfax in 1600. Fairfax "Englished" the poem, translating it into English Heroic Verse (ABABABCC) and used English cultural references, metaphors, and allusions. The poem continued to be retranslated, with major editions by poets like Elizabeth Singer Rowe (1725), James K. King (1884), and Ralph Nash (1987). The Nash edition, the only one remaining in print, belongs to a group of translations from the late 1970s to mid-1980s that translated poetry into English prose. In doing so, a good deal of the poetic or figurative language is lost. Nash addresses this problem in his introduction. He states that he is more interested in preserving Tasso's story than his language and so chose to use prose, which is easier to read, and more like a narrative. Nash's translation is very readable and focuses on the storyline, but it does lose the fire and beauty of the earlier, poetic translations. The following examples from the Nash prose translation (1987) and the Fairfax poetic translation (1600) illustrate this point:

> "Solyman, Solyman, reserve to a better time your sluggish slumbers; for the country where you reigned is yet a slave, under the yoke of foreign peoples. Can you sleep on this earth and not call to mind that it holds the bones of your unburied men? Where so great a token of your shame remains, are you lazily awaiting the new day?"

> "O Soliman! Thou far-renowned king,
> Till better season serve, forbear thy rest;
> A stranger doth thy lands in thraldom bring;
> Nice is a slave, by Christian yoke oppress'd;
> Sleepest thou here, forgetful of this thing,
> That here thy friends lie slain, not laid in chest,
> Whose bones bear witness of thy shame and scorn,
> And wilt thou idly here attend the morn?

The prose translation is easier to read and understand, but the poetic translation has a better rhythm and use of figurative language.

HISTORICAL CONTEXT

Italian Renaissance

Tasso is considered the last of the major Italian Renaissance poets. The Italian Renaissance, which began, traditionally, with the Fall of Constantinople in the fifteenth century, was a period of renewed literary, architectural, and artistic creativity that slowly spread across Europe. The Italian Renaissance launched artists like Michelangelo, Leonardo Da Vinci, and Titian; writers like Castiglione, Petrach, and Machiavelli; and artisans like Amati, the teacher of Stradivarius. There was a renewed sense of cultural identity, religious clarity, and pride in nationality. Literature was to be written in Italian rather than Latin. At the same time, educated people were to be knowledgeable about everything from art to warfare, from politics to dancing, and were expected to be able to express this knowledge and these abilities effortlessly. The Italian Renaissance collapsed under its own weight soon after Tasso died, ushering in the Baroque Period, but for its time, the Renaissance was the most important cultural, artistic, and political movement.

The Crusades

The Crusades were a series of military campaigns ordered by the then universal European Church in Rome against the ever-expanding Turkish/Ottoman Muslim Empire between the eleventh and the sixteenth centuries. Although there were Crusades as late as the seventeenth century, the major Crusades were in the eleventh, twelfth, thirteenth, and fourteenth centuries. The First Crusade, called for by Pope Urban II in 1094, was arguably the most successful. The Ottoman Turks had captured Jerusalem and forced all pilgrims to pay travel taxes. The Turks were Muslim, a monotheistic religion similar to Judaism and Christianity, but for the Medieval Roman Catholic Church, the Muslims were just another group of pagans, like the Jews. Godfrey of Bouillon was selected to head the multinational force to re-take the city with the holiest of Christian shrines, the Church of the Holy Sepulcher (Christ's tomb) and Mount Calvary (where Christ was crucified). The leaders of the First Crusade secured the cooperation of the Orthodox Church in the Byzantine Empire and so were able to invade Palestine and conquer Jerusalem. The city was quickly retaken by the Turks in the early twelfth century, thus launching the Second Crusade, lead by Philip of France and Eleanor of Aquitaine, and the Third Crusade, lead by Philip III of France and Richard I of England. However, by that time, the Crusades had deteriorated into European fights with the European kings making deals with the Turkish generals to betray one another. Throughout these military campaigns, the morality of killing thousands of people in the name of God was never addressed. The immorality and increasing length of

COMPARE
&
CONTRAST

- **18th Century:** During the Renaissance and throughout most of Western history since then, women have not been allowed to fight in armies. In fact, women are legally barred from enlisting in the military for most of American history. Europeans, as well, made military service by women illegal.

  19th Century: Florence Nightingale founds the nursing corps of the British Army during the Crimean War. Clara Barton assembles a similar unit in the United States during the American Civil War.

  20th Century: Women have made significant strides towards increasing their numbers and presence in all branches of the military. Women not only serve in the general corps of the army, navy, and marines, many can be found in high-ranking supervisory positions. In the last half of the twentieth century, a handful of women braved established military and societal codes to integrate branches and schools that had been exclusively male. Despite these vast changes, some countries in Europe and the Middle East, while allowing women to serve in the military, keep women out of combat service.

- **16th Century:** Religious intolerance is predominant at the time that Tasso is writing. The Protestant Reformation began a century earlier with the writings of Jon Huss and Martin Luther's break with the Catholic Church in Rome. Italy remained predominately Catholic and, with the power of Spain and France, started the Counter Reformation and the Inquisition. There is a great deal of animosity between Catholics and Protestants.

  20th Century: While there are still some hotbeds of religious tension, a majority of the European countries adhere to policies of religious tolerance. In the United States, laws mandate freedom of religion. The greater public's acceptance of varied religious practices continues to grow as more and more people are encouraged to integrate outside their cultural backgrounds and come in contact with those of differing faiths.

- **16th Century:** Most Europeans during this century believe in magic, mystical practices, and philosophies to explain things they can not understand. The Catholic Church has forbidden most scientific exploration because it threatens their view of God's connection to the Universe.

  17th Century: In 1609, Galileo makes the first complete astronomical telescope. Using his new telescope, Galileo notices that the moon has an uneven, mountainous surface and that numerous stars make up the Milky Way Galaxy. In 1610, he discovers the four largest satellites of Jupiter, the first satellites of a planet other than Earth to be detected. His investigations support the Copernican theory of the solar system; however, this theory was denounced as dangerous to faith. Galileo was warned not to uphold it or teach it.

  19th Century: Charles Darwin establishes Darwinism, which is the theory of evolution. Darwin meticulously documents observations that lead him to question the generally held belief in the specific creation of each species. Darwin observed species undergo a continuing struggle to survive and adapt. His theory of evolution hinges on the fact that species need their variations to adapt to their environments, allowing them to survive and reproduce. His monumental *Origin of Species* is published in 1859.

  20th Century: This century saw an explosion of scientific, astronomic, medical, and technological advances. From Einstein's famous theorem, to the landing of the first man on the moon and the proliferation of information technology, man's understanding of the world within and around him is greater than it has ever been. What has not changed from Tasso's age is that the more people learn the more they understand how much is unknown, pushing them to continue posing questions and seeking their answers. Magic, for many people, has become relegated to a world of sideshow demonstrations, consisting of card tricks, illusions, and fortune tellers.

the Crusades lead to a number of social, political, and religious reforms including the end of serfdom, the rise of the nation-state, and the Protestant Reformation.

The Renaissance Art Epic

The Renaissance Art Epic is a narrowly defined literary genre that involves a mixture of political and religious ideology with traditional heroic poetry and romance elements to express new ideas about life, social ideas, and religious truths. There are two basic types of Art Epics: Religious and Secular. The Religious Art Epic uses biblical or religiously based material as its starting point such as John Milton's *Paradise Lost*, while Secular Art Epics focus on heroic traditions or invented storylines like Ludvico Ariosto's *Orlando Furiouso* and Edmund Spencer's *The Faerie Queene*. The Renaissance Art Epic, regardless of its type, always uses old ideas about the heroic past like national pride, fighting ability, and the transformation of the hero through a death of some kind, wedded with elements of romance such as female characters, love (whether sexual or courtly), and the supernatural. The epics also usually used heroes out of the distant past whose stories could be manipulated and embellished. The point of Art Epic was to show contemporary readers how to live a true, honest, and productive life through historical example. It was also a place for the poet to display his (the overwhelming majority of authors were male) poetic skill in rhyme, rhythm, poetic imagery, and figurative language. The Art Epic fell out of favor as the dominant form of non-dramatic literary expression by the end of the eighteenth century, as novels became more popular to read at home. However, the poets who created the Renaissance Art Epic are still regarded as some of the best poetic crafters ever.

CRITICAL OVERVIEW

Gerusalemme Liberata was a great critical success when it was published in 1581. Tasso was hailed as the greatest poet in all of Europe for combining the Heroic, the Romance, and the Moral tales in one poem. The early English translations spoke highly of Tasso's moral plan and his political allegory. Italian critics, who had originally hated the poem, claimed Tasso as the poetic successor to Dante and Virgil. This praise did not make Tasso happy, partly because he did not believe it and partly because he felt the poem had too much erotic and supernatural content. The poem did not provide Tasso with economic security because there were no notions of copyright, but its popularity did help secure Tasso the post of Poet Laureate of Rome in 1594. Tasso's reputation and the poem's critical impact continued to grow after his death.

The English poets seemed to be more heavily influenced by Tasso and *Gerusalemme Liberata* than were French, Spanish, or Italian poets. Edward Fairfax's translation in 1600 brought numerous new readers to the poem and poets such as Edmund Spencer, Rachel Speght, and Margaret Cavendish credited Tasso with teaching them how to write poetry. John Milton, Thomas Gray, and various Victorian poets continually referenced Tasso's work as a model for writing epic poetry.

The idea of the moral duty of the poet was very popular among literary circles in Europe during the seventeenth and eighteenth centuries and Tasso was regarded as the shining example of a poet with his readers' best interests at heart. Both French and English literary critics favored Tasso over Ariosto since Tasso's message of honor, truth, and victory through God's help seemed a better influence than Ariosto's tales of lust and sex. John Dryden preferred Tasso as an epic poet and recommended him to several young poets including Mary, Lady Chudleigh, John Oldham, and Anne Killigrew. Elizabeth Singer Rowe, the most popular epic poet in eighteenth century England, also recommended reading and translating Tasso's *Gerusalemme Liberata* as a way of learning how to write epic poetry, both in terms of style and content.

The French critics were not as admiring as the English, however. Nicholas Boileau argued that, although Tasso was the master at instructing his readers, he found the didacticism too overpowering and the plot dull in places. He also did not like poetry with heavy moral messages, but he praised Tasso for his use of figurative language and the sustained cadence of his writing. Anne Dacier, a prominent French intellectual and translator of Homer's epics also liked Tasso's style and his use of language. She did not mind his use of real history since he chose a time and place unknowable to most of his audience and could, therefore, delight and instruct them without really telling them outright lies.

Gerusalemme Liberata continued to fare well in the eighteenth century and it continued to be translated and to influence other poets, holding a place in European Literary history as the finest Italian Art Epic. As the popularity of epic poetry declined in the nineteenth century, Tasso was still ranked among the most influential poets of the Renaissance, but his work was no longer read with the regularity it had been in the seventeenth and eighteenth centuries. Tastes in poetry, especially epic poetry, were changing toward a more satirical view of the heroic Warrior Code. In the twentieth century, epic poetry was abandoned almost entirely as a genre, with critics like E. M. Tillyard arguing that epic poetry died with Milton's *Paradise Lost*. While Tillyard credits Tasso with creating a masterpiece, he dooes not consider *Gerusalemme Liberata* as a must read work. Recently, a new interest has developed among scholars in epic poetry. Critics like Barbara Lewalski and David Quint argue that epic poetry needs to be reread in social and political terms. They examine these aspects of Tasso's poem as do post-colonial theory critics, mining the poem for what Tasso has to say about the creation of empire and religious interaction between peoples. *Gerusalemme Liberata* has always been and will continue to be an influential poem and the finest example of the Religious Renaissance Art Epic.

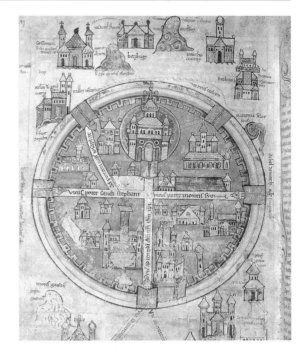

Medieval map of Jerusalem, depicting how the city looked at the time the poem takes place.

CRITICISM

Michael Rex

In the following essay, Rex explores how Tasso uses and manipulates images of femininity in traditional art epic terms.

Gerusalemme Liberata has rightly been called the finest Renaissance art epic written in terms of style, action, message, and characters. Torquato Tasso successfully combines elements of the heroic epic with elements of the medieval romance. One of his major contributions to the art epic are his female characters. Traditionally female epic characters fall into one of two kinds: the prize object and the Amazon. The prize objects are usually characters that are hyper-feminine; they cannot defend themselves, they are usually the reward for some heroic act by the male characters, and they provide the majority of the narrative action. The Amazons, on the other hand, tend to be women who cease to be women; they are warriors who refrain from anything feminine and fight, act, and generally behave just like men. Both prize objects and Amazons are incredibly beautiful. These definitions are open to numerous mutations, but the idea of women as the source of tension in epic literature is a predominant feature of the genre. While Tasso uses these types of

female characters in his poem, he subtly twists these definitions, trying to give his women more credibility and human focus. Although these powerful characterizations of women are, in epic terms, evil, i.e. bad guys, they are redeemed by the power of love. Tasso's three main female characters, Clorinda, Erminia, and Armida, reshape the traditional definitions of epic femininity and recast the role of women in Renaissance society.

Clorinda is, perhaps, the most traditional of Tasso's women. She is the typical epic Amazon in that she dresses in armor, fights the enemy, and detests anything feminine. However, she is different from the Amazons in epic literature before her. She, unlike the Amazons in Boiardo's and Ariosto's epics, is on the wrong side. Clorinda is a Persian princess who arrives in Jerusalem just before Godfrey and his Christian knights lay siege to the city. Her reputation as a warrior proceeds her and the Saracens seem to have no problems with her taking command of the troops. This appears odd given Renaissance society's reluctance to view women as anything but silent, chaste, and obedient. However, at the time Tasso was writing the poem, there were several powerful women rulers who led troops into

WHAT DO I READ NEXT?

- In the 1990s, Robert Fagles produced the most celebrated poetic translations of Homer's *The Iliad* and *The Odyssey*. These highly readable translations tell the stories of the Greek victory at Troy and Odysseus's ten-year voyage home. In European literature, these poems started it all.

- *The Aeneid* by Virgil, first century A.D., is Rome's answer to Homer's epics. A cross between political propaganda and high literature, Virgil's poem tells the story of an escaped Trojan prince and his adventures while searching for a new homeland. *The Aeneid* is available in multiple prose and poetic translations including editions by John Dryden (1680) and Allen Mandelbaum (1972).

- Dante Alighieri's three-part Medieval masterpiece, *The Divine Comedy*, ranks as one of the most widely read and influential epic poems ever written. Dante has Virgil guide the main character through Hell and Purgatory, while Beatrice (his childhood sweetheart) guides him through Heaven. In each place, Dante describes famous historical and literary characters that spend eternity in the various stages of the afterlife. It, too, exists in numerous translations.

- *The Tale of Genji*, 1100 A.D., by Murasaki Shikibu, tells a story of romance, political intrigue, and court life in Medieval Japan. Written by an aristocratic Japanese woman, the story revolves around Genji's rise to power, fame, and wealth, while detailing a culture that is foreign to most Western readers. A full translation by Edward Seidensticker appeared in 1976, which he later abridged in 1990 for a paperback edition.

- Thomas Malory's 1472 *Le Morte d'Arthur* remains the single best collection of the tales of King Arthur. While not an epic in strict terms, since it is in prose and not poetry, the work combines all of the previous tales, bringing them into a cohesive whole. From the appearance of Merlin to the Sword in the Stone to the death of Arthur at the hands of his illegitimate son, Mordred, Malory's work is the stuff legends are made of.

- Matteo Maria Boiardo's *Orlando Innamorato*, 1480, marks the beginning of the Renaissance Art Epic. This tale of chivalric love and romance takes an obscure French hero, Orlando, and makes him travel in endless pursuit of the woman he loves through lands filled with magic, fairies, and monsters. Never fully translated into English until Charles Ross in 1995, the work remains a great under read classic.

- The most influential Renaissance poem is Ludovic Ariosto's massive *Orlando Furioso*, written between 1499 and 1525. This huge poem uses Boiardo's character, Orlando, to relate a leisurely tale of sex, chivalry, and love. The poem has been translated numerous times, including the 1591 version by John Harrington and the 1975 translation by Barbara Reynolds.

- Edmund Spenser's *The Faerie Queene*, 1596, is the English answer to the Italian Renaissance epic poem. The scale is vast, the plan simple: Spenser envisioned a tale for each of the virtues and the vices, fourteen in all, as a way to entertain and instruct his readers. He sought to challenge the Italian poets and his work has remained popular for over four hundred years.

- John Milton, himself an admirer of Spenser, wrote the ''greatest'' religious epic in *Paradise Lost*, (1664) which chronicles the beginning of the world. Adam and Eve are his heroes, but his creation of Satan is much more interesting and many Romantic poets, including Lord Byron and Percy Shelley, thought Satan was the hero of the poem. Milton's description of Eden as the Bower of Bliss comes directly out of Tasso's poem.

- *The Voyage to the Isle of Love* is generally regarded as the last Renaissance Art epic written in English. Published in 1684 by Aphra Behn, the poem chronicles the adventures of Lysander as he pursues the love of his life, Aminta. She followed *Voyage to the Isle of Love* in 1688 with an unfinished epic entitled *A Return to the Isle of Love*.

battle, including Mary, Queen of Scots, the Italian-born French queen Catherine De Medici, and England's Elizabeth I. So, in his characterization of Clorinda, Tasso might be arguing for a more inclusive role for a limited class of women.

However, his manipulation of Clorinda's character does not end with making her the commander of the Saracen army. Tasso also makes her the love interest of the Christian knight Tancred, whom she has never met. This is a traditional epic/romance convention. However, he twists this idea as well. Clorinda is never informed of Tancred's love until she is dying, slain by his sword in battle. The affair is completely one sided. Tasso is commenting on the inequities of European society and literary tradition that insist that a woman should accept whoever declares "love" for her, merely because the man has fallen in love. Tasso's Amazon, unlike those in Boiardo and Ariosto, does not revert to a normal woman when love enters the picture. Neither does she kill herself for love, as Virgil's Amazon, Dido, does. While Clorinda is redeemed, in a religious sense, by Tancred, she does not submit to his wooing and remains true to her own code of conduct.

This divergence from the traditional form is also seen by the fact that Tasso also makes Clorinda a Christian by birth, but a Saracen by culture. The revelation that she was born a Christian does not change Clorinda's commitment to the Saracen cause. In fact, she seems to ignore the possible conflict of interest and proceeds to wreak the most damage against the Christians by burning their siege engines. Tasso makes the argument that just being born into a certain race, culture, or religion does not solidify one's "membership" in that group. To soundly consider oneself within a group, one must embrace its traditions, practices, and beliefs. Because Clorinda never practiced a Christian tradition, she did not consider the Christians she battled as her people. Tasso's view on this issue takes on greater meaning in light of the religious and ethnic wars that were tearing Europe apart during the Renaissance.

Erminia, however, does not fit neatly into either major category. She is a Syrian princess who is in love with the man who destroys her family and home, Tancred. She loves him because he protected her when the Christians sacked Antioch. She, too, is on the wrong side, narratively speaking, in love with the enemy. But, Erminia is not really an Amazon, nor is she only a Prize object. Tasso creates a complex character who wants to help her people, yet feels torn between her duty and her desire. She

> " Although these powerful characterizations of women are, in epic terms, evil, i.e. bad guys, they are redeemed by the power of love."

loves Tancred, but he does not know that she exists. She tells Aladine the names of all the Christian knights as they assemble around Jerusalem and she watches the battle between Tancred and Argantes. Although she is a Saracen and a woman, she is horrified when Tancred is wounded in the combat and longs to go and comfort him. This is the typical emotional state of a Prize object. However, Erminia realizes that she cannot venture outside the city walls as a woman; she needs a disguise. Unlike a true Amazon, Erminia borrows Clorinda's armor instead of a man's armor, suggesting that she wants the strength of an Amazon, but lacks the inner fiber to pull off the role. She acts like a typical Prize object as she flees from the Christian soldiers, who think she is Clorinda, but this role becomes highly ironic when the reader realizes that her main pursuer is Tancred. Erminia wants Tancred to pursue her, but when this happens, she panics and rejects the prize object role. Erminia's fate is rather cloudy at the end of the poem. She is tending Tancred's wounds, but he is still grieving for the loss of Clorinda and Tasso leaves their story unfinished. By playing with this character, Tasso exposes the dangerous situations and problems faced by real women in his era.

By far the most interesting and creative female character in *Gerusalemme Liberata* is the Saracen enchantress, Armida. She is gorgeous, wicked, evil, and marries the hero in the end. Armida enters the story as Satan's ploy to destroy Godfrey's army, thus taking on the traditional role of woman as evil temptress in the religious literature of the period. Here too, though, Tasso does not let these traditional definitions of femininity go unaltered. Godfrey is portrayed as the best and most chivalric knight in all of Europe, and one of the main rules of knighthood was that knights were to give aid to whomever asked them for it, especially women. However, Godfrey refuses to grant Armida's request, so Godfrey is as much to blame for what happens as is Armida herself.

Armida enjoys playing the role of Prize object. She uses her sexuality and her beauty to seduce over fifty knights from Godfrey's army including Rinaldo, Godfrey's best fighter. Armida seduces and takes Rinaldo to her enchanted castle out in the Atlantic Ocean. There she entertains him with sex, food, wine, and beautiful things. Under Tasso's pen, the Prize object becomes the sexual aggressor. When Rinaldo decides to return to Godfrey's camp, he and Armida reverse roles. He is now the Prize object and she the pursuer. Although Armida has destroyed her palace and gone after Rinaldo, she still sees herself as the ultimate prize. She offers herself in marriage to any man who will bring her the prize she wants: the severed head of Rinaldo.

Even after all of this, the sexual freedom, the difference in religion, the contract on his life, Rinaldo still loves Armida. This love is not one sided as is the case with Tancred, Clorinda, and Erminia. Armida and Rinaldo have spent a good deal of time together, getting to know one another. Yes, her beauty and his handsome features drew them together at first, but there was no talk of marriage four hours after meeting as there is in most fairy tales and epic romances. Rinaldo and Armida discover that they truly love each other after the battle for Jerusalem is over and the Christians have won. Ironically, the least honorable female character in the poem, Armida, "wins." She converts to Christianity and gets her man. Through her marriage, Armida becomes the "successful" woman in the poem, according to Renaissance standards, rather than the honorable Clorinda or the long-suffering Erminia. Tasso re-writes the social code of conduct for women with the creation of Armida. By making her the only successful woman in the poem, Tasso argues for female agency, the freedom of sensual choice, and the redeeming power of romantic love.

The wild women of Tasso's *Gerusalemme Liberata* challenge the traditional definitions of real Renaissance women and the literary women of epic and romance. Tasso is not satisfied with creating flat, static characters that can be easily defined or manipulated. Instead he plays with the traditional forms of the Prize object and the Amazon to create women characters who leap off the page and into the imagination.

Source: Michael Rex, for *Epics for Students*, Gale, 2001.

Patrick Cheney

Patrick Cheney compares the similarities and differences between Spenser's Dance of the Graces *and Tasso's* Dance of the Sylvan Nymphs.

The two major annotated editions of *The Faerie Queene* both overlook Tasso's Dance of the Sylvan Nymphs in the *Gerusalemme Liberata* as a source for Spenser's Dance of the Graces. Yet the similarities between the two Dances are striking. The scenes for both Dances, Mount Acidale and the Enchanted Forest, are Venusian paradises. Both scenes depict music, dancing nymphs who are really conjured spirits, an artist figure animating the Dance, and dancers who vanish through a hero's action. More specifically, both feature Dances animated by a magician in which one hundred spirit-nymphs move around a figure of beauty in the center.

In Book VI, canto x, of *The Faerie Queene*, Spenser's hero Calidore stumbles upon Mount Acidale, a paradise sacred to Venus. Mount Acidale features a "spacious plaine" atop a hill that is "bordered with a wood," through which flows a "gentle flud". Calidore, hearing "the merry sound / Of a shrill pipe", marches to the forested edge of the plain until he spies

> An hundred naked maidens lilly white,
> All raunged in a ring, and dauncing in delight.
> All they without were raunged in a ring,
> And daunced round; but in the midst of them
> Three other Ladies did both daunce and sing,
> The whilest the rest them round about did hemme,
> And like a girlond did in compasse stemme:
> And in the middest of those same three,
>   was placed
> Another Damzell.

Spenser's Dance features a series of concentric circles: a hundred nymphs in an outer ring surround the Three Graces, who in turn surround the Fourth Grace at the very center. All are spirits animated by the magician-poet Colin Clout, who plays his pipe to create the "enchaunted show". Calidore, "Much wond[ring] … at this straunge sight … / resolving, what it was, to know", steps forward, causing all the dancers to vanish.

Thus far critics have found a variety of sources for the ingredients of Spenser's complex Dance. Among the most commonly cited sources for Spenser's information on the Three Graces themselves are Hesiod's *Theogony*, Seneca's *De Beneficiis*, Servius' *In Vergilli Carmina Comentarii*, Boccaccio's *De Genealogia Deorum*, and Natalis Comes' *Mythologia*. However, according to D. T. Starnes, "all that Spenser wrote about the three

Graces" could have come from two handbooks of mythology, Thomas Cooper's *Thesaurus Linguae Romanae & Britannicae* and Charles Stephanus' *Dictionarium Historicum, Geographicum, Poeticum*, which conveniently synthesize Hesiod, Seneca, Servius, and Boccaccio in a manner resembling Spenser. Among the most commonly cited sources for Spenser's information on the Fourth Grace is Homer's Pasithea in the *Iliad*, as well as the mythological handbooks of Comes, Cooper, Stephanus, and others. The only two sources cited for an artist or magician creating the magical vision are Chaucer's *Wife of Bath's Tale*, which features an old witch animating a dance of twenty-four maidens for a knight of King Arthur's court; and Book II of Boiardo's *Orlando Innamorato*, which features three naked ladies dancing around a youth who is making music. Although these sources shed much light on Spenser's Dance, none of them provides a precedent for Spenser's use of a "hundred" dancers in his outer ring—a feature consistently overlooked in all of the commentary.

Such a precedent is found in Tasso's Dance of the Sylvan Nymphs. In Canto XVIII of the *Gerusalemme Liberata* Tasso's hero Rinaldo enters the Enchanted Forest to cut down the charmed myrtle tree, which is traditionally sacred to Venus. His doing so will enable the Christian army to use the wood for engines designed to free Jerusalem. Tasso depicts the Enchanted Forest as being "lietamente ombroso" ("sweet with pleasant shade"), featuring "un fiume trapassante e cheto" ("a quiet, still, transparent flood"). As Rinaldo progresses through this beautiful paradise, he hears "un suono in tanto / che dolcissimamente si diffonde" ("a sound that strange, sweet, pleasing was"). Attracted to the music, he moves forward to "un mirto ... in gran piazza" ("a myrtle in an ample plain"), where he witnesses a "maggior novitate" ("a marvel great and strange"):

> Quercia gli appar, che per sé stessa incisa
> apre feconda il cavo ventre, e figlia:
> e n'esce fuor vestita in strana guisa
> ninfa d'etá cresciuta (oh meraviglia!);
> e vede insieme poi *cento* altre piante
> *cento* ninfe produr dal sen pregnante.
> Quai le mostra la scena, o quai dipinte
> tal volta rimiriam dèe boscareccie,
> nude le braccia, e l'abito succinte,
> con bei coturni e con disciolte treccie:
> tali in sembianza si vedean le finte
> figlie de le selvatiche corteccie;
> se non che in vece d'arco e di faretra,
> chi tien leúto, e chi vïola o cetra.
> E cominciâr costor danze e carole;

> e di sé stesse una corona ordiro,
> e cinsero il guerrier, sí come sòle
> esser punto rinchiuso entro il suo giro.
> Cinser la pianta ancóra; e tai parole
> nel dolce canto lor da lui s'udiro.
> (emphasis added)
> [An aged oak beside him cleft and rent,
> And from his fertile hollow womb forth ran
> (Clad in rare weeds and strange habiliment)
> A nymph for age able to go to man;
> An *hundred* plants beside, even in his sight,
> Childed an *hundred* nymphs, so great, so dight;
> Such as on stages play, such as we see
> The Dryads painted, whom wild Satyrs love;
> Whose arms half naked, locks untrussed be,
> With buskins laced on their legs above,
> And silken robes tuck'd short above their knee;
> Such seem'd the Sylvan daughters of this grove,
> Save that, instead of shafts and boughs of tree,
> She bore a lute, a harp or cittern she;
> And wantonly they cast them in a ring,
> And sung and danc'd to move his weaker sense;
> Rinaldo round about environing,
> As centres are with their circumference:
> The tree they compass'd eke, and 'gan to sing,
> That woods and streams admir'd their excellence.]

Afterwards, the guardian of the grove, the enchantress Armida, appears. She has magically animated the hundred nymphlike spirits, to tempt Rinaldo from cutting down the tree, in order to help the pagan army defeat the Christians. But Rinaldo, infused with the Holy Spirit after his prayer on Mount Olivet, and armed with the divine wisdom of both the wise old magician from Ascolona and Peter the Hermit, refuses to be moved by Armida's enchantments and cuts the tree down. "Qui l'incanto forní, sparîr le larve" ("Then fled the spirts all, the charms all ended").

The similarities between the two Dances are striking enough to suggest that Spenser may have had Tasso's Dance in mind when creating his own. One reason the new source is significant is that for

" The similarities between the two Dances are striking enough to suggest that Spenser may have had Tasso's Dance in mind when creating his own."

the first time we have a Dance similar in details to Spenser's that presents a precedent for a hundred nymphs dancing within a magical vision. Another reason the source is significant is that the juxtaposition of the two Dances offers us another instance of how Spenser adapts literary materials to his romantic epic. For, although both Dances present artistically created visions of beauty designed to enchant the senses of man, the differences between them are equally important. Armida's dancers, for example, are wantonly clad ("nude le braccia, e l'abito succinte"), revealing them to be the embodiments of seduction and the false appearance of reality, as the simile from the theatre in Stanza 27 further suggests. Hence, Armida uses this Dance as a vision of beauty designed to deceive Rinaldo—to tempt him to abandon his divinely ordained quest. Rinaldo's ability to disperse the magical illusion thus reveals the power of divine wisdom concerning the spirit of God to dispel the illusion of the false beauty of nature and man (woman).

Spenser, by contrast, inserts the Graces into the Dance (as it were), and converts the half-dressed nymphs into "naked maidens lilly white," so that "without guile / Or false dissemblaunce all them plaine may see, / Simple and true from covert malice free". The outer appearance and the inner reality of Spenser's dancers are the same: chaste, graceful beauty. For, unlike Armida, Colin Clout is a good magician who creates beautiful visions that inspire heroes on their quests. For Spenser, the Dance becomes an embodiment of the true spiritual beauty that, however evanescent, nonetheless is the source guiding man to the fulfillment of his true destiny. Spenser's borrowing from Tasso thus reveals his syncretic habit of mind at work: he creates Colin's Dance of Grace out of Armida's Dance of Disgrace.

Source: Patrick Cheney, "Spenser's Dance of the Graces and Tasso's Dance of the Sylvan Nymphs," in *English Language Notes,* Vol. 22, No. 1, September, 1984, pp. 5–9.

Charles H. Carman

Charles Carman argues that Lodovico Cardi's painting "The Liberation of Jerusalem" is an interpretation of Tasso's Gerusalemme Liberata.

The National Gallery of Ireland in Dublin has a painting of *The Liberation of Jerusalem* in its collection. One enters the carefully arranged and brilliantly colored composition through the most prominent figure on a rearing horse who signals the onslaught enacted to the right. In sharp contrast is the relaxed and somewhat melancholy allegory of victory reclining in the foreground. By combining a keen historical accuracy with an allegorical figure to suggest the context and purpose of action, the painter reveals himself to be acutely sensitive to Torquato Tasso's epic poem *Gerusalemme liberata.* Before pursuing this relationship, however, there is a question of authorship to resolve.

Currently attributed to Ambrose Dubois, the painting actually belongs to the *oeuvre* of Lodovico Cardi, 'Il Cigoli.' Through comparisons with known works by Cigoli this painting can be attributed securely and dated with relative precision ca. 1590. The soldier at the lower right with his back to us grasping the bottom rung of the ladder, for example, is almost identical in pose to the tormentor in Cigoli's *Martyrdom of St. Lawrence* of 1590. Both he and his companion shooting an arrow are similar in pose, body type, proportion, and clothing to the soldier in Cigoli's *Resurrection* of 1591. And the ramparts of this Jerusalem are sufficiently close to the walls of Jerusalem in Cigoli's *St. Heraclius Carrying the Cross* of 1594 to confirm common authorship.

Stylistically the static posed quality in some of the principal figures immediately calls to mind Cigoli's teacher Santa di Tito. In fact Cigoli's *Liberation* is based partially on a version by Santi of 1589 that was executed as part of the decorations for the marriage of Ferdinand de' Medici and Christine of Lorraine, known to us from an engraving. Cigoli's portrayal of the city and his concentration of elements is quite different, yet there are two obvious points of comparison: one, the placing of a similar grouping of soldiers raising a ladder at the foreground right; and two, the practically complete adoption (by Cigoli) of Santi's foreground left soldier, shooting his crossbow (which Cigoli uses), for the soldier shooting an arrow at the right.

Cigoli, too, participated in the commission of 1589 where he painted a scene of *The Defeat of Manfred by Charles of Anjou.* Almost every painter of note in Florence participated in this commission and their works were placed on one of three triumphal arches (Cigoli's on the first and Santi's on the third). These celebrated the entry of Christine of Lorraine into Florence by depicting famous deeds of the Florentines (first arch), her wedding (second arch), and the glory of the houses of Lorraine and Guise (third arch). Cigoli's *Liberation,* though different in subject and composition, also owes something to his *Defeat of Manfred.* He has selected from the group fighting at the foreground right in the *Defeat* the horse and rider in the foreground left of the *Liberation*: an image lively enough to fit the subject but sufficiently subdued to serve a role more appropriate to the content of Tasso's poem.

The prominence of the mounted soldier suggests that he is Godfrey of Boulogne, leader of the Christian army. Beginning in stanza 49 of canto 18 of the *Jerusalem Liberated* the flight of a dove is described as it wings over the camp towards the walls only to be intercepted (stanza 50) by a falcon causing it to fall and land in Godfrey's lap. In stanzas 51 and 52, we learn that the dove bore a message for the Saracen prince, telling of Egyptian troops coming to relieve the siege and defeat the Christians. Taking this good fortune as a sign from heaven, Godfrey commences the attack. Though the dove is actually let go (stanza 53), we assume it is retained on top of Godfrey's staff to identify him and signify divine authority of the mission.

The figure's posture on horseback and his backward glance also help to identify him as Godfrey. In stanza 65, after describing the preparation for the battle and the Saracens' fear of the siege towers (seen in the distant middle ground), Tasso tells us:

> The Syrian people now were no wit slow
> Their best defences to that side to bear
> Where Godfrey did his greatest engine show,
> From thence where late in vain they placed were;
> But he who at his back right well did know
> The host of Egypt to be 'proaching near,
> To him call'd Guelpho and the Roberts twain,
> And said—On horseback look you still remain....

Tasso continues in the next stanza:

> And have regard, while all our people strive
> To scale this wall where weak it seems and thin,
> Lest unawares some sudden host arrive,
> And at our backs unlook'd-for war begin.
> This said, three fierce assaults at once they give,
> The hardy soldiers all would die or win;
> And on three parts resistance makes the King,
> And rage ' gainst strength, despair ' gainst hope
>   doth bring....

These stanzas point out that Godfrey is still on horseback, that in looking back he appears to anticipate the approaching Egyptians and that he is commanding the general mobilization of troops and siege towers for scaling the walls.

The success of this battle depends on the return to camp of Rinaldo who, released from the magical grip of Armida, leads the attacking forces. His bravery in leading the assault against the Saracens is succinctly described in stanza 77 where we read:

By combining a keen historical accuracy with an allegorical figure to suggest the context and purpose of action, the painter reveals himself to be acutely sensitive to Torquato Tasso's epic poem <u>Gerusalemme liberata</u>"

> One died, another fell, he forward went,
> And these he comforts and he threat'neth those,
> Now with his hand outstretch'd the battlement
> Well nigh he reach'd, when all his armed foes
> Ran thither, and their force and fury bent
> To throw him headlong down, yet up he goes;
> A wond'rous thing, one knight whole armed bands,
> Alone, and hanging in the air, withstands!

Cigoli captures Tasso's image of Rinaldo emerging from the chaos of the assault miraculously unscathed and poised to conquer. All but obscured at first glance, we find Rinaldo immersed in the battle, standing atop the ladder in the middle ground about to thrust his spear as if in response to Godfrey's commanding gesture.

Conforming with the poem's epic nature, Cigoli suggests events that lead up to and, by implication, extend beyond their current activity. Godfrey looks back anticipating the arrival of the Egyptians, and at the same time he gestures forward towards the walls and Rinaldo, who is on the threshold of victory. We are suspended in a moment of battle that carries with it the sensuous weight of the entire poem, the strain, terror, romance, and heroism of the whole Christian endeavor.

Also like Tasso, in his allegory accompanying the poem Cigoli describes the figures' hierarchical relationships to one another. Godfrey is understood most fully through his effectiveness as a leader—a purer, wiser man of control who ties the past to the present through his knowledge and action. Likewise, Rinaldo's depiction invokes his total life in the poem, culminating in his immersion in battle in obedience to his destiny and Godfrey's command. For Tasso, Godfrey as commander represents rational control. Rinaldo represents a more irrational nature that is subjected to obedience. If Godfrey is mind, a higher state, Rinaldo is the embodiment of passion that acts on what the mind, the intellect, commands. While Rinaldo had exhibited passion in a less acceptable, sensual fashion by yielding to Armida as well as by relinquishing his responsibility to nobility (of purpose), he is now in battle reunited with his proper natural role, obedience to intellect.

Tasso is heroic and he is melancholic. This Cigoli captures in the allegorical figure whose expression betrays the fear and sadness of these men who know devastation as well as glory. Her sadness is the embodiment of reflection and so Tasso ends his canto in stanza 105 following the battle:

> The conquerors at once now enter'd all,
> The walls were won, the gates were open'd wide;
> Now bruised, broken down destroyed fall
> The ports and towers that battery durst abide:
> Rageth the sword, death murd'reth great and small,
> And proud 'twixt woe and horror sad doth ride;
> Here runs the blood, in ponds there
>   stands the gore,
> And drowns the knights in whom it liv'd before.

But remorse cannot be the final tone of the poem. However much one senses the irony of bloody conquest, the main theme is Christian victory wherein all apparent contradictions are resolved. The painting celebrates this victory under the aegis of faith and divine supervision in a manner consistent with the Counter Reformation emphasis on faith and action (works), a meaning revealed through the allegorical figure.

The combination of her various attributes, cornucopia, conch shell, and triangle does not yield to precise interpretation, yet the figure can be interpreted to suggest a thoroughly Counter Reformatory meaning. To begin with, there is a prototype for the reclining figure. She resembles Eve in her posture and expression, as seen, for example, on Ghiberti's 'Gates of Paradise' and in numerous paintings of the fourteenth century. The figure of Eve in turn is related to the Earth Mother. Eve as Earth Mother is especially fitting here because she is associated with the Church. Like the Church, Eve is the mother of all living things. She is biblically responsible for future generations of mankind and her name in Hebrew is interpreted as meaning 'all living things.' It would follow then that Eve as the Church would also symbolize Jerusalem, even Jerusalem as the new Church. Clearly this is the subject of the painting in general, the saving of Jerusalem, or the purification and restitution of the Church in a Counter Reformatory sense. Eve then, may be interpreted as an allegory of the liberation of Jerusalem, the subject of the painting.

The attributes can be interpreted to support this thesis. If the shell and the cornucopia with grain are seen as basic elements, earth and water, they reenforce the notion of the figure as Eve/Earth Mother. Furthermore in the context of the painting's subject matter they can be interpreted as symbols of the sacraments of Eucharist (bread) and Baptism (water), the latter held on the side of the embattled citizens of Jerusalem soon to be availed of the opportunity of conversion. The triangle likewise suggests something compatible with this interpretation. The obvious meaning would be the Trinity. But an explanation of the tilted, almost inverted angle is less apparent. Possibly it is meant to conform with the compositional directives, the angle of the action, the charge forward and the scaling of the walls. If so, as a central symbol of the mystery of faith, the Trinity here would draw even greater attention to the Counter Reformation doctrine of the relationship of man's action and its success through faith. Placed in the center of the allegory of victory it reminds us of man's real means of achievement through the action and dedication to God of Godfrey and Rinaldo.

Cigoli, like Tasso, conceives the subject within the historical terms of the Counter Reformation. He casts the heroism, which subsumes the adventure and romance of the episodes of individuals, in the context of the larger struggle of the Church to assert its doctrine, to fight the heresy of Luther and the threat of the pagan Turks. Any painter undertaking a depiction of the liberation of Jerusalem subsequent to the publishing of Tasso's poem would presumably have this concept in mind. Let us consider two comparable examples dating around the same time or slightly earlier. One by Santi di Tito has already been mentioned; the other is by Bernardo Castello, who illustrated early editions of Tasso's poem. Santi's work contains many elements in common with Cigoli's, as we have seen. It lacks conviction, however. One is given only a fleeting impression of battle. His organization of the composition into parallel receding planes is disjunctive. It does not unite the main elements of the composition, which represent opposing forces, in a way that suggests anything more than the description of parts of a battle. The viewer is effectively shut off from the painting, kept out of it. Yet one is treated to a feast of detail that stretches back into the distance exploring minute hill towns or castles that disappear into a vast sky.

Castello, too, arranges his composition into a series of planes that conform essentially to the picture plane. They recede into the distance parallel to one another, the first comprising the mass of attacking soldiers and the second the massive architecture of the city. There is no engaging activity, only the proportionally small foreground soldiers on horseback and the few distant figures running onto the ramparts. At no point does the viewer enter the space of the painting to foster sufficiently a feeling of involvement. In Cigoli's attack one moves into the space diagonally along the ramparts and battlefield. The action is close and consequently personal. One is caught between the soldiers scaling the walls and the charging horse. Cigoli provides an intimate view of the battle, not the entire scene as if viewed from a safe distance.

Ellis Waterhouse in his article 'Tasso and the Visual Arts' defines the prevalent unimaginative approach to Tasso. While referring to the tradition for illustrating *Orlando Furioso* , he says:

> ... it is therefore all the more curious that painters seem hardly to have illustrated Tasso at all during his lifetime—apart from the two series of engravings for the illustrated editions of the *Gerusalemme*, which mainly show the 'historical' incidents of the poem and are not in the least influenced by Tasso's description of the passions.

Elsewhere in his article, Waterhouse partially locates the special quality that links Cigoli more closely to Tasso:

> The mannerists constantly placed their figures in poses contrary to normal usage, but they were organized so predominantly in the interest of the whole pattern that their individual contribution to the narrative tended to be vague and imprecise. This was exactly the opposite of Tasso. In painting it was not until the 1590's, above all in the style of the Carracci, who were working on the decoration of the Galleria Farnese in Rome at the time of Tasso's death, that a reaction against this kind of mannerism set in, in favor of significant action.

It is precisely Cigoli's grasp of the personal as well as the essentially historical nature of the characters that reveals his faithfulness to Tasso's interpretation of the epic. It is the passion of Tasso's figures that he strives so successfully to re-create. And certainly the transformation into 'significant action' of vague, imprecise, and anecdotal contributions to narrative content characterizes Cigoli and distinguishes him from his contemporaries, before, I might add, the Carracci were working in Rome.

As a model for achieving his coherency with Tasso it would seem that Cigoli adheres to the humanist theory of *ut pictura poesis*, 'as in painting so in poetry' (and vice versa). Central to this theory (adopted from antique sources and developed in the fifteenth and sixteenth centuries) is the notion that painting, like poetry, should be subject to the principles of clear style, convincing expression, and edifying purpose. In spite of the prevalence of this theory at the end of the century, few artists utilized its potential, as we have seen in the previous comparisons. Rensselaer Lee, in discussing the principles, evolution, and applicability of *ut pictura poesis* in the sixteenth century, points out that artists dealing with Tasso's *Gerusalemme* 'eschewed the serious main action of the poem that had to do with the siege and capture of Jerusalem under the crusader Godfrey Boulogne, and chose for the most part only those amorous and idyllic episodes wherein the lyric element is strong, and Tasso's idosyncratic vein of tender melancholy finds unfettered expression." He is commenting on the popularity of Tasso's poem among artists of the seventeenth century and their lack of concern with the moralistic and didactic aspects of the theory that were stressed by the Counter Reformation. But we are safe in saying that such a concern existed in the late sixteenth century. The instructional emphasis in *ut pictura poesis* served during Cigoli's time as a theoretical standard by which art might be measured and might convey historical significance. Cigoli's painting which we have discussed here is eloquent testimony to this.

Source: Charles H. Carman, "An Early Interpretation of Tasso's *Gerusalemme liberata*," in *Renaissance Quarterly,* Vol. 31, No. 1, Spring, 1978, pp. 30–38.

C.P. Brand

C.P. Brand presents an examination of Tasso's style and language in Gerusalemme Liberata.

Structurally the *Liberata* is a fusion of the heroic epic and the chivalrous romance, and represents a conscious attempt at the perfection of a literary form. Few poems have been less 'spontaneous' in the conventional sense: years of reading, thought, discussion, correspondence, even formal declaration of principles preceded and accompanied the composition of the poem. For Tasso the peaks of literary achievement had been reached by Homer and Virgil in the epic and his aim was to rival, where possible to excel them. It is typical of Tasso's approach to art, to style and language to build on the great achievements of the past, and he deduced his principles for epic poetry very largely from the *Iliad*

Crusaders attacking Jerusalem.

and the *Aeneid*, and from the classical literary theorists, particularly Aristotle and Demetrius.

His epic thus treats an heroic theme of large scale, the siege and capture of Jerusalem in 1099 by Godfrey of Boulogne and his allies; it deliberately plunges 'in medias res' with the approach to Jerusalem, ignoring the previous exploits of the crusaders; it has a single unified theme, to which the episodes are subordinated; it adopts a serious magniloquent tone throughout—so that De Sanctis complained that 'from first to last he blew the trumpet'; and its characters and action are very widely inspired by classical precedent, with 'maraviglie', 'agnizione', 'peripezie', etc. The councils of the supernatural forces controlling the action, the quarrel and withdrawal of the leading Christian knights on whose eventual recall the success of the campaign depends; the night expedition of two enemy warriors, the espionage mission of Vafrino, the troop reviews, the battles and duels—these and many other incidents are often closely reminiscent of passages from Homer and Virgil. At the same time the heroic ideal is adapted to the claims of the time: a period of history is chosen which allows the celebration of the Christian faith, which is no less prominent here than are the Greek gods in Homer; and the contemporary critics of 'empty fictions' are met with references to

the chronicles and a substratum of historical fact. This is the structure of the heroic epic devised by Tasso.

However, Tasso had no wish to renounce the chivalrous romance completely. His plan as outlined above might seem.a deliberate attack on the romances, with their light-hearted humorous approach, loose structure, popular language and indifference to historical and geographical reality; and indeed Tasso's approach is in a degree negative. He opposes forcefully the 'defects' of the romances, but he cannot deny their appeal, and indeed feels it himself. Ariosto's remarkable popularity beside Trissino's failure was not to be ignored. The heroic ideal is adulterated therefore with the charms of the romances—notably the loves and enchantments—and Tasso admits his compromise from the beginning. He begs pardon of his Christian muse for his adorning the truth:

> … e tu perdona
> s'intesso fregi al ver, s'adorno in parte
> d'altri diletti, che de' tuoi, le carte.
> Sai che là corre il mondo ove più versi
> di sue dolcezze il lusinghier Parnaso,
> e che 'l vero condito in molli versi,
> i più schivi allettando ha persuaso.

So in the accepted romance tradition the pagan Armida wreaks havoc in the Christian ranks by her seductive charms, and two other pagan beauties, an Amazon (Clorinda) and a stay-at-home (Erminia), are at the centre of other digressive incidents. Nor are the wizards and witches of the romances absent, and the crusaders even suffer at one stage from being turned into fish. The camouflage of these obvious 'diletti' is thin—the loves are mildly allegorical, an obstacle in the path of Christian duty; and the enchantments are remotely controlled by Christian powers, by God and his angels or Beelzebub. But the connection with the romances of chivalry is seen everywhere—not only in the form, where the traditional octave rhyme and canto structure are employed, but in the chivalrous spirit of the crusaders, who will take no unfair advantage of an unhorsed or disarmed opponent, and in many details of the action: even the favourite Italian knight Rinaldo reappears as a crusading ancestor of Tasso's patrons, the Estensi.

This compromise between the heroic, serious, didactic elements on the one hand and the fanciful and romantic on the other is typical of Tasso's approach to so many things: it constantly appears in his letters in his attempts to placate his critics and at the same time to safeguard his own wishes; in his search for peace and independence and yet his hankering for the court and its excitement; in his writings it is also evident in his aim to reconcile Aristotle and Plato, in his frequent reference to or intimation of sources, and his attempts at almost every literary genre, epic, lyric, dramatic, dialogue, discourse—as though he stands in no one camp but in all. So that he has seemed to many critics a man of the Renaissance struggling to conform to the spirit of the Counter-Reformation in which he had the misfortune to be born, while to others he is of the very essence of his time or even a herald of the Seicento. It is this very imprecision of mind, this drifting between schools and genres and feelings which contributes so effectively to Tasso's originality as a poet and which has preserved his reputation through the changing trends of the centuries, so that he has appealed to Secentisti and Arcadians, Romantics and Classicists.

This is, however, a difficult and dangerous course for a poet who may juxtapose but fail to blend the contrasting components. Thus the *Liberata* has been condemned by many critics since De Sanctis for failing to reconcile the heroic and the romance elements. The strictly heroic elements have been considered uninspired, accepted by a reluctant poet because of the climate of religious and literary opinion. Tasso is held to have been unmoved by the Crusade as a glorious feat of arms, or at least unable to convey his emotion; and to be lacking in religious faith, for which he substituted the formal ceremony and pomp of the Counter-Reformation; thus the attempt to create a heroic religious epic failed. On the other hand, where the poet was in sympathy with his material was in the love episodes and the enchantments—here, it was said, his fancy had free play and here the poet found inspiration for his best work, in the enchanted wood and the garden of Armida, the death of Clorinda and the loves of Erminia and of Olindo. So the *Liberata* has been thought of as an epic poem in which the strict epic elements fail, while the romance, lyrical moments keep the poem alive—hence Momigliano's view, repeated by Fubini, of a new poetic technique, 'per cui la poesia si raccoglie in alcuni momenti culminanti e sembra tacere per lungo spazio'.

While there is certainly an element of truth in this view, it errs through oversimplification and the aesthetic judgement has been biased by long-standing historical fallacies—that the heroic and religious elements were alien to the poet who accepted unwillingly the dictates of Inquisitors and literary dictators—and perhaps by a distaste for psychologi-

> "This compromise between the heroic, serious, didactic elements on the one hand and the fanciful and romantic on the other is typical of Tasso's approach to so many things. . ."

cal half-tones. (Is Tancredi a hero or isn't he? Is Armida a wicked sorceress? Is Goffredo the ideal prince?) The search for a biographical explanation has contributed to the distinction between epic and lyric, between heroic and romance, as though the poem were a document of the everyday life of the poet (who was neither heroic nor religious but who *was* superstitious and amorous) whereas it is really a reflection of a complex world of fears and aspirations which pervades the heroic and religious material no less than the romantic. However, the distinction between the two bodies of material, the heroic epic and the romance, is a useful one and will serve to illustrate what has been said.

Tasso's theme then is the celebration of a great and glorious feat of arms, and to dismiss the military and heroic elements as unpoetic concessions to literary tradition or popular taste or Counter-Reformation missionary zeal is to misread the poem. The military action is important to Tasso—it is not merely a structure on which to hang his romantic episodes. The poet is fascinated by action, perhaps precisely because he was not himself a man of action. His military experience is nil, but his imagination is stirred by the clash of arms and the emotional tensions aroused by the prospect of death. The very techniques of fighting interest him intensely, particularly the parry and thrust of the duel; he is expert in the arts of the sword, and the accuracy of his accounts of single combats is legendary. The duel is no longer the monotonous hacking of the chivalrous romances but a contest of skills and characters, a moving interplay of minds as of bodies. The duel between Tancredi and Argante in Canto VI is a good example of this, from the cautious taking of stance to the first feint inducing the aggressive Argante to make his overbold thrust;

Tancredi parries swiftly, wounds his opponent and reassumes his stance. Argante, arrogant, always victorious, can scarcely believe that he is wounded and in his rage and pain rushes wildly on to Tancredi's sword again:

> Il fero Argante, che se stesso mira
> del proprio sangue suo macchiato e molle,
> con insolito orror freme e sospira,
> di cruccio e di dolor turbato e folle;
> e portato da l'impeto e da l'ira,
> con la voce la spada insieme estolle,
> e torna per ferire, ed è di punta
> piagato ov'è la spalla al braccio giunta.

Now the pagan throws discretion to the winds and rains blows on the lighter Tancredi who anxiously defends himself; and only the oncoming darkness puts an end to the dramatic conflict. The duel between Rinaldo and Gernando in Canto V is also dramatic, not only in the vivid representation of the action, but particularly in the picture of the inferior Gernando who in his moment of fear trembles, but puts on a bold face and meets his opponent resolutely. Thus the clash of arms uncovers the deepest resources of character.

The broader canvas of the military campaign is also treated with considerable narrative skill. Tasso is interested in every aspect of the conflict—the costumes, weapons, supplies, troop dispositions and tactics. The instruments of war assume a personality of their own, the sword for example which is thrust into the supplicating face of the young Lesbino:

> Senso aver parve e fu de l'uom più umano
> ilferro, che si volse e piatto scese.

The massive siege-tower participates in the action almost as though a character ('primo terror de le nemiche genti') and sets off a chain of colourful and moving incidents: it is damaged in the first assault, and brought back by the Christian knights, but its wheels break and it sways furiously in the darkness while Goffredo puts guards round it and sets men to work to repair it. Through the night the besieged Muslims can hear the sound of the workmen and see the gleam of their torches—hence the sortie of Clorinda and Argante to fire it and the lengthy attempt on the enchanted forest for more wood. The firing of the tower becomes a colourful and thrilling incident as the pagans flee leaving the blazing structure behind them:

> Vedi globi di fiamme oscure e miste
> fra le rote del fumo in ciel girarsi.
> Il vento soffia, e vigor fa ch'acquiste
> l'incendio e in un raccolga i fochi sparsi.
> Fère il gran lume con terror le viste
> de' Franchi, e tutti son presti ad armarsi.

> La mole immensa, e sì temuta in guerra,
> cade, e breve ora opre sì lunghe atterra.

The tension of this night sortie is conveyed by Tasso with great skill: the two fleeing assailants reach the walls of the city with the Christians in pursuit; the gates are opened to receive them, and then hastily shut, and in the confusion Clorinda is shut out—but in the darkness she is able to mingle with her opponents and slip away. The splendour of troops in battle-array, the noise and confusion of the battle-field, the murmurings of a riotous army, the eloquence of leaders, the crafty subtleties of ambassadors—all these are brilliantly shown, not indeed with the accuracy of the historian, but with the feeling of a poet who imagines and relives the event with the help of the chroniclers and the poets of the past.

Thus in spite of his historical documentation Tasso's battles are often dream landscapes through which his knights pass in a frenzy of heroism. Ariosto, who knew something of campaigning from first-hand experience, has a scene in which his knights tramp reluctantly out into the rain to do battle with a tired wayfarer. Tasso will not suffer this denigration of the heroic ideal: he believes in the high motives of his crusaders. His account of the noble Goffredo pressing forward through the battle to attack Soliman is effective poetically precisely because it is a dream of heroism, a baroque painting where the outlines are forgotten: Goffredo seems to fly on, as he leaps over 'i confusi monti … de la profonda strage': all is vague and confused—blood and dust, danger and death.

Arms and heroism are not then alien to Tasso's poetic inspiration, but it is more often the heroism of failure which moves him than the glory of success, and more often the horror of violence than the splendour of armed might. Tasso is fascinated by violence and has scenes of slaughter which shock by a grim realism of imagery and sound:

> e'l ferro ne le viscere gli immerse.
> Il misero Latin singhiozza e spira,
> e con vomito alterno or gli trabocca
> il sangue per la piaga, o per la bocca.

Elsewhere the horror of death is conveyed in a vague generic impression, as in his description of the uneasy still of the strewn battle-field:

> Non v'è silenzio e non v'è grido espresso,
> ma odi un non so che roco e indistinto:
> fremiti di furor, mormori d'ira,
> gemiti di chi langue e di chi spira.

It is easy to place these scenes of horror against the background of Tasso's own anxious and fearful mind—his practical inexperience of battle does not debar him from the poetry of violence and of death. Indeed Tasso's own passivity seems to bring into his heroic action an element of humanity which is rare in the chivalrous epic. There is often an inner life behind the act of heroism which the unhappy, unheroic Tasso knew only too well: Sofronia, the shy 'matura vergine' suffers martyrdom in her exposure to the public gaze before ever the fire is lit around her; the timid Erminia's heroism is to don Clorinda's armour and to dare to ride out, past the guards, in spite of her fears, into the hostile night; Gernando foresees his death at Rinaldo's hands and trembles inwardly with fear while he assumes a bold face.

The most moving poetry of defeat however is in the deaths of the two pagan leaders, Solimano and Argante. They are both fanatical warriors, relentless in battle, unwilling to acknowledge superior force; but the ferocity of each is softened by a moment of self-pity or of introspective gloom which heightens the heroism of their death. Argante pauses before his final fatal duel with Tancredi to look back at the falling Jerusalem: Tancredi taunts him with cowardice and Argante suddenly rises superior to Tancredi's taunts in a few deeply pondered words:

> Penso—risponde—a la città del regno
> di Giudea antichissima regina,
> che vinta or cade, e indarno esser sostegno
> io procurai de la fatal ruina,
> e ch'è poca vendetta al mio disdegno
> il capo tuo che 'l Cielo or mi destina.

It is with Argante, the noble loser, that our sympathies lie, and his ultimate death, brought about by the violence of his own blow, is that of a 'grande vinto', and has become legendary:

> Moriva Argante, e tal moria qual visse:
> minacciava morendo e non languia.
> Superbi, formidabili e feroci
> gli ultimi moti fur, l'ultime voci.

Solimano too reveals a moment of weakness in his tears for the dead Lesbino. When he falls finally stunned by Rinaldo's blow he is suddenly aware of his approaching defeat and death, and cannot bring himself to defend his life, but dies silently under the attack:

> non fugge i colpi e gemito non spande,
> nè atto fa se non se altero e grande.

It is by virtue of this intensely personal reaction to the theme of arms and heroism that Tasso's choice of subject is justified poetically. Yet the element of subjectivity is constantly minimized by Tasso in his 'lettere poetiche', while the historical accuracy is emphasized. The choice of an historical theme is made in accordance with the poet's belief in the importance of verisimilitude. He states in the *Discorsi dell' Arte Poetica* that the theme of the epic poem is best taken from history, because if the reader thinks that the material is false, he will not be so easily moved to anger, terror or pity. Historical truth is thus a means of gaining the close participation of the reader.

A good deal of historical research therefore went into the *Liberata*. Tasso made use of William of Tyre, Paolo Emilio, Roberto Monaco, indeed any historical information that came his way, without distinguishing the more reliable sources from the derivative. The crusade of 1096–99 organized by Urban II, is then an historical fact, and from the chronicles Tasso draws many of his characters: Goffredo and his brothers Eustazio and Baldovino, Tancredi, Pietro the hermit, Dudone, Odoardo, Ottone Visconti, Guglielmo Embriaco and others; and many details and episodes are also taken from historical sources: the expulsion of the Christians from Jerusalem, the geographical descriptions of the city, the underground tunnel, the death of Sveno, the Arab attack, the drought, and many details of the battles—the dove-messenger intercepted by the Christians, the use of siege-towers, of deception, smoke, even the weather of the day of the final battle. More often hints in the chronicles are the basis for Tasso's own inventions. Clorinda, an invented character, is justified by a statement in an anonymous chronicle that the Saracen women fought against the Crusaders. Ottone's duel with the invented Argante is based on a duel between Ottone and a pagan mentioned by William of Tyre. The Sofronia-Olindo episode is invented on the basis of a report of the self-sacrifice of a Christian youth following the discovery of a dead dog in a Jerusalem mosque and threats of punishment of the Christians for profanation. Tancredi's love for Armida is justified by Tasso in a letter where he claims that the chronicles describe him as 'excessively fond of the embraces of the Saracen women'. Similarly Tasso is able to defend the supernatural elements by reference to the beliefs of the time, 'the history of this war being full of miracles, it wasn't suitable for the poem to be any less wonderful'.

In many cases however the chronicles were a hindrance to the poet. They often did not conform to the heroic ideal which he was celebrating because they showed up the vices of the crusaders: he has tried, he says, to gloss over or excuse the defects of the Christians. He pretends therefore that the faults of Raimondo were due to his old age, and those of Tancredi to his youth, although he knows that this is not historically true. For structural reasons he felt the need to bring the anti-Christian forces under a more unified command, and he makes Solimano subordinate to the King of Egypt and the Arabs, while Argante is made the rival of Solimano, in imitation of Homer and Virgil—but he has doubts about this: some critics, he says, might like him to keep to historical truth, but he would prefer not to do so.

Tasso is therefore no enthusiast for historical truth and frequently ignores it or consciously exaggerates it. So the three years of campaigning are increased to six; Ugone who has deserted is declared to have died; Goffredo, not in fact elected to leadership until after the conquest of Jerusalem, is here made the ideal prince from Canto I; and the invasion by the Egyptian army is made to occur several months earlier than it really did in order to produce a grand climax to the poem. Thus Tasso's frequent references in letters and discourses to his historical sources are often a cover for his own artistic inclinations—an excuse for the inventions of his own imagination which he feared that moralizing and pedantic critics might censure.

Tasso's theories did not require the epic to reproduce historical truth, but to celebrate 'l'impresse d'una eccelsa virtù bellica, i fatti di cortesia, di generosità, di pietà, di religione'. It is from his belief in the illustrious nature of the epic and in universal truth that so many of the defects of the poem spring. In accordance with these principles Tasso strives, often uncritically, after certain ideals of character and action. He wishes to impress on us the noble, grave, serious nature of his heroes and he is not content to let this arise from their actions, but blows the trumpet when they appear. Goffredo more than any other character suffers from this. He is not in fact a very compelling or admirable leader, and resorts to the drawing of lots and a hypocritically contrived dignity to cover his insecure control of his army—but Tasso bolsters him up with pompous epithets: in the first canto alone he is 'il gran capitano', 'il pio Goffredo augusto in volto ed in sermon sonoro', 'il provido Buglion' with 'volto placido e composto'. This arid and meaningless labelling is applied to nearly all his main characters: Rinaldo 'venerabile e severo', Clorinda's 'regal sembianza', Armida's 'regal sdegno', Erminia 'altera e gentile', Dudone 'di virilità grave e maturo'; and of the Caliph of Egypt, who, history tells us, was a youthful twenty-five, Tasso declares:

> e ben da ciascun atto è sostenuta
> la maestà de gli anni e de l'impero.

The attempt to sustain a lofty tone is thus intruded into the action where often it serves only to accentuate an uninspired passage. The lance, which Goffredo avoided by ducking, strikes the faithful Sigiero, whose fidelity must be stressed:

> nè gli rincresce, del suo caro duce
> morendo in vece, abbandonar la luce.

It is notable in the hyperbolic feats of arms where the exhausted muse resorts to ever hollower epithets:

> …egli fe' cose
> incredibili, orrende e monstruose.

—and it leads the poet into complicated and unnatural situations, as in the Sofronia episode. The historical origin was a dead dog thrown into a mosque—but a dead dog was hardly worthy of the heroic epic. Tasso looks for a substitute and thinks of the Palladio stolen by Ulysses and Diomedes in the *Iliad*. By a violent contortion of probability he then makes the pagans steal the Christian image of the Virgin to protect them, so that a Christian could be expected to steal it back, and a truly noble act of heroism may replace a rather pedestrian one.

The search for heroic gravity here as elsewhere leads Tasso too often to the classics, as though the presence of a Homeric detail, by the force of association, will ensure dignity and gravity. Particularly in matters of style Tasso repeats constantly the formulas and devices of the 'stile magnifico' which Aristotle and Demetrius had declared appropriate to the epic, and the pursuit of this stylistic ideal leads him into many faults. It is above all his attempt to avoid the commonplace and everyday which is so difficult to reconcile with his professed attention to historical truth. Everyday words are replaced by high-sounding periphrases, such as that describing Erminia in the shepherd's cottage making cheese:

> e da l'irsute mamme il latte preme
> e 'n giro accolto poi lo stringe insieme.

In many cases a vacuous genetic language results, or a pedantic paraphrase of a commonplace expression:

> …e Gabriel s' accinse
> veloce ad esseguir l'imposte cose.

A similar lameness results from a mechanical amplification, which aims at solemnity but sounds very like padding:

> e drizza a l'Oliveto il lento moto
> monte che da l'olive il nome prende,
> monte per sacra fama al mondo noto.

It is often Tasso's fear that his material is not sufficiently heroic which prompts him to resort to rhetorical devices. Erminia's indecision between her desire to help the wounded Tancredi and her fears of leaving the besieged city is poetically inspiring, but Tasso must relate it to his heroic theme by a high-sounding personification:

> e fan dubbia contesa entro al suo core
> duo potenti nemici, Onore e Amore.

This pompous and literary style is particularly inappropriate in the mouths of some of his characters, who are compelled to use a language and literary reminiscences remote from their experience, so that we find the phraseology of classical philosophy on the lips of the pagans, and the crusading soldiers praying at the sight of Jerusalem in Dantesque tones.

In this examination of the attempt to create an heroic epic, one important element has not yet been mentioned: it is the concern with 'meraviglia', a word which constantly appears in statements about the epic, and which recurs not infrequently in the *Liberata* itself:

> percote l'alta pianta. Oh meraviglia!
> manda fuor sangue la recisa scorza.

Its close association with classical precedent ('mirabilia') is apparent from Tasso's declared aim of over-going antiquity:

> Già ne l'aprir d'un, rustico sileno
> meraviglie vedea l'antica etade,
> ma quel gran mirto da l'aperto seno
> imagini mostrò più belle e rade.

In the *Giudizio sulla Gerusalemme Conquistata* he claims that he is in some ways more 'meraviglioso' than Homer. Elsewhere he insisted that it was the poet's aim to arouse wonder—this was essential in the heroic epic—but at the same time he must be true to life. The fictions of the classical epics, based on a false religion and therefore incredible, should now be replaced by the supernatural structure of Christianity, God and his angels, Beelzebub and his devils. In this way not only the marvels of antiquity but also the enchantments of the romances could be reconciled with the Christian religion—or such was Tasso's intention.

The suitability of supernatural elements arousing wonder in a poem intended to celebrate heroic ideals is clear: heroes are superhuman by virtue of their alliance with supernatural forces, and only by superhuman strength can the opponents of heroes rise to meet them. This is true of the classical epics no less than of the romances—indeed the continued popularity of magic throughout the ages might well have made it indispensable now. But it is no cold spirit of literary emulation that interests Tasso in the 'marvellous'. He was himself fascinated by the supernatural throughout most of his life, in fact until the comparative calm of his last years. Lacking a firm religious faith, he was unable to reconcile the world as he knew it with his own inner consciousness. Science could not explain all the marvels of the world, and what escaped the control of reason and will seemed to him a sort of diabolical force. Hence his fascination with magic forces, which led him at one stage to believe that he was himself bewitched.

The 'meraviglie' of the *Liberata* therefore respond both to a theoretical literary programme and to an intimate personal necessity. Their failure always to coincide seems to explain the uncertain inspiration of the supernatural elements in the poem. Thus the reproduction of classical miracles in a Christian setting is often incongruous: the Christian guardian angel of Goffredo heals his wounds by plucking herbs on Mount Ida and dropping them unobserved in the dressing that is prepared for him. Beelzebub's method of disturbing the duel between Argante and Raimondo is to form an image of Clorinda ('Mirabil mostro') who urges Oradino to shoot an arrow at Raimondo, and the latter's guardian angel is only just in time to reduce the force of the shot—a complex and unconvincing intrigue inserted under Homeric influence. Equally uninspired is the episode in which, in imitation of the *Iliad*, *Odyssey* and *Aeneid*, Solimano enters Jerusalem in a magic chariot enveloped in a cloud that makes him invisible. He also uses an underground tunnel, mentioned in the chronicles—which seems hardly necessary for one so magically equipped.

Indeed the miracles of the Christian religion are reconciled only with difficulty with the needs of the story. The mysterious appearance of two hermits by Sveno's dead body and their command that for the sake of revenge his sword should be taken to Rinaldo, is a strangely un-Christian scene. So too is the picture of the hermit Pietro, whose devout trance ('Pieno di Dio, rapto dal zelo') enables him to recount the glories of the house of Este. The attempt to 'Christianize' the supernatural structure of the poem is generally a failure—the struggle between Christians and Moslems is related to a contest between God and the devil the outcome of which is only too obvious; and the miracles by which God answers the prayers of the faithful are too mechanically obvious and too zealously advertised:

Oh glorioso capitano! oh molto
dal gran Dio custodito, al gran Dio caro!
A te guerreggia il Cielo; ed ubidenti
vengon, chiamati a suon di trombe, i venti.

Elsewhere and most frequently the supernatural is a mechanical afterthought, superimposed on an action which is already psychologically justified: Gernando's arrogant dislike of Rinaldo is adequately explained before ever the 'maligno spirito d'Averno' unnecessarily creeps into his breast. Tasso's approach is perhaps illustrated by his treatment of Tancredi's failure in the enchanted wood: before the tree which he must fell but which takes on the appearance of his lady Clorinda, he is caught in an agony of indecision likened in a telling simile to a nightmare; but Tasso regretted this human weakness in his hero and proposed to change the passage by introducing an enchantment. The change was not made, however, on this occasion and Tancredi's humanity does not suffer.

In spite of this Tasso succeeds in innumerable ways in convincing the reader that the hand of God does indeed hang over the action—a sense of fatality, which must be God's providence, drives the characters on their courses. This is particularly moving in the case of Clorinda. On the evening of her sortie to fire the siege-tower her nurse senses the perils that await her and tells her the story of her youth—her miraculous preservation from dangers, the warnings conveyed in a dream that she should be baptized. Now at least she should take heed. Clorinda listens attentively for she too has had forebodings, but she will not abandon the faith in which she has been brought up and she goes off, completes her task and is attacked by Tancredi. The end is preordained, and is forecast with melancholy resignation:

Ma ecco omai l'ora fatale è giunta
che 'l viver di Clorinda al suo fin deve,

and fatally wounded she accepts baptism and dies at peace.

…In questa forma
passa la bella donna e par che dorma.

There are moments too when the presence of God and his angels urging on the battling Christians seems to blend the earthly and the supernatural forces into an irresistible power—as in the assault on Jerusalem, where Goffredo lifts his eyes to heaven and sees the dead Christian heroes with the heavenly host fighting for the Christian cause.

Where, however, the supernatural most frequently inspires Tasso to passages of great poetic feeling is where it coincides with his own anxious sense of the mystery of the world, in the expression of vague haunting fears and strange visions of fascinating but unattainable scenes of beauty and peace. The nightmarish horrors of his own clouded mind reappear in the devilish forces which beset the Christians, in Pluto's terrifying appearance, and the swarming demons:

Venieno innumerabili, infiniti
spirti, parte che 'n aria alberga ed erra,
parte di quei che son dal fondo usciti
caliginoso e tetro de la terra;

and the murky landscapes:

Ma già distendon l'ombre orrido velo
che di rossi vapor si sparge e tigne.

The enchanted wood is a study in fear: Tancredi, like Tasso, does not dare to confess his fear—only the uncomplicated Rinaldo is unmoved by the terrors. These are imprecise pictures where the image has no place in space or time, no rational explanation; their fascination is in their lack of rationality. The mysterious haunting music of the wood springs from an unknown source:

di novo s'udia quella gioconda
strana armonia di canto e di querele;
ma il coro uman, ch'a i cigni, a l'aura, a l'onda
facea tenor, non sa dove si cele:
non sa veder chi formi umani accenti,
nè dove siano i musici stromenti.

Together with the fear of unknown dangers goes the dream of only half-visualized scenes of happiness and confidence. The Christian knights Carlo and Ubaldo are carried to the distant Fortunate Isles in a boat that sails but seems to fly, impelled by an unknown force, the description of which is vague, generic, significant for the sound rather than the visual imagery—'porta seco non so che di vago e di curioso', Tasso said of it. Here in a remote and misty dream are set the gardens of Armida, on a dark and uninhabited mountain amid snow and shadows. Dante's supernatural world is so precise that it can and has been mapped with geometrical accuracy. We could hardly even begin to map the gardens of Armida. Tasso, sensitive as he was to the poetry of Dante's vision, goes beyond him in the expression of these vague and dreamlike experiences that belong not in the concrete world of action and reality, but in the only half-conscious workings of his own mind. This is a new note in Italian literature and a foreshadowing in some ways of the poetry of the Romantics.

The fascination of magic is only one element in Tasso's preoccupation with the supernatural which arises, as we have suggested, out of an intimate sense of the mystery of the universe and of man's part in it, and a dissatisfaction with the rational explanations of science. This concern with a reality beyond the normal world of the senses is, in my view, of a religious nature and identifies Tasso as a man of serious religious aspirations. Many critics have been unable to find in the *Liberata* what they term the 'true religious sense', and have dismissed the religious passages as cold, formal, expressive of the letter of the Counter-Reformation, preoccupied with ceremony and display. Donadoni was extremely critical: Tasso's religious sense seemed to him negative and insincere, not really religious at all, but a weariness of the world, something external and formal.

It is undeniable that the spirit of the Council of Trent pervades the poem—this is in a sense a document of the Counter-Reformation in which the religious ideals of the new age are displayed in the medieval context of the crusades: the resistance of the Church to the heretical empire of the over-powerful Turks as to the heresies of the Reformation was a contemporary necessity in which Tasso sincerely believed and which certainly motivated his choice of subject. It is part of Tasso's epic ideal that his poem should celebrate 'l'illustre della religione', and he brings to his work a seriousness of religious interest not to be found in Pulci or Ariosto. The poet's fears of Inquisitorial censorship certainly influenced his treatment of the subject, but there is every reason to believe that his conformity was not a violent suppression of his own inclinations; it has been aptly said that the Counter-Reformation was *in* him.

Whether or not one accepts this view it is clear that two different themes of a religious nature recur in the *Liberata*. On the one hand there is the personal, intimate sense of mystery, loneliness and weakness which seeks for God as an explanation and consolation; and on the other is the consciousness of the collective force of the Church and the delight in its ceremonial and liturgy. These are not conflicting themes, although Tasso often fails to reconcile them in his poetry just as he had not yet succeeded in reconciling them in his life. The first is nearly always poetical in expression. Rinaldo on Monte Oliveto is alone, beyond Church, priests, ritual—he looks up at the night and marvels at the incorruptible beauties of nature and is ashamed of his own wickedness. His penitence is the result of that sense of mystery and wonder which was Tasso's

own experience and which he interpreted in a broadly Platonic rather than Christian way:

> Fra se stesso pensava: 'Oh quante belle
> luci il tempio celeste in se raguna!
> Ha il suo gran carro il dì, l'aurate stelle
> spiega la notte e l'argentata luna;
> ma non è chi vagheggi o questa o quelle,
> e miriam noi torbida luce e bruna
> ch'un girar d'occhi, un balenar di riso,
> scopre in breve confin di fragil viso.'

A sense of the weakness of man and the futility of human effort recurs in the journey of Carlo and Ubaldo to the Fortunate Isles:

> Giace l'alta Cartago: a pena i segni
> de l'alte sue ruine il lido serba.
> Muoiono le città, muoiono i regni,
> copre i fasti e le pompe arena ed erba,
> e l'uom d'esser mortal par che si sdegni:
> oh nostra mente cupida e superba!

So the 'mago di Ascalonia' condemns his own folly of thinking that his learning could ever measure the creations of God; and Ugone contrasts in his exhortation to Goffredo the beauty of the heavens with the loneliness of man on earth:

> Quanto è vil la cagion ch'a la virtude
> umana è colà giù premio e contrasto!
> in che picciolo cerchio e fra che nude
> solitudini è stretto il vostro fasto!

Here then the unhappiness of the human lot is religious in origin, a sense of the greatness of God's creation which man can never fully experience on this earth, an aspiration to a beauty and mystery beyond the senses. In contrast with the loneliness, the weakness and fears of the poet, which receives poetic form in the gloomy horrors of darkness, is the glowing light that dispels fear, as in Goffredo's vision of Ugone:

> Pareagli esser traslato in un sereno
> candido e d'auree fiamme adorno e pieno;
> e mentre ammira in quell'eccelso loco
> l'ampiezza, i moti, i lumi e l'armonia,
> ecco cinto di rai, cinto di foco,
> un cavaliero incontra a lui venia.

Alongside this rather pondered philosophical faith should be set the simple acceptance of Christ which brings peace—the acceptance of Clorinda who has not questioned the Moslem faith in which she was brought up (and is free from the introspective anxiety of some of the Christians), but who asks for baptism and dies in peace without second thoughts. Her calm acceptance of death is the Christian ideal of peace in God; and her faith has the power to stir the errant Tancredi, who has set the love of a pagan woman above his duty as a Christian:

> In queste voci languide risuona

un non so che di flebile e soave
ch'al cor gli scende ed ogni sdegno ammorza,
e gli occhi a lagrimar gli invoglia e sforza.

The simplicity of this scene where the spiritual awakening of Tancredi is an intimate and personal drama that takes place within himself and without the external pressure of the Church has been contrasted by an Italian critic with the coldly formal sermon preached at him by Pietro the Hermit shortly after:

Questa sciagura tua del Cielo è un messo.

It is as though Tancredi is not to be entrusted with the working out of his own spiritual welfare, which must be placed in the hands of the Church. Similarly Rinaldo's moving experience on Monte Oliveto is reinforced by another formal sermon from Pietro. This concession to the spirit of the times is probably not insincere. Tasso was not content with the reconciliation of Plato and Aristotle with which he interpreted the real world and his own reactions to it. He felt the need of a creed, and the formalities of worship— hence his eagerness to consult the Inquisitors. He was seriously afraid of hell and only too eager to conform, so that the ceremonial of the poem, the confessing, baptizing, praying, preaching, parading correspond to an inner prompting in the poet. The love of colour and pageantry inspires some fine passages, particularly the procession to Monte Oliveto:

Va Piero solo innanzi e spiega al vento
il segno riverito in Paradiso,
e segue il corso a passo grave e lento
in duo lunghissimi ordini diviso.

At times, however, this religious mission is cold and unmoving. Tasso works too hard to raise the tone in obedience to the principles of magnificence and gravity which dictate his treatment of the military theme, and a formal pomp and display destroy the sense of religious devotion. God and his angels gaze down from a theatrically contrived stage setting, with Fate and Nature, Motion and Time, Place and Fortune carefully disposed around them. The religious struggle becomes a cold political battle in which the Christians' prayers are mechanically answered and those of their opponents ignored, while an unflinching love of blood and revenge moves the ministers of God and Tasso himself:

O giustizia del Ciel, quanto men presta
tanto più grave sovra il popol rio!
Dal tuo secreto proveder fu desta
l'ira ne' cor pietosi, e incrudelio.
Lavò co 'l sangue suo l'empio pagano
quel tempio che già fatto avea profano.

Appropriate as this may have been to the spirit of the Crusade, we feel neither interest nor sympathy for this political conflict reported in so partisan a manner.

Above all, the religious inspiration falls foul of a cold didactic sermonizing tendency which is the formal side of the Counter-Reformation. Sofronia reads the amorous Olindo a chilling lecture on his sins:

Amico, altri pensieri, altri lamenti,
per più alta cagione il tempo chiede.
Chè non pensi a tue colpe? e non rammenti
qual Dio prometta a i buoni ampia mercede?

—and most of Pietro's speeches are set in the same key. A severe Inquisitorial morality enters the medieval scene:

…in cima a l'erto e faticoso colle
de la virtù riposto è il nostro bene.
Chi non gela e non suda e non s'estolle
da le vie del piacer, là non perviene.

This didactic note in the *Liberata* sounds forced and superficial. It is not an integral part of the poem, and the attempt to strengthen it in the *Conquistata* proved quite unsuccessful. Indeed there is good external evidence of Tasso's purely formal attempts to add more weight to his poem in his Allegory, which was not composed until after the poem was written and first appeared only with the Bonnà editions. Tasso himself declared in a letter to Gonzaga that when he first began his poem the idea of an allegory was quite remote from his mind, but that when he had come more than halfway he began to think about an allegory, as something that might help him to meet his critics. The formal Allegory is thus an afterthought. This does not mean that symbolic meanings did not occur to Tasso as he wrote— in view of the derivative nature of so much of the material this would hardly have been possible. The tests of the enchanted wood are clearly a means of purification, and the garden of Armida a picture of the seduction of the senses; but the essence of these episodes is in their literal, not their allegorical senses, which is stressed, as Tasso admits, because of 'la strettezza dei tempi'; and in fact the Allegory was welcomed widely as justification for the amorous material, and helped to smooth the poem's path, not least in England.

The elements examined so far may all be considered essential features of the serious heroic epic: that is to say from the adaptation of the classical epics to the spirit of the Counter-Reformation Tasso evolved a poem celebrating an heroic and religious ideal of character, based on an historical theme and interpreted according to classical principles of verisimilitude and 'meraviglia'. In adopting this programme Tasso was conforming, sometimes more, sometimes less willingly, to the ideas of his time—to the literary Aristotelianism and Catholic severity of the late sixteenth century in Italy. His constant theorizing on the epic and his anxious self-abasement before the Inquisition are characteristic of his age, even more than they are of the man, and while Tasso was able to mould the ideals of the time to his own temperament, so that in the heroic and Christian ideal and the techniques of verisimilitude and 'meraviglia' he translates aspects of his own inner life, the inspiration here is uncertain and unequal just because of the pressure of external forces.

An epic constructed exclusively according to this formula could not satisfy Tasso because it would not allow him sufficient place for himself. He makes this clear in the *Arte Poetica* in his insistence on the poet's 'licenza del fingere'. The theme chosen should be sufficiently remote in time to allow the poet to invent as he sees fit, and the material should not be too extensive if the author is not to be forced to leave out 'gli episodi e gli altri ornamenti, i quali sono al poeta necessarissimi'. The episodes, which deal mainly with love and enchantments, have long been admired as the most personal and inspired parts of the poem. At the same time they are the traditional components of the chivalrous romance and were still of great popular appeal, so that Tasso in introducing his serious epic suggests that the introduction of elements not strictly sanctioned by his Muse is a sop to popular demands.

The distinction between the essential, serious, epic elements in his poem and the non-essential, romance, 'soave licor', is then something of which Tasso is so conscious as to feel the need of an explanation and apology from the very beginning. However, this attempt to forestall moral and religious objections is far from convincing and the simile of the medicine administered to the sick child (a conventional literary one), like so many of Tasso's similes, sounds quite inappropriate in its context (although it certainly comes directly from the experience of the unhealthy Tasso who would take no medicine that wasn't sweet). In fact it is in the 'sweets' of his poem that he seems most inspired, the love stories, the enchantments and the pictures of nature which are as though interludes in the serious action of the epic. The enchantments which, as we have seen, corresponded to a demand of Tasso's own personality, could be related, although rather loosely, to classical principles of 'meraviglia'.

The love episodes on the other hand were remote from classical precedent. Dido and Circe provided no more than a hint. In the relationship of Sofronia and Olindo, Tancredi and Clorinda, Erminia and Tancredi, Rinaldo and Armida, Tasso was able to express many aspects of the psychology of sexual love which he knew from his own experience or observation; and here he felt freer to develop and embroider his subject as his imagination moved him, unencumbered by historical sources, and not seriously hindered by principles of epic gravity.

His conception of love, as of heroism and of religion, is strongly influenced by his own deep-rooted anxiety and melancholy. It is not the happiness and tranquillity of reciprocal passion physically fulfilled or spiritually sublimated which stirs Tasso's imagination—any more than uninhibited courage or untroubled faith. It is love as an unknown, unreciprocated devotion or as frustrated physical desire—a mysterious fated power that cannot be resisted. The loves, all of which are finally legalized or 'spiritualized', are full of human weaknesses and suffering. Thus Olindo loves Sofronia from afar without daring to declare his 'cupidi desiri'. He is young and modest; she is 'matura', beautiful, chaste, retiring, taking no interest in her beauty and avoiding admirers. For centuries readers have interpreted this episode as a camouflage for the youthful Tasso's love for the mature Leonora d'Este, and while this has now been abandoned one cannot doubt that the incident springs from the poet's own experience. It is written from the viewpoint of Olindo; the reader, like the young lover, does not know what Sofronia feels:

> …ed ella
> o lo sprezza, o no 'l vede, o non s'avede.

But the unhappy Olindo is able to reveal his love by offering the supreme sacrifice of his own life to save Sofronia when she is bound to the stake—it is the adolescent dream—but he is bound to the same stake and in his despair dares to confess his love and his sensual desire:

> oh fortunati miei dolci martiri!
> s'impetrarò che, giunto seno a seno,
> l'anima mia ne la tua bocca io spiri.

To complain that Olindo's declaration is too sudden, or his language too rash in view of the flames at his feet, is to miss the point of this adolescent vision. The sense of outrage to the immaculate, unapproachable Sofronia in her exposure to the public gaze and then to the physical contact and immodest language of Olindo is indicative of the conflicting emotions in the mind of the young lover who both loves and resents, reveres and desires. The last-minute release by Clorinda brings the dream to a happy ending rather abruptly and in a few hasty lines we learn that Sofronia's modesty is overcome by Olindo's loving sacrifice, and Olindo's desires are legitimized by marriage. The antithetical language is a conscious attempt to reflect the tense conflict of the action: contrast the highly artificial style of the frenzied Olindo at the stake:

> Quest'è dunque quel laccio ond'io sperai
> teco accoppiarmi in compagnia di vita?

with the simple words of the calm Sofronia:

> Mira 'l ciel com'è bello, e mira il sole…

Erminia's love for Tancredi, like Olindo's for Sofronia, is undeclared and unreciprocated. She is a child indulging a dream. When Tancredi conquered her father's kingdom his courteous treatment of the captive princess conquered her too, and reluctantly she left her 'prigion diletta' to go with her mother to Jerusalem where she lives in her memories:

> Ama ed arde la misera, e sì poco
> in tale stato che sperar le avanza
> che nudrisce nel sen l'occulto foco
> di memoria via più che di speranza;
> e quanto è chiuso in più secreto loco,
> tanto ha l'incendio suo maggior possanza.

When Tancredi is wounded in his duel with Argante she longs to go out and help him, but her duty is to care for her opponent. The long debate with herself before she finally puts on Clorinda's armour and rides out is spoilt by Tasso's exaggerated concern with the verisimilitude of this incident, but it contains some moving poetry, notably the picture of the tender girl donning the hard armour, her gazing across the Christian camp in the starry night, and her flight from the hostile guards:

> Fuggì tutta la notte, e tutto il giorno
> errò senza consiglio e senza guida,
> non udendo o vedendo altro d'intorno,
> che le lagrime sue, che le sue strida.

She takes refuge with the shepherds and then disappears until the end of the poem where she and Vafrino find the senseless body of Tancredi and in her care of his wounds, bound with her own hair, she is able at last to show her love. It is another dream of the anguished lover, and the ending is deliberately left uncertain. Erminia is lodged near the wounded Tancredi, and we hear no more of her. Later Tasso feared that he might be criticized for this apparently happy ending and he declared his intention of making her become a nun. The essence of her story is in the pathos of her undeclared love which might well have finished in the cloister but is not, I think, spoilt by this inconclusive ending. She may be thought to have won Tancredi's love by her unselfish devotion or to have outlived her childish dreams in this brief contact with reality. Neither interpretation mars the delicacy of Tasso's portrait.

Tancredi's love for Clorinda is not only unhappy in that it is not returned, but is sinful in that it is for a pagan opponent and distracts him from his duty as a soldier of Christ. There is a note of despair and confusion in his conduct before ever he fights Clorinda, and in his masochistic surrender to the confident Amazon and his dazed contemplation of her when he should be fighting Argante, Tasso comes close to depicting his own dreamy passivity;

> Ecco io chino le braccia, e t'appresento
> senza difesa il petto: or chè no 'l fiedi?

—and in the mental anguish to which his killing of Clorinda brings him, Tancredi is beset by all the horrors of Tasso's own moral confusion—the terrors of the darkness and his fear of solitude—

> Vivrò fra i miei tormenti e le mie cure,
> mie giuste furie, forsennato, errante;
> paventarò l'ombre solinghe e scure
> che 'l primo error mi recheranno inante,
> e del sol che scoprì le mie sventure,
> a schivo ed in orrore avrò il sembiante.
> Temerò me medesmo; e da me stesso
> sempre fuggendo, avrò me sempre appresso.

In this torment the memory of Clorinda's simple faith and her pardon cannot help him, and only the rebuke of the priest and his fear of hell bring him to his senses, but even then only slowly. The parallel with Tasso's own experience is notable. In spite of the ill-digested Petrarchan and Virgilian reminiscences, Tancredi stands out as a moving and original portrait of the introspective tragic lover—he anticipates the anguish of the lovers of Romantic times when his popularity reached its peak.

Rinaldo's love for Armida is different from those of Olindo, Tancredi and Erminia, in that it is, until his awakening by Carlo and Ubaldo, entirely sensual. He is excused morally in that his downfall is entirely the result of enchantment. This episode was suggested to Tasso particularly by Homer's Circe, Ariosto's Alcina, and Trissino's Faleria, and certainly attracted him for the possibilities it offered in the depiction of physical and natural beauty and sensual pleasure. But his imagination is checked by moral considerations, and he is careful to stress the allegorical significance of the incident, and to try to improve morally on his models. Rinaldo is in the mould of Achilles, young, impetuous and resentful of authority, and his break with Goffredo and departure from the Christian camp is in the Homeric and romance tradition—but Tasso is concerned to show the moral development of Rinaldo who is to represent an ideal of Christian virtue. His love for Armida is the central experience in his education—he is made to see the dangers of excessive self-confidence, which caused him to fall a victim to Armida's wiles, while Carlo and Ubaldo, with the instruction of Pietro (the Church) and the 'mago di Ascalona' (scientific knowledge in conformity with religion), are able to resist the enchantments and bring him to his senses by showing him his reflection in a shield (reason). Rinaldo is thus able to leave Armida and to return to the Christian fold where he repents of his past ways, confesses, prays and is then able to overcome the enchantments of the forest—from an egoistic and headstrong youth he has become a modest God-fearing man. The reconciliation with Armida at the end of the poem is due partially at least to Tasso's desire for moral perfection in Rinaldo, who does not desert his seductress, as Aeneas had deserted Dido, but forgives and converts her.

In spite of the didactic and allegorical elements, however, the seduction of Rinaldo in the garden of Armida is perhaps the most inspired passage in the whole poem; it hinges on a theme prominent in Tasso's poetry, sensual love. But here once more is the poetry not of fulfilment but of anticipation—not sensual satisfaction but erotic desire. Armida from the beginning reveals all the artful wiles of the court lady who keeps her admirers in a frenzy of anxious expectation: she is the complete flirt, such as might have tormented and delighted the youthful Tasso at Ferrara. Her enchanted garden stimulates the senses without satisfying them. Tasso lingers lovingly over his picture of the bathing girls, and even Carlo and Ubaldo stop to watch them, knowing they are sinful. The sense of sinfulness, the frustrating veil of the running water, the long swathing hair, emphasize the erotic delight:

> e'l crin, ch'in cima al capo avea raccolto
> in un sol nodo, immantinente sciolse,
> che lunghissimo in giù cadendo e folto
> d'un aureo manto i molli avori involse.
> Oh che vago spettacolo è lor tolto!

Even Rinaldo in Armida's embrace is anxious and unsatisfied in the frustration of a merely sensual love that is never calmed:

> Sovra lui pende; ed ei nel grembo molle
> le posa il capo, e 'l volto al volto attolle,
> e i famelici sguardi avidamente
> in lei pascendo si consuma e strugge.
> S'inchina, e i dolci baci ella sovente

> liba or da gli occhi e da le labra or sugge,
> ed in quel punto ei sospirar si sente …

Their passion is selfish: Armida wants to be worshipped and served, and Rinaldo forgets his duty in his attempt to satisfy his senses—but Rinaldo's love is spiritualized by his return to duty and Armida is redeemed by his love and forgiveness. However, this new, spiritual love is barely hinted at—it does not move Tasso because it lies outside his experience. What does move him is a world of alluring and unattainable female charm, and he succeeds, as few poets have done before or since, in expressing in his poetry the fascination and the frustration of the senses.

In the love episodes, then, Tasso's inner experience finds poetic expression, but to isolate the loves from the rest of the epic and to claim that here the poet's self is revealed free from the restricting influence of literary or moral pressure is far from the truth. Literary influences are strong here and the moral severity of the Counter-Reformation frequently intrudes. These are not, however, totally external, unwelcome impositions—they were part of the poet's own mind and imagination. He saw Armida as a Circe-Dido-Alcina-Faleria figure, and he felt the sinfulness of sensual love. So the love-stories are woven into the action as essential components of the heroic Christian epic, and Tasso insisted on the correctness of his decision, which he was prepared to defend, he said, on the authority of Aristotle: epic and romance were not, he maintained, separate genres.

As a background to the loves and feats of arms, the religious miracles and romantic enchantments, Tasso paints in a highly subjective and largely original natural scene. His nature descriptions are rarely superfluous ornaments or interludes: they are an adjunct to the action and emphasize its emotional tones. Trees and winds, sunshine and storm take on human attributes and reflect the mood of the characters or of the author. As in the *Aminta* therefore the natural background blends easily into the human action. The wind takes a part in the narrative, almost like a chorus, threatening in the storm, plaintive with Erminia by the brook, gentle and soothing in the Isles of Fortune, evoking sobs and sighs in the trees of the enchanted wood; and when the wind ceases the silence itself befriends the actors:

> Senza risposta aver, va per l'amico
> silenzio de le stelle a l'alte mura.

The trees and plants also participate: the great myrtle speaks with Clorinda's voice, and a chain of flowers binds Rinaldo (as the tree bound Silvia in the *Aminta*). The fascination of the garden of Armida is that around the sensuous lovers the trees and plants and animals repeat the human abandon:

> Raddoppian le colombe i baci loro,
> ogni animal d'amar si riconsiglia:
> par che la dura quercia e 'l casto alloro
> e tutta la frondosa ampia famiglia,
> par che la terra e l'acqua e formi e spiri
> dolcissimi d'amor sensi e sospiri.

But this apparently natural scene is really contrived. Here where we find Tasso's most elaborate nature description the subject is not a landscape but a garden, a work of art not of nature; and this garden is conditioned by the human action. It is a confusion of overluxuriant growth, but a baroque confusion, consciously disordered.

The natural scene is therefore treated extremely subjectively. It is difficult to speak of love of nature in Tasso: to him nature is kindly or hostile, attractive or repellent, not of itself, but according as one comes to it in peace or in anxiety, elated or afraid. Night, for example, may be friendly and comforting or mysterious and threatening. It is frequently associated with fear of the darkness, with the nightmares of the fevered mind and the unseen powers of evil:

> Ma quando parte il sol, qui tosto adombra
> notte, nube, caligine ed orrore
> che rassembra infernal, che gli occhi ingombra
> di cecità, ch'empie di tema il core.

The darkness, however, may be friendly: the confident mind has no such fears—the enchanted wood is 'lietamente ombroso' to the converted Rinaldo. The night may also be comforting when the darkness is dispelled by stars or moonlight, and Tasso has some superb pictures of its calm and beauty which, in spite of frequent literary reminiscences, still seem fresh and immediate in their fusion of sound and image:

> Era la notte, e 'l suo stellato velo
> chiaro spiegava e senza nube alcuna,
> e già spargea rai luminosi e gelo
> di vive perle la sorgente luna.

The light, the dawn, the sunshine, on the other hand, accompany the triumphant progress of the powers of goodness—in subtle ways Tasso parallels the progressive lightening of the sky with the advance of the Christian army, for example, or with Rinaldo's spiritual awakening:

> Così pregava, e gli sorgeva a fronte
> fatta già d'auro la vermiglia aurora
> che l'elmo e l'arme e intorno a lui del monte
> le verdi cime illuminando indora.

Each of the elements of nature is thus felt rather than described. Botanical, zoological and geographical knowledge is at a minimum—the few conventional similes of wild life are pallid beside Dante's—but nature evokes a deep emotional response. Deserts are vast solitudes; mountains are remote, fraught with difficulties and threatening. Water in particular fascinates Tasso, often as a kind of symbol of human restlessness: it may be cruel and harsh in the turbulence of flood, rushing anxiously on in the mountain stream, seeking the peace of the sea where at last it is calm:

> … dove il fiume
> queta in letto maggior l'onde correnti.

It is mysterious and fascinating: although transparent it conceals the bathing girls, and although clear and beautiful its depths hold strange poisons:

> ma dentro a i freddi suoi cristalli asconde
> di tosco estran malvagità secreta.

Nature is neutral therefore: natural pnenomena reflect or symbolize human predicaments. Tasso's idyll does not betoken a romantic faith in the healing powers of mother nature. In the *Aminta* the refuge of a natural golden age is known to be illusory: and in the *Liberata* the simple pastoral life, for all its charms, cannot hold Erminia. It is a refuge from the city, from action and intrigue, but Erminia, like Tasso, could not settle in the rustic tranquillity; and the idyll of Armida's garden is blatantly false.

Stylistically this intensely subjective view of nature is brought out by a frequent use of personification to which the reader becomes so habituated that he hardly notices it. Night 'embraces' the earth, 'yields' to day, 'comes from the womb of its mother'; the sun 'threatens', the mountain 'hides its face'; the wind 'plays' with the waves; the dawn 'appears at its balcony'; the silence is 'friendly'; the stars 'cruel', the moon 'miserly'. And as Tasso's view is so personal and emotional, hardly observing but rather feeling the object, a simple generic vocabulary gives the barest outline of the scene, which is filled in with a picture in sound, so that readers are conscious of a music or harmony in Tasso's poetry that is difficult to define, but has stimulated so many composers to set his verse to music. The effectiveness of these passages has been variously attributed to the great care with which Tasso analysed the effects of aspirants and sibilants, long and short vowels, single and double consonants in the rhyme words, etc.; to his clever use of traditional literary images for their associative effect; and to the intensity of his emotional life. The result is that strange vitality of the written word which recalls and at the same time brings added poignancy to experience.

Thus each of the major motives of inspiration in the poem, arms, religion, magic, love, nature, while drawn from traditional literary sources, is interpreted subjectively and in large part originally. The unifying factor is not the narrative theme which is split into often conflicting romance and classical elements, but the poet's own personality, which by means of his style colours his heterogeneous material. The subjectivity and originality of Tasso's style makes his poetry among the most difficult for translators, and the non-Italian reader may miss much of the subtlety of the poet's effects. As so often in Tasso, there is a confusing combination of traditional with original: he studied and analysed carefully the stylistic devices of the classical epic, which reappear profusely in his poetry; yet he uses them subjectively to express new and intimate themes, outside the classical originals; and he goes beyond the rhetorical techniques in his attempt to convey indeterminate hinterlands of experience which he could not particularize or rationalize.

The formal basis of Tasso's style is classical rhetoric: his analysis of style into sublime, mediocre and lowly, and his enunciation of the features of the sublime style is close to Aristotle's *Rhetoric* and Demetrius' treatise on *Style*, and is largely based on examples drawn from Homer and Virgil. Thus in his pursuit of sublimity he avoids the language of everyday life and particularly recommends the use of a learned literary vocabulary with 'foreign' words and Latinisms—hence 'destra' is used for 'mano', 'piaghe' for 'ferite', 'lumi' or 'luci' for 'occhi', 'atro' for 'oscuro'. Compound forms replace simple ones, 'dibattendo' for 'battendo', 'discorrere' for 'scorrere', 'dimostrare' for 'mostrare', etc.; and certain high-sounding epithets are much abused— 'grande, alto, nobile, generoso, magnanimo', etc. The word-order is frequently changed from normal prose-usage to give dignity and solemnity— sometimes effectively, sometimes with a hollow pompousness:

Allor sen ritornar le squadre pie
per le dianzi da lor calcate vie.

Repetition anaphora, syntactical symmetry give added weight:

quindi son l'alte mura aperte ed arse,
quindi l'armate schiere uccise e sparse.

Antithesis, hyperbole and enumeration highlight the scene:

su 'l morto il vivo, il vincitor su 'l vinto.

e fatto è il corpo suo solo una piaga.
Qui mille immonde Arpie vedresti e mille
Centauri e Sfingi e pallide Gorgoni.

Prosaic phrases or words are replaced by periphrasis, so that a ship is a 'curvo pinto', the navel 'la 've primo s'apprende nostro alimento': and abstract qualities are personified: 'Amor, Cortesia, Confusione, Sdegno', etc.

This basis of classical rhetoric does not, however, check the individuality of the poet's style. Even in the comparatively neutral passages which set the scene Tasso impresses on us his own reaction to the physical world. He starts from Aristotelian principles:

necessària è in lui (il poeta epico) l'energia, la quale sì con parole pone innanzi agli occhi la cosa che pare altrui non di udirla ma di vederla.

This does not in practice lead to minute and objective descriptions, but to a personal view in which the poet selects a detail (his own view): Guelfo and Ubaldo see the enchanted boat of fortune appear—a speck, the stern, and finally the pilot:

vider picciola nave, e in poppa quella
che guidar li dovea fatal donzella

Similarly the return of the messenger sent out by Argante to challenge the Christians is described as if seen from the city walls:

… tornò il re d'arme al suo viaggio
per l'orme ch'al venir calcate furo.

The visual aspect is often explicitly stressed by the poet, so that his description becomes a picture or even a stage-setting:

Degne d'un chiaro sol, degne d'un pieno
teatro, opre sarian sì memorande:

—and a carefully contrived word-order presents startling 'coups de théâtre' as when Erminia finds the wounded Tancredi:

Salta di sella e gli discopre il viso,
ed:—Oimè,—grida—è qui Tancredi ucciso.

There is similarly a great attention to sound: a lengthy section in the *Arte Poetica* analyses the sound effects of different letters and their combinations. Thus there is the simple mimicry of the clash of battle, winds and waves, trumpets—even, in a rare humorous aside, of ducks:

stuol d'anitre loquaci in secca riva
con rauco mormorar lieto l'attende …

There is also the subtle reinforcement of an image by phonetic means: the vastness of a sea, or of a desert:

… a portar guerra

a i gran regni del mar e de la terra.
E in quelle solitudini arenose …

Notable too is the precision of the lines describing Argante,

… che se stesso mira
del proprio sangue suo macchiato e molle,

so that he sees his blood ('macchiato') before he feels it ('molle'). All these devices indicate an intensity of experience which gives vitality often to the most unpromising material.

However, it is not only his 'participation' in the physical sensation which gives Tasso's style its subjective character. Behind the formal narrative we are constantly made aware of the emotional response of the poet to his story—his reaction of wonder, excitement, anxiety, horror. This is apparent of course in his frequent and feeling intrusion into his own narrative:

Il padre, ah non più padre! (ahi fera sorte,
ch'orbo di tanti figli a un punto il face!)

Thus Tasso establishes a bond with his characters: his sympathy, sorrow, wonder, accompany them, as when Tancrediun wittingly wounds Clorinda:

Misero, di che godi? ….

or when Armida swoons at Tancredi's departure:

Chiudesti i lumi, Armida: il Cielo avaro
invidiò il conforto a i tuoi martiri.

There are, however, many less obvious ways in which Tasso's style is coloured by his emotional reaction to his material. The personification of natural objects, referred to above, is one of these: the moon feels Tasso's horror at the incantation of Ismeno:

e la luna si turba e le sue corna
di nube avolge, e non appar più fora.

The dawn feels his relief at the defeat of evil:

l'alba lieta rideva …

Latinisms are used to express emotional tones for which the normal terms are too hackneyed or too pallid: 'flebili atti' ('lagrime'), 'sincero' ('puro'), 'padri' ('genitori'), etc. Syntactical variations reinforce the intensity of expression: as of Erminia 'che già sente palpitarsi il petto' (in place of 'si sente palpitare'), where the displacement of the reflexive pronoun strengthens the 'feeling' and increases the intimacy of the dependent infinitive 'palpitare'. Another characteristic device is the use of the pronoun in place of the reflexive particle, as to convey the tenderness of Erminia's invocation to

the Christian tents: 'Raccogliete me dunque …' (for 'accoglietemi').

There is also a tendency to emphasize the psychological effect, so that often the psychological precedes the physical description, as in the lines on the wounded Tancredi, where the vital 'despair' has pride of place:

… come il move
suo disperato di morir desio,
squarcia le fasce e le ferite …

Erminia has only been presented to the reader as 'bella' before she makes her first 'action', a sigh—she is to be a sigh throughout the poem. And Olindo has almost no physical characteristics other than being a 'giovinetto', but many psychological ones: 'cupidi desiri', 'modesto', 'brama assai, poco spera e nulla chiede'.

A result of this marked lyricism and preoccupation with the emotional situation rather than the physical fact is that there is often a vagueness in Tasso's narrative which is reflected in his style. The details which do not contribute to the psychological situation are often ignored or hastily passed over: so that we do not know how Clorinda recognized the innocence of Sofronia and Olindo; nor do we know the end of Erminia's story, or of Armida's. This is partially attributable to Tasso's desire for 'magnificenza', his fear of lowering the tone of his poem by realistic and unpoetical detail. Thus the particular is replaced by the universal:

Tosto, ciascun, da gran desio compunto,
veste le membra de l'usate spoglie.
(il) buon Tancredi e … chi vien con esso.

In many such cases the generic vocabulary sounds weak and flat, but more often the lack of physical detail is an advantage, and the vague phrases achieve their effects by their sound alone. This is particularly true of Tasso's treatment of magic, where the supernatural effects are cloaked in a mysterious reticence. How do Guelfo and Ubaldo pass from the bed of the river to the shore?

Gli accoglie il rio ne l'alto seno, e l'onda
soavemente in su gli spinge e porta.

Nor are we given any close description of Armida's garden which is an uncharted profusion of growth, of twisting paths and screens, half cultivated, half wild. Mystery would seem to be a conscious aim of Tasso—he feels the poetry of the unknown or the half-hinted truth. Female beauty is invariably half-concealed, mysterious and alluring:

stassi l'avaro sguardo in se raccolto,
e i tesori d'amore e i suoi nasconde.

The reader never knows how the image of the Virgin disappeared from the mosque in Canto II:

> ch' incerta fama è ancor se ciò s'ascriva
> ad arte umana od a mirabil opra.

Situations are presented often not from the all-seeing gaze of the poet, but from that of the hesitating, fearful, hopeful participant: thus Sofronia is seen from Olindo's viewpoint, and the fleeing Armida, after the defeat of the pagan army, from the viewpoint of the pursuing Rinaldo, or the spectator's:

> Al fin raccolta entro quel caro laccio,
> che le fu caro forse …

Tasso's 'forse' leave the matter in doubt.

In his attempt to convey these psychological subtleties Tasso often uses an irrational and illogical language, sometimes consciously ambiguous: characteristic is his 'non so che', which abandons the attempt to be rational.

> In queste voci languide risuona
> un non so che di flebile e soave.
> Non sai ben dir s'adorna o se negletta …

—hence too his self-corrections:

> non scese no, precipitò di sella.

Thus grammatical categories are blurred, ambiguities add shades of meaning, and literary allusions also add their overtones—as in the picture of Gildippe and Odoardo who take on something of Dante's Paolo and Francesca:

> E son que' duo che van sì giunti in uno.

Tasso has not generally been given credit for this personal and largely original style—indeed, stylistically he has often been criticized as contributing to and encouraging the 'corrupt' taste of the Seicento. There is certainly some truth in this view, but it can only be accepted with reservations. Tasso's poetry has affinities with that of the Secentisti, but it is still far removed from them and it is as well to stress the differences. The first is quantitive. 'Secentismo' evolved out of the poetic styles of the Cinquecento—it is characterized not by new devices, but by the intensification of traditional techniques: antithesis, hyperbole, personification, inversion, play on words, periphrasis, etc., which occur with moderate frequency in the poets of the sixteenth century and with unrestrained profusion in the 'Secentisti'. Such devices are used with infinitely greater restraint by Tasso. Secondly the Secentisti exaggerated the forms of expression until the original inspiration and feeling were often lost and the means of expression became all important: the aim of the poet, said Marino, was to shock. This

is not perhaps so remote from Tasso's principle that the poet should arouse 'maraviglia', but in Tasso's poetry the conceit normally arises directly out of its poetic context—it is functional in that it reflects a condition or situation in the narrative; it exists in order to draw attention, not to itself, but to an unusual concept.

If there are moments when the charge of 'Secentismo' seems justified, such moments most often occur when Tasso is striving to maintain the illustrious tone which he believed essential in the epic. Sometimes his play on words is hollow and artificial: Clorinda's nurse explains her mother's fear that the birth of a white baby to coloured parents might have aroused her father's suspicions:

> ch'egli avria dal candor che in te si vede
> argomentato in lei non bianca fede.

There are some intellectually contrived antitheses, as of Rinaldo resisting Armida's entreaties that he should not abandon her:

> resiste e vince: e in lui trova impedita
> Amor l'entrata, il lagrimar l'uscita.

—and an excessive symmetry of syntax, as of Olindo:

> brama assai, poco spera, e nulla chiede:
> nè sa scoprirsi, o non ardisce: ed ella
> o lo sprezza, o no 'l vede, o non s'avede.

The word-order is sometimes displaced to the point of obscurity:

> Tu lo mio stabilire e in tempo corto
> puoi ridrizzar il tuo caduto seggio.

There are too some exaggerated and inapt metaphors, of which the most criticized perhaps is the description of Erminia relating her woes to the fields:

> e secretari del suo amore antico
> fea i muti campi e quel silenzio amico.

Most of Tasso's conceits fall within these categories, and are usually a combination of two or more of these devices: antithesis, word-play, metaphorical extremes, parallelism of syntax, and displaced word-order.

The greatest concentrations of conceits are in a few emotionally tense and confused situations—the Sofronia-Olindo episode, the death of Clorinda, Erminia's love for Tancredi, and Rinaldo in Armida's garden—and here the formal devices are used carefully with relation to their context. Thus the contrast between Sofronia's restraint and reticence and the reactions of her lover and the general public is stressed in antithetical word-play:

Ahi! tanta amò la non amante amata.
… e pianta da ciascun, non piagni.

Tancredi's emotional *volte-face* when he kills his opponent and discovers it is Clorinda justifies the antithetical

… a dar si volse
vita con l'acqua a chi co 'l ferro uccise.

Equally justified is the complicated play on the lover's eyes as mirrors of his lady's beauty, continued for several stanzas in the account of Rinaldo resting on Armida's lap:

Volgi,—dicea—deh volgi—il cavaliero
—a me quegli occhi onde beata bei.

This is no mere playing on words: it responds closely to the situation of the vain self-loving Armida gazing in her mirror, and the adoring Rinaldo who is no longer anything in himself, but merely a reflection, or an echo of his lady:

chè son, se tu no 'l sai, ritratto vero
de le bellezze tue gli incendi miei.

Erminia's antithetical style similarly responds to her inner conflict, as a Moslem loving a Christian:

Ella l'amato medicar desia,
e curar il nemico a lei conviene.

—and her play on words in describing her lover to the enemy king is essential to her situation:

Ahi quanto è crudo nel ferire! a piaga
ch'ei faccia, erba non giova od arte maga.

So too Tasso's distortions of word-order have a carefully considered poetic effect, as in conveying the love-sick Erminia's longing for Tancredi:

O belle a gli occhi miei tende latine!

—or Goffredo's veneration for Jerusalem:

Queste sacre e dal Ciel dilette mura.

One should not therefore label the *Liberata* a predominantly Secentista poem, or consider the conceits impurities in a generally pure work. Tasso endeavoured in his style to convey the force and delicacy of his reaction to the story he had to tell, and the conceits are an almost inevitable accompaniment of this subjectivity of style. Far from priding himself on new and startling effects, Tasso condemned the excesses of the 'concettisti' and shunned their obscurity—and when he himself moved towards greater clarity and simplicity of style his verse was generally found to be pallid and monotonous, as we shall see later.

Source: C.P. Brand, "The Epic: The 'Gerusalemme Liberata,'" in *Torquato Tasso: A Study of the Poet and of His Contribution to Literature,* Cambridge University Press, 1965, pp. 79–118.

SOURCES

Bakhtin, Mikhail Mikhailovich, "Epic and Novel" in *The Dialogic Imagination*, University of Texas Press, 1981.

Boileau, Nicholas, *The Art of Poetry*, translated by John Dryden, Rentley, 1683.

Clark, John, *A History of Epic Poetry*, Haskell, 1973.

Cook, Patrick, "The Epic Chronotope from Ariosto to Spenser," in *Annali D'Italianistica*, Vol. 12, 1994, pp. 115–142.

Dacier, Anne, Letters, "Preface to Homer," and Notes to *Iliad*, in *Madame Dacier: Scholar and Humanist*, edited by Fern Farnham, Angel Press, 1976.

Dryden, John, *Essays of John Dryden*, edited by W. P. Ker, Clarendon Press, 1926.

Dubois, Page, *History, Rhetorical Description and the Epic: From Homer to Spenser*, Brewer, 1982.

Feeney, D.C., "Epic Hero and Epic Fable," in *Comparative Literature*, Vol. 38, 1986, pp. 137–158.

Lewalski, Barbara, "The Genres of *Paradise Lost*: Literary Genre as a Means of Accommodation," in *Milton Studies*, Vol. 17, 1983.

Rowe, Elizabeth Singer, *Letters Moral and Entertaining in Prose and Verse*, Robert Johnson, 1805.

Quint, David, *Epics and Empire: Politics and Generic Form From Virgil to Milton*, Princeton University Press, 1993.

Tasso, Torquato, *Discourses on the Heroic Poem*, translated by Mariella Cavalchini and Irene Samuel, Clarendon Press, 1973. Translation of *Discrsi dell' Arte e del Poema Eroico*, 1594.

Tillyard, E. M. W., *The English Epic and Its Background*, Oxford University Press, 1966.

FURTHER READING

Bowra, C.M., *Heroic Poetry*, MacMillan, 1952.
    Bowra explores the features of epic poetry from the ancients through early modern times.

Broaddus, James, *Spenser's Allegory of Love: Social Vision in Books III, IV, and V of The Faerie Queene*, Fairleigh Dickinson University Press, 1995.
    This work explores how love, both romantic and patriotic, works in Spenser's poem.

Cavanagh, Sheila, *Wanton Eyes and Chaste Desires: Female Sexuality in The Faerie Queene*, Indiana University Press, 1994.
    Examines the uses of female sexuality in understanding how Spenser creates female characters.

Curran, Stuart, "The Epic" in *Poetic Form and British Romanticism*, Oxford University Press, 1986.

Curran explores how poetic form influenced and shaped Romantic poetry. This essay focuses on epic poetry and its features.

Dennis, John, *Advancement and Reformation of Modern Poetry*, Richard Parker, 1701, Garland, 1971.
Dennis discusses all types of poetry and how these poetic forms developed, spending a good deal of time on epic and heroic poetry.

Gutschera, Deborah, "'A Shape of Brightness': The Role of Women in Romantic Epic," in *Philological Quarterly*, Vol. 66, 1987, pp. 87–108.
Discusses the role of women and female characters in Renaissance epic.

Hayley, William, *An Essay on Epic Poetry*, J. Dodsley, 1782.
This major essay, written in poetic form, calls on British poets to write new epics. He creates not only a definition for epic poetry, but a tradition as well. In addition, Hayley specifically tells women to write epic poems.

Murrin, Michael, *The Allegorical Epic: Essays in Its Rise and Fall*, University of Chicago Press, 1980.
Murrin explores the Renaissance epic and its allegorical elements.

Treip, Mindele Anne, *Allegorical Poetics & The Epic: The Renaissance Tradition to Paradise Lost*, University Press of Kentucky, 1994.
Treip chronicles the epic poets, their poems, and their times.

Wacker, Norman, "Epic and the Modern Long Poem: Virgil, Blake, and Pound," in *Comparative Literature*, Vol. 42, 1990, pp. 126–143.
Wacker makes comparisons between Renaissance epics and Victorian long narrative poems.

Le Morte d'Arthur

THOMAS MALORY

1469

Although *Le Morte d'Arthur* is thought to have been written in 1469, the first known publication was in 1485, by William Caxton. Caxton's edition was divided into 21 books and 506 chapters. In 1934 another manuscript was discovered in the Fellows Library of Winchester College. The text of this second manuscript is more fully developed in sections than the earlier known edition and it is divided into ten parts, forming five larger sections. This later manuscript was published in 1947 as *The Works of Sir Thomas Malory*. This second text, with the divisions into five books, is the text most commonly used text today.

In composing this work, Malory took a body of legends, mostly French in origin, and adapted them to English life, with an English perspective. Malory's sources, dating from 1225–1230, are largely a selection of courtly romances about Launcelot. These stories purport to be historical accounts of King Arthur and his knights and of their quest for the Holy Grail. In addition to the French sources, Malory added material from a fourteenth century English alliterative poem, the *Morte Arthur*. Although it is probable that a real Arthur did exist (it is a common name), there is little actual historical basis for the stories, which are largely legend and folklore. Many scholars have attempted to prove the veracity of the work, but the attraction of Malory's work has always been the text itself, with its emphasis on courtly love, honor and virtue, valor and devotion, magic and miracles. *Le Morte d'Arthur* was imme-

diately popular with readers and critics and has remained so. It has been an influential source for many writers, including Edmund Spenser's *The Faerie Queene* and Alfred Tennyson's *Idylls of the King.*

AUTHOR BIOGRAPHY

The authorship of *Le Morte d'Arthur* has long been in dispute, although for practical purposes, the actual identity of Thomas Malory is now less important than the literary folklore that surrounds this individual. Traditionally, this text has been credited to Thomas Malory, a knight, who was born in about 1410 in Warwickshire, England. As a young man, Malory is said to have served with the Earl of Warwick's forces in Calais, and later, succeeded to his father's estate in 1433 or 1434, probably when he was in his twenties. Shortly after, Malory married, although there is little reliable information about his personal life with his wife, Elizabeth. There is evidence of one child, a son, Robert, although there may have been more. There are, however, accounts of Malory's imprisonment, which followed what appeared to be a fairly respectable existence. After inheriting his father's estate, and a second estate a few years later, Malory led a quiet, and by most accounts, affluent life. But for some reason, in 1450, Malory turned to crime. The list of his crimes is appalling, including multiple rapes, robberies, and attempted murder. After a prison escape, Malory turned to robbing churches, and was again arrested, this time serving three years. When he was released, Malory returned to crime, was imprisoned again, and again escaped. However, he was evidently in prison once again when Edward IV issued a pardon for prisoners that specifically excluded Malory. Malory died in 1471 and is buried in Newgate, just outside London.

Malory is credited with writing *Le Morte d'Arthur* during the last years of his imprisonment. Scholars and historians who dispute Malory's authorship do so on the grounds that he was little more than a common thief, and was therefore, not capable of composing such an important work. There is no way to assert with complete accuracy, if this Thomas Malory, or any other Thomas Malory, was actually the author of this work, but Malory's criminal record is not an indicator of his literary capabilities. *Le Morte d'Arthur* is filled with battles, chivalry, jealousy, and lust. These are all ideas that

Malory, the knight turned criminal, would know about, and with which he would be familiar. The statement at the end of the book says that *Le Morte d'Arthur* was completed in "the ix yere of the reygne of kyng edward the fourth." That date corresponds to the period between March 4,1469 and March 3, 1470, near the end of Malory's imprisonment and life. *Le Morte d'Arthur* was finally printed in 1485 by William Caxton. There is no evidence that Malory wrote any other texts.

PLOT SUMMARY

I. The Tale of King Arthur

The birth of Arthur results from King Uther's deceptive bedding, which is really a rape, of Arthur's mother, Igrayne. Merlin, who arranges with Uther for the satisfaction of his lust, is promised the child that results. After Arthur's birth, Merlin sends the child to live with Sir Ector. Two years later, Uther dies, and Merlin secures the dying king's promise that Arthur shall be king. With Uther's death, the kingdom is in disarray with several of the barons struggling to gain control. Merlin and the Archbishop arrange for a gathering of the lords. When the lords arrive, they find a sword buried in a stone. Upon the stone are the words, "whoso pulleth out this sword from this stone and anvil is duly born king of all England." None of the men present can budge the sword, but Arthur, who mistakes the sword for the sword mislaid by Kay, easily pulls the sword free. However, the lords do not wish to be ruled by a boy and resist proclaiming Arthur king. Eventually, however, the lords agree, and as king, Arthur is successful, ruling equitably and cautiously.

When Arthur has himself crowned king of Wales, the husbands of Uther's three daughters, who are themselves kings, arrive for the coronation. But instead of arriving to celebrate with Arthur, Kings Lot, Nantres, and Uriens arrive to make war. Although Merlin tells the three kings of Arthur's heritage and arranges a truce, Merlin returns to Arthur telling him to attack because destiny is with him. After his easy victory over his enemies, Arthur meets and falls in love with Guinevere. Arthur also creates a child, Mordred, with Lot's wife, whom Arthur does not realize is his sister. Soon, Merlin appears disguised first to tell Arthur that he is Uther's son, and later, to tell Arthur that he has lain with his sister and created a child who will destroy him. When Arthur loses his sword in battle against

Sir Pellanor, Merlin leads Arthur to the Lady of the Lake, where Arthur promises a later gift in return for his sword, which will protect him, as long as he wears it. In a final effort to secure his kingdom and himself, Arthur orders the deaths of all highborn children born on May Day, but the reason for this order, Mordred, survives. And instead, Arthur incurs the wrath of his lords. Merlin has had a part in every event that has shaped Arthur's life although he does not yet know this.

The story now shifts to an emphasis on revenge, as a magical sword is used by a newly released prisoner, Sir Balyn, to slay the Lady of the Lake. When Sir Balyn attempts to win back Arthur's favor, he accidentally kills Launcelor of Ireland, one of Arthur's men, and is responsible for the suicide of Launceor's sister. Soon another battle with King Lot ensues, and Pellanor kills the king, and Arthur manages a great victory over his enemies. Merlin warns Arthur that he must guard his scabbard, and that the woman to whom he gives it, will steal it. Arthur gives it to Morgan le Fay, his sister, who gives the scabbard to her lover. After many battles, Balyn dies in battle with his brother, the two having killed one another by mistake. Merlin fixes Balyn's sword so that no man can use it except for Launcelot or Galahad.

Against Merlin's advice, Arthur married Guinevere. Her dowry is the Round Table, which seats 150, the seats of which Merlin fills with as many knights as he can find. One of the new knights is Lot's son, Gawain. After some minor skirmishes, Arthur establishes the new code for the knights of the Round Table. The new code demands that the knights be merciful, righteous in their battles, and honorable toward women.

II. The Tale of Arthur and King Lucius

This book recounts the battles between Arthur and Lucius of Rome. Lucius has demanded tributes from Arthur, who refuses. Arthur promises war and is supported by his knights, who are eager for an honorable war. Although Lucius is warned of Arthur's strength, he chooses to attack anyway. Leaving his grieving Guinevere behind, Arthur leaves England for Normandy. The battles begin earlier than planned, after Gawain and King Bors precipitate a clash with the Romans. In spite of their lack of preparedness, Arthur's forces destroy the enemy with Gawain emerging as a heroic figure. Arthur next sends Launcelot and Cador to deliver the Roman prisoners to Paris but Roman forces ambush them. Launcelot proves himself a hero, and the

small force defeats the Romans. Lucius' men beg him to end the war, but the Romans choose to attack yet again. This time, Arthur vows to take no prisoners, killing every one of his enemies in the battle. Arthur is crowned king of Rome, where he apportions the city's wealth. Soon Arthur and his men return to England and their wives.

III. The Tale of Sir Launcelot du Lake

After his victory in Rome, Launcelot returns to England, an honored and heroic knight. This book relates Launcelot's adventures, which embody the ideal heroic knight and the code of the Round Table. In the first of the episodes related here, Launcelot is asleep under a tree when Morgan le Fay and three other ladies find him. She uses magic to return him to her castle, where the women demand that he must choose one of them or he will die. Launcelot is saved when he promises to help Sir Bagdemagus in a tournament. On his way to the tournament, Launcelot fights and wounds another knight, who has attacked him as he rested. After he wins the tournament, Launcelot is guided to Tarquin, who had earlier captured Launcelot's nephew. Launcelot kills Tarquin and has all of the prisoners released. He next kills a thief and rapist who had been attacking women, before moving on to Tentagil castle, where Arthur was conceived, and where Launcelot kills the giant that had been attacking women. As his adventures continue, Launcelot gives his armor to Sir Kay to protect him, and when a maiden seeks his help, Launcelot willingly risks his life to do so. He even agrees to help a lady who deceptively attempts to have him killed. Soon, everyone knows of Launcelot's many heroic deeds.

IV. The Tale of Sir Gareth

Gareth is another of Lot's son and the brother of Gawain. He is the perfect knight, more humble and pure than all the other knights. When this book begins, he is working as a kitchen boy and has adopted the name, Beaumains. Sir Kay is angered that this kitchen boy, whom he has always distrusted, is made a knight and that he is given an adventure, which is to help the maiden, Lynet. However, when Sir Kay follows him, Gareth seizes Kay's spear and shield. After several adventures and the defeat of many criminal types, Gareth proves his worthiness to be a knight of the Round Table. Finally after a tournament in which Gareth, unknowingly, fights his brother Gawain, Gareth is married to Lyonesse to whom he has been a devoted suitor.

V. The Book of Sir Tristram de Lyones

The book recounts the adventures of Sir Tristram, who at eighteen meets Isolde and falls in love with her. Unfortunately, he is bound to deliver Isolde to King Mark, whom Tristram serves. The love potent prepared for King Mark and Isolde, is instead, consumed by Tristram and Isolde, who consummate their relationship. Isolde marries King Mark, but she and Tristram will remain lovers. King Mark eventually realizes what Tristram and Isolde are doing, and the two lovers flee the castle. Eventually, King Mark is able to capture Isolde, and a wounded Tristram leaves Cornwall. In Britain, Tristram meets and marries another woman, Isolde le Blaunche Maynes, but he will not consummate the union. Tristram hears that Launcelot has condemned Tristram's betrayal of his lady.

After he again returns to Cornwall, Tristram is exiled by King Mark. Soon, Tristram encounters Arthur's knights, assists Launcelot, when Morgan le Fay threatens his life, and enters a tournament. Fighting under another name, Tristram nearly wins the tournament (Launcelot wins but declares Tristram the rightful winner), but is wounded and flees to the forest. After a series of adventures, Tristram and Launcelot fight one another, although neither knows the other. Soon, the two men arrive in Camelot, where Tristram is made a knight of the Round Table. Because of Tristram's success, King Mark is more jealous than ever. He plots to have Tristram killed, but even fails at this, and when his kingdom is at risk, King Mark is forced to ask Tristram for help. Once the kingdom has been saved, King Mark writes to Arthur accusing Guinevere of faithlessness. For the remainder of this book, Tristram, Launcelot, and various other knights engage in tournaments and adventures designed to reveal their valour and strength.

VI. The Tale of the Holy Grail

Previously, Launcelot had been tricked into an affair with Elaine, the daughter of King Pelles. The child of that affair is Galahad. At the beginning of this book, there is a report that a sword has been found in a floating stone. The sword is engraved with a legend that the sword belongs to the best knight in the world, but there is also a warning that any man who tries to pull it out and fail, will suffer a serious wound from it later. Gawain tries after Arthur orders him to do so, and Percival also tries to share in Gawain's curse. Galahad arrives and successfully pulls out the sword. Soon all of Arthur's knights vow to go on the Grail Quest. Galahad soon wins a white shield marked with a red cross. The story behind the shield claims that it has healing powers. Galahad undergoes many tests on his journey, and by successfully passing these tests, he proves his virtue, humility, generosity, and worthiness. Galahad is the Christ-figure, who refuses to kill his enemies, but is content to drive them off. Meanwhile, Launcelot is undergoing his own tests. As a result, he learns that he has been motivated in his successes, not by love of God, but by love of Guinevere. Launcelot regrets his sins and vows to become a better man.

Percival, Launcelot, Gawain, and Bors each continue their separate search for the Grail Quest. Each man has visions while sleeping that reveals his sins. Like the other knights, these three knights are also having no luck in their search, since, as their dreams reveal, each one is too sinful to succeed. Each man understands that he is too filled with pride and lacks the humility and devotion to God that is required to succeed. Launcelot tries to enter the Grail chamber but is struck down just when he catches a glimpse of it. He lies in a coma for twenty-four days before recovering. Galahad, accompanied by Percival and Bors finds the Grail. Galahad prays and is granted his wish of choosing his time of death. After this event, Galahad performs many miracles.

VII. The Book of Sir Launcelot and Queen Guinevere

After the Grail Quest, this book reverts to Launcelot's more human qualities and to a life less perfect than Galahad's. Launcelot has forgotten all the promises he made during the Grail Quest and quickly turns to his love for Guinevere. Launcelot must rescue Guinevere after Meliagrance captures her. Thereafter, Launcelot is less circumvent in his loyalty and love for the queen. Launcelot has been forced to choose between King Arthur and Queen Guinevere, and he has chosen the queen.

VIII. The Death of King Arthur

It is clear to everyone that the queen and Launcelot are involved in an adulterous love affair. Arthur, who has ignored this for some time, can no longer ignore what has become knowledge, and he orders Guinevere's death. As Guinevere is about to be burned, Launcelot arrives to rescue her, killing everyone who was ready to participate in her burning, including Gawain's brothers. The pope intervenes, and Launcelot returns Guinevere to the king and is banished. Gawain insists that he and Arthur attack Launcelot. This occurs and Launcelot wins, but refuses to kill Gawain. While Arthur and Gawain have been pursuing Launcelot, Mordred, Arthur's incestuous son, seizes the throne and the queen. Arthur and Gawain return to fight Mordred, and Gawain dies. While discussing a truce, an error is made, and the battle resumes. Arthur kills Mordred, but in doing so, receives a fatal wound. Arthur orders Excalibur thrown into a lake and his body is placed on a barge. Guinevere and Launcelot each turn to God in their grief and each soon dies. Sir Constantine becomes King, the Round Table disperses, and the knights simply wander off into other directions.

CHARACTERS

Agravaine

Agravaine is one of Gawain and Gareth's brothers and is also a nephew of Arthur. Along with his brother, Gaheris, Agravaine participates in Mordred's plots and in the murder of his mother.

Archbishop of Canterbury

It is the Archbishop, who in concert with Merlin, arranges for the gathering of the lords. This results in Arthur's successfully pulling Excalibur from the stone, and the lord's acceptance of him as their king.

Arthur

Arthur is the child of Igrayne and Uther. Arthur was promised to Merlin as payment for his father's pact with the magician. After his birth, Arthur is placed in the care of Sir Ector and his son, Kay. When he is able to remove the sword from the stone, Arthur become king of Britain. He is wise and strong and is able to restore peace and tranquility to the kingdom. However, not everyone approves of Arthur and he must fight many battles. Finally to secure his kingdom, Arthur orders the death of all highborn sons. This action costs Arthur much support, but illustrates how far he will go to keep his kingdom intact. Arthur places great value on the friendship and loyalty of his men. Arthur forms the Round Table, a forum for knightly loyalty and fealty to crown. He also establishes a code of behavior, demanding that the knights be merciful, righteous, and honorable. One of Arthur's great strengths is the loyalty his men demonstrate for him. Even when Arthur makes a mistake in battle, his men quickly muster the strength to save both Arthur

and his kingdom. He loves his knights so much that he ignores the love between Guinevere and Launcelot, until forced to act. His love for Launcelot is greater than his love for his queen. When he is forced to acknowledge his queen's love for Launcelot, he orders Guinevere burned and Launcelot banished, and only undertakes to fight Launcelot because Gawain insists upon it. Arthur dies in battle with Mordred, but not until after he has killed the usurper. With Arthur's death, the Round Table dissolves, and the knights scatter.

Isolde la Blaunche Maynes

This Isolde is Tristram's wife, the Princess of Brittany. Tristram refuses to consummate the marriage and make this Isolde unhappy.

Lamorak de Galis

Lamorak is a knight famous for his valor and his strength. Only Launcelot and Gawain are stronger, but he is unarmed when Gawain and his brother kill him because he has an affair with their mother. Gawain cannot achieve greatness because of his role in Lamorak's death.

Bors de Ganis

Bors is one of the knights who accompanies Galahad on the Grail Quest. Like Percival, Bors is one of the purest of the knights, filled with humility and valor. He is rewarded for his purity when he is permitted to join Galahad in locating the Grail. Bors witnesses Galahad's death and ascension into heaven. He returns to the Round Table and describes his visions.

Sir Ector

Sir Ector is given Arthur to raise. He is one of Arthur's brave and honorable knights who willingly goes into battle for Arthur.

Elayne

This Elayne is the daughter of King Pelles. Launcelot is tricked into an affair with this lady and they have a child, Galahad. She loves Launcelot, although he rejects her.

King Evelake

King Evelake is an ancient ruler. He has been promised that he will live long enough to see the virtuous knight who will complete the Grail Quest. He is 400 years old when he dies after witnessing Galahad's successful completion of the quest.

MEDIA ADAPTATIONS

- *Knights of the Round Table*, (1953 MGM, 106 min.) starring Robert Taylor, Ava Gardner, and Mel Ferrer and directed by Richard Thorpe, was nominated for Academy Awards in Best Art Direction/Set Direction and Best Sound.

- *First Knight*, (1995 Columbia, 134 min.) starring Sean Connery, Richard Gere, Julia Ormond, and John Gielgud and directed by Jerry Zucker was panned by the critics as unintentionally funny with a plot similar to a Harlequin Romance.

- *Camelot*, (1967 Warner Brothers, 150 min.) starring Richard Harris, Vanessa Redgrave, David Hemmings, Franco Nero, and Lionel Jefferies and directed by Joshua Logan, received Academy Awards for Best Art Direction/Set Direction, Best Costume Design, and Best Score. This film also won Golden Globe Awards for Best Actor, Best Song, and Best Score.

- *King Arthur and His Knights*, (1998 Greathall) narrated by Jim Weiss. Weiss is a storyteller whose work appeals to children. He uses song to tell several of the episodes from King Arthur's life.

- *Le Morte D'Arthur*, (1998 Blackstone) narrated by Frederick Davidson, containing eleven (two-hour) cassettes, is a reading of selections from Malory's text.

- *Le Morte D'Arthur*, (1997 Highbridge) narrated by Dereck Jacobi, contains six cassettes, and offers an abridgement of Malory's text.

- *Le Morte D'Arthur*, (1963 Argo) is a dramatization starring Harry Andrews, William Squire, Joan Hart, and Tony White.

- *Le Morte D'Arthur: Launcelot and Guinevere*, (1972 Caedmon) narrated by Siobhan McKenna, includes selections for Malory's story.

Gaheris

Gaheris is one of Gawain and Gareth's brothers and is also a nephew of Arthur. Along with his brother, Agravaine, Gaheris participates in Mordred's plots and in the murder of his mother. Gaheris is ordered by Arthur to participate in the execution of Guinevere, although he is opposed and attempts to escape this duty. Gaheris is murdered by Launcelot during his rescue of Guinevere.

Galahad

Galahad is the son of Launcelot. He is the best of the knights, the only one capable of succeeding in the Grail Quest. He is virtuous and great enough to draw Balin's sword from the floating stone. Galahad soon wins a white shield, marked with a red cross. The shield gives him healing powers, which Galahad will need on his journey on the Grail Quest. Galahad represents a Christ-like figure. He will have many adventures on his journey and encounter many enemies, but Galahad refuses to kill his enemies, content only to drive them off. Galahad rejects pride and greed and refutes all the seven deadly sins. Only Galahad is sinless, as is required to touch the magnificent sword and crown that he encounters on his journey. After he finds the Grail Quest, Galahad is able to perform many miracles, protected from all dangers by God and faith. Galahad is motivated only by his love of God. Eventually, Galahad sees a vision of Christ and asks to join Christ in heaven. He dies, and Percival and Bors see Galahad raised into heaven.

Gareth

Gareth first enters in disguise, as a humble kitchen boy, Beaumains. But he is the brother of Gawain and proves himself a brave and virtuous knight. Gareth is one of the most gentle of the knights and one of the most virtuous. He is also patient and strong, the ideal of the Round Table knights. Gareth has many adventures and consistently proves himself worthy of the Round Table. Unlike many of the other knights, Gareth rejects the idea of vengeance, the spilling of blood that all the other knights appear to embrace. Gareth is ordered by Arthur to participate in the execution of Guinevere, although he is opposed and attempts to escape this duty. Launcelot, who rescues Guinevere from a sentence of death, murders Gareth. Gareth's death leads Gawain to seek revenge and leads to his death, as well.

Gawain

Gawain is Arthur's nephew, the oldest child of King Lot. He is one of the most virtuous of the knights and one of the most just. Gawain emerges as a hero after he helps Arthur defeat Lucius. He errs when he beheads a lady and when he murders the unarmed Lamorak. Gawain is a heroic figure, but is really as a secondary figure in the tradition of the loyal sidekick, loyal to Launcelot. He takes the heroic central figure in *Sir Gawain and the Green Knights*. Ultimately, it is Gawain's sin as murderer that prevents his complete success. When Launcelot murders his brothers, Gawain vows revenge, and this action leads to Mordred seizing the kingdom and the queen while Arthur and Gawain are fighting Launcelot. Gawain dies in battle, but before he dies, he admits to Arthur that his desire for revenge has led to all this calamity.

Guinevere

Guinevere is the daughter of Leodegrance and the wife of Arthur. Guinevere's dowry is the Round Table, which is filled with knights loyal to Arthur. She also represents the idea of courtly love, providing a reason for many of Launcelot's heroics. Thus Guinevere's role is central to Arthur's success, but she is also largely responsible for his defeat. When Meliagrance kidnaps her, Launcelot appears to rescue her. Her obvious love for Launcelot leads Arthur to condemn Guinevere to death. Launcelot again rescues her as she is about to be burned. Later, with Arthur in pursuit of Launcelot, Mordred seizes Guinevere for his wife. After Arthur is killed, Guinevere enters a nunnery. After her death, she is buried next to Arthur.

Igrayne

Igrayne is the wife of the Duke of Cornwall and the mother of Arthur. She conceives Arthur after Uther comes to her bed, disguised as her husband.

Igrayne has already been widowed when the disguised Uther visits her bed, and she later marries her husband's murderer.

Isolde

Isolde is the daughter of Angwyssh. She heals Tristram when he is wounded. Tristram loves Isolde, but King Mark claims her as his bride. When Tristram assumes the role of delivering Isolde to King Mark, the two inadvertently drink the love potent intended for King Mark and Isolde, and fall in love. They consummate their love, and Isolde continues to love Tristram even after her marriage to King Mark.

Kay

Kay is the son of Sir Ector and Arthur's foster brother. When he loses his sword, Kay sends Arthur to find it, and Arthur mistakenly pulls the magic sword from the stone. Kay is loyal to Arthur and is wounded in the battle against Lucius. Arthur is equally loyal and tolerates Sir Kay's disparaging treatment of Gareth, although Kay is clearly wrong about Gareth's abilities.

Lady of the Lake

The Lady of the Lake assists Merlin in his goals. She demands a promise of Arthur when she returns his sword to him. When she reappears to demand her promise, it is to demand the head of Sir Balyn or of the maid who brought Balyn's sword. Balyn recognizes the Lady of the Lake as the woman who murdered his mother and he decapitates her.

Launcelot du Lake

Launcelot is the greatest of Arthur's knights, except for those who succeed in the Grail Quest. He gets his first real chance to distinguish himself in the battle against Lucius, when Launcelot steals Lucius' banner. Launcelot returns to England a hero after the war in Rome. He has many adventures and proves that he is virtuous and heroic. The queen is particularly impressed with Launcelot's heroic adventures. At this point, Launcelot represents the ideal in knightly behavior, except in one area. He is clearly working to serve the queen, rather than the king. Launcelot appears to forget that he is a member of Arthur's Round Table, not Guinevere's. Launcelot joins the Grail Quest, but he has too many sins to succeed. Launcelot's knightly deeds have all been in honor of Guinevere, not God. When

Launcelot finally sees the Grail, he is struck down and lies in a coma for twenty-four days, and when he awakens, returns to Camelot. Launcelot forgets that it was his love for Guinevere that prevented him from succeeding in the Grail Quest, and he quickly returns to his old ways with Guinevere. When Melliagaunce kidnaps Guinevere, Launcelot rescues her, and he rescues her again when she is about to be burned for adultery. His loyalty is to Guinevere and it is this misguided loyalty that helps lead Arthur to his death. After the death of Arthur, Launcelot enters the priesthood and soon dies.

Launceor of Ireland

Launceor is one of Arthur's knights. After he is humiliated by Balyn's success, he rashly attempts to defeat Balyn and is killed. Launceor's death results in severe punishment for Balyn, who will die killing his own brother.

Elayne le Blanc

Elayne is the maid of Astolat who loves Launcelot and who dies when he will not love her. After her death, her body is placed on a barge, with a letter telling her story placed in her hand.

Morgan le Fay

Morgan is Uther's third daughter. She enters school in a nunnery, becomes a necromancer, and later, marries King Uriens. Morgan le Fay attempts to steal Arthur's sword and have him murdered. She is treacherous and evil, willing to murder anyone who gets in the way of her ambition.

Percival le Galois

Percival is one of the more virtuous knights, who also accompanies Galahad on the Grail Quest. Percival is raised in the woods and is lacking in everything that would be expected of a knight. However, his desire for the Round Table is so great that he willingly sacrifices to be a knight. Percival's desire to go on the Grail Quest means that he must repent of the pride that led him to the Round Table and to the desire to be better than Galahad. Galahad has many adventures on his journey and several visions before he joins Galahad in discovering the Grail. After Galahad's death, Percival becomes a religious hermit and does not return to the Round Table.

Balyn le Sauvage

Balyn is a knight who is fated to kill his brother. In response, Merlin puts the magic sword into a stone and it remains there until the greatest knight of the realm can pull it out.

Linet

Linet is a damsel who seeks Arthur's assistance. When the disguised Gareth is assigned to help her, she mocks him. However, it is this quest that proves Gareth's worthiness to join the Round Table.

Lot

Lot is one of the kings who marries Uther's daughter. Although King Lot is the leader of Arthur's enemies, he is the most heroic of these men. He is both noble and brave and is a worthy opponent for Arthur. Two of his sons, Gareth and Gawain, become the most noble and virtuous of the Round Table knights. In order for Arthur's kingdom to be secure, Lot must finally die. He is killed in battle by Sir Pellanor, who will die when Gawain avenges his father's death.

Lucius of Rome

King Lucius demands tributes from Arthur, but a distracted Arthur refuses, which leads to a war. Lucius loses decisively, but he refuses to accept defeat and ignores advice to withdraw. Lucius is finally killed and the battle can end.

Mark

Mark is the king of Cornwall who, in his jealousy of Tristram, insists upon marrying Isolde, the woman Tristram loves. King Mark plots to have Tristram murdered but needs him to save his kingdom. Arthur's knights trick King Mark and generally make a fool of him, but he is really unable to do much to defend himself. An inept ruler, King Mark needs the man he hates the most—Tristram—to defend his kingdom. Mark is jealous of anyone who achieves success, even his own brother, whom he has murdered.

Melliogrance

Melliogrance is a traitor who kidnaps Guinevere. When she will not yield to his demands, he accuses her of treason with Launcelot. In a fight with Launcelot, Melliogrance is defeated and dies.

Merlin

Merlin is a master manipulator, who masters Arthur's conception and who, unseen, directs much of the action. As a great sorcerer, he is responsible for the creation of the Round Table. Merlin is both prophet and magician. Merlin arranges a truce between Kings Lot, Nantres, and Uriens, but then betrays the kings when he orders Arthur to attack. When Arthur loses his sword in battle, Merlin takes Arthur to the Lady of the Lake to retrieve it. Merlin provides Arthur with prophesies and he fixes the sword of Balyn so that only Launcelot or Galahad can use it, and when Arthur's life is threatened, Merlin steps in and saves the king. Merlin is opposed to Arthur's marriage to Guinevere, but is ignored. Merlin is able to assume disguises and appears before Arthur disguised as both a young boy and an old man. Merlin is directly responsible for everything that happens to Arthur. Although it initially appears that Merlin represents God, it soon becomes clear that he does not, and since he does not represent God, he must, according to the medieval world, represent the devil. Merlin meats his downfall when he falls in love with Nineve, who refuses to be bedded by Merlin but is willing to study his tricks. When she has learned his magic, Nineve has Merlin sealed alive in a cave where he must remain since only she can set him free.

Mordred

Mordred is the son of Arthur's incestuous relationship with his sister. He is an evil knight, who plots to seize the crown and Arthur's queen. His actions result in a battle in which Arthur kills him. But Arthur is also killed and the Round Table is dissolved and the knights scatter throughout the kingdom.

Nantres

Nantres is a second king who marries one of Uther's daughters. He joins with his other brothers-in-law to fight against Arthur and is defeated.

Nineve

Nineve is the maid Pellanor brought to court, the damsel of the lake. Merlin falls in love with her and fails to see that she is using him to learn his secrets. Nineve uses magic to seal Merlin in a cave, where he must remain since no one but Nineve can free him. She uses her magic to save Arthur's life and generally uses her magic for good.

Palamides

Palamides is Tristram's enemy and Isolde's admirer. Eventually, he is forced to admit that

Tristram is a worthy knight, and Palamides becomes Tristram's admirer, as well.

Pellanor

Pellanor, the knight of the Questing Beast, kills Lot and is himself killed by Lot's son, Gawain. This series of murders is only one of the many that occur, in an epic that focuses largely on revenge.

Pelles

King Pelles' identity is often unclear, although some times he is the Fisher King of the grail legends. He arranges for Galahad to be conceived and is cured when Galahad achieves the Grail Quest.

Uther Pendragon

Uther is the king of primeval England. He lusts for Igrayne, who is the wife of the Duke of Cornwall. When his attempts to bed Igrayne fail, Uther's forces attack Cornwall's, and the king then beds Igrayne under the guise that he is her husband. With Igrayne's husband dead, Uther is free to marry the widow. The next two years are filled with wars and dissention for Uther, who eventually falls sick. As he lies dying, Merlin succeeds in convincing Uther to declare his child, Arthur, king.

Tristram

Tristram's story has many parallels to that of other characters. Like Arthur, Tristram is born after his father's death and is raised by a foster parent. Like Launcelot, who loves Guinevere, Tristram also loves the wife of his king. In spite of the poor treatment afforded Tristram by his king, he continues to be loyal to King Mark, returning to defend him and to save his kingdom. His love for Isolde is unabated, and even though he marries another woman of the same name, he refuses to betray the woman he loves and will not consummate the marriage. Tristram has many more adventures where he successfully proves his strength and valor as a knight.

THEMES

Courtly Love

There are many examples of courtly love in *Le Morte d'Arthur*, including the story of Sir Gareth, his defeat of the Red Knight, and his winning of the Lady Lyonesse as his wife. Gareth represents the ideal love, one that ends in marriage and is, above all else, honorable. But the story of romantic love and chivalry that most often comes to mind is the story of Sir Launcelot and Queen Guinevere, a love that is clearly adulterous. After his introduction into the text, it is clear that many of Launcelot's heroic actions are designed to please the queen. He is clearly her favorite, and justifiably so, since in all of his adventures, Launcelot is brave, honorable, and strong. Because Launcelot fights to please and honor Guinevere, and not God, he is excluded from the quest for the Holy Grail. This image of courtly love changes when Launcelot is called upon to fight to save Guinevere's life. In the first instance, Guinevere is unjustly accused of murder, and a disguised Launcelot becomes her champion, overcoming Sir Mador and freeing the queen. According to romantic tradition, a knight entering a tournament might also wear a lady's token to express his love. Sir Launcelot wears the token of Elayne of Astalot, but does so only to enhance his disguise. Later, he wears the queen's token, thus making public his love for her. Another aspect of courtly love is the knight's rescue of his lady. Launcelot has already rescued Guinevere once, but when she is kidnapped, he rescues her again from Melliagaunce, her kidnapper. Launcelot then fights and kills Guinevere's oppressor. But because of these events, Guinevere is judged guilty of adultery and treason and is sentenced to be burned. Again, Sir Launcelot rescues his lady, but as a result, sets into motion events that will lead to the destruction of Arthur and of the Round Table. Sir Launcelot and Queen Guinevere's courtly love was far more than a harmless romantic interlude.

Honor

When Arthur establishes the code for the knights of his Round Table, one important element is honor. Arthur's knights owe him honor, but, more importantly, they owe honor to God. Most of the knights waver on this last requirement. For nearly all of the knights, their adventures, battles and tournaments, are fought to honor their king, or more immediately, themselves. Gawain fights for personal and family honor, and Launcelot fights for the queen's honor. Because of this, almost all of the knights fail in their quest for the Holy Grail. Only Galahad, Bors, and Percival place honor of God ahead of personal honor, vanity, and pride. Therefore, only these three knights are permitted to complete the quest for the

TOPICS FOR FURTHER STUDY

- Religion plays a significant role in Malory's epic, often as allegory. Discuss some of the images of Christianity that are present and explore their influences on Arthur's court and Round Table.

- Contrast the images of legitimate love between Gareth and his wife and the adulterous love between Launcelot and Guinevere. What do you think Malory is saying about the role of legitimate love in his readers' lives?

- Discuss Arthur's Round Table code to which his knights must adhere. Which knights do you think most closely follow Arthur's desires? And which knights most seriously deviate from these expectations?

- Discuss the features of the epic genre, paying special attention to which features are present in Malory's text.

- Explore the role of revenge in Malory's text and how this motif ultimately leads to the destruction of Arthur's Camelot.

Grail. Malory makes individual character an important element of his story, and how each character conducts himself, in an honorable fashion, is a key point in the text.

Fate and Destiny

Thanks to Merlin's prophecies and his magic, many times the readers are told of a prophecy that includes death and destruction. Characters are fated to meet one another on the battlefield or in tournaments, and fated to win or die based on an action that occurred much earlier, and for which, they may hold no responsibility. For example, Balyn easily draws out the sword affixed to a scabbard worn by the damsel. By doing do, he is fated to kill his dearest friend, his brother. In another example, the burial spot of Launcelor is fated to be the sight of the battle between Launcelot and Tristram, two knights who love one another and who would not willing fight one another, but who are destined to do so. This fate or destiny is not attributed to God or other spiritual matters, but instead to characters present in the text. Both Merlin and the Lady of the Lake act as representatives of fate, manipulating the characters and their actions to create a fate they predict.

Obedience

Obedience is an element of the duty and responsibility that all knights owe to their king and God. Obedience to Arthur is a part of every knight's code, even when obedience results in certain death. There are several examples of obedience to Arthur's commands, where to do so will bring harm to the knight. One such example occurs at the beginning of the quest for the Holy Grail, when Arthur learns of the sword in the floating stone. Arthur learns that the legend promises that only the best knight in the world can claim the sword, and if any others try to pull out the sword, they will be cursed. Launcelot refuses Arthur's order to try, but Gawain willingly obeys Arthur's order because Arthur is his king and he has commanded it. In another section, Arthur orders Guinevere to be put to death. In this instance, Gawain refuses to obey his king's command, but his brothers, who also object, are present. As a result, Gareth and Gaheris are murdered by Launcelot during his rescue of the queen.

Revenge

Much of the action in this epic revolves around revenge. The eye for an eye motif runs through the individual character's stories. For instance, Sir Pellanor kills King Lot, and Lot's son, Gawain, to avenge his father's death, will later kill Pellanor. In another example of revenge, Gawain and his brother, Gaheris, murder Lamerok, whom they accused of an adulterous relationship with their mother. This feud, between Lamerok and the sons of King Lot, has motivated many of the sons' actions before culminating in death. Finally, it is Gawain's insistence that his brothers be avenged that leads to the destruction of the Round Table. Because Arthur and Gawain are pursuing Launcelot, they leave Britain and the queen unattended and Mordred seizes both. Had Gawain been able to pass on the need for blood revenge, the battle in which he and Arthur were destroyed, would not have happened. Ultimately the theme of revenge, most particularly the familial blood revenge, runs throughout the epic and leads to the destruction of all that Arthur had created.

STYLE

Character

The actions of each character are what constitute the story. Character can also include the idea of a particular individual's morality. Characters can range from simple stereotypical figures to more complex multi-faceted ones. Characters may also be defined by personality traits, such as the rogue or the damsel in distress. Characterization is the process of creating a lifelike person from an author's imagination. To accomplish this the author provides the character with personality traits that help define who that person will be and how that person will behave in a given situation. Most of the characters in Malory's epic are derived from characters who appeared in his sources. But, Malory has also changed some of the characters, giving them more depth, such as Launcelot, who is transformed from a minor character in the sources to a major character in Malory's epic.

Epic

An epic is a long narrative poem that presents characters and events of high position. There may be a central heroic figure, as in the case of Arthur in Malory's *Le Morte d'Arthur* . There is frequently a muse who inspires the writer to create a work that is inspired and magnificent in its scope. The epic most frequently recounts the origins of a nation or group of people. *Le Morte d'Arthur* recounts the story of King Arthur, but it also establishes a history for the English people, providing a source of national pride. Epics usually share certain features: a heroic figure who is imposing in his greatness; a vast setting or great nation; heroic deeds; supernatural forces, such as miracles, gods, or angels; elevated diction and style; and an objective narrator. *Le Morte d'Arthur* is not an epic in the tradition of *The Odyssey*, instead fitting more loosely into the genre of the romantic prose epic.

Fiction

Fiction is any story that is created out of the author's imagination, rather than factual events. Sometimes the characters in a fictional piece are based on real life, but their ultimate form and the way they respond to events is the creation of the author. In *Le Morte d'Arthur*, the story is purported to be historical and real, but actually it is based on a series of legends and folktales and has little basis in actual facts. Although the actual story is not taken from Malory's imagination, it is taken from the imaginations of his sources, and thus, it retains its fictional basis.

Foreshadowing

Foreshadowing is a device in literature to create expectation and tension in the story. This device is one way to build anticipation and keep the reader interested in the story, or even worried about a character's future or well-being. There is much foreshadowing in Malory's epic, primarily through the use of prophesy, which predicts death and destruction.

Genre

Genres are a way of categorizing literature. Genre is a French term that means "kind" or "type." Genre can refer to both the category of literature such as tragedy, comedy, epic, poetry, or pastoral. It can also include modern forms of literature such as drama, novels, or short stories. This term can also refer to types of literature such as mystery, science fiction, comedy or romance. *Le Morte d'Arthur* is a romantic epic.

Plot

This term refers to the pattern of events. Generally plots should have a beginning, a middle, and a conclusion, but they may also sometimes be a series of episodes connected together. Basically, the plot provides the author with the means to explore primary themes. Students are often confused between the two terms; but themes explore ideas, and plots simply relate what happens in a very obvious manner. In *Le Morte d'Arthur*, Malory has expanded on the original sources, which were really just a series of legends, to create a chronologically based plot, which covers events over a duration of many years. The plot depicts the birth of Arthur, his succession to the crown, and the formation of the Round Table. The plot also depicts the many adventures of the knights, particularly the quest for the Holy Grail. But the themes include adherence to the knightly code of behavior that Arthur institutes and devotion to king and God.

Romantic Epic

A romantic epic is a long narrative poem that combines the medieval romance and the classical epic. The poets who created romantic epics used many of the features of the classical epics but combined these features with stories of love and both romantic and religious. Malory deviates slightly from the conventional, substituting prose for verse.

Malory also combines the Grail Quest with romantic courtly love to add dimension to the romantic epic.

Setting

The time, place, and culture in which the action of the play takes place is called the setting. The elements of setting may include geographic location, physical or mental environments, prevailing cultural attitudes, or the historical time in which the action takes place. The location for *Le Morte d'Arthur* is mostly Britain, but the time is understood to be many years earlier, perhaps as early as the six century, during the Anglo-Saxon period.

HISTORICAL CONTEXT

A Time of War

Life in fifteenth century England was certainly turbulent during the period in which Malory is writing *Le Morte d'Arthur*. The century began with Henry V deciding to invade France. Henry found ways to justify his choice, claiming a hereditary entitlement to France and a desire to unite Europe under a Christian flag. These righteous claims allowed Henry to claim God's endorsement of this attack. As it turns out, Henry had need of God. Miserable weather and rampant dysentery hampered his invasion, but eventually Henry achieved great victories and succeeded in his quest to unite France and England. Henry emerged from these battles as a legend, having defeated the French at Agincourt, against almost impossible odds. The heavily armored French army, which was weighted down in the muddy field, quickly fell victim to the English archers, who deftly stayed out of the mud as they attacked from a distance. As a result, the French sustained thousands of lost lives and the English only a few. Henry gave credit to God, for having been party to the English victory. More importantly, Henry's exploits assumed a level more often associated with myth, and certainly reminding his people of the earlier British Legend, King Arthur, whose exploits on the battlefield were also legendary. To seal the comparisons, Henry also died soon after his victories, although not in battle as Arthur had, but of the dysentery that had plagued his men during the earlier campaign.

COMPARE
&
CONTRAST

- **Fourteenth Century:** In 1419, England's Henry V conquers all of Normandy, wining a battle at Agincourt, in which the heavily outnumbered English soldiers defeat the French. Henry's glorious win is considered as a sanction from God for having undertaken the war. Some scholars think that Henry's glorious exploits in battle serve for Malory's depiction of Arthur.

  Late Twentieth Century: Neither the English or the French are seen as great military forces, and indeed, both have fought on the same side all during this century. The twentieth century has not witnessed a military hero of the stature of either Henry or Arthur, although General Eisenhower perhaps comes closest.

- **Fourteenth Century:** In 1428, the University of Florence begins to teach Greek and Latin literature, as a way to emphasize moral values. When this occurs, the early Greek and Roman epics, *The Odyssey* and *The Aeneid* are again taught. This results in a greater interest in the ancient epics and leads to the creation of many new epics within the next two hundred years, including Thomas Malory's *Le Morte d'Arthur*, Edmund Spenser's *Faerie Queene*, and John Milton's *Paradise Lost*. These authors were all interested in using the epic form to establish moral values and to promote the importance of religious faith as a positive influence.

  Late Twentieth Century: Most modern authors have little interest in creating epics. Instead, many people use mass media as a moral compass and as a way to model behavior. However, the religious epics of Malory, Spenser, and Milton continue to be very popular as literature. In particular, sections from Malory's epic are often depicted on film as either romance or action entertainment.

- **Fourteenth Century:** The Hundred Years War between England and France that began in 1377 continues throughout most of the century, only ending in 1453 with England's defeat. After the glorious victories of Henry V, there is little for the British to cheer about. In bringing a heroic figure such as Arthur to life, Malory once again offers the English a reason to remember their past glories and a reason to hope again that their country will find real glory on the battlefield.

  Late Twentieth Century: During World War II, the British refuse to capitulate to the Germans, becoming one of the few European countries to withstand the force of the Axis. Although they are certainly outnumbered and suffer heavy losses during the Blitz, the British prove once again that they have the strength to survive, often calling upon a proud heritage to give the people continued hope for victory.

- **Fourteenth Century:** Civil war, between the Yorkists (wearing white roses) and the Lancastrians (wearing red roses) lasts for thirty years. The War of the Roses, as it is called, tears at the fabric of England, whose resources are directed toward war rather than the improvement of the country. The civil war is particularly destructive as English soldiers kill English soldiers. Meanwhile, many people are starving and little developmental progress is made. Malory's epic clearly illustrates the destruction from murder and chaos that occurs when revenge and death take precedence over constructive actions.

  Late Twentieth Century: Unlike England's experience with the War of the Roses, most nations have found that war is an economic boon, providing more employment and often leading to the development of technology that has peacetime applications. For instance, war has led to improvements in medicine and in airplane design. War also leads to increased production and an increase in the countries gross national product; accordingly, war can provide one way for a country to emerge from an economic depression.

During Malory's lifetime, English life had been marked by dissention and war. The monarchy squandered the country's wealth by waging wars, when what England needed was an emphasis on recovery and stability. Except for the brief period of glory that the English found with Henry V, there had been little to cheer the people during the past hundred years or more. The Peasant's Revolt of 1381, which had been caused by the imposition of a Poll tax, had offered no lasting lessons for the monarchy. The revolt has been squashed in less than a month and it had failed as a social revolution, and so the problems that had led to the revolt were ignored. The Peasant's Revolt had been about much more than the Poll tax. There had been a shortage of laborers, and thus a shortage of food since the last serious outbreak of plague in the middle of the fourteenth century, which killed a third of England's population. The people were starving, and the aristocracy's solution was to raise taxes and fight among themselves for the crown. In short, the medieval period was a time of social unrest and disorder. In spite of severe economic conditions, the Hundred Years War raged in the background, until finally the French drove the English from their territories. Back in England, the aristocracy were more involved with the getting and keeping of land and wealth, rather than the social revolution that the country so desperately needed.

Late Medieval Life

As an adult, Henry VI established Eton College and King College, Cambridge. These actions revealed the king's interest in education. But education served the aristocracy and not the people. To add to the problems, the king's relatives had been engaging in almost constant feuds since the date of his birth, finally erupting into civil war in 1453 with the birth of Henry's heir. This event led to a war that would last thirty years. During this period, the crown shifted several times between the Yorkist faction and the Lancastrians. Each side of the war had both their dissenters and their supporters, but both of these groups were quick to shift their allegiance if it appeared that the battle had been lost or, perhaps, won. During all this fighting, there was little change for the English peasant. The feudal system of life offered little benefit to anyone, except the aristocracy. The peasant owned neither himself nor his property. Absolute control resided with the landowner, who simply increased demand of his

workers when he needed additional capital outlay, as owners frequently did. There were no accommodations for illness or death. As the poor suffered, the wealthy became even richer. This condition culminated in another peasant's revolt in 1450 and the peasant's march on London. Although there was some small blood shed during this revolt, there was little practical change. The influence of the Hundred Years War and the English civil wars led to increased lawlessness. There were many thefts, more than in any other period. Merchants were dishonest, selling shoddy goods and cheating their customers. The law was corrupt, with bribery too commonplace to ignore. The seas were filled with pirates and the highways with robbers. Greediness and a desire for even more money motivated much of what passed for English society. There was little to stop the common criminal, except the efforts of those citizens who retained some core of decency.

In spite of all this corruption, many people, mostly those who were poor and who lived as peasants, maintained the honestly and goodness that sustained England through this period. For the people of the late medieval period, the Catholic Church was the center of their lives. Its teaching guided all their actions, and its rules provided people with a pattern upon which to base all behaviors. The teachings of the church and its masses were in Latin, which few except the most learned could understand. Thus, the church held a position of authority that could not be challenged. Its representatives were charged with interpreting the word of God to the people, who trusted in their clergy. The people relied on the church to provide their moral compass, and although there was much corruption in the church, its authority still helped to maintain order. The Catholic Church still maintained a strong hold on England at the beginning of the sixteenth century. But the fist stirrings of the Reformation were being felt in Europe, and by the early sixteenth century, the Catholic church's rule in England had ended.

The end of the fifteenth century marked the end of the medieval period in England. The sixteenth century brought with it the first of the Tudor kings and a period of relative peace following the civil wars that had plagued England during much of the preceding century. Although it was still present in smaller, yearly outbreaks, the threat of the Black Death, plague, had finally decreased. In short, England at the beginning of a new century had become a good place to live. The first of the Tudor kings, Henry VII, formed alliances with neighboring countries and trade flourished in London. The cloth for which English sheep were so famous became an important commodity for trade in Europe. But the coming of trade changed the face of England. Instead of a country largely composed of an agrarian culture, England, and especially London, became an important center of trade. Land for agricultural use was enclosed, and displaced rural families fled to the larger cities, where crowding, unemployment, and plague were a greater problem. The feudal order was ending, as well, as knights on horseback, who became obsolete after Henry V, proved that there was a more efficient way to win a battle. Literacy increased, too, as moveable type made books and other printed material more available and literacy increased as more people learned to read.

The Move to the Renaissance

Fifty years before Malory's death, and after Henry the fifth's early death, his heir became his infant son, Henry VI, and control of the government lay in the hands of the infant's uncles. The plotting and fighting that resulted eventually led to civil war. There are clear comparisons to Arthur's death, which led to the dissolution of the Round Table and the end of that period of greatness in England's prehistory. With Henry V dead, the period of England's greatness was also diminished. England lost the newly won France and did not emerge as a stable and strong country again until Richard III's defeat at Bosworth Field in 1485, when Henry VII, the first of the Tudor kings, would bring England back to that former glory. But Thomas Malory could not predict that the world outside his prison would change so drastically as he sat writing in his prison in 1469. Instead, what awaited England was the end of the medieval period and the beginning of the English Renaissance, which could only come about with the end of war and the establishment of peace.

CRITICAL OVERVIEW

Malory's epic *Le Morte d'Arthur* deviates from traditional romantic epics in that it is a prose work,

rather than a poem. This choice may reflect Malory's own talents and preference for the prose format. There is little knowledge of Malory's education, but it is doubtful that he had any serious education. Prior to Gutenberg's success in 1454, there were few books, and so there is no reason to think that Malory had any practical access to the epic tradition, as it evolved from works such as *The Odyssey* or *The Aeneid*. These Greek and Roman epics had virtually disappeared from public view until the Renaissance made them more widely accessible. There is no evidence that Malory wrote any other works, but that does not diminish his accomplishment in writing *Le Morte d'Arthur* . With this work, Malory functions as a compiler, compiling all the stories associated with the Arthurian legends and assembling them in one book. As a compiler, Malory also places the stories in a more straightforward chronological format, which makes the work more accessible to the reader.

Initially, many of Malory's readers focused on proving or disproving the historical veracity of his work. In the initial printing, William Caxton devoted a considerable portion of his preface to arguing that Malory's work proved that King Arthur really did exist and that his exploits really were true. Caxton ignored the fact that Malory had no scholarly sources for his text. He had performed no research, and in fact, none existed that would have aided him. Instead, Malory relied upon the early French legends and a fourteenth century alliterative poem for information. None of these details bothered Caxton, who demonstrated that he had all the makings of a good salesman as he marketed the book to readers. Caxton's assertions in the text's preface made little difference anyway since the book helped to establish a national heritage, and that was more important than any search for the truth.

Malory's text does suggest that the English were in need of the many important morals emphasized by *Le Morte d'Arthur*. Arthur's establishment of the Round Table indicates a need for a code of conduct that will govern the land. His knights are bound by honor, both to king and God, ideas that are equally important to Malory's readers. Sir Galahad succeeds in the quest for the Holy Grail because he is pure and without sin. He never forgets that he serves God before he serves his king. While most modern readers would recognize that Malory is suggesting a moral code, not all of Malory's early readers embraced this view. In *The Scholemaster*,

Roger Ascham condemns the morality of Arthur's knights:

> In our forefathers tyme, when Papistrie, as a standyng poole, couered and ouerflowed all England, fewe bookes were read in our tong, sauyng certaine bookes of Cheualrie, as they sayd, for pastime and pleasure, which, as some say, were made in Monasteries, by idle Monkes, or wanton Chanons: as for example, *Morte Arthure:* the whole pleasure of which booke standeth in two speciall poyntes, in open mans slaughter, and bold bawdrye: in which booke those be counted the noblest Knightes, that do kill most men without any quarell, and commit fowlest aduoulteres by sutlest shiftes.

In addition to the obvious attacks on the Catholic Church, which were common in many English texts printed after the Reformation, Ascham is leveling criticism on the knights' behavior. Interestingly, this is the same criticism Malory implies. Only the purest of the knights—Galahad, Bors, and Percival—succeed in the Grail Quest. The implication is clear: those knights who engage in adulterous behavior or who use their strength or talent with a sword in an unjust or murderous manner, will not be rewarded with God's blessing. Ascham apparently misses this point, but he undoubtedly was not alone. Although Malory's epic was popular as entertainment, quasi-history, or even a model of morality, it was not regarded as serious literature for some time. Eventually, *Le Morte d'Arthur* took a place in the literary canon and was recognized as a major influential work. While Malory's book influenced many of the poets who followed him, such as Spenser and Tennyson, it also created an interest in the world of Knights, jousts, and courtly love. In this century, the Knights of the Round Table have spawned several films and even a musical. And finally, comparisons during the John Kennedy presidency to Arthur's Camelot, recalled the excitement and perfection of Arthur's rule, and later after it had ended, the brevity of his world.

CRITICISM

Sheri E. Metzger

Metzger has a Ph.D., and specializes in literature and drama at the University of New Mexico, where she is a Lecturer in the English Department and an Adjunct Professor in the University Honors

Fourteenth-century tapestry depicting King Arthur.

Program. In this essay, she discusses how Le Morte d'Arthur *fulfills the requirements of the epic tradition while incorporating all the aspects of a domestic drama into the story line.*

Historically, the epic genre derives from the Greek tradition and is the oldest form of Greek literature, existing before drama or history developed. As it evolved from its Greek roots, the epic form was a continuous narrative poem that celebrated the achievements of one or more heroic individuals. Most frequently, the hero or heroes were important personages historically or traditionally. Their exploits, as recounted in the epic, were useful in establishing a national identity. For example, Homer uses Odysseus' journey and triumphs as a way to counter the current dismal picture of Greek life. *The Odyssey* reminded Homer's listeners of Greece's former greatness, and his stories offered hope that Greece would arise once again as a mighty force. Similarly, Virgil used *The Aeneid* to provide Rome with a glorious national history—something they needed very badly at that time. Thomas Malory does much the same thing with his story of Arthur and his Round Table. In *Le Morte d'Arthur*, Malory provides a history of greatness for Britain's past and

WHAT DO I READ NEXT?

- *Knighthood in the Morte d'Arthur*, 1985, by Beverly Kennedy, examines knighthood as found in several medieval texts.

- *The Idylls of the King*, 1833, by Tennyson, is a poetic presentation of the story of Arthur, from his meeting with Guinevere to the time of his death.

- *History of the Kings of Britain*, 1136, by Geoffrey of Monmouth (reprinted in 1977 by Viking Penguin), is an epic work that begins with the founding of Britain. This book provides a history of Arthur, and may have served as one of Malory's sources.

- *The Evolution of Arthurian Romance: The Verse Tradition from Chretien to Froissart*, 1998 by Beate Schmolke-Hasselmann (originally published in German in 1985), is a study of Arthurian verse romance. In it the author argues that scholars need to redraw the lines on the literary and linguistic map of medieval Britain and France.

- Edmund Spenser's, *The Faerie Queene*, 1590-1596, incorporates many of the ideas and characters from Malory's work, including King Arthur and the search for the ideal, in this case the Faerie Queene.

- *The Scolemaster*, 1570, by Roger Ascham (reprinted in 1996 by Thoemmes Press) provides Ascham's theories on education and includes his concerns about the moral influences of some books.

- *The Sword in Anglo-Saxon England: Its Archaeology and literature*, 1995, by Hilda Ellis Davidson, is a study of the archaeological evidence on the importance of the sword and of sword making in medieval literature. This book includes many illustrations.

- *Early Medieval*, 1994, by George Henderson, explores the connections between art and civilization, covering the period from the fifth century to about the tenth.

- *Early Medieval Architecture*, 1999, by Roger Stalley, examines the development of medieval architecture by exploring the social and religious influences of the period.

- *The Arthurian Legends: An Illustrated Anthology*, 1992, by Richard Barber, contains a collection of all the many Arthurian legends, each set into its literary and historical context.

---

the hope of greatness for the future. Thus, it is not important whether Odysseus, Aeneas, or Arthur actually existed; instead, it is the need for a sense of national identity and the promise of the future that is in important in the classical epic genre.

The epic is ideally suited for the purpose of providing a national identity because it is most frequently used to recount the origins of a nation and to provide a sense of national pride. *Le Morte d'Arthur* offers the vast setting that is required: the creation of a nation and an early history of Britain. There are also the Knights of the Round Table, always prepared to do heroic deeds or set out on a divinely inspired quest. Malory includes supernatu-

ral forces in the personas of Merlin and the Lady of the Lake. The quest for the Holy Grail also provides an element of the supernatural, in the miracles, and in the creation of Galahad as a Christ figure. This latter element clearly demonstrates an adaptation of the classical epic style to the Christian era. However, Malory's most important deviation from the classical epic is his use of prose, instead of verse, to tell Arthur's story. Greek and Roman epics use narrative verse, and both Edmund Spenser and John Milton will use narrative verse in their great epics, but Malory probably lacks the education and intimate knowledge of Greek epic, with which Spenser and Milton are familiar. Perhaps because he does not know the exact formula, Malory creates a new style of epic, blending the classical epic to the French prose tradition, injecting the French courtly romances into the heroic proportions of the classical epic. What Malory creates is a domestic epic, one that recounts the creation of a great king, providing both the battles and the victories to support Arthur's greatness, but also including the domestic tragedy that leads to the destruction of both the heroic figure and all that he created.

There is yet one other way in which Malory modifies the classical epic form. Instead of just one heroic figure, Malory creates several. Gawain, Gareth, and Galahad are each heroic figures in their own way, each one having a significant role in the epic, and yet, not the central role. The commanding heroic presence is, of course, King Arthur. But he is nearly upstaged by the heroic presence of Sir Launcelot. In his essay, "The English Prose *'Morte,'*" C. S. Lewis notes that there are many elements of *Le Morte d'Arthur* that make it an epic. Although Lewis observes that Malory's heroes commit many barbaric acts, they also have a morality that guides them. Lewis calls this "the civilization of the heart," which provides "a fineness and sensitivity, a voluntary rejection of all the uglier and more vulgar impulses," that creates the heroic figure. If Arthur more closely fits the classical definition of the heroic protagonist, larger than life and of mythical heritage, Launcelot is the human counterpart. With Galahad assuming the Christ role, Launcelot is left to be Adam, a flawed but certainly human creation. Lewis observes that even Launcelot claims to be no better than lesser men, capable of sinning, as he does with Guinevere. Launcelot and Arthur present two disparate images of epic heroes. Together, these two men create an imposing presence, saving damsels in distress, performing good deeds, and winning battles. But one mortal woman undoes them, whom both love: Guinevere.

Thomas Malory's *Le Morte d'Arthur* offers something few other epics offer—an emphasis on women and the domestic sphere as a way to find salvation, as a way to complete a man's journey. However, some scholars would argue that it is the domestic sphere that hampers women in Malory's text and prevents them from enjoying the success that men enjoy. In her study of patriarchal marriage and courtly love, MaryLynn Saul argues that women in *Le Morte d'Arthur* are portrayed as sexually insatiable, overly aggressive, needy, and more concerned with acquiring property than with male happiness. Arthur, on the other hand, is portrayed as

> " Whether he knew it or not, Thomas Malory created the first steps toward making domestic romance a legitimate topic of poets, playwrights, and novelists."

loyal to his men, rather than to any woman. But this is the way a classic epic hero is expected to behave. Odysseus and Aeneas always put loyalty to their men and to the mission before the needs of their women. In this respect, Arthur is performing as he should perform. Saul also points that when love affairs go badly, "the woman may find herself receiving all the blame." As an example, Saul cites Launcelot's many love affairs, which Saul says work to serve his ego. Saul declares that "the benefit of loving Launcelot goes not to the women but to Launcelot, who receives their praise and gains in reputation by the number of women who love him." However Launcelot's ego is in keeping with what Lewis observed—Launcelot's humanity and humanness; his propensity to sin is one of his most important defining characteristics. Although Saul is critical of the way Malory treats women, comparing his treatment to the patriarchal system in place during the medieval period, she concludes that medieval women, and probably medieval men, are captive to the social structure that governs their behavior. Thus, she seemingly excuses the very behavior she criticizes.

Not all critical studies of *Le Morte d'Arthur* find the women characters at such a disadvantage. In his essay on Guinevere, Edward Donald Kennedy argues that Guinevere escapes the typical outcome of other feminine characters. Guinevere, says Kennedy, can give Launcelot something that no male character can: salvation. She sacrifices her happiness with Launcelot to prevent his sinning with her, to save his soul. Kennedy reminds his readers that Launcelot's love for Guinevere kept him from succeeding in the Grail Quest. Now in his love for the queen, he promises to devote his life to God, just as she has. Kennedy argues that Malory includes this final scene between the lovers as a way to provide Launcelot with a chance for salvation.

After Guinevere is buried next to Arthur, Launcelot blames himself for their deaths. Like Aristotle's tragic hero, Launcelot is to be pitied because, in his grief over his mistakes, he is as human as any of Malory's readers. As Kennedy says, "[Malory] would not have had to read Aristotle to know that good people often make terrible mistakes and to realize it only after it is too late to do anything about it." The role of savior might have gone to Galahad, who, as the Christ figure, should have been able to save his father. Kennedy observes that "on the Grail Quest women had been depicted as a stumbling block on the road to salvation." Launcelot failed to find salvation from the quest because of his love for Guinevere, but now in their final scene together, Guinevere provides what Launcelot could not have otherwise achieved. Kennedy says that Guinevere emerges as a hero when she does what the male heroes could not: lead Launcelot to salvation. His choice to reject the secular life and marriage and, instead, embrace the church was the clearest way to redemption in the medieval world. Guinevere succeeds where men have failed, as a woman who leads Arthur's greatest knight to choose God.

Unlike Homer's *Odyssey* or Virgil's *Aeneid*, Malory creates a human woman in the image of the epic goddesses, a woman of complexity who is capable of leading a man to redemption. Where Odysseus has the goddess Athena to assist him in his journey, and Aeneas has the goddess Venus to led help when needed, Launcelot has only the love of an ordinary mortal woman. In a way, this change toward the mortal reflects the Christianizing of the World. In the pre-Christian world, Odysseus and Aeneas journey toward their homes or toward a new home. But in the Christian world, the journey is toward salvation. This is but one way that Malory adapts the epic tradition to fit his purposes and to fit the requirements of the Christian era.

Two hundred years after Thomas Malory composed *Le Morte d'Arthur*, John Milton used the traditional epic form to explore a domestic romance, between man and woman in *Paradise Lost*. Milton's use of the epic is more pure to the genre than that of Malory, but, like Malory, Milton saw the connection between the epic and the domestic. Malory took the love triangle between Arthur, Guinevere, and Launcelot and turned a domestic tragedy into an epic romance. Appearing as it does at the end of the fifteenth century, *Le Morte d'Arthur* straddles the move from the Medieval Period into the English Renaissance. Malory's text was, then, the last old and the first modern domestic

tragedy of this period. In the five hundred years since *Le Morte d'Arthur* appeared, the domestic tragedy has become a staple of theatre and fiction, while in the twentieth century, Malory's text has adapted effortlessly to both novel and film. Whether he knew it or not, Thomas Malory created the first steps toward making domestic romance a legitimate topic of poets, playwrights, and novelists.

Source: Sheri E. Metzger, for *Epics For Students*, Gale, 2001.

Sarah Kay

In her chapter "Adultery and Killing in La Mort le roi Artu,*" Sarah Kay analyzes the unique representation and use of adultery in* La Mort *as it relates to the taking of life, not property, and how its treatment becomes important to poignant actions in the work.*

Insofar as adultery is considered wrongful, in medieval texts, it is often because it is connected in some way with an offence against property. This is either because of the importance laid on legitimate inheritance (which in turn requires wives to be faithful to their husbands), or because of the tendency to see women as themselves a form of property. In *La Mort le roi Artu* (*The Death of King Arthur*), however, adultery is presented in relation not to property but to the taking of life. How and why this is so is what this chapter will explore.

The *Mort* is the last work in the great early thirteenth-century compilation known as the *Prose Lancelot*, and describes the decline and fall of Arthur's kingdom. The adultery between Arthur's queen Guenevere and his greatest knight Lancelot plays a key role in this apocalyptic narrative, since it leads to the estrangement of Lancelot and Arthur. When Arthur pursues Lancelot abroad, he entrusts his kingdom to Mordred, who usurps it for himself; Arthur feels unable to call on Lancelot to assist him against Mordred, and so his army perishes along with Mordred's.

In the early part of the *Mort*, Arthur is induced by court spies to ask himself repeatedly whether Lancelot and Guenevere are guilty of adultery. But he is also called upon to approve legal challenges against both of them for wrongful killing. For both have caused death, in episodes which present striking parallels. The victims in both cases are knights who have similar names (Guenevere kills Gaheris, Lancelot kills Gaheriet), and both are commemorated by inscriptions put up by members of the court. The brother of each victim wants to avenge his death: Mador de la Porte obliges Arthur to put Guenevere on trial; Gawain's love for Lancelot turns to implacable hostility as he pressures Arthur to go to war against Lancelot, and eventually challenges him to single combat. Then again, each of the killings could be described as accidental. Guenevere hands Gaheris a poisoned fruit which was prepared by someone else (Arvalan) and intended for Gawain; she was completely unaware that it was poisoned. Similarly Lancelot strikes down Gaheriet, who is his dear friend, without recognising him in the confusion of rescuing the queen. Finally, when each of the avenging brothers (Mador, Gawain) obtains a judicial duel (or approximation to one, in Gawain's case), he is pitted against Lancelot who fights first on behalf of the queen and then on his own behalf, and on both occasions wins. Although much of the romance is about efforts to ascertain whether or not Lancelot and the queen are lovers, attempts to entrap them are not successful. Thus Lancelot and the queen are never required legally to defend themselves as adulterers, only as killers. The killings, it seems, function as a displacement of the crime of adultery, and also as a narrative metaphor for it.

This metaphorical dimension is established textually by the close association that exists in each case between the question of adultery and the alleged wrongful killing. In the first case, that of Guenevere and the poisoned fruit, the link is established from the outset. Arthur has returned to court from the castle of his sister Morgan, who has shown him Lancelot's paintings which reveal his love for Guenevere. And so for Arthur 'there was never a time again when he was not more suspicious of the queen than he had been, because of what he had been told'. Only two sentences later those suspicions find an object, as Arvalan hands the fruit to Guenevere and Gaheris dies. Meanwhile, Lancelot has been dismissed from the court by the queen as a result of a misunderstanding, a fact which causes Boors to curse the love between them. The interweaving of these episodes associates the themes of love and death.

A similar convergence of these two themes occurs in the case of Lancelot's accidental killing of Gaheriet. It is causally linked with the adultery plot, since it takes place while Lancelot is rescuing the queen from execution. When later Lancelot hands her back to Arthur, he seeks to justify himself with respect both to the queen, and to the death of Gawain's brothers, so that the issues of adultery and the killing are linked again: 'Sire, behold the queen,

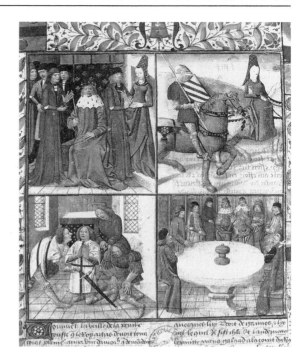

Illustrations from a fifteenth-century manuscript representing the legend of King Arthur.

whom I return to you, who would earlier have been killed as a result of the disloyalty of members of your household, had I not taken the risk of rescuing her. [...] And it is better that they should perish in their treachery than that she should die'. He goes on: 'If I loved the queen with foolish passion, as you were given to understand, I would not give her back to you, not for months, and you would not win her back by force'. But Gawain pulls the discussion back to Lancelot's guilt for Gaheriet's death: 'You can be sure that you will not lack for war [...] for you will have it, and mightier than you ever did before, and it will last until my brother Gaheriet, whom you wrongfully killed, will be avenged on your own body; and I would rather see your head cut off than have the whole world'.

These links between adultery and killing shift the ground on which the adultery is considered. Most characters in the text want to know whether Lancelot and the Queen are committing adultery as a matter of fact, not how to judge them if they are. For Arthur, adultery calls for automatic condemnation. Gawain, Guerrehés and Gaheriet prefer that he should not know, rather than cause enmity in the court. We readers, however, know that the couple

> The equation between adultery and killing, which seems so sinister and guilt-ridden, conveys in fact a curious innocence which makes it difficult to evaluate."

are lovers; our problem, rather, is what attitude to adopt to this. As the story goes on, an increasing number of characters know the truth about their relationship, and some (such as Lancelot's kin) are clearly loyal to them. But no character, whether in the know or not, discusses the question which is uppermost in the reader's mind, namely how we should view their adultery. On the contrary, there is a gap between the discourse that maintains, of Lancelot, that he is the best knight in the world because of his love for the queen, and the discourse lamenting that, because of his love for the queen, a terrible cataclysm will engulf the Arthurian kingdom. If the text seeks to evaluate the fact of their relationship, it does so via the thunderous silence between these two positions. In the matter of the killings, however, the facts are agreed between readers and characters; it is their evaluation which is in question for all of us together. Both the judicial duels address the question of whether the killers are guilty of a disloyal and treacherous act. That is, they ask with respect to the killings what the reader might ask with respect to the adultery. In this way, the metaphorical importance of the killings becomes both more obvious, and more interesting.

The Guenevere trial considers disloyalty and treachery from the point of view of intention. Before the combat, Mador makes his formal accusation to Lancelot: 'Sir knight, I am ready to prove that she killed my brother disloyally and treacherously', a charge Lancelot rebuts with an important change of wording: 'And I am ready [...] to defend her on the ground that she never intended disloyalty or treachery'. Lancelot's formulation is, for Gawain, an illumination of Guenevere's innocence. Arthur agrees that this new perspective makes it likely Guenevere's champion will win. And Guenevere herself repeats the winning formula: 'I never in-

tended disloyalty or treachery,' she says. Win Lancelot duly does; the queen is exonerated. If, as I have argued, the trial is a metaphorical displacement of anxiety about adultery, can we infer from Guenevere's acquittal that she is also to be exonerated sexually because she 'never intended disloyalty or treachery'? Is the text driving a wedge between intention and result, and inclining us to base our moral judgements on the former not the latter? The fact of Gaheris's death is undeniable, but Guenevere has been found innocent because she did not mean to cause it; likewise, although her adultery has dire political consequences, since she did not intend them, should she be acquitted of responsibility for them too?

One could feel more confident about making this inference if the text were more committed to the concept of intention. When members of the court first find Gaheris's body, the question of intent is raised, and Guenevere protests her ignorance that the fruit was poisoned, but Arthur counters: 'Whatever the circumstances in which you gave it to him, the outcome is evil and intolerable, and I greatly fear that you will suffer more for it than you imagine'. No one believes Guenevere to be innocent or is prepared to dishonour himself defending her. The consensus view is unambiguously expressed by Gawain: 'for we know very well that the queen killed the knight, as she stands accused; I saw it and so did many others'. Even Lancelot who did not see it believes her to be guilty: 'for I know truly, from what I have heard, that I shall be on the side of wrong and Mador on the side of right'. He fights only because he loves the queen, and her reputation is hitherto unblemished. The outcome, not the intent, of her deed is what mesmerises everyone's attention.

So Lancelot's all-important formulation at the trial, which wins support and eventual acquittal for the queen, is curiously inadvertent; while the switch of position by Gawain and Arthur is almost somnambulistic. In fact, the text seems more inclined to dull the distinctions between intent, outcome, and responsibility than to illumine them. This obfuscation reaches a peak when Arthur, shortly afterwards, reproaches Gawain for having withheld the truth of the queen's adultery from him. Gawain's reply, 'Indeed, my treachery never did you any harm', is simply mind-boggling. Has he forgotten what treachery is? His use of the term implies that he meant no ill, had no ill effect, and bears no responsibility: the word becomes empty of meaning.

Throughout the *Mort,* the capacity of the characters to form, or respond to, intention is extremely limited. The text contains several examples of unintended killing or wounding apart from the two cases I am concerned with. They include Lancelot being wounded twice (by Boors who failed to recognise him at the Winchester tournament, and a huntsman who missed his intended quarry in the forest); and Arthur killing his last-but-one survivor by hugging him too hard. On each occasion questions of intent and moral responsibility are dimly raised but they never get anywhere. Thus Boors tells Lancelot that he ought not to be blamed for wounding him since Lancelot was fighting incognito, and Lancelot agrees but nevertheless remains full of reproaches. Elizabeth Edwards has described the characters in medieval prose romance as resembling 'a distinctive mark, or graving, on the surface of the text [… which is] of insufficient capacity to accommodate more than one code at a time'. In the *Mort,* they seem able to focus either on intent or on outcome but not on both at the same time, as they would need to do in order to evaluate the ethical significance of one *vis-à-vis* the other. Guenevere's trial may involve the question of intent, but it no more succeeds in making it a determinate issue than these other episodes do. We cannot infer from it that intent defines the moral horizon of action in the *Mort.* Does the text, then, have anything clearer to say on the question of justice?

When Mador enters the judicial duel, he does not know who his opponent is. Only when he has been defeated does Lancelot declare his identity. Mador then protests to the king: 'Sire, you have deceived me, setting my lord Lancelot against me'. In the Gawain-Lancelot encounter over the death of Gaheriet, the question is again raised whether the outcome of a trial depends less on what is being fought over than on who is fighting. Gawain sends a messenger to challenge Lancelot to single combat. The messenger thinks he must be mad to fight such a 'good and seasoned knight' and Arthur, repeating these same words, also fears that Gawain cannot win, but Gawain insists that justice will be done, for right makes a weak knight prevail, whereas wrong makes a strong one lose. In the course of the combat Gawain's strength grows and ebbs, so that he seems first likely to win, then headed for defeat. Does he lose because his strength declines, or because he was wrong to fight in the first place?

The Gawain-Lancelot combat echoes the concerns of the Guenevere trial. Once again, the charge involves killing 'treacherously and disloyally'. Dif-

ferent opinions are expressed as to which of the two, Gawain and Lancelot, is on the side of right, and Lancelot himself, acting as his own champion, is as diffident about the justice of his cause as he was when fighting for Guenevere. He prepares himself for the duel by confession and vigil, 'for he was very afraid lest ill befall him against lord Gawain, on account of the death of his brothers whom he had killed'. But rather than foregrounding the status of intent in relation to the notion of right, what is at stake here is the status of right itself. What is it and how do you know when you have it? Many of the *Mort*'s critics seem persuaded either that Lancelot clearly has justice on his side, or that he clearly does not. R. H. Bloch, for example, writes: 'Lancelot's victorious support of a merely adequate cause against Mador and a patently indefensible one against Gawain can only be interpreted as the triumph of might over right'. Convinced that Lancelot's causes are undeserving, Bloch is obliged to see the *Mort* as a world in which belief has been lost in the efficacy of an immanent God to achieve justice through human intermediaries. For other critics, however, Lancelot is just as obviously in the right, as borne out by his victories.

Such critical responses, it seems to me, make too much sense of a text which (just as in the murky issues of intent and outcome) clouds and inhibits judgements; the critics are reliant on notions of right and justice being transparent whereas in the *Mort* they are at best dimly lit, at worst wholly opaque. For justice in the *Mort* is linked to an irresolvable problematic of how far the world is governed by providence and how far by chance or fortune; and how far we could possibly know which, or what that meant. This is a problem on which, as Karen Pratt has shown, the characters can shed no light.

> They are constantly 'reasoning why'—hence the frequent references by them to God, Fortune, Destiny, and their own guilt or sin. Yet they never reach a conclusion. This is because not only is it not man's place to reason why, it is also a futile activity, since it is evident that the world of the flesh is subject to laws which are far less just and predictable than those that govern the salvation of an individual's soul.

It is also a problem from which the text as a whole retreats into secular gloom, reflecting 'the equivocal attitude of so many secular writers in the Middle Ages towards the problem of explaining history and the rise and fall of great civilisations'. Thus while it is true that Lancelot emerges from his second duel having apparently demonstrated to Gawain's satisfaction that he did not kill Gaheriet 'treacherously and disloyally', this duel does not clarify our ethical attitude towards Lancelot either as a killer, or as a lover. It merely leaves the whole field of ethical inquiry darker and more impenetrable.

So far I have considered the trial scenes of Guenevere and Lancelot as metaphors—inconclusive ones—for how readers might attempt to put them on trial for adultery. I now want to examine the crime with which they are charged. Why are they represented as killers? What do adultery and killing have in common?

The deaths for which Lancelot and Guenevere are tried (even if they are not found guilty) are only two among the indefinitely many to which their adultery might be said to contribute. For the *Mort* portrays an increasingly violent world, its conflicts aggravated by the rift between Lancelot and Arthur. The text opens with a series of tournaments, but these soon give way to genuine warfare in the wake of the attempted entrapment of the lovers and Lancelot's rescue of Guenevere. Arthur finds himself at war, successively, with Lancelot, the Romans, and Mordred. Armies are wiped out as civilisations crumble. Fighting dominates the text, and killing becomes necessary and unavoidable, simultaneously appalling and banal. (Bresson's 1974 film *Lancelot du Lac*, based on the *Mort*, excellently captures the frenzied meaninglessness of violence in this text.) In identifying the lovers as killers, then, the text both integrates their adultery to the *Mort*'s cataclysmic canvas, and represents it as (literally) lethal.

The sinister and guilt-laden implications of this contrast markedly with the role of the philtre in the *Tristan* story, guarantor of the lovers' innocence. As the philtre marks equality between Tristan and Iseut, so the striking parallels between the deaths of Gaheris and Gaheriet signal the parity between Lancelot and Guenevere. But while the *Tristan* lovers drink the love-potion together, Guenevere, as if in reminiscence of Eve's role in the Fall, offers a poisoned fruit to someone else. And while the *Tristan* potion is a presage of the lovers' eventual death, in the *Mort* the lovers themselves are oddly immune to the fatality they are associated with. In fact, their killings are a curious reversal of the anticipated story-line, namely that *they* should be the ones to be killed. As in other Celtic-influenced texts, the penalty for adultery in the *Mort* is death, but Arthur is prevented from executing Guenevere. The couple might have shared the fate of other literary adulterers (such as Iseut) who die of their own accord, as though in acknowledgement of

society's condemnation of them, but they do not. Like all the major characters in the *Mort*, Lancelot and Guenevere are at times so overwhelmed by grief or anger that they are convinced they will die, but only the maid of Escalot, much earlier in the text, is as good as her word and actually dies from her grief whereas Lancelot and Guenevere don't. Instead the plot effects a curious exchange between killing the lovers and having them kill others. Their enemies (except for Morgan) predecease them, dying violent deaths, whereas Guenevere does not die until very nearly the end and Lancelot outlives virtually everyone. In a text where death is so commonplace, the lovers are almost magically protected from it.

Not only that; the lovers also avoid deliberate killing. Lancelot does not kill Mador; he deliberately saves Arthur's life; and he refuses to kill Gawain ('I could not do it [...] for my heart to which I belong could not agree to it on any account'. Although the best knight in the world, he actually kills very few people. The crimes of which he and Guenevere are accused consist in killing outside socially prescribed norms; it is not the deaths but the aberrant circumstances of them that lead to their being perceived as 'treacherous and disloyal', and if Lancelot had lost his two fights he would have been made to die a socially sanctioned death. Killing, the text seems to suggest, is inevitable and universal, and yet society polices it in such a way that accidental killing calls for legal investigation whereas killing on purpose does not. Adultery, likewise, is love in the wrong place, and thus perhaps only an arbitrarily censured instance of universal and inevitable behaviour. The guilt involved is one of social convention, not absolute value.

Indeed, the 'guilt' of the 'adultery killings' in the *Mort* begins to look quite innocent when one compares them with what could be called the 'incest killings', the reciprocal slaying of Mordred and Arthur. Mordred, the text reveals, is both son and nephew to Arthur, a child incestuously conceived with his sister. In Arthur's absence Mordred usurps his throne and tries to marry his wife, thus compounding treachery with attempted bigamy and further incest. Despite repeated warnings that this war will bring his reign and his kingdom to an end, Arthur seeks out Mordred and each deals the other his death-blow. Here is a striking instance of how sexual crime and killing can be linked: this tight-knit family drama crystallises Freudian preoccupation by economically combining transgression of the two most sacred taboos: parricide and incest.

By contrast, both Lancelot and Guenevere (their adultery apart) show exemplary love and respect for Arthur and his authority. By sparing Arthur's life Lancelot avoids Mordred's parricide and by handing Guenevere back voluntarily desists from sexual transgression. As Méla says, because '[Lancelot] chooses to live henceforth in a state of unfulfilled desire out of respect for the Name of the Father [...] the essential achievement of *La Mort Artu* is to have integrated love for the king into Lancelot's love for the queen'. Compared with the meaningful deaths of Arthur and Mordred, the killings for which Lancelot and Guenevere are tried are impressively insignificant. Their victims are neither figures of oppression (such as a father) nor are they rivals. There is no psychodrama involved: on the contrary Gaheris, recipient of the poisoned apple, has no connection whatever with the adultery plot, while Gaheriet was doing his best to keep out of it. Gaheris is the medieval equivalent of today's 'innocent bystander', unheard of until killed. Gaheriet is slightly more prominent, but still a relatively minor figure. Each is simply the wrong person in the wrong place at the wrong time.

The random character of these deaths in contrast with the Arthur-Mordred confrontation seems to indicate that anyone could die at any time. And the fact that they die by accident corresponds with the lovers' lack of control over the rest of their lives. The lovers' killings, in other words, can be read as a projection of their own mortality and frailty, a condition they share with the other characters in the text. Here at last the literal and the metaphorical converge: death is literally about human mortality and frailty, while adultery is their ethical expression. The poisoned fruit serves as a textual marker of this convergence, since the Genesis intertext links sexuality with human weakness and death.

This essay has grappled with the lack of clear interpretation available to readers of the *Mort*. We are offered the trials as metaphors for our inquiry into adultery; and yet they don't lead very far, and when one trial is over, we start again with the other and a further set of questions. The equation between adultery and killing, which seems so sinister and guilt-ridden, conveys in fact a curious innocence which makes it difficult to evaluate. I think, however, that the way that the point eludes the reader *is* the point, and that we are invited, in reading this text, to contemplate a depressing portrayal of human limitation. This is a penumbral text which, as it narrates the demise of civilisation, looks back (via

the episode of the poisoned fruit) to the time before civilisation began. In the intervening shadows, lacking the light of Eden or of heaven, we are uncertain about the ethical significance of intention and responsibility, guilt and sin, justice and truth. Love and death are worked together in a pessimistic duo, ingrained in the shallow experience of humanity, arbitrarily treated by society, fraught with violence, subject to uncontrollable intent and unpredictable outcome, and resistant to moral judgement.

Source: Sarah Kay, "Adultery and Killing in 'Le Mort le Roi Artu,'" in *Scarlet Letters: Fictions of Adultery from Antiquity to the 1990s*, edited by Nicholas White and Naomi Segal, MacMillan Press Ltd, 1997, pp. 34–44.

Donald C. MacRae

In discussing La Mort le Roi Artu, *Donald McRae argues that while destiny is a major theme in the story, the theme of free choice plays an equal if not more important role and describes how this idea drives many of Arthur's actions and the consequential events of his decisions.*

In his *Etude sur la Mort le Roi Artu,* Jean Frappier has suggested that the "... thème de Fortune—du Destin—est sans doute le thème majeur de *La Mort Artu*" ("... theme of Fortune—of Destiny—is undoubtedly the major theme of *La Mort Artu*"). Elsewhere he restates this conviction when he refers to the "... cercle de fatalité qui pèse sur son [Arthur's] royaume terrestre" ("circle of fatality that weighs heavily upon his [Arthur's] terrestrial kingdom"). Everything, he insists, gives the impression of tragic inevitability so that at times Fortune even seems to acquire a force all its own: "... le destin est comme l'âme du roman; le thème en est traité avec assez de force et de profondeur pour que la *Mort Artu* ... puisse faire penser par endroits aux tragiques grecs ou au drame élisabéthain" ("destiny is, as it were, the soul of the romance. The theme is treated with enough force and profundity that the *Mort Artu* reminds one in places of Greek tragedy or Elizabethan drama"). There is no doubt about the importance of fate in the *Mort Artu*, but to suggest, as Frappier and others have done, that the role of this one motif is so striking that it dominates all others would seem to place too great an importance upon its function to the detriment of other important themes in the story. Indeed, consideration of the work essentially as a fate-tragedy is to ignore, or at least to play down, certain essential characteristics which contribute not only to the superb psychologi-

A nineteenth-century woodcut illustration depicting King Arthur being transported to Avalon after his death.

cal portraits of which the mediaeval author has proved himself a master, but also to the very structure of the romance itself.

Without denying the slow but inexorable rotation of the Wheel of Fortune in turning the tide in the affairs of men, Eugène Vinaver, however, argues convincingly for a much more complex and subtle pattern of cause and event leading to the final catastrophe. In his discussion on the poetry of interlace, he draws attention not just to "… one major cause, but [to] … several concurrent causes," citing in addition to this theme: the withdrawal of

divine protection from both Arthur and Lancelot; conflicts arising out of the divided loyalties which Lancelot feels toward Guinevere on the one hand and Arthur and Gauvain on the other, as well as Mordred's incestuous birth. These, he indicates, are a part of the intricate setting, the vast design, without which there can be neither plot nor characterization. This complex fabric provides a "… continuous and constantly unfolding panorama stretching as far into the past as into the future—such are the things that hold the reader spell-bound as he progresses through these interwoven 'branches' and themes." Destiny, he asserts, is inextricably linked with character, and destiny means "... the convergence of simultaneously developed themes, now separated, now coming together, varied, yet synchronized, so that every movement of this carefully planned design remains charged with echoes of the past and premonitions of the future." Vinaver's arguments are eminently reasonable, accounting, as they do, for the complexity and apparent confusion of the many themes of the *Mort Artu* and lifting it above the state of a mere fate-tragedy to which the others would seem to relegate it.

There is, however, one essential theme which Vinaver does not take into account and which plays a major role in the development of character and plot in the *Mort Artu*. I refer to a critical measure of free choice, granted to Arthur in particular, which permeates the story from beginning to end. It is this measure of free choice which lies behind all of Arthur's decisions, influencing and directing his behaviour in the various situations in which he finds himself. If, to the thirteenth-century mind, his fall from grace is unavoidable "... as a result of Arthur's rise to excessive heights of success and fame" the introduction of this theme of free choice clearly provides a tangible and logical foundation for the inevitability of that process. In this fact lies "... the convergence of simultaneously developed themes" to which Vinaver has referred. There is absolutely nothing inconsistent in that. However, the role of free choice is not a simple one in the *Mort Artu*. The King's inability or, more frequently, his unwillingness to distinguish between the appearance and the reality of a given situation directly affects his subsequent course of action. Consequently, this clouds his vision and prevents him from choosing wisely and correctly. When one realizes that the decisions which Arthur must make are invariably imposed upon him during a time of crisis in the story, it is relatively easy to understand how the effect of these decisions gradually builds up to the tragic battle on the Salisbury Plain where not only King Arthur but also the entire Kingdom of Logres are destroyed. This, then, is the essential theme of the romance to which we have referred: confronted by a need to make a decision in a moment of crisis, Arthur is unwilling or unable to see the situation as it really is and invariably chooses the wrong course of action. It is not Fate acting wilfully and arbitrarily, but Arthur himself, who is ultimately responsible for his own demise.

In the opening pages of *La Mort le Roi Artu*, King Arthur is confronted by the insistence of his

" . . .it is important to stress that the prophecies that Merlin makes there are inevitable only insofar as Arthur's own behaviour makes them so."

nephew, Agravain, that his Queen, Guinevere, is involved in an adulterous affair with Lancelot del Lac. Even though the situation is a recurrence of an earlier illicit relationship which Lancelot has vowed to terminate *[Queste del Saint Graal],* Arthur is outwardly struck by disbelief and, at least initially, refuses to pay heed to the accusations. In spite of the fact that Agravain's suspicions are well-founded, the King's angry rejections of this contention as totally without justification would seem to indicate the impossibility of such a relationship. Arthur seems certain that Lancelot could never betray their friendship in so base a way, and yet, in virtually the same breath, he belies this apparent conviction and vacillates: "... et certes se il onques le pensa, force d'amors li fist fere, encontre qui sens ne reson ne peut avoir duree" ("and indeed if he ever did, he was compelled by the force of love, which neither common-sense nor reason can resist"). Aware of the inherent dangers in Agravain's accusation, Arthur vehemently denies the possibility of such behaviour on Lancelot's part, but in spite of his protestations, he knows there may well be something in his nephew's words. Thus, he immediately leaves himself this opening, but in so doing, he contradicts his own certainty in the matter.

This is but the first hint of many such instances in which the King proves himself at best indecisive and hesitant, at worst weak and pitiful. He is ill at ease in this situation, and his anger that he must do something is clearly evident. Thus when Agravain pursues the matter further and suggests that Arthur have the two lovers closely watched in order to prove the validity of these accusations, Arthur finds himself in a dilemma from which there is no easy escape. Although he has the choice whether or not to act upon Agravain's information, he closes his eyes to the truth of the matter because he is immediately and painfully aware of the consequences for the Kingdom should they prove to be true. Arthur does not want to know the truth and this is why he neither approves nor disapproves of Agravain's plans, for any confrontation with Lancelot del Lac at this particular moment would hardly be in the best interests either of Arthur or of the Kingdom of Logres. The quest for the Holy Grail has just been brought to a conclusion, but only at the cost of the lives of many of Arthur's knights. Indeed, aware of the crisis now facing them, and in a last desperate attempt to bolster the failing morale of a sadly-depleted Round Table, the King has just announced a tournament. Conflict with Lancelot at this time would surely spell disaster to his hopes for a rebirth of his Kingdom. It is abundantly clear to him that the well-being of the Round Table is directly dependent upon the choice he must now make. Consequently Arthur avoids taking the firm course of action necessary to discover the truth for himself, and at the risk of his honour, he is forced to close his eyes to the reality of Agravain's accusations, all the while trying to convince himself that they are not true.

That night there follows a period of deep soul-searching during which the King must wrestle with his problem. Ultimately, his predicament being what it is, he is able to persuade himself that there is no truth to Agravain's contention and therefore no need for action on his part, and yet, in spite of this, his actions in leaving the Queen behind when he goes to the tournament, "… por esprouver la mençonge Agravain" ("to put Agravain's accusation to the test"), clearly show that he is deceiving himself in order to avoid coming to terms with reality.

Although this psychological aspect of Arthur's character is important in itself, it has further implications for the structure of the romance. His moments of weakness, his vacillations and self-deception invariably occur in times of crisis during which the necessity for decisive action, the hallmark of the young King Arthur, is of the utmost importance. Here, as elsewhere, Arthur is faced by a freedom of choice between two distinct alternatives: the one centered in reality, the other in the illusion of reality. It is the latter, however, the deception of appearances, assuming the form of deliberate distortion or misinterpretation of the facts and half-truths, which invariably holds sway at these crucial moments in the story and ultimately brings about the final hours of the Round Table on the Salisbury Plain.

If the hatred of Agravain for Lancelot has been the impetus for Arthur's dilemma, his meeting with his sister, Morgan, further complicates the situation. Like Agravain, she, too, is motivated by hatred, but her means of revealing to Arthur the deceit of the two lovers whom she would destroy is even more carefully and deliberately planned. The proof with which she thus confronts him with all the supernatural powers at her disposal is, therefore, all the more difficult for him to ignore. Even the circumstances of the King's arrival at Morgan's castle would seem to suggest something more than mere chance; the subsequent systematic way in which she sets about to convince Arthur to take action against Lancelot and Guinevere would tend to reinforce this assertion. After his stay in Tauroc, Arthur enters the forest in which Morgan once imprisoned Lancelot del Lac. As he does so, he feels unwell and shortly thereafter he and his company have lost their way. The suspicion that the supernatural powers of Morgan are already at work is strengthened by the sound of the horn. Although it is later made clear that the King is tired after a long ride from Tauroc, the fact that no further issue is made of Arthur's illness suggests that it was a transitory state, probably induced by the supernatural powers of Morgan herself and followed up by the sound of the horn and the dazzling display in the castle itself. Clearly Morgan has laid the groundwork for her plan most carefully.

At first she tells him no more than is necessary for her purposes until such time as she is prepared to reveal her identity to him and to allow him to discover the pictures on the wall of the room to which he has been brought. Having once examined these pictures and deciphered them, Arthur is forced to consider the truth of the message they convey. Significantly, he is not yet prepared to accept the reality of the evidence that they present, for once he has recovered from the initial shock of his discovery, he immediately questions their authenticity. The consequences of the situation and the need for a decision, however, are obvious to him; his own honour and the well-being of the Kingdom of Logres are at stake. And so, in the light of Morgan's carefully prepared arguments which corroborate the message of the pictures on the wall, Arthur declares that he sees "toute aparissant" ("clearly") and that he is more convinced than ever of the need to act. In spite of the overwhelming evidence before him and in spite of his apparent resolve to take the steps that the situation demands, Arthur still refuses to admit the truth to himself and continues to seek a way out of the unpleasant circumstances which a deliberate decision on his part would bring about. "Et *se* il est einsi …" (53:59: the italics are my own; "*If* it is as …" [p. 73]). And again:

> "Je en ferai tant … que *se* li uns ainme l'autre de fole amor, si com vos me dites, que ge les ferai prendre ensemble ains que cis mois soit passez, *se* il avient que Lancelos viegne a court dedens celui terme." (the italics are my own)

> ("I shall make sure … that *if* one loves the other adulterously as you say, I shall have them caught together before the end of the month, *if* Lancelot should return to court by then.")

Putting his crown on the line, he promises punishment to both, *if* they are guilty. It is obvious that Arthur has a choice how he will react: the tragic truth of the matter is that whichever way he moves, he stands to lose. Should he fail to take action to avenge his shame, his own position as King would be jeopardized, his authority a sham and his honour degraded. If, however, Arthur were to move against Lancelot he is certain that the reverberations of his actions would be sufficient to bring about the final destruction of the Round Table as he knows it. This is for him the greatest fear of all.

This latter consideration should not be underestimated. Subtle but repeated references to the glories of the past punctuate the entire text and make obvious the concern of an old man for a world—the only one he has ever lived for—which is slowly but surely crumbling about him. Nowhere is this more clearly stated than in the scene in which Gauvain and Arthur come upon the boat containing the corpse of the maid of Escalot. Gauvain remarks to the King:

> "Par foi … se ceste nacele est ausi bele dedenz com dehors, ce seroit merveilles; a poi que ge ne di que les aventures recommencent."

> ("In faith … if that boat is as beautiful inside as it is outside, it would be a marvel; it is almost as if adventures were beginning again.")

Both are aware that they are living in the twilight of the Round Table.

When Arthur finally leaves Morgan and returns to Camelot, he is surprised to learn that Lancelot has spent but one day at court. As a result he becomes confused why this should be so if he loves the Queen adulterously. More than willing to accept the situation at face value, Arthur immediately finds in this just cause to doubt the words of both Agravain and Morgan:

> "… et c'estoit une chose qui moult metoit le cuer le roi a aise et qui moult li fesoit mescroire les paroles que il ot oïes …."

> ("This was a thing which went a long way to set the king's mind at rest and which led him to discount what he had heard….")

His escape from reality is short-lived.

If one were to apply Jean Rychner's linguistic analysis of the *Mort Artu* to this situation in order to substantiate these arguments even further, the willingness of the King to close his eyes to the truth would become adequately clear. Rychner suggests:

> Entre le pn sj sans conjonction [sujet pronominal: i.e., le pronom personnel, il, ele, et le pronom démonstratif cil, cele] et le pn sj avec conjonction on peut être sensible à la même différence qu'entre sj nm [sujet nominal] et 'et' + sj nm: plus de calme et de ponderation d'un coté, et de l'autre plus de familiarité et de vivacité.

> (Between the pronominal subject without a conjunction [i.e., the personal pronoun, *il*, *ele*, and the demonstrative pronoun *cil*, *cele*] and the pronominal subject with a conjunction, one can be aware of the same difference that exists between a nominal subject and "and" + nominal subject: more calm and equilibrium on the one hand, and on the other more intimacy and vivacity.)

Elsewhere he refers to the "… entrée plus vive et plus dramatique …" ("more lively and dramatic opening") of such phrases, and "Le syntagme en 'et il' de même sujet est habituellement prospectif et pourvu d'une suite" ("The syntagma in "et il" of the same subject is usually prospective and provided with a continuation"). The thrust of the story is, therefore, clearly in the direction of this clause rather than the preceding one and thus toward Arthur's attempts to discredit what he has heard and seen. He continues to close his eyes to the truth in the hope that the threatened confrontation with Lancelot will somehow disappear. The presence of the "et" which introduces this section looks ahead to the continuing attempts of the King to avoid making an unwanted decision.

The episode of the poisoned fruit follows and Lancelot is called upon to prove the innocence of the Queen in the death of Gaheris. Once he has done so, however, he falls more hopelessly in love with her: "Et se Lancelos avoit devant ce amee la reïne, il l'ama orendroit plus qu'il n'avoit onques mes fet a nul jor, et ele ausint lui…." ("And if Lancelot had loved the queen before, from now on he loved her more than he had ever done in the past, and so did she him"). Unfortunately, their lack of discretion makes this illicit relationship obvious to almost everyone and ultimately leads to yet another crisis.

To some extent this crisis provides an interesting contrast with the initial Arthur-Agravain episode, for this time, Agravain finds himself on somewhat firmer ground. By now, the gravity of the situation is clear and he deliberately allows Arthur to overhear the conversation between himself and his brothers. Once he has captured the King's attention, he then allows both Gaheriet and Gauvain to parry Arthur's questions in order to cover up the truth about Lancelot and Guinevere. In spite of the King's anger, neither will yield to Arthur's pressure and tell him what they have been discussing. Significantly, he reacts to their refusal in a totally irrational way, demanding to know their secret, first, on the oaths they have sworn to him, and then, threatening them on pain of death if they should fail to inform him. In spite of these angry words, neither Gaheriet nor Gauvain gives in and both leave the King's presence; Arthur does nothing about it. Left in the room with the others, Arthur asks them, begs them and finally, beside himself with rage, stands ready to strike Agravain dead with a blow from his sword. No longer in control of himself, Arthur shows signs of cracking under the strain of his dilemma. However, as soon as Agravain has finally told him what he wants to know, Arthur recoils from the truth he fears; subconsciously, he does not really want to hear the truth: "Comment, fet li rois, me fet donc Lancelos honte? De quoi est ce donc? Dites le moi…" ("What," said the king, "is Lancelot dishonoring me? What are you talking about? Tell me…"). One would almost think that he was hearing this news for the first time! When Agravain assures him of the facts, Arthur turns pale, and as earlier in the initial Agravain scene, as well as in the scene with Morgan, falls silent, lost in deep thought. He can no longer take refuge in appearances; the truth is out and the reality of the situation known: "…car il set bien de voir que, se Lancelos est pris a cest afere et il en reçoit mort, onques si grant tormente n'avint en ce païs por la mort d'un seul chevalier" "He knew perfectly well that if Lancelot were caught in adultery and put to death, there would be such torment in the country as had never before been caused by the death of a single knight". Once again in a position to make a choice (although admittedly the options open to him are not very attractive) Arthur is so emotionally involved because of the faithlessness of his wife, the deception of a friend, and the certain downfall of all his kingdom that he can hardly act with a clear and rational mind. Accepting the treacherous advice of Agravain, he rejects his loyal nephew, Gauvain, and from this point onward, acting out of "desmesure" ("lack of moderation"), he swears revenge upon Lancelot and the Queen. Unlike Morgan, who finds herself forced to remind Arthur constantly of the steps he must take, Agravain no longer needs to goad him into action. He merely capitalizes on a situation from which Arthur cannot escape. Once the oath has been sworn to him, there can be no turning back—the crisis which must inevitably lead to bloodshed has been reached.

The death of Gaheriet, a direct result of Agravain's hatred for Lancelot, is significant, falling as it does almost exactly in the middle of *La Mort le Roi Artu*. Once again, appearances play an essential role in the progress of the plot and lead to an irreversible turning point in it. Gaheriet's death is a simple case of mistaken identity, for he is not who he seems to be or Lancelot would never have slain him willingly. This single event, originating in appearances, irrevocably alienates Gauvain and sets him off on his senseless quest for revenge upon Lancelot. This, in turn, marks the beginning of the end and that which Arthur fears more than anything else: a confrontation between himself on the one hand, and Lancelot and Ban's kin on the other. The King is quite aware of the inevitable consequences of such a conflict for the Kingdom of Logres.

Lancelot's love for the Queen, while obviously important in itself, finds its real significance, not in adultery, but in the fact that it threatens to bring about the confrontation which Arthur has sought to delay as long as possible. The King is prepared to close his eyes to the truth, to accept the appearances of the situation, as long as he can postpone the inevitable. The pity he betrays when he sentences Guinevere to death is indicative of the genuine love he still has for the Queen, while the anger he shows at Lancelot's good fortune in the tournament at Karahés is a reflection of his frustration that the very knight he loves most should be the catalyst in his dilemma. Indeed, there are times, in particular when Lancelot's actions seem to contradict the reality of the situation, when Arthur's vacillations would seem to suggest that he could almost live with the shame of the Queen's adultery if only he could somehow avoid the impending conflict with Lancelot. Let there be no mistake; it is not because Arthur fears Lancelot, but because he loves him and because he is quite aware of the consequences of his choice that he finds himself on the horns of a dilemma. From a structural point of view, it is important to note that the adulterous love affair plays a less significant role in the second half of the story than the first, although that aspect of it which would lead to confrontation is retained and developed, not in the love affair itself, but in Gauvain's passionate hatred of Lancelot. The thread of unity in the work is thus maintained.

As we have seen, the love affair aggravates the dilemma in which Arthur finds himself by slowly but surely forcing a confrontation between Arthur and Lancelot del Lac. The "desmesure" of Gauvain takes up where this adulterous relationship leaves off and continues inexorably to force Arthur into a conflict which he knows will ultimately destroy himself and, more significantly, the Round Table. Gauvain's obsession for revenge plays an important role in the second half of the *Mort Artu* not only as an end in itself, for that is certainly important, but also insofar as it contributes to the death of Arthur and with him, the downfall of the entire Kingdom of Logres.

The death of Gaheriet is significant for our discussion of appearances and reality, for out of it arise the hatred and irrational behaviour of Gauvain, who, in a state of shock at the news of his brother's death, is unable to see the situation as it really is. Blaming Lancelot for slaying Gaheriet willingly, he does not realize that it was a case of mistaken identity and that Lancelot would never have killed the man he loved so much. Gauvain should have known this, but his inability to recognize the truth of the matter leads him to an "idée fixe"—a fatal aspect of "desmesure." He derives his very "raison d'être" from the thought of revenge upon Lancelot, and this grows so out of proportion that he cannot see clearly nor make rational decisions. He neither can nor will recognize the truth. Motivated by blind passion which originates in mistaken observations, Gauvain's subconscious quest for his own death which so dominates the second half of the romance begins, bringing with it the realization of Arthur's fears of an end to the glorious days of the Round Table. Overwhelmed by grief, he mistakenly lays the blame for his brother's death and his own sorrow on Fortune, for therein would seem to lie the source of the problem. But he fails to see that Agravain's hatred—a hatred which he, himself, has already warned against—has contributed directly to Gaheriet's death and that he is mistaken in his accusation of Lancelot. Gauvain, in emotional shock, is therefore deceived by the appearance of things.

When Gauvain lays the blame for his tragic loss upon the whims of Fortune, he is making a serious error, for Fortune is only the apparent cause of his troubles. Indeed, she almost becomes the scapegoat

for his own weaknesses, since the real source of his dilemma lies within himself, in his "fol apel," his irrational behaviour, his inability to see things as they really are. But it is easier and perhaps more human for Gauvain to blame Fortune rather than himself. In this, the mediaeval author of the *Mort Artu* measurably broadens the scope of his characterization of Gauvain.

Arthur's reaction to Gaheriet's death is also significant, for even though the King has retreated somewhat into the background in a scene devoted primarily to insight into Gauvain's behaviour, the author has found it essential to re-emphasize those elements that retain the thread of unity throughout the work. As one might expect, Arthur views the events of the past few hours less in terms of the death of Gaheriet, himself, than in terms of his own personal loss. Still preoccupied with himself and his own dilemma, he considers Gaheriet's death an extension of his own problems. Since these problems, at least as far as he is concerned, find their origin in Lancelot, the King accuses him and holds him directly responsible. The inevitable confrontation has drawn closer; there can be no turning back once the oath of vengeance has been sworn from his followers. Thus, at this most critical of moments, both Gauvain and the King are confronted by a choice and both are incapable of acting rationally. The former, blinded by his emotional shock and his desire for revenge, and the latter, obsessed by his fears that the end of the Round Table is in sight, both fail to distinguish reality from appearances.

If King Yon's pleas for moderation are readily discounted, in particular at the urging of Mordred whose own motives are suspect, it is hardly likely that Lancelot's offer of explanation and submission to the will of the court can be accepted either. Once again, men are deluded and deceived by the appearance of things and are therefore vulnerable to the baseness of such men as Mordred. Consequently, they reject truth and reason. Repeated warnings have no effect: "…vos en seroiz destruiz er menez a mort, ou li sage home par maintes fois sont deceii" "You…will be destroyed and brought to death as a result of this war; you know that death often deceived wise men"; and Gauvain is admonished for his foolishness. Although the main thrust of the story is now, at least temporarily, carried by Gauvain, whose actions at times overshadow those of Arthur, the author of the *Mort Artu* never really loses sight of the King as the central figure in the story. Arthur continues to display the weakness that characterized him in the first half of the romance, wavering back and forth between love and hatred, admiration and contempt for Lancelot. Whenever the latter makes a chivalric gesture (quite in contrast to Gauvain's behaviour) by sparing Arthur's life or by willingly returning his Queen, Arthur's resolve begins to vacillate, much to the anger of his nephew. The King still hopes against hope that conflict can be avoided. Had he indeed the courage of his convictions, recognizing the senselessness of a war between his forces and Ban's kin, he would then reject those unreasonable demands that Gauvain is making upon him, but instead, he allows himself to be swayed by the apparent truth of Gauvain's arguments. "Puis que Gauvains le velt…il me plest bien" "Because that is what Gawain desires…it is what I want too".

Thus the human weakness inherent in his own character inevitably leads to the tragedy Arthur would avoid. Finding himself in a situation for which there is now no satisfactory solution, he is obviously aware of the consequences of continued confrontation with Lancelot, and yet, by refusing to draw the line, he brings about his own destruction and that of the Round Table with him. In this he parallels Gauvain who is also accused of pursuing his own death. By this time, Arthur's passive acceptance of the inevitability of the conflict becomes clearer and he becomes an almost pitiful figure. He has had several opportunities to make a clear decision, but he has failed to avail himself of them. Now he almost seems to believe that only death can relieve him of his burden and so he is no longer willing to struggle against a situation he thinks he cannot control. Perhaps he is right. The events which have been set in motion could have been stopped only by a firm stand by the King himself and this is something beyond the capabilities of the older Arthur of *La Mort le Roi Artu.*

In the scene involving Arthur and Gauvain and the old woman, the King and his nephew are both criticized for their foolishness. To the King she says: "Saches veraiement que c'est grant folie et que tu crois fol conseil…" "I can tell you truly that it is a great madness and that you are ill-advised". Gauvain, too, does not escape her remarks: "…vous porchaciez si durement vostre damage que vous jamais ne reverrés le roialme de Logres sains ne haitiés" "You are so resolutely pursuing your own destruction that you will never again in good health see the kingdom

of Logres". Her warnings represent the reality, the truth, of the situation in which they find themselves, but Arthur's weakness, indeed by now the loss of his desire to live, coupled with Gauvain's stubbornness, close their ears to her words. Arthur is still unsure of himself and Gauvain continues to cling stubbornly to the apparent truth that Lancelot deliberately killed his brother. In his anger and grief, Gauvain is unable to distinguish between appearances and reality and pursues his foe to the end, dragging with him Arthur and the remnants of the Round Table to their destruction. Not even Lancelot's magnanimous offer of penance can dissuade him. Thus "desmesure," "outrage," and "desreson" ("irrationality"), the most serious sins a knight could commit, bring about his death.

These are the root causes of the tragedy; man himself by his excesses, and not Fortune as an active force intervening in the affairs of men, is responsible. Although Gauvain blames his problems on Fortune, he does so mistakenly. It will be some time yet before he realizes that he does have a measure of control over his own destiny. But that moment will come and when it does, the moral lesson of the author will be clear: in spite of the seriousness of his sins, there is still hope for the true penitent which Gauvain ultimately becomes. Seeing the error of his ways, Gauvain recognizes his own guilt—not Fortune's—in this tragic situation. Rising above self-indulgence and ego, he soon attains the Kingdom of Heaven. When his quarrel with Lancelot is over, resulting as it does in the subsequent death of Gauvain, a man the King held most dear, there remains virtually nothing more for Arthur in this life. His loved ones and his Kingdom are gone. The fight with Mordred which must now follow serves only to wipe away the final remnants of a once glorious society.

It is significant at this point in the story that Arthur has not yet reached the level of awareness and understanding which Gauvain finally attains and still cannot recognize that the source of his problems lies within himself and his inability to see the reality of things. As Gauvain did before him, therefore, he, too, mistakenly shifts the blame for his own shortcomings upon the vicissitudes of Fortune:

> Hé! Fortune, chose contrere et diverse, la plus desloial chose qui soit el monde, por quoi me fus tu onques si debonere ne si amiable por vendre le moi si chierement au derrien? Tu me fus jadis mere, or m'ies tu devenue

marrastre, et por fere moi de duel morir as apelee avec toi la Mort, si que tu en deus manieres m'as honni, de mes amis et de ma terre. Hé! Mort vileinne, tu ne deüsses mie avoir assailli tel home comme mes niés estoit qui de bonté passoit tout le monde.

("Ah! Fortune, contrary and changeable, the most faithless thing in the world, why were you ever so courteous or so kind to me if you were to make me pay so dearly for it in the end? You used to be my mother; now you have become my stepmother, and to make me die of grief you have brought Death with you, in order to dishonour me in two ways at once, through my friends and through my land. Ah! base Death, you should not have attacked a man such as my nephew, who surpassed the whole world in goodness.")

Arthur, to whom the weight of the plot now shifts, still must learn that Fortune, whom he blames for his predicament, is only the manifestation, the apparent cause of his troubles. In a sense, Fortune functions as a kind of symbol here. This becomes adequately clear in the scene in which she takes Arthur up on her wheel and tells him the real reason for his impending downfall. Arthur has just been admonished in another dream by the crowd following Gauvain. They tell the King that his nephew, as a true penitent, has indeed attained the Kingdom of Heaven: "…et fei aussi comme il a fet…" "follow his example". In other words, overcome foolish earthly pride, and salvation will be guaranteed. But Arthur does not. Instead, he commits himself even more completely to the inevitable battle on Salisbury Plain. Lifting him up on her wheel, Fortune warns him of the consequences of his actions, the direct result of his own unwillingness to see the truth: "Mes tel sont li orgueil terrien qu'il n'i a nul si haut assiz qu'il ne le coviegne cheoir de la poesté del monde" "But such is earthly pride that no one is seated so high that he can avoid having to fall from power in the world". The baseness of human actions, then, which overwhelms knightly virtue, and not the whimsical intervention of blind fate, leads to the rude awakening that Arthur experiences in his dream. There is no suggestion that the King could not have retained his lofty position even longer if he had acted in accordance with the chivalric code of behaviour. Arthur's worst fears, the final destruction of his Round Table, are about to be realized; the climax has been reached. He knows this but he also believes that he has come too far to turn back. Like Gauvain immediately before his fateful battle with Lancelot, he continues to deceive himself by trying to convince himself that victory is possible and that there is an apparent hope for him. The Battle of Salisbury Plain puts an end to these illusions.

From the initial scenes of the *Mort Artu*, the main thread of this story has dealt with the downfall of Arthur and with him the destruction of the Round Table. The events which began with Merlin, his prophecies and his relationship to Arthur at the beginning of the Vulgate Cycle (Sommer: Vol. II) have now come full circle. But it is important to stress that the prophecies that Merlin makes there are inevitable only insofar as Arthur's own behaviour makes them so. These events are destined to occur because they must, for after all, they are a part of the traditional story which the mediaeval author has inherited from his predecessors; but with a remarkable degree of sophistication, that same author has introduced a tangible motivation beyond that of Fate or Fortune to justify their occurrence. Arthur's own weakness and unwillingness to see the truth provide the story with another dimension—another of the "branches" to which Vinaver refers. When he finally does realize that the tragic end is near, he cannot go back. It is too late.

Source: Donald C. MacRae, "Appearances and Reality in *La Mort le Roi Artu*," in *King Arthur: A Casebook*, edited by Edward Donald Kennedy, Garland Publishing, Inc., 1996, pp. 105–19.

R. Howard Bloch

In their joint article, Lynette R. Muir and Howard Bloch focus on the duel between Lancelot and Gauvain in La Mort le roi Artur, offering their separate interpretations of the oaths sworn by the combatants before that duel and how each pertains to judicial law in the Arthurian court.

I

In his recent article, 'From Grail Quest to Inquest', Professor Bloch has analysed the legal aspects of the two trials by combat described in the *Mort Artu* with special reference to the picture they give of the workings of feudal justice in the early thirteenth century. Professor Bloch has earned the gratitude of all Arthurians by his sensitive and minute analysis of the legal background and implications of these two duels which provide a major part of the structural framework of the romance. In his discussion of the second duel, however, that between Lancelot and Gauvain, there seems to me to be some misinterpretation of the French text in the matter of the exact form of the oaths sworn by the combatants before the battle so that it

Richard Harris as King Arthur and Vanessa Redgrave as Lady Guinevere in Camelot, *a 1967 film dramatization of the legend of Arthur.*

seems worth looking at this particular question in more detail.

When the terms of the battle are discussed outside Gaunes, Gauvain reminds Lancelot that: 'vos savez bien que entre moi et vos avons enprise une bataille si grant comme de traïson mortel por la mort de mes freres que vos oceïstes en traïson, desloiaument, ce savons nous bien tuit; et si en sui apelerres et vous deffenderres'. The use of the past tense indicates that Gauvain is here referring back to his original challenge to Lancelot, after the reconciliation between Arthur and Guinevere. On that

occasion however, the term *traïson* was not used: 'A la guerre ne poez vos faillir … tant que Gahereiz mes freres, que vos oceïstes malvaisement, sera vengiez de vostre cors meïsmes', Lancelot did not reply to this first attack but the challenge was taken up by Bors: 'Si avez dit que messires ocist desloiaument vostre frere … je deffendroie mon seigneur encontre vostre cors, si que, se g'estoie veincuz en champ, que messires Lancelos fust honniz, et se ge vos pooie recreant fere, que vos fussiez maubailliz comme faus apelerres'. Gauvain accepted Bors's challenge but the king 'refusa d'ambes deus les gages et dist que ceste bataille ne seroit otroiee en nule maniere'. In this original challenge, then, the point at issue was the killing of Gaheriet only, but in the confrontation near Gaunes, Gauvain talks of the death of 'mes freres', that is Agravain *and* Gaheriet. Gauvain adds on this latter occasion an offer that if he be defeated, Arthur will swear not to continue the siege: 'einz leront del tout le siege et s'en iront arriere en leur païs?' Lancelot's answer is, firstly, to try to forgo the battle even if he were judged a coward thereby: 'tout soit il ore issi que ge ne la porroie lessier que la honte n'en fust moie et que l'en nel me tornast a coardise'. Secondly, Lancelot offers reparation on a noble scale: he and all his kin, save the two kings, Lionel and Bors, will swear fealty to Gauvain; in addition Lancelot himself will set off alone, barefoot and in rags, for an exile of ten years, and should he die during that time, his kin will hold Gauvain innocent of his death. Lastly, Lancelot is ready to swear an oath 'seur seinz que onques au mien escient n'ocis Gaheriet vostre frere et que plus m'en pesa qu'il ne fu bel'. The crux of this last oath is that it does not raise *at all* the question of the death of Agravain. Gauvain mentions brothers, *mes freres*, Lancelot mentions one brother, *vostre frere*. (It is surely significant in considering this whole quarrel, that Gauvain never attacks Bors for having killed his third brother Guerres.) Gauvain refuses Lancelot's offer completely and repeats his accusation, this time formally: 'Lors tent son gaje et dist au roi: "Sire, veez me ci prest de prouver que Lancelos ocist desloiaument mes freres"'. Lancelot does not formulate his reply in legal terms, he merely accepts the battle: '"Vez ci mon gage por moi deffendre" … et li rois reçoit les gages d'ambedous'. Gauvain's own cousin Yvain claims that Gauvain is in the wrong: 'Sire, pour coi avés vous emprise ceste bataille, et encore a tort, car il se deffendra a son droit', and later he and the king agree that right is not on their side: 'ci ot si grant offre [that made by Lancelot] qu'aprés ceste chose je ne puis veoir par devers nos se desreson non … por ce que je voi par dela le droit et par deça le tort'. Lancelot himself is uneasy and makes his confession: 'car moult doutoit qu'il ne li mescheïst envers monseigneur Gauvain por la mort de ses freres qu'il avoit ocis'. Lancelot does not, however, even here admit the accusation of *traïson*.

In the light of these quotations, it is surely not possible to accept that in this battle 'Gauvain's accusation, unlike that of Mador, has a strong basis in fact. Lancelot did kill his brother *with harmful*

> " The essential distinction between manslaughter and murder (traïson), under feudal law, centres around the issue of challenge."

intent and in a deceitful manner' (my italics). The brother referred to here, is Agravain, whom, Bloch claims, Lancelot slew in a premeditated attack from ambush. Bors, at the time, declared it was an open attack after challenge: 'onques en traïson n'oceïstes ses freres, mes en apert, en tel leu ou il avoit plus de cent chevaliers'. Bloch may be right in claiming premeditation since Lancelot certainly declares his intention of killing Agravain if he can, but it seems arguable if an attack that can be seen coming, can be considered legally a secret and therefore treacherous killing: 'chascuns monte seur son cheval, et pranent escuz et lances; si tornent cele part ou il voient le feu. Et quant cil qui es prez estoient *les virent venir*, si s'escrierent tuit ensemble: "Veez ci Lancelot! fuiez! fuiez!"' (my italics). If the killing of Agravain is only possibly treachery, there can be no doubt at all that the killing of Gaheriet was not merely not premeditated, it was quite unintentional: 'Lancelot, qui aloit les rens cerchant, *nel connut mie*' (my italics). Indeed, Lancelot is deeply distressed when he learns what he has done: 'Moult fu Lancelos courrouciez par la mort de Gaheriet, car ce estoit uns des chevaliers del monde que il plus amoit'. It is, therefore, incorrect to claim that 'Lancelot killed Gaheriet with evil intent according to the medieval formula of *traïson*'.

Professor Bloch deduces from this battle that 'the combatants' fatigue at the end of this second struggle reflects an exhausted method of ascertaining judicial truth' but it seems rather that the whole incident represents an excellent example of the *duel judicaire*. Gauvain's cause is bad, but he genuinely believes it good, and this gives him the power to prolong the battle for a full day against the hitherto invincible Lancelot:

> Si te di bien que, se je n'i veïsse mon droit apertement, je n'assamblasse oan a lui por la meillor cité del monde, … Mes ce sevent bien tuit que torz et desloiautez feroit del meillor chevalier del monde

mauvés … et ce est la chose par coi je douteroie moins Lancelot, car je sai bien que li tors en est siens et li drois en est miens; par coi ne toi ne autres ne devez avoir poor de moi, car en toz leus aïde Nostre Sires au droit: c'est ma fiance et ma creance.

After such a declaration it seems unreasonable to claim that: 'Mador's and Gauvain's accusations engender a crisis of belief in the efficacy of the *Dei judicio*'. It is true that this form of trial only proves the point made on oath, but that after all was what it was intended to do. It would be wrong to criticise or to hold that the author of the *Mort Artu* wanted to criticise the system of judicial combats for not doing something it was never designed to do. Gauvain, believing he was right, attacked Lancelot and was defeated because he was, in fact, wrong. He, himself, admitted this on his death-bed: 'Se ge veïsse celui que ge sei au meilleur chevalier del monde et au plus cortois et ge li peüsse crier merci de ce que ge li ai esté si vilains au derrien, il m'est avis que m'ame en fust plus a ese aprés ma mort'.

The changing attitude of the thirteenth century towards judicial combat is indeed reflected in Arthurian romance, though not, I would suggest, in this combat. In the prose *Tristan*, however, there is an example of a trial by battle in which the winner is later proved to have been in the wrong. King Arthur is deeply distressed when this discovery is made and we are told that after this battle the combatants in future duels had to swear an oath *sur seinz* that their cause was good: a manifest attempt to prop up what had been shown to be an inadequate method of achieving justice, 'car devant ce que cele aventure avint n'avoit l'en fet nul serement, ne il n'en fesoient nul se il ne leur plesoit'. The incident is summed up by the author in terms that could not have been used in the *Mort Artu:* 'et cil qui por Dieu et por droit se combatoit i fu ocis; ainssi ala li tort devant le droit en l'ostel le roi A. en la plus loial cort et en le plus droituriere qui a celui tens fust en tot le monde'.

II

In response to Dr Muir's remarks I should like to make the following points. First of all, in contracting the battle outside Gaunes, Gauvain refers not to 'his original challenge to Lancelot, after the reconciliation between Arthur and Guinevere', but to his challenge of the preceding day: 'Va t'en leanz en la cité de Gaunes et di a Lancelot del Lac, s'il a tant de hardement en soi qu'il ost deffendre que il mon frere n'oceïst en traïson, je sui prez del prouver encontre son cors que il desloiaument et en traïson l'ocist'. Although Dr Muir is correct in assuming

that the word *traïson* is not used in the original defiance some months prior to the eventual trial by combat, she fails to point out that Gauvain twice repeats the accusal of *traïson* in establishing the wagers of battle on the day before actual confrontation. Again, Dr Muir is right in observing that Gauvain speaks at the time of his brothers' death of only one brother, but the fact that he also speaks in the encounter near Gaunes of 'mes freres' serves to support the contention that Gauvain's challenge harks back to the self-contained episode of Gaunes and not to the peace concluded before the walls of 'La Joyeuse Garde'.

Second, the fact that Lancelot, in responding to the challenge, only claims to have slain Gaheriet unwittingly—'vos jurai seur seinz que onques au mien escient n'ocis Gaheriet vostre frere'—does not mean that he did not kill Agravain intentionally. In fact, the evidence at the time of slaying is just the opposite, and Lancelot's response may be a shrewd verbal manoeuvre to avoid the issue of intent altogether. His subsequent uneasiness when praying for God's help may be caused by his own sense of guilt, for he includes in his prayers reference to the death of Gauvain's three brothers and not just Gaheriet. In any case, the use of verbal trickery within the judicial ordeal is an increasingly common theme in twelfth-century and thirteenth-century literature; see, for example, *Le Roman de Renart* and Béroul's *Roman de Tristan*.

Third, Yvain claims that Gauvain is wrong not because of the righteousness or weakness of his case, as Dr Muir maintains, but because Lancelot is the stronger knight: 'Haés vous si durement vostre vie, qui avez emprise bataille encontre le meillour chevalier del monde vers qui nus Hom ne pot onques durer en bataille qui ne fust honis au daerrain?'. Yvain's recrimination is a cynical recognition, in contrast with Gauvain's belief in the efficacy of the *judicium Dei,* that might makes right. Like the Lancelot of the first battle, Yvain perceives the extent to which an ordeal of immanence can be manipulated by human intention. Yvain's and Arthur's recognition that 'right is not on their side' does not refer to the question under judicial dispute, but to Gauvain's stubborn refusal to accept Lancelot's magnanimous offers of compromise. The expiatory pilgrimage and homage were, incidentally, standard means of reconciliation without recourse to the duel.

Fourth, Bors's claim that the death of Gauvain's brothers is justifiable because it was witnessed 'by more than a hundred knights' represents an attempt to stretch the definition of justifiable homicide; it is yet another instance of the manipulation of judicial institutions through the clever use of language. The essential distinction between manslaughter and murder (*traïson*), under feudal law, centres around the issue of challenge. I refer the reader to the following passages from thirteenth-century customals not cited in my article:

> Murtres si est quant aucuns tue ou fet tuer autrui en *aguet apensé* … (Beaumanoir, *Coutumes*) Et murtre si est, quant home est ocis nuitantre, porquoi il ne viegne apenséement à la meslée, ou en trives ou en *agait de chemin*, ou en menière que il ne voie le cop venir, ou quant il est sorpris que il n'a poer de soi deffendre. (*Li Livre de Fostice et de Pletz*)

Ironically, the Gauvain of Chrétien's *Perceval* finds himself accused of treacherous homicide for 'having slain without challenge':

> Ainz l'apele de felonnie
> Et dist: "Gauvains, tu oceïs
> Mon seignor, et si le feïs
> Issi que tu nel desfïas.
> Honte et reproce et blasme i as,
> Si t'en apele de traïson.

Ganelon, accused of treason at the end of *La Chanson de Roland*, denies the charge on the grounds that he challenged Roland publicly and not in secret.

Thus, Agravain's death is not 'possibly treachery', as Dr Muir contends: the circumstances of its enactment—a premeditated attack without challenge from a hidden location—make it morally and materially an act of murder. This is all the more significant because the circumstances surrounding criminal wrongdoing matter much more, under feudal law, than the question of criminal intent. It mattered not *why* one killed another, but *how* he did it. Premeditation was deduced in an *a posteriori* fashion from the character of the crime. In other words, Gauvain's cause is not 'bad', as Dr Muir asserts; it is an essentially justifiable cause. His deathbed confession harks back to his earlier refusal of Lancelot's offers of peace and compromise rather than to the legality of his suit: 'Sire (Arthur), se vos avez perdu Lancelot par ma folie, si le recouvrez par vostre savoir'.

Finally, though Gauvain does manage to 'prolong the battle for a whole day against the hitherto invincible Lancelot', he does eventually lose. Moreover, he is only able to sustain the fight as long as he does because his opponent refuses to exert his full martial strength and because of the solar myth attached to Gauvain's prowess but irrelevant with respect to judicial right.

In conclusion, I do not reproach the author of *La Mort le roi Artu* for 'criticizing the system of judicial combats for not doing something it was never designed to do'. Rather, I credit him, along with Chrétien, Béroul, Marie de France, the authors of *Perlesvaus*, *Le Roman de Renart*, and the prose *Tristan*, for his awareness of the insufficiencies, pitfalls, and paradoxes of feudal judicial procedure during a period of profound legal transformation.

Source: Lynette R. Muir and R. Howard Bloch, "Further Thoughts on the 'Mort Artu,'" in *Modern Language Review*, Vol. 71, Issue 1, January, 1976, pp. 26–30.

R. Howard Bloch

In this essay, R. Howard Bloch draws a parallel between the collapse of the Arthurian world and the decline of feudalism in France in the years after La Mort le roi Artu was composed, arguing that both were brought about by the "crisis of values and institutions."

For a novel which begins in earthly splendour and spiritual plenitude *La Mort le roi Artu* ends in a curious spectacle of chaos and decline. This final sequel of the enormous thirteenth-century Lancelot-prose cycle contains what should have been the golden age of Arthur's court, knighthood having returned to the native soil of Camelot after the distant Grail quest. Instead, it proclaims the twilight of the Arthurian world, the steady disintegration of the courtly and chivalric ideals which are the very stuff of romance. Of the hundred thousand knights who gather for the last battle of Arthur's reign—'la derreniere qui i sera au tens le roi Artu'—only four survive the end of an empire and the end of an age: 'Einsi commença la bataille es pleines de Salesbieres dont li roiaumes de Logres fu tornez a destrucion, et ausi furent meint autre, car puis n'i ot autant de preudomes comme il i avoit eü devant; si en remestrent aprés leur mort les terres gastes et essilliees, et soufreteuses de bons seigneurs, car il furent trestout ocis a grant douleur et a grant haschiee' The wasting of Logres and the depletion of its ruling class of 'preudomes' and 'bons seigneurs' is, to a limited extent, attributable to those who least desire it. Lancelot's adultery with the Queen, Gauvain's thirst for vengeance, Arthur's blindness and weakness all contribute to the chain of catastrophe that drives the novel towards its apocalyptic finale. And yet none justifies, ultimately, the collapse of a kingdom, its noble families, ruler and all that surrounds them. Rooted far deeper than personal foible or folly, the decline of Arthur's world reflects a crisis of values and institutions—in particular judicial procedures—that is traceable to the decline of feudalism in France in the century and a half that preceded the poem's composition. The kingdom of Logres is, in its form, a mirror-image of the feudal world: a collection of independent political states structured around ties of fealty, clannish loyalty to family as part of the vendetta ethic, archaic practices of private war and trial by battle. A system that offers no distinction between private and public domains, Arthurian kingship resembles the feudal monarchies of the late Carolingians and early Capetians as seen from the increasingly national perspective of a Philippe-Auguste or Saint Louis. From this point of view, the death of Arthur and destruction of the Round Table along with its baronage of 'bons seigneurs' looks like the failure of feudal organization to deal with the problems of a new more centrally oriented era.

The first real test of the strength of the realm comes about quite unexpectedly. At dinner one evening Gauvain's enemy Arvalan prepares a piece of poisoned fruit which he offers to Guinevere, believing that she will, in turn, offer it to Gauvain. To Arvalan's surprise the Queen hands the fatal dessert to a third knight, Gaheris de Karaheu, who dies 'as soon as it passes his neck': 'La reïne prist le fruit qui de la traïson ne se gardoit; si en dona a un chevalier qui estoit compains de la Table Reonde et avoit non Gaheris de Karaheu; … et si tost comme il en ot le col passé, il chaï morz erranment voiant la reïne et touz cels qui furent a la table'. Arthur reacts to Gaheris's death with astonishment and sadness but takes no cognizance of the event in terms of criminal action. Arvalan disappears entirely from the author's tale. The Queen, in spite of the fact that many have witnessed her part in the deed, is not indicted; and Gaheris, after an honourable burial, is soon forgotten. Forgotten, that is, by all except his brother Mador de la Porte. Upon arrival in Camelot for the next assembly, Mador learns of Gaheris's death and proceeds to Arthur's court where, long after the infraction has taken place, redress is first mentioned in connexion with Guinevere's crime. He pronounces publicly the formal accusation of murder: 'Sire, or vos requier ge comme a roi que vos me faciez droit de la reïne qui en traïson a ocis mon frere; et se ele velt noier et mesconoistre, que ele traïson n'ait fete et desloiauté, je seroie prez del prouver contre le meilleur chevalier que ele i vodra metre'. Arthur warns the defendant that if convicted she will be in sorry straits—'vos est alee'—then adjourns for a period of forty days during which time she will be free to seek a champion: 'aucun prudome qui por vos entrast en champ et qui vos deffendist'.

The criminal procedure under which Guinevere is indicted for the murder of Gaheris is not unknown within the Western legal tradition. Prevalent in Greece and Rome, it disappeared during the latter days of the Empire and reappeared in Germanic feudal custom; portions are preserved in the judicial institutions of England and the United States. According to this and similar 'accusatory' methods of legal process, a criminal action can only be initiated by the victim of an offence or, as under feudal law, the family or liege lord of the offended party. Every citizen is, under an accusatory mode of indictment, eligible to become the plaintiff in a judicial proceeding, but no action can be undertaken independently of private pleas for recognition. In other words, neither the civil apparatus of the state nor its representative agent, the judge, has the power to proceed against offenders like Guinevere without the formal appeal of a Mador to the justice of Arthur's court.

For the well-armed and well-trained warrior aristocracy of the feudal era trial automatically implied physical combat. Almost any accusation punishable by mutilation or death featured the judicial duel as its primary mode of proof. Even in minor actions, where testimony is sometimes permitted, the only means by which testimonial evidence might be contested is by challenging the witness to battle. In both cases the burden of proof rests upon the shoulders of the defendant, who is forced either to accept the challenge or stand guilty as accused. Arthur explains the situation to Mador and the Queen: 'Mador, la querele la reïne doit estre menee a fin par tel maniere que, s'cle en ce jor d'ui ne treuve qui la vueitle deffendre, l'en fera de son corps ce que la cort esgardera. Or remanez ceanz jusques a eure de vespres; etse dedenz celui terme ne vient avant qui por lui empraigne ceste bataille vos est quires de l'apel et ele est encolpee'. As far as Guinevere is concerned the absence of a defender is tantamount to conviction. Mador's charge—'apel'—which works by definition against the accused, conforms historically to the procedure of indictment in use well after the novel's composition. Beaumanoir outlines in the *Coutumes de Beauvaisis* the correct method of accusal: 'De tous cas de crime l'en puet apeler ou venir a gages se l'acuseres en veut fere droit acusacion selonc ce qu'apeaus se doit fere, car il convient que cil qui est apelés s'en defendre ou qu'il demeurt atains du fet duquel il est apelés'. For Beaumanoir as for Arthur, accusation—'apeler'—

is equivalent to a wager of battle—'gages'—as long as the proper judicial formula—'droite acusacion'—has been observed. Failure to defend oneself or to provide for representation carries the force of confession.

Despite the obvious seriousness of arriving for trial without a defender, Guinevere nonetheless experiences a great deal of difficulty in locating a champion. Because of the clear and evident nature of her offence none of the knights who would have ordinarily undertaken her cause will do so against Mador. Lancelot's clan is absent from court. Arthur is prohibited by his role as justiciar from openly advocating the Queen's defence, although he does later seek without success a supporter on her behalf. Both Arthur and Guinevere have lost all hope of finding an advocate by trial time, when Lancelot, who has heard meantime of the Queen's predicament, arrives at court, defeats Mador and simultaneously redeems the defendant's honour and her favour. Lancelot's victory and vindication of his mistress corresponds generally to our own ideas of justice. The passage from false accusation to ultimate acquittal serves to reaffirm the efficacy of a judicial system in which the innocent are cleared in the end despite intervening moments of hesitation or doubt. Yet the seemingly just correlation of innocence and acquittal obscures a number of logical dilemmas concerning Arthur's support of the Queen, Lancelot's espousal of her cause and the impunity with which the true culprit escapes. Instead of assuring the integrity of the feudal mode of justice, Guinevere's exculpation calls into question the philosophic and pragmatic bases of trial by battle.

The *duel judiciaire* belongs to the series of ordeals common to any primitive sense of justice in which legal process remains indistinguishable from divine process, human will from godly will, positive law from divine law. Historically, it came to France from the Germanic tribes mentioned by Tacitus and Caesar though there is some evidence of its practice by the Gauls before the northern invasions. The efficacy of the *Deo judicio* rests upon a belief in the immanence of supernatural powers within the natural sphere. As in the *Chanson de Roland* where the contests between Charlemagne and Baligant, Thierry and Pinabel, are clearly linked to a transcendent contest between good and evil, all physical combats between mortal opponents reflect a superhuman struggle. For Homer the immanence of justice was often the result of capricious disputes between semi-human divinities; medieval man was much more likely to picture the judicial duel in terms of a

> At no point do the archaic legal mechanisms of immanent justice prevent the violence of private grievance from menacing and destroying the integrity of the realm."

conflict between the forces of Satan and those of a Christian God. Underlying both outlooks is the assumption that nature remains incapable of indifference to the outcome of earthly events and that the judicial process represents but one expression of a constant dialogue between nature and man.

The role of human judgement in criminal actions, is, under an immanent legal mode, reduced to a bare minimum, the assumption being that God alone judges and that men, having acted either innocently or with guilt, then become the passive objects of divine scrutiny. The cognitive decisions that we associate with the active binding judgeship of the Roman *praetor* or modern magistrate have little meaning for the feudal judge. Unable to disregard the law and unable to indict of his own accord, he presides to pronounce sentence and ensure the fairness of the proceedings. Much like the referee in a sporting event, he possesses sufficient discretionary power to apply the rules that have applied in the past without the authority to change them through the precedent of his decisions. Free to fix the fine details of Guinevere's trial, the forty day adjournment to find a champion, Arthur is nonetheless obliged to establish the conditions under which a direct encounter between plaintiff and defendant can take place. That encounter, the judicial ordeal, represents an attempt to elicit supernatural intervention in human affairs. Both the unilateral ordeals of trial by fire, water, burning oil, or coal and the bilateral 'ordeal of the cross' and combat seek to force God to show his hand in cases where the righteousness or the culpability of the parties is not apparent. Justice becomes manifest through the burns that either heal or fester, the bearers of the cross who endure or falter, the combatants who kill or are killed, the entire process dependent upon the theoretical premise that the Lord does not abandon the just man and that he punishes those who have failed him. Before facing Lancelot in battle Gauvain professes his faith in the unerring justness of the *duel judiciaire*: 'Mes ce sevent bien tuit que torz et desloiautez feroit del meillor chevalier del monde mauvés, et droiz et loiautez feroit del plus mauvés et seür et preu'. Whether or not Gauvain's cause is, in fact, just, he believes that right and force are sufficiently allied to insure judicial fairness.

The strictness of the rules governing combat and the obligation on the justiciar's part to apply them are meant to facilitate God's work in making his judgement evident. The accusation and denial, acceptance of the wagers of battle, swearing of oaths that accompany the actual physical match are conducted according to precise formulas whose slightest infraction can invalidate the entire proceeding. By the twelfth century the rituals have been christianized to such an extent that trial has become a sacrament. At the end of *Roland* Thierry and Pinabel visit church, hear mass, take confession and offer pious gifts before battle. Lancelot too confesses his sins in an all night vigil before meeting Gauvain (p. 184.11). The premise that God judges according to the comparative moral status of the two contestants makes it a matter of utmost importance to enter combat as free as possible from any trace of lingering sin. Ritualization—blessing of relics and arms, swearing of oaths, hearing of mass and confession—is aimed at establishing a direct rapport between the divine judge and the human instruments of his judgement. Cases are submitted to God for his decision, *per duelli probationem*; the ceremonial trappings ensure his participation. Thierry declares to Pinabel, 'Deus facet hoi entre nus dous le dreit!' Harold decrees before the Battle of Hastings, 'Dominus inter me et Willelmum hodie quod justum est descernat'. Both are aware that God alone judges the petty quarrels of men and that his judgement often surpasses their understanding.

Representation in battle by a champion was an ancient Germanic prerogative (*sunnis* or *avoué*) by which direct participation of the parties involved in litigation can, under certain circumstances, be waived. Mentioned in the Frankish capitularies and the sixth-century *Lex Burgondionem*, provisions for substitution in the judicial duel are a constant feature of medieval procedure. In *Roland* representation is automatic: Ganelon's trial hinges upon the appearance of Thierry to substantiate Charlemagne's accusation. According to Beaumanoir, if a defendant is missing a limb, is over sixty years of age, has a sickness that prevents excitement or a chronic illness (*quartaine* or *tierçaine*), he has the right to find a champion to fight in his place. The *Coutumes de Beauvaisis* also contains a specific proviso for women: 'li quins essoines, si est se fame apele ou est apelee, car fame ne se combat pas'. Hence, Arthur, as judge, is perfectly warranted in permitting Guinevere a stand-in for the actual trial by battle. His position becomes considerably less tenable through his active solicitation of support. Where the Queen acquiesces to the lack of champion Arthur first turns to the knights of the Round Table who baulk at the idea of defending a cause in which defeat is a foregone conclusion: 'car il sevent bien que la reine a tort et Mador a droit'. He next approaches Gauvain who refuses on the grounds that no loyal knight would enter combat with the knowledge of his party's fault, not even if the party were his own mother: 'car nos savons bien que la reïne ocist le chevalier dont ele est apelee'.

What stands out most clearly in Arthur's attempt to find a champion for Guinevere is his hesitancy to let the process of divine justice run its natural course. The king is not content to trust the matter of God's judgement to the invisible mechanism of infallible providence, but feels compelled to hasten the progress of providence with his own interventions. Nor is he secretive about his reasons for wanting to protect the Queen: Arthur's personal commitment to the woman he loves leads him to disregard her evident guilt. And whereas the judge within an immanent accusatory system should remain neutral once he has established a direct confrontation between parties, Arthur confuses his public role as justiciar with his private role as husband. Mador accuses him after the trial of having manipulated the proceedings: 'Sire, vos m'avez deceü qui encontre moi avez mis monseigneur Lancelot'.

In the long run, the efficacy of the judicial duel depends upon the faith of those who participate in it, a faith that God's will ultimately protects the innocent and punishes those who perjure themselves in his presence. The fear of perjury in the name of a bad cause explains Gauvain's and the other knights' reluctance to respond to Arthur's call for help. Lancelot, however, reacts differently to the news of the Queen's dilemma. Fully aware of her guilt, he nonetheless consents to champion what is commonly acknowledged to be a faulty cause:

> Certes, fet Lancelos, s'ele me devoit haïr a touz jorz
> en tel maniere que ge ne trouvasse jamés pes a li, si ne
> voudroie ge pas qu'ele fust deshonoree a mon vivant;
> car c'est la dame del monde qui plus m'a fet d'enneur
> puis que ge portai armes; si me metrai en aventure por

li deffendre, non mie si hardiement come j'ai fet en autre bataille, car ge sei bien veraiement, a ce que g'en ai oï dire, que li torz en sera meins et li droiz Mador.

Lancelot's acceptance has been attributed by some to shock and momentary weakness. Be that as it may, his decision seems more conscious than a transitory slip. He states explicitly that he will defend the Queen not because he believes in her essential righteousness, but because of her past reputation. In reflecting upon his decision Lancelot accepts the prospect of entering battle 'half-heartedly' due to the certainty of her guilt: 'car ge set bien veraiement … que li torz en sera meins et li droiz Mador'. And in so doing, the greatest knight of Logres shows himself clearly willing to undertake what amounts to an adequate but not wholly valid judicial cause. His readiness to perjure himself and thus to compromise with the *sine qua non* of feudal justice, a belief in the omnipotence of the divine judge, has far-reaching implications. For Lancelot the absolute certainty of God's vengeance no longer poses a serious threat. His attitude is much closer to an Aristotelian vision of a universe created by God but existing apart from his continual presence than to an immanent universe in which the divine being penetrates every object and events. Lancelot's action implies a world in which human and divine will function independently of each other, a world from which the gods have withdrawn, leaving humans responsible for the consequences of their deeds.

Further doubt concerning the efficacy of the immanent legal system emanates from the trial itself. According to the *Deo judico*, every effort is made not only to force the parties into a situation of direct confrontation, but to establish a clear-cut contradiction between their respective allegations, the assumption being that one of the two will, of necessity, be guilty of perjury. Accusations are therefore repeated orally, publicly and according to set formula. Denial also takes place in accordance with a fixed pattern requiring verbatum—*verbo ad verbum*—refutation of the charges.

At Guinevere's trial Mador repeats the allegation originally pronounced upon arrival in Camelot. Lancelot refutes it word for word: 'Sire chevaliers, ge sui prez de prouver qu'ele desloiaument et en traïson a ocis mon frere.—Et ge sui prez, fit Lancelos del deffendre qu'ele n'i pensa onques desloiauté ne traison'. Mador's accusal and Lancelot's denial carry us a long way from Gaheris's death and the common knowledge of the Queen's part in it. Mador maintains that Guinevere not only killed his brother, she did so knowingly and treacherously: 'desloiaument et en traïson a ocis mon frere'. In fact, the accused at no point denies having handed the fatal piece of fruit to Gaheris despite her disavowal of any knowledge of the poison. Yet the formulary accusation opens the delicate question of intention behind criminal behaviour. The Queen's case hinges upon a subtle distinction between intentional misdeed and the absence of intent, a difference that often escapes the ken of primitive legal methods and that becomes especially muddled in the judicial apparatus of Arthur's court.

In spite of his initial concern about the motive surrounding Guinevere's act, Arthur seems to be singularly indifferent to the notion of intention. He says nothing when Mador first accuses her of wilful murder, nor when she questions her accuser's use of the words 'treason' and 'disloyalty', nor at the time of the acceptance of the wagers of battle along with the repetition of the original charge. It is not until the final accusation has been pronounced and the combatants have left for the battlefield that the error becomes apparent. Gauvain points out to Arthur the weakness of the plaintiff's allegation: 'Or creroie ge bien que Mador fust en mauvese querele; car comment que ses freres moreust, je jurroie seur seinz au miens escient qu'onques la reïne n'i pensa desloiauté ne traïson; si l'en porroit tost max avenir, se li chevaliers avoit en lui point de proesce'. With Gauvain's sudden awareness of the inaccuracy of Mador's charge the Queen's originally indefensible position becomes justifiable once again. Lancelot's cause, through the unconscious mishandling of judicial formula, unexpectedly becomes the right cause, as Mador's carelessness with words during the proceedings neutralizes Arthur's clumsiness prior to trial.

The outcome of Guinevere's case points to a judicial system that succeeds despite itself. Its fragile triumph, coming as it does after a series of fortunate errors of judgement and procedure, can be attributed to Lancelot's willingness to risk perjuring himself and to Mador's misconception of the events surrounding Gaheris's death. At root, the weakest point in the entire process centres around the issue of criminal intent. Arthur's court, like most feudal courts, does not possess the investigatory apparatus—system of inquest, testimony, witnesses, written proof and documentary evidence—to determine the motivation behind wrong-doing, much less to apprehend the offender when his action is not apparent.

In many ways, Guinevere's offence constitutes what in modern jurisprudence is a case of accident or neglect, a special category of infraction under medieval law. For the jurist of the Middle Ages the perpetrator of a criminal act, however innocent his intentions, was nonetheless liable for his misdeed. Negligence as we know it did not enter the picture. Harm done a stranger with unguarded weapons was, under Anglo-Saxon law, attributable to the owner of the arms. Borrowing or stealing arms was a frequent means of obscuring evidence and thereby deflecting guilt. The medieval law of *deodand*, showing traces of the Roman noxal actions, specifies that where injury is inflicted the nearest object—animate or inanimate—bears the responsibility and should by rights be handed over to those obliged to avenge the crime. Damage done to humans by dogs or other animals is ascribable to the owner 'according to a scale of compensation increasing after the first bite' The *Coutume de Tourraine et Anjou* prescribes a fine of 100s. Id. payable by the master of an animal that causes the death of a man. And in England, if two men are at work in a forest and one lets a tree accidentally fall upon the other, the tree belongs to the victim's kin. When injury occurs under the jurisdiction or protection of the king's forest the blameworthy object is automatically transmitted to the royal agent of justice. Both instances acknowledge that where one brings about the death of another he is, like Guinevere, liable regardless of intent.

Pragmatic to an extreme degree, feudal law offers solutions to obvious situations and punishes misdeeds of a general kind without regard to the motivation or circumstances surrounding the crime. Harm inflicted upon one's fellow man constitutes criminal action, but where no harm is done no crime has been committed. The thoughts of a man were not to be tried, nor was attempted offence any offence at all. For medieval man the idea of guilt does not exist apart from actual infractions against specific individuals. He possesses no concept equivalent to the Roman *culpa* or the modern sense of negligence within the criminal sphere. On the contrary, feudal justice had no use for such abstract precepts, its immediate goal being the cessation of hostilities between private parties, its long range aim the prescription of indemnities to be paid the injured party or his family. Without injury there is no need for reparation; and when retribution is required, the amount of compensation is determined by the victim's social status and the fixed tables of payment, the *wergeld* or *relief d'homme*. At no stage does the need arise to consider the offender's motive or intent.

Although archaic Germanic law provided for only one degree of homicidal guilt, with little distinction between premeditated and accidental manslaughter, it did possess limited means of differentiating a few cases of aggravated slaying known as *morth* (Latin *murdrum*, Old French *murdre*). The term *morth* designated an unemendable crime involving concealment of the victim's body. Salic law, for example, specifies that if a dead man's corpse has been hidden in a well or in the branches of a tree, the deed falls into the category of *morth*, or *homicide odieux*. Otherwise, it constitutes plain manslaughter, *homicide simple*, for which the tariff of compensation is considerably lower. Allemand and Frisian law set the price of murder at nine times the figure set for an ordinary slaying.

The essential distinction between homicide and murder hinges, throughout the Middle Ages and up until the fourteenth century, upon the idea of open as opposed to hidden misdeed. Glanvill defines *murdum* as a 'killing seen by none'—'Dou autem genera homicidii. Unum est quod dicitur murdrem, quod nullo vidente'. The *Très Ancien Coutumier de Normandie*, written about ten years after Glanvill's death in 1190, classifies murder among the irreparable crimes occurring under the cover of darkness. The thirteenth-century *Livre de Fostice et de Plet* is even more precise: slayings carried out at night automatically constitute murder: 'homicide fet nuitantre fet murtre'. Thus for Germanic custom, Glanvill, the *Très Ancien Coutumier*, and the *Fostice et Plet* the notion of murder necessarily implies treachery, or killing in which the guilty party, through ruse or surprise, takes unfair advantage of his victim.

Treacherous homicide comprises, on the one hand, any slaying not enacted openly, that is not the result of direct conflict between the slain man and his slayer. Saint Louis incorporates both the concept of night-time deed and that of unfair advantage in the definition of murder found in the *Établissements*. For Louis, murder was synonymous with death in bed, or in any way that does not involve a fight: 'Murtres si est d'ome ou de fame quant l'en la tue en son lit, ou en aucune meniere por coi ce ne soit en mellée'. Murder implies trickery, the denial of a fair chance at self-defence. As such, it entails an automatic death sentence without the obvious benefit to the killer of trial. All that Louis required to admit the possibility of legal process was that the slayer show by the presence of scars inflicted prior to the victim's death proof that open conflict did, in fact, occur.

The notion of murder comprehends, on the other hand, the idea not only of treachery, but of surprise. A murdered man has been taken unawares either in his sleep or in a contest without formal challenge or equality in the means of confrontation. When Charlemagne accuses Ganelon of treason the defendant denies the charges on the grounds that his defiance of Roland was made publicly and not in secret:

> Jo desfiai Rollant le poigneor
> Et Oliver e tuiz lur compaignun
> Carles l'oïd e si nobilie baron.
> Venget m'en sui, mais n'i ad traïsun.
> (*Roland*)

Ganelon's distinction between treason, a punishable misdeed, and vengeance, a justifiable one— 'Venget m'en sui, mais n'i ad traïsun'—centres around the visible nature of his action. The challenge to the emperor's nephew took place in the open, that is to say within the hearing range of all concerned: 'Carles l'oïd e si nobilie baron'. Instead of denying the accusation Ganelon makes a virtue of the openness of the deed which, by feudal standards, did not constitute criminal offence. Feudal law recognizes only two sorts of homicide, vengeance and treason, overt and covert slaying. The fine distinctions that Bracton later draws between killing in self-defence, in execution of a death sentence or in apprehending a man who is himself a criminal, in short, the circumstances that give each act its particular character, are completely ignored. It matters little why one man kills another, but how he does it. Abidance by the rules of public challenge suffices to render homicide legal, and all killings conducted properly are essentially justifiable.

When Mador accuses Guinevere of having killed his brother 'treacherously' he is, in effect, accusing her of premeditated murder. She must have, according to his allegation, been aware of the poison hidden in the piece of fruit and intended to trap Gaheris with her gastronomic deceit. Yet the reader knows what Lancelot only suspects: that the Queen is completely innocent of any premeditation and that her part in the slaying is the product of accident. Not even a case of the old Germanic *homicide simple*, Guinevere's crime constitutes what today is considered involuntary manslaughter, an ambiguous mixture of guilt in deed and innocence of intent that defies the legal mechanism of Arthur's court. Structured around a well-defined and undeviating series of binary options, feudal procedure has no means of assimilating events like Gaheris's murder that cannot be reduced to a strict *either/or* proposition. In the first place, there exists no regularized method of prosecution, a fault shared by all purely accusatory systems. Guinevere's act either escapes any sort of public notice, as during the period prior to Mador's arrival in Camelot, or she finds herself charged with intentional wrongdoing; the Queen either eludes prosecution altogether, or is indicted for murder with evil intent. And whereas the author of *La Mort* possesses a language in which to recount such ambiguous happenings as accidental death, Arthur's court has no legal language in which to couch such equivocal phenomena. The formula of accusation together with the inflexible contradictory response disclose the insufficiency of a judicial process that has no way of affirming the reality of an event, its simple occurrence, without at the same time confirming conscious motivation, an act of will on the part of those involved. The failure of the justice of the Round Table reaches far beyond a mere lack of familiarity with problematic criminal action to a lack of discourse by which to assimilate partial, relative, non-exclusive truths and therefore to give adequate legal meaning to Guinevere's misdeed.

The breakdown of procedure during the Queen's trial would not offer such incontrovertible evidence of a more general crisis of legal institutions were it not for the novel's second judicial combat, that which pits Lancelot against Gauvain before the walls of Gaunes. Here, trial by battle has been agreed upon as a suitable means of resolving the blood-feud following the death of Gauvain's three brothers, in particular Gaheriet. Gauvain, like Mador, adopts the standard accusatory formula under which all homicide becomes premeditated homicide: 'Lancelot, fet messire Gauvains, messires le rois est ci venuz por fere ce que vos m'avez requis; vos savez bien que entre moi et vos avons emprise une bataille si grant comme de traïson por la mort de mes freres que vos oceïstes en traïson, desloiaument, ce savons nos bien tuit; si en sui apelerres et vos deffenderres'. Lancelot responds in the appropriate manner, with a direct denial of the charges: 'vos jurai sur seinz que onques du mien escient n'ocis Gaheriet vostre frere'. Once again the question put to legal test is not whether the accused did, in reality, perpetrate the act of which he stands accused, but whether his actions were intentional. Gauvain insists upon the premeditated quality of the deed—'vos oceïstes en traïson'—while Lancelot disavows any conscious intent—'du mien escient n'ocis vostre frere'.

The issue under judicial dispute occurs during the quarrel over Guinevere's execution after her capture in *flagrante delicto*. In the struggle to save her Lancelot's men kill Gauvain's brothers. Boort maintains that the original conflict took place openly, in an area where there were more than one hundred knights, and that the resulting deaths were therefore justified: 'onques en traïson n'occeïstes ses freres, mes en apert, en tel leu ou il avoit plus de cent chevaliers'. Lancelot's cousin thus establishes the traditional opposition between treacherous and overt wrongdoing. In looking back at the actual incident being judged, however, it seems clear that Lancelot did, in fact, literally ambush the party accompanying Guinevere to the stake. As the Queen's escort approaches the place of execution he waits, hidden in the woods, for a message from court: 'Tant alerent parlant entre Agravain et Gaheriet qu'il aprouchierent del feu. Et Lancelos, qui fu enbuschiez a l'entree de la forest a toute sa gent...'. When Lancelot hears that his mistress has been condemned to die he singles out Agravain, the man responsible for the entrapment of the lovers, as the prime target of attack: 'Or doint Dex que, si onques oi priere de pecheeur, que ge truisse premierement Agravain qui m'a cest plet basti'. Lancelot's lying in wait at the entrance to the forest—'embuchiez a l'entree de la forest'—bears the mark of the original sense of ambush (Latin *am-būsca*) implying a concealed attack 'from the woods'. His designation of Agravain as the object of assault reveals a degree of premeditation that cannot be denied. The crime of which Gauvain accuses Lancelot combines the Roman notion of aforethought with the germanic concept of surprise attack or *guet-apens*.

Thus Gauvain's accusation, unlike that of Mador, has a strong basis in fact. Lancelot did kill his brother with harmful intent and in a deceitful manner. The episode in question reveals none of the uncertainty that surrounds Guinevere's case; and yet the outcome is even more ambiguous. Lancelot wins the judicial duel, but he wins on the grounds of a technicality long after his opponent has been, for all intents and purposes, physically vanquished. Arthur, acting in his capacity as judge and upon an appeal from the defendant, puts an end to the fight: 'Lancelot, Gauvains ne lera pas la bataille, s'il ne li plest; mes vos la poez lessier, se vos voulez, car ja est eure passee; si avez bien fet ce que vos devez'. Through his reference to the hour that has come—'ja est eure passee'—Arthur invokes the medieval judicial custom according to which any defendant who manages to fend off his accuser until evening stands acquitted. The *Grand Coutumier de Normandie* defines the *terminus ad quem* of judicial battle with the appearance of stars in the sky. Lancelot sets the limit at the hour of vespers in a last-minute plea to end the struggle: 'et dedenz vespres qui apele home de traïson doit avoir sa querele desresniee et sa bataille veincue, ou il a perdue sa querele par droit' (p. 201.12). Lancelot scores, then, what amounts to a technical knockout in a present-day prizefight. His victory is neither complete, as against Mador, nor the product of his efforts alone; for with Arthur's intervention the application of human procedure, positive law, succeeds where divine justice has failed.

Having undertaken what was a dubious cause in Guinevere's defence and a patently poor cause in his own case, Lancelot emerges victorious from both encounters. The first can be justified in terms of a sudden reversal due to inappropriate judicial formula; the second, however, can only be explained as the triumph of superior physical force. Unlike the *Chanson de Roland*, where God intervenes at crucial moments to save the hero and thus reaffirm men's faith in his abiding presence, the two trials of *La Mort* only serve to undermine credence in the fundamental tenets of feudal justice: that the righteous, though not necessarily the most powerful, man emerges victorious and that human error and chance play no part in the functioning of the legal process. The *Deo judicio* no longer punishes wrongdoing, nor does it vindicate injury swiftly and clearly. It has failed in its chief capacity, which is the designation of intrinsic but unobvious guilt through an irreducible contradiction of parties. Trial by combat has ceased, even, to distribute justice fairly. Arvalan and Lancelot, the guilty parties in the two legal actions, elude prosecution; Mador and Gauvain fail to obtain redress.

The ineffectiveness of trial by battle can, in Mador's case, be ascribed to the formulary weakness of the system, and in Gauvain's to the substantive failing of the duel itself. A more inherent defect lies at the epistemological root of immanent justice. Stated simply, the outcome of the ordeal by battle exists independently of the notion of cognitive truth. The justice of Arthur's court depends upon the observance or non-observance of a series of fixed rules—formulas of accusation and denial, adjournment, representation, wagers and termination of combat—that matter much more than the collection and assessment of information concerning the criminal act. In fact, within a feudal accusatory system the only means of challenging the truthfulness of the proceedings is to prove that the rules have not been applied with sufficient rigour, that the judge has either refused to hear a case brought before him or that he has mishandled the precepts at his disposal. Both require an additional wager of battle, tendered this time against the judge by the party that questions his probity. Neither involves reference to the original deed whose truthfulness or falsity is never really tested. Arthur initiates no investigation at the time of Guinevere's crime, he calls no witnesses and holds no inquest during her trial; nor does anyone present at the original accusation raise the question of what, in point of fact, occurred at the time of Gaheris's death. The attempt to recreate faithfully the reality of past events remains a non-essential concept within the feudal legal system, whose only concern is the prevention of their recurrence. At best a means of regularizing and codifying single hand-to-hand conflicts, the *duel judiciaire* represents a symbolic re-enactment of the original deed brought before the court. It can in no way be confused with the endeavour to recapture the basic truth of the crime: the coherence of its etiology, strategy, and resolution.

Founded upon the weakest of fragmentary evidence, the truth of events stands, under the procedure at Arthur's disposal, only loosely bound to the process of rational human thought. Judicial truth, that involved in the trial itself, is witnessed by the presence of the barons at court, affirmed by the judge, who receives the accusations and pronounces sentence, and risked by the parties who expose themselves to divine wrath. The barons are, in this respect, the repository of collective truth, the customs of the community as expressed by the judge. The memory of the latter represents, in turn, a storehouse of appropriate rules intended to provoke a manifestation of higher truth. Logically, an accusal and wager of battle, once pronounced, can either be accepted or refused; if rejected, the accused stands guilty as charged; if accepted, the allegation may still be either true or false. Assuming that it were true, then the defendant would supposedly lose the judicial duel; and if false, then and only then would the judgement of the gods fall upon the accuser. As is evident, the act of accusal coupled with the agreed upon conditions of confrontation occupy the centre of the trial. It is only at the final stage of arbitration that a distinction is theoretically

drawn between innocence and guilt and that divine wrath punishes the offender. Until the conclusion of battle the opposition between falsehood and truth plays a relatively minor role in the proceedings.

In Guinevere's case the deed of which she is accused did take place, although her indictment is, strictly speaking, false because of the innocence of her intentions. The wager of battle is accepted by Lancelot who, as defendant, defeats Mador. In the second judicial test the infraction did again occur, but the accusal is essentially true this time, since Lancelot killed Gaheriet with evil intent according to the medieval formula of *traïson*. Once more the defendant, Lancelot again wins the *duel judiciaire*. Thus both trials of *La Mort* begin from the same initial premise: the occurrence of the act submitted to the court. Yet in both cases the link between the truth of the misdeed and the outcome of the *Deo judicio* is at some point severed. Mador disturbs the progression at the outset through the inaccuracy of his accusal; from that moment on it is no longer a question of the veracity of the events surrounding the Queen's wrongdoing. With Gauvain's suit the alliance of justice and truth is not disrupted until the battle itself when the plaintiff loses despite the truth of his allegations. Here, the victory of a defendant faced with a true accusation can only be taken as a failure of divine judgement and hence of the entire set of assumptions underlying immanent justice. The combatants' fatigue at the end of this second struggle reflects an exhausted method of ascertaining judicial truth.

For the knight-warrior caste of the feudal era the judicial duel was a privilege of class, a symbolic means of terminating personal quarrels like that of Lancelot and Gauvain in the absence of any more effective civil mechanism. As such, the right to participate in the *duel judiciaire* was considered a seigneurial prerogative inseparable from the general maintenance of arms incumbent upon the holding of land in fief. With the reconstitution of the national monarchy of the twelfth and thirteenth centuries, however, the archaic feudal mode of proof came under heavy attack from several quarters: the Church, the northern municipalities, and especially the late Capetian and Angevin kings of France. Suppression of the *Deo judicio* along with the appearance of a coherent system of judicial appeal stood at the heart of the royal programme of administrative centralization aimed at creating direct legal ties between king and subject; in this way, the crown hoped to undermine the local seigneurial jurisdiction of a former age. It was with this objective in mind that Saint Louis in the late 1250s prohibited the ordeal of battle within the royal domain. In its place he substituted the old Frankish practice preserved throughout the Middle Ages in canonical courts, the *enquête*: 'Nous deffendons les batailles partout nostre domoine en toutes quereles, mais nous n'ostons mie les clains, les respons, les contremanz, ne touz autres erremanz qui ont esté accostumé en cort laie jusques à ores, selonc les usages de divers païs, fors tant que nos en ostons les batailles; et en leu de batailles nos metons *prueves de tesmoinz et de chartes*'. The proof by witnesses and written documents—'preuves de tesmoinz et de chartes'—that Louis prescribes as an alternative to trial by combat implies a radically different concept of the goals and methods of criminal procedure. Justice will henceforth focus not upon the payment of reparation to the injured party, but the establishment of legal truth. Intended to recreate the reality of past events as they actually happened, the inquest suddenly introduces the notion of rational truth, human rather than divine, into the centre of the judicial process. The pivotal position formerly occupied by customary rules of accusation and denial followed by divine intervention is now filled by the judge's obligation to render cognitive legal decisions independent of any system of higher causality. Under an inquisitional system man and not God determines innocence and guilt according to comprehensible logical criteria.

The primary basis for judgement by inquest is the collection of information regarding the act or issue in question through the sworn statements of witnesses. Normandy possessed an inquisitory procedure in use before the Conquest and certainly before the re-annexation of the Duchy in the early thirteenth century. As a matter of course a defendant had the right to refuse a wager of battle, insisting instead upon an examination of the merits of his case by loyal and credible men of the vicinage under oath to appraise the facts as objectively as possible. The presiding judge then transmitted their decision to the duke. Where a question of custom or possession arose the wise men of the community gathered to determine the precedent practice or title. In criminal cases a man arrested on suspicion of serious offence might be asked to submit to an inquiry into the deed of which he is accused. An *enquête du pays* would be ordered. Twenty-four neighbours likely to know about the infraction were summoned individually before four knights and a bailiff who questioned them and committed their testimony to

writing. The resulting account of criminal action sworn to by many witnesses constituted an act of public notoriety equivalent to capture of the accused party in *flagrante delicto*.

The canonical inquest or *Inquisitio generalis* represented a standard principle of procedure long prior to its re-introduction within the public sphere. Throughout the Middle Ages the bishop or other high church official could force members of the clergy or laymen to disclose known ill-doers from among the populace; an indictment elicited in this manner automatically led to trial. The *visitatio* of the bishop for the purpose of hearing complaints from the community at large was reinforced by the presence of a permanent judicial officer, the *promotor* or prosecutor, charged, in addition to the general populace, with the denunciation of notorious offenders. The ideal method of *processus per inquisitionem* as outlined by the Fourth Lateran Council (1215) first required the establishment of the *infamia* or infraction either by the *promotor* acting on his own or the judge acting upon the plea of a third party. Witnesses were then called and testimony recorded by a notary. At that point the defendant was summoned, informed of the charge against him and permitted to produce his own witnesses whose testimony was to be weighed against that of the opposing side. After hearing both depositions the judge decided between the two adversaries.

The differences between the feudal accusatory system of Arthur's court and the inquisitory system utilized by the Church and eventually adopted by the civil authorities are enormous. In the first place, the inquisitory judge or his affiliate has the power to proceed against offenders like Guinevere and Lancelot without the formal complaint of a Mador or Gauvain. The accused is, moreover, obliged to submit to the court's jurisdiction with no possibility of refusing the wager of battle tendered against him. The trial itself no longer implies a direct confrontation between opposing parties, but a mediated encounter through a third party who hears the testimony of both sides independently and thus arrives at a satisfactory solution. Finally, the inquest represents a secret judicial process conducted behind the closed doors of the judge's or *promotor*'s chambers. The oral public character of the feudal court, its authority conferred by the presence of the barons, gives way to a privately conducted investigation whose main objective is the constitution of a written dossier. In Paris an inquest directed by the highest court of the land, the *Parlement*, began with a written demand to the *Chambre des Enquêtes* which issued a letter of justice authorizing legal action; the court then summoned the adverse party whose deposition under oath (*serment de calomnie*) was recorded by the *greffier* . If the defendant could prove his innocence through existing documents, he was acquitted. If not, the court appointed trained commissioners to collect the information needed for the inquest and, where necessary, to travel to the place of infraction. This board of inquiry recorded the sworn testimony of witnesses, as in the *enquête du pays*, sealing their declarations along with any other relevant evidence in a sack to be returned to Paris. A dossier compiled in this fashion was expedited to the *Grand Chambre* of the *Parlement* where its contents were examined and an *arrêt* or decision finally pronounced.

The end product of the inquisitory system—the dossier—denotes an attempt to uncover the truth of a crime, to capture, in essence, the guilty party in the act of offence by assembling the facts surrounding the alleged wrongdoing. More importantly, the designation of guilt where infraction is not apparent is no longer a matter for God alone to judge according to an infallible logic invisible to humans and *a posteriori* to the deed in question, but a matter to be determined by the scrupulous ordering of past events into a coherent scenario of action. Justice, under this second mode of procedure, does not exist independently of the notion of truth, which constitutes its chief *raison d'être*. The *enquête* seeks to transcribe the memory of the crime into concrete intelligible form.

The author of *La Mort* offers no remedy for the failure of feudal judicial institutions—entrapment in *flagrante delicto*, vendetta, private war, and trial by combat—to resolve the disputes arising naturally between the members of any given social group. On the contrary, they complicate and extend them. Mador's and Gauvain's accusations engender a crisis of belief in the efficacy of the *Deo judicio*. The capture of Lancelot and Guinevere in the act of adultery provokes the gratuitous slaughter of Gauvain's three brothers. Their deaths initiate the endless cycle of vendetta and war that sets one half of the kingdom against the other and that leads, in the end, to the usurpation of kingship by Arthur's bastard son. At no point do the archaic legal mechanisms of immanent justice prevent the violence of private grievance from menacing and destroying the integrity of the realm. *La Mort Artu* represents, from this perspective, a declaration of bankruptcy of the most cherished values and institutions of the feudal world two centuries after the beginning of the end of feudalism in France. Private war and its symbolic termination in trial by combat suffice within a society of small independent political units; they fail to provide adequate responses to the problems of a larger political body, the national monarchy of Saint Louis and his successors.

A novel without explicit resolution of the dilemma that it portrays, *La Mort* does contain, in the opening paragraph of the text, an implicit antidote to the drama of social decline:

> 1. 'Aprés ce que mestres Gautiers Map ot mis en escrit des *Aventures del Seint Graal* assez soufisanment si com li sembloit, si fu avis au roi Henri son seigneur que ce qu'il avoit fet ne devoit pas soufire, s'il ne ramentevoit la fin de ceus dont il avoit fet devant mention et conment cil morurent...; et por ce commença il ceste derrienne partie. Et quant il l'ot ensemble mise, si l'apela *La Mort le Roi Artu*.'

> 2. 'Quant Boorz fu venuz a cort en la cité meïsmes de Kamaalot de si lointeignes terres comme sont les parties de Jerusalem, assez trouva a court qui grant joie li fist;... Et quant il ot aconté le trespassement de Galaad et la mort Perceval, si en furent tuit moult dolent a court;... Lors fist li rois metre en escrit toutes les aventures que li compaignon de la queste del Seint Graal avoient racontees en sa court.

In Henry II's invitation to Walter Map to record the tragic 'end of those he has already mentioned' and in Arthur's command to put into writing the 'adventures recounted by the companions of the Holy Grail Quest', we detect the basic formula of inquest: the commission by the ruler in a position of legal authority to transcribe the reality of the past. Evoking the image of Henry II, the man responsible in large part for the transformation of English jurisprudence from a feudal to a national system, and Walter Map, himself a jurist and man of letters, the text itself can be regarded as the transcription of a legendary oral past into concrete written form. The author's effort to register the truth of the tale (*li contes*) that constantly escapes him—'Mes atant lesse ore li contes ... En ceste parti dit li contes'—coincides with Arthur's own search for the truth of the Queen's adultery. Both recognize the possibility of a logical ordering of objects and events, the existence of rational human truth separable from the immanence of divine truth, upon which the legal and literary discourse of the modern world depends.

Source: R. Howard Bloch, "From Grail Quest to Inquest: The Death of King Arthur and the Birth of France," in *Modern Language Review*, Vol. 69, Issue 1, January, 1974, pp. 40–55.

SOURCES

Ascham, Roger, *The Scolemaster*, rev. ed., Thoemmes Press, 1996.

Caxton, William, "Caxton's Preface," in *The Works of Thomas Malory, Vol. I*, edited by Eugene Vinaver, Clarendon Press, 1947.

Kennedy, Edward Donald, "Malory's Guinevere: 'A Woman Who Had Grown a Soul,'" in *Arthuriana*, Vol. 9, No. 2, Spring, 1999, pp. 37–45.

Lewis, C. S., "The English Prose 'Morte,'" in *Essays on Malory*, edited by Walter Oakeshott, et. al., Clarendon press, 1963, pp. 7–28.

Saul, MaryLynn, "Courtly Love and the Patriarchal Marriage Practice in Malory's *Le Morte d'Arthur*," in *Fifteenth Century Studies*, Vol. 24, 1998, pp. 50–62.

FURTHER READING

Archibald, Elizabeth and A.S.G. Edwards, editors, *A Companion to Malory*, D. S. Brewer, 1996.
    This book is a compilation of essays that focus on several of the themes and ideas present in Malory's text.

Benson, L.D., *Le Morte d'Arthur*, in *Critical Approaches to Six Major Works: Beowulf through Paradise Lost*, edited by R. M. Lumiansky and Hershel Baker, 1968, pp. 112–120.
    This article is a discussion on the thematic unity of Malory's text, which uses as its example the story of Gareth.

Caxton, William, "Caxton's Preface," in *The Works of Thomas Malory, Vol. I*, edited by Eugene Vinaver, Clarendon Press, 1947.
    This text is from the original preface that appeared in the 1485 publication of Malory's epic.

Cole, Harry, "'Forgiveness as Structure:" The Book of Launcelot and Queen Guinevere,'" in *Chaucer Review*, Vol. 31, No.1, 1996, pp. 36–44.
    This article examines the purpose and function of the section of Malory's epic that focuses on the story of Launcelot and Guinevere.

Fenster, Thelma S., editor, *Arthurian Women: A Casebook*, Garland, 1996.
    This book is a compilation of essays that focus on the women in Malory's text.

Field, P. J. C., *The Life and Times of Sir Thomas Malory*, D. S. Brewer, 1993.
    Field's book is an attempt to understand Malory and to establish the real identity of the author of this epic.

Gaines, Barry, *Sir Thomas Malory: An Anecdotal Bibliography of Editions, 1485–1985*, AMS Press, 1990.
    Gaines' book is a discussion of many of the different editions of Malory's text that have appeared over the years. Gaines' book also includes books based on the Arthurian legends, as well as children's editions.

Kennedy, Edward Donald, "Malory's Guinevere: 'A Woman Who Had Grown a Soul,'" in *Arthuriana*, Vol. 9, No. 2, Spring, 1999, pp. 37–45.
    This article argues that Guinevere, who also led to Launcelot's failure in seeking the Grail, was ultimately the reason his soul was saved.

Lewis, C. S., "The English Prose 'Morte,'" in *Essays on Malory*, edited by Walter Oakeshott, et. al., Clarendon press, 1963, pp. 7–28.
    This essay examines several of what Lewis claims are key paradoxes in Malory's text.

Lynch, Andrew, *Malory's Book of Arms*, D. S. Brewer, 1997.
    Lynch's book provides a narration and discussion of the combat sequences in Malory's text.

Malory, Sir Thomas, *Le Morte d'Arthur*, Bramwell House, 1962.
    This edition of Malory's text has been translated into modern English, with the intent that the text be more accessible to the casual reader than previous editions.

Putter, Ad, "Finding Time for Romance: Medieval Arthurian Literary History," in *Medium Aevum*, Vol. 63, No.1, Spring, 1994, pp. 1–16.
    Putter's article is a discussion of the historical basis of the Arthurian legend, using Geoffrey of Monmouth's *History of the Kings of Britain*.

Saul, MaryLynn, "Courtly Love and the Patriarchal Marriage Practice in Malory's *Le Morte d'Arthur*," *Fifteenth Century Studies*, Vol. 24, 1998, pp. 50–62.
    This article explores the historical basis of medieval marriage as depicted in Malory's text.

Les Misérables

VICTOR HUGO

1862

When Victor Hugo's novel *Les Misérables* first came out in 1862, people in Paris and elsewhere lined up to buy it. Although critics were less receptive, the novel was an instant popular success. The French word "misérables" means both poor wretches and scoundrels or villains. The novel offers a huge cast that includes both kinds of "misérables." A product of France's most prominent Romantic writer, *Les Misérables* ranges far and wide. It paints a vivid picture of Paris's seamier side, discusses the causes and results of revolution, and includes discourses on topics ranging from the Battle of Waterloo to Parisian street slang. But the two central themes that dominate the novel are the moral redemption of its main character, Jean Valjean, an ex-convict, and the moral redemption of a nation through revolution. Victor Hugo said: "I condemn slavery, I banish poverty, I teach ignorance, I treat disease, I lighten the night, and I hate hatred. That is what I am, and that is why I have written *Les Misérables*." The novel is a critical statement against human suffering, poverty, and ignorance. Its purpose is as much political as it is artistic.

AUTHOR BIOGRAPHY

As a novelist, poet, political activist, and painter, Victor Hugo was a central figure in the Romantic movement of nineteenth-century France. Both his

family and his times influenced Hugo's social views and politics, which included a deep concern with human rights, social injustice, and poverty as the root of evil. Born in Besançon, France, in 1802, Hugo grew up in the years of Napoleon Bonaparte's empire. In 1815, the empire collapsed at the battle of Waterloo, which Hugo describes in detail in *Les Misérables,* and a constitutional monarchy was established. His father was a general in the Napoleonic army with republican sympathies while his middle-class mother had royalist leanings. The young Hugo spent a large part of his childhood in Paris with his mother. He also traveled through Europe in his father's wake and glimpsed the Napoleonic campaigns. After attending school in Paris, he married his childhood love, Adèle Foucher, in 1822.

In that same year, Hugo published his first volume of poetry, the beginning of a long and diverse literary career that also included drama and novels. He was acquainted with many major figures on the intellectual and artistic scene. His political convictions changed over time as various French governments rose and fell, however his belief in human rights was consistent. In a letter to a friend describing why he wrote *Les Misérables,* Hugo said: "If the radical is the ideal, yes, I am a radical. . . . A society which admits poverty, a religion which admits hell, a humanity which sanctions war, seems to me an inferior society, an inferior religion and humanity, and it is towards the higher society, the higher humanity and religion that I turn: society without a king, humanity without frontiers, religion without a book. . . . I condemn slavery, I banish poverty, I teach ignorance, I treat disease, I lighten the night, and I hate hatred. That is what I am, and that is why I have written *Les Misérables.*''

The 1840s to the 1860s were an active time for the writer. He was elected to the Académie Française in 1841 and to the peerage in 1845 in recognition of his literary achievements. The late 1840s marked a period of serious political involvement for Hugo. He spoke up in the Chamber of Peers, criticizing the legal system and the treatment of the poor, themes to which he returned in *Les Misérables.* Disillusioned with monarchism, he publicly espoused republicanism and participated in the revolution of 1848. These experiences gave him firsthand knowledge of what barricade fighting was like, which he used in the novel. Louis Napoleon, the elected president of the newly established republic, seized power in a coup d'état in 1851. Hugo criticized the new ruler and ended up in exile, first in Belgium,

then later on the Isle of Guernsey in the English Channel, where he remained until 1870. Here he wrote most of *Les Misérables.*

Les Misérables was first published in 1862, appearing simultaneously in cities across Europe. In spite of a mixed critical reaction, the novel, with its championing of the poor and disenfranchised, was an immediate popular success in France and abroad. It sealed Hugo's reputation as a legend.

Upon his return to France in 1870, he received a hero's welcome. He continued to write for the rest of his life, but abstained from politics. After his death in 1885, Victor Hugo lay in state under the Arc de Triomphe and was buried in the Pantheon, in the heart of his beloved city, Paris.

PLOT SUMMARY

Les Misérables is the story of four people, Bishop Myriel, Valjean, Fantine, and Marius who meet, part, then meet again during the most agitated decades of nineteenth century France. It also tells the story of the 1832 revolution and describes the unpleasant side of Paris. The novel is in essence a plea for humane treatment of the poor and for equality among all citizens.

Part I—Fantine

The year is 1815 and Napoleon has just been defeated at Waterloo. Bishop Myriel lives a quiet life as a just man, who is especially sympathetic toward the poor, bandits, and convicts. One day a strange man asks for shelter at his home and, with his usual compassion, the bishop gives him room and board. This man is Jean Valjean, who has just been released from prison after serving a lengthy, unjust sentence, during which he tried to escape numerous times. Valjean is angry, hurt, and re-vengeful. His soul has "withered" and all but died. The bishop urges him to replace anger with good-will in order to be worthy of respect: "You have left a place of suffering. But listen, there will be more joy in heaven over the tears of a repentant sinner, than over the white robes of a hundred good men. If you are leaving that sorrowful place with hate and anger against men, you are worthy of compassion; if you leave it with goodwill, gentleness, and peace, you are better than any of us."

Valjean listens. Nevertheless, he decides to rob the good bishop. During the night, he runs away with the bishop's silver. He is caught and brought back to the bishop who tells the police that he himself gave Valjean these precious objects. Later Bishop Myriel tells Valjean, ''you belong no longer to evil, but to good. It is your soul I am buying for you. I withdraw it from dark thoughts and from the spirit of perdition and I give it to God!'' Valjean is stunned. After he steals a coin from a little boy, he has an epiphany: ''he could see his life, and it seemed horrible; his soul, and it seemed frightful. There was, however, a gentler light shining on that life and soul.''

Fantine is a seamstress unjustly fired once her employer learns about her scandalous past. Abandoned by her lover, she is hungry, destitute, and unable to care for her daughter, Cosette. First she sells her hair, then her teeth before finally prostituting herself. At this stage of the story, Fantine has "endured all, borne all, experienced all, suffered all, lost all, wept for all. She is resigned, with that resignation that resembles indifference as death resembles sleep." She leaves Cosette when her daughter is two years old to the care of the Thénardiers, who run a tavern in the outskirts of Paris. Cosette is poorly treated by the couple and their two daughters. The Thénardiers view Cosette as if she is their domestic slave all the while demanding more and more money for Cosette's care. Fantine must continue selling her body to pay for Cosette's keep.

Valjean assumes a new identity, Mr. Madeleine, becomes a good citizen, a rich industrialist, and ultimately mayor. Valjean saves Fantine from the police headed by Javert once he discovers she was fired from the very factory under his care. He wants to redeem her, but it is too late. Fantine is sick and dies very soon.

At the same time, Champmathieu is falsely accused of being Valjean by the police officer Javert, whose lifelong goal is to find the escaped convict Valjean. Javert was a "formidable man" whose mother was a fortune-teller and whose father was in the galleys. "His stare was cold and as piercing as a gimlet. His whole life was contained in these two words: waking and watching." After a long night of hesitation—to accuse Champmathieu would save him from Javert, to keep silent would send an innocent man to death—Valjean decides to confess his true identity to save the wrongly accused man:

> He declared that his life, in truth, did have an object. But what object? to conceal his name? to deceive the

Victor Hugo

police? was it for so petty a thing that he had done all that he had done? had he no other object, which was the great one, which was the true one? To save, not his body, but his soul. To become honest and good again. To be an upright man! was it not that, above all, that alone, which he had always wished, and which the bishop had enjoined upon him!. . . To deliver himself up, to save this man stricken by so ghastly a mistake, to reassume his name, to become again from duty the convict Jean Valjean; that was really to achieve his resurrection, and to close for ever the hell from whence he had emerged! to fall into it in appearance, was to emerge in reality! he must do that! all he had done was nothing, if he did not do that! all his life was useless, all his suffering was lost. He had only to ask the question: "What is the use?"

When the unyielding Javert arrests him, Valjean escapes, beginning a long hunt.

Part II—Cosette

He does not go too far. Fantine has told him about Cosette. He goes to the Thénardiers' and saves the little girl from her terrible life. They settle in Paris, where they constantly have to hide from Javert's eye. They finally find shelter in a convent, the Petit-Picpus, where they spend five happy years of redemption: "Everything around him, this quiet garden, these balmy flowers, these children, shouting with joy, these meek and simple women, this silent cloister, gradually entered into all his being, and his soul subsided into silence.... His whole heart melted in gratitude and he loved more and more."

Part III—Marius

Marius is a young student, and like many other young men of his generation, he is passionately interested with Napoleon: "Napoleon had become to him the people-man as Jesus was the God-man." In Paris he meets a group of young radical students, the Friends of the ABC, who are very much like him and who convert him to republicanism: "my mother is the republic." One day, he spots in a park a young girl, walking with her father. "She was a marvelous beauty. The only remark which could be made . . . is that the contradiction between her look, which was sad, and her smile, which was joyous, gave to her countenance something a little wild." He sees her again the next day, and the following until, six months later, he falls in love with her. It is the fifteen-year-old Cosette.

Part IV—Saint Denis

Cosette has noticed Marius and falls in love with him, but she does not want Valjean to know about it. One day Marius writes to her and they secretly meet: "these two hearts poured themselves into each other, so that at the end of an hour, it was the young man who had the young girl's soul and the young girl who had the soul of the young man." Valjean suspects nothing until he accidentally intercepts one of Marius' letters.

Part V—Jean Valjean

Marius is an active participant. Workers and republican students are on the barricades, opposing the police and the army of the monarchy. Many of the revolutionaries are killed in the struggle. Valjean discovers Marius and Cosette's love, but still saves Marius's life on the barricades. He carries the wounded and unconscious young man through the Paris sewers. He has one last confrontation with Javert, his old nemesis, who is at his mercy. He decides to let him go. Moved by this gesture and appalled at himself, Javert kills himself: "Terrible situation! to be moved! To be granite, and to doubt! to be ice and to melt! to feel your fingers suddenly open! to lose your hold, appalling thing!... The projectile man no longer knowing his road, and recoiling!" Still, many died, including Gavroche, a little Parisian boy whose courage inspired the fighters of the barricades.

Cosette restores Marius to health, and they decide to get married. On the wedding day, Marius meets Valjean who tells him who he really is, a convict still hunted by the police and that Cosette does not know anything about his unsavory past. However, Valjean does not tell Marius that he saved his life during the insurrections. Marius wants to help him win his pardon, he refuses: "I need pardon of none but one, that is my conscience." Marius decides to stay silent, but he is horrified by the revelations. Valjean stops visiting the young couple. Soon, Marius learns that he was saved by him and, accompanied by Cosette, rushes to Valjean's home. It is too late, Valjean is dying. "There is scarcely anything else in the world but that: to love one another." He was buried under a blank stone.

CHARACTERS

Bahorel

A member of the ABC Society, a revolutionary group, Bahorel is also a student. But he has no respect for authority and is a real troublemaker, liking nothing better than a good fight.

Mademoiselle Baptistine

The unmarried sister of the Bishop of Digne, she lives with him and runs his household. She is a gentle, respectable woman who does good works.

Bishop of Digne

See Charles Myriel

Bossuet

A member of the ABC Society, a revolutionary group, Bossuet is a law student. He is cheerful but unlucky; everything he undertakes seems to go wrong.

Combeferre

Combeferre is a member of the ABC society, a student, and a philosopher of revolution. He has a scientific mind and dreams of the inventions of the future and how they will benefit the human race.

Cosette

Cosette is the illegitimate daughter of Fantine, a Parisian ''grisette'' (working woman) whose lover, Félix Tholomyès, abandons her when she is pregnant. Valjean rescues Cosette from the Thénardiers, and she becomes the love of his life and the motiva-

MEDIA ADAPTATIONS

- Recorded in 1988, *Les Misérables* is available from Dove Books on Tape in an abridged version read by Christopher Cazenove.

- *Les Misérables* was adapted for the stage as a musical by Alain Boubliĺ and Claude-Michel Schonberg, with the lyrics composed by Herbert Kretzmer. In 1995, the tenth anniversary concert in Royal Albert Hall, London, was released as a movie by Columbia Tristar Home Video. The musical is also available as a sound recording from Geffen in 1987. This version features the original Broadway cast.

- *Les Misérables* was made into a film in 1935, starring Fredric March, Charles Laughton, Cedric Hardwicke, Rochelle Hudson, and John Beal. Directed by Richard Boleslawski, this adaptation is detailed and faithful to the novel, except for a changed ending. Considered a classic, the film received Academy Award nominations for Best Cinematography and Best Picture.

- There are many French film adaptations of the novel. A version released in 1957 stars Jean Gabin, Daniele Delorme, Bernard Blier, Bourvil, Gianni Esposito, and Serge Reggiani. Directed by Jean-Paul LeChanois, the film is in French with English subtitles.

- A version directed by Glenn Jordan was made for television in 1978, starring Richard Jordan, Anthony Perkins, John Gielgud, Cyril Cusack, Flora Robson, Celia Johnson, and Claude Dauphin.

- An animated version of *Les Misérables* appeared in 1979, produced by Toei Animation Company.

- A 1994 film version of the novel transposed its setting to early twentieth-century France. Directed, produced, and adapted by Claude Lelouch, the movie, starring Jean-Paul Belmondo, Michel Boujenah, Alessandrea Martines, and Annie Girador, received a Golden Globe award for Best Foreign Film.

---

tion for his goodness. She is raised and educated in a convent. When she and Valjean move out into the real Paris, she turns into a beautiful young Parisian woman and falls in love with Marius Pontmercy.

Courfeyrac

A member of the ABC Society, a revolutionary group of students and workers, Courfeyrac becomes Marius' friend and takes him in.

Enjolras

Enjolras is a leader of the ABC Society, a secret revolutionary society composed of students and workers. Marius first meets him there and ends up fighting with him on the barricade. The only son of rich parents, Enjolras is a student of the Revolution and has "a nature at once scholarly and warlike." He is indifferent to women and pleasure, but pas-

sionate about justice. Enjolras defines what he is fighting for in a speech on the barricade: "'Citizens, no matter what happens today, in defeat no less than in victory, we shall be making a revolution. [. . . Equality] means, in civic terms, an equal outlet for all talents; in political terms, that all votes will carry the same weight; and in religious terms that all beliefs will enjoy equal rights. Equality has a means at its disposal-compulsory free education. The right to learn the alphabet, that is where we must start.'"

Fantine

Fantine is a Parisian "grisette," or working woman, who falls in love with a student, Félix Tholomyès. Just after Félix breaks off their relationship, she gives birth to a daughter, Cosette. From that point forward her life is a downward spiral. She gives up her child to the mercenary Thénardiers and finds a job in her home town, but is dismissed when her supervisor finds out about her past. She struggles to make ends meet, selling everything she has: her hair, her teeth, and herself (becoming a prostitute). Fantine represents society's cruelty to the poor and its degradation of poor women in particular. Only Valjean shows her any kindness.

Père Fauchelevent

When Fauchelevent, an elderly carrier, gets caught beneath the wheels of his own cart, Valjean rescues him and afterward finds work for him as a gardener in a Paris convent. In doing so, Valjean risks giving away his identity to Javert, who is already suspicious, by showing his great strength. But Fauchelevent pays Valjean back by taking him and Cosette in when he is on the run from the police. Fauchelevent, an educated peasant, is both shrewd and good-willed. He recognizes his debt and finds the means to repay it.

Feuilly

A member of the ABC Society of revolutionaries, Feuilly earns his living as a fan-maker and is self-educated.

Mademoiselle Gillenormand

Monsieur Gillenormand's eldest daughter is a prudish, narrow-minded old woman who runs her father's household.

Monsieur Gillenormand

Monsieur Gillenormand, Marius' grandfather and caretaker, is a relic of the past. He had his heyday in the decadent Ancien Régime, the pre-Revolutionary monarchy, in which the nobility dominated France. He still looks back to those days with nostalgia and regret. Gillenormand believes that in modern times people lack the gift of living life to the fullest and enjoying all its pleasures. He raises Marius to believe that the Revolution ''was a load of scoundrels.'' When Marius discovers that his father was a Revolutionary hero, it causes a bitter break between them.

Théodule Gillenormand

Théodule is Gillenormand's great-nephew and a lieutenant in the army. He is a vain young man and a favorite of his Aunt Gillenormand. He tries to become Gillenormand's favorite when Marius is out of the picture, but he can't replace Marius in the old man's affections.

Grantaire

Although Grantaire belongs to the ABC Society, a revolutionary group of students and workers, he is a cynic and a hedonist and does not believe in the ideals of revolution. But he does believe in one thing: Enjolras, whom he regards with love and admiration.

Javert

Inspector Javert is nearly as renowned a character as Jean Valjean, perhaps due to the dramatized versions of *Les Misérables*, which have tended to cast it as more of a detective story than a morality tale. Javert serves as Valjean's nemesis throughout the novel, continually threatening to expose his past and bring him under the control of the law. In this exaggerated, nearly fanatical devotion to duty and his lack of compassion, Javert represents a punitive, vengeful form of justice.

Hugo suggests that Javert's "respect for authority and hatred of revolt" are rooted in his past, for he was born in a prison. As if to compensate for this fact, he has spent his life in faithful service to law enforcement. When Valjean saves Javert by helping him escape from the revolutionaries, Javert's rigid system of behavior is upset, for he realizes that Valjean, a criminal who has not yet been officially punished, has performed an act of great kindness and courage. Javert previously would have overlooked such an act and arrested the criminal, but his recognition proves more than he can bear. Unable to resolve his inner conflict, Javert drowns himself in the Seine.

Joly

A member of the ABC Society, Joly is studying medicine. He is something of a hypochondriac.

Monsieur Mabeuf

An elderly churchwarden, he befriends Marius' father Pontmercy, and Marius becomes friends with Mabeuf after his father dies. He is a gentle man whose main interests in life are his garden and his books, but he becomes very poor and has to sell all of his books. Impoverished and without hope in life, Mabeuf joins the rebels, courageously climbs to the top of the barricade to plant a flag, and is shot by the militia. His age and gentleness make his courage even more remarkable, showing that revolution can come in any form.

Madame Magloire

Madame Magloire is the personal maid of Mademoiselle Baptistine and the Bishop of Digne's housekeeper.

Charles Myriel

Myriel is a kind and generous bishop who gives Jean Valjean aid when everyone else refuses him. Searching for a place to spend the night, the ex-convict finds that he is a branded man and no inn will let him stay. His last resort is the home of the bishop, who takes him in and treats him as an honored guest. After Valjean steals the silverware and caught by the police, the bishop protects him by insisting that the silver was actually a gift. Afterward, he says to Valjean, ''[You] no longer belong to what is evil but to what is good. I have bought your soul to save it from black thoughts and the spirit of perdition, and I give it to God.'' The bishop's selfless act inspires Valjean to change his life.

Colonel Pontmercy

A hero of the Napoleonic wars, he marries Gillenormand's youngest daughter and has a son, Marius. The villainous innkeeper, Thénardier, drags Pontmercy to safety from the battlefield of Waterloo. Although Marius does not meet his father, Pontmercy watches him from afar in church and loves his son. He leaves Marius a note telling him to adopt the title of Baron (Napoleon gave it to Pontmercy on the field of battle); and to do Thénardier every good in his power. Marius worships his father as a hero and is strongly influenced by his political beliefs.

Marius Pontmercy

Marius is a young law student who falls in love with Cosette. He also saves Valjean from a plot against his life by the innkeeper-turned-criminal, Thénardier. In turn, Marius is saved by Valjean while fighting on the barricade. He is the son of Georges Pontmercy, a colonel and war hero under Napoleon. But Marius' grandfather, Monsieur Gillenormand, despises Georges and takes Marius into his own home to raise him.

Marius is at a stage of life where he doesn't know yet what he believes. His image of the world keeps opening up as he encounters new points of view. When Marius discovers his father's identity, he worships him as a war hero and adopts a pro-Napoleon stance opposed to his grandfather's royalism. He gets into a quarrel with Gillenormand and storms out of the house to make his way through Paris as a starving student. Marius falls in with a group of students, led by Enjolras, who share his republican beliefs. At first he is reluctant to give up his belief that conquest and war are the greatest ideals of a nation. But he begins to have doubts when the students present him with a new ideal, freedom: ''Having so lately found a faith, must he renounce it? He told himself that he need not; he resolved not to doubt, and began despite himself to do so.'' When unrest stirs Paris in 1832 and his friends take up arms, he joins them on the barricades. But it is more out of desperation, because he fears he has lost Cosette, than out of political conviction. He is lured there by the voice of the street girl Eponine telling him that his friends await him.

Jean Prouvaire

Prouvaire is a member of the ABC Society of students and workers. A wealthy student, he is interested in social questions, but is also a poet and lover with a romantic side.

Eponine Thénardier

The poor daughter of the Thénardiers, Eponine falls in love with Marius and becomes jealous of his love for Cosette. She is torn between wanting to help him and wanting to keep him away from Cosette. She courageously saves his life on the barricade by stepping between him and a bullet and dies in his arms. Her life is an example of poverty's degradation: ''What it came to was that in the heart of our society, as at present constituted, two unhappy mortals [Eponine and her sister] had been turned by extreme poverty into monsters at once depraved and innocent, drab creatures without name or age or sex, no longer capable of good or evil, deprived of all freedom, virtue, and responsibility; sould born yesterday and shrivelled today like flowers dropped in the street which lie fading in the mud until a cartwheel comes to crush them.''

Gavroche Thénardier

Gavroche is a Parisian urchin (street child), the son of the villainous Thénardiers. Lively and clever, he lives by his wits. He dies by them as well and proves his courage, getting shot by soldiers when he is teasing them on the barricade. His fate is interwoven with that of Marius, Cosette, and the Thénardiers. The novel presents him as an essential representative of Paris: "He had neither hearth nor home, nor any regular source of food; yet he was happy because he was free. By the time the poor have grown to man's estate they have nearly always been caught in the wheels of the social order and become shaped to its requirements; but while they are children their smallness saves them."

Madame Thénardier

The coarse wife of the innkeeper Thénardier, she takes in Fantine's daughter, Cosette. But she treats her like a Cinderella, feeding and clothing her poorly and making her do the worst work in the household. She helps hatch a plot to entrap Valjean and steal his fortune, but instead ends up in prison. The narrator states that she is naturally cruel and scheming and offers her as an example of those who commit crimes not because they are driven to it, but because it suits them.

Monsieur Thénardier

The unscrupulous innkeeper and his wife take care of Cosette, but treat her poorly. He embarks on a life of crime, getting involved with the worst criminals in Paris, and attempts to entrap and rob Valjean. Although he ends up in prison, he escapes. He helps Valjean escape from the sewers when Valjean is trapped there with Marius. Thénardier plays a central part in the plot. He does good in spite of his evil intentions, not knowing what the consequences of his own actions will be.

Felix Tholomyès

A wealthy, rakish student, he is Fantine's lover for a while and then abandons her. Their affair ruins Fantine. She becomes pregnant and cannot earn enough to save herself and her child. The narrator says of the relationship: "For him it was a passing affair, for her the love of her life."

Jean Valjean

The chief protagonist, Jean Valjean, is an ex-convict who struggles to redeem himself morally and to find acceptance in a society that rejects him as a former criminal. Valjean's redemption through his many trials is the central plot of *Les Misérables.*

The child of a poor peasant family, he loses both his parents as a young child and moves in with an older sister. When her husband dies, Valjean supports her and her seven children by working as a tree pruner. Unable to feed the family on his earnings, he steals a loaf of bread from a baker and ends up serving nineteen years in prison for his crime. Finally free, he finds that he cannot find lodging, work, or acceptance in the outside world. As an ex-convict he is at the bottom of the social order.

But Valjean has a transforming experience when he meets the Bishop of Digne, who accepts and shelters him regardless of his past, even after Valjean tries to steal from his household. Here Valjean learns the lesson of unconditional love, a reason for living that sustains him through all of his trials. And they are many. He lives on the run from two forces: the justice of the law, represented by Javert, a police detective who doggedly pursues him, and his own conscience, which leads him to make difficult choices between what is right and what is easiest.

Valjean starts a new life as the mayor of Montreuil sur Mer. He is the savior of this manufacturing town, rebuilding its industries and economy and sustaining the population with new jobs. But he lives on the run from his dogged pursuer, Javert, and in his first moral trial he has to give himself up to keep an innocent man from going to prison in his place. He escapes again and lives the rest of his life as a fugitive.

The harshness of the society in which he lives presents great obstacles to Valjean's moral redemption. Only the transforming power of love lets him overcome them. He loves a young girl, Cosette, daughter of the prostitute Fantine, and raises her as his daughter. Most of his good acts center on her welfare: saving the life of her lover, Marius; protecting her, whatever the cost to himself; even giving up Cosette after she marries, so that she will not be sullied by connection to an ex-convict. His love for her teaches him how to act in the world at large. In all of his actions he strives to be honorable and generous.

THEMES

Change and Transformation

The most important theme the novel examines is that of transformation, in the individual and in society. Jean Valjean, the chief protagonist, is transformed from a misanthropic and potentially violent ex-convict to a man capable of heroic love and self-sacrifice. The force that transforms him is love. The

Bishop of Digne offers Valjean unconditional love, trusting the former criminal with his life and giving him all that he can. Valjean finds inspiration for an entirely new life from this example. He learns to put another person first when he raises Cosette as his own daughter, and he endures moral trials, such as risking his life to rescue Marius, who loves Cosette and whom Valjean hates. On the broader scale, the workers and students on the barricade fight for social transformation, to create a new France without injustice and poverty.

Human Rights

Closely related to the theme of transformation is that of human rights. This is what the barricade is about and what the students, workers, and downtrodden poor of Paris want. The novel offers many examples of the violation of human rights. Valjean steals a loaf of bread because he has hungry children to feed. The law punishes him for nineteen years because of this petty crime, and Valjean finds little peace at the end of his term. The police inspector Javert pursues him almost to the grave for the theft of a coin. Fantine loves a man who abandons her, and she ends up as a prostitute. She sacrifices her child, her looks, and her body just to survive. Even worse, when she does defend her human dignity and accuses a bourgeois gentleman of assault, the police arrest her. As the novel presents it, the aim of revolution is to create a society in which all individuals have equal rights, in which poverty itself is undesirable, not marginalized citizens.

Class Conflict

The central struggle is also a class conflict: revolution mobilizes the have-nots against the haves. The working-class of Paris is presented as an ominous force, ready to throw up a barricade at a moment's notice. The barricade is where the life-and-death struggle of the disenfranchised and the government takes place. The students and workers join and fight to create a new and better nation, even at the cost of their lives. Enjolras, their leader, puts it eloquently when he says: "'[This] is the hard price that must be paid for the future. A revolution is a toll-gate. But mankind will be liberated, uplifted and consoled. We here affirm it, on this barricade.'"

Justice and Injustice

Another major question the novel deals with is whether the legal institutions of the state exact true justice. While he is in prison, the convict Jean Valjean considers the question of whether he has been treated fairly. Readers must wonder if his crime, stealing a loaf of bread to feed his family, really merits the punishment he receives, four years of imprisonment that stretch to nineteen when he tries to escape. Valjean asks himself "whether human society had the right to . . . grind a poor man between the millstones of need and excess—need of work and excess of punishment. Was it not monstrous that society should treat in this fashion precisely those least favored in the distribution of wealth. . .?" He comes to the conclusion that, although he did commit a reprehensible crime, the punishment is out of proportion, and he develops an intense hatred for society as a whole. Fantine meets the same fate when she defends herself against attack. As a prostitute, she is on the bottom rung of society; the law offers her no protection. Only respectable people with money appear to have any legal rights.

Meaning of Life

Valjean's great discovery, the one that transforms him, is that the meaning of life lies in love. His love is twofold, both the generalized love for one's fellow creatures that the Bishop of Digne shows toward him and the specific love for another person that he feels for Cosette. Summing up this philosophy at the end of his life, Valjean says to Cosette and Marius, "Love one another always. There is nothing else that matters in this world except love."

STYLE

Structure

In some ways the novel is structured traditionally. It has a rising action, that is the part of the narrative that sets up the problems that are to be resolved. This consists of Valjean's life up to the point when he saves his enemy Marius by carrying him through the sewers of Paris to safety. The climax, or turning point, when the conflict reaches its peak, is the suicide of the police detective Javert. Caught between his rigid belief in the absolute power of law and his conclusion that he has a moral obligation to break the law and free his savior, Valjean, Javert solves his dilemma by killing himself. The denouement, or winding-down of the story, which describes the outcome of the primary plot problem as well as resolving secondary plots, includes Marius's recovery, the marriage of Cosette and Marius, the revelation of Valjean's true story, and the young couple's visit to Valjean's deathbed.

But the narrative's many departures from the main plot are important to the novel as well. The novel includes separate sections on the sewers of Paris, the criminal underworld, the convent, Parisian street slang, the battle of Waterloo, revolutionary societies, and the barricades. Hugo is telling more than the story of one man; he is telling the story of Paris. His digressions, although they do not forward plot development, give the reader information about the novel's themes, such as human rights, justice and injustice, class conflict, and the city. He's primarily concerned not so much with narrating a story, but with critiquing society and presenting his notions of reform.

Point of View

The story is told from a third-person omniscient point of view. Omniscient narrators have a god's-eye or all-knowing view, knowing more than their characters do. The narrator breaks in several times to equate himself with the author. For example, at the beginning of the Waterloo episode, the narrator says: "On a fine May morning last year (that is to say, in the year 1861) a traveller, the author of this tale, walked from Nivelles in the direction of La Hulpe." And in describing Paris, he states: "For some years past the author of this book, who regrets the necessity to speak of himself, has been absent from Paris." Although generally there is a distinction between the author and the narrator of a work, this device blurs the boundary. The novel is a vehicle of expression for the author's social views. Whenever the narrator is not describing the actions, thoughts, and speech of the characters, the voice of authority emerges. This includes the discussion of Parisian street urchins, the sewers, the underworld, and the barricades. The narrator pulls back from the characters to look at the broader scenario. Here is a typical example of this device, describing the barricade: "And while a battle that was still political was preparing in that place that had witnessed so many revolutionary acts; while the young people, the secret societies, and the schools, inspired by principle, and the middle-class inspired by self-interest, were advancing on each other to clash and grapple . . . there was to be heard the sombre growling of the masses: a fearful and awe-inspiring voice in which were mingled the snarl of animals and the words of God, a terror to the faint-hearted and a warning to the wise, coming at once from the depths, like the roaring of a lion, and from the depths like the voice of thunder."

Setting

The setting for most of the novel is Paris around 1830, a character in its own right. The narrative devotes almost as much space to it as to the protagonist, Valjean. It is a dark, gloomy, and sinister place, full of plague-carrying winds and polluting sewers, rotting old districts and slums. Its secretive aspect is a blessing, though, for Valjean, who seeks refuge in dark corners. The narrow alleys lend themselves, too, to the building of barricades. The narrative also presents Paris as a microcosm, reflecting the world as a whole: "Paris stands for the world. Paris is a sum total, the ceiling of the human race. . . . To observe Paris is to review the whole course of history. . . ." Paris also has its places of beauty and tranquillity, such as the Luxembourg Garden on a fair day, but even here discontent lurks, in the form of two hungry boys wandering in search of food.

The novel presents Paris in all its wretchedness and grandeur. The urban environment has power over those who live in it. Some characters, such as Thénardier, an innkeeper who gets involved with the worst criminal elements of the city, are corrupted by Paris's temptations and hardships. Others, like Gavroche, the street urchin who is Thénardier's son, demonstrate courage and compassion in spite of their circumstances. For Valjean, Paris is both a refuge and a testing-ground. Hugo ranges over many aspects of the city in his portrayal of it, from the convents to the argot, or slang, spoken on the streets, from the heart of the city to its half-tamed outskirts, from rooftops to sewers. The sewer system of Paris symbolizes the dark underside of the city, where its secret history is stored: "that dreadful place which bears the impress of the revolution of the earth and of men, in which the remains of every cataclysm is to be found, from the Flood to the death of Marat." (Marat was a leader of the French Revolution who was assassinated.) Most of all, the citizens of Paris make up its character. The novel presents a sprawling picture of the people: criminals, orphans, students, the middle class, and others.

Symbolism

The novel employs symbolism, the use of one object to represent another, on a grand scale. Paris stands in for the world. Gavroche symbolizes the heroism of the average individual. The city sewers represent the seamy underside of Paris, filled with scraps of history, both good and evil, that have been discarded and forgotten, but not destroyed. The sewers also represent Valjean's passage through hell to redemption. He carries Marius to safety on his back through their passages like a martyr bearing a cross. A pair of silver candlesticks, stolen from the Bishop, serves for Valjean as a symbolic reminder of where he has come from and how he should act. Such leitmotivs, or recurring themes, woven through the text add depth and meaning.

Romanticism

Romanticism was an artistic and intellectual movement of the late eighteenth and early nineteenth century that put the individual mind at the center of the world and of art. Romanticism valued emotional and imaginative responses to reality, the individual's interior experience of the world, which it perceived as being closer to truth. It evolved partly as a reaction to the Enlightenment's emphasis on restraint, simplicity, logic, and respect for tradition. *Les Misérables* is a characteristic Romantic work in both theme and form. In theme, the novel assaults the traditional social structure, glorifies freedom of thought and spirit, and makes a hero of the average individual, such as Gavroche the street urchin, who dies with courage on the barricade. In form, the novel values content over structure, offers passionate rhetoric rather than classical restraint, and ranges freely over many subjects.

HISTORICAL CONTEXT

Romanticism

Romanticism was an intellectual and artistic movement that swept Europe and the United States in the late-eighteenth to mid-nineteenth centuries. This movement was preceded by the Enlightenment, which emphasized reason as the basis of social life. The Enlightenment also promoted universal, formal standards, dating back to Greek and Roman classicism, for greatness in art. The artists, philosophers, writers, and composers of the Romantic movement rejected these standards and instead valued the individual imagination and experience as the basis of art and source of truth. Nature, the state

of childhood, and emotion, rather than logic or scientific investigation, were considered the primary sources of eternal truth.

Victor Hugo was one of the leading writers of the Romantic movement in France, and *Les Misérables* was one of its major works. The novel is Romantic in style and theme. It is written in a sweeping, emotional manner, taking the experience of the individual as the starting-point for discovering truths about French society.

Revolution

France in the nineteenth century was in a constant state of political and social unrest. In 1789, the newly formed National Assembly created a document called the "Declaration of the Rights of Man," establishing the right to liberty, equality, property, and security, and adding that every citizen had a duty to defend these rights. After King Louis XVI was executed on January 21, 1793, a period of confusion and violence followed. Many people, the innocent along with the guilty, were executed in the aftermath of the Revolution.

With the bloody departure of the monarchy, the legislature appointed a five-man Directory to power in 1795. But conspirators, including Napoleon Bonaparte, staged a coup d'état, or surprise overthrow of the state, in 1799. Napoleon became dictator and remained in power until he was completely defeated at the Battle of Waterloo in 1815. This is when Hugo's novel *Les Misérables* begins.

From 1815 until 1830, France was ruled by Louis XVIII and then Charles X under the Second Restoration. During this time the French used a constitutional monarchy where the king governed alongside of a elected parliament. This was a comparatively tranquil and prosperous period, but it ended in the Revolution of 1830, when Charles X published ordinances dissolving Parliament, limiting voting rights to land owners, and abolishing freedom of the press. Charles was forced from the throne and replaced by Louis Philippe, the "citizen king," who had fought in the French Revolution. This was a triumph for the middle class, but it left the working-class and poor out in the cold.

The insurrection of 1832, the first Republican uprising since 1789, started to stir at the burial of Lamarque, a Revolutionary hero. Republicans shouted, "Down with Louis Philippe!" The barricades went up, and a violent clash ensued. The

COMPARE & CONTRAST

- **1830s:** Under public pressure, French legislators reform prisons to some extent. They abolish some of the more barbaric forms of punishment that were practiced under the *Ancien Régime,* such as torture and hanging, and offer education for petty offenders.

  1850s: As a result of unemployment caused by industrialization, crime rates rise in France and the prison population increases. Inmates are not allowed to speak to each other. Riots and suicides take place in prisons.

  Today: Because of economic conditions in France, prison populations are on the rise again, with an increase in the number of convicts serving time for drug related crimes. With a prison population that is steadily increasing, overcrowding is a problem, and many inmates find themselves sharing a cell with as many as five other prisoners.

- **1830s:** France is beginning to become an industrialized nation, a process that will transform its economy, workplace, working class, and political landscape.

  1850s: Increasing industrialization brings wealth to France as well as increased unemployment. Lack of work drives thousands of poor women to prostitution and many of the urban poor to crime.

  Today: After rapid consolidation of industries in the 1970s, many French manufacturing jobs were eliminated, resulting in high levels of unemployment. Currently, many young people have difficulty finding permanent work. However, recent changes in the French school system have expanded educational opportunities for students, in an effort by the government to create an employable workforce.

- **1830s:** Antigovernment protesters set up barricades in Paris after Charles X publishes three ordinances calling to abolish freedom of the press, dissolve Parliament, and limit voting rights to 25,000 landed proprietors. The 1830 revolution successfully removes Charles from the throne; succeeding him is Louis Phillippe.

  1850s: A bloody protest occurs in Paris in 1848, removing Louis Phillippe from power and creating a provisional government that extends the right to vote and sets up national workshops to combat unemployment. After another violent clash, this government is in turn replaced by the Second Republic, with an assembly dominated by the middle class.

  Today: After violent student protests and nation-wide strikes in May of 1968, new French leaders shifted towards a more liberal form of government, trying to balance a market economy while preserving social-democratic principles. Today, France is joining with other European nations to create the European Union, a community that will share a common currency and create a formidable trading bloc.

---

forces on the barricades, composed mainly of students and workers, lacked public support, and the rebellion was put down by government forces.

In 1848, a new wave of revolution swept across Europe, triggered by the political unrest of bourgeois liberals and nationalists, crop failures several years in a row, and economic troubles. In France, Louis Philippe was driven from his throne. After a bloody struggle between the working-class and the middle-class provisional government in Paris, the Second Republic was established, with a mainly middle-class national assembly and Louis Napoleon, who was related to Napoleon I, as president.

Hugo was sympathetic to the 1848 revolution, became a representative in the assembly, and initially supported Louis Napoleon. However, in 1851 the president assumed control of France in a military coup d'état, and in 1852 the population voted to disband the republic and reestablish the empire. Hugo was disillusioned with both the French people who were willing to exchange freedom for stability and with Napoleon III, who had traded in his republican opinions to become a dictator. Criticizing the government and Louis Napoleon publicly, he was forced to leave France, first for Belgium and then for the Channel Islands. *Les Misérables,* which Hugo composed from the late 1840s to 1862 during his exile, integrated his feelings about the political situation, his memories of the barricades of 1848, and his republican ideals. The novel denounces the degradation of the urban working-class and society's mistreatment and neglect of the poor, especially women and children.

Industrialization

The continuing industrialization of France in the 1850s and 1860s created wealth for the country, but it also created unemployment as machines replaced manual laborers in many jobs. This in turn led to an increase in crime. Poor working women also turned to prostitution as a means of survival. They worked under the scrutiny of a Police Morals Bureau, which considered them corrupt. The character of Jean Valjean was drawn from a historical person, a petty thief named Pierre Maurin who spent five years in prison for stealing bread for his sister's children. Hugo draws a clear distinction in the novel between those who choose crime because they are corrupt and those who are driven to it by poverty and desperation. On the one hand, there is Thénardier, who is by nature "highly susceptible to the encroachments of evil." On the other, there is Valjean, who stole only to save his family, and Fantine, who suffered for protecting her own child. The narrator blames society's indifference and injustice for the situation of those who fall in the latter category.

CRITICAL OVERVIEW

Publishers bid against each other for the right to publish *Les Misérables,* no doubt sensing that the novel would be a gold mine. It had been awaited for years. The author's exile to Guernsey only increased his international reputation and the suspense of waiting for his next major work. Hugo received an unheard-of 300,000 francs as the advance payment for the novel. But the publishers more than realized their investment when the book came out.

Les Misérables appeared in 1862, published by LaCroix of Brussels and Paris. It appeared simultaneously in Paris, London, Brussels, New York, Berlin, St. Petersburg, and other European capitals. Published initially in five parts, divided into ten volumes, the novel was released in three separate installments in April, May, and June. Hugo's family and friends gave it a huge build up in the press, advertising its release for a month in advance in all the major papers of Europe. Rumors that it might be banned in France built up the suspense even more. The book-buying public gave it an enthusiastic reception. Booksellers in Paris lined up to buy the second installment in such great numbers that police were needed to manage the crowd. It was an enormous success for its publishers and its author. Adèle Hugo, the author's wife, wrote that groups of workers shared the cost of the ten volumes in order to pass it from hand to hand and read it. The critic Saint-Beuve commented that Hugo "had snatched the greatest popularity of our time under the nose of the very government that exiled him. His books go everywhere: the women, the common people, all read him. Editions go out of print between eight in the morning and noon."

The critical reception, on the other hand, was mixed. Some of his contemporaries perceived Hugo's style as long-winded, digressive, melodramatic, and full of unlikely coincidences. Others found his sweeping, passionate prose, championing of social issues, and ideals of justice and morality inspirational.

On the negative side, many critics disliked the novel's digressions from the main plot, especially the long account of Waterloo. Adolphe Thiers, a historian, expressed the strong opinion that the novel was "detestable. The spirit is bad, the plan is bad, and the execution is bad." The writer Barbey D'Aurévilly found the novel vulgar and full of improbabilities, and criticized it for its socialist views. Hippolyte Taine, a critic and historian, thought the novel was insincere and its success was a flash in the pan.

On the positive side, the poet Charles Baudelaire offered praise for the work's poetic and symbolic qualities. The English novelist George Meredith, though he thought it was drawn in oversimplified terms, called it "the masterwork of fiction of this century—as yet. There are things in it quite wonder-

Frederic March as Jean Valjean in the 1935 film version of Les Misérables.

ful." The great Russian novelist Fyodor Dostoevsky considered *Les Misérables* superior to his own *Crime and Punishment,* and saw Hugo as a champion of the idea of spiritual rebirth. Walter Pater was of the opinion that Hugo's works were among the finest products of the Romantic movement.

In the first half of the twentieth century, Hugo's reputation as a novelist waned. This was in part because of changes in the taste of writers and readers. First the Realist, then the Modernist writers swept through the literary scene, and it is characteristic of most such movements that they debunk what has come before in the effort to break new ground. *Les Misérables* in particular achieved its blinding success partly because of the moment in time when it was released. It was the long-awaited work of a national hero returning from exile, and that historical moment passed, along with Hugo's great influence over national opinion.

But many writers, including André Gide and Jean-Paul Sartre, acknowledged his lasting influence. Hugo's works are still widely read today, and he has his modern defenders. The literary critic Victor Brombert, for example, comments: "The dramatic and psychological power of Hugo's novels depends in large part on the creation of archetypal

figures. . . . The sweep of his texts and the moving, even haunting images they project are a function of the widest range of rhetorical virtuosity." *Les Misérables* has passed into modern legend in its well-known and popular adaptations for the movies and the stage, and it is arguably the most important Romantic novel of the nineteenth century.

CRITICISM

Anne-Sophie Cerisola

In the following essay, Cerisola, a former teacher at the Lycee Francais de New York and a current instructor at New York University, outlines some of the biographical background that led to Hugo's great work; Cerisola also discusses the author's ambition of creating not only a great story, but also a novel that would be an epic of its time, thus explaining the story's complicated narrative approach.

Victor Hugo took seventeen years to write *Les Misérables,* his vast fresco of individual and collective destinies, which was published in 1862 when he was sixty years old. The novel is the parallel story of the redemption of Jean Valjean and France—and to a larger extent, the story of humanity's political and social progress. Above all, Hugo intended *Les Misérables* to be a novel about the people, and for the people, and he largely succeeded.

When *Les Misérables* was published, it appeared simultaneously in Paris, London, Budapest, Brussels, Leipzig, Madrid, Milan, Naples and was translated into many other languages. The novel's phenomenal success has continued ever since, and understandably so: it is a gripping story well told. As the critic Kathryn Grossman put it, "a plot as full of twists and turns as the treacherous labyrinths—sewers, conscience, streets—Hugo describes." Grossman also reminds us, "in France, Hugo's supporters had prepared the event with a massive publicity campaign. [The book] appeared first in serial form on April 3, 1862. Yet the magnitude of the public's response surprised even the most committed Hugo partisans. According to reports at the time, no one had ever seen a book devoured with such fury: public reading rooms rented it by the hour. By April 6, the book was sold out in Paris."

The novel's power derived from its simple message. Man was not inherently evil, he was made

WHAT DO I READ NEXT?

- Victor Hugo's other major works include the novel *The Hunchback of Notre Dame*, published in 1831, and the poetry collection *Contemplations,* released in 1856, which he wrote at about the same time as *Les Misérables.* Some critics consider the latter, written after the drowning death of his daughter, his best poetry.

- Fyodor Dostoevsky's *Crime and Punishment*, first published in 1866, tells the story of Raskolnikov, a man who commits a brutal murder and then cannot escape either his own conscience or the detective who pursues him.

- Published in 1940, *Native Son*, a novel by Richard Wright, is the story of Bigger Thomas, a poor black boy raised in the Chicago slums. Wright describes how Bigger's fear of white society, and its fear of him, turns him into a criminal.

- *In the Belly of the Beast* is an insider's account of prison life written by the controversial Jack Henry Abbott, a convict. Abbott was released after he published the book in 1991, at the urging of a group of writers including Norman Mailer. Shortly thereafter, he killed a man in a bar brawl and was sentenced to life imprisonment.

- Marie Henri Beyle Stendhal offers a detailed account of the battle of Waterloo in *The Charterhouse of Parma,* published in 1839. The main theme of this novel is the struggle of the individual against a conformist society.

- Charles Baudelaire's 1857 *The Flowers of Evil* is a collection of poems centered on life in Paris. One of the major poetry collections of the century, it bridged the Romantic and Modernist movements. Six of the poems that were considered too erotic and decadent were banned in France until 1949. Baudelaire was Hugo's contemporary and often reviewed his work.

---

so by an unjust society. In the preface to the novel, Hugo wrote emphatically: "So long as the three problems of the age—the degradation of man by poverty, the ruin of woman by starvation, and the dwarfing of childhood by physical and spiritual night—are not yet solved . . . books like this cannot be useless." Jean Valjean was the perfect illustration of this principle. Valjean was not by nature a criminal. The motive which led him to steal bread, the origin of his fall, was not evil. He was seeking to provide food for hungry children, his sister's offspring, only out of desperation. But his years of prison have hardened him. "He had for his motives," says Hugo, "habitual indignation, bitterness of soul, the profound feeling of iniquities endured, and reaction even against the good, the innocent, and the just, if such exist." The story of his conversion is exemplary. As Monsieur Madeleine of Montreuil-sur-mer, he is the good industrialist, the admirably just and efficient mayor, the caring philanthropist. Forced back into his true identity by the revelation of the imminent exile to the galleys of the innocent Champmathieu, who has been identified as Jean Valjean, he reluctantly fights again with his demons. From this ordeal, minutely analyzed in the chapter, "A Tempest in a Brain," he emerges triumphant, saves Champmathieu in time and goes again to the galleys. After his escape, his life is a long record of care and self-sacrifice to Cosette, his adopted daughter. Even with Marius and his love for Cosette, Valjean is able not only to dominate his jealousy but to save the life of Marius (the famous episode of the sewers) and make possible Marius's marriage with Cosette.

Moreover, Hugo draws constant analogies between Valjean's spiritual progress and humanity's striving toward freedom and social justice. The fight for justice and freedom is led by Marius's group of radical friends, the "Friends of the Underdog," and in particular Enjolras, whose speech on the barricades echoed most of Hugo's ideas:

"the nineteenth century is grand, but the twentieth century will be happy. Men will no longer have to fear, as now, a conquest, an invasion, a usurpation, a rivalry of nations with the armed hand . . . they will no longer have to fear famine, speculation, prostitution from distress, misery from lack of work, and the scaffold, and the sword, and the battle, and all the brigandages of chance in the forest of events. . . . Men will be happy. . . . Oh! the human race shall be delivered, uplifted, and consoled! We affirm it on this barricade."

However, the young radicals die on the barricades and, as one critic noted, Hugo sometimes seems pessimistic about the outcome of the fight, "The dismal, lurid, grotesque imagery with which Hugo consistently depicts les misérables drives home a powerful point. Despite all the talk about progress, nothing has changed for a large swath of humanity. Conditions may have improved for some individuals and their offspring. But each new generations of the poor and uneducated faced the same physical, psychic, and moral disintegration."

Because he wrote *Les Misérables* late in his life, Hugo also wanted to leave a personal testimony on his own political fights. One of the central characters in the novel, Marius, passes through an intellectual evolution closely similar to the author's. At first strongly royalist, then Bonapartist, later Republican. He fights for his convictions on the barricades. Hugo was born in 1802 to a royalist mother and a republican father who was one of Napoleon's generals. By the time he was a year old his parents were not living together anymore. Seeking fulfillment in and through art, as he was often left by himself. As one of his biographers noted, "Hugo was terribly precocious. He began writing complete plays, echoing his fondness for popular drama, at the age of fourteen; he devoured Walter Scott's historical novels as soon as each translation rolled off the press; and he penned his first work of fiction—whose black rebel hero foreshadowed Jean Valjean—when he was sixteen; finally, he composed poetry that gave him national recognition, including a royal pension, before he had turned eighteen."

At first aesthetically and politically conservative, within years he backed the new school of innovators—Lamartine, Musset, Nodier, Vigny—who were labeled *romantics*. In 1830 his first play, *Hernani*, broke completely with dramatic conventions. Hugo became the leader of this group of writers, most of them democrats in a regime that killed civil liberties. However, only the 1848 Revolution—the model for the insurrection described in the novel—spawned a republic, which Hugo supported vigorously. He was even elected to the Parliament, on the left. The Republic did not last long. Louis-Napoleon Bonaparte, whom Hugo had first supported, overthrew the young republic three years later in 1852 and became emperor. Hugo, who never hid his own republicanism, had to flee abroad to avoid arrest. It is from exile that he wrote *Les Misérables*.

Since his earlier work, Hugo believed in the importance of the illusion of reality, what he called verisimilitude. Very often in the novel, Hugo pretends that he is copying from notes left by Myriel or Valjean. He quotes pseudo newspaper articles and letters that came into his possession: everything must suggest authenticity. Indeed, he always worked a great deal on sources, and at least two characters of the novel, bishop Myriel and Valjean, were inspired from real people whose story Hugo had read. Finally, Hugo was careful to have each character speak according to the language of his or her social class. So much so that when the novel came out he was accused by some critics of being "low." For example, Gavroche, the street urchin, always speaks slang, including to the two little orphans he has just met and for whom he buys some bread.

Finally, like *The Hunchback of Notre-Dame*, Hugo's earlier historical novel, *Les Misérables* multiplies the digressions—on Waterloo, on slang, on the sewers—in an effort to give the historical background of the story. According to one critic, "stripped of all its digression, *Les Misérables* would still be an interesting book, containing an essentially great lesson, but it would be much less a book extraordinarily representative of the nineteenth century. In its final form it gives us not only the lesson of Valjean, but it gives us some of the great deeds and ideas of the century." Hugo justified himself by saying he wanted to create a contemporary work of fiction that would rival such great national verse epics as Homer's *Iliad* and *Odyssey* and John Milton's *Paradise Lost*.

The strong political content of the novel divided the critics of the time. While popular opinion was virtually unanimous, the many critical assessments—by about one hundred and fifty reviewers in 1862 alone—fell into two camps. Political, social, and religious conservatives assailed the author's intellectual integrity, his motives, his intentions: to blame society for human suffering was, according to them, to deny individual responsibility and to undermine existing institutions. The more progressive, republican critics, on the other hand, defended the novel as profoundly moral. Imbued with the New Testament notions of grace, charity, and self-sacrifice, the novel depicted the struggles of human conscience with temptation and the eventual triumph of duty over passion, of freedom over nature.

Critics were also uncertain about the genre and the composition of the book. Indeed, Hugo's ambitious goal complicated the structure of the book. There is very little linearity and numerous echoes and parallels, while the narration goes back and forth in time. The effect is a little disorienting for the reader who has problems following the narration, as if Hugo was playing with his reader's patience. Adding to this unconventional composition, it defies any attempt at classification. The mingling of literary styles—*le melange des genres*–was a hallmark of French romanticism since the 1820s. As a consequence, *Les Misérables* is a blend of epic, myth, dramatic and lyrical components; grotesque and sublime; satire and romance; comedy and tragedy; realism and romanticism which led many critics to describe the novel as a "monster." Maybe it is, and yet, it still makes people dream.

Source: Anne-Sophie Cerisola, for *Epics for Students*, Gale, 2001.

Laurence M. Porter
"The Masterpiece: Les Miserables" is an essay that provides an overview of various positions that Hugo focuses on in his epic.

The Masterpiece: *Les Misérables*

Hugo's Social Views

Admired for his poetry and respected for his theater, which provided the main impetus for the militant romantic movement from 1827 through 1838, Hugo as a novelist has been severely underrated. *Les Misérables* (The Underclass) in particular may be more than his masterpiece: it may be "the great French novel" of the nineteenth century. Its sweep rivals Melville's *Moby Dick*, Tolstoy's *War and Peace*, and Manzoni's *The Betrothed*.

After completing his great visionary poem cycles, Hugo turned eagerly to writing *Les Misérables* (1862). He finished the vast novel in 14 months. Its initial inspiration was probably his *Dernier Jour d'un condamné à mort* (The Last Day on Death Row, 1829). There Hugo dramatized the plight of prisoners in the galleys at Toulon, especially one sentenced to five years for stealing a loaf of bread. Hugo insists on extenuating circumstances, notably,

on the brutalization of the poor by society. "There but for the grace of God go I," might be his hypogram, the matrix of his meaning. With it he, like his contemporary Charles Dickens, deconstructs the simplistic dichotomy of innocence and crime that allows us to evade social responsibility. Hugo's attribution of near-satanic resentment to Jean Valjean seems overblown when we consider his behavior. His only actual crimes are two acts of petty larceny, plus a third of which he is falsely accused (stealing a loaf of bread, a coin, and some apples), but Hugo is making the point that he made in *Claude Gueux*: harsh law enforcement breeds the monsters it wants to eliminate.

Hugo himself had been a prisoner of conscience since 1851, remaining in voluntary exile because he refused to accept Napoleon III's empire. Compensating for his exile in his thoughts, he makes a mental return to Paris, where he situates his epic novel, *Les Misérables*. The loving precision of his detailed Parisian topography there combines the realistic with the nostalgic. Frequently he describes a vanished scene and adds that he's not sure what one would find there now. "[The author] doesn't need to say he loves Paris; Paris is the birthplace of his intellect. Today demolitions and reconstructions have made the Paris of his youth, that Paris he religiously bore away in his memory, a Paris of former times. But let him speak of that Paris as if it still existed. He doesn't know the new Paris, and he is writing with the [image of the] former Paris before his eyes, an illusion that is precious to him". Hugo's reminiscences of Paris often carry an implied symbolic commentary on how ephemeral neighborhoods and monuments can be. For example, see the passages concerning "l'éléphant de la Bastille". The beast of the Bastille prison that swallowed innocent people before the Revolution has been transformed into an avatar of the whale that God sent to preserve Jonah. Napoleon I had had that monumental plaster elephant statue built—it stood on the site of the former Bastille from 1814 to 1846—to embody the idea of the might of the French people, but "God had made of it something greater; He housed a child there". Today (in 1862) that grotesque reminder of Napoleon has vanished, Hugo observes. Similarly, the narrow, crooked streets near the Corinth Restaurant, where the rebels of 1832 led by Enjolras made their last stand behind a barricade at the social climax (as opposed to the climax of the personal drama) of *Les Misérables*, have been straightened and widened until no trace of the original site remains.

The Plot

The plot of Hugo's sprawling, sentimental novel focuses on the redemption of the convict Jean Valjean: first through a bishop's Christian love for him, and then by Valjean's love for the orphan girl Cosette. Although he literally cannot live without her, he eventually relinquishes her to the man she loves.

Elements of the detective story (the police investigator Javert's unrelenting search for Jean Valjean, and depictions of the underworld) remind one of nothing so much as a Dickens novel such as *Oliver Twist* or *Our Mutual Friend*. Both Hugo's and Dickens's major theme is that poverty dehumanizes. Some, like the criminal anti-father Thénardier, become indifferent not only to the sufferings of their victims but even to the survival of their own children. When his two youngest boys disappear, he makes no effort to locate them. And he does not care whether his older daughter Éponine will be killed by other members of his gang for interfering in a burglary. Others such as the police detective Javert, born to a prostitute in prison, and without any family himself, react with uncompromising moral brutality toward the accused.

Dickens and Hugo want to excite our compassion. But their benevolence is paternalistic, and their modest proposals for the voluntary, partial redistribution of wealth—as in Dickens's *A Christmas Carol*—could not threaten well-to-do readers. Aside from his steadfast opposition to capital punishment, Hugo offers no practical solutions for reforming the police, the courts, or the prisons. He simply tries to stimulate our moral sensibilities as Fantine's misadventures and steadfast love for her child stimulated the moral sensibilities of Jean Valjean. Hugo intends the reformed convict to serve as a model for us as Valjean comes to know God, whom Hugo equates with conscience. His message is that of the Gospels: "Inasmuch as ye have done it unto one of the least of these my brethren, ye have done it unto me" (Matt. 25:40). Eventually, Hugo will explicitly compare Valjean to Christ.

A poor young tree pruner at the outset of the story, Jean Valjean is supporting his widowed sister and her seven children. One winter, lacking work, and fearing that his relatives will starve, he breaks a bakery window to steal a loaf of bread. He is sentenced to five years in the galleys at Toulon. Four times he tries to escape. Each time he is recaptured, and his sentence is eventually extended to 19 years.

His incarceration began in 1796, when Napoleon (who is just his age) first assumed a share of governmental leadership. Valjean's release in 1815 corresponds to that of the French people, freed from the tyrannical leadership and bloody wars of Napoleon I. The individual spiritual drama reflects French history.

Valjean has become deeply embittered against society because of his excessively harsh punishment. After his release, this attitude is promptly aggravated: his ex-convict's yellow passport makes everyone scorn and reject him. Only a saintly bishop, Monseigneur Myriel, is willing to give him lodging for the night. But Valjean cannot resist stealing the bishop's last remaining luxuries, his silver place settings. Valjean flees in the night. He is arrested and brought back, but the bishop saves him from imprisonment by saying he had given the place settings to Valjean. The bishop then adds two silver candlesticks, which his guest had "forgotten." As Jean Valjean is released, and about to set off again, the bishop whispers in his ear that he has purchased Valjean's soul with his gifts, and that Valjean has promised him henceforth to embrace the good.

Hugo's depiction is not simplistic; the bishop's beneficent influence will work progressively but intermittently on Jean Valjean. On the road north, impulse and residual rage lead Valjean to steal a coin from a little chimney sweep (a crime that will pursue him for the remainder of the novel), but then he repents and resolves to lead a virtuous life. He cannot forget the bishop's act of kindness. "He fought against this heavenly indulgence with his pride, which is like the stronghold of evil within us". An inner voice tells Valjean that he must choose between virtue and crime. He is obliged to judge himself; he exclaims: "Je suis un misérable!" [I am an abominable man!]. The inner image of the bishop's virtue makes the old self-image of the hardened, vengeful criminal fade away as if Jean Valjean could contemplate Satan illumined by the glow of paradise.

Incognito in a northern village, Valjean becomes the benevolent mayor "Monsieur Madeleine." His name alludes to Mary Magdalene, the archetype of repentance. With Madeleine's career, Hugo illustrates a paternalistic "trickle-down" theory of social progress: all redistribution of wealth is voluntary. He ensures the prosperity of an entire community by inventing a superior method for manufacturing glassware. Despite his modest protests, in time he is elected mayor. His period of achievement in this role, from 1815 to 1824, coincides with the first and relatively more liberal period of the French Restoration under Louis XVIII.

Meanwhile Fantine, a young working woman impregnated and then abandoned by her cynical Parisian lover, has returned to her hometown to find work. Hugo has not received due credit for anticipating the naturalist movement in the chapters devoted to her life both in Paris and in her hometown. I would define naturalist literature as treating the working classes seriously and tragically while emphasizing the influences of heredity and environment. Naturalism tends to depict drudgery. In the Paris scenes, however, Hugo depicts the *grisettes* (young women who wore gray smocks at their jobs, and who were stereotypically easy targets for seduction) at play rather than at work. And he emphasizes the inequities of their sexual exploitation by middle-class men in a way Zola, with his sexual insecurities, could not (cf. Zola's *Nana*, 1880, depicting female sexuality as a monstrous source of social corruption).

To be hired, Fantine—although a devoted mother—must conceal her illegitimate child, Cosette. Fantine innocently lodges the child with the evil Thénardier couple and their pampered daughters, Éponine and Azelma. Unknown to Fantine, Cosette is starved, overworked, beaten, and terrorized. When the manager of M. Madeleine's glassworks factory learns of Cosette, he fires Fantine. She must turn to prostitution to support her child.

Eventually M. Madeleine learns of this situation and promises to reunite Fantine with her child and to care for them both. Ordering her release when she is unjustly accused of assault, he alienates the local police inspector, Javert, who has already sensed something suspicious about M. Madeleine. And soon his conscience compels him to denounce himself when an innocent vagrant, Champmathieu, is falsely accused of stealing apples, mistaken for Jean Valjean, and about to be sentenced to life in the galleys. (This episode may reflect the historical Hugo's decision to "go public" with his opposition to the coup d'état of Napoleon III, knowing that he would therefore face a possible lifetime in exile, when it would have been much more comfortable and convenient to keep silence.)

Valjean has time to hide the fortune he made legitimately in glassware, but the rigid Javert will not allow him to bring Cosette to Fantine before she dies. Jean Valjean returns to prison in 1824, the year when the reactionary monarch Charles X took power.

On the spiritual plane, Valjean's renunciation of his freedom saves him from self-righteousness, the first danger of loving one's fellow humans: having done good, one feels superior. One must learn to relinquish this prideful, alienating sense of superiority.

Considered in isolation, the generalizations with which Hugo characterizes the moral dynamics of his novel later in the story make its outcome seem inevitable: "The book the reader holds at this moment is from end to end, as a whole and in its details, whatever may be the interruptions, exceptions, or momentary weaknesses, the march from evil to good … from the void to God. The point of departure: matter; the point of arrival: the soul. The hydra at the beginning, the angel at the end". In its details, however, Hugo's moral vision remains too complex to let us assume that even the most saintly influences or the firmest resolve makes anyone's regeneration a certainty. When Valjean begins actively practicing Christian charity, this new vocation provides him with the rationalizations—based on the importance of his service to others—that almost overwhelm him. The obscure old tree pruner Champmathieu seems expendable, whereas if "M. Madeleine" is arrested, as Valjean knows, the community he has nurtured will collapse. The accidental delays he encounters while rushing to the final session of Champmathieu's trial tempt Valjean to give up his attempt at exonerating his substitute. He could say he had tried everything in vain (the possibility of his disclosing his identity *after* Champmathieu's sentencing never is raised).

To escape once more from prison, Valjean feigns a drowning accident; believed dead, he returns to Paris, where all the major characters will converge. With a note from Fantine authorizing him to take Cosette, he reclaims her from the Thénardiers. He brings her to hide with him in Paris. But Javert has been reassigned there and recognizes him. Pursued by Javert, Valjean finally manages to find a haven in a convent as an assistant gardener. (The regular gardener who lets him stay is a man whose life Valjean once saved.)

Valjean raises Cosette like a daughter, and they love each other deeply. He is consoled by the thought that she will always stay with him because she will grow up ugly. Through Bishop Myriel, Valjean learned of virtue; but through practicing virtue, he risks falling prey to pride. The accident or providential intervention (the many apparent coincidences in Hugo's novel constitute an indirect attempt to persuade us that God intervenes in human affairs, while preserving the imperatives of human commitment and responsibility in the overt rhetoric of the narrator) that leads Valjean to the safe shelter of the convent saves him from pride: he must compare his involuntary sufferings as a victim of social inequities and as a convict to the voluntary, altruistic suffering of the nuns. Their example foreshadows Valjean's voluntary self-sacrifice.

Through Cosette, he has learned of love; but his love remains selfish. It is indispensable for him. The narrator speculates that Jean Valjean might have needed Cosette's daughterly love to persevere in virtue. As mayor, he had learned much more than before about social injustice; he had been sent back to prison for doing good; he needed the support of Cosette's dependency to keep him morally strong. She is schooled in the convent. To prevent her pursuing a false religious vocation, Valjean leaves after seven years, and they live in seclusion. Meanwhile, the Thénardiers as well have come to Paris to join the underworld.

Becoming a beautiful young woman, Cosette attracts the attention of a poor young man, Marius. He has been estranged from his royalist grandfather because of his loyalty to his deceased father, a heroic colonel under Napoleon. By moving across Paris, Jean Valjean manages to elude Marius. As yet unrecognized by Thénardier, however, Jean Valjean nevertheless attracts his attention by generously giving alms. With the aid of the formidable Patron-Minette gang, Thénardier tries to kidnap Cosette to hold her for ransom. By coincidence, Marius lives next door to the Thénardiers. Learning of their plan to kidnap and torture Jean Valjean to force him to write a letter that will lure Cosette into their ambush, Marius denounces them to Javert. But then he learns that Thénardier is the man who had saved his father's life at Waterloo (inadvertently reviving him by stealing the valuables from his unconscious body, left for dead). The dying wish of Marius's father is that his son will find and repay Thénardier. Therefore Marius feels a sacred obligation to help him under any circumstances.

Thénardier's daughter Éponine has fallen in love with Marius. She and her family had persecuted Cosette when she stayed with them as a paid boarder and, in effect, as a slave. Now, although Cosette never becomes aware that Éponine has moved to Paris, the roles have been reversed. Devoted without hope of reward, and self-effacing, Éponine helps Marius find Cosette again. Cosette and Marius fall helplessly in love and meet at night in Cosette's garden for a chaste but passionate romance. When Thénardier's gang stakes out Valjean's isolated new residence—without realizing that it belongs to their former intended victim—Éponine drives the gang away and anonymously warns Valjean to move. Valjean plans to flee to England. An accident prevents Cosette from telling Marius where she is going. In despair at not finding her at home, he plans to seek death on the barricades of the insurrection of 1832. As he joins his republican friends there, a sudden political illumination makes his commitment to their cause authentic.

Meanwhile Jean Valjean has discovered the imprint of Cosette's desperate note to Marius on her blotter. He hates Marius for threatening to take away the only person he has ever loved; Valjean must now overcome the second trap of loving. When you love, you can feel a claim on those you love; you must renounce possessiveness and set them free. After an intense inner struggle, Valjean goes to the barricade to protect Marius. Realizing that Marius and she love each other, "he who had finally come to believe himself incapable of wishing anyone ill, there were times when he felt reopening and rising up against that young man those old depths of his soul where there had once been so much rage".

The loss of the person one loves, Hugo says later, is the cruelest, the only true ordeal. Having discovered that Cosette adores Marius in turn, Jean Valjean "felt right down to the roots of his hair the enormous reawakening of selfishness, and his ego howled within his spiritual abyss". That man who had devoted so much effort to spiritual perfection looked within his soul and saw the specter of hatred there. Hugo does not reproduce the inner debate that leads Valjean at last to the barricade to watch over Marius and eventually to save his life—binding his wounds, carrying him to safety and to medical treatment, and in effect hiding him from prosecution or summary execution for treason. Conscience has its mysteries, Hugo implies.

Éponine simultaneously illustrates a poignant but limited version of sacrifice. Knowing Marius cares only for Cosette, in the name of his friends she summons him to the barricade where they will be fighting, hoping he will die there. But she wants to die first. Disguised as a young worker, she saves Marius by throwing herself in front of a bullet aimed at him.

Meanwhile, behind the barricade, Javert has been unmasked as a police spy. Valjean asks permission to be the one to execute him but then secretly sets him free. When the barricade falls to the government troops and Marius collapses wounded and unconscious, Jean Valjean manages to escape through the sewers. He risks drowning or suffocation in the muck as he carries Marius for four miles on his shoulders. At the locked exit, Valjean meets Thénardier, who has taken refuge there from Javert. Thénardier does not recognize Valjean. He thinks that Valjean has killed Marius for his money, and demands all Valjean's cash in exchange for opening the sewer gate with his skeleton key so that Valjean can escape. Thénardier hopes to distract the waiting Javert by giving him a substitute fugitive. But Javert, who owes Valjean his life, feels morally obligated to let him go. Torn by his unresolvable conflict between religious and legal duty, Javert kills himself.

Marius is nursed back to health by his grandfather, reconciles with him, and marries Cosette. Valjean has given them all his fortune. The moral climax of the novel is Jean Valjean's inner struggle during the wedding night. Should he confess to Marius that he is an escaped convict and withdraw from Cosette's life to spare the young couple the shame of his possible denunciation and arrest? "He had reached the ultimate crossroads of good and evil. That shadowy intersection lay before his eyes. Once again, as it had already happened to him at other painful and critical moments, two paths lay before him: one was tempting, the other fearsome. Which should he take? The fearsome path was advised by the mysterious finger that we all see every time we stare into the darkness. ... We can never find an end to conscience. ... It is bottomless, since it is God". Hugo, like the romantic Lamartine in his epic poem *Jocelyn,* implies that human love tempts us to become isolated in the egotism of earthly happiness. It is sacrifice, not human love alone, that brings us closer to God.

On the next day, Valjean confesses secretly to Marius that he is not Cosette's father, and that he is an escaped convict. Marius, believing that Valjean's fortune was stolen, does not touch it. And believing that Valjean killed Javert at the barricade, Marius only reluctantly allows him to see Cosette in the anteroom to his grandfather's house. Realizing he is unwelcome to Marius, Valjean stops coming, stops eating, and wastes away.

Now Thénardier unwittingly serves as the instrument of Providence. He comes to Marius to extort money from him by revealing the "secret" that his father-in-law is an escaped convict who has recently killed a man (meaning Marius himself). Inadvertently he reveals that Valjean neither made his fortune illegally nor killed Javert: indeed, he is the one who saved Marius. The latter discharges his debt of honor to Thénardier, sending him to America, where he will become a slave owner. Marius and Cosette rush repentantly to Valjean's bedside; they arrive too late to save him. But they beg his forgiveness and he dies happy in one of the most pathetic scenes in literature, which is also an optimistic rewriting of the death scene in Balzac's *Le Père Goriot (Old Goriot).*

The Archetype of Inversion

Throughout *Les Misérables*, Hugo frequently suggests the archetype of Inversion. They who humble themselves shall be exalted. Jean Valjean socially humbles himself in others' eyes by confessing his identity as an escaped convict. He physically lowers himself by descending into the sewers of Paris to carry the wounded, unconscious Marius away from the barricades. But this physical descent exalts him spiritually. As many commentators have remarked, his dark night of the soul will lead to his total regeneration as well as to a reconciliation with his grieving, admiring son-in-law and adopted daughter.

The archetype of Inversion shapes characters and destinies other than Jean Valjean's in *Les Misérables* . In its negative form, Inversion means that what had seemed good, proves bad. Hugo invokes this form of the archetype to characterize the police agent Javert when he learns that M. Madeleine, who earlier had humiliated him, is really the ex-convict Valjean. "A monstrous Saint Michael," Javert is both imposing and hideous: "The honest, pitiless joy of a fanatic in the middle of committing an atrocity preserves some kind of lugubriously venerable radiance.... Nothing was as poignant and as fearsome as that figure, where one could see what you might call all the evil of the good". The sinister, deformed grandeur of Thénardier's visionary painting of Napoleon may be another example of this phenomenon, of a spider's ambition to rival the sun. It seems as if Thénardier, by capturing the emperor's image, were trying to appropriate for himself the soul of Napoleon's genius.

In its positive form, Inversion means that what seemed bad, proves good. The Beatitudes from Christ's Sermon on the Mount (Matt. 5:2–12), and the Passion itself (Matt. 27–28; Mark 15–16; Luke

23–24; John 19–20), are outstanding examples. Appropriately for his tidy structural sense, Hugo frames his epic novel with nesting layers of inversions. At the beginning and the end, we learn that humility can lead to spiritual exaltedness (in Bishop Myriel, then in Jean Valjean). In fact, the novel is framed by two rejections of Jean Valjean as a convict (by society in general, and then by his son-in-law, Marius). In the middle, Javert's bad excess of goodness is followed by his shocked awareness of the possible goodness of badness as he learns of Jean Valjean's moral sublimity. He then intuits "some sort of justice according to God, working counter to justice according to human beings … the monstrous could be divine".

Near the end, having won his last spiritual battle by confessing his past to Marius, Jean Valjean speaks for the author as he explains that "to respect myself, I must be despised. Then I hold my head high. I am a convict who obeys his conscience. I know all too well that it's not plausible. But what can I do? It's so". The word "ressemblant" echoes Hugo's pirouette at the beginning of the novel as he concludes his idealized moral portrait of Bishop Myriel—"We don't claim that it's plausible; we'll say only that it's a good resemblance". This subtle, nearly subliminal association of the two men reminds us of Myriel's enduring moral influence on Valjean. Switching from the author's voice to the hero's voice in the second of these scenes makes the novel's moral import more immediate at the climax. Hugo had summed it up not many pages earlier: "For those of us who prefer martyrdom to success, John Brown is greater than George Washington". His motto might be Rousseau's: "Vitam Impendere Vero" [to sacrifice one's life for the (cause of) truth]. This resolve is the essence of the moral sublime.

Unlike his contemporaries Baudelaire, Rimbaud, and Verlaine, Hugo has received little credit for preparing the religious revival in French letters during the first half of the twentieth century. Like Claudel (who detested Hugo), Mauriac, or Bernanos 30 to 90 years after him during the Catholic Renaissance, Hugo in 1862 dramatizes his heroes' relentless pursuit by conscience, meaning our instinctive awareness of God. "To write the poem of the human conscience, were it only the conscience of a single person … would be to blend all epics into a higher, definitive epic. … There you find, underneath an external silence, battles between giants as in Homer, struggles with dragons and hydras and clouds of phantoms as in Milton, visionary spirals as in Dante.

What a shadowy thing is this infinity that every person bears within".

Artistic Self-Consciousness: The Art of Hugo's Digressions

The plot summary of *Les Misérables* suggests a melodramatic thriller by Dumas *père* or Eugène Sue. Hugo adopts many conventions from that genre: the evil master of disguises, the mysterious fugitive, daring escapes, self-sacrifice in the name of love. And for whatever reasons, critics seem inclined to condemn as symptoms of Hugo's superficiality the same such motifs and devices that they accept without question and even admire when reading Balzac or Stendhal. But artistic self-consciousness in Hugo is no less intricate than in other great writers; his political experience often is broader than theirs; and his range of characterization (although his novels lack self-confident, assertive women such as Stendhal's Mathilde or Lamiel, Balzac's Eugénie Grandet, or the villainous Cousine Bette) is unquestionably richer. An overview of Hugo's novelistic imagination provides a good starting point for an attempt to do him justice. He combines elements from other traditions into a structure more imposing than those traditions themselves: he possesses a preeminently synthesizing imagination.

This gift shows in the generalizations and aphorisms one finds on nearly every page of *Les Misérables*. Consider the introductory story of the bishop of D———. Hugo observes in passing that "true or false, what is said of people often has as large a place in their lives and especially in their destinies as what they do". And two pages later: "It seems a woman must be a mother to be venerable [instead of merely 'respectable']". Again, "there is always even more wretchedness at the bottom of society than fellow-feeling at the top". Hugo's generalizations, like La Rochefoucauld's two centuries earlier, reflect the traditional belief in a "human nature" that remains invariable, and that implicitly makes the universe revolve around human beings. But Hugo always roots his aphorisms solidly in a social context. He sees people as a medley of potentialities; he emphasizes personal responsibility; yet he understands that the outcome of people's lives often depends on chance, on Providence, or on how they are treated by others. The distinction between the two writers becomes clearer through a brief comparison. Consider La Rochefoucauld's famous maxim: "L'hypocrisie est un hommage que le vice rend à la vertu" [Hypocrisy is a form of respect that vice pays to virtue]. It describes an abstract, unvarying relationship among abstract nouns—hypocrisy, vice, virtue. As we see in the foregoing examples, Hugo, in contrast, describes relationships among real people (what is said or felt about them by others) and the contingencies of individual existences: social (one's reputation), biological (e.g., being a mother), and financial (wealth or poverty). At the same time, in his political subtext, he implicitly urges the French bourgeoisie to stop supporting Napoleon III through their passive acquiescence to the empire, and to strive for the restoration of the republic.

Hugo's historical and cultural digressions set the stage for the characters, explain the limits of their possibilities, and often hint at, foreshadow, or symbolize what he sees as an overarching spiritual odyssey of Fall and Redemption. Unless we sin in thought or deed, as even Bishop Myriel (his name a near-anagram of *lumière*—light or illumination) will do, we cannot benefit from grace and ascend nearer God. William Blake's scandalous slogan "Damn braces; bless relaxes," like Johann Wolfgang von Goethe's concept of Faustian striving and erring as essential to spiritual progress, are earlier, condensed versions of Hugo's theme. These writers do not rebel against God; they reject society's image of a God who demands self-righteousness and conformity.

The most important of Hugo's excursuses within *Les Misérables* are 10 sections concerning (1) "L'Année 1817" (The Year 1817); (2) "Histoire d'un progrès dans les verroteries noires" ("The History of an Improvement in the Manufacture of Small Glassware "); (3) "Waterloo" (2.1); (4) the Convent of the Perpetual Adoration; (5) the street urchin; (6) the underworld; (7) King Louis-Phillipe; (8) slang; (9) the origins of the insurrection of 5–6 June 1832; and (10) and the sewers of Paris. These sections contrast social irresponsibility with social responsibility (1, 2), material pomp and spiritual grandeur (3, 4), the symptoms of social dysfunction in the child and in the adult (5, 6), the summit and the nadir of society (7, 8), and political and metaphorical analyses of social corruption (9, 10). Critics who erroneously believe that Hugo is always tugging at our sleeve and bellowing a moral message in our ear—that he can communicate only through bombast—should ponder the tacit social commentary conveyed by his careful structuring of these 10 digressions. Each of the first three sections of the novel contains two; the one exception—three digressions in part 4 and only one in part 5—can be

explained by Hugo's desire to prepare a climax with a story uninterrupted for the last 200 pages.

"The Year 1817" characterizes the immoral frivolity of the early Restoration period. The remainder of the first part details the horrific consequences of such behavior for the single mother Fantine. The second digression, on the manufacture of glassware, explains how responsible, enlightened capitalism can enrich an entire society—although blind social prejudice against unwed mothers prevents Fantine from benefiting. Throughout, the contrast between reputation and reality underlines social injustice. Hugo shows as much as he tells his opposition to the sexual double standard, and to treating prostitutes as criminals while their clients go free. The wealthy young men of 1817 who abandon their mistresses are respected; their victims are not. Fantine as a streetwalker is despised; M. Batambois, who assaults her by shoving snow down her dress, seems exempt from the law: later, indeed, we find him serving on a jury. Jean Valjean, the escaped convict, is considered a menace to society: but disguised as M. Madeleine, only he can ensure the prosperity of an entire community.

In part 2, Napoleon's self-aggrandizement, disastrous for France, contrasts with the nuns' total self-abnegation. Hugo implies that both attitudes are excessive; but from Jean Valjean's viewpoint, the nuns provide a startling lesson in self-sacrifice beside which his sufferings as a convict appear relatively mild. Part 3 compares the present of abandoned children to their future: the generous-spirited street urchin Gavroche, not yet brutalized by hunger and cold, to the immoral, savage underworld that he eventually would have little choice but to join.

Part 4 contrasts the summit of society, the king, whose conspicuous display creates an icon of social value, with the concealed base whose members are linked by their slang. In a particularly supple movement of thought, Hugo first seems to use a naive reductio ad absurdum to recommend slang as a legitimate object of study. All trades and professions, he says, have their own slang. But then, in a characteristic pirouette, he distinguishes *argot* from other jargons as the language of extreme poverty and a "langue de combat," a means of aggression through language. Language is an aspect of culture, however, Hugo claims, and studying it serves civilization. Through a further distinction, he avoids limiting thieves' cant to one dialect. Several interesting passages treat the differences between slang from different regions of Paris. The author, who claims to know them all, indirectly claims the gift of tongues that ensures universal communication. Nothing human, he implies, no language, high or low, is alien to him. His linguistic virtuosity recalls that of Bishop Myriel, who from the beginning is admired and has access to all his flock because he knows the patois from the various regions of southern France. These gifts of tongues recall Pentecost; the apostolic mission that followed; and, by association, a spiritual meaning latent in the novel.

The last pair of digressions depicts the insurrection of 1832 as resulting from social unrest caused by the unfair treatment of workers, and juxtaposes it with a discussion of the sewers, the physical underpinning of Paris and its culture. Hugo draws an implicit parallel. Unless the sewers are studied, rebuilt, and cleaned out, he argues, they will overflow into the streets above as they have done before. Unless we pay attention to the people, they will rise in rebellion. Flushing fecal matter into rivers poisons our environment and wastes a precious potential resource, Hugo claims; likewise, he implies, locking the poor in prisons poisons society and wastes great potential resources. The naïveté of our wishing always to remain clean and decent by suppressing human waste products is exposed when they contaminate the remainder of society.

Flushing away human wastes symbolizes attempting to conceal all social problems through incarceration—and creating the specious impression that society is making progress by merely changing the words used to refer to our instruments of control. Hugo skewers the euphemistic pseudo-progress that claims to be advancing toward humanitarianism while changing nothing but the words—or worse yet, the arrangement of the words—that describe social conditions: "Formerly those harsh places where prison discipline isolates an inmate were composed of four stone walls, a stone ceiling, a stone floor, a folding bed, a barred skylight, a door reinforced with iron, and were called *dungeons*; but the dungeon came to be considered too horrible; now it's made of an iron door, a barred skylight, a folding bed, a stone floor, a stone ceiling, and four stone walls, and it's called a *punitive detention cell* ".

Syllepsis: A Signpost to Mystery

Hugo's synthesizing imagination associates the material with the spiritual by using syllepsis as a signpost to mystery. This figure of speech uses the same word with two radically different meanings in different contexts; the archetype of Inversion, a more fully developed equivalent of syllepsis, suggests that apparently contrasting values are actually the same phenomenon viewed from opposite directions. Hugo prepares us to understand his first prominent use of syllepsis in *Les Misérables* by introducing it with its expanded form, thematic inversion. Impoverished from having given alms, Bishop Myriel rides into the town of Senez on a donkey. He sees that the mayor is scandalized by his humble mount and hears several bourgeois laughing at him. "I see why you are scandalized," Myriel retorts, "you think it's quite prideful for a poor priest to ride a mount that was Christ's [entering Jerusalem on Palm Sunday]. I assure you that I did so from necessity, not vanity". A page later, Myriel introduces syllepsis through a pun. Teasing his servant Madame Magloire for calling him "Votre Grandeur" [Your Greatness], he asks her to bring him a chair so that he can reach a book on a high shelf, because "my Greatness/height [ma grandeur] doesn't reach to that board".

The same interplay of material and spiritual reappears in a double meaning when Jean Valjean, at Champmathieu's trial at the time of the Restoration, notices a crucifix on the wall of the courtroom. There had been none when he was tried in 1796: "When he was sentenced, God [the physical representation of Christ; the spirit of God] had been absent". Again, when Cosette and Marius are married on Mardi Gras, a carriage full of ribald maskers hired by the government watches their wedding procession go by, and one of them observes "a false *noce* [wedding procession]. *We* are the real *noce* [bawdy orgy]". The riffraff in the carriage consider their material celebration more authentic than a spiritual one. Still later, when Marius offers to use his grandfather's influence to secure a pardon ("grâce") for Jean Valjean, the ex-convict answers, "I need only one kind of pardon/grace, that of my conscience". Human and divine law contrast.

The predominant syllepsis, of course, is that of the title: "misérable" means both "a member of the underclass" and a morally degenerate person. Poverty often brutalizes people, as Hugo is well aware, but he carefully distinguishes material from spiritual disgrace. Once a character identifies himself as a "misérable" (it is only men who do so in this novel), the term already reveals a self-awareness that anticipates regeneration. Once you acknowledge that you are a reprobate in Hugo's world, you wish to start becoming something better. In the context of the novel, the title connotes both the spiritual hypocrisy of blindly condemning others and the enlightenment of morally condemning one-self, which is the starting point on the road of redemptive contrition. Sinners all, we are invited to emulate Jean Valjean. Key words have exceptional importance in Hugo because of the organic worldview that he shares with many fellow romantics: like chromosomes in a living cell (a concept, of course, unknown at the time) each part of Creation reflects the whole, and all is evolving toward an ultimate atonement with God.

By naming four of the five parts of the work after individuals—Fantine, Cosette, Marius, "L'Idylle rue Plumet et l'épopée rue Saint-Denis" (The Love Story of Plumet Street and the Epic of Saint-Denis Street), and Jean Valjean—Hugo links social love-lessness (our lack of *caritas* or commiseration) to our individual, imperative need for love. In order, the four characters named are the working woman fallen to the status of a prostitute to be able to support her daughter; the daughter, rescued from the abusive Thénardiers by Jean Valjean; the young man who loves her, and who as an admirer of Napoleon has been rejected by his monarchist grand-father; and the redeemed ex-convict. The first and last of the four individual names refer to persons of the older generation (symbolizing the social past), who die because they have no one to love them; the middle two names designate people of the younger generation (symbolizing the social future), who survive because they are loved. The remaining section, on " L'Idylle" (meaning, in French, "love story" or "love interest"), deconstructs the simplis-tic dichotomy of past and present by contrasting self-absorbed young love with idealistic self-sacri-fice in the interests of humanity. We need to be loved both as humans and as ourselves.

Hugo and the Idealistic Novel

A useful starting point for vindicating the aes-thetic merits of *Les Misérables* is a provocative distinction made by Naomi Schor in her attempt to rehabilitate the novels of George Sand. Schor di-vides nineteenth-century French novels into two contrasting strains, the realistic and the idealistic. She claims that the idealistic tradition, familiar at the time and whose chief representative was Sand, has been largely forgotten. Sand's originality, Schor claims, marginalized her.

Valuable as Schor's concept has been in reviv-ing interest in Sand, it unfortunately tempts her readers to slip back into a gender-based essentialism: women can be altruistic, but men cannot. Schor

wants to dramatize Sand's achievement, and to that extent her formulations are entirely legitimate; but her view is too limiting in the larger contexts both of romanticism and of the nineteenth century. Balzac, Senancour, Gautier, and even Zola wrote idealis-tic novels; Stendhal's contain idealistic strands; Flaubert's *Trois Contes* correspond to this genre, and there his "Un cœur simple" (A Simple Heart), a tale of obscure sainthood, was inspired by, and written *for*, George Sand.

Enumerating examples and counter-examples, however, will not explain Hugo. More important is that *Les Misérables* deconstructs the opposition of real and ideal by synthesizing them. Hugo's novel repeatedly refers to Providence, grace, prayer, re-demption, and the afterlife. The immortality of the soul is suggested by scenes in which, shortly after they have died, both Fantine and Éponine can understand comforting words said to them, or feel a chaste kiss, and thus can be at peace. Indeed, *Les Misérables* ends by explicitly affirming the after-life, with this sentence referring to Jean Valjean: "No doubt, hidden in shadow, some great angel stood with wings unfurled, waiting for the soul."

Supererogation, the transference of merit be-yond what is required for one's own salvation (in French, *réversibilité*, as in the title of Baudelaire's poem in *Les Fleurs du Mal*), provides a guid-ing thread in *Les Misérables*. Supererogation is a dynamic mode of Inversion, a way of integrat-ing belief in free will with a providentialist fatal-ism. The first example in the work occurs in the "Conventionnel" G—— (a representative of the assembly that dissolved the monarchy, and of which a majority excluding G—— condemned Louis XVI to death). He humbles Bishop Myriel, who recognizes the moral excellence of his devotion to humanity and kneels before him to ask his blessing. "Nobody could say that his encounter with that mind [le Conventionnel's] did not play a role in [the Bishop's] approach to perfection". The blessing is later transferred—so to speak—from Myriel to Valjean, saving the ex-convict from further hatred and crime: "Jean Valjean, my brother, you no longer belong to evil, but to good. It's your soul I am purchasing for you, I'm drawing it away from dark thoughts and from the spirit of perdition, and I'm giving it to God". Valjean symbolically transfers his own excess of merit to the dying Fantine, assuring her that since her motivation for prostituting herself was her pure wish to provide for her daughter, she remained innocent in the eyes of God. And in the final scene, the repentant Marius, kneeling at the dying Valjean's bedside to ask his blessing, recalls the initial scene between the Conventionnel and Myriel.

Hugo broadly signals the presence of supererogatory merit in his characters. First he compares Bishop Myriel to Christ: "When examples were lacking he invented parables, going straight to the point with few words and many images, with the very eloquence of Jesus Christ, full of conviction and persuasive force". Not long afterward, the as yet unredeemed Valjean is sleeping in the bishop's house. When Valjean wakes in the middle of the night, Hugo explains that his unusual last name probably came from the colloquial contraction "v'là Jean" [There's John]. The phrase recalls Pilate's *ecce homo* [There is the man], spoken when he has Christ wearing the crown of thorns brought out to the Jewish priests who have accused him (John 19:5): it suggests a person condemned according to one law, and destined for suffering, but who will be redeemed according to a higher law. At the moment, Valjean outwardly remains quite unregenerate, but the bishop's kindness has already begun to work within his soul.

Hugo picks up the comparison between Valjean and Christ during another night, years later, when the ex-convict struggles against the temptation to allow Champmathieu to be condemned in his place: "Thus this unfortunate soul struggled in anguish. Eighteen hundred years earlier, the mysterious being in whom all the holiness and all the suffering of humanity are summed up had, also, while the olive trees shivered in the fierce wind of the infinite, for a long time pushed aside the fearsome chalice that appeared to him trickling with shadows and overflowing with darkness in the starry depths". Hugo reintroduces the image of the chalice in the title of book 7, part 5, "La Dernière Gorgée du calice" (The Last Draught from the Chalice), and affirms Jean Valjean's total transformation unequivocally from Marius's point of view: the young man begins to recognize Valjean's absolute, self-sacrificial goodness: "The convict was becoming transfigured as the Christ".

Hugo blurs the distinction between Providence and will (in a narratologist's language, between "event" and "act") because he believes that these forces work together. As he describes it, the whole story hinges on the slightest circumstance: if Mme Thénardier had been standing instead of sitting when Fantine first saw her, Fantine would have noticed the innkeeper's colossal size, like that of a strong woman in a carnival, and hesitated to confide her daughter Cosette to her: "A person who is seated instead of standing, destinies hinge on such things". The outcome of the Battle of Waterloo similarly depends on a combination of unpredictable circumstances. Again by chance, Jean Valjean takes refuge with Cosette in what proves to be a convent, where the gardener owes Valjean his life. And destiny brings Cosette and Marius together, Hugo says in so many words; once they are ready, they fall in love at a glance.

Chance seems to reflect a hidden divine intentionality preserving the possibility of freedom, whereas necessity results from human evil and error. But we are mistaken if we hold God, rather than ourselves, responsible for political events. The cynic Grantaire whimsically complains: "Well now, so there's going to be another revolution? I'm astonished that the good Lord should have such limited resources. At every moment, He has to set about greasing the tracks of events again. Something's sticking, it's not working. Quick, a revolution. The good Lord's hands are always black with that nasty sort of grease". But where society is concerned, Enjolras, the idealistic leader of the insurrection of 1832, adopts a more responsible, proactive view. "The law of progress is that monsters give way to angels, and that Fatality dissipates in the face of Fraternity". Suffering, violence, and injustice will be eliminated by *philia,* by a community of active mutual concern. Hugo, nevertheless, offers a realistic image of political change: one finds only a few committed militants on either side; others are drawn in through love, affection, anxiety, greed, or hatred.

Once he has been redeemed, Jean Valjean's attitudes are shaped by his overarching faith in Providence, by an active passivity that blends act and event. His conviction that God is with him is explicit in the sewers, and the narrator endorses his view. "Sometimes happenstance compels us to assume duties," he says during his confession to Marius as he tries to explain how a brutal convict could become a loving father to an orphan girl. The melodramatic convergence of the destinies of the orphan Pip and the escaped convict Magwitch in Dickens's *Great Expectations* (1861; see chapters 54 and 56), comes to mind: there too, the orphan appreciates his benefactor's devotion only as the latter dies.

Hugo's own faith in Providence appears in the parallels he implies. Devoting his life to Cosette allows Jean Valjean to atone for his crime toward another child, the little chimney sweep. "M. Madeleine" cannot fully assuage his guilt by giving alms to chimney sweeps who pass through his town. The opportunity for a definitive expiation—first rescuing Cosette and later accepting her loss—is presented to him as if by accident. Marius is redeemed when he manages to arrive at his surrogate father-in-law's bedside before Jean Valjean dies, whereas he did not arrive at his real father Pontmercy's bedside on time, being too indifferent to check into the coach schedules. Such interconnected motifs contribute to the structural rhetoric of the implied author, whose plot seems to reflect a divine plan. Each structure in *Les Misérables* always contains a strand of actual or potential redemption.

The Realism of Hugo's Moral Vision

So far we have been characterizing Hugo's idealism. In general, critics are aware of it, if not of its place in a broad tradition. But they have been less aware of his realism, and still less aware of how realism and idealism in Hugo are interconnected. He is not vapidly optimistic; his concept of Providence always preserves a dimension of human responsibility that can alter an outcome. The three "fatalities" he identifies in the preface to *Les Travailleurs de la mer* (that of nature in *Les Travailleurs de la mer*, that of religious dogma in *Notre-Dame de Paris*, that of social inequities in *Les Misérables*) are expressions of unreasoning instinct (recall that for Hugo, nature is sentient). Humans must remain in an unenlightened state to be able to exercise free will and work out their redemption. Hugo's moral complexity appears when he describes how Jean Valjean learns to read and write while in prison. Although Hugo associates education with the light that dispels darkness, he acknowledges that education can reinforce evil by empowering the evildoer: "He went to school at age forty, and learned to read, to write, to do arithmetic. He sensed that to strengthen his intellect was to strengthen his hatred. Sometimes, education and enlightenment can serve as an extension [like an extra leaf in a table] for evil". On the contrary, even the arch-villain of the novel, unlike the villain of melodrama, might not have become irremediably bad:

> Thénardier was one of those dual beings who sometimes pass among us unrecognized and disappear without having become known, because destiny has shown only one side of them. The fate of many people is to live half-submerged in this way. In a calm, monotonous situation Thénardier had everything necessary to act like—we won't say, to be—what society has generally agreed to call an honest businessman, a

solid middle-class person. Simultaneously, given certain circumstances, certain shocks that could stir up his lower self, he possessed all the qualities needed to become a scoundrel. He was a shopkeeper with a monster inside.

Hugo depicts his characters' moral progress realistically: revelation comes to them in stages, not total and instantaneous like the vision to Saul on the Damascus Road (Acts 9:1–20). Jean Valjean illustrates spiritual progress; Marius, political enlightenment. Raised an unreflective royalist (like Hugo himself, who lends some of his life story to this character), Marius discovers too late how much his father had loved him. He learns to admire Napoleon, the master whom his father served. "His ideas underwent an extraordinary change. The phases of this change were numerous and successive". Many people in his generation, Hugo adds, underwent similar transformations in their political outlook. Marius now realizes that the republic restored their civil rights to the masses, and that the empire restored the rights of France in Europe. He could not but approve. What had seemed the fall of the monarchy now appeared to him the rise of France. What had seemed sunset proved to be the dawn.

When Marius begins associating with the republican "Amis de l'A B C" (Friends of the Alphabet/of the "Abaissé" [the oppressed masses; the pun implies that education fosters social progress]), he is startled by their lack of veneration for Napoleon. "Having abandoned his grandfather's opinions to adopt those of his father, he had believed himself settled in his mind; now he suspected, uneasily and without daring to admit it to himself, that he was not. The angle from which he viewed everything was again beginning to shift". At length he forces the issue, addressing his new friends with a lyrical encomium of the emperor: "To vanquish, dominate, strike like thunder, to be in Europe a kind of nation gilded by glory, to sound a titanic fanfare in history, to conquer the world twice, by conquest and by dazzling others, that is sublime; and what could be grander?—To be free, said Combeferre". Hearing this retort, Marius feels what the earth must feel when it is pierced by an iron rod so that the grain of wheat may be deposited in it, Hugo explains: only the wound. The quickening of the seed and the joy of bearing fruit come only later. The adversity of poverty will temper his soul.

The crucial moment of Marius's political evolution arrives as he prepares to join his friends at the barricade. He mistakenly thinks Cosette has abandoned him; he wishes to die. But he feels shame when imagining how his father would feel: a hero, who had often risked his life for France, would abhor the son who contributed to plunging his country into civil war. Stimulated by imminent death, Marius has a sudden illumination. Because of the insurrection he will join, "France will bleed, but liberty will smile". A war against injustice cannot be defined by national boundaries. "In short, to reestablish social truth [human equality], to restore the throne [of France] to freedom, to restore the people to the people, to restore sovereignty to humanity … what cause more just, and in consequence, what grander war?".

When the novel ends, Marius has just learned to recognize the spiritual grandeur of Jean Valjean, but he has not yet learned to apply that lesson to society: "He found it self-evident that certain violations of written law should be followed by eternal punishment, and he accepted, as an instrument of civilization, social damnation. He was still at that point, except that his opinions would inevitably evolve later, since he was naturally good, and fundamentally composed entirely of latent progress". After the death of Marius's political companions on the barricade, he never mentions them again. Has he forgotten them and their cause? Hugo leaves Marius morally unfinished in the novel, as he leaves the work of revolution politically unfinished. By selecting the abortive uprising of 1832 as his subject, Hugo avoids a triumphalist perspective that would leave us satisfied that no further progress toward justice was necessary. Such open-endedness solicits our involvement in the society and politics of the future. Losing a battle—the situation in which the exiled Hugo finds himself—does not mean losing the war. Enjolras's metaphor that a revolution is a toll implies not only that rebellion has its costs but also that when you have paid them, you have not yet crossed the bridge.

Hugo's Political Views

Regarding social progress in general, Hugo is optimistic. He shows Jean Valjean, alias M. Madeleine, reading at every meal. Hugo himself once claimed that 20 years of good free mandatory education would be the last word and raise the dawn. Having become a utopian socialist like M. Madeleine, Hugo thinks that salaries will increase naturally as do profits, and that the dynamism of capital expansion will naturally resolve the problems of workers' conditions. To be fair to Hugo, one must

realize that in 1862 an organized proletariat had not yet formed, although it was foreshadowed by a workers' uprising in Lyons in 1832. Labor union movements as such had not yet developed. Hugo still thinks that guidance and enlightenment must descend on the people from "above," from the intelligentsia.

Hugo often plays with the reader, drawing us into making hasty, conventional judgments that seem to agree with his. He then withdraws from such positions with a pirouette, leaving us to confront our own superficiality. After admitting that the rabble (*la canaille*) sometimes fights blindly against the common good, he says that he uses words such as "rabble" only with pain and respect, "for when philosophy gets to the bottom of the facts to which such words correspond, it often finds greatness next to wretchedness there. … The rabble followed Jesus Christ".

Nor does he blindly espouse one political solution as definitive. Instead, his trenchant political analyses reveal the aporias, the unresolvable difficulties one encounters by adopting either of two opposed positions, which as it happens are those of liberal Democrats and conservative Republicans in the United States today:

All the problems that the Socialists address can be reduced to two main problems. First problem: To produce wealth. Second problem: To distribute it.…

England resolves the first of these two problems. She creates wealth admirably well; she distributes it badly … [She has] an ill-composed grandeur made up of every material element but lacking any moral element.

Communism and land reform believe they can solve the second problem. They are mistaken. Their [egalitarian] distribution kills [incentive for] production. Sharing equally eliminates the spirit of competition. And consequently, the desire to work. It's a distribution accomplished by the butcher, who kills what he divides.

Hugo suggests a balance of these two extreme solutions, socialism and mercantilism.

Thus he characteristically deconstructs naively categorical views that risk blocking compromise and solution. He contests the dichotomies of middle class and lower class, of police and criminals. He argues that the bourgeoisie is simply the materially satisfied portion of "the people," and that on the other hand the mob can betray the best interests of "the people" through unthinking violence. He explains that Javert's unreasoning moral rigidity prevents him from realizing that the police are always infiltrated by criminal double agents such as Claquesous, who disappears from the police wagon while on the way to prison: "Did that sphinxlike man have his forepaws in crime and his hind paws in authority? Javert wouldn't hear of such combinations, but there were other inspectors on his squad, perhaps more knowing than he although he outranked them, and Claquesous was such a villain that he could be a very fine agent".

Similarly, Hugo attacks the divine-right monarchists for criticizing the king because he is insufficiently royalist, and the pope because he is insufficiently papal. Such fanatical supporters undermine their cause. They prevent their leaders from making the adaptive compromises that would allow them and the institutions that they represent to survive.

Insofar as he represents the working classes enslaved by the ancien régime, Jean Valjean had in Hugo's eyes been too brutalized and debased to enter the current of historical progress through militant political action. But his destiny prefigures an eventual reconciliation of social classes foreseen by Hugo: the ex-convict presides over the marriage of Cosette—the proletarian daughter of a prostitute—and Marius, the aristocrat adopted by the bourgeois Gillenormand. Nevertheless, Cosette herself does not participate in, or even know about, the insurrection. Hugo implies that we must await Cosette and Marius's children (foreshadowed by the courageous street urchin Gavroche killed fighting on the barricades) to find a full embodiment of the spirit of the new France.

Why choose the obscure revolt of 1832 rather than the glorious revolution of 1830 as the historical crux of the novel? Hugo was struck by the historian Louis Blanc's account of the 1832 uprising. He borrowed most of his facts from Blanc. Creating a practical manual for revolutionaries or celebrating a particular historical triumph interested Hugo less than providing a symbolic illustration of the French people struggling toward the light. From the viewpoint of eternity, as Hugo sees things, minor events (such as 1832) as well as major ones (such as 1830) may reveal the intentions of Providence. The self-sacrifice of Enjolras and his friends will serve to mobilize others. Like Berthold Brecht, Hugo does not want to serve up a cathartic, triumphalist (as the French say) vision of history: he prefers to imply that much work remains to be done.

Source: Laurence M. Porter, "The Masterpiece: *Les Miserables*," in *Victor Hugo,* Twayne Publishers, 1999, pp. 127–50.

Angelo Metzidakis

Les Miserables is interpreted by author Angelo Metzidakis as a "selective reading of French history."

In *Les Misérables*, Hugo presents a very selective reading of nineteenth-century French history in order to convince the bourgeoisie of the Second Empire of the virtues of republicanism. Hugo's historical commentary underscores the unwitting role that the bourgeois class had played in the development of republicanism in France as a means to persuade his readers that conscious opposition to the government of Napoleon III would serve their own interests as well as those of France as a whole. Hugo's reading of French history contains an implicit critique of the Second Empire during the early 1860s. By praising various aspects of political life during the Restoration and the July Monarchy in his novel, Hugo makes oblique references to specific changes in contemporary political life which he deplores. In this way, he educates his readers with respect to their political opportunities in the hope that they will renounce their tacit collusion with the regime of Napoleon III by taking action through the political process.

The bulk of Hugo's commentary centers on two dates: 1814, the year of Napoleon's first abdication and of the first Bourbon Restoration and, 1830, the year of the July Revolution and of the rise to power of Louis Philippe. Both of these dates represent stages of political transition during which the powers of the throne were diminished in favor of the bourgeoisie which, in each case, prolonged the monarchy for the sake of national stability.

In a discussion on the result of the July Revolution, Hugo draws a parallel between the events of 1814 and 1830 in order to underscore the bourgeois role in them:

> Qui arrête les révolutions à mi-côte? La bourgeoisie. Pourquoi? Parce que la bourgeoisie est l'intérêt arrivé à la satisfaction. Hier c'était l'appétit, aujourd'hui c'est la plénitude, demain ce sera la satiété. Le même phénomène de 1814 après Napoléon se reproduisit en 1830 après Charles X. On a voulu, à tort, faire de la bourgeoisie une classe. La bourgeoisie est tout simplement la portion contentée du peuple. Le bour-

The storming of the Bastille, one of the most significant events in the French Revolution. Eponine and many other revolutionaries died in defense of the Bastille and the freedom it symbolized.

geois, c'est l'homme qui a maintenant le temps de s'asseoir. Une chaise n'est pas une caste. Mais, pour vouloir s'asseoir trop tôt, on peut arrêter la marche même du genre humain. Cela a été souvent la faute de la bourgeoisie. On n'est pas une classe parce qu'on fait une faute. L'égoïsme n'est pas une des divisions de l'ordre social.

Hugo describes 1814 and 1830 as "halts," moments during which the bourgeoisie consolidated its gains and forces in view of further progress at some more auspicious moment in the future. At the time, republicanism was seen as a threat against which a weakened throne was a safeguard. It seemed that the monarchy would preserve liberal policies that would assure national stability.

Hugo's commentary on 1814 and 1830 has negative implications for the political situation in which the original readers of *Les Misérables* found themselves. Although the aspirations of the bourgeoisie in the early 1860s had not changed, the government of Napoleon III was no longer the guarantor of liberalism and stability. As the Second Empire had already begun its gradual decline, government opposition grew on many fronts. For example, the industrialists were alienated by Napoleon III's free trade agreements with Britain, and the Catholics were furious with his military involvement in Italian affairs which touched off the "Roman Question". Faced with such growing opposition, Napoleon III changed his despotic policies for more liberal ones in order to gain support. Unfortunately, his politically motivated liberalism only gave more ground to the Opposition and fostered political activity among the French.

Having intimated that support of Napoleon III is no longer in the interest of the bourgeoisie, Hugo shifts the focus of his historical criticism to the early years of the Second Empire. Two of Hugo's remarks, one concerning the Bourbons, the other Louis Philippe, are of particular interest in this context since they amount to indirect accusations of Napoleon III's rule during the authoritarian phase of the Second Empire which had entered into its so-called "liberal" phase only a few years prior to the publication of *Les Misérables*. Given this time frame, the reader cannot possibly ignore Hugo's intent.

In his first critical remark, Hugo favorably stresses the relative liberties that prevailed during the Restoration until the signing of the July Ordinances:

> [C]'est sous Louis XVIII et Charles X que vint le tour de parole de l'intelligence. Le vent cessa, le flambeau se ralluma. On vit frissonner sur les cimes sereines la pure lumière des esprits. Spectacle magnifique, utile et charmant. On vit travailler pendant quinze ans, en pleine paix, en pleine place publique, ces grands principes, si vieux pour le penseur, si nouveaux pour l'homme d'état: l'égalité devant la loi, la liberté de la conscience, la liberté de la parole, la liberté de la presse, l'accessibilité de toutes les aptitudes à toutes les fonctions. Cela alla ainsi jusqu'en 1830.

The "flambeau de l'intelligence" that shone on France from on high is Hugo's main concern here. He is referring to the "sacred" tribune of the Chamber of Deputies in which long parliamentary debates were fought between the Liberals and the Ultraroyalists during public sessions throughout the Restoration. Napoleon III suppressed such free debate during which the will of the people, as expressed by the Liberals, was heard and not without effect. Clearly, by extolling selected aspects of past political life, Hugo is emphasizing the fact that the first nine years of the Second Empire was a period of dictatorial rule during which the legislature was gagged and powerless.

❝It should be remembered, however, that the bourgeois reader of <u>Les Misérables</u> needed no . . . reminders since many of the practices of the despotic regime were still in recent memory: wide press censorship, unconstrained government spending, official lists of approved candidates for elections, and the arbitrary arrest and deportation of many persons suspected of antigovernment activity after Orsini's attack on Napoleon III.❞

Furthermore, the history of the tribune from the French Revolution until its destruction by Louis Napoleon's coup d'état is detailed in the fifth book of *Napoléon le Petit* entitled "Parlementarisme". One typically Hugolian sentence from the ninth chapter of this book, "La Tribune détruite," suffices to revive Hugo's incisive criticism of Napoleon III which is shrouded under the veil of historical commentary in *Les Misérables*:

> Donc 'le parlementarisme', c'est-à-dire la garantie des citoyens, la liberté de discussion, la liberté de la presse, la liberté individuelle, le contrôle de l'impôt, la clarté dans les recettes et dans les dépenses, ... la liberté de conscience, la liberté des cultes, le point d'appui de la propriété, le recours contre les confiscations et les spoliations, la sécurité de chacun, le contrepoids à l'arbitraire, la dignité de la nation, ... tout cela n'est plus.

It should be remembered, however, that the bourgeois reader of *Les Misérables* needed no such reminders since many of the practices of the despotic regime were still in recent memory: wide press censorship, unconstrained government spending, official lists of approved candidates for elections, and the arbitrary arrest and deportation of many persons suspected of antigovernment activity after Orsini's attack on Napoleon III.

A second indirect accusation of Napoleon III is found in Hugo's appreciation of Louis Philippe's apparent good faith in his ascendance to the throne:

> Louis-Philippe était entré dans l'autorité royale sans violence, sans action directe de sa part, par le fait d'un virement révolutionnaire, ... dans lequel lui, duc d'Orléans, n'avait aucune initiative personnelle. Il était né prince et se croyait élu roi. Il ne s'était point donné à lui-même ce mandat; il ne l'avait point pris; on le lui avait offert et il l'avait accepté; convaincu, à tort certes, mais convaincu que l'offre était selon le droit et que l'acceptation était selon le devoir.

Hugo's characterization of Louis Philippe dramatically underscores the extent of Louis Napoleon's bad faith while preparing the rise of the Second Empire: once elected President of the Second Republic, on the strength of his Napoleonic ancestry, he intended to remain in power, no matter what the cost. He began by manipulating the "Parti de l'Ordre" in order to crush the democratic movement of the Republicans. After failing in his attempt to revise the Constitution so as to permit his reelection, his last recourse was the coup d'état. After having exploited this chaotic situation by evoking the threat of the "spectre rouge," Louis Napoleon polled the Frenchmen on an exacting plebiscite: "Le peuple français veut le maintien de l'autorité de Louis-Napoléon Bonaparte et lui délègue les pouvoirs nécessaires pour faire une constitution." That is how Louis Napoleon legitimized his cause, procured his new mandate, and became Napoleon III on the first anniversary of the coup d'état which conveniently coincided with the date of the great battle of Austerlitz.

Hugo's limited presentation of the Restoration and of the July Monarchy makes the bourgeois readers aware of their unwitting participation in France's political transformations. Their political strength grew under the rule of the "legitimate" Bourbons and continued to do so under the "illegitimate" duc d'Orléans, "le roi citoyen," the bourgeois king. One very real aspect of their power was the national guard which was organized in March 1831. It was a bourgeois army, a type of police force, whose function was to protect Louis Philippe's regime from its adversaries. When its support of the July Monarchy ended in 1848, the regime collapsed. What followed was the troubled Second Republic during which the interests of the French people were split into two antagonistic groups: the bourgeois, along with the peasants, versus the workers, the truly afflicted class. The former group was horrified by the latter, while the latter hated the former. This marks the beginning of the counterproductive or, to use more lenient language, the "irresponsible" role of the bourgeois in French society. From this point on, Hugo's moral instruction of the bourgeois, his plea for the spirit of revolution and Christianity in the service of the ideal—and therefore of the people—is applicable.

In Les Misérables, Hugo's interest in the Second Republic is limited to a discussion of the socialist insurrection of June 1848. The complexity of this situation, which required bourgeois participation, is clear in the following passage: "Juin 1848 fut ... un fait à part, et presque impossible à classer dans la philosophie de l'histoire. ... [C]ette émeute extraordinaire où l'on sentit la sainte anxiété du travail réclamant ses droits. Il fallut la combattre, et c'était le devoir, car elle attaquait la République. Mais, au fond, que fut juin 1848? Une révolte du peuple contre lui-même". Although the "duty" of the bourgeois was to save the Republic from mounting socialist protest and disorder, these stringent measures could have been avoided had the government had the will to initiate legislation that could have eased the poverty-stricken condition of the workers. The need for such legislation was chronic because the French economic crisis, which had begun during the July Monarchy, worsened during the Second Republic, especially after the February Revolution. Socialist agitation had brought commerce to a virtual standstill.

In order to discredit the Socialists—and, in particular, Louis Blanc, theoretician of *L'Organisation du travail*—the provisional government intentionally founded a warped version of the "Ateliers nationaux". When these workshops proved to be obvious failures, the government closed them, ordering indigent workers either to join the army, or to leave for work in the provinces. The barricades of the June Revolt, "l'acropole des va-nu-pieds," arose from this tragic situation. The bourgeois and the peasants were ready for order, even if it meant Louis Napoleon's order: the suppression of the Republic and of its ideals. They would be content if material order were restored, but would they remain content if moral order were not also restored in the long run? The question of moral grandeur, inspired by the contemplation of the ideal, is crucial to Hugo's argument against the premises of the Second Empire. Hugo does not situate this grandeur with the bourgeois position, but rather with the socialist one. The Socialists were directly concerned with the social issues that the politically oriented bourgeoisie wanted to ignore. By analyzing the abortive revolt of 1832 and the temporarily successful one of 1848, Hugo presents his reader with the ideal side of the socialist position. He disengages its lofty goals from its violent acts by characterizing the insurrectionists as "essayeurs de l'avenir" whose aim was to build a truly equitable republic in which global growth would be uninhibited by artificial means.

Hugo's advocacy of the ideals of the revolution of 1848 constitutes a call for political action that seems to have been heard by his readers of the Second Empire. The legislative elections of 1863, approximately one year after the publication of *Les Misérables*, established a sizeable anti-Empire group within the government thanks to the growing idea of an "union libérale". This wide-ranging shift in public opinion, gradual though it was, raised the moral consciousness of the bourgeois who, during the regime of silence, had rather apathetically concerned themselves with material considerations.

The reason for Hugo's interest in the bourgeois reader, especially in the young generation that had matured during the Empire, is quite simple. This group, having been given a certain education and culture, was the most receptive to what he called the peaceful "philosophie de la révolution" which is, in short, ideal republicanism. Up until Napoleon III's rise to power, republican ideals were associated with the violent anarchy and militant socialism surrounding 1832 and 1848. During the period that preceded the Second Empire, the workers who revolted, "les barbares de la civilisation," received "la souterraine éducation de l'émeute" which was, judging from Enjolras' speech to the insurgents of 1832, a course in the force of the ideal without any concern for its implementation through peaceful means. The bourgeois, among others, was to receive later a similar form of education beginning with the brief, but violent repression that followed the coup d'état. The education of the bourgeois in the value of the ideal was to be much slower and, so to speak, more reasoned than had been the case for the insurgents of the Republic.

The role of *Les Misérables* in the "subterranean" education of the bourgeois can be seen in Hugo's evaluation of the political and social climate of France in the early 1830s. To a great extent, this historical description is applicable to the 1860s, with the difference that the bourgeois is called upon to act "appropriately" against the Empire:

> Entre l'attaque du passé et l'attaque de l'avenir, l'établissement de juillet se débattait. ... Une harmonie voulue à contre-sens est souvent plus onéreuse qu'une guerre. De ce lourd conflit, toujours muselé, mais toujours grondant, naquit la paix armée, ce ruineux expédient de la civilisation suspecte à elle-même. ... Cependant, à l'intérieur, paupérisme, prolétariat, salaire, éducation, pénalité, prostitution, sort de la femme, richesse, misère, production, consommation, répartition, échange, monnaie, crédit, droit du capital, droit du travail, toutes les questions se multipliaient au-dessus de la société; surplomb terrible. En dehors des partis proprement dits, un autre mouvement se manifestait.

Clearly, "la paix armee" is an indictment of Napoleon III's "peaceful" Empire which began warring early on; for example, the Crimean War in 1854, the war in Italy in 1859, and the beginning of the ruinous Mexican Involvement in 1861–1862. Furthermore, the economic factors concerning monies, credits, capital investment, and the like, all point to Napoleon III's financial ventures which, although having done much for the nation's economy and prestige, did much less for the workers. This produced a cleavage between the bourgeois and the workers, the "misérables" of the Second Empire, that is referred to indirectly in the previous passage by the relative terms: "paupérisme, ... salaire, éducation, pénalité, prostitution, sort de la femme, richesse, misère." In the 1860s, all of these factors taken together produced a new movement in France, a movement that was to form a coalition that would cut across party lines, namely the Opposition. If Hugo addressed the bourgeois element of this growing opposition, he did so in the hope that its members would channel their efforts and influence towards the building of the Republic that they had once scorned, the same Republic that the majority of the Opposition was still against.

Hugo's selective rereading of French history in *Les Misérables* presents a multifaceted analysis of the republican ideal that goes far in the education of its bourgeois reader. While it is true that the social question posed by the "misérables" has a moral dimension that transcends the time frame of the novel, Hugo's political intent—his credo—is very specific and posits the political inevitability of the Republic. In short, Hugo maintains that if bourgeois readers become politically active, they will thereby reconcile their power with their moral obligations, and thus join the revolutionary movement of which they are part with the truly Christian fervor (in Hugo's sense) that blind "égoïsme" had previously dampened. Conversely, if they do not act, they will be an "obstacle" to be done away with when the Republic is at hand. This is Hugo's message to his readers of the Second Empire, and this is precisely the wider, political point of view to which he alludes at the end of his preface to *Les Misérables*: "… en d'autres termes, et à un point de vue plus étendu encore, tant qu'il y aura sur la terre ignorance et misère, des livres de la nature de celui-ci pourront ne pas être inutiles".

Source: Angelo Metzidakis, "On Rereading French History in Hugo's *Les Miserables*," in *The French Review,* Vol. 67, No. 2, December, 1993, pp. 187–95.

T. W. M.

In the following excerpt from a review of Part 1 of Les Miserables, *this anonymous reviewer gives the story unqualified praise.*

[*Les Misérables*] is the greatest and most elaborate work of Victor Hugo's fruitful genius…. A novel, in the ordinary acceptation of that term, [*Fantine*] is *not*. The ordinary novel, according to Carlyle, is a "tale of adventures which did *not* occur in God's creation, but only in the Waste Chambers, (to be let unfurnished,) of certain human heads, and which are part and parcel of the Sum of No-things; which, nevertheless, obtain some temporary remembrance, and lodge extensively, at this epoch of the world, in similar still more unfurnished chambers." These productions have wonderful plots and still more wonderful machinery. *Fantine* has simply dramatic situations, and therefore *Fantine* is no novel. *They* are remarkable for many words and few ideas; every page of *Fantine* contains some beautiful thought, poetically expressed, or some brilliant passage upon Life, Law, Religion, or Philosophy; hence *Fantine* is not a novel. People with waste chambers, (to let unfurnished,) need not read it; it was never written for them. But to the thinker it will be a solace and delight, albeit its lessons may excite some saddened reflections in sympathetic minds.

We have stated that *Fantine* had not the plot of the ordinary novel; but dramatic situations, instead. Let us add, that the work is composed of a series of brilliant pictures, boldly touched off by a master-hand, as in the case of the great works of Niccola Poussin and Claude Loraine…. There is not in the literature of fiction a finer portraiture than that given of [M. Charles François Bienvenu Myriel, Bishop of D—]. His every trait of character, objective and psychological, is elaborately depicted. It is, for several pages of the book, a lone sketch, nothing to heighten the interest thereof save two old virtuous ladies of his household; who are about as important to the theme, as the occasional and indifferent tree in some of Raphael's paintings. It is quite as powerful and much more elaborate, yet not quite so fearful or mysterious, but far more genial and beautiful in type than, Byron's grand portrait of *Lara*; and equally well sustained in power throughout. But the character of Lara is dark and gloomy; that of M. Myriel radiant with spiritual beauty. We are permitted to look, not only upon the objective form and actions of the man, but as if his mind were spread open to view, we have a full revelation of his psychology—we gaze into the divine depths of his immortal soul. Indeed so beautiful is the moral portraiture of that simple but good man, that one of our contemporaries has pronounced such a being an impossibility! We cannot think so—and if mistaken, our historic lessons, standard of ideal virtue, and belief in the true, beautiful and good, must have rested upon shifting sands…. But conceding the supposed fact, that we err—surely it is highly creditable to the genius of M. Hugo, that out of the depths of his contemplation he could create an Ideal Character, so perfect as to be an impossibility in humanity; a concession which, however, must greatly reflect upon, and detract from, the boasted grandeur of the human soul.

But, be this as it may, two personages of opposite opinions are brought in contact with the Bishop—one, a Senator, and the other, a Conventioner, persecuted by the ruling power which succeeded to the French Revolution. The former is a kind of little Atheist—a scoffer at the established forms of religion, after the manner of Voltaire. The latter is a bold intellectualist; a master of the syllogistic forms of logic; a dogmatic denunciator of legitimacy and royalty; and a mystic in Deism. In detailing the particulars of M. Myriel's interviews with these men, Victor Hugo has carried to its highest point of delicacy, that civilization in Art, which pervades modern French authorship. The Atheist's sneers against revealed religion, is treated with respectful silence, or returned only with Christian pity. The bold sallies and loud declamations of the old Conventioner, are met with pastoral humility until he is half subdued. And when death is about to close his eyes, the good Bishop is his only friend—the only witnesser of his spirit's flight. It is as if the Lion had made of the Lamb its confidant and friend. This is the place to remark, however, that Senator and Conventioner, are simply machinery whereby lessons upon life, history, and morality are promulged; as with many of the seemingly nonessential characters in Goethe's *Faust.* ...

[We] do not hesitate to pronounce [*Les Misérables*] the ablest novel—after Goethe's *Welhelm Meister*—of this century.

Certain supercilious young gentlemen, of most questionable principles, and certain publicists of still more questionable morals, think it fashionable and brilliant to decry *Les Misérables* as an immoral book; simply because they have not the brains to understand it. To us, it is a Bible in the fictitious literature of the nineteenth century. To them, it is merely a translation of a French novel; and all France is but *their* second Sodom: we know that France is *not* morally worse than America. To them, it is a production by Victor Hugo; to us it is a protest of genius against universal crimes—the plea of one who advocates, in the face of obloquy and contumely, the cause of the Life-Wretched. To them, it is a proclamation of war against society; to us, it is a grand sermon in behalf of primitive Christianity—a splendid endeavour to have Christendom permeated by the rules and regulations of the "Church and House Book of the Early Christians," and of the "Law-Book of the Ante-Nicene Church." To them, it is massive, grand, unusual, and incomprehensible; to us, it is beautiful as the *Iliad* of Homer—real as a play by Shakespeare. *Les Misérables* is an event—it is a new jewel in the literary crown of our century....

[*Les Misérables*] should awaken the conscience of society from its dismal lethargy of evil. For it is profound, straight-forward, and marvelously eloquent. "But then, it is a French novel"—say its critics. So much the better, is our response; because it is greater than all of the English novels, gathered together and massed into one, which have appeared during the past quarter of a century. "But," repeat its critics, "it contains exaggerations." No doubt of it; we admit the fact. But are there not exaggerations in all novels? Was there ever one printed that contained them not? Are there not ... more absurdities and vulgar caricatures in [Dickens's] *Great Expectations,* than there could be found in so many of such books as *Les Misérables,* as would sink the Great Eastern? *A French novel*! Is this phrase used as a term of reproach, applicable to the literature of

> ".. .every page of <u>Fantine</u> contains some beautiful thought, poetically expressed, or some brilliant passage upon Life, Law, Religion, or Philosophy; hence <u>Fantine</u> is not a novel."

the most civilized and cultivated empire upon the globe? If so, is the novel, or its ignorant assailant, to be blamed—and which? Why the latter. Who is the French Novelist, and what is the French Novel? The one, is a scholar of genius and refinement; the other, a reflex of life and society. What English writers—what American writers—can be compared with such authors, in points of power and art, as Victor Hugo, Alfred de Musset, Alphonse Karr, Edmund About, Emile Souvestre, Octave Feuillet, Alexandre Dumas, Michelet and Sue? Here are no contortionists—no forced humorists—no retailers of vulgar and far-fetched wit—no writers of dreary, idealess wilderness-pages; but gentlemen of power, large and well digested observation, polished wit, noble satire, keen irony, and great Philosophy.... [To] such as find fault with Hugo's humble characters, we would say: first remove Reynold's Dunghill, or clean out Dickens's Augean stables. If they think that the Frenchman crushes society, why, let them the more enjoy Thackeray's crunching and mastication of it. Or if they dislike Jean Valjean, because he was a reformed criminal, then let them revel in the irreclaimable hideousness of Bulwer's Villains. For there are no graceless scamps or vagabonds in the chambers of M. Hugo's mind. His most infamous creation has some principle of homogeneity left; but the vagabond of one English novel, like the sinner of Jonathan Edwards' theology, is past redemption. In short, the French novel is civilization; the English novel affectation—semi-nude barbarism. It is not, however, much to the credit of our vaunted enlightenment, that the greatest of recent Fictions—this very *Les Misérables* —should have been but poorly received by the press.... [It] is safe to say, at the least, that another so grandly brilliant a book, of its class, will not appear in the lifetime of the youngest of this generation!

Source: T. W. M., Review of "Les Miserables-Fantine," in *The Southern Literary Messenger,* July, 1863, pp. 434–46.

Edward Sagarin

In the following excerpt, Sagarin argues that Valjean fails as a symbol of redemption because his crime—stealing a loaf of bread for his sister's children—was an act of altruism.

[What delineates Jean Valjean in *Les Misérables*] is the essential innocence of the man. If he were innocent only in the sense of having been falsely accused, his would be a different tale, and probably one with far less significance for us. Jean Valjean does indeed commit the act that sends him to the galleys and that is the beginning of his downfall. Hugo's supreme indictment of society—for this *is* an indictment of society (he was a forerunner of Zola and other novelists who saw themselves as social critics)—lies in the nature of the act which his hero has perpetrated and for which he is imprisoned. Literally, Jean Valjean is guilty of stealing a loaf of bread.

It would appear that such an act would ordinarily evoke only sympathy and hence require no further mitigation in order for an author to exculpate his "criminal" and to paint him as the purest and most saintly of all beings (one is almost compelled to use quotation marks around *criminal,* so that Hugo's relentless efforts to remind the reader of Valjean's goodness are rendered with integrity). To this end, the taking of the loaf of bread is an almost perfect transgression, and the breaking of the law is justified or at least extenuated by the forces of hunger, poverty, and the execrable social conditions that followed the counterrevolution in France. But Hugo goes even further than this, and in so doing betrays a weakness not only in the literary work but in the social criticism: it is not for himself and his own stomach that Jean Valjean commits a theft. He does not even so much as expect to taste a morsel of the stolen bread. It is for his sister's children, young, fatherless, and hungry, that he becomes a thief. So two factors are here at work, and as they follow the reader throughout the five volumes that make up this novel, they detract from each other rather than act symbiotically to strengthen the motifs: there is the social indictment, and there is the criminal as saint.

Starting with the criminal as victim, Hugo continues with the criminal (or more accurately the exconvict) as the embodiment of virtue. He is the penitent incarnate, but he has never done wrong and has nothing for which to repent. Over and over he redeems himself. Without a blemish on his past, however, the redemption is ill-placed. What emerges, from the viewpoint of the social critic, and in contrast with other great literary images of the transgressor, is a series of unintended ambiguities, with messages not as clearly drawn as are even the one-dimensional characters who inhabit the novel.

If Jean Valjean is going to be painted as pure and saintly, and he is, the theft from the bishop and a subsequent incident with a little boy from whom he takes a coin are the blemishes—these, and not the stealing of the loaf of bread. Through the many years to follow until the last moments of his life, and through the countless pages and the episodes, coincidences, acts of strength, heroism, and sacrifice, there will be nothing but these two acts that are short of Christlike purity. What is Hugo telling us, then, when so good a person as his hero steals first from the bishop and then from the boy Gervais? That it is prison that brings out all that is worst in man, that turns the potentially best into the most wretched, that leaves one bitter and angry, seeing all humanity, even a man of God and a child, as enemy....

In the message of Hugo, it is kindness, in its most extreme and unexpected form, that alone can bring reform or even instant rehabilitation, not through guilt or expiation but through rebirth and resurrection. Love, Victor Hugo is telling us: love, and the wretched mass of humanity will be redeemed. Man is essentially good, more than good, he is pure and heavenly, he needs only to be shown the other cheek and he will embrace and kiss it, not rebuff and repel it. Jean Valjean is the embodiment of this, but how universal, or how convincing even in his own instance, is a matter of dispute....

[After Jean Valjean's encounters with the bishop and Gervais, we] are given a glimpse of a man in the process of conversion, of the forces of good and evil struggling within him, each seeking victory over the other, the classic theological battle for possession of a man's soul between the devil and God's angels....

[Hugo catches] his character in the very act of change, at the moment of duality when he is traveling from evil to good and both are present as adversary forces. He is neither one person nor the other, neither the convict hardened, gloomy, and bitter against the world nor the redeemed man who has had a vision of the beauty that resides in the good and is beckoned to it. He is neither in the pure sense, because he remains both, as anyone at a moment of change must be. For Hugo, he is one of the two persons (or personalities) in his impulses, instincts, and habits, and he is the other in the intellect which is freeing him (or seeking to do so) from the nineteen years of the constant formation of an evil self. When his intellect sees what his habits have brought him to, he recoils, he denies that it is he (the eternal evasion of responsibility, it was not I, it was something in me, something that drove me), he repents and seeks to undo the act. It is Schopenhauer's eternal enmity between the worlds of will and idea, and it is a forerunner of Freud and the struggle between the unconscious and the intellect. In Valjean, the idea and the intellect will triumph.

Now he must run, run endlessly, for as a second offender, he will, if seized, be returned to the galleys for life. Hugo implies some condemnation of the judicial and penal systems, their harshness and cruelty, but essentially they are tangential to his story and even occasionally interfere with it. The galleys are not filled with Jean Valjeans but with men whose delicts are far more serious than the theft of a loaf of bread, and there is not a great deal that Hugo has to say about these men or their conditions of servitude. Here and there a word suggests suffering and cruelty, but Hugo seems to have known little about the actual conditions prevailing for prisoners, and his book falls short as an important indictment. If it is not an example of successful rehabilitation, for there was no evil in the protagonist but only in the society that condemned him, it nevertheless contradicts the strongly believed tenet that prison itself corrupts. All that is necessary for Jean Valjean to make his way in society is to conceal that he is an exconvict and, as the event with the child makes him, a fugitive as well.

Had Valjean been a different person, or had there been others from the galleys like him, he might have symbolized what Hugo seems haltingly to be suggesting at times: the criminals are the saints, and their jailers are the sinners. But Thénardier and many others are evil criminals, and aside from Valjean himself there are none that epitomize goodness. Only one man has risen, and in the end he is one who had never fallen.

André Maurois has written glowingly of this work. He praises its literary qualities, the excellent prose, the historical frescoes (the description of the Battle of Waterloo, and a more detailed one of the barricades on the streets of Paris in 1832). It is, however, a narrow view, for while *Les Misérables* has these virtues, Maurois ignores its faults—how ill-drawn the characters are, how absurd the plot,

how unsubtle the unweaving of the story, as one compares it with the works of the giants of the French novel who came just before Hugo and during his lifetime: Balzac, Stendhal, Gautier, and particularly Flaubert. But then Maurois finds in it great moral qualities, the painful quest of heroism and sanctity.... It is an interesting evaluation, and heroism and sanctity are indeed here present—frequently, selflessly, passionately, unmistakably. No reader can fail to discern the message. There is satisfaction in finding in another these qualities that one cannot attain oneself, but a reader must wish that there really were base passions in Valjean, and that he had actually conquered them and not merely overcome a momentary bitterness that arose because of the inhuman treatment he was accorded following the theft of the single loaf. If only there had been sin, there might have been redemption. Valjean never rises from the basest passions because he had never descended. The thefts of the bishop's silver plates and of the child's two-franc coin, which he sought to return: these and the loaf of bread are all that we have against him; for these he must spend a lifetime of expiation.

Yet there is expiation. I am not sure, as Maurois contends, that this is the sort of book that gives one "greater confidence in life and in himself." Maurois writes of *Les Misérables* that it speaks more to man of "his liberty than of his slavery." Yes and no, but it depends largely upon the willingness of the reader to suspend confidence in the universality of almost all other characters and utilize the hero as symbol of humanity. For Valjean does have liberty to rise, despite the pursuit by Javert, innumerable social pressures, and the social conditions that caused hunger and virtual thralldom.

Victor Hugo evidently gave great importance to the loaf of bread, and *Les Misérables* has left a legacy to the language of irony, that in the world of unequals he who steals a million dollars becomes a prime minister or an industrial tycoon while he who steals a loaf of bread ends up in prison. Jean Valjean spent nineteen years as a galley slave for his theft, about which Hugo writes in one of the passages in which he departs from his role of novelist and becomes essayist, social commentator, or historian:

> This is the second time that, during his essays on the penal question and condemnation by the law, the author of this book has come across a loaf as the starting-point of the disaster of a destiny. Claude Gueux [in the short story "*Claude Gueux*"] stole a loaf, and so did Jean Valjean, and English statistics prove that in London four robberies out of five have hunger as their immediate cause....

Here is Hugo as the critic of society: it is a world populated by prisoners of starvation, and it drives good men to crime. It is a world of cruelty and injustice, and it determines the destiny of men such as Jean Valjean. His, the author's and the hero's, is a cry from the depths of despair. Yet the message of Hugo actually is that all that is good in man cannot be destroyed by the prison air…, not *all* that is good, and not in *all* good men. It can only be driven beneath the surface as one hardens in the struggle for survival.

If this is a story, or even the story, of man rising to heights from the lowest depths, it is also a story of man seeking to escape from a past, to conceal it, to find a manner of starting life anew without pursuit from others and without the cloak that must be worn if one's stigma is to remain invisible. In the first instance, one almost wishes that the rise to heights were to places somewhat less lofty. Maurois is understating when he draws attention to the inability of the reader to fulfill a similar quest for heroism and sanctity. The fact is that Jean Valjean is just too good to be true, and this becomes literal for the reader who cannot immerse himself only in the man as symbol and wants to see him as a living person and to be confronted with greater verisimilitude with his fate.

Hugo's artistry, nonetheless, with all its short-comings, does present us with an individual who captures our interests; very much as in the old-fashioned cinemas that were continued from week to week, as the hero or heroine hung from the cliffs while the enemy was in hot pursuit, so we read breathlessly and applaud inwardly as Jean Valjean narrowly escapes doom.

Jean Valjean is a sympathetic symbol, but more than a symbol. At times he does emerge as a meaningful personality, even if no one else in the novel has the same good fortune. As symbol, however, Valjean is never at the lowest depths, never has been, and here Hugo fails us. Essentially, Valjean was not converted, especially since his first crime had not been anything other than an act of sacrifice, of altruism, of goodness. Raskolnikov [in Dostoevsky's *Crime and Punishment*] did murder, he killed the pawnbroker and her sister with a hatchet; he planned the murder, and his was an act of baseness. And … Lord Jim [in Conrad's *Lord Jim*] did abandon ship, as no captain or mate ever should, leaving aboard the sinking vessel the men under his command in contravention of his vows and the moral order of the sea. Moll Flanders [in Defoe's *Moll Flanders*] stole and stole and stole. But what Hugo has given us is more of a condemnation of society (as his aside on the subject of four out of five English crimes would indicate), and for that reason his novel cannot rank as a study in human redemption. There was really no crime, or so little of one. Valjean had never been a Raskolnikov; Raskolnikov could never have been canonized by Dostoevsky.

Like Lord Jim, Jean Valjean is seeking to escape from a past, but there the analogy ends. Lord Jim never wants to be faced by anyone who has learned of his misdeed because it was an act of infamy; it is really from himself that he wishes to find refuge. An impossible task: there are no worlds without mirrors. So while Lord Jim's secret protects him from inner persecution, Valjean's secret must guard him from the outer world, for two reasons: first, because the world will demand a penalty if he is apprehended and his identity disclosed; and second, because the world will never cease condemning an exconvict…. [In the world of Hugo, man,] once condemned, is forever condemned; he may be released from the bagnes, the galleys, the walls and bars, but he remains always in prison once he has been there. There is no Christian world that forgives anyone, not even this man for whom there is nothing to forgive. One pays forever, and at best can live only by concealment. The biography is there and cannot be rewritten, but it does not have to be told, or it can be falsified (and the two are essentially one). In this sense, if there is a message that Hugo wants us to learn from the life of Jean Valjean, the book is still very much alive. Ask any exconvict, in France or the United States and probably most other countries of the world, and they will tell you that the world of Jean Valjean remains almost unchanged among us. If these exconvicts were to be sanctified, it would give them as little solace as it did Hugo's central figure, for where is the audience that would believe the glorifiers, or perform the canonization rites, except perhaps a century and a half after their death?

The departures that the author takes from his novel in order to offer social commentary often have only tangential reference to the plots and subplots of the book, but they are significant in themselves. Hugo is, as it were, reminding himself that he is writing a story of the wretched, not of one individual, and even if the two clash it does not concern him. "All the crimes of the man begin with the vagabondage of the lad," he states…, although it was hardly true of Jean Valjean and there is little evidence of it in the criminal underworld elements with whom Valjean comes into contact at certain points in his adventures.

A passage that refers to the underworld, the literal criminal underworld though it might be equally applicable to the world of fear of exposure in which Jean Valjean lives, summarizes perhaps as well as any in this novel what Hugo has to say about crime:

> The social evil is darkness; humanity is identity, for all men are of the same clay, and in this nether world, at least, there is no difference in predestination; we are the same shadow before, the same flesh during, and the same ashes afterward; but ignorance, mixed with the human paste, blackens it, and this incurable blackness enters man and becomes Evil there....

It is more than Jean Valjean that Hugo is discussing when he writes that the social evil is darkness, it is humanity. If only humanity could accept the brotherhood of man, know that we come from nothing and will return to nothing, that the short time between need not be wretched for the millions of poor, *les Misérables,* then we could live in harmony and love on earth. Have no illusions: we are not predestined, Calvinism notwithstanding, to eternal damnation or endless bliss. We all have the same future, the darkness of the grave, and if we could lift ourselves from the ignorance that does not accept this, we could bring light into a world of somber shadows. This is Hugo's hope for salvation, but it is a meager hope, and in the end only Jean Valjean finds this salvation, only one unusual soul among millions of ordinary folk. Our sins are greater than thefts of loaves of bread for the hungry and the young, and we will not be able to fulfill en masse the hopes that Hugo expresses so eloquently in this passage.

Source: Edward Sagarin, "Jean Valjean: For Stealing a Loaf of Bread," in *Raskolnikov and Others: Literary Images of Crime, Punishment, Redemption, and Atonement,* St. Martin's Press, 1981, pp. 60–76.

SOURCES

Brombert, Victor, *Victor Hugo and the Visionary Novel*, Harvard University Press, 1984.

Josephson, Matthew, *Victor Hugo: A Realistic Biography of the Great Romantic*, Doubleday, 1942.

Richardson, Joanna, *Victor Hugo*, St. Martin's, 1976.

FURTHER READING

Grant, Elliot, *The Career of Victor Hugo*, Harvard University Press, 1945.
    A very basic and useful study of Hugo's main novels and poetry.

Grant, Richard B., *The Perilous Quest: Image, Myth, and Prophecy in the Narration of Victor Hugo*, Duke University Press, 1968.
    Hugo liked to describe himself as a "prophet" among men, as a translator of myths. This book analyzes this theme by looking at Hugo's major novels.

Grossman, Kathryn M., *Les Misérables: Conversion, Revolution, Redemption*, Twayne, 1996.
    Aimed specifically toward students, Grossman praises the novel as a book that "enables us to escape into the adventures of others: it brings us back to ourselves."

Houston, John Porter, *Victor Hugo*, Twayne, 1988.
    Good introduction to Hugo's life and work.

Ward, Patricia, *The Medievalism of Victor Hugo*, Pennsylvania State University Press, 1975.
    Hugo was fascinated by the mysteries and secrets of medieval times. Although *Les Misérables* cannot really be called a Gothic novel, some of its episodes, like the sewers episode, belong to the genre.

Lord of the Rings

J. R. R. TOLKIEN

1954—1955

In 1997, *Lord of the Rings* was voted, to the chagrin of some critics, the greatest book of the twentieth century in a poll run by major British booksellers. Despite some negative criticism, *Lord of the Rings* has been a steady best-seller since the first volume was published in 1954, and a campus craze in the sixties and early seventies. The extensive fantasy sections in today's bookstores, from Terry Brooks to Terry Pratchett, are all its children, as are, if George Lucas is to be believed, the Star Wars films.

On the surface, a combination of popular acclaim and critical disquiet is a baffling response to the work of an Oxford professor saturated in the study of language development and early medieval literature. Still, it is perhaps this crossing of characters and situations common to epic and folktale with a judicious use of novelistic technique that accounts for both its popularity with the reading public and the hostility of some critics, whose literary culture is too centered in the avant-garde to be comfortable with a work that reaches so deeply into medieval literature and which rejects, however thoughtfully, moral relativism. Despite its roots in medieval literature, *Lord of the Rings* places its characters and its readers on a collision course with modern moral dilemmas of knowledge and power. Tolkien poses these modern problems with absolute ethical principles and a belief in both an overarching providence and the importance of human choice. These ethical absolutes are, however, at least partially expressed in terms of a new type of hero, one which does not

supplant the old epic hero but which complements it. Although Tolkien always insisted that *Lord of the Rings* was not allegorical, it is apparent that the Ruling Ring and the destruction of the natural world that flows from the desire for its power are a reflection of Tolkien's concern for humanity's ability to destroy both itself and the earth. That Tolkien chooses a course of total rejection of such knowledge and power is perhaps one of the unconscious sources of some critics' reaction to the work. Such a rejection strikes at the heart of the concept of progress as it has developed in western civilization.

AUTHOR BIOGRAPHY

J. R. R. Tolkien was born January 3, 1892 in South Africa, where his father was a banker. His father died in 1896 while Tolkien, his mother, and younger brother were visiting family in England. To economize, his mother moved the family to a village near Birmingham where she began Tolkien's education in French, German, and Latin, as well as botany and drawing. Here Tolkien fell in love with the English countryside. Mother and sons were received into the Catholic church in 1900. Tolkien was deeply religious; beneath the surface of the *Lord of the Rings* is a deep sense of God's providence. His mother died when Tolkien was eleven. They had moved back and forth from country to city, but her death meant a final move into the industrial city of Birmingham. There, at sixteen, he met his future wife, Edith Bratt. His guardian, worried by an infatuation in a teenager studying for an Oxford scholarship, insisted that he break off contact until he was twenty-one. A similar period of working and waiting is a defining circumstance in Aragorn's life, who must not hope to marry Arwen, daughter of Elrond, until he has restored his ancestors' kingdom.

Tolkien, from his first lessons in Latin, had shown a facility for languages and a deep curiosity about their inner working. As well as learning Latin and Greek at school, he taught himself Old English and Gothic. Tolkien soon went from inventing Gothic words to filling out the surviving vocabulary, then to inventing a language. This love of languages, together with a love of the countryside, was to be the genesis of Middle Earth and its history.

At Oxford, Tolkien specialized in Philology, the study of the development of languages over time. As his studies were drawing to a close, World

War I broke out. His experience of battle and the deaths of nearly all his closest friends stayed with him in his writing and his criticism of early texts. After the war, he worked on the Oxford English Dictionary, then taught at the University of Leeds. In 1925 he was back in Oxford where he taught until retirement. Alongside his academic work, he continued to write the 'history' of Middle Earth, the world of his invented languages, discussing it with friends like C. S. Lewis. In 1936 he published *The Hobbit*, a story written for his children. An incident in *The Hobbit*, the finding of the Ring, becomes the point of departure for *Lord of the Rings*.

Lord of the Rings was written during the Second World War and the beginning of the Cold War. Although he insisted the trilogy was not an allegory, he and it were not untouched by events of the time. The atomic bomb intensified his misgivings about modern technological progress and the corruption of power. His concept of the heroic, already affected by his experience in World War I, shifted further away from the traditional in the context of a world now capable of destroying itself. The publication *The Lord of the Rings* in 1954–55 was greeted with bitter criticism from some members of the literary establishment, but sales were steady into the mid-sixties when the trilogy became a cult best seller. Tolkien, meanwhile, worked to prepare *The Silmarillion*, the pre-history of Middle Earth. He died in England on September 2, 1973, and the work was published posthumously in 1977.

Of his critical writing, *Beowulf: The Monsters and the Critics, On Fairy Stories*, and the short study *Ofermod*, printed with the short play *The Homecoming of Beorthnoth Beorthelm's Son*, all reflect the interaction of his scholarship and his creativity, as well as his profound concern with ethics.

PLOT SUMMARY

Overview

In *Lord of the Rings*, the inhabitants of Middle Earth join to save themselves from enslavement by the malevolent Sauron. Centuries before, Sauron forged a Ring, putting much of his power into it, to control through a series of lesser rings, men, dwarves, and elves. Some men fell into his power, but an alliance of men and elves defeated him, and the Ring was cut from his hand. It should have been destroyed, but a human prince, Isildur, took it. Isildur was slain, and the Ring fell into a river.

J. R. R. Tolkien

There, the hobbit-like Deagol eventually found it. His friend Sméagol killed Deagol for the Ring. From Sméagol it passed to Bilbo Baggins, who, innocent of its powers and dangers, takes it back to his home and eventually leaves it to his cousin and heir Frodo Baggins. Once it is understood what the Ring is, and that Sauron is trying to recover it, it becomes clear that it must be destroyed. It can, however, only be destroyed in the same fire in which it was forged, the volcano Orodruin deep in Sauron's realm. It appears a rash and hopeless mission, requiring that the last forces of Middle Earth fight and act as a decoy while sending Sauron's ultimate weapon back into the heart of his realm. The very unlikelihood of the mission confuses Sauron. The Ring is destroyed in an act of providential irony, but not without enormous loss and a fundamental change to Middle Earth.

The Hobbit

The *Lord of the Rings* is preceded by a prologue, *The Hobbit*, which introduces the Hobbits, Middle Earth, and Sauron's Ring. Bilbo Baggins, on a superficially unrelated adventure finds, steals, or wins—actually a little of all three—a magic ring. His first act while wearing the ring is to spare the life of its previous owner, Gollum, despite the creature's murderous intentions. Bilbo uses the ring throughout the rest of the book to help his companions, raising their estimation of him from something like an awkward piece of baggage to a statesman, if not quite a hero. Returning home, he finds that his reputation will never recover from his adventure and that he does not care.

The Fellowship of the Ring: Book 1

Gandalf the Wizard, an old family friend of Bilbo and his companion in *The Hobbit,* suspects Bilbo's ring is Sauron's lost Ring. Bilbo's advanced age and vigor are unusual even for a hobbit, and the Ring has begun to fill him with unease. Bilbo leaves the Shire, bequeathing the Ring, on Gandalf's advice, along with the rest of his estate to his cousin and heir Frodo. Eventually, Gandalf returns and makes a final test that convinces himself and Frodo that the Ring is Sauron's. Sauron has built up his power and is searching for his Ring. He sends his most terrible servants, the Ringwraiths, to find it. Frodo, his servant Sam, and cousins Merry and Pippin barely manage to elude them with the help of Aragorn, the heir of the ancient kings who had fought Sauron in the past. Frodo nearly falls under Sauron's power when he puts on the Ring and is wounded by a Ringwraith.

The Fellowship of the Ring: Book 2

The hobbits and Aragorn reach Rivendell with the Ringwraiths closing in. There a council of men, elves, dwarves, and hobbits is held. They decide the Ring is too dangerous either to use or to hide. It must be destroyed. Frodo offers to take and destroy it in the fire where it was forged. With him go Gandalf, Aragorn, and Boromir, son of the Steward of Gondor, for mankind; Legolas, son of Mirkwood's Elf-king, for the elves; Gimli, son of Gloin of the Lonely Mountain for the dwarves; Sam, Merry, and Pippin for the hobbits. Gandalf leads them until, thwarted in their attempt to cross the mountains, he takes them underground through the mines of Moria. There he falls in battle to an evil creature from the earth's depths. Aragorn takes over leadership of the band, guiding them to the elven kingdom of Lórien where its queen Galadriel tests their resolve and gives each a gift, then sends them down the river Anduin to the Rauros falls. There they must decide whether to turn east towards Sauron's realm or go with Boromir to the aid of Minas Tirith, capital of Gondor. Already they realize Gollum is following them. When it becomes clear Frodo will continue the apparently hopeless quest to destroy the Ring, Boromir tries to take the Ring. Frodo, horrified at the Ring's effect, leaves the others. Sam insists on coming with him. Orcs from Mordor and from the renegade wizard Saruman attack while the rest search for Frodo and Sam. Boromir dies trying to protect Merry and Pippin from the Orcs who have been told to capture hobbits.

The Two Towers: Book 3

Gimli, Aragorn, and Legolas return at Boromir's horn call, but arrive only in time for Boromir to confess to trying to take the Ring and to beg Aragorn to save his people. Aragorn, Legolas, and Gimli start in pursuit of the Orcs. The three are overtaken by a troop of horsemen, the Riders of Rohan, led by Eomer, nephew of their King. Eomer tells them that he and his men overtook a band of Orcs at the edge of the great forest of Fangorn and slaughtered them. He lends them horses to search for their friends on the condition that they come to his uncle's court afterwards to justify his help. The hobbits, however, have escaped and met Treebeard the Ent, the master of the forest. Hearing their story, Treebeard decides the time has come to move against Sauruman who has begun to imitate Sauron, destroying or enslaving everything within his reach. Aragorn, Gimli, and Legolas reach the forest where Gandalf, sent back from the dead to finish his work, meets them. He tells them that the hobbits are safe and have found allies: the Ents. They travel to the court of Theoden, king of Rohan. The wizard turns the king from the despair induced by the insinuations of Grima, the king's councilor, Saruman's agent. They and the Ents help Rohan fight off Saruman's invasion, and then go with Theoden to confront Saruman, now besieged by the Ents. There they are reunited with Merry and Pippin. Saruman refuses to give up his bid for power; Gandalf breaks his staff. Grima throws a palantír, one of the last three seeing stones, brought from the lost land of Númenor at Gandalf. Pippin, overcome by curiosity, looks into the stone and is seen by Sauron, who thinks he is the Ringbearer. Gandalf gives Aragorn, heir of the kings of Númenor, the palantír and rides with Pippin to Minas Tirith in Gondor. Merry becomes King Theoden's squire.

The Two Towers: Book 4

Frodo and Sam are found by Gollum, whom Frodo befriends, almost winning him over from his malice. Gollum leads them through the desolation around Mordor, but they discover that they cannot enter its "Black Gate." Gollum offers to show them another, hidden way. As they journey there, a scout-ing party under command of Boromir's younger brother, Faramir, catches them. Faramir learns of the Ring and their plans, but resists any temptation to seize it. He gives them supplies and warns them that Gollum's secret way, the Spider's Pass, is more dangerous than Gollum has said. They follow Gollum, however, having no other choice. A monstrous spider, Shelob, bites Frodo. Sam thinks he is dead and takes the ring to complete Frodo's task. Just as he is about to cross into Mordor, Sam overhears Orcs bickering and realizes that Frodo is not dead. He attempts to follow the Orcs carrying off the unconscious Frodo, but collapses.

The Return of the King: Book 5

Pippin and Gandalf reach Gondor and meet Denethor, the ruling steward. Denethor questions Pippin closely about his dead son. He is not happy with what he hears. He resents Aragorn and believes the Ring should be used to defeat Sauron. Pippin, who admired Boromir, offers his sword to Denethor who accepts him as one of his guardsmen. Meanwhile Aragorn has been joined by a small band of his kinsmen. He takes leave of King Theoden and rides for the Paths of the Dead to demand the help of a ghostly army cursed to have no peace until they fight against Sauron. Gimli and Legolas go with him. Longing for glory and in love with Aragorn, Éowyn, niece of Theoden and regent in his absence, begs Aragorn to let her come with him. Aragorn is miserable. He knows she loves him, but he has spent his whole adult life trying to win Elrond's permission to marry his daughter Arwen. He also understands she is frustrated by woman's work. He refuses Éowyn's pleas and tries to convince her that her role as regency is vital. When Theoden sets out for Gondor, Éowyn, disguised, rides with the army. Merry, who had been ordered behind by the king, comes with her.

At Gondor, meanwhile, Denethor, aged prematurely by watching events distorted by Sauron in the palantír of Minas Tirith, falls further into despair. When Faramir, whom he berated for not seizing the Ring, is brought back wounded, he slips into madness. The Riders of Rohan arrive at Minas Tirith and attack the besieging army. In the battle, the Chief Ringwraith, mounted on a flying beast, attacks Theoden and kills his horse, which falls, killing the king. Éowyn, who has stayed close to him through the fighting, comes between the Ringwraith and her dying uncle and, with Merry's help, kills him. Eomer finds his uncle in time to be named king and receive Theoden's last message for Éowyn. Finding

Éowyn apparently dead, he goes into a rage and charges through the enemy, overstretching his lines, but bringing them within sight of Aragorn, who is arriving with the fleet he has liberated from Sauron. Denethor has seen the approach of the fleet in the palantír and, thinking it is Sauron's, decides to kill himself and Faramir. Pippin, looking for Gandalf, meets a guard, Beregond, whom he sends to try to delay Denethor. With the help of Pippin and Beregond, Gandalf rescues Faramir, but Denethor commits suicide. The battle won, Aragorn refuses to officially enter the city for fear of stirring up dissension, but comes secretly to nurse Faramir, Éowyn, and Merry. With Minas Tirith secured for the moment, the leaders decide to send a small force under Aragorn to Mordor to draw Sauron's attention away from the Ringbearer. When they reach the gates of Mordor, they are met by the "Mouth of Sauron" who shows them Sam's sword, an elven cloak, and Frodo's armor.

The Return of the King: Book 6

Sam rescues Frodo from the Orcs, helped by their in-fighting and the power of Galadriel's gift. He hands Frodo back the Ring, and they travel on, still shadowed by Gollum. They abandon their few possessions as they abandon their hope of doing anything more than destroying the Ring. The landscape grows increasingly bleak as they approach the volcano, Orodruin. Frodo grows weaker and Sam carries him when he can no longer walk. Gollum catches up with them and knocks both of them down. Frodo rises with sudden strength and orders Gollum out of his path: "Begone and trouble me no more! If you touch me ever again, you shall be cast yourself into the Fire of Doom,'' and walks up the path to the fire. Sam, left alone with Gollum, almost kills him, but, having known briefly the burden of the Ring, cannot out of pity. He follows Frodo and sees him, at the fire's edge, claim the Ring for himself. Gollum attacks Frodo, they struggle and Gollum bites off Frodo's ring finger and, dancing with glee, topples into the flames destroying the Ring.

At the gate of Mordor, the little army is at bay. Eagles arrive just as the armies of Mordor are thrown into panic with the destruction of the Ring. Gandalf sends the eagles to rescue the hobbits. Nearly two weeks later, Sam and Frodo wake in Aragorn's camp. They are reunited with the rest of the Fellowship and formally honored. The army returns to Minas Tirith, where Faramir and Éowyn have fallen in love during their convalescence. Aragorn is crowned. On Midsummer's Day, Aragorn

and Arwen are married. They and the Fellowship escort the body of Theoden back to Rohan for his burial. Éowyn and Faramir are betrothed. Arriving at Orthanc, they discover Treebeard has allowed Saruman to leave. Accompanied by Gandalf, the hobbits travel on to Rivendell, meeting Saruman and Grim on the way. The hobbits visit with Bilbo and travel on to learn the Shire has not escaped unscathed. Gandalf leaves them telling them to hurry. Entering the Shire, they find that Lotho Sackville-Baggins and then Saruman under the name of "Sharkey" have turned the Shire into a police state and the beginnings of an ecological disaster. They rouse their fellow hobbits to see off the men who have terrorized them, but discover that Grim has murdered Lotho, and that Sharkey is Saruman. Frodo tries to keep them from bloodshed and will not allow the hobbits to harm Saruman. The miserable Grim, who is in turn killed, murders Saruman. Merry, Pippin, and Sam re-enter the life of the Shire as acknowledged heroes. Sam marries Rose Cotton; the newlyweds live with Frodo in Bag End. Frodo, however, does not recover from his ordeal. Just three years after they had fled the Shire with the Ring, Sam accompanies Frodo to the Havens where together with Bilbo, Gandalf, Galadriel, and Elrond, he takes ship for the west. With Merry and Pippin, Sam watches as the ship sets sail and then returns home to his wife and baby daughter.

CHARACTERS

Aragorn

The last descendant of the kings of the west, Aragorn, named Estel (Hope) by his mother, was born in the northwest of Middle Earth. (Aragorn is variously known as Strider, Thorongil, Estel and Elessar.) There his kinsmen and people had dwindled to a small clan of hardy, relatively long-lived men and women. His father was killed soon after his birth; Aragorn was raised in Rivendell, the last secret hope of his people. He has spent his adult life, like the other men of his people, as a Ranger, protecting the northwest lands of Middle Earth (particularly the Shire, since the finding of the Ring) from the threat of Sauron. He has ridden under an assumed name with the riders of Rohan and fought under an assumed name—Thorongil—in Gondor.

Aragorn is not a fairy-tale hero. His hard, hunted life has made him grim and, at times, a little tart. His ability and experience have not left him without self-doubt. His personal life, particularly his love for Arwen, has been mothballed for decades. He hardly refers to that love, and only retrospectively do some of his actions, for example, singing the Lay of Beren and Luthien, reveal its true, almost painful intensity. Despite this, his capacity for true friendship defines him as much as his actions. He is capable of great tenderness and understanding, born of intuition honed by experience. Gandalf relies on him. Bilbo treats him with the avuncular fondness with which he treats his own young cousins. Eomer of Rohan trusts him very nearly on sight, something Aragorn has not often experienced. Aragorn responds to this with a brother's love for Eomer and his sister Éowyn. Éowyn falls briefly in love with him. His struggle to put their relationship on a footing which will neither deny respect for her ability nor compassion for her situation, but which will not mislead her as to his true feelings, is an often overlooked indicator of Aragorn's personality. When she finds her real love in Faramir, there is a palpable release of tension between Aragorn and Éowyn. Aragorn, the only child, has found in Eomer and Éowyn something like a family. Finally united to Arwen, there is a certain unbuttoned happiness about him that he will carry to his death.

Arwen

A half-elf and Elrond's daughter, like all elves, she is for all practical purposes immortal. Arwen (also known as Undomel 'Evenstar') is called 'Evenstar' because of her resemblance to her great-grandmother, Luthien 'Morningstar,' who also renounced immortality for the love of a mortal man. She has waited for Aragorn through all his labors and marries him shortly after the end of the War of the Ring, assigning her right to pass over the sea to the uttermost west to Frodo should he wish. After Aragorn's death, she goes back to her mother's home of Lórien and, the elves all departed, dies alone.

Arwen's character and meaning are elusive, but in the end, hidden away in the Appendices, supremely tragic. The true female counterpart of Frodo, she is wounded by the necessary choice between father and lover, immortality and mortality, just as Frodo is by the experience of the Ring. Although she assumes mortality, she dies utterly elven in her attitude.

Bilbo Baggins

A Hobbit who accompanies a group of dwarves on an attempt to kill a dragon and reclaim their

MEDIA ADAPTATIONS

- *The Road Goes Ever On: A Song Cycle* are poems by Tolkien, with music by Donald Swann, recorded on Caedmon Records in 1967. *Poems and Songs of Middle Earth* were also recorded in the same year. William Elven performs.

- 'The Ballad of Bilbo Baggins' was recorded by Leonard Nimoy.

- *Lord of the Rings* was made into an animated film released in 1978, directed by Ralph Bakshi.

- *The Lord of the Rings*, directed by Peter Jackson, is to be released as three separate live action movies beginning in 2001. There is a trailer/preview available on the internet.

- ''Harvard Lampoon'' published a parody of *The Lord of the Rings* entitled *Bored of the Rings* in 1969.

home and treasure. All this happens, although not quite the way they expected, and largely through Bilbo's growing self assurance and the help of a ring Bilbo finds, steals, or wins—actually a little of all three—that renders its wearer invisible. Bilbo brings the ring back with him and occasionally uses it, largely to avoid meeting his more obnoxious relatives. It has, however, other effects. He enjoys extended life and vigor, but also begins to feel it "growing on his mind." The ring is the Ring, the great ruling Ring of Sauron, holding a power that devours and corrupts sooner or later all that carry it. He relinquishes it to Frodo, his heir, and goes off to Rivendell. He eventually passes over the sea into the west with Frodo, Elrond, Gandalf and Galadriel. Bilbo is the first author and compiler of the Red Book of Westmarch, "source" of Tolkien's history of Middle Earth.

Frodo Baggins

Cousin and adopted heir of Bilbo, he is left a clearly magic ring along with the rest of Bilbo's property and warned not to use it. After a number of years, Gandalf comes to perform a final test that identifies the ring as the One Ring of Sauron, whose power and influence is so great and so corrupting that it cannot be safely used. Attempting to protect the Shire and his people, Frodo and three companions, Sam, Merry, and Pippin flee with it while being pursued by the Sauron's servants the Ringwraiths. At the Council of Elrond, he offers to take it to Mount Doom and destroy it. He struggles to perform the task, slowly being devoured by the power of the Ring until, at the edge of the volcano's crater, he chooses to claim the Ring for himself. At that moment, Sauron is aware of him and is distracted from the little army lead by Aragorn. Before he or Frodo can act, Gollum bites off Frodo's finger to steal back the ring and, dancing with glee, falls backwards into the fire, destroying the Ring. Frodo is doubly maimed by his sufferings while carrying the Ring and by his final failure to resist and destroy it. He can find no peace in his return home and takes up Arwen's offer to pass over the sea into the west in her place.

Balin

One of Bilbo's dwarf companions, Balin goes to restore the ancient Dwarf kingdom of Moria where he is killed by Orcs.

Beregond

A man of the Guards of the Citadel, he and Pippin save Faramir from death at the hands of Faramir's father, Denethor. To do this, Beregond leaves his post and kills three of his comrades, who attempt to stop him, following orders from Denethor. Beregond's dilemma is an exemplum of divided loyalties and competing moral imperatives among which each person must choose and act. His trial is one of Aragorn's first acts as the newly crowned king of Gondor, shifting from warleader to judge.

Bergil

The son of Beregond who guides Pippin about Minas Tirith and fetches the herb Athelas, which Aragorn uses to save Merry, Éowyn, and Faramir.

Black Captain

See Witch King of Angmar

Black Riders

See Ringwraiths

Fredegar Bolger

Fredegar, also known as Fatty, is another of Frodo and Bilbo's cousins. He tries to keep up the pretense that Frodo is still in Buckland for as long as possible. He raises Buckland against the Ringwraiths and later leads guerilla warfare against Sharkey's rule, emerging from the Lockholes in Michel Delving a much thinner Hobbit.

Tom Bombadil

A character something like Kipling's Puck of Pook's Hill, he has a power that can be asserted over nature, but it is not certain that he has any role in guarding or tending it as the Ents have. The Ring has no power over him. At times, he seems like a vision of what man would have been if Adam had not fallen in Eden.

Boromir

Boromir is the eldest son of Denethor and the last ruling steward of Gondor. He is a masterful man, who loves the glory of battle, and, like his father, thinks only in terms of preserving the status quo in Gondor. He insists on traveling to Rivendell to find out the meaning of his brother's dream. He becomes one of the Fellowship of the Ring, but is clearly uncomfortable with the decision to unmake the Ring and with the pretensions of Aragorn. He attempts at the Rauros Falls to take the Ring from Frodo. When Frodo flees, Boromir is stricken immediately with remorse for his action. A company of Orcs attacks the band, dispersed by Frodo's flight. Boromir is mortally wounded defending Merry and Pippin from the Orcs. He confesses to Aragorn that he attempted to take the Ring and begs him to go to Gondor to save his people.

Meriadoc Brandybuck

See Merry

Bregalad

Bregalad (also known as Quickbeam) is one of the youngest of the Ents or shepherds of the trees. He makes up his mind with most un-Entish speed and, having made up his mind that Saruman must be stopped, is excused from the Entmoot or parliament to play host to Merry and Pippin.

Barliman Butterbur

Owner of the Prancing Pony Inn in Bree, often patronized by Gandalf. He forgets to send on Gandalf's letter to Frodo warning him to leave the

Shire. He thinks Aragorn is at best a dubious character.

Celeborn

The husband of Galadriel, Celeborn is the ruler, with his wife, of the elves of Lórien. He is a somewhat shadowy figure compared to his wife. His reactions to men and events seem less shrewd than hers.

Círdan

Círdan is the elf lord who originally wore one of the three rings of the elves, and who rules the Grey Havens from which the elves depart to the lands of the Valar in the west. Círdan provides the ships that make the voyages. He departs with the other leaders of the elves and the Ringbearers Frodo and Bilbo.

Farmer Cotton

A farmer from near Bywater, and a local leader, he and his sons rally to five hobbits returned from the War of the Rings and help them clear the Shire of the interloping men under the leadership of Saruman, now called Sharkey. His daughter Rose marries Sam Gamgee.

Rose Cotton

Daughter of Farmer Cotton, she marries Sam Gamgee the year after he returns from the quest to destroy the Ring.

Dain

Dain (also known as Ironfoot), the Dwarf king of the Lonely Mountain, dies fighting beside King Brand of Dale against the forces of Sauron in the Ring War.

Denethor

The last ruling steward of Gondor. He is very much in the mold of the ancient men of the west. His resemblance to Aragorn is mentioned at more than one point. Nevertheless, he pays only lip service to the essential nature of the stewardship. It is clear he would not relinquish, with any good grace, his rule to the true king should he return. He is contemptuous when speaking of Aragorn. In the Appendices in the last volume of *Lord of the Rings*, there are suggestions that Denethor's attitude may have been affected by an earlier meeting of the two men. Aragorn, under the name of Thorongil, fought as a captain in the wars of Gondor under Denethor's father, Ecthelion II. Denethor resented Thorongil's ability, success, and his father's regard for the stranger from the north. Since Denethor is a "farseeing" man, the reader is left to ponder whether Denethor realized from the beginning who Thorongil was. Denethor's relationship with Gandalf is equally poisoned. He resents his patronage of Aragorn and his influence over his own younger son, Faramir. When Denethor realizes that his younger son Faramir has allowed Frodo to continue on his attempt to destroy the Ring instead of bringing it to him, he flies into a cold rage. Denethor bitterly drives him back into battle. There, Faramir, fighting desperately to cover a retreat, is wounded and falls under the influence of the poisonous Black Breath. Mad with despair for Gondor and grief for his dying son, Denethor commits suicide, attempting to kill his son with him. Faramir is saved by the desperate action of Beregond and Merry, but all attempts to save Denethor fail.

Dernhelm

See Éowyn

Dunhere

Dunhere is the Lord of Harrowdale and one of the lords of Rohan at the muster.

Eomer Eadig

See Eomer

Elanor

Sam Gamgee's oldest daughter, named for a flower of Lórien. According to the Appendices, she marries Fastred Fairbairn. It is in their family that the Redbook of Westmarch, represented as Tolkien's source, was handed down.

Elessar

See Aragorn

Elladan and Elrohir

The sons of Elrond who have long fought alongside the Rangers and come with them to meet Aragorn in Rohan and fight under his banner.

Elrond

The son of Eärendel the Mariner, son of Idril Celebridal and Tuor, and Elwing, daughter of Luthien Tintúviel and Beren. He was a master of ancient learning, a careful councilor, and his house in Rivendell in the northwest of Middle Earth was a citadel against the rising power of Sauron. At the end of the first Age, the Valar, the spirits who rule earth under the one divinity Iluvater, gave Elrond and Elros, his brother, the choice of belonging to the people of their female grandparents, the immortal elves, or of joining the mortal humans of their male grandparents. Elrond chose to be an elf and like the elves he had the right to pass into the deathless lands of the west. His children also were allowed the choice of mortality in Middle Earth or passing into the uttermost west. Elros chose mankind and remained with the people of his grandfathers', the Edain. He was granted a life span longer than most humans, and this longer life span was inherited, although diminished, by his descendants of whom Aragorn was one. Aragorn and Arwen, Elrond's daughter, were deeply in love. Elrond, although he sheltered and encouraged Aragorn, opposed the match because he knew it would mean the loss of his daughter to mortality.

Ents

Ents are great tree-like beings, among the oldest senescent beings on Middle Earth. Slow and careful of speech and judgement, when aroused they are capable of enormous destruction. They care for all trees, and it is in defense of their trees that they attack Saruman at his fortress Isengard. They and the Huorns turn the tide of the battle at Helm's Deep.

Entwives

Female Ents, they were more interested in fruit trees than in forest trees and were famous for their gardens. They seem to have been instrumental in teaching mankind agriculture. They chose to live in cultivated lands rather than with the male Ents who preferred the wild woods. Eventually the Entwives were lost to the Ents. The Ents searched for them, but found only their broken gardens.

Eomer

Eomer (also known as Eomer Eadig) is Third Marshal of Rohan and the son of King Theoden's beloved younger sister, Theodwyn. Orphaned as a young boy, his uncle takes him and his sister Éowyn into his home and raises them as his own. Eomer and his sister have had to endure seeing the king made old and feeble before his time by the evil counsel of Grima Wormtongue. Since his only son Theodred had died in fighting against Saruman's army, Theoden, dying on the battlefield before Minas Tirith, named Eomer his heir. Confronted

with Aragorn on his hunt for Merry and Pippin, he immediately recognizes Aragorn's qualities and worth and takes the great risk of his uncle's anger to lend him and his companions, Legolas and Gimli, horses. This is the beginning of a deep friendship between the two. Finding his sister, as he thinks, dead beside their uncle, he leads a reckless charge that cuts across the Pellenor Fields within sight of Aragorn's ships coming to the aid of the city.

Estel
See Aragorn

Éowyn

Sister of Eomer, Éowyn (also known as Dernhelm) has been like a favorite daughter to her uncle. She stood by him while Grima made an old man of him and has had to resist Grima's advances. The best description of her is Háma's, "She is fearless and high hearted. All love her." She falls in love with Aragorn at first sight, recognizing in him all the qualities of a leader. Her uncle makes her regent of the Mark in his absence at the suggestion of Háma. When she realizes Aragorn cannot love her as she wishes, she disguises herself as a young warrior and, with Merry as her companion, rides off to war with her uncle. When the Chief of the Ringwraiths confronts her uncle on the battlefield, killing his horse, she comes between them and with the help of Merry kills the Wraith, who it was foretold would never die by a man's hand. Éowyn and Merry are overcome by the Black Breath, only to be saved along with Faramir by Aragorn's nursing and herb lore. Recovering together while the armies move towards Mordor, Faramir comes to love her deeply. She accepts him and the task of rebuilding the ravaged province of Ithlien. They are formally betrothed after her uncle's funeral. She never mentions her own great deed, but almost her first words to her brother after coming out of her coma are, "You shall make him [Merry] a knight of the Riddermark for he is valiant."

Undomel 'Evenstar'
See Arwen

Fangorn
See Treebeard

Faramir

The younger son of Denethor, Faramir is a scholarly man, but, nonetheless, a formidable warrior. Although his father has always and obviously preferred his older brother, he and Boromir were always close. Faramir admires Gandalf and attempts to learn as much as he can from him. Unlike his brother and father, he is not tempted by the Ring and makes good his boast that he would not stoop to pick it up if he found it on the road when he finds Frodo and the Ring in his power. Instead, he gives what help he can to Frodo's quest. Broken-hearted by his father's anger against him and worn out by incessant fighting, he is seriously wounded and infected with the Black Breath while trying to cover his men's retreat to Minas Tirith. His father, mad with despair, attempts to kill him, but Merry, Beregond, and Gandalf save him. Aragorn is able to cure him by force of will and herb lore. While recuperating, he falls in love with Éowyn whom he marries. Aragorn gives him Ithilien to restore.

Fatty
See Fredegar Bolger

Bill Ferny
A Breelander man in league with the Ringwraiths. He is in the Shire when the companions return.

Galadriel
A powerful elf woman who, with her husband Celeborn, rules Lórien, a land where the ravages of time, or the effects of the waves of evil that have swept over Middle Earth, are held at bay by the power of her Ring. Galadriel is a political being, despite her sylvan trappings. She first summoned the White council, and she attempted to have Gandalf made its head. She has long desired the Ring, but when offered it by Frodo, draws back from her desire having carefully considered what the ends of her actions would be. Her keen understanding of individuals is not practiced coldly. Her quick and penetrating understanding and sympathy for Gimli and his world-view and sorrows win her a deep and enduring love. It in turn enlarges Gimli's sympathy and understanding in all his dealings. She is Arwen's grandmother and clearly favors the match with Aragorn.

Gaffer Gamgee
Gaffer is Sam's father, the gardener at Bag End.

Sam Gamgee
The youngest son of Bilbo and Frodo's gardener, Gaffer Gamgee. He is acting gardener of Bag End when he is caught eavesdropping on Frodo and

Gandalf. A practical, long suffering soul, there is a streak of the sublime in him, longing to come in contact with the higher sensibilities of the Elves, meeting obstacles with unconscious heroism. He emerges as a hero on the level of Aragorn, specifically mirroring many of the qualities of Faramir.

Gamling the Old
Gamling the Old is the Commander of the men of Rohan holding Helm's Deep.

Gandalf the Grey
Gandalf the Grey, also known as Mithrandir, Grey Pilgrim, Gandalf Greyhame and Gandalf Stormcrow, is a wizard, one of five sent from the west to Middle Earth to help in the fight against Sauron. The wizards were not to dominate, but to encourage and aid in the fight against Sauron. Although Saruman was head of the White council and the chief of the order of wizards, Círdan gave Gandalf his own Ring when he arrived from out of the west. He traveled incessantly, trying to keep some sort of watch and alliance against Sauron. He is sensitive to the movement of providence, even if he does not know what the pattern of providence is. He dies fighting a Balrog in Moria and returns to Middle Earth only briefly to see the struggles against Sauron to their conclusion and leaves within two years for the west.

Mithrandir Gandalf
See Gandalf

Ghân-buri-Ghân
Leader of the 'Wild Men,' an indigenous primitive people, in the forest of Drúadan. He leads the riders of Rohan through secret paths and brings them news of the Siege of Gondor. Aragorn confirms their possession of the forest and bans others from entering it without their permission.

Gimli
Son of Bilbo's companion, Gloin, Gimli represents the Dwarves among the Fellowship of the Ring. His friendship with Legolas and love for Galadriel brings a new rapprochement between the long estranged peoples.

Glorfindel
Glorfindel is the Elf prince who rides out from Rivendell to find and help Frodo and his companions. His horse carries Frodo and the Ring to safety.

Goldberry

Goldberry is the wife of Tom Bombadil.

Gollum

Gollum, also known as Sméagol, is a Hobbit-like creature who came into possession of the Ring by murdering his friend Deagol who had found it. He sneaks away into the mountains where, after centuries, he loses the Ring to Bilbo. He is still drawn to the Ring, desiring it and hating it. He helps Frodo and Sam half out of a pathetic desire for friendship, half out of addiction to the Ring. At the edge of the crater of Mount Doom, he bites off Frodo's finger to steal back the Ring. Dancing with glee, he falls backwards into the fire, destroying himself and the Ring, fulfilling Gandalf's belief that his fate is bound up with that of the Ring and that mercy to him would be repaid.

Sméagol Gollum

See Gollum

Gorbag

Gorbag is a commander of a body of Orcs who capture Frodo.

Great Captain

See Witch King of Angmar

Grey Pilgrim

See Gandalf the Grey

Gandalf Greyhame

See Gandalf the Grey

Grima

Grima, also known as Wormtongue, is Counsellor of Theoden in the pay of Saruman. It is he who throws the Palantir of Orthanc. He finally murders Saruman.

Grishnakh

An Orc of Mordor who attempts to spirit Merry and Pippin away before the final battle with the Riders of Rohan.

Háma

The warrior who keeps the door to Meduseld, the house of King Theoden. He allows Gandalf to take his staff into the hall, which is instrumental in the fall of Grima, a spy of Saruman. It is Háma who tells Theoden that Éowyn is the person that the people will want as their regent. Háma is killed by the Orcs at the battle at Helms Deep. Theoden refers to the mutilation of his body by Saruman's men when he refuses to be swayed by Saruman's offers of help and power.

Her Ladyship

See Shelob

Hirgon

Hirgon is the messenger who brings the red arrow of summons from Gondor to Theoden. He is killed by Orcs on his return journey.

Holdwine of the Mark

See Merry

Huorns

A large group of Ents who have grown wild and treeish. They are extremely dangerous to meet un-accompanied by an Ent. They annihilate the army of Saruman at Helm's Deep.

Gildor Inglorion

The elf whose people meet Frodo, Sam, and Pepin on their flight from the Shire. He invites them to stay the night with them, which briefly frustrates the Ringwraiths. He sends word through other elf bands which eventually reaches Elrond and Rivendell.

Ioreth

A talkative nurse in the House of Healers in Minas Tirith. She reminds Gandalf that 'The hands of the king are the hands of a healer.' This message brings Aragorn to the beds of Eowyn, Faramir, and Merry.

Ironfoot

See Dain

Legolas

The son of the King of the Mirkwood elves, he represents the elves among the Fellowship. He and Gimli become inseparable friends.

Lieutenant of the Tower

The Lieutenant of the Tower, also known as The Mouth of Sauron, is not a Ringwraith, but a living man, a sorcerer of the same people as the men of the West, but of those who worshipped Sauron for the sake of his wicked knowledge. He confronts Aragorn, Gandalf, and the combined armies of

Gondor and Rohan at the gates of Mordor with Sam's sword and Frodo's mail.

Farmer Maggot

A substantial hobbit in the Marish, a district of the Shire. He once set his dogs on Frodo for trespassing on his land after mushrooms, but welcomes him and his companions to his home and helps them to the crossing of the Brandywine River, despite being approached by one of the Ringwraiths.

Merry

Merry, also known as Meriadoc Brandybuck and Holdwine of the Mark, is Frodo's younger cousin. Later the Master of Buckland, he is slightly older and more serious than his cousin Pippin. He and Pippin were almost not allowed to join the fellowship, but their presence, on Gandalf's advice, turns the tide of events on at least three occasions. Meriadoc offers his services to Theoden, and trying to stay near the king in battle, takes the help of a young warrior who turns out to be Éowyn. Together they kill the Nazgûl. With Pippin, he spearheads the scouring of the Shire.

The Mouth of Sauron

See Lieutenant of the Tower

Nazgúl

See Ringwraiths

The Necromancer

See Sauron

The Nine

See Ringwraiths

Old Man Willow

A malevolent tree who infects the whole of the old forest east of the Shire. He attempts to kill the hobbits.

Pimple

See Lotho

Pippin

Pippin, also known as Peregrine and later, the Thain of the Shire, is the youngest and most thought-less of Frodo's companions. He makes the same impression on events as his cousin Merry, saving the life of Faramir.

Quickbeam

See Bregalad

Rangers

The Rangers are the remnants of the men from Númenorean kingdom of Arnor in the northwest of Middle Earth. They have kept watch over the Shire as well as the rest of the lands north and west of Gondor since the fall of the northern Kingdom over a thousand years before the action of the *Lord of the Rings*.

Rhadagst the Brown

A wizard, particularly interested in bird-lore. He is innocently used by Saruman to capture Gandalf.

Ringwraiths

Ringwraiths, also known as Black Riders, The Nine, and Nazgul, are the nine human kings enslaved by the nine rings forged by Sauron 'for mortal men doomed to die.' They are lead by the witch king of Angmar.

Lobelia Sackville-Baggins

Bilbo and Frodo's cousin by marriage, her husband Otho was Bilbo's heir until he adopted Frodo. Lobelia had never forgiven Bilbo for coming back from his adventure just as she was about to move into his eminently desirable Hobbit hole, Bag End.

Lotho Sackville-Baggins

Otho and Lobelia's son, Lotho (also known as Pimple), was used to gain a foothold in the Shire. He is murdered (and possibly eaten) by Grima.

Saruman the White

Saruman the White, also known as Sharkey, is one of the wizards sent from over the sea, and the one master of 'realpolitik' in the narrative. He has become obsessed with creating a power base from which he might rule Middle Earth. He has become enslaved to Sauron, although he hardly seems to realize it. Escaping from the wreck of his ambition in Orthanc, he makes his way to the Shire, taking over Lotho Sackville-Baggins's regime and intensifying it.

Sauron

Sauron, also known as The Necromancer, is a being of incredible power, he has tricked elves, men, and dwarves to their destruction even when he has not actually enslaved them. His malevolence and hunger for power is insatiable. To this end, he forged the great Ring to control a series of others that he distributed among men and dwarves. Into this ring, he put a greater part of his own power. Lost to him, it diminishes him. Destroyed, it will make him impotent.

Shagrat

Shagrat is an Orc officer who captures Frodo.

Sharkey

See Saruman the White

Shelob

Shelob, also known as Her Ladyship, is the great, all-devouring, primeval spider who guards the secret entrance to Mordor. She wounds Frodo, but is wounded in turn by Sam with his knife made by the men of the west for the battles against the Witch King of Angmar.

Snaga

Snaga is an Orc of Shagrat's command.

Gandalf Stormcrow

See Gandalf the Grey

Strider

See Aragorn

Theoden

Theoden is King of Rohan. He is an exceptionally gentle and loving man in spite of being the warrior king of a warrior people. His relationship with Merry, more father than lord, is a thumbnail sketch of what his relationship with his people must have been. He falls into a despair brought on by Grima's poisonous take on events and people, but his cure is quick and complete.

Thorongil

See Aragorn

Peregrine Took

See Pippin

Treebeard

The oldest of the Ents or shepherds of the Trees, Treebeard (also known as Fangorn) can remember the first age. He sees the world largely in terms of his trees, but realizes the interconnectedness of the trees' welfare with that of all those who desire to follow the good in Middle Earth. His meeting with Merry and Pippin is the catalyst for his decision to call out the Ents in defense of their trees and take Saruman in hand.

Uglúk

A Captain of the Isengard Orcs, Uglúk's men capture Merry and Pippin. He is brought to bay at Fangorn and is killed in single combat with Eomer.

Witch King of Angmar

The Witch King of Angmar, also known as the Black Captain or the Great Captain, is leader of the Nazgúl, a renegade Númenórean who finally broke the power of the northern kingdom of Arnor and forced Aragorn's people into the role of Rangers.

Wormtongue

See Grima

THEMES

The Ring: Absolute Power Corrupts Absolutely

Lord Acton in the 1880s wrote, "Power Corrupts; absolute power corrupts absolutely." When Sam urges Galadriel, "I think my master was right. I wish you'd take his ring. You'd put things to rights. You'd make some folk pay for their dirty work," Galadriel answers, "I would—That is how it would begin, but it would not stop at that, alas!" While many earlier philosophers and writers would have agreed, such a clear and unequivocal vision of the intrinsic dangers of power could only come with the sharply increasing ability of humans to control and destroy not only themselves, but the earth itself. The Ring is the embodiment of the will to power. It exists only to dominate. It corrupts, driving a wedge between the wearer and his own nature, let alone

TOPICS FOR FURTHER STUDY

- J. R. R. Tolkien's lifelong interest in Philology, the study of change and development in language, is one of the foundations of his narrative. Research a study of comparative languages, particularly as it applies to a language family that interests you culturally.

- Tolkien's *Lord of the Rings* has attracted the work of many illustrators. Tolkien himself was a gifted amateur illustrator and a number of his illustrations for his stories have been published. Study Tolkien's illustrations and discuss the ideas, artistic movements, and individual artists that you believe may have entered into his style.

- Tolkien served in the trenches in World War I during the Somme offensive. Look at both his biography and at narratives of the battle of the Somme and attempt to find reflections of his experiences in *Lord of the Rings*.

- For a time in 1965–66, Tolkien and his publishers were involved in a battle with Ace books over their unapproved paperback edition of *Lord of the Rings*. Investigate the history of copyright laws, and discuss the long running problems of British authors with American copyright laws.

- Some critics have noticed the similarity between the society Tolkien drew in the Shire and the social ideas of William Morris. Study the ideas of Morris about work, art, and society, and discuss the extent to which the picture Tolkien draws of the Shire agrees or diverges from those ideas.

---

every other being, no matter how dear. Tolkien expresses this corruption in the language of addiction where everything is sacrificed to the insatiable desire for the Ring/Power.

Providence

Near the beginning of *Lord of the Rings* when Gandalf tries to explain the Ring to Frodo he says: "It was the strangest event in the whole history of the Ring so far: Bilbo's arrival, just at that time, and putting his hand on it, blindly, in the dark. . .There was more than one power at work. . .The Ring was trying to get back to its master. When its master was awake once more and sending out his dark thought . . . Behind that there was something else at work, beyond any design of the Ring-maker. I can put it no plainer than by saying that Bilbo was *meant* to find the Ring and not its maker." Critics have often remarked that there is nothing which amounts to religion in *Lord of the Rings* and no mention of God. A providence, however, hovers over the narrative, a beneficent power working through events and through individual willed actions, good and (ironically) bad, to bring about the destruction of the Ring and the end of Sauron. This providence does not give happily ever after, as it relies on the speaking people, it leaves them with the cumulative results of their choices, but it does not leave them alone. Elves, men, dwarves, Ents and Hobbits must act, but providence ensures that their actions are not without results. The victory of the good cannot restore what was lost nor even preserve all that was saved. Nevertheless, the far greater, unthinkable evil is averted.

Mercy and Pity

Pity in the *Lord of the Rings* presupposes understanding, sympathy, and a recognition of a moral imperative to alleviate rather than cause pain. In action, it seems to be closer to empathy than to the common modern use of the word pity, which in common usage, has now overtones of contempt. Acts of mercy born of sympathetic pity are clearly subsumed into the providential purpose. Gollum is spared again and again by the pity of others, notably Bilbo, Frodo, and Sam. In the end, this mercy saves not Gollum, who cannot reject the addiction of evil, but those who have been merciful.

Death and Deathlessness

While most readers and critics concentrate on the absolute corruption of power, Tolkien wrote that *Lord of the Rings* was about death and deathlessness. The importance of the theme often comes as a surprise to even the most assiduous readers of the trilogy, although in the context of the larger history of Middle Earth, it emerges with greater clarity. Nevertheless, the juxtaposition of the effectively immortal elves with mortal men, (not to mention dwarves and hobbits) confront the reader at every turn. Sauron's initial temptation to men was based on the fear of the unknown and an unspoken jealousy of the elves. It is the attempt to seize immortality that destroys the island kingdom in the western sea Númenor, the preoccupation with death and ancestors that leaves Minas Tirith under-populated. Tolkien has the inhabitants of Middle Earth call death a "gift" and insinuates death is a welcome natural movement from earth to the presence of earth's creator. It is probably only in the context of the larger body of Tolkien's writings—notably the *Silmarrillion* and *The Book of Lost Tales*—that its ubiquity and centrality becomes apparent. Even more than men, the landscape of Middle Earth itself is again and again described in terms of loss, change, and decay. The juxtaposition of the immortal and changeless elves with a flawed and transitory environment indicates the elves are in an uncertain and ambiguous position. Perhaps the false mutable world is more surely the "long defeat" of which Galadriel speaks.

Moral Absolutes

Tolkien has been accused of seeing events in black and white, but throughout the trilogy, it is clear that while moral absolutes are the touchstone of actions, they do not prescribe specific and unvarying action. They are the weights against which the characters must balance competing 'right actions.' Merry and Pippin both swear oaths of allegiance. Both of them consciously break those oaths in pursuit of a higher good, "but," as Rosebury wrote, "it is precisely these kinds of departure from a facile and predictable structuring of ethical action which exemplify the work's moral subtlety and openness to contingency." Tolkien drew his characters in terms of moral and imperfection and intellectual limitation. Even Gandalf's character reflects a strong sense of the imperfections of humanity. Tolkien's wisest characters in the stories maintain this wisdom with a balance of restricted knowledge. Frodo demonstrates this when he quotes the proverb, "Go not to the elves for counsel, for they will say both no and yes." The elf Gildor replies, "Elves seldom give unguarded advice for advice is a dangerous gift, even from the wise to the wise, and all courses may run ill."

STYLE

Point of View

Tolkien in the Prologue to *Lord of the Rings* adopts a common literary convention: he has 'translated' it from Bilbo and Frodo's own Red Book of Westmarch. For long stretches of *Lord of the Rings* the point of view is third person, but there are important flashes of omniscience. These flashes derive from a complex set of circumstances rooted in the convention of translation from an autobiographical account, not a wavering of approach. What a character is thinking is usually revealed by means of words or actions. Where omniscience occurs, the mind involved is usually Frodo's. In the narrative of the debate before the company leaves Lórien, Boromir's thought is revealed by his words and actions, while the reader is taken into Frodo's mind. A more complex example occurs when Frodo's struggle with the eye of Sauron is reported. When Frodo puts on the Ring, the narrator becomes fully omniscient, but the ground has been carefully prepared for this effect of the Ring. If readers will accept that the 'real' authors are part of the action and one of those authors has the heightened awareness born of the Ring, it will not be strange to find that at times that we know the mind of Frodo, Sam or even, at the end, the reaction of Sauron himself.

Setting

Tolkien wrote of Middle Earth in the Prologue to *Lord of the Rings*: "Those days, the Third Age of Middle Earth are now long past, and the shape of all lands have been changed; but the regions in which the Hobbits lived are doubtless the same as those in which they still linger: the North-West of the Old World, east of the Sea." The landscapes Tolkien brings his characters through and describes in such loving detail are clearly European, suggesting landscapes from the arctic Norway to the shores of the Mediterranean. It is a sparsely inhabited, pre-industrial world, with scattered self-sufficient communities. Along with his care in describing the landscape and mapping the larger topography of Middle Earth, is the careful chronology and the accurate astronomical data that suggests he set his narrative in a time which was not long ago in astronomical terms.

Despite this, the landscape of Middle Earth reca-pitulates epic landscapes back to Homer. The movement of battle across the Pelennor Fields can be compared to the *Iliad*. Lórien draws on both the island of Circe and the land of the Phoenicians. Medusel is modeled on Heorot from *Beowulf*.

Allusions

Tolkien's allusions are self-contained. They are drawn exclusively from within the history he created for Middle Earth. Possibly because the *Silmarillion* was not published and seemed unlikely to be published at the time he was writing the *Lord of the Rings*, even these allusions are kept to a minimum.

Imagery

Tolkien's imagery is rooted in the traditional. There has been some critical disquiet at his use of black and white, but careful reading demonstrates that it is complex and heavily nuanced. The corrupt wizard Saruman's color is white, Aragorn's banner is white on a black field and he wears black armor. Grey is a privileged color, elven cloaks are grey, Gandalf's color is grey. Similarly some critics have equated Tolkien's use of the 'industrial' landscape with class hatred or dislike for the urban industrial proletariat, an idea which is as far from his opinions as it was from Blake's when he wrote of 'dark satanic mills.' Two images are worth particular attention. One is of a great wave rearing up over fields, houses and trees, drowning the land of Númenor, the reflex of a dream Tolkien had from childhood. The second is Tolkien's complicated use of trees and forests running the full gamut of positive and negative meaning, from the trees of the Valar to Old Man Willow.

Quest or Anti-Quest

The *Lord of the Rings* has been discussed as a quest at least since Auden. Gandalf himself announced, "The realm of Sauron is ended. The Ringbearer has fulfilled his quest," as Mordor and its armies collapse. A quest, however, presupposes something or someone that is sought. Circumstances and enemies will have to be overcome, but even if this involves the destruction of evil beings or places, the destruction is not the quest, only the means by which the quest is achieved. In *Lord of the Rings* only Sauron and his forces and Gollum are strictly on a quest, seeking the Ring. Frodo and his companions have the Ring. Their journey has only one purpose, to destroy it, ending Sauron's threat. Even

Aragorn, who apparently turns to save Gondor and take up his responsibilities, offers himself to his followers as bait to distract Sauron away from the Ringbearer. In this, *Lord of the Rings* is closely related to Mary Shelley's *Frankenstein*, in which Victor Frankenstein struggles to destroy his creation that has proved to be deeply flawed and uncontrollable.

Fantasy

Although all fiction writers, "make things up," fantasy involves this act of 'subcreation'—creating a world or vision of the world that has an inner consistency and honesty—to a much greater extent. Fantasy worlds are drawn with sharper outlines and clearer colors. At its best, fantasy draws the audience to fresh awareness of reality. The reader believes not because the genre requires suspension of disbelief, but because the consistency and coherence of the imaginary world compels belief. The *Lord of the Rings*' success is based in equal measure on delineation of a physical world and thoroughness in creating Middle Earth's historical cause and effect. Fantasy requires enormous discipline on the part of the writer or it will slide into sentimental wish fulfillment. A writer of fantasy can allow their characters almost unlimited range of experience, but must be rigorously selective in the character's reaction to them. It is a characteristic of the most successful type of modern fantasy that it extends the range of reaction by skewing the expected characters. In this, Tolkien took a lead, introducing an almost Dickensian invention.

HISTORICAL CONTEXT

Introduction

Tolkien is often approached with the expectation that he was a typical child of late Victorian and Edwardian England, and deeply embedded in the British intellectual establishment. He was in some ways, however, atypical. His Catholicism, passion for Philology, profound love and respect for the earth, and distrust of the benefits of technology, particularly that of the internal combustion engine, made him a potentially uneasy member of his society. Even as the atomic bomb was being developed, the Ring was emerging in his narrative as the technology that cannot be harnessed, but must be destroyed, the source of unlimited power that cor-

COMPARE & CONTRAST

- **Early Twentieth Century:** Tolkien's secondary school education is centered on the language and literature of Greece and Rome. He is expected not only to be able to read and write both languages, but to be able to speak them with some fluency. Debating in Latin was common, and in Classical Greek not unknown.

  Today: Science and technical subjects have moved to the heart of the curriculum in English-speaking countries, and few students receive a similarly thorough training even in their mother tongue.

- **Early Twentieth Century:** The society that Tolkien depicts is an essentially self-sufficient one, in which families grow their own food and most goods are produced locally by craftsmen. Trade, when mentioned, is usually in luxuries: wine, pipeweed, and dwarf-made toys. In Tolkien's own childhood in the English countryside, this life-style would have not have seemed like the stuff of fairy-tales, but very close to people's own experience.

  Today: Nearly all goods are mass-produced, often on a world-wide scale of distribution, and even the production of meals from basic ingredients is being superceded by ready prepared foods.

- **Early Twentieth Century:** There is a strong antipathy among many British people towards Catholics. Mrs. Tolkien's conversion distances her and her children from both her own and her husband's family. Her sister, who is converted at the same time, is forced by her husband to renounce her new faith.

  Today: Britain has a large population of Sikhs, Muslims, and Hindus whose religious views and observances are generally treated with respect and who are legally protected from discrimination.

---

rupts and destroys even the best and highest. His picture of the Shire, which works as a society because justice and law are internalized rather than imposed, while admittedly ideal, is an ideal that has more in common with the Jeffersonian ideal of democracy than Imperial or Post-Imperial Britain. Far from being an imperialist, Tolkien was the champion of the local, wherever it was, as is clear from Aragorn's treatment of Rohan, the Woses and the Shire. He identified deeply with the West Midlands of England and spent much of his scholarly life working on its medieval texts, which he felt preserved a literary language and a sense of worth and identity through the dark days of Norman French domination.

Philology

Tolkien's passion for language emerged in his earliest Latin lessons with his mother. Philology as it developed in the early nineteenth century, after the discovery of Sanskrit and its great grammarians by western scholars, was one of the intellectual success stories of the first half of the century. The discovery of a family of languages stretching from Ireland to India and the pattern of their development, the history fossilized in words and their changes of pronunciation and meaning can be compared to the great developments in cosmology in the twentieth century. Indeed Philology could be described as the particle physics of literature. Philology allowed scholars to comprehend patterns of thought deep in the past. At its best, Philology sensitizes the reader to nuances and subtle shifts of word meaning, which are the manifestations of conceptual development. At its worst, it can strike those outside the area as an arid and endlessly refining word game. Philology, properly done, is hard work and requires a facility for languages and a willingness to expend infinite care upon a text. Even at Oxford in Tolkien's time, Philology was under attack by members of the faculty who thought literature and their students should not be bogged down in what they perceived as minutia.

The Destruction of the Countryside and the Fallibility of Progress

In the "Scouring of the Shire" chapter of *The Return of the King*, Frodo, Sam, Merry, and Pippin return to find Sharkey (Saruman) and his men have been busy destroying the Shire, building ugly buildings, cutting down trees, and fouling the water and air. This is only the beginning on a smaller scale of a process the reader has already seen on an almost unimaginable scale in Mordor and in mimicry of Mordor at Isengard. Tolkien was deeply distrustful of the ideas of progress, which seemed to be driving his world. Unlike most of his colleagues, he had experienced the real face of industrialization. He had lived in some of the worst parts of industrial Birmingham. He wrote in incomprehension of colleagues, who described the enormous car factories growing up around Oxford as the real world, as if there was something essentially unreal about fields and trees. He mourned for a large tree that had been cut down by a neighbor apparently simply for having the temerity to be alive and big. He was also acutely aware of the uses made of technology and the impulse that often drove its development. In *The Hobbit*, he wrote, "It is not unlikely that they (Orcs) invented some of the machines that have since troubled the world, especially the ingenious devices for killing large numbers of people at once, for wheels and engines and explosions always delighted them, and also not working with their own hands more than they could help; but in those days and those wild places they had not advanced (as it is called) so far." He wrote of the prisoners and slaves that they made to work "until they die for want of light and air." Nevertheless, the Ring transcends a mere symbol for the atom bomb and Sauron has no true historical counterpart. They are embodiments of the idea of evil in which historical evils only participate, symbols of a situation in which men and women in the mid-twentieth century, like Frodo, found themselves with the possession of a power over nature. This possession is a threat over humanity so immense that even the contemplation and desire of its use corrupts. It is not enough that it be kept out of the hands of the evil, because it will betray the good into evil.

The Lord of the Rings and Catholicism

Tolkien's Catholicism was deeply felt. His devotion to Christ present in the sacrament of the Lord's Supper was both traditional and fervent. He was by no means, however, the typical conservative Catholic, and his Catholicism did not put him in an intellectual straight jacket. Even if we did not know

that he was a supporter of the Ecumenical movement and faulted the Church for its paternalistic attitude, the very ability to create a narrative and world that does without traditional biblical narrative would suggest it.

The Experience of the Twentieth Century, Old English Literature, and Heroism

Tolkien did not reject the idea of the heroic, but redefined it over a number of years. His understanding and treatment of the heroic was born out of an interaction between two Old English texts and the realities of the twentieth century. Looking at the Old English epic *Beowulf* in the context of the 1930s, he concentrated on the existence of radical evil and the necessity of opposing that evil even if in the face of inevitable defeat. By the 1950s, the effects of the almost inevitable pride of the traditional hero had come to loom large in Tolkien's thought and writing on the Old English poem The Battle of Maldon, in which the narrator suggests that Earl Beortnoth gives the Vikings an advantage out of pride, and therefore, throws his men's lives away in subordinating good sense to a notion of 'good form.' It is the heroism of obedience and love, of service, which has become the truly heroic in his mind.

Such a view of heroism is not new. It was traditionally the mode of representing the sacrifice of Christ and underlay the idea of king as shepherd of his people. It was a heroism that Tolkien had witnessed and taken to his heart in the horrors of his service in World War I. The renunciation of power is essential to Tolkien's view of heroism and to his perception of the changes brought about by mankind's ability to destroy itself and all earthly creation. The truly heroic required restraint, selflessness, and concern for the good of all. It required even the renunciation of glory. It is important that Aragorn insists that attention should be directed away from him to the Ringbearers and to Gandalf and it is important that Frodo seems almost relieved that he is not honored in the shire, and Sam hardly realizes his fame.

CRITICAL OVERVIEW

In 1997, the *Lord of the Rings* was voted the greatest book of the twentieth century in a poll run by a major British bookstore chain. The results were greeted with chagrin by some critics and writers who felt this vote slighted serious literature. Their reaction was a reprise of many of the initial reviews. Tolkien criticism has been deeply divided in the nearly half century since the Wilson and Auden reviews at the time of its publication. Their reviews, it seems, set the agenda for Tolkien criticism. Writer after writer has chased sources, refuted the accusation of ethical flatness, lack of character development, and escapism. Writer after writer has struggled with their revulsion of a work that has a cult following, which belongs supposedly to a minor and marginal genre (fantasy), that superficially at least seems entirely outside the mainstream of twentieth-century literature.

Wilson, in his famous (or infamous) 1956 review "Oo, Those Awful Orcs," would not give serious consideration to a work that was both generically and stylistically mixed. He rejected the sense of relativism and irony, which for many contemporary critics was the only possible stance for a serious writer and an intelligent audience, and would only be rejected out of escapism. Faced with a major literary figure, Auden (a former student of Tolkien's), who not only took the work seriously, but praised it, Wilson felt it necessary to politely excuse the poet's taste. To be fair, it cannot be denied that escapism is part of the lure of *Lord of the Rings* when one looks at the thousands of fantasy novels its success has spawned in the last thirty years. It is equally fair to say that the critics that have found Tolkien's normative ethics congenial, particularly those approaching him as a Catholic author, have seldom produced anything much above the trite. A full study of late nineteenth-century and twentieth-century Catholic theology and Tolkien's understanding and reaction to it has yet to be written.

It has been suggested this lack of critical sympathy is the result of a lack of sympathy with or knowledge of the early medieval literature behind Tolkien's work. But most readers of *Lord of the Rings* are not specialists in early medieval literature, although many present day members of departments of Old and Middle English literature came to the subject from *Lord of the Rings*. Despite Isaacs' request for analytical and formalist approaches in 1968, the reader will still find, as Rosebury did, too much substitution of classification for analysis. Rosebury unerringly put his finger on perhaps the central problem of Tolkien criticism: "The truth is that it is difficult to write well about Tolkien because of the distinctive nature of his merits . . . yet if he is to be praised effectively, the praise must be justified in terms of which bear an intelligible

relation to other writers. . . . Analysis and evaluation are always comparative." Tolkien criticism still seems to be too much in the hands of, as Carpenter says, the "deplorable cultus" of which Tolkien himself complained. Numerous books and articles appear to be written by authors who have not really digested their research, who do not seem to realize that the one thing a Tolkien critic does not need to do is to retell the story for the reader. Too many books and articles have been written by critics who feel it their duty to insist *Lord of the Rings* is not literature, and if it is, it certainly is not good literature, often making sweeping pronouncements on style or characterization, which cannot be defended in the light of close reading.

There has been good Tolkien criticism. Purtill handles myth, morality, and religion in *Lord of the Rings*. He makes a beginning on the question of the essential nature of modern fantasy, linking it appropriately with science fiction. He is one of the very few critics to even advert to the often overlooked theme of immortality in *Lord of the Rings*. Nevertheless, he is capable of simple mistakes of facts and leaves the reader with the feeling they have experienced a good beginning, but that there is much more to be done.

Rosebury and Shippey, however, have easily produced the two best critical studies of *Lord of the Rings*, both appropriately published in the centenary year of the author's birth. Shippey's work will probably be the standard work on the northern European sources of Tolkien, as well on the particularly unfortunate animus that existed and so often continues to exist between the critics and scholars working on either side of the great watershed of the Renaissance. Rosebury's study, besides its technical excellence, commends itself in that it is perhaps the first written by a critic who, while clearly appreciating Tolkien both on an emotional and aesthetic level, makes no grandiose claims for high position in English literature. Even for a reader who would rank Tolkien a good deal higher than Poe, Rosebury's choice of comparison, such relative balance is reassuring. Rosebury, unlike so many enthusiastic admirers of Tolkien, takes the trouble to apply the sort of close reading Tolkien the scholar applied to texts. He gives a detailed and satisfying account of the methods Tolkien used in creating the fullness of his world in words. He moves then from method to the aesthetic as well as philosophical meaning of this fullness of breadth and detail. Continuing his pattern of close reading, he discusses the prose style and the infinite pains in word choice and sentence structure in *Lord of the Rings*. No author who can command the interests of two such critics can possibly be dismissed as minor.

CRITICISM

Helen Conrad-O'Briain

In the following essay, Conrad-O'Briain suggests that Tolkien's treatment of women is far more sensitive than critics have generally allowed.

Tolkien has been accused of being perfunctory in his treatment of his female characters and excused as being merely a man of his times. Looking closely at the characters in *Lord of the Rings*, however, it could be argued that Tolkien returned to possibilities for female participation which the epic traditionally afforded, but which were long overlooked in criticism. Tolkien's own relationships with women were obviously largely a product of his time. The early death of his mother, his marriage to a woman who was uncomfortable in Oxford intellectual circles, and the attitude of C. S. Lewis, whose misogyny was only overcome by a late marriage, all affected Tolkien. It is wrong, however, that it always affected him for the worse. Tolkien had been a student of Joseph Wright, the philologist who had married a former student. She not only worked alongside her husband, but made Tolkien and many other students comfortably at home. His final scholarly collaborator was a woman, Simone d'Ardenne, a former student who became a professor at Liege. This promising collaboration, thwarted in part by the World War II, only ended because of his increasing involvement with his fiction.

"My friend . . . you had horses, and deeds of arms, and the free fields; but she, born in the body of a maid, had a spirit and courage at least the match of yours. Yet she was doomed to wait upon an old man, whom she loved as a father, and watch him falling into a mean dishonoured dotage; and her part seemed to her more ignoble than that of the staff he leaned on." These lines from *The Return of the King* are a recognition of spirit that has nothing to do with gender, and the effects of a gender-based division of opportunities on ability. From a man born in the reign of Victoria, who spent most of his life in the men's club atmosphere of the Oxford colleges, it suggests an unexpected, but genuine, sensitivity.

The women in *Lord of the Rings* reflect the broad generic background that Tolkien co-opted

Manuscript page from Beowulf. *Tolkien's story contains ancient and archetypal patterns of events and characters derived from Old English models like* Beowulf.

into his novel. They range from the comic Lobelia Sackville-Baggins who could, except for her furry feet, wander through the door at Blandings without more than a passing groan from Lord Emsworth, to Galadriel, who one suspects has more than a little in common with the hero, Athena. Between them are Mrs. Maggot and Rose Cotton, who could be out of the kinder moments of Hardy, and Goldberry, who like her husband seems to represent the earth as it might have been. There is Arwen, elusive, and in the end, hidden away in the Appendices, supremely tragic. The true female counterpart of Frodo, she is wounded by the choice between father and lover, immortality and mortality, just as Frodo is by the experience of the Ring. Although she assumes mortality, she dies utterly elven in her attitude. The individual reader is almost forced to react to it on a purely subjective level.

Three women, however, are pivotal in *Lord of the Rings*: Ioreth, Eowyn and Galadriel. Each of them is not only important to cause and effect in the narrative, but each gathers up important thematic threads.

WHAT DO I READ NEXT?

- Tolkien's first published fiction in 1937 was *The Hobbit*, subtitled *or There and Back Again*. It was written as a freestanding children's story within the world of Middle Earth. It became, however, with significant revisions of the Ring finding episode, the prelude for the whole of *Lord of the Rings*.

- Although J. R. R. Tolkien's *The Silmarillion* was published posthumously in 1977, he was working on it as early as 1917. It is a narrative of the Elder Days, beginning with Eru, the One, Ilúvatar, the creator, and ending with the downfall of Númenor and the changing of the world so that there was no longer a straight passage to the Deathless lands. Unlike *The Hobbit* or the *Lord of the Rings*, it makes little or no use of modern novelistic conventions. Christopher Tolkien writes in the Foreword that the material "became the vehicle of his profoundest reflections. In his later writing, mythology and poetry sank down behind his theological and philosophical preoccupations: 'from which arose incompatibilities of tone.'"

- Tolkien's *Farmer Giles of Ham* published in 1949 includes a gentle send-up of scholarship and ironic observations on the perennial faults of central government in a hilarious tale of a talking dog, a short-sighted giant, a clever but unlucky dragon, and a hero more astute than heroic, but no less effective for it.

- Tolkien's "On Fairy Stories," a revision of his Andre Lang Lecture of 1938 at the University of St. Andrews, was first published in 1947 in "Essays presented to Charles Williams." It is more generally available in the collections *Tree and Leaf* or *The Tolkien Reader*, and is a reflection on his thinking about what he was trying to achieve in *Lord of the Rings*.

- *Grimm's Teutonic Mythology*, translated by J. S. Stallybrass, (4 volumes, 1882–88) from the original work by the Brothers Grimm of fairytale fame, is a rich collection of the fragments of the lost mythology and legend from the Germanic past.

Ioreth is the lineal descendant of Juliet's nurse, if less earthy, certainly, and, if she could be stopped for the question, unlikely to suggest deception and bigamy as the answer to any problem. But for all the comedy of her character, Ioreth performs and embodies a vitally important cluster of functions. She might be called the tenth muse, the muse not of a particular genre, but of those all-important literary functions: preservation and transmission. She is muse as philologist. It is she who remembers that "the hands of the king are the hands of the healer." She and her kind remember the old rhymes and words and ponder them, "'kingsfoil' . . . 'tis a strange name, and I wonder why 'tis called so; for if I were a king I would have plants more bright in my garden." Her garrulousness is comic, but it is more than comic; it is deeply characteristic. She must repeat what she remembers, what she has heard, what she has experienced. She is a repository, transmitter commentator. On Aragorn's triumphal re-entry into Gondor, she begins the transmutation/transposition of event into literature "Would you believe. . ." Old wives tales, or the material of epic? But as Charles M. Schulz famously had Linus van Pelt remark "some of those old wives were pretty smart." There may be a formal minstrel's "Nine fingered Frodo and the Ring of Doom," but anyone who has read Tolkien's "On Fairy Stories" will know perfectly well the version Tolkien would expect to sink deep into the hearts and minds of the west like a grain of sand in an oyster. However comic Ioreth is, she is not mere comic relief, to a philologist, she is the *beau ideal* of the Brothers Grimm. Ioreth is a moral reality check. She wrenches the narrative away from the dash and superficial glories of battle, the grandeur that never bears close scrutiny, to the real purpose of the fight outside the walls. As she says, "All I hope is that those murdering devils do not come to this House and trouble the sick." Battles are a means to an end and nothing more. It is characteristic of Tolkien to place so much weight on a minor character, albeit in highly specific areas.

Eowyn the Lady of the Golden House and Galadriel the Lady of the Golden Wood, while superficially unlike, are, in fact, intensely alike. Their differences are of degree not kind. To see Eowyn, one intuits in the *Lord of the Rings*, is to see Galadriel in her youth. This suspicion is confirmed in the *Silmarrillion* and the *Unfinished Tales*. Tolkien wrote that Galadriel was "tall and valiant among the contending princes . . . she yearned to see the wide unguarded lands and to rule there a realm at her own will." In *Unfinished Tales*, "she was strong of body, mind, and will, a match both the loremasters and athletes of the Eldar . . . she had a marvellous gift of insight into the minds of others."

Eowyn is her mortal equivalent, a Galadriel for the fourth age. At her first meeting she looks at Aragorn and "she was suddenly aware of him: tall heir of kings, wise with many winters, greycloaked hiding a power that yet she felt." If Theoden is slow to recognize her as the equal of any man of his house, other men are not. When Theoden asks who he shall leave in charge of the Mark and protests that his nephew who cannot be spared from the host is the last of his house, the warrior Hama replies, "I said not Eomer . . . And he is not the last. There is Eowyn, daughter of Eomund, his sister. She is fearless and high-hearted. All love her. Let her be as Lord to the Eorlingas, while we are gone." Eowyn and Galadriel, both in their own way, have fought the long defeat: Eowyn, the premature dotage of her uncle; Galdriel, the flawed and mutable nature of Middle Earth. Both were looking for a stage for their talents, Galadriel in Middle Earth, Eowyn on the battlefield. Both of them in defying an injunction bring themselves into danger, but nevertheless, fight the good fight. Both Galadriel and Eowyn end up rejecting their original desires. Galadriel, offered the Ring and all the power she has ever desired, rejects it and accepts that she will depart and go into the west. Eowyn gives up the glory of battle for another life, but not quite the life that she has flown. Feminist readers may complain of Eowyn's change of heart, but to describe this as merely a move from the "masculine" (and, therefore, high status) arena of warfare to the "female" (and, therefore, low status) forum of marriage and the restoration of

> " Three women, however, are pivotal in Lord of the Rings: Ioreth, Eowyn and Galadriel. Each of them is not only important to cause and effect in the narrative, but each gathers up important thematic threads."

Ithilien, is to willfully misread the episode and the characters involved.

Eowyn is not a minor character. She does not represent the young woman who learns her place or even moves from infatuation with death and glory to life's quieter victories. She carries first the burden of representing the woman who can move across the stereotypical roles of male and female—she does this even before she disguises herself—and her ability to cross these boundaries is acknowledged by the institutions of her society. In this, she replaces Galadriel in the second half of *Lord of the Rings* as the woman who crosses the traditional boundaries by virtue of her character, a character and ability that cannot be denied. But Eowyn draws more meaning to her character.

Eowyn points two ways in her speech to Aragorn. She bluntly sweeps aside all the rhetoric of the glory of war and idealized, romantic womanhood: "All your words are but to say you are a woman, your part is in the house. But when the men have died in battle and honour, you have leave to be burned in the house, for the men will need it no more." The lines pivot on "honour"; there is no glorious immortality of fame for the non-combatants. Aragorn may plead with her to recognize her duty and valor all the greater, for being uncelebrated, but Eowyn now equates the war with her one chance of being with Aragorn. Although her infatuation with him is only a symptom of her desire to excel in a way her society has traditionally recognized. It is in this context that the stage is set to place Eowyn with Merry and Beregond. Eowyn makes a conscious decision to disobey orders, to leave her post. Her dereliction of duty is perhaps the most reprehensible, since a people depend upon her. Tolkien's treatment of this is sympathetic, partially because it fits into his scheme of providence: she and Merry kill the chief Ringwraith, partially because he is essentially sympathetic to her frustration. Her dereliction of duty is never alluded to by any of the characters or by the narrator. Even more important is what lies behind Merry's belief that "There seemed to be some sort of understanding between Dernhelm and Elfhelm, the Marshall who commanded the *éored* in which they were riding." Is Elfhelm acquiescing merely in Merry's presence or does he know and sympathize with her more?

Eowyn is not thinking of glory, however, when she stands between her dying uncle and the Witchking. She is acting out of pure love to protect the man who has raised her as if she were his own child. Her change of heart, however, does not begin then. It begins when there is an alternative offered that is worthy of her. She does not marry Faramir because she cannot have Aragorn, neither does she betray her abilities. The opposite is true. Faramir has been carefully developed to offer an alternative measure of courage and honor, heroism focused on more than warfare, to include creating and conserving. Faramir's own nature and his talents have been consistently placed in opposition to mere military prowess. Tolkien does not create a female character who must learn to accept a female role. Rather, he creates a female character who comes to love a man who like her can cross the traditional boundaries of gender roles. And when she finds him, they will banter like Benedict and Beatrice, on the walls of Minas Tirith.

Source: Helen Conrad-O'Briain, for *Epics for Students*, Gale, 2001.

James Obertino

In J. R. R. Tolkien's The Fellowship of the Ring, *Obertino examines Gandalf's sacrifice and its relation to the bible.*

The death of Gandalf is a moment of transcendent heroism in *The Fellowship of the Ring*, yet Celeborn, reflecting on it later, remarks, "And if it were possible, one would say that at last Gandalf fell from wisdom into folly, going needlessly into the net of Moria". An understanding of the strongly overdetermined etymology of Moria helps to clarify the significance of Gandalf's death and the question of his fate and folly. Moria's roots would have to include *mors* (Latin for death), as well as *Moira* (Greek for fate) and *moria* (Greek for madness, late

Latin for folly). Celeborn's remark unwittingly stresses the thematic linkage of fate (*Moira*) or "net" (a frequent image for fate) and folly (*moria*). The drumbeats that sound within the earth before and after Gandalf's death seem to stress fate: "doom, doom". It is, however, also possible to see, as Celeborn does, Gandalf's death as perhaps foolish or unnecessary, as his fall at the Bridge of Khazad-dum (emphasis supplied) may imply. But is Gandalf's leading the company into Moria, where he dies, as foolish as Celeborn implies?

In fact, far from "going needlessly" into Moria, Gandalf first considers other tactical options and even tries one-the ascent of Caradhras-as an alternative to the underworld journey. To go around the mountains would endanger the quest by prolonging it and open the company to further observation from the air and interference by the enemy. The company attempts to climb over the mountains but is rebuffed by Caradhras itself. By the time Gandalf recommends the descent, Moria is the only reasonable option available. Later in Lothlorien, Galadriel sees this more clearly than her husband Celeborn: "Needless were none of the deeds of Gandalf in life". Nevertheless, even Frodo, who was present during the deliberations that took the company into the earth, seems to have doubts about whether Gandalf's death was wise: "In Khazad-dum, his wisdom died". Frodo's lament suggests that he may see his friend's death, a result of the descent into Moria, as foolish.

A way to reconcile Gandalf's fate (in the sense of unavoidable death) with a wisdom that also addresses the issue of folly is found in the New Testament, and especially Corinthians. The Christian precept "Greater love hath no man than this, that a man lay down his life for his friends" (John 15:13) pairs love with the willing self-sacrifice of death, and the god-hero of Christendom would for Tolkien be the principal exemplar of self-sacrifice for love. The path of martydom or "the wisdom of the Cross" is foolishness to the non-Christian (I Cor 1.18), who prefers the "fleshly wisdom" (2 Cor 1.12) that serves oneself and not others. Following the slain hero and often expecting themselves to be slain, the early Christians turned upside down the conventional wisdom that seeks self-preservation above all else. Thus St. Paul notes, "God" has "made foolish the wisdom of this world" through the folly of freely chosen self-sacrifice (I Cor 1.20–23). To refuse to give one's life and instead to follow the way of the world by pursuing a longer life and more pleasure for the flesh was, in the view of the marginalized early Christians, a colossal error: "The wisdom of this world is foolishness with God" (1 Cor 3.19). To see Gandalf's sacrificial death as perhaps foolish is a temporary lapse of judgment on Celeborn's and Frodo's part, perhaps useful to remind the reader that the flesh and its wisdom make their strong demands despite what real wisdom compels one to do. But Gandalf must not be measured by the wisdom of the world, as his rebirth makes clear. Gandalf fits the Pauline model, for his death to save others and preserve Frodo's quest shows a foolishness that is "wiser than men" (1 Cor 1.25).

The place of Gandalf's death—Moria—in addition to having the associations noted earlier also echoes Moriah in Genesis 22.2, the land where Jahweh commands Abraham to take Isaac to sacrifice him "as a burnt offering on one of the mountains." Gandalf is pulled by the burning Balrog into the depths of a mountain. While Jahweh relents in the matter of the sacrifice of Isaac, God the Father in the New Testament does not in demanding the sacrifice of his only begotten Son. Another dissimilarity between the Genesis Moriah and the trek into Moria is that circumstances, rather than the voice of God, dictate the journey in Tolkien and the stand at the bridge. But Gandalf's self-sacrificial death is in accord with the precept of obedience to the higher good that the Genesis story endorses. His death also reveals the same strategy of renunciation Gandalf recommends Frodo take in bearing the Ring into the center of darkness that is Sauron's home and there throwing it into the cracks of Doom, because Sauron will not expect the Ring-bearer to willingly give it up and throw it away. About this strategy Gandalf remarks, "It is wisdom to recognize necessity, when all other courses have been weighed, though as folly it may appear to those who cling to false hope". The paradox that wisdom may be found by going before one's time into the earth and that only a crazy person would go there to find it is also seen in *The Aeneid*, where the Sibyl calls Aeneas's quest into Hades a fantastic project, or "insanus labor". But Tolkien goes beyond the Roman model of catabasis because Gandalf, unlike Aeneas, actually dies in the underworld. Gandalf's apparently foolish, yet ultimately wise, death through sacrifice, for both his friends and the good of all Middle Earth, is folly to those who refuse to see the goodness of the gesture, but through redemptive self-surrender "God has made foolish the wisdom of this world" (1 Cor 1.20). That this sacrifice occurs in Moria (Moriah) is especially appropriate.

> "The Christian precept 'Greater love hath no man than this, that a man lay down his life for his friends' (John 15:13) pairs love with the willing self-sacrifice of death, and the god-hero of Christendom would for Tolkien be the principal exemplar of self-sacrifice for love."

Source: James Obertino, "Tolkien's *The Fellowship of the Ring*," in *The Explicator*, Vol. 54, No. 4, Summer, 1996.

Ralph C. Wood

J. R. R. Tolkien's Lord of the Rings *recounts a pre-biblical period of history from a point of view that is distinctly Christian. In this article, Wood discusses Christian aspects in this epic.*

J. R. R. Tolkien's *Lord of the Rings* is a massive epic fantasy of more than a half-million words. It is also a hugely complex work, with its own complicated chronology, cosmogony, geography, nomenclature and multiple languages, including two forms of elvish. The plot is so grand, moreover, that it casts backward to the formation of first things while glancing forward to the end of time. How did this huge and learned work—written by an obscure Oxford philologist—become a classic?

The answer has to do with Tolkien's central characters. They are humanoid creatures called hobbits, and their unlikely hero has the unheroic name of Frodo. During the 1960s, so many American youths were drawn to these diminutive creatures that Tolkien became something of a cult figure. "Frodo Lives" was a popular graffito of the time. T-shirts declared that "Tolkien is Hobbit-Forming." No doubt there was something escapist about this hobbit-habit. Perplexed by our nation's carnage in Vietnam and by the ultimate threat of a nuclear inferno, a whole generation of young Americans could lose themselves and their troubles in the intricacies of this triple-decker epic. Indeed, the

Tolkien was influenced by Anglo-Saxon history and the adventures of its main characters, the Vikings.

ents frees us from bondage to the pseudo-reality that most of us inhabit: a world deadened by bleary familiarity. Fantasy, Tolkien observed, helps us recover a sense of wonder about ordinary things: "stone, and wood, and iron; tree and grass; house and fire; bread and wine."

Despite the eucharistic hint, Tolkien's work is not self-evidently Christian. As C. S. Lewis observed when it was first published, the Ring epic is imbued with "a profound melancholy." The ending is tearfully sad. Frodo is exhausted by his long quest to destroy the Ring of coercive power that had been fashioned by the monster Sauron. Though the victory has been won, Frodo cannot enjoy its fruits. And so he sails away to the elven realm, leaving his companions behind. Sauron and his minions of evil may have been defeated, but the triumph is only temporary. Evil will reconstitute itself in some alarming new form, and the free creatures of Middle Earth will have to fight it yet again.

The word "doom"—in its Anglo-Saxon meaning of damning judgment as well as final fate in ruin and death—pulses like a funereal drumbeat throughout the entire work. Toward the end of volume I, the elf Legolas offers a doom-centered vision of the world. It sounds very much like an elvish and Heraclitean version of entropy. "To find and lose," says Legolas, is the destiny "of those whose boat is on the running stream.... The passing seasons are but ripples in the long long stream. Yet beneath the Sun all things must wear to an end at last." Though elves are so long-lived that they seem immortal to humans and hobbits, the tides of time will sweep even them away. A deeply pagan pessimism pervades all three of the Ring books.

Yet it is a mistake to read Tolkien's work as sub-Christian. Tolkien, the finest *Beowulf* scholar of his day, had a thesis about the Anglo-Saxon epic that may be applied to his own fiction. *Beowulf* is a pagan work, Tolkien argued, exalting the ancient Scandinavian and heathen virtue of an unyielding, indomitable will in the face of sure and hopeless defeat. Yet it was probably written by a Christian, Tolkien contended, who infused it with Christian concerns: "The author of *Beowulf* showed forth the permanent value of that pietas which treasures the memory of man's struggles in the dark past, man fallen and not yet saved, disgraced but not dethroned." In a similar way, *The Lord of the Rings* recounts a prebiblical period of history—a time when there were no Chosen People, no incarnation,

rumor got about—a wish seeking its fulfillment, no doubt—that Tolkien had composed *The Lord of the Rings* under the influence of drugs.

Yet *The Lord of the Rings* has outlasted its cult status. Repeated readings do not exhaust its potential to deepen and define our moral and spiritual lives. Young and old alike keep returning to it for both wisdom and delight. True fantasy, Tolkien declared in his 1939 essay "On Fairy-Stories," is escapist in the good sense: it enables us to flee into reality. The strange world of hobbits and elves and no religion at all—from a point of view that is distinctly Christian.

This judgment may seem strange because there is little that is Christian about *The Hobbit*, Tolkien's first fantasy work, published in 1937. It is a standard quest-story about the seeking and the finding of a tremendous treasure, a delightful "there and back again" tale concerning the adventures of Bilbo Baggins. But by the time he published *The Lord of the Rings* in 1954 and 1955, Tolkien had deepened and widened his vision, especially concerning the nature of heroism. The hobbits prove to be perennially attractive characters because they are very unconventional heroes. They are not tragic and death-defying warriors like Ajax or Achilles or Beowulf; they are frail and comic foot soldiers like us. The Nine Walkers—four hobbits, two men, an elf, a dwarf and a wizard—constitute a company not of the noble but of the ordinary.

They all learn, in a proleptically Christian way, what every mortal must confront: that we no sooner find our lives than we have to give them up. Unlike Bilbo, Frodo his nephew is called not to find but to lose, indeed to destroy, his great gem: the Ring of Total Control. It is a task that he does not seek but reluctantly accepts. Yet Frodo proves to be a fit bearer of the Ring. Not only does he possess native powers of courage and resistance; he is also summoned by a mysterious providential grace. The destruction of the Ring is nothing less than Frodo's vocation. And the epic's compelling interest lies in our discovery of how, just barely, Frodo remains faithful to his calling. In so doing he does far more than save his beloved Shire from ruin. Frodo learns—and thus teaches—what for Tolkien is the deepest of all Christian truths: how to surrender one's life, how to lose one's treasure, how to die, and thus how truly to live.

Early in the narrative, Frodo recalls that his Uncle Bilbo, especially during his latter years, was fond of declaring that

> ... there was only one Road; that it was like a great river: its springs were at every doorstep, and every path was its tributary. "It's a dangerous business, Frodo, going out your door," he used to say. "You step into the Road, and if you don't keep your feet, there is no knowing where you might be swept off to."

Tolkien's work is imbued with a mystical sense of life as a journey that carries one, willy-nilly, beyond the walls of the world. To get out of bed, to answer the phone, to open the door, to fetch the mail—such everyday deeds are freighted with eternal consequence. They immerse us in the river of

> **" Tolkien's work is imbued with a mystical sense of life as a journey that carries one, willy-nilly, beyond the walls of the world. . .everyday deeds are freighted with eternal consequence. They immerse us in the river of time: the 'ever-rolling stream' which, in Isaac Watts's splendid rendering of the 90th Psalm, 'bears all its sons away.'"**

time: the "ever-rolling stream" which, in Isaac Watts's splendid rendering of the 90th Psalm, "bears all its sons away." Whether engaged in great or small acts of courage or cowardice, we are traveling on the path toward ultimate joy or final ruin.

For Tolkien the Christian, the chief question—and thus the real quest—is how we are to travel along this Road. The great temptation is to take short-cuts, to follow the easy way, to arrive quickly. In the antique world of Middle Earth, magic offers the surest escape from slowness and suffering. It is the equivalent of our machines. They both provide what Tolkien in a letter called immediacy: "speed, reduction of labor, and reduction also to a minimum (or vanishing point) of the gap between the idea or desire and the result or effect." The magic of machination is meant for those who lack patience, who cannot wait. Sauron wins converts because he provides his followers the necromancy to coerce the wills of others, the strength to accomplish grand ends by instant means.

The noble prove to be most nobly tempted. Gandalf, the Christlike wizard who lays down his life for his friends, knows that he is an unworthy bearer of the Ring—not because he has evil designs that he wants secretly to accomplish, but rather because his desire to do good is so great. Lady Galadriel, the elven queen, also refuses the Ring of Force. It would make her enormous beauty mesmerizing. Those who had freely admired her loveliness would have no choice but to worship her. Perhaps alone among modern writers, Tolkien understood that evil's subtlest semblance is not with the ugly but with the gorgeous. "I shall not be dark," Galadriel warns, "but beautiful and terrible as the Morning and the Night! Fair as the Sea and the Sun and the Snow upon the Mountain! Dreadful as the Storm and the Lightning! Stronger than the foundations of the earth. All shall love me and despair!"

The one free creature utterly undone by the lure of total power is Saruman the wizard. Like Judas, he is impatient with the slow way that goodness works. He cannot abide the torturous path up Mount Doom; he wants rapid results. Since the all-commanding Sauron is sure to win, Saruman urges Gandalf and his friends to join forces with the Dark Lord. Those who face defeat can survive only by siding with the victor, using his coercive power to achieve their own noble aims: "We can bide our time, we can keep our thoughts in our hearts, deploring maybe evils done by the way, but approving the high and ultimate purpose: Knowledge, Rule, Order; all the things we have so far striven in vain to accomplish, hindered rather than helped by our weak or idle friends."

Saruman is doubly blind. He fails to see that laudable designs, when achieved by compulsive force, become demonic. Neither does he perceive the hidden strength of the hobbits. The chief irony of the entire epic is that hobbitic weakness is the solution to the problem of Absolute Might. The hobbits are worthy opponents of Sauron because their life-aims are so modest. Wanting nothing more than to preserve the freedom of their peaceable Shire, they have no grandiose uses for the Ring. Their meekness uniquely qualifies them to destroy the Ring in the Cracks of Doom. This is a quest that can be accomplished by the small even better than the great. In fact, the figure who gradually emerges as the rightful successor to Frodo is the least likely hobbit of them all, the comically inept and ungainly Samwise Gamgee.

In the unlikely heroism of the small and the weak, Tolkien's pre-Christian world becomes most Christian. Their greatness is not self-made. As a fledgling community of faith, the Nine Walkers experience a far-off foretaste of the fellowship that Christians call the church universal. Their company remarkably transcends both racial and ethnic boundaries. Though it contains representatives from all of the Free Peoples, some of them have been historic enemies—especially the dwarves and the elves. No shallow commitment to diversity binds them together. They are united by their hatred of evil, and even more by their ever-increasing, self-surrendering regard for one another. Through their long communal struggle, they learn that there is a power greater than mere might. It springs not from the force of will but from a grace-filled fellowship of kindred minds and souls.

Perhaps we can now understand what Tolkien meant when he called *The Lord of the Rings* "a fundamentally religious and Catholic work." Its essential conflict, he insisted, concerns God's "sole right to divine honor." Like Milton's Satan, Sauron will not serve such a deity. He is intent upon his own supremacy, and he reads all others by his own light. He believes that anyone, having once possessed the power afforded by the Ring, will be determined to use it—especially the magical power to make its wearer invisible. He assumes that Frodo and his friends will seek to overthrow him and to establish their own sovereignty. Sauron's calculus of self-interest blinds him to the Company's strategy. Under Gandalf's leadership, they decide not to hide or use the Ring, but to take it straight back into the Land of Mordor—Sauron's lair—to incinerate it.

Not for want of mental power is Sauron deceived. He is a creature whose craft and power are very great, as his fashioning of the Ring proves. Sauron also embodies himself as a terrible all-seeing Eye. He can thus discern the outward operation of things, but he cannot discern the inward workings of the heart. Sauron's fatal lack is not intelligence, therefore, but sympathy. He cannot "feel with," and so he is incapable of community. The ores, the evil creatures whom Sauron has bred to do his will, constantly betray each other and feud among themselves. Tolkien thus holds out the considerable hope that evil cannot form a fellowship: there is no true Compact of the Wicked, but there is a real Company of the Good.

The animating power of this Company is the much-maligned virtue called pity. Frodo had learned the meaning of pity from his Uncle Bilbo. When he first obtained the Ring from the vile creature called Gollum, Bilbo had the chance to kill him but did not. Frodo is perplexed by this refusal. 'Tis a pity, he maintains, that Bilbo did not slay such an evil one. This phrase angers Gandalf, and prompts him to make the most important declaration in the entire epic:

"Pity? It was pity that stayed his hand. Pity, and Mercy; not to strike without need. And he has been well rewarded, Frodo. Be sure that [Bilbo] took so little hurt from the evil, and escaped in the end, because he began his ownership of the Ring so. With Pity."

"I am sorry," said Frodo. "But … I do not feel any pity for Gollum … He deserves death."

"Deserves it! I daresay he does," [replies Gandalf]. "Many that live deserve death. And some that die deserve life. Can you give it to them? Then do not be too eager to deal out death in judgement … The pity of Bilbo will rule the fate of many—yours not least.

"The pity of Bilbo will rule the fate of many" becomes the motto of Tolkien's epic. It is true in the literal sense, because the Gollum whom Bilbo had spared so long ago is the one who finally destroys the Ring. The saying is also true in a spiritual sense. Gandalf the pagan wizard describes the nature of Christian mercy. As a creature far more sinning than sinned against, Gollum deserves his misery. He has committed Cain's crime of fratricide in acquiring the Ring. Still, Gandalf insists on pity, despite Frodo's protest that Gollum should be given justice. If all died who deserve punishment, none would live. Many perish who have earned life, and yet who can restore them? Neither hobbits nor humans can live by the bread of merit alone.

The unstrained quality of mercy makes *The Lord of the Rings* an enduring Christian classic despite its pagan setting. As a pre-Christian work, it is appropriately characterized by a melancholy sense of ineluctable doom and defeat: the night that comes shall cover everything. Such profound pessimism must not be disregarded. It has its biblical equivalent, after all, in the dark omen of death found in Ecclesiastes 12:5: "man goeth to his long home."

Yet this gloomy saying is not the ultimate word. Near the end of their wearying quest, Frodo and Sam are alone on the slopes of Mount Doom. All their efforts seem to have failed. Even if somehow they succeed in destroying the Ring, there is no likelihood that they will themselves survive, or that anyone will ever hear of their valiant deed. Amid such hopelessness, Sam—the bumbling and unreflective hobbit who has gradually emerged as a figure of great moral and spiritual depth—beholds a single star shimmering above the dark clouds of Mordor:

> The beauty of it smote his heart, as he looked up out of that forsaken land, and hope returned to him. For like a shaft, clear and cold, the thought pierced him that in

the end the Shadow was only a small and passing thing: there was light and high beauty for ever beyond its reach.… Now, for a moment, his own fate, and even his master's ceased to trouble him. He crawled back into the brambles and laid himself by Frodo's side, and putting away all fear he cast himself into a deep and untroubled sleep.

Sam discerns that light and shadow are not warring in uncertain battle. It is the gleaming star that defines the darkness. These hobbits cannot name their source, but they know that Goodness and Truth and Beauty are the first and the last and the only permanent things.

Source: Ralph C. Wood, "'Traveling the one road': *The Lord of the Rings* as a …," in *The Christian Century,* Vol. 110, No. 6, Feb. 24, 1993, pp. 208–11.

Tom Shippey

T. A. Shippey talks about the symbolism of J. R. R. Tolkien's characters from The Lord of the Rings *through* The Council of Elrond.

The gist of what has been said in this chapter is that *The Lord of the Rings* possesses unusual cultural depth. 'Culture' is not a word Tolkien used much; it changed meaning sharply during his lifetime, and not in a direction he approved. Still, one can see a deep understanding of its modern meaning of 'the whole complex of learned behaviour … the material possessions, the language and other symbolism, of some body of people' in chapter 2 of Book II of *The Fellowship of the Ring*. This marks a jump-off point for the characters, whose objective is disclosed within it. It was also I suspect a jump-off point for Tolkien, since after that he was no longer writing his way through landscapes he had travelled before. It is therefore perhaps not surprising that as with the house of Beorn in *The Hobbit* 'The Council of Elrond' should provide a sudden introduction to archaic and heroic worlds confronting and overwhelming modern, practical ones. The later work is, however, many degrees more complex than its earlier analogue, being indeed an interweaving of at least six major voices besides minor ones and reported ones; as well as telling a complex tale in complex fashion what all these voices do is present, in our language, a violent 'culture-clash'.

This comes out most in the speeches and scripts impacted *inside* Gandalf's monologue of pages 269–78, the fifth and longest from a major speaker (the others coming from Glóin, Elrond, Boromir, Aragorn, Legolas). Within that monologue Gaffer

> Elrond has seen 'many defeats, and many fruitless victories,' and in a way he has even given up hope, at least for his adopted people the elves; but this does not make him change his mind or look for easy options."

Gamgee functions as a kind of base-line of normality—and, concomitantly, of emptiness. 'I had words with old Gamgee', Gandalf reports, 'Many words and few to the point':

> '"I can't abide changes," said he, "not at my time of life, and least of all changes for the worst." "Changes for the worst," he repeated many times.
>
> '"Worst is a bad word," I said to him, "and I hope you do not live to see it."'

It is indeed a bad word, especially when all the Gaffer has to complain about is the Sackville-Bagginses; Denethor uses it as well, much later, but again with ominous effect. As for 'abide', as used by Gaffer Gamgee it has almost no semantic content at all; in context it means 'bear, tolerate, put up with', but in that sense is simply untrue. The Gaffer *can* abide changes; he just has. He means only that he doesn't like them. But there is a moral for him in the history of the word, which has the frequent early sense of 'to await the issue of, to wait (stoically) for, to live to see'. In this last sense the Gaffer *could* 'abide' changes, and he does. Right at the end he moralises, stubborn as ever, 'It's an ill wind as blows nobody any good, *as I always say*' (my italics), 'And All's well as ends Better'. At least he has learnt to eschew superlatives. But his language in Gandalf's monologue conveys an unwelcome reminder of psychological unpreparedness.

However there is another modern voice in Gandalf's monologue to act as vehicle for cultural contrast: this is Saruman's. He has hardly been mentioned before, and the question whether he is good or bad is more difficult to decide than with most. But when he is introduced by Gandalf, we know what to think very soon; the message is conveyed by style and lexis. Saruman talks like a politician. 'We can bide our time', he says, using a fossilised phrase:

> 'we can keep our thoughts in our hearts, deploring maybe evils done by the way, but approving the high and ultimate purpose: Knowledge, Rule, Order, all things that we have so far striven in vain to accomplish, hindered rather than helped by our weak or idle friends. There need not be, there would not be, any real change in our designs, only in our means.'

What Saruman says encapsulates many of the things the modern world has learnt to dread most: the ditching of allies, the subordination of means to ends, the 'conscious acceptance of guilt in the necessary murder'. But the way he puts it is significant too. No other character in Middle-earth has Saruman's trick of balancing phrases against each other so that incompatibles are resolved, and none comes out with words as empty as 'deploring', 'ultimate', worst of all, 'real'. What is a 'real change'? The *OED*'s three columns of definition offer nothing appropriate; the word has got below dictionary level. As we all know, 'real' is now a word like 'sincere' or 'genuine', a word whose meaning its speaker asks you to take for granted, a politician's word, an advertiser's word. 'Real change' shows Saruman up with even greater economy than 'changes for the worst' does Gaffer Gamgee.

By contrast with these familiar styles and voices several of the other participants in the Council come over as archaic, blunt, clear-sighted. Gandalf himself uses an older vocabulary than usual, as if to authenticate himself, and Elrond's speech, as is only suitable for one so old, is full of old-fashioned inversions of syntax and words like 'weregild', 'esquire', 'shards'. Its burden is to state the Northern 'theory of courage', as Tolkien called it in his British Academy lecture, whose central thesis is that even ultimate defeat does not turn right into wrong. Elrond has seen 'many defeats, and many fruitless victories', and in a way he has even given up hope, at least for his adopted people the elves; but this does not make him change his mind or look for easy options.

The heroic note is struck most firmly, however, by the dwarf Glóin, or rather by his report of the dialogue between Sauron's messenger and that exemplar of stubbornness King Dáin. The messenger offers 'great reward and lasting friendship' in return for information about hobbits, or for the Ring. If Dáin refuses, he says:

> "... things will not seem so well."

'At that his breath came like the hiss of snakes,
 and all who stood by shuddered, but Dáin
 said: "I say neither yea nor nay. I must
 consider this message and what it means
 under its fair cloak."
'"Consider well, but not too long," said he.
'"The time of my thought is my own to spend,"
 answered Dáin.
'"For the present," said he, and rode into
 the darkness.

We get exchanges like this several times in *The Lord of the Rings*, mostly involving dwarves: Elrond and Gimli swap grim proverbs in the next chapter, Théoden King silences Merry in similarly abrupt style in Book V chapter 2 . . . Whatever it is, it comes over in Dáin's speech as a force: words imply ethics, and the ethics of the spokesmen of Middle-earth fit together, beneath surface variation. None of them but Saruman pays any attention to expediency, practicality, *Realpolitik*, 'political realism'.

Any one of the counsellors in this chapter would bear similar analysis. Gandalf's account of Isildur makes a point through its combination of ancient words and endings ('glede', 'fadeth', 'loseth', etc.) with sudden recall of the words of Bilbo and Gollum. 'It is precious to me, though I buy it with great pain'; the 'reality of human nature' persists. More subtly Aragorn and Boromir strike sparks off each other through their ways of speech as well as their claims, Aragorn's language deceptively modern, even easy-going on occasion, but with greater range than Boromir's slightly wooden magniloquence. There is even significance in Aragorn letting his rival have the last word in their debate, with a clause which is perfectly in line with modern speech—'we will put it to the test one day'—but also relates easily to the vaunts of ancient heroes, like Ælfwine's *nú mæg cunnian hwá céne sý* in *The Battle of Maldon*, 'now who is bold can be put to the test'. Still, the overriding points are these: the 'information content' of 'The Council of Elrond' is very high, much higher than can be recorded by analyses like this; much of that information is carried by linguistic mode; nevertheless most readers assimilate the greater part of it; in the process they gain an image of the 'life-styles' of Middle-earth the solider for its occasional contrasts with modernity. Language variation gives Tolkien a thorough and economical way of dramatising ethical debate.

A part of the answer is that the Rohirrim are not to be equated with the Anglo-Saxons of history, but with those of poetry, or legend. The chapter 'The King of the Golden Hall' is straightforwardly calqued on *Beowulf*. When Legolas says of Meduseld, 'The light of it shines far over the land', he is translating line 311 of *Beowulf*, *líxte se léoma ofer landa fela*. 'Meduseld' is indeed a Beowulfian word for 'hall'. More importantly the poem and the chapter agree, down to minute detail, on the procedure for approaching kings. In *Beowulf* the hero is stopped first by a coastguard, then by a doorward, and only after two challenges is allowed to approach the Danish King; he and his men have to 'pile arms' outside as well. Tolkien follows this dignified, step-by-step ceremonial progress exactly. Thus in 'The King of the Golden Hall' Gandalf, Aragorn, Legolas and Gimli are checked first by the guards at the gates of Edoras (= 'enclosures'), and then by the doorward of Meduseld, Háma. He too insists on the ceremony of piling arms, though Tolkien's characters object more than Beowulf does, largely because he is a volunteer and in any case fights by choice bare-handed. There is a crisis over Gandalf's staff, indeed, and Háma broods, reflecting rightly that 'The staff in the hand of a wizard may be more than a prop for age'; he settles his doubts with the maxim 'Yet in doubt a man of worth will trust to his own wisdom. I believe you are friends and folk of honour, who have no evil purpose. You may go in.' In saying so he echoes the maxim of the coastguard of *Beowulf*, 'a sharp shield-warrior must know how to tell good from bad in every case, from words as well as deeds. I hear [from your words] that this warband is friendly … I will guide you.'

The point is not, though, that Tolkien is once more writing a 'calqued' narrative, but that he is taking advantage of a modern expansive style to spell out things that would have been obvious to Anglo-Saxons — in particular, the truths that freedom is not a prerogative of democracies, and that in free societies orders give way to discretion. Háma takes a risk with Gandalf; so does the coastguard with Beowulf. So does Éomer with Aragorn, letting him go free and lending him horses. He is under arrest when Aragorn re-appears, and Théoden notes Háma's dereliction of duty too. Still, the nice thing about the Riders, one might say, is that though 'a stern people, loyal to their lord', they wear duty and loyalty lightly. Háma and Éomer make their own decisions, and even the suspicious gate-ward wishes Gandalf luck. 'I was only obeying orders', we can see, would *not* be accepted as an excuse in the Riddermark. Nor would it in *Beowulf*. The wisdom of ancient epic is translated by Tolkien into a whole sequence of doubts, decisions, sayings, rituals.

The Riders gain life from their mixture of homely, almost hobbitic familiarity with a strong dash of something completely alien. Éomer is a nice young man, but there is a streak of nomad ferocity in the way he and his men taunt Aragorn and company with their narrowing circle of horses and Éomer's silent advance 'until the point of his spear was within a foot of Aragorn's breast'. They behave like mail-shirted Red Indians. And like a Middle-earth Deerslayer Aragorn 'did not stir', recognising the nomad appreciation of impassivity. A certain craziness shows itself in the Rohirric psychology at other points, as Éowyn rides in search of death and Éomer, sure he is doomed to die, laughs out loud for joy. The Dunlendings have heard that the Riders 'burned their prisoners alive'. Tolkien denies it, but there is something in his description that keeps the image alive.

For all this there is, once more, a visual correlative, and it is the first flash of individuality Éomer is given; he is 'taller than all the rest; from his helm as a crest a white horsetail flowed'. A horsetail plume is the traditional prerogative of the Huns and the Tartars and the steppe-folk, a most un-English decoration, at least by tradition. Yet it comes to prominence several times. Across the chaotic battlefield of Pelennor it is 'the white crest of Éomer' that Merry picks out from the 'great front of the Rohirrim', and when Théoden charges at last, opposing hornblast and poetry to horror and despair, behind him come his knights and his banner, 'white horse upon a field of green', and Éomer, 'the white horsetail on his helm floating in his speed'. As it happens, there is a word for both Éomer's decoration and the Riders' collective quality, but it is not an English word: it is *panache*, the crest on the knight's helmet, but also the virtue of sudden onset, the dash that sweeps away resistance. This is exactly the opposite of English 'doggedness', and is a virtue traditionally regarded with massive suspicion by English generals. However *panache* in both the abstract and concrete senses help to define the Riders, to present them as simultaneously English and alien, to offer a glimpse of the way land shapes people. Théoden's kindly interest in herbs and hobbits (they would have had him smoking a pipe, given time) co-exists with his peremptory decisions and sudden furies. It is a strange mixture but not an implausible one. There must have been people like that once, if we only knew.

Source: Tom Shippey, *The Road to Middle Earth,* Grafton, Harper Collins, 1992, pp. 107–116.

SOURCES

Adams, Robert M., "The Hobbit Habit," in *Tolkien New Critical Perspectives*, edited by Neil D. Isaacs and Rose A. Zimbardo, University Press of Kentucky, 1981, pp. 168–175.

Aldritch, Kevin, "The Sense of Time in Tolkien's *The Lord of the Rings*," in *Tolkien A Celebration: Collected Writings on a Literary Legacy*, Harper Collins, 1999, pp. 86–91.

Auden, W. H., "The Quest Hero," in *Tolkien and the Critics*, edited by Neil D. Isaacs and Rose A. Zimbardo, University of Notre Dame Press, 1968, pp. 40–61.

———, "At the end of the Quest, Victory," in *New York Times Book Review*, January 22, 1956, p. 5.

Basney, Lionel, "Myth, History, and Time in *The Lord of the Rings*," in *Tolkien New Critical Perspectives*, edited by Neil D. Isaacs and Rose A. Zimbardo, University Press of Kentucky, 1981, pp. 8–18.

Beagle, Peter S., "Tolkien's Magic Ring," in *The Tolkien Reader*, Ballantine Books, 1966, pp. ix–xv.

Bradley, Marion Zimmer, "Men, Halflings, and Hero-Worship," in *Tolkien and the Critics*, edited by Neil D. Isaacs and Rose A. Zimbardo, University of Notre Dame Press, 1968, pp. 109–127.

Brewer, Derek S., "*The Lord of the Rings* as Romance," in *J. R. R. Tolkien, Scholar and Storyteller: Essays in Memoriam*, Cornell University Press, 1979, pp. 249–64.

Caldecott, Stratford, "Over the Chasm of Fire: Christian Heroism in *The Silmarillion* and *The Lord of the Rings*," in *Tolkien A Celebration: Collected Writings on a Literary Legacy*, Harper Collins, 1999, pp. 17–33.

Carpenter, Humphrey, *J. R. R. Tolkien: A Biography*, Allen and Unwin, 1977.

Christensen, Bonniejean, "Gollum's Character Transformation in *The Hobbit*," in *A Tolkien Compass*, edited by Jared Lobdell, Open Court, 1975, pp. 9–28.

Coulombe, Charles A., "*The Lord of the Rings*—A Catholic View," in *Tolkien A Celebration: Collected Writings on a Literary Legacy*, Harper Collins, 1999, pp. 53–66.

Curry, Patrick, "Modernity in Middle Earth," in *Tolkien A Celebration: Collected Writings on a Literary Legacy*, Harper Collins, 1999, pp. 34–39.

Dowies, William, "The Gospel of Middle Earth according to J. R. R. Tolkien," in *J. R. R. Tolkien, Scholar and Storyteller: Essays in Memoriam*, Cornell University Press, 1979, pp. 265–285.

Fairburn, Elwin, "J. R. R. Tolkien: A Mythology for England," in *Tolkien A Celebration: Collected Writings on a Literary Legacy*, Harper Collins, 1999, pp. 73–85.

Flieger, Verlyn, "Frodo and Aragorn: The concept of the Hero," in *Tolkien New Critical Perspectives*, pp. 40–62.

Fuller, Edmund, "The Lord of the Hobbits,'' in *Tolkien and the Critics*, edited by Neil D. Isaacs and Rose A. Zimbardo, University of Notre Dame Press, 1968, pp.17–39

Gasque, Thomas J., "Tolkien: The Monsters and the Critics," in *Tolkien and the Critics*, edited by Neil D. Isaacs and Rose A. Zimbardo, University of Notre Dame Press, 1968, pp. 151–163.

Grant, Patrick, "Tolkien: Archetype and Word,'' in *Tolkien New Critical Perspectives*, edited by Neil D. Isaacs and Rose A. Zimbardo, University Press of Kentucky, 1981, pp. 87–105.

Guntun, Colin, "A Far-off Gleam of the Gospel: Salvation in Tolkien's *The Lord of the Rings*," in *Tolkien: A Celebration*, edited by Joseph Pearce, Trafalgar Square, 1999.

Harvey, David, *The Song of Middle Earth : J. R. R. Tolkien's Themes, Symbols and Myths*, Allen and Unwin, 1985.

Helms, Randel, *Tolkien's World*, Thames and Hudson, 1974.

Hughes, Daniel, "Pieties and Giant Forms in the *The Lord of the Rings*," in *Tolkien New Critical Perspectives*, edited by Neil D. Isaacs and Rose A. Zimbardo, University Press of Kentucky, 1981, pp. 72–86.

Huttar, Charles A., "Hell and the City: Tolkien and the Traditions of Western Literature," in *A Tolkien Compass*, edited by Jared Lobdell, Open Court, 1975, pp. 117–142.

Isaacs, Neil D., "On the Need for Writing Tolkien Criticism," in *Tolkien New Critical Perspectives*, edited by Neil D. Isaacs and Rose A. Zimbardo, University Press of Kentucky, 1981, pp. 1–7.

———, "On the Possibility of Writing Tolkien Criticism," in *Tolkien and the Critics*, edited by Neil D. Isaacs and Rose A. Zimbardo, University of Notre Dame Press, 1968, pp. 1–11.

Isaacs, Neil D. and Rose Zimbardo, ed., *Tolkien and the Critics*, University of Notre Dame Press, 1968.

———, *Tolkien New Critical Perspectives*, University of Kentucky Press, 1981.

Jeffrey, David L., "Recovery: Name in the *The Lord of the Rings*," in *Tolkien New Critical Perspectives*, edited by Neil D. Isaacs and Rose A. Zimbardo, University Press of Kentucky, 1981, pp. 106–116.

Kaufmann, U. Milo, "Aspects of the Paradisiacal in Tolkien's Work," in *A Tolkien Compass*, edited by Jared Lobdell, Open Court, 1975, pp. 143–52.

Keenan, Hugh T., "The Appeal of the *The Lord of the Rings*: A Struggle for Life," in *Tolkien and the Critics*, edited by Neil D. Isaacs and Rose A. Zimbardo, University of Notre Dame Press, 1968, pp. 62–80.

Kocher, Paul, *Master of Middle Earth the Achievement of J. R. R. Tolkien*, Thames and Hudson, 1973.

———, "Middle Earth: An Imaginary World?" in *Tolkien New Critical Perspectives, Tolkien New Critical Perspectives*, edited by Neil D. Isaacs and Rose A. Zimbardo, University Press of Kentucky, 1981, pp. 117–132.

Lewis, C. S., "The Dethronement of Power," in *Tolkien and the Critics*, edited by Neil D. Isaacs and Rose A. Zimbardo, University of Notre Dame Press, 1968, pp. 12–16.

Lobdell, Jared, ed., *A Tolkien Compass*, Open Court, 1975.

Manlove, C. N., *Modern Fantasy—Five Studies*, Cambridge University Press, 1975.

McGrath, Sean, "The Passion according to Tolkien," in *Tolkien A Celebration: Collected Writings on a Literary Legacy*, Fount, Harper Collins, 1999, pp. 172–182.

Moorman, Charles, "The Shire, Moedor, and Minas Tirith," in *Tolkien and the Critics*, edited by Neil D. Isaacs and Rose A. Zimbardo, University of Notre Dame Press, 1968, pp. 201–17.

Murray, Robert, "J. R. R. Tolkien and the Art of the Parable," in *Tolkien A Celebration: Collected Writings on a Literary Legacy*, Harper Collins, 1999, pp. 40–52.

Nitzsche, Jane Chance, *Tolkien's Art*, Macmillan Press, 1980.

Noel, Ruth S., *The Mythology of Middle Earth*, Thames and Hudson, 1977.

Parks, Henry B., "Tolkien and the Critical Approach to Story," in *Tolkien New Critical Perspectives*, edited by Neil D. Isaacs and Rose A. Zimbardo, University Press of Kentucky, 1981, pp. 133–149.

Pearce, Joseph, "Tolkien and the Catholic Literary Revival" in *Tolkien A Celebration: Collected Writings on a Literary Legacy*, Harper Collins, 1999, pp. 102–140.

———, *Tolkien A Celebration: Collected Writings on a Literary Legacy*, Harper Collins, 1999.

Perkins, Agnes and Helen Hill, "The Corruption of Power," in *A Tolkien Compass*, edited by Jared Lobdell, Open Court, 1975, pp. 57–68.

Plank, Robert, "'The Scouring of the Shire': Tolkien's View of Fascism," in *A Tolkien Compass*, edited by Jared Lobdell, Open Court, 1975, pp. 107–116.

Purtill, Richard L., *J. R. R. Tolkien, Myth, Morality, and Religion*, Harper and Row, 1984.

Raffel, Burton, "*The Lord of the Rings* as Literature," in *Tolkien and the Critics*, edited by Neil D. Isaacs and Rose A. Zimbardo, University of Notre Dame Press, 1968, pp. 218–46.

Reilly, Robert J., "Tolkien and the Fairy Story," in *Tolkien and the Critics*, edited by Neil D. Isaacs and Rose A. Zimbardo, University of Notre Dame Press, 1968, pp.128–150.

Rosebury, Brian, *Tolkien a Critical Assessment*, St. Martin's Press, 1992.

Ryan, J. S., "Folktale, and the Creation of a Story," in *Tolkien New Critical Perspectives*, edited by Neil D. Isaacs and Rose A. Zimbardo, University Press of Kentucky, 1981, pp. 19–39.

Sale, Roger, "Tolkien and Frodo Baggins," in *Tolkien and the Critics*, edited by Neil D. Isaacs and Rose A. Zimbardo, University of Notre Dame Press, 1968, pp. 247–88.

Salu, Mary and Robert T. Farrell, *J. R. R. Tolkien, Scholar and Storyteller: Essays in Memoriam*, Cornell University Press, 1979.

Schall, James V., "On the Reality of Fantasy,'' in *Tolkien A Celebration: Collected Writings on a Literary Legacy*, Harper Collins, 1999, pp. 67–72.

Scheps, Walter, "The Fairy Tale Morality of *The Lord of the Rings*," in *A Tolkien Compass*, edited by Jared Lobdell, Open Court, 1975, pp.43–56.

Shippey, T. A., "Creation from Philology in *The Lord of the Rings*," in *J. R. R. Tolkien, Scholar and Storyteller: Essays in Memoriam*, Cornell University Press, 1979, pp. 286–316.

———, *The Road to Middle Earth*, Harper Collins, 1992.

Spacks, Patricia Meyer, "Power and Meaning in *The Lord of the Rings*," in *Tolkien and the Critics*, edited by Neil D. Isaacs and Rose A. Zimbardo, University of Notre Dame Press, 1968, pp. 81–99.

Tinkler, John, "Old English in Rohan," in *Tolkien and the Critics*, edited by Neil D. Isaacs and Rose A. Zimbardo, University of Notre Dame Press, 1968, pp. 164–69.

Tolkien, J. R. R., *The Silmarillion*, edited by Christopher Tolkien, Houghton Mifflin, 1977.

———, *Unfinished Tales*, edited by Christopher Tolkien, Unwin Paperbacks, 1982.

West, Richard, "The Interlace Structure in *The Lord of the Rings*," in *A Tolkien Compass*, edited by Jared Lobdell, Open Court, 1975, pp. 77–94.

West, Richard C., *Tolkien Criticism: An Annotated Checklist*, Kent State University Press, 1970.

Wilson, Edmund, "Oo, Those Awful Orcs," in *Nation*, April 14, 1956, p. 182.

Zimbardo, Rose A., "The Medieval-Renaissance Vision of the *Lord of the Rings*," in *Tolkien New Critical Perspectives*, pp. 63–71.

———, "Moral Vision in the *The Lord of the Rings*," in *Tolkien and the Critics*, edited by Neil D. Isaacs and Rose A. Zimbardo, University of Notre Dame Press, 1968, pp.100–108.

FURTHER READING

Beagle, Peter S., "Tolkien's Magic Ring," in *J. R. R. Tolkien, The Tolkien Reader*, Ballantine Books, 1966, pp. ix–xv.
    An excellent, if non-technical and short, introduction to *The Lord of the Rings* by another celebrated writer of fantasy.

Rosebury, Brian, *Tolkien a Critical Assessment*, St. Martin's Press, 1992.
    An excellent extended study of Tolkien's style, and an antidote to a lot of extremely bad criticism.

Shippey, T. A., *The Road to Middle Earth*, Harper Collins, 1992.
    One of the finest pieces of Tolkien criticism yet written, it is unsurpassed for the sources of *The Lord of the Rings* and the influence of Philology upon Tolkien's work.

Tolkien, J. R. R., "On Fairy Stories," in *The Tolkien Reader*, Ballantine Books, 1966, pp. 3–82.
    Written while Tolkien was beginning the *Lord of the Rings*. It is a critical theory and justification for the trilogy.

Pharsalia

MARCUS ANNAEUS
LUCAN(US)

65

The *Pharsalia* has been described by Ahl as "a political act as well as a political poem." Written when Nero's true nature could no longer be denied, it is a harrowing portrait of the disintegration of Rome, civil war, and the triumph of a single will. Lucan's unfinished epic was a subject of criticism even as he wrote it. In Petronius's *Satyricon*, a bitterly satiric novel written by another victim of Nero, a character complains that it is not a true epic, but a history, because it did not incorporate divine motivation. Even more important to later readings of the poem was the historian Tacitus's negative portrait of the poet in the *Annales*. From that day to this, Lucan has suffered from Tacitus's portrait and confusion about his approach.

Lucan's ability to paint the terrifying and the unearthly and to produce a pithy quotable line has not endeared him to all critics, but he has never lacked readers. The only copy of a secular poem copied between 550–750 A.D. that survives is a fragment entitled *Pharsalia*. His partisan portraits of Cato, Brutus, and Marcia made them models for medieval clerics and eighteenth century revolutionaries. His treatment of the witch Erictho and her necromancy made a fundamental impression on the western mind. Lucan's influence surfaces in the narratives of witch trials as well as in horror literature. Despite Lucan's references to fate, his use of human will as the source of action and events, rather than divine, is more immediately understandable to modern readers. His vision of dismembered bodies

and fractured boundaries holds a mirror up to a century that has descended more than once into horror and chaos.

AUTHOR BIOGRAPHY

Of all the poetry Marcus Annaeus Lucanus, better known to English readers as Lucan, wrote during his short life, only his unfinished epic *Pharsalia* survives. The little known about Lucan comes from two biographies that circulated in some manuscripts of *Pharsalia* and from the historian Tacitus's *Annals*. Lucan was born in Cordova in Spain on November 3, A.D. 39. He committed suicide at the order of the emperor Nero on April 30, A.D. 65. The grandson of a famous rhetorician, Seneca the Elder, and the nephew of philosopher, writer, and financier Seneca the Younger, Lucan was brought to Rome as a baby. There he received the usual upper class Roman education in literature and public speaking. He also studied Stoic philosophy. His talent for public speaking had already gained him fame in his teens. Nero, his uncle Seneca's student, encouraged him at first with political appointments, but later the emperor forbade him to plead in the courts, publish his poetry, or even to give private readings. Traditionally, this, rather than a political motive, has been given as the reason Lucan joined a plot to assassinate Nero. Recent scholarship has tended to reject this.

It is uncertain whether Nero's change of attitude towards the poet came from his jealousy of Lucan's talent or his fear of Lucan's philosophical and political beliefs that talent increasingly served. Lucan had written a poem that suggested Nero's involvement in setting the great fire of A.D. 64, which destroyed so much of Rome. It is likely that Lucan's part in a plot to assassinate Nero and to restore the Roman republic was influenced both by his philosophic and political beliefs and his frustration at being denied both the political forum of the law courts and an audience for his poetry. Lucan was, however, by all accounts, one of the main conspirators. Stoicism stressed rationality, control of emotions and inner freedom. It taught the existence of a continuum of order embracing both natural law and human ethics. Stoicism's beliefs and ideals not only permeate *Pharsalia*, they put its followers on a collision course with a ruler like Nero. Despite this, when the plot was discovered, Lucan broke down and implicated other conspirators, including his innocent mother. He was al-

lowed, like his uncles and father to commit suicide. For a Roman and a Stoic, suicide was a dignified and rational way of meeting a hopeless situation and also legally saved his estate for his young widow, Polla. Polla, it seems, never remarried, and celebrated his birthday at least until A.D. 89.

PLOT SUMMARY

Overview

The unfinished *Pharsalia* narrates the Roman Civil War's first phase, which ended almost thirty years later in the victory of Caesar's grandnephew Octavius (Augustus), over the forces of Mark Anthony and the Egyptian queen Cleopatra at the naval battle of Actium. It breaks off with Caesar trapped in Alexandria by the Egyptians.

Book One

Lucan begins his epic with themes and images that will run through his work, 'of legality conferred on crime,' images of self-slaughter and self-induced ruin brought on by Rome's own power and her citizens' corruption by wealth and greed. Peace was maintained as long as Crassus, the wealthiest man in Rome, and Julia, daughter of Caesar and wife of Pompey, lived to hold Caesar and Pompey apart. Their deaths left them unencumbered rivals. Caesar, despite a vision of Rome begging him to turn back, defies the senate and crosses the Rubicon, the river of Italy. He takes Ariminum. Curio comes to urge him to take up arms against Pompey and the Senate. Caeser addresses his troops looking for their support. They are wavering when the senior centurion Laelius speaks, pledging absolute loyalty to Caesar even if it means turning his sword on brother, father, or pregnant wife. They swear their allegiance to Caesar. Fear runs before his army; citizens and senators flee Rome. Portents appear. The senior Etruscan augur sees in the entrails of a sacrificed bull the full horror of the republic's collapse. The astrologer Figulus sees it in the stars. The book ends with a Roman matron filled with the spirit of prophecy running frantically through the streets of Rome prophesying the civil war.

Book Two

Mothers and wives besiege the altars with prayer. The men prepare for war. An old man who had lived through their horrors recalls the civil war between Marius and Sulla. His picture of the butchery in

Rome will be matched by the horrors of the sea fight at Massila (Marseille). Brutus goes to Cato for advice. Cato tells him he intends to join Pompey's side to protect the republic. Marcia, Cato's former wife, arrives from the funeral of her husband, Cato's friend whom she had married at Cato's request to give the man children. Marcia and Cato marry again. Pompey marches to Capua while Caesar comes down the Italian peninsula, driving all before him. Domitius is surrounded in Corfinium, and handed over to Caesar by his own men. Caesar releases him. Domitus hurries to join Pompey. Pompey withdraws to Calabria, and sends his son to rouse the whole Roman world before setting sail for Greece.

Book Three

Pompey sails for Greece. Sleeping, he has a vision of his dead wife Julia, Caesar's daughter. She reproaches him for his marriage to Cornelia, and brings him a prophetic warning of the underworld's preparations for the Civil War. Caesar is vexed at Pompey's retreat. He sends Curio to secure the grain producing islands of Sardinia and Sicily. He leads his troops to Rome. There the tribune Metellus opposes his rifling of the treasury. Cotta convinces Metellus to give way. Meanwhile, the known world flocks to Pompey. Caesar leaves Rome and marches towards Massilia. There he insists that the city join him in the Civil War. They ask to be allowed not to involve themselves in an internecine Roman war. Caesar lays siege to Massilia. He leaves for Spain, ordering that the siege be kept. The Greeks defeat the Romans at the landward walls. The Romans attack by sea, in a ferocious battle. Men die horrible deaths, their bodies broken and unrecognizable. Massilia falls.

Book Four

Caesar enters Spain where Afranius and Petreius lead the senatorial army. He pitches his camp opposite the senatorial camp. Rains and the melting snows cause a flood and starvation. With the improving weather the two armies move their camps. The camps are now so close soldiers recognize their friends and relatives across the lines. For a short while the ties of blood and friendship seem likely to turn the running tide of war. Petreius, however, goads his men back to warfare, killing the very men whom they had welcomed. Caesar rejoices that he now has the moral high ground. He besieges the republican force in the arid hills until thirst breaks them. Afranius leads his dying men out to sue for peace. He asks only that they not be compelled to fight in Caesar's army. Caesar grants this; the soldiers depart to enjoy the blessings of peace. Caesar's fleet in the adriatic suffers a set back, although in the courage of Vulteius and his men choosing suicide to cheat the republican forces of victory, they achieve a moral victory. Curio, meanwhile, has sailed for Africa and reaches the ruins of Carthage. He expects luck because he pitches his camp at the ruinous camp of Scipio Africanus, conqueror of Carthage. When battle with the North African princes comes, however, his men are slaughtered and he commits suicide. The narrator regrets that Pompey profited by such a defeat. The book ends with a summation of Curio's career and character. A man of enormous talents and patriotism, he had betrayed his country and his promise: Sulla, Marius, Cinna, and all the Caesar's bought their country. Curio sold it.

Book Five

Winter has come. In Epirus, the Senate sits in session preparing for war. Appius, a senator learned in religious matters, travels to Delphi to consult the oracle. The priestess tries to avoid her duty, but is forced by Appius and the god, Apollo. She speaks but is "not permitted to reveal as much as she is suffered to know," since "the endless chain of events is revealed" to her. Her prophecy to Appius is true but misleading. He finds the peace in Euboea she foretold, in his grave. Caesar faces down a mutiny. He hurries to Rome and is voted consul. He then rushes to Brundisium. There at first the fleet is becalmed. Eventually, he reaches Greece. Mark Antony is slow to join him with his men. Caesar attempts to sale back to Italy in a small fishing boat, but surviving a ferocious storm, returns to his army in Greece. The storm over, Antony's forces arrive. Pompey recognizes that the war is about to come to a head. He sends Cornelia to the island of Lesbos for safety. Both are grief stricken at parting.

Book Six

The armies encamp on neighboring heights. They move, trying to gain advantage. Caesar plans a great entrenchment to hem in Pompey's troops without their knowing it. Pompey realizes his plan and disperses his troops to stretch Caesar's armies. Pompey's forces are well provisioned, but suffering from disease; Caesar's are unable to re-provision because Pompey holds the coast. Pompey attempts to break out. He is nearly successful, but is held at bay by Scaeva, one of Caesar's centurions. Pompey then breaks out at the seacoast. Caesar rushes to fight him, but suffers a defeat. Pompey does not follow up his initial advantage, but as Caesar withdraws Pompey intends to harry his flight. Pompey is urged to return to Rome, but refuses to do so before he can disband his army. Pompey marches towards Thessaly. Lucan recounts the evil things that have originated in Thessaly. The rivals pitch their camps. Sextus, the son of Pompey, urged by fear, decides to consult the senior witch, Erictho. Sextus finds her working on a spell to keep the war at Philippi. The witch is pleased to help and immediately searches for a suitably fresh corpse and forces it to speak, promising safety from any future necromancy. The soldier describes the dead heroes and villains of Roman history mourning or rejoicing over the battle's outcome. He urges the Pompeians to go bravely to death; they will be admitted to Elyssium, the fields of the blessed.

Book Seven

The morning of Pharsalia dawns. Pompey wakes from a dream in which the citizens in Rome acclaimed him. The army urges a speedy engagement and accuses Pompey of hanging back. Cicero (in his one appearance in the *Pharsalia*), eager to return to the forum, urges Pompey to engage the enemy: "his eloquence gave force to an unsound argument." Pompey has a premonition of the disaster to come. He knows that whichever side wins, horrors and cruelty will follow. The auspices cannot be taken; the bull bolts into the fields and cannot be caught. Caesar, ready for a day of foraging, sees his chance. Caesar urges his army on, telling them the opposing army is full of foreigners; most of the lives they must take are not Roman. Caesar also speaks of his inclination to clemency compared to Pompey and the senate, praying the gods to "give victory to him who does not feel bound to draw the ruthless sword against beaten men, and does not believe that his fellow citizens committed a crime by fighting against him. None of you must smite a foe in the back, and every fugitive must pass as a countryman." Pompey dreads the approach of Caesar's army, and understands his dread as a bad omen. He harangues his troops, urging them to think of Rome, the aged senators, the mothers of families, Romans yet to be born entreating them to secure their freedom. The battle takes place. The slaughter still leaves the world desolate. Liberty was lost there to generations yet unborn, who had no chance to fight for themselves. The battle turns against the republican army. Pompey leaves the battle, fearing that otherwise the army will stay to be slaughtered. Caesar allows his

soldiers to pillage Pompey's deserted camp and denies burial to the dead.

Book Eight

Pompey takes a ship to Lesbos to rejoin Cornelia. She sees Pompey's approach and immediately recognizes the signs of defeat and collapses. The people of Lesbos offer Pompey a secure base. Filled with gratitude, he declines. All grieve the departure of Cornelia who has won their affection with her goodness. Pharsalia's survivors rally to Pompey. He sends King Deiotarus in disguise to see if he can raise the east to their aid. Finally, at Syhedra, he addresses the senators. He asks to whom they should turn for aid, Libya, Egypt, or Parthia. He rejects the first two and suggests Parthia. Lentulus rejects this with disdain because it is un-Roman and against the essential nature of their campaign to preserve liberty. Lentulus urges them to seek aid in Egypt. Egypt meanwhile learns of their approach and takes council. Old Acoreus urges loyalty to their benefactor, Pompey. Pothinus urges the young pharaoh to kill Pompey who will bring Caesar down upon them. Achillas is sent to meet Pompey and kill him. He offers to bring Pompey ashore in his boat. The Romans are suspicious, but Pompey chooses to die rather than to reveal fear. Cornelia begs to accompany him and is refused. Once in the boat, Pompey is murdered; his head is brought to the Pharaoh. Cordus cremates Pompey's body on the seashore, and buries the ashes in hope of retrieving them for Cornelia.

Book Nine

Pompey's spirit soars to heaven. Cato and Brutus are now the leaders of a senatorial party which "after the death of Magnus was the party of freedom." Cornelia grieves, urging her stepsons to carry on the war. Cato gives Pompey a somewhat ambiguous funeral oration, rallies the army and sets sail for Cyrene, which he takes. He and his army set out for Libya. Unable to reach it by sea, he marches over land through the desert, suffering thirst and then poisonous snakes. He refuses to consult the great oracle of Ammon Zeus. A number of his men die spectacularly horrific deaths from snakebites and he refuses with disdain a drink of water from one of his men. Cato shares his men's sufferings and encourages them even at their deaths. Finally, the Psylli protect his army against the snakes. Eventually, they reach Leptis. Caesar, meanwhile, has been tracking Pompey. He visits the site of Troy. Caesar prays to the gods to give him prosperity and promises to restore Troy. He reaches Egypt where he is presented with Pompey's head. Caesar at least feigns horror.

Book Ten

Caesar arrives in Egypt. He visits the tomb of Alexander, giving the narrator the chance to redirect his reader's view of Alexander's achievements, casting an equally unflattering light on Caesar's. Cleopatra seduces Caesar. He pursues his affair with her while the senatorial forces regroup. During a great feast given by Cleopatra in Caesar's honor, Lucan introduces three traditional categories of information about Egypt, the great wealth of the country, its long history, and finally the mystery of the Nile's floods and source. Pothinus, who plotted Pompey's murder, now moves against the other Roman who threatens Egyptian independence and his own position. He convinces the young Pharaoh (Ptolemy) to surprise Caesar, ridding him at one stroke of both the internal (Cleopatra) and external threat to his throne. Pothinus does not follow up his initial advantage. Caesar, energetic and resourceful, takes Ptolomy hostage, and sets fire to the Egyptian fleet, which threatens him. The fire spreads to the city itself. Caesar beheads Porthinus and seizes the city's great Lighthouse, closing Alexandria to shipping. He is preparing to evacuate his army on his own ships when he is brought to bay on the causeway linking the lighthouse to the city by fresh Egyptian forces. The book breaks off with another appearance of the heroic Scaeva.

CHARACTERS

Achillas

The Egyptian official who kills Pompey on the order of the Pharaoh Ptolomy and his council. He is later executed by the Egyptian princess Arsinoe.

Arruns

The oldest of the Etruscan seers, he is called to Rome in Book I to perform the traditional rites of divination. When he inspects the internal organs of the bull sacrificed to the gods, he discovers that "What we fear is unspeakable, but worse will follow."

Brutus

A Roman senator and follower of Stoicism. He is a descendant of Brutus the first Consul who drove the tyrant king Tarquin Superbus out of Rome and

founded the Republic. At first, he intends to join neither side to avoid the guilt of civil war and to free himself to deal with the winner, whether Pompey or Caesar, until Cato convinces him to join Pompey's camp. He sets himself of being the enemy. Brutus was with Cassius, the leader of the group that assassinated Caesar in 44 B.C.

Caesar

The 'antihero' of *Pharsalia*, a Roman general and politician from an ancient Roman clan who claim descent from Iules, son of the Trojan prince Aeneas and the grandson of the goddess Venus. Caesar is fortune's man, but he also makes the most of fortune. He grabs every advantage with both hands. When fortune wavers, he makes his own. He was a master of military engineering. His personal bravery and consideration for his men made him popular with the men in the ranks. The historical Caesar was noted for his clemency, but Lucan plays this down at every turn.

Cato

The moral center—if not the hero—of the *Pharsalia*, Cato has been traditionally seen as the embodiment of Stoic ideals in the service of the Roman state, although Lucan, according to some critics, seriously undercuts his fulfillment of these ideals. Johnson quotes a Stoic text that suggests that Cato is a caricature of every virtue except the one that makes the others palatable: humility. Cato joins Pompey to keep before him the ideals of the Roman republic and the rule of law, so that if he wins he will not think he has won Rome for himself. Ahl describes Cato as more a symbol than a hero, "urging men to fight for themselves, not for someone, or even something, else." Ahl goes on to note some strikingly Christian echoes in his portrait, notably his desire to be a scapegoat, to 'devote' himself to the gods in self-sacrifice to save the Roman people and their institutions: "This blood redeem the people, this death pay the penalty of whatever Rome's corruption deserves." Unfortunately this is couched in terms of his being the only person who cares about the republic. There is also something jarring about his image of himself as a father mourning his lost son in reference to the Republic; surely the more acceptable image would have been of the son mourning the father.

Cicero

Conspicuous by his almost complete absence from the poem, he was the greatest orator and one of the most important politicians in Rome for nearly forty years. Never a military man, he worked for most of his political life to bring about an equitable consensus among all good citizens, *consensus omnium bonorum*. Cicero was not present at the battle, but Lucan gives him a speech which in context drips with irony to shame Pompey into battle. He insists that Pompey, always the favorite of fortune, fighting in a cause the gods will favor, make use of the luck that has always been his.

Cleopatra

The sister and queen of the young Ptolomy, king of Egypt. She throws her lot in with Caesar, and distracts him from his duties in pursuing war. For Lucan, civil war appears to be preferable to dallying with Cleopatra.

Cornelia

The widow of Crassus's son who died at Carrhae with his father, massacred by the Parthians (the inhabitants of modern Iran). She married Pompey after the death of his wife Julia. The reaction of the people of Lesbos when she leaves the island with her husband presents a picture of a truly lovable woman. She believes herself to be a source of her husband's bad luck.

Crassus

With Pompey and Caesar, Crassus dominated Roman politics until he and his son, Cornelia's first husband, were slaughtered along with their legions in an attempt to conquer the Parthians, the inhabitants of what is now Iran.

Curio

One of the tribunes of the people. These were officials whose duty it was to look after the rights of ordinary citizens. Once a defender of law and liberty, he urges Caesar to defy the Senate and fight his fellow countrymen. He is, for Lucan, even viler than Caesar. Caesar bought his country's liberty, but Curio sold it. He is a potent symbol of Roman strengths and talents diverted from the good of the commonwealth to personal aggrandizement. His death is described in terms of a sacrifice to the unquiet shades of Carthage.

Deiotarius

A client king, ruler under Roman patronage of part of Asia minor, he is a loyal friend to Pompey and the republican cause. Disguised as a beggar, he is sent by Pompey in the aftermath of the battle of Pharsalia on a secret mission to the king of the Parthians in modern Iran.

Lucius Ahenobarbus Domitius

Lucius Ahenobarbus Domitius is an ancestor of Nero. Lucan treats him with some respect, not because he wishes to flatter Nero, but because he was the one major republican to actually die in battle at Pharsalia.

Erictho

The chief Thracian witch who is more than happy to oblige to contact the god at Delphi. She is the most notorious of the famous Thracian witches; in fact, she has gone beyond their traditional witchcraft to invent spells of her own. In many ways, she is the female equivalent of Caesar.

Figulus

An astrologer whose readings of the stars confirms the terrible, if enigmatic, prophecies of Arruns. Peace will only bring the endless loss of freedom. He urges the Romans not to pray for an end of the bloodshed because when it ends, their freedom will too.

Gnaeus Pompeius

Pompey's eldest son. His father sends him to raise soldiers and allies all over the Roman world.

Iuba

The king of Libya, who destroys the army of Curio. He is an image of the timeless enmity between Rome and Carthage.

Julia

The daughter and only child of Caesar and the wife of Pompey. She was the child of his beloved first wife Cornelia who died young. When the civil war begins, she is dead, and Pompey is married to another Cornelia, the widow of Crassus' son who died with his father fighting the Persians. At the beginning of Book III, she appears in the guise of a fury (a spirit who punishes kin murder) in a dream to Pompey to prophesy his death and the carnage of the civil war. She resents Pompey's quick remarriage, and tells him that in battle she will appear to him as a constant reminder that the war is, as Lucan wrote at the beginning of *Pharsalia*, not merely between fellow countrymen, but kinsmen.

Laelius

The senior centurion of Caesar's army, his speech in Book I convinces the army to follow Caesar into civil war. Laelius's attitude of unwavering loyalty to Caesar rather than to his country or even his family represents a disastrous change in the late Roman republic. Soldiers' loyalty to a charismatic patron commander rather than to Rome fueled the rise of dictator warlords like Sulla and Marius in Pompey and Caesar's youth, as well as Pompey and Caesar themselves. In Lucan's childhood, the continuing loyalty of the legions to Caesar's family had frustrated an attempt to restore the republic after the murder of the Emperor Caligula. Their preference for the rule of one man rather than the Senate continued after the death of Nero.

Lagus

See Ptolemy

Publius Cornelius Lentulus

Publius Cornelius Lentulus is one of the consuls for 49 B.C. He convened the senate at Epirus and commanded the left wing of the republican forces at Pharsalia. In Book 8, he takes the lead in quashing the idea that the Parthians should be called into the war.

Magnus

See Pompey

Marcia

Cato's wife and the mother of his three children. Cato divorced her so that his childless friend Hortensius could marry her and father a family. In Book II, Hortensius has just died. Marcia comes to Cato from Hortensius' funeral and asks him to marry her again so she can be with him in his struggle for Rome and die his wife. Some commentators see Marcia as a symbol of Rome.

Marius

Roman general, dictator, and husband of Caesar's aunt. He was the opponent of Sulla.

Metellus

The tribune of the people who attempts to stop Caesar from breaking into the public treasury to pay his soldiers. Lucan undercuts his stand by observing that it was only his love of money that made him incapable of fear.

Old Roman Man

In Book 2, an old man recounts the sorrows and horrors of the civil war and proscriptions in the time of Sulla. He is the counterpart of the matron inspired with prophecy in Book 1. His description of the murder, mutilation, and inhumane treatment of the dead will be paralleled in every battle of the civil war.

Pompey

Pompey (also known as Magnus) is a successful general and politician who has managed to almost live down his connection with the vicious dictator Sulla. There sometimes appears to be two Pompeys. The first is a man as bloodstained and hungry for power as Caesar. The second is the leader of the fight for *libertas*, not the perfect hero, but as Cato says of him, good in terms of his evil times. Pompey is a man who needs love and admiration. His actions are reactions to the demands others place upon him, of others' perceptions of him. His love for his wife ought to be admirable, but like everything he does in the poem, somehow annoys.

Porthinus

The chamberlain of the young Egyptian king and the power behind the throne. He suggests the murder of Pompey and attempts to kill both Caesar and Cleopatra in the palace at Alexandria. He argues: "If a man would be righteous, let him depart from a court. Virtue is incompatible with absolute power. He who is ashamed of cruelty must always fear it." He is executed by Caesar.

Ptolomy

Ptolemy, also known as Lagus, is the young king of Egypt and brother of Cleopatra. Some writers see in him at least a partial portrait of Nero. The variant name is derived from his ancestor, the first Macedonian king of Egypt.

Roman Matron

Book 1 ends with a series of three prophecies of war. The first two are made by men trained in the reading of the future, Arruns in the Etruscan manner observing the internal organs of sacrificed animals, and Figulus, an astrologer. The final and most clear and violent prophecy is spoken by a Roman matron who is possessed by Apollo, the god of prophecy. While the others are professionals who have been asked to read the signs, her words represent the direct intervention of the divine in human affairs. As a matron (the mother of a family), Apollo's choice of her to be his mouthpiece is particularly poignant. Not only will she naturally fear for the men of her two families, but a defining point in early Roman history was the intervention of the Sabine women to end a battle between their Roman husbands and Sabine fathers and brothers.

Scaeva

A Roman centurion, the paramount example of *virtus* perverted. He single handedly holds off Pompey's army while Caesar brings up reinforcements. Caesar sees Scaeva in the last lines of the *Pharsalia*. It has often been assumed that this must be a vision, but Masters, in his argument that the poem as we have it is complete, although not thoroughly revised, points out that the historical Scaeva survived his much exaggerated wounds at Dyrrachium.

Pompeius Sextus

The younger of Pompey's two sons. He decides out of fear to consult Erichtho. It has been suggested that he is meant as a portrait of Nero.

Sulla

The first of the Roman dictators in the modern sense of the word as opposed to the traditional Roman sense of a man given special constitutional powers for a limited period in times of national crisis. His rule was infamous for massacres and wave after wave of political murders.

THEMES

Libertas

Libertas for a Roman citizen meant a web of rights and obligations. Particularly important to the Roman sense of self was the freedom, theoretically, to have a voice in shaping Roman law and policy. They acknowledged only the law and the lawfully constituted magistrates whose power derived from their will. It is easy to dismiss *libertas*, particularly in the late republic, as merely aristocratic privilege. From the *Pharsalia,* it is clear that Lucan is aware of the shortcomings of *libertas* (1.158–82).

Lucan's *libertas* may appear limited or naive to some, but it has touched a chord with every period to which the liberty of the individual to live a considered and self-controlled life in an orderly and humane society has been recognized as a supreme good. It is unfair to speak of his concept of *libertas* as being restricted to one class. Lucan displays the imaginative sympathy to recognize the nobility and *virtus* (courage) of anyone who yearned for the right and the honorable. He carefully draws attention to the Massilians who have left the Romans behind in the practice of their own virtues. They emerge, as no Roman does, clothed in the qualities of the early republic. They are resolute, true to their friends, desiring only to behave with piety towards gods and men.

Suicide and Fratricide

Lucan begins the *Pharsalia* by reminding his audience that the Roman civil war is worse than civil, it is fratricidal. Pompey and Caesar were, as he repeats at every turn, son-in-law and father-in-law, kin against kin. Rome turns its sword upon itself. The speech of the Centurion Laelius is chilling not only for the fanaticism it places in the service of an amoral leader, but also for the complete breakdown of the social contract and common humanity. Laelius will turn his sword against the gods, his father, his brother, even his pregnant wife out of loyalty to Caesar. He has lost the sense of the wounds each such blow would inflict upon him. This sort of war involves all participants in guilt; no man's hands, however righteous his cause, are free from the blood of his brother, his fellow citizen.

Lucan never allows his readers to forget the suicidal nature of the conflict. Even the grammatical structure of Lucan's sentences serves to carry the theme. Again and again the logical object of a sentence is made the grammatical subject as in 4.561–2 "their breasts dashed against the steel, and their throats struck the hand." Lucan uses this because it is a profound expression of the paradox of civil war, where every blow struck wounds the one who strikes even more than the one who receives it.

Nevertheless, suicide has its positive side for Lucan. It is the final weapon against the tyranny of men and events. No one can be forced to endure any evil, if they do not fear death. Death removes a man from all compulsion. It is also, in the sense of the Roman concept of *devotio*, the means whereby a man offers his life to the gods for the good of the people. The word *devotio* paradoxically and appropriately means both consecrating and cursing. These meanings are reflected in Cato's wish to offer his life to the powers of heaven and hell, to atone for his country's sins.

TOPICS FOR FURTHER STUDY

- Compare the rise and personalities of American Populist politicians in the first half of the twentieth century to the *Populares* of the late Roman Republic.

- Lucan's circumstances have been repeated more than once in the twentieth century. Compare his experiences with those of writers working under twentieth century dictatorships.

- In Book X, Lucan has one of his characters discuss the source of the Nile. Research the search for the source of the Nile up to its discovery in the nineteenth century.

- Lucan has both his narrator and Julius Caesar himself mention his reform of the calendar. Research the development of the modern calendar. Look in particular for its importance for the development of mathematics and astronomy.

- In Book III, Caesar sends troops to invade Sicily and Sardinia to control the supply of grain. Grain from these two islands and later from Egypt would have a profound effect on Roman history. Research the effects of the introduction of this cheap wheat on Italy or the effects on Europe of a similar introduction of cheap wheat from North America in the later nineteenth century.

- Robert Graves called Lucan the ''father of the costume film.'' Compare Lucan's use of atmospheric landscape, the supernatural, or the representation of brutality to their use in films.

- Lucan's portrait of Erichtho and her magic is one of the foundation texts in the development of the western ideas of the witchcraft. Look at historical witch hunts and trials and compare the beliefs and accusations to material in Lucan's text.

Fortune, Fate, and Chance

Lucan makes little distinction between fortune and fate. They both correspond roughly to the modern use of "fate," but they are not exactly interchangeable. Servius wrote, "Birth and death are the provinces of fate; all that lies between is the province of fortune." Ahl explains this remark as meaning that Fate is used to suggest the definite and definable order of the world, the ultimate boundaries of life on individuals, nations, and the universe itself. Death is the only certainty in life, and therefore, it is the only thing over which the individual has control and it is the ultimate weapon in defense of freedom. Lucan attributes to natural law the existence of inevitable moral entropy. The empire's own growth brought it to the state where collapse was inevitable.

Chance is only a cause for which men do not understand the reason. Fortune is chance controlled by a higher power. Because it favors certain individuals, fortune appears to have a rudimentary personality. This favor, however irrational or im-

moral, is a series of occurrences that has a pattern. Fate in the opening of the *Pharsalia* is described as *invidia*, jealous. This might be too little to allow it to be described as a personification, but it recalls the Greek belief that the gods would never allow mankind or its institutions to blur the distinction between the human and the divine through too much success.

Virtus

Virtus is the word behind the modern English "virtue." But while the modern English word tends to mean what is practiced, the Latin focused on the practice. That is *virtus* did not refer to individual virtuous states, like honesty, prudence, humility, but to the strength that carries out right action. The difference between *pietas* and *virtus* is the difference between sterile and unthinking dedication to the *mos maiorem* or traditional customs and values and the conscious thoughtful commitment to discovering and following the good. The suicide of Vulteius and his men is a classic example of the Stoic use of death, but their virtue is thrown away on a man who will reduce men and women to a society where death is the only freedom. The Centurion Scaeva is the embodiment of martial courage and devotion to duty. He withstands the onslaught of an army, but his *virtus* is corrupted because it is directed towards the victory of a tyrant over *libertas*. Caesar's mercy on this view is a punishment to the one who receives it.

STYLE

Epic Features

Lucan composed his epic in Virgil's shadow. But he absorbed and transformed Virgil and the whole epic tradition back to Homer. He was forced to jettison the traditional gods, not so much by the use of his Stoic education, but because the Virgilian epic and Julio-Claudian propaganda had so closely associated the traditional pantheon with Caesar. His choice and development of the witch Erictho and of the image of Anateus are good examples of his subversion of the Virgilian epic.

Point of View

It is important to distinguish between Lucan and his narrator. Lucan the poet depicts situations and characters so that we look at them one way, while the narrator insists we look at them in another. It is an interesting, if pointless question to ask how the point of view would have changed if the conspiracy against Nero had succeeded.

Setting

The action of *Pharsalia* sweeps back and forth across the Roman world. The choice of setting was dictated largely by history, but the specific treatment of places is atmospheric, pulled between the traditional associations of wild places and city. City equals family and society. Wilderness is danger and horror, the result of the breakdown of society and family.

Imagery and Symbolism

The leading images of the *Pharsalia* are those of shattered boundaries and dismembered bodies. The horrific treatment of men's bodies forces the reader to place both sides before the bar of common humanity. Civil war must destroy even what the republican cause hopes to save. Persistent images of disintegration are a symbol of the violent disintegra-

tion of the Roman state and the bonds between friends, kinsmen, and brothers. This is buttressed by the repeated reference to friends and kinsmen, seeing each other across the battle lines.

Related to the image of broken bodies is the image of the broken boundary. Under this category is the crossing of the Rubicon and the deaths of Crassus and Julia who had at the same time joined Pompey and Caesar and kept them from confrontation. Lucan places Crassus and Julia in a continuum with two emotionally potent episodes in Roman history: Romulus's murder of his brother for defiantly jumping over the lines of Rome's unbuilt walls and the Sabine women's throwing themselves between the opposing forces of their husbands and fathers. The first preyed on the Roman mind with a sense of fratricidal bloodguilt. The second was a bracing example of woman's *virtus* in the service of duty born of love. Cato in Book 2 pulls together this imagery when he wishes that he could stand between both armies and intercept every blow.

The battle between Curio and Iuba is described in terms of gladiatorial combat. Lucan's focus on the gladiatorial combat hinges on the original function of these combats as funeral games and sacrifices to the dead. Curio's death is described as an offering to the dead of Carthage.

Lucan's landscapes and their symbolism are firmly within the traditional Latin literature. Fear of the wild, often expressed in terms of forests and mountains, seems to have been embedded in the Roman psyche. Cities represent the natural law of humanity, family, and social cohesion. The wilderness is a place of war, of the breakdown of human society, even on the most basic level of the family.

Digressions

Lucan often inserts apparently extraneous descriptive or narrative passages in the *Pharsalia*. These digressions draw on a well-developed practice in public speaking and are paralleled in the epics of Lucan's contemporaries, Statius and Silius. Lucan's intensity as he tells his main story leaves little space for the delight and technical virtuosity that audiences expected. Lucan's delight and technical virtuosity are placed almost entirely in his digressions and allow his audience to regroup emotionally. Despite their apparent lack of justification in the work as a whole, internally, they are carefully composed. They had to display a thorough knowledge both of their subjects and of their traditional literary treatment. Stylistically, they are dramatic and concrete with neatly turned phasing and pointed moral or philosophical reflection.

The digressions are in fact far more integrated into the narrative proper than is often admitted. The birds-eye view of Brundisium begins with its foundation as a refuge for peaceloving fugitives. The focus narrows line by line from Italy to its extreme southeast corner, to the city itself, the hills behind, the harbour, and to the ships at anchor before opening out again to the sea. The movement of vision recapitulates Pompey's flight through Italy to the refuge of Brundisium and foresees his flight overseas. The description creates not only a sense of place, but more importantly draws the narrative movement into ironic focus.

Rhetoric

Quintillian called Lucan, grandson of the greatest teacher of public speaking in Rome, a better model for a public speaker than for a poet. His poem exploits all the tools of rhetoric, not only in the formal speeches, but also throughout the *Pharsalia*. Rhetoric has a bad connotation for many people, although like all tools, it is morally neutral. Rhetoric is simply the means by which a speaker or writer, but usually a speaker in Rome, can explain a position or idea, and/or convince an audience to adopt a particular attitude towards what has been explained. The duty of the orator or, indeed, of any writer was to teach, to move, and to entertain. The writer must assemble materials, *inventio*, carefully organize it, *dispositio*, and use language to its best advantage, *elocutio*. He must carefully plan out the introduction and development of his themes, *divisio*, reduce them to apt and striking comments, short, often ironic, but always didactic, *sententiae*. Finally, he must present his facts in a particular light, or *color*, so that his audience will at least experience them from his point of view.

HISTORICAL CONTEXT

Lucan's World

Lucan set his epic more than a century before his own time. To understand why Lucan should feel so strongly about events that not even his grandfather could have remembered, it is necessary to understand the circumstances in which the young poet found himself, circumstances which were the direct result of the defeat of the senatorial cause. While the empire at large was reasonably well-

governed with peace, prosperity and even justice, the upper classes of Rome and Italy suffered the caprices of immediate absolute rule under a series of men who were not immune to either the temptations of their power or the paranoia attendant upon it. Even allowing for the possibility of a certain amount of sensationalism in our sources for events in Rome between Augustus and Nero, it is clear that Rome was a place of enormous uncertainty and real danger for anyone whose place in society involved them in public life. Disengagement was not always a protection because it could be interpreted as a sign of disapproval and disloyalty.

Senatus Populusque Romanus

The tradition of participation in government and public service were vital elements in the formation of the Roman character. The Roman republic was theoretically ruled by the Senate and the People or, in Latin *Plebs*, but was effectively governed by the Senate, three hundred men chosen for life and drawn in general from the landed aristocracy. The senate's position derived from custom rather than any specific law. Its capable handling of affairs, particularly during the life or death struggles with Carthage and the complex situations Rome found itself in with Greece, meant that the Roman people were willing to leave foreign affairs and problems of finance to the Senate.

In 287 B.C., the *Lex Hortensia* had recognized the sovereign authority of the Roman people and had enacted that their resolutions *plebescita* should have the force of law for the whole community. Democracy went no further in Rome, partly because of the expertise that the Senate provided, and partly because the common people were content to leave matters in their hands. Furthermore, the people's representatives, the tribunes, were responsible for bringing in a considerable amount of legislation through the Tribal Assembly and were always at hand to keep an eye on the senate, whose acts they could veto.

The Collapse of a System

Lucan never idealized the Roman Republic in its last days. Wealth and widespread slavery, the products of her vast conquests, exacerbated some problems and created others that would have in earlier times been resolved by compromise among a people whose chief characteristic was pragmatism. Much of Roman politics was family-based and a relatively restricted small group of noble families

COMPARE & CONTRAST

- **Roman Empire:** The Roman Empire, at its height, stretches from modern Iraq to Scotland. The concept of such a superstate has never lost its hold of the western imagination; the modern European union could be described as a subconscious attempt to recreate a lost ideal.

  Modern Day: Latin imperial culture changed the linguistic and cultural face of Europe, providing a bedrock for the development of western culture, whatever way individual societies built on it. Today, former colonial peoples in Africa and the Indian sub-continent have embraced much of the literary and cultural heritage of the former imperial powers and have adapted and transmuted it even as Europeans earlier treated the culture bequeathed them by the Roman empire.

- **Roman World:** Lucan's world is dominated by the figure of an absolute ruler, whose actions can be curbed only by his own moral sense or assassination. In the twentieth century, nations as diverse as Haiti, Germany, and Cambodia have experienced the same terrifying situation.

  Modern Day: Lucan placed one of the most frightening speeches ever written in the mouth of Caesar's senior centurion. In it, he pledges that he will forget all ties of affection and even common humanity to follow Caesar's orders. There is a chillingly prophetic quality to Lucan's lines. They catch the attitude that made the most vicious regimes of the last century possible.

controlled the consulship, the state religion, and the senate. Loyalty to family and a desire to protect and increase its power became, in the absence of a powerful external enemy, many senators' first aim. Among the people at large, the Tribal Assembly came to represent almost exclusively the wishes of city *plebs*, although, if sufficiently aroused, the generally more conservative small farmers would come in to vote. After the *Lex Claudia* barred senators from taking part in banking or commerce in 218 B.C., a third class arose. The *equites* were originally *plebs* who could afford to serve as mounted soldiers. After senators were barred from trade, they became the entrepreneurial class in Rome, agitating for more influence on government policy. The *equites* were in a position to benefit from Rome's expansion, and their interests became more and more a pretext for further expansion. Enormous wealth flowing into Rome from its conquests upset the traditional economy based on the small farmer. The wealthy could afford slaves to cultivate their land; the small farmer could not. Grain flowing in from large slave cultivated estates in Sicily and Sardinia exacerbated the problem of a class who had suffered enormous losses of manpower in the fight against

Carthage. Furthermore, this wealth introduced not only pleasurable distractions to Rome's ruling class, but the possibility of bribing the urban *plebs* to ensure the outcome of elections. Into this changing world in which power was becoming more closely linked with privilege than with duty, two factions emerged in the Senate: The *Optimates* and the *Populares.*

Optimates and Populares

It is wrong to think of the *Optimates* as a reactionary senatorial party and the *Populares* as a democratic or reform party; neither was there any real class distinction between them. All were senators; among the most notorious *Populares* were men of the most ancient families. Whatever their motives and intentions, the real distinction between them is one of method. The *Optimates* controlled the Senate, and by blocking the policies of other senators, led them to seek support from the Tribal Assembly. Some *Populares*, like the Grachi brothers, were genuine reformers concerned about the effects of the growing disparity between rich and poor citizens, but many, if not most, sought personal power.

Stoicism

Stoicism, particularly as it was adapted by the teacher Panaetius of Rhodes, appealed to many Romans because it provided a philosophical basis for such traditional Roman ideals as *virtus* (courage), *pietas* (dutiful love and loyalty), and *gravitas* (seriousness). In Roman Stoicism, a person seeking wisdom and right living could feel love, loyalty, and friendship. They were expected to concern themselves with humanity and, therefore, were not to exclude themselves from political life. In matters of religion, the Roman Stoics, like Stoics in general, rejected the traditional gods of mythology, but believed that God was reason immanent in the universe; divine reason gave men and woman an ethical impulse. Stoicism could be hard and self-sufficient, but the call to follow reason struck a chord in the Roman character.

Taste and the Age of Nero

Morford stressed that Lucan was a product of the age of Nero. Literature had been in the doldrums since the death of Augustus, partly because of the daunting greatness of the works of writers like Virgil, Horace, and Ovid, and partly because of imperial hostility. The first century was an age of scholarship. When we read Lucan on Etruscan forms of divination, on the details of necromancy or on snakes, we must not forget the emperor Claudius's work on Etruscan divination or the elder Pliny's *Natural History*. When education was primarily literary and rhetorical, the treatment of works like the *Aeneid* suggested that epics should be more or less overtly learned. Nero intended to launch a cultural revival. His literary ambitions, combined with a petty nature and an autocratic style of government, meant that true literary activity, which requires freedom of the critical as well as the creative facility, was impossible. A revival of the republicanism that was never far buried in Roman hearts and minds was inevitable. Nero simply did not have the character to compete with Rome or with a philosophy for men's allegiance.

CRITICAL OVERVIEW

Lucan wrote with his already claustrophobic world closing in on him. He wrote as if he could not possibly believe that the conspiracy against Nero would succeed; he was no longer rallying his time, but all time to the cause of *libertas*. Criticism of *Pharsalia* has regularly spilled over into criticism of the man who implicated his own mother in the plot against Nero. Political circumstances have set the critical agenda for the *Pharsalia* even more than changes in literary taste. But can this really be wrong when the *Pharsalia* is above all, political literature?

Even while Lucan was at work on his epic, there was critical unease about the suitability of his treatment. It was not that he chose to handle a historical narrative but that he did not make the gods the prime movers in events. Virgil's *Aeneid* had co-opted the Roman gods literally into the Julian clan to which Julius Caesar belonged. He had enshrined in his magnificent poetry their belief that they were descended from Iules, son of Aeneas, son of the goddess Venus and grandson of Jupiter himself. Lucan sidestepped this by replacing divine wills with fate and human will. His contemporary, Petronius, criticized the decision, but his criticism is placed in the mouth of such a sleazy character that the traditional assumption that the criticism is serious may be wrong. Nevertheless, the idea that the *Pharsalia* was history rather than epic because of its treatment of causation, is repeated again and again in antiquity and the Middle Ages.

Although Lucan's portrait of Julius Caesar is at odds with that of many medieval writers, he was popular with readers. Four hundred manuscripts of his epic survive, including a fragment that represents the only surviving copy of any secular poem made between c. 550 and c.775 A.D. It was translated into Old Irish and was used by at least one Icelandic saga writer. Lucan was quoted by Aldhem in seventh-century England and in twelfth-century France by Heloise. In the sixteenth century, Christopher Marlowe published a translation of Book 1; Shakespeare adapted its opening lines in *Julius Caesar*; Ben Johnson used a speech from Book 8 in his play *Catiline*. Lucan's politics found him admirers at the end of the eighteenth century. Ahl wrote that he "codified the political rhetoric of liberty."

The later nineteenth century and the first half of the twentieth century were not so good for Lucan. Both imperialist and socialist ideologies were against him, as well as the steady retreat of classical studies and the overwhelming position of Virgil, both in the curriculum and in criticism. As Greek and Latin's position in western education slowly contracted, Lucan was no longer a standard author. Lucan's idea of liberty and his ambiguous treatment of the imperial nation state lost its hold in both England and Germany. In Germany, national unity had fi-

Julius Caesar. The Roman civil wars chronicled in The Pharsalia *destroyed the republic and brought the legendary leader to power.*

nally arrived under a German Caesar. To the English speaking world, caught between *pax Britannia* and manifest destiny, Julius Caesar and Augustus were the leaders of a benign empire, taking chaos by the scuff of the neck. Attacks on Lucan became personal and vicious. His political ideals were irrelevant; his dedication to them hypocritical; he informed on his own mother. His poetry was lost in the politics; though it is fair to say he brought this on himself by producing one of the most intensely and single-mindedly political poems ever written.

It is a measure of the strength of the Virgilian ideal that when Brisset began Lucan's rehabilitation it was by denying he was a republican. It has been the twentieth century's experience of tyranny and the broken bodies of its victims that has turned the critical tide. Lucan's experience has come home. In the last three decades, interest in Lucan has grown, and it has been positive. Johnson's studies of the characters of Erichtho, Cato and Pompey are not only deeply perceptive, (and often devastatingly funny), they are written by a scholar who makes straight for the heart of the *Pharsalia*. Lucan's "disgusting exaggeration" is neither disgusting nor

exaggeration. We should be horrified, but our horror should spring from our lacerated common humanity, not from broken canons of literature. Bartsch reads the *Pharsalia* very much as a document for our time. Her quotations from Arendt and from the experiences of the concentration camps are apt, but her own prose often comes between her and her meaning, let alone her audience. Masters on the other hand provides at least the beginning of the commentary on the *Pharsalia* which it has lacked, the historical background, the sources, the manipulation of history and of the literary tradition, which alone will save the modern reader from flattening Lucan's narrative into mere reportage.

CRITICISM

Helen Conrad-O'Briain

In the following essay, Conrad-O'Briain looks at the Pharsalia *in terms of Roman ideals and education.*

The Romans were deeply practical, and they were also deeply superstitious. Their sense of self was defined in part by the participation in Roman tradition which required strict attention to the details of worship and to the phenomena by which the gods communicated with men. It was also defined, at least for the literate upper classes, by a view of history and of service which was embedded in their language, literature, and which dominated their education. *Romanitas* [the idea and ideal of "Roman-ness"] was not a matter of genes, but of language and outlook. *Romanitas* could be and was taught from the Euphrates to the Irish Sea, from the edge of the Sahara to the lowlands of Scotland. The effects of that teaching remain to this day, so much a part of western thought and institutions that they hide in plain sight. The American pledge of allegiance is pure *Romanitas*. Any Roman hearing it would have instinctively sympathize with the concepts and the way in which they are expressed.

Liberty that comes of recognizing that without law only the strong are free was *Romanitas*' essential, if often betrayed, ideal. Virgil enshrines it in the *Aeneid*. Other nations would produce greater art, literature and science, but Rome shall rule and crown peace with law, to spare the humble and to fight the proud to the end. A fine ideal, perhaps, but real? Ideals always take a battering in real life. Human nature hasn't changed between Lucan's or

WHAT DO I READ NEXT?

- Virgil's *Aeneid*, written between 27–17 B.C., is the essential Latin epic. Like Lucan's *Pharsalia*, it was unfinished at its author's death. It quickly became a school text. Lucan would have studied the poem in great detail. His own epic has been compared, usually unfavorably, to Virgil's since his own lifetime.

- Caesar's own *De bello civili* offers his view of the Roman civil war. Like his account of his campaigns in Gaul (modern day France and the Rhineland), it is written in the third person, and while understandably self-serving, is disarmingly direct and matter-of-fact.

- Tacitus's *Annals*, written early in the second century A.D., is the history of the Roman emperors from the death of Augustus to Nero. Tacitus's natural sympathies were republican, but he still believed that good men could and should serve their countrymen even under a tyrant.

- Cicero's *Pro Marcello* (In Defence of Marcellus), *Pro Ligario* (In Defence of Ligarius), and *Pro Rege Deiotaro* (In defence of King Deiotarius) are the so-called Caesarian speeches, given before Caesar in the aftermath of his triumphant return to Rome. Cicero attempts to save his clients from the wreckage of the republican defeat and to influence Caesar's attitude and actions in his new position of master of Rome and her empire.

- Cicero's *Epistulae ad Atticum* (Letters to Atticus) are the very private and often shockingly witty letters of a republican senator to his closest friend. Many of the letters were written during the period of the civil war. The great characters of the *Pharsalia* are reduced to an even more fallible human scale by a brilliant prose writer, himself exasperating and charming by turns.

- Shakespeare's *Julius Caesar* takes up the story of the Roman civil wars, covering Caesar's assassination and the deaths of the leaders of the final conspiracy, Brutus and Cassius. Shakespeare's treatment balances itself between two heroes, Caesar and Brutus.

---

his heroes' days and this. A craze for power and insatiable greed brought down the Roman republic.

For the upper classes in Rome, at least, the first century of the empire was more often than not a claustrophobic horror; normal decency and humanity were stood on their head. But the ideal remained, and there were always men and women who tried to follow it, even if to quote Cato on Pompey, they "were inferior to our ancestors." Some of them, like Cicero, died defending the republic, some of them died, like Lucan, in conspiracies against madmen, or even like Scribonius and Paetus, simply against the idea of an emperor. Others, like the Plinies, Agricola, even emperors, Titus, Trajan, Antonius, Marcus Aurelius, simply tried to do their duty by those around them, with whatever abilities they had. For what else was a Roman to do? A Roman defined

himself by public life, by public service, by the mutual respect and aid of patron and client, of friend and kinsman. He was a public being. To live retired, far away from public life was the fate of the old, the exiled or the extremely eccentric.

And what were the Roman's tools in living out this ideal? The spoken and written word was his tool, more important than the short sword carried by every Roman soldier from new recruit to legate. To persuade, to explain, to use this power effectively for the good of the state and for one's friends and dependants was the duty, and purpose, the life's blood of every good Roman. His whole education was based on language and the uses of language. He was taught to take texts apart and see how and why they worked. He learned to pick and chose his material, to catch the emotions of his audience. He

> The spoken and written word was his tool, more important than the short sword carried by every Roman soldier from new recruit to legate. To persuade, to explain, to use this power effectively for the good of the state and for one's friends and dependants was the duty, and purpose, the life's blood of every good Roman."

learned the importance of the right word, the exact example, the telling anecdote. He learned or tried to learn how to swing an angry crowd, a wet, footsore knot of soldiers, or a group of grave, experienced old men behind him. Everything an educated Roman knew was directed by the use he would make of it in public life. Every educated man was educated to be a statesman, or at least a politician. For some the arena would be the senate and the great law courts in Rome, but throughout the empire, in Roman colonies and in local market towns, Roman citizens and provincials alike were repeating the same process and living on their own local stages the same lives.

This is the background of Lucan's *Pharsalia* and of Lucan himself. The ideal, the education, the defining mode of life had claimed him. He was from a provincial family that had made good, and that had made good by producing the greatest teacher of public speaking of his day, his grandfather Seneca the Elder. His uncle the younger Seneca had become a senator, the tutor and the advisor of an emperor. Lucan had inherited all the sparkling talent of his family. He could persuade, he could move, he could catch the eye and the mind. So why is Lucan the suicide, the failed conspirator, the author of an unrevised if not unfinished (Masters, 1992, 216–259) epic? Because of the ideal and because of the nature of *Romanitas* and Roman education, because he found that the lack of real

libertas could not be replaced by private integrity and interior freedom, and it was self-delusion to believe otherwise. Lucan believed that liberty and participation in the making and defining of law were at the heart of *Romanitas*.

He found himself in the Rome of Nero in a place where he was excluded from the work which defined his existence as a Roman, the only existence which he desired or could even imagine. It was not that Nero had barred him from defending clients in the law courts, from giving public readings of his poetry. That was only the result of Lucan's realizing that the Roman system could not and did not work as long as it was headed by a man above the law, whose only curb was his own sanity or the assassin's sword. Perhaps his view of events were colored like those of the republican senators a century before, the resentment of a young man who felt that he should be at the center of real power, where the decisions were made, though he could have been there had he been willing.

As Bartsch (1997) reminds us, Lucan believed in his tools, just like every writer who takes on a totalitarian regime does. If those tools had served to establish the imperial ideal, to defend the status quo, he would wrench them back and stand them on their head. Did Nero want a golden age of poetry? Lucan would give him poetry to match the world he had created in Rome, horror for horror. Did Nero want to be a god? Well then how could he complain if a poet begged him not to unbalance the heavens with his divine weight, when everyone including the pudgy young emperor knew that the gods were known by their great size (Ahl, 1996, 26).

Rhetoric and rhetoricians have always had bad press. There is something rather unsavory, in many peoples' minds, about learning and planning the art of persuasion, of getting your views across, but rhetoric is only a tool. It can be used for good or for evil. The woman who, through careful presentation of facts and an appeal to the penalties of the law (and with a few judicious and emotive references to human suffering), convinces investors to force their company to clean up its toxic waste dump is praised, but she is using the same tools as her sister successfully defending an unsavory client. In Lucan's eyes, the gods had been hijacked, the sword had been seized by this obscenity of rule, but the words, the formidable arsenal of rhetoric, was still his.

So Lucan wrote a rhetorical epic. He had to persuade, and he had to persuade quickly and thoroughly before the words, drained of their real meaning by imperial propaganda, were lost to him too. He must transmit the claustrophobia and despair of his world to his audience, make them face the unthinkable so that they would do the unthinkable, reject the Julio-Claudians and all their works and all their empty glories. From the opening lines of the poem he drums it home. Jealous fate may have resented the power of the Roman people, but those people, the greater and the lesser, were eager tools in the hands of fate. This cooperation is what gave us civil war, and ultimately Nero, with Roman blood spilt by Roman hands, while Rome was still ringed with enemies. And what were these Roman deaths like? Worse still, how died the noble Massillians, more Roman in their attitudes than the Romans themselves? They died, bodies broken, smashed beyond recognition.

In Lucan's work the gods of Rome predict no happy culmination to Jupiter's plans. They predict only the crime and pollution of civil war and the death of the *libertas* that was to be Rome's great gift as a nation to all men. Where is the piety of the divine Julio-Claudians when their founder treats the gods and Rome like nothing more than the spirits of his household shrine? Julius Caesar's manic energy, his ability to seize events and make his will the fate of the weak, are a reproach, not only to every one of the republican figures who oppose him, but to Lucan's audience.

Lucan creates a world crashing down, a world in which his audience are still dazed survivors walking around in the ruins. It is a world in which decency survives, but that decency is presented in a way which give the Roman people little comfort. The Roman women who crowd the altars, the picture of traditional piety, the Roman men who take up their weapons against their own countrymen and kin, seem powerless to cry halt. They allow themselves to be led rather than to bring their own collective power to bear on events. Cornelia, the pattern of a Roman matron, the pattern of a Roman, drawing foreigners to admiration by her *virtus*, is the personification of the bad fortune. Lentulus is eloquent in his denunciation of paying a price for victory which will be a defeat of their ideals, but his eloquence sets in motion the chain of events which will lead to Pompey's death and the disintegration of the republican will to fight. With Cato, Lucan kills any comfortable hope that personal freedom and integrity can be maintained under the rule not of the law, but of one man. Cato has no illusions, he will not retire into philosophic consolation. He will not live with a selfish illusion of freedom, while he

can commit the final rebellion of death. And if the good are impotent, the bad are busy making the better side worse. One after another, Lucan draws the portraits of Roman senators who sell their birthright, who shame their class and country. The gifted Curio sells his country's freedom. Appius wakes the long silent oracle of Delphi simply to find out, at a time when the senate cannot even meet in Rome, how things will go for him. The great Pompey's younger son, crawling to a witch rather than the gods, watches one of his father's own men dragged unwillingly from the safety of death to learn what cannot help him.

Why does Lucan force his audience down the road of claustrophobic despair, cutting of each possibly retreat, thwarting the efforts and gifts of every decent character, leaving power in the hands of the two characters who single-mindedly pursue power, for whom no act is too vile, who will sacrifice kin and force the gods to do their bidding—Caesar and his female counterpart, Erichtho? How similar they are, ever hungry for battle, ever inventive in finding new ways to force the events or the gods to do their bidding. The answer may lie, if it lies anywhere, at the end of Lentulus's speech in Book 8, "*Quantum, spes ultima rerum, libertatis habes*" "A last hope, how much freedom you have." Forced to see the cause and the plain face of their predicament, perhaps they will finally seize events like a Caesar.

Source: Helen Conrad-O'Briain, for *Epics for Students*, Gale, 2001.

Shadi Bartsch

Author Shadi Bartsch discusses the importance of Lucan's major themes in this excerpt.

The previous two chapters have presented the grounds for a grippingly negative interpretation of the *Civil War*. This reading has had a powerful pull for recent readers of the epic; indeed, the present critical climate has rendered it one of the most compelling positions on the poem. The collapse of the autonomous individual amid the wreck of linguistic systems and subject-object relations, the hopelessness of meaningful narrative in a meaningless world, the impossibility of representing the trauma of Romans killing Romans—"Shun this part of the war, O mind, and leave it in darkness, and let no time learn of such evils from my poetry, that so great is the license granted to civil war"—all these are undeniable aspects of Lucan's epic world, and for readers of our times I think they are more than undeniable: they ring true with an evocation of the particular horrors of the twentieth century. Lucan's attempt to convey what he would represent as the unspeakable physical and psychological brutalities of the civil wars of the first century B.C. fastens, uncannily enough, upon the actual truths of what happens to the human subject *in extremis* and on the realities of the societal and psychic results of the totalitarian agenda, and so he produces a picture that has curious resonances in the history of our own century. Certainly Nazi Germany and Stalinist Russia have rendered unhappily familiar such regimes' assault on moral standards, the surveillance of citizens, the spread of fear, the paradoxes that arise from the overturning of norms of law and human behavior. We know well that terror is the tool of all such regimes—"the essence of totalitarian government," in Hannah Arendt's words. And Arendt, along with Czeslaw Milosz, Alexander Solzhenitsyn, and other voices from the past, all attest to totalitarianism's focus on "the destruction of a man's rights, the killing of the juridical person in him … the murder of the moral person in man". Suddenly the darkest visions of the human imagination become alive in history, and, with them,

> it becomes evident that things which for thousands of years the human imagination had banished to a realm beyond human competence can be manufactured right here on earth … The totalitarian hell proves only that the power of man is greater than [one] ever dared to think, and that man can realize hellish fantasies without making the sky fall or the earth open.

I bring up this analogy here because it is difficult for readers of Lucan not to be struck by parallel after parallel between the visions of his imagination and our own history. As I have noted, even the figure of the restless, madly self-confident Julius Caesar, that demonic and charismatic force "who felt he had accomplished nothing while anything still remained to be done", seems tailor-made to evoke, for us, a crucial feature of such regimes—the charisma invested in the figure of the leader and the exaggeration of his powers of agency. Henderson remarks that Caesar himself seems to represent the very principle of "subjectivity as active agency" in this poem in which other subjectivities are faring less well; similarly with Hitler, who himself and whose regime was associated with energy and agency: Arendt notes the "perpetual motion mania of totalitarian movements which can remain in power only so long as they keep moving and set everything around them in motion." Moreover, Hitler's regime identified itself with the forces of nature and history: its rise to power was supposedly inevitable and inexorable, its present existence temporally eternal, as evidence by the well-known Nazi projection of the "Thousand Year Reich" and "revolutionary immortality," and the National Socialists' belief that they were children of the gods—like Lucan's Julio-Claudians, claimers of spurious divinity. Finally, Arendt notes the moral cynicism of the leaders: "would-be totalitarian rulers usually start their careers by boasting of the past crimes and carefully outlining their future ones … The propaganda value of evil deeds and general contempt for moral standards is independent of mere self-interest, supposedly the most powerful psychological factor in politics." These men believe everything is permitted to them: Lucan's Caesar, anyone? The Third Reich meets the Pax Romana.

Our knowledge of Stalinist and fascist regimes aside, I think we read Lucan's epic with another, still darker piece of recent history as our lens. I am referring here to the Holocaust: not only to its unnarratability, but to the scattered testimony of its survivors and the deliberate and crushing destruction of the very idea of the human that was so successfully carried out by its Nazi perpetrators. Here, too, Lucan's grim visions may become for us more than the fancy of a long-dead poet striving for the expression of evil, precisely because the inexorable disintegration of subjectivity, the sense of the futility of language, the complete loss of agency, are not themes alien to our times: we know that these developments are possible as the goals of those who would destroy millions of their fellow beings. The topic is a difficult one, and far beyond my powers: here I would just like to remind my readers of how some scholars and writers have *tried* to talk about the Holocaust, and to suggest that Lucan's view of a world gone mad may mean more than he could have guessed to his readers.

Source: Shadi Bartsch, *Ideology in Cold Blood: A Reading of Lucan's Civil War,* Harvard University Press, 1997, pp. 66–8.

Matthew B. Roller

In this essay, the author examines the uses of divided communities in Lucan's Bellum Civile.

Lucan's *Bellum Civile* is riven with ethical contradictions. It is not simply that different voices within the poem disagree about the proper moral evaluation of particular actions and patterns of behavior;

such disagreement is widely present in ancient epic. Rather, these voices, including the narrative voice itself, are collectively enmeshed in a web of competing ethical discourses and modes of valuation that are more or less equally authoritative yet irreconcilable. Thus actions can be evaluated in more than one ethical framework—not only by different voices embracing alternative modes of valuation, but even by a single voice as it applies now one evaluative framework and now another. This paper will contend that these competing ethical discourses, and the contradictory moral judgments that derive from them, are necessary features of the condition of civil war as Lucan represents it. For these discourses and judgments are based in competing, irreconcilable conceptions of the Roman community. Indeed, the fracturing of ethical discourse in Lucan may constitute a literary strategy for representing civil war: the warring of two groups within society is reflected in the competition between alternative ethical discourses. Finally, I consider some of the ideological ramifications of Lucan's literary choices. For by portraying specific modes of discourse as he does, and by making them compete in certain ways, Lucan makes his civil war a context in which he can recreate, explore, and participate in the ideological struggles of his own day.

I. Traditional Roman Ethical Discourse

Before turning to Lucan, however, I must describe crucial features of the received ethical system of the late republican and early imperial aristocracy. I call this system "traditional" because these aristocrats regarded it as passed down from their ancestors, the *maiores*, unchanged since time immemorial. Its values consisted in particular conceptions of proper behavior, closely linked with an interest in status and position: praise was bestowed for behavior that enhanced the position of the aristocracy with respect to other groups, and of individual aristocrats with respect to other aristocrats. These behavior patterns and status concerns were encoded in the familiar moral vocabulary of the Latin language: *virtus, pietas, fas, ius, fides, laus, honor, gloria, nobilitas, dignitas* (along with their opposites), and so on. Although the content of these terms was always subject to contestation, all Roman aristocrats nevertheless operated with regard to this mapping of ethical space—that is, all accepted the validity of the moral categories in which the terms *nobilis, pius, fidus*, etc., designate positive value. Thus their collective acceptance of this mapping— their judging of others according to these catego-

> The collapse of the autonomous individual amid the wreck of linguistic systems and subject-object relations, the hopelessness of meaningful narrative in a meaningless world, the impossibility of representing the trauma of Romans killing Romans . . . all these are undeniable aspects of Lucan's epic world. . ."

ries, and their own desire to be judged positively according to them—was part of their acculturation, hence partially constituted their identity, as aristocrats within Roman society and as Romans with respect to non-Romans. Looked at another way, the ethical categories defined by the traditional Roman moral vocabulary collectively provide a template for the structure of the Roman community, for they mark out its boundaries, articulate its internal relations, and define degrees of distinction within it; in other words, they define positions in society for people to occupy. Thus the use of these moral terms not only reflects social forms and structures, but also formalizes, confirms, and helps to reproduce those structures.

Another crucial feature of this ethical system is that moral value is social and external. The community as a whole, not its constituent individuals, is the basic unit of social organization, and moral value exists only with reference to the community as a whole. This communal, external frame of reference has three aspects. First, a person's moral value is determined entirely by the judgments of other members of the community, not by his own self-judgment. Second, moral value is allocated (i.e., praise and blame bestowed) on the basis of observed actions, not on the basis of any internal, privately accessible states of mind. Third, these actions are evaluated in terms of the effect they have on the community as a whole—that is, for the degree to

Marcus Portius Cato. Cato is the central figure in the events of Book 8, when he is forced to assume leadership of the Republicans after Pompey's death.

which they further the community's agendas and reproduce its ideologies.

A consistent, coherent ethical discourse—praising and blaming, and deploying value terms with reference to the actions of others—therefore requires a notionally coherent, well-defined community to serve as the social basis for moral valuation. As an illustration, consider the semantics of the value terms *virtus, pietas,* and their opposites. *Virtus* means "behavior appropriate to a man"; most commonly it is attributed to a soldier who has displayed notable valor in battle, or to a magistrate for outstanding service—in each case, actions performed in the public eye for the benefit of the community. Meanwhile *pietas,* along with its opposite *impietas,* defines a category of action encompassing duty toward family, community, and the gods. Taken together, these two moral categories of action project a well-defined community, and articulate coherently certain aspects of that community's inter- and intramural relations: its members owe one another the various duties and obligations associated with *pietas,* but they must also display *virtus* by fighting bravely against non-members who threaten

it from without. Indeed, in such a community these categories overlap, for one who fights well (demonstrating *virtus*) thereby also defends his family and community (demonstrating *pietas*).

Civil war, however, divides the community and turns it against itself, abolishing the social boundaries and bonds that make these moral categories consistent. Hence *pietas* and *virtus* become inconsistent, even contradictory: a soldier who demonstrates *virtus* by fighting the adversary effectively can also be judged *impius* for harming other members of his own community; likewise, if he refuses to fight (so as not to kill fellow-citizens), he fails his comrades-in-arms and may be accused of cowardice. For when the community has split into two warring factions, the view that one's opponents are *cives* (fellow-Romans, i.e., members of one's own community) and the view that they are *hostes* (foreign enemies, therefore not members of one's own community) are available simultaneously. These alternative conceptions of civil war—that it is or is not a conflict within a single community—authorize competing ethical discourses which in turn provide competing, often contradictory, value judgments on particular actions and therefore motivate sharply divergent actions in a given situation. And so it is in Lucan's *Bellum Civile.* In the sections below I examine representations of piety and valor (and the deployment of ethical terms generally) in Lucan, arguing that various voices in the poem contradict not only one another, but also themselves. But I contend that there is a systematic logic to these contradictory value judgments: they arise from these alternative conceptions of the community in civil war, the competing views that one's opponent is a *civis* and a *hostis.*

II. The "Communitarian" Viewpoint

Of the two views of civil war articulated in Lucan, I first discuss what I call the *communitarian* view: the idea that the conflict at hand takes place within a single community that, despite this conflict, remains fundamentally intact. The very term *bellum civile* privileges this view, implying as it does that the belligerents are all fellow-citizens, members of a single community. In the first eight lines of the poem the narrative voice describes the conflict from this viewpoint. It expresses the Romans' behavior metaphorically as a person turning a sword against his own vitals (*populumque potentem/in sua victrici conversum viscera dextra*), it apostrophizes both factions collectively as *cives,* and it portrays them as identical and interchangeable ("kindred battle-lines," "standards opposed to hostile standards, equal eagles, and javelins threatening javelins"). On this view the conflict is inherently criminal, for slaughtering other members of one's community—massively violating the obligations and duties one owes one's fellow-citizens—is manifestly impious. Thus the narrative voice condemns the conflict as a crime, as sacrilege, and as madness (*scelus, nefas, furor*). Furthermore, on this view of the conflict there is no place for martial valor (*virtus*), for there is no foreign enemy against whom it can properly be displayed. The communitarian view of the conflict thus authorizes a particular pattern of action, and a corresponding ethical discourse: violence against the adversary is condemned; avoidance of violence is praised.

Throughout the poem, the communitarian view is most clearly articulated and enacted by Pompey himself, and to a lesser extent by his followers. This view, however, involves an unavoidable contradiction: if Pompey regards the Caesarians as members of the community, as people who have claims upon his *pietas,* how can he also advocate violence against them? This contradiction leaves its traces in many of Pompey's speeches. Consider his speech to his troops at 2.531–95, Pompey's first words in the poem. Here he represents his clash with Caesar primarily as a dispute within a single community. At 2.539–40 he denies that the conflict is a *proelium iustum* (which I take to be equivalent here to *bellum iustum*, a phrase specifically associated with warfare against a *hostis*) and insists rather that it is the "anger of a vengeful fatherland"—anger directed, implicitly, at a recalcitrant member of itself. Elaborating this claim, he goes on to compare Caesar to other Romans who took up arms against the state: Catiline, Lentulus, Cethegus, Cinna, Marius, Lepidus, Carbo, even Spartacus; significantly, he does not compare Caesar to a foreign foe such as Hannibal, a paradigm that others have already applied. Also, at the end of the speech he explicitly calls the conflict a *bellum civile*. In accordance with the communitarian view, throughout the speech he condemns Caesar's assault on his fatherland as criminal, sacrilegious, and mad: he associates with Caesar words such as *scelus, pollutus, nefas, rabies, furens, furor,* and *demens.* But embedded in this communitarian presentation of the conflict are jarring notes, traces of the inherent contradiction noted above. At 2.532–33, for example, he calls his troops the "truly Roman band" (*o vere Romana manus*) whose warmaking is authorized by the Senate, and contrasts this authorization with Caesar's "private arms."

> " These alternative conceptions of civil war—that it is or is not a conflict within a single community—authorize competing ethical discourses which in turn provide competing, often contradictory, value judgments on particular actions and therefore motivate sharply divergent actions in a given situation."

This portrayal seems to eliminate the Caesarians from the ranks of "Romans," rather than include them. Similarly, at 2.533 he urges his soldiers to "pray for a fight" (*votis deposcite pugnam*)—hardly consistent with the violence-averse communitarian view. These inconsistencies suggest that Pompey cannot in fact reconcile the communitarian view with advocating violence. Perhaps these inconsistencies also account for the speech's poor reception, for his men do not applaud, nor show enthusiasm for battle.

Pompey's actions, on the other hand, do accord generally with the communitarian view and its associated value system: for the most part he does try to avoid killing his opponents and hence to avoid the *impietas*—the violation of duties and obligations—that such action, on the communitarian view, entails. At 6.118–39, when Pompey first attempts to break out of the encirclement at Dyrrachium—the first time Pompey himself sends his troops into battle—his sudden onslaught scares the Caesarians *literally* to death: "That his victory might owe nothing to the sword, fear had finished off his stunned enemies. They lay dead in the place they ought to have stood—the only thing their *virtus* had the strength to do. Already there was nobody left to receive wounds, and the storm-cloud bringing so many weapons was squandered" (*ne quid victoria ferro/deberet, pavor attonitos confecerat hostes./ quod solum valuit virtus, iacuere perempti/debuerant quo stare loco. qui volnera ferrent/iam derant, et nimbus agens tot tela peribat*). The narrator implies that Pompey remains undefiled by civil bloodshed because his victory is technically non-violent: fear itself does the killing before Pompeian weapons can draw blood.

A second episode at Dyrrachium more clearly shows Pompey's communitarian behavior, but reveals a further contradiction inherent in this ethical stance. Pompey has surrounded a portion of Caesar's army and could end the war on the spot if he annihilates them—but he restrains his men's swords:

> Totus mitti civilibus armis
> usque vel in pacem potuit cruor: ipse furentes
> dux tenuit gladios. felix ac libera regum,
> Roma, fores iurisque tui, vicisset in illo
> si tibi Sulla loco. dolet, heu, semperque dolebit,
> quod scelerum, Caesar, prodest tibi summa tuorum,
> cum genero pugnasse pio. pro tristia fata!

> All the blood in civil conflict could have been shed, even to the point of peace: but the leader himself restrained the furious swords. You would have been happy, free from kings and master of yourself, Rome, had Sulla conquered for you in that place. It grieves us, alas, and will always grieve us, that the pinnacle of your crimes benefits you, Caesar: you have done battle with a son-in-law who is *pius*. Oh, cruel fate!

Pompey is declared *pius*—a positive value judgment—because he restrains his men's swords (suppressing their *virtus*) and so preserves Caesar. In this respect he differs from Sulla and especially from Caesar himself, who commits a *scelus* in fighting his own son-in-law. Yet the adjective *pius* here is also ironic, as the exclamation *pro tristia fata*! signals: for thanks to Pompey's current *pietas*, the mutual communal slaughter will continue and the state will eventually be enslaved (*libera regum,/ Roma, fores iurisque tui* …). So Pompey's pious action not only comes at the expense of *virtus*, but also, on the communitarian view itself, begets further *impietas* in the long run—continued mutual slaughter within the community, then subjection to a *dominus*.

The ethical contradictions involved in the communitarian view are further elaborated early in Book 7. On the morning of the battle of Pharsalus, Pompey's troops, overcome by a "dire frenzy" and hence eager to join battle, accuse their leader of being "slow and cowardly" for pursuing a strategy of delay: *segnis pavidusque vocatur/ac nimium patiens soceri Pompeius* …. That is, they imply that his strategy betrays a lack of *virtus* and that he is overly concerned with matters of *pietas* (his duty toward his father-in-law). In reply Pompey con-

cedes that battle can no longer be postponed, in part because the "prods of martial valor" are inciting his soldiers (*si modo virtutis stimulis iraeque calore/ signa petunt*). But he also labels his soldiers' desire to fight as "madness for criminality" and suggests that victory without bloodshed is desirable in civil war (*quis furor, o caeci, scelerum? civilia bella/ gesturi metuunt ne non cum sanguine vincant*. Since *scelus* here refers to killing one's kin and fellow-citizens, Pompey is implying that *pietas* justifies his strategy of delay and avoidance; thus he counters his soldiers' implied judgment that he lacks *virtus*. This passage once again demonstrates that using violence is ethically incompatible with maintaining a communitarian view of the conflict: the desire to be evaluated positively in the category of martial valor (*virtus*) urges battle, while consideration for community obligations (*pietas*) demands abstention from battle.

Nevertheless, Pompey does attempt to bridge this gap, and to render *virtus* and *pietas* consistent. Addressing his soldiers just before the battle, he seeks to motivate them to fight effectively by invoking images of fatherland, wives and children left behind:

> "quem flagitat" inquit
> "vestra diem virtus, finis civilibus armis,
> quem quaesistis, adest. totas effundite vires:
> extremum ferri duperest opus, unaque gentis
> hora trahit. quisquis patriam carosque penates,
> qui subolem ac thalamos desertaque
>   pignora quaerit,
> ense petat: medio posuit deus omnia campo.''

> "The day your *virtus* demands," he says, "the end to civil conflict that you have sought, is at hand. Pour out all your strength: a final work of arms remains, and a single hour draws together all nations. Whoever longs for his fatherland and dear *penates,* whoever longs for his offspring and wife and relatives left behind, let him seek them by the sword: god has set everything in the middle of the field."

Later he adduces still other images of the community in need, asking his men to imagine Roman matrons urging them to battle from the walls of the city, Roman senators abasing themselves before them, and the city itself making an appeal—that is, he appeals repeatedly to his soldiers' sense of duty to family and community, to their desire to be judged *pii*, in an effort to motivate them to fight with valor (*virtus*; *totas effundite vires*). He even refers to the Caesarians as *hostes*. Yet in the context of the upcoming battle, his rhetorical strategy is self-contradictory and doomed to fail: for what will his troops do when they see their own fathers, sons, and brothers on the other side? That is, how can they fight vigorously (demonstrating *virtus*) on the moral basis that Pompey has provided for them (that of acting piously), when the purported *hostes* facing them are the very people to whom they are bound by obligations of *pietas*? Again, Pompey cannot resolve the fundamental contradiction inherent in his communitarian view: for this view is consistent with a strategy of avoidance and delay in civil war, but not with violent conflict. Nor do his soldiers deal effectively with this contradiction. For although we are told that his speech kindles their desire to display *virtus*, it turns out (as we shall see in section IV) that their desire to be judged *pii*, upon which this desire for *virtus* is presumably founded, will indeed undermine their will to fight as soon as they recognize their friends and relatives on the other side.

III. The "Alienating" Viewpoint

Petreius, in the fraternization scene, is the one Pompeian who systematically rejects the communitarian viewpoint and so avoids the contradictions that plague Pompey. In a speech urging his men to kill the Caesarians who have entered the Pompeian camp, Petreius rhetorically excludes the Caesarians from the community. He calls them *hostes* and insists that the Pompeian troops owe loyalty only to their own side, which he identifies with the state as a whole: "heedless of your fatherland, forgetful of your own standards …" (*immemor o patriae, signorum oblite tuorum*). His value judgments support this construction of the community: he calls his men's fraternization "outrageous betrayal" (*proditio nefanda*) and implies that they have violated the trust placed in them (*fides*) in giving up the fight against the Caesarians. Petreius' ethical language contrasts sharply with the communitarian language of the narrator in his description of the fraternization: there, *nefas* is predicated of killing one's adversary and *fides* of preserving and cherishing him. Petreius' words are persuasive; his soldiers, reluctant at first, are finally induced to abandon the communitarian view and slaughter their Caesarian guests.

Petreius' viewpoint, which I call the *alienating* view, is not "perverse"—an adjective that scholars regularly apply to this line of thought—nor is it merely a travesty or inversion of communitarian values: it has a systematic logic of its own. It is the view that one's opponent is a *hostis,* a foreign enemy, whose behavior both excludes him from the community of Romans and threatens that community. Therefore making war on him is both pious and

valorous. On this view, the conflict at hand is not a *bellum civile* at all, but rather a *bellum externum*; it is fundamentally no different from a war against (say) the Parthians or a German tribe. The alienating view is well-represented throughout Lucan's poem, but it is much more commonly associated with the Caesarians than with the Pompeians.

This view is first articulated at the initial crisis point in the poem, Caesar's arrival at the Rubicon. As Caesar stands on the bank of the river, a vision of the Roman state itself, the *patria*, appears to him and says, "Where beyond are you aiming? Where are you carrying my standards, soldiers? If you come with legal sanction, and as citizens, this far only is permitted" (*quo tenditis ultra?/quo fertis mea signa, viri? si iure venitis,/si cives, huc usque licet*). This image of the nation itself embodies the values of the community as a whole, telling Caesar that he will be violating the proper Roman way of doing things (*ius*) and hence will be excluded from the body of *cives,* if he crosses the river with his army: he will, in other words, alienate himself. Caesar responds by forcefully asserting his membership in the community: he invokes the Trojan *penates* of his own house, the fire of Vesta, and Jupiter in two different forms—all symbols of the Roman community and his membership in it—asking them to favor his undertaking. In this way he affiliates his actions with the interests of the community; he implies that he is *pius*. Indeed, he explicitly denies that he is attacking the *patria* itself: "It is not you whom I am harrying with furious arms" (*non te furialibus armis/persequor*). He does concede the application of the term *hostis* to himself, but insists that the blame for his behavior will ultimately fall upon his adversaries: "He, he will be guilty, who made me a *hostis* to you" (*ille erit, ille nocens, qui me tibi fecerit hostem*). The violation of *ius* and *pietas* will then be theirs, not his, and his own claim to membership in the community will be vindicated.

Caesar here resists being made the object of alienating discourse, though soon he will take up this discourse himself for use against the Pompeians. Initially, however, he makes no effort to exclude them from the community. Addressing his soldiers in Book 1, he justifies war by arguing that Pompey's extraordinary power must be abolished and by claiming that he is looking out for his soldiers' welfare. These arguments seem rather *ad hoc*; he fails to articulate a systematic moral basis for going to war—as he could do, for example, by tarring his opponents as *hostes*. For this reason his speech fails to persuade: "he finished speaking, but the crowd, doubtful, murmured to itself with indistinct mumbling. *Pietas* and their ancestral *penates* broke their resolve, despite being fierce with slaughter, and their inflamed spirits" (*dixerat; at dubium non claro murmure volgus/secum incerta fremit. pietas patriique penates/quamquam caeda feras mentes animosque tumentes/frangunt*). His men regard their opponents as members of the community, and thus considerations of *pietas* preclude the assault Caesar urges.

But among Caesar's centurions is one Laelius, who wears an oak wreath indicating that he once saved the life of a fellow-citizen in battle. The wreath signifies the community's collective judgment that he has displayed both *virtus* and *pietas* — since his heroic action falls into the ethical categories of both "martial valor" and "service to the community." As such he is an authoritative moral voice: it is he who provides a systematic moral basis for Caesar's war effort and thus resolves the soldiers' concerns about *pietas*. Specifically, he grants Caesar the authority to define the community of Roman citizens as he wishes, simply by indicating whom his soldiers should attack: "nor is anyone a fellow-citizen of mine if I hear your trumpets against him, Caesar" (*nec civis meus est, in quem tua classica, Caesar,/audiero*). If the community so defined excludes the soldiers' blood-relations and spouses, so be it, says Laelius: "If you order me to bury my sword in my brother's breast or my father's throat or in the belly of my pregnant wife, even if my right hand is unwilling, I will nevertheless do it all" (*pectore si fratris gladium iuguloque parentis/condere me iubeas plenaeque in viscera partu/coniugis, invita peragam tamen omnia dextra*). He also declares himself willing to plunder and burn the temples of the gods, and even to destroy the city of Rome itself, if Caesar requests it. In these statements Laelius disavows each significant aspect of *pietas* as normally understood: he forswears his obligations to the gods, to the state and community at large, and to his family. Indeed, he obliquely acknowledges the normative force of this conception of *pietas* when he concedes that his own right hand may be unwilling: he implies that he must struggle to overcome an ingrained aversion to slaughtering kin. But this acknowledgment merely emphasizes the radical nature of the alienating view he articulates. The point is that, on this view, his kin are no longer members of the community, and *pietas* is not owed to them. For only those alongside whom one fights are fellow-citizens, and those against whom one fights are not. It is this view of the community that his ethical language is tailored to fit. To judge from the soldiers' reactions, Laelius' speech succeeds where Caesar's speech failed: now that Laelius has addressed their concerns about *pietas* by redefining the community, the soldiers pledge to follow Caesar into "any war to which he should summon them".

In the next few books Caesar and the Caesarians regularly assert, and act in accordance with, the alienating view of the conflict. In a description of Caesar's march south through Italy at 2.439–46, we are told that Caesar rejoices in shedding blood continuously, in taking the towns by force, and in devastating the fields; he regards the defenders as *hostes*. Furthermore, he is ashamed to go by an undefended route, lest he "appear to be a citizen" (*concessa pudet ire via civemque videri*). In his actions, in his characterizations of the belligerents, and in the moral judgments on the action embedded in his emotional reactions (*gaudet, iuvat,* and *pudet*), Caesar manifests the alienating view of the conflict: he and his opponents are foreign enemies in relation to one another; hence it is right, good, and a source of joy to destroy them violently.

Scaeva's behavior and ethical discourse (6.140– 262) are also rooted in the alienating view. Rallying the defeated Caesarians after Pompey's attack at Dyrrachium, he speaks as follows: "'To what point,' he said, 'has impious fear, unknown to all the weapons of Caesar, driven you? … with *pietas* gone, young men, will you not stand your ground out of anger, at least?'" ("*quo vos pavor*" inquit "*adegit/impius et cunctis ignotus Caesaris armis? … non ira saltem, iuvenes, pietate remota/stabitis?*"). In accusing them of *pavor* (the opposite of *virtus*) and *impietas*—i.e., of failing to fight well against a foreign enemy and thereby neglecting their obligations to their community—he implicitly constructs a community consisting of Caesarians only and excluding the Pompeians. Indeed, he refers to the Pompeians as *hostes* at 6.156, and the narrator maintains this characterization of the Pompeians in the lines that follow (*hostes, hosti, hostem*)—that is, Scaeva can be seen as the focalizer of these words, and of the description of his actions generally as told by the narrator. Toward the end of his *aristeia*, however, Scaeva briefly adopts communitarian discourse and behavior to create a deception: his *virtus* subsides (*virtute remota*) and he addresses the Pompeians as *cives*, asking them to spare him. When Aulus draws near, Scaeva stabs him in the throat, reigniting his *virtus* (*incaluit virtus*) and restoring the alienating pattern of action and valuation. His fellow-Caesarians share this view, and therefore, as representatives of his community and hence a judging audience for his spectacular public performance, they "praise him as the living image of outstanding Martial Valor" (*vivam magnae speciem virtutis adorant*). They also dedicate his weapons to Mars, presumably a mark of their *pietas*. But again, his actions are valorous, and theirs are pious, only on the alienating view, in which the Pompeians are regarded as *hostes* and therefore violence against them is right, appropriate, and divinely sanctioned.

The final strong statement of the alienating perspective occurs in Caesar's speech in Book 7, just before the battle of Pharsalus is joined. A crucial passage in this speech is the following:

> vos tamen hoc oro, iuvenes, ne caedere quisquam
> hostis terga velit: civis qui fugerit esto.
> sed, dum tela micant, non vos pietatis imago
> ulla nec adversa conspecti fronte parentes
> commoveant; vultus gladio turbate verendos.

> But this I ask you, young men, that no one wish to strike the enemy in the back: consider anyone who flees a fellow-citizen. But, while the weapons gleam, let no vision of *pietas* move you, nor your parents if you see them facing you: churn up with your sword those faces demanding reverence.

Here Caesar progressively nuances the notion of "enemy" (*hostis*). First, opponents who flee are not enemies at all; on the contrary, he formally and explicitly defines those who flee as members of the community (*civis qui fugerit esto*). This definition provides a social, hence ethical, basis for sparing them: one should not seek to kill a member of one's community; to do so would be impious. Against those who stand and fight, however, Caesar urges his soldiers to fight vigorously. Even if they are your parents, he says, you must not let *pietas* move you; you must mangle their faces regardless. The claim that those who stand their ground do not warrant pious treatment, regardless even of kinship, implicitly excludes them from the community; it is this subset of the Pompeians who comprise the "real" *hostis* against whom martial valor must be displayed. Here Caesar takes up Laelius' earlier suggestion that the community (as the Caesarians see it) be defined in terms of whom Caesar chooses to attack. Also like Laelius, Caesar's language acknowledges the existence of the communitarian viewpoint: in speaking of parents as "demanding reverence" (*verendi*), he concedes that the duties of *pietas* would normally be owed to them. But here too, in his explicit rejection of the traditional social

bases for morally judging peoples' actions, Caesar emphasizes the innovativeness of his alienating view.

IV. Discourses and Armies in Conflict

I have argued that the military and political competition between Caesar and Pompey also entails a competition between two different articulations of the Roman community and hence between two different ethical discourses regarding the conflict. Another passage from Caesar's speech in Book 7 discusses the stakes of the latter competition in particular.

> haec [*sc.* est illa dies] fato quae teste probet,
>   quis iustius arma
> sumpserit; haec acies victum factura nocentem est.
> si pro me patriam ferro flammisque petistis,
> nunc pugnate truces gladioque exsolvite culpam:
> nulla manus, belli mutato iudice, pura est.

> This [*sc.* is the day] that certifies, with fate as witness, who took up arms more justly; this battle is going to make the loser guilty. If it is for me that you attacked your fatherland with sword and fire, fight fiercely now and clear your guilt by the sword: no hand is pure, if the judge of the war is changed.

Caesar declares here that he is fighting Pompey for control of the content and application of the Roman ethical vocabulary. The victor, he says, will appropriate the (currently contested) term *ius* for his own cause and assign the term *nocens* to the vanquished. Therefore he urges his soldiers to fight fiercely (*nunc pugnate truces*), i.e., to display *virtus:* the blame incurred by their assault on the fatherland (*si...patriam ferro flammisque petistis*), the impiety of attacking one's own community, will be cleared if and only if that attack is successful (*gladioque exsolvite culpam*). For the victor establishes himself as *iudex belli*, meaning that the allocation of value terms (such as *ius*, *nocens*, *culpa*, and *purus*, in this passage) will be entirely at his disposal. Only in victory, then, can Caesar enforce his own articulation of the community and thus make authoritative the ethical discourse based on that articulation. The definition of the community, and consequently the moral interpretation of history, belongs to the victor. In the meantime, however, the moral interpretation of events is up for grabs. Contestation over the assignment of value terms is in fact a major theme of the poem, as the first sentence of the poem declares (*iusque datum sceleri canimus ...*). Indeed, in many ancient civil war narratives, control of the ethical vocabulary is at stake: it is a commonplace that civil war produces multiple moral perspectives, resulting in contestation over the allocation of moral terms.

We have seen, then, that in the communitarian view of the conflict—which Pompey repeatedly champions, despite its internal inconsistencies—there is no *hostis*, hence no social or ethical basis for displaying *virtus*. The obligations of *pietas* are owed to the Caesarians, as well as to everyone else. Therefore Pompey cannot provide a moral context in which his soldiers can fight the Caesarians effectively. On the other hand, Caesar's predominantly alienating view, which excludes from the community all who actively oppose him, creates an ethical space in which his soldiers can display *virtus* as well as *pietas*. We now turn to the narrative of the battle of Pharsalus, to see how these differing social and ethical constructions of the conflict translate into action.

As the battle-lines approach each other on the plain, the soldiers on both sides size up the opposition:

> quo sua pila cadant aut quae sibi fata minentur
> inde manus, spectant. vultus, quo noscere possent
> facturi quae monstra forent, videre parentum
> frontibus adversis fraternaque comminus arma,
> nec libuit mutare locum. tamen omnia torpor
> pectora constrinxit, gelidusque in viscera sanguis
> percussa pietate coit. ...

> ... they look to see where their weapons will fall, or what hands threaten doom against them from the other side. That they might know what terrible deeds they were about to do, they saw the faces of their parents confronting them opposite and the weapons of their brothers close at hand, and they did not see fit to shift their ground. Nevertheless, a numbness froze all their breasts, and their blood congealed cold in their vitals because of the outrage to *pietas*. ...

When they see their brothers and fathers opposing them, they realize the violence they are doing to *pietas* (*percussa pietate*): their breasts go numb, their blood runs cold, and the start of the battle is deferred. For the moment, the communitarian perspective dominates—despite the fact that Caesar urged his men away from that perspective and that Pompey's speech kindled his soldiers' desire to display *virtus*. But soon Crastinus hurls the first lance and the battle is on. The Pompeians quickly have difficulties: they are too crowded to wield their weapons effectively; they can only hide behind a wall of shields. Meanwhile, Caesar's troops attack furiously. An extremely one-sided battle ensues, in which the Caesarians do all the killing: "One battle-line endures civil war, the other wages it; from that side the sword stands cold, but from Caesar's every guilty blade is warm" (*civilia bella/una acies patitur, gerit altera; frigidus inde/stat gladius, calet omne nocens a Caesare ferrum*). This one-sidedness is emphasized again thirty lines later: "what followed was no battle, but war is waged on one side with throats, on the other with the sword; nor does this battle-line have as much strength to kill as that one has capacity to perish" (... *nulla secutast/pugna, sed hinc iugulis, hinc ferro bella geruntur;/nec valet haec acies tantum prosternere quantum/inde perire potest*). Ultimately, then, the soldiers on each side act in accordance with the ethical frameworks that their commanders provided in advance. Pompey's soldiers seemingly do not fight at all; they do not commit the impiety of killing family members and countrymen. Meanwhile, Caesar's troops fight well, displaying *virtus* by killing those who, on Caesar's definition, are excluded from the community. There are hints, however, of a latent communitarian perspective among the Caesarians, for even as they kill kin and countrymen their reactions sometimes suggest that they feel qualms; they also have nightmares afterward in which they perceive their actions as a "savage crime" (*saevum scelus*).

V. The Narrator

In my discussion of conflicting definitions and discourses, I have largely neglected the most authoritative voice in the poem, the narrative voice. Like all epic narrators, Lucan's is, at one level, omnipotent and omniscient: he can move the narrative instantly from one location to another, expand or compress time at will, and so on. But other narrators, particularly Homer and Virgil, generally do not put forward strong opinions: they tend to remain ethically and emotionally detached from the events they narrate and gain credibility precisely by virtue of their self-effacement. Lucan's narrator, on the other hand, as many scholars have remarked, is deeply engaged with the poem's action. He often takes obtrusive, partisan stances on the events he narrates and therefore seems scarcely less opinionated than the voices of Pompey, Caesar, and other characters. Accordingly, the ethical stances he takes, and the value judgments he passes, may seem no more (or less) credible and authoritative than those of the other characters.

This claim that Lucan is an active, partisan spectator of the events he narrates is unquestionably true in certain respects. However, an exclusive focus on overt interventions misses subtler, less obtrusive, but equally important ways in which the narrator can present and manipulate his own narrative. For instance, the narrator may be completely subsumed in someone else's viewpoint, adopting the ethical stance and conception of community of the character or group whose story he is narrating at the moment: that is, the character or group in question focalizes the narrator's description of its actions. One such passage is the narrative of Scaeva's deeds: here the narrator regularly refers to Scaeva's Pompeian foes as *hostes*, just as Scaeva does; also, the taunting address to the Pompeians, denying that ordinary weapons can stop him, could be seen as Scaeva's own boast.

At a more visible and self-assertive level, the narrator adopts an ethical stance at odds with that of the character or group whose actions he narrates—a situation I call "hostile narration." For example, he heaps condemnation upon the Caesarians as he relates their occupation and plundering of the Pompeian camp after Pharsalus; he emphasizes in particular the bonds of kinship and community that they have violated—though from the Caesarians' own (alienating) perspective they have seized an enemy camp, and on that view their actions are morally right. Here, then, the narrator adopts a communitarian ethical stance as he relates actions done in accordance with an alienating view.

At his most obtrusive—the narrative mode that scholars have repeatedly noted and studied—the narrator actually interrupts the narrative and gives a more or less extended evaluative commentary on the action *in propria voce*. A striking case is, where the narrator, in a direct address, tells Scaeva that his alienating view of the community is false. For while Scaeva calls the Pompeians *hostes*, vigorously fights them, and deploys ethical language accordingly (e.g., *pietas* is owed only to fellow-Caesarians), here the narrator insists that they are not a foreign enemy such as the Teutoni or Cantabri (evidently the "true" *hostes*); hence there can be no triumph and no proper dedication of spoils to Iuppiter Tonans. Consequently his *virtus,* grotesquely misdirected, has gained him nothing but a *dominus*. A final example of this most assertive obtrusion of the narrative voice is his denunciation of the consequences of Pharsalus:

> maius ab hac acie quam quod sua saecula ferrent
> vulnus habent populi; plus est quam vita salusque
> quod perit: in totum mundi prosternimur aevum.
> vincitur his gladiis omnis quae serviet aetas.
> proxima quid suboles aut quid meruere nepotes
> in regnum nasci? pavide num gessimus arma
> teximus aut iugulos? alieni poena timoris
> in nostra cervice sedet. post proelia natis
> si dominum, fortuna, dabas, et bella dedisses.

The peoples of the world have a wound from this battle greater than their own age could bear; it is more than life and safety that passes away: we are laid low for the whole eternity of the universe. Every age is

conquered by these swords, and will be slaves. Why did the next generation, or the one after that, deserve to be born into tyranny? Did we ply our weapons in a cowardly manner, or shield our throats? The penalty for someone else's cowardice sits upon our necks. Fortune, if you gave a master to those born after the battle, you might also have given them a chance to fight.

This passage indicts both parties: the Caesarians for seeking to impose a "master" (*dominus*) upon the state and thus to "enslave" everyone else (*serviet, in nostra cervice*); but also the Pompeians for their cowardice, their failure to fight that enabled the Caesarian victory. Thus the narrator rejects the inevitable consequences of the communitarian perspective: in condemning the Pompeians for *pavor* and *timor*—i.e., a lack of *virtus*—he adopts an alienating ethical discourse. Essentially, he implies that the Caesarians *are* a valid target for martial valor (hence they are *hostes* and are excluded from the community) and suggests that the Pompeians would have served the community better by taking such a view themselves.

These examples of the narrator's moral judgments on the actions he narrates were of course chosen with malice aforethought, for I wished to demonstrate his inconsistency, on several axes, in the face of competing views of the community and competing ethical discourses. First, as in the Scaeva episode, at one level the narrator may implicate his own viewpoint with that of a character (Scaeva focalizes the narrator's alienating discourse: see section III above), but at another level sharply distinguish his own viewpoint from the character's (explicitly rejecting Scaeva's view, and embracing a communitarian discourse instead: see the previous paragraph). Second, he can enthusiastically reject each faction's principal viewpoint: by lamenting the Pompeians' cowardice (quoted above), he indicts the communitarian view that underlay their collapse; then, just one hundred lines later, he provides a hostile narration of the Caesarians' plundering of the Pompeian camp (i.e., he takes a communitarian ethical stance) and in so doing rejects the alienating perspective that justifies the Caesarians' actions. Finally, he can equally enthusiastically embrace each faction's principal viewpoint. In an apostrophe to Pompey after the battle, the narrator tells the defeated general "it was worse to win" (*vincere peius erat*)—presumably validating Pompey's communitarian perspective, according to which the killing in this conflict is criminal. And even Caesar's alienating perspective is praiseworthy, under the right circumstances: when

Afranius surrenders the Pompeian army in Spain, Caesar sends these troops home unpunished and unconscripted. For on the alienating view, these men, being *hostes*, have committed no crime in fighting, nor do they owe any military duty to their conquerors.

The narrator, then, is inconsistent in that he does not systematically embrace one or the other competing conception of community and its corresponding ethical discourse. Rather, he moves back and forth between them, at one point or another judging the actions of each side by the moral standards of each ethical discourse. Masters, discussing the narrator's vacillation between the Pompeian and Caesarian causes, speaks of Lucan's "fractured voice" and suggests (rightly, I think) that its inconsistency necessarily follows from the poem's subject matter. The present discussion reveals a similar connection between subject and form, for we have seen that the cleft in the community—the defining contradiction of civil war—is reproduced first in a divided ethical discourse and second in the narrator's conflicting moral evaluations. Consequently, in failing to adopt one view over the other, the narrator not only narrates the civil war, but performs it as well: he allows the alternative ethical discourses and views of community to compete through his own voice just as they compete through the words and actions of the characters. This unresolved competition also shows that neither discourse, and neither conception of the community, by itself can adequately embrace the conflict that is the poem's subject. Indeed, the opening phrase of the poem, "war more than civil" (*bella ... plus quam civilia*), may also suggest in retrospect that both available ethical frameworks are inadequate to the subject. For we have seen that the phrase *bellum civile* sometimes conveys specifically the communitarian view on the conflict. Therefore, the phrase "more than civil" may imply that the communitarian view does not quite fit. However, this phrase may also imply "less than (or not exactly) external," in which case the alienating view is also inadequate. On this reading, the words *plus quam*, like the aporetic competition between ethical discourses, marks the lack of a comprehensive view and the need for a third way.

But despite these contradictions, the narrator is not without direction: through the poem as a whole he does seem to adopt (and praise) the communitarian view, and engage in its corresponding ethical discourse, more often than he embraces the alternative. Perhaps we should reflect this differential prefer-

ence by labeling communitarian discourse "dominant" or "normative" in the poem and alienating discourse "oppositional" or "subversive." But the latter is not thereby swept under the rug: it remains a coherent, visible, persistent, and powerful discourse, emerging repeatedly in the statements and actions of many characters—Pompeians as well as Caesarians—and in the narrative voice. I also see little evolution: there is no move toward a reconciliation of these discourses, nor does either one seem to become more favored or prominent, or less so, over the course of the poem. These discourses simply coexist, in somewhat unequal authorial favor, ever competing and conflicting with each other, inescapable artifacts of civil war itself.

A possible third way does appear in Book 9, where Cato is at the center of an entirely different mode of ethical discourse. Here Cato and *virtus* are closely associated—but this *virtus* seems to have little to do with martial valor, for there is no fighting in this section of the poem; nor is it ever in tension with *pietas*, as it often is elsewhere. Rather, it is linked repeatedly with endurance, toil, and overcoming difficulty. The Stoic connection is easy to make: it is a commonplace of imperial Stoicism that moral virtue, though of course independent of indifferent externals such as pain, suffering, and death, is best displayed—and may even be strengthened—by being exercised in their presence. In this and other respects, the ethical discourse centered on Cato is strongly Stoicizing.

But Stoic ethics differs radically from both alienating and communitarian ethical discourse. The latter two are fundamentally the same, being alternative versions of the traditional, external, community-based mode of evaluation. They operate identically with respect to the underlying conception of community and differ only insofar as that underlying conception differs. In Stoic ethics, however, moral value is internal and resides in states of mind that are accessible primarily to oneself. Things that are externally observable, such as the actual results of one's plans and actions, are regarded as beyond one's control and therefore without moral value. The community therefore has no role in moral evaluation. Thus, Cato's Stoicism potentially offers an escape from the competing, irreconcilable discourses discussed above: it provides a universal moral standard, invariant over all conditions of peace and war, unity and disunity, as the basis for a reconstituted, unitary ethical discourse. However, at 9.950 the narrator turns his attention back to Caesar; Cato and his Stoic ethics do not reappear in the poem. How Lucan might have developed this alternative system subsequently, and how it might have interacted with the poem's other ethical discourses, we will never know.

VI. *Lucan and Early Imperial Aristocratic Ideology*

Several times in the poem Caesar articulates an ideological reconstruction of the Roman community and its ethical discourse. This reconstruction, which he can impose if he wins, will establish his alienating view of the community as the normative basis for ethical valuation, thereby removing all moral opprobrium from himself and depositing it upon his adversaries. Yet within the poem itself no such reconstruction occurs. Lucan at no point allows Caesar's alienating view and its ethical discourse to dominate; also, voices that move toward Caesar's view in the last three books (after Pharsalus) are presented unsympathetically. Historically, however, Caesar did attempt such a reconstruction, and we can recover its general outlines. Once we have done so, we will be able to consider the ideological consequences of Lucan's disallowing that reconstruction and of his projecting the particular image of civil war that he does from the cultural context of Neronian Rome.

Raaflaub (1974), in his survey of the terms used by the Pompeians and Caesarians, shows that the historical Pompeians generally claimed to be defending the commonwealth (*res publica*) and that they called Caesar and his followers such things as "depraved men," "bandits," and "condemned criminals" (*perditi, latrones, damnati*); whether they called them *hostes* is unclear. Thus the Pompeians appear to have engaged in an alienating discourse, marginalizing Caesar within the community or even expelling him from it—though the evidence for their rhetoric is extremely sparse, coming almost exclusively from letters of Cicero (*et al.*) dating from B.C. 50–48. On the other hand, Caesar and the Caesarians generally labeled the conflict a "civil disagreement," "secession" (*civilis dissensio, secessio*), or the like, they labeled the Pompeians "personal enemies" or "opponents" (*inimici, adversarii*) rather than using the alienating term *hostes*. They seem, then, to have embraced a communitarian view, or at least avoided inflammatory, alienating language. The evidence for the Caesarian viewpoint is much more plentiful, coming from Caesar's *Commentarii*, Hirtius' *Bellum Gallicum VIII*, and portions of Cicero's Caesarian speeches (especially *Lig., Marc., Deiot.*). But these

sources, in contrast to the Pompeian ones, postdate the bulk of the civil war and therefore must be seen, whatever their truth value, as representations of the conflict that serve Caesar's interests in the aftermath. Indeed, the advantages for Caesar of presenting his cause this way, for public consumption and for posterity, are manifest: by embracing a communitarian discourse, he can seek (or claim to seek) reconciliation with the vanquished, and to reintegrate them into the community of which they have always been a part. This, then, is Caesar's ideological reconstruction of the civil war, the history he as victor gets to write that allows him to mobilize support and consolidate power.

Another means of access to the historical Caesarians' re-presentation of their cause following their victory is through the symbolism of Caesar's triumphs. It is a commonplace, in Lucan and elsewhere, that a civil war cannot produce a triumph, and there are at least two reasons, inherent in the ceremony's form and symbolism, why this is so. First, the triumphal procession symbolically subjects the non-Roman to the Roman: it includes a display of spoils, pictures of towns captured, and a parade of notable prisoners led in chains before the *triumphator*'s chariot. Second, the triumph is inherently expansionist in its celebration of military conquest: Valerius Maximus states that a victory won in reconquering territory previously conquered but subsequently lost does not qualify for a triumph. A victory in civil war is incompatible with a triumph on both these counts, for neither are the vanquished non-Romans, nor does the victory expand the empire. Now, Caesar sent no word of his victory at Pharsalus to the senate—a necessary step, along with being proclaimed *imperator*, for a commander who hopes for a *supplicatio* or triumph. Indeed, says Dio, Caesar not only did not triumph, but did not wish to appear to take pleasure in this victory. His refusal to seek a triumph, then, also implies a communitarian viewpoint, and so coincides with the viewpoint taken in the literary sources—the view that Pharsalus was part of a civil war, a conflict within a single community.

This interpretation of Caesar's non-triumph for Pharsalus is confirmed by an analysis of the triumphs Caesar did celebrate. In his quadruple triumph of B.C. 46, celebrating victories in Gaul, at Zela, at Alexandria, and at Thapsus, Caesar mixed conflicts that were manifestly external (the first two) with those that were arguably civil—yet the very act of celebrating triumphs was to portray all four alike as *bella externa*. The triumph for Thapsus involved a systematic manipulation of symbolism, as the sources point out: for although his principal military opponents in Africa were Cato and Metellus Scipio, his triumphal procession prominently displayed the younger Juba, son of the Numidian king who supported Cato and Sepia. Thus Caesar emphasized the foreignness of the force opposing him and so constructed Thapsus symbolically as a battle between Romans (his own troops) and non-Romans. After his victory at Munda, however, Caesar went even further: according to Plutarch, he caused outrage by triumphing unambiguously over other Romans. For (says Plutarch) he had previously avoided seeking recognition for victories in civil war, and his fellow-countrymen were grieved that he now celebrated a triumph for destroying Pompey's family rather than for defeating foreigners. Caesar, then, used triumphal imagery to represent each conflict *after* Pharsalus as a *bellum externum*, and to exclude those opponents from the community. These representations may have persuaded no one (certainly not Plutarch). But the point is that Caesar made the attempt, and in the most public and visible way: we must regard these performances as part of his attempted ideological reconstruction.

Lucan, however, disallows this Caesarian ideological reconstruction in two ways. First, the poem portrays no systematic remobilization of discourse to Caesar's advantage, before or after Pharsalus: it insists on presenting an endlessly divided community, forever bollixed up in competing, irreconcilable discourses. In this respect Lucan differs from other Augustan and Julio-Claudian authors, who at least acknowledge that many ideological resources have been organized in support of the imperial regime. Second, and more strikingly, Lucan switches the modes of discourse that each faction embraced historically: it is Lucan's Pompeians, not his Caesarians, who generally regard their opponents as members of their own community, and his Caesarians who, in their rhetoric and actions, tend to exclude their opponents. This reversal enables Caesar's victory within the poem, but also precludes him from duplicating the historical Caesar's ideological reconstruction.

Lucan's resistance to Caesarian ideology must itself be ideologically important. What interests does Lucan's construction of civil war serve, given that its ethical structuring substantially contradicts that of the dominant (i.e., Caesarian) historical tradition? Also, what is the ideological significance, within the social and political context of Neronian Rome, of a Roman aristocrat's evincing so powerful an interest in fractured communities and competing, irreconcilable ethical discourses? I suggest that Lucan, along with other contemporary authors, perceives a divided community and competing ethical discourses in the Rome of his own day. For like Caesar himself, Caesar's heirs, the *principes*, have the power to organize novel discourses that serve their own interests. One example is the discourse of flattery, in which the traditional grounds for praise and blame are disregarded or transmuted so as to create a uniform front of praise. Flattery distorts and undermines the aristocracy's fundamental, received mode of valuation, and so threatens the social cohesion and group identity that traditional ethical discourse provides them.

Seneca's advocacy of Stoic ethics implicitly addresses this problem and provides the aristocracy with one possible solution. For, as noted in section V, an ethical discourse systematically grounded on an internal standard (states of mind) elides all the problems that traditional discourse, being social and external, encounters in the face of a divided evaluative community. On this reading, Seneca's support for Stoic ethics is ideological in that it supports the interests of the aristocracy as a whole in its power struggle with the *princeps*. For by reconstituting a unitary evaluative community, Seneca's Stoic ethics negates an important aspect of the *princeps'* power—the power to organize ethical discourse to his own advantage.

Lucan, meanwhile, examines divided communities and competing discourses in the framework of the civil war, which is at once the origin of the principate and also a moment at which these issues are particularly prominent and sharpened. By refusing to allow his Caesar to mimic the historical Caesar's ideological reconstruction, Lucan resists the reorganizations of community and discourse to Caesar's (and the principate's) advantage. But at the same time he fails to reject Caesar's program decisively; he makes no systematic attempt to stamp out the irruption of Caesarism into aristocratic ethics. Thus he leaves competing articulations of the community and competing discourses forever in conflict, with no resolution in sight. It is, I think, a dark view of the aristocracy's position: Caesar and the principate ensure a perpetual, irreparable fracturing of their community and destroy even the possibility of talking meaningfully (i.e., morally) about the regime itself or any other matter.

Source: Matthew B. Roller, "Ethical Contradiction and the Fractured Community in Lucan's *Bellum Civile*," in *Classical Antiquity,* Vol. 15, No. 2, October, 1996, pp. 319–47.

C.M.C. Green

The author, C.M.C. Green, portrays the necessity of the murder in Lucan's Book 3.

Lucan created the relationship between Pompey and Caesar, it has been argued, on the pattern of the relationship of Agamemnon and Achilles. Thus it is through an acknowledgment of his Greek literary ancestry that Lucan constructs the opening of his epic. The rivalry between the great leader and the young warrior provides the explosive, psychological beginnings (*hae ducibus causae* ...) of the action of the *Bellum Civile,* shaping the conflict as one which, while between individuals, remains even less personal than that between Agamemnon and Achilles. Yet, though Achilles threatens, he does not in the end take his men home and abandon Agamemnon. Their personal quarrel is resolved, and thus subordinated to their obligations in the greater battle against the Trojans. Caesar, enraged with Pompey's arrogance, *does* take his troops home; the Iliadic pattern is violated, so that the Greek epic pattern will no longer serve the Roman epic poet. We must now consider what paradigm Lucan sets in its place.

The battles, purges, and proscriptions of the Civil Wars had left lasting scars on the Roman people. Those Roman writers—historians and poets alike—who survived the end of the Republic knew too well the wounds that lay beneath the polished surface of Augustan peace. In their attempts to reconcile who the Romans were with what they had done, several authors—Horace and Livy especially—had turned to a well-established Republican tradition that found in the myth of Romulus's murder of Remus the seeds of the later civil conflict. When Lucan in turn, not quite a century later, had to confront Caesar's armies on the march toward Rome, he could thus accept and adapt for his epic an already fully developed mythic connection.

He extended the mythic significance yet further, however, by exploiting the religious paradigm of combat and murder for kingship that had once been practiced by Latin communities, a paradigm exemplified by the *rex nemorensis*, the king of the wood. The *rex* and his cult were still extant in Lucan's time, and were not the only source for such a kingship ritual. It is the purpose of the present article to set out the evidence for Lucan's use of such a paradigm, and then, using this as a guide, to reassess Book 3 of the *Bellum Civile* in the terms that it dictates. The choice of Book 3 is logical: it is here that the themes of sacred place, sacred combat,

Nero, the fifth emperor of Rome. Nero fancied himself a literary man and sought the company of gifted poets such as Lucan. Lines 33-66 of The Pharsalia *are an ode Nero, with whom the poet fell in and out of favor throughout his career.*

and the necessary murder are most clearly presented. It is my further purpose to demonstrate that seeming inconsistencies in the nature of the gods in Lucan's epic can be at least partially resolved if we understand that the gods must remain aloof, outside the action, while the ritual takes place, even though they themselves have instituted the ritual of kingship murder, and will, when it is completed, receive the murderer as their ritually validated priest-king. I will conclude by suggesting ways in which this paradigm, if accepted, begins to clarify various puzzling choices Lucan has made elsewhere in the epic, as regards his narrative of events, his development of character, and the recurrent images of lightning, tree, and blood sacrifice owed to the gods.

I

The need to find not just an explanation for the Civil Wars, but an explanation of the Roman people, is given anguished voice in one of Horace's epodes:

> ❝ Rome was not only founded by a murderer, but her first citizens were exiles, fugitive slaves, murderers, and every other kind of violator of civil and religious law: men like Romulus, and Caesar, and their followers. <u>In her end is her beginning.</u>❞

Quo, quo scelesti ruitis? aut cur dexteris
aptantur enses conditi?
parumne campis atque Neptuno super
fusum est Latini sanguinis?

Where, villains, where are you rushing? Why are once-sheathed swords at the ready in your right hands? Has not enough Latin blood been shed on land and sea?

He demands an answer—*responsum date!*—and the response given is one that has been shaped to this very purpose by two centuries of Republican writers:

sic est: acerba fata Romanos agunt
scelusque fraternae necis,
ut immerentis fluxit in terram Remi
sacer nepotibus cruor.

So it is: harsh fates and the crime of a brother's murder drive the Romans on, just as when the blood of undeserving Remus flowed onto the earth, a curse upon his descendants.

Fratricide and civil war were the private and public faces of the same crime; they had come to be seen as the inescapable legacy of Romulus's murder of Remus to protect his *regnum* over Rome. This is not just a poet's figurative language. For Livy, Romulus and Remus present the same lesson:

Intervenit deinde his cogitationibus avitum malum, regni cupido, atque inde foedum certamen coortum a satis miti principio.

These plans [for the foundation of Rome] were interrupted by the wickedness that had marked their grandfather, greed for kingship (*regni cupido*), and thence, from a peaceful enough beginning, a loathsome competition grew.

That the murder of Remus was the direct and fated result of the conflict between the brothers over

regnum formed an essential part of the Republican tradition. It can be traced back to Ennius's account of Romulus and Remus—*curantes magna cum cura tum cupientes / regni dant operam simul auspicio augurioque* ("Having a great concern, indeed, a greed for kingship, they gave their attention at once to the auspices and the augury" and *sic expectabat populus atque ore timebat / rebus utri magni victoria sit data regni* ("Thus their followers were waiting, with fear in their faces for the state, to see to which of the two men would victory of the great kingship be given,"). Lucretius, *DRN* 3.68–72, links civil war and fratricide. "Romulus' victory was only secured by a crime and that crime of fratricide continued to reassert itself throughout Roman history. The evils of the Civil Wars were seen as a legacy of Romulus' acts …."

It is hardly surprising that Lucan is, in turn, as powerfully affected by this view as were his predecessors. His *sententia* defining the cause of the Civil War as the competition between two men for the *regnum* of Rome—*nulla fides regni sociis, omnisque potestas / impatiens consortis erit* ("kingship has no loyalty to its allies, and every power / will be intolerant of a colleague"—is completed by the paradigm of that first murder:

… nec gentibus ullis
credite, nec longe fatorum exempla petantur:
fraterno primi maduerunt sanguine muri.

… You need look to no foreign peoples, nor seek examples of these fates far away: the first walls were soaked in a brother's blood.

The first walls of Rome, then, were stained with human blood in a fight for *regnum*. In *nulla fides regni sociis* ("kingship has no loyalty to its allies"), Lucan is very particularly naming the same type of rule as the one over which the *fides* of Pompey and Caesar—allies in the first Triumvirate—will fail. The point of this *sententia* is lost if we understand *regnum* here to mean no more than "tyranny" (as Duff has it), a Greek-derived and *polis*-based concept, rather than "kingship," which both reflects the sense of the Latin root and maintains crucial historical associations, including Lucan's reminder that kingship preceded and was a step toward the creation of Rome as a *civitas*. Not the abstract concept of "tyrannical power," not even the political reality of the "first Triumvirate," but rather *kingship itself* is unmistakably Lucan's meaning. This is further emphasized by his conscious echo of Ennius's line, *nulla sancta societas / nec fides regni est* ("There is no sacred alliance, no loyalty in kingship"), a line we know precisely because Cicero used it to illustrate the nature of Caesar's *regnum*. The belief (or fear) that Caesar actually wanted to make himself king in Rome was one of the principal justifications for his assassination.

Caesar and Pompey, then (not brothers, but father- and son-in-law), are striving for the same prize that Romulus and Remus sought. The whole structure of Lucan's epic emphasizes this, for everywhere the military conflict is subordinate to, and a violent reflection of, the personal struggle between two men. Murderous conflict, whether manifested in civil war or assassination, is an inseparable part of the kind of power for which Pompey and Caesar compete. This power is inseparable from place. *Regnum,* for Caesar and Pompey, is not sovereignty as an abstract notion, but kingship in Rome. Lucan concludes the paradigm of the conflict between Romulus and Remus with a comparison of Rome, the victor's prize, now and then:

> nec pretium tanti tellus pontusque furoris
> tunc erat: exiguum dominos commisit asylum.

> … and at that time, land and sea were not the prize for such a great frenzy: a robbers' hideout brought the leaders to battle.

This comparison serves to re-emphasize the parallel between Romulus's act and Caesar's, and to remind us that the pathology is the same, whether Rome is the capital of a great empire or a small clearing on the Capitol. Lucan chose the *asylum* to symbolize the earliest, and smallest, physical entity of Rome, and this reminds us that the asylum on the Capitoline hill was originally the haven of escaped slaves, criminals, and others excluded from, or hostile to, political order. Rome was not only founded by a murderer, but her first citizens were exiles, fugitive slaves, murderers, and every other kind of violator of civil and religious law: men like Romulus, and Caesar, and their followers. *In her end is her beginning.*

II

The asylum at Rome was not unique. Other Latin communities had similar sacred areas of refuge for exiles or escaped slaves. The most famous, partly because it was the longest lasting, and partly because Virgil's use of one element of the ritual associated with it guaranteed it a place in Servius's commentary on the *Aeneid,* was the grove of Diana above Aricia, the site of the cult of the *rex nemorensis*. While the cult of the king of the wood may have been peculiar to Aricia, there is evidence that a similar kind of rite was—at least for a time—practiced at Rome. More importantly for our pres-

ent purposes, there is evidence that the cult of the *rex nemorensis* was thought, in Lucan's time, to be directly associated with rites that affected the succession to the imperial throne. Let us review, first, the cult itself, then the relationship of this cult to the Roman kings in the sixth century B.C., and, finally, the evidence for Lucan's knowledge of it and its significance for his narrative.

In the mountains above the city of Aricia there was a grove, sacred to Diana and ruled over by a priest-king. He was an escaped slave who had won his exalted position by slaying his predecessor. The priest-king's life was dedicated to protecting the goddess's sacred tree, and he had to be ready, night and day, to fend off challengers with his sword. We do not have a full description of the rite, but from Servius's account we know that any challenger to the reigning priest-king had also to be a fugitive, and to declare his challenge by cutting off the golden bough. If the challenger succeeded in this first test, there was then (though surely not immediately) a mortal combat fought between the two. One of them must die, and the survivor became the next priest-king. Thus the sacred grove is a refuge for fugitives, of whom the priest-king has been one. As priest he is the goddess's servant, and perhaps her husband. As king, he serves as her protector, and the protector of the sacred tree. His successor must challenge him by cutting off the golden bough which grows on her sacred tree. The cut bough requires the priest to meet the challenger in sacred, mortal combat The victor is the new priest-king.

To clarify Lucan's use of the rite, it is particularly important to emphasize several aspects of the ritual that may otherwise escape our notice. The assault on the tree is a sacrilege committed against the goddess herself, and both the reigning king and the challenger must have committed this crime. The defeated one is the sacrificial victim, the victor is the anointed priest, and the combat is a test of the goddess's will, which can only be ascertained by the outcome of the combat. Most important of all, the entire ritual is instituted by the goddess herself—that is, the sacrilege, the murder, and the victor's ascension to priesthood are all equally part of the ritual and are all therefore equally sacred.

Possession of Diana's grove made Aricia enormously wealthy, a condition that prevailed without doubt well into the first century B.C., and quite possibly on into Lucan's own day. Indeed, in the time of the kings at Rome, Aricia was a greater power than Rome, and an equal to the most important cities in central Italy. She shared control with Alba Longa of the source of the Ferentine river (*caput aquae ferentinae*), the gathering place for the leaders (*proceres*) of the Latin tribes, where Turnus confronted Tarquinius, who, by his behavior to the rest of the Latin leaders, earned his sobriquet *Superbus*. During the fifth century B.C., Aricia, like the other Latin cities, was defeated by the Romans—several times, in fact—but preparations for her permanent eclipse by Rome had been made, almost a century earlier, by Servius Tullius, who held the last legitimate Roman kingship, and who appropriated Aricia's cult of Diana as an assertion of Rome's claim to political, as well as religious, leadership of the Latin people:

> Saepe iterando eadem perpulit tandem, ut Romae fanum Dianae populi Latini cum populo Romano facerent. Ea erat confessio caput rerum Romam esse, de quo totiens armis certatum fuerat.

> Through constant effort, he (Servius) finally got his way, with the result that the Latins and the Romans together created a shrine to Diana at Rome. This was an admission that Rome was their common capital (*caput rerum*), a question over which they had so many times gone to war.

Livy concludes his account with the story of a magnificent heifer, a prodigy. Imperial power would belong to the state whose citizens sacrificed this heifer to Diana, according to the soothsayers (*ibi fore imperium*). Among the gods, while Jupiter certainly represents Rome's will to *imperium,* Diana, clearly, is the divinity who has the power to guarantee it. No wonder Servius was anxious to establish her cult in Rome.

Servius's sanctuary of Diana on the Aventine (there well may not have been a temple at first) imitated several important aspects of the cult at Aricia. First, the festal day was the same as that at Aricia—August 13. Slaves celebrated a holiday on this day: they could participate in the rite (not a common practice), and the cult was particularly sacred to them. Indeed, according to Festus, temple was a sanctuary for escaped slaves. Moreover, the *success* of Servius's appropriation of the cult was as important as the move itself, for it testified to divine authorization for Rome's expanding power, a very forceful confirmation in the early period when belief was strong and rationalism and syncretism had not yet drained divinity of its present *numen*.

Though in Republican times the Aventine cult did not include the "ghastly priest," the priest may indeed have been part of Servius's foundation. There is evidence that Servius Tullius, as king, was himself Diana's priest. According to a tradition that could not be denied—despite the openly expressed dismay of historians such as Livy and Dionysius of Halicarnassus—Servius Tullius was born a slave. He succeeded Tarquinius Priscus upon that king's violent death, and accomplished this through the intercession of Tarquinius's queen. As an old man, Servius was himself physically attacked and removed from the throne by his son-in-law, Tarquinius Superbus.

There is a curious, and for this discussion revealing, chronological problem here. Tarquinius was supposed to be the son of Tarquinius Priscus, and was also young and vigorous enough to throw the elderly Servius downstairs, even though he had to be at least forty-four (the number of years Servius reigned, according to Livy) and—if he was married to Tullia when Servius became king—was probably a good deal older than that. The important fact—that a young successor made a physical attack on the aging king—confounds the chronology, and reminds us that not Tarquinius's claim to the throne, but the physical attack, was what was crucial to the story.

After the attack, Servius, the story goes, was murdered by Tarquinius's agents. The event is described in vivid and telling detail by Livy. Tullia, who is both sister and wife to Tarquinius, summons her husband out of the Curia and is the first to call him "king." Then she goes to the top of the Cyprian Way, where there was a shrine to Diana, and directs her carriage to turn right onto the Urbian Way. Servius is lying, dead, across the road. She orders the driver to drive over the body, spattering herself with the blood of her father, a crime so terrible that it has given the name to the street—the "Accursed Street." This horrible story is concluded by Livy thus: *ceterum id quoque ad gloriam accessit quod cum illo simul iusta ac legitima regna occiderunt* ("this, too, accrued to his glory, that with him just and lawful kingship disappeared," Livy).

If we ignore the anachronistic *color* of contemporary politics that Livy and Dionysius apply to make sense of this, we see that it is remarkably like a ritual such as the one practiced by the *rex nemorensis*. Indeed, the oddest "facts," which, however much they are explained, are never explained away—Servius the slave; Tullia the daughter, sister, wife; the mysterious shrine to Diana on the Esquiline; Servius's blood on Tullia; the tradition that Tarquinius Superbus was not only "the son" but was also "the young, vigorous man" capable of heaving another man down steps, despite the chronological impossibility; the strange vanishing of any helpers for the king as soon the young man proves his superior prowess—these are elements most appropriate, not to a political *coup*, but to a ritual combat for kingship.

It is not necessary to determine whether such a rite was ever actually practiced by Romans in Rome. It is enough that the tradition existed, was associated with a Roman king, Servius Tullius, and could be thus interpreted in Lucan's time. There is, fortunately, evidence suggesting that the rites of Diana were of more than a little interest to those around Lucan. Crispus Passienus, step-father to Nero, orator, Stoic, and friend of Seneca, was much concerned with Diana's cult. Pliny reports that Passienus formed an attachment to a certain exceptional tree in a grove near Tusculum, a grove which "by the ancient religious practices from Latium was sacred to Diana." Passienus would embrace and kiss the tree, sleep under it, and pour wine over it.

But of far greater importance for Lucan's understanding of the rites of Diana, as they relate to the history of Rome, is Claudius's curious use of the rites at a significant point in the chronic crisis of imperial succession. Tacitus records that Claudius ordered "expiatory rites (*piacula*) to be celebrated by the priests in the grove of Diana," and these rites were to be conducted according to "ceremonies from the rules of King Tullius," when he was persuaded that Lucius Junius Silanus Torquatus, betrothed to his daughter Octavia, was guilty of incest with his (Silanus's) sister Junia Calvina. Tacitus also reports that this order caused considerable derision, as Claudius himself at that very time was proposing an incestuous marriage to his own niece, Agrippina. According to the life attributed to Vacca, Lucan was an augur. Such a priesthood attests Lucan's interest in, and access to, the religious traditions of the Romans, Etruscans, and—surely—the Latins.

Thus, the rite of Diana (and this purification of incest—if that is what it was—must relate to the part of the rite in which the Iphigenia-priestess "married" her "brother") has reappeared in precisely the context that supports our reading of Lucan's reference, and assures us that while the allusion may have been arcane, it did not require information unavailable to the audience for whom Lucan wrote. Tacitus's account of Claudius's efforts, at once learned and inept, to protect himself from a palace

coup provides a connection that links Servius Tullius, the rite of Diana at Aricia, a purification ceremony conducted publicly at the grove (*lucum Dianae*), and the imperial household during Lucan's lifetime.

III

Now, when we turn to Book 3 of Lucan's epic, we can see, with much greater understanding, the metaphorical landscape Lucan paints for Caesar as he approaches Rome, foreseeing his destiny as Rome's master and, eventually, as a Roman deity. Caesar, descendant of Venus and King Iulus, looks down from Alba Longa, the seat of the first kings of Rome, his ancestors. He has crossed over high Anxur and marsh-ridden Pometia—cities whose defeat had increased the power of Rome in Latium, and the power of Capitoline Jupiter. He has also passed the grove of Diana and the sacred *regna* of her cult. He has traveled up the Via Triumphalis to the sanctuary of Jupiter Latiaris, the second most powerful Jupiter in Latium:

> ... miratusque suae sic fatur moenia Romae:
> "tene, deum sedes, non ullo Marte coacti
> deseruere viri? pro qua pugnabitur urbe?
> di melius, quod non Latias Eous in oras
> nunc furor incubuit nec iuncto Sarmata velox
> Pannonio Dacisque Getes admixtus: habenti
> tam pavidum tibi, Roma, ducem Fortuna pepercit
> quod bellum civile fuit."

> ... he marveled at the walls of his Rome and spoke thus: "Have men, not compelled by warfare, deserted you, the abode of the gods? For what city *will* there be war? The gods have willed the better end, that the frenzied East has not fallen on Latin shores, nor the swift Sarmatians with their Pannonian allies, nor the Getes and the Dacians combined. When you have so timorous a leader, Rome, Fortune has spared you, because the war has been civil."

Caesar speaks directly to issues which we have raised: Rome is the abode of the gods—not least of Jupiter and the appropriated Diana—whom he will soon join as Iuppiter Iulius or as Divus Iulius; the walls which Romulus and Remus fought over for *regnum* are there before him; his fight with Pompey over these same walls awaits him—but Pompey has not stayed to fight. The central lines turn our attention to the peripheries of the Roman world, to the nightmare of barbarians descending on an undefended city, not only in order to heighten Rome's vulnerability—with or without Pompey she was at risk—but even more to prepare for the irony of the final clause. The barbarians are not a threat, because this is a civil war—a war between citizens (no barbarians allowed) and (thus far) an unpretentious, unfought war, since one of its two principal combatants (*tam pavidum ... ducem*—so timorous a leader) has left town, retreating with unseemly haste. Thus the barbarian threat is bracketed, contained, and then *diffused*, by the civil conflict over Rome. Our attention is focused directly on City and leaders, the irreducible ingredients of the Civil War.

The war will be fought, despite Pompey's desertion. Central to this conflict is the shedding of human blood. Lucan signals very clearly and early that blood shed in the war is a human sacrifice owed to the gods, for Cato—the voice of morality, if not the hero of the epic—tells Brutus that *because the gods demand it*, the war will not end until the full measure of blood is shed:

> sic eat: immites Romana piacula divi
> plena ferant, nullo fraudemus sanguine bellum.

> Let it be so. May the merciless gods accept Roman expiations in full measure; let us not defraud the war of a single drop of blood.

Thus the war constitutes the expiations (*piacula*) that these merciless gods (*immites divi*) require. It is surely no accident that we have here a distinct echo of Horace's Epode 7 (*sic est: acerba fata Romanos agunt ...*) quoted above. The bloodshed of war, the human sacrifice of *Pharsalia*, form a tragic, but essential, part of the mortal combat for *regnum*—ritualized in the cult of the *rex nemorensis*, mythologized in Romulus and Remus, incorporated in one way or another in the Roman city by the Latin king Servius Tullius, and realized once again in Caesar and Pompey.

So Caesar, on the Alban Mount, looks down on the walls of Rome, walls that were built, according to tradition, by Servius Tullius. Pompey has fled. Fortune has spared Rome, with her timorous leader, *because* this is a civil war, just as Lucan says. Like Servius Tullius, Pompey is weakening daily, because this is the kind of war it is, a combat for kingship. With right on his side, with Cato's support, with all the Senate in his train, he is nevertheless still the leader who is being displaced. The comparison of Caesar, the vigorous, violent, enraged young fighter, with Pompey, the older, wearier, frightened leader, is of course a recurrent theme throughout the epic; but now it has a new, and brilliantly *Roman*, resonance, as befits a Roman epic.

IV

Thus, with Caesar poised above the fatal walls, let us consider now what significance the allusion to

the rite of the *rex nemorensis* might have for our understanding of Lucan's deeper poetic purpose within the often perplexing conjunction of events in Book 3. The narrative is as follows: Caesar approaches Rome (which Pompey has chosen not to defend) and there loots the temple of Saturn. The catalogue of Pompey's forces—regal, massive, and from every corner of the earth—follows. The scene shifts to Roman Gaul, specifically the territory of Massilia. When Massilia refuses to take sides in the war, Caesar begins a ruthless siege. In Lucan's account, the siege-works Caesar has devised in order to mount his attack against the city are of major importance. In order to get enough wood to build the works, a sacred grove must be cut down. The soldiers are afraid to commit such a sacrilege; Caesar is not, delivering the axe-blow to an oak even as he declares, proudly, "Be confident that I have committed the sacrilege!" The Massiliotes, indeed, are confident Caesar will be punished for his assault on the gods. Instead, Caesar, unharmed, departs for Spain, and the scene shifts, without explanation, from a siege to a naval battle. This *naumachia*, gory and utterly Lucanian, concludes the book. The victory of the naval battle goes to the (Caesarian) Romans rather than the (Greek) Massiliotes, but no mention is made of the fall of Massilia itself.

The challenger to the *rex nemorensis* must first cut down the bough from the sacred tree in the sacred grove. The Arician grove was, even in historic times, very dense and dark despite the fact that a substantial complex of temples had grown up around it—physical evidence for the continuation of thriving religious business at Aricia—and the hillsides were studded with suburban villas. The tree and the priest were linked in an extraordinary union, no doubt reflecting a very early period of Italic religion in which the tree *was* an aspect of the goddess, and the priest both her protector and consort. The priest's duty was to defend the tree from injury; yet the man who would be king of the wood was compelled to do just that—he had to commit sacrilege in order to gain his sacred status in service to the goddess. Nevertheless, the sacrilege can only occur if it is divinely approved, for, as the Sibyl tells Aeneas, the bough may be cut only if the fates summon the challenger to this task. The fated injury to the tree commits the reigning priest-king to mortal combat.

In this light we must rethink what exactly is represented in Book 3 by Caesar's decision to level the sacred grove, and indeed by the grove itself:

Lucus erat longo numquam violatus ab aevo
obscurum cingens conexis aera ramis
et gelidas alte summotis solibus umbras.
hunc non ruricolae Panes nemorumque potentes
Silvani Nymphaeque tenent, sed barbara ritu
sacra deum. structae diris altaribus arae
omnisque humanis lustrata cruoribus arbor.

There was a grove, from the earliest time undefiled,
encircling with interlaced boughs a murky space and
shadows chilled because the sunlight from above was
warded off. The rural Pans, the Silvani, rulers of the
forest, and the Wood-Nymphs do not hold sway in
this grove, but sacred ceremonies of the gods, barbarous in their observance. Shrines with dreadful altars
have been erected and every tree has been ritually
purified with human blood.

The words should bring us back to the passage
in which Lucan's first allusion to Scythian Diana
appears:

… et quibus immitis placatur sanguine diro
Teutates horrensque feris altaribus Esus
et Taranis Scythicae non mitior ara Dianae.

[At the departure of Caesar's troops, those Gauls also
rejoiced] who satisfy the merciless Teutates with
dreadful blood, and Esus, horrific with his savage
altars, and Taranis, whose altar is no more merciful
than the altar of Scythian Diana.

In Gaul, the Druids have their *barbaricos ritus
moremque sinistrum / sacrorum* ("barbarian rites
and baleful tradition of religious ceremonies" and
nemora alta remotis / incolitis lucis ("you [who
practice these rites] inhabit high forests and remote
groves"). The groves in Gaul and Massilia are
hauntingly alike. But we mistake the likeness if we
do not perceive the shadow of Diana and her grove
at Nemi following all these allusions. "Scythian" is
a common epithet for Diana of Aricia and reflects
the barbarism of the goddess, shared in the shrines
at Aricia where the *rex nemorensis* is killed, in Gaul
where the altars and trees drip with human blood, in
Aulis where, as Artemis, she demanded the sacrifice
of Iphigenia and thus precipitated events leading to
the Trojan War, and in Scythia where her demand
for human sacrifice is central to the *Iphigenia
Taurica*. The patron deity of Massilia was Artemis;
the Romans knew—and were quite proud of—the
close connection between their cult statue of Diana
on the Aventine (brought in, as we have seen, from
Aricia by Servius Tullius, according to Livy the last
legitimate king at Rome) and the cult of Artemis
among the Massiliotes. Thus this grove outside
Massilia stands in much the same relation to the
great cult of Artemis, established by the Phocaean
settlers, as does the cult of Diana of Aricia to the cult

of Diana on the Aventine. Indeed, the Massiliotes,
like the Romans, were in the habit of using their cult
as a tool of cultural imperialism, for Strabo notes
that not only did they establish in their colonies cults
of Artemis identical to their own, but also they
taught the Iberians the ancestral rites of Ephesian
Artemis, so that they sacrificed according to Greek
ritual. So Artemis/Diana—together with the intimate connection of cult imperialism, cult imitation,
and cult syncretism—draws together Rome, Aricia,
Massilia, and this nameless grove beyond the walls.

When Caesar approaches the grove to cut down
a tree, then, he is not approaching just any act of
sacrilege, but an acting out of the specific sacrilege
required of the challenger to the *rex nemorensis*.
That he may complete the sacrilege without retribution is a sign that his challenge is acceptable to the
goddess. In Book 1, he declared himself Rome's
own soldier, able to protect her everywhere on earth:

non te furialibus armis
persequor: en, adsum victor terraque marique
Caesar, ubique tuus (liceat modo, nunc
        quoque) miles.
Ille erit ille nocens, qui me tibi fecerit hostem.

… I do not attack you with frenzied warfare; behold
me, victor on land and sea, Caesar, everywhere—
were it allowed, even now—your soldier. He will
be the one, he will do the harm, who makes me
your enemy.

His first command, that the wood must fall by
the stroke of the blade (*ferrum* is equally the blade
of a sword and of the axe) recalls, quite deliberately,
the language of battle. The soldiers quail, unwilling
to test the unknown gods within the grove. Caesar

… primus raptam librare bipennem
ausus et aeriam ferro proscindere quercum
effatur merso violata in robora telo:
"iam ne quis vestrum dubitet subvertere silvam,
credite me fecisse nefas."

… he was the first who dared to seize and wield the
two-headed axe and to slash the lofty oak with his
steel; as his weapon sank into the profaned wood he
said: "Let none of you now hesitate to topple the
grove; be confident that *I* have committed the sacrilege."

As is well recognized by now, the axe in the oak
"is doubtlessly intended by the poet as an allusion to
the initial comparisons of Pompey to an old oak at
1.136 and of Caesar to lightning at 1.151–57." Yet
Lucan is after something far more important than
just a bit of poetic craft. Of course the oak is
Pompey. The priest-king and his tree are one. The
cutting of the tree is not only the act of challenge to
which there is no answer save mortal combat, but

also symbolizes the fate of the loser. Caesar's great cry, *be confident that I have committed the sacrilege*, thus becomes more than just another random act of excess by one prepared to defy the gods as well as man. When he takes the axe to the oak, Caesar proclaims that he *is* the challenger; he is the soldier (*tuus … miles*) of the city and the gods of Rome. He must take responsibility for his crime, because it is *only* through that crime that he can attain his *regnum*.

Lightning, the divine weapon against a tree, symbolizes the power and the will of both Caesar and Jupiter. Jupiter is represented, embodied, celebrated, in both lightning, which strikes the oak, and the oak that is struck. It is through the rite of the *rex nemorensis* that we can understand how Lucan dares to use the symbols of Jupiter for both combatants. This rite is a procession of paradoxes, which both begins and ends with a crime: the cutting of the tree, the killing of the priest. Once the essential rite has begun, the challenger is as *sacer* as the priest, and will become no less so for the crimes he must commit. Caesar and Pompey are both *sacer*, and their acts—the cutting of the tree, the shedding of blood (both in murdering and in dying), the winning of *regnum*—are also *sacer*.

The two similes of oak and lightning for the protagonists introduce the Roman pattern and the imagery of the ancient Latin rite into Lucan's epic. To identify Pompey as an oak is to identify him as a sacred tree:

> …stat magni nominis umbra,
> qualis frugifero quercus sublimis in agro
> exuvias veteris populi sacrataque gestans
> dona ducum nec iam validis radicibus haerens
> pondere fixa suo est, nudosque per aera ramos
> effundens trunco, non frondibus, efficit umbram,
> et quamvis primo nutet casura sub Euro,
> tot circum silvae firmo se robore tollant,
> sola tamen colitur.

> … he stands, the shadow of a great name, like a lofty oak in an overgrown clearing, bedecked with the ancient armorial spoils of the people and the consecrated offerings of generals; holding on now not with vigorous roots, it stands fixed by its own weight, and sending forth denuded branches through the air, it casts a shadow, not with leaves, but with its trunk; and though it sways, about to fall beneath the first East wind, and round about so many trees with sound timber rise up, even so it alone is worshipped.

But it is also essential to realize that the violation of the tree, the strike of lightning, the murder of Pompey, are equally sacred—and necessary—acts.

Lightning is as sacred as the oak. Its swiftness, its violence, the destructiveness of its power, form part of its message from Jupiter to mortals. For lightning to strike the oak is to injure the oak: thus, the lightning inflicts *sacra vulnera*. The thing injured, the instrument of the injury, and the injuries themselves are all sacred. Pompey's death is the death of the protector of the oak—the oak which, as the terrible combat begins, is a shade of itself, ready to fall, but not fallen. The vulnerability of the oak reflects Pompey's role in the ritual of the war; his character and the moral value of his position are extraneous. The strike of lightning is the divine and fatal wound, which does not deny, but reaffirms, the oak's sacredness. Thus Pompey's death, if not at Caesar's hands, at least to fulfill Caesar's destiny, is a *necessary* murder—necessary to their sacred obligations as the sacrificial victim and the sacrificing priest.

These wounds—the lighting or the axe striking the tree, the death of Pompey, the civil war that engulfs Rome—are all sacred wounds. They are all part of the Roman expiations that must, as Cato has said, be completed before the unmerciful gods are satisfied.

Once we see this, the speech of the Massiliotes assumes its proper significance in the poem. The Massiliotes try to reason their way out of involvement in this terrible rite. First they acknowledge their ancient ties to Rome; next they promise their aid in any external war. Then they address the heart of the matter:

> at, si funestas acies, si dira paratis
> proelia discordes, lacrimas civilibus armis
> secretumque damus. tractentur vulnera nulla
> sacra manu.

> … but, if you [Pompey and Caesar], at odds between yourselves, are preparing fatal battle-lines, dreadful battles, we offer tears for civil warfare and stand aside. The sacred wounds may not be touched by any hand.

They will stand aside, for the sacred wounds—the blood sacrifice of civil war—must not be touched by any hand. The combat is between Caesar and Pompey, between their followers and their armies. These two (men, sides, armies) must fight to the death; outsiders may not interfere. The odd and perplexing phrase *secretum damus* (lit: we grant seclusion)—which the scholiast is surely right to gloss as *secernimus nos a vobis* (we separate ourselves from you)—may well have actually been part of the rite, an utterance made at the moment the combatants engaged, and the bystanders had to withdraw until one or the other was dead. In ritual combat, it is obvious, neither party could under any circumstances receive outside help. What the Massiliotes have not understood is that in every respect, whether as combatants or not, they still share a common destiny—*communia fata*—with the Romans: Rome is the *caput mundi*, the head of the world, and her fate is the fate of the civilized world, the *imperium Romanum*. The Massiliotes may not hold themselves apart from the war. Thus, Lucan neglects entirely to assign any cause to Caesar's assault on Massilia beyond the fundamental cause: the Civil War itself. Massilia, who shared a copy of her statue of Artemis with the Romans, is the first to demonstrate the universal nature of the Roman Civil War.

The metaphor of the sacred wound, as the Massiliotes' speech would lead us to suspect, is paramount to the meaning of Book 3. The sacred wounds are the wounds to the divine tree, the murder of Pompey, the wounds suffered by all those who fight, and the wounds to the body politic. They are sacred in the most fundamental way, for the violator, no less than the violated, is set apart: both are *sacer*, both are part of a sacred rite. They form the metaphor with which Lucan shapes his epic view of the events of the Civil Wars. Though sacrilegious in the extreme, these wars were nevertheless necessary to the divine order (which had already made Rome mistress of the known world) and, therefore, sacred in their very horror.

Now we can approach the naval battle, which, again, Lucan has created out of very meager historical material. After the act of sacrilege, after the sacred wounding, there is a struggle. The remarkable *naumachia* of Book 3 has a specific function: it is the inevitable consequence of sacrilege, but, as Caesar departs for Spain before it takes place, it is a substitute for the real struggle, a metaphor which foreshadows that struggle and conveys further just what Lucan, and the Massiliotes, mean when they speak of "sacred wounds."

Within the *naumachia*, Lucan explores the meaning of the sacred wounds on three levels. First, there is the wounded and soon-to-be-wrecked ship of state, metaphorically implicit in the naval battle. Then there is the wounding of the body politic, sustained through the descriptions of the wounded bodies of men. Finally, the blood and wounds themselves become agents in the destruction. The

sacra vulnera are the purest aspect of the bloody expiations of civil war. The half-dead fall into the sea and drown drinking their own blood. Javelins thrown haphazardly find bodies to wound in the water. Consider "daring Catus":

> … terga simul pariter missis et pectora telis
> transigitur: medio concurrit corpore ferrum,
> et stetit incertus, flueret quo vulnere, sanguis,
> donec utrasque simul largus cruor expulit hastas
> divisitque animam sparsitque in vulnera letum.

> … he is pierced, through the back and the chest at the same time, by weapons launched together; the steel points meet in the middle of his body and the blood stops, unsure—from which wound should it flow?—until the bloody flood drives out both spears at once, and splits his soul and drenches his wounds with death.

The blood of the double wound itself becomes almost a divine agent, overpowering the two weapons and dividing his soul in its drive to spread death on the gaping double wounds. One of two twin brothers, after losing first his right and then his left hand, dies protecting his twin—the whole is split and the pair (hands, twins) is sundered. Lycidas is rent in two, the upper half from the lower. And so forth.

The concluding metaphors sum up the nature of the struggle (which, up to then, has been *anceps*, "of double meaning" as well as "undecided"). There is a victory, but the victors and the vanquished cannot be distinguished, either through their ships, or through the bodies of the dead themselves:

> … Graiae pars maxima classis
> mergitur, ast aliae mutato remige puppes
> victores vexere suos; navalia paucae
> praecipiti tenuere fuga. quis in urbe parentum
> fletus erat! quanti matrum per litora planctus!
> coniunx saepe sui confusis vultibus unda
> credidit ora viri Romanum amplexa cadaver,
> accensisque rogis miseri de corpore trunco
> certavere patres.

> … the most part of the Greek fleet is sunk, but some ships with changed oarsmen carried their own conquerors; a few in headlong flight made it to the docks. What weeping of parents there was in the city! How many lamentations of mothers along the shores! Often a wife believed the Roman corpse she embraced was her own husband with the features disfigured by the sea; and wretched fathers fought over headless bodies on funeral pyres already aflame.

The metaphor of the damaged ship of state— one that in victory has the "wrong" crew in charge—is then transferred to the wounding of the body politic; the bodies are unrecognizable, and (defeated but living) Massiliote wives often embrace Romans

The remains of the Roman Forum, the center of the city and the scene of public meetings, law courts, and gladiatorial combats.

(victorious but dead) by mistake. Worse, the wounds have severed the heads of the fighters from their bodies, and a further war is incited between fathers for possession of these headless corpses on burning pyres. Rome, in the throes of civil war, is a foundering ship. She is a body without a head, a body fought over by Senatorial fathers (*Patres Conscripti*), in blind desperation, unable to identify their sons among the slaughtered of both sides, while the funeral pyres for the Republic are already aflame.

And it will be the dead body of Pompey, headless on another shore, abandoned by all, that will complete the first series of murders and make Caesar master of Rome, Rome, the *caput mundi*.

Surely, now, we can see that, far from being an unexpected anticlimax, the concluding line and a half of Book 3 resonates with meaning: *at Brutus in aequore victor/primus Caesareis pelagi decus addidit armis* ("but Brutus, victorious at sea, was the first to confer the honor of a sea-battle to Caesar's arms"). Lucan thus names Decimus Brutus, the commander of the Roman navy. It was Decimus Brutus who, on the Ides of March, urged Caesar not to disappoint the meeting that had for some time been waiting for him and thus assured that the plot could go forward. Decimus Brutus and his brother Marcus were two of the assassins who inflicted the twenty-three stab wounds. But more than the particular man, it is the name that matters, for the name itself carries a monumental metaphorical burden. One Brutus drove out the kings from Rome: two more Bruti will in their turn add honor to this ancient struggle, by taking on their responsibility for yet another sacred wound when they kill Caesar. By preparing the way for Octavian, these new Bruti bring back the kings—as the Caesars.

Through all this, the inability to see, to identify, to know for certain, is at the core of the dilemma, not just of the Massiliotes, but of the Romans, of all human beings. Thus the Massiliotes defend their refusal to choose sides; men would not dare even to aid Jupiter in the battle of the gods, they say, because humans cannot know what is meant to happen—which means they cannot know which side it is right to join:

> non tamen auderet pietas humana vel armis
> vel votis prodesse Iovi, sortisque deorum
> ignarum mortale genus per fulmina tantum
> sciret adhuc caelo solum regnare Tonantem.

> The piety of men would not, even so, dare to aid Jupiter either by arms or by prayers, and only by the lightning bolts would the human race, ignorant of the destinies of the gods, be aware that the Thunderer alone still reigned in heaven.

Lucan first implicitly compared the Civil War with the battles of Gods and Giants in his proem, and he there equated the coming of Nero with the triumph of Jupiter in that battle. Since then Caesar has regularly been identified with the lightning that the Massiliotes claim will tell them Jupiter has won. Caesar is the lightning and makes his first petition to Rome's gods beginning with Jupiter Tonans; Augustus founded the temple to Jupiter Tonans; Nero is equated with Jupiter Tonans. When Lucan again describes the Civil War in terms of this conflict, we should pay attention to the connection between the two. If the Civil War resembles the battle of the Gods, and Nero's reign (described with—to us—repulsive flattery) is the result of the Civil War, then his reign must be equated to Jupiter's—a triumphant, but at the time unknowable, consequence of the upheaval and violation of the divine order. Lucan may have changed his mind, and at the end he may have seen Nero as one more in the series of sacrilegious *Caesariani;* but his support for Piso does not in the least argue a romantic desire for a return to the ways of the Republic. If any trust at all is to be placed in Tacitus, then the conspiracy was

designed to produce, not a refashioning of the failed Republic, but a *princeps* preferable to Nero: one who would justify the *scelera* and *nefas* that had so devastated Rome for a century or more. There is an undeniable emotive power that lies always with the defense of the Republic as exemplified by Cato; that is not sufficient reason to ignore the patent factuality (if one is going to believe in the gods at all) of the first half of that famous line: *the victorious cause pleased the gods, the vanquished, Cato.* The Republic—Rome defeated—was pleasing to Cato, but Rome herself—greater, always, than the man or men who ruled her—is the *victrix causa*. If Augustus was to found the New Rome, then the Old Rome must pass away.

V

We return thus to the sacred grove, the lightning, and the tree, noting Lucan's insistence that the divinities of the sacred grove at Massilia are all the more terrifying because they are unrecognizable and unknown:

> … simulacraque maesta deorum
> arte carent caesisque extant informia truncis.
> ipse situs putrique facit iam robore pallor
> attonitos; non vulgatis sacrata figuris
> numina sic timeant: tantum terroribus addit,
> quos metuunt, non nosse, deos.

> the grim images of the gods are crudely rendered and they stand there as shapeless blocks formed from the felled trees. The very neglect and the grayness of their rotting wood is what terrifies; men would not thus fear sacred powers rendered in familiar shapes: so much it adds to their terror, not to know the gods they fear.

Similarly, the gods of his epic are unrecognizable, lacking *vulgatae figurae*—familiar shapes. Since Feeney's recent study, it can no longer be argued that the gods are absent in Lucan's epic. It is the traditional characterization of them, the literary equivalent of anthropomorphic representation, that Lucan avoids, as Feeney so persuasively demonstrates. Here, at 3.413–17, Lucan has presented his justification for this—not that people no longer believed in the gods, nor that gods were inappropriate for a "historical" epic, but that he understood, as a poet, how the events of the Civil War became all the more terrifying because the victims could neither escape the slaughter, nor ascertain which side would own the *victrix causa*. There was no interpretation to be made, no omen or augury or prophecy which could guide humans through these horrifying disasters. Such disorder must seem contrary to divine order until the outcome demonstrates the new order: as the Massiliotes say, they must wait for signs (the thunderbolts) to know who won: "only by the lightning bolts would the human race, ignorant of the destinies of the gods, be aware that the Thunderer alone still reigned in heaven."

The fact that Lucan's own designs for divine matters remain, apparently, even more impenetrable is, surely, due to the incompleteness of the poem: he has not been obscure in the work as we have it. He has already spoken clearly in Book 1: if there was no other way to bring about Nero's reign (and his eventual godhead: "nature will allow you to be whatever god you desire", then not just civil war, but all its consequences, including the devastation of Italy, were not too high a price to pay—*scelera ipsa nefasque / hac mercede placent* ("these very crimes and sacrilege are welcome at this price").

Still, we do not have the outcome, and therefore lack a decisive statement of the poet's intentions. This offers ironic, if accidental, confirmation of everything Lucan says: until we know how it is supposed to end, the purpose of it all remains desperately confusing.

As in the battle of the Gods, however, so in the rite of the *rex nemorensis:* humans are left ignorant of the outcome of the struggle instituted by Diana, whether that is the sacrifice of Iphigenia, or the battle between the *rex nemorensis* and his challenger. The goddess cannot signal her preferences, nor interfere in the struggle between challenger and priest; that the priest defends her, while the challenger commits a deep sacrilege against her, remains irrelevant to her divinity, which had itself created the rite of sacrilege, struggle, and murder. Only the outcome, not the nature, of the struggle determines who is Diana's true defender; thus, in several ways and at several levels, Lucan is telling us that the outcome, not the nature, of the struggle will determine who is to be Rome's true leader.

There is one last section of Book 3, the catalogue of Pompey's troops, that now falls into place, not merely as a generic epic convention, but as a further realization of Lucan's specifically Roman epic. Now the apparently contradictory character of Pompey is resolved. His lack of vigor represents not Lucan's comment on the man's character, nor his judgment of the validity of the Republican cause, but his understanding of Pompey's position as the ruler about to be deposed by the vigorous young challenger. Pompey is the dying oak, the only one honored among the surrounding vigorous forest, bearing the honors of the people, and ready to be toppled. Like Servius Tullius, *prope exsanguis* ("al-

most white from fear") after he had been thrown out of the Curia by Tarquinius Superbus, Pompey is timorous—*pavidus* (6)—after Caesar threatens to make war on him. Like Servius, *semianimis regio comitatu domum se reciperet* ("only half conscious, with his royal escort he was retreating homeward"), Pompey flees and in the east gathers his "royal escort". Lucan is at pains, in Book 3, to maintain Pompey as leader of an army of kings ("never did so many kings obey a single leader"). But he will have lost the great royal company following him when he flees to Egypt. There, like Servius, Pompey will indeed die alone, with his head covered—at once priest and victim, a Roman sacrifice made to the merciless gods.

Conclusion: "The Necessary Murder"

Lucan created the relationship between Pompey and Caesar on the pattern of the relationship of Agamemnon and Achilles. Onto this powerful inherited epic form he grafted the paradigm which held a place of mythological honor for Romans as the story of Romulus and Remus, who fight to the death over the walls of Rome. For both poets and historians in the generations preceding Lucan, this myth of murderous combat initiated the historical process which they believed led Rome into the Civil Wars. Behind that myth was a Latin ritual whose traces could be discerned in the accepted histories of Rome's kings, and which was formalized and preserved from the earliest days as a religious rite in which the *rex nemorensis*, the priest of the goddess Diana in the grove near Aricia, fought to the death any challenger who could first cut off a bough of the sacred tree.

In Book 3, Caesar crosses through the heart of Latium, and passes and masters (*superare*), among three other cults, the *regna* of Diana at Aricia. The rites of Arician Diana—the sacrilege of wounding the tree, the armed battle to the death, and the murder of the priest-king by his challenger—are Lucan's reminder to his readers of a religious and historical paradigm, rooted in Latin tradition and Roman culture, through which he is assimilating the Civil War to a rite that was undeniably *Latin* and *Roman*. It provided a pattern for a *necessary* sacrilege against the gods, a *necessary* struggle and a *necessary* murder, all leading to a conclusion in which the transgressor, the murderer, becomes the divinely appointed priest-king *precisely because he was successful* in his sacrilege and murder. The monstrous events of the Civil War, both the individual deaths and the destruction of the Republic, become—like the story of Romulus and Remus—a part of the destiny of Rome.

Beyond that, the paradigm of the *rex* offers Lucan a perspective that is necessary for his epic: it becomes possible for him to cast the struggle between Pompey and Caesar as a struggle between individuals—not factions, not parties, not families; yet, even though it is acted out between individuals, it surpasses the limited nature of a merely personal political feud. Rendering the conflict in these terms permits Lucan to keep the specific, historical, and unpoetic causes of the war to one side (though it cannot be doubted that he understood them) and concentrate rather on the tragic processes through which history, as he saw it, worked. Caesar and Pompey thus retain their epic character, and are not contaminated by the limiting, trivializing nature of factional politics. The challenge, the fight, the murder and the triumph are all sacred acts, terrible, barbarous and violent though they may be. Their sum makes up the divinely appointed expiations owed to a dire goddess; it is through a crime that the victorious *rex nemorensis* obtains, as Orestes had done before him, purification for his crime.

In particular, it is through the paradigm of the *rex nemorensis* that the relationship of the specific events of Book 3 can now be understood to make a related, dramatic, whole. Pompey's abandonment of Rome, which has ended Book 2, opens the way for Caesar's triumphal advance through Latium to Rome. In turn, because he is retreating, because he is in eclipse, because he is the dying oak, Pompey loses strength, conviction, and power as he goes. The royal panoply of kings and armies who are catalogued in forces supporting Pompey simultaneously calls attention to his diminishing personal powers, as the surrounding vigorous forest calls attention to the leafless oak, and, by contrast, cast him ever more vividly as a king, and a leader among kings; for this is his role—Pompey is Rome's dying priest-king, bedecked with the ancient honors of his people. He is the oak, Caesar is the lightning; both lightning and oak are symbols of the power of Jupiter—and of Rome—and it is the very nature of that power to destroy and renew itself. All this is the preparation for Caesar's great act of sacrilege, when he cuts down an oak in the sacred grove outside Massilia. He claims the crime, for it is only through the crime that he can approach and challenge the reigning priest—Pompey.

In their speech to Caesar, the Massiliotes introduce the parallel of the battle of Gods and Giants, and argue that, as mere mortals, they cannot discern which side in the war is the right (religiously right, rather than morally right) side to join. They beg Caesar to allow them to stay neutral, for as outsiders they cannot choose between Caesar and Pompey, and may not touch the sacred wounds. Caesar's sacrilege is sacred; his purification is conditional upon the fulfillment of the sacrifice of the reigning priest, which is a sacred wounding. The imagery of the sacred wound overwhelms the end of Book 3. Caesar has cut the sacred tree; Pompey is weakening; blood must be shed. The Massiliotes discover that when Rome is convulsed in a civil war, the whole civilized world is drawn in; they are not outsiders after all. At that moment in the ritual when the combatants would first engage, Lucan brings Book 3 to a close with a sea-battle, wherein he works out all the terrible metaphors of civil war: man(kind) is torn in two; the ship (of state) is battered and no one knows which side has won command; the body (politic) is headless, and the fathers (of the country) are fighting over the dismembered and unrecognizable remnant. The gods are implacable and bloody, and the expiation they demand is a human sacrifice—those who will die in the war.

Despite this, however, the fact of the Civil War and what it meant remains unchanged. Neither the failures that lead to Pompey's defeat nor Caesar's guilt in transgressing the laws of the Republic and murdering his fellow citizens is altered one whit by Lucan. It is a cold, unsentimental and even, seemingly, amoral view. It is perhaps the view of an artist who has himself been scarred by the lethal combat for *regnum* in the palace of the Caesars; one who has learned the devastations of the war and the horrors of those who dare not, who *may* not choose the "right" side, from his own grandfather's account of the war, and from the consciousness that his family had survived only because they were adept at trimming their sails to the prevailing Roman storm. It may be cynical, or it may be a young man's attempt to frame a justification for his own as well as for the imperial family—but it is not an unreligious (or irreligious) view. The gods of the Romans—particularly "Scythian" Diana—may be cruel and incomprehensible, but they *are* gods. Rome and her people are still the rulers on earth. This is part of the paradox of Lucan's creation: the war that seems to prove the gods' withdrawal is in fact the terrifying convulsion that renews the greatness of Rome. That this civil conflict is unbearably murderous, immoral, and against divine law, *yet required by it*, is a paradox that lies at the root of Lucan's view of the war and its leaders. The murder, the slaughter, the blood, are all necessary. Cato has spoken the truth. The war constitutes the expiations that the gods, without mercy, require.

It may perhaps be helpful to turn, finally, to a poet in our own time, writing about another civil war:

> Today the inevitable increase in the chances
>   of death;
> The conscious acceptance of guilt in the neces-
>   sary murder;
> Today the expending of powers
> On the flat ephemeral pamphlet and the bor-
>   ing meeting.
> ....
> The stars are dead; the animals will not look:
> We are left alone with our day, and the time
>   is short and
> History to the defeated
> May say Alas but cannot help or pardon.

Lucan—one of the young poets "exploding like bombs"—has created in his epic the "conscious acceptance of guilt in the necessary murder." When we consider his deep emotional attraction to Pompey, Cato, their cause, and the great Roman Republic, we must not mistake this for political partisanship. *Rome herself* commanded Lucan's deepest loyalty. When all is done, to Pompey and Cato, to Brutus and the Republic, Lucan—as a poet of history—"to the defeated / May say Alas but cannot help or pardon."

Source: C.M.C. Green, "'The Necessary Murder': Myth, Ritual, and Civil War in Lucan Book 3," in *Classical Antiquity,* Vol. 13, No. 2, October, 1994, pp. 203–233.

SOURCES

Ahl, Frederick M., *Lucan: An Introduction*, Cornell University Press, 1976.

———, "Form Empowered: Lucan's *Pharsalia*," in *Roman Epic*, Routledge, 1993, pp. 125–142.

Bartsch, Shadi, *Ideology in Cold Blood: A Reading of Lucan's Pharsalia*, Harvard University Press, 1998.

Bowersock, G. W., *Fiction as History: Nero to Julian*, University of California Press, 1994.

Boyle, A. J., *Roman Epic*, Routledge, 1993.

Fornara, Charles William, *The Nature of History in Ancient Greece and Rome*, University of California Press, 1983.

Gillespie, Stuart, *The Poets on the Classics: An Anthology*, Routledge, 1988.

Gotoff, Harold C., *Cicero's Caesarian Speeches: A Stylistic Commentary*, North Carolina University Press, 1993.

Johnson, W. R., *Momentary Monsters: Lucan and his Heroes*, Cornell University Press, 1987.

Kaster, Robert Andrew, "Servius and *Idonei Auctores*," in *American Journal of Philology,* Vol. 99, 1978, pp. 181–209.

Lucan (Marcus Annaeus Lucanus), *Lucan: The Civil War (Pharsalia)*, translated by J. D. Duff, Harvard University Press, reprint, Harvard University Press, 1988.

Masters, Jamie, *Poetry and Civil War in Lucan's Bellum Civile*, Cambridge University Press, 1992.

Morford, M. P. O., *The Poet Lucan Studies in the Rhetorical Epic*, Bristol Classical Press, 1996.

Reynolds, L. D., *Texts and Transmission: A Survey of the Latin Classics*, reprinted with corrections, Clarendon Press, 1986.

Sanford, Eva Mathews, "Lucan and his Roman Critics," in *Classical Philology,* Vol. 26, 1931, 233–57.

Scullard, H. H., *From the Gracchi to Nero: A History of Rome from 133 B.C. to A.D. 68*, 3d ed., Methuen and Co. Ltd., 1970.

Tacitus, *The Annals of Imperial Rome*, translated by Michael Grant, revised edition, Penguin Books, 1996.

Tarrant, R. J., "Lucan," in *Texts and Transmission: A Survey of the Latin Classics*, pp. 215–218.

FURTHER READING

Ahl, Frederick, "Form Empowered: Lucan's *Pharsalia*," in *Roman Epic*, Routledge, 1993, pp. 125–142.
    Perhaps the best short critical analysis of the *Pharsalia* available. Ahl ends with a powerful overview of Lucan's place as the poet of *libertas*.

Boyle, A. J., *Roman Epic*, Routledge, 1993.
    An-up-to-date survey of the Latin epic from its beginning to the Latin epics of the Renaissance. A specialist in a particular author or period writes each chapter. The articles are scholarly without being either dry or difficult.

Gotoff, Harold C., *Cicero's Caesarian Speeches: A Stylistic Commentary*, University of North Carolina Press, 1993.
    The introduction to the Latin texts of the speeches is useful even to those who are not familiar with Latin. It investigates the nuances of discourse and the interplay of events and personalities during the civil war and Caesar's subsequent return to Rome.

The Song of Igor's Campaign

ANONYMOUS

1185

The Song of Igor's Campaign is one of the classics of medieval epic literature and the only surviving example of the epic form written in Russia. It was written between 1185 and 1187, shortly after the events it describes took place. The epic relates the unsuccessful expedition of Prince Igor of Novgorod-Seversk, in Russia, against the nomadic tribes known as the Kumans, who had been raiding Russian lands in the southeast. Igor is defeated and captured but he eventually escapes and returns to Russia.

The manuscript of *The Song of Igor's Campaign* was discovered in 1795 and first published in 1800. The one surviving manuscript was then destroyed in the fire of Moscow in 1812. Fortunately, a copy had been made for Russia's Catherine the Great. However, there are many corrupt passages where the anonymous author's meaning is unclear.

The Song of Igor's Campaign has always been treasured for its literary quality. It is dense with imagery, simile and metaphor, and shows great structural variety. To the tale of Igor's military campaign, the author adds reminiscences of Russia's past. He employs laments, panegyrics (passages which lavishly praise a person), omens and dreams. *The Song of Igor's Campaign* is also notable for its poetic view of nature, in which animals, vegetation and natural forces react to and even shape the actions of humans. The author's psychological insight into his characters has also been admired.

The major theme of the work is the author's passionate plea for unity amongst the Russian princes, who had a history of feuding among them. The author believes that disunity leads to disaster for Russia. A melancholy feeling therefore pervades the epic. Although the author makes Igor's defeat seems more important than it was historically, his words proved prophetic. Early in the next century Genghis Khan's Mongol army conquered Russia and subjugated it for 200 years.

AUTHOR BIOGRAPHY

The author of *The Song of Igor's Campaign* is unknown. Scholars believe the epic was the work of one man, not the accumulated effort of many, but anything else said about the author is speculation. From the text it appears that the author was very familiar with military life, and it is possible that he took part in Igor's campaign. The anonymous author also knew about hunting, and had detailed knowledge of the flora and fauna of the prairies. He was learned in books and oral tradition and was well acquainted with the genealogies and histories of the Russian noble families. It is possible, then, that he may have been a court poet, or a close companion of a prince.

When *The Song of Igor's Campaign* was discovered in 1795, some suspected it might be a forgery. However, few question its authenticity today. Scholars point out that the Old Russian language in which the *Song* is written is used with great skill, and no one in the eighteenth century had the knowledge or the poetic genius to forge a work of such high quality. This is the same verdict that Alexander Pushkin, the foremost Russian poet, reached at the time the manuscript was discovered. He said there was not enough poetic ability in the entire eighteenth century to forge even a small part of *The Song of Igor's Campaign*.

PLOT SUMMARY

Lines 1–70: Invocation

The epic begins with a tribute to Boyan, an eleventh century Russian bard who paid tribute in

song to the military exploits of Russian princes. Nothing is known of Boyan other than the allusions to him in the *Song*. The author praises Boyan's poetic inspiration and names three princes who were subjects of Boyan's songs: the great ruler Yaroslav, prince of Kiev from 1019 to 1054; Mstilav, who was known as Mstilav the Brave, and Roman, who was killed by the Kumans in 1079. The author then says he will tell of events that happened in his own time, not in the past, and he introduces his subject: he will describe how Igor led the Russian forces against the Kumans in defense of Russian land. Then follows another brief apostrophe (direct address) to Boyan, in which he imagines how Boyan might sing of Igor's military campaign.

Lines 71–150: Preparations for Battle

Igor's brother Vsevolod joins Igor. Vsevolod speaks in affectionate words of his brother, and tells Igor to saddle his horses, for his own are ready. Vsevolod then praises his own soldiers as having been bred for battle from an early age. They are masters in the pursuit of honor for themselves and glory for their prince. Next, Igor addresses his army. He tries to inspire them with heroic words about how it is nobler to die in battle than to be taken captive. Filled with ambition, he says he wants to drink from the water of the River Don, which is at the Kuman frontier. But as Prince Igor mounts his horse and rides into the prairie, there are various ominous signs in nature. These include howling wolves and the song of a bird (daeva) traditionally associated with misfortune. But the Prince is so eager for battle he does not notice them.

Line 151–180: Early Russian Success

The action now moves immediately to the battlefield. On the first day of battle, the Russians are victorious. In the early morning, they slaughter their enemies, and take away booty such as beautiful cloths and garments. They also capture young Kuman women and bring them back as part of the spoils of war.

Lines 181–230: Russian Adversity

The second day of battle day begins with ominous signs from nature. When battle commences, the fortunes of the previous day are reversed. The Russian army is surrounded on all sides by the enemy; they retreat. As the earth groans under the weight of the conflict, the Russians fight bravely and inflict heavy casualties on the opposing side. Igor is not mentioned directly, but his brother Vsevolod is twice singled out for praise of his courage and prowess.

Lines 231–266: Rebuke of Igor's Grandfather

As the battle rages, and the signs are bad for the Russians, the author takes a digression. He goes back to the events of former times, and criticizes the princes of that era for their feuding. He singles out two individuals in particular. First he names Oleg, Igor's grandfather, whom he blames for the internal wars that destroyed the unity of Russia. Historically, this was Oleg Svyatoslavich of Chernigov. Next he reminds his readers of the downfall of Prince Boris, who died in battle but whose name was tarnished because he too warred against other Russian princes. He also failed to listen to the advice of Prince Oleg, who advised him to surrender. This period, the author says, was disastrous for Russia. Death was everywhere, and the peaceful farming of the land was interrupted.

Lines 267–298: Russian Defeat

Returning to the battle, the author says it was the greatest battle of all time. The Russians fight on in the lands of their enemy, but by noon of the third day they are defeated. The two brothers are parted, but their fate is not yet disclosed. The defeat takes place on the shores of the River Kayala, which was a tributary of the Donets river, which was itself a tributary of the River Don.

Lines 299–350: Lamentations

In a long section, the author laments that in the wake of Igor's defeat, unhappy times have now come to Russia. The remaining princes quarrel among themselves, and Russia is subject to invasion on all sides. Grief and sorrow spread across the land as the victorious invaders demand tribute (money) from each household.

Lines 351–390: Igor Rebuked

The narrator then criticizes Igor and his brother for permitting, by their defeat, the evil forces to gather strength. He points out that Prince Svyatoslav, the Prince of Kiev and one of the most powerful of the Russian rulers, had always triumphed over the Kuman enemy. Svyatoslav is the cousin of Igor

and Vsevolod. Svyatoslav had even captured the Kuman leader and taken him to Kiev as a prisoner. Historically, this occurred in 1184, a year before Igor's campaign. The narrator says that the peoples of Europe—Germans, Venetians, Moravians and Greeks—praise Svyatoslav. This praise is because the victory over the Kumans kept open the trade routes between Russia and southwestern Europe. But now all that has changed. Many reproach Igor for allowing the Kumans to capture so much Russian wealth. It is at this point that the narrator reveals for the first time that Igor was not killed in the battle, but was taken prisoner.

Lines 391–410: Prince Svyatoslav's Dream

The narrator relates the dream of Prince Svyatoslav of Kiev. It is full of ominous signs. He dreams he is covered by a black shroud, drinking wine that makes him sorrowful. Strangers from a foreign land pour pearls onto his chest (pearls were a traditional symbol of tears). And all night he hears the ravens calling.

Lines 411–450: The Prince's Dream Explained

The Prince's *boyars* (nobles) explain the dream to him. They tell him the story of Igor's ill-fated expedition, of how the forces of darkness overcame the forces of light. The victorious enemy is likened to a brood of panthers marauding across Russian lands, celebrating their revenge. Glory has faded from Russia and only shame is left.

Lines 451–490: Svyatoslav Speaks

Svyatoslav replies in words that give more insight into why the narrator rebuked Igor in the previous section. The Prince says that Igor and Vsevolod acted too rashly. Although they showed courage, they were too ambitious, and that was why they failed.

Lines 491–590: The Bard Appeals to Russian Princes

The narrator now appeals, one by one, to the surviving Russian princes. He asks them to unite in defense of Russia. First he addresses Volodimir, who has been wounded trying to repel the Kumans as they attack the city of Rim, on the river Sula. Then he appeals to the powerful Vsevolod, Prince of Suzdal, for assistance. Next he turns to Rurik and David, noting their military prowess and appealing for their help in avenging the Russian defeat. He

Prince Vsevolod I of Kiev. The author of Song of Igor's Campaign *makes a plea for unity amongst the Russian princes of the Middle Ages, who were constantly feuding.*

makes a similar appeal to Yaroslav of Galich (Igor's father-in-law), whose troops have proved their mettle. Then Roman and Mstislav are evoked as mighty warriors who have subdued Hins, Lithuanians, Yatvangians, and Kumans. Ingvar and Vsevolod, and three unnamed sons of Mstislav, are next. The author calls on them to protect the prairies and avenge the Russian land.

Lines 591–610: Tribute to Izyaslav

The narrator recalls the bravery of the warrior Izyaslav, who was killed in battle in 1162 against the Lithuanians. Izyaslav fought alone, without his two brothers, Bryachislav and Vsevolod, and this is honored by the author as a sign of Izyaslav's courage.

Lines 611–630: Reproach of Yaroslav and Vseslav

Yaroslav, the subject of an appeal by the author in lines 523–41 is now rebuked. (There is some doubt amongst scholars about whether this may in fact be a different Yaroslav). Along with the descendents of Vseslav, he is held responsible for the invasions of Russia by the Kumans. The invasions happened because of the feuding between the Russian princes.

Lines 631–686: The story of Vseslav

Vseslav of Polotsk (d. 1101) conquered Novgorod in 1067, but was then defeated at the river Nemiga by Yaroslav's three sons. (Novgorod had traditionally been ruled by the House of Yaroslav.) In 1068 Vseslav became Prince of Kiev for seven months. He had a reputation for being a magician. These facts explain many of the references and expressions in this section. Vseslav is said to cast lots for a maiden; the maiden is the city of Kiev. He touches the golden throne with his staff—an allusion to the brevity of his reign. At night he has the ability to envelop himself in a blue mist as he travels, or to take on the form of a wolf-signs of his power as a magician. Lines 645–48 allude to Vseslav's victory at Novgorod, and the following lines (649–58) to his defeat at Nemiga.

Lines 659–686: Assessment of Vseslav

The narrator elaborates on the nature of Vseslav and his magical powers. He ruled his territories by day but at night he prowled like a wolf. He managed to travel all the way from Kiev to Tmutorakan in one night—an incredible journey since Tmutorakan is more than 700 miles southeast from Kiev! Then when the bells of the Church of St. Sophia in Polotsk tolled matins (morning services) for him, he could hear them in Kiev, 350 miles south. Despite the fact that Vseslav was physically strong, and a magician, he still suffered personal catastrophes. The author quotes the bard Boyan as having said of Vseslav that no one can escape the judgment of God. This section concludes with another short passage mourning the fate of Russia. It looks back to the glory days of Vladimir I and then in regret to the present, in which Russian forces are divided against themselves.

Lines 686–730: Lament of Yaroslovana, Igor's Wife

Igor's wife, Yaroslovana, stands on the walls of the city of Putivl and laments for her lost husband. She says she will fly like a cuckoo to the river Kayala and wipe the wounds from Igor's body. The remainder of her lament is divided into three parts, each of which apostrophizes (addresses directly) an inanimate force. First, she asks the wind why it chose to blow the weapons of the enemy in the direction of the Russian army. Why could it not just blow on the seas, setting the ships in motion? Then she addresses the river Dnieper. She says that since the river had the power to pierce the stone hills that run through the land of the Kumans, it can also respond to her request and return her husband to her. The last part of her lament is addressed to the sun. She asks the sun why it sent its hot rays onto her husband's warriors, scorching them on the battlefield when there was no water available.

Lines 731–770: Igor Escapes

One night Igor escapes from his Kuman captors. At midnight, on the other side of the river, a friendly Kuman named Ovlur provides him with a horse at midnight. Igor swims across the river, leaps on the horse, and speeds away. Ovlur accompanies him. The account of the escape is brief, but it follows the description given in the chronicles of the period. According to the chronicles, Igor's guards were enjoying a boisterous night drinking fermented mare's milk, and this gave Igor his chance to slip away.

Lines 771–802: Igor Speaks to the River Donets

The River Donets tells Igor that he will receive glory, and Russia will receive joy. In return, Igor praises the river. He says it carried him on its waves and he has enjoyed the green grass on its banks and the mists that enveloped him in the shadows of its trees. He compares it favorably to the river Stugna, which is a tributary of the Dnieper, south of Kiev. It was in that river that Prince Rostilav (paternal ancestor of Igor's wife) was drowned in 1093, after a battle with the Kumans.

Lines 803–830 : Igor Pursued by the Enemy

Two Kumans, Gzak and Konchak, pursue Igor on horseback, but soon realize they cannot capture him. Gzak suggests that they kill Igor's son, Vladimir, whom they still hold captive. Kochak replies with a suggestion that they enmesh Vladimir in the charms of a beautiful woman (presumably so that he will not be able to escape). Gzak replies that if they do that, they will end up with neither the woman nor Vladimir. Then he adds that the birds will start to beat them on their own territory. (The conversation between the two Kumans is difficult to interpret, and no commentator has satisfactorily explained these puzzling lines.)

Lines 831–861: Igor Returns to Russia

The author quotes a passage from a song by the bard Boyan, in which Boyan says it is hard for a body to be without a head—that is, for a land to manage without its king or leader. After pointing out how badly Russia misses Igor, the author describes the effect of Igor's return to Kiev. The sun shines and maidens sing, cities and whole countries rejoice. Igor goes immediately to the church called the Blessed Virgin of the Tower. The *Song* ends with a song of praise in honor of Igor, his brother Vsevolod and his son Vladimir, and to all the Christian knights of Russia who are fighting the pagans.

CHARACTERS

Boris

Boris was a Russian prince who died in 1078. He was the grandson of Yaroslav I. He is used by the author as an example of princely folly (lines 245–50).

Boyan

Boyan was a minstrel and poet who sang in former days about the exploits of the Russian princes. He does not appear directly in the epic, but is invoked several times by the author, who praises his skill as a bard. Boyan is a "nightingale of the times of old."

David of Smolensk

David (d. 1198), brother of Rurik, fought the Kumans in 1183, alongside Rurik's forces. The author urges him and his brother to avenge the defeat of Igor.

Euphrosyne

Euphrosyne is Igor's wife. She is also called Yaroslavna. She appears late in the epic and sings a lament to the wind, the river and the sun in which she reveals her deep love for her husband. She also expresses compassion for Igor's fallen warriors.

Gzak

Gzak is a Kuman warrior who pursues Igor after he has escaped.

Igor, Prince of Novgorod-Seversk

Igor is the prince who leads the Russians in their attack on the Kumans. He is depicted as courageous and manly, imbued with a warlike spirit. He cares deeply for glory and for battle, and has the ability to inspire his men. "It is better indeed to be slain / than to be enslaved," he tells them (96–7). He is prepared either to triumph in battle or die in the process. Igor is also devoted to his brother Vsevolod and very concerned for his welfare in the battle. But on the negative side, he is so eager to pursue his military goals that he fails to see warning signs in nature. Later in the poem he is condemned for being too ambitious. Nonetheless, he is held in high esteem by Russians, because when he escapes from captivity and returns to Russia, the whole Russian land rejoices. Igor is also a family man, with a wife and son who accompany him into battle.

Ingvar of Galich

Ingvar is a prince (d. 1202) to whom the author appeals for assistance in avenging the Russian defeat.

Izyaslav

Izyaslav was killed in the Battle of Gorodets in 1162, against the Lithuanians. He is recalled as a brave warrior.

Konchak

A companion of Gzak, Konchak is a Kuman warrior who pursues Igor after Igor's escape.

Mstislav of Peresopnits

Mstislav (d. 1224), fighting alongside Roman of Galich, conquered many other nations, and is highly praised by the author.

Mstislav of Tmutorakan

Mstislav (d. 1036) was the brother of Yaroslav I. He is referred to in lines 26–28 as a great warrior.

Oleg, Prince of Chernigov and Tmutorokan

Oleg, also known as Oleg Malglory, was Igor's grandfather, who died in 1115. He does not appear directly in the epic, but the author recalls him and some of his deeds. Oleg is blamed for initiating feuds with other Russian princes.

Ovlur

Ovlur is Igor's servant, and he assists Igor in his escape from captivity.

Roman of Galich

Roman (d. 1205) was a powerful warrior. Linked with Mstislav of Peresopnits, he is praised by the

MEDIA ADAPTATIONS

- *Prince Igor*, an opera written in 1890 by the Russian composer Alexander Porfir'yevich Borodin, is based on in *The Song of Igor's Campaign*. Borodin added to the tale some episodes and descriptions from two Russian chronicles.

- In the 1920s, Russian artist Ivan Golikov painted a series of lacquer miniatures illustrating *The Song of Igor's Campaign*. These are considered to be masterpieces of this Russian art form. According to M.A. Nekrasova, ''A distinctive and expansive rhythm conveys the determined spirit of the Russian warriors . . . . The colour blue . . . is always threatening. Blue flashes of lightning rend the clouds on the morning of the battle at the Kayala river; Svyatoslav sees a blue wine containing deadly poison in his dream; and the werewolf Vseslav is shrouded in blue mist. Golikov makes extensive use of this symbolic meaning of the colour, especially when depicting the eclipse of the sun over the heads of Igor's army.'' More information on this genre can be found at the Web site, ''Russian Lacquer miniatures,'' http://www.miniature.ru/index16.htm [June 11, 2000].

---

author for subduing many other nations, including Hins, Lithuanians and Kumans.

Roman of Tmutorakan

Roman (d. 1079) was the brother of Igor's grandfather. He is referred to once in the epic, in lines 26–28.

Rostislav

Rostislav of Pereyaslval was a prince who was drowned in the River Stugna, a tributary of the River Dnieper, in 1093, during a retreat after a battle with the Kumans.

Rurik of Belgarod

Rurik (d. 1215) was a Russian prince hailed by the author for his military prowess. In 1183, he fought a battle with the Kumans. The author appeals to him for help in avenging Igor's defeat.

Svyatoslav III

Svyatoslav III (d. 1194) is Igor's first cousin. He is the Prince of Kiev and the most powerful of the Russian nobility. The author presents him as an ideal, wise ruler. He is feared by the Kumans and has won victories against them, capturing their leader. For these exploits he is widely praised by many peoples and nations. In words described as "golden," Svyatoslav rebukes Igor for behaving rashly and neglecting his duty and causing sorrow for his prince.

Vladimir of Putivl

Vladimir is Igor's son, who at the age of twelve accompanies his father into battle. He is mentioned only in passing, when two Kuman warriors consider whether to kill him because Igor, his father, has escaped. At the end of the epic, the author includes Vladimir in his final words of praise to the Christian knights who fight the pagans.

Volodimir, Prince of Pereyaslavl

Volodomir was wounded as he repelled a Kuman attack on Pereyaslavi. He died of his wounds in 1187.

Vseslav of Polotsk

Prince Vselav of Polotsk (d. 1101) was thought to be a magician. He travels surrounded by blue mist, and is described as a werewolf. He won a victory over Novgorod, lost a battle at the River Nemiga, and ruled for a short period in Kiev. The bard Boyan said of him, "Neither the guileful not the skillful, / neither bird [not pard],/ can escape God's judgment'' (676–78).

Vsevelod, Prince of Suzdal

Vsevelod later became Vsevelod III (d. 1212). One of the most powerful princes of the time, he is praised by the author for the mighty strength of his forces. (He is not to be confused with Igor's brother, Vsevelod.)

Vsevolod

Vsevolod is the brother of Ingvar. The author appeals to him and his brother to come to Russia's aid.

Vsevolod, Prince of Trubchevsk and Kursk

Vsevolod is Igor's brother. He is called Wild Bull or Fierce Bull and is a formidable warrior. It is Vsevolod who urges Igor to begin the military campaign. His troops are ready to ride off to the Kuman lands even before Igor's men are fully prepared, and he is deeply proud of the valor and martial skill of his men. His golden helmet gleaming, he fights valiantly, standing his ground even when the tide turns against the Russians. Immersing himself totally in the battle, he forgets everything else, even his home and his wife. Although he kills many of the enemy, he is eventually taken prisoner. He is hailed at the end of the epic as one of the warriors fighting the pagans.

Yaroslav I

Yaroslav I, known as the Wise, was Igor's great-great-grandfather. He is referred to in line 25 as one of the men praised by Boyan. He is also referred to as great. Yaroslav ruled Kiev from 1019 to 1054.

Yaroslav of Galich

Yaroslav (d. 1187) was the father of Igor's wife, Euphrosyne, and therefore Igor's father-in-law. He is praised as a great military leader who has expanded his lands and defeated the Hungarians.

THEMES

Patriotism

The love of Russia's homeland and the desire to fight to preserve it is a continual theme in the *Song*. Early in the epic it is made clear that Igor leads his troops "in the name of the Russian land" (line 50).

As Igor's army sets off on its mission, the author imagines glory ringing in Kiev, trumpets blaring in Novgorod-Seversk and banners raised in the city of Putivl. In other words, the whole of Russia is rejoicing in patriotic pride at this expedition.

Patriotism is again evoked in the phrase "the sons of Rus" (148) to describe Igor's army as they approach the battlefield. (Rus is the ancient name of Russia.) Their collective identity as Russians is presented as more important than their individual genealogies. In the midst of the battle Igor's men are "brave sons of Rus" (209), and when they fall, they die in defense of the Russian land (298). It is clear that for a warrior, no destiny could be higher than this.

Love of country is again suggested by the poignant refrain "O Russian land, / you are already behind the culmen!" (Culmen means hill.) This is first uttered as Igor and his men enter the Kuman lands. It suggests the affection the author and by extension the warrior feel for Russia, and how acutely they are aware of the fact that they have journeyed to a distant, foreign land.

The tone of melancholy that pervades the epic is linked to the fate of Russia. Sometimes this is in the form of nostalgia for a lost, glorious past. For example, the author laments that as a result of Igor's defeat, "The Russian land shall moan / recalling her first years / and first princes!" (679–81).

Although there are some laments for individuals, as when the Russian women mourn the fact that they will not see their husbands again (331–38), these are quickly followed by a more generalized lament for the Russian nation: The city of Kiev mourns, as does Chernigov and the entire land of Russia. It is this patriotic sorrow caused by the fall of Russia that dominates the author's mind, and it is patriotism that fuels his desire for the Russian defeat to be avenged.

Duty and Responsibility

The author does not present the defeat of Igor as the result of bad luck or the evil tricks of the enemy. As the epic unfolds it transpires that Igor only has himself to blame for the catastrophe. Although the author is sympathetic to Igor, and Igor's courage is never in question, he is rebuked for being too concerned with personal glory at the expense of his national duty. Historically, Igor and the three other princes embarked on their military adventure without the support of the other Russian rulers. This is why in the epic, Svyatoslav III, Igor's cousin,

TOPICS FOR FURTHER STUDY

- Epics such as *The Song of Igor's Campaign* often glorify war, or at least view it as a legitimate, even laudable, way of pursuing political goals. Examine how attitudes towards war, and what war itself involves, have changed in recent times, especially since the Vietnam War. Are our heroes today warriors like Igor, or have we come to value different virtues? If Igor's campaign had taken place today, for example, what would have been the reaction of the world to the conduct of the Russians after they were victorious on the first day of battle? (Lines 151–70.)

- Russians treasure *The Song of Igor's Campaign* as part of their literary and national heritage, yet the epic records not a great victory but a catastrophic defeat. Research and examine other examples in history of how a great defeat has been enshrined in a nation's mythology and given a positive meaning. Examples might include the way Serbian nationalism has been fueled by a defeat suffered by Serbian forces in Kosovo in 1380; and the way the British turned the evacuation of their troops from Dunkirk in France in 1940 into a kind of moral victory. An example from American history might be the heroic but doomed defense of the Alamo against Mexican forces in San Antonio, Texas, in 1836. Is there something about a brave defeat that moves us more than a great victory?

- Kievan Rus was torn apart by internal conflict between rival principalities. No single group had the power to dominate the others. When the Soviet Union was formed following the Russian revolution in 1917, what methods did the communist government use to try to ensure that a vast country, full of disparate ethnic groups, would remain loyal to the Soviet state?

---

censures him. Svyatoslav had defeated the Kumans only two year earlier, in 1183, and Igor's defeat undid all the Russian gains. Igor's honor is tarnished, therefore, because he acted too rashly. Caught up in martial fervor, he declared, according to words the author places in the mouth of Svyatoslav, "Let us be heroes on our own, / let us by ourselves grasp the . . . glory" (480–81).

The moral is that the needs of the nation must be put before personal needs and ambitions. It is a matter of fulfilling one's duty. The author links this theme of Igor's lack of responsibility to occasions in the past when Russian princes have neglected their duty and quarreled amongst themselves. The effect has always been disastrous. These incidents form the substance of many of the laments in the epic. For example, Igor's grandfather Oleg "forged feuds with the sword" (235), and Prince Boris is rebuked for "vainglory" (pride and boastfulness) which he paid for with his life. And according to the author, the feuds associated with Yaroslav and all the descendents of Vseslav (d. 1101) are directly responsible for the invasion of Russia by the Kumans.

Given the author's interpretation of the political events of previous years, it is not surprising that he devotes nearly one-sixth of the entire epic (lines 491–630) to an appeal to the various Russian princes for a unified front to defeat the invaders and restore Russia's glory.

Nature and its Meaning

As in many medieval epics, nature plays an active role in the plot. The natural world is neither neutral nor inanimate. It reacts to human actions. When Igor sets off for battle, there are warning signs in nature: an eclipse of the sun and a storm at night. Nature already knows the outcome of the battle, and these signs might be interpreted as a warning to Igor. But he ignores them, and during the battle nature itself seems to turn against him. For example, the direction the wind blows in causes the enemy arrows to devastate the Russian army. After

Igor's defeat, however, nature mourns. The grass droops and trees bend to the ground in sorrow. And when it is time for Igor to escape, nature assists him. The magpies and ravens keep silent, and this allows Igor to hear the sound of the woodpeckers, who with their tapping guide Igor to the river from which he can make his escape.

STYLE

Epic Features

The Song of Igor's Campaign contains many of the elements of the traditional epic. It is about a heroic figure, Igor, who is of national significance for Russia. The setting is vast, stretching across the great expanse of Russian lands, and the author augments this effect by recalling many battles from the past and naming the places where they were fought. The action involves feats of courage in battle, and the omniscient point of view adopted by the author allows him to tell of events widely apart in time and place. This also allows him to convey the inner feelings of some of the characters through dialogue and description. Finally, epics usually begin with an invocation to a muse, and this is echoed in the *Song*: the author starts by recalling the skill of the earlier bard, Boyan.

However, many aspects of the traditional epic are not present in the *Song of Igor's Campaign*. Supernatural beings take no part in the action. The *Song* relates events in the immediate not the distant past, and is therefore more directly historical than other medieval epics. It is also much shorter and more concise than the traditional epic, and it is written not in verse of elevated language, but in what scholars of the Russian language describe as a cadenced (rhythmic) prose. Nor is the *Song* entirely a narrative work. The story of Igor's campaign, his capture and escape, takes up less than half of the epic. The remainder consists of lyrical lamentations for Russia, omens, dreams, exhortations by the author to other Russian princes, and nostalgic flash-backs to events in Russia's past.

Metaphor

The author gives a hint at the beginning of the metaphoric style of his work. He writes that when Boyan wanted to recall some deed of old, "He set ten falcons upon a flock of swans, / and the one first overtaken, / sang a song first" (21–24). Seven lines later, the author explains his metaphor: Boyan did not literally do this, the ten falcons were his ten fingers and the flock of swans were the strings of his musical instrument.

Many more metaphors are used in the epic. One of the most striking is the metaphor of battle as farming. For example, Oleg "sowed the land with arrows" (236). The metaphor is repeated in lines 278–79, where the earth "was sown with bones / and irrigated with gore." The crop that these seeds produce is "grief" throughout Russia. The metaphor recurs in extended form when the author recalls the fate of Vseslav at the battle at the river Nemiga. Warriors' severed heads are "spread sheaves," the threshing implements are steel swords, and the threshing floor is where lives are laid out. Souls are "winnowed" from bodies and the banks of the river are sown with bones (651–58).

Simile

Similes are frequent. A simile is a figure of speech in which a comparison is made between two unlike things that resemble each other in one aspect. In this epic, the comparisons are usually made between humans and animals or birds. Boyan is compared to a nightingale and an eagle; warriors on both sides are likened to gray wolves; the Kumans as they advance are like "dispersed swans." When Igor's wife laments his fate, she is compared to a cuckoo, and when Igor escapes from captivity, he speeds to the reeds by the river "like an ermine," settles on the water "like a white duck," then runs "like a demon wolf" and flies "like a falcon" (751–59). The effect of these similes is to suggest the close connection between the human and the natural world, which is one of the themes of the epic.

Imagery

The author makes full use of color imagery. Red and gold are the most prominent colors. Igor's men carry vermilion shields (vermilion is a brilliant red color), and the Kuman standards, or flags, are also vermilion. The battle scene features "bloody effulgences" at dawn (a red sky) and "crimson pillars" (a metaphor for Igor and his brother as they go down to defeat, perhaps suggesting the setting sun).

Gold is used always with references to the nobility. Igor has golden stirrups and a golden saddle; his brother Vsevelod has a golden helmet. Princes have "golden thrones"; Svyatoslav's tower is "gold-crested" and his words are golden. In

Russian art of the period, gold symbolized glory and magnificence.

The Kumans are associated with black ravens and black clouds. The color blue is used to describe not only the river Don but also the wine of sorrow that Svyatoslav drinks and the mist that surrounds the sorcerer Vseslav.

Hyperbole

Another technique used by the author is hyperbole, a figure of speech which employs exaggeration to heighten an effect. When Igor's brother Vsevolod describes his own warriors he emphasizes that they have been well trained for battle. A series of hyperbolic statements follow. His men were "swaddled under war horns, / nursed under helmets, / fed from the point of the lance" (79–81). The point is that his men have been bred for warfare since an early age. Then when the author appeals to Vsevolod, Prince of Suzdal, for assistance, he says Vsevolod's men are so powerful they can scoop the river Don dry using only their helmets (502–03). Similarly, Rurik and David were so effective in battle that their helmets floated on blood; Yaroslav has hurled heavy missiles over the clouds (529), and the iron breastplates of Roman and Mstislav make the earth rumble (553). In each case the exaggeration heightens the dramatic effect: great power is available for Russia if the princes would only use it.

CRITICAL OVERVIEW

The Song of Igor's Campaign had an influence on Russian literature long before it was rediscovered in 1795. The manuscript known as the Zadonshchina, which commemorates the victory in 1380 of a Russian army over the Mongols, is based on the earlier epic in structure and poetic detail. The Zadonshchina was written about 1385.

In the modern era, *The Song of Igor's Campaign* has had an influence on Russian literature that is felt to the present day. It has been called a national classic, the greatest achievement of the Kievan period in Russian literature (1030–1240). The anonymous author has been called the equal of Alexander Pushkin (1799–1837), Russia's greatest poet. Pushkin himself had plans to translate the epic into modern Russian, although he never fulfilled his desire. Poets of the Romantic era were inspired by the *Song*'s lyrical beauty and depth of feeling. In the

This illustration depicts Moscow clergy as they would have looked at the time the work takes place.

nineteenth century, Nikolay Gogol used imagery taken directly from the *Song* in his short stories.

The reputation of the epic continued to grow in the twentieth century. Scholars spent much time on research, trying to produce the most accurate text possible. This was necessary because the one extant manuscript and the first printed version of 1800 contain many corrupt or obscure passages that have proved difficult to elucidate.

The Song of Igor's Campaign was first translated into English in 1902, by Leo Wiener, and again in 1915, by Leonard A. Magnus. Another translation appeared in 1943, by Bernard Guilbert Guerney, who wrote of the epic: "It is not only higher in poetic content but infinitely more readable than the *Nibelunglied* and the *Chanson de Roland* [*Song of Roland*]." Vladimir Nabokov made a fourth translation in 1960, and called the work "a magnificent literary masterpiece." Nabokov's literal translation is considered to be the most accurate, although Nabokov sacrifices some of the poetic devices of the original, such as the frequent alliteration.

In the Soviet Union, Soviet poet Pavel Antokolsky, as quoted by Kuskov, wrote in *Pravda* in 1938, "[*The Song of Igor's Campaign*] is an eternally flowering trunk extending branches laden with fruit into the future. Therefore we hear direct and indirect echoes of this work in many monuments of our culture and art."

In 1941, Russia was invaded by the German Nazis. During those dark times of World War II, *The Song of Igor's Campaign* struck a deep chord with the Russian people. They were inspired by the epic's call for Russia to unite to defeat the enemy.

It is unlikely that *The Song of Igor's Campaign* will ever fall into disfavor or lose the reverence with which the Russian people regard it. Many educated Russians know parts of it by heart. In 1980, Russian literary scholar Vladimir Kuskov called it an "immortal work of Russian and world literature." It has frequently been translated into modern Russian in many different forms of prose and poetry, including free verse and more structured forms of meter and rhyme.

CRITICISM

Bryan Aubrey

In the following essay, Aubrey discusses the epic in the light of mythologist Joseph Campbell's description of the "monomyth."

There has not been a great deal of detailed critical work in English on *The Song of Igor's Campaign*. It is often discussed fairly briefly in surveys of early Russian literature, and critics usually note the historical background, the poetic language and symbolism, and the political theme of Russian unity. Occasionally, a few parallels have been noted between *Song* and other medieval epics, such as the Western European *The Song of Roland* and the Germanic epic, the *Nibelunglied*.

However, *The Song of Igor's Campaign* differs from the typical medieval epic. *The Song of Roland* has its origins in events four centuries before the work was written; similarly, the historical events underlying the twelfth century *Nibelunglied* go back to the fifth and sixth centuries. Both of these epics contain miraculous or supernatural elements, such as the miraculous sword wielded by Siegfried to kill a dragon in the *Nibelungleid*, and the equally miraculous sword Durandal, as well as the magic horn, possessed by the knight Roland in the *Song of Roland*.

In contrast to these, *The Song of Igor's Campaign* remains much closer to historical events, having been written within a year or two of their occurrence. The author shows little interest in the kind of supernatural events that play an important role in other epics. There are few magical happenings in *The Song*, and those apply to a peripheral character from the past, Vseslav, who is used by the author as a bad example of princely conduct.

The Song of Igor's Campaign is also far less deeply imbued with Christian values and symbolism than the *Song of Roland*. In the latter work, Roland is helped by the direct intervention of the Archangel Gabriel; Charlemagne and his knights embody the Seven Cardinal Virtues of Christian moral theology, and the pagans embody the Seven Deadly Sins. In contrast, although *The Song of Igor's Campaign* was written two centuries after the conversion of Russia to Christianity, the Christianity it exhibits does not seem to be central to the author's way of interpreting the world. It is true that the Kumans are described as infidels and pagans, and the epic concludes with a passage praising the Christian knights, but the Christianity extends no deeper than that. The author's purpose is more political than religious, and the gods he prefers are the pagan gods of mythology, not the Christian God, who is mentioned only twice. And one of those references (in line 733) may be, according to translator Vladimir Nabokov, a corrupt passage, possibly altered by a Christian transcriber. The original word may have been *Stribog*, the god of the winds. Stribog is one of four pagan gods mentioned; the others are *Dazhbog*, the god of abundance, *Hors* or *Horus*, the god of the sun, and *Troyan*, whose function is not known but who is invoked four times.

Although there are differences between *The Song of Igor's Campaign* and other epics of the period, *Song* nonetheless contains certain elements that can be elucidated by an approach known as archetypal criticism. This is a method of analyzing literary texts in terms of recurring symbolic or structural patterns (archetypes) that appear in the literature and mythology of many diverse cultures. One of the best known archetypal approaches was developed by mythologist Joseph Campbell in his book, *The Hero With The Thousand Faces*, which was first published in 1949 and became a bestseller in the 1980s. Campbell noticed that many mythological stories, although different in surface details, followed a similar underlying pattern. He called this pattern the "monomyth." In the monomyth, a hero

WHAT DO I READ NEXT?

- Historian John Keegan's *The Face of Battle*, 1995, is a riveting account of what it must have been like for the soldiers who actually fought in a medieval battle. The example he uses is the battle of Agincourt in 1415 between English and French armies, in which the weapons used did not differ much from those used by the armies of Igor and the Kumans. Keegan also discusses the Battle of Waterloo in 1815 and the Battle of the Somme in 1916.

- Leo Tolstoy's *War and Peace* (1869), one of the greatest novels ever written, is another epic of war on Russian soil, describing how the Russians beat back the French invasion of 1812.

- *Borderland: A Journey through the History of Ukraine*, by Anna Reid (1999), is a journalist's exploration of present-day Ukraine that gives a picture of its tragic past and its hopes for the future.

- Serge A. Zenkovsky's *Medieval Russia's Epics, Chronicles, and Tales*, 1963, includes some extracts from the *Primary Chronicle* of Kievan Rus. The most interesting pieces are ''The Apostle Andrew Comes to Russia,'' ''The Founding of the City of Kiev,'' ''The Beginning of the Russian State and the Arrival of Rurik,'' ''Vladimir Christianizes Russia'' and ''Yaroslav the Wise.''

- *Slovo*, the newsletter of the Slavic Interest Group (vol. 5 issue 1, Fall, 1999), http://www.uwplatt.edu/~goldschp/news16.html [June 11, 2000], features an interesting article, ''Wild Animals in Ancient Rus,'' by Peotr Alexeivich Novgorodski. It describes the wild animals that were common in Europe's primeval forests a thousand years ago, including those mentioned in *The Song of Igor's Campaign*. Some of these are now extinct. The auroch, for example, was a wild ox that Igor's brother Vsevelod derived his nickname from (''Wild Bull''). It became extinct in the seventeenth century.

---

journeys to an unknown or unfamiliar realm, undergoes many trials, which may include a symbolic death and rebirth, and then returns to his society to bestow a boon on his fellow man.

Archetypal criticism and the concept of the monomyth are useful for understanding parts of *The Song of Igor's Campaign*. They may also explain something of why this epic has held the respect and won the admiration of readers over a long period of time—it sets out in symbolic fashion the process of human renewal or psychic growth.

First, the hero Igor hears what Campbell calls the "call to adventure." He journeys beyond the territories he is familiar with, leaving Russia far behind, as is conveyed in the refrain, "O Russian land, / you are already beyond the culmen." Since a *culmen* is a hill, this phrase conveys the sense that Igor and his men have completely cut themselves off from their own world. Indeed, the battle takes place "in the field unknown, midst the Kuman land" (276).

Before this, the author has linked Igor symbolically with the sun. Vsevolod refers to his brother as "one bright brightness" (73) and only eighteen lines later, as the warriors assemble, Igor notices that the "bright sun" is eclipsed. This temporary "death" of the sun foreshadows the fate of Igor, who is like a sun to his men. The metaphor of Igor as sun is continued in the short battle scenes. He and Vsevolod are "two suns"; they are "crimson pillars" that are extinguished and veiled with darkness as they sink into the sea. These are images that suggest the setting of the sun on the horizon. Light is covered by darkness.

It is remarkable that Igor now disappears from the action of the epic completely, until his escape over three hundred lines later. The author does not disclose his fate. In terms of the monomyth, Igor is

> In the monomyth, a hero journeys to an unknown or unfamiliar realm, undergoes many trials, which may include a symbolic death and rebirth, and then returns to his society to bestow a boon on his fellow man."

in the condition Campbell describes as "the belly of the whale," where he is completely enveloped in the unknown. This is a symbolic loss of self, a sleep, or even a death, that contains the seeds of the hero's rebirth. Seen in this light, the simple phrase "Igor sleeps,"—which appears when the author finally returns to Igor—suggests a significance beyond its immediate context. Igor may be asleep, but he is now ready to wake up: "Igor keeps vigil" is the very next line.

When the hero is ready to return to his society, the monomyth often features what Campbell calls the magic flight, in which the hero receives supernatural aid on his journey home. Sometimes the flight includes a sea journey at night.

Igor's escape resembles a magic flight. His relationship to natural and supernatural forces clearly undergoes a change at this point in the narrative. The winds whip up at night, and God (perhaps it is the god of the wind) shows him how he can return to Russia. This is a contrast to the adverse way the wind blew during the battle, which helped to ensure Igor's defeat. Now, as Igor makes his break for freedom, he is more at one with nature than he had been before, and similes drawn from nature (ermine, duck, wolf, falcon) are used thick and fast to describe him. Swimming across rivers plays a role in his escape, and he also engages in a charming dialogue with the River Donets, in which each praises the other. This relaxed exchange on the banks of the river is quite different from Igor's calamitous experience at the swift-flowing River Kayala where he met his defeat. And nature has even more to offer Igor as he tries to escape his pursuers. Magpies and ravens fall silent, enabling the woodpeckers to guide Igor to the river with their tapping.

All this is suggestive of rebirth, an effect reinforced by Igor's destination when he finally reaches Russia. He does not return to his home in Novgorod-Seversk. Instead, he goes straight to Kiev, the capital city of Russia, where he is to present himself at the "paternal golden throne" (736). This is the throne of Prince Svyatoslav. In the epic, Svyatoslav is presented as the ideal ruler, who rebukes Igor for his rashness and his willingness to put the quest for personal glory above his duty to Russia and the other princes, especially Svyatoslav himself. The implication of Igor's journey to Kiev is that during his captivity—his time "in the belly of the whale"— Igor has learned from his mistake. Now he recognizes where his duty lies, and he seeks to make amends. And as Igor reenters Russia, the author appropriately returns to the sun image, which is also a metaphor for the prince himself: "The sun shines in the sky: / Prince Igor is on Russian soil" (841–42).

Igor's rebirth, then, consists of his growth beyond pride and personal ambition into a leader who accepts his place in the social hierarchy and who knows how to act in a way that brings the support of nature. In terms of the monomyth, this is the boon that Igor brings to his people. The author points out that the body cannot function without the head, and so a people cannot function without their leader (835–40). It follows from this that the influence of the head is felt throughout the body, just as the influence of the sun is felt throughout the body of the earth. Now that Igor, Russia's son/sun, has risen once more, his own growth can, or should be, Russia's too.

Not all the components of the monomyth are present in *The Song of Igor's Campaign*, but examining the epic within that framework shows that it possesses an inner, psychological dimension alongside the political one.

Source: Bryan Aubrey, for *Epics for Students*, Gale, 2001.

Tatiana Fefer

In the following essay, Tatiana Fefer claims that Slovo O Polku Igoreve (Song of Igor) *is not an epic, but a "sophisticated lyrical work."*

The *Slovo o polku Igoreve* is not only the most famous work of medieval Russian literature, but after nearly two hundred years of study it remains among the most mysterious. Much of its symbolism has never been satisfactorily interpreted. Many of its "dark" places continue to remain obscure and hopelessly out of reach, and as a result, the author's original idea remains open to considerable speculation. Although the *Slovo* is still generally identified as an epic, some scholars, such as D. S. Lichačev (Lichačev 1978) have in recent decades began to modify the traditional views, recognizing the significance of the work's lyrical undertone. Unfortunately, however, even this change of viewpoint has failed to bring about any satisfactory re-interpretation.

The aim of this paper is to continue where Lichačev left off and to demonstrate that the *Slovo* is not an epic, as it is generally believed, but a highly sophisticated lyrical work. This study offers a new and challenging interpretation of the text, made possible by paying greater attention to the work's poetic idea and composition and by taking a closer look at its author's mode of reasoning and philosophical outlook; it also brings into focus small and often overlooked details of the text which prove to be highly significant.

One basic error that most scholars commit when dealing with the *Slovo o polku Igoreve* is their nearly unavoidable adoption of a patronizing attitude toward its ancient author. Almost unanimously, they see him as a talented but somewhat confused man who cannot quite decide whether to call his work a tale or a song, and in what exact manner he should sing it. In the past two hundred years, many men of letters recognized the superior poetic talent of the author but saw an apparent lack of logic in the development of the plot, and as a result took up the task of helping him with the tale, often rearranging words and whole passages, and supplying the old author with their own literary ideas along the way. Numerous translations and interpretations, both in prose and in verse, produced the work we have today—obscure, nearly devoid of meaning, absurd in places, and as this study will attempt to show, with its original essence all but lost.

To gain insight into the poetic idea of the *Slovo*, it is important to take on a willingness to see its author as a sophisticated and complex poetic mind, capable of creating stylistic nuances of both irony and cynicism, whose seemingly illogical composition of the original text is deliberately and purposefully designed.

In my reading I used a Musin-Puškin text, as well as its Ekaterininskij copy recognized by many as the least damaged versions of the work. Both

> "...*Slovo* may be much less muddled and incomprehensible than we are taught to believe; and the key to a new understanding lies not in rearranging words and the sequence of events, but simply in one's willingness to trust the logic and wisdom of the author, in whose tale a historical event of the ill-fated campaign of Igor' serves as a stylistic metaphor for the esoteric struggle within the poet's psyche."

appear in Gudzij's edition. The English translation of the *Slovo* is adopted in part from Serge Zenkovsky. My comments are placed in square brackets.

The key to understanding this complex work lies mainly in its opening passage, in which the seemingly insignificant particle "bo"... translated in modern Russian as "ved'" ("it is known" or "it is believed") provides a stylistic nuance of irony which has escaped the attention of most scholars, but is of particular importance. ... With this detail in mind, the opening passage can be briefly interpreted as follows:

> Wouldn't it be nice, brethren, to commence the grievous tale of Igor's campaign according to the conventional style? To begin following the accepted stories of our time, and not according to the whim of Bojan? For he [it is believed] is a sorcerer [and that means he is not to be entirely trusted]; when he wants to compose a song, [they say, he can do magical things:] he can soar over a tree with his thoughts, run as a grey wolf over the land, fly as an eagle below the clouds. [And while doing these magical things,] he would recall the feuds of former times. Then [they say] he would let loose ten falcons upon a flock of swans [...]. [But, in fact, all this is not true. He was neither a sorcerer nor did he do any of these magical things. In reality,] brethren, Bojan would [simply] lay his wise

fingers upon the living strings and they would sound on their own…

Oh Bojan, if you sang about this campaign while soaring like a nightingale over the tree of *wisdom*, if you used your *mind* to fly under the clouds […], then you would sing Igor's song like this: "[…] [i.e., in a very loud, harmonious and heroic fashion. But Bojan did not use his *rational mind* or *wisdom* to create a conventional epic, instead, he followed his *feelings* and free poetic *inspiration*.]

As a result, instead of the traditionally expected picture of glory, he sees a nightmare, a dark and disturbing dream, deep within his soul. His poetic creation is not the harmonious song of a nightingale but a cacophony of mysterious sounds. In his song, . . . jackdaws caw in the dark, foxes bark, eagles screech, frightening battle cries of the devil's children are mixed with the groaning of the earth itself; and Div, a mysterious bird-like deity, cries its ominous warnings. Even when the poet hears trumpets, they sound not gloriously, but mournfully, after the lonely death of prince Izjaslav.

Thus, since the irony of [his utterance] was not taken into account, the author's artistic method was misunderstood both by his contemporaries and by modern scholars alike. Both compare him to a sorcerer, which he quite obviously was not, and both fail to recognize in *wisdom* and *thought* the opposition to *free feeling* of one's heart. It appears that *wisdom* and *rational thinking*, in Bojan's understanding, are connected with the generally accepted and easily recognizable artistic clichés, loud and heroic; while pure artistic inspiration, on the other hand, is heard in the esoteric melody of the strings sounding on their own and following nobody's rules.

Therefore, in addition to the obvious plot, the author of the *Slovo* touches the purely poetic dilemma: can a poet let his inspiration roam freely (in a pagan fashion) or does he have to rationally choose what to think and what to feel? According to the introduction, the essence of the *Slovo* could be seen as a lament of an independent poetic mind trying to come to terms with rigid rules, both artistic and moral. The underlying theme of the work could be seen as a reflection of the inner struggle between the rational and the intuitive, between mind and body, between pagan values and Christian values. The latter would also explain the seemingly casual combination of pagan and Christian elements in the work, which proved to be difficult to interpret for many scholars. Thus, the explicit story of the historically-based battle of Igor' can be seen as a mere

outer surface of this multi-layered inner conflict, concealed by symbolism.

Another important aspect of the *Slovo* is that many of its structural and stylistic elements suggest a dream—rather than a true-to-life recounting of the historical events—lying at the centre of the poem. The "unreality" of the setting is stressed by the ever-present atmosphere of darkness that envelops virtually the entire work, in which supposedly historical events unfold without any apparent chronological order. Indeed, the author himself points at this dream-like state as the source of his vision of the battle of Igor, the picture and sounds of which are evoked in the poet's imagination at the break of dawn. . .

. . .In the dark of night or in twilight, in a solitary state between dream and awakening, it seems that dark and uncensored feelings roam within the poet's psyche, following their own logic. When the rational mind is eclipsed by a dream-like state, these feelings sometimes transcend into the realm of the subconscious and find their expressions in pure symbols. Thus, it is interesting to point out that in the *Slovo*, the sun never fully appears in the course of Igor's campaign; the mysterious atmosphere of darkness, on the other hand, is repeatedly stressed by the author. In keeping with this transcendental state, the dark tale is not presented by the direct succession of events; the themes and scenes interchange chaotically; events from the past, future and present casually come together, while the poet perceives their course as natural, seemingly unaware of anything unusual or illogical in their manifestation. Such a psychological perception of events most often takes place in the realm of dreams, when a restless mind tries to sort out past occurrences or project itself into the future in search of answers to its own anxieties.

Closely interwound, both the obvious and the esoteric plot of the *Slovo* deal essentially with the same issues of moral and spiritual doubts. Apparently, one of the key dilemmas facing both the poet and his hero is the difficult task of choosing between two sets of moral values, Christian and pre-Christian, and abandoning one in favour of another. The irreconcilable contradictions within the poet's psyche and his inability to adequately deal with the problem, it seems, deeply affect his consciousness, and as a result, become projected into the plot. In the beginning of the *Slovo* the author sets out to tell the whole Christian history of Russia . . .but in fact, he cannot find a single happy event to tell about—only feuds, wars and hunger. The Christian God, it seems, did not bring the promised peace. Left alone with his feelings, the author cannot suppress his frustation and clear longing for the old days when they were all. . .children of the sun-god, strong and united; and he is looking for the answer to the question of why this life ended. Perhaps the old gods themselves are staging their revenge for being abandoned: "Ni chytru, ni gorazdu, ni pticju gorazdu suda božia ne minuti." Possessing an uncommon mind, Bojan obviously has the ability to see sorrowful events coming long before they take place or before anyone else can see them, and the pagan feelings of bad premonitions and dark symbols make the outcome of the events evident to him before they actually happen. . . (ironically, the same pagan gods, summoned by Jaroslavna, later help the hero to escape).

It is quite obvious that within his heart the poet bitterly blames others for his troubled state. His feelings tell him explicitly that the princes and their feuds are responsible for the lost happiness of the bygone days. . . This idea of doom and longing for the past is further emphasized by Svjatoslav's lament, in which the hero weeps for his vanished youth that can never be returned. In Svjatoslav's dream, he blames the treachery of [those in his dreams], whoever they were, for his sorrow: they appeared as friends, but in reality they were enemies and should never have been trusted. Symbolically, they dress him in a black shroud, they pour for him blue wine mixed with sorrow, from their empty quivers they pour large pearls and comfort him. Although the exact literary identity of [those in his dreams] has never been clearly established by the researchers of the *Slovo* (most often they are referred to as *foreigners* or *translators*), their historical Greek connection is mentioned in one of Nestor's chronicles. . .

. . .Consequently, one cannot entirely discount the idea of a subtle connection between the acceptance of Christianity by Russia from the Greeks and the symbolism of Svjatoslav's dream, which shows the hero's initial mistake in judgement and later regret. This supposition would also logically correspond to the general idea of the *Slovo*. Significantly, in his call for help, Svjatoslav appeals to the princes with the voice of the old gods. . .

. . .Characteristically, the struggle of the princes among themselves. . .presents a certain parallel to the inner struggle within the poet's psyche—the irreconcilable contradictions between the consciously adopted Christian moral values and the concealed (yet quite apparent to the reader) inner pagan desires. Thinly veiled by symbolism, the erotic undertone of Igor's passion is easily recognizable. Perhaps it is also evoked by the old gods who make Igor' forget the Christian values which teach one to resist carnal temptations. The hero's inner fire is translated in the text into a symbolic obsessive need to drink water from a helmet or to break his lance at the end of the enemy's field. . .

. . .The words "pochot" and "iskusiti" traditionally have erotic connotations in the Russian language. Consequently, Igor's statement. . .which was found illogical by some scholars because it was pronounced by Igor' before he left for the war, appears clearer considering that Igor's inner battle was all but lost. He was, indeed, a prisoner of his own body. . . .

. . .Regardless of the divine warnings, they cannot turn back. Unwittingly, perhaps, the poet is questioning the very virtues of conventional morality. His apparent cynical attitude finds its stylistic expression in the text in the lament of the Russian wives who casually equate husbands with money. . .

. . .Ironically, "mysliju smysliti" and "dumoju sdumati" (of the dear beloved) is a tautology referring to a rational, cerebral process, while the intuitive affectionate gesture of a gentle touch is reserved for gold and silver.

Free-roaming feelings uncensored by the rational mind apparently bring uneasiness and fear to the poet in the images of beasts, mysterious birds, nightmarish chases, bloody scenes, strange voices and sounds from unknown sources. The voice of Div or the devil's children resound in the twilight atmosphere of lonely contemplation. Typical of a distressed human being, the poet's uneasy thoughts wander chaotically from one subject to another and find their parallel in the doomed fate of Russia or in frustration concerning Igor and all his relatives, which, perhaps, reflects Bojan's personal feelings of guilt and a wish to blame somebody else for his own pagan weaknesses. . . .

. . .Seeing the *Slovo* in this light also clarifies perhaps the darkest and most often misinterpreted part of the whole work—the sentence just prior to its glorious conclusion. . .

. . .Bojan expressed his wishes to be like the old-time bard of Svjatoslav [...] [because he realized that] it is difficult for the head to be without shoulders [i.e., to have only rational mind without a heart], but it is

Artist's rendering of medieval Russian nobles like those in the story.

wretched to have a body without a head [i.e., to be ruled entirely by your emotions and physical desires without control of the conscious mind].

This appears to be the main idea of the entire work and it brings the *Slovo* to its surprising but logical finale: in the bright morning sunshine, Igor, although Christian asceticism was not in his nature, nevertheless goes to church, perhaps with the purpose of asking God to forgive him for his sins and give him renewed inner strength.

It can be concluded, therefore, that the *Slovo* may be much less muddled and incomprehensible than we are taught to believe; and the key to a new understanding lies not in rearranging words and the sequence of events, but simply in one's willingness to trust the logic and wisdom of the author, in whose tale a historical event of the ill-fated campaign of Igor' serves as a stylistic metaphor for the esoteric struggle within the poet's psyche.

Source: Tatiana Fefer, "The *Slovo O Polku Igoreve*: A Poetic Dream," in *Russian Literature,* Vol. 42, 1997, pp. 17–24.

Robert Mann

The author of this essay, Robert Mann, explores the meaning of the beginning stanzas of the Igor Tale.

No satisfactory solution has yet been proposed for the problems presented by the following passage near the beginning of the *Slovo o polku Igoreve*:

> Let us, brothers, begin
> this tale
> from old Vladimir
> to the present-day Igor,
> who pulled out his mind with his fortitude
> and sharpened it with the valor of his heart,
> filled with the battle spirit,
> led his valiant regiments
> against the Polovtsian land
> for the Russian land.

Why does the narrator propose to begin "from Vladimir" when Vladimir plays no role at the beginning of the tale? And what is meant by "beginning from Vladimir to Igor"?

Likhachev's argument that this line defines the chronological limits of the events dealt with in the tale is weak in at least two respects. First, Vladimir is mentioned only in passing, and the *Igor Tale* can hardly be said to deal with him. Second, no similar syntactic constructions in Old Russian have been found to support Likhachev's idea.

Taking words from a passage in the *Zadonshchina* and from a similar passage in the *Slovo o pogibeli russkoi zemli,* the only known literary work before the *Zadonshchina* that closely resembles the *Igor Tale* stylistically, Roman Jakobson reconstructs the passage this way:

> Let us, brothers, begin this tale,
> because the princes have been sad for the
> Russian land from old Vladimir
> to the present-day Igor. ...

Although I think Jakobson is correct in viewing the lines in question as defective, the line he chooses to insert is unjustified both stylistically and textologically.

These lines are linked only by their position before an *ot ... do* construction and by thematic similarity. There are no lexical parallels between the two lines to justify Jakobson's choice of words. In addition, the subordinate conjunction *zane zhe* ("because") has no place in the *Igor Tale*, a paratactic work with very little subordination. As a subordinating conjunction of reason, *bo* ("for") is used throughout the tale.

One can deduce a more likely reconstruction if one compares the unintelligible lines of the *Igor Tale* with the related *Zadonshchina* passage as it appears in all of the copies and in a more complete context.

In three of four copies, the *ot ... do* construction contains a number which gives the line a clear meaning. Only copy *K-B*, like the *Igor Tale*, lacks the number and is as meaningless in this respect as the *Igor Tale* passage.

The line from the *Slovo o pogibeli russkoi zemli* on which Jakobson bases his reconstruction was cited above.

The problem with basing a reconstruction on the final lines of this text is that the work is probably only a fragment of a larger composition. The final lines may be incomplete, and the words "A v ty dni bolezn' krestiianom" ("But in these days there is trouble for Christians") may express a complete thought independent of the passage following, which contains the *ot ... do* construction. Either a number or a phrase establishing spatial or temporal boundaries, as in the *Zadonshchina*, may be missing in the manuscript. That this is indeed the case is suggested by a passage in the sixteenth-century *Stepennaia kniga* which is styled after the *Slovo o pogibeli russkoi zemli* or a related work.

As in the *Zadonshchina*, the *ot ... do* construction serves to connect historical reference points. The passages differ only in that a time span is used as a connector in the *Zadonshchina*, while the *Stepennaia kniga* focuses on the place from which the princes rule. This suggests that the mysterious passage in the *Igor Tale* lacks a phrase or number specifying spatial or temporal boundaries. Because it is more closely related to the passage in the *Zadonshchina* than to the one in the *Stepennai kniga*, it is likely that the *Igor Tale* formerly contained a number at this point in the narrative, as in the *Zadonshchina*. Letters with a bar, or *titlo*, were used in Old Russian to represent numbers. They could easily become unintelligible if they were copied poorly or if a scribe forgot to include the *titlo*. This could eventually lead to the deletion of the number, which is most likely what has happened in the *Igor Tale* as well as in copy *K-B* of the *Zadonshchina*. Before it was distorted, the *Igor Tale* passage probably read:

> Let us, brothers, begin
> this tale.
> From old Vladimir it was 170 years
> to the present-day Igor,
> who pulled out his mind with his fortitude. ...

Compare the opening words of the Primary Chronicle: "Se nachnem" povest' siiu" ("Now let us begin this tale"). These words are followed by a lengthy passage which establishes geographical reference points. Later the chronicle sets up chronological reference points with a long series of *ot ... do* constructions, which are preceded by the words: "temzhe otsele pochnem i chisla polozhim ("thus let us begin from here and place dates").

It is worth noting that neither of the two numbers contained in the *Zadonshchina* copies exactly corresponds to the number of years which elapsed between the Battle on the Kalka and the Battle of Kulikovo (one hundred fifty-seven years). However, the number 170, which appears in copy *U*, exactly coincides with the number of years between the death of Vladimir the Great in 1015 and Igor's campaign. This even points to the remote possibility that the choice of numbers in the *Zadonshchina* might have been influenced by the *Igor Tale*.

Source: Robert Mann, "A Note on the Text of the *Igor Tale*," in *Slavic Review*, Vol. 39, No. 2, June, 1980, pp. 281–285.

SOURCES

Anonymous, *The Song of Igor's Campaign*, translated by Vladimir Nabokov, Random House, 1960.

Campbell, Joseph, *The Hero with a Thousand Faces*, 2d ed., Princeton University Press, 1968.

Cizevskij, Dmitrij, *History of Russian Literature: From the Eleventh Century to the End of the Baroque*, Moulton & Co., 1960.

Guerney, Bernard Guilbert, *A Treasury of Russian Literature*, Vanguard Press, 1943.

Kuskov, Vladimir, *A History of Old Russian Literature*, Progress Publishers, 1980.

Zenkovsky, Serge A., ed., *Medieval Russia's Epics, Chronicles, and Tales*, E. P. Dutton, 1963.

FURTHER READING

Lindstrom, Thais S., *A Concise History of Russian Literature*, Volume 1, New York University Press, 1966.
> The first chapter contains a useful account of the origins of Kievan Rus, and gives an informative overview of *The Song of Igor's Campaign*.

Mirsky, D. S., *A History of Russian Literature*, edited and abridged by Francis J. Whitfield, Alfred A. Knopf, 1973.
> A good one-volume history of Russian literature from the earliest days to the twentieth century.

Thompson, John M., *Russia and the Soviet Union*, 4th edition, Westview Press, 1998.
> The first chapter, "Ancient Russia and the Kievan State," gives a good overview of the development of Kievan Rus and its political and social structure.

Táin Bó Cúailnge

ANONYMOUS

1185

The setting of the *Táin Bó Cúailnge* has tradition-ally been identified as the first century A.D. The earliest extant manuscript of any version of the work was written in the early twelfth century in the great monastery of Clonmacnoise overlooking the Shannon River. Sometime between these two dates, the *Táin Bó Cúailnge* came into existence.

It has been a basic assumption of Irish literary studies that the *Táin Bó Cúailnge* was written to be the *Aeneid* of Ireland. Nevertheless, despite con-tinuous references to the characters and events of the *Táin Bó Cúailnge*, it is probably true that the stories of the Irish hero Finn Mac Cumhghaill (Finn Mac Cool), his son Oisín, and his warrior band, the Fianna, were more popular until the nineteenth century. Then, Irish nationalism interacting with contemporary scholarship began to look to the *Táin Bó Cúailnge* as the major source for a sense of Irish identity. National and cultural worth was judged against the classical past and the dominant English language culture. It was important that Ireland had a vernacular epic.

The Irish literary revival at the turn of the nineteenth and twentieth centuries introduced the *Táin Bó Cúailnge* to a world audience. Lady Au-gusta Gregory, patroness of the young W. B. Yeats, published retellings of the stories clustered around the hero of the *Táin Bó Cúailnge*, Cúchulainn. Yeats wrote a series of plays based on the stories of

Cúchulainn and Deirdre (Dierdriu) and the *Táin Bó Cúailnge* entered the western literary heritage.

AUTHOR BIOGRAPHY

The twelfth-century manuscript called the *Book of Leinster* preserves a note stating that at one time none of the poets of Ireland knew the full *Táin Bó Cúailnge*. Two pupils of the poet Senchán Torpéist set out to find a copy that had been taken out of Ireland to exchange for a copy of the *Cuilmenn*, the Irish name for the *Etymologiae* of Isidore of Seville, the greatest digest of learning of the early middle ages. On their way, they happened upon the grave of Fergus, one of the great heroes of the Ulster cycle of tales. His spirit came and recited the whole *Táin Bó Cúailnge* to them. The note's scribe, however, added an alternative version: some people said Senchán himself learned the whole story from some of the descendants of Fergus adding, "this seems reasonable."

The existence even in such a note is characteristic of the history and scholarship of *Táin Bó Cúailnge*. The *Táin Bó Cúailnge* survives in several versions. The *Book of the Dun Cow*, or *Lebor na hUidre*, copied in the twelfth century and the *Yellow Book of Lecan*, copied in the late fourteenth century preserve an older, shorter version, perhaps as old as the seventh or eighth century. This version is often described by scholars as 'mutilated' and 'interpolated' with alternative and sometimes contradictory versions of events. Other scholars suggest that these 'additions' are the author's own attempt to acknowledge variant material, and that this early version should be seen as a collection of materials relating to the great cattle raid of the Cooley peninsula. The *Book of Leinster*, copied in the twelfth century, preserves a fuller, more unified version. The compiler of this later version of the *Táin Bó Cúailnge* attempted to clear up inconsistencies and repetitions and produce a polished narrative. The elaborate style, however, suffers in comparison with the older version, despite its variants and additions.

There is no real consensus as to exactly when the original author of the *Táin Bó Cúailnge* wrote, or even if it is essentially the version that survives in the *Book of the Dun Cow*. Older scholars pushed the composition back as far as they might on linguistic grounds, but recently it has been strongly suggested that the *Táin Bó Cúailnge* was consciously composed to have the feel of an ancient work.

There are good modern editions with translations of both the *Book of the Dun Cow* and *Book of Leinster* by Cecile O'Rahilly. In 1969, the poet Thomas Kinsella produced a translation of the *Táin Bó Cúailnge* working from the earliest version with additions from the later versions. It is this version that is generally used by non-specialists.

PLOT SUMMARY

How Conchobor was Born and Became King of Ulster
Nes asked the druid Cathbad what the hour was lucky for. He replied it was lucky for conceiving a king, and swore that a son conceived then would be famous in Ireland forever. Nes and Cathbad therefore had relations. The son she bore was Conchobor. Cathbad raised him.

Fergus was King of Ulster, and he wished to marry Nes. She would only accept him if he allowed her son Conchobor to be king for a year. Conchobor was allowed to become king for a year, but Nes was clever. At the end of the year, she had persuaded the Ulstermen to not accept Fergus back.

How the Men of Ulster were Cursed with Labor Pains
Crunniuc mac Agnomain was a wealthy widower. One day, a fine woman walked into his house and stayed. The place flourished under her care. One day, there was great fair in Ulster. Crunniuc went, but the woman, being pregnant, did not. She warned him to be cautious in his speech, but he boasted at the fair that his wife could run outrun the king's chariot horses. The king immediately demanded she do so. The woman was fetched. She begged the crowd for compassion because she was going into labor, but to no avail. She told the king her name was Macha and that a curse would come on Ulster for what she was forced to do. She raced the chariot. As they reached the finish, she gave birth to a son and a daughter shrieking that every man who heard her scream would have labor pains when Ulster needed them most. All the men of Ulster there that day and their sons for nine generations after suffered the curse, except Cúchulainn and his father.

The Story of Deirdriu

Cathbad predicted that the daughter of the king's storyteller Fedlimid would be the most beautiful woman in the world and the cause of death in Ulster. The warriors wanted to kill her, but Conchobor had her raised in secrecy until she should be old enough to marry him. The girl, Deirdriu, met Noisiu, Uisliu's son, however, and fell in love with him. They ran off together with his brothers and eventually settled in Scotland. There they were threatened by the king who wanted Deirdriu himself. Conchobor offered them safe conduct home. Fergus, Dubthach, and Conchobor's son Cormac went surety (to stand in promise) for him. Conchobor had the brothers killed, Noisiu by the spear of Eogan mac Durthacht, who also killed Fergus's son Fiacha when he tried to protect Noisiu. Fergus, Dubthach and Cormac fled to the court of Connacht. Deirdriu killed herself.

The Birth of Cúchulainn

Deichtine, Conchobor's sister, was driving her brother's chariot as they hunted a great flock of destructive birds. When night fell, they came to a little house where a woman was about to give birth. Deichtine helped her deliver a baby boy. When morning came, everything had disappeared except the baby. Deichtine took the baby home with her, but he died. Deichtine was heartbroken. One of her servants brought her a drink of water. While she drank, a tiny creature flew into her mouth. She swallowed before she noticed it. That night, she dreamed a man came to her. He said he was Lug mac Ethnenn, a prince of the *Síde*, one of the magical beings who live in the fairy hills. The boy she had nursed was his son. She was now carrying him. He was to be called Sétanta. It soon became obvious Deichtine was pregnant so her brother married her off to Sualdam mac Roich. She was so upset at marrying him pregnant that she vomited up the being she had drunk. Soon, she was pregnant again by Sualdam. She had a boy. They named him Sétanta. Although the tradition of Cúchullain's birth is contradictory, a rational explanation for his birth has never been expected.

The Pillow Talk

Medb and Ailill, the queen and king of Connacht, were talking in bed about who between them was the richer. Their possessions were counted; they were equal except that Ailill had a beautiful bull, Finbennach, the calf of one of Medb's cows that had gone over to Ailill's herd rather than belong to a woman. Medb asked Mac Roth if there was any bull its equal in Ireland. There was only one: the Donn Cúailnge in Ulster. Mac Roth was sent to borrow the bull for a year with the offer of a generous reward. Dáire, its owner, was pleased to lend the bull on such generous terms. Unfortunately, one of the messengers drank too much and announced that if the bull had not been lent, they would have taken it by force. Dáire was enraged and ordered them to leave.

The Muster of the Connacht Army

Ailill and Medb muster their army and wait for a favorable omen before setting out. The poetess and prophetess Feidelm tells Medb that the army will suffer enormous losses at the hands of Cúchulainn, repeating again and again, "I see them bloody. I see them red."

The Army Encounters Cúchulainn

Fergus, given command of the army, leads it astray to give the Ulstermen time to recover from their curse. Cúchulainn feels the imminent approach of the army and asks his father, Sualdam, to warn the people. Playing for time, Cúchulainn leaves a challenge to the Connacht army, but the army circumvents it. Again, he attempts to slow them down with a challenge: he placed a forked branch in the river and impaled the heads of four of the advancing warriors on it with a challenge that the army cannot pass until someone pulls the branch out with one hand. Fergus meets the challenge.

The Boyhood Deeds of Cúchulainn

Ailill asks Fergus Cúchlainn's age. When told that Cúchulainn is only seventeen, Medb scoffs that he could not be much of a warrior yet. Fergus recounts his boyhood deeds, including the story behind his name change. As a small boy, he killed a fierce watchdog that attacked him, and then guarded its owner's property until a new one could be reared. Hence came the name Cú Chulainn 'the hound of Culann.'

Cúchulainn's Challenge and the First Series of Combats

Cúchulainn puts a log in the army's path with a challenge that they dare not continue until a warrior leaps it in a chariot. Cúchulainn reluctantly kills his boyhood friend Fráech who had been sent against him. Fergus leaps the oak with his own chariot. Cúchulainn fights and kills all who come against him. The army pillages Ulster. Ailill suspects that Fergus and Medb are having an affair, and he sends his chariot driver to spy on them. He finds them sleeping together and steals Fergus's sword from its sheath. He returns with the sword to Ailill and confirms his suspicions. Ailill seems pleased by this: 'She is justified. She does it to keep his help on the raid.' He then tells the charioteer to keep the sword safe.

Bargain of the Single Combats

Cúchulainn takes his stand at the river Cronn, calling upon air, earth, and the river to help him. Maine, the son of Ailill and Medb, and thirty horsemen reach the river and Cúchulainn kills them all. These massacres continue until Fergus and Lugaid mac Nois Allchomaig organize terms of engagement favorable to Cúchulainn.

The Escape of the Bull, the Bargain of the Single Combats, and the Morrígan

Medb sets out with a third of the army to find the bull and lay waste to Ulster. Cúchulainn meets her cowherd Buide mac Báin with the stolen Bull of Cooley. Cúchulainn kills Buide, but Medb's men get the bull to their camp. Cúchulainn fights warrior after warrior. In the midst of his struggles, the Morrígan, in the shape of a young woman, comes and offers herself to him. He spurns her. She swears to hinder him. He promises to wound her. She will carry the marks forever unless he gives her a blessing. He continues to fight whatever champions they send against him. When Lóch, his foster brother fights him, three times the Morrígan hinders him and is wounded. Fergus encourages Briciu to taunt the flagging Cúchulainn to keep his anger up in the fight. Cúchulainn feels his own need for help. He kills Lóch, but is exhausted. The Morrígan appears now as an old woman milking a cow. He asks for a drink of milk. She gives him three and with each he blesses her and she is healed. Medb organizes an ambush, but Cúchulainn kills the warriors. She offers her daughter to him, but he cuts the girl's hair and leaves her on a pillar stone.

Respite for Cúchulainn

Laeg spots a fine-looking man coming towards them. Cúchulainn recognizes him as one of the *síde*. The man identifies himself as Cúchulainn's father from the fairy hills, Lug mac Ethnenn. Cúchulainn admits, "My wounds are heavy. It is time they were let heal." Lug tells him to sleep. He tends his son's

wounds. While Cúchulainn sleeps, the boys of Ulster come to his aid and are, to Cúchulainn's sorrow, slaughtered after a brave fight. Cúchulainn orders out his sickle chariot, 'every angle and corner, front and rear was a tearing place,' and in a frenzy, rages through the army encamped against him.

The Single Combat of Ferdia and Cúchulainn and the Fight of Cethern

An Ulster warrior, Oengus, comes and hurls stones at the Connacht army until he is slain. Trying to find another warrior to fight Cúchulainn, Medb approaches Fergus. He refuses to fight his foster son. However, he faces Cúchulainn, asking him to retreat a step before him if he gives ground at another time when asked by Cúchulainn. He agrees. There is more fighting in which Cúchulainn is victorious. Fíacha mac Fir Febe, an Ulster exile, goes to Cúchulainn's aid in one fight. Medb works on Cúchulainn's foster brother and closest friend, Ferdia, telling him Cúchulainn has slandered him. The two fight over four days. Finally, Cúchulainn gives Ferdia a mortal wound, but laments over his lost friend. The Ulster warrior Cethern arrives, attacks the army and then retreats to Cúchulainn with a litany of his wounds. He kills doctor after doctor until Conchobor's doctor Fingin arrives. He examines his wounds from a safe distance, and tells him he can either stay still for a year and live or have three days of strength to fight before dying. He chooses the latter and dies fighting.

Fintan and the Death of Finnabair

Fintan, father of Cethern, arrives to avenge his son. His other son is taken prisoner and returned on condition that Fintan not attack Ailill's army until the final battle. Rochobad Rigderg arrives to help Cúchulainn, but Ailill arranges a trap for Rochobad, baited with Finnabair, who has told her parents how much she loves him. Her parents agree to allow Finnabair and Rochobad to sleep together if Rochobad gives them a truce until Conchobor arrives.

The Warning of Súaldaim and the Muster of the Men of Ulster

Súaldaim goes to his son's aid. Cúchulainn sends him to warn the Ulstermen to come immediately if they hope to punish the invaders. Súaldaim reports "men are slain, women carried off, and cattle driven away." He falls and is decapitated by his own shield, but his head repeats the warning. Conchobor vows to crush the raiders and bring back their booty.

Ailill asks Mac Roth if he can see the Ulstermen approaching. He says they are coming on like a lightning filled mist. He goes out again and sees the Ulster camp and comes back with descriptions of the men and troops he has seen. Fergus identifies them for the king. A truce is arranged until the next morning. The Morrígan appears to prophesy the coming slaughter.

The Battle of the Armies and of the Two Bulls

The battle begins. Ailill and Medb beg Fergus to join the fight and give him back his sword. He cuts through the Ulstermen and confronts Conchobor, but is restrained by Cormac who begs him to remember his own people. Cúchulainn leaves his sick bed, arms and confronts Fergus, demanding that he keep his promise to retreat before him. Fergus takes the Ulster exiles out of the battle. The men of Leinster and Munster follow them. Cúchulainn catches up with Medb, but spares her. Fergus observes that the outcome of the battle is what one would expect when the herd follows a mare.

The following morning the survivors gather to watch the fight between the two bulls. The Donn Cúailnge defeats Finnbennach, littering the landscape with pieces of Finnbennach's body. The places where they fight give rise to place names (places where important events occurred). The Donn Cúailnge finally dies at Druim Tairb.

CHARACTERS

Aengus

An Ulster warrior who turned aside the whole Connacht army, pelting them with flagstones. The Connacht army eventually overwhelmed and killed him.

Aife

A woman warrior living on the island of Britain. When Cúchulainn defeats her, he spares her life on the understanding that she will give hostages to his teacher Scáthach and bear him a son. She is to name the boy Connla and send him to Cúchulainn when he is big enough to wear the gold thumb ring Cúchulainn leaves for him. He tells her the boy must never reveal his name to any man, never give way to any man, and never refuse any man combat.

MEDIA ADAPTATIONS

- While the character of Cúchulainn has proved a potent image in the expression of Irish identity in the last century and a half, there have been remarkably few media adaptations. Yeats wrote a series of plays using material from the Ulster Cycle, although not from the *Táin Bó Cúailnge* proper. *On Bailie's Stran* was first performed on 27 December, 1904, Dublin; *The Green Helmet* was first performed on February 1910, Dublin; *Deirdre* was first performed on 24 November, 1906; *At the Hawks Well* was first performed on April 1, 1916, London; *The Only Jealousy of Emer* was first performed in Amsterdam, 1922; and *The Death of Cuchulain* was produced after Yeat's death in Dublin in December, 1949.

Ailill

Medb's husband and the owner of the white bull, Finnbennach. He is a cynical man who generally accepts his wife's decisions, but seems curiously detached throughout the *Táin Bó Cúailnge*.

Amargin

Amargin is the husband of Finnchaem and father of the hero Conall Cernach.

Brown Bull of Cúailnge

See Donn Cúailnge

Cathbad

A Druid and the father of Conchobor. Because he is a druid, Cathbad has prophetic powers.

Conall Cernach

Cúchulainn's cousin and foster brother. Connall is one of the Ulster exiles with Medb's army.

Cú Chulainn

See Cúchulainn

Conchobor

The son of Ness and Cathbad the druid. Conchobor was conceived because his mother learned from Cathbad that the hour was propitious for the conception of a king. Conchobor is the most celebrated king of the Ulster cycle. The character of Conchobor is deeply ambivalent. On one hand, his Ulstermen idolize him. But on the other, he has lost some of the finest men of his kingdom through duplicity.

Connla

The son of Aife and Cúchulainn. Cúchulainn told Aife that the boy must never reveal his name to any man, never give way to any man and never refuse any man combat. When he comes to Ulster these promises prove Connla's death. He refuses to give his name or give way. He matches Condere mac Echach in eloquence, stuns Conall Cernach and ties him up with his own shield strap. Cúchulainn goes out to fight him. Emer recognizes that the boy must be her husband's son and pleads with him not to kill his own child. Cúchulainn insists, however, that he must kill him for the honor of Ulster. He kills Connla with a weapon that Scathach had taught only him to use. Cúchulainn acknowledges his dying son, and the boy greets the hero of Ulster and dies.

Cormac Connlongas

Conchobor's son. Cormac is one of the Ulster exiles with Medb's army.

Cúchulainn

Cúchulainn is the son of Conchobor's sister, Deichtine. Both the human Sualdam mac Roich and a *sídh* prince are identified as his father. He is the Achilles of the Táin, fated to die young, but to leave a glorious memory. He holds off the combined forces of the other three provinces of Ireland and the Ulster exiles while the warriors of Ulster suffer the effects of Macha's curse. Cúchulainn, young, mercurial, and glorious, does what he can do and what only he can do, while all around him is deceit, treachery and chaos. Many of his fantastic deeds can be paralleled in Greek and Latin accounts of Celtic champions and warrior society.

Deichtine

Conchobor's sister and wife of Sualdam mac Roich. She is the mother of Cúchulainn by a strange series of events that lead the *Táin Bó Cúailnge* to

identify both the human Sualdam mac Roich and a *sídh* prince as his father.

Derdriu

Derdriu is often compared to Helen of Troy. Cathbad predicted before her birth that she would be the most beautiful of women and the destruction of Ulster. Conchobor ordered that she be raised in complete seclusion until she was old enough to become his wife. Derdriu, however, falls in love with Noisiu, Uisliu's son. He tries to refuse her because of the prophecy and the king's decree, but she put him under a magical compulsion or *geasa*, and they ran away together with his brothers and their followers. Eventually, Fergus, Dubthach and Cormac, Conchobor's son, give them their word that they could come safely back to Ulster and make their peace with the king. Conchobor had, however, tricked them all and had Noisiu and his brothers murdered. Fergus, Dubthach and Cormac burnt the king's stronghold at Emain Macha and went into exile with their warriors. Derdriu committed suicide rather than be given to Noisiu's murderer, Eogan mac Durthacht.

Donn Cúailnge

A bull belonging to Dáire mac Fiachna. Medb tried to buy and then to steal the bull so that her wealth would match Ailill's.

Dubthach

One of the Ulster warriors who stood surety (to stand in promise) for the return of Uislliu's sons. Dubthach went into Ulster with Fergus and Cormac.

Emer

The daughter of Forgall Monach. She becomes Cúchulainn's wife.

Etarcomol

A foster son of son of Ailill and Medb. Fergus was against Etarcomol coming along on the parley to establish the single combats, but took him there under his protection. Etarcomol picks a fight with Cúchulainn, who tried to avoid killing him, out of courtesy to Fergus, but must kill him in the end.

Fedelm

A poetess and prophetess of Connacht. She returns from study in Britain and meets Medb's army about to set out on the cattle raid. Medb demands that she prophesy the expedition's outcome. The girl predicts their slaughter at the hands of Cúchulainn.

Finnchad Fer Benn

Finnchad is called the Horned Man because of the silver horns he wore. He is Conchobor's son and was sent to call up the warriors of Ulster.

Finnabair

Finnabair is the daughter of Ailill and Medb. She had been promised to one warrior after another to induce them to fight Cúchulainn. She is eventually even offered to Cúchulainn and was sent to him in the disguise of her father. Cúchulainn saw through the disguise, cut off Finnabair's hair, and thrust a pillar stone under her cloak and tunic, shaming her without defiling her. She is said to have committed suicide when she learned of the killing of so many princes on her account. In a variant tradition, she goes off with Cúchulainn at the end of the *Táin Bó Cúailnge*.

Finnbennach

The bull of Ailill's herd and a calf of one Medb's cows. This bull would not stay with a woman's herd and switched sides.

Finnchaem

Finnchaem is the sister of Conchobor and Deichtine. She was Conall Cernach's mother and Cúchulainn's foster-mother.

Horned Man

See Finnchad Fer Benn

Ferchu Loingsech

A Connachtman who had never accepted the rule of Ailill and Medb. He proposed to his band that they kill Cúchulainn and win their favor. All twelve attacked Cúchulainn but were killed.

Crunniuc mac Agnomain

Crunniuc is the husband of Macha. His boasting of his wife leads to her race against the king's chariot and her curse on the men of Ulster.

Buide mac Báin

Medb's cowherd. Cúchulainn kills him.

Bricriu mac Carbad

A mean-minded man who loved stirring up trouble; it was said of him that if he heard something unfavorable about any decent person he could not rest until he had told it. He was chosen to judge between the two bulls because it was well known that 'he favoured his friend no more than his enemy.' He was killed by the bulls.

Ferdia mac Damáin

Cúchulainn's foster brother and closest friend. He was the son of a king of Connacht. He did not want to fight Cúchulainn, but Medb shamed him into fighting by telling him that Cúchulainn had boasted, "he wouldn't count it any great triumph if his greatest feat of arms were your downfall." They fight for four days, and Cúchulainn finally defeats Ferdia with the *gae bolg*, a terible javelin only he can use. He laments his friend. His beautiful lament for Ferdia is one of the high points of the *Táin Bó Cúailnge* with its repetition of the highest praise for Ferdia's ability.

Eogan mac Durthacht

Eogan is the king of Fernmag. He came to make peace with Conchobor and was chosen to kill Noisiu and his brothers.

Dáire mac Fiacha

The owner of the Bull of Cooley. He was going to lend the bull until he learns that had he not accepted Medb's offer, the bull would have been taken by force.

Fiacha mac Fir Febe

Fiacha is the son of Conchobor's daughter. He was one of the Ulster exiles with Medb's army. Fergus sent him to bring news of the fight when Gaile Dána and his twenty-seven sons and his sister's son simultaneously attacked Cúchulainn's with their poisoned weapons and fists. Fiacha broke the compact of the Ulster exiles and went to the hero's aid. To protect the Ulstermen from Medb's wrath, Cúchulainn and the two sons of Ficce killed all twenty-nine.

Lugaid mac Nois Allchomaig

Lugaid is the king of Munster. He goes to parley with Cúchulainn on several occasions on the behest of Aillil. He is on good terms with Cúchulainn. At his request his brother Láréne is the only man who escapes alive from single combat with Cúchulainn.

Laeg mac Riangabra

Laeg is Cúchulainn's charioteer. He was the hero's confidant, counselor, and right-hand man.

Sualdam mac Roich

Cúchulainn's mortal father who died when he cut his head off on the rim of his own shield trying to rouse the warriors of Ulster.

Mac Roth

Mac Roth is the messenger of Ailill and Medb. He is sent to borrow the Bull of Cooley from Dáire mac Fiacha.

Noisiu mac Uislenn

Noisiu is Derdriu's lover and one of the finest men in Ulster. He tries to escape the love of Derdriu but she puts a *geasa* on him, binding him to do as she requires. Despite a safe conduct from Conchobor, the king of Ulster, he and his brothers were murdered by Eogan mac Durthacht on Conchobor's orders, despite Fergus's own son throwing himself across Noisiu to save him.

Lug macEthnenn

Cúchulainn's *síde* father, he comes to take his son's place holding the ford against the invading army when Cúchulainn is on the edge of collapse from his wounds and lack of sleep.

Macha

Macha is the daughter of Sainrith mac Imbaith. She gave birth to twins after the race against the King of Ulster's chariot. She curses the men of Ulster with labor pains for their cruelty towards a woman in childbirth. Her story not only explains why Cúchulainn had to stand alone against the combined forces of three provinces of Ireland, but also explains the name of the royal fortress, Emain Macha, "the twins of Macha."

Medb

Medb is the daughter of the High King of Tara who gave her the province of Connacht for her own. Originally, Medb was the goddess of sovereignty, the patroness of every true king. In the *Táin Bó Cúailnge*, she is a cold, amoral, power-hungry woman who treats her own daughter as a commodity to be bargained with for a moment's advantage. Her own adulteries are merely a form of leverage. She is, however, one of the most fully realized and internally consistent of the characters.

Morrígan

Morrígan is the goddess of war. She was a presence on the battlefield but did not participate in combat. She caused panic in the Connacht army and attempted to seduce Cúchulainn. It is worth noting in reference to the setting of most of Cúchulainn's fights that she was traditionally associated with fords where she would be seen washing the clothing of those fated to die in a coming battle. This manifestation has passed into Scottish Highland folklore as the *Bean-nighe*, who is seen washing the clothing of those about to die.

Nes

The mother of Conchobor by the druid Cathbad. She marries Fergus on the understanding that her son Conchobor can be king for a year, ensuring that his children will be the children of a king and giving them both status and a place in the succession. She then manipulates the situation to ensure that the warriors of Ulster will not allow Fergus to resume the throne.

Scáthach

A woman warrior and prophetess of Albu, the island of Britain. She completes Cúchulainn's education as a warrior. He defeats her greatest enemy, the woman warrior Aife, by whom he has a son, Connla. Scáthach prophesied to him that he would have a short life, but everlasting fame.

Setanta

See Cúchulainn

Warped One

See Cúchulainn

White Horned

See Finnbennach

THEMES

The Breakdown of Social Order

Cúchulainn is the focus of a valiant attempt to preserve his society. Around him, the basic relationships of the early Irish social order are snapping: the ties between kin, between foster brothers, between men and women, between kings and subjects are broken. It is characteristic of medieval Irish thought that this anarchy flows from rulers. Conchobor has driven out his own kin through deceit, treachery,

TOPICS FOR FURTHER STUDY

- The artifacts that are described in the *Táin Bó Cúailnge* have often been compared to the artifacts and the decorative style of the La Tène culture. Research the La Tène style in Europe, Britain, and Ireland and its persistence in Irish art.

- Early medieval Ireland produced more than a vernacular literature. It had an enormous effect on Western literary culture, even on the basic level of how a text is presented on the page. Investigate the development of word division, punctuation, and page layout in early Irish and Irish-influenced manuscripts.

- The excavation at Navan Fort, the site of Emain Macha, has uncovered an Iron Age complex that is probably religious in nature. The interpretive center is an integral part of an initiative in Northern Ireland to give a sense of cultural inclusion to both communities in Northern Ireland. Research the differing attitudes of Northern Nationalists and Unionists in relation to the *Táin Bó Cúailnge*.

- The *Táin Bó Cúailnge* is full of incidents that explain place names. Research the place names in your own locality to establish what lies behind them.

and murder. Medb counsels the murder of faithful allies and manipulates men into breaking the sacred bonds of fosterage and kinship. Between them, they have compromised Fergus, a hero as great Cúchulainn, and left widows, orphans, and grieving parents across Ireland.

Heroism

Bravery is at the heart of the *Táin Bó Cúailnge*. Facing physical dangers in combat is of the utmost importance. The highest expression of such heroism is the hero alone; Cúchulainn standing against the enemies of Ulster with only the most intermittent and qualified aid is perhaps the most rarefied example in western literature. Whatever flaws Cúchulainn may have, his physical courage and the motives that fuel it cannot be despised. Cúchulainn has made a decision based on his understanding of his ability and training, his sense of obligation to his Ulster kin and to Ulster society as a whole, and on the desire to purchase immortal fame.

Kingship and the Sovereignty Goddess

At the end of the final battle, there is an exchange between Medb and her erstwhile lover and champion, Fergus. "Medb said to Fergus, 'We have had shame and shambles here today, Fergus.'

'We followed the rump of a misguided woman,' Fergus said. 'It is the usual thing for a herd lead by a mare to be strayed and destroyed.'" The negative attitude toward women has been a recurring subject in the *Táin Bó Cúailnge* criticism, but it is not as crude as it is sometimes portrayed because women exercising power are not uniformly presented in a negative light. Medb, daughter of the High King of Tara, who brings a whole province with her on her marriage, is the sovereignty goddess made mortal. When the land is poorly ruled or without a king, the goddess had the form of an old woman; when joined to a just and capable king, she had the shape of one young and beautiful. Imperious, coldly amoral, and incapable of love, she may be an argument against women being allowed political power, but her character clearly reflects the kings with which she has contact. Ailill, Conchobor, and the disposed Fergus are all deeply flawed. Her lack of battle-prowess and ethical sense and her murderous treachery and sexual appetite mirror the flaws of the three royal men.

Mythology

No pagan god or ritual is mentioned as such in the *Táin Bó Cúailnge*. At most, characters swear "by the gods" or by "the oath of my people." The ancient gods and customs have been so thoroughly neutralized that it is often only through comparative mythology or information from classical writers that mythological material can be identified as such. Nevertheless, the epic has been carefully searched for pre-Christian gods and cult since the mid-nineteenth century. Various characters have been identified as gods, various episodes and actions have been identified as being reflections of pre-Christian worship and belief. Lug mac Ethnenn, who identifies himself to Cúchulainn as 'your father from the *síde,'* is the *Táin Bó Cúailnge's* version of the Celtic god of light. The battle of the bulls has been identified by some scholars as a distant reflection of a myth of a sacrificed bull from which the world was made. The pains of the Ulstermen, lasting from the *Samhaim* (November 1) to *Imbolc* (February 1), which are the months of winter in Ireland, are similarly identified as a symbol of winter sleep. Perhaps the most easily recognizable cluster of mythological material centers around Cúchulainn himself. His conception and birth are miraculous and providential. His ability to function during the winter when the Ulstermen are laid low suggests a powerful force of nature. All these things, however, have been transformed from divine action or intervention to something more akin to magic.

Topography and Place Names

A major element in the *Táin Bó Cúailnge* is the attention given to the setting of the action. This is not in the usual form of verbal description, which allows the audience to 'see' the setting. Instead, the setting is established as a story behind a place name. Incidents often appear to be included simply to explain the name of a minor ford or wood. Some stories may have been invented simply to provide such an explanation. The great battle between the men of Ulster and the forces of Medb and Ailill at the end of the *Táin Bó Cúailnge* is treated in far less detail than the circuitous route of the dying bull, Donn Cúailnge, leaving behind him a scatter of place names.

This preoccupation with place names and their meanings and origins is not confined to *Táin Bó Cúailnge.* A whole genre of place name narratives exists in Irish literature, the *dinnsenchas.* This native genre was reinforced by the importance of biblical place names in explaining the Bible in early Christian writings and by the use of place name narratives in classical literature, particularly in Virgil's *Aeneid.* It is possible that identification of a story with a place was a device for remembering a particular character or event.

The place name narratives in the *Táin Bó Cúailnge* cannot be dropped out of the narrative without changing its meaning and character. First, they anchor the action, however fantastic, in the reality of the Irish countryside. Second, they all seem to share in establishing the action of the epic as of such importance that this raid and its heroes have made an indelible mark on Ireland. Third, they effectively confirm the author's status with his audience by his apparently exact and detailed knowledge of every cairn, every wood in the path of the raid, and the combat of the bulls. This use of place name stories as an indication of learning is reflected in the *Táin Bó Cúailnge* when Cúchulainn, on his first day as a warrior, is instructed in place name lore by Ibor, Conchobor's charioteer.

War and Peace

Despite its concentration on the martial achievements of Cúchulainn, the *Táin Bó Cúailnge* does not glorify warfare nor treat cattle raiding as merely a commonplace nuisance. Cúchulainn's grief over the death of Ferdia is only the most striking of his laments, and his reaction to the sound of the final battle ("anger destroys the world") is telling. The *Táin Bó Cúailnge* was composed in a society that was attempting in some small measure to limit violence.

STYLE

Epic Features

An epic is a long narrative in which a crisis must be met and overcome, whether in the form of warfare or a quest. An epic almost always represents the summation of a culture's ideals at the point of when those ideas are in flux. The *Táin Bó Cúailnge* certainly qualifies as an epic because it is a long and complex narrative, treating a serious subject, the survival of a people in the terms of their ability to protect themselves, the integrity of their borders, and their means of survival. The action is centered on an outstanding hero, Cúchulainn, in whose hands lies the fate of his people. Around him are equally magnificent and compelling characters, subsidiary only in reference to Cúchulainn. The action springs from the clash of Medb and Ailill who are almost god-like in their detachment. The progress of the action is vitally affected by earlier decisions of Ulster kings: the command to Macha to race the king's chariot, despite her appeals, and Conchobor's treachery towards the sons of Uisliu. The first results in the warriors of Ulster being stricken with labor pains so that they cannot defend their homes; the second results in the desertion of many of their greatest warriors, splitting even the king's own family.

Point of View

The narrator in all versions of the *Táin Bó Cúailnge* sounds like a modern researcher. He is well informed about places, actions, and conversations, but anchors his story in remarks like, "They say it is here that Dubthach chanted," or, "Others say that the bird and the squirrel were both perched on Medb's shoulders." The narrator claims to do nothing more than report, noting the existence of alternate traditions and stories. In place of the help of the muses with their divine knowledge, there is, in one version, the ghost of Fergus or at least the traditions preserved by his descendants. Even when the narrator describes a character's mood, that mood is only what is apparent from either the character's plain admission or actions.

Inconsistencies

The earliest recession of *Táin Bó Cúailnge* notes a number of variant versions of the narrative. This reference to variant versions raises questions concerning the state and purpose of the text. Is it a reconstituted version of an original that cannot be exactly established from among the variants or is it a file of materials for the composition of an epic? Both opinions are worth considering.

Plot

The plot of the *Táin Bó Cúailnge* is remarkably thin, particularly when one strips away the preliminary material. There is the muster and march of the army of Medb and Ailill, punctuated by prophecies of doom. These actions are then followed by a long series of fights at a ford, which resolve into one long vindication of Ulster and the prowess of Cúchulainn. The fight of the two armies, when it finally comes, is punctuated with the confrontation of Fergus with Conchobor and of Cúchulainn with Medb. It ends with the final fight of the bulls. The self-cancelling victory of the Bull of Cooley over the Bull of Connacht is an ironic mirror of the waste of the human battle. The confrontations of the human battle reaffirm basic decency: Cúchulainn will not kill a woman and Fergus stops himself short of killing a kinsman.

Imagery and Symbolism

Imagery in the *Táin Bó Cúailnge* has been described as Kelly suggests, "limpid." Her example, the description of the prophetess Fedelm, consists of concrete description in short sentences using only two comparisons in describing fourteen separate items. Looking at similar descriptions, the Fedelma description emerges as unusual in having even two comparisons. There is, however, a famous extended description that functions essentially as a metaphor using the messenger/interpreter, watchman/interpreter technique. Mac Roth, Medb's messenger reports a scene of unnatural phenomena that functions as a metaphor of the army of Ulster since Fergus is able to read these phenomena for what they really are—the effects of the army of Ulster on the march. The basic symbols of the *Táin Bó Cúailnge* are hound/wolf, cow/bull, and horse. In general, the first is largely reserved for Cúchulainn, but is connected with a social type: the young warrior. The second is used of humans in general, but more particularly in the comparison of cows and women. Finally, horses are used as symbols of kingship. This symbol is exploited ironically when a mare is used to characterize Medb's incompetence as a leader of men. An image that passes into symbol in Cúchulainn's lament for Ferdia is the gold brooch that Medb gave to Ferdia as part of the inducement to fight his foster brother. In Cúchulainn's grief, the brooch is transformed into a symbol of all that Ferdia was.

Style and Prosody

The *Táin Bó Cúailnge* is unusual in the epic tradition in that it is written largely in prose with inset passages of syllabic verse. Some of these passages, for example, the prophecy of the Morrígan, the unrhymed, alliterative *rosc(ad)* or *rhetoric* gives the impression of being older than the surrounding prose text. It has been suggested, however, that they are the products of poets who are trying to compose in what they thought was an ancient style. This text was probably not an attempt to confuse the audience about the age of their compositions, but to create the proper atmosphere of antiquity and give an exalted and heroic quality to the characters who spoke them.

Description and Narrative

The *Táin Bó Cúailnge* uses a number of narrative/descriptive techniques, for example, the watchman device. The watchman device is when a character whose knowledge and sense has been established and who is involved in the events gives action, scene, or character descriptions. A variation of this device has an uninformed but carefully observant character relaying a description to a knowledgeable character who then identifies what is observed.

HISTORICAL CONTEXT

The Reinvention of Early Irish History

The *Táin Bó Cúailnge* floats within a period of over a thousand years. At one end is the generally assumed date of the essential action and characters of the first century A.D. At the other is the date of the earliest manuscript written in Clonmacnoise on the Shannon River in the first quarter of the twelfth century. Between these two dates is the great watershed of Irish history: the introduction of Christianity.

Christianity and Roman culture, because of the proximity of the Roman empire in Britain, had begun to affect Ireland from at least the third century. Their influence was strengthened with the mission of St. Patrick in the second half of the fifth century. At that point, the Irish had already developed a script of their own: Ogham. This script shows signs of having been affected by a high-level understanding of Latin grammatical and linguistic theory. Within a century of St. Patrick's death, Ireland was producing good Latin scholars and fervent Christian missionaries. Irishmen were laying the basis for modern page presentation and the spread of literacy, both in Latin and vernacular across Western Europe. Meanwhile, Ireland was in constant turmoil as new tribal and family groups like the Ui Neill remade not only the political landscape but the landscape of history, reinterpreting the past to establish political legitimacy. While the myth of the high kingship was being invented, the whole pre-Christian history of Ireland, or more properly, the pre-Patrician history of the island and it peoples, was overhauled. This was partially an attempt to integrate the Irish into the mainstream Mediterranean culture and Christian salvation history. It also represented an attempt to provide a basis for native Irish law acceptable to the new religion and learning. There was also an attempt at cultural one-upmanship. If the Jewish nation boasted of Moses, the Greeks of Homer and Plato, and the Franks and Romans of descent from Troy, the Irish would claim to be the descendants of a pharaoh's daughter, the foster mother of Moses. At some point in this intellectual and social ferment, *Táin Bó*

Cúailnge as we have it in the earliest collection began to take shape.

Cattle and Cattle Raiding

Across Irish history, certain constants of Irish life emerge: endemic warfare, disunity, and cattle rearing as the basis of the economy. It is in this atmosphere that cattle raiding emerged almost as an institution and continued until the final imposition of English rule. The *Táin Bó Cúailnge* is only the most famous tale of a cattle raid. The names of thirteen such tales survive. The tale type and its popularity were a reflection of social reality. For most of Ireland's history, indeed up until the last twenty years, cattle rearing for meat, milk, butter, and hides was the mainstay of the economy. Prices in early medieval Ireland were expressed in cattle and slave girls at a ratio of seven cows to one slave. The integrity of a community vis-a-vis its neighbors were demonstrated by the successful cattle-raid. A king's authority was expressed in terms of the ability to enforce a tax of cattle over a given area. Cattle-raids were used regularly as a tool of local politics by both the native Irish and the Anglo-Norman settlers and were a constant fact of Irish life into the seventeenth century.

The Ulster Cycle

The *Táin Bó Cúailnge* is the centerpiece of the Ulster cycle of eighty heroic sagas, one of several cycles of medieval and early medieval Irish stories, the most famous being the Fianna cycle centered on the figure of Finn Mac Cool and his son Oisín. It is by far the longest of any of these early Irish tales. While the Fianna cycle was more generally popular up to the nineteenth century, Irish language poetic eulogies used stories, images, and characters from the Ulster cycle to great effect. Native works on word meanings and place names also drew heavily on the cycle.

Historical Fiction and the Place and Date of Composition

As part of a larger effort to integrate Irish history into biblical salvation history and place their past on a footing with that of Greece and Rome, medieval Irish scholars placed the action of the *Táin Bó Cúailnge* around the time of Christ. They worked tirelessly to ensure that their proofs for its date corresponded to accepted notions of chronology and historical evidence. O'Rahilly, a recent editor of the three versions of the *Táin Bó Cúailnge* believed that the earliest version of the work was

COMPARE
&
CONTRAST

- **The setting of *Táin Bó Cúailnge:*** Hurling plays an important role in the Ulster society. Not only does it serve as a great social event, it emphasizes the qualities and traits of courage and physical aptitude that the society admires.

  1999: Mentioned at several points in the Ulster cycle of stories, hurling is the Irish national game and is promoted, with several other native sports, by a national association: the Gaelic Athletic Association. It is played in nearly every school in Ireland. Local club teams feed their best players into county teams, which then compete on the national level. County and provincial finals are as hotly contested as any ancient raid. The All Ireland Hurling Champions were County Cork in the men's game and County Tipperrary in the women's game.

- **The setting of *Táin Bó Cúailnge:*** Cattle and the care and breeding of livestock is another important aspect of Ulster society. The number and quality of livestock a person maintains reflects highly on his or her character. This importance explains why Medb and Ailill emphasize the quality of their catttle during their pillow talk.

  2000: Cattle rearing still dominates Irish agriculture. Irish butter and beef is exported all over the world. Irish cheese makers have developed an international reputation in the last twenty years. Although artificial insemination is used almost exclusively on modern Irish farms, the pursuit of the best bull is still important; league tables of available bulls are published in farming journals.

Most cattle reared in Ireland are now from breeds developed on mainland Europe, but a native breed, the small, hardy, Kerry Cow is still bred.

- **The setting of *Táin Bó Cúailnge:*** Although Medb is queen, she still is only second in power to Ailill. Throughout the Ulster cycles, she has to resort to her powers of cunning and manipulation to assert her dominance in society.

  2000: In contrast to the treatment of Medb in the *Táin Bó Cúailnge*, the last two Irish presidents have been women. Both were formerly professors of law at Trinity College Dublin. Ironically, the first, Mary Robinson, is a Connacht woman, while the present incumbent, Mary MacAleese, is from Ulster.

- **The setting of *Táin Bó Cúailnge:*** Place names play a key role throughout the Ulster cycles. Place names spring from the locations where specific battles or important events took place. At the end of the epic, the bulls do battle. The places where the Donn Cúailnge and Finnbennach fight are remembered by the people present and throughout the generations.

  2000: Although some of the place names in the *Táin Bó Cúailnge* cannot be identified in the modern landscape, most of the action of the raid can still be followed across the modern landscape. The Cooley peninsula is in County Louth where *Táin* walks are regularly held. Louth is still an area of cattle rearing, although the port of Duddalk is important for bulk shipping.

---

written in the seventh century but composed three centuries earlier. But the language of the *Táin Bó Cúailnge* has been deeply affected by the introduction of Christianity and Latin. Further, archaeological study of artifacts, particularly of swords and their use suggests that the constant reference to beheading and the descriptions of the use of swords in general can only be explained in terms of the long

sword, introduced during the Viking period. It would be nearly impossible to perform the actions recounted with the much shorter Iron Age or early Christian period swords. On this basis, the author of the *Táin Bó Cúailnge* should be seen as consciously attempting to recreate a past for which there were broad outlines but few particulars. To recreate that past, the author relied on whatever information could be gleaned from native Irish sources, undoubtedly including the memory of the warfare that lead to the downfall of the ancient Ulaid. The author would also have adapted information about other ancient peoples known through Latin texts, people who were understood as living at a similar level of civilization, perhaps including information from Roman writers on British and continental Celtic peoples of the first century B.C. and the first century A.D. It is also possible that this recreation was affected by pagan peoples that Irish missionaries had encountered in their work. The poetic speeches inserted in the prose narrative were once thought to be extremely early. Recently, however, it has been shown that writers working in the eighth century and later were capable of producing consciously archaic texts. It would be appropriate for an author attempting to recreate a period long past to attempt to reproduce what he and his audience would recognize as linguistically old-fashioned. Thus, if a modern writer set her story in the sixteenth century, she might attempt conversation using words and meanings of words familiar to her audience from Shakespeare. In the last thirty years, a number of scholars have attempted to assign a particular place and situation and even an author to the *Táin Bó Cúailnge*. As yet, no suggestion has gained general acceptance. It is fairly clear, however, that the *Táin Bó Cúailnge* must be one of the earliest sagas to reach a stable form because so many other of the tales depend on it in one way or another. It must also have been in existence by the ninth century since the story of its being exchanged for Isidore's *Etymologiae* and being recovered from the ghost of Fergus is preserved in the *Triads of Ireland*.

CRITICAL OVERVIEW

The *Táin Bó Cúailnge* appears alien, primitive, and unimaginably ancient. There are unmistakable signs that this atmosphere is a sophisticated construction of the past, making its historicity a scholarly donné (a thing in a literary work that is taken for granted or expected by virtue of the genre or milieu in which it is contained) well into the twentieth century. As B. K. Lambkin notes, the clarity of perception of its earliest critic, the scribe of the twelfth century *Book of Leinster* who said, "But I who have written this story, or rather this fable, give no credence to the various incidents related in it. For some things in it are deceptions of demons, others poetic figments; some are probable, others improbable" was forgot-

ten in a desire to have a reliable historical source. It was its apparent 'primitiveness' that caught the imagination of nineteenth-century scholars whose obsession with the presumed and desired antiquity of the *Táin* quickly became part of the Irish strain of nineteenth century romantic nationalism. Scholarship under its influence, and not only in Ireland, often justified itself in the search for the pure, unsullied national character of a people. As editor Barbara Hillers notes, even the greatest nineteenth century scholars approached the Ulster cycle of tales as history and its characters as real people. The *Táin Bó Cúailnge* was a rich source of historical, mythological, and linguistic information. As Gerard Murphy notes, the question of literary technique hardly entered into their consideration, its artlessness was a positive virtue, if only as a proof of its great antiquity, their origin in "the youth of the world, before the heart had been trained to bow before the head or the imagination to be troubled by logic."

The critical situation of the *Táin Bó Cúailnge* is somewhat better than Irish saga literature as a whole. According to Cathasaigh, there are good modern editions with translations. Yeats' dramatic adaptations of the Ulster tales never achieved the popularity of his lyrics, but Kinsella's 1969 translation has opened the work up to a wider audience whose interests are more exclusively literary than philological, mythological or historical. Ironically, it is further historical and archaeological research picking up anachronisms in the text that has shifted interest to the author's artifice and learning in projecting the aura of an archaic pagan past. This has been furthered by the emergence of a strain of historical-political readings according to N. B. Aitchison, moving interest away from the period it depicts to that of its original audience. This movement towards the analysis of the *Táin Bó Cúailnge* as highly ironic political satire has been further complicated by the fault line that has opened up across the fields of early Irish literature and history in the second half of the twentieth century. On one side are the so-called "nativist" critics who have traditionally emphasized the pagan and Indo-European material fossilized in medieval texts. They dominated the study of early Irish history and literature until the later twentieth century. On the other side are the "revisionists," beginning with Carney, who emphasize the quick and thorough assimilation of classical and Christian literary culture among the Irish and its profound influence on Irish vernacular literature. Carney's explanation of the *Táin Bó Cúailnge's* origins with its even-handed recognition of both native and classical Christian material is worth recapitulating. The *Táin Bó Cúailnge*, like the Irish sagas in general, shows in its vocabulary that it was given the form we find in the manuscripts after Christianity was introduced. The essential narrative and characters go back to a more or less remote pre-Christian past. This nucleus of characters and action, however, were like the grain of sand in an oyster's shell. They attracted the author's total literary experience ranging across classical and Christian literature as well as native material, particularly the *senchus*, the stories that explained place names or how certain peoples came to be in a particular part of the country. The *Táin Bó Cúailnge* also attracted both popular characters from other legends into its narrative and popular types of narrative episodes.

It is understandable that students of language, history, and archaeology have monopolized the *Táin Bó Cúailnge's* study, because only by taking them into account can criticism have validity. Nevertheless, whatever criticism has done, if, as Carney suggested, the original author of *Táin Bó Cúailnge* was attempting to give Ireland the equivalent of the *Aeneid*. Scholars and poets in the last 150 years have worked tirelessly to ensure it that position in the history of Irish literature and in the popular imagination.

Medb (also known as Maeve), Queen of Connacht, who made a raid on the Ulaid (Ulstermen) to carry off the great bull of Cooley.

CRITICISM

Helen Conrad-O'Briain

In the following essay, Conrad-O'Briain looks at the Táin Bó Cúailnge *as an elaborate literary creation, with particular emphasis on the author's use of place.*

Students of the *Táin Bó Cúailnge* in particular and the early Irish literature in general have often neglected treating it as literature. Patricia Kelly at the beginning of "The *Táin* as Literature" saw as the main obstacles to literary analysis the scholarly preoccupation with mythology, history, and prehistory, and a "primitive" quality that Murphy in *Saga and Myth in Early Ireland* attributed to their origin in "the youth of the world, before the heart had been trained to bow before the head or the

imagination to be troubled by logic." Research is making this explanation of the peculiar quality of the *Táin Bó Cúailnge* more and more difficult to accept. Work on all the elements of the texts suggests that the "primitive" character of the epic is a carefully constructed one, using biblical and classical as well as native material to build up a picture of the past that accorded with what might be called an anthropology of pagans. This construction was surprisingly positive for three reasons. First, these pagans were their ancestors; second, they were the source of a formidable body of native law that must be preserved; third, their society had been relatively amenable to conversion. What was the purpose of this reconstruction? Recent readings of the *Táin Bó Cúailnge* are still driven by history, with suggestions or assumptions of a political allegory touched by bitter irony. But no single time, place, or situation, no one key for this allegory has, however, achieved even general acceptance. Despite Kelly's belief that "a reliable verdict of the artistic failure or success of the *Táin Bó Cúailnge* is only possible if the texts aims have been correctly identified," it is still valid to look at the text as something that should

WHAT DO I READ NEXT?

- P. W. Joyce's *Old Celtic Romances*, first published in 1879 and recently re-printed, is one of the first and most influential collections of translations of Irish tales. ''The Children of Lir'' is perhaps the best-known story in the collection, which leans towards romance and magic rather than heroic battle.

- ''The Death of Aife's Only Son'' is included in Kinsella's translation of the *Táin Bó Cúailnge*. It is a tragedy worthy of the Greek drama. Cúchulainn is caught up in an inevitable tragedy of his own making. In this tale, unlike in the *Táin Bó Cúailnge*, a woman's advice represents wisdom and the finest prompting of human love. Emer, Cúchulainn's wife, out of love for him and for his son by another woman, pleads with him to acknowledge and spare his son, Connla.

- W. B. Yeats' cycle of plays (*On Bailie's Strand, The Green Helmet, Deirdre, At the Hawks Well, The Only Jealousy of Emer*, and *The Death of Cúchulain*), based on Cúchulainn's exploits, transpose the hero into a world of late nineteenth and early twentieth romantic, nationalistic and aesthetic sensibilities, but nevertheless, demonstrate the enduring appeal of the Ulster Cycle.

- It may be a reflection of a continuing Irish preoccupation with the land, reflected in the place name stories of the *Táin Bó Cúailnge*, but the landscapes of few countries have been as well or lovingly described as Ireland's in Frank Mitchell and Michael Ryan's *Reading the Irish Landscape*. The authors bring the geological and environmental history of the island forward from the earliest rocks to the present day pressures on the Irish environment.

- The first volume of *Clonmacnoise Studies*, edited by Heather King, is a collection of wide-ranging studies of the monastery where the earliest extant manuscript of the *Táin Bó Cúailnge* was written. Taken together, they are a window on the world, both physical and intellectual, in which the author, scribe, and audience lived.

- Paul Saenger's *Space Between Words: The Origins of Silent Reading* is a demanding text, but for anyone interested in the development of western literacy and the way information is presented in text, the first ninety-nine pages are worth any difficulty they may present.

---

on one level explain itself. That is, the author has produced a work that says what it says in general terms that is a story that has generally applicable insights into the human condition.

Whether the first recession represents a learned Christian re-interpretation of the past for a complex political purpose, or as O'Corrain suggested, a file of material to be worked up for various purposes at a later date, it, like the later recessions must reflect the tastes and preoccupations of its contemporary audience. If the reader finds a theme, particular motif, or image used continuously throughout a work, it suggests that that theme, motif, or image is important. It is there because it embodies something important or fundamental, and it does it better than

anything else the author can imagine. A reader must grasp how such things work both individually and as patterns in the work as a whole. However unappealing a literary device might be to a modern audience, for instance the use of proverbs or elaborate genealogical passages, they demand attention. They cannot be dismissed because they are not the modern choice.

Living far from the places named, with no sense of connection to the individual commemorated in any given place name, few modern readers can see an immediate purpose or pleasure from the place name narratives in the *Táin Bó Cúailnge*. But, they cannot be dismissed as meaningless or awkward. Carney suggests that they were the element most likely to be derived from the purely native tradition, but that the writers were using them in a radically new way. The function of these *dinnsenchus*, to use the Irish term, was to preserve historic lore attached to a place. They existed as independent, self-sufficient narratives and were gathered into collections at an early date. They were not originally part of any dramatic, least of all fictional, narrative. Their superficially pointless ubiquity in the *Táin Bó Cúailnge* must then represent a decision by the author to use them, outside of the immediate tradition of both the heroic tale and the place name narrative. When Carney identified the place name stories as native, he was right in recognizing that they reach back into the pre-Christian past and that they played a part in Irish literature and cultural life that cannot be exactly paralleled in any other country. But other literatures have used place name narratives and referred to the meaning of place names. Virgil's *Aeneid* used stories attached to place names to make his poem more than simply a glorification of the Emperor Augustus' Julian clan or even of Rome. Instead, his lingering descriptions of the places, people, and their origins, while fewer and more developed than those in the *Táin Bó Cúailnge*, created a broader theme of Italy over which the specific action of his poem runs. Scripture scholars and preachers regularly stressed the meaning of place names in the Bible, connecting them with the larger spiritual meaning of the individual actions that had occurred in each. It is not surprising that the most important study of the topography of the bible lands in the middle ages was written by the Irishman, Adomnán. All this must have fed into an already active native interest and genre, suggesting the possible ways short narrative attached to a place might be used to refer to something connected to, but outside of themselves. The author of the *Táin Bó Cúailnge* then had an important body of material in which his audience had a cultivated interest. Clearly, the author used this material.

There has been a tendency among readers to concentrate on the lack of a particular type of topographical or landscape use in the *Táin Bó Cúailnge*. The *Táin Bó Cúailnge* does not have the sort of landscape description, beloved by the romantics and Victorians, which concentrates on the individual and particular. The essential function of these landscapes is to create atmosphere, as for example in the description of Dartmoor in *The Hound of the Baskervilles*. The author of the *Táin Bó Cúailnge* was perfectly capable of creating such a landscape. Landscape as modern readers gener-

> " The author does not use individual landscapes to create atmosphere. It is the sum total of all the short topographical narratives together that creates the effect. The land is connected in sympathy with its people."

ally expect it to be introduced into a narrative appears spectacularly not as an actual landscape, but as a description and simile for the vast Ulster army finally coming to Cúchulainn's aid. Its use in the passage not only shows that it was not lack of ability that stopped the writer, but it gives the army a feeling of a force of nature, echoing Cúchulainn's calling of the land of Ulster to rise and fight the invaders with him.

The most usual form in which natural features enter the narrative is purely topographical, taking the audience and characters to rarely described features of the landscape: woods, fords, plains, standing stones. It does this fifty-eight times in Recession 1, slightly more in the second recession. The author does not use individual landscapes to create atmosphere. It is the sum total of all the short topographical narratives together that creates the effect. The land is connected in sympathy with its people. When Cúchulainn intercepts the raiding army of Medb and Ailill he says: "I summon air and earth; but I summon now above all the Cronn river . . . and the water reared up to the treetops." Standing at the ford, a naturally defensible place but also a boundary with all the deep significance of a boundary, Cúchulainn calls upon the country to stand by him to protect their people. The landscape names become the trophies of the earth; fame, or at least memory, is shared by both place and warrior. These features are very much where the action is. They are defined and named by a moment of history, but that moment of history is about the trees, the fields, the standing stones as well as men and women. Every fight is about protecting Ulster, whether the Ulster of water and earth or flesh and blood. Here a collection of *dinnsenchus* has been subjected to a new organizing principle. Suddenly, not only the place names but the endless series of individual combats begin to make sense. One great story, one great threat, one great champion to meet it, has emerged from their total. One combat would not have made Cúchulainn the champion of Ulster any more than one clan or province would have made Medb's army the formidable force it was. It is the cumulative effect tinged with irony. Cúchullain's rings his province with the graves of her enemies. Boundary burials are usually of one's own protecting ancestors or heroes; here, they are of one's enemies. Cúchulainn sets the boundary not for Ulster, but for those who have attacked her.

Source: Helen Conrad-O'Briain, for *Epics for Students*, Gale, 2001.

Patricia Kelly

The following essay considers various characteristics and puzzling questions that the Táin presents.

Creative Literature or Functional Writing?

What then of *Táin Bó Cúailnge?* While the earliest references to the events of the tale occur in a genealogical context, as early as the eighth century the Ulster Cycle would seem to have acquired a literary autonomy. For instance, the originally independent saga *Táin Bó Fróich* (Fróich's cattle-driving) was adapted in the eighth century to function as a foretale to the greater *Táin*. Motifs of the cycle are already parodied in two eighth-century tales, *Scéla Muicce meic Dathó* (The story of Mac Da Thó's pig), and *Fled Bricrenn* (Bricriu's feast).

While Recension II of the *Táin* conforms more to modern expectations of an aesthetic creation, presenting a smooth narrative in a unified style, the focus of this article will be on Recension I, which, it is hoped to show, is more than 'a mass of workshop fragments, not yet assimilated or amalgamated'. Recension II will occasionally be drawn on where it supplies extra material or helps to clarify the terse account of the earlier version.

The Boyhood Deeds of Cú Chulainn

The young boy expresses the heroic ethos memorably when he declares that he values everlasting fame more than life 'Provided I be famous, I am content to be only one day on earth'. Much of the action of the *Táin* shows Cú Chulainn living out his heroic ambitions. He fulfils his early promise when he compensates for the Ulstermen's inability to defend their province, and wards off the Connacht offensive in a series of single combat encounters. A mimetic interpretation of the *macgnímrada* episode would view it as a depiction of the initiation of a young man into warrior status as a fully integrated member of his *túath* (kingdom), and Cú Chulainn's characterisation in the body of the narrative as an exemplification of the warrior ideal. But Cú Chulainn's heroic biography also has mythological resonances, and these are reflected in this section by the scene in which the triumphant returning warrior is greeted by the bare-breasted Ulster women. This has been explained as a reflex of Cú Chulainn's original role as the vigorous young male who brings about the renewal of the year in an old seasonal vegetation drama.

The preceding episode is an even better indication of how densely-layered the meaning of an ostensibly straightforward narrative can be. 'The death of the smith's hound', explains how the boy Sétantae acquired his adult name: forced to kill the fierce hound of Culann the smith-hospitaller in self-defence, he undertakes to substitute temporarily as a guard-dog, and accepts Cú Chulainn 'the hound of Culann' as his new name. Greene describes this as a 'simple well-told story' and signals disapproval that 'scholars have looked for deeper meanings'. That the story can be appreciated at the surface level of plot is undeniable, but in view of the sophistication of many early sagas, as recent scholarship has demonstrated, it seems implausible that the 'national epic' should be an anomalous case of naiveté. And indeed it has been shown that there is more to this 'simple story' than is immediately apparent.

Given the literary convention that tales set in the distant past were primarily of relevance to the time and milieu in which they were redacted, it is clear that a knowledge of social idiom and particularly of the legal system is crucial to a deeper understanding of early Irish saga. The role of the warrior was obviously vital to that society. A number of recent studies have illuminated the institution of the *fían(n)*, 'an association of propertyless and predominantly young, unmarried warrior-hunters on the fringes of settled society'. The *Männerbund* culture of such sodalities of young men is well attested in Germanic and Greek traditions, so that here we have a trace of Ireland's pagan inheritance. The *fían*'s wild life was expressed in the wearing of wolf-skins or wolf-heads, which is reflected in the proliferation of names incorporating elements meaning 'wolf': such an element is *cú*, which signifies both the canine and lupine kind. Members of a *fían* were traditionally credited with the ability to experience ecstatic distortions. Both these features, the canine/lupine aspect and the distortion, are expressed in the warrior-hero of the *Táin*: Cú Chulainn's name marks him as a 'hound' or 'wolf', and the contortions he undergoes in his *ríastrad* are mentioned frequently. With this background knowledge, *Aided con na cerda* can be read as a predictable stage in Cú Chulainn's martial career. By killing the hound Sétantae appropriates its martial spirit. The symbolism of the episode and its wider societal implications would presumably not have been lost on an early Irish audience.

The Táin Bó Tale Type

On the subject matter of this tale type Mac Cana says: 'The *tána* are the literary reflex of a social practice which was not merely Irish, but Celtic and Indo-European, and which is found elsewhere among cattle-rearing peoples ... For the Celts the successful cattle-raid was an assertion of the integrity of the tribal community *vis-à-vis* its neighbours and a vindication of its leader's claim to primacy over his people ... It is no mere accident, therefore, that the greatest of Irish tales, *Táin Bó Cúailnge* ... belongs to the category of the *tána*'. What was at stake in *Táin Bó Cúailnge* on the political level was therefore the continued independence of the kingdom of Ulster. Such a conflict could easily provide the stuff of narrative, but surely does not exhaust the literary meaning of the tale. That something more than a normal, albeit major, cattle raid is involved is shown by the fact that the defeat of Ailill and Medb does not end the tale: the climax is not the battle between Connacht and Ulster forces, but the fight of the two bulls and their ensuing deaths. As the various encounters between Cú Chulainn and his adversaries leave an abiding mark on the landscape in the form of new place names, so too the battle of the bulls gives rise to a new onomastic inventory. The rivalry of the two bulls and the cosmogonic significance of the final scene, in which the physical landscape is recreated, is thought to reflect the original mythological nucleus of the tale. Between these two poles, the mimetic and the mythic, must lie the literary significance of the tale.

The other *Táin Bó* tales may give an indication of what is involved in a literary presentation of the cattle-raid. They all function as fore-tales (*remscéla*) to *Táin Bó Cúailnge*, the motivation for the raid being of no great political importance, but merely to provide food for the duration of the larger foray. None of the raids is conducted by a reigning monarch, or against such a major political opponent, and

The Druid warns Queen Medb about Cu Chulainn's impending attack against the Connacht Army.

as one would expect, the protagonist is always a man. Finally, as Carney noted there is often a love interest: the driving off of cattle goes hand in hand with the acquisition of a woman. I suggest that these two narrative strands are figuratively linked, via a metaphor which equates cattle with humans, and particularly women with cows.

This metaphor is memorably exploited in a famous passage from another Ulster Cycle tale, *Longes mac nUislenn* (The exile of the sons of Uisliu). The beautiful Deirdre, who is being raised in seclusion as a future consort for Conchobar, meets and is smitten by Noísiu, a handsome young warrior. Their conversation is couched in figurative language:

—'A fine young heifer that is going by,' he said.

—'The heifers are bound to be fine where there are no bulls,' she answered.

—'You have the bull of the province: the king of Ulaid,' Noísiu 'said.

Thus the identification of cows and women in the plot of the *táin bó* genre is supported in the language by a metaphor in which terms for cattle can denote humans. In *Táin Bó Cúailnge*, of course, the roles of male and female are reversed. It is a

> This stunning image is expressed with all the eloquence and brevity of the most admired passages of early Irish prose, but the other narrative responses to the task of describing the battle need not therefore be denied structural validity and artistic intent."

woman who is the initiator of the raid, and her primary objective is not cattle-herds, but a particular prize bull, the Donn Cúailnge, the 'bull of the province' of Ulster, i.e. the Ulster king, Conchobar. The choice of a female protagonist therefore brings about a variation on the normal *táin bó* pattern, and the interpretation of Medb's anomalous behaviour is seen as crucial to the understanding of this tale.

Medb: Sovereignty Goddess or All-too-human?

Medb's role in the *Táin* is pivotal. She identifies herself at the outset as the chief instigator of the foray: 'it is I who have mustered this hosting', and remains the driving force throughout the narrative. Her decisions are carried even against the advice of Ailill and Fergus. She has a major say in the choice of warriors sent against Cú Chulainn and the rewards they are promised. In her marriage she is the dominant partner: Ailill is a complaisant husband, virtually conniving in her cuckoldry of him with Fergus, as a means of securing Fergus's support in their expedition. It is she who quells the disturbance in the ranks caused by the attack of the war-goddess and the dire prophecy of Dubhthach. She leads a sub-expedition of her own for a fortnight to Dál Riata. At the end of the tale she participates actively, and initially with success, in the actual fighting.

While much in the presentation of Medb's character has the impact of a tour-de-force of verisimilitude, her exercise of power is unlikely to reflect the reality of early Irish society. Ó Corráin comments: 'On the political level, women never inherited political power as such and never governed as independent sovereigns or rulers, though, of course, strong-minded women had a powerful influence on the political activities of their husbands. Indeed, Medb … is the archetypal strong woman—determined, domineering and wanton—and we need not doubt that there were many like her in real life'. Kelly points out that 'the annals provide no instances of a female political or military leader. Indeed, the male imagery which surrounds the office of kingship … would seem to preclude even the possibility of a female ruler.' The imagery of kingship is well-attested in the literature of all periods. Its fundamental element symbolizes the land as a woman, with whom the prospective king must mate if his reign is to be legitimate. Various reflexes of this mythic female have been identified, but Medb is considered 'the outstanding figure of the territorial goddess in Irish literature'. One of the ways the goddess signalled acceptance of a would-be king was to offer him a drink: this aspect is conveyed in Medb's very name, which has been explained as a derivative of the word *med* 'mead', meaning 'the intoxicating (or intoxicated) one'. Medb Lethderg of Tara who is considered to be the original sovereignty goddess, of whom her namesake, the queen of Connacht in the Ulster Cycle, is a literary reflex. Medb Chrúachna's divine aspect is only 'vestigial in Recension I of the *Táin*, but Recension II is more explicit when it has her stipulate the qualities she demands in a husband: he should be *cen néoit, cen ét, cen omon* 'without meanness, without jealousy, without fear'. Absence of jealousy is necessary 'for I was never without a man in the shadow of another' (i.e. without one lover quickly succeeding another). This was once seen as a reference to the loose morals of pre-Christian Ireland, but Medb's promiscuity has been more plausibly explained as a reflection of her original role as the mythic sovereignty figure, union with whom is constantly sought by candidates for the kingship.

For all that some contexts do identify Medb as a classic sovereignty figure, this aspect is certainly not to the fore in *Táin Bó Cúailnge*. O'Rahilly notes that here 'she is no longer a goddess but a masterful woman, with the inevitable result that her character has sadly degenerated, so much so that at times she is no better than a strong-willed virago with unconcealed leanings towards a multiplicity of husbands and paramours.' I suggest that O'Rahilly's view of Medb's 'degeneracy' is shared by her literary creator, and that it is a central purpose of the *Táin* to depict her in a thoroughly unflattering light.

Medb's conduct of her expedition is shown to be severely wanting. She makes an inauspicious start when she rejects the vision of the prophetess Fedelm, whom she has asked 'How do you see the fate of the army?' Fedelm replies three times, chillingly, ' *Atchíu forderg, atchíu rúad*' 'I see it bloody, I see it red'. Twice Medb disputes the veracity (*fír*) of this prediction, and finally dismisses it as of little significance (*ní bá a aní sin trá*). She proposes to kill the crack regiment, the Gaileóin, lest they gain all the credit for the success of the raid, or eventually turn against the Connacht forces and defeat them. Ailill remarks laconically: '*Ní chélam as banchomairle*' 'I shall not deny that is a woman's counsel'. That following a woman's advice can only have negative results is a topos in many texts, and in a later scene Fergus pleads with Ailill not to heed the 'foolish counsels of a woman' (*banairle baetha*) when Medb predicts victory. She airily discounts Fergus's lengthy eulogy of Cú Chulainn. When the river Cronn floods, Medb rejects the possibility of travelling upstream to its source to find a passage, but sets the troops three days and nights digging up the mountain to make a pass through it, since that will remain as a permanent insult to the Ulstermen. The Connacht leaders repeatedly violate the warriors' honour code (*fír fer* literally 'truth of men', usually translated 'fair play') against Ulster warriors, but Medb is the only one who personally recommends this course: *Brister fír fer fair* 'Let terms of fair play be broken against him'. Other characters make negative comments which reveal her reputation. When she plans a 'mock peace' (*sída celci*) to lure Cú Chulainn to a meeting unarmed, his charioteer warns: *At móra glonna Medbi … Atágur lám ar cúl aci* 'Many are Medb's treacherous deeds … I fear that she has help behind the scenes'. Although she fights actively, and initially with success, in the final pitched battle, in the end she is in the ignominious position of having to beg Cú Chulainn to spare her.

The last scene in which Medb appears shows her viciously disparaged as a woman for aspiring to military leadership. Her admission to Fergus that their forces are routed elicits this savage riposte from him: '*Is bésad…do cach graig remitét láir, rotgata, rotbrata, rotfeither a móin hi tóin mná misrairleastair*' 'That is what usually happens … to a herd of horses led by a mare. Their substance is taken and carried off and guarded as they follow a woman who has misled them.' The implication is that a 'stallion' would have been a more suitable choice of leader, and Fergus's patronymic mac

Roeich 'son of great horse' marks him out as an ideal candidate. The final verdict of the narrative on Medb is therefore that she has usurped a man's function, and this is what has doomed the expedition from the start.

The positioning of this comment of Fergus's at a crucial point in the tale suggests that this aspect is of greater importance to the overall meaning of the *Táin* than has been acknowledged. Frank O'Connor noted 'the rancorous anti-feminist irony that occurs again and again through the story', and declared his conviction that 'the purpose of the original author would seem to have been to warn his readers against women, particularly women in positions of authority'. O'Connor's thesis is considered 'clearly extreme' by O'Leary, though even he concedes that 'distrust of women is by no means an insignificant theme' in the tale.

A further indication that Fergus's jibe may provide a clue to part of the central message of the *Táin* is that it echoes a phrase which occurs at other significant points in the narrative. The phrase is *tóin mná*, which has also been rendered less delicately as 'the rump of a woman' or 'a woman's buttocks'. The first use of the term in the tale certainly requires the literal translation. When the Morrígan in the guise of a beautiful young woman tries to distract Cú Chulainn from his task he dispatches her brusquely: *Ní ar thóin mná dano gabus-sa inso* 'it is not for a woman's body that I have come'. Conall Cernach taunts Fergus by implying a dishonourable motive for his Connacht allegiance: '*Baramór in bríg sin,*' ar Conall Cernach, '*for túaith 7 cenél ar thóin mná drúithi*' 'Too great is that force which you exert against (your own) people and race, following a wanton woman as you do,' said Conall Cernach. The editor's discreet rendering notwithstanding, the sexual innuendo is again clear.

Medb is therefore not just a 'heavily rationalized' reflex of the sovereignty goddess, but a negative manifestation of the figure. Granted, the classic 'straight' version of the myth of the sovereignty woman can depict her as mentally deranged or physically unattractive or deformed; but this when she is bereft of a suitable lover. The negative depiction of Medb in the *Táin* has also been interpreted in this light: 'It is of the essence of the myth that the beautiful sympathetic goddess is transformed into a harpy or a harridan whenever the cosmic plan is out of joint—as when usurpers or unworthy pretenders lay claim to her favours—and in this instance the monastic redactor has chosen to present her as a lusty and overbearing autocrat with a puppet husband'. Medb however retains all her beauty, and the focus of the text is not on Ailill's failings as a spouse, though of course they are a precondition for his wife's excesses. Of Medb's two male partners, it is Fergus who comes off the worst in the *Táin*; but he is rehabilitated as an honourable figure at the end.

One realization of the goddess which might be seen to merit the 'harpy or harridan' formulation is Sín, in *Aided Muirchertaig meic Erca* (The death of Muirchertach mac Erca). Sín is 'a diabolical sovereignty woman who bewitches the Tara monarch [Muirchertach], causes him to abandon his former wife, and leads him to conflict and death' (McCone 1990, 133). Here again, however, the narrative does not put the burden of blame on Muirchertach's inadequacy as king: 'Sín leads a hitherto flawless sovereign astray out of personal malice' (*ibid*). O'Hehir (1983, 168) characterizes this tale as an 'anti-goddess story, reversing the pagan polarities' and attributes it to a 'Christian redactor bent on discrediting otherworld goddesses as queens'. *Aided Muirchertaig meic Erca* can thus be seen as an inversion of the 'normal' sovereignty goddess story pattern, and this strengthens the case for reading the *Táin* in a similar way.

There is some support therefore for the view that the characterisation of Medb as a negative paradigm of the sovereignty goddess is a serious thematic concern of *Táin Bó Cúailnge*. Its author takes the matter a step further, however.

As we have seen, Medb does not confine herself to traditionally female spheres of activity. And the narrative judges her in accordance with the traditional criteria for the male role she aspires to. This can be seen in the legal implications of a number of incidents.

As mentioned above, in the final battle Medb is reduced to asking Cú Chulainn for his protection. He complies *úair nád gonad mná* 'because he used not to kill women' (4117). Medb, however, is a would-be combatant and should maintain the warrior ethos she seeks to embody. And 'pleading for quarter' is listed by the laws among the seven things which 'reveal the falsehood of [one party in] a duel' (Kelly 1988, 212–213). That doing so amounts to an admission of cowardice is shown by a contrasting instance where a defeated adversary asks a favour of Cú Chulainn. The full import of the scene is spelled out in Recension II: the dying Lóch asks that his body be let fall in such a way as to allay any suspicion that he was killed in flight. He justifies his plea: *Ní ascid anacail nó midlachais iarraim-se fort* 'No favour of quarter do I ask nor do I make a cowardly request', and Cú Chulainn concurs: is *láechda ind ascid connaigi* 'it is a warrior's request you make' (*TBC II* 2005–2010).

Themes

In keeping with the view that *Táin Bó Cúailnge* is epic or heroic literature, the main thematic concern has been formulated as 'the celebration of the martial heroism of Cú Chulainn; of his courage and ingenuity, his mastery of the martial arts, his unswerving loyalty'. Certainly the greatest bulk of the tale is devoted to Cú Chulainn's exploits, and he is depicted in a wholly favourable light. This rubs off on the Ulaid, who are the victors in the contention. Some scholars however dispute the apparent corollary that the whole heroic age in general is also being celebrated. Radner notes that the tale emphasises the negative effects of war, summarised in Cú Chulainn's statement on hearing the clamour of the final battle: *conscar bara bith* 'anger destroys the world'. 'Thematically', she argues, 'the Ulster Cycle as a whole tends to present the tragic breakdown of those relationships on which early Irish society was founded: the relationships between host and guest, between kindred, between foster-brothers, between men and women, between lords and clients and kings and overkings, between the human world and the gods. Behind the immense vitality, humor and imagination of the Ulster stories is a picture of society moving to dysfunction and serf-destruction'.

Yet the blame for the breakdown of social order is not laid impartially on both sides, or on all participants. As far as 'societal' virtues such as *goire* 'filial piety' and *condalbae* 'love of kin, patriotism' are concerned, as exemplified in the behaviour of the Ulster characters, they prove resilient in the end. Fergus's kin-love (*condalbae*) causes him to sabotage the Connacht venture, he can be prevailed upon to desist from attacking the Ulaid in the final battle, and his ties of fostership with Cú Chulainn preclude their engaging in direct combat. The Ulaid are presented as strongly motivated by *condalbae* in relation to Conchobar's grandson. It is Medb who sets foster-brothers, foster-fathers and foster-sons against each other, who offers her daughter as a bribe to any likely opponent of Cú Chulainn, and who seduces Fergus into disloyalty to his kin.

The most negative point about the Ulaid is their inability to support Cú Chulainn through the winter months, and Radner makes the attractive suggestion that their mysterious sickness, the *ces noínden*, is 'the tangible and persistent symbol of a radical flaw in the Ulstermen'. Aitchison also notes the ambiguous tone in the depiction of Ulster glory, but his conclusion that the Ulster Cycle is anti-Ulaid propaganda is informed less by the *Táin* than by other Ulster tales. In the *Táin* the Ulaid are certainly not singled out for criticism, but I would agree that whole-hearted approval of war is withheld. The tale does not dwell indulgently on descriptions of the large-scale battle, and the final encounters, between Fergus on the one hand and Conall Cernach and Cú Chulainn on the other, pass off without human casualties. This I would interpret as a reflection of a general pacifist stance, which would accord well with a hypothesis of clerical authorship.

The immediate catalyst for the chaos and killing is the cattle raid itself. Though such raiding may have been 'the most typical and abiding event recorded in the annals down the centuries' and 'a commonplace, not to say routine, experience to every individual in the population', there is evidence that efforts were made by the Church to put a stop to it, or to alleviate the destruction it could entail. Killing plough oxen and stealing milch kine are said to be among the three most serious offences which Patrick proscribed. The canons of Adamnán, no later than the ninth century, lay down that 'cattle seized in a raid are not to be taken by Christians whether in trade or as gifts'. An ecclesiastical *Cáin* attributed to a sixth-century nun Dar Í enjoined 'not to kill cattle'. The annals record its promulgation four times between 810 and 826. This concern with the destructive potential of cattle-raiding is perhaps only implied in the narrative message of *Táin Bó Cúailnge,* but may have found more explicit literary reflection elsewhere in the Ulster Cycle: a passage in *Táin Bó Regamna* has been interpreted as advice to Cú Chulainn to give up cattle-raiding.

As the instigator of the cattle raid, Medb is the primary culprit, who as a woman has unjustifiably arrogated power and status to herself. It is her challenge to male superiority, the bedrock of a patriarchal society, which upsets the natural balance and destabilises society. One of the thematic concerns of the tale, then, is the perennial question of the relative roles in society of men and women. More specifically, it concentrates on Medb's unseemly aspirations towards the supreme male role, that of the king.

Style and Structure

It is generally agreed that one of the best features of early Irish storytelling is the terse, fast-paced style, consisting of taut, almost elliptical, sentences or phrases. It is deployed to striking advantage in conversation, lending passages of direct speech a staccato-like effect. As an example I quote from the touching exchange between Cú Chulainn and his mother in the first section of the *macgnímrada*:

> "Cú Chulainn asked his mother to let him go to join the boys.
>
> 'You shall not go,' said his mother, till you be escorted by some of the Ulster warriors.'
>
> 'I think it too long to wait for that,' said Cú Chulainn. 'Point out to me in what direction is Emain.'
>
> 'To the north there,' said his mother, 'and the journey is hard. Slíab Fúait lies between you and Emain.'
>
> 'I shall make an attempt at it at all events.' said Cú Chulainn"

In general, the older the text, the more economical the prose. A comparison with the Recension II version of the above scene may serve to illustrate the development in style between the ninth and twelfth centuries:

> "'It is too soon for you to go, my son,' said his mother, 'until there go with you a champion of the champions of Ulster or some of the attendants of Conchobar to ensure your safety and protection from the youths.' The effect is smoother, but tends to the verbose.

In another instance from Recension I, the succinctness of Medb's speech is a perfect vehicle for the stark message it conveys. She feels threatened by the superiority of the Gaileóin. Ailill tries to divine her intentions:

> 'Well then, what shall be done with them,' asked Ailill, 'since neither their staying nor their going pleases you?'
>
> 'Kill them!' said Medb.

The limpid quality prevails even in descriptive passages, as in the following extended word portrait of the prophetess Fedelm, which consists largely of verb-free nominal phrases:

> 'She had yellow hair. She wore a vari-coloured cloak with a golden pin in it and a hooded tunic with red embroidery. She had shoes with golden fastenings. Her face was oval, narrow below, broad above. Her eyebrows were dark and black. Her beautiful black eyelashes cast a shadow on to the middle of her cheeks. Her lips seemed to be made of partaing. Her teeth were like a shower of pearls between her lips. She had three plaits of hair: two plaits wound around her head, the third hanging down her back, touching her calves behind. In her hand she carried a weaver's

beam of white bronze, with golden inlay. There were three pupils in each of her eyes. The maiden was armed and her chariot was drawn by two black horses'.

An eleventh-century addition to Recension I, which contains a description of Cú Chulainn's hair, provides a contrast and highlights the later tendency to heap up adjectives: 'Fair was the arrangement of that hair with three coils in the hollow in the nape of his neck, and like gold thread was each fine hair, loose-flowing, bright-golden, excellent, long-tressed, splendid and of beautiful colour, which fell back over his shoulder. A hundred bright crimson ringlets of flaming red-gold encircled his neck'.

Some stretches of direct speech in the *Táin* are in a rhythmical alliterative style called *rosc(ad)* or *retoiric*. Their syntax is frequently marked, and they have therefore often been held to belong to an older linguistic stratum of the text. Corthals points out, however, that in the *Táin* such passages are fully integrated into the surrounding 'straight' prose as regards narrative content. Rather than reflecting a chronological divide, they exemplify one of the possible varieties in the 'supple stylistic continuum' of early Irish writing. A lengthy stretch of *roscad* occurs in the exchange between Ailill, Fergus and Medb after the love-making scene. Another context which features this style is the Morrígan's prophecy to the bull. The style here is even more highly marked, through the use of metre for the words of the actual prophecy, contained in the two central lines below, which are linked by alliteration to the surrounding rhetorical prose (alliterating consonants in boldface):

'…I have a secret which the Black one will find out: 'If he will (=would) eat in May (?) the very green grass of the bogland, he would be overpowered (and driven) out of his field by fire (and) contest of strong warriors.' The flowering splendour of the host seduces the Bodb'.

Another variation in style is brought about by an alternation between prose and syllabic verse. Some sections have no syllabic verse at all, e.g. the *macgnímrada*, while the eleventh century Fer Diad episode (2567–3142) features almost a half-and-half distribution between these two modes. After this episode the remaining thousand or so lines are entirely in prose, with some short passages of *roscad*.

The narrative technique also features diversity. A popular means of ringing the changes on conventional exposition is the 'watchman device'. This consists of description presented by a knowledgeable participant in the events (the 'watchman'), rather than by an omniscient narrator. The device

has not found favour with the taste of modern scholars, who have dismissed instances in other texts as 'long and tedious', or 'repetitive and wearisome'. With an effort of empathy, however, it is possible to see some virtue in its employment in the *Táin*.

If it is correct to suggest that it is no concern of the tale to glorify war, the author is faced with the problem of how to create a credible battle scenario without direct description of the carnage. He conveys a sense of the strength of the defending army in the lengthy account of the approach of the Ulster warriors as viewed by the Connachtmen. The use of the watchman device here is far from mechanical: a reconnaissance man is sent out and returns with descriptions of individual warriors, who Fergus, their one-time comrade, is asked to identify. His answers are not stereotyped, and his personal reactions are varied. Another sophisticated use of the technique furnishes a *post hoc* and indirect account of bloody combat in 'The hard fight of Cethern'. The wounded Ulsterman Cethern will not suffer any physician near him, so the diagnosis of his injuries is conducted at a distance: he describes the warriors who wounded him, and here it is Cú Chulainn, all too familiar with the Connacht adversaries, who identifies them. In contrast, the account of Cú Chulainn's own participation in the final fray is a gem of understatement:

'It was midday when Cú Chulainn came to the battle. When the sun was sinking behind the trees in the wood, he overcame the last of the bands, and of the chariot there remained only a handful of the ribs of the framework and a handful of the shafts round the wheel'.

This stunning image is expressed with all the eloquence and brevity of the most admired passages of early Irish prose, but the other narrative responses to the task of describing the battle need not therefore be denied structural validity and artistic intent.

The structure of the opening scenes of the *Táin* has evoked unanimous critical approval. Some of the best literary effects here have been analysed by Carney. In the initial portion, some eight hundred lines, from the mustering of the Connacht forces to the end of the *macgnímrada*, he detects the hand of a literary personality, 'not a mere story-teller'. The *pièce-de-résistance* is undoubtedly the 'Boyhood deeds'. After the advance of the Connachtmen has been held up by some displays of Cú Chulainn's prowess, the forward movement of the narrative is interrupted with a flashback to enable the exiled Ulstermen to recall the most striking martial feats of his precocious childhood. The build-up to this flash-back is also impressive. The narrator's attention is initially directed entirely to the Connacht side. The prophecy of Fedelm soon casts an ominous shadow on their proceedings. Cú Chulainn only slowly comes into focus: he is first referred to, but not named, in the prophecy of Dubthach (194), as the army traverses the centre of the country. When they reach the east, Fergus sends him a warning. From then on, Cú Chulainn's presence is increasingly felt, until he kills four of the vanguard of the invading army and sets their heads up on spits to confront the Connachtmen when they arrive. It is at this point that Ailill and Medb inquire about their formidable opponent, and the Ulstermen each contribute their memories of his 'boyhood deeds': this sets the scene for the ultimate triumph of the Ulster defence, and reinforces the sense of foreboding which dogs the Connacht forces throughout. Such 'tricks of presentation' Carney (*ibid* 71) considers to be evidence of a wholly literary sophistication, of a quality rare even in the early texts.

The remainder of the tale has not received anything like the same accolades. Greene's judgement (1954, 32) that 'the long series of single combats becomes wearisome and the story tails off badly' is probably representative of modern scholarly opinion. For Carney (1955, 67) the decline in the quality of the narration sets in with the very first of the single combats, the interpolated 'Death of Fróech'. Admittedly 'after this point … there are a greater number of incidents which are merely of antiquarian interest' (*ibid*), but perhaps there are some points of significance encoded in the placenames or personal names in the single encounters which may yet be elucidated. However that may be, O'Rahilly concedes that 'the skill with which these encounters are varied in circumstance and detail is remarkable'.

Source: Patricia Kelly, "The *Táin* as Literature," in *Aspects of the Tain,* edited by J. P. Mallory, December Publications, 1992, pp. 69–95.

David Greene

This lecture by David Greene regarding Táin Bó Cúailnge *relates the story's origins, history, and its many versions, providing a sense of this story's national and international appeal.*

People who deal with early Irish literature, usually refer to *Táin Bó Cúailnge* simply as 'the *Táin*'. This

Cu Chulainn carries Ferdiad across the river.

is partly a handy abbreviation, but it is also the usage in Irish literature and it tells us something about the story; it is the original *Táin*, and the other stories whose titles begin with *Táin Bó* are all either later stories or old ones which have been re-worked to bring them into relationship with the *Táin* as *remscéla*—preliminary stories. . . .

And why was this black bull of Cooley so badly wanted? Well, one of the versions of the *Táin*—not the oldest—gives us a nice rational interpretation. Ailill, king of Connacht, and his wife Maeve, chatting in bed one night, begin to argue about what each of them brought into the marriage. The argument grows so heated that they decide to compare their property on the spot, and, for every treasure that Ailill can produce, Maeve can find one to match it—except for one, a fine bull called Finnbheannach—Whitehorned—which had originally belonged to Maeve but had refused to be a woman's property and had joined the king's herd. When Maeve realises this, the rest of her wealth isn't worth a penny to her and she swears to get as good a bull for herself. The only one which is known to be good enough is the black bull of Cooley, owned by a certain Dáire. Maeve immediately sends messengers to Dáire to offer him the

> "*. . .even to the present day, the native genius has felt more at home with short stories than with long works of complicated construction; certainly there is nothing in the fragmentary Táin we have that would allow us to suspect the existence of a planned and developed prose epic. . .*"

most generous terms for the bull, and all goes well until the Connacht emissaries get drunk and are overheard boasting that if the bull were not given freely they would take it by force. Tempers rise, negotiations are broken off, and war is the only possible solution.

It's a human enough incident, very well told in the Book of Leinster. . .but I don't think it's part of the original story. At the very end of the *Táin* the two bulls, the white one from Connacht and the black one from Ulster, sweep aside the fighting men and finish the war for themselves; the Connacht bull is defeated and the black bull makes his way home triumphantly to Cooley before he, too, dies of his wounds. It is plain that these are no mere animals, but heroic and god-like creatures; we have memories here, however altered, of a cult of bull-gods, such as is well known from the ancient civilisations of the Mediterranean.

The *Táin*, then, like the rest of the Ulster sagas, preserves pre-Christian traditions—but of what period? The German scholar Windisch and the English archaeologist Ridgeway were struck, over fifty years ago, by the resemblances between the chariot-fighting warriors of the *Táin* and the Celts of Britain and Gaul described by classical writers in the first century B.C., and Windisch pointed out, reasonably enough, that this way of life could have survived considerably longer in Ireland, free from Roman observers and Roman invaders. But, while the Romans seem to have regarded the Gauls as fairly civilised people, the contemporary Irish were not so

acceptable; the chariots in the *Táin* were often decorated with newly acquired human heads, and scholars educated in the classical tradition felt that the *Táin* stories would be more fittingly placed in a vague and distant past. . . .

This view lingers on; it's only a year or so since I read an article which said that 'it is an acknowledged fact that the *Táin* cycle embodies memories of the Celtic way of life and of Celtic beliefs in the centuries from 500 B.C. to 100 A.D.' I think that talking in terms of Celts, and more especially of Celtic gentlemen, is liable to distract our attention from the main point. We know that Celts came to Ireland, since Irish is a Celtic language, and we know that early Irish society has many points in common with that of Celtic Gaul, as well as more distant relationships with early Rome and India. But that Irish society, and the literature it produced, are neither Indo-European nor Celtic, but simply Irish, and must be studied on that basis. Certain elements belonging to the coherent society portrayed in the *Táin*—totem and tabu, headhunting, fighting from chariots—are unknown in early Christian Ireland and cannot, therefore, be inventions of literary men influenced by Latin learning; we need not go too far in the other direction, however, and regard them as memories of an infinitely remote past. You may remember that some of the antiquarian writers after the end of the Old Irish period like to put the death of Conchobhar Mac Neasa, the king of Ulster in these stories, as coincidental with the death of Christ, but that is, of course, just a conjecture or invention. Remembering that writing was little known in Ireland before the fifth century, and writing in Irish not much before the seventh, we have to ask ourselves how long we should allow for an oral tradition which would preserve all these archaic features, free from any admixture of Christian lore. Not too long, I would suggest; the most important fact that occurs to me is that the same antiquarian writers put the abandonment of Emhain Mhacha, the capital of the Ulstermen in all these tales, somewhere about the middle of the fourth century. It's a common enough device to choose, as the subject of a national epic, a people or kingdom which has no longer any real political existence—it prevents any charges of undue favouritism against the literary men. If the Ulaid, this warlike people who gave their name to the whole province, if they preserved what we might call the *Táin* way of life up to the fourth century, and then were overwhelmed by an alliance of their enemies, it is not impossible that, just before the coming of Christianity and writing, the stories about them should have become part of the stock-in-trade of the literary men. These stories would hardly have been popular in the first flush of missionary enthusiasm—not popular, that is to say, with the propagators of the new learning. But in no country did the church make its peace with the old learning as quickly or as thoroughly as in Ireland; the elegiac poem in the old bardic style on St. Columba, who died in 597, is sufficient proof that a complete understanding had been arrived at by that date. And I think we might accept one more deduction from the antiquarian writers and say that the alleged finding of the *Táin* by the poet Seanchán Torpéist in the seventh century—he had to call up Fergus from the dead to tell it—that this finding of the *Táin* is just the antiquarians' way of saying that it then became respectable to write it down.

Not only writing down this traditional material, but re-arranging it as well. Most of our early sagas are quite short—about the length of this lecture, say. But even the earliest version of the *Táin* is about ten times that length and the Book of Leinster version longer still; they are no longer stories, but literary works. This, I suppose, was partly due to the fact that the story-tellers now had pen and vellum and could spread themselves, and there's probably a good deal of truth in the suggestion of Thurneysen that the *Táin* in its present form has been influenced by the Aeneid; the writers were out to provide Ireland with a national epic.

I find that I have been talking as though this seventh century *Táin* had been preserved, but the fact of the matter is that we can only deduce its existence from later evidence. . . .

. . .Our earliest literary manuscripts in Irish are as late as the twelfth century. One of these, Leabhar na hUidhre, or the Book of the Dun Cow, contains the earliest version of the *Táin* known to us, and there is another copy of the same version in the Yellow Book of Lecan. But this version is not a straightforward story at all; it is a compilation by somebody who was interested in collecting as much of the varying traditions of the *Táin* as possible. He does not attempt to conceal the fact; he interjects remarks such as 'They say it is here that Dubhthach sang the lay', 'But other books have the following version', 'According to another version, however', and so on. These are the remarks a modern editor would reserve for footnotes or a preface; here they are jumbled in with the text and, as they suggest, we often find two versions of the same incident told one after the other.

This arises, of course, from the popularity of the story. Once it had been established as the national epic, it became the common property of saga-writers who remoulded it to the taste of their period. We have plenty of parallels from other literatures; you will remember Professor Stanford's researches on the figure of Ulysses throughout the ages, and the play by Giraudoux, called Amphitryon 38, because it was the thirty-eighth handling of the theme, by the dramatist's own reckoning. From this point of view we can regard Yeats's use of Irish saga themes in his verse plays as a perfectly legitimate continuation of a process that had been going on since the beginning of Irish literature. But, to return to the *Táin*, it is sad that we do not possess one of the early versions in its entirety, instead of having to piece a story together from the very varied material gathered together by the industrious compiler. . . .

. . .The original material of the *Táin* lay in the rivalry between the divine bulls, with which the story still begins and ends; Cú Chulainn's part, originally just an incident in the story, has been enormously expanded, in two ways. The first was to describe, not just one or two of his fights on the ford, while delaying the Connacht troops, but all of them, and in great detail; the most famous of these, the fight with Fer Diad, although occurring in the earliest version, is still so late in style and language as to show beyond doubt that it cannot be a great deal older than the twelfth century manuscript in which it is written down. You remember the story: Fer Diad, Cú Chulainn's old friend and comrade, is plied with drink and women, threatened with satire, and cajoled with promises of wealth, until he promises to fight Cú Chulainn, by whom, of course, he falls. Cú Chulainn's lament over him has been well rendered by Sigerson:

'Every other combat and fight that ever I have made was to me but a game or a sport, compared to the combat and the fight of Ferdia. And he spake these words:
Play was each, pleasure each,
Till Ferdia faced the beach …'

This is fine stuff, as is the quarrel between Ailill and Maeve to which I have already referred, but it is not part of the original story, and neither, in all probability, are most of the fights on the ford, the best of which are by the same hand as wrote the 'boyish deeds'—the Prose-writer, as O'Connor calls him because, though his language is much older than that of the Fer Diad episode, it is not interspersed either with verse or with rhetorics—those passages in obscure alliterative rhythmic language which are characteristic of the older sagas and which we find in long passages between Ailill, Maeve and Fergus in the *Táin*. The language is barer here and the background more barbarous; take the death of Etarcomol, who forces a fight on Cú Chulainn against Fergus' advice:

> Loeg said to Cú Chulainn: 'The chariot is back again and it has turned its left side to us'. 'That is not an obligation that can be refused', said Cú Chulainn, 'we will go down to the ford to meet it and see about it'. 'I do not wish what you ask of me', said Cú Chulainn. 'You must do it', said Etarcomol. Cú Chulainn cut the sod from under his foot, so that he fell with the sod on his belly. 'Get away from me', said Cú Chulainn, 'I don't want to have to clean my hands on your account. I would have you cut into many pieces long ago had it not been for Fergus'. 'We will not part this way', said Etarcomol, 'I will bring away your head or leave my head with you'. 'That is what will happen', said Cú Chulainn and struck with his sword under his two armpits, so that his clothes fell off him, but his skin was not touched. 'Go away now', said Cú Chulainn. 'No', said Etarcomol. Cú Chulainn swept him then with the edge of his sword and took his hair off as though it had been shaved with a razor. And, since the boor was still tiresome and persistent, he struck him on the top of the head and split him to the navel.

We can imagine how popular this murderous sort of slap-stick was with early Irish audiences, especially when connected with the great name of Cú Chulainn, and they were given plenty of it. But the second and greater triumph of the Prose-writer was his introduction of the stories of the hero's boyhood, given as the reminiscences of Fergus and the other Ulster exiles with Connacht forces—exiles, you will remember, since the death of Deirdre and the sons of Uisliu. This is the technique familiar to us in the modern cinema as the 'flash-back', and it is used here with remarkable effect, with little naturalistic touches such as 'that took place in the presence of Bricriu here', and 'I met him in the door of the lios and I badly wounded' and 'nine of the boys dashed past Conchobhar and myself, who were playing chess'. It is more than a little surprising to find so sophisticated a style allied to very primitive, not to say barbarous material; the language of these stories shows that they can hardly have been written much before the ninth century, but there is no admixture at all of classical or ecclesiastical elements. They are one of the happiest examples of the process I have mentioned before, the remoulding of a traditional theme; extraneous though they may be to the action of the *Táin*, they came to form an integral part of it—indeed, to modern taste, by far the most attractive part. . . .

. . .For example:

I haven't had enough of my game yet, uncle Conchobhar', said the boy, 'I will go after you'. When they all reached the feast Culann said to Conchobhar, 'Is anyone coming after you?' 'No', said Conchobhar; he did not remember that he had told his foster-son to follow him. 'I have a fierce dog', said Culann, 'there are three chains on it, and three men on each chain. Let it be loosed to protect our cattle and let the lios be closed?' The boy comes along then. The dog makes for him. He kept on his game meanwhile; he was throwing his ball and throwing his hurling stick after it so that it struck the ball. This shocked Conchobhar and his people so that they were unable to move; they thought they could not reach him alive, even if the lios had been open. When the hound reached him, he threw away his ball and stick and seized the hound with his two hands, one on its throat and the other at the back of its head, and swung it against a pillar-stone which was nearby, so that every limb of it sprang asunder. The Ulstermen rushed towards him, some over the wall, others through the door of the lios, and he was placed in Conchobhar's arms. They raised a great clash of arms, because the son of the king's sister had nearly been killed.

Well, the smith comes along then, and while rejoicing over the boy's escape, laments the death of the dog which protected his wealth, and Sétanta offers to take its place until another dog can be reared; and Cathbhadh, the druid, says 'Cú Chulainn shall be your name'. . . .

. . .For the *Táin,* taken as a whole, can hardly be called an artistic success; if it's really intended as an imitation of the Aeneid, it's a very bad one. Of course, we have to make allowances for the fact that the earliest version we possess is the merest hotch-potch; how much we would give for a sight of those *alii libri*, those other books to which the compiler so often refers! But, even to the present day, the native genius has felt more at home with short stories than with long works of complicated construction; certainly there is nothing in the fragmentary *Táin* we have that would allow us to suspect the existence of a planned and developed prose epic—nothing to suggest that the *Táin* was ever otherwise than jerky and episodic. I have suggested that later revisers threw the original story of the contest between the two bulls considerably out of proportion by devoting more and more attention to the attractive figure of the hero Cú Chulainn. And yet the *Táin* ends, as it begins, with the bulls, with the picture of the Black Bull of Cooley making his way home from Connacht with the carcase of his broken rival on his horns.

Source: David Greene, "The *Táin Bó Cúailnge*," in *Irish Sagas*, edited by Myles Dillon, Stationary Office, Dublin, 1959, pp. 94–106.

SOURCES

Aitchison, N. B., "The Ulster Cycle: Heroic Image and Historical Reality," in *Journal of Medieval History*, 13, 1987.

Carney, James, *Studies in Irish Literature and History*, Dublin Institute, 1955.

Hillers, Barbara, "The Heroes of the Ulster Cycle," in *Ulidia, Proceedings of the First International Conference on the Ulster Cycle of Tales*, edited by J. P. Mallory and Gerard Stockman, December Publications, 1995, pp. 99–106.

Kelly, Patricia, "The *Táin* as Literature," in *Aspects of the Táin*, edited by J. P. Mallory, December Publications, 1992, pp. 69–102.

Kinsella, Thomas, trans., *The Táin*, Oxford University Press, 1969.

Lambkin, B. K., "Navan Fort and the Arrival of 'Cultural Heritage,'" in *Emania: Bulletin of the Navan Research Group*, No. 11, 1993, pp. 61–4.

———, "The Ulster Cycle, The Navan Centre, and the Improvement of Community Relations in Northern Ireland," in *Ulidia, Proceedings of the First International Conference on the Ulster Cycle of Tales*, edited by J. P. Mallory and Gerard Stockman, December Publications, 1995, pp. 281–90.

Murphy, Gerard, *Saga and Myth in Ancient Ireland*, Published for the Cultural Relations Committee of Ireland by Colm O Lochlainn, 1955.

O'Corrain, Pádraig, "The *Táin*: A Clue to its Origins," in *Ulidia, Proceedings of the First International Conference on the Ulster Cycle of Tales*, edited by J. P. Mallory and Gerard Stockman, December Publications, 1995, pp. 31–7.

Yeats, W. B., *Selected Plays*, edited by Richard Allen Cave, Penguin Books, 1997.

FURTHER READING

Dillon, Myles, ed., *Early Irish Society*, Published for the Cultural Relations Committee of Ireland by Colm O Lochlainn, 1954.
In need of updating, but there is still no introduction so well suited to the student. Dillon loved his subject, and his love is infectious.

———, ed., *Irish Sagas*, Thomas Davis Lectures, Published for Radio Éireann by the Stationary Office, 1959.
Another classic from the Thomas Davis Lectures, each scholar retells and discusses one of the Irish legendary tales. It is almost impossible to put this little book down.

Kelly, Patricia, "The *Táin* as Literature," in *Aspects of the Táin*, edited by J. P. Mallory, December Publications, 1992, pp. 69–102.
A clearly written introduction to the literary qualities of *Táin Bó Cúailnge*. Studies of the Táin Bó Cúailnge as literature are few and far between. Kelly's discussion goes some way to make good this lack, particularly for the student.

Kinsella, Thomas, trans., *The Táin*, Oxford University Press 1969.
This is the most useful translation for the non-specialist. It introduces the reader to all the beauties as well as all the scholarly puzzles of the *Táin Bó Cúailnge*. There are careful, but not overwhelming notes, including the identification of manuscript sources of the additional material. Louis le Brocquy's brush drawings make it one of the high points of twentieth century book illustration.

Mallory, J. P., "The World of Cú Chulainn: The Archaeology of *Táin Bó Cúailnge*," in *Aspects of the Táin*, edited by J. P. Mallory, December Publications, 1992, pp. 103–59.
This study will prove useful in two ways. First, it is an absolutely vital study for our understanding of the development and historical source of the *Táin Bó Cúailnge*. Second, it is a nearly flawless example of how literature and archaeology ought to be used to illuminate one another.

ÓUiginn, Ruairi, "The Background and Development of the *Táin Bó Cúailnge*," in *Aspects of the Táin*, edited by J. P. Mallory, December Publications, 1992, pp. 29–68.
Another excellent essay from the Mallory collection. ÓUiginn gives a thorough and clear overview of the theories of how the *Táin Bó Cúailnge* of the manuscripts came into being.

The Tale of Genji

LADY MURASAKI SHIKIBU

1000

Murasaki Shikibu's epic-length novel, *The Tale of Genji*, probes the psychological, romantic and political workings of mid-Heian Japan. The novel earned Murasaki Shikibu notoriety even in the early 11th century, some six hundred years before the printing press made it available to the masses. Court society, which served as the subject of the novel, sought out chapters. Ladies-in-waiting and courtiers even pilfered unrevised copies, according to legend. Some thousand years later, Murasaki Shikibu and her novel continue to delight an enthusiastic audience. Stamps, scrolls, comic books, museums, shower gel, movies, parades, puppet plays, CD-ROMS: Murasaki Shikibu and her creation *Genji* have achieved National Treasure status in Japan and admiration all over the world.

The tale spreads across four generations, splashed with poetry and romance and heightened awareness to the fleeting quality of life. Murasaki Shikibu's tale of love, sex, and politics explores a complex web of human and spiritual relationships. This focus on characters and their emotional experience, as compared to plot, makes the novel easily accessible to the modern reader. It explains, in part, why many scholars consider *Genji* to be the world's first great novel.

Readers through the ages have especially admired Murasaki Shikibu's depiction of the Heian court society's deep aesthetic sense. Beauty—in flesh, flowers, sunsets, musical notes—moved and

influenced the society. The title character, Genji, flourishes in this atmosphere. He is a master of speech, poetry, music, manners, dress.

Many Japanese scholars cite as an influence Chinese poet Po-Ch-I's classic narrative poem, *The Song of Unending Sorrow*. Murasaki Shikibu writes in her diary of reading the poet's work to the empress. She also refers to it several times in *The Tale of Genji*. Importantly, the novel also marked Japan's liberation from Chinese influence. According to Richard Bowring in *Landmarks of World Literature: The Tale of Genji*, "Japan had just emerged from a time of substantial Chinese influence and was going through one of its periodic stages of readjustment, during which alien concepts were successfully naturalized. *The Genji* is thus the product of a native culture finding a truly sophisticated form of self-expression in prose for the first time."

The Tale of Genji has had a pervasive influence on later Japanese and world-wide art. It has inspired Noh theater, waka poetry, scroll paintings, pop music and dances. It has had an especially profound influence on Japanese literature. Court fiction for hundreds of years after openly modeled itself after Genji. Present-day writers, including Kawabata Yasunari in his 1968 Nobel Prize acceptance speech, still cite *The Tale of Genji* as a great influence.

AUTHOR BIOGRAPHY

Murasaki Shikibu wrote the long novel *The Tale of Genji*, a diary, a collection of short lyric poems, and assorted poems found only in royally commissioned anthologies.

Very little is known for certain about her life. Much of her biography is gleaned from *Murasaki Shikibu Diary* and a set of autobiographical poems she left behind. She may have been born as early as 973, but possibly as many as five years later. She died some time between 1013 and 1031. Accepted wisdom has it that Murasaki Shikibu died around her fortieth year.

Murasaki Shikibu was born in the Japanese capital of Kyoto. Her father, Fujiwara Tametoki, was a member of a minor branch of the nation's most powerful family. Heian Japanese custom deemed it bad manners to record the names of well-born ladies. Shikibu refers to her father's post in the Board of Rites. Murasaki, which literally means

"violet," probably refers to the character in her own novel. Before she began writing *Genji*, she seemed to have been known as To Shikibu.

Murasaki Shikibu's mother died when she was still a child. Her father was a well-known scholar, and other ancestors were accomplished poets. She grew up in her father's house, where she was educated alongside her brother. Murasaki Shikibu profited from her family's artistic and scholastic pedigree, as well as from the circumstances of her education. She learned all the feminine arts which would have been expected of her, but also developed a great command of Chinese and Japanese literature, as well as Buddhist writings. These pursuits were generally reserved for men.

Murasaki Shikibu married at about the age of twenty, but her husband died a year later. She had one daughter. Murasaki Shikibu probably began writing *Genji* before 1005, when she was appointed lady-in-waiting to Shoshi, the consort of Emperor Ichijo. Shoshi's father, Michinaga, had surrounded Shoshi with a brilliant group of court ladies, and Murasaki Shikibu may have been included because parts of *Genji* had already been circulated and admired. Her activities at Shoshi's court are detailed in the diary, which primarily deals with the birth of two sons to the empress between the fall of 1008 and the beginning of 1010.

Living among aristocrats, Murasaki Shikibu probably was privy to gossip of real court people. That knowledge, along with her cultured upbringing and sensitivity to human nature, helped Murasaki Shikibu to create a masterpiece of literature.

Long-standing debates about the chapter orders and whether the work is of a single author will likely never be solved. Except for fragments, the earliest surviving texts are from at least two centuries after the date of composition. The book circulated in the court in Murasaki Shikibu's days, not in complete manuscript form but rather as chapters. Thus, it's unlikely readers experienced the chapters in the chronology Murasaki Shikibu intended. The proper chapter order debate is complicated by the fact that some chapters discuss events that happened at the same time, instead of advancing the plot chronologically.

Serious scholars do not question that Murasaki Shikibu wrote most—if not all—of *The Tale of Genji*. However, the discrepancies in style and tone, as well as poetic technique, have convinced some that isolated chapters were written by somebody else. The final ten chapters , in which the mood turns noticeably more pessimistic, are the subject of the most skepticism.

PLOT SUMMARY

Chapters 1–41

The Emperor and Kiritsubo give birth to the he novel's hero, Genji, in 11th century Japan. Kiritsubo, the Emperor's true love, is of the lower ranks of court. The slander and petty jealousy of the other palace wives contribute to the mental anguish which results in her early death, when Genji is but three years old.

Genji from the start impresses everybody with his unparalleled beauty. He is exceptional in every way. He is raised in the court. Despite his father's unflinching devotion, indeed because of it, the boy receives the name Genji, which classifies him as a commoner. The Emperor knows that without influential maternal relatives, Genji's position as a crown prince (or a son picked to become future Emperor) would be tentative, especially after his own death. Since the Kokiden faction will most certainly cause his son problems, it seems more practical to secure for him a court ranking (a political but not royal position) and to encourage his studies. A Korean soothsayer's prediction that the boy will never become emperor plays a part in this decision.

Genji, or Minamoto, roughly translated means ''commoner.'' It carries negative connotations, that the bearer of the name has been dispossessed of a potential birthright because of an embarrassment or scandal. But the name Hikaru Genji, by which he becomes known, means "the shining prince."

The Emperor's grief over Kiritsubo is eased when he meets her look-alike, Fujitsubo. She becomes the Emperor's official consort, and Genji grows up in her presence. Genji is drawn to Fujitsubo for much the same reasons as his father. The Emperor seeks a substitute for his wife, and Genji seeks a mother. Right after Genji's coming-of-age ceremony, at the age of twelve, Genji is married off to the Minister of the Left's daughter, Aoi. She is a Fujiwara. Aoi turns out to be cold and unsympathetic, and Genji spends most of his time at the Palace in his mother's apartments (though he is now denied access to her). His inattentiveness to his wife inspires resentment from his father-in-law. Aoi's

brother, To no Chujo, becomes both Genji's close friend and bitter rival.

Five years pass between the first and second chapters. At the age of seventeen, Genji is already an experienced lover. His countless affairs occupy much of his time and energy. He seems to have a penchant for difficult situations, that or he is too weak to avoid them. Genji seduces Yugao, a former mistress of To no Chuo's, and she dies of a mysterious ailment shortly after. Lady Rukujo's living ghost seems to be responsible. Though this is Lady Rukujo's first appearance, it is understood that her jealousy (she is one of Genji's many partners) is the root cause.

Genji, now eighteen, discovers Murasaki in the hills north of Kyoto. He is there seeking a cure for a persistent illness. Though just a girl of ten, Murasaki looks hauntingly like Fujitsubo. She turns out to be her niece. A series of negotiations in which Genji tries to adopt her fail. He won't be denied, though, and before her father, Prince Hyobu, can make his proper claim, Genji spirits her away to his household. He begins her education, grooming her to be his future romantic partner. Meanwhile, Genji's persistent efforts to be with Fujitsubo finally come to fruition. She becomes pregnant as a result of their one sexual encounter, but the son's real heritage must remain secret. Fujitsubo resolves not to allow Genji even the slightest access to her in the future, though the Emperor, unaware of the clandestine relationship, sometimes brings the two together. Everybody assumes the son, who eventually will be Emperor Reizei, to be the current Emperor's. Genji is filled with shame because he betrayed his father and fears that the secret will be revealed.

Genji's captivation with the young Murasaki further alienates him from Aoi. Meanwhile, he becomes involved with one of Kokiden's sisters, Oborozukiyo, who is engaged to the heir apparent (one of the crown princes). This is another very dangerous liaison because Kokiden sees Genji as a threat to her son, the crown prince.

Aoi becomes pregnant. As her pregnancy progresses, her health fails. Lady Rukujo again seems to be the culprit. Their baby is named Yugiri. When Aoi dies, Genji goes into a deep mourning, despite the couple's weak relationship. He consummates his relationship with Murasaki, thus making the transition from her father figure to her husband. The Emperor, Genji's father, dies, and the power shifts to the Minister of the Right and Lady Kokiden. As

Genji's power and influence decline, he seems to mature. But then the Minister of the Right catches his daughter, Oborozukiyo, and Genji in the act of making love. Lady Kokiden is determined to punish Genji.

Feeling the force of Kokiden's wrath, Genji decides to go into a self-imposed exile in Suma. By now Genji has entered his twenty-sixth year. He is surrounded in the rustic seaside retreat by only a few attendants. The capital denizens almost all grieve the loss of Genji, who by now is well-known for his many gifts and charm. Genji at first maintains hearty correspondence with many friends, but after a while only Murasaki and To no Chujo ignore Kokiden's wishes to have him left alone. Genji increasingly longs to return. During a fierce storm Genji dreams that his dead father has told him to put out to sea. Coincidentally, or by divine intervention, depending on one's reading, the ex-Governor of Harima visits Genji. The entourage goes to Akashi. The ex-Governor promotes a relationship between Genji and his daughter. The affair is consummated shortly before the young emperor officially pardons Genji, who heads home.

Back in the capital, Genji's half brother, the emperor, abdicates his thrown to Fujitsubo's son (secretly Genji's, too). Genji is restored to the court. Akashi has a baby girl back in Akashi. Genji's genuine sympathy for women is shown through several incidences: he agrees to raise the dying Lady Rokujo's daughter and also helps the safflower princess out of miserable conditions. Genji's sensitivity and artistic talents are further displayed during a painting contest. He wins hands down by displaying works he painted during his exile. Though just thirty-one years old, Genji already begins contemplating his retirement.

Genji's domestic life now takes the forefront. He builds a series of elaborate complexes to house his many love interests and children. While he is less reckless than in his youth, Genji continues to pursue new affairs, such as with his cousin Princess Asagao. Murasaki begins to worry that Genji has grown tired of her. Fujitsubo dies and a period of mourning follows.

Yugiri (Genji's son with Aoi), now twelve, enters court life. Yugiri is prevented from pursuing a relationship with To no Chujo's second daughter Kumoi-no-kari (his cousin). Genji gets a larger estate and finally all his wives can share the same address. He covertly manages to bring Yugao's daughter (by To no Chugo) to his palace, in part so that she might avoid a bad marriage. Now thirty-six, Genji seems content. He remains loyal to his many female relations.

Tamakazura, Yugao's daughter, becomes popular among suitors. Genji, too, begins to fall in love with her, but is rejected. Genji thinks of revealing her identity to To no Chugo, but then begins tutoring her on the koto and decides to leave things as they are. Yugiri feels a pang of desire but thinks Tamakazura is his sister. Then he eavesdrops on Genji acting in an unfatherly-like manner to her. To no Chujo meanwhile discovers a long-lost daughter, a most inelegant woman, living in Omi.

When it comes time for Tamakazura's initiation ceremony, Genji reveals her true parentage to To no Chujo. With this fact now well known, Tamakazura's relationships begin to change. She soon marries Higekuro, unhappily. Higekuro's former wife, Murasaki's stepsister, goes into a jealous fit and pours burning incense all over him.

Now thirty-nine, Genji prepares for his Akashi daughter's initiation ceremonies. The magnificent ceremony reminds To no Chujo that his own daughters have not been as successful. He rues his decision to separate his daughter Kumoi from Yugiri, who by now has achieved distinguished rank. At a memorial service for his late mother, the late Princess Omiya, To no Chujo approaches Yugiri about a reconciliation. Subsequently, at a wisteria-viewing party, the two resolve their differences. That very night, Yugiri consummates his relationship with Kumoi, and soon they move into the refurbished Sanjo mansion.

The retired Emperor Suzaku wants to become a Buddhist monk. He convinces Genji to marry his favorite daughter, Nyosan, so that she'll be well taken care of. Her installation at Rokujo worries Murasaki, who resolves not to show any signs of jealousy. Nyosan is of higher birth than Murasaki but is unrefined in every other way, and again Genji appreciates his true love all the more. Kashiwagi is intent on having an affair with Nyosan.

Meanwhile, the little Akashi princess has a baby boy. During her labor, she meets her old grandmother and learns that she was not born in the capital. This fact, which marks her as being of unsophisticated ancestry, serves to humble her.

Murasaki beseeches Genji to let her become a nun, but he refuses. Genji gives Nyosan music lessons to prepare for a performance honoring the retired Emperor Suzaku's fiftieth birthday. Murasaki again refuses to be jealous, and Genji contrasts her disposition to that of Aoi and Lady Rokujo. Murasaki falls ill, the work of Lady Rokujo's dead ghost. Once the ghost is lured into the open, Genji says prayers to appease her anger. Murasaki begins to get better.

While Genji is occupied with Murasaki, Kashiwagi seduces and impregnates Nyosan. Genji discovers the truth of the matter, and Kashiwagi's shame overwhelms him. He falls ill and dies before seeing his son. Nyosan delivers a boy who looks nothing like Genji and then becomes a nun. Yugiri takes responsibility for the care of his friend Kashiwagi's wife, Ochiba. Yugiri, who has been a near model of the faithful husband, soon makes unwanted advances toward Ochiba. When he returns to Kumoi, a letter arrives from Ochiba's mother. In order not to raise Kumoi's suspicions, Yugiri refuses to open it. Ochiba's mother assumes her daughter has been jilted, and soon after dies. Ochiba blames Yugiri, who alternately tries to console and seduce her. Kumoi, hurt and angered at her husband, takes her two daughters and moves back to her father's house.

In Genji's fifty-first year, Murasaki begins formal preparations for her death. She dies. Genji's grief is unbearable. He enters seclusion at Nijo, disperses his property, and destroys his old letters. His death scene is not rendered, but starting with Chapter 42 the story shifts to the third generation.

Chapters 42–54

Nine years have passed. Kaoru, distinguished by a strong and distinct odor, declines to pursue any romantic relationships, though he is desired by many court women. He becomes curious about the circumstances of his mother's flight to the nunnery. Niou does pursue romantic relationships. He, in fact, deliberately competes with Kaoru.

Kobai, To no Chujo's oldest surviving son, takes over as head of the Fujiwara clan. He has married Prince Hotaru's widow, Makibashira. They have a son together, Hotaru's first. He tries, as is tradition in the Fujiwara clan, to marry his daughters into the imperial family. Higekuro has died and left Tamakazura with two daughters. He has instructed her to marry them into the imperial family. After some competition for the daughters, the retired Emperor Reizei, who has long been interested

in Tamakazura, accepts Himegimi as a replacement. She bears him two children. His other women, Chujo and Akikonomu, become jealous. The present emperor, angry that he wasn't given first choice of daughters, settles for Wakagimi. This turn of events turns people against Tamakazura, who is accused of arrogance in thrusting two daughters into the imperial line.

Prince Hachi, the Eighth Prince, is introduced. Living in exile, his wife, late in her life, gives birth to two daughters then dies. He lives a pious life in a meager cottage at Uji, though his parental responsibilities prevent him from taking religious vows. Kaoru begins studying Buddhist scriptures with Prince Hachi. They become fast friends. Kaoru becomes attracted to Prince Hachi's eldest daughter. On a subsequent visit, Kaoru learns from Ben-no-kimi, daughter of the late Kashiwagi's nurse, the true story of his birth.

Prince Hachi dies shortly after giving his daughters final instructions to beware of casual suitors. Kaoru, upset that he failed to properly honor his true father, longs to become a monk. Kaoru and the two daughters mourn the loss, and so does Niou, though he obviously wants to use the occasion to seduce the princesses. Kaoru catches a glimpse of the women through a screen and is impressed by their beauty. Kaoru pursues the elder princess and promotes Niou to the younger. The elder, though, interprets her father's final wishes to mean that she should make no attachments at all. She tries to convince Kaoru to marry her younger sister. But Kaoru helps Niou, a known philanderer, to seduce the younger sister. They marry in secret. Around the same time, Niou takes another wife. He barely manages to spend any time with Nakanokimi. The elder daughter, Oigimi, becomes distraught over her role in the disastrous affair. She grows ill and dies.

Kaoru comforts Nakanokimi and comes to think of her as a replacement for Oigimi. Though Kaoru never consummated his relationship with the elder sister, he mourns for her as deeply as he would for a beloved wife. Nakanokimi respects this sensitivity. Niou plans to move Nakanokimi to the capital. Kaoru refuses to become involved with Yugiri's daughter Rokunokim because of his infatuation with Nakanokimi.

Nakanokimi becomes pregnant. Kaoru continues to console her. He begins to wish he'd taken Nakanokimi as his own when he had the chance. Niou suspects that his friend and his wife's relationship is no longer platonic. Nakanokimi, to avoid future jealousy, directs Kaoru to pursue Ukifune, an illegitimate half sister who looks like Oigimi. He does. Even though Kaoru marries above his station, he obsesses over Ukifune.

Ukifune's mother carefully supervises her daughter's interests while her husband thinks mostly of his own daughters. A guard lieutenant withdraws his proposal to Ukifune when he learns that she isn't a blood relative to the powerful governor. Ukifune, humiliated, is stored away at her half sister Nakanokimi's house. Niou, finding her alone, nearly manages to force himself upon her. Ukifune's mother, in the name of security, takes her to an unfinished cottage. Kaoru finally manages a meeting with Ukifune and soon takes her to his villa at Uji, where he begins her social education.

Niou learns of Ukifune's situation. One night, in the darkness, Ukifune confuses Niou for Kaoru. He spends the night and the next day with her. Soon, Niou is as obsessed with her as Kaoru. They both send her letters professing their love and laying out plans to take her to a secret hideaway. Niou kidnaps Ukifune, who falls in love with him. Ukifune becomes depressed over her situation, burns her love letters and throws herself in the Uji River. Her body is discovered downstream, at the grounds of an abandoned mansion.

On the grounds of a nunnery, Ukifune recovers her health. An exorcism helps her recovery. She refuses to engage in even polite exchanges with a suitor. As she recovers her memory, she realizes that Kaoru is of greater worth than Niou. She convinces the bishop to administer her vows and so renounces the world.

Kaoru learns of the situation. Much disturbed, he goes to the nunnery to talk with Ukifune. She refuses to acknowledge anybody, even her brother who delivers a message from Kaoru.

CHARACTERS

Lady Akashi

Daughter of a provincial governor turned priest, Genji woos her during his exile. She is daunted by his elevated position and refinement, but eventually succumbs and becomes one of Genji's secondary wives. Her daughter is adopted by Murasaki and eventually becomes empress.

MEDIA ADAPTATIONS

- A CD-ROM introduces the novel through picture scroll reproductions, photographs, illustrations, and narration. It was produced in 1999 by the Futitsu Software Corporation, out of San Jose, CA.

- An animated version of *The Tale of Genji* was produced in 1987 as a joint production of Asahi Publishing, the Asahi National Broadcasting Company, and Nippon Herald Films. Directed by Girsaburo Sugii, whose previous work includes *Night on the Galactic Railroad* and *Street Fighter II*, the film won accolades from the Japan Film Appreciation Society. It will be released on video in the fall of 2000.

- A Tale of Genji museum opened in Uji, near Kyoto, in 1998. In its first eight months it had 120,000 visitors.

- The last part of Saeko Ichinohe's three-part dance, *The Tale of Genji* premiered at New York's Lincoln Centre in early 2000.

Akikonomu

Akikonomu is the daughter of Prince Zembo and the Lady of Rokujo. She serves as high priestess of the Ise shrine and later, with Genji's backing, becomes the Reizei Emperor's (Genji's son) wife. She eventually becomes Empress. Genji inappropriately tries to seduce her.

Lady Aoi

Genji's first principal wife, Lady Aoi marries him when he is twelve and she is somewhat older. She is portrayed as cold and curt, and the two never seem compatible. Genji incurs the resentment of her family by his prolonged absences from her home at Sanjo. She is the only daughter of the Minister of the Left at the opening of the novel. Like her brother, Genji's friend To no Chujo, she is his child by his principal wife, Princess Omiya. At a lustration ceremony, Lady Aoi pushes her carriage past Lady

Rokujo's. This move humiliates Rokujo, and in turn inspires her spirit to take possession and kill Aoi. After her death, Genji mourns profusely. This deep mourning period may be explained by Genji's feelings of guilt, both for being a bad husband and for causing her premature death. Before Aoi dies, she gives birth to their son, Yugiri.

Princess Asagao

Princess Asagao is daughter of Prince Momozono, who was a brother of Genji's father. She is thus his first cousin. He pursues her from time to time, but without success.

Bennokimi

The daughter of Kashiwagi's late nurse, Bennokimi holds the true story of Kaoru's birth. She finally, after many years, tells Kaoru everything and hands over a packet of Kashiwagi's old love letters to his mother, Princess Nyosan.

Bishop Of Yokawa

The Bishop of Yokawa performs the exorcism that enables Ukifune to recover from her seemingly fatal illness. Later, he cuts her hair and allows her to take vows. He regrets having done this after he realizes Kaoru's attachment to the woman.

Chujo

The name means "captain." Several female servants bear this name, probably taken from their fathers' rank. One is the servant of the wife of the Governor of Iyo. In a subsequent chapter, a different Chujo seems to be a servant of the Lady Rokujo.

To no Chujo

To no Chujo is not only Genji's brother-in-law, but also his best friend and frequent rival. Like Genji, To no Chujo possesses great charm, beauty, and refinement in the arts. He has much success in his romantic pursuits. However, he is always seen as just a step below his rival in all areas: a poor man's Genji. He is the eldest son of a Minister of the Left and Princess Omiya, and the brother of Lady Aoi. He is the father of Kashiwagi, Kobai, Kumoi, and (by Yugao) Tamakazura. His principal wife is a daughter of a Minister of the Right.

Chunagon

A series of ladies in waiting bear this name. In Chapter 7, a Chunagon is mentioned as an attendant of Lady Aoi, and he later sleeps with her. The same or another Chunagon serves as Genji's intermediary in a correspondence with Oborozukiyo.

Fujitsubo

After the death of Kiritsubo, the Emperor (Genji's father) marries her look-alike, Fujitsubo. Fujitsubo is the sister of Prince Hyobu, and thus the aunt of Murasaki. Though she ranks as a secondary wife, Fujitsubo is clearly his favorite. She serves as a substitute not only to the Emperor for the loss of his wife, but also to Genji for the loss of his mother. Genji recklessly pursues Fujitsubo and finally seduces her. As a result, she bears a son, the future Reizei Emperor, whom the world thinks of as the Emperor's child. She and Genji shamefully protect the terrible secret. She becomes a nun to impede Genji's persistent advances. Her death at the age of thirty-seven sends Genji into a long period of mourning.

Genji

The son of the Emperor and Kiritsubo, Genji is marked from his birth as extraordinary in every way. Because of weak maternal backing (Kiritsubo was of the lower ranks of court), the Emperor deems Genji a commoner. Ironically, the Korean fortuneteller who predicts, and thus helps seal, this fate also deems the boy, "The Shining Genji." Genji's natural beauty, combined with his cultivated skills in all the arts, makes him incomparably charming. It explains, in part, Genji's great success with women. He marries Lady Aoi at an early age but never has a meaningful relationship with her. He pursues Fujitsubo, his father's principal wife after Kiritsubo, and eventually impregnates her. Their offspring, the future Emperor Reizei, is passed off as the son of the Emperor. This and other similar events demonstrate the way future generations repeat the mistakes of their ancestors. Genji grooms Murasaki to be his perfect wife. Murasaki, like Fujitsubo, represents a substitute for his dead mother. Along the way, Genji has countless other romantic affairs and never forgets his women. He often gets into trouble as a result of inappropriate interludes, especially with Oborozukiyo. This affair leads to his exile in Suma. As he grows older, Genji's complexes grow to accommodate his many wives, concubines, old loves, and many children. This loyalty seems to arise from Genji's great sympathy for humanity. But in the spirit of *mono no aware*, Genji also understands too deeply the fleeting quality of earthly things. Through it all, Genji's one true love remains Murasaki. Soon after her death, Genji too passes away, and the implication seems to be that society from that point on is in decline.

Prince Hachi

A younger stepbrother of Genji's, Prince Hachi enters the novel at the very end. While living an ascetic existence in exile, Prince Hachi's wife gives birth to two daughters and then dies. Prince Hachi, already quite old, must give up plans to become a priest to assume his new parenting responsibility. He lives a saintly existence in a cottage near Uji. He and Kaoru become friends and study Buddhist scripture together. On his deathbed, he appoints Kaoru guardian of the Uji princesses

Prince Higekuro

Prince Higekuro successfully wins his bid for Genji's ward Tamakazura, to unsatisfactory results. Tamakazura seems to hold no fondness for Prince Higekuro and marries him out of fate. Prince Higekuro's principal wife, Murasaki's stepsister, is a supposed mad woman whose father, Prince Hyobu, becomes angry with Prince Higekuro and wants his daughter and all their children to return to his home. The principal wife dumps ashes all over Prince Higekuro, thus ending any attempt at reconciliation. The act of jealousy is attributed to spirit possession. Prince Higekuro's father was a Minister of the Right. His sister Shokyoden becomes the principal wife and empress of the Susaku emperor, so he is an uncle of the emperor reigning at the novel's end.

Himegimi

The daughter of Prince Higekuro and Tamakazura, the beautiful Himegimi attracts many suitors. Emperor Reizei wins her mother's approval, in part because Prince Higekuro wanted his daughters married into the imperial line. She bears Emperor Reizei two children, a second daughter and first son, and in the process causes jealousy among his other wives, Chujo and Akikonomu.

Prince Hotaru

A younger half-brother of Genji, Prince Hotaru unsuccessfully courts Tamakazura, who is so shy that she lets her attendant Saisho handle all correspondence. Finally, Genji convinces her to bring a bag of fireflies (hotaru) into her bedchamber, which gives off enough light for Prince Hotaru to get a glimpse of her. This is where he gets his name.

Prince Hyobu

Prince Hyobu is the son of a former emperor and brother of Fujitsubo. Genji's love, Murasaki, is Prince Hyobu's child by a concubine. A daughter of his principal wife becomes the principal wife of Prince Higekuro.

Kaoru

A son of Genji's second principal wife, Princess Nyosan, he learns as an adult that his true father is not Genji but Kashiwagi. He looks nothing like Genji. He feels guilt and a sense of failure for not having properly honored his true father. His rivalry with his cousin Prince Niou is the main topic of the last quarter of the novel. Kaoru is not inclined toward romantic pursuits until he meets Prince Hachi's daughters, Oigimi and Nakanokimi. He seems to have Genji's sympathetic nature, but not his skill with women. Though both of the Uji princesses are beautiful, he falls in love with Oigimi, who dies without succumbing to his advances. He transfers his love to Nakanokimi, but out of loyalty promotes Niou as her husband. He instead consoles Nakanokimi over Niou's long absence. Upon Nakanokimi's advice, he transfers his love one more time, to her stepsister Ukifune. This final affair ends even more disastrously than the others do. As Kaoru and Niou vie for possession of Ukifune, the fragile woman becomes overcome with shame. After a failed suicide attempt, Nakanokimi ends up in a nunnery, where she refuses to communicate with Kaoru or any potential suitor.

Kashiwagi

A son of To no Chujo, Kashiwagi possesses some of the fine skills of the earlier generation, especially with the koto [a musical instrument]. His principal wife is Princess Ochiba, a daughter of the Susaku Emperor. He is a suitor for Genji's ward Tamakazura. He seduces Genji's second principal wife, Princess Nyosan, and is the true father of Genji's son Kaoro. When Genji discovers the secret, he becomes sick with shame and dies young.

Kiritsubo

Genji's mother, the Emperor's favorite consort, is extremely beautiful but from the lower ranks of court society. The Emperor's other ladies exhibit malicious jealousy toward Kiritsubo, which causes her to fall ill and die. Due to her class standing, Kiritsubo's son Genji faces a future with no strong maternal backing. This contributes to the Emperor's decision to deem his son a commoner. Both the Emperor and Genji will search far and wide for Kiritsubo's substitute, a dynamic that leads, in the case of Fujitsubo, to much regret.

Kobai

After Kashiwagi's death, Kobai is To no Chujo's eldest surviving son. He takes over as head of the Fujiwara clan upon his father's death. Kobai has two daughters from his first principal wife, and his union with Makibashira finally produces a son. In true Fujiwari fashion, Kobai attempts to marry his daughters into the imperial family. He sends notes on a branch of rose plum, which is how he gets his name.

Kogimi

The brother of the Lady of the Locust Shell, the beautiful Kogimi serves as messenger between Genji and his sister.

Kokiden

Genji's wicked stepmother, Kokiden, the Emperor's principal wife, sees Genji as a threat to her own eldest son's future. Her jealousy and hunger for power lead her to treat Genji as a foe. Kokiden's son is indeed made crown prince while Genji settles for commoner status. Under the reign of their son, the Susaku Emperor, she and her father, a Minister of the Right, are very powerful. A sister apparently marries Prince Hotaru. A younger sister, Oborozukiyo, marries the Susaku emperor. Kokiden's relentless rage over Genji's affair with Oborozukiyo leads to his self-imposed exile.

Koremitsu

The son of Genji's old nurse goes on confidential missions for Genji.

Lady Kumoi

Lady Kumoi becomes Yugiri's principal wife after a long period in which their match is prevented by her father, To no Chujo. They consummate their love after a wisteria-viewing party. There seems to be a parallel between this affair and Genji's with his cousin Asago, except here Yugiri is more successful. Her name is taken from the lines of one of her own poems, "wild goose in the clouds," that tells of her longing for Yugiri.

Lady of the Bedchamber

See Naishi

Lady of the Evening Faces

See Yugao

Lady Of The Locust Shell

While she is wife of the governor of Iyo, Genji persists in his unwanted advances toward The Lady of The Locust Shell (also known as Utsusemi) until finally he manages to seduce her. He is attracted by her quiet and sullen temperament. This begins a long relationship. Early in the novel, when she gives him the slip, Genji winds up sleeping with her stepdaughter, the wife of the governor of Kii. After the death of her husband, she suddenly becomes a nun.

Lady Of The Orange Blossoms

Genji takes charge of The Lady of the Orange Blossoms after the death of her younger sister Lady Reikeiden, who was a consort of Genji's father. She helps raise Genji's son Yugiri and To no Chujo's daughter Tamakazura. She is considered "no great beauty."

Makibashira

Makibashira marries Kobai after the death of her first husband, Prince Hotaru.

Lady Murasaki

Lady Murasaki first enters the novel as a ten-year-old child. She is the daughter of Prince Hyobu, and thus Fujitsubo's niece. Genji discovers her in the northern hills on a mission to receive treatment for a persistent illness. Her resemblance to Fujitsubo gives rise to Genji's obsession for her. Genji's desperate and persistent pleas to adopt her are finally approved, but at the same time Prince Hyobu decides to take charge of her. Genji steals Murasaki away to begin her education, which amounts to a long, careful grooming to become his perfect lover. At fourteen, she becomes one of Genji's secondary wives and his favorite. She embodies the ideal Heian woman, sophisticated, loyal, and of an even temperament. She dies at almost the same time of the year as Aoi, causing Genji such despair that he's unable to tend to the funeral arrangements. Her name is from a plant that produces a lavender dye. Her prominence in the novel probably accounts for its author being known as Murasaki Shikibu.

Naishi

Naishi, also known as the elderly Lady of the Bedchamber, acts as aggressor toward Genji, which makes him very uncomfortable. Genji and To no Chujo inadvertently enter her bedchamber at the same time and make light of the situation by staging a mock fight.

Nakanokimi

The youngest daughter of Prince Hachi, Nakanokimi is seduced by Prince Niou, who immediately becomes preoccupied with another wife. His long absences from Nakanokimi seem to confirm his reputation as a philanderer and mark their relationship as a disgrace. Her sister dies from the shame of having promoted the relationship against her father's wishes. With Nakanokimi pregnant in Uji, Prince Niou marries Rokunokimi.

Prince Niou

The third son of Emperor Kinjo and the Akashi Empress, Prince Niou hopes to succeed his brother to the throne. He thwarts his own hopes through scandalous behavior. Prince Niou, who is extremely elegant, engages in a friendly rivalry with Kaoru. He wins Nakanokimi, whom Kaoru also loves, if after the fact. His marriage to Yugiri's daughter Rokunokimi prevents him from spending time with Nakanokimi even during her pregnancy. Eventually, he suspects Kaoru has become involved with Nakanokimi. Always the rival, Prince Niou's crassness leads to his pursuit of Ukifune and her eventual misery.

Nun of Ono

After finding the sickened body of Ukifune, the Nun of Ono nurses Ukifune back to health.

Princess Nyosan

A daughter of the Susaku Emperor, Princess Nyosan (also known as the Third Princess) becomes Genji's second principal wife. Murasaki, who is of lower birth, worries when Princess Nyosan moves into the Rokujo mansion. Princess Nyosan gives birth to Kaoru, who would seem to be Genji's son but is actually the product of an illicit affair with Kashiwagi. Genji learns of the affair through a letter left carelessly out in the open.

Oborozukiyo

A younger sister of Kokiden, Oborozukiyo is engaged to the heir apparent (the Susaku Emperor). Genji seduces her after failing to gain admittance to Fujitsubo's chambers. Her father, the Minister of the Right, catches her and Genji in the act. Their affair inspires Kokiden's wrath and earns Genji exile.

Ochiba

After her first husband, Kashiwagi, dies, Ochiba (also known as the Second Princess) is attended to by Yugiri. She is shocked when, at the height of her mother's illness, Yugiri tries to hoist himself on her. Ochiba's mother writes Yugiri, but he does not respond due to an awkward situation with his wife. The mother equates the lack of response to a public jilting; she has a relapse and dies. Yugiri continues to pursue Ochiba.

Oigimi

Oigimi interprets her father's (Prince Hachi) dying wish (a warning against frivolous suitors) to mean that she and her younger sister Nakanokimi should reject all proposals. Partly for this reason, she rejects Kaoru's persistent advances. Trying to do what is best for the future, Oigimi tries to deflect Kaoru's interest to Nakanokimi. When the affair seems to end in disgrace, Oigimi starves herself to death in a scene reminiscent of Murasaki's death.

Omyobu

Omyobu is one of the women who attend Fujitsubo.

Lady Reikeiden

A one-time minor wife of Genji's father, Lady Reideiden has fallen on hard times. Genji is interested in her younger sister, the Lady of the Orange Blossoms.

Reizei Emperor

The son of Fujitsubo, the Reizei Emperor abdicates early, after he learns that he is the child of Genji rather than of Genji's father. His principal wife and empress is Akikonomu. His other ladies include Chujo and later Himegimi.

Lady Rokujo

The widow of Prince Zembo, Lady Rokujo is a longtime mistress of Genji. She is apparently an older women whom Genji tires of after their initial liaison. Her jealousy is so strong that her wandering spirit kills Yugao and Aoi and attacks Murasaki, among others. Distracted by jealousy and anxiety over Genji, Lady Rokujo accompanies her daughter Akikonomu in her move to court as a Shinto priestess at Ise. On her deathbed, Lady Rokujo begs Genji to look after her beautiful daughter. The character gets her name from the branches of the tree on which Genji ties love notes.

Rokunokimi

Yugiri's daughter Rokunokimi is first promoted as a wife to Niou, and then to Kaoru. Niou finally accepts Yugiri's proposal just as his other wife Nakanokimi becomes pregnant in Uji.

Safflower Lady

Genji and To no Chugo engage in a friendly rivalry for the affections of the Safflower Lady, also known as Tayu. When Genji glimpses the Safflower Lady, he is not impressed but visits her anyway out of sympathy. It turns out she has a big red nose. In addition, she lacks culture, which is exhibited in the poorly made Chinese robe she gives Genji as a present. In a rare example of insensitivity, Genji, in a poem, compares her unkindly to a safflower, a flower with a bright red bloom. He makes jest of her in a private moment with Murasaki by painting his own nose red. Later, a more mature Genji shows his compassion when he saves the Safflower Lady from miserable conditions. Genji helps repair the mansion she inherited from her father and then moves her to his own, better, living quarters.

Second Princess

See Ochiba

Shokyoden

Shokyoden is the sister of Prince Higekuro, principal wife of the Susaku Emperor, and mother of the emperor reigning at the end of the novel.

Shonagan

Shonagan is the nurse of Murasaki. Her name is the same as that of a famous contemporary of the author's, Sei Shonagan, a sharp-tongued woman who wrote the *Pillow Book*.

Suzaku Emperor

The Suzaku Emperor is Genji's brother, the son of their father and his principal wife, Kokiden. He succeeds his father and is succeeded by the Reizei Emperor, who is succeeded in turn by the Susaku emperor's son (by the sister of Prince Higekuro), who is reigning at the end of the novel. His daughter Princess Nyosan (by Genji no Miya) becomes Genji's second principal wife. Another daughter (by Lady Ichijo) is the principal wife of To no Chujo's son,

Kashiwagi. Another wife is his maternal aunt, Oborozukiyo, who deceives him with Genji.

Tamakazura

The daughter of To no Chujo and his mistress Yugao, the whereabouts of Tamakazura remains unknown for years. After she flees an aggressive and unattractive suitor, Genji finds Tamakazura and brings her to his mansion at Rokujo. Genji keeps her existence secret from her father and commissions the Lady of the Orange Blossoms to raise her. He makes advances toward Tamakazura, but she rebuffs him. He finally marries her off to Prince Higekuro, with whom she has several sons and two daughters. When Tamakazura finds imperial matches for both daughters, court ladies accuse her of being presumptuous. This causes her great depression. Her unsuccessful suitors include To no Chugo's son, Kashiwagi and Genji's younger brother, Prince Hotaru. Tamakazura and Genji's discussion about fiction is one of the most memorable scenes in the novel.

Tayu

See Safflower Lady

Third Princess

See Princess Nyosan

Ukifune

A stepdaughter to the Emperor, Ukifune gets thrown over by a guard's lieutenant when he discovers she's not a blood relation. Ukifune's mother is intent on arranging a suitable match for her daughter. Kaoru expresses interest in Ukifune, but before he can claim his prize, Niou finds her alone at her half sister Nakanokimi's house. In an attempt to divert disaster, Ukifune's mother moves her daughter to an unfinished cottage. Kaoru finds her and moves her again, to his own villa at Uji, where she begins koto lessons. Niou covertly visits Ukifune and manages to trick her into intimate relations. The two rivals bombard Ukifune with ardent and aggressive pledges. Ukifune's affections are divided, and her shame and indecision are so great as to cause her to leap into the Uji River. She is found alive and taken into a nunnery, where she takes her vows and maintains a distance from the world, in particular men.

Ukon

Used for several female attendants, including one of Yugao's maids. Genji supports her for many years. She is instrumental in bringing Tamakazura to Genji's palace.

Utsusemi

See Lady of the Locust Shell

Yugao

Yugao, also known as the Lady of the Evening Faces, is the former mistress of To no Chugo, by whom she has a daughter, Tamakazura. To no Chujo abandons Yugao because, as he says in his rainy night conversation with Genji, she is too meek and forgiving. Genji later and by coincidence notices the flowers or "evening faces" outside her house, and investigates the hidden delights inside. Unlike To no Chujo, Genji is attracted to Yugao's gentility. Yugao briefly becomes Genji's mistress, but she is quickly killed by the jealous spirit of the Lady of Rokujo. Out of sympathy, Genji employs Yugao's maid Ukon and asks her to find the daughter Tamakazura, whom he raises under his protection.

Yugiri

The son of Genji and Aoi, Yugiri, like Genji, rises through the ranks to eventually become an important minister of state. Yugiri suffers from the policies of Genji and his uncle To no Chujo, who act to prevent him from making the mistakes of their own youth. As a low-ranking court member, he studies the classics. Yugiri for some years feels oppressed by his father's decision not to promote him more rapidly. His childhood friendship with his cousin Lady Kumoi grows into romance, but her father, To no Chujo, initially prevents their match. Eventually, as Yugiri rises in station, the match is approved and Lady Kumoi becomes his principal wife. At the behest of his friend, Kashiwagi, Yugiri accepts the responsibility to care for Ochiba (Second Princess). Once a relatively faithful and devoted husband, Yugiri starts to feel smothered by Lady Kumoi and their many children. He pursues Ochiba. Lady Kumoi, upset, leaves with their daughters to go home to her father. Yugiri compares his own ill fortune to Genji's good fortune with women.

THEMES

Overview

Murasaki Shikibu's epic-length novel, *The Tale of Genji*, probes the psychological, romantic and political workings of mid-Heian Japan. The tale spreads across four generations, splashed with poetry and romance and heightened awareness to the fleeting quality of life.

Evanescence

The theme of evanescence unifies much of the action. Evanescence means, literally, "to dissipate or disappear like vapor," according to *The American Heritage Dictionary of the English Language, Third Edition*. The characters in *The Tale of Genji* appreciate beauty to an extreme degree, an aesthetic known in Japan as *miyabi*. But this appreciation is tempered by an understanding of the impermanence of all things, especially life. The theme of surface phenomenon as illusory repeats itself throughout Buddhist doctrine. It is this prevailing attitude that gives the novel a tone of underlying sorrow, which can be translated into another Japanese term, *mono no aware*, or, loosely, "the pity of things."

Many characters throughout the novel, with this idea of fleeting human beauty and life in mind, take religious vows. Fujitsubo, Genji's old nurse, Ukifune, and others attempt to leave the material world. Murasaki and Genji seriously consider taking vows, though they ultimately don't follow through. These characters demonstrate their understanding that the time and things of Earth quickly give way. Murasaki depicts Genji as a complex character with a keen awareness of the sorrow of his existence.

The Law of Karma

The concept of moral causality is used to explain events of the novel. Fate is related to past lives. Good actions will be rewarded and bad actions will be punished. In this formula, there is no escaping justice. For example, Kaoru seems to be the victim of severely bad luck. He knows, though, that he surely did something to bring on this ill fortune. "His thoughts on the road were of long ago. What strange legacy had brought him and the Eighth Prince together? A bond from an earlier life, surely, had tied him to this family and its sad affairs, and made him see to the needs of this last foundling, even."

Genji, of course, is highly sensitive to the cause-and-effect quality of his actions. His regret often predicts future retribution. He also worries about others. "The bishop talked of this ephermal world and of the world to come. His own burden of sin was heavy, thought Genji, that he had been lured

TOPICS FOR FURTHER STUDY

- In *The Tale of Genji,* a great importance is placed on art. People gain respect and admiration based on their musical, painting, and writing ability. How does this value system compare to that of contemporary America?

- Describe the political system in Heian-era Japan. Who were the decision-makers and how did they come to power? Explain the fundamental differences between that system of government and a democracy.

- The characters in *The Tale of Genji* are highly sensitive to the seasons. Make a list of poetic references to each of the four seasons: five each for spring, summer, winter, and autumn. Judging by the context of these references, what broad assumptions can you make about the characteristics of these seasons?

- The law of karma assumes that actions in past lives influence circumstances in the present life. How does this spiritual law serve to govern morality? How does it function compared to modern legal systems, which also serve to influence human behavior?

- What kinds of rights and privileges did court women have in the society depicted in *The Tale of Genji*? You can use the author as an example.

- What could women in this society do to preserve and increase these rights?

---

into an illicit and profitless affair. He would regret it all his life and suffer even more terribly in the life to come."

According to William J. Puett, in *Guide to The Tale of Genji,* "To the Heian mind karma neatly accounted for the apparent inequities in the world: why one man, despite his virtue, seemed to have nothing but troubles to live with, or why another was blessed with continuous satisfaction. It was also employed to explain such strong emotional affinities as when one falls in love at first sight, for people once bonded together in a previous life were likely to be pushed together by force of karma."

Substitution

Throughout *The Tale of Genji,* male characters seek consolation for lost or unattainable loves in women of similar composition. Genji's father, the Emperor, is inconsolable after the death of Kiritsubo until he finds a woman, Fujitsubo, who almost exactly resembles her. Genji himself falls in love with Fujitsubo, a mother replacement. Later, he falls in love with Murasaki because of her resemblance to Fujitsubo. His interest in Yugao and her daughter Tamakazura stems from one love. Late in the novel, Genji's supposed son Kaoru loves Oigimi, and then her younger sister Nakanokimi, and then a half-sister Ukifune. In Kaoru's desperate and endless search for Oigimi, the reader sees the need for substitution as being almost beyond the character's control.

Richard Bowring, in *Landmarks of World Literature,* writes, ". . .in *The Genji* this substitution is largely effected on the principal of similarity. Desire as original sin will always win out, so that when the first object of desire proves to be out of reach, attention is naturally transferred to the next best thing."

Jealousy

In the Heian society of *The Tale of Genji,* men take multiple wives. A woman's relative standing is measured in part against her relationship to her husband. Jealousy, then, is a natural part of the order. It also, in the novel's world vision, kills.

The novel opens with a case of jealousy as a murderous weapon. Kiritsubo, the Emperor's favorite, becomes the subject of malicious gossip. All the Emperor's other women resent her. A sensitive and beautiful woman, Kiritsubo finally wins her plea to go home. "Fearing that even now she might be the victim of a gratuitous insult, she chose to go off without ceremony, leaving the boy behind." She dies an emaciated wreck of her former self.

Several episodes of spirit possession come about due to jealousy. Lady Rukujo's spirit takes possession of Aoi, Yugao, and Murasaki. The first two women die as a result, and Murasaki gets very ill before her recovery.

According to Doris G. Bargen, in *Yugao: A Case of Spirit Possession in The Tale of Genji*, "Jealousy is traditionally regarded as the major force behind spirit possession in the Genji because female grievances are revealed to be rooted in the polygynous [sic] system which constantly threatens women's status and lowers their self-esteem in the very sensitive matter of sexual relations."

Higekuro's wife, too, acts in a way attributed to spirit possession. She flies into a jealous rage at the news that she likely will be ousted from her position as principal wife by a new mistress. She dumps ashes all over her husband's head. Though contemporary readers no doubt understand her rage, Heian readers, especially male, would disapprove of such jealousy. Women were to welcome their competition, almost as family. In fact, Genji loves Murasaki all the more for her resistance to jealousy.

Supernatural Events

Other supernatural events infuse the novel with a mystical quality. The Korean fortune teller of the opening chapter figures in the Emperor's decision to give his son commoner's status. Genji's malaria is cured my an old mountain sage who is more exorcist than physician. The storm in Suma serves as a sign that Genji should move to Akashi. The Suzaku Emperor's dream of Genji's father leads to an eye ailment. These and other supernatural events are meant to be interpreted literally.

Social Decline

In a novel that covers four generations, no character can compare with Genji. Even in his lifetime Genji is seen as a throwback to a better time. The Emperor calls Genji's wonderful *Dance of the Blue Waves*, the "only one worth seeing." Time and again, the author makes the point that there is no comparison to Genji. The insinuation is that as time marches on there is an inevitable decline in the social order. Genji possesses unparalleled

beauty. His skill in the arts, his social graces, his inconceivable refinement—everything he does is unmatched. Genji is the peak. Everything after Genji is downhill.

According to Edward G. Seidensticker in the introduction to his English translation of the novel, "A widely held belief in Heian Buddhism was that the religion itself, like everything else, was caught in an irreversible process of decline. The last sad stage, in which forms would remain when faith was gone, was expected to begin several centuries after the death of the historic Buddha. One chronology held that this event would occur in the eleventh century. So, with the Buddhist law itself entering an inferior age from which there could be no recovery, there could be no hope for improvement in the affairs of man, so ephermal and insignificant by comparison."

In Genji's last appearance, he is, "handsomer than ever, indeed almost unbelievably handsome. For no very good reason, the holy man was in tears." And then in the next chapter, nine years later, "The shining Genji was dead, and there was no one quite like him." The novel then follows Niou and Kaoru, the first a quick-witted man of action, the latter a sensitive and introspective soul. Neither can measure up to the standards set by Genji. According to J. Thomas Rimer, in *A Reader's Guide to Japanese Literature*, "Together they might have equaled Genji; separately, they seem limited, inadequate."

Excessive Desire

Love in Japanese really means longing. Love, then, is a loss of self control. Genji is peerlessly handsome, incomparable in everything he does—whether painting, dancing, or composing poetry. He lacks all restraint in his pursuit of earthly pleasures, though. This is a Buddhist sin. Genji understands he should not pursue Fujitsubo, Oborozukiyo, and many other women, but still he does it. This weakness defines the human condition in *The Tale of Genji*.

STYLE

Genre

The Tale of Genji does not meet many of the classical requirements of an epic. Merriam-Webster's *Encyclopedia of Literature* defines epic as, "Long narrative poem in an elevated style that celebrates heroic achievement and treats themes of historical, national, religious or legendary significance." It goes on to report, "The main aspects of epic convention are the centrality of a hero—sometimes semi divine—of military, national, or religious importance; an extensive, perhaps even cosmic, geographical setting; heroic battle; extended and often exotic journeying; and the involvement of supernatural beings, such as gods, angels, or demons, in the action."

The Tale of Genji is written in prose, not verse. The hero and the setting are completely mortal, more realistic than cosmic. It is a time of peace and tranquility.

The quintessential epic tales—such as Homer's *Iliad* and *Odyssey*—tell of great war heroes. Genji never brandishes a weapon, nor does he ever receive notice for his bravery. Rather, Genji distinguishes himself in love. His self-exile to Suma fits into the epic mold: the hero goes abroad, where he confronts and passes a series of potentially fatal tests. His hero status is achieved through national recognition of his talents in arts, manners, and beauty.

Narrative Technique

In a work of fiction, the narrator, or teller of the story, is distinct from the author. The narrator is the voice through which the author speaks.

Murasaki Shikibu's distinct narrative technique establishes a framework for the whole story. Since she wants to chronicle life in this idealized society, Murasaki Shikibu must convincingly portray the characters, setting, and action. Here, the fictional world is represented as true to the historic world. The first sentence reads, "In a certain reign. . ." This immediately provides a vague historical context to the story. Though the narrator, at this point, does not overtly come through the pages, she is already establishing trust with her reader. Later, the author intrudes upon the narration, lending it a conspiratorial tone, as if she is revealing something of herself to the readers. "I had hoped, out of deference to him, to conceal these difficult matters; but I have been accused of romancing, of pretending that because he was the son of an emperor he had no faults. Now, perhaps, I shall be accused of revealing too much."

At times, the author intrudes upon the narration to comment on her rationale for leaving out certain details, on her mood, on her writing process. Otherwise, the narrator remains unobtrusive, more or less objective though not omniscient. Richard Bowring, in *Landmarks of World Literature,* explains, ". . .it

is probably that Murasaki Shikibu retained the somewhat raw technique of open narrative intrusion in order to play with her audience, to remind them that they were not reading gossip and that *Genji* was not to be seen in the same light as its predecessors."

Plot

Genji's rise, followed by his decline, give the first 41 chapters a raw outline. In general, though, *The Tale of Genji* does follow traditional plotting techniques. Most stories have a beginning, middle, and end. Typically, plots exhibit causality and unity. In *The Tale of Genji*, the action, which covers four generations, is more episodic, meaning the action shifts from one to another incident of seemingly equal weight. Even Genji's death, which would seem of monumental importance, receives very little dramatic attention. He dies and the action picks up nine years later with a shift in focus to the next generation.

Certainly, there is tension in the novel. Genji's many affairs, and their potential consequences, stir the reader's curiosity. There is little attempt to maintain this tension, though. William J. Puett, in *Guide to the Tale of Genji,* writes, "A story may begin in one chapter, recede for several more, then break out in a chapter further on, while other subplots are developing at their own, very practical rate with similarly measured thrusts. Plots overlap and tangle in a complicated and totally realistic fashion."

It is difficult to say how much of the plotting can be attributed to the author's technique, and how much might be explained by the shuffling of chapters over the years.

Character Development

In the course of such a long novel, the reader learns about major characters both through narrative commentary and their action in various scenes. Murasaki Shikibu promotes her readers' understanding of characters in ways that seem related to her times. For example, characters are often described in terms of their parentage. In introducing Genji, the narrator first tells the reader all about his mother. This Heian method is known as *ab ovo*.

Other times, the narrator refers to new characters as if they've already been presented. Lady Rokujo appears for the first time in Chapter 4, though from the context it seems as if the reader should already know something of her biography. It is another five chapters before this character directly participates in the story. Again, it is impossible to know if this was a convention used by Murasaki Shikibu, or if it was the result of chapters being lost or shuffled.

Use of Poems

Sprinkled through the novel are nearly 800 poems. These poems illuminate the importance of artistic achievement in Heian society and also the conventions of courtship. Beyond that, the use of the poems highlights the relationship between spiritual and human. References to nature infuse many of the poems. The accumulate effect—"august clouds," "wailing groves," "river of tears"—is to equate nature with a higher power. In a line like, "The dew does not rest long upon the leaves," there is a very clear connection between nature and human existence.

Keene writes of the poems, ". . .they contribute not only to the beauty of the style but also to the creation of a lyrical mode of narration."

Tone

The author's attitude toward her subject matter can be deduced from the tone of the words in *The Tale of Genji*. This relates closely to two of the novel's major themes, evanescence and social decline. A melancholy and generally pessimistic tone communicate the premise that the material world, especially life, is fleeting, and that society is in perpetual decline. This melancholy can be detected in the scene where Genji first meets Murasaki. "She was weeping, and a vague sadness had come over Genji too. The girl gazed attentively at her and then looked down. The hair that fell over her forehead was thick and lustrous." The novel is filled with regret and sadness, especially in the final few chapters. The darker tone of the post-Genji chapters shows a world in definite decline. "Nothing more was to be done, clearly, and the boy feared that he was beginning to look ridiculous. Saddened and chagrined at his failure to exchange even a word with his so grievously lamented sister, he started for the city."

Style

Style refers to the author's unique arrangement of ideas, her use of diction, her manner of composing sentences, using figures of speech, imposing a rhythm. In essence, it refers to the qualities of her craft that make her work distinct. Murasaki Shikibu employed a somewhat ornate style of writing, in keeping with the aristocratic society of which she wrote. The author went into elaborate and meticulous detail of costumes, scents, habits.

HISTORICAL CONTEXT

Heian Era (794–1186)

The era gets its name from the capital, which in 794 moved from Nara. It occupies the area today known as Kyoto. Heian means "peace and tranquility." The capital was built to accommodate almost exclusively the emperor and the ranked hierarchy of the court. The scope of *The Tale of Genji*, then, is the refined aristocrats and not the society at large. All that was considered noble, beautiful, and worthwhile resided in the capital. Therefore, Genji's exile to the mountains and his relationship to a country woman would be seen as vulgar.

Genji, adept at all the most refined arts, epitomizes the idealized Heian aristocrat. In a culture that ranked beauty above all else, Genji possessed almost overwhelming charm. His true love, Lady Murasaki, represents the idealized Heian woman. The tale opens during the reign of Emperor Daigo (897–930), an age considered to be the high point of Heian civilization. The novel moves ahead some seventy years to Murasaki's own time. The tenth son of Emperor Daigo, Minamoto no Takaakira, might have been a model for the character Genji. Like Genji, he was made a commoner, was exiled (in 969), and later was restored to the capital.

The Heian court was weakened by the rise of military powers outside the capital, and in the twelfth century several revolts occurred. But Genji made a lasting impression on Japanese culture. Donald Keene, in *Seeds in the Heart*, says, "During the centuries after the completion of *The Tale of Genji* the court life it so superbly evoked was overshadowed by the rise to power of the samurai class, and at times its existence seemed to be imperiled; but the fierce warriors who threatened the way of life at the court generally did not remain immune to its charms, and they turned with respect and a kind of nostalgia to *The Tale of Genji*."

Heian Literature

The literature of the era was dominated by women. The proliferation of literature, and especially of the long novel, was made possible by a new, purely phonetic, writing system. The Buddhist Kobo Daishi, who had studied Sanskrit in India, introduced a phonetic alphabet. Hirgana consists of

COMPARE & CONTRAST

- **Heian (Classical) Period (800–1186):** About the time of the First Crusades, Japan's Heian Era, which was depicted so skillfully in *The Tale of Genji*, is coming to its end. This marks the end of a period of great material prosperity, of learning and the arts. As suggested in *The Tale of Genji*, the ruling classes are not so interested in the arts of government and war. They stay enclosed in a tight circle of high refinement and pleasure. Literature is largely the work of women. The *The Tale of Genji* is written towards the end of the Heian period.

  Kamakura Period (1186–1336): This period is associated with the decline of learning under the rule of the Shogun, who values mainly warlike accomplishments. Ties to China, which had strongly influenced the poetry and arts represented in *The Tale of Genji* are mostly severed. Under the much more masculine culture of the Shogun, the contributions by women to the literature of this period are insignificant.

  Modern-day Japan: Modern-day Japan little resembles the feminine court society of the Heian culture. Japan has a democratic government that represents all Japanese people, not just those related to and living near the emperor. The outside world knows of Japan more as an economic superpower than a center of the arts. (Though current Japanese artists and writers are indeed numerous and highly influential.) Nor does modern Japan resemble the Shogunate days of the Kamakura Period. The current Japanese constitution restricts the government from building up military power and from waging war, and Japan is highly connected to other countries and cultures. Both men and women contribute to the great body of current Japanese literature. Kenzaburo Oe recently won the Noble Prize for Literature.

---

simple, cursive strokes in which each character represents a single syllable. Hirgana is easier and faster to write, and doesn't require a knowledge of Chinese characters. In the Heian period, women generally used hirgana and men used kana. Murasaki, however, wrote Genji in kana, making it accessible to men.

According to Richard Bowring, in *Landmarks of World Literature*, "Japanese prose had to wait for its true beginnings until the phonetic script had become fully established, because to write Japanese exclusively in Chinese characters was an extremely cumbersome business."

Love and Marriage

Court ladies were rarely seen by men; they were hidden behind curtains, doors, or screens. Men fell in love not based on looks, but rather from the sound of a woman's music or the words of her poem. A glimpse of a woman, though, might send a man into a swoon of longing.

Women painted false eyebrows on their foreheads in place of their real eyebrows, which they shaved off. Their teeth were blackened. Their faces: were pudgy and powdered white. A slight plumpness was considered beautiful. Hair was the most admired physical trait, custom dictating that a woman's hair be at least as long as she was tall.

Clothing and scents were also carefully thought out. Court women's robes were layered and arranged so that various color shades and combinations could be admired in the long, dangling sleeves. Sometimes, a man could glimpse a sleeve jutting out from behind a screen or carriage door, in a style referred to as idashi-guruma. Over time, robes were delicately incensed and perfumed to create a distinctive fragrance, and a person of good breeding could easily recognize the woman by her scent.

William J. Puett, in *Guide to the Tale of Genji*, notes, "For the denizens of the capital, the actual world of daily activities was, by comparison to ours, largely nocturnal, where time was solely governed by the flow of events. People slept, ate, and committed their other quotidian duties around their social activities, which more often than not were conducted at night, till just before dawn. Even the design of the buildings and furniture required that, for the most part, the courtiers lived out their lives in a state of semi-darkness. . . ."

Polygamy, or the practice of having more than one spouse at a time, was common practice. The first, major, marriage was arranged by family, and subsequent, lesser, marriages could be made by any combination of arrangements. After marriage husbands and wives generally lived apart, like Genji and Aoi, with the husband making occasional visits. Sexual relations with close family members, like with Genji and Fujitsubo, were not considered taboo. The problems in such relationships involved politics (tampering with the imperial succession) more than anything.

Politics

The Fujiwara clan, headed by Fujiwara no Michinaga (966–1027), dominated Japanese politics. Michinaga used a carefully-designed network of marital arrangements to maintain control. He was brother-in-law to two emperors, uncle to one, uncle and brother-in-law to another, and grandfather to two more. Women were critical in the successful manipulation of these marriage politics. Women had income, property and other rights that made them more privileged than women of later eras.

The Arts

Heian women were expected to be educated at home in calligraphy, embroidery, painting, and other feminine arts. Men were to learn the Chinese classics and the histories in preparation for official careers. All members of court were expected to be accomplished musicians on a variety of instruments. In the novel, there is frequent mention of the koto, but also the lute and the flute. The 13-string koto was considered a feminine instrument. Genji was a master of the 7-string koto, which went out of fashion, historically, about the time of his fictional demise.

During the Heian period (794–1185), poetry became increasingly involved with the court. There were many poetry competitions, know as uta-awase,

held under the sponsorship of the emperor or some other member of the imperial family. Poetry was often written on assigned topics. Judges heavily weighed how well a poem fulfilled the specifications. Court members composed the poetry, but never used court life as a subject. Poetry was often used to decorate paintings.

That *The Tale of Genji* gained high regard in Heian times and beyond is evidenced in its pervasiveness throughout the arts. In the last century of the Heian period, the illustrated narrative handscroll, the *emaki*, came to prominence. Dating from about 1130, the illustrated *Tale of Genji* represents one of the high points of Japanese painting. This system of pictorial conventions conveys the emotional content of each scene.

Religion

At least three religions impacted Heian culture: Shinto, Buddhism, and Confucianism.

In Buddhist thinking, life is characterized by suffering, which is created by desire, pleasure, attachment to this world, and rebirth. If nothing is done to end the cycle of rebirth, it will continue forever. The law of karma determines whether the cycle of rebirth is broken. Nirvana, the divine state, is possible for all human beings, but only when a person is free from human desire. Taking vows was seen as a way toward achieving nirvana. Failure, in the Buddhist mindset, is never final because compassion is central to its beliefs.

The native religion of Japan, Shinto, literally, means "the way of the Gods." All that is beautiful in nature is deified. The right to rule was tied to Shinto beliefs. Shrines were built for the exclusive use of the imperial family and were used in connection with imperial succession. Shinto, then, was important for public concerns, and Buddhism, private. The Sumiyoshi shrine, which is central to Genji's exile, plays an important part in his return to the capital and the birth of a future empress.

Confucianism remained an essential part of formal education, but like Buddhism was primarily a male preserve. Prior to *The Tale of Genji*, Japanese culture was heavily influenced by the Chinese, and so naturally Confucianism played a role. According to "The Oxford Companion to Politics of the World," Confucian thought is characterized by a spirit of humanism, rationalism, and moralism. It relies on human experience—rather than religious doctrine—to uphold its beliefs. It places *ren*, meaning humanity or love, above all other values. During Murasaki

Shikibu's time, Confucianism remained an essential part of formal education, and, like Buddhism, was primarily a male preserve. In Confucian belief, the ideal society could be realized because each individual had the capacity for self-actualization and the state was obligated to aid in their cultural and intellectual growth.

Publishing

The printing press did not come to Japan until the 17th century. Murasaki Shikibu wrote *The Tale of Genji* in handbooks with an inkstone and brush. Court people were probably employed to copy it as she went along. The court people who formed her audience sometimes copied chapters as they read them.

CRITICAL OVERVIEW

Ever since its birth, *The Tale of Genji* has been almost universally applauded by literary critics and readers, with some exceptions. Medieval writers deemed it inferior because prose was considered a feminine form. Japanese purists into the 20th century have lambasted the novel's decadence as immoral.

Donald Keene, in *Seeds of the Heart*, points to the oldest work of criticism of Japanese fiction as an indication of early praise. *Mumyo Zoshi* (*Story Without a Name*, c. 1200) is cast in the form of conversation among various literary ladies about their favorite books. They all take it for granted that *The Tale of Genji* is the supreme work of fiction. One of them says, "The more I think of it, the more I am convinced that to have created this *Tale of Genji* was such an extraordinary achievement it could not have been accomplished without divine aid. I believe it was a genuine miracle granted by the Buddha in response to the author's prayers."

Soon after its appearance, *The Tale of Genji* became essential reading for the upper class. In the last part of the 12th century, digests of it were required reading for poets. *The Tale of Genji* continues to be regarded as an integral part of a Japanese student's curriculum. *The Economist*, in an article published Christmas Day 1999, wrote, "In Japan today, *The Tale of Genji* is as natural to the culture as Mount Fuji and the cherry-blossom season. High

schools teach sections of the ancient text, in its classical Japanese, to prepare pupils for university entrance. Novelists challenge themselves by writing modern translations. . . ."

Motoori Norinaga, writing in the eighteenth century, dispelled commonly accepted Buddhist and Shinto interpretations of the novel. Norinaga insisted that the good and evil of *The Tale of Genji* did not stem from religious traditions but rather from a quality of *mono no aware*, or a delicate awareness of the pathos of the human condition.

The novel's broad and long-lasting appeal can be attributed, in part, to its focus on character. The first English translation was published in six volumes between 1925–32. Keene, writing in *The Pleasures of Japanese Literature*, says, "Ever since Arthur Waley's translation appeared in the 1920s, readers have been astonished by its seeming modernity. Waley himself discussed the resemblance that reviewers had found between Murasaki Shikibu's work and those of Proust, Jane Austen, Boccacio, and Shakespeare."

Indeed, comparisons to Marcel Proust, Jane Austen, and William Shakespeare happen throughout the body of criticism, as well as comparisons to Henry Fielding and Samuel Richardson. Keene speculates, "Murasaki Shikibu devoted her greatest attention to the elements of human life that have changed least over the centuries. Because the emotions of her characters are so easily intelligible, we sometimes obtain a startling impression of modernity, and it is easy to overlook even the aspects of life in Heian Japan that differ most conspicuously from our own."

CRITICISM

Donald Evans

In the following essay, Evans examines the reasons why Murasaki Shikibu's thousand-year-old novel remains so accessible and appealing.

Image a white-faced, black-toothed woman. Painted eyebrows crest either side of her forehead. Her hair falls down to the floor. She hides behind a screen, just the ornate sleeves of her robe in plain view. On the other side, a carefully-scented man. At home waits his wife, and his other wife, a couple of

Painting of a scene from The Tale of Genji.

concubines, a pseudo-adopted daughter who some-day will be his lover. But for now—as he sends off a love haiku via messenger—his passion swells for this woman whose koto he heard as he sat under the cherry blossoms.

Ever since the first installment of Arthur Waley's English translation appeared in 1925, critics of Mirasaki Shikibu's eleventh-century Japanese novel *The Tale of Genji* have remarked on its seeming modernity. Even today, readers find the novel far more accessible than other dated classics. White-faced women, modern? Polygamous men, modern? Haiku poetry? Kotos?

Nearly a thousand years and a continent separate the contemporary American reader from the Japanese society of Murasaki Shikibu's *The Tale of Genji*. Homer, Milton, Chaucer, through Shake-speare—the study of these great writers happens tentatively, and only with an arsenal of study guides. Genji, somehow, has a more timeless quality. Why?

Edward G. Seidensticker, in a 1993 introduc-tion to a reissue of his own English translation, writes, "The Genji describes the highest levels of Heian society, so high that the governor who was god to the rustics out in the provinces could himself be treated like a rustic buffoon. Yet all the important characters fall within the ordinary range of human experience."

Content, in this case the focus on characters and their psychological and emotional experience, is the main ingredient in Murasaki Shikibu's recipe for an ageless story. Craft, especially the author's decision to portray an entirely realistic world, makes the recipe come out right. The modern reader has a warehouse of emotional experience in which to relate to any story. In so many antiquated tales, though, the circumstances, the characters, and the setting seem so foreign as to be absurd. The footnote is the clumsy, cumbersome antidote to this problem.

Writers of long ago—due to standard literary conventions, social norms, political pressure, and other now largely-defunct expectations—seldom invented worlds that seemed true to their time even during their time. It could be that Murasaki Shikibu benefited from her rare circumstances: an intellec-tual and artistic woman working in a form domi-nated by women, living in a culture that regarded art above all else. She makes no apologies for her novel or the behavior of its characters. Murasaki Shikibu uses precise, detailed descriptions to make her Japa-nese aristocratic society come to life. The reader develops an immediate trust for the narrator, lets the narrator guide her through the book. The customs,

WHAT DO I READ NEXT?

- Murasaki Shikibu's *The Diary of Lady Murasaki*, translated by Richard Bowring in 1996, primarily deals with the birth of two sons to the empress between the fall of 1008 and the beginning of 1010.

- Sei Seishonagon's *The Pillow Book*, written around 1000 A.D., is a series of jottings and essays that chronicles life in the Heian court. Characterized by the author's extreme wit, the book was translated into English by Ivan Morris in 1971.

- *The Ten Thousand Leaves*, the first great anthology of Japanese poetry, was written in the first half of the eighth century and translated into English by Ian Hideo Levy in 1981. It represents the best surviving example of a native Japanese literary tradition.

- *Tales of a Time That is Now*, a collection of more than 1,000 Buddhist and secular tales from India, China, and Japan, appeared around 1120. It is particularly notable for its rich descriptions of the lives of the nobility and common people in the Japan society of that time.

- *Tale of the Bamboo Cutter*, from an unknown author in the early 10th century, is considered the ancestor of all romances. It is the story of the exquisitely beautiful Kaguya-hime, who was born inside a bamboo stalk.

- Chinese poet Po-Chu-I's classic poem *The Song of Unending Sorrow* was much admired in Heian Japan. It tells of Emperor Hsuan Tsung's love for the beautiful Yang Kuei-fei.

---

manners, and style might seem odd to, say, an American teenager living in New York City. But they always make sense in context. Once the reader trusts the world, then she can also trust the emotions. The object that inspires the emotion—an old shoe, a kite, a white-faced woman—becomes, in a sense, arbitrary.

The title character Genji invites compassion. He is deemed, from his early childhood, a commoner, somebody who will be held down by his lack of birthright. He is a hero in the vein of all the mutt heroes to come. Yet, Genji defies the word common. His natural beauty combines with the other skills he cultivates in dance, song, poetry, music, painting. Nobody compares to his prowess in any of the arts, of which romance seems to be one. So Genji is at once a mutt and a thoroughbred, a character accepted by almost everybody.

Perhaps Genji's great compassion comes from his disadvantaged birth. Throughout the novel, the hero repeatedly shows affection, even respect, for characters well below his station. When he stumbles across a down-on-her-luck Safflower Lady, Genji,

by now the highest aristocrat, instinctively wants to help. He restores to order her disheveled mansion and brings the red-nosed woman to his own mansion.

One thousand A.D. or two thousand, it doesn't matter: decency, kindness, and especially humility hit home.

It starts with beauty. America's cultural obsession with beauty is well documented: pretty faces and perfect tans and washboard abs dot the advertising landscape. Billboards smile, and television ads blink, and web sites pop up: all the pitch men and starlets reek of beauty. Though the Heian era's definition of beauty differs from Y2K America's definition, the obsession remains the same.

"[Genji] was wearing several soft white singlets with an informal court robe thrown loosely over them. As he sat in the lamplight leaning against an armrest, his companions almost wished that he were a woman." One can almost imagine that very sentence, with an updated wardrobe, in the pages of a Hollywood gossip rag. As American fans marvel over the minutia of a star's life, so too does Murasaki Shikibu marvel over the minutia of her star's life.

She mentions Genji's dazzling looks at every turn. "The chrysanthemums in Genji's cap, delicately touched by the frosts, gave new beauty to his form and his motions, no less remarkable today than on the day of rehearsal." "A slight flush from drink made Genji even handsomer than usual." ". . .the messenger was able to observe Genji at close range. He was moved to tears of admiration by what he saw." One almost couldn't cast Genji in a Hollywood production. Tom Cruise, too short. Mel Gibson, too macho. Jackie Chan, not enough charm. Genji's kind of beauty is rare indeed.

Genji obtains hero status much like so many American heroes gain pop culture stardom. Genji's reputation spreads far and wide..Murasaki Shikibu seems intent on exploring his inner workings. The modern American can easily understand Genji's accomplishments without understanding the finer points of the culture. The context is Genji's ranking: first, by far. One need not know what a koto is or what it sounds like to know that Genji's skill in using it is astonishing. One need not appreciate the Heian culture's sense of beauty to understand that Genji sends women into a swoon.

To describe Genji as merely a lover is to cheapen his overall effect. At his core, Genji, it is true, is a romantic. He lusts after countless women, no single one able to suppress his great sexual appetite. He goes to great lengths to conduct clandestine affairs: he travels far, he uses disguises, he employs messengers and enlists allies. Even when he suffers from malaria, Genji musters the strength to pursue the child Murasaki. During his exile he manages to find a new partner.

In the course of Genji's amorous adventures, he risks everything: his reputation and social standing, the continued happiness he has with his true love, standing with the Gods. He does not come through it unscathed. Genji's self-imposed exile, to cite the most dramatic instance, is the result of an unwise affair.

Genji's exhilaration, the recklessness of his infatuations, predates by hundreds of years Shakespeare's Romeo and Goethe's Faust. It predates Tristan. The modern era is filled with such stories of reckless, hopeless romance. Importantly, Genji is not a cad. Unlike Don Juan, his interest is never in the conquest. Unlike Don Giovanni, who humiliates Donna Elvira for belaboring their affair, Genji never forgets any woman he has loved. He sees to the needs of the Safflower Lady with her big red nose,

> Murasaki Shikibu uses precise, detailed descriptions to make her Japanese aristocratic society come to life. The reader develops an immediate trust for the narrator, lets the narrator guide her through the book."

and pretends to maintain an interest in her. He educates rather than chastises Omi for her crassness. Though Genji hoists himself on his share of women, such as the frightened Yugao, he redeems himself through a genuine interest in their lives.

Genji's narrator relates, "There were no ordinary, common women among those with whom he had had even fleeting affairs, nor were there any among them in whom he could find no merit; and so it was, perhaps, that an easy, casual relationship proved durable. There were some who changed their minds and went on to other things, but he saw no point in lamenting what was after all the way of the world."

The famous rainy night conversation, in which Genji and To no Chujo debate the characteristics of the ideal woman, is noteworthy. To a modern reader, the discussion presents an array of chauvinistic viewpoints. Again, though, Genji's magnetic personality helps bridge this cultural gap. According to William J. Puett, in *Guide to the Tale of Genji*, ". . . each character in the discussion does emerge as a distinct personality and, most of all, Genji's sensitivity and open-mindedness are seen by comparison."

The sexual politics of the novel might present the greatest difficulty for a contemporary American reader. For somebody whose legal and moral system deems it inappropriate for a boss to ask an underling on a date, it must seem wrong indeed for a man to scoop up a woman in a moment of lust and literally carry her off to his home. Male dominance might have been a fact of life in Heian society, but that doesn't mean the modern reader will want to tolerate it. Why do they, then?

Before long, Genji has a complex for his women so enormous as to anticipate suburban sprawl. Construction crews seem constantly at work making new living quarters for the latest concubine, wife, or casual conquest. Always, the reader senses that Genji does not abide by the usual rules of male chauvinism. He cares.

Donald Keene, in *Seeds in the Hearts*, writes, "Genji responds perfectly to each woman. He is a genius at lovemaking, and if he had lived in a society where monogamy was strictly enforced or if, deciding that Murasaki was an ideal wife, he had never looked at another woman, the world would have been the poorer. Unlike Don Giovanni, he not only woos and wins each lady but he makes each feel sure of his love, and each is content with her small part of his life."

Genji's sensitivity, his sympathy, his loyalty continue, today, to be respected qualities. These characteristics are easily seen against any backdrop, even Heian era Japan. Genji's flaws, his mistakes, seem to accentuate these qualities. For every mistake, he seems all that much more in touch with the complicated fabric of his life as it collides with other lives.

Genji's underlying humanistic tendencies give him a more rounded and identifiable profile than the archetypal hero. He betrays family and friends. He regrets poor decisions. Even in his betrayals, maybe because of them, he appreciates his impact on the world around him. He is able to laugh at himself.

When Genji and To no Chujo meet in the elderly Lady Naishi's bedchamber, it is a most embarrassing moment for The Shining One. "Still ignorant of the latter's identity, Genji thought of headlong flight; but then he thought of his own retreating figure, robes in disorder, caps all askew." As the scene progresses, and the two rivals engage in mock battle, Genji swallows his pride. "Somewhat rumpled, they went off together, the best of friends." It's not the only time Genji gets caught with his pants (or robe, as the case may be) down. The Minister of the Right catches Genji and Oborozukiyo in the act. A derobed Genji can be read figuratively as a character exposed to the world. A hero with insides.

Genji, as the embodiment of *mono no aware* [a sensitivity to things], is acutely aware of the fleeting quality of life. Though Genji has a tremendous lust for life, he understands his time as a flicker in space. "But he was also obsessed with evanescence. . . .

He wanted to withdraw quietly and make preparations for the next life, and so add to his years in this one." This mindset derives from Buddhist philosophy. But the origins, again, are irrelevant. People through the ages, in whatever capacity or form suits them best, have had to deal with the reality of death. Genji's great sadness over the loss of Fujitsubo, Aoi, and especially Murasaki seems extremely modern. He mourns what was, even as he anticipates what will be.

"There seemed to be nothing in the least false about Genji's own tears, which gave an added elegance and fineness of feature."

The fact that Genji has invaded the pop culture, especially in Japan, but also here in America, suggests that the modern reader can easily cast Genji as a modern hero. There is a popular Genji comic book. An animated film. A Murasaki Shikibu stamp. A Genji museum in Kyoto. A sandalwood and musk-scented Genji shower gel. Many, many web sites.

Those readers who especially admire Murasaki Shikibu's great achievement, who appreciate *The Tale of Genji* as great literature, might take offense at such treatment. After all, to lump the refined and incomparable Genji in with Pokemon and Brittany Spears seems like a grand insult. But in modern American society, such recognition constitutes flattery. It means that *The Tale of Genji*, far removed in time and place from its birth, has not lost its appeal.

Source: Donald Evans, for *Epics for Students*, Gale, 2001.

The Economist

In this essay, the author illustrates how The Tale of Genji *was the birth of the modern novel.*

1001–19

The modern novel was born at the imperial court of Japan.

Almost exactly 1,000 years ago, a young woman in a small town in Japan began to write the story of an imagined prince who had just about everything—brains, looks, charm, artistic talent and the love of well-born ladies. He was Genji, "the shining one", so dear to his father, the emperor, that the latter reduced his rank to that of a commoner, to spare him the malice at court.

Born in the first chapter of *The Tale of Genji*, the prince reinvents himself as the most powerful commoner in the kingdom. When last seen, by now aged 52, he is planning to seclude himself in a mountain temple. Further chapters concern his supposed son Kaoru, troubled to find out that his adored father is not his natural father at all.

Today, *The Tale of Genji* is acknowledged as the world's first modern novel, and its writer, Murasaki Shikibu, not just as a pioneer but as one of enormous talent, not least in her use of irony. This long book is peopled by dozens of well-wrought characters, sophisticated figures in an aristocratic society that values celebrity and ambition. It has often been compared to Proust's *Remembrance of Things Past*. Both works "explore memory and passing time. The psychology of the characters is complex; the central drama is their internal conflict," says Haruo Shirane, professor of Japanese literature at Columbia University, in New York.

Murasaki's characters and their setting reflect the reality around her. Genji's seduction of court women is also political opportunism. He fathers at least one emperor and an empress. In the late Heian era (893–1185), when the book is set, the ruling Fujiwara clan of upper- class commoners (to which Murasaki belonged) would send their daughters to court at Kyoto, hoping that one would give birth to a crown prince and ensure their control of the imperial power.

Little is certain about Murasaki Shikibu. The name itself is a pen- name. She may have lived from around 975 to 1025. Until her marriage she perhaps lived in the province on the Japan Sea where her bureaucrat father had been appointed governor. She married probably in 998; had a daughter; was widowed in about 1001; and probably then began "Genji". She kept a diary, which reports her arrival at court—thanks to both her connections and her talent—in 1005 or 1006.

There, in Kyoto, an attendant to Empress Akiko, she was Lady Murasaki, "pretty yet shy, unsociable, fond of old tales", as her diary puts it. Everyone wanted to read the story of Genji. The young empress was the first to see the work-in-progress, which Murasaki did not complete until about 1019.

She wrote the novel in her own hand; court amanuenses copied it as she went along. Ladies-in-waiting and courtiers sought it out, even stealing unrevised pages from her room. Although Murasaki read Chinese, and indeed instructed Akiko in its ideograms, she wrote her book in the Japanese phonetic kana syllabary. That was one reason

The ghost of Lady Yugao drifts through the gourd garden in this woodblock print of a scene from chapter four of the story.

for its appeal. Educated men studied Chinese; few women did.

The Tale of Genji soon became essential reading for the upper class. In the late 12th century, digests of it were required reading for poets. At last, in the 17th century, when the printing press came to Japan, the book was available to the masses. Murasaki's style became the Japanese model for writing, if not for morality: her hero's active sex life, and the luxury of the ancient court, as she represents it, were deplored as decadent by Japanese purists into the 20th century.

In Japan today, *The Tale of Genji* is as natural to the culture as Mount Fuji and the cherry-blossom season. High schools teach sections of the ancient text, in its classical Japanese, to prepare pupils for university entrance. Novelists challenge themselves by writing modern translations. The most recent, by a Buddhist nun, 76-year-old Jakucho Setouchi, came out in ten volumes, the final one in 1998. Between them, they have sold over 2m copies. Other well-read modern versions by Akiko Yosano, a poet, and by two novelists, Junichiro Tanizaki and Fumiko

> *She wrote the novel in her own hand; court amanuenses copied it as she went along. Ladies-in-waiting and courtiers sought it out, even stealing unrevised pages from her room."*

Enchi (who supposedly lost her eyesight working on *Genji*), also are in print.

Spin-offs from the book, serious and less so, are legion. A CD-ROM about it has sold 15,000 copies. Internet websites abound, most created by academics. Several films have been drawn from it. The late 1980s brought a successful pop group calling themselves Hikaru Genji—Shining Genji. An animated Genji film came out in 1987, following a television series. A Tale of Genji museum opened in Uji, near Kyoto, in 1998. In its first eight months it had 120,000 visitors, mostly middle-aged or elderly women. This year, the last part of Saeko Ichinohe's three-part dance *The Tale of Genji* was premiered at New York's Lincoln Centre.

Modern translations of the novel have been published in Chinese, German, French, Italian and English. Arthur Waley, a British scholar also known for his translations of Chinese literature, published his version from 1925 to 1933. It was his limpid prose that brought *Genji* to western readers, as they re-examined Japanese culture after the second world war. An American author-translator, Edward Seidensticker, produced a fuller translation in 1976, using a matter-of-fact voice akin to Murasaki's own. His is the preferred version in the United States today.

Source: "The Tale of Murasaki Shikibu," in *The Economist*, Vol. 353, Issue 8151, December 25, 1999, p. 106.

Doris G. Bargen

In the following excerpt, Bargen considers the social implications of the episodes of spirit possession in The Tale of Genji, *suggesting that "they can be viewed as a female protest against the polygyny of Heian Society."*

The Japanese national classic, Murasaki Shikibu's *Genji monogatari*, is chiefly valued for its exquisitely drawn psychological character portrayals and detailed realistic descriptions of tenth century Heian court life. Yet the work also contains highly dramatic episodes and animated scenes of spirit possession. One of the most memorable scenes occurs in a minor episode in which Higekuro's wife dumps ashes on her husband's head. She is violently enraged by the prospect of being ousted from her position as principal wife by a new mistress, and she is possessed. According to the Heian practice of polygyny, she was expected to tolerate another woman joining the household, and therefore her indignant and undignified behavior is perceived as that of a madwoman:

> Suddenly she stood up, swept the cover from a large censer, stepped behind her husband, and poured the contents over his head. There had been no time to restrain her. The women [in attendance] were stunned.

> The powdery ashes bit into his eyes and nostrils. Blinded, he tried to brush them away, but found them so clinging and stubborn that he had to throw off even his under robes. *If she had not had the excuse of her derangement* he would have marched from her presence and vowed never to return. It was a *very perverse* sort of spirit that possessed her.

Higekuro's wife's case is the exception to the rule which takes spirit possession seriously and requires that it be treated with respect. Inasmuch as spirit possession "permits the expression of things that cannot be said ordinarily or directly," it is, as a technique of communication, eminently suited to the general cultural preference for elegant indirections and subtleties in Heian Japan (A.D. 794–1185). Thus it is the very directness of the distraught woman's physical attack on Higekuro that renders her blunt action comic. Precisely because her behavior is undisguised and straightforward, and thereby unconventional, it paradoxically appears as an instance of the infuriated lady's "derangement." This particular madcap version of possession is counterproductive; direct action defeats its own purpose.

The relative simplicity of this comic possession contrasts with the extraordinary complexity of a series of possessions which involve the eponymous hero of *The Tale of Genji*. In the first of them, Genji's affair with Yugao is suddenly terminated when Yugao is possessed. Her death puzzles Genji and his puzzlement leads us to speculate about the phenomenon of spirit possession and its relation to

The back of the 2,000-yen bill, issued in July 2000 to commemorate the millennium, features an illustration from The Tale of Genji.

gender and courtship conventions at the peak of the Heian period (c. 950–1050). These speculations enable us to understand spirit possession as a female protest against the polygyny of Heian Society.

A few readers have begun to speculate about *The Tale of Genji's* four major possession cases. William H. McCullough has pointed to "the havoc wreaked upon Genji's lovers and wives by the possessing spirit of the very possessive Lady RokujŌ," whose spirit he sees as "one of the principal unifying elements" in the *Genji*. McCullough draws several useful conclusions. First, the victims

of spirit possession in Heian times—indeed in most cultures, and especially in polygynous societies— are women. Second, the spirit who attacks is most typically that of a dead person, and third, the spirit's motive is jealousy. These insights are valuable, but, in light of the questions raised by anthropologists, they merely lay the foundation for an investigation into the very complex interaction between the possessed, the possessor and society.

The phenomenon of spirit possession is an old and universal one, but anthropological research into the subject is relatively new. The opinion that spirit

" It is mainly women who are possessed because they and other peripheral groups oppressed by the dominant group release their tensions and frustrations in this way. Their protest, however, is not directed straightforwardly at the dominant group, but indirectly, through the mysterious esoteric language of spirit possession."

manifestations of possession can usually be traced to grave psychological disturbances or conflicts.

Certain peculiarities about the phenomenon of spirit possession—such as the elements of ecstasy and self-enhancement in the state of dissociation or speaking in different voices—have raised important questions about the meaning of spirit possession. Who are the possessed in relation to the possessor and the witnesses? What public statement does the intensely private and esoteric experience of spirit possession make about the society in which it occurs? In other words, what do the spirits' complaints and wishes, voiced either directly through the possessed, or indirectly through a medium, say about the values of the society? How successful is possession as a psychological strategy?

It is mainly women who are possessed because they and other peripheral groups oppressed by the dominant group release their tensions and frustrations in this way. Their protest, however, is not directed straightforwardly at the dominant group, but indirectly, through the mysterious esoteric language of spirit possession. Joan M. Lewis has aptly described the nature of this protest as "oblique aggressive strategy."

Jealousy is traditionally regarded as the major force behind spirit possession in the *Genji* because female grievances are revealed to be rooted in the polygynous system which constantly threatens women's status and lowers their self-esteem in the very sensitive matter of sexual relations. Thus it is a conspicuous fact that the mainly female authors of Heian tales and diaries voice complaints that are universal to polygynous societies, namely, that competing wives, concubines and mistresses become the agents or victims of jealousy. And to the extent that Heian aristocratic women enjoyed exceptional freedom and economic independence, they made bold to express psychological conflicts in a variety of ways. However, from a pool of diverse grievances, scholars have singled out jealousy as the symbol—or source—of women's rebellious rejection of their assigned role in society.

As the case of Higekuro's wife demonstrates, openly violent, aggressive behavior was viewed with contempt in an elitist society that prided itself on its refined esthetics and an exquisite code of manners in harmony with the society's hierarchical structure. Therefore hostile and aggressive feelings could not easily find expression. They must be repressed or find their own culturally accepted idiom. Higekuro's wife's behavior was not respect-

possession is *not* simply a primitive, pathological practice of superstitious peoples is even more recent. Since the pioneering work of Oesterreich (1921), the many varieties of spirit possession have been divided into two basic categories: voluntary (self-induced) and involuntary (spontaneous). Similarly, the response has been twofold: spirit possession is either thought to be desirable or undesirable. In the latter case, exorcism is deemed necessary. In the most problematic case, then, someone involuntarily enters an "altered state of consciousness" that is considered undesirable or is feared by society at large. It is important to note that spirit possession is not merely a conflict between the possessed and the possessor; it is also a test of the values of the whole society. These values are usually, but not always, represented by exorcists who employ a medium to approach the possessed and drive out and identify the spirit. With identification of the spirit and the promise to meet its wishes, the spell is broken, the victim and the spectators are relieved and, curiously, life goes on much as it had, until the next seizure occurs. Unlike witches, the possessed are not persecuted or punished.

When such dramatic occurrences are placed in the realm of fiction, they must be understood within their literary context. While in reality altered states of consciousness can have purely physical causes, as, for example, the hardships of pregnancy, nutritional deficiencies or the use of drugs, the literary able because of the violation of options available to women under intense psychological pressures. These options encompassed a wide range of activities, such as religious austerities or devotion to the arts. Spirit possession was a woman's most dramatic strategy.

Yugao's possession is the first of the major possession cases. It is prototypical and symptomatic of the cause and purpose of possession, even though its technical apparatus is minimal: there are no exorcists, no mediums and consequently no public ritual. The only spectator, aside from a lady-in-waiting who merely confirms but does not perceive the possessing spirit, is Genji, the woman's lover. Although spirit possession constitutes the climax of an intensely private love affair, its larger social implications cannot be ignored. What especially distinguishes this possession from the others is its direct termination in death.

For many critics of the *Genji*, spirit possession is virtually synonymous with death. Yet between the first and the last case a remarkable progression takes place. While possession and death are practically synchronic events in the first case, in the next three cases the fatal consequences of spirit possession are postponed or avoided completely. Consequently, a note of hope is sounded in the last case: a suicide attempt is converted into spirit possession, which is transformed in turn into an act of artistic affirmation. Ukifune, the last of the heroines in the *Genji*, sublimates her self-destructive desires into spirit possession and then resolves her psychological crisis through the therapeutic composition of poetic memoirs.

Yugao, however, is seized by a spirit, and dies. The mystery of the sudden possession and its tragic end challenges the witness's analytic powers. The events before and after the climax of the affair—the possession—are viewed mainly from Genji's male perspective. His biased interpretation complicates and psychologically charges this famous episode.

Crucial to an understanding of the affair between the son of an emperor and an aristocratic lady of relatively low rank are the lovers' secretive motivations that lead to the mysterious, supernatural event of spirit possession. The mystery of this affair is largely due to the lovers' sustained incognito. One singular aspect of Heian courtship ritual was that the lover frequently had no inkling of his or her sexual partner's physical appearance and identity before the consummation of the affair. Esthetic responsiveness was all that mattered and furtive

glimpses of the prospective lover were ever so much more enticing than full visibility. In the case of Genji and Yugao, however, the couple's tantalizing secretiveness continues beyond their initial encounters and into the phase of intimacy. Why? The lovers' previous adventures determine their response to each other, and provide a clue to the tragedy that results from their departure from courtship routines.

Yugao's unhappy love affair with Genji's best friend TŌ no ChujŌ bears directly on her subsequent relations with Genji.

An orphan without the parental backing necessary for marriage, Yugao was at the mercy of her former lover and had no choice but to forgive him for his frequent neglect. However, after three years of mistreatment, her patience was exhausted. When TŌ no ChujŌ's wife dealt the last blow by humiliating her, Yugao resolved to disappear, to live without her lover's support, and to take with her the daughter she had borne him—a strategy that contained elements of self-assertion, protest and self-sacrifice. Her inaccessibility revives TŌ no ChujŌ's interest. In the famous "Rainy-Night Discussion," he confides to Genji the story of his lost love. Genji is intrigued and, through a fortuitous turn of events, begins to court Yugao, whom he does not initially recognize as the lost lady described by his friend. She is caught in a psychological conflict between lovers which provokes her to terminate the new relationship with a strategy that is the logical, forceful extension of the first: spirit possession and death.

Genji's discovery of Yugao is serendipitous. He is attracted by a humble flower whose name is the sobriquet of the woman of lower rank with whom it is symbolically associated: Yugao. When Genji comes upon the woman, he is captivated by the Yugao flower, its mystery deepened by the poem penned on the fan that accompanies it. Genji pursues this enticing flower-woman despite the fact that he is married to Aoi (TŌ no ChujŌ's sister) and is still interested in his first passion (Lady RokujŌ) and in other ladies of high rank. Much later when Genji has taken not only the flower but also the woman, he fully realizes what he had merely suspected: he has coveted his best friend's love.

While Yugao sees herself in two triangular situations—as a rival of TŌ no ChujŌ's wife for his love and as the object of an implicit rivalry between Genji and TŌ no ChujŌ—Genji perceives quite a different triangle. Aware of his own promiscuity, he imagines his neglected ladies consumed by jealousy over the new mistress. From his perspective, the figural constellation seems initially to involve several females and one male. Genji's subsequent awareness of Yugao's identity complicates matters considerably. The ominous thought crosses Genji's mind: "Might she be the lady of whom TŌ no ChujŌ had spoken that rainy night?" The possibility of identifying Yugao with TŌ no ChujŌ's unassertive lady is so disturbing that it is, at first, entirely repressed: "Genji did not know who the lady was and he did not want her to know who he was."…

As his love becomes like "madness," Genji grows increasingly reflective about his fascination with Yugao: "What was there about her, he asked himself over and over again, that drew him to her?" The lady, in addition to her profound excitement, is unduly worried and through her anxiety betrays the fact that she is experiencing this affair in the traumatic context of the previous one: "She was frightened as if he were an apparition from an old story." While the bittersweet memory of the "old story" with TŌ no ChujŌ causes her to repress the source of her pain, the mystery of her new incognito lover evokes once more the half-forgotten past which casts its ominous shadow on the present and well into her daughter's future. It is unacknowledged triangular complications of this kind that trigger spirit possession.

Genji alludes lightheartedly to the uncanny mystery of their bond. The metaphor used for their reciprocal seductiveness is the fox: "Which of us is the mischievous fox spirit?" As the fox in Japanese folklore induces sexual passion by taking either male or female shape, the image is appropriate and occurs in other possession scenes. Approaching the height of his passion, Genji is again reminded of TŌ no ChujŌ's unassertive lady. Although he intuitively recognizes a strong resemblance between his friend's lost love and Yugao, his behavior indicates that he still resists identifying the two.

It is at this point that the first crisis in their love affair occurs. During their harvest-moon love-making at Yugao's residence, Genji fascinated at first, but soon exasperated, by the epitome of lower-class life, the "plebeian voices in the shabby houses down the street," which he finds "genuinely earsplitting." Such a difference in the lovers' sensibilities would ordinarily have been unthinkable in Heian court life, but here dark romantic passion overpowers conventional etiquette. Genji manages to resolve the crisis. Inspired by a pious old man, he makes a modest vow to Yugao and takes her, against her wishes, to a desolate, isolated villa. This forced move triggers their second crisis, and it is lethal for her.

Yugao may seem unreasonably "frightened, and bewildered," but the fears that she experiences as she approaches the climax of the relationship concern a power no less than nemesis. Of lower rank than her former and her present lovers, she must consider herself fortunate to be favored by such high-ranking courtiers. At the same time, she has learned to be distrustful of uneven matches. Yugao, whose self-confidence the earlier affair has already impaired, suffers from anxiety about a similarly abrupt end to passionate love.

The move to Genji's desolate villa is an ambiguous statement that both threatens and elates Yugao. On the one hand, Genji's earlier plan to establish her at NijŌ, his main residence, was rather quickly abandoned in order to avoid all risk of public scandal. In this sense, Yugao interprets the isolation of their affair as her lover's refusal to acknowledge her and as an omen of inevitable rejection. On the other hand, "Memories of past wrongs quite left her" when she considers how much she must mean to a disguised lover willing to risk his own peace of mind at a neglected residence where "devils" might come forth. The lovers oscillate between psychological stress and the joys of passion, but the trauma of her first love intensifies Yugao's conflicts to a degree not experienced by Genji.

At the deserted villa, in the dead of night, Yugao becomes possessed. It is important to note that the phenomenon is described from Genji's perspective. Because of his successful repression of all thoughts concerning Yugao's affair with TŌ no ChujŌ, he interprets the possession as an expression of *his* imagined triangular conflict, i.e., simply as the result of female jealousy. However, for Genji's other women to have been jealous of the new mistress required their knowledge of her existence. Since the affair had been kept a secret, none of them knew of the new affair and each of them had reason to attribute Genji's neglect to attentions paid to one of the others rather than to the unknown Yugao. Yet critics have unanimously adopted Genji's preliminary interpretation of jealousy. In fact, in their exclusive focus on Lady RokujŌ, they have been more definite than he. And they have ignored the function of the possession and its meaning for the afflicted female protagonist.

Time and setting help induce Yugao's extreme mental and physical agitation: "The girl was trembling violently. She was bathed in sweat and as if in a trance, quite bereft of her senses." Genji too is entering an altered state of consciousness—albeit on a quotidian scale—that of sleep. While sleeping, he has a nightmare of "an exceedingly beautiful woman" who berates him for neglecting her in favor of Yugao. Genji awakens just as this specter of one of his neglected ladies is turning to snatch his beloved away from his bedside. He has been jolted from sleep by Yugao's violently restless possession trance. His first thought is for himself: he does *not* at once conclude that *Yugao* is possessed: "He awoke, feeling as if he were in the power of some malign being." This moment has gone virtually unnoticed by scholars because Genji reaches for his sword, symbolic of male power, and quickly dispells his fears for himself. Nonetheless it is important to see that the drama of Yugao's possession is so powerful that Genji feels compelled to share her altered state and continues to do so, in a form of "possession once removed," even after she has died.

While Genji's waking, dozing and sleeping during that fateful night are minutely described in reference to Yugao's crisis, the heroine's perspective is dramatized in far less detail. It is through Genji's feverishly involved perspective, at crucial times bordering on the hallucinatory, that Yugao's rapid psychological and physical decline are first assessed. Genji's frame of mind is, therefore, at least as pertinent to our understanding of Yugao's tragedy as her own history of anxieties. In fact, the violent dénouement of the love affair forces the hero into the role of interpreter. Due to the suddenness of Yugao's death and the absence of an exorcist who might have lent the seal of authenticity to the mysterious, Genji must psychologically master his lover's possession and death without the aid of esoteric magic rituals.

It is only when Genji's "rationalizations" include his role in the drama of spirit possession that he gradually learns to come to terms with Yugao's death. With a certain amount of self-pity, Genji acknowledges his share of guilt: "He was being punished for a guilty love, his fault and no one else's ... he would gain immortality as the model of the complete fool." Torn between the conflicting emotions of grief for the lost lover and a terror akin to that of a murderer who must dispose of a dead body, Genji's breakdown seems inevitable. His suffering does not end when his confidant Koremitsu takes care of practical matters. Indeed, he further implicates himself by lying to the suspicious TŌ no

ChujŌ about the cause of his absence from court and his present inaccessibility. Not surprisingly, emotional distress is accompanied by psychosomatic symptoms, such as headaches, lack of appetite and fever. Again, only his confidant can help him by suggesting practical ways of doing penance, instead of passively "torturing" himself.

Although Genji risks discovery of his involvement in Yugao's fate, he feels compelled to pay his last respects to his departed lady. At a mountain temple he overcomes some of his own grief by commiserating with her lady-in-waiting. Yet, exhausted from guilt and shame, and perhaps from a momentary sense of relief at having completed this tragic affair, he falls from his horse, like a fool. It is as if this accident were the worst fate liable to afflict a courtier who has been romantically involved with a woman of lower rank.

Back at NijŌ he must endure the aftereffects of stress in a twenty-day crisis. His readjustment is slow and painful: "For a time he felt out of things, as if he had come back to a strange new world.... He spent a great deal of time gazing into space, and sometimes he would weep aloud." Since "gazing into space" was a common expression of Heian women's "immobile existence," Genji's form of suffering gives him the appearance of a woman possessed. In short, Genji now reenacts a milder version of Yugao's trauma which the court, despite their ignorance of Yugao's tragedy, diagnose as akin to possession: "He must be in the clutches of some malign spirit, thought the women."

From Genji's standpoint, Yugao's tragedy can be traced back to his offenses against several women, thus evoking the possessing spirit of jealousy, the stock explanation for female hysteria. That this spirit might attack him as well as any preferred lover is vaguely sensed by the female public's assessment of Genji's psychological state. Yet males in Heian culture generally fancied themselves not only aloof from but even immune from the untidy, specifically female emotion of jealousy. Hence Genji remains fixed on the "exceedingly beautiful woman" of his nightmare as the victimizer of Yugao.

Although the possessing spirit is never named, a significant detail (foot) noted by one reader, most critics have identified the "exceedingly beautiful woman" as RokujŌ. But the image of the beauty is a collective image, an allegory of Genji's betrayed ladies. To single out RokujŌ "whose sense of rivalry" becomes a serious threat only in the second possession case, or to speculate about others such as Aoi, is equally beside the point.

The emphasis of the author is not on solving the riddle of the spirit's identity but on analyzing the male response to the complex phenomena. The critics have neglected the role which TŌ no ChujŌ plays in Yugao's possession and in Genji's guilty reaction to it. While the affair with RokujŌ is over as far as Genji's is concerned, Yugao's affair with TŌ no ChujŌ lies in the immediate past and is, moreover, the very affair confided to Genji in the "Rainy-Night Discussion." As accomplices in love, Genji and Yugao have both, each in his or her own way, betrayed TŌ no ChujŌ. It can plausibly be argued that this betrayal contributed to Yugao's possession and death and to Genji's profound misery. The wrong done to TŌ no ChujŌ is, after Yugao's death, followed by Genji's continuing offenses. Not only does the hero dishonestly cover up the affair, but he also blocks TŌ no ChujŌ's paternal rights until ChujŌ's daughter by Yugao is nearly grown. Genji is, in fact, claiming to be doing penance by caring for Yugao's child, but his charitable intentions appear rather selfish in the light of his friend's frustrated natural privileges. No wonder, then, that Genji develops a painful conscience. After the 49th-day services for Yugao, Genji is in a bad way: "His heart raced each time he saw TŌ no ChujŌ." He concludes that the secret affair with Yugao was actually an "unfortunate contest of wills." Once again, Genji is haunted by the nightmarish dream "of the woman who had appeared that fatal night." This dream had originally functioned to repress Genji's guilt toward TŌ no ChujŌ, and it continues to do so.

The problem, however, is that Genji's initial interpretation of the nightmare and the possession, and his subsequent guilt about his betrayal of TŌ no ChujŌ, ignore the one person who suffers firsthand from the casual behavior of both men: Yugao. Genji's other women and his best friend are all quite unaware of Yugao's affair with Genji. In short, only Yugao, the most vulnerable of all the people involved, had been in a position to know all the relevant facts. If anyone had a motive for the oblique aggressive strategy of spirit possession, it was she, the otherwise helpless woman who had been victimized once and was fearful of a second victimization by a second lover. Unfortunately for Yugao, her feverish attempt at spirit possession fails because Genji is simply unable to realize that she, a woman made vulnerable by her lower rank, is the person most likely to use the only psychological weapon available to her in her unequal position vis-à-vis Genji, TŌ no ChujŌ, and their high ranking aristocratic wives and concubines. Ironically, then, after a moment of fear that he himself might be possessed, he interprets her possession and death neither as an obliquely hostile act nor as an appeal for sympathy and reassurance; he can do no better than to assume egoistically that Yugao's trauma is the result of female rivalry over him. His halting efforts to fathom TŌ no ChujŌ's and his own complicity in Yugao's fate cease. His perceptions are too gender-bound to see that the complex relations between men and women in polygynous Heian society are reflected in the superimposed triangular constellations of his affair with Yugao. Consequently, his guilt remains diffuse. In later years, it intensifies. When his wife Aoi and his favorite concubine Murasaki become possessed, Genji's sympathy for his women grows, but his intellectual response remains clouded by the mores of the times. Finally, spirit possession cannot change the social structure, and male-female relations remain as they were.

Yugao, the female heroine, is doomed to lose in her nonverbal oblique aggressive strategy; in her case, spirit possession is a self-destructive protest. Yet at the end of the Yugao chapter, the author of the *Genji*, herself a lady at the Heian court, verbalizes the heroine's grievance against the hero by making a direct appeal to the reader. *Monogatari* conventions, which required the hero of a romance to be an idealized prince, are flouted. In short, Murasaki Shikibu refuses to make concessions to public taste: "I had hoped, out of deference to him [Genji], to conceal these difficult matters; but I have been accused of romancing, of pretending that because he was the son of an emperor he had no faults. Now, perhaps, I shall be accused of having revealed too much." Yugao's case of spirit possession is an oblique criticism of male behavior toward women in polygynous society. Unlike subsequent possessed heroines, who are more eloquent, this unassertive lady has, quite literally, no voice to express her fears. Her spirit possession neither castigates the men who toyed with her nor does it calm her agitated mind. She may nonetheless have scored a victory. The shock of her spirit possession left Genji vaguely, uncomprehendingly, uneasy. In the attempt to penetrate the mystery of his dream and her possession, he is compelled to rehearse—again and yet again—the drama of her death.

Source: Doris G. Bargen, "Yugao: A Case of Spirit Possession in 'The Tale of Genji,'" in *Mosaic,* Vol. XIX, No. 3, Summer, 1986, pp. 15–24.

Mary Dejong Obuchowski

In this excerpt, Mary Dejong Obuchowski explores the influence of Japanese religious eclecticism on The Tale of Genji.

In the lengthy and complex Japanese novel, *The Tale of Genji*, Buddhist priests attend court ceremonies, women disappointed in love become nuns, jealous spirits possess the bodies of Genji's wives and mistresses, and folk superstitions work their way into the most dramatic of adventures. These varied and apparently conflicting religious elements pose some questions about the dominant religious attitudes in the story. Are the various practices exclusive, and are they ever at odds with each other? How do knowledge of religious rites and understanding of the associated beliefs illuminate both the plots in the novel and the themes that dominate it?

Rather than maintaining distinct identities, these religious beliefs and their related customs tend to come together in Japan.

In order to approach these questions, one may look at religious practices in Japan to illustrate the eclectic nature of the general attitudes toward Buddhist, Shinto, folk, and even Christian beliefs. A historical context shows them most clearly. The folk religions, indigenous to Japan, came first, before history. The mythological beginnings of Japan, imbedded in folk tales, were transmitted, preserved, and undoubtedly transmuted by storytellers until they were permanently committed to writing in the *Kojiki* and *Nihongi* in the eighth century as the official history of Japan. Shinto priests kept the manuscripts for many centuries more, and the myths solidified into part of the Shinto orthodoxy. Folk legends outside these documents still hover around shrines and landmarks, especially in rural areas, and recently anthologists have compiled amazing numbers of such stories and variations of them. Shinto became the national religion and remains in its "pure" form at the state shrines at Ise and elsewhere. After 1945, however, the government declared state and religion separate. It denied the belief in the emperor as divine in heritage and act, though many adults today still consider Hirohito to be ordained by the gods. The role of religion nationally remains controversial.

Buddhism arrived in Japan in the eighth or ninth century through China and Korea. At first a threat, it merged into the established religion by a creed known as *Ryobu*, or two-way Shinto. The practices mingled, and Buddhism became increasingly Japanese as new sects such as Zen groups and followers of Nichiren emerged. Christianity first came via Portugese Jesuits in the fifteenth century. Toccata Hidetada declared it illegal in the seventeenth, and his son, Tokugawa Iemitsu, who also closed Japan to outsiders, had Christians pursued and persecuted. They went underground, and preserved their icons in disguise; artifacts purportedly Buddhist but containing secret Christian symbols appear from time to time. Missionaries arrived again in the nineteenth century when Japan reopened itself to foreigners.

Rather than maintaining distinct identities, these religious beliefs and their related customs tend to come together in Japan. Of course, they exist officially in relatively pure forms, but many supposedly Shinto Shrines bear decorations in Buddhist style. A wedding may have both Christian and Buddhist ceremonies, and when a baby is born, his parents might take him to a Shinto shrine for a ritual visit. Legally, funerals must proceed according to Buddhist conventions. Even young Japanese consciously or unconsciously maintain respect for their ancestors as well as for family honor. Most homes keep small altars which display pictures of deceased parents, often with incense burners beside the portraits. A missionary at a theological seminary told me about a Christian student who, after his ordination, went directly to a cemetery to "tell" his ancestors.

In the eleventh century, when Murasaki Shikibu was writing *The Tale of Genji*, Christianity had not yet reached Japan, but *Ryobu* Shinto had already assimilated much of what was Buddhist in ritual and architecture as well as belief, and folk superstitions were only more present than they are today in the intensity of their reality to the Japanese. Therefore, when one examines religion in the novel, he must consider its eclectic nature. In the novel, most of the religious ceremonies at the court appear to be Buddhist. The installations, coming of age rites, purifications, and prayers for success or prevention of trouble seem to follow these conventions. Exorcisms, though Shinto in origin, are performed by Buddhist priests. On the other hand, a religious conflict occurs when Lady Rokujo's daughter becomes Vestal Virgin at Ise. Rokujo accompanies her to that royal Shinto shrine. When she returns, however, Rokujo feels a definite struggle, even a sense of guilt at having violated the Buddhist faith by observing the Shinto rites, and decides to become a Buddhist nun ....

Lady Rokujo is also a primary figure in one of the most complicated tangles of religion and superstition and the occult that occur in the story. With her, Genji has his first adult affair of consequence. As the liaison progresses, she becomes irritable, demanding, and jealous, the last with some reason. While Genji is trying to disentangle himself from this "older" woman (she is in her middle twenties, he in his teens), he meets a mysterious girl. She is called Yugao, after a flower translated as "evening face," because of her lovely, fragile appearance, their nocturnal meetings, her shadowy background, and the terrifying nighttime circumstances which bring about her death. As this affair proceeds in great secrecy, neither party revealing name or history, a spirit suddenly possesses Yugao and kills her. Since the whole situation is so clandestine (the body is disposed of quickly and silently), and Genji is prostrated by grief for weeks afterward, no one investigates the cause of Yugao's death. Twice on the night of the disaster, however, Genji has seen at their bedside a dreamlike figure of an angry woman who is undoubtedly responsible.

Some years later, Genji's proud and estranged wife, Aoi, develops the symptoms of a similar possession after she gives birth to Genji's only legitimate son. Because the circumstances of her illness are more public, unlike the secrecy with Yugao, Aoi is subjected to prayers and incantations to remove the spirit which is debilitating her, although no one is absolutely certain that she is really possessed. She dies, and Rokujo seems to be the only person jealous enough of Genji to be responsible. Rukujo acknowledges that on occasion her body and spirit do feel detached from each other, and though she emphatically intends Aoi no harm, she may not be able to control the hatred she cherishes toward Genji's wife. She admits to herself that she has retained a deep sense of injury against Aoi since that lady's servants rendered Rokujo an unintentional insult during Aoi's pregnancy. In Japanese folk literature, spirits of the jealous, both living and dead, may enter the object of that hatred and kill that person: this belongs to the most ancient of recorded beliefs. Still later in the novel, Genji's beloved consort Murasaki falls prey to an identical malady (though she is not pregnant), and Genji again calls in quantities of priests to force the spirit

out. At length, a medium induces the spirit to identify itself as Rokujo, who has died several years before, and it answers that it had caused the deaths of both Yugao and Aoi. It tries unsuccessfully to persuade Genji to call off the priests. Murasaki partially recovers for a while but later dies anyway, and Genji follows soon after. It is interesting in this context to note that the beliefs regarding possession are folk beliefs, the priests are Buddhist, and the acts of exorcism are Shinto: nowhere is there any indication that those beliefs and practices should be exclusive, nor, in spite of the failure of the rites, that any is more powerful than the others.

Both folklore and Buddhism subscribe to the theory that a spirit of a person longing for a loved one at the time of his death will not be able to rest. Hence, Rokujo's spirit remains active after she dies. Similarly, in Book Five, Hachi no Miya, a half-brother of Genji, is urged to stop mourning his wife in order that he, a priest himself, might be at peace after his own death. He dies, still longing, mourned by his two daughters. The story proceeds in a different direction, enhanced by more folk superstitions. One of the girls, Agemaki, is courted by Genji's supposed son, Kaoru. She resists all of his advances and offers, and she tries to turn his affections toward her younger sister, Kozeri. Genji's grandson, Niou, however, begins an affair with Kozeri first, and carries her off as his mistress. Worn out by resisting Kaoru and worrying about the future of her sister, Agemaki wastes away and dies. Heartbroken by the loss of both girls, Kaoru locates a half-sister of theirs, Ukifune, becomes intimate with her, and prepares to set her up near him. Niou, single-minded and voraciously competitive in regard to women, again moves faster and visits her secretly. When Ukifune finds that Kaoru has learned about her infidelity, she attempts suicide by jumping into a rushing river, and her household gives her up as dead. A group of travellers find her and nearly run away because they fear that she is a fox-spirit. According to folklore, foxes are notorious shape-changers. They may assume the form of beautiful maidens and seduce men, or they may perpetrate other kinds of mischief. Apparently a good deal of trouble had occurred in the locality where Ukifune appeared, for an old man reported,

> "Oh yes, it's a fox that has done that ... They're always doing odd things just here. It's their favorite tree. Only last autumn one of them carried off a child or two and brought it to this very spot. And when I came running up, do you suppose that fox took any notice of me? Not at all." "What a dreadful thing!"

said one of the priests. "The child, I suppose, was dead?" "No, it wasn't," said the old man rather testily, "it was alive. Fox isn't a fellow to do any real harm. He just likes to give people a bit of a fright sometimes; that is all."

Nevertheless, the travellers decide Ukifune is really human and nurse her, though she lies half-conscious for months, not revealing her identity. Her rescuers feel, of course, that she must be possessed, and request a priest to exorcise her. The spirit he contacts makes a significant admission:

> "I, too, in my day was a master of magic such as yours. But I died with something on my mind. Not much—a trivial resentment; but it was enough to hold me back, to keep me drifting hither and thither, back and forth between this world and the next. I walked into a house. It was full of beautiful women. One of them [Agemaki?] I destroyed. Then I bided my time, and presently this girl here gave me the chance I sought. Day after day, night after night, she lay moaning and weeping, and calling for death to come. At last, one evening when it was very dark, I saw her get up and leave the house. I followed her, and when she was alone, I did my work."

Later, the priest states an additional theory of his own: that because she was found in a clump of trees, Ukifune may have been a *tengu*, or tree-spirit. *Tengu* are also shape-changers and causers of mischief, and even as recently as 1860, official documents contained warnings against them. Ukifune, still pursued by Kaoru and yet another suitor, retreats from these complications by becoming a nun. The story, then, incorporates a number of folk myths and creatures as well as possession and exorcism.

Many of the superstitions and folk beliefs have bases in common sense, as a matter of fact. Possession explained many illnesses that medical science has more clearly defined in recent years. Custom dictated, however, that a person weakened by sorrow or guilt was more vulnerable to wandering spirits than a happy and stable one might be, as in any illness. The possessing spirit was generally one of an unhappy, grieving, or jealous individual, as is the case with Rokujo and with the spirit that worked upon Agemaki and Ukifune; hence the concern that a person be done with worldly attachments before he dies. Themes of the damage caused by jealousy, shame, and guilt run through the novel like threads of different colors but of similar texture. Genji and his descendants alike compromise their happiness and that of their offspring by repeating mistakes engendered by passion or willfulness.

The cluster of stories surrounding Rokujo establishes one dominant theme: that hatred kills, directly or indirectly. The jealousy in her destroys the three most important women in Genji's life, and his death is surely linked with that of Murasaki. It works inversely in the case of Rokujo's final illness; her hostility may well have provoked it. Genji has tried desperately to placate her, even to arranging the marriage of her daughter to the heir apparent. She finally seems to accept his attempts to make amends and his apologies at her deathbed, but her spirit still runs its destructive course afterward.

In fact, it becomes increasingly clear through the novel that one is fundamentally responsible for his feelings and desires as well as for his acts, and that religious belief has firm grounding in common sense. In Buddhist as well as Christian thought, the sins of the father are visited on the sons, and the corruption may affect or express the condition of his country. For example, Genji has an affair with his beautiful stepmother, Fujitsubo, who has a baby, Ryozen. The child is apparently Genji's step-brother but really his son. The boy becomes Emperor while still a small child and comes painfully to find that he was born out of divine succession. The priest tells him, "… the Powers Above are manifesting their displeasure; for, as you have been taught, it frequently happens that the sins of one generation are visited upon the next." He knows that by continuing as Emperor he is violating religious and ancestral traditions. According to Waley's note, "In sacrificing at the Imperial tomb (as if in honor of his father), etc., he was committing an outrage upon the dead." Moreover, this time is one of political and astrological unpleasantness. Public dismay coupled with irregularities in astronomical and weather conditions seem to portend displeasure on the part of the Sun God, from whom the Emperor of Japan is supposed to descend. Now that Ryozen is of sufficient age to understand the problem of his birth and its possible consequences, he worries about whether or not to resign. Genji feels acutely his own guilt in the matter, but attempts to persuade his son to continue as Emperor, because if the reason for his resignation became known, it would appall the Japanese people, who had never known the line of succession to be broken before. The political effects might be drastic. Nevertheless, after some years Ryozen quietly resigns with the excuse of poor health. Thus, the religious belief in divine succession is intertwined with issues of practical responsibility and the consequences of guilty knowledge.

Further links between the effects of sexual misconduct, the physical ravages of guilt or shame, and the kind of understanding that leads to forgiveness come up in a parallel situation. In his later years, Genji takes on an unwelcome marriage of convenience with a niece, Nyosan, in whom he (surprisingly, for Genji) has little interest. He neglects her outrageously. A nephew of his, Kashiwagi, falls in love with Nyosan and seduces her, and she bears his son, Kaoru (mentioned earlier in connection with Agemaki and her sisters). Kashiwagi, a young man who makes heavy demands on himself and who is anxious to be right and perfect in whatever he does, breaks down completely, overwhelmed by grief and guilt at having betrayed his friend and idol, Genji. When Genji finds that Nyosan is pregnant, knows that the child is not his, and suspects Kashiwagi, he is angry only at first. Remembering that he behaved in an almost identical fashion toward his father and that his child by Fujitsubo had been a constant source of discomfort and guilt, he regains his compassion. Consequently, Genji acts kindly toward his nephew, but Kashiwagi feels terrible remorse and imagines that Genji must be justly angered at both himself and Nyosan, and declines rapidly in health. Moreover, he feels that death would remove his "treachery" from Genji's memory, and in his last days confesses to Genji's legitimate son, Yugiri, "for if I died with it on my conscience I should be held back from Salvation in the life to come." His self-hatred finally destroys him. As Fujitsubo had done before her, Nyosan becomes a nun: her shame, too, drives her out of the world.

Genji is a character of sufficient magnitude and intelligence to sustain successful affairs with a score or more women; to seduce his father's wife and to father an emperor out of succession; to survive exile (provoked because of still another affair with another emperor's prospective consort) and return to political prominence; and to develop enough self-knowledge and conscience to forgive the nephew who philanders with his wife. He is a gifted musician, dancer, calligrapher, poet, and diplomat, among many other accomplishments. With every woman he seduces or even desires, he maintains a gentle consideration for the remainder of her life; he even employs or grants places in his household to several former favorites (who get along amazingly well), and he never forgets one or deliberately treats any unkindly. Genji's descendants inherit a number of his physical assets but lack, however, his self-consciousness and moral strength. As the story about Agemaki and her sisters indicates, Genji's grandson, Niou, and supposed son (really his great nephew by two routes), Kaoru, expend themselves

on affairs with women without putting similar energy into other accomplishments. Nothing particularly distinguishes either young man except charm and good looks. Niou stands out only in his appetite for new affairs, from which he quickly tires: he may have more than Genji, but he does not exhibit the concern that Genji has lavished on his ladies, even the old and unattractive ones. He vies with his more serious cousin, Kaoru, trying to reach first any woman Kaoru might have been courting. (Genji and his cousin, To no Chujo, Kaoru's real grandfather, had carried on a lighthearted rivalry as youths: Yugao, for example, attracted them both.) Kaoru, indeed, inherits some of the moral sensitivity that appears in both Genji and Kashiwagi, his real father, but he finds himself unable to act upon it and wastes his time in ceaseless worry and indecision. After his successive failures with Agemaki, Kozeri, and Ukifune, he, too, wants to leave the world and take up the religious life, but he never manages to decide to do so.

In religious as well as practical terms, a person not only bears the responsibility of his own acts and inclinations, he also passes on those predilections and their consequences. For example, Genji's affair with his father's consort grants him understanding when his own wife is seduced. Genji's grandson, Niou, inherits his ability to carry on numerous affairs, and they both have liaisons with women who are really possessed or supposed to be. Though Genji passes on his charm and beauty to his descendants, he cannot prevent them from repeating his errors; though he can understand Kashiwagi, he remains unable to extricate him from the consequences of his affair; and though Genji's relationship with Yugao is one of the most profound in his life, that of Niou (and Kaoru as well) with the lady Ukifune dwindles off into nothingness.

Thus, the religious elements of court ritual, exorcism and folk superstition, and themes of jealousy, guilt, and responsibility turn out to be so closely intertwined as to be inseparable. Possession and other folk beliefs work together with the practical realities of jealousy and hatred and the destruction they work on both the object and the source of those emotions, as in the stories about Rokujo. They point up the physical as well as the spiritual consequences of anger and depression. Adherance to Shinto and Buddhist ritual becomes intimately connected with politics in the case of the Emperor Royzen's tenure. Belief that crosses religious boundaries, as in the recurrent emphasis that a man's errors affect his children, is Buddhist in the context of *The Tale of Genji* but universal in its implications.

Source: Mary Dejong Obuchowski, "Religious Threads and Themes in 'The Tale of Genji'" in *CLA Journal,* Vol. XX, No. 2, December, 1976, pp. 185–94.

SOURCES

Bargen, Doris G., "Yugao: A Case of Spirit Possession in The Tale of Genji," in *Mosaic: A Journal for the Interdisciplinary Study of Literature*, Vol. XIX, No. 3, Summer, 1986, pp. 15–24.

Bowring, Richard, *Landmarks of World Literature: The Tale of Genji*, Cambridge University Press, 1988.

Economist, Vol. 353, No. 8151, December 25, 1999, p. 106.

Encyclopedia of Literature, Merriam-Webster's, Merriam-Webster, 1995.

Keene, Donald, *The Pleasures of Japanese Literature*, Columbia University Press, 1988.

———, *Seeds in the Heart: Japanese Literature from Earliest Times to the Late Sixteenth Century*, Henry Holt & Co., 1993.

Puett, William J., *Guide to The Tale of Genji*, Charles E. Tuttle Co., 1983.

Rimer, Thomas J., *A Reader's Guide to Japanese Literature: From the Eighth Century to the Present*, Kodansha International, 1988.

Seidensticker, Edward G., Introduction to English translation of *The Tale of Genji*, Everyman's Library, 1992.

Shikibu Murasaki, *The Tale of Genji*, English translation by Edward G. Seidensticker, Everyman's Library, 1992.

FURTHER READING

Collcutt, Martin, Marius Jansen, and Isao Kumakura, *Cultural Atlas of Japan*, Phaidon, 1988.
    An overview of Japan's cultural history and physical environment. Illustrations include depictions of Heian court, its culture, and society.

Field, Norma, *The Splendor of Longing in the Tale of Genji*, Princeton University Press, 1987.
    Includes a glossary of character names that helps establish their various names and relationships to each other. A thorough analysis of women and poetry in Japanese society.

Goff, Janet, *Noh Drama and The Tale of Genji*, Princeton University Press, 1987.
    Translations of select works that were inspired by Murasaki Shikibu's novel.

Hempel, Rose, *The Golden Age of Japan, 794–1192*, Rizzoli, 1983.
    This book focuses on art and culture in the Heian period and includes many photos and pictures.

Miner, Earl, Hiroko Odagiri, and Robert E. Morrell, *The Princeton Companion to Classical Japanese Literature*, Princeton University Press, 1985.
    Covers Japanese literature from its beginnings through the end of the Tokugawa period (1868). Includes a glossary of literary terms, a listing of major authors and works, and essays on literary history.

Morris, Ivan, *The World of the Shining Prince*, Knopf, 1972.
    An overview of the Heian period, including glossaries of characters and historical figures.

Puett, William J., *Guide To The Tale of Genji*, Charles E. Tuttle Co., 1983.
    A condensed guide to the lengthy novel, plus insight into historical, cultural, geographic, and artistic aspects of the culture.

Rimer, Thomas J., *A Reader's Guide to Japanese Literature*, Kodansha International, 1988.
    This work illuminates wide-ranging classics from poetry to essays, fiction to dramatic texts.

War and Peace

LEO TOLSTOY

1866

War and Peace is a historical novel that chronicles the tumultuous events in Russia during the Napoleonic war in the early nineteenth century. Focusing on an aristocratic way of life that had already started to fade at the time that Leo Tolstoy wrote the book in the 1860s, it covers a comparatively short span of time—fifteen years—but it renders the lives of disparate characters from all segments of society with vivid, well-realized details. The story captures a generation on the brink of change, with some defending the existing class structure with their lives while others realize that the old way of life is disappearing. Part history lesson, part grand romance, part battlefield revisionism, and part philosophy lecture, *War and Peace* has captivated generations of readers with its gripping narrative and its clear, intelligible understanding of the human soul.

AUTHOR BIOGRAPHY

Leo Tolstoy was born to an upper-class Russian family on September 9, 1828, at the family's estate in Tula province, Russia. His father was Count Nikolay Tolstoy, a nobleman and prestigious landowner. Tolstoy's mother died when he was two years old. Tragically, his father died when Leo was

nine, leaving the young boy to be raised in the home of his aunts. He went to the University of Kazan when he was sixteen, studying Oriental languages and then law, but he left in 1847 without completing his degree.

In 1851 he went to the Caucasus to live with his brother, and began writing his first novel *Childhood*. Published in 1852, it was followed by *Boyhood* (1854) and *Youth* (1856). During this time he served in the army at Sevastopol, fighting the Crimean War. His experience as a soldier in that war provided much of the experience that he drew upon in writing *War and Peace*.

After the war, Tolstoy returned to his family estate. In 1859 he started a school on his estate for peasant children. In 1861, after the emancipation of the serfs, Tolstoy served as Arbiter of the Peace, a temporary local judiciary position. The following year, after the deaths of two his brothers, he married Sophia Behrs, the daughter of a Moscow physician, and began an educational magazine, *Yasnaya Polyana*, which I. S. Aksakov called a "remarkable literary phenomenon" and "an extraordinarily important phenomenon in our social life." Tolstoy edited the journal for a little more than a year.

After that, a second phase of his literary career began, the phase that produced his two greatest masterpieces, *War and Peace* and *Anna Karenina*. He retired to his estate with his new wife, wrote, hunted, farmed, and socialized with his country neighbors. At the end of the 1860s, though, he found himself at a spiritual crisis, brought about by the deaths of several of his children and other relatives. He questioned the meaning of life and was not sure about whether he could or should go on. He drifted away from the Russian Orthodox Christianity he had been raised in and focused on a more rational world view that eliminated the need for church intervention between humanity and God. This religious conversion left him at odds with many members of his family, especially his wife.

Impacted by his evolving philosophical outlook, his later works of fiction were less ornamental and more direct. They include the novellas *The Death of Ivan Ilych*, *Master and Man*, and *Memoirs of a Madman*. Tolstoy also produced many philosophical works and religious tracts. His 1888 religious essay *What is Art?* is still considered an important treatise on art and morality. Tolstoy died on November 20, 1910 of pneumonia.

Leo Tolstoy

PLOT SUMMARY

Book I

War and Peace is a massive, sprawling novel that chronicles events in Russia during the Napoleonic Wars, when the French Emperor Napoleon Bonaparte conquered much of Europe during the first few years of the nineteenth century. Bonaparte unsuccessfully tried to expand his dominion into Russia, only to be turned back in 1812. The novel opens in July of 1805, with Russia allied with England, Austria, and Sweden to stave off Bonaparte's aggressive expansion.

A member of a dissolute, upper-class crowd, Pierre Bezukhov is a troublemaker who criticizes governmental policies. At night he frequents drunken card parties with a fast crowd, including Anatole Kuragin and Fedya Dolokhov, whom Tolstoy describes as "an officer and a desperado." Another member of the group, Prince Andrew, is a patriot who is determined to defend his country and aristocratic way of life. The novel soon introduces the Rostov family as they prepare a celebration for their youngest daughter Natasha.

The illegitimate son of a well-known, wealthy aristocrat, Pierre's life changes when his father dies and recognizes him as his son. Therefore Pierre is heir to his large fortune. Prince Andrew leaves to fight in the war against the French, leaving his pregnant wife with his father and sister Mary. Natasha's brother, Nicholas, gets into trouble in the army for threatening a superior officer whom he has caught cheating; later, in battle, Nicholas runs away from the enemy and realizes that he is the coward and cheat. Suddenly popular, Pierre marries Helene Kuragin. Her brother, Anatole, proposes to Mary, but her father will not allow her marriage. Prince Andrew is wounded in battle and left for dead at the end of Book I.

Book II

Nicholas Rostov is in love with his cousin Sonya, and she loves him; unfortunately, the family needs him to marry somebody with money because their wealth is dwindling. Pierre, reacting to rumors about an affair between his wife and Dolokhov, challenges him to a duel. When Pierre wounds Dolokhov he runs away, questioning his own morals, and in an inn he meets an old acquaintance who introduces him to the Freemasons, a secret society that does good deeds. Pierre becomes an enthusiastic member, separating from Helene and arranging to give away his belongings to help humanity.

Prince Andrew returns from the war on the same day that his wife dies giving birth to their son. Nicholas encourages Sonya to accept Dolokhov's marriage proposal, but she refuses. Soon after his father puts him on a budget of two thousand rubles, Nicholas gambles with Dolokhov and loses forty-three thousand rubles, which the family has to sell more property to pay. While Pierre is busy freeing his serfs from their commitment to him, in accordance with his new Masonic beliefs, Prince Andrew is setting up new economic policies that will allow them to be self-sustaining after they earn their freedom.

In 1808 a truce is called in the Napoleonic war. Prince Andrew becomes disheartened with the difficulties of dealing with the army bureaucracy and Pierre becomes disenchanted with being a Mason. In 1809, when Natasha is sixteen, Pierre falls in love with her. So does Andrew, and he proposes to the young lady. However, Andrew's father will not give his consent and tells him to wait a year before marrying. Andrew returns to the army. Meanwhile, Nicholas' mother convinces him that he cannot marry Sonya—he must marry someone rich.

Impatiently waiting for Andrew to return, Natasha lets Anatole court her, secretly giving in to his charm. He makes plans to run away with her, but fails to tell her that he is already married in secret to a girl in Poland. The elopement is broken off when he comes to fetch her and is met by a huge doorman; like a coward, he runs away. Word of this gets back to Andrew, and he breaks the engagement. Natasha tries to poison herself but is unsuccessful. Pierre visits her and confesses his love.

Book III

The war begins again in 1812, when the French army moves into Russia. The novel narrates Napoleon's thoughts and impressions of the campaign, and then switches to Tsar Alexander, going back and forth between them. During the fighting, Nicholas comes to realize that his earlier cowardice was just a normal reaction to war and he forgives himself. Recovering from her suicide attempt, Natasha starts to attend morning mass and gains peace and serenity. Her younger brother, Petya, joins the army, but cannot find a way to tell his family.

As the French army advances toward their estate in the country, Mary's father has a stroke. After he dies, Mary rides into the town nearby to prepare to evacuate her household servants. When she sees the peasants starving she offers them all of the grain stored on the family estate, but they become suspicious and think it is some sort of trick to get them to leave their land. They are on the verge of rioting against her when Nicholas rides up, saves her, and falls in love with her.

People flee Moscow to avoid the oncoming French army. Pierre travels out to Borondino, which is the last place where the French can be stopped. Much of Part III is concerned with different views of the Battle of Borondino—from Napoleon, Andrew, Pierre, and Kutuzov.

After the Russian defeat, Moscow has to be evacuated. Natasha insists that the wagons taking her family's belongings need to be emptied in order to bring some injured soldiers too. One of the injured soldiers turns out to be Andrew, who, seeing Natasha for the first time since their engagement was broken off, forgives her.

In deserted Moscow, Pierre comes up with a crazed scheme of assassinating Napoleon. Taken into custody by a French captain, he saves the man's life when Pierre's servant is going to shoot him, and, after being given the comforts of good food and drink he forgets his assassination attempt. He races into a burning building to save a peasant's child, then assaults a French soldier who is molesting a woman, for which he is arrested.

Book IV

Pierre's wife dies while he is a prisoner of the French army. During a long march, Pierre becomes even more at peace with himself. He meets Platon Karataev, a peasant who owns nothing but has a joyful outlook, and decides to be more like him.

Mary finds out that her brother, Andrew, is still alive. She travels to where Natasha and her family are caring for him, and the two women take turns nursing him until he dies.

Kutuzov, the Russian general, is pressured to overtake the fleeing French and kill them, but he knows his army does not have the energy. Petya Rostov admires Dolokhov's daring when he accompanies him on a scouting party into the French camp. The next day, they attack the French: Pierre is freed when the French soldiers flee, but Petya is killed. As the French menace fades, Pierre rejoins the Rostov family and he and Natasha console each other over their grief: she has lost her brother, Petya, and her lover Andrew; he has lost many friends in the fighting. They fall in love.

First Epilogue

Nicholas and Mary marry, as do Pierre and Natasha. They all live at Bald Hills, the estate left to Mary by her father. On December 6, 1820, Pierre arrives home from a trip to Moscow, where he has been meeting with a secret organization. Pierre and Nicholas disagree about a citizen's responsibility to the state, but everyone is happy living together—especially Andrew's son Nicholas, who idolizes Pierre.

Second Epilogue

Tolstoy discusses his view of history and how the weaknesses of the historian's methods fail to distinguish between those actions undertaken by free will and those that are caused by circumstance.

CHARACTERS

Elizabeth Bolkonskaya

Elizabeth is Prince Andrew's wife. She dies while giving birth to their son, Nicholas.

MEDIA ADAPTATIONS

- The quintessential adaptation of *War and Peace* is the six-and-a-half hour film done in Russia in 1968, which was directed by Sergei Bondarchuk. It is available on videocassette with either dubbing or subtitles from Continental Distributing.

- *War and Peace* is available on audiocassette, in a 45-tape package, from Books on Tape, Inc. The novel is read by Walter Zimmerman.

- There was another cinematic adaptation in 1956 by King Vidor, starring Audrey Hepburn, Henry Fonda, Herbert Lom, Vittorio Gassman, and Anita Ekberg.

- In 1994 the British Broadcasting Company did a six-part miniseries adaptation with Colin Baker, Faith Brook, Alan Dobie, and Anthony Hopkins. The series is available from BBC Video.

- The novel has been adapted to an opera by Sergei Prokofiev, renowned for his production of *Peter and the Wolf*. The opera version of Tolstoy's story was first produced in Leningrad at the Malay Theater on June 12, 1946.

Mary Bolkonskaya

Mary is the sister of Prince Andrew. She is a devoutly religious woman who stays devoted to her father even though her devotion nearly ruins her life. Early in the book she is engaged to Anatole Kuragin, but her father objects, and she finds that she cannot ignore his objection. While Andrew goes off to war, Mary stays on the family estate, watching after her father and Andrew's son, Nicholas Bolkonsky. Her father, Prince Nicholas Bolkonsky, becomes more and more verbally abusive in his old age, and Mary becomes more involved with the religious pilgrims who stop at their estate. When Nicholas Rostov stops at Bolkonsky, he protects her from the peasants and they fall in love. After her father's death she is immersed in guilt, feeling that he was not so bad after all and that it was awful of her to not be with him in his last moments. She ends up marrying Nicholas.

Prince Andrew Bolkonsky

Prince Andrew is a dashing, romantic figure. For much of the book, he and Natasha are in love, but are separated by the war. In the beginning he is married to the pregnant Anna Pavlovna, "the little princess," and is active in the army. At the Battle of Austerlitz, he is wounded and listed as dead for a while, but he shows up alive just as his wife dies while giving birth to their son, Nicholas. When he falls in love with Natasha Rostov, he asks her to marry him right away, but his domineering father tells him to wait for a year to see if their love will endure. He is wounded at the Battle of Borodino and again news comes that he is dead, but while Moscow is being evacuated wounded soldiers are brought to the Rostov house and Andrew is one of them. Nastasha stays with him through the evacuation, but he eventually dies. In the end, he reaches a new level of spiritual enlightenment.

Napoleon Bonaparte

Napolean is the Emperor of France. Napoleon mistakenly thinks that his army's progress is due to his own skill, not taking into account the role of fate. On the eve of the great Battle of Borodino, for instance, he is more concerned with a painting of his infant son than with devising an effective battle plan for his troops.

Pierre Buzekhov

Pierre is the central character of this novel and its moral conscience. When he first appears, he is a loud, obnoxious man only interested in himself and the next party. Pierre is forced to change when his father dies: after some uncertainty over the will, it is determined that the old Count did recognize Pierre as his son. Suddenly rich and titled as Count Buzekhov, Pierre finds himself very popular. He marries Princess Helene Kuragin.

After hearing rumors of an affair between Helene and Dolokhov, Pierre challenges him to a duel. After wounding him, Pierre escapes, and while he is traveling across the country he is invited by an old acquaintance to join the Freemasons, a secret society. As a Mason, Pierre releases his servants and spends millions on charitable endeavors, often without knowing that he is being swindled. He is still married to Helene, but they lead different lives, and he finds himself attracted to Natasha Rostov. As the battle is waged against the French outside of Moscow, Pierre hangs around curiously asking questions of the officers; after his return to Moscow, he plans to kill Napoleon. He is captured after saving a child from a burning building, and is taken as a prisoner when the French march back to Paris.

After the war, when he is freed, Pierre marries Natasha. They have children, and at the end of the novel he is involved in a secret society that gathers against the government's knowledge to overthrow the social structure that kept men as serfs. The society described resembles the one that led the Decembrist uprising that was to take place in Russia five years later.

Vasili Dmitrich Denisov

Denisov is the model of a professional military man. Angered at the inept bureaucracy that is not getting provisions to his troops, Denisov rides off to the division headquarters and threatens a commander, which gets his troops their food but makes Denisov subject to court martial. Returning from the division headquarters, Denisov is shot by a French sharpshooter. When Nicholas Rostov tries to visit him at the hospital the place is quarantined with typhus, with only one doctor for four hundred patients. Eventually, the court martial is averted, but Denisov retires from the service disillusioned. At the end of the book he is staying with the family of Count Nicholas at their estate.

Fedya Dolokhov

Dolokhov comes off as a rogue, a man of small means who manages to impress society's elite and get ahead by using his social position. As a gambler, he wins thousands off Nicholas Rostov. As a lover, he fights a duel with Pierre Bezukhov over rumors about Dolokhov and Pierre's wife. He is wounded in the duel, but that makes him even more of a romantic figure. He proposes to Sonya, but she rejects him. While the Russian forces are chasing the French army out of the country, Dolokhov makes the bold move of riding into the enemy camp in disguise on a scouting mission; young Petya Rostov idolizes him for his courage.

Boris Drubetskoy

Drubetskoy's rise in the military is due to the social machinations of his mother, who is a wealthy society widow and not afraid to ask, or even peg, highly-placed officers to give her son a good position in the army.

Platon Karataev

Platon is a Russian soldier who gives spiritual comfort to Nicholas.

Anatole Kuragin

Anatole is a scoundrel. His role in the book is to break up the engagement of Natasha and Prince Andrew. He starts paying attention to her out of a sense of adventure, considering her as another in his string of conquests. When he proposes to her and arranges to elope with her, even his friend and companion Dolokhov finds the scheme ridiculous. Anatole is already married in Poland, and the priest and witnesses that he arranges for the wedding are gambling friends willing to go along with a hoax. The wedding plans fail to transpire when, approaching the house, Anatole is asked in by a huge door-man, and he runs away instead. Later, at a field hospital with an injury, Prince Andrew is put on a stretcher next to Anatole, the man who ruined his wedding plans, who is having his leg amputated. Anatole later dies of complication from that operation.

Helene Kuragin

Helen is Anatole's sister and she is every bit as devious as he is. When Pierre inherits his father's fortune, she marries him. After he fights a duel with Dolokhov over her honor, they lead separate lives. Helene is known in Petersburg polite society. She converts to Roman Catholicism, and, under the pretense that to the church her marriage to Pierre is invalid, plans to marry one of her two suitors. When she dies, it is from a botched operation to cure an illness that is not clearly described in the book, indicating that it might be an abortion: "They all knew very well that the enchanting countess' illness arose from an inconvenience resulting from marrying two husbands at the same time, and that the Italian's cure consisted in removing such inconvenience."

Kutuzov

The commander of the Russian Army, the novel follows Kutuzov through some of his decision-making process, especially focusing on his wisdom in ignoring the popular decision that he should attack the French army as it was fleeing back home.

Nataly Rostov

See Natasha Rostov

Natasha Rostov

In the course of the story, Natasha (also known as Nataly) grows from a petulant child to a mature woman who knows the sorrows of war. Natasha is pretty and flirtatious, and the young soldiers are smitten with her. When she and Andrew are engaged, she is delighted to feel like a grown-up, but as time goes by she grows impatient. Kuragin, convincing her that she is in love with him, arranges to elope with her, even though he is already secretly married. When Andrew learns about it, he breaks up with her. She tries to poison herself, in shame.

Later, when Moscow is being evacuated, Natasha is the one who convinces her parents to leave some of their fine possessions behind so that they can take some wounded soldiers. When she finds out that Prince Andrew is one of the wounded, she writes to his sister Mary and together they nurse him until his death. Natasha marries Pierre after he is the only person who she can talk to about Andrew's death.

Nicholas Rostov

Presented as a typical example of a nobleman, Rostov lived a wasteful life with little intellectual or spiritual depth. Early on he joins the army because he needs the money. He loses great sums of money gambling. Passing by the town near the Bolkonsky estate, he finds the peasants accusing Mary of trying to steal their land by making them evacuate. His aristocratic sensibilities are offended; unarmed, he makes the mob rulers quiet down and turn away. At the end of the book he is a retired gentleman, arguing with his brother-in-law Pierre that he should leave the government alone to handle the situation of the serfs properly.

Peter Rostov

The youngest member of the Rostov family, Peter is mostly forgotten in the background, playing childish games, until, at age sixteen, he enlists in the army. He is killed in the same attack that frees Pierre from the retreating French forces.

Sonya

Sonya is a pathetic figure, always in love but too meek to do anything about it. She is a cousin of and lives with the Rostov family, and early in the book she and Nicholas Rostov pronounce their love for one another. His family, in bad financial shape, object and hope that he will find a woman with a better dowry to offer. Sonya is Natasha's confidante, and stands by her during her various disastrous love affairs.

THEMES

Class Conflict

Although there is not much open conflict between members of the different classes of this novel, there is an underlying tension between them. Members of the older generation, such as Countess Rostova and Prince Nicholas Bolkonsky, verbally abuse the peasants who are under their command. In a patronizing manner, they openly discuss how lost the peasants would be without their guidance. At the same time, there are characters like Platon Karataev, a poor man who leads a simple and happy life.

The closest the novel comes to an open class conflict is when Mary is confronted by peasants at Bogucharovo, near her family's estate, as she is planning to evacuate before the French arrive. Tolstoy is clear about the fact that they act, not out of resentment for the social privilege Mary has enjoyed at their expense, but because of their fear that they have no leader. They are starving, but will not accept the grain that Mary offers them because they fear angering the French. The greatest danger that they pose to her is blocking her horse when she plans to leave. When Nicholas arrives they automatically fall under his spell and comply with his demands without hesitation, apparently in recognition of his superior breeding and intelligence. He orders the leaders of the insurrection bound, and several men in the crowd offer their belts for that purpose; "How can one talk to the masters like that?" says a drunken peasant to his former leader as he is being led away. "What were you thinking of, you fool?"

Duty and Responsibility

The greatest motivation for the noble families in this novel is their duty to the serfs in their care. In other words, the upper classes believe that they have the responsibility to care for their serfs, looking after them as one would look after children. This assumption stems from the common perception that the serfs were not intelligent enough to survive without their help. To do this is an important part of the code of honor; any nobleman that violates this trust is recognized and punished by his peers.

In fact, this code of conduct controls almost every aspect of upper-class life. It dictates how a gentleman should act in any given situation; to deviate from it invited the censure of one's peers. After the drunken revelers at a poker party throw a policeman in the canal, the act is derided as improper for well-bred gentlemen:

> And to think it is Count Vladomirovich Bezukhov's son who amuses himself in this sensible manner! And he was said to be so educated and clever. That is all that his foreign education has done for him!

Later, Bezukhov, undergoes a series of transformations that raise his sense of social responsibility. He joins the Freemasons with the idea of working among society's elite to help the poor. He visits the army at the Battle of Borondino and tours the field; half-crazed, he decides he should get a gun and shoot Napoleon. In peacetime, he works with a secret organization to rearrange the social order and free the serfs from their oppression.

Art and Experience

Any historical novel such as *War and Peace* raises questions about the interplay between fiction and reality. The battle scenes in this novel are commended for their realism, but Tolstoy did not actually experience these battles; instead, they are drawn from his exhaustive research of the war against France and his own experiences in the Crimean War. At the end of the novel, Tolstoy dispenses of the fictional story altogether and talks directly to the reader about how historians impact history. Reality is too large and complex for humans to comprehend, Tolstoy contends, and so historians cannot cover all of the diverse aspects of historical events.

Success and Failure

A large part of what drives Tolstoy in the novel is his rejection of conventional historical perceptions of the war: Napoleon, who eventually lost in Russia, is viewed as a shrewd commander today, while the Russian commander, Kutuzov, is dismissed as a blunderer. As Tolstoy perceived the situation, those detractors who considered the Russians as failures because they did not destroy Napo-

TOPICS FOR FURTHER STUDY

- Find out about the music that would have been played at Russian society gatherings in the 1800s and 1810s. Play some samples for your class. What role did music play in nineteenth-century Russia? Identify the most important Russian composers during that time.

- Compare the protests in America during the Vietnam War in the late 1960s and early 1970s to the Decembrist uprising, which Pierre is involved with at the end of the book. What were the Decembrists protesting? Were there any similarities in the way the Decembrist and Vietnam protests were organized?

- The Society of Freemasons, which is so influen-

tial in Pierre's life, is still an active organization. Investigate the modern-day Masons. Considering the fact that it is still a secret organization, how much information can you find out about them? How have their practices and goals changed from the time of Tolstoy's novel?

- During World War II, Russia was an ally of America and Great Britain. Yet for most of the twentieth century, America and Russia were bitter rivals. Research the relationship between the two countries at the time of the novel and report on it. What is America's relationship to Russia today?

---

leon's army were not accounting for the army's weakened condition. Moreover, those who credited Napoleon with brilliant strategy were not taking into consideration his good luck. In the end, Tolstoy reminds readers of the role of chance involved in life, and the sometimes small difference between success and failure.

STYLE

Structure

Since *War and Peace* was first published, critics have discussed the ambiguous structure of the novel. Some contend that Tolstoy raced through the book, putting down ideas as they came to him; therefore, any structure in the story is accidental. As evidence of this, they point to the final chapters, which seem if the author's attention was distracted and he followed his interests rather than doing what the novel would require for completion. Some critics consider the free-floating structure to the appropriate device for the ideas that Tolstoy was trying to convey about free will, and they credit him with

utilizing a structure that permitted him to balance necessity with chance.

Some critics perceive a clear pattern to the overall book: the alternation of chapters about war with chapters about peace; the symmetry and repetition in the amount of time spent on the march to Moscow and the march from it; in the scenes of blithe society and the scenes of existential angst; and in the scenes about love and the scenes about death. The question of whether Tolstoy planned the patterns that can be found in his book or whether they were coincidences is an issue that will be debated throughout history.

Setting

In the early nineteenth century, Russia was going through a tumultuous and transitional time. The old feudal system was disappearing. Conventional ideas of honor were losing ground to pragmatic ideas from the Enlightenment. Military victories were seen as a result of luck. Tolstoy took advantage of these unique circumstances to set his sprawling tale of love, war, and changing political and social ideas. It took genius to recognize the potential of this setting and exploit it, but his philosophical case was helped greatly by the fact that this was a situation rich in possibility.

Hero

Prince Andrew is a hero in a conventional sense: he overcomes initial fear in battle to ride bravely against the enemy, and he has a beautiful woman waiting for him at home, dreaming of his return. He has qualities, though, that are less than heroic, such as a fear of commitment. He is all too willing to accept his father's demand that he put off his marriage for a year. During that time, Natasha is drawn to another man, Anatole, who almost ruins her socially. In the end, Andrew remains an idealized hero by dying a soldier's death after he has been reunited with his beloved.

On the other hand Pierre is more of a modern hero. He is not a warrior, but a thinker: the struggle he fights is with his conscience, after he is made rich with an unexpected inheritance. He is not a dashing figure, and he bears his love for Natasha silently instead of declaring it. Yet in the end, he is the one wins her hand.

Narrator

Toward the end of the story, Tolstoy increasingly addresses the reader directly, stepping out from behind the persona of the third-person narrator who has told the stories of the characters. Throughout the novel, there are breaks from the action where the theoretical aspects of war are discussed. Sometimes these are written like textbooks, describing troop movements; sometimes the important figures of the war are discussed as characters, describing their specific movements and thoughts. At the end, the narration directly addresses the reader, referring to thoughts presented as having come from "I," apparently abandoning the structure of the story to talk about philosophy. The narrator becomes a character who hijacks the novel by the second and last epilogue, lecturing his audience about his theories of historical truth.

HISTORICAL CONTEXT

The Napoleonic Wars

In 1789, the French Revolution swept through France, marking one of the true turning points in Western civilization. In part, this revolt was inspired by the success of the American Revolution, which had rejected the old English monarchy and established a new country based on democratic principles. Mostly, though, the French Revolution was a protest against the widespread abuses of the French aristocracy, who lived in decadence while the lower classes had to endure higher taxes and economic restrictions. When the peasants realized that the French government was going to use force against protesters, they became violent. The violence escalated as the people systematically began to eliminate anyone of aristocratic lineage. After a long fight, King Louis IX was beheaded in Paris in 1793. There followed a two-year period called the Reign of Terror, during which the revolutionary leaders executed more than 17,000 people.

During this time, France's enemies tried to take advantage of the situation. As a result, France was constantly at war. Out of all of this confusion, conservative elements in the government supported the rise of military commander Napoleon Bonaparte, whose solution to the government's instability was to take control. He was appointed First Consul by the constitution of 1799, and in 1802 he appointed himself that position for life. In 1804, a new constitution appointed him Emperor, a title which was to pass down to his heirs.

Napoleon's influence was seen in almost all aspects of French social life. However, his true interest was in waging war. As England and France had always been enemies, he aimed to conquer England; but since England was the most powerful and important country in the world at that time, his plans were foiled. He turned his attention to Russia. The Treaty of Tilsit, which he signed with Russia's emperor Alexander I in 1807, divided Europe into half: the French controlled Holland, Westphalia, Spain, and Italy. By 1809 Napoleon was the ruler of most Europe, except for Russia and England. In 1812 he invaded Russia with 500,000 troops, a situation depicted in *War and Peace*.

Emancipation of the Serfs

From the 1600s until the middle of the nineteenth century, the Russian economy had been based upon an economic principle of serfdom. Serfs were agricultural laborers, legally bound to work on large estates and farms. Moreover, serfs were owned by the people who owned the land they worked on. The serf could buy his freedom or work it off, but this happened rarely (serfs were always males; female peasants were attached to spouses or parents and, likewise, the property of the landowners). Landowners had a responsibility to take care of their serfs, and in hard times they might have to in-

COMPARE & CONTRAST

- **1805:** America is a country that is still developing an identity after winning its independence from England in 1783. A second war against England will be fought in 1812–1814.

  1866–1869: In the aftermath of the Civil War, America undergoes a period known as the Reconstruction.

  Today: America is a stable country. It is considered the dominant economic and military power in the world.

- **1815:** News of Napoleon's defeat at Waterloo is reported four days later by London's *Morning Chronicle*, which scoops the competing British newspapers.

  1866: Telegraph communication is the most common way to communicate over long distances. In America, Western Union controls 75,000 miles of wire, becoming the first great monopoly.

  Today: News events are available instantly from all corners of the globe, thanks to the Internet.

- **1807:** Former Vice President Aaron Burr is arrested for his part in a scheme to form an independent nation of Mexico and parts of the Louisiana Territory.

  1868: President Andrew Johnson faces an impeachment trial, charged with dismissing the Secretary of War, a violation of a year-old law prohibiting removal of certain cabinet officers without the consent of Congress. Opposition forces ended up one vote short of the number necessary to impeach him.

  Today: President Bill Clinton is impeached by the Senate for crimes related to a sex scandal. After his acquittal, his approval ratings are higher than ever.

- **1805–1815:** Napoleon Bonaparte is the Emperor of France. He assumed that position after his rise to military power during the French Revolution.

  1866–1869: Naploean III is Emperor of France, having named himself emperor in 1852. A nephew of Napoleon Bonaparte, he was elected president in 1848 and then seized dictatorial power.

  Today: France is a republic; the people democratically elect a president.

- **1805:** The Russian population is approximately thirty-three million people.

  1866: The population of Russia has increased to approximately seventy-six million people.

  Today: Russia has a population of approximately 149 million people.

---

cur losses to make sure that their serfs were all adequately fed.

This social system was always fraught with tension. As in *War and Peace*, when the war broke up society and forced landlords to flee their land, open rebellion was only avoided by those serfs who felt loyalty to the tradition. In America, the slave system that was in place at the same time was justified by theories of one race being inferior to another, but the Russian system had even less justification for saying why one human had a right to rule over another. Many members of the aristocracy realized this, and in the years after the Napoleonic Wars they banded together to form the secret societies that would lead the Decembrist uprising.

The Decembrist uprising was the first real revolution of modern Russia. In 1817 landowners started forming secret societies, patterned on societies such as the Masonic Order. These societies, such as the Society of Russian Knights and the Union of Welfare, started as gentlemen's clubs; but as they grew in number their rhetoric became more revolutionary. When Tsar Alexander I died unexpectedly in December of 1825, there was confusion about who was to assume power, and in the temporary confusion about who was to be the next ruler the members of the uprising were able to gather three thousand soldiers to their cause. Alexander's successor, Tsar Nicholas, gathered fifteen thousand soldiers; the result was a massacre in Senate Square. Members of the secret societies were gathered up and jailed. After trials, the leaders were executed and over a hundred received jail sentences, but revolutionaries in Russia since then have acted in the names of the Decembrists.

Not surprisingly, Nicholas' reign was conservative in its nature and intolerant of dissent, but even he realized that the days of the old aristocracy were disappearing. He appointed commissions to study the question of serfdom. In 1855, when his son Alexander II took power, it was clear that the country was headed for chaos, that the serf system would not survive. He had a committee work for four years on the right way for Russia to evolve beyond the serf structure with the least change.

The system that Alexander announced with his Imperial Manifesto Emancipating the Serfs arranged for land to be divided: landlords were to keep half of their land, and communes, or *mirs*, were to distribute the other half equally between the serfs. The peasants had a forty-nine year period to pay back the cost of their land. This proclamation was read at churches throughout Russia in February of 1861, two years before Tolstoy began writing *War and Peace*. These reforms still left the former serfs, now peasants, under the control of a government ruled by an aristocracy. The issues of freedom and of class continued to boil in Russia, and eventually led to the Russian Revolution in 1917.

CRITICAL OVERVIEW

Much of the earliest critical reaction to *War and Peace* focused on how well Tolstoy had accurately portrayed historical events in Russia. Although Tolstoy took great pains to research the historical documents, he did not feel obliged to stick firmly to the common historical interpretations. Still, since many critics had lived through the events described, while many others had grown up hearing about them, it was difficult for critics to not talk about how Tolstoy's version related to their own. In general, they found the novel to be quite accurate.

Some critics took exception with the way that Tolstoy had presented the military commanders as less instrumental in the outcome of the war. At the other extreme were those critics who faulted Tolstoy for failing to improve the social consciousness of the time. Edward Wasiolek explains that radical critic Dmitry Pisarev commented that the first half of the book, which was all that was published before his death, was "a nostalgic tribute to the gentry."

Wasiolek also relates the comments of N. K. Strakhov, whose criticism of the novel he describes as "the best criticism on *War and Peace* at the time, and possibly the best in Russian since." He credits Strakhov for his appreciation of the psychology of the novel and for recognizing the fact, which is commonly accepted today, that Tolstoy's greatness was in being able to render a full character in just a few words. Strakhov appreciated the novel, but he could not fully account for its greatness: as he noted, "among all the various characters and events, we feel the presence of some kind of firm and unshakable principle on which the world of the novel maintains itself."

The ambiguity of that "firm and unshakable principle" was what earned the book a lukewarm reception when it was translated into English. Matthew Arnold, in his review for *Fortnightly Review*, noted that Tolstoy wrote about "life" but not "art." Perhaps the most lasting criticism by an English-speaking author was that of novelist Henry James. In his introduction to the book *The Tragic Muse*, as in the introductions to most of his works, James considered philosophical matters of art. Considering Tolstoy and Alexandre Dumas, the French author of *The Three Musketeers* and *The Count of Monte Cristo*, James wondered, "What do such large loose baggy monsters, with their queer elements of the accidental and the arbitrary, artistically *mean*?" He went on to assert that "there is life and life, and as waste is only life sacrificed and thereby prevented from 'counting,' I delight in a deep-breathing economy and organic form."

After the Communist Revolution in Russia in 1917, Tolstoy's literary reputation was maintained by people who had known him (he died in 1910) and a few stalwart fans. Because of his work with the impoverished during the last decades of his life, and the familiarity that the leaders of the revolution had with his works, his reputation was kept intact. Lenin, for instance, considered him in 1918 to be more significant than any artist Europe produced, a

Vladislav Strzhelchik as Napoleon in the 1968 film version of War and Peace.

judgement that carried great importance, considering the totalitarian power exerted by the new Communist government. It was not long before Tolstoy studies went beyond personal reminiscences to intellectual scholarship in Russia. At a time when many other important Russian authors were banned because of their views, Tolstoy was embraced as a foresighted nobleman who wrote about the value of common people and the arbitrary nature of class distinctions.

Today, Tolstoy's career is divided into two eras: the spiritualism of the later novellas and the sweeping romances of the earlier novels, such as *War and Peace* and *Anna Karenina*. Critics perceive within *War and Peace* one phase of his life leading into the other: how the prodigious novelist of the 1860s and 1870s evolved into the thoughtful spiritual man he was by the turn of the century. There is no question of Tolstoy's greatness today.

CRITICISM

David Kelly

David Kelly is an instructor of creative writing and literature at College of Lake County and Oak- *ton Community College in Illinois. In the following essay, Kelly discusses why the people most likely to avoid reading* War and Peace *are the ones who would probably enjoy and benefit from it most.*

It would be difficult to question the quality of Leo Tolstoy's *War and Peace*. Although most critics would not go as far as E. M. Forster did in *Aspects of the Novel*, proclaiming this to be the greatest novel ever written, all would swear to its overall excellence. As with any work, critics consider different ideas about its relative merits and weaknesses, no matter how revered.

Still, with such universal acclaim, no one ever feels the need to ask why *War and Peace* isn't read more often—anyone who has ever looked at it on a bookshelf, taking up the space of four or five average novels, knows at a glance the secret of its unpopularity. It's huge. All across the world *War and Peace* is mentioned in pop culture, but usually it is discussed in terms of how difficult the speaker's education was, or would have been, if they had actually gone ahead with things like reading big novels.

Literary critics tend to skip quickly past this issue of the book's enormous size, although the general public can never get past it. In the literary

WHAT DO I READ NEXT?

- Thomas Hardy was an English author who lived at approximately the same time as Tolstoy. One of the crowning achievements of his later life was a long poem, *The Dynasts*, written between 1903 and 1908. It is an epic drama with nineteen acts and 135 scenes that are impossible to produce for the stage. The work focuses on England's role in the Napoleonic Wars.

- Tolstoy's other great masterpiece is *Anna Karenina*, his 1877 novel about an aristocratic woman's illicit affair with a count.

- Henri Troyat's biography, *Tolstoy*, was published in 1967 by Doubleday and Co. It chronicles the life and times of this intriguing author.

- Russian writer Ivan Turgenev was a friend of Tolstoy. Contemporary critics consider his 1862 novel *Fathers and Sons* to be his greatest work.

- Patient readers who can work their way through this novel's mass may be ready for *Moby Dick*, Herman Melville's 1851 opus about a whaling ship captain and the object of his obsession, the great white whale of the title.

- *Crime and Punishment* is considered to be the masterpiece of Fyodor Dostoyevsky's literary career. It was published in 1866, the same year as the first installment of *War and Peace*.

world, bringing up a book's length is as tasteless as mentioning its price—both being worldly concerns, not artistic considerations. Unfortunately, the result is a huge gap between the values of critics and the values of readers, especially students. Many students find the page count intimidating, and would be just as happy reading three hundred pages of nonsense as a thousand worthwhile pages. This is where the jokes about *War and Peace* come in, reinforcing the idea that it is not only unimportant, but is ridiculous. Students end up making their decision about whether or not to read it without ever looking at a page, judging the book by the distance between its covers. To students who do not care for literature this book seems the most dreaded of all possibilities.

Actually, this is the book that students who do not like literature have been asking for. It is not too clever, too wound up in an artistic style, to be appealing to the general reader. We all feel life's pace—its mix of chance and fate—and some people find themselves particularly irritated by the way that life is compressed to fit into a book of a few hundred pages. They sorely miss the rich incidental details that are trimmed off on the edges of the writer's frame. Young readers, who are dissatisfied with

books that don't represent life, need a book like this: one that can take bends, back up, or plow straight ahead, according to what happens in the world we know—not according to some literary theory. Ernest J. Simmons' classic examination of *War and Peace* quoted an anonymous reader saying it best: "if life could write it would write just as Tolstoy did."

Of course, all writers write about life in their own way, but what makes this case different is that *War and Peace* is successful at reflecting a true pace of life without having to dwell upon how poignant it is or oversell its own sensitivity. It is not difficult to understand. The book has something in it to remind readers of all of their own experiences. Working with such a long form gives Tolstoy freedom to follow the lives of his characters as they zig and zag, as they live out their intentions or fall to fate's control.

Freedom is what *War and Peace* is about, although Tolstoy does not formally declare this intention until nearly twelve hundred pages are done. By that time, after we have felt the looseness of his style, the emphasis on freedom of the mind is no surprise. The feeling of freedom takes time to establish. A novel that is tightly plotted can get to its point in a few sentences, but these are the books that raise the suspicions of those wary readers who hate the artificiality of art. For an author like Tolstoy to follow the rhythms of life, especially the easygoing lives of the leisured class, means taking time.

The idea of freedom, which Tolstoy talks about in the Second Epilogue, is evident in the way that this book came to be, having ended up a far, far different thing than it was when he first thought of it. It originally spanned over fifty years—at the pace *War and Peace* as we know it unravels, that would come out to nearly five thousand pages. When the idea first came to Tolstoy, the character Pierre Bezukhov was to be a veteran of the Decembrist uprising, returning to Moscow in 1856 after being exiled in Siberia for thirty years for his part in the uprising. That led the story back to 1825, but writing about the uprising raised the broader question: Who were these revolutionaries? They were Russian noblemen who had tried to overthrow the government to gain freedom for the country's peasants. What gave them the idea to act against their own self-interests? Searching for the answer to that question took Tolstoy even deeper into the past.

Eventually, the sections taking place in 1856 and 1825 were dropped from the novel. Instead, the action begins in 1805, when the major characters are young adults and the Russian aristocracy is first being politicized by the threat of Napoleon, and concludes in 1820, when Pierre is just starting to discuss the ideas that later led to the Decembrist uprising. This flexibility led the book in directions that could not have been anticipated when Tolstoy started it—directions that the readers do not see coming. Reluctant readers might not buy the idea that the book is a "thrill-ride," but it certainly plays out unlike any other novel, which in itself should cut short most objections to reading it.

To get the full effect readers need to take their time unraveling this book, which is not the same thing as saying that it is difficult to understand. The language is not difficult, and the situations are clear enough, but the wealth of details just will not be understood as quickly as busy people want. Of course, there will always be readers who think that any novel that does not happen in their own towns within their own lifetimes is irrelevant to their life. They foolishly think that human nature has somehow become different as the times have changed, or that it is significantly different from one place to another. There isn't much that will change these

> **"** Actually, this is the book that students who do not like literature have been asking for. **"**

people's minds, because they will always find excuses to hate reading.

It is one of the great ironies of literature that many people will not touch *War and Peace* because they do not consider themselves to be fans of history. They feel that history is not real or relevant. These people could have sat down with Leo Tolstoy and, language problems aside, gotten along just fine. He disliked history, too—at least, the way that historians present it. The novel's long, winding road leads to its Second Epilogue, where Tolstoy addresses the problems with historical interpretation of the past and how he thinks events should be recorded as time passes. It is almost beyond worth mentioning to say that anyone who feels that she or he cannot understand history has not had it presented to them in the right way before. They might have been told about "heroic" deeds that were obviously done out of desperation, not good character, or heroic figures with despicable personal lives, or "common" people who are more interesting than the focal subjects of history. Over generalization makes historians liars, a fact that bothered Tolstoy as much as it bothers people who feel that reading stories based in the past are not worth the effort.

Sometimes people feel that they are not qualified to read *War and Peace* because they do not know enough about its time and setting. The book certainly mentions a lot of historical detail, but it also explains the significance of the details. If it did not explain the references within the novel, it would not have to be so frighteningly long—that is what all of those hundreds of pages are for. All one should do before starting is to take out a map, find France, find Moscow, and know that in 1812 the French army marched across Europe and Russia to Moscow, then quickly turned around and marched back to France. Any further knowledge of the events of the time—why they advanced, why they retreated, who the principle actors were—would be nice, but it is not necessary.

" . . .War and Peace is successful at reflecting a true pace of life without having to dwell upon how poignant it is or oversell its own sensitivity. It is not difficult to understand. The book has something in it to remind readers of all of their own experiences."

There will always be people who do not want to read—whatever their reasons, and there are millions of them, they feel that reading is not worth their time, and, if you haven't heard it all your life, *War and Peace* takes time to read. But it is not much more reader-friendly than books a fraction of its size. It is not much more difficult to figure out what is going on than it is to catch up with the characters on a soap opera, and it is, in the end, a better experience: soap operas do not consider the questions of reality and freedom that make non-readers shun novels in the first place.

Source: David Kelly, for *Epics for Students*, Gale, 2001.

Laura J. Olson

Laura Olson explores Tolstoy's views on the aesthetic power in females with ambivalence, which implies that the essence of femininity is used for nurturing and not for power.

Among the critical innovations that have shaped studies of the nineteenth-century realist novel in recent decades, one of the most striking has been the shift away from questions of representation to broader, ideological concerns. In this context, feminist readings of Russian realism have been especially compelling. Feminist criticism on Tolstoy in the 1980s and 1990s, for example, has shown that his novels often display a misogynistic attitude toward women. As Amy Mandelker recently pointed out, feminist critics have blamed him for mistreat-

ing his own wife, turning his character Natasha into a boring housewife, and killing his Anna, while elevating the meek Dolly, Kitty, and Mar'ia to the status of saints.

By contrast, the importance of a strong feminine principle in Tolstoy's fiction has also been noted by critics, most notably Vera Sandomirsky Dunham, who have spoken of Tolstoy's contribution to the "strong-woman motif" in Russian literature. While both positions offer important insights into Tolstoy's works, a more complex understanding of his novels emerges when they are considered in the European literary context in which myths of femininity developed. The romantic underpinnings of Tolstoy's conceptions of gender are particularly important. In this article I trace the ways in which Tolstoy's *War and Peace* frames mythic femininity in terms of romantic aesthetic principles.

Femininity in this novel is linked to myths of the folk and national character. This cluster of mythic concepts—femininity, the folk, and Russianness—is used in the novel to evoke a return to spontaneity and to critique the author's intellectual, aristocratic milieu—a quintessentially romantic literary project. Yet despite its complex myth-making about these concepts, the novel does not fully embrace any of them. Instead, it rewrites femininity, folk spirit, and Russianness into a utopia of the bourgeois family.

Recent American scholarly work on the role of gender in English romantic literature enables us to identify some of the myths in Tolstoy's novel. Critics have shown that male romantic authors strive for a mythic wholeness by evoking androgyne or envisioning a union with the Eternal Feminine. According to Diane Long Eviler, Anne K. Mellor, and others, the drive to mythologize femininity in the European romantic tradition comes from a sense of a split between genders. Masculinity implies aggressiveness, rationality, and individual competence, and is associated with culture, while femininity implies passivity, intuitiveness, feeling, nurturing, and unity with others, and is associated with nature. Often, the male author sees himself as limited by his masculinity and desires to be whole. He typically expresses this desire in the form of androgynous descriptions of male characters, or by positing an idealized union with the feminine through a female character. Such a character is defined in relation to the male, and she may take on any of a number of roles: mother, lover, sister, muse, and femme fatale, depending on which feminine characteristics the male author wants to appropriate.

In my analysis Natasha Rostova plays all these roles at various times. She is a gentry child, a "sister," who becomes a "lover" to several male characters. She is also a muse figure: for both the characters who love her and the narrator, she functions as a spontaneous source of aesthetic power and closeness to the folk roots of the people. Finally, after a moral fall in which she comes perilously close to attracting men in the manner of a femme fatale, she undergoes a transformation to a fertile matron, a mother. Her story of metamorphosis may be juxtaposed to a different figuration of femininity in the novel, the depiction of androgyny in Platon Karataev. If Natasha embodies metamorphosis, Karataev represents stasis and is purely a symbolic presence meant to inspire and teach by example. The images of both Natasha and Karataev combine traits of femininity with Russianness and connection to folk roots, but as we will see, the depiction of femininity in Natasha emerges as more central to the novel and at the same time more problematic.

Karataev: The Folk as Feminine

If romantic authors saw the feminine principle as attractive because it provided an antidote to what they perceived as rational, alienated masculinity, then folk culture offered an equally powerful counteragent. The idealization of the folk was closely linked with the theory of the unconscious genius. For Schiller and others, the best art came from those who did not create consciously, but from "necessity," in a natural or "naive" way. In Herder's thought, the national culture would remain incomplete and indistinct unless the folk culture was given its due importance. Urging travellers to foreign nations to pay more attention to the "infantile" music of the people, Herder writes that "the music of a nation, in its most imperfect form ... displays the internal character of the people." For the romantic poet, one of the ways to possess such spontaneity and innocence was to draw upon folk culture, either by imitating a folk style or by depicting folk themes or characters. Doing so provided not only aesthetic power but also a link with the national culture and an alternate point of view from which to regard the alienated, industrializing society.

In *War and Peace* Tolstoy, like many romantic authors, mythologizes the folk in order to critique Western morality. The portrait of the peasant

> "Through Natasha. . .male characters and even the narrator himself can approach a union with an unself-conscious spiritual power."

Karataev is the most striking image of the folk in the novel and one of the most often cited representations of the folk in Russian literature. Central to the ideological structure of the narrative, his function is to teach and inspire Pierre by example; thus the wandering, lost aristocratic hero finally finds his true path by way of this unself-conscious peasant. While both Karataev and Pierre embody the feminine characteristic of passivity, Pierre's passivity is different, for it grows out of a lack of directness and connectedness. Pierre lacks a family and seeks community by allowing members of various groups—the Petersburg high society and the Freemasons—to influence him. By contrast, Karataev is pictured as connected to family, people, and animals, even though he is in prison alone. The peasant serves as the embodiment of wholeness and connectedness without attachment, the Tolstoyan ideal of Russianness and a model of how to achieve true happiness. If Pierre is the generous but childlike and incompetent "Ivanushka-Durachok" (Ivan the Fool) of the Russian folktale, Karataev is the representative of the feminine power, associated with nature and the family, which enables the hero to triumph over the masculine forces associated with wealth and ambition (personified by the evil elder brothers in the folktale, and by the evil aristocratic society in the novel). Indeed, after meeting the peasant, Pierre is able to disconnect himself from the corrupt Petersburg aristocracy and the Freemasons, and to establish a family community.

The portrait of Karataev performs a useful function in the narrative because it represents certain aspects of peasant culture (and femininity) in symbolic form. Through the Karataevan rejection of rationality, separateness, alienation, and the divided nature of the gendered self, the author's own Western, aristocratic, intellectual milieu is criticized. In its place a romantic myth of wholeness, connection, and lack of ambitious desire is constructed. This myth is related to femininity through the depiction of this male character as symbolically feminine. There are two aspects of the description of this character that bear discussing in this context: the language used to describe the character's appearance and manner of speaking, and the points made by the narrator about the character's sense of morality.

In the description of Karataev a cluster of epithets underlines the connection between folk culture and femininity. The narrator speaks of Karataev's "affection" and the "simplicity" in his "singing" (*pevuchyi*) voice; his voice is also described as containing the "singing gentleness" of "old Russian peasant women." In another passage the sounds he emits when singing are termed "almost feminine." The character's manner of speaking and singing is emphasized in the description as the source of his folk spontaneity, a fact that underlines the connection to romantic ideology. For it is precisely the folk's verbal production, including its music, that is mythologized by the descendants of Herder's aesthetic.

Another epithet, "round" (*kruglyi*), used repeatedly to describe Karataev's physical being, can also be interpreted as a marker of femininity and to point to the character's androgyny. The circle is a universal symbol of woman, not only because of the shape of the womb, belly, vulva, and breasts, but also because mythic woman is symbolic of unity, the embracing of separateness and difference by an enveloping whole. This adjective becomes significant not only through its repetition (six times in one paragraph alone) but also through its strangeness for a Russian reader: it is particularly striking in such juxtapositions as "Platon Karataev forever remained in Pierre's mind as a most vivid and precious memory, and the very personification of all that was Russian, good and round (*vsego russkogo, dobrogo i kruglogo*)." The repetition of "round" and its use here as the equivalent of a philosophical concept underscore the poetic and symbolic dimension of the description. It could be argued that the manner in which Karataev enters the narrative is just as round and symbolic as the character himself: Karataev is the only important character in the novel to appear, as it were, out of nowhere, occupy nine chapters, and then "disappear" (Karataev is killed by soldiers "offstage," out of the reader's direct gaze).

Karataev's mythic femininity is not only associated with the character's appearance and manner;

it also plays an important role in *War and Peace* because it is connected with an ideal of how to live one's life. The narrator's commentary makes clear that Karataev is to be held up as an example for Pierre, and by extension, for the reader as well. The ideal rejects the self-conscious, isolated self (represented in the novel by Pierre) as the center of all knowledge and morality. Instead, it posits a self founded on the basis of connection and community (Karataev). In this sense the portrayal of Karataev offers a critique of the Western individualized view of the self. The distinction between alienation and connection that is set up in the passages about Karataev gestures toward the psychological difference that informs the masculine/feminine opposition in Western culture. That psychological difference has recently been articulated by feminist psychologists Carol Gilligan and Nancy Chodorow, who reject the universality of the Freudian claim that the ego is defined by separation from others.

Although Tolstoy's novel predates Freud, it is in Freud that we find the canonical definition of a bourgeois, individualistic self. For Freud, the primary relation of self to other is one of assertion and aggression. Gilligan's and Chodorow's critiques of Freud are similar to Tolstoy's critique of the individuated self in that both show an alternative psychology: Tolstoy in the Russian folk, Gilligan and Chodorow in women. An examination of Gilligan's and Chodorow's conclusions indicates that we can profitably apply the category of a feminine subjectivity to Tolstoy's depiction of the folk.

Gilligan and Chodorow show Freud's purportedly universal conception of subjectivity to be in fact gendered, that is, male. They argue that women's psychology lacks a base of separation and aggression and is instead founded on connection. This sense of self gives rise to a morality that privileges interconnectedness over the limitation of aggression. Gilligan calls this female morality an "ethic of care" and imagines the interconnectedness as a web, contrasted with the male perception of the world as hierarchy.

The description of Karataev foregrounds the qualities which Chodorow and Gilligan identify as feminine: the manner in which the peasant expresses affection and love for other beings makes clear that he does not objectify them. During the scene when Pierre first encounters Karataev, the peasant's affection for him, expressed through voice and gestures, nearly makes Pierre cry. The narrator notes that although the peasant loves everyone around him, he would not be grieved if he had to part from these people. He stands for a radical rejection of individuality; if his is an "ethic of care," it is generalized care, a mothering of all beings. His stories about right and wrong behavior indicate that he places high value on the lives and comfort of others, and no importance on individual pride, self-worth, or ambition. In speaking of his forced enlistment in the army, he does not complain of the wrong done him or of his own suffering, but sees the problem in terms of the amount of suffering saved by his serving instead of his younger brother, who has five children. The issue is not the black-and-white one of right or wrong, but one of the relative distribution of pain and well-being. In this sense Tolstoy stages the female morality that Gilligan synthesizes by comparing the biblical story of Abraham, who was ready to sacrifice his son in order to demonstrate his faith, and the story of "the woman who comes before Solomon and verifies her motherhood by relinquishing truth in order to save the life of her child."

In a similar manner, Karataev's way of speaking indicates he has little need to demarcate himself as a separate individual who might have significance for others or who might claim certain rights or privileges. He uses his own nickname, "little falcon" (*sokolik*), to address Pierre, as if to erase the concept of "individual" and to express fluid boundaries between subjects. This is underlined in a passage presenting both functions of the nickname in quick succession as Karataev introduces himself and then addresses Pierre: "They called me Falcon in the service. How can you help from pining, Falcon!" Another aspect of Karataev's speech indicating a lack of a well-delineated individual self-consciousness is his constant and spontaneous use of proverbs, which he loosely attributes to a community of "old folks" (*tak-to starichki govarivali*). In this manner his own speech and sense of morality are characterized as belonging to a group rather than being the product of an individual's mind and thus to his credit. The narrator's analysis emphasizes Karataev's lack of individuation: "his life, as he looked at it, held no meaning as a separate entity. It had meaning only as a part of a whole of which he was at all times conscious."

To be sure, in his description of Karataev's sense of community, nonviolence, and lack of competition, Tolstoy is drawing on a common myth of the Russian folk, one particularly favored by the

Slavophiles. But it is clear that the very qualities attributed to the folk are also attributed by Tolstoy to femininity, and he connects the two in the peasant by describing Karataev's androgynous character, repeating epithets associated with femininity, and embodying in him an alternative to the male-associated behaviors of competition and aggression. In the depiction of Karataev, Tolstoy constructs a romantic myth of wholeness, connection, and lack of ambitious desire. The implied critique of Tolstoy's intellectual and social milieu remains implicit and symbolic in *War and Peace,* but in *Anna Karenina* it is made explicit in the depiction of Levin's forays into intellectual and political activity. That milieu is more concerned with the conventions of rational argument and with political and social power than the moral issues of human well-being.

Karataev acts as a central locus of maternal feminine power despite the fact that he is male and that the female characters in the novel also embody many of these traits. As my analysis of the story of Natasha will show, she—indeed, any female figure—is not able to provide a reliable and stable source for the positive characteristics associated with femininity that we spoke of in relation to Karataev. This is in part because of the demands of realism —a main character in a realist novel cannot stand for a purely philosophical concept such as femininity; she must also bear negative traits that serve to create the illusion of her "humanity." Yet the negative traits assigned to female characters are themselves quite significant, for even in romantic texts (where the symbolic nature of the characters may be foregrounded), the power that females bring to the male is potentially threatening: the feminine can be "a usurping, castrating power, to be suppressed, not exalted." In the fictional world of *War and Peace,* to be female means to be either excessively susceptible to temptation (Natasha); or excessively chaste and didactic (Mar'ia). The kind of symbolic femininity exemplified by Karataev is best given to a male character since there are no narrative demands placed upon him: he does not marry, fall in love, or attract sexual attention, but can remain a symbolic, philosophical presence in the novel. That is, he can remain outside the main thread of the narrative yet still retain life-changing significance for one of the main characters and symbolic force for the reader. By contrast, a female character with aesthetic and/or symbolic power must be woven into the plot and "tamed" through marriage. Because of the dangers of female aesthetic and sexual power, a female does not provide as pure a receptacle for positive feminine qualities as does an androgynous male.

Yet despite the fact that her feminine qualities are not always viewed positively, Natasha serves a central function in the novel in that she provides a link with the spontaneous folk spirit while still remaining a full-fledged character with faults, feelings, and a biography. Importantly, that biography emphasizes her aristocratic roots. The critique of modern Western alienation and the celebration of androgyny that are contained in Tolstoy's depiction of Karataev are, in the final analysis, inadequate. Although Pierre can experience and receive the peasant's wisdom, he cannot unite with it or fully integrate it into his aristocratic way of life. (Similarly, in *The Cossacks* the aristocratic hero Olenin is unable to merge with the Cossack society he so admires.) Through Natasha, however, male characters and even the narrator himself can approach a union with an unself-conscious spiritual power. Natasha is necessary to the narrative because she closes the gap between aristocracy and folk; this was a common role for heroines in nineteenth-century Russian literature. In this context the transformation that Natasha undergoes in her union with Pierre provides a means of taming Nature, of incorporating the spirit of the ancient folk roots into a modern, socially acceptable image of Russianness.

Natasha's Russianness and Romantic Aesthetics

Natasha's association with the Russian national character and with the folk roots of Russian culture is brought out most clearly in the scene in which she dances a Russian folk dance. This performance is one of several depicted in the novel in which Natasha, through her singing and dancing, inspires male characters to achieve moments of insight into the meaning of life. In all instances, Natasha's singing is described in terms that underline her connection with a wellspring of authentic feeling. The male characters who witness her performances can access that feeling only through her performances: they realize that this—the unschooled beauty of Natasha's singing, and its intimation of some higher power at work—is what life is about. Thus, characters who are otherwise bound by convention and rationality achieve release from those shackles. In this particular instance, the narrator of the novel is inspired:

> Where, how, and when could this young countess, who had had a French emigre for governess, have

imbibed from the Russian air she breathed the spirit of that dance? Where had she picked up that manner which the pas de chale, one might have supposed, would have effaced long ago? But the spirit and the movements were the very ones—inimitable, unteachable, Russian—which "Uncle" had expected of her.

This passage is striking because the narrator rarely uses rhetorical questions. The effect is to indicate spontaneity on the part of the speaker, as if his emotions had gotten the better of him and he broke into an exclamation. Natasha's charm is infectious.

The source of Natasha's charm is attributed not to Natasha herself but to her "Russianness." In ascribing Natasha's Russian nature to a "spirit" which she had "sucked" into herself from the Russian air, Tolstoy uses terms similar to the ones romantic writers used to indicate the national character of a work of art or of an artist. The metaphor of the "tree" or "plant," which incorporated the raw materials at its disposal into a living whole, was important in romantic theories of creativity. For Herder, the plant conveyed the idea of the development of a national art in the soil of its own time and place. The poet was, like a seed growing into a plant, unself-conscious and unaware of his own potential powers. We can see similar ideas of artistic ability in the romantic use of Shakespeare as a model of the formation of the natural genius. Carlyle writes that Shakespeare's was an "unconscious intellect":

> Shakespeare's Art is not Artifice; the noblest worth of it is not there by plan or precontrivance. ... Such a man's works, whatsoever he with utmost conscious exertion and forethought shall accomplish, grow up withal unconsciously, from the unknown deeps in him;—as the oak-tree grows from the Earth's bosom, as the mountains and waters shape themselves. ... How much in Shakespeare lies hid ... like roots, like sap and forces working underground!

Just as Shakespeare stands for a certain type of artistic creation for Carlyle, so Natasha symbolizes an aesthetic value for Tolstoy. Despite the somewhat self-conscious tendencies in Natasha—her desire to please or to gain attention—her performances have unconscious, hidden roots. It is important to note, however, that even though Natasha represents the entry of folk culture into the aristocratic milieu and the bubbling of the unconscious into the conscious, she is not Carlyle's Shakespeare, not a true artist. She is merely a conduit for these forces, which are perceived and visualized by a male figure. In this sense she is cast as a muse figure, who could enable the otherwise rational male narrator to produce great art.

Female artists—often singers—commonly acted as muses in romantic fiction. The historical novels of Scott often contained a female character who possessed the ability to convey feeling through singing. In *Waverly* the wild Highlander Flora's "translation" of a bard's Celtic ballad leads the hero to fall in love with her, while also giving the author justification for a two-page description of the "grandeur" of the craggy waterfall which serves as the setting of Flora's romantic performance. But if both Scott and Tolstoy favor female characters as a source of inspiration and power, they also reject them, in the final analysis, as too dangerous. In *Waverley*, although the hero is in love with the wild Flora, he does not marry her. Rather, the other heroine, the domestic and aristocratic Rose, wins the hero's heart and hand in the end. Tolstoy combines the two types of heroine into Natasha: while the first Natasha displays a deep connection with the untamed spirit of the antiquarian culture, this spirit is domesticated and made safe in the Natasha the reader encounters at the end of the novel.

The Fortunate Fall and the Romantic Critique of Culture

Natasha's transformation fits the pattern of another important myth in romantic culture, the myth of the fortunate fall. The myth is a reinterpretation of Christian mythology, in which Adam's loss of paradise is viewed as a blessing since it guarantees the incarnation of God in Christ and the eventual restoration of man to an even greater paradise. As M. H. Abrams has shown, this idea was reworked in secular form by Schiller, who presented man's fall as a descent from instinct into culture and morality. Man's loss of his instinctiveness makes evil possible, but it also gives him a conception of good. In the future paradise envisioned by Schiller, the spontaneity of the original state of "instinct" is restored to man and he is whole again; his moral action will come from his heart rather than from his self-conscious rationality. The myth of Natasha's fall follows this pattern: there is an initial image of the unity of the self with itself and with others, a subsequent transformation into a state of disharmony, disequilibrium, and unwholeness through a moral fall, and an eventual reintegration into a more solid and secure whole in the end.

Tolstoy's reconception of the fortunate fall makes clear that the fall was inevitable from the beginning. It had to happen, not because Natasha is "bad," but because she is "too full" of life, as her mother remarks early in the novel. The wild, primitive Russianness symbolized by Natasha contains the seeds of its own downfall. Such raw aesthetic power, such sensuality and passion, must be restrained by being joined, in the end, with Culture and Rationality. But before it can be joined, it must experience a split.

The split occurs through the metaphor of the theater, a model that Rousseau had used to criticize French immorality and artificiality. In *Lettre a d'Alembert* Rousseau likened the social game of seduction to the theater's seduction of the public. Similarly, in Tolstoy's conception Natasha's sexual seduction by Anatole is paralleled by her eventual seduction by the theatrical presentation, through the mediation of the audience's reaction.

Along with the narrative dynamic of Natasha's moral fall, in this scene a romantic critique of classicist aesthetics and rationalist theories of mind is accomplished. Through the defamiliarizing use of the spontaneous and naive Natasha as focalizor, the opera is reduced to its bare mechanics. The scene is presented as if Natasha has never been to the theater before (although in fact we are told she has), as if she were truly a child or a peasant. Her fresh, unconventional vision permits the narrator to uncover the falseness of the illusion she is witnessing. Because only Natasha has retained her innocent perspective, no one in the audience except her sees that the "trees" in the stage set are simply painted cardboard, that the "girl" singing onstage is a fat woman in a red corsage and white skirt, and that the "lover's" declaration of love occurs after waiting for the right beat in the music. Natasha's perception foregrounds the mechanical parts that make up the illusion of the opera. She does not see the whole spectacle, nor does she succumb to the calculated illusion itself. This criticism of the opera as completely rational, involving nothing but materials, skill, and timing, recalls romantic critiques of the classical model of artistic production. In the romantic view, art had to be inspired in order to be true art. Tolstoy makes a similar critique: such a mechanistic conglomeration of parts is lacking the soul that unifies the parts and makes the thing true art.

Natasha's vision is rebellious: she refuses to submit to the illusion being presented before her eyes. The act of seeing in this manner is portrayed as unconscious, passive (because motivated by her mood and situation), and active (because it involves turning away from the normal interpretation, of which Natasha is aware). Her rebellion against this type of art is not only aesthetic but moral: "She felt … ashamed." Her own moral position is superior to that of the people she is observing: "She felt … amused at them." Thus ironic distance is depicted as a strong moral position. Indeed, throughout *War and Peace,* narrative irony is often the vehicle for moral judgments. The scene at the opera shows how the loss of that ironic distance causes spiritual death. Thus, the scene naturalizes the novel's own aesthetic tactics. If the innocent Natasha before her fall is capable of an ironic vision, that is because it is the privileged vision of Nature itself. By contrast, Natasha's joining with the vision of the group (*le monde*) by the end of the scene signals her departure from the novel's critical stance, hence her association with Culture and her corruption. In this assessment, the moral distance pictured in these scenes as a "boundary," which Natasha feels to be absent or transgressed in her dealings with Anatole, is symbolic of the "good" moral guidance provided by the institution of the family. On the other hand, the absence of any moral boundaries is identified with the evil and hypocritical aristocracy, who engage in trickery in order to manipulate the limitations society puts on sexual activity.

Natasha's "fall" during and after the opera episode lies in her gradual loss of the distanced aesthetic and moral vision, and her acceptance of the evil and hypocritical vision of "the crowd." After seeing that everyone in the theater wears a false expression of delight, she thinks, "I suppose it has to be like this!" a phrase which had been used earlier to indicate Pierre's passive acceptance of the guidance of the morally corrupt Prince Vasilii and Anna Mikhailovna. As a result of her observations of the crowd, Natasha loses the aesthetic distance necessary to censure the art on stage; she also loses the moral distance necessary to judge Anatole's acts as wrong.

As Natasha becomes unable to judge, it becomes clearer and clearer that the narrator is in fact presenting the view of the opera, and that this is in fact a mature view. The narrator introduces it under the guise of the girl, but is unable to sustain that illusion. During the four acts described in this manner, the descriptions grow further and further away from Natasha's perception and become more representative of the narrator's vocabulary and satiric aims: in Act 3 we are given the ironic informa-

tion that one of the actors received sixty thousand rubles for his skill; in Act 4, the narrator speaks of "chromatic scales and diminished sevenths" in the music. The process that is occurring before the reader's eyes is the loss of Natasha. The reader loses her as rebellious artist; society gains her as submissive actress in the drama that ends in spiritual death.

If Natasha is the victim of an aesthetic game whereby a fresh perspective is needed in order to see what is rotten in Culture, it is clear that outside the context of the novel, the reader is the winner, in that s/he gains the insight that Natasha loses. The reader is drawn along with the heroine to the brink of her disaster and left to watch her fall. S/he does not fall, but only glimpses the truth to which Natasha must now be temporarily blinded. What for Natasha is a fall into Culture is the reader's simultaneous fall out of Culture. The act of perception the reader is made to engage in—the vision of the truth about uninspired, fetishized "art"—is not itself mechanistic or automatic; it is creative, rebellious.

The Domestication of Femininity: The Bourgeois Family in Aristocratic Russia

Such rebellious aesthetic power in a female character is viewed ambivalent by male authors, as we have said. In *Waverley*, the male protagonist rejects the wild and rebellious Flora because she is too dangerously idealistic: she "will never love mortal man." Nor is Flora symbolic of Nature: Rose, with her formal garden and careful attention to Waverley's wishes, is deemed more "natural." Flora analyzes Rose's superior character in a statement that could be used to describe the position of woman in the bourgeois family: "Her very soul is in home, and in the discharge of all those quiet virtues of which home is the centre. Her husband will be to her what her father now is—the object of all her care, solicitude, and affection. She will see nothing, and connect herself with nothing, but by him and through him."

Whereas Scott has his hero switch love objects to resolve the dilemma of the too-powerful woman, Tolstoy "kills" the wild spirit of Natasha. Scott's novel focusses on the transformation of the hero from a starry-eyed and rebellious romantic to a more well-grounded, sensible young man who respects authority. He compares the two female characters, who remain essentially the same throughout the novel. By contrast, Tolstoy's novel juxtaposes two male lovers and shows the "development" of the female. The first male lover, the cold and rational Andrei, is done away with in order to make room for the more feminine (sensitive, passive, emotional) and thus spiritually fertile Pierre. Pierre himself grows from conformity to authentic desire. Meanwhile, the heroine, Natasha, is made into the perfect object of Pierre's desire in a domestic incarnation in the First Epilogue of the novel. As if she has experienced a spiritual death and rebirth as the result of her fortunate fall, she emerges as a reduced self, evaluated as better than her previous "too full" self. That new self is represented in the Epilogue of the novel by the picture of Natasha as a "fertile female" (*plodovitaia samka*).

The positive result of Natasha's fall is her ability to cripple her own dangerous energies: because she now knows good and evil, she can identify the "evil" remnants of culture in her own personality and excise them, leaving a half-self which is all the more readily bound to another being for fulfillment. Her singing is now deemed an unnecessary evil, a remnant of the influence of French culture:

> Natasha did not follow the golden rule preached by so many clever people, especially the French, which lays down that a girl should not let herself go when she marries.... Natasha, on the contrary, had instantly dropped all her witchery, in the armoury of which she had one extraordinarily powerful weapon—her singing. She gave up even her singing just because it was such a great attraction.

Natasha's musical performance, which had earlier been associated with her naturalness and even Russianness, is discarded as belonging to the evil, rational West. What is embraced in place of this charm is a relationship with Pierre in which Natasha puts her talents to work reading the thoughts and predicting the desires of her mate.

He experienced the rare happiness men know when women listen to them—not clever women who when they listen are either trying to assimilate what they hear for the sake of enriching their minds and, when opportunity offers, repeating it, or to apply what is told them to their own ideas and promptly bring out the clever comments elaborated in their own little mental workshop; but the happiness true women give who are endowed with the capacity to select and absorb all that is best in what a man shows of himself. Natasha, without knowing it, was all attention: she did not miss one word, one inflection of the voice, no twitch of a muscle in his face nor a single gesture. She caught the still unspoken word on the wing and took it straight into her open heart, divining the secret import of all Pierre's spiritual travail.

What had been aesthetic power in Natasha is now used for nurturing. In this couple all sense of a separate self disappears as each member sees him or herself reflected in the spouse. The secret of the "fulfillment" that Pierre has discovered in Natasha is the infantile one of having all his needs met by an Other who determines and predicts his desires, as if he cannot fulfill them or express them himself. Natasha is a mother to Pierre: indeed, the narrator reports that Pierre's current elevated self-esteem comes from his complete identification with his female Other. "Pierre was able to feel a comforting and assured conviction that he was not a bad fellow after all, and this he felt because he saw himself mirrored in his wife." The passage is remarkable for its use of language similar to that of contemporary theories of self-formation in the infant. In the Tolstoyan conception of mirroring, it is the role of the female Other to provide the male's self-conception by allowing him to see himself in her, to view her as a part of himself. This is a moral conception: what the male receives is not just a self without boundaries, but a conception of the self as "good." Here the important function of Natasha's self-censorship becomes apparent: she must clean herself of all "evil" in order to permit the male's mirrored self-conception to appear "good" and hence valuable to him. To have a good wife means to have a good self; this identification allows Pierre total gratification at the cost of his freedom. The metaphor of the mirror captures the sense in which the male subject of romantic texts imposes a structure on the female Other, reducing her to a reflection of himself. As Lucien Frappier-Mazur has argued, the romantic quest involves the "sanctification of woman as mother and mediatrix"; she is "immobilized in timeless perfection," and, although she shows the way for the hero's quest, she never quests herself.

At first glance, the picture of this couple seems to provide an ideal of family unity and to recall the criticism of the separate, alienated self offered by Karataev's altruism. But in fact what we are presented with is a closed world, the bourgeois ideal of domesticity. In the traditional aristocratic family, matches were made for economic reasons, and the family existed to protect property and reinforce the hierarchical social structure. A sense of privacy or individual self-fulfillment was absent, and children were raised by strangers (foreign tutors and governesses, and peasant serfs). By contrast, in the new configuration Tolstoy offers, the members of the couple choose each other for reasons of personal fulfillment, they create a private life for themselves, and they devote themselves to raising children (Natasha breastfeeds her infant).

As John Lukacs has argued, a bourgeois spirit does not require a middle class; it is an ideology which crops up in Europe from 1450 to 1950, wherever comfort, conformity, and the peaceful life of the interior and of the family are privileged. The ideology particularly resides in romantic thinking, despite the aristocratic background of most romantic writers. Hoeveler points out that in a time of industrial and political revolutions, domesticity can seem to provide a refuge from corruption and alienation. In this context woman is redefined as an "Angel in the House."

The First Epilogue to *War and Peace* defines a bourgeois utopia within the context of the Russian aristocracy. Natasha builds a secure nest in which each person's self is defined by his or her relation to her, the center of the home, the fulfiller of desires. Conflict does not exist because the mother mediates all desire. The family members are protected from the ravages of Culture, of the outside world; their freedom from intervention by the state or by social pressure is ensured in this private sphere. The husband works outside the home, trying to promote reform of the political system according to liberal principles of equality and freedom. In truth, these individuals are no more "free" than they would be in a traditionally aristocratic, patriarchal family; the father is still the head of the family and the mother and children mold their behavior to suit his needs. But this model family lives in accordance with bourgeois liberal thought, which dictates that the individual can "find the greatest degree of happiness and fulfillment" through privacy.

This utopian conception of the family has no place for the autonomy of individuals (women in particular) or the nonclinging love of a Karataev. Karataev is mentioned by the pair as a moral yardstick against which they ought to measure their lives: Natasha asks, "What would Karataev have said?" and Pierre answers that he would have approved of their family life. But in fact there is no Karataevan acceptance and love of all human beings here; rather, there is a mother's desire to claim power in the family by doing away with all desire unless it is her desire, that is, interpreted and sanctioned by her.

The Eden depicted in this resolution of *War and Peace* means to define a space that is marked as Natural, as opposed to the Culture of the Petersburg salons. But if the novel assigns the category of Culture to that which is associated with aristocracy and foreignness, and Nature to the family, the home, and that which is Russian, it overlooks the conventional nature of the structures that make up this paradise. This is characteristic of what Roland Barthes identifies as the bourgeois myth, in which the conventions of the bourgeois way of life are covered by an aura of "humanity," as if they were timeless, biologically necessary. Leo Bersani's assessment of the resolution of the novel runs along these same lines. Arguing that essentially all nineteenth-century realist fiction subscribes to a myth of the coherence and legibility of human psychology, Bersani uses *War and Peace* as an example of a text that represents the author's blindness to his own simplification of psychology and human desire. Despite the author's remonstrations against systematization in history writing, he himself reduces the complex spiritual quest of the novel to a picture of an "exclusive, self-contained social unit." Bersani writes: "The transcendence of culture into nature turns out to be an obedient retreat into a given social form—a retreat which conveniently provides a biological alibi for social conformity."

One wants to ask, with Bersani, whether this limited view of personal happiness is the culmination of the wisdom that the characters have gained throughout this rich novel. In *War and Peace* the quest for self-definition on the level of both the individual and the nation occurs in warlike relations with an Other. How, then, can the novel resolve this quest with such a utopia of peace? In this utopia, both on the individual and national level, the "self" no longer needs to be defined, for it exists in perfect harmony with its neighbors. It seems too simple, too convenient a solution.

A Myth of National Strength

The utopian ending, however, is perfectly in tune with the aims of the novel, if we view these as the establishment of a mythology that would help to locate Russia's strengths as the nation endured the economic and political upheavals of the 1860s. *War and Peace* transplants issues and concerns of the 1860s to the 1810s and 1820s. As radicals like Chernyshevsky called for an emancipated woman, Tolstoy countered with something equally new, for Russia—the bourgeois domestic woman. In arguing for a different solution of the woman question, Tolstoy clothes his ideal woman in the timeless garb of myth. He chooses the earlier period not only because it is a time of relative innocence and of national pride but also because it is in the past: one of the essential qualities of myth is the sense that what we do now has been done before and will be done again. By identifying Russianness with femininity through Natasha, Tolstoy is doing more than providing an antidote to the pessimism of the 1860s—he is prescribing a way out of Russia's current crisis of values, educating a generation.

A myth of national glory, national cohesiveness, and family cohesiveness is worked out in the pages of *War and Peace*. Russianness lies in the spontaneous national spirit which stubbornly remains even after exposure to foreign influence, that which Kutuzov, Karataev, Pierre, and Natasha all possess. Even though the strength of the nation lies precisely in its feminine submissiveness and flexibility, that submissiveness does not invite conquerors or masters (that is, it does not encourage the development of a strong state), but instead simply withstands the subsequent blows of invading foreign cultures. Russia is not only the strong-willed Natasha before her fall; it is also the story of the fall itself, the brush with foreign evil forces that allows the subject to emerge even stronger than before. We may see Natasha's fall as an allegory for Russia's near "rape" by invading foreigners. In the case of both the girl and Russia, the lapse into weakness is the source of strength; passivity is the cause of victory. Just as Natasha undergoes a long sickness during which she loses all traces of the spark that had attracted Anatole, Russia abandons and burns Moscow in the dead of winter, leaving the enemy nothing to eat and nothing to fight. Russia's passive acceptance of the penetration of its "mother" city enables it to overcome its foes.

The final recovery after the fall of both the fictional heroine and the nation is depicted as an inevitable, natural, Russian phenomenon. Natasha's recovery is described in terms of spring shoots of green growing in her; similarly, the Muscovites' abandonment of and return to their city is compared to ants' spontaneous return to the site of their wrecked hive. Both involve an inner strength—instinct—that guides and allows the character or culture to heal itself. In this scheme, some kind of disaster, mishap, or sickness is necessary in order to prove the strength of the subject. Natasha's and Russia's spontaneity and naturalness is not visible

or valuable until it is challenged by an encounter with rationality in the form of Western (represented here by French) culture.

The natural quality of this sickness-and-recovery series of events is emphasized in the novel's cyclical and peaceful conclusion: Natasha's fall culminates in her purposeful creation of a non-conflict domestic utopia. Here, people's lives—that is, history—are no longer to be defined as a series of distinct, individual, and significant events, but as a cyclical repetition of births, marriages, and deaths. History is biology. The First Epilogue gestures at the cyclical nature of history by showing children being raised by characters whom we previously knew as children, and by suggesting that the new generation of children embodies the same traits (they even carry the same names) as their elders. The ending hints at a seemingly endless repetition of the personalities and events in the book: they will reproduce themselves.

Even though the picture of the family offered here is bourgeois, it reinforces the connection between aristocracy and folk in Russian culture. In Russian culture the peasant woman was associated with fertility and child-rearing. By referring to Natasha as a "fertile female," Tolstoy implies she is like the Mother Earth of folk tales and songs. By depicting her breast-feeding her infants, he underlines her connection with peasant earthiness. Thus, while Natasha no longer acts as a muse-like conduit of folk spirituality and aesthetics, she offers an image of organic femininity.

Here we have not so much an embracing of the Russian folk spirit as a way of transplanting certain aspects of the folk culture to the aristocratic culture. Tolstoy's stance was common among Russian intellectuals of the period: Laura Engelstein sees a similar move among liberal sociologists during the post-Reform era. These critics rejected the patriarchal family structure as a vestige of serfdom, but they did not accept the radical individualism of the modern urban family, either. Instead, "they seized on the peasant woman's reproductive prowess, a product of female subordination and cultural dependency, as a Rousseauian alternative to the self-indulgent, sterile urban world to which they themselves belonged but which they could not justify in moral terms." In Tolstoy's case we can see some of what Geoffrey Hartman has identified as the romantic drive to overcome the inevitable alienation and sense of separation that results from an intellectual, analytical relation to the world. Writing requires a distanced, intellectual relation to the world; mythic thinking offers a respite from that distance. For modern writers the experience of alienation arising from this dilemma is common: "The mind which acknowledges the existence or past existence of immediate life knows that its present strength is based on a separation from that life." Revisiting the past is a crucial step toward the goal of recovering wholeness, for the past represents a former version of the alienated self.

Source: Laura J. Olson, "Russianness, Femininity, and Romantic Aesthetics in *War and Peace*," in *The Russian Review,* Vol. 56, No. 4, October, 1997, pp. 515–31.

A. V. Knowles

The following overview illustrates the experience of reading War and Peace.

When Tolstoi first thought of writing *War and Peace* he gave it the title *Three Eras*, referring to the years 1856 (when the hero returns home from exile after the death of Tsar Nicholas I and the Crimean War), 1825 (the year of the Decembrist Revolt and the reason for the hero's exile and 'the period of [his] delusions and misfortunes'), and 1812 (the Battle of Borodino and Russia's defeat of Napoleon). His moral integrity then forced him to consider Russia's 'failures and shame' and start earlier, in 1807 (Treaty of Tilsit) and then 1805 (Battle of Austerlitz). In effect he ended up with only the last three and when the first 38 chapters were published in *The Russian Messenger* in 1865 the editors entitled them *1805*. In 1866 it was to be called *All's Well That Ends Well* and only in the following year was its final title decided. The novel was completed in 1869. Tolstoi, however, refused to call it a novel, or even a historical chronicle. It was 'what the author wished and was able to express in the form in which it is expressed' and he justified this unsatisfactory definition by stating that all Russian literature which rose above the mediocre did not fit into any of the conventional categories of novel, story, or poem, citing Pushkin's *Eugene Onegin* (*Evgenii Onegin*), Lermontov's *A Hero of Our Times* (*Geroi nashego vremeni*), Gogol's *Dead Souls* (*Mertvye dushi*) and others, including his own *Childhood*.

Leaving to one side whether or not it is a novel, more particularly a historical novel, it is clearly anti-historical in intent. The vast, panoramic canvas includes 'real' historical characters—Tsar Aleksandr

I, Napoleon, the Austrian emperor, generals, diplomats, politicians, and so on—but it also presents a philosophy of history. 'History would be a fine thing', he wrote, 'if only it were true'. He studied relevant documents, books, archives, and personal recollections of the period, and distrusted them all. History to Tolstoi was the sum total of what individuals thought and did; the 'great men' of history had little or no influence over events, the changes and evolutions noted by historians were illusions, and there was no such thing as progress or historical advancement. At the Battle of Borodino Pierre Bezukhov sees only a succession of incomprehensible acts: Napoleon deludes himself in thinking his orders are carried out or that there is such a thing as a grand strategy; Kutuzov, as much idealized as Napoleon is satirized, knows all this, sleeps through councils of war, and lets things take their inevitable course; and the outcome depends basically on the morale of the troops. And here the book's title is significant in a way other than epitomizing one of the most obvious features of Tolstoi's style—the use of contrast. It is as if he wants to point up the fact that all those great events and important people that have always been thought to be the stuff of history are quite irrelevant. What is crucial are the lives of the thousands of ordinary people, their personal joys and disappointments, their births and their deaths, their loves and hates, their feelings, thoughts, short-comings, and ambitions. That is reality and everything else is a harmful illusion.

Nevertheless it is in his characterization, not in his philosophizing or beating the reader over the head with his own idiosyncratic though stimulating ideas, that Tolstoi's greatness as a writer really lies. If they had the choice most readers might choose to forget the 'war' and cherish and admire the 'peace'. The reader lives with Tolstoi's characters as with those of no other writer. All the 900 or so are sharply individualized and stand out clearly when they appear (even the dogs are differentiated). Albeit with a vast historical backcloth, *War and Peace* is based on the stories of three families: the Bolkonskiis—the old aristocratic Prince, a crusty 'Voltairean', his daughter Maria, and son Andrei; the Moscow gentry Rostovs—the gentle, conservative Count, the motherly countess, and their children Nikolai and the utterly charming and delightful Natasha; and the wealthy Bezukhovs, especially the Tolstoian 'seeker of the truth' Pierre. There are also their numerous relations and friends. The lives of these families are shown in all their variety, at dinner parties and in conversation at home, at grand

Napoleon Bonaparte. The French emperor's nineteenth-century military campaigns provide the historical backdrop for the novel.

balls at the Imperial Court, at entertainments with mummers at Christmas, on country estates, at hunting parties, in intrigues, social climbing, drunken escapades of army officers, their births, marriages, and deaths, love affairs, financial matters and the endless complications, joys, and heartbreaks of everyday life.

The world Tolstoi creates is bright, healthy, and happy. There are none of the grotesques of Gogol' or the abnormalities of Dostoevskii. His characters are generally likeable and even the horrors of war are treated with such an epic sweep and magisterial

overview that death, injury, and even the futility of it all are lessened. The mood of *War and Peace* is largely serene. Tolstoi, although historically fatalistic, is optimistic about the human condition. His love of life shines through even its darkest pages and his praise of the value of family life is unstinting and unsurpassed. His acceptance of life in all its vicissitudes is contagious, yet it is accompanied by a search for meanings and his searing psychological analysis exposes everything false. His prejudices, however, are not disguised. He prefers the country to the town, Russia to the West, the submissive

> On finishing the book the reader, as an early admirer of Tolstoi put it, should have experienced not a work of fiction, but life itself."

personality to the ambitious or pretentious, and ultimately peace to war. On finishing the book the reader, as an early admirer of Tolstoi put it, should have experienced not a work of fiction, but life itself.

Source: A. V. Knowles, "War and Peace: Overview," in *Reference Guide to World Literature,* edited by Lesley Henderson, St. James Press, 1995.

William W. Rowe

William W. Rowe presents an analysis of the major characters in War and Peace.

Tolstoy's longest and perhaps greatest novel underwent several false starts and numerous revisions. Behind it lay two intentions. For many years Tolstoy had wished to write an accurate account of early nineteenth-century European history, and so decided to write about a man returning in 1856 from exile in Siberia after taking part in the abortive Decembrist uprising of 1825. As he explained in an unpublished foreword to the beginning of the novel, he soon found it necessary to trace his hero back to 1805, and the first thirty-eight chapters appeared in early 1865, in the *Russian Messenger,* under the title *1805.* A year later, Tolstoy wrote Fet that he hoped to finish the work by 1867 and publish it under the title *All's Well That Ends Well.* He made so many changes, though, that the last chapters appeared only in 1869.

War and Peace is first of all a celebration of life. In this work more than any other, Tolstoy succeeded in achieving what he termed (in a famous unposted letter of July–August, 1865) "the aim of an artist": "to make people love life in all its countless inexhaustible manifestations." An astonishing multitude of vividly individualized characters promotes this end; even the dogs, as the critic Nikolay Strakhov noted, are individualized. The novel also provides a patriotic view of Russian

history beginning in 1805 and extending beyond Napoleon's invasion of 1812, seen through a very special lens of Tolstoyan determinism. In some respects, it is a heroic epic in the tradition of Homer's *Iliad.* Though the historical sections of *War and Peace* are successfully interrelated with the fictional ones, the work sprawls so idiosyncratically as to cause Henry James to label it a "loose baggy monster."

Tolstoy anticipated objections to the form of his work. "What is *War and Peace?"* he proleptically addressed its first readers. "It is not a novel, still less an epic poem, still less an historical chronicle. *War and Peace* is that which the author wished to and could express in that form in which it found expression. Tolstoy repeatedly insisted that the best works of Russian literature had their own unique and necessary form. And there was considerable truth in this: Pushkin's masterpiece *Eugene Onegin* is subtitled "a novel in verse"; Gogol's great novel *Dead Souls* is subtitled "an epic poem"; Lermontov's novel *A Hero of Our Time* consists of five separate but interconnected stories; and so on.

Who is the hero of *War and Peace*? Here too there can be no easy answer. A good case can be made for the Russian people, or for Russia itself. More narrowly, the hero of Tolstoy's novel has been considered a combination of Prince Andrew and Pierre, as two sides of the author himself, or even tripartite person (including Nicholas). Yet we should not forget Natasha, a central figure intimately related to the other main characters. One critic has even seen *War and Peace* as "a gigantic novel of education, centering not on one protagonist but on five" (the above four plus Princess Mary). Another critic, after naming these five, contends that none of them is "the hero" of the novel, which is deliberately "decentralized" in order to create an illusion of the essence of life. However, if one looks for "a hero and a heroine," Pierre and Natasha stand out for a variety of reasons.

Pierre and Natasha

The impishly enchanting Natasha was generally modeled upon Tolstoy's younger sister-in-law, and in many respects the kindly, bearlike Pierre recalls Tolstoy himself. It is they who celebrate life the most fully in *War and Peace* and most strikingly display a virtue that may be termed spontaneous altruism. Moreover, Pierre and Natasha are linked by numerous similar traits, attitudes, and circumstances long before they come together at the end of the novel.

To begin with, each is disastrously involved with a Kuragin. Pierre's marriage to Helene almost results in his death (in a duel with Dolokhov); Natasha's infatuation with Anatole almost results in her death (by suicide). Both amorous involvements are officially "engineered" by Kuragins, Prince Vasily and Helene. Also, Dolokhov causes evil behind the scenes of both relationships, as Helene's presumed lover and as Anatole's resourceful accomplice. Both Pierre and Natasha initially wonder if their infatuations are somehow wrong, after which they rather strangely yield to the Kuragins: Pierre tells himself that his marriage to Helene is predestined; Natasha rationalizes that Helene's good husband Pierre probably approves of her involvement with Anatole. Moreover, both amorous involvements are appropriately punctuated by exclamations in the French language. When Pierre submits to Helene, he rather awkwardly blurts out " *Je vous aime* !". When Anatole singles out Natasha, he exclaims "*Mais charmante!*". As R. F. Christian has observed, the use of French "of or by a Russian" in *War and Peace* "very often has a suggestion of sophistication, artificiality, even mendacity." This falsity is appropriately reflected by the backgrounds of each episode. Helene's parents wait impatiently for Pierre to propose, spying on him and finally pressuring him into it. Natasha and Anatole are attracted to each other against a backdrop of opera which travesties his intended abduction of her and which is deliberately rendered artificial by Tolstoy's technique of "making strange." This Gallicized falsity contrasts with the normally natural Russianness of both Natasha and Pierre. Natasha's natural Russianness is repeatedly emphasized when she does a Russian dance; Pierre's, when he decides that he is predestined to kill Napoleon.

Pierre and Natasha succumb in similar ways: both are startled by the "terrible nearness" of the Kuragins, and both feel that protective "barriers" have been removed. After Pierre's duel, when Helene viciously insults him, he is likened to "a hare, surrounded by dogs, who lays back its ears and continues to crouch down before its enemies". When Natasha, after failing to elope with Anatole, learns that he was already married, she is likened to "a wounded, cornered animal who looks at the approaching dogs and hunters".

The "natural, Russian" Natasha and Pierre thus give in to the "false, French" Kuragins, but after much suffering they both emerge somehow stronger and ready to rebuild their lives. This process recapitulates in miniature the abandonment of Moscow

" *War and Peace* is first of all a celebration of life. In this work more than any other, Tolstoy succeeded in achieving what he termed. . . 'the aim of an artist': 'to make people love life in all its countless inexhaustible manifestations.' An astonishing multitude of vividly individualized characters promotes this end; even the dogs,. . .are individualized."

to the French Army, a decision so inevitable, Tolstoy insists, that "every Russian" might have predicted it. In all three cases, Tolstoy's imagery is aptly similar. At great length, Tolstoy likens the burned, abandoned city of Moscow to a bee hive charred and cleansed by fire. At the end of the novel, Natasha declares that Pierre has been morally cleansed as if by a steam bath, and he too finds a great change in her, barely recognizing the woman in a black dress with dark eyes and a thin, pale, stern face. In all three cases, the imagery has a remarkably positive aspect. The stern woman in the black dress seems "dear, kind, marvelous" and even "kindred" to Pierre; Natasha finds Pierre "pure, smooth, fresh" after his moral steam bath; the charred ruins of Moscow "astonish" Pierre with their "beauty".

Natasha and Pierre are uniquely similar in their combination of sensitivity, spontaneity, altruism, and effectiveness. Indeed, the most significant similarity between them is their readiness to help people in distress. However, Pierre displays the quality of spontaneous altruism only after considerable Tolstoyan searching, whereas Natasha exhibits it from the very first. Early in the novel, for example, when Sonya bursts into tears because Vera has said unkind things about her, Natasha immediately embraces, comforts, and kisses her. Sonya brightens up with shining eyes, like a kitten ready to play again. Natasha displays the spontaneous ability to console others most fully when Petya dies and she quite literally comforts her mother back to life, supporting the almost insanely aggrieved woman with healing love and tenderness for three days and nights.

Perhaps still more remarkable is the selfless efficiency with which Natasha works to help others. When her mother cruelly accuses Sonya of ingratitude and of scheming to catch Nicholas, relations between those three become almost unbearably strained. However, we learn from a one-sentence paragraph that Natasha set to work to bring about a reconciliation and succeeded admirably. Most striking of all, though, is what Natasha accomplishes during the evacuation of Moscow. First, she arranges for some of the wounded soldiers to stay in the Rostovs' house. Then it is Natasha alone who blocks the monstrous decision to cart away household goods when the wounded could be taken instead. The servants, we are told, crowd around Natasha, unable to believe her strange instructions, but soon they joyously and energetically work to transport the wounded soldiers, and it all seems not strange to them now, but inevitable.

After Pierre becomes a Freemason, he gives large sums of money to their cause and tells Prince Andrew: "only now, when I live, at least, when I try to live (Pierre modestly corrected himself) for others, only now do I understand all the happiness of life". This formulation resembles earlier ones to be found in Tolstoy's works—for example, in *A Landowner's Morning* and *The Cossacks*—with one qualification: Pierre's modest correction suggests that his happiness in helping others is less self-centered than Nekhlyudov's or Olenin's. Pierre thus draws closer to answering the Tolstoyan question of how we should live. Though Prince Andrew replies, "Yes, if only it were so!"—we then learn that he has now begun "a new inner life".

After Natasha, failing to elope with Anatole, has attempted suicide, Pierre talks with her, and she is suddenly struck by his "timid, tender, heart-felt" voice. He then warmly offers her his friendship and sympathy. Natasha declares herself unworthy, and Pierre is himself amazed at his next words: "If I were not myself, but the handsomest, most intelligent and best man in the world, and if I were free, I would this very moment ask on my knees for your hand and your love!" Natasha sheds "tears of gratitude and tenderness," and it is clear that Pierre's spontaneous generosity has set her recovery in motion. Pierre later saves an enemy officer, protects an Armenian girl, and rescues a child from the Moscow fire; these acts parallel Natasha's efficient helping of the wounded soldiers. Together, Pierre and Natasha display a greater degree of spontaneous altruism than any other principal characters in Tolstoy's works, with the possible exception of Kitty in *Anna Karenina*.

From the very beginning of the novel, Pierre and Natasha are associated by suggestions of childhood and fairy tale—like pleasure. During the opening soiree scene Pierre is likened to "a child in a toyshop," and we first see as if under a cap of invisibility, Natasha at age thirteen when she rushes recklessly in with her doll. She then hides in the conservatory "as if under a cap of invisibility," a Russian fairy-tale image; Pierre soon pretends to be Napoleon, piercing an "invisible" enemy with his sword.

In their childlike enthusiasm, both are inspired to emulate others early in the novel. When Dolokhov, for a bet, drains an entire bottle of rum while precariously balanced on a window ledge, Pierre watches like a frightened child. His expression combines a faint smile of excitement with terror and fear: "Why is it so long?" he wonders. "It seemed to him that more than half an hour had gone by." Pierre twice averts his eyes, the second time telling himself "that he would never open them again." But when he does, and sees that Dolokhov has won, Pierre insists on emulating him, even without a bet. "I'll do it! Bring me a bottle!" he repeatedly shouts.

Also early in the novel, Natasha hides in the Rostovs' conservatory, pleased that Boris is looking for her. At this point Nicholas and Sonya (who is jealous and upset at him) meet nearby, and Natasha excitedly eavesdrops upon their reconciliation. Sonya sobs, and Nicholas takes her hand: "Natasha, not stirring and not breathing, watched from her hiding place with shining eyes. 'What will happen now?' she wondered." Nicholas asks Sonya's forgiveness and kisses her: "Oh, how nice!" Natasha thinks. When they leave, she calls Boris to her "with a meaningful and sly expression" and proposes that he kiss her doll. He hesitates. Natasha's flushed face expresses both triumph and fear: "'And would you like to kiss me?' she whispered almost inaudibly, looking up at him from under her eyebrows, smiling, and almost crying from excitement." When Boris still hesitates Natasha jumps up on a tub and kisses him full upon the lips. As the scene ends, she counts on her fingers the years remaining until she will be sixteen and Boris can ask for her hand in marriage.

During this entire episode, Natasha seems disarmingly innocent. Her conduct is hardly above reproach—she spies upon two lovers and makes bold advances to Boris—and yet the childlike wonder with which she looks on ("What will happen now?") and her joy at the lovers' reconciliation ("Oh, how nice!") render her slyness forgivable, and even quite appealing. As in the episode with Pierre and Dolokhov, life is seen as an exciting game to play and to experience fully. Both Pierre and Natasha are anxious at whatever cost to experience the intensity of what they have just witnessed. Both display a compelling desire to plunge into the tide of life.

The intensity of Natasha's and Pierre's experiences is indirectly—but all the more powerfully—conveyed by the momentary impairment of their sight and hearing. Thus after Pierre's confrontation with Helene, he "did not hear and did not see anything"; and when he tries to kill Napoleon, "he did not hear anything and did not see anything around himself". When Natasha learns that Petya has been killed she "did not see, did not hear"; as she enters the ballroom at her first ball, "the steady hum of voices, footsteps, and greetings deafened Natasha; the light and glitter blinded her still more".

The intensity of the immediate experience is irresistible: early in the novel both Pierre and Natasha give their "word of honor" only to break it later. First, Pierre emphatically gives Andrew his word not to go to Anatole Kuragin's, then recalls that he had already promised Anatole. Besides, he reasons, "words of honor" are "conventional things with no definite meaning, especially if one considers that by tomorrow he may have died"—and goes anyway. Natasha gives her "word of honor" not to tell anyone that Nicholas has been wounded—and immediately rushes to tell Sonya about it. Upon seeing Sonya's reaction, however, Natasha embraces her, bursts into tears, and explains that Nicholas, only slightly wounded, writes that he is "now well" and promoted to the rank of officer.

Especially as viewed against the backdrop of apparently predestined historical events in *War and Peace,* Natasha's and Pierre's parallel circumstances tend to suggest that they are fatefully related. Early in the novel Natasha, still aglow after kissing Boris, sits opposite Pierre at dinner. Her glance, filled with love for Boris, sometimes rests on Pierre: "and the look of this funny, animated girl made him want to

laugh without knowing why". Soon thereafter, Natasha herself exclaims: "that fat Pierre who sat opposite me is so funny!". "How happy I feel!" she adds. Much later, at the Bergs' party, we learn that Pierre "happened to sit opposite Natasha" when she has just fallen in love with Prince Andrew. "What has happened to her?" Pierre wonders. These parallels seem still more fateful after Natasha becomes engaged to Prince Andrew: "Pierre was avoiding Natasha. It seemed to him that his feeling for her was stronger than a married man's should be for his friend's fiancee. And some kind of fate continually brought him together with her".

Long before Pierre realizes that he loves Natasha, he is uniquely sensitive to her feelings, and she to his. After Pierre's duel with Dolokhov, everyone in the Rostov house likes Dolokhov except Natasha, who "insisted that he was an evil person, that in the duel with Bezukhov, Pierre was right and Dolokhov was guilty, that he was unpleasant and unnatural". Talking with her mother at night, Natasha then reveals a deeper affection for Pierre than perhaps she consciously realizes. Having playfully dismissed Boris as "narrow" and "grey," Natasha abruptly declares that Pierre is "dark blue with red". Her mother, laughing, remarks that Natasha flirts with Pierre too, but Natasha denies it, insisting that Pierre is a "fine" person, "dark blue with red."

Since Pierre and Natasha are associated from the first in a separate dimension of childlike enthusiasm and imagination, it is appropriate that she here reveals a preference for him in what appears to be a rather silly game of childlike perception. Natasha's ostensibly playful notion of "red with blue" is mysteriously echoed by Sonya in a game of predicting the future. First, Sonya pretends to see Prince Andrew "lying down" with a "happy" expression, thus unwittingly predicting the circumstances of his death. Asked what came afterwards, Sonya replies: "something blue and red". She therefore becomes one of Tolstoy's most remarkable unlikely prophets by also predicting Natasha's marriage to Pierre. The "red and blue" prediction was obviously important to Tolstoy, for Natasha and Sonya discuss it much later, confusing the details but marveling at its accuracy.

Andrew

If Pierre and Natasha embody an intense celebration of life, Prince Andrew suggests by indirection a cyclical affirmation of the life force. From the beginning he is pointedly contrasted with his close friend Pierre. Andrew, we are told, "combined in the highest degree all those qualities which Pierre lacked and which can best be expressed by the concept, strength of will". Pierre admires Andrew's self-control and is astonished by his capacity for work and study. Later, we learn that Andrew's stern father (modeled on Tolstoy's maternal grandfather) recognizes only two virtues: activity and intellect. His sister Mary, however, accuses Andrew of "a kind of intellectual pride".

If we return to the distinction Tolstoy made when he was writing *Childhood* between "from the head" and "from the heart," we will recall that he preferred the latter, despite its apparent crudeness. We may therefore suspect that Andrew's cool intellect and strength of will, so generously envied by warm-hearted Pierre, are, in a sense, weaknesses masquerading as strengths. This is by no means clear at first: Pierre's naivete and rather irresponsible naturalness seem to contrast quite unfavorably with Andrew's sophisticated self-control. Yet for this very reason, Pierre is more open to personal development, especially since he lives more by the heart than by the head. Their attitudes toward Napoleon provide a revealing contrast: Pierre imagines himself to be Napoleon in a make-believe game; Andrew admires Napoleon as a master military strategist. Pierre's character, Tolstoy suggests, is not yet formed, whereas Andrew's, in taking shape, has acquired a hard surface crust; for most of his life he is enviably protected from other people, but also sadly isolated from them. Prince Andrew easily sees through others (at least, enough for his own purposes), but until he is mortally wounded he lacks the capacity for a full and open relationship with others that would necessarily render him somewhat vulnerable.

Primarily for these reasons, Andrew, throughout the novel, remains oddly static. Each lesson he learns leaves him in need of another. Each time his protective surface crust is penetrated—whether by loss or by love—it seems to close over once again. John Hagan has observed that Prince Andrew goes through "five distinct cycles of death and rebirth," arranged "so that what is metaphorical in the first four becomes literal reality in the fifth." The first cycle, Hagan suggests, begins with Andrew's fall at the battle of Austerlitz (his wound is described as if it were mortal, and Andrew's father tells everyone that his son is dead). Andrew's prior conceptions of Napoleon and military glory "die" at this point, yet he also discovers "peace" in the lofty, infinite sky, which suggests a "rebirth." The second cycle commences with his wife Lise's death, when Andrew's

guilt causes "a second spiritual death of his own." This time, Hagan finds, the rebirth consists of two parts: Andrew's brief turning to God (in his conversation with Pierre at the ferry) and his turning to Nature and Natasha (climaxed by the nocturnal window scene at Otradnoe). The famous old oak mirrors Andrew's feeling that life is over, and then his regeneration when he observes its transformation. Cycle three begins with Andrew's "fatal" involvement with the rationalist Speransky and ends with a new, stronger feeling of love for Natasha and his proposal of marriage. She then begins cycle four by attempting to elope with Anatole; it ends with Andrew's vigorous condemnation of war in conversation with Pierre before the battle of Borodino. In the fifth cycle Andrew literally dies, but does so with the conviction that "death is an awakening."

It should be noted that the first two cycles are composed of what Tolstoy terms at one point the "best moments" of Andrew's life. Upon seeing that the bare old oak at Otradnoe has suddenly become gloriously green, Andrew recalls these "best" moments: "Austerlitz with that lofty sky, his wife's dead, reproachful face, Pierre at the ferry, and that girl thrilled by the beauty of the night, and that night, and the moon". The first of these four moments comprises the entire first cycle; the last three, the composite second one. How, we may wonder, can Lise's dead reproachful face constitute a "best" moment? Moreover, would Tolstoy have considered the main elements of the last three cycles—including the painful blow of Natasha's attempted elopement—to be Andrew's best moments as well?

In attempting to answer the first question, Edward Wasiolek has observed that Lise's reproachful face causes Andrew to understand for the first time "that he has violated by his judgment the sacredness of her being." Wasiolek notes that the other three moments involve the sky, which reminds Andrew that "life within him is infinite" as he "catches a glimpse of something that is not circumscribed by his understanding." The connection is thus the fact that Andrew senses the limitations of his intellect during each moment. All this is helpful, but the crucial criterion of a "best" moment seems to be that a period of heightened consciousness—no matter how disillusioning or painful—leads to positive personal growth. Moreover, Prince Andrew's four moments of growth seem still more unified if we return once again to Tolstoy's distinction between the head and the heart. During the first two moments Andrew realizes, at least briefly, the danger of living "from the head." He realizes that his intensely rational approach (to Napoleon, military glory, and his own wife) is inadequate and wrong. During the last two moments, Andrew recognizes the importance of living "from the heart." His turning to God with Pierre at the ferry leads him to begin "a new inner life," and his turning to Nature, inspired by Natasha's joyful enthusiasm at the window, reinforces this internal rebirth. All four moments, however ostensibly disparate, form two halves of a consistent, unified process of personal growth. Andrew's long-standing and all-consuming commitment to living from the head, however, renders this growth incomplete for most, if not all, of his life.

We may now attempt to answer the question about Andrew's other "best" moments. Cycle three (his disenchantment with the rationalist Speransky and his increased love for Natasha) clearly fits the pattern of movement from the head toward the heart. The end of the fourth cycle—Andrew's condemnation of war—aptly echoes the end of cycle one. The beginning of cycle four, Natasha's attempted elopement, is far less obviously a "best" moment, yet in a very real sense this echoes the beginning of cycle two: by agreeing to postpone his engagement to Natasha, Andrew treats her in much the same coldly rational way that he did Lise. Wasiolek goes so far as to insist that it is not Natasha who betrays Andrew, but he her, and there is some truth in this. Still, if Natasha's attempted elopement is to be a "best" moment for Andrew, he must realize his error sufficiently to achieve significant personal growth—and this he never quite seems to do. Not long before his death, Andrew derives "comfort" from thinking that "love is God" and that as a particle of love, he will, at death, return to the eternal source. "But," as Tolstoy rather pointedly remarks, "these were only thoughts". Andrew, we may infer, still lives too much from the head. Finally, however, a "veil" that has obscured Andrew's "spiritual vision" is lifted: his last days are "an awakening from life," and he realizes that "death is an awakening."

Apart from the concepts of "cycles" and "best moments," Andrew may be profitably seen also in terms of his relationship to Pierre. The goal of "living for oneself" that Andrew expounds to Pierre contrasts sharply with the latter's answer about "living for others". It is therefore rather ironic that Andrew in fact carries out with great efficiency all the reforms that Pierre vainly attempts on his estates. Andrew's advice to Pierre ("don't marry, my friend, don't marry!") is ironically echoed by Pierre's

advice to Andrew that he "marry, marry, marry" Natasha. And this is part of another symmetry: each friend (with far-reaching results) directs the other toward Natasha. Pierre urges Andrew to ask Natasha to dance; Andrew brings Pierre to Natasha and tells her to rely on him alone.

Prince Andrew is framed by a window or a door at several crucial moments of his life. Important episodes featuring doors and windows associate Andrew with life and death—and, symmetrically, with Pierre. Early in the novel, they are both excited by episodes at open windows: Pierre, by Dolokhov and the rum bottle; Andrew, by Natasha and the beautiful night. Whereas Pierre is inspired to defy death, Andrew is inspired to begin a new life. Tolstoy eventually uses the image of a shattering window to describe the exploding shell that fatally wounds Prince Andrew. Much earlier, when Andrew returns to his wife, Lise, a strong wind blows out a candle through a window, in a prefiguration of her death. Someone later holds a door shut against him as his son is born. Hagan has related this door, behind which struggle life and death, to the door through which Andrew's own death later seems to force itself. That door, which exists only in a dream resembling a vision and admits Andrew's death, may be linked to the metaphorical door that seems to open on rusty hinges when Pierre is finally united with Natasha to begin a new life.

War and Peace with Women

Anna Mikhailovna is said to "conquer" a position next to Prince Vasily as she fights for Boris's advancement, and she literally engages in a tug of war with Catiche for the old Count Bezukhov's portfolio. As Anna Pavlovna maneuvers Pierre into desiring Helene, she is said to be "in the excited condition of a commander on a battlefield". And when Anatole arrives at Bald Hills, Andrew's pregnant wife, Lise, "like an old war horse that hears the trumpet, unconsciously and forgetting her condition, prepared for the accustomed gallop of coquetry".

Tolstoy was not kind to women in *War and Peace*. "Selfish, vain, stupid, trivial in every way—that's women when you see them as they really are," Andrew tells Pierre. "Women are especially harmful," Dolokhov tells Nicholas, "countesses or cooks, it's all the same—I have yet to meet a woman who was not a creature for sale". Vera is spiteful; Helene is both superficial and predatory. Julie Karagina debases love through calculation: for example, there is something tendentiously despicable about the way Julie's face gleams "with triumph and self-satisfaction" as she forces her fiance, Boris, to vow "that he loved her and had never loved any woman more than her. She knew that for the Penza estates and the Nizhegorod forests she could demand this, and she got what she demanded".

Natasha, on the other hand, is a truly delightful heroine, at least until the epilogue. Charmingly spontaneous and generous, she enlivens all those with whom she comes into contact. Her enthusiastic love of life helps others even when she is not aware of their presence: thus when Prince Andrew overhears her rapturous exclamations at the window about the beauty of the night, his despair gives way to a host of youthful thoughts and hopes arising in his soul. Natasha can melt the layers of pride and cynicism Andrew has built around himself. Even after her attempted elopement, he recalls "that spiritual force, that sincerity, that openness of soul".

Yet when we meet her in the epilogue, after seven years of marriage to Pierre, we find a very different Natasha. Now "stouter and broader", she neglects her hair and her clothing. She has purposely abandoned all her enchanting ways, including her singing, precisely because they were seductive. Here one may cite from *Family Happiness* Sergey Mikhailich's instructing Masha in the "undesirability" of coquettishness, and from *Anna Karenina* Levin's squirming with painful embarrassment when he sits opposite a girl who wears a low-cut dress for his benefit.

Having eradicated her sparkling charm, Natasha now centers her entire being upon her family: "her husband, whom she had to hold so that he would belong undividedly to her and to the home—and the children, who had to be carried, born, nursed, and brought up." Natasha's jealousy is a common object of family amusement. She strictly controls Pierre, who dares not even smile when he talks with another woman. In return, Natasha places herself "on a footing of slave to her husband." She tries to anticipate his every wish, yet she uses his own words against him if he seems to be changing his mind. Pierre's "joyous" sense of his own identity as "not a bad man" results from "seeing himself reflected in his wife".

Unattractive as this mutual absorption and mutual enslavement may appear, it is an almost inevitable development of what Tolstoy then considered a highly satisfactory marriage. For him, a good wife was nurturing and supportive, yet constraining and somehow sexless. Ruth Benson puts it, "Tolstoy's own and his heroes' search for moral purity" were "constantly threatened" by "woman's selfish interests and particularly her sexuality." Only total absorption in marriage and family could disarm the dangerous weapon of female sexuality. The more earthy vitality a young girl radiated, the more necessary it was that she be quickly herded into the safe confines of family life.

The young Natasha fairly bursts with undirected energy. Significantly, she is called "gunpowder" early in the novel. As her performance of a Russian peasant dance pointedly suggests, society had failed to squelch in her that primitive force of nature which is not separate from female sexual energy. Hence, grave danger: the same capacity for total abandonment makes Natasha susceptible to the depravity of the Kuragins—which in turn leads to her suicide attempt. As Barabara Monter has observed of Anna Karenina: "Anna's vitality, the essence of her attractiveness, is made up in large part of sexuality, and with Tolstoy sexuality fulfills only itself and leads away from life. Thus we have the paradox of Anna who is so alive ending in suicide."

Natasha's realization of her near doom and of the value of the man she has abandoned tames her sensuality, as does her association with that spiritually elevated, Tolstoyan wife and mother, Princess Mary. Nevertheless, her transformation in the epilogue is quite startling and rather tendentious. Tolstoy remarks that only the old countess understood the change: she "knew by her maternal insight that all Natasha's bursts of impulsiveness had their origin merely in the need of having a family, of having a husband". After Natasha's marriage, her face has "none of the ever-burning fire of animation that had formerly constituted its charm," and she withdraws from society, which finds her "neither attractive nor amiable."

Tolstoy's treatment of Natasha reflects Russian religious and social tradition. Before Peter the Great initiated the custom of having upper class women appear at court and social functions, they were severely restricted, spending their entire lives in separate, prison-like quarters called the *terem*. Still earlier, Byzantine Christianity had brought to Russia a dual image of woman: Mary the Virgin Mother and Eve the temptress. The concept of sex as sin carried over into marriage. The icons had to be covered during marital relations, and ablutions had to be performed afterwards. The popular "Parable of Feminine Evil" by the Byzantine church father St. John Chrysostom described women as "insinuating, cunning, stealthy; slanderers, ensnarers, heretics, wolverines, serpents, scorpions, vipers…," words resembling the pronouncements of Prince Andrew and Dolokhov quoted above.

Helene incorporates what Tolstoy most hated and feared in women: the combined power of beauty and sensual corruption. Her body seems covered by a veneer from all the glances that have passed over it, he writes, clearly implying that it has thus been greatly cheapened. Her "nakedness" is a dangerous weapon for evil: in the opening salon scene her "full shoulders, bosom and back" are "very much exposed," and Pierre looks at her "with almost frightened, rapturous eyes." In the novel *Resurrection*, the hero sees a shapely streetwalker who is quietly confident of her "vile power". In "D'iavol" ("The Devil"), a married man is so tortured by desire for his former mistress that he commits suicide—or, in an alternate ending, kills the mistress. The hero of "Otets Sergii" ("Father Sergius"), in a feverish state, chops off one of his fingers in order to resist a woman who is trying to seduce him. At first Father Sergius suspects that "the devil has assumed a woman's form," as he has "read in the *Lives of the Saints*". Then, as she undresses in the next room, "he heard everything. He heard the silk fabric rustling as she took off her dress, how she stepped on the floor with her bare feet; he heard her rubbing her legs with her hand." In *War and Peace*, as Pierre decides that Helene is destined to be his wife, "he was conscious of the warmth of her body, the fragrance of perfume, and the creaking of her corset when she breathed … he saw and sensed the entire charm of her body, which was covered only by her garments". At this point, Tolstoy says, she has "power over him already."

Princess Mary is in some ways Helene's exact opposite. She is thrice removed from the prospect of causing or succumbing to moral corruption—by her life in the country, by her plainness, and by her spirituality. Her somber life consists of duties, prayer, and surreptitious communication with wandering pilgrims. She considers her longings for earthly love an inspiration of the devil. Conscious that she has suppressed her personal dreams, she achieves a sort of peace until fate intervenes in the person of Nicholas. The development of their relationship allows the fruit of her virtuous life, her inner beauty, to radiate from within her: "All her struggles to improve her inner being, her sufferings, her striving for goodness, her submissiveness, love, self-sacrifice—all this now shone in those radiant eyes, in her delicate smile, and in every trait of her gentle face".

She becomes an ideal Tolstoyan woman—not only a devoted wife and mother, but an inspiration to her mate and the embodiment of high spirituality. She achieves greater happiness than she had thought possible, yet senses that there is "another sort of happiness, unattainable in this life".

Other Fictional Characters

Nicholas Rostov, modeled upon Tolstoy's father, also exhibits several of the author's own traits: "his strength and health, his pagan love of nature, his exaggerated sense of honor and his passion for hunting," as Henri Troyat writes. Yet as Dmitry Pisarev commented in 1868, Nicholas tends to prefer "not to think," to escape from serious problems by ordering a second bottle of wine. Compared with Prince Andrew and Pierre, who engage in a more deeply Tolstoyan quest for truth, Nicholas seems less concerned by the question of how we should live. He is also more limited in his options, restricted by his early promise to Sonya and subsequently by his own and his father's financial losses.

Nicholas's inability to aid Alexander at Austerlitz immediately precedes and pointedly parallels Andrew's disenchantment with Napoleon. Tolstoy carefully prepares us for both episodes by stressing Andrew's admiration for Napoleon in a conversation he has with his father at Bald Hills, and by emphasizing Nicholas's fervent admiration of the emperor as he reviews Kutuzov's army. Three days later, he even has the Tolstoyan feeling that the emperor can discern what is occurring inside his, Nicholas's, own soul. After this, though, the two admired figures are rather didactically shown to have feet of clay. Nicholas sees the emperor alone and despondent; Andrew, wounded but inspired by the lofty sky of Austerlitz, hears the words of "his hero" Napoleon "as he might have heard the buzzing of a fly". There is an important difference, however. Whereas Andrew seems to gain strength and serenity from the incident, Nicholas's "despair" at having failed to aid Alexander is "all the greater as he felt that his own weakness was the cause of his grief".

Whereas Andrew gains spiritual inspiration from the sky, Nicholas is moved, in a similar moment of heightened consciousness, to love life more keenly but also to fear death. As he gazes at the waters of the Danube and the gloriously beautiful sky, Nicholas feels that death is both "above" and "around" him. Much later, when he captures a young, blue-eyed French soldier almost by accident, Nicholas learns that he has earned the St. George Cross. "So others are even more afraid than I am!" he realizes in amazement.

Nicholas, though good, is rather weak; Dolokhov is not a good man but a strong one. The climactic encounter in which Dolokhov assertively wins 43,000 roubles from Nicholas points up this symmetry. Dolokhov coldly and deliberately sets his goal at 43,000 because his and Sonya's ages total 43, and she has refused him because of Nicholas. After Nicholas's enormous loss, it becomes less likely that he will marry Sonya, who has no fortune of her own.

Dolokhov, a dashing but faintly sinister figure, causes considerable harm to others throughout the novel, seemingly almost without trying. His feat of draining a bottle of rum in the window inspires Pierre, who has been drinking heavily, to insist upon similarly risking death. Much later Dolokhov's daring quite literally inspires Petya Rostov to his death. And the fact that Petya is moved to kiss Dolokhov just before this may remind the reader that Dolokhov had vowed the very deepest friendship to Nicholas not long before depriving him of 43,000 roubles.

Dolokhov indirectly brings both Pierre and Natasha close to death. As he goads Pierre into challenging him to a duel, his mocking smile seems to say: "Ah, this is what I like!". Later on, Dolokhov apparently also takes pleasure in masterminding Anatole's furtive wooing and attempted abduction of Natasha, which leads to her near ruin and attempted suicide. The love letter which he composes for Anatole is so well done that Natasha, reading it "for the twentieth time," thinks: "Yes, yes, I love him!".

Dolokhov is a complex figure: his code of behavior, which seems to allow such dangerous sport, also requires honor of him. For example, after he is wounded in the duel with Pierre he bursts into tears because his "adored angel mother" may not survive the shock, and he later begs Pierre's forgiveness, declaring that he is glad of the opportunity to do so. These incidents complicate Dolokhov's character and obscure his sinister role in the novel.

Bazdeev and Platon Karataev represent two symmetrically positive forces. However, the influence of Bazdeev is comparatively superficial and temporary, whereas Platon's is more permanent and profound. Pierre meets them at two of the lowest points in his life; after his painful confrontation with Helene and after he has watched in horror as the French execute prisoners. Each time, Pierre is struggling in despair with questions about the meaning of life and death. Bazdeev treats him paternally; Platon, maternally. Thus Bazdeev repeatedly accompanies his observations with a "gentle, fatherly" smile, and Pierre is several times likened to a child. Platon comforts Pierre "with the gentle singsong caressing tones that old Russian peasant women use," and is "sad that Pierre has no parents, especially a mother." There is no one "dearer than your own mother!" he says, and soon he sings in a "gentle, almost feminine" way. Pierre involuntarily submits to the comforting voices of Bazdeev and Karataev, both of whom suggest that God's great plan is beyond our understanding.

Bazdeev persuades Pierre to become a Freemason, after which he earnestly urges his new beliefs upon Andrew in their conversation at the ferry. Andrew realizes, however, that although Pierre's concern is heartfelt his ideas have little practical wisdom. His initiation into the Society of Freemasons, moreover, is described in a tolerant but parodic manner. Tolstoy himself considered Freemasonry (a secret, philanthropical, and somewhat mystical movement that existed in Russia from the mid-eighteenth century until its suppression under Nicholas I) admirable enough in its aims but rather ridiculous in action.

The peasant Platon Karataev's first name is the Russian form of Plato, and it is tempting to associate him with the peasant Platon from whom the Tolstoyan figure Levin (in *Anna Karenina*) derives spiritual inspiration. Pierre finds comfort in Platon's "roundness," and he relates to Pierre one of Tolstoy's favorite stories, "God Sees the Truth But Speaks Not Soon." In this tale a merchant undergoes brutal torture and ten years of hard labor in Siberia for a murder he did not commit. When the man who had framed him confesses, the merchant responds: "God will forgive you. We are all sinners before God. I suffer for my own sins." When a pardon and compensation finally arrive from the tsar, we are told that God had already forgiven the merchant: he had died. It was not "the story itself," writes Tolstoy, but its "mysterious meaning" and the "rapturous joy" on Platon's face as he told it that joyfully suffused Pierre's soul. This statement becomes somewhat clearer if one recalls that Platon is described as "unable to understand the meaning of words apart from their context." His life, as he saw it, "had meaning only as a particle of a whole that he continually sensed". Just as the merchant in Platon's story is "forgiven" by his return to the source of divine love, so Platon naturally feels that his own life is a particle of that source, as Pierre himself realizes at Platon Karataev's death. Pierre's visionlike dream of the "globe of drops" encapsulates this understanding: "In the center is God, and each drop tries to expand in order to reflect Him as widely as possible. It grows, merges, shrinks, is destroyed on the surface, sinks to the depths, and again floats forth. Here now it is Karataev who has spread out and disappeared". Like Platon himself, Pierre intuitively grasps a concept that Prince Andrew had articulated, on his deathbed, but in a form Tolstoy had declared "only thoughts."

Two critics have persuasively related Pierre's dream of the globe of drops to "the Taoist doctrine that at death one is re-absorbed into the total flow." Pierre's vision of his own immersion in water "so that it closed over his head," they observe, is similarly associated with his realization that Platon has died. In a broader sense, they note, the "round" and "almost feminine" Platon may be likened to sages "in touch with the Tao that is the Mother of all and the stream of history." It may thus accord with Tolstoy's theory of historical causation that our limited "freedom is the ability to become coincident with this sensed flow." Natasha, Pierre, and Kutuzov sense a current in their lives and flow with it; Prince Andrew resists; while Napoleon—in Tolstoy's version of history—blindly bucks the tide.

Napoleon and Tolstoyan Determinism

When Tolstoy wrote *War and Peace*, he had long been convinced that historians distort historical truth. The distortion, he believed, was most evident in treatments of famous people thought to have shaped the course of history. Characteristically pushing his view to extremes, Tolstoy decided that so-called great people actually have very little influence on historical events: "A tsar," he insisted in *War and Peace,* "is the slave of history". At another point he likens Napoleon to a carved figure on the bow of a ship, which, savages think, powers and directs the vessel—and to a child who, grasping the ribbons and braid that decorate the inside of a carriage, thinks he is driving it.

These and similar extreme views are clustered in the second epilogue of the novel, where Tolstoy discusses "the will of historical persons". He argues that such persons, as well as the orders they give, depend on historical events rather than vice versa. An event will not take place, Tolstoy explains, no matter how many orders are given, without the existence of other causes; when an event does occur, we are too ready to seek out individuals whose orders seem in retrospect to have caused it. As Frank Seeley has observed, such reasoning blurs the distinction between "cause" in the sense of "sufficient condition" and "cause" in the sense of "necessary condition." Tolstoy, however, was intent upon drawing another distinction: "Morally, the cause of an event appears to be those in power; physically, it is those who submit to the power". He stubbornly adheres to this position throughout the novel. The military campaign of 1812, he claimed, appeared to depend upon "the will of Napoleon and Alexander," but in order for their will to be carried out "it was necessary that millions of men, in whose hands was the real force, the soldiers who fired or transported provisions and cannons—it was necessary that they consent to carry out the will of these weak *sic* individuals and that they be led to do so by an innumerable quantity of complex, diverse causes". Or, more simply put, "at the battle of Borodino Napoleon did not shoot at anyone or kill anyone. All that was done by the soldiers. Thus it was not he who killed people".

The evacuation and burning of Moscow (instead of its ceremonious surrender to the French) understandably evokes an emotional reaction from most Russians. In Pushkin's famous phrase, Moscow prepared "not revelry, not a welcoming gift" but "a conflagration for the impatient hero." Tolstoy himself carefully anticipates this moment by describing Napoleon as self-centered and supremely confident of his own power: "Everything outside of him," Tolstoy writes, "had no meaning for him because everything in the world, it seemed to him, depended entirely on his will". Then, as Napoleon is about to occupy Moscow, Tolstoy takes evident pleasure in having him dream of being magnanimous to its humble citizens as they surrender. As Tolstoy explains, the French generals faced a twofold problem: how to tell Napoleon the terrible news that the Russians would not surrender, but, still worse, how to keep him from appearing ridiculous. When the French army finally abandons Moscow and retreats in disarray, Tolstoy compares its movements to the reflexive spasms of a mortally wounded animal. It is then that he likens Napoleon to a child who, while playing with the decorations inside a carriage, is convinced that he is driving it.

Tolstoy calls the evacuation and burning of Moscow "just as inevitable as the retreat of the army without fighting beyond Moscow after the battle of Borodino". "Every Russian," he adds, "could have predicted what happened, not by reasoning but by a feeling inside of us and in each of our fathers." In an unpublished foreword to the first chapters of *War and Peace*, Tolstoy expressed the secret hope that Russia's triumph of 1812 "was not accidental, but lay in the essence of the character of the Russian people and army." Of the one-eyed Kutuzov—who is often called "blind" in the novel but whose patient strategy crucially contributes to Russia's triumph—Tolstoy writes: "For the representative of the Russian people—after the enemy had been destroyed and Russia had been placed on the pinnacle of her glory—for this Russian there was nothing left to do as a Russian. For the representative of the people's war, nothing remained except death. And he died". The facts do not support the contrast between Tolstoy's Kutuzov, a simple, unaffected, wise Russian general who passively submits to events, and his Napoleon, a stupid, arrogant French poseur who believes he can impose his will on history. However, this contrast illustrates Tolstoy's views on the role of so-called great men in history, as well as his aggressively elaborated theory of determinism.

This theory is painstakingly developed in the second epilogue. Our actions, Tolstoy contends, are far less free than we suppose. A person who commits a criminal act, he explains, may have been driven to do so for a variety of reasons. If, Tolstoy insists, we could understand the almost infinite chain of causes and circumstances leading up to and attending a particular action, it would be clear that the action was inevitable. As an illustration, he analyzes the simple action of moving one's arm. Free as the action may seem, he argues, it is necessarily limited in three respects. First, there are physical limitations—the structure of one's arm and any obstacles in its path. Second, the action is temporally limited: in retrospect, Tolstoy claims, we realize that no different action could have occurred at that exact same instant. (Even though the action seems free as we perform it, he suggests, it later appears less so in proportion to the time that has elapsed since then and the consequences stemming from it.) Finally, Tolstoy reasons, we are limited by causes (even the desire to perform an action without a cause is itself a cause). He therefore declares: "In order to imagine a perfectly free person, one not subject to the law of necessity, we must imagine him alone, *outside of space, outside of time,* and *outside of dependence upon causes.* "

Tolstoy then differentiates between reason, which expresses the laws of necessity (though they in their totality are beyond our comprehension) and conscious awareness, which expresses what we perceive as the freedom of our actions. In his opinion, our consciousness "tells" us that we are not outside of space but are outside of time and outside of causes, since we "feel" that we ourselves are the cause of every manifestation of our lives. That which we term free will, he concludes, is actually a natural, predictable force, like electricity or gravity; it is similarly subject to laws, but in this case laws that we fail to discern. Just as we have had to admit that, despite appearances, the other planets do not orbit the earth, so "we must renounce our non-existent freedom and acknowledge a dependence that we do not perceive".

Though one can disagree with some of Tolstoy's arguments, especially those on temporal limitation, it is virtually impossible to disprove his conclusion, with its self-substantiating emphasis upon the limited, illusory nature of human consciousness. A vastly superior, "infinite" consciousness, capable of perceiving literally all circumstances leading up to and surrounding an action, could perhaps indeed see the action as predictable, even inevitable.

The creator of a literary work may be said to have a godlike perspective on the destinies of his characters. Of course, the author also controls these destinies—as invisibly or visibly as his intentions and abilities permit. Throughout *War and Peace*, Tolstoy adheres to his theory of determinism as convincingly and artistically as possible: he depicts both historical and fictional events as apparently inevitable while preserving for his characters their illusion of free will. The novel opens with the suggestion that Napoleon is the "Antichrist"; within a few pages Lise asks Pierre, who is discussing Napoleon, if he believes that assassination shows greatness of soul. All of this ironically anticipates Pierre's subsequent conviction that he is predestined to assassinate Napoleon, who, he has decided, is the Antichrist. Still later, however, Tolstoy suggests that Pierre was "destined" *not* to kill Napoleon.

Other events are explicitly described as inevitable—the duel between Pierre and Dolokhov begins, for example: "It was evident that the affair so lightly begun could already not be prevented but was taking its own course independent of the will of men and had to happen".

Similar views permeate what one critic has termed "the novel's crucial scene." Captured in Moscow by the French, Pierre watches them execute prisoners in the belief that he too will be shot: "He had only one wish—that the frightful thing that had to happen should happen quickly". The French soldiers do in fact hurry, "as if to finish an essential but unpleasant and incomprehensible task." Having decided to shoot the prisoners in pairs, bound to a post, they begin. Pierre turns away, but upon hearing sounds "louder than the most terrible thunder claps," he looks around to see smoke and soldiers with pale faces doing "something" beside a nearby pit.

They position the next pair. "Pierre again did not want to look and turned away; but again a horrible explosion struck his ears." Again he sees smoke and soldiers with pale, frightened faces doing "something" near the post. He also notices that all those present, even the French, seem to experience the very same horror as he. "But who is really doing this?" he wonders. "They are all suffering just the same as I. Who, then? Who?"

Next a young factory worker is led to the post alone; Pierre, the sixth, is spared in order to witness the final execution, although he fails to realize this. No longer able to turn away, he cannot "take his eyes off" the young victim: "A command must have been heard; after the command, the shots of eight rifles must have resounded. But Pierre, much as he later tried to remember, did not hear the slightest sound of the shots." This third execution resembles in its numbing horror a silent film strip. During the first two, Pierre could not look but was shocked by the sound of the shooting. This time, however, he watches in frozen silence: "He only saw the factory worker for some reason suddenly sinking down upon the ropes." Here Tolstoy characteristically employs the technique of "making strange": for a brief but vivid moment, we wonder why, "for some reason," the young worker's body sinks down upon the ropes that bind him. Once again Pierre sees soldiers with pale, frightened faces doing "something"—this time next to the factory worker, and the reader again envisions soldiers moving the dead from post to pit. Even the smoke functions similarly, as one pictures what created it. Of course, this entire episode is also "made strange" by the fact that Pierre has never before witnessed such horrors, which seem the more terrible for their apparent inevitability. A grim note of inevitability also echoes in the memories that haunt him later: "Whenever he closed his eyes, he would see before him the factory worker's face, especially dreadful in its simplicity, and, in their agitation, the still more dreadful faces of the involuntary murderers".

A revealing comparison between the artistic techniques and moral and philosophical concerns of Tolstoy and Dostoevsky may be obtained by juxtaposing this scene with the observations on execu-

tions made by Prince Myshkin in *Idiot* (*The Idiot*). (Whereas Dostoevsky, like Tolstoy's Pierre, had fully expected to be executed himself on one occasion, Tolstoy had been horrified, like Dostoevsky's Myshkin, by a guillotining he had witnessed in France.) Myshkin says he was particularly shocked that the victim, a strong, brave man, "cried, white as paper." What causes a man "who has never cried," he wonders, to cry from fright? "What happens at that minute to the soul, what causes it such convulsions?" It is "an outrage to the soul," Myshkin concludes, to kill a person because he has killed. "I saw this a month ago, and it is still before my eyes. About five times I've dreamed of it."

Like Pierre, Myshkin is haunted by visions of the execution, but in his case they have also been internalized as dreams. A similar but more basic difference is that whereas Pierre watches in frozen horror, Myshkin probes the victim's inner experience. Even the "pale, frightened" faces of Tolstoy's executioner-soldiers are transferred in Dostoevsky to the victim ("white as paper"). Still more important, Pierre's question "Who is doing this?" is formulated by Myshkin as "How can one person do this to another?" And this leads to the crucial comparison. Whereas Dostoevsky characteristically arraigns a world in which such atrocities can exist, Tolstoy sees them, in *War and Peace*, as grimly inevitable: beyond our control ("the frightful thing that had to happen"), beyond our comprehension ("an essential but unpleasant and incomprehensible task"), and even beyond our direct responsibility ("the involuntary murderers").

Source: William W. Rowe, "Leo Tolstoy," in *Twayne World Authors Series Online,* Twayne Publishers, 1986, Chapter 4.

SOURCES

Arnold, Matthew, "Count Leo Tolstoy," in *Fortnightly Review*, December, 1887.

Christian, R. F., *Tolstoy's "War and Peace": A Study*, Clarendon Press, 1962.

Fodor, Alexander, *Tolstoy and the Russians: Reflections on a Relationship*, Ardis Press, 1984.

James, Henry, "Preface to *The Tragic Muse*," in *The Art of the Novel*, C. Scribner's Sons, 1934.

Simmons, Ernest J., *Tolstoy*, Routledge & Kegan Paul, 1973, p. 81.

Wasiolek, Edward, *Tolstoy's Major Fiction*, University of Chicago Press, 1978.

FURTHER READING

Berlin, Isaiah, "Tolstoy and Enlightenment," in *Mightier than the Sword*, MacMillan & Co., 1964.
An influential assessment of the often-repeated charge that Tolstoy was a good fiction writer but a flawed philosopher.

Christian, R. F., *Tolstoy's* War and Peace*: A Study*, The Clarendon Press, 1962.
A comprehensive and recommended study of the novel.

Citati, Pietro, *Tolstoy*, Schocken Books, 1986.
Written by an Italian literary critic, this is a short biography that introduces students to the key elements in Tolstoy's life and works.

Crankshaw, Edward, *Tolstoy: The Making of a Novelist*, The Viking Press, 1974.
Traces Tolstoy's development as a novelist.

Crego Benson, Ruth, "Two Natashas," in *Women in Tolstoy: The Ideal and the Erotic*, University of Illinois Press, 1973.
Examines the conflict between Tolstoy's portrayal of Natasha as a strong complex heroine and his tendency to see women only as objects of beauty.

Debreczeny, Paul, "Freedom and Necessity: A Reconsideration of *War and Peace*," in *Papers on Language and Literature: A Journal for Scholars and Critics of Language and Literature*, No. 2, Spring, 1971.
Debreczeny's understanding of Tolstoy's basic philosophy allows him to read the diverse aspects of the novel as one continuous, homogeneous narrative.

Greenwood, E. B., "The Problem of Truth in *War and Peace*," in *Tolstoy: The Comprehensive Vision*, St. Martin's Press, 1975.
Explores Tolstoy's interest in the problem of historical truth.

Johnson, Claudia D., *To Kill a Mockingbird: Threatening Boundaries*, Twayne, 1994.
A book-length analysis of the novel that provides historical and literary context as well as discussion of key themes and issues.

Morrison, Gary Saul, *Hidden in Plain View: Narrative and Creative Potentials in "War and Peace,"* Stanford University Press, 1987.
Discusses the structure of the novel.

Sampson, R. V., "Leo Tolstoy: 'God Sees the Truth, But Does Not Quickly Reveal It'," in *The Discovery of Peace*, Pantheon Books, 1973.
Sampson examines several key writers who have influenced the history of the moral debate about war.

Simmons, Ernest J., "War and Peace," in *Introduction to Tolstoy's Writings*, The University of Chicago Press, 1968.
In this chapter in a book about the Tolstoy's major works, Simmons provides a stylistic and thematic analysis of the novel.

Glossary of Literary Terms

A

Abstract: Used as a noun, the term refers to a short summary or outline of a longer work. Used as an adjective, abstract refers to concepts not knowable through the five senses. Examples of abstracts (n) include the synopsis that appear in front of the critical essays in each *Epics for Students* entry. Examples of abstract concepts (adj) include "idea," "guilt" "honesty," and "loyalty."

Accent: The emphasis or stress placed on a syllable in poetry. Traditional poetry, including epic poetry, commonly uses patterns of accented and unaccented syllables (known as feet) that create distinct rhythms. Much modern poetry uses less formal arrangements that create a sense of freedom and spontaneity. The opening line of the Dorothy Sayers translation of *The Divine Comedy*: "Midway this way of life we're bound upon" has five accents: on the second syllable of the first word ("-way) and on "way," "life," "bound," and the last syllable of the last work ("–on").

Allegory: A narrative technique in which characters represent things or abstract ideas and are used to convey a message or teach a lesson. Allegory is typically used to teach moral, ethical, or religious lessons but is sometimes used for satiric or political purposes. Examples of allegorical works include Dante's *Divine Comedy* and John Bunyan's *The Pilgrim's Progress*.

Alliteration: The repetition of vowel sounds as a poetic device.

Allusion: A reference to a familiar character, real person, event, or concept, used to make an idea more easily understood. Describing someone as a "Romeo" makes an allusion to William Shakespeare's famous young lover in *Romeo and Juliet*.

Analogy: A comparison of two unlike things. An analogy appears in Book 9 of *The Aeneid,* when the sounds of battle are described in one translation as being "like a great shower from the west drumming on the earth in the rainy season ... or like hailstones dropping from the clouds into the sea when the south wind in blowing."

Antagonist: The character in a narrative or drama who works against or stands in opposition to the hero or protagonist. An example of an antagonist is Ganelon in *The Song of Roland.*

Anthropomorphism: The presentation of animals or objects in human shape or with human characteristics. The term is derived from the Greek word for "human form." The fables of Aesop and many of the animated films of Walt Disney feature anthropomorphic characters.

Anti-hero: A central character in a work of literature who lacks traditional heroic qualities such as courage, physical prowess, and fortitude. Anti-heros typically distrust conventional values and are unable to commit themselves to any ideals. They generally feel helpless in a world over which they have no control. Anti-heroes usually accept, and often celebrate, their positions as social outcasts.

Antithesis: Direct opposite. In literature, the use of antithesis as a figure of speech results in two statements that show a contrast through the balancing of two opposite ideas. Technically, the second portion of the statement is the ''antithesis''; the first portion is the ''thesis.'' An example of antithesis is found in the following portion of Abraham Lincoln's ''Gettysburg Address'': ''The world will little note nor long remember what we say here, but it can never forget what they did here.''

Apocrypha: Writings tentatively attributed to an author but not proven or universally accepted to be their works. The term was originally applied to certain books of the Bible that were not considered inspired and so were not included in the ''sacred canon.'' Geoffrey Chaucer, William Shakespeare, Thomas Kyd, Thomas Middleton, and John Marston all have apocrypha. Apocryphal books of the Bible include the Old Testament's Book of Enoch and New Testament's Gospel of Peter.

Apostrophe: A statement, question, or request addressed to an inanimate object or concept or to a nonexistent or absent person. Requests for inspiration from the muses in poetry are examples of apostrophe.

Archetype: In literature, a universal type of recurring image, character, plot device, or action. This term was introduced to literary criticism from the psychology of Carl Jung. It expresses Jung's theory that behind every person's ''unconscious,'' or repressed memories of the past, lies the ''collective unconscious'' of the human race: memories of the countless typical experiences of our ancestors. These memories are said to prompt associations that trigger powerful emotions. Examples of literary archetypes include the theme of birth and death and the figure of the war hero. The term is used more generally to mean the first or best example of its kind: Gilgamesh and Enkidu are sometimes described as the archetypal best friends, for example.

Argument: The argument of a work is the author's subject matter or principal idea. Examples of defined ''argument'' portions of works include John Milton's *Arguments* to each of the books of *Paradise Lost.*

Assonance: The repetition of similar vowel sounds in poetry.

Audience: The people for whom a piece of literature is written. Authors usually write with a certain audience in mind: for example, children, members of a religious or ethnic group, or colleagues in a professional field. The term ''audience'' also applies to the people who gather to see or hear any performance, including plays, poetry readings, speeches, and concerts.

B

Ballad: A short poem that tells a simple story and has a repeated refrain. Ballads were originally intended to be sung. Early ballads, known as folk ballads, were passed down through generations, so their authors are often unknown. Later ballads composed by known authors are called literary ballads.

Blank Verse: Loosely, any unrhymed poetry, but more generally, unrhymed iambic pentameter verse (composed of lines of five two-syllable feet with the first syllable accented, the second unaccented). Blank verse has been used by poets since the Renaissance for its flexibility and its graceful, dignified tone. John Milton's *Paradise Lost* is in blank verse, as are most of William Shakespeare's plays.

C

Cadence: The natural rhythm of language caused by the alternation of accented and unaccented syllables.

Caesura: A pause in a line of poetry, usually occurring near the middle. It typically corresponds to a break in the natural rhythm or sense of the line but is sometimes shifted to create special meanings or rhythmic effects.

Character: Broadly speaking, a figure in a literary work. The actions of characters are what constitute the plot of a story, novel, or poem. There are numerous types of characters, ranging from simple, stereotypical figures to intricate, multifaceted ones. In the techniques of anthropomorphism and personification, animals—and even places or things— can assume aspects of character.

Chronicle: A record of events presented in chronological order. Although the scope and level of detail provided varies greatly among the chronicles surviving from ancient times, some, such as the *Anglo-Saxon Chronicle,* feature vivid descriptions and a lively recounting of events. During the Elizabethan

Age, many dramas—appropriately called ''chronicle plays''—were based on material from chronicles.

Classical: In its strictest definition in literary criticism, classicism refers to works of ancient Greek or Roman literature. The term may also be used to describe a literary work of recognized importance (a ''classic'') from any time period or literature that exhibits the traits of classicism.

Classicism: A term used in literary criticism to describe critical doctrines that have their roots in ancient Greek and Roman literature, philosophy, and art. Works associated with classicism typically exhibit restraint on the part of the author, unity of design and purpose, clarity, simplicity, logical organization, and respect for tradition.

Climax: The turning point in a narrative, the moment when the conflict is at its most intense. Typically, the structure of stories, novels, and plays is one of rising action, in which tension builds to the climax, followed by falling action, in which tension lessens as the story moves to its conclusion.

Colloquialism: A word, phrase, or form of pronunciation that is acceptable in casual conversation but not in formal, written communication. It is considered more acceptable than slang.

Concrete: As a literary term, concrete is the opposite of abstract, and refers to a thing that actually exists or a description that allows the reader to experience an object or concept with the senses.

Conflict: The conflict in a work of fiction is the issue to be resolved in the story. It usually occurs between two characters, the protagonist and the antagonist, or between the protagonist and society or the protagonist and himself or herself.

Consonance: Consonance occurs in poetry when words appearing at the ends of two or more verses have similar final consonant sounds but have final vowel sounds that differ, as with ''stuff'' and ''off.''

Convention: Any widely accepted literary device, style, or form. An authorial aside, in which an omniscient narrator reveals something to the reader that the characters in the literary work do not yet know, is an example of a literary convention.

Couplet: Two lines of poetry with the same rhyme and meter, often expressing a complete, self-contained thought.

Criticism: The systematic study and evaluation of literary works, usually based on a specific method or set of principles. An important part of literary studies since ancient times, the practice of criticism has given rise to numerous theories, methods, and ''schools,'' sometimes producing conflicting, even contradictory, interpretations of literature in general as well as of individual works. Even such basic issues as what constitutes a poem or a novel have been the subject of much criticism over the centuries.

D

Dactyl: See *Foot*

Denotation: The definition of a word, apart from the impressions or feelings it creates in the reader.

Denouement: A French word meaning ''the unknotting.'' In literary criticism, it denotes the resolution of conflict in fiction or drama. The *denouement* follows the climax and provides an outcome to the primary plot situation as well as an explanation of secondary plot complications. The *denouement* often involves a character's recognition of his or her state of mind or moral condition.

Dialogue: In its widest sense, dialogue is simply conversation between people in a literary work; in its most restricted sense, it refers specifically to the speech of characters in a drama. As a specific literary genre, a ''dialogue'' is a composition in which characters debate an issue or idea.

Diction: The selection and arrangement of words in a literary work. Either or both may vary depending on the desired effect. There are four general types of diction: ''formal,'' used in scholarly or lofty writing; ''informal,'' used in relaxed but educated conversation; ''colloquial,'' used in everyday speech; and ''slang,'' containing newly coined words and other terms not accepted in formal usage.

Didactic: A term used to describe works of literature that aim to teach some moral, religious, political, or practical lesson. Although didactic elements are often found in artistically pleasing works, the term ''didactic'' usually refers to literature in which the message is more important than the form. The term may also be used to criticize a work that the critic finds ''overly didactic,'' that is, heavy-handed in its delivery of a lesson.

Dissonance: A combination of harsh or jarring sounds, especially in poetry. Although such combinations may be accidental, poets sometimes intentionally make them to achieve particular effects. Dissonance is also sometimes used to refer to close but not identical rhymes. When this is the case, the word functions as a synonym for consonance.

Drama: In its widest sense, a drama is any work designed to be presented by actors on a stage. Similarly, "drama" denotes a broad literary genre that includes a variety of forms, from pageant and spectacle to tragedy and comedy, as well as countless types and subtypes. More commonly in modern usage, however, a drama is a work that treats serious subjects and themes but does not aim at the grandeur of tragedy.

Dramatic Monologue: See *Monologue*

E

Eclogue: A poem featuring rural themes and structured as a dialogue among shepherds. Eclogues often took specific poetic forms, such as elegies or love poems. Some were written as the soliloquy of a shepherd. In later centuries, "eclogue" came to refer to any poem that was in the pastoral tradition or that had a dialogue or monologue structure. The form takes its name from Virgil's *Eclogues,* also known as *Bucolics.*

Epic: A long narrative poem about the adventures of a hero, usually a person of great nationalistic, historic, or legendary importance. The setting is vast and the action is often given cosmic significance through the intervention of supernatural forces such as gods, angels, or demons. Epics are typically written in a classical style with elaborate metaphors and allusions that enhance the symbolic importance of a hero's adventures.

Epic Simile: See *Homeric Simile*

Epilogue: A concluding statement or section of a literary work. In dramas, particularly those of the seventeenth and eighteenth centuries, the epilogue is a closing speech, often in verse, delivered by an actor at the end of a play and spoken directly to the audience.

Episode: An incident that forms part of a story and is significantly related to it. Episodes may be either self-contained narratives or events that depend on a larger context for their sense and importance.

F

Fable: A prose or verse narrative intended to convey a moral. Animals or inanimate objects with human characteristics often serve as characters in fables.

Feet: See *Foot*

Fiction: Any story that is the product of imagination rather than a documentation of fact. Characters and events in such narratives may be based in real life but their ultimate form and configuration is a creation of the author.

Figurative Language: A technique in writing in which the author temporarily interrupts the order, construction, or meaning of the writing for a particular effect. This interruption takes the form of one or more figures of speech such as hyperbole, irony, or simile. Figurative language is the opposite of literal language, in which every word is truthful, accurate, and free of exaggeration or embellishment.

Figures of Speech: Language that differs from customary conventions of construction, meaning, order, or significance for the purpose of a special meaning or effect. There are two major types of figures of speech: rhetorical figures, which do not make changes in the meaning of the words, and tropes, which do. Types of figures of speech include simile, hyperbole, alliteration, and pun, among many others.

Flashback: A device used in literature to present action that occurred before the beginning of the story.

Foil: A character in a work of literature whose physical or psychological qualities contrast strongly with, and therefore highlight, the corresponding qualities of another character. In *The Song of Roland,* for example, the cautious Olivier serves as a foil to the hot-blooded and impetuous hero Roland.

Folk Ballad: See *Ballad*

Folklore: Traditions and myths preserved in a culture or group of people. Typically, these are passed on by word of mouth in various forms—such as legends, songs, and proverbs—or preserved in customs and ceremonies. This term was first used by W. J. Thoms in 1846. *The Kalevala* incorporates many elements of traditional Finnish folklore.

Folktale: A story originating in oral tradition. Folktales fall into a variety of categories, including legends, ghost stories, fairy tales, fables, and anecdotes based on historical figures and events.

Foot: The smallest unit of rhythm in a line of poetry. In English-language poetry, a foot is typically one accented syllable combined with one or two unaccented syllables. There are many different types of feet. When the accent is on the second syllable of a two syllable word (con-*tort*), the foot is an "iamb"; the reverse accentual pattern (*tor*-ture) is a "trochee." Other feet that commonly occur in poetry in English are "anapest", two unaccented syllables followed by an accented syllable as in in-ter-*cept*, and "dactyl", an accented syllable followed by two unaccented syllables as in *su*-i-cide.

Foreshadowing: A device used in literature to create expectation or to set up an explanation of later developments.

Form: The pattern or construction of a work which identifies its genre and distinguishes it from other genres.

G

Genre: A category of literary work. In critical theory, genre may refer to both the content of a given work—tragedy, comedy, pastoral—and to its form, such as epic, poetry, novel, or drama. This term also refers to types of popular literature, as in the genres of science fiction or the detective story.

Georgic: A poem about farming and the farmer's way of life. The genre is named after Virgil's *Georgics,* written before the *Aeneid.*

H

Half Rhyme: See *Consonance*

Hamartia: In tragedy, the event or act that leads to the hero's or heroine's downfall. This term is often incorrectly used as a synonym for tragic flaw.

Hellenism: Imitation of ancient Greek thought or styles. Also, an approach to life that focuses on the growth and development of the intellect. "Hellenism" is sometimes used to refer to the belief that reason can be applied to examine all human experience

Heptameter: See *Meter*

Hero/Heroine: The principal sympathetic character (male or female) in a literary work. Heroes and heroines typically exhibit admirable traits: idealism, courage, and integrity, for example. Epic heroes and heroines include Aeneas in the *Aeneid,* Gilgamesh in *The Epic of Gilgamesh,* and Kriemhild in the *Nibelungenlied.*

Heroic Couplet: A rhyming couplet written in iambic pentameter (a verse with five iambic feet).

Heroic Line: The meter and length of a line of verse in epic or heroic poetry. This varies by language and time period. For example, in English poetry, the

heroic line is iambic pentameter (a verse with five iambic feet). In French, it is the alexandrine (a verse with six iambic feet); in classical literature, dactylic hexameter (a verse with six dactylic feet).

Heroine: See *Hero/Heroine*

Hexameter: See *Meter*

Historical Criticism: The study of a work based on its impact on the world of the time period in which it was written.

Homeric Simile: An elaborate, detailed comparison written as a simile many lines in length.

Humanism: A philosophy that places faith in the dignity of humankind and rejects the medieval perception of the individual as a weak, fallen creature. Humanists typically believe in the perfectibility of human nature and view reason and education as the means to that end.

Hyperbole: In literary criticism, deliberate exaggeration used to achieve an effect.

I

Iamb: See *Foot*

Idiom: A word construction or verbal expression closely associated with a given language. Idioms pose particular problems to translators.

Image: A concrete representation of an object or sensory experience. Typically, such a representation helps evoke the feelings associated with the object or experience itself. Images are either "literal" or "figurative." Literal images are especially concrete and involve little or no extension of the obvious meaning of the words used to express them. Figurative images do not follow the literal meaning of the words exactly. Images in literature are usually visual, but the term "image" can also refer to the representation of any sensory experience.

Imagery: The array of images in a literary work. Also, figurative language.

In medias res: A Latin term meaning "in the middle of things." It refers to the technique of beginning a story at its midpoint and then using various flashback devices to reveal previous action. This technique originated in such epics as Virgil's *Aeneid.*

Induction: The process of reaching a conclusion by reasoning from specific premises to form a general premise. Also, an introductory portion of a work of literature, especially a play.

Intentional Fallacy: The belief that judgments of a literary work based solely on an author's stated or implied intentions are false and misleading. Critics who believe in the concept of the intentional fallacy typically argue that the work itself is sufficient matter for interpretation, even though they may concede that an author's statement of purpose can be useful.

Interior Monologue: A narrative technique in which characters' thoughts are revealed in a way that appears to be uncontrolled by the author. The interior monologue typically aims to reveal the inner self of a character. It portrays emotional experiences as they occur at both a conscious and unconscious level. images are often used to represent sensations or emotions.

Internal Rhyme: Rhyme that occurs within a single line of verse.

Irony: In literary criticism, the effect of language in which the intended meaning is the opposite of what is stated.

L

Lay: A song or simple narrative poem. The form originated in medieval France. Early French *lais* were often based on the Celtic legends and other tales sung by Breton minstrels. In fourteenth-century England, the term ''lay'' was used to describe short narratives written in imitation of the Breton lays.

Literal Language: An author uses literal language when he or she writes without exaggerating or embellishing the subject matter and without any tools of figurative language.

Literature: Literature is broadly defined as any written or spoken material, but the term most often refers to creative works. Literature includes poetry, drama, fiction, and many kinds of nonfiction writing, as well as oral, dramatic, and broadcast compositions not necessarily preserved in a written format, such as films and television programs.

M

Measure: The foot, verse, or time sequence used in a literary work, especially a poem. Measure is often used somewhat incorrectly as a synonym for meter.

Metaphor: A figure of speech that expresses an idea through the image of another object. Metaphors suggest the essence of the first object by identifying it with certain qualities of the second object.

Meter: In literary criticism, the repetition of sound patterns that creates a rhythm in poetry. The patterns are based on the number of syllables and the presence and absence of accents. The unit of rhythm in a line is called a foot. Types of meter are classified according to the number of feet in a line. These are the standard English lines: Monometer, one foot; Dimeter, two feet; Trimeter, three feet; Tetrameter, four feet; Pentameter, five feet; Hexameter, six feet (also called the Alexandrine); Heptameter, seven feet (also called the ''Fourteener'' when the feet are iambic). The most common English meter is the iambic pentameter, in which each line contains ten syllables, or five iambic feet, which individually are composed of an unstressed syllable followed by an accented syllable.

Monologue: A composition, written or oral, by a single individual. More specifically, a speech given by a single individual in a drama or other public entertainment. It has no set length, although it is usually several or more lines long.

Mood: The prevailing emotions of a work or of the author in his or her creation of the work. The mood of a work is not always what might be expected based on its subject matter.

Motif: A theme, character type, image, metaphor, or other verbal element that recurs throughout a single work of literature or occurs in a number of different works over a period of time.

Muses: In Greek mythology, nine goddesses, the daughters of Zeus and Mnemosyne (Memory). Each muse patronized a specific area of the liberal arts and sciences. Calliope presided over epic poetry, Clio over history, Erato over love poetry, Euterpe over music or lyric poetry, Melpomene over tragedy, Polyhymnia over hymns to the gods, Terpsichore over dance, Thalia over comedy, and Urania over astronomy. Poets and writers traditionally made appeals to the Muses for inspiration in their work. John Milton invokes the aid of a muse at the beginning of the first book of his *Paradise Lost*, and Homer's *Odyssey* beings ''Tell me, Muse, the story of that resourceful man.''

Myth: An anonymous tale emerging from the traditional beliefs of a culture or social unit. Myths use supernatural explanations for natural phenomena.

They may also explain cosmic issues like creation and death. Collections of myths, known as mythologies, are common to all cultures and nations.

N

Narration: The telling of a series of events, real or invented. A narration may be either a simple narrative, in which the events are recounted chronologically, or a narrative with a plot, in which the account is given in a style reflecting the author's artistic concept of the story. Narration is sometimes used as a synonym for "storyline."

Narrative: A verse or prose accounting of an event or sequence of events, real or invented. The term is also used as an adjective in the sense "method of narration." For example, in literary criticism, the expression "narrative technique" usually refers to the way the author structures and presents his or her story.

Narrative Poetry: A nondramatic poem in which the author tells a story. Such poems may be of any length or level of complexity. Epics are examples of narrative poetry.

Narrator: The teller of a story. The narrator may be the author or a character in the story through whom the author speaks.

O

Objectivity: A quality in writing characterized by the absence of the author's opinion or feeling about the subject matter. Objectivity is an important factor in criticism.

Omniscience: See *Point of View*

Onomatopoeia: The use of words whose sounds express or suggest their meaning. In its simplest sense, onomatopoeia may be represented by words that mimic the sounds they denote such as "hiss" or "meow." At a more subtle level, the pattern and rhythm of sounds and rhymes of a line or poem may be onomatopoeic.

Oral Transmission: A process by which songs, ballads, folklore, and other material are transmitted by word of mouth. The tradition of oral transmission predates the written record systems of literate society. Oral transmission preserves material sometimes over generations, although usually with variations. Breton lays, Native American legends, French *fabliaux,* and many national epics (including the Anglo-Saxon *Beowulf,* the Finnish *Kalevala* and the Mali *Sundiata*), are examples of orally transmitted literature.

Oration: Formal speaking intended to motivate the listeners to some action or feeling. Such public speaking was much more common before the development of timely printed communication such as newspapers.

P

Parable: A story intended to teach a moral lesson or answer an ethical question.

Pastoral: A term derived from the Latin word "pastor," meaning shepherd. A pastoral is a literary composition on a rural theme. The conventions of the pastoral were originated by the third-century Greek poet Theocritus, who wrote about the experiences, love affairs, and pastimes of Sicilian shepherds. In a pastoral, characters and language of a courtly nature are often placed in a simple setting. The term pastoral is also used to classify dramas, elegies, and lyrics that exhibit the use of country settings and shepherd characters.

Pathetic Fallacy: A term coined by English critic John Ruskin to identify writing that falsely endows nonhuman things with human intentions and feelings, such as "angry clouds" and "sad trees."

Pen Name: See *Pseudonym*

Persona: A Latin term meaning "mask." *Personae* are the characters in a fictional work of literature. The *persona* generally functions as a mask through which the author tells a story in a voice other than his or her own. A *persona* is usually either a character in a story who acts as a narrator or an "implied author," a voice created by the author to act as the narrator for himself or herself.

Personification: A figure of speech that gives human qualities to abstract ideas, animals, and inanimate objects.

Plagiarism: Claiming another person's written material as one's own. Plagiarism can take the form of direct, word-for-word copying or the theft of the substance or idea of the work.

Plot: In literary criticism, this term refers to the pattern of events in a narrative or drama. In its simplest sense, the plot guides the author in composing the work and helps the reader follow the work. Typically, plots exhibit causality and unity and have a beginning, a middle, and an end.

Sometimes, however, a plot may consist of a series of disconnected events, in which case it is known as an "episodic plot."

Poem: In its broadest sense, a composition utilizing rhyme, meter, concrete detail, and expressive language to create a literary experience with emotional and aesthetic appeal. Typical poems include epics, sonnets, odes, elegies, *haiku,* ballads, and free verse.

Poet: An author who writes poetry or verse. The term is also used to refer to an artist or writer who has an exceptional gift for expression, imagination, and energy in the making of art in any form.

Poetics: This term has two closely related meanings. It denotes (1) an aesthetic theory in literary criticism about the essence of poetry or (2) rules prescribing the proper methods, content, style, or diction of poetry. The term poetics may also refer to theories about literature in general, not just poetry.

Poetry: In its broadest sense, writing that aims to present ideas and evoke an emotional experience in the reader through the use of meter, imagery, connotative and concrete words, and a carefully constructed structure based on rhythmic patterns. Poetry typically relies on words and expressions that have several layers of meaning. It also makes use of the effects of regular rhythm on the ear and may make a strong appeal to the senses through the use of imagery.

Point of View: The narrative perspective from which a literary work is presented to the reader. There are four traditional points of view. The "third person omniscient" gives the reader a "godlike" perspective, unrestricted by time or place, from which to see actions and look into the minds of characters. This allows the author to comment openly on characters and events in the work. The "third person" point of view presents the events of the story from outside of any single character's perception, much like the omniscient point of view, but the reader must understand the action as it takes place and without any special insight into characters' minds or motivations. The "first person" or "personal" point of view relates events as they are perceived by a single character. The main character "tells" the story and may offer opinions about the action and characters which differ from those of the author. Much less common than omniscient, third person, and first person is the "second person" point of view, wherein the author tells the story as if it is happening to the reader.

Polemic: A work in which the author takes a stand on a controversial subject, such as abortion or religion. Such works are often extremely argumentative or provocative. Classic examples of polemics include John Milton's *Aeropagitica* and Thomas Paine's *The American Crisis.*.

Prologue: An introductory section of a literary work. It often contains information establishing the situation of the characters or presents information about the setting, time period, or action. In drama, the prologue is spoken by a chorus or by one of the principal characters.

Prose: A literary medium that attempts to mirror the language of everyday speech. It is distinguished from poetry by its use of unmetered, unrhymed language consisting of logically related sentences. Prose is usually grouped into paragraphs that form a cohesive whole such as an essay or a novel.

Protagonist: The central character of a story who serves as a focus for its themes and incidents and as the principal rationale for its development. The protagonist is sometimes referred to in discussions of modern literature as the hero or anti-hero.

Pseudonym: A name assumed by a writer, most often intended to prevent his or her identification as the author of a work.

Pun: A play on words that have the same or similar sounds but different meanings.

Pure Poetry: poetry written without instructional intent or moral purpose that aims only to please a reader by its imagery or musical flow. The term pure poetry is used as the antonym (opposite) of the term "didacticism."

Q

Quatrain: A four-line stanza of a poem or an entire poem consisting of four lines.

R

Refrain: A phrase repeated at intervals throughout a poem. A refrain may appear at the end of each stanza or at less regular intervals. It may be altered slightly at each appearance.

Resolution: The portion of a narrative following the climax, in which the conflict is resolved.

Rhyme: When used as a noun in literary criticism, this term generally refers to a poem in which words sound identical or very similar and appear in parallel positions in two or more lines. Rhymes are classified into different types according to where they fall in a line or stanza or according to the degree of similarity they exhibit in their spellings and sounds. Some major types of rhyme are ''masculine'' rhyme, ''feminine'' rhyme, and ''triple'' rhyme. In a masculine rhyme, the rhyming sound falls in a single accented syllable, as with ''heat'' and ''eat.'' Feminine rhyme is a rhyme of two syllables, one stressed and one unstressed, as with ''merry'' and ''tarry.'' Triple rhyme matches the sound of the accented syllable and the two unaccented syllables that follow: ''narrative'' and ''declarative.''

Rhyme Royal: A stanza of seven lines composed in iambic pentameter and rhymed *ababbcc.* The name is said to be a tribute to King James I of Scotland, who used it in his poetry.

Rhythm: A regular pattern of sound, time intervals, or events occurring in writing, most often and most discernably in poetry. Regular, reliable rhythm is known to be soothing to humans, while interrupted, unpredictable, or rapidly changing rhythm is disturbing. These effects are known to authors, who use them to produce a desired reaction in the reader.

Rising Action: The part of a drama where the plot becomes increasingly complicated. Rising action leads up to the climax, or turning point, of a drama.

Romance: A broad term, usually denoting a narrative with exotic, exaggerated, often idealized characters, scenes, and themes.

S

Scansion: The analysis or ''scanning'' of a poem to determine its meter and often its rhyme scheme. The most common system of scansion uses accents (slanted lines drawn above syllables) to show stressed syllables, breves (curved lines drawn above syllables) to show unstressed syllables, and vertical lines to separate each foot.

Semiotics: The study of how literary forms and conventions affect the meaning of language.

Sestet: Any six-line poem or stanza.

Setting: The time, place, and culture in which the action of a narrative takes place. The elements of setting may include geographic location, characters' physical and mental environments, prevailing cultural attitudes, or the historical time in which the action takes place.

Simile: A comparison, usually using ''like'' or ''as,'' of two essentially dissimilar things, as in ''coffee as cold as ice'' or ''He sounded like a broken record.''

Slang: A type of informal verbal communication that is generally unacceptable for formal writing. Slang words and phrases are often colorful exaggerations used to emphasize the speaker's point; they may also be shortened versions of an often-used word or phrase.

Spondee: In poetry meter, a foot consisting of two long or stressed syllables occurring together. This form is quite rare in English verse, and is usually composed of two monosyllabic words.

Sprung Rhythm: Versification using a specific number of accented syllables per line but disregarding the number of unaccented syllables that fall in each line, producing an irregular rhythm in the poem.

Stanza: A subdivision of a poem consisting of lines grouped together, often in recurring patterns of rhyme, line length, and meter. Stanzas may also serve as units of thought in a poem much like paragraphs in prose.

Stereotype: A stereotype was originally the name for a duplication made during the printing process; this led to its modern definition as a person or thing that is (or is assumed to be) the same as all others of its type. Stereotypical characters who appear in both ancient and modern literature include the bragging soldier, the wise old advisor, the young people who fall madly in love at first sight, and the nagging wife.

Structure: The form taken by a piece of literature. The structure may be made obvious for ease of understanding, as in nonfiction works, or may obscured for artistic purposes, as in some poetry or seemingly ''unstructured'' prose. Examples of common literary structures include the plot of a narrative, the acts and scenes of a drama, and such poetic forms as the Shakespearean sonnet and the Pindaric ode.

Style: A writer's distinctive manner of arranging words to suit his or her ideas and purpose in writing. The unique imprint of the author's personality upon his or her writing, style is the product of an author's way of arranging ideas and his or her use of diction, different sentence structures, rhythm, figures of speech, rhetorical principles, and other elements of composition.

Subject: The person, event, or theme at the center of a work of literature. A work may have one or more subjects of each type, with shorter works tending to have fewer and longer works tending to have more.

Subplot: A secondary story in a narrative. A subplot may serve as a motivating or complicating force for the main plot of the work, or it may provide emphasis for, or relief from, the main plot. The efforts of retired Major Plunkett to assimilate himself into the culture and history of his adopted home of St. Lucia is a subplot of Derek Walcott's *Omeros*.

Suspense: A literary device in which the author maintains the audience's attention through the build-up of events which are intended—but may fail—to result in a specific outcome.

Syllogism: A method of presenting a logical argument. In its most basic form, the syllogism consists of a major premise, a minor premise, and a conclusion.

Symbol: Something that suggests or stands for something else without losing its original identity. In literature, symbols combine their literal meaning with the suggestion of an abstract concept. Literary symbols are of two types: those that carry complex associations of meaning no matter what their contexts, and those that derive their suggestive meaning from their functions in specific literary works.

T

Terza Rima: A three-line stanza form in poetry in which the rhymes are made on the last word of each line in the following manner: the first and third lines of the first stanza, then the second line of the first stanza and the first and third lines of the second stanza, and so on with the middle line of any stanza rhyming with the first and third lines of the following stanza.

Textual Criticism: A branch of literary criticism that seeks to establish the authoritative text of a literary work. Textual critics typically compare all known manuscripts or printings of a single work in order to assess the meanings of differences and revisions. This procedure allows them to arrive at a definitive version that (supposedly) corresponds to the author's original intention.

Tone: The author's attitude toward his or her audience may be deduced from the tone of the work. A formal tone may create distance or convey politeness, while an informal tone may encourage a friendly, intimate, or intrusive feeling in the reader. The author's attitude toward his or her subject matter may also be deduced from the tone of the words he or she uses in discussing it.

Tragedy: A drama in prose or poetry about a noble, courageous hero of excellent character who, because of some tragic character flaw or *hamartia*, brings ruin upon him- or herself. Tragedy treats its subjects in a dignified and serious manner, using poetic language to help evoke pity and fear and bring about catharsis, a purging of these emotions. The tragic form was practiced extensively by the ancient Greeks.

Tragic Flaw: In a tragedy, the quality within the hero or heroine which leads to his or her downfall. Some critics have charged that Roland's excessive pride, which prevents him from calling for help until it is too late, is the tragic flaw of the hero of *The Song of Roland*.

Trimeter: See *Meter*

Triple Rhyme: See *Rhyme*

Trochee: See *Foot*

U

Unities: Strict rules of dramatic structure, formulated by Italian and French critics of the Renaissance and based loosely on the principles of drama discussed by Aristotle in his *Poetics.* Foremost among these rules were the three unities of action, time, and place that compelled a dramatist to: (1) construct a single plot with a beginning, middle, and end that details the causal relationships of action and character; (2) restrict the action to the events of a single day; and (3) limit the scene to a single place or city. The unities were observed faithfully by continental European writers until the Romantic Age, but they were never regularly observed in English drama. Modern dramatists are typically more concerned with a unity of impression or emotional effect than with any of the classical unities.

V

Verisimilitude: Literally, the appearance of truth. In literary criticism, the term refers to aspects of a work of literature that seem true to the reader.

Versification: The writing of verse. Versification may also refer to the meter, rhyme, and other mechanical components of a poem.

Z

Zeitgeist: A German term meaning "spirit of the time." It refers to the moral and intellectual trends of a given era.

Cumulative Author/Title Index

Nationality/Ethnicity Index

American
Pound, Ezra
The Cantos: V2

English
Malory, Thomas
Le Morte d'Arthur: V2
Milton, John
Paradise Lost: V1
Spenser, Edmund
The Faerie Queene: V2

Finnish
Lönnrot, Elias
Kalevala: V1

French
Hugo, Victor
Les Misérables: V2

Greek
Homer
Iliad: V1
Odyssey: V1

Italian
Dante, Alighieri
Dante Divina Commedia (The Divine Comedy): V1
Tasso, Torquato
Gerusalemme Liberata: V2

Japanese
Shikibu, Murasaki
The Tale of Genji: V2

Malian
Kouyaté, Djeli Mamoudou
Sundiata: V1

Roman
Lucretius
De rerum natura: V2
Virgil
Aeneid: V1

Russian
Tolstoy, Leo
War and Peace: V2

South African
Tolkien, J. R. R.
Lord of the Rings: V2

Spanish
Lucan(us), Marcus Annaeus
Pharsalia: V2

West Indian
Walcott, Derek
Omeros: V1

Subject/Theme Index